GLOBAL MARKETING

Visit the *Global Marketing, fifth edition* Companion Website at **www.pearsoned.co.uk/hollensen** to find valuable **student** learning material including:

- Full versions of the video case studies
- Multiple choice questions to test your learning
- Annotated links to relevant sites on the web
- An online glossary to explain key terms
- Flashcards to test your knowledge of key terms and definitions
- Classic extra case studies that help take your learning further

Fifth Edition

GLOBAL MARKETING
A DECISION-ORIENTED APPROACH

Svend Hollensen

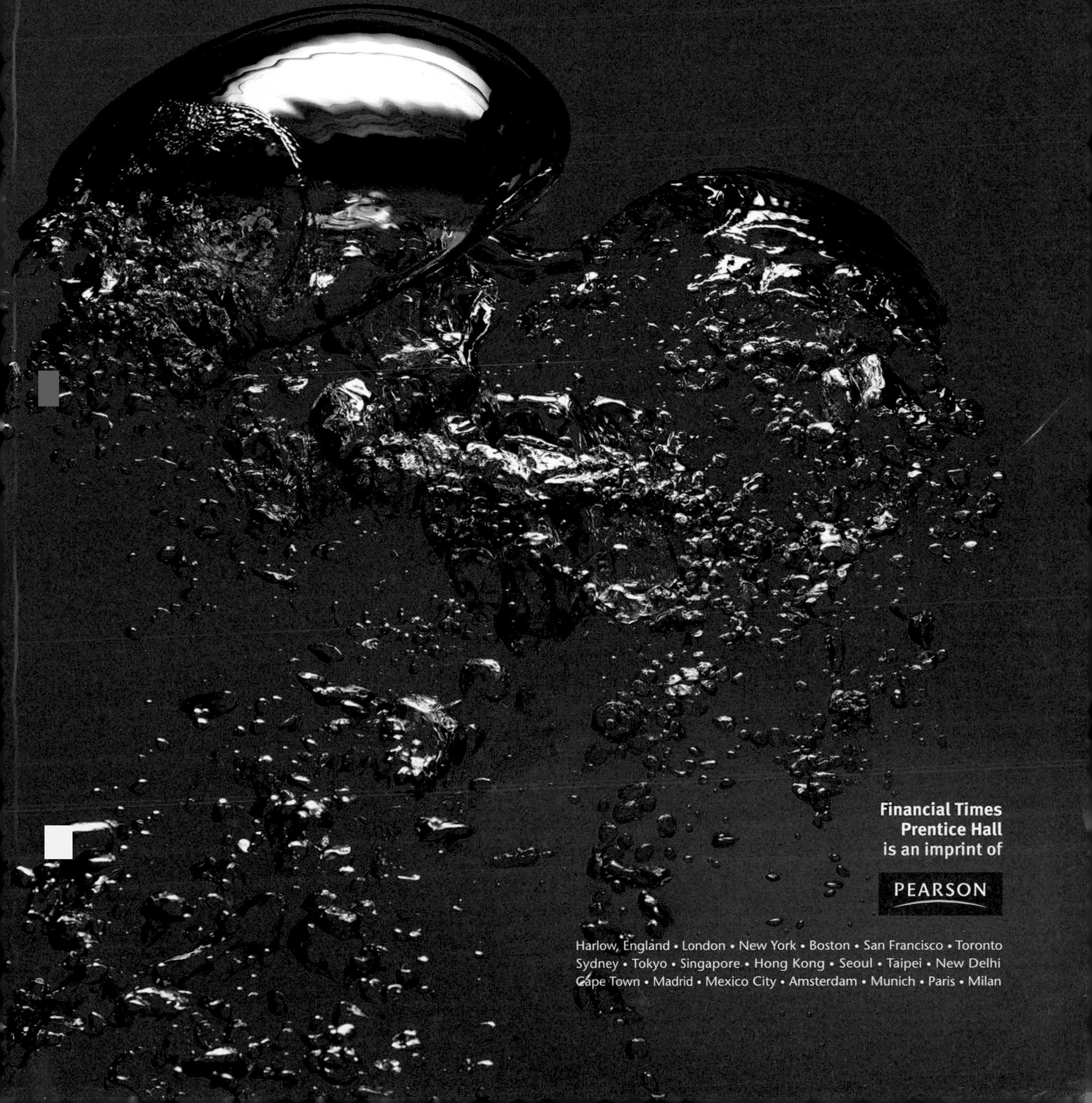

Financial Times
Prentice Hall
is an imprint of

PEARSON

Harlow, England • London • New York • Boston • San Francisco • Toronto
Sydney • Tokyo • Singapore • Hong Kong • Seoul • Taipei • New Delhi
Cape Town • Madrid • Mexico City • Amsterdam • Munich • Paris • Milan

Pearson Education Limited
Edinburgh Gate
Harlow
Essex CM20 2JE
England

and Associated Companies throughout the world

Visit us on the World Wide Web at:
www.pearsoned.co.uk

———————

First published 1998 by Prentice Hall
Second edition published 2001 by Pearson Education Limited
Third edition published 2004
Fourth edition published 2007
Fifth edition published 2011

ISBN 978-0-273-72622-7

British Library Cataloguing-in-Publication Data
A catalogue record for this book is available from the British Library

Library of Congress Cataloging-in-Publication Data
Hollensen, Svend.
  Global marketing : a decision-oriented approach / Svend Hollensen. –
5th ed.
    p. cm.
  ISBN 978-0-273-72622-7 (pbk.)
1. Export marketing.   2. Export marketing–Case studies.   I. Title.
  HF1416.H65 2010
  658.8′4–dc22

                                            2010009888

10 9 8 7 6 5 4 3 2
14 13 12 11 10

Typeset in 10/12pt Minion by 35
Printed and bound by Rotolito Lombarda, Italy

BRIEF CONTENTS

CONTENTS

SUPPORTING RESOURCES

Visit **www.pearsoned.co.uk/hollensen** to find valuable online resources:

Companion Website for students

- Full versions of the video case studies
- Multiple choice questions to test your learning
- Annotated links to relevant sites on the web
- An online glossary to explain key terms
- Flashcards to test your knowledge of key terms and definitions
- Classic extra case studies that help take your learning further

For instructors

- PowerPoint slides that can be downloaded and used for presentations
- Extensive Instructor's Manual with sample answers for all of the case study question material, including the extra case studies on the Companion Website
- Answers to the questions in the book that accompany the video case studies
- Testbank of question material

Also: The Companion Website provides the following features:

- Search tool to help locate specific items of content
- E-mail results and profile tools to send results of quizzes to instructors
- Online help and support to assist with website usage and troubleshooting

For more information please contact your local Pearson Education sales representative or visit **www.pearsoned.co.uk/hollensen**.

PREFACE

Globalization is the growing interdependence of national economies – involving primarily customers, producers, suppliers and governments in different markets. Global marketing therefore reflects the trend of firms selling and distributing products and services in many countries around the world. It is associated with governments reducing trade and investment barriers, firms manufacturing in multiple countries and foreign firms increasingly competing in domestic markets.

For many years the globalization of markets, caused by the convergence of tastes across borders, was thought to result in very large multinational enterprises that could use their advantages in scale economies to introduce world-standardized products successfully.

In his famous 1994 book, *The Global Paradox*, John Naisbitt has contradicted especially the last part of this myth:[1]

> The mindset that in a huge global economy the multinationals dominate world business couldn't have been more wrong. The bigger and more open the world economy becomes, the more small and middle sized companies will dominate. In one of the major turnarounds in my lifetime, we have moved from 'economies of scale' to 'diseconomies of scale'; from bigger is better to bigger is inefficient, costly and wastefully bureaucratic, inflexible and, now, disastrous. And the paradox that has occurred is, as we move to the global context: The smaller and speedier players will prevail on a much expanded field.

When the largest corporations (e.g. IBM, ABB) downsize, they are seeking to emulate the entrepreneurial behaviour of successful SMEs (small- and medium-sized enterprises) where the implementation phase plays a more important role than in large companies. Since the behaviours of smaller and (divisions of) larger firms (according to the above quotation) are convergent, the differences in the global marketing behaviour between SMEs and LSEs (large-scale enterprises) are slowly disappearing. What is happening is that the LSEs are downsizing and decentralizing their decision-making process. The result will be a more decision- and action-oriented approach to global marketing. This approach will also characterize this book.

In light of their smaller size, most SMEs lack the capabilities, market power and other resources of traditional multinational LSEs. Compared with the resource-rich LSEs, the complexities of operating under globalization are considerably more difficult for the SME. The success of SMEs under globalization depends in large part on the decision and implementation of the right international marketing strategy.

The primary role of marketing management, in any organization, is to design and execute effective marketing programmes that will pay off. Companies can do this in their home market or they can do it in one or more international markets. Going international is an enormously expensive exercise, in terms of both money and, especially, top management time and commitment. Due to the high cost, going international must generate added value for the company beyond extra sales. In other words, the company needs to gain a competitive advantage by going international. So, unless the company gains by going international, it should probably stay at home.

The task of global marketing management is complex enough when the company operates in one foreign national market. It is much more complex when the company starts operations in several countries. Marketing programmes must, in these situations, adapt to the needs and preferences of customers that have different levels of purchasing power as well as different

---

[1] Naisbitt, J. (1994) *The Global Paradox*, Nicholas Brearly Publishing, London, p. 17.

climates, languages and cultures. Moreover, patterns of competition and methods of doing business differ between nations and sometimes also within regions of the same nation. In spite of the many differences, however, it is important to hold on to similarities across borders. Some coordination of international activities will be required, but at the same time the company will gain some synergy across borders, in the way that experience and learning acquired in one country can be transferred to another.

Objectives

This book's value chain offers the reader an analytic decision-oriented framework for the development and implementation of global marketing programmes. Consequently, the reader should be able to analyze, select and evaluate the appropriate conceptual frameworks for approaching the five main management decisions connected with the global marketing process: (1) whether to internationalize, (2) deciding which markets to enter, (3) deciding how to enter the foreign market, (4) designing the global marketing programme and (5) implementing and coordinating the global marketing programme.

Having studied this book, the reader should be better equipped to understand how the firm can achieve global competitiveness through the design and implementation of market-responsive programmes.

Target audience

This book is written for people who want to develop effective and decision-oriented global marketing programmes. It can be used as a textbook for undergraduate or graduate courses in global/international marketing. A second audience is the large group of people joining 'global marketing' or 'export' courses on non-university programmes. Finally, this book is of special interest to the manager who wishes to keep abreast of the most recent developments in the global marketing field.

Prerequisites

An introductory course in marketing.

Special features

This book has been written from the perspective of the firm competing in international markets, irrespective of its country of origin. It has the following key features:

- a focus on SMEs as global marketing players;
- a decision/action-oriented approach;
- a value chain approach (both the traditional product value chain and the service value chain);
- a value network approach (including different actors vertically and horizontally);
- coverage of global buyer–seller relationships;

- extensive coverage of born globals and global account management (GAM), as an extension of the traditional key account management (KAM);
- presents new interesting theories in marketing, for example, service value chain, value innovation, blue ocean strategy, social marketing, corporate social responsibility (CSR), global account management, viral branding and sensory and celebrity branding;
- aims to be a 'true' global marketing book, with cases and exhibits from all parts of the world, including Europe, the Middle East, Africa, the Far East, North and South America;
- provides a complete and concentrated overview of the total international marketing planning process;
- many new up-to-date exhibits and cases illustrate the theory by showing practical applications.

Outline

As the book has a clear decision-oriented approach, it is structured according to the five main decisions that marketing people in companies face in connection with the global marketing process. The 20 chapters are divided into five parts. The schematic outline of the book in Figure 1 shows how the different parts fit together. Global marketing research is considered to be an integral part of the decision-making process, therefore it is included in Chapter 5, so as to use it as an important input to the decision about which markets to enter (the beginning of Part II). Examples of the practice of global marketing by actual companies are used throughout the book, in the form of exhibits. Furthermore, each chapter and part end with cases, which include questions for students.

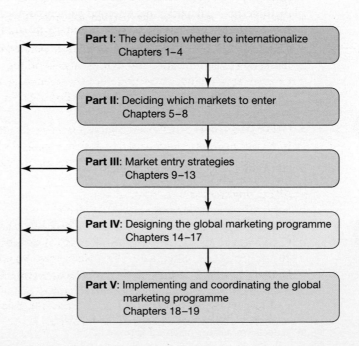

Part I: The decision whether to internationalize
Chapters 1–4

Part II: Deciding which markets to enter
Chapters 5–8

Part III: Market entry strategies
Chapters 9–13

Part IV: Designing the global marketing programme
Chapters 14–17

Part V: Implementing and coordinating the global marketing programme
Chapters 18–19

| Figure 1 | Structure of the book |

What's new in the fifth edition?

- Chapter 1 – the glocalization concept is expanded and the 'de-globalization' concept is introduced as a reverse globalization process.
- Chapter 4 – based on a new definition of customer perceived value (CPV) this chapter now contains a new comprehensive section on value net, which is a company's value creation in collaboration with suppliers and customers (vertical network partners) and complementors and competitors (horizontal network partners). Furthermore this chapter introduces the sustainable value chain, where it is explained how CSR (corporate social responsibility) influences the international competitiveness of the company.
- Chapter 5 – in this chapter a new section shows what pitfalls are connected with doing market research in India.
- Chapter 6 – new updated information on the EU and furthermore this chapter discusses the BOP (bottom of the pyramid) strategy as a new business opportunity in the world market.
- Chapter 8 – a new section about 'trickle-up' strategies (the opposite of the 'trickle-down' or waterfall approach) explains how some multinational companies are taking low-cost products developed for emerging markets and adapting them for developed countries.
- Chapter 9 – a new exhibit explains the principles of choosing the 'right' entry mode for Konica Minolta Printing Solutions.
- Chapter 12 – this chapter now includes a completely new section subsidiary growth strategies. It also explains the motives for Wal-Mart's withdrawal from the German market.
- Chapter 14 – this chapter explains the 'time-to-market' strategies, and introduces the different parameter strategies that a company can follow in the different stages of the product life cycle (PLC).
- Chapter 15 – introduces an international pricing taxonomy: the local price follower firm, the global price follower firm, the multilocal price-setter firm and the global price leader firm.
- Chapter 16 – introduces the 'banana split model', which shows how much of the retail value of a product (e.g. a banana) stays with each actor in the value chain.
- Chapter 17 – this chapter now includes a new comprehensive section on integrated marketing communication through social networking.
- Chapter 18 – includes a section about a seven-stage cross-cultural negotiation process, including a discussion about the so-called BATNA (best alternative to a negotiated agreement).
- Chapter 19 – now contains even more extensive coverage of global account management (GAM), including three models for handling the organizational set-up of GAM. Furthermore this chapter now also contains an overview model of the total international marketing planning process.
- All existing cases are now up-to-date.
- Seventeen completely new cases are available:
  Chapter cases (13 new cases): Build-A-Bear Workshop (case 1.1), LifeStraw (case 2.1), Classic Media (case 3.2), Nintendo Wii (case 4.1), Ziba Design Consultancy (case 5.3), G-20 and globalization (case 6.1), Tata Nano (case 8.1), Hello Kitty (case 11.1), Polo Ralph Lauren (case 12.1), Syngenta Crop Protection (case 13.1), Vaseline (case 15.3), Morgan Motor Company (case 17.2) and Henkel (case 19.2).
  End-of-part cases (4 new cases): Zara (case I.1), Bajaj Auto (case II.1), Raleigh Bicycles (case III.1), Sony Music Entertainment (case V.1)

Pedagogical/learning aids

One of the strengths of *Global Marketing: A decision-oriented approach* is its strong pedagogical features.

- Chapter objectives tell the reader what they should be able to do after completing each chapter.
- Real-world examples and exhibits enliven the text and enable the reader to relate to marketing models.
- End-of-chapter summaries recap the main concepts.
- Each chapter contains two case studies, which help the student relate the models presented in the chapter to a specific business situation.
- Questions for discussion allow students to probe further into important topics.
- Part cases studies – for each part there are five comprehensive case studies covering the themes met in the part. To reinforce learning, all case studies are accompanied by questions. Case studies are based on real-life companies. Further information about these companies can be found on the Internet. Company cases are derived from many different countries representing all parts of the world. Tables 1 and 2 present the chapter and part case studies.
- Multiple choice questions.
- Video library, including questions.

Table 1	Chapter case studies: overview (The video case studies can be downloaded at **www.pearsoned.co.uk/hollensen**)					
Chapter	Case study title, subtitle and related websites	Country/area of company headquarters	Geographical target area	Target market		
				B2B	B2C	
Chapter 1 Global marketing in the firm	Case study 1.1 **Build-A-Bear Workshop (BBW)** How to manage the global comeback www.buildabear.com	USA	USA, World		✓	
	Case study 1.2 **Arcor** A Latin American confectionery player is globalizing its business www.arcor.com.ar	Argentina	World		✓	
	Video case study 1.3 **Nivea** (8.56) www.nivea.com	Germany	World		✓	
Chapter 2 Initiation of internationalization	Case study 2.1 **LifeStraw** Vestergaard-Frandsen transforms dirty water into clean drinking www.vestergaard-frandsen.com	Switzerland	World (developing countries)	✓	✓	
	Case study 2.2 **Elvis Presley Enterprises Inc. (EPE)** Internationalization of a 'cult' icon www.elvis.com	USA	World		✓	
	Video case study 2.3 **TOMS Shoes** www.tomsshoes.com	USA	World (developing countries)		✓	

Table 1	*Continued*				
Chapter	**Case study title, subtitle and related websites**	**Country/area of company headquarters**	**Geographical target area**	**Target market**	
				B2B	**B2C**
Chapter 3 Internationalization theories	Case study 3.1 **Cryos** They keep the stork busy around the world www.cryos.dk	Denmark	World	✓	✓
	Case study 3.2 **Classic Media** The internationalization of 'Postman Pat' www.classicmedia.tv	UK	World		✓
	Video case study 3.3 **Reebok** (9.09) www.reebok.com and www.adidas-group.com	USA	World		✓
Chapter 4 Development of the firm's international competitiveness	Case study 4.1 **Nintendo Wii** Nintendo's wii takes first place in the world market—can it last? www.nintendo.com	Japan	World	✓	✓
	Case study 4.2 **Senseo** Creating competitiveness through an international alliance www.senseo.com	Netherlands/USA	World	✓	✓
	Video case study 4.3 **Nike** (14.03) www.nike.com	USA	World		✓
Chapter 5 Global marketing research	Case study 5.1 **Teepack Spezialmaschinen GmbH** Organizing a global survey of customer satisfaction www.teepack.com	Germany	World	✓	
	Case study 5.2 **Tchibo** Expanding the coffee shops' business system in Eastern Europe www.tchibo.com	Germany	Germany	✓	
	Video case study 5.3 **Ziba** www.ziba.com	USA	USA, World	✓	✓
Chapter 6 The political and economic environment	Case study 6.1 **G-20 and the economic and financial crises**: what on earth is globalization about? Massive protests during a meeting in London 2009 www.g20.org www.londonsummit.gov.uk	USA	World	✓	✓

| Table 1 | Continued |

Chapter	Case study title, subtitle and related websites	Country/area of company headquarters	Geographical target area	Target market B2B	B2C
	Case study 6.2 **Sauer-Danfoss** Which political/economic factor would affect a manufacturer of hydraulic components? www.sauer-danfoss.com	Denmark, USA	World	✓	
	Video case study 6.3 **Debate on globalization** (15.44) No website available	USA	USA	✓	✓
Chapter 7 The sociocultural environment	Case study 7.1 **Lifan** A Chinese sub-supplier and brand manufacturer of motacycles is aiming at the global market www.lifan.com/en	China	World	✓	✓
	Case study 7.2 **IKEA catalogue** Are there any cultural differences? www.ikea.com	Sweden, Holland	World		✓
	Video case study 7.3 **Communicating in the global world** No website available			✓	✓
Chapter 8 The international market selection process	Case study 8.1 **Tata Nano** International market selection with the world's cheapest car	India	World (emerging countries)	✓	✓
	Case study 8.2 **Philips Lighting** Screening markets in the Middle East www.philips.com	Holland	World		✓
	Video case study 8.3 **Hasbro** (9.42) www.hasbro.com	USA	World		✓
Chapter 9 Some approaches to the choice of entry mode	Case study 9.1 **Jarlsberg** The king of Norwegian cheeses is seeking new markets www.jarlsberg.com	Norway	World	✓	✓
	Case study 9.2 **Ansell condoms** Is acquisition the right way for gaining market shares in the European market? www.anselleurope.com www.lifestylesplay.com	Australia, Belgium	Europe, World		✓
	Video case study 9.3 **Understanding entry modes into the Chinese market** (16.33) No website available	World	China	✓	

Table 1	Continued				
Chapter	Case study title, subtitle and related websites	Country/area of company headquarters	Geographical target area	Target market B2B	B2C
Chapter 10 Export modes	Case study 10.1 **Lysholm Linie Aquavit** International marketing of the Norwegian Aquavit brand www.linie-aquavit.com	Norway	Germany, the rest of the World	✓	✓
	Case study 10.2 **Parle Products** An Indian biscuit manufacturer is seeking agents and cooperation partners in new export markets www.parleproducts.com	India	World	✓	✓
	Video case study 10.3 **Honest Tea** (8.25) www.honesttea.com	USA	World, USA		✓
Chapter 11 Intermediate entry modes	Case study 11.1 **Hello Kitty** Can the cartoon cat survive the buzz across the world? www.sanrio.com	Japan	World	✓	✓
	Case study 11.2 **Ka-Boo-Ki** Licensing in the LEGO brand www.kabooki.com	Denmark	World	✓	✓
	Video case study 11.3 **Marriott** (9.36) www.marriott.com	USA	World	✓	✓
Chapter 12 Hierarchical modes	Case study 12.1 **Polo Ralph Lauren** Polo moves distribution for South East Asia in-house www.ralphlauren.com	USA	World, Asia	✓	✓
	Case study 12.2 **Durex condoms** SSL will sell Durex condoms in the Japanese market through its own organization www.durex.com	UK	World	✓	✓
	Video case study 12.3 **Starbucks** (13.04) www.starbucks.com	USA	World	✓	✓
Chapter 13 International sourcing decisions and the role of the subsupplier	Case study 13.1 **Syngenta Crop Protection** A world market leader in crop protection is defending its position www.syngenta.com	Switzerland	World	✓	
	Case study 13.2 **LM Glasfiber A/S** Following its customers' international expansion in the wind turbine industry www.lmglasfiber.com	Denmark	World	✓	

Table 1 *Continued*

Chapter	Case study title, subtitle and related websites	Country/area of company headquarters	Geographical target area	Target market	
				B2B	B2C
	Video case study 13.3 **Eaton Corporation** (9.52) www.eaton.com	USA	World	✓	
Chapter 14 Product decisions	Case study 14.1 **Danish Klassic** Launch of a cream cheese in Saudi Arabia www.arla.com (regarding the Puck brand)	Denmark	Saudi Arabia Middle East	✓	✓
	Case study 14.2 **Zippo Manufacturing Company** Has product diversification beyond the lighter gone too far? www.zippo.com	USA	World	✓	✓
	Video case study 14.3 **Swiss Army** (9.07) www.swissarmy.com	Switzerland	USA, World		✓
Chapter 15 Pricing decisions and the terms of doing business	Case study 15.1 **Harley-Davidson** Does the image justify the price level? www.harley-davidson.com	USA	USA, Europe		✓
	Case study 15.2 **Gillette Co.** Is price standardization possible for razor blades? www.gillette.com	USA	World	✓	✓
	Video case study 15.3 **Vaseline** www.vaseline.com	USA	USA, World		✓
Chapter 16 Distribution decisions	Case study 16.1 **De Beers** Forward integration into the diamond industry value chain www.debeers.com	South Africa, UK, Luxembourg	Europe, World	✓	✓
	Case study 16.2 **Nokia** What is wrong in the US market for mobile phones – can Nokia recapture the number 1 position from Motorola? www.nokia.com	Finland	USA	✓	✓
	Video case study 16.3 **DHL** (10.53) www.dhl.com	Germany	World	✓	

Table 1	Continued				

Chapter	Case study title, subtitle and related websites	Country/area of company headquarters	Geographical target area	Target market B2B	B2C
Chapter 17 Communication decisions	Case study 17.1 **Helly Hansen** Sponsoring fashion clothes in the US market www.hellyhansen.com	Norway	USA	✓	✓
	Case study 17.2 **Morgan Motor Company** Can the British retro sports car brand still be successful after 100 years? www.morgan-motor.co.uk	United Kingdom	World (Europe and United States)	✓	✓
	Video case study 17.3 **BMW Motorcycles** (12.04) www.bmwmotorcycles.com www.bmw.com	Germany	USA, World	✓	✓
Chapter 18 Cross-cultural negotiations	Case study 18.1 **Mecca Cola** Marketing of a Muslim cola to the European market www.mecca-cola.com	United Arab Emirates (UAE)	Europe, Middle East	✓	✓
	Case study 18.2 **Toto** The Japanese toilet manufacturer seeks export opportunities for its high-tech brands in the United States www.toto.jp/en/	Japan	USA	✓	✓
	Video case study 18.3 **Dunkin' Donuts** (10.30) www.DunkinDonuts.com www.dunkinbrands.com	USA	World		✓
Chapter 19 Organization and control of the global marketing programme	Case study 19.1 **Mars Inc.** Merger of the European food, pet care and confectionery divisions www.mars.com	USA	World	✓	✓
	Case study 19.2 **Henkel** Should Henkel shift to a more customer-centric organization? www.henkel.com	Germany	World	✓	✓
	Video case study 19.3 **McDonald's** (36.55) www.mcdonalds.com	USA	World	✓	

Table 2	Part case studies: overview				
Part	Case study title, subtitle and related websites	Country/area of company headquarters	Geographical target area	Target market	
				B2B	B2C
Part I **The decision whether to internationalize**	Case study I.1 **Zara** The Spanish retailer goes to the top of world fashion www.inditex.com/en	Spain	World	✓	✓
	Case study I.2 **Manchester United** Still trying to establish a global brand www.manutd.com	UK	World, USA	✓	✓
	Case study I.3 **Bridgestone Tyres** European marketing strategy www.bridgestone.com	Japan	Europe	✓	✓
	Case study I.4 **Cereal Partners Worldwide (CPW)** The number 2 world player is challenging the number 1 – Kellogg Company www.cerealpartners.com	Switzerland, USA	World		✓
Part II **Deciding which markets to enter**	Case study II.1 **Bajaj Motor Company** The Indian motorcycle manufacturer internationalizes its business www.bajajauto.com	India	Emerging countries		✓
	Case study II.2 **Female Health Company** The female condom, Femidom, is seeking a foothold in the world market for contraceptive products www.femalehealth.com	USA	World (governmental organizations)	✓	✓
	Case study II.3 **Tipperary Mineral Water Company** Market selection inside/outside Europe www.tipperary-water.ie	Ireland	Europe	✓	✓
	Case study II.4 **Skagen Designs** Becoming an international player in designed watches www.skagendesigns.com	USA (Denmark)	World	✓	✓

Table 2	*Continued*				

Part	Case study title, subtitle and related websites	Country/area of company headquarters	Geographical target area	Target market	
				B2B	B2C
Part III Market entry strategies	Case study III.1 **Raleigh Bicycles** Is the iconic bicycle brand still having a chance on the world market? www.raleigh.co.uk	UK	World	✓	✓
	Case study III.2 **IKEA** Expanding through franchising to the South American market? www.ikea.com	Sweden, Holland	South America (Brazil)	✓	✓
	Case Study III.3 **Autoliv airbags** Transforming Autoliv into a global company www.autoliv.com	Sweden, United States	World	✓	
	Case study III.4 **IMAX Corporation** Globalization of the film business www.imax.com	Canada	World	✓	✓
Part IV Designing the global marketing programme	Case study IV.1 **Absolut Vodka** Defending and attacking for a better position in the global vodka market www.absolut.com www.pernod.net	France, Sweden	World, Eastern Europe		✓
	Case study IV.2 **Guinness** How can the Irish iconic beer brand compensate for the declining sales in the home market? www.diageo.com www.guinness.com	UK, Ireland	World	✓	✓
	Case study IV.3 **Dyson Vacuum Cleaner** Shifting from domestic to international marketing with the famous bagless vacuum cleaner www.dyson.co.uk www.dysonairblade.co.uk	UK	USA, the rest of the World	✓	✓
	Case study IV.4 **Triumph Motorcycles Ltd** Rising from the ashes in the international motorcycle business www.triumph.co.uk	UK	World		✓

Table 2	*Continued*				
Part	Case study title, subtitle and related websites	Country/area of company headquarters	Geographical target area	Target market	
				B2B	B2C
Part V Implementing and coordinating the global marketing programme	Case study V.1 **Sony Music Entertainment** New worldwide organizational structure and the marketing, planning and budgeting of Pink's new album www.sonymusic.com	USA, Japan	World	✓	✓
	Case study V.2 **OneCafé** A 'born global' penetrates the coffee industry	Sweden	World	✓	✓
	Case study V.3 **Philips Shavers** Maintaining shaving leadership in the world market www.philips.com	Holland	World	✓	✓
	Case study V.4 **Vipp AS** An SME uses global branding to break into the international waste bin business www.vipp.dk	Denmark	Europe		✓

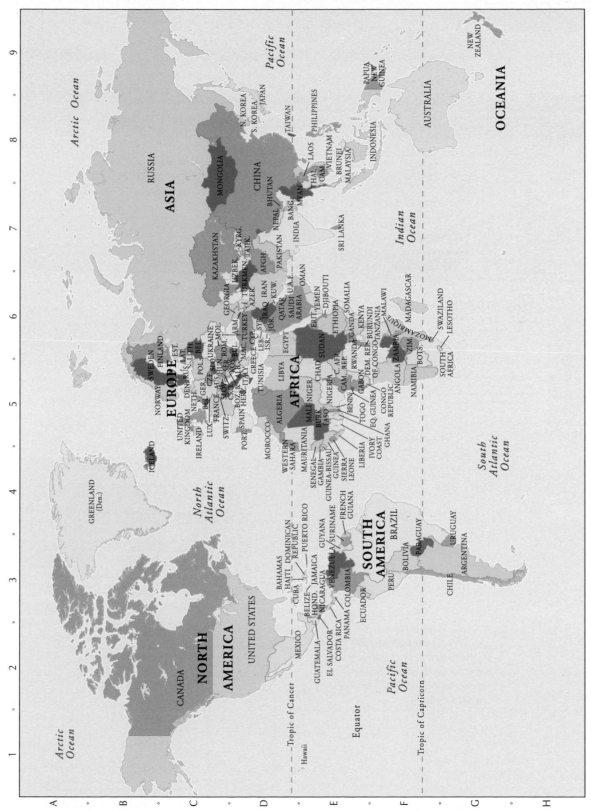

GUIDED TOUR

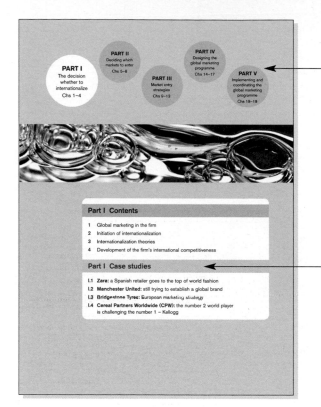

Flowcharts show how each part of the book fits into the five stages of the global marketing process.

A wealth of longer **Case Studies**, drawn from a wide range of countries, products and industries, enhance the end of each part of the book.

An **Overview** outlines the topics, Case Studies and learning objectives in each chapter, showcasing what you should expect to learn.

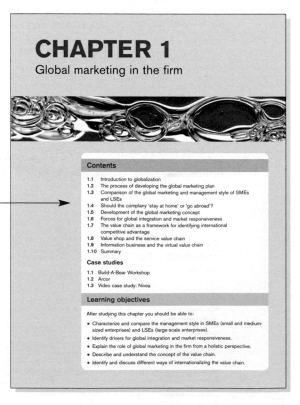

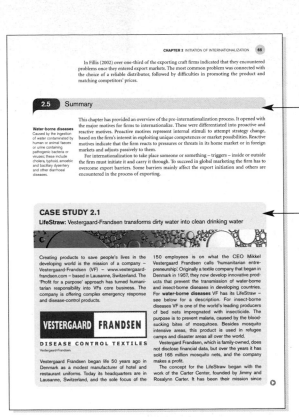

The chapter **Summary** highlights the key concepts and issues, along with a concise checklist of the topics covered.

Two insightful **Case Studies** conclude each chapter, providing a range of material for seminars and private study by illustrating the real-life applications and implications of the topics covered in the chapter.

Marginal definitions highlight the key terms in each chapter. A full glossary can be found at the end of the book and on the *Global Marketing* website at: **www.pearsoned.co.uk/hollensen**

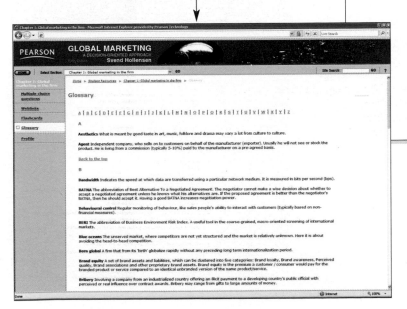

New and engaging **Exhibits** analyse and discuss specific companies to show how the theories in the chapter are used by well-known brands in the business world.

After reading the chapter, take your learning further by watching a Video Case Study from a leading international company on the *Global Marketing* companion website at **www.pearsoned.co.uk/hollensen** and answering the questions.

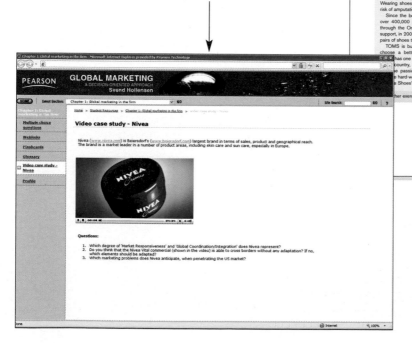

Test yourself at the end of each chapter with a set of **Questions for Discussion**. Then try answering the self-assessment **Multiple Choice Questions** that accompany each chapter on the *Global Marketing* Companion Website at **www.pearsoned.co.uk/hollensen**.

The **References** list sources book journals articles and websites that will help develop your understanding and inspire independent learning.

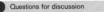

ACKNOWLEDGEMENTS

Writing any book is a long-term commitment and involves time-consuming effort. The successful completion of a book depends on the support and generosity of many people and the realization of this book is certainly no exception.

I wish to thank the many scholars whose articles, books and other materials I have cited or quoted. However, it is not possible to acknowledge everyone by name. In particular I am deeply indebted to the following individuals and organizations. I thank you all for your help and contributions:

University of Southern Denmark

- Management at University of Southern Denmark provided the best possible environment for writing and completing this project. I would especially like to thank the Head of the Department of Border Region Studies, Elisabeth Vestergaard, for her support during the writing process.
- Colleagues provided encouragement and support during the writing process. I would especially like to thank the Secretaries, Charlotte Lund Hansen, Angela Hansen, Janne Øe Hobson and Project Coordinator, Simon Kleinschmidt Salling, at the Department of Border Region Studies for their helpfulness and support during the writing process.
- The library at University of Southern Denmark provided articles and books from different worldwide sources.

Reviewers

- Reviewers provided suggestions which were useful in improving many parts of the text.
- In the development of this text a number of reviewers have been involved, whom I would like to thank for their important and valuable contribution: Henrik Agndal, Jönköping International Business School; Grahame Fallon, University College Northampton; Ronald Salters, Fontys Eindhoven.
- Professor Alkis Magdalinos contributed with many necessary corrections and suggestions for improvement in different sections of the book.

Case contributors

- Wim Wils, Fontys Eindhoven, for Case 8.2: Philips Lighting.
- Sjoerd Drost, Product manager, Philips Shavers, for Case V.3: Philips Shavers.
- Jon A. J. Wilson, Senior Lecturer in Advertising and Marketing Communications, University of Greenwich, London, for Exhibit 17.5.

I also wish to acknowledge the help from the following firms whose managers have provided valuable material that has enabled me to write the following cases. I have been in direct personal contact with most of the case companies and thank the managers involved for their very useful comments. Especially, I would like to thank:

Chapter cases:

- Build-A-Bear Workshop, Denmark for Case 1.1 on BBW.
- Family Vestergaard-Frandsen for Case 2.1 on LifeStraw.
- Cryos, Aarhus, Denmark for Case 3.1 on Cryos.
- Entertainment Rights, London, UK for Case 3.2 on Postman Pat.
- Teepack Spezialmaschinen GmbH, Düsseldorf, Germany for Case 5.1 on Teepack Spezialmaschinen.
- IKEA, Sweden for Case 7.2 on the IKEA Catalogue.
- Jarlsberg, Norway for Case 9.1 on Jarlsberg.
- Arcus AS, Oslo, Norway for Case 10.1 on Lysholm Linie Aquavit.
- Sanrio, Europe for Case 11.1 on Hello Kitty.
- Ka-Boo-Ki, Ikast, Denmark for Case 11.2 on Ka-Boo-Ki.
- Polo Ralph Lauren, USA for Case 12.1 on Polo Ralph Lauren.
- Syngenta, Switzerland for Case 13.1 on Syngenta.
- Morgan Motor Company, UK for Case 17.2 on Morgan Motor Company.
- Henkel, Germany for Case 19.2 on Henkel.

Part cases:

- Inditex, Spain for Case I.1: Zara.
- Bridgestone/Firestone, Bruxelles, Belgium/Tokyo, Japan for Case I.3: Bridgestone Tyres
- Bajaj family, India for Case II.1: Bajaj Motor Company.
- Skagen Designs, Reno, USA and Copenhagen, Denmark for Case II.4: Skagen Designs
- Raleigh Bicycles, UK for Case III.1: Raleigh Bicycles.
- Autoliv AB, Stockholm, Sweden for Case III.3: Autoliv airbags
- IMAX Corporation, Toronto, Canada for Case III.4: Imax Corporation
- The Absolut Company, a division of Vin & Sprit AB, Stockholm, Sweden for Case IV.1: Absolut Vodka
- Sony BMG, New York, USA for Case V.1: Sony Music Entertainment
- OneCafé International AB, Sweden for Case V.2: OneCafé
- Philips Shavers, Eindhoven, Holland for Case V.3: Philips Shavers
- Vipp A/S, Copenhagen, Denmark for Case V.4: Vipp.

I would also like to thank The Tussauds Group, especially Global Marketing Director Nicky Marsh from London and Cathy Wong, External Affairs Consultant from Shanghai for their contribution to Exhibit 14.4.

I am also grateful to the following international advertising agencies, which have provided me with examples of standardized and/or localized advertising campaigns:

- J. Walter Thompson (JWT Europe), London who contributed with a European ad for LUX soap.
- Hindustan Thompson (HTA), Bombay, India who contributed with an ad for Kellogg's Basmati Flakes in India and an ad for LUX soap in India.

I would also like to thank LEGO and Langnese (special thanks to Silke for her efforts to get the Magnum ad) for their contributions to different examples in the book.

I am grateful to my publisher, Pearson Education. I would like to thank Editorial Director Matthew Smith, Acquisitions Editor Rachel Gear, Desk Editors Sarah Wild and Mary Lince and Marketing Manager Oliver Adams for their help with this edition.

I also extend my greatest gratitude to my colleagues at the University of Southern Denmark for their constant help and inspiration.

Finally, I thank my family for their support through the revision process. I am pleased to dedicate this version to Jonna, Nanna and Julie.

Svend Hollensen
University of Southern Denmark, Sønderborg,
Department of Border Region Studies, Denmark
May 2010

svend@sam.sdu.dk

PUBLISHER'S ACKNOWLEDGEMENTS

We are grateful to the following for permission to reproduce copyright material:

Figures

Figures 1.2, 1.14, 2.3, 2.4, 11.3, 12.2 from *Essentials of Global Marketing*, FT/Prentice Hall (Hollensen, S. 2008), Pearson Education Ltd; Figure 1.3 from The strategy concept I: five Ps for strategy, *California Management Review*, Vol. 30, No. 1, pp. 11–24, Fig. on p. 14 (Mintzberg, H. 1987), Copyright © 1987, by The Regents of the University of California. Reprinted from the *California Management Review*, Vol. 30, No. 1. By permission of The Regents; Figure 1.4 from Rethinking incrementalism, *Strategic Management Journal*, 9, pp. 75–91 (Johnson, G. 1988), Copyright 1988 © of John Wiley & Sons Ltd. Reproduced with permission; Figure 1.6 from A framework for analysis of strategy development in globalizing markets, *Journal of International Marketing*, Vol. 5(1), p. 11 (Solberg, C. A. 1997), reprinted by permission of American Marketing Association; Figure 1.10 reprinted with the permission of The Free Press, a Division of Simon & Schuster, Inc., from *Competitive Advantage: Creating and Sustaining Superior Performance* by Michael E. Porter. Copyright © 1985, 1998 by Michael E. Porter. All rights reserved; Figure on page 66 from *World's Water 1998–1999* by Peter H. Gleick. Copyright © 1998 Island Press. Reproduced by permission of Island Press, Washington, DC; Figure 3.1 adapted from *International føretagsekonomi*, Norstedts (Forsgren, M. and Johanson, J. 1975) p. 16, with permission from Mats Forsgren; Figures 3.2, 3.3 from Internationalization: evolution of a concept, *Journal of General Management*, Vol. 14, No. 2 (Welch, L. S. and Loustarinen, R. 1988), reproduced with permission from The Braybrooke Press Ltd; Figure 3.6 from *Strategies in Global Competition*, Croom Helm (Hood, N. and Vahlne, J. E. eds 1988) p. 298, Internationalization in industrial systems by Johanson, J. and Mattson, L. G., with permission from Taylor & Francis; Figure 3.7 adapted from *Internationalization Handbook for the Software Business*, Centre of Expertise for Software Product Business (Âijö, T., Kuivalainen, O., Saarenketo, S., Lindqvist, J. and Hanninen, H. 2005) p. 6; Figure 4.5 adapted from Competitive advantage: merging marketing and competence-based perspective, *Journal of Business and Industrial Marketing*, Vol. 9, No. 4, pp. 42–53 (Jüttner, U. and Wehrli, H. P. 1994), with permission from Dr. Hans P. Wehrli; Figure 4.6 from Exploiting the core competences of your organization, *Long Range Planning*, Vol. 27, No. 4, p. 74 (Tampoe, M. 1994), Copyright 1994, with permission from Elsevier; Figure 4.9 reprinted from *European Management Journal*, Vol. 26, Issue 4, Weber M., The business case for corporate social responsibility: a company-level measurement approach for CSR, pp. 247–61, Copyright 2008, with permission from Elsevier; Figure 5.5 from *Marketing Research*, 7th ed., Wiley (McDaniel Jr., C. and Gates, R. 2007) p. 283, Copyright © 2007, reproduced with permission of John Wiley & Sons, Inc; Figure 5.8 from *Marketing Research: An International Approach*, FT/Prentice Hall (Schmidt, M. I. and Hollensen, S. 2006) p. 587, Pearson Education Ltd; Figure 6.3 from Czinkota/Ronkainen. *Global Marketing*, 1E. © 1996 South-Western, a part of Cengage Learning, Inc. Reproduced by permission. www.cengage.com/permissions; Figure 7.3 from *International Marketing: A Cultural Approach*, Pearson Education Ltd. (Usunier, J.-C. 2000); Figure 8.6 from *European Business: An issue-based approach*, Pearson Education Ltd. (Welford, R. and Prescott, K. 1996); Figure 8.11 from Keegan, Warren J.; Green, Mark, *Global Marketing*, 2nd, © 2000. Electronically reproduced by permission of Pearson

Education, Inc., Upper Saddle River, New Jersey; Figure 8.12 from *International Marketing Strategy*, 2nd ed., Prentice Hall (Bradley, F. 1995), Pearson Education Ltd; Figure 8.13 from Market expansion strategies in multinational marketing, *Journal of Marketing*, Vol. 43, Spring, p. 84 (Ayal, I. and Zif, J. 1979), reprinted by permission of American Marketing Association; Figure 11.6 adapted from *Strategiske allianser i globale strategier*, Norges Eksportråd (Lorange, P. and Roos, J. 1995) p. 16, reprinted by permission of Index Publishing/Norwegian Trade Council; Figures 11.7, 11.8 from *Strategies for Joint Ventures* (Harrigan, K. R. 1985), reprinted by permission of K. R. Harrigan; Figure 12.3 reprinted by permission from Macmillan Publishers Ltd: *Journal of International Business Studies*, Vol. 25, No. 1, pp. 45–64, Toward a theory of international new ventures, by Oviatt, B. M. and McDougall, P. P., copyright 1994, published by Palgrave Macmillan; Figure 12.4 from Organisational dimensions of global marketing, *European Journal of Marketing*, Vol. 23, No. 5, pp. 43–57 (Raffée, H. and Kreutzer, R. 1989), Emerald Publishing Ltd., www.emeraldinsight.com; Figure 12.5 from Why are subsidiaries divested? A conceptual framework, *Working Paper No. 3–93*, Fig. 2 (Benito, G. 1996), reprinted by permission of Institute of International Economics and Management, Copenhagen Business School; Figure 13.1 adapted from Alihankintajarjestelma 1990-luvulla [subcontracting system in the 1990s], *Publications of SITRA*, No. 114, p. 22 (Lehtinen, U. 1991), reprinted by permission of Sitra; Figure 13.3 from A total cost/value model for supply chain competitiveness, *Journal of Business Logistics*, Vol. 13, No. 2 (Cavinato, J. L. 1992), Council of Logistics Management; Figure 13.4 adapted from Interactive strategies in supply chains: a double-edged portfolio approach to SME, *Subcontractors Positioning Paper, presented at the 8th Nordic Conference on Small Business Research* (Blenker, P. and Christensen, P. 1994), reprinted by permission of Per Blenker; Figure 13.5 from *Strategies for International Industrial Marketing*, Croom Helm (Turnbull, P. W. and Valla, J. P. 1986), with permission from Taylor & Francis; Figure 13.6 from Relationship marketing from a value system perspective, *International Journal of Service Industry Management*, No. 5, pp. 54–73 (Jüttner, U. and Wehrli, H. P. 1994), Emerald Publishing Ltd., www.emeraldinsight.com; Figure on page 457 adapted from Standardisation: an integrated approach to global marketing, *European Journal of Marketing*, Vol. 22, No. 10, pp. 19–30 (Kreutzer, R. 1988), reprinted by permission of Emerald Group Publishing Ltd; www.emeraldinsight.com; Figure 14.3 from *Marketing Management: A Relationship Approach*, 2nd edition, FT/Prentice Hall (Hollensen, S. 2010) Fig. 11.7, Pearson Education Ltd; Figure 14.4 from *Marketing Management: A Relationship Approach*, FT/Prentice Hall (Hollensen, S. 2010) Fig. 7.5, Pearson Education Ltd; Figure 14.7 after Competitive analysis using matrix displays, *Long Range Planning*, Vol. 17, No. 3, pp. 98–114 (McNamee, P. 1984), copyright 1984, with permission from Elsevier; Figure 14.8 from *International Marketing: Analysis and Strategy, 2nd Edition*, 2nd ed., Macmillan (Onkvisit, S. and Shaw, J. J. 1993) p. 483, reprinted by permission of Sak Onkvisit; Figures 14.10, 14.11 from New products: cutting the time to market, *Long Range Planning*, Vol. 28, No. 2, pp. 61–78 (Töpfer, A. 1995), Copyright 1995, with permission from Elsevier; Figure 14.14 adapted from *International Marketing: Analysis and Strategy*, 2nd ed., Macmillan (Onkvisit, S. and Shaw, J. J. 1993) p. 534, reprinted by permission of Sak Onkvisit; Figure 14.20 adapted from Environmentally responsible logistics systems, *International Journal of Physical Distribution and Logistics Management*, Vol. 25, No. 2, p. 23 (Wu, H. J. and Dunn, S. C. 1995), Emerald Group Publishing Ltd; Figure 15.3 from Hax, Arnoldo C.; Majluf, Nicholas S., *Strategic Management: An Integrative Perspective*, 1st, © 1984. Electronically reproduced by permission of Pearson Education, Inc., Upper Saddle River, New Jersey; Figure 15.4 from Kotler, Philip, *Marketing Management: Analysis, Planning, Implementation and Control*, 7th, © 1991. Electronically reproduced by permission of Pearson Education, Inc., Upper Saddle River, New Jersey; Figure 15.5 from Pricing conditions in the European Common Market, *European Management Journal*, Vol. 12, No. 2, pp. 163–70, p. 168 (Diller, H. and Bukhari, I. 1994), Copyright 1994, with permission from Elsevier; Figure 15.7 from The European pricing bomb – and how to cope with it, *Marketing and Research Today*, February, p. 26 (Simon, H. and Kucher, E. 1993), Copyright ESOMAR; Figure 15.9 from *International Marketing Strategy: Analysis, Development and Implementation*, Thomson Learning (Phillips, C. *et al.*

1994) p. 454, with permission from Cengage Learning; Figure 16.2 from *Marketing Management: An Overview*, The Dryden Press (Lewison, D. M. 1996) p. 271, with permission from Dale M. Lewison; Figure 16.4 adapted from *Marketing Management: An Overview*, The Dryden Press (Lewison, D. M. 1996) p. 279, with permission from Dale M. Lewison; Figure 16.8 from *International Marketing and Export Management*, 2nd ed., Pearson Education Ltd. (Albaum, G. *et al.* 1994) p. 419; Figure 16.9 adapted from *Food, Inc. – Corporate concentration from farm to consumer*, UK Food Group (Vorley, B. 2003) Fig. 7.2, p. 52, with permission from UK Food Group; Figure 16.11 from *International Marketing*, Heinemann (Paliwoda, S. 1993) p. 300, reprinted with permission from Butterworth-Heinemann Publishers, a division of Reed Educational & Professional Publishing Ltd; Figure on page 700 from Sauer-Danfoss, Inc; Figure 19.12 from *International Marketing: Planning and Practice*, Macmillan (Samli, A. C. *et al.* 1993) p. 421, with permission from Professor Coskun Samli.

Maps

Map on page xxix from Daniels, John; Radebaugh, Lee; Sullivan, Daniel, *International Business, 12th*, © 2009. Electronically reproduced by permission of Pearson Education, Inc., Upper Saddle River, New Jersey.

Screenshots

Screenshot on page 97 from Cryos International – International Departments, http://dk.cryosinternational.com/about-us/international-departments.aspx, with permission from Cryos International – Denmark ApS; Screenshot on page 97 from http://dk.cryosinternational.com/clinics/products.aspx, with permission from Cryos International – Denmark ApS; Screenshot on page 199 from www.teepack.com, reprinted by permission of Teepack Spezialmaschinen GmbH & Co. KG; Screenshot on page 248 from Pocari Sweat website, www.pocarisweat.info, Otsuka Pharmaceutical Co., Ltd; Screenshot on page 435 from www.ikea.com, reprinted by permission of Ikea Ltd; Screenshot on page 443 from www.autoliv.com, reprinted by permission of Autoliv; Screenshot on page 512 from www.zippo.com, reprinted by permission of Zippo Manufacturing Company.

Tables

Table 2.1 adapted from *International Marketing and Export Management*, 2nd ed., Addison Wesley (Albaum, G. *et al.* 1994) p. 31, reprinted by permission of Pearson Education Ltd; Table 3.1 adapted from First steps in internationalisation: Concepts and evidence from a sample of small high-technology firms, *Journal of International Management*, Vol. 7, Issue 3, p. 197 (Jones, M. V. 2001), Copyright © 2001, with permission from Elsevier; Table 4.1 from Composite strategy: the combination of collaboration and competition, *Journal of General Management*, Vol. 21, No. 1, pp. 1–23 (Burton, J. 1995), reprinted with permission from The Braybrooke Press Ltd; Table on page 135 from http://www.vgchartz.com/hwcomps.php?weekly=1, with permission from Brett Walton, VGChartz; Table on page 138 adapted from *Coffee machines: recommendations for policy design, Report* 7th August, Topten International Group (Nipkow, J. and Bush, E. 2008); Table on page 138 adapted from Euromonitor International, www.euromonitor.com; Table 6.1 from Big Mac Index, *The*

Economist, 4 February 2009, © The Economist Newspaper Limited, London (4.2.09); Table 7.2 adapted from *International Marketing Strategy: Analysis, Development and Implementation*, Thomson Learning (Phillips, C., Doole, I. and Lowe, R. 1994), with permission from Cengage Learning; Table 7.4 from *Going International*, Random House (Copeland, L. and Griggs, L. 1985) p. 62, reprinted by permission The Sagalyn Agency; Table 10.1 from *Entry Strategies for International Markets: Second Revised and Expanded Edition*, Jossey Bass (Root, F. R. 1998) pp. 90–91, Copyright © 1998, reproduced with permission of John Wiley & Sons, Inc; Table 11.3 adapted from *International Market Entry and Development*, Harvester Wheatsheaf/Prentice Hall (Young, S., Hamill, J., Wheeler, S. and Davies, J. R. 1989) p. 233, Pearson Education Ltd; Table 13.1 from Relationship marketing from a value system perspective, *International Journal of Service Industry Management*, No. 5, pp. 54–73 (Jüttner, U. and Wehrli, H. P. 1994), Emerald Publishing Ltd., www.emeraldinsight.com; Table on page 458 from *Essentials of Global Marketing*, FT/Prentice Hall (Hollensen, S. 2008) p. 299, Table 1, Pearson Education Ltd; Table 14.3 adapted from The international dimension of branding: strategic considerations and decisions, *International Marketing Review*, Vol. 6, No. 3, pp. 22–34 (Onkvisit, S. and Shaw, J. J. 1989), Emerald Publishing Ltd., www.emeraldinsight.com; Table 14.4 from The future of consumer branding as seen from the picture today, *Journal of Consumer Marketing*, Vol. 12, No. 4, p. 22 (Boze, B. V. and Patton, C. R. 1995), Emerald Group Publishing Ltd; Table 15.5 adapted from *International Marketing Analysis and Strategy*, 2nd Edition, Macmillan (Onkvisit, S. and Shaw, J. J. 1993) p. 799, courtesy of Sak Onkvisit; Table 17.3 from *International Marketing Strategy: Analysis, Development and Implementation*, Thomson Learning (Phillips, C. *et al.* 1994) p. 362, with permission from Cengage Learning; Table 17.5 from Guidelines for managing an international sales force, *Industrial Marketing Management*, Vol. 24, p. 138 (Honeycutt, E. D. and Ford, J. B. 1995), Copyright 1995, with permission from Elsevier; Table 19.1 adapted from *Principles and Practice of Marketing*, 3rd ed., McGraw-Hill (Jobber, D. 1995) © 1995 McGraw-Hill, with the kind permission of the McGraw-Hill Publishing Company; Table 19.2 from *International Marketing: Planning and Practice*, Macmillan (Samli, A. C. *et al.* 1993) p. 425, with permission from Professor Coskun Samli; Table 19.3 adapted from Kotler, Philip, *Marketing Management: Analysis, Planning, Implementation and Control*, 9th, © 1997. Electronically reproduced by permission of Pearson Education, Inc., Upper Saddle River, New Jersey.

Text

Exhibit 2.3 from *Essentials of Global Marketing*, FT/Prentice Hall (Hollensen, S. 2008) pp. 47–48, Pearson Education Ltd; Extract on page 99 from *Open Your Own Cryos Sperm Bank*, Cryos International, with permission from Cryos International – Denmark ApS; Case study 4.2 from case study about Senseo written by Svend Hollensen, Senseo; Case Study 9.1 from case study about Jarlsberg written by Svend Hollensen Tine BA; Case Study 11.1 adapted from Top Cat: how 'Hello Kitty' conquered the world – Japan's new tourism ambassador by Esther Walker, *The Independent*, 21 May 2008, http://www.independent.co.uk/news/world/asia/top-cat-how-hello-kitty-conquered-the-world-831522.html, copyright The Independent, www.independent.co.uk; Case Study 12.1 from case study written by Svend Hollensen using Polo Ralph Lauren Press Releases, Annual Report 2009, Polo Ralph Lauren; Exhibit 13.1 from Network sourcing: A hybrid approach, *Journal of Supply Chain Management* (formerly *International Journal of Purchasing and Materials Management*), 5 April, pp. 17–24 (Hines, P. 2006), Copyright © 2006, 1995 Institute for Supply Management, Inc., with permission from John Wiley & Sons, Inc; Extract on pages 462–463 from Developing global strategies for service businesses, *California Management Review*, Vol. 38, No. 2 (Lovelock, C. and Yip, G. S. 1996), Copyright © 1996, by The Regents of the University of California. Reprinted from the *California Management Review*, Vol. 38, No. 2. By permission of The Regents; Exhibit 14.3 from *Essentials of Global Marketing*, FT/Prentice Hall (Hollensen, S. 2008) p. 311, Exhibit 11.1,

Pearson Education Ltd; Exhibit 14.8 from Roundup – A global brand for multiple markets, Monsanto Europe S.A.; Case Study 15.3 from History of Vaseline, http://www.vaseline.co.uk, with the kind permission of Unilever; Extract on page 561 from *International Marketing Management*, 5th ed., South-Western, a division of Thomson Learning (Jain, S. C. 1996) p. 523, with permission from Professor Subhash C. Jain; Extract on page 563 from *International Marketing and Export Management*, 2nd ed., Pearson Education Ltd. (Albaum, G. *et al.* 1994) p. 419; Extract on pages 572–73 adapted from *Food, Inc. – Corporate concentration from farm to consumer*, UK Food Group (Vorley, B. 2003) p. 53, with permission from UK Food Group; Exhibit 17.5 from Exhibit written (including interviews conducted by) Jonathan A. J. Wilson, with permission from Jonathan A. J. Wilson, Senior Lecturer (Advertising & Marketing Communications), University of Greenwich, London UK.

Photographs

The publisher would like to thank the following for their kind permission to reproduce their photographs:

(Key: b-bottom; c-centre; l-left; r-right; t-top)

The Absolut Company: 627t, 627b, 632; Alamy Images: Bildagentur-online 16, david pearson 287t, J.F.T.L. Images 100, P Cox 287b, Thomas J. Peterson 246, Justin Kase z02z 571; Ansell: 329; Arla Foods: 509l, 509r, 510l, 510c, 510r; Bajaj Auto: 283, 296, 297; Build A Bear: 40, 41; Copyright © Inditex: 146, 147; Corbis: Pawel Libera 668; Courtesy of Cadbury plc: 617; Courtesy of Dyson: 641, 647; Courtesy of Philips Consumer Electronics: 292, 731, 735l, 735r, 736l, 736r, Jaap Vliegenthart (photographer) 737; Courtesy of Procter & Gamble UK: 546; Courtesy of Syngenta: 422, 423tr, 423l, 423cr, 423br; Courtesy of Unilever Danmark A/S: 547; Diageo plc: 596, 634, 636; DK Images: Tony Souter 129; Ducati: 497, 498; Elvis Presley Enterprises: © Elvis Presley Enterprises, Inc. Used by permission 68; Fisherman's Friend is a registered trademark of Lofthouse of Fleetwood Ltd.: 344; Getty Images: ROBYN BECK/AFP 245, Bob Riha Jr/WireImage 133, Hassan Ammar/AFP 511, Kevin Lee/Bloomberg 56, SAUL LOEB/AFP 230, Tiffany Rose/WireImage 69, WireImage 723; Gleeson group: 304; Helly Hansen: 620; Henkel: 717l, 717r; IMAX Corporation: 450; Inter IKEA Systems BV: 256l, 256r; Courtesy of J. Benjamin, The Network Agency: Joachim Hansen 598; © 2010 The LEGO Group. Used with permission.: 14, 382, 609b, 611; Madame Tussauds: 479l; Madame Tussauds Shanghai: 479r; Manchester United Ltd.: 152; McDonalds Corporation: 24t, 24c, 24b; Mecca Cola: 678; Monsanto Company: 488; Morgan Motor Company: 621, 622l, 622r; Nivea and Beiersdorf UK Ltd.: 47; Nokia UK: 582; One Laptop per Child: 279; OneCafe International: 727, 728tl, 728tr, 728cl, 728cr, 728bl, 728br, 729l, 729r, 730l, 730r; Parle Products Pvt. Ltd: 352; Press Association Images: Ann Heisenfelt/AP/EMPICS 545, Martin Keane/PA/EMPICS 716; Raleigh International Ltd: 429, 431, 433, 434; Ralph Lauren Fragrances: 400; Rex Features: 20th Century Fox/Everett 591; Sanex: 278; Sanrio License GmbH: 379, 381; Sauer-Danfoss Ltd: 231t, 231b; Senseo: 142; Skagen: 309, 311; Tchibo: 200; The Female Health Company: 300; The Nestlé name and image is reproduced with kind permission of Société des Produits Nestlé S.A.: 163, 489, 618; Tine: 328, 610tl, 610tr, 610bl, 610br; TOTO: 680; Vestergaard-Frandsen: 65, 67; Vipp Inc.: 740t, 740b, 741; www.arcus.no: 351; www.lm Glasfiber.com. Copyright LM Glasfiber A/S: 426; Zinkia Entertainment: Pocoyo Series © Zinkia Entertainment, S.A. 30; Zippo: 513.

In some instances we have been unable to trace the owners of copyright material, and we would appreciate any information that would enable us to do so.

ABBREVIATIONS

ACs	advanced countries
APEC	Asia Pacific Economic Cooperation
ASEAN	Association of South East Asian Nations
B2B	business to business
B2C	business to consumer
BATNA	best alternative to a negotiated agreement
BDA	before–during–after
BERI	Business Environment Risk Index
BMI	Business Monitor International
BOP	bottom of the pyramid
BT	British Telecommunications
C2B	consumer to business
C2C	consumer to consumer
C&F	customs and freight
CATI	computer-aided telephone interviews
CDMA	code division multiple access (wireless mobile)
CEO	chief executive officer
CFR	cost and freight
CIF	cost, insurance and freight
CIP	carriage and insurance paid to
CMM-SEI	Carnegie Mellon University's Software Engineering Institute
COO	country of origin
CPT	carriage paid to
CRM	customer relationship management
CSR	corporate social responsibility
DAF	delivered at frontier
DDP	delivered duty paid
DDU	delivered duty unpaid
DEQ	delivered ex-quay
DES	delivered ex-ship
DMR	digital remastering
DSS	decision support system
ECB	European Central Bank
ECSC	European Coal and Steel Community
EDF	Environmental Defense Fund (USA)
EDI	electronic data interchange
EEA	European Economic Area
EEC	European Economic Community
EFTA	European Free Trade Area
EMC	export management company
EMEA	Europe, Middle East and Africa
EMU	European Economic and Monetary Union
EPAC	electronically power-assisted cycles
EPRG	ethnocentric, polycentric, regiocentric, geocentric
EU	European Union: title for the former EEC used since the ratification of the Maastricht Treaty in 1992

EURATOM	European Atomic Energy Community
EXW	ex-works
FAB	flavoured alcoholic beverages
FAS	free alongside ship
FCA	free carrier
FDA	Food and Drug Administration (USA)
FDI	foreign direct investment: a market entry strategy in which a company invests in a subsidiary or partnership in a foreign market (joint venture)
FHI	Family Health International
FMCG	fast-moving consumer goods
FOB	free on board: the seller quotes a price covering all expenses up to the point of shipment
GA	global account
GAM	global account management
GATT	General Agreement on Tarrifs and Trade
GDP	gross domestic product
GEL	General Electric Lighting
GNI	gross national income
GNP	gross national product: the total 'gross value' of all goods and services produced in the economy in one year
GPC	global pricing contract
GRP	gross rating point
GSM	global system for mobile communications (wireless mobile)
GWD	guinea worm disease
HLL	Hindustan Latex Ltd
HOG	Harley Owners Group
IDR	intermediation–disintermediation–reintermediation
IMC	integrated marketing communications
IMF	International Monetary Fund
IMS	international market selection
IMUSA	Independent Manchester United Supporters Association
IPI	industrial products tax
IPLC	international product life cycle
ISO	International Standards Organization
ISP	internet service provider
IT	information technology
KAM	key account management
KSF	key success factor
L/C	letter of credit
LCC	low-cost car
LDCs	less developed countries
LSEs	large-scale enterprises
LTO	long-term orientation
M&A	merger and acquisition
MIS	marketing information system
MNCs	multinational corporations
MNE	multinational enterprise
MSRC	manufacturer's suggested retail price
NAFTA	North American Free Trade Agreement: a free trade agreement to establish an open market between the United States, Canada and Mexico
NASSCOM	National Association of Software and Service Companies
NICs	newly industrialized countries
NPD	new product development
NSB	National Standards Board

OE	operational effectiveness
OECD	Organization for Economic Cooperation and Development: a multinational forum that allows the major industrialized nations to discuss economic policies and events
OEM	original equipment manufacturer (outsourcer)
OLI	ownership-location-internalization
OPEC	Organization for Petroleum Exporting Countries
OTC	over the counter
OTS	opportunity to see
PDA	personal digital assistant
PEST	political/legal, economic, social/cultural, technological
PLC	product life cycle: a theory that characterizes the sales history of products as passing through four stages: introduction, growth, maturity, decline
POS	point of sale
PPP	purchasing-power parity
PR	public relations
QDF	quality deployment function
R&D	research and development
RM	relationship marketing
RMC	regional management centre
ROA	return on assets
ROC	Registrar of Companies (India)
ROI	return on investment
RTD	ready to drink
SBU	strategic business unit: a single business or a collection of related businesses that can be planned separately from the rest of the company
SGVC	sustainable global value chain
SMEs	small and medium-sized enterprises
SMS	short message service
SRC	self-reference criterion
STD	sexually transmitted disease
STP	software technology park
TC	transaction cost
TF	trade fair
TLC	technological life cycle
TMWC	Tipperary Mineral Water Company
TPMS	tyre pressure monitoring system
TQM	total quality management
TTM	time to market
ULCC	ultra low-cost car
UNAIDS	Joint United Nations Programme on AIDS
URL	uniform resource locator
USAID	United States Agency for International Development
USP	unique selling proposition
VAT	value added tax
VER	voluntary export restraint
WHO	World Health Organization
WTO	World Trade Organization (successor to GATT)
WWF	World Wildlife Fund

ABOUT THE AUTHOR

Svend Hollensen is an Associate Professor of International Marketing at University of Southern Denmark (Department of Border Region Studies). He holds an MSc (Business Administration) from Aarhus Business School. He has practical experience from a job as International Marketing Coordinator in a large Danish multinational enterprise as well as from being International Marketing Manager in a company producing agricultural machinery.

After working in industry Svend received his PhD in 1992 from Copenhagen Business School.

With Pearson Education he has published *Marketing Management – A Relationship Approach* (the second edition was published in 2010) as well as *Marketing Research – An International Approach* (2006), together with Marcus Schmidt. *Essentials of Global Marketing* was published in 2008. *Global Marketing* has been translated into Russian and Chinese. An Indian edition (co-authored with Madhumita Banerjee) was published in September 2009 and a Spanish edition (co-authored with Jesus Arteaga) was published in May 2010.

Svend has also worked as a business consultant for several multinational companies, as well as global organizations such as the World Bank.

The author may be contacted via:

University of Southern Denmark
Department of Border Region Studies
Alsion 2
DK-6400 Sønderborg
Denmark
e-mail: svend@sam.sdu.dk

PART I
The decision whether to internationalize
Chs 1–4

PART II
Deciding which markets to enter
Chs 5–8

PART III
Market entry strategies
Chs 9–13

PART IV
Designing the global marketing programme
Chs 14–17

PART V
Implementing and coordinating the global marketing programme
Chs 18–19

Part I Contents

Part I Case studies

PART I
The decision whether to internationalize

Introduction to Part I

It is often the case that a firm going into an export adventure should have stayed in the home market because it did not have the necessary competences to start exporting. Chapter 1 discusses competences and global marketing strategies from the value chain perspective. Chapter 2 discusses the major motivations of the firm to internationalize. Chapter 3 concentrates on some central theories that explain firms' internationalization processes. Chapter 4 discusses the concept of international competitiveness from a macro level to a micro level.

CHAPTER 1
Global marketing in the firm

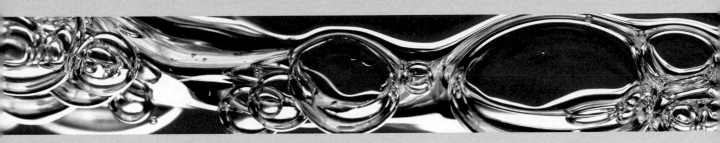

Contents

Case studies

Learning objectives

After studying this chapter you should be able to:

- Characterize and compare the management style in SMEs (small and medium-sized enterprises) and LSEs (large-scale enterprises).
- Identify drivers for global integration and market responsiveness.
- Explain the role of global marketing in the firm from a holistic perspective.
- Describe and understand the concept of the value chain.
- Identify and discuss different ways of internationalizing the value chain.

1.1 Introduction to globalization

After two years (2008–10) in economic crisis mode business executives are again looking to the future. As they are re-engaging in global marketing strategy thinking, many executives are wondering if the turmoil was merely another turn of the business cycle or a restructuring of the global economic order. However, although growth in the globalization of goods and services has stalled for a period, because international trade has declined along with demand, the overall globalization trend is unlikely to reverse (Beinhocker *et al.*, 2009).

In 2005 Thomas L. Friedman published his international bestselling book '*The world is flat*' (Freidman, 2005). It analyses globalization, primarily in the early twenty-first century, and the picture has changed dramatically. The title is a metaphor for viewing the world as a level playing field in terms of commerce, where all players and competitors have an equal opportunity. We are entering a new phase of globalization, in which there will be no single geographic centre, no ultimate model for success, no surefire strategy for innovation and growth. Companies from every part of the world will be competing – for customers, resources, talent and intellectual capital – with each other in every corner of the world's markets. Products and services will flow from many locations to many destinations. Friedman mentions that many companies in for example the Ukraine, India and China provide human-based sub-supplies for multinational companies, from typists and call centres to accountants and computer programmers. In this way these companies in emerging and developing countries are becoming integral parts of complex global supply chains for large multinational companies, like Dell, SAP, IBM and Microsoft.

Globalization
Reflects the trend of firms buying, developing producing and selling products and services in most countries and regions of the world.

Internationalization
Doing business in many countries of the world, but often limited to a certain region (e.g. Europe).

In the face of this **globalization** and the increasingly interconnected world many firms attempt to expand their sales into foreign markets. International expansion provides new and potentially more profitable markets, helps increase the firm's competitiveness and facilitates access to new product ideas, manufacturing innovations and the latest technology. However, **internationalization** is unlikely to be successful unless the firm prepares in advance. Advance planning is widely regarded as important to the success of new international ventures (Knight, 2000).

1.2 The process of developing the global marketing plan

As this book has a clear decision-oriented approach, it is structured according to the five main decisions that marketing people in companies face in connection with the global marketing process (Figure 1.1). The nineteen chapters are divided into five parts, according to these five subsequent decisions.

In the end, a firm's global competitiveness is mainly dependent on the end result of the global marketing stages: *the global marketing plan* (see Figure 1.2). The purpose of the marketing plan is to create sustainable competitive advantages in the global marketplace. Generally, firms go through some kind of mental process in developing global marketing plans – in SMEs this process is normally informal; in larger organizations it is often more systematized. Figure 1.2 offers a systematized approach to developing a global marketing plan, based on Figure 1.1's five subsequent decision stages, which are further illustrated by the most important models and concepts explained and discussed throughout the chapters.

It is advisable to return to Figure 1.2 throughout the book.

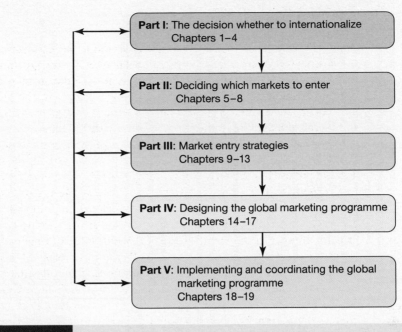

| **Figure 1.1** | The five-stage decision model in global marketing |

1.3   Comparison of the global marketing and management style of SMEs and LSEs

LSEs

According to the EU definition LSEs (Large-Scale Enterprises) are firms with more than 250 employees. Though LSEs account for less than 1 per cent of companies, almost one-third of all jobs in the EU are provided by LSEs.

SMEs

SMEs (Small and Medium-sized Enterprises) occur commonly in the EU and in international organizations. The EU categorizes companies with fewer than 50 employees as 'small', and those with fewer than 250 as 'medium'. In the EU, SMEs (250 employees and less) comprise approximately 99 per cent of all firms.

The reason underlying this 'convergence' is that many large multinationals (such as IBM, Philips, GM and ABB) have begun downsizing operations, so in reality many **LSEs** act like a confederation of small, autonomous, entrepreneurial and action-oriented companies. One can always question the change in orientation of **SMEs**. Some studies (e.g. Bonaccorsi, 1992) have rejected the widely accepted proposition that firm size is positively related to export intensity. Furthermore, many researchers (e.g. Julien *et al.*, 1997) have found that SMEs as exporters do not behave as a homogeneous group.

Table 1.1 gives an overview of the main qualitative differences between management and marketing styles in SMEs and LSEs. We will discuss each of the headings in turn.

Resources

● *Financial.* A well-documented characteristic of SMEs is the lack of financial resources due to a limited equity base. The owners put only a limited amount of capital into the business, which quickly becomes exhausted.
● *Business education/specialist expertise.* Contrary to LSEs, a characteristic of SME managers is their limited formal business education. Traditionally, the SME owner/manager is a technical or craft expert, and is unlikely to be trained in any of the major business disciplines. Therefore specialist expertise is often a constraint because managers in small businesses tend to be generalists rather than specialists. In addition, global marketing expertise is often the last of the business disciplines to be acquired by an expanding SME, finance and production experts usually precede the acquisition of a marketing counterpart. Therefore it is not unusual to see owners of SMEs closely involved in sales, distribution, price setting and, especially, product development.

Tools used in different stages (references to the book)

	Process stages	Description

Introduction:
The international marketing plan is based on a firm's mission (purpose of the business) and vision (where do we want to go). Developing an international marketing plan is the systematic process involving the assessment of market opportunities combined with the internal resources, the determination of marketing objectives, and the plan for implementation of the international marketing mix. The plan describes all the marketing activities that the firm should perform during a specified time period (usually one to three years).

The 'nine strategic windows' model:
This model uses industry globalism and the firm's preparedness as criteria for deciding if the firm should go abroad or rather stay at home

Benchmarking – competence profile:
The customer perceived value of the different competitor offerings along the value chain provide the necessary input for determining where the firm has got its core competence and where further capabilities should be developed

SWOT-analysis:
Strengths and Weaknesses (inside your company)
Identify internal strengths and weaknesses of your company. For example education-level, international experience and reputation in your area of expertise is most likely a strength

Opportunities and Threats (from outside)
Identify and rank by order of importance, any threats or opportunities your business may face from outside influences.

The whole issue is to find the right match between the internal and external analysis, i.e. where in the global market can we use our special firm competences?

Estimation of total market: Numbers of buyers × average consumption per year

Segmentation: Relevant segmentation/screening criteria
B2C markets: Demographic: age, income, occupation
Psychographic: lifestyle, preferences, etc.
Geographic: Countries, regions
Behavioural: heavy, medium, light users

B2B markets: Demographic: size of firm, type of industry
Economic: Buying power of customers

Process stages

Introduction:
Purpose of the international marketing plan

Should the company go international or not?

What are the competences of the firm and how should they be utilized internationally?

External analysis:
- Political forces
- Economic forces
- Socio-cultural forces
- Market size
(Chapters 5 and 6)

Internal analysis:
Identifying firm competences ⇨ International competitiveness (*Chapter 4*)

Match

SWOT-analysis

Internal	Strengths	Weak-nesses
External	Oppor-tunities	Threats

IMS = International Market Selection

PART I:
THE DECISION TO INTERNATIONALIZE

The 'nine strategic windows' model:

		Industry globalism		
		Local	Potentially global	Global
Preparedness for internationalization	Mature	3. Enter new business	6. Prepare for globalization	9. Strengthen your global position
	Adolescent	2. Consolidate your export markets	5. Consider expansion in international markets	8. Seek global alliances
	Immature	1. Stay at home	4. Seek niches in international markets	7. Prepare for a buyout

Chapter 1

Benchmarking – competence profile

Value chain functions

Upstream
Economies of scale (in production)
Product development
Internal logistics
etc.
Downstream
Market knowledge
Personal selling
After-sales service
etc.

Very strong 5.0 | Above average 4.5 | 4.0 | 3.5 Average 3.0 | 2.5 | Below average 2.0

Customer wants

Critical success factor

Core competence of the firm

Firm A
Firm B

Large gap

Early warning

Chapter 4

PART II:
DECIDING WHICH MARKETS TO ENTER

Total market:

Countries entering the screening process

Segmentation/ Screening

See Screening process in Chapter 8

- Geographical market: region (Western Europe, Eastern Europe, Far East, North America etc.) country or area in a country
- Customer type: end-customer, middlemen, OEMs, Global Accounts (GAs)

Competitor analysis:

You'll discover your company's competitive advantage – the reason customers do business with you instead of your competition. By observing the actions of your competitors, you might learn more about your market. For example, does a successful competitor offer reduced prices in a specific market? If so, what might that tell you about the market's spending habits. If you find that your market is saturated with capable competitors ('red ocean'), you can avoid the costly mistake of selecting a target market without adequate demand for your offer. You can then redirect your efforts toward something that will generate more profit with the existing resources base in your company ('blue ocean strategy').

Marketing objectives:

Meeting marketing objectives should lead to sales. (If not, you need to set different marketing objectives). They should be clear, measurable, and have a stated time frame for achievement.

With other words the objectives should follow the SMART-concept: **S**pecific, **M**easurable, **A**chievable, **R**ealistic, **T**imeable

Setting your marketing objectives and finalizing the remaining components of your marketing plan may serve as a reality check: Do you have the resources and competences necessary to accomplish your objectives?

Example: Increase market share in target market from now (t_0) 5% to 15% in three years (t_3) – Is that realistic?

Entry mode strategy:

Once the firm has set its target objectives in target markets the next step is to choose the best way to enter the market. The chosen entry mode can be regarded as the first decision level in the vertical chain that will provide distribution to the next actors in the vertical chain at the national level.

Following characteristics are connected to the three types of entry modes (seen from the manufacturer's perspective):

- Export modes (agent, distributor): low control, low risk, high flexibility
- Intermediate mode (joint venture, strategic alliance): shared control and risk, split ownership
- Hierarchical modes (own subsidiary): high control, high risk, low flexibility

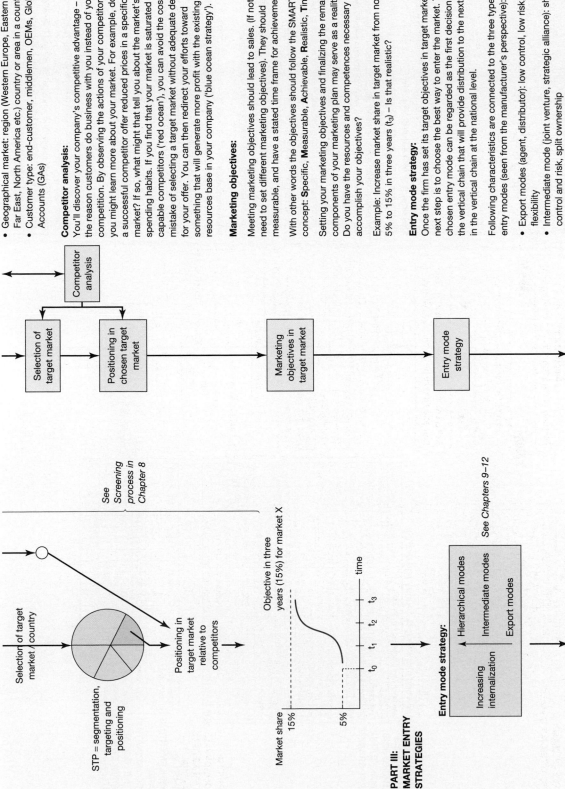

PART III: MARKET ENTRY STRATEGIES

Figure 1.2   Development of the global marketing plan

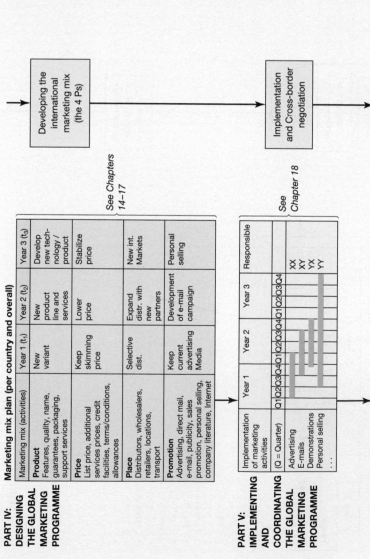

Development of the marketing mix:

The international marketing mix section of your plan (the 4 Ps or alternatively the 7 Ps) outlines your game plan to achieve your marketing objectives internationally. It is, essentially, the heart of the marketing plan. The marketing mix section should include information about:

- Product – your offering: product(s) and services
- Price – what you'll charge customers for regarding delivered products and services
- Promotion – how you will promote or create awareness and interest for your product in the marketplace
- Place (distribution) – how you will bring your product(s)/services together with your customers? How can you create extra value by developing relationships with your customer?

Implementation:

To translate the strategy into action (organizing):

- Assemble the 4P-mix for each product/service (SBU)
- Organize the marketing effort
- *Who* is responsible for the implementation of the activities?
- *When* will the activities take place?
- Internal marketing plan: Sell the the marketing plan inside the organization before going outside. Are there any internal barriers that should be considered?

Cross-border negotiation:

The most fundamental gap influencing the negotiation climate between buyer and seller is the *cultural distance*, represented by differences in communication and negotiation behaviour, the concepts of time, space and work patterns, and the nature of social norms. The cultural distance can be reduced by cultural training and market research.

Developing the international marketing mix (the 4 Ps)

See Chapters 14–17

Implementation and Cross-border negotiation

See Chapter 18

PART IV: DESIGNING THE GLOBAL MARKETING PROGRAMME

Marketing mix plan (per country and overall)

Marketing mix (activities)	Year 1 (t_1)	Year 2 (t_2)	Year 3 (t_3)
Product Features, quality, name, guarantees, packaging, support services	New variant	New product line and services	Develop new technology / product
Price List price, additional services prices, credit facilities, terms/conditions, allowances	Keep skimming price	Lower price	Stabilize price
Place Distributors, wholesalers, retailers, locations, transport	Selective dist.	Expand distr. with new partners	New int. Markets
Promotion Advertising, direct mail, e-mail, publicity, sales promotion, personal selling, company literature, Internet	Keep current advertising Media	Development of e-mail campaign	Personal selling

PART V: IMPLEMENTING AND COORDINATING THE GLOBAL MARKETING PROGRAMME

Implementation of marketing activities	Year 1				Year 2				Year 3				Responsible
(Q = Quarter)	Q1	Q2	Q3	Q4	Q1	Q2	Q3	Q4	Q1	Q2	Q3	Q4	
Advertising													XX
E-mails													XY
Demonstrations													YX
Personal selling													YY
...													

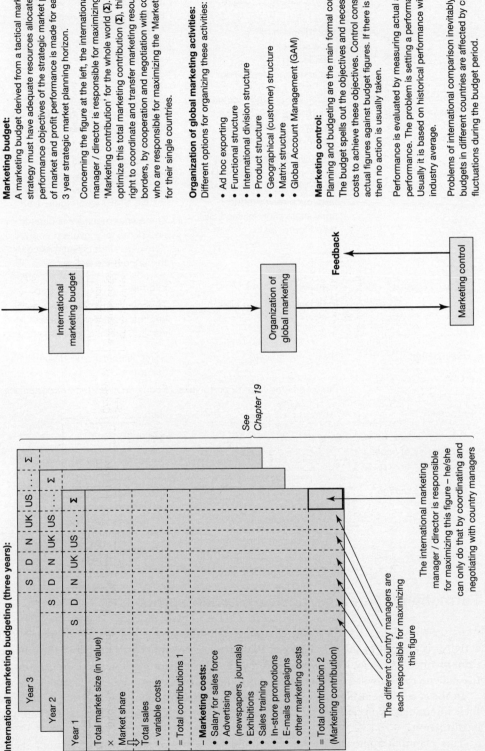

Marketing budget:
A marketing budget derived from a tactical marketing strategy must have adequate resources allocated to meet the performance objectives of the strategic market plan. An estimate of market and profit performance is made for each year of a 3 year strategic market planning horizon.

Concerning the figure at the left, the international marketing manager / director is responsible for maximizing the total 'Marketing contribution' for the whole world (Σ). In order to optimize this total marketing contribution (Σ), this person has the right to coordinate and transfer marketing resources across borders, by cooperation and negotiation with country managers, who are responsible for maximizing the 'Marketing contribution' for their single countries.

Organization of global marketing activities:
Different options for organizing these activities:

- Ad hoc exporting
- Functional structure
- International division structure
- Product structure
- Geographical (customer) structure
- Matrix structure
- Global Account Management (GAM)

Marketing control:
Planning and budgeting are the main formal control methods. The budget spells out the objectives and necessary marketing costs to achieve these objectives. Control consists of measuring actual figures against budget figures. If there is tolerable variance then no action is usually taken.

Performance is evaluated by measuring actual against planned performance. The problem is setting a performance standard. Usually it is based on historical performance with some kind of industry average.

Problems of international comparison inevitably occur like how budgets in different countries are affected by currency fluctuations during the budget period.

Figure 1.2 *Continued*

Source: Hollensen, S. (2008) *Essentials of Global Marketing,* FT/Prentice Hall, pp. 6–9.

Table 1.1	The characteristics of LSEs and SMEs	
	LSEs	**SMEs**
Resources	Many resources	Limited resources
	Internalization of resources	Externalization of resources (outsourcing of resources)
	Coordination of – personnel – financing – market knowledge, etc.	
Formation of strategy/ decision-making processes	Deliberate strategy formation (Mintzberg, 1987; Mintzberg and Waters, 1985) (see Figure 1.3)	Emergent strategy formation (Mintzberg, 1987; Mintzberg and Waters, 1985) (see Figure 1.3)
	Adaptive decision-making mode in small incremental steps (logical incrementalism) (e.g. each new product: small innovation for the LSE) (see Figure 1.4)	The entrepreneurial decision-making model (e.g. each new product: considerable innovation for the SME) (see Figure 1.5)
		The owner/manager is directly and personally involved and will dominate all decision-making throughout the enterprise
Organization	Formal/hierarchical	Informal
	Independent of one person	The owner/entrepreneur usually has the power/charisma to inspire/control a total organization
Risk-taking	Mainly risk-averse	Sometimes risk-taking/sometimes risk-averse
	Focus on long-term opportunities	Focus on short-term opportunities
Flexibility	Low	High
Take advantage of economies of scale and economies of scope	Yes	Only limited
Use of information sources	Use of advanced techniques: – databases – external consultancy – Internet	Information gathering in an informal manner and an inexpensive way: – internal sources – face-to-face communication

Formation of strategy/decision-making processes

As is seen in Figure 1.3, the realized strategy (the observable output of an organization's activity) is a result of the mix between the intended ('planned') strategy and the emergent ('not planned') strategy. No companies form a purely deliberate or intended strategy. In practice, all enterprises will have some elements of both intended and emergent strategy.

In the case of the deliberate (planned) strategy (mainly LSEs), managers try to formulate their intentions as precisely as possible and then strive to implement these with a minimum of distortion.

This planning approach 'assumes a progressive series of steps of goal setting, analysis, evaluation, selection and planning of implementation to achieve an optimal long-term

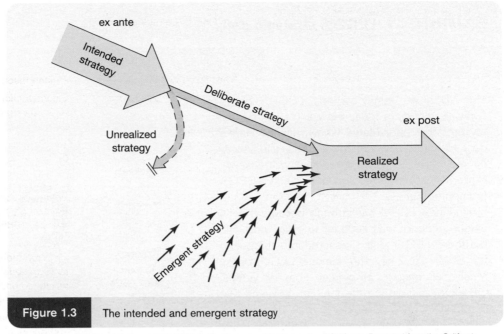

| **Figure 1.3** | The intended and emergent strategy |

Source: Mintzberg (1987, p. 14). Copyright © 1987, by The Regents of the University of California. Reprinted from the *California Management Review*, Vol. 30, No. 1. By permission of The Regents.

direction for the organization' (Johnson, 1988). Another approach for the process of strategic management is so-called *logical incrementalism* (Quinn, 1980), where continual adjustments in strategy proceed flexibly and experimentally. If such small movements in strategy prove successful then further development of the strategy can take place. According to Johnson (1988) managers may well see themselves as managing incrementally, but this does not mean that they succeed in keeping pace with environmental change. Sometimes the incrementally adjusted strategic changes and the environmental market changes move apart and a *strategic drift* arises (see Figure 1.4).

Exhibit 1.1 gives an example of strategic drift.

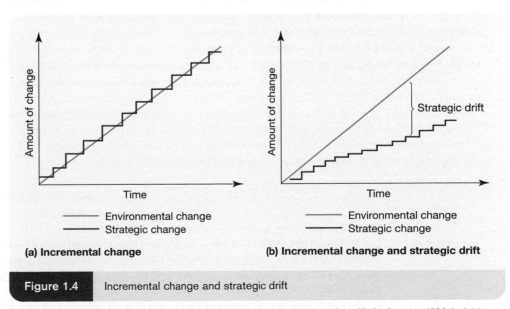

| **Figure 1.4** | Incremental change and strategic drift |

Source: Johnson, G. (1988) 'Rethinking incrementalism', *Strategic Management Journal*, 9. pp. 75–91. Copyright 1988 © of John Wiley & Sons Ltd. Reproduced with permission.

EXHIBIT 1.1   LEGO'S strategic drift

The Danish family-owned LEGO group (www.lego.com) is today the world's fifth largest toy producer after Mattel (known for the Barbie doll), Hasbro (known for Trivial Pursuit and Disney figures, via a licensing agreement with Disney), Nintendo (computer games) and SEGA (computer games).

Until now LEGO has strongly believed that its unique concept was superior to other products, but today LEGO feels pressured into competing for children's time. The famous LEGO bricks receive increasing competition from TV, videos, CD-ROM games and the Internet. It seems that in LEGO's case a 'strategic drift' has arisen, where LEGO management's blind faith in its unique and pedagogical toys has not been harmonized with the way in which the world has

© 2010 the Lego Group. Used with permission.

developed. Many working parents have less and less time to 'control' children's play habits. Spectacular computer games win over the 'healthy' and pedagogical toys that LEGO represents. This development has accelerated and has forced LEGO to re-evaluate its present strategy regarding product programmes and marketing.

The company suffered heavy losses in 1998 and 2000 and was forced to shed jobs, but in 2002 LEGO showed some solid profits, however in 2003 they suffered a net loss of approximately €190 million.

LEGO was trying to extend its traditional concepts and values into media products for children aged between 2 and 16. These new categories – including PC and console software, books, magazines, TV, film and music – aim to replicate the same feelings of confidence and trust already long established among children and their parents.

LEGO kits came as themed playsets under licensing deals with Harry Potter, Bob the Builder, Star Wars and Disney's Winnie the Pooh. It also went high-tech with products such as Mindstorms, and its popular Bionicles toys will appear in a full-length animated feature film. After the huge loss in 2003 (announced at the beginning of 2004) LEGO is now returning to its former concept. In order to ensure increased focus on the core business, in the autumn of 2004 the LEGO Group decided to sell off the LEGOLAND Parks. It will focus more on building bricks as its main product, concentrating on small kids' eagerness to assemble. This strategy had already paid off in 2005. The LEGO Group's net profit improved considerably from a loss of €242 million in 2004 to a profit of €29 million in 2005 and this even improved to €300 million in 2009. With focus on the re-establishment of a strong core business with classic construction toys the LEGO Group expects to maintain its market position in 2010 and the coming years as a financially stronger and more competitive toy company, though it is a relatively small company in the global toy market.

Source: adapted from different public media.

On the other hand, the SME is characterized by the entrepreneurial decision-making model (Figure 1.5). Here more drastic changes in strategy are possible because decision-making is intuitive, loose and unstructured. In Figure 1.5 the range of possible realized strategies is determined by an interval of possible outcomes. SME entrepreneurs are noted for their propensity to seek new opportunities, and this natural propensity for change, inherent in entrepreneurs, can lead to considerable changes in the enterprise's growth direction. Because

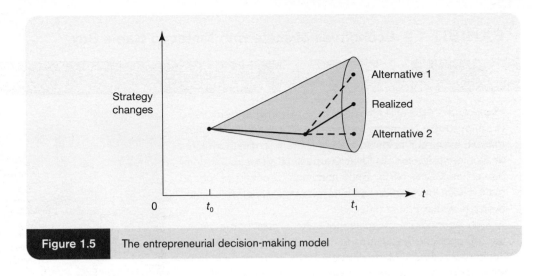

| Figure 1.5 | The entrepreneurial decision-making model |

the entrepreneur changes focus, this growth is not planned or coordinated and can therefore be characterized by sporadic decisions that have an impact on the overall direction in which the enterprise is going.

Organization

Compared to LSEs the employees in SMEs are usually closer to the entrepreneur, and because of the entrepreneur's influence these employees must conform to his or her personality and style characteristics if they are to remain employees.

Risk-taking

There are, of course, different degrees of risk. Normally the LSEs will be risk-averse because of their use of a decision-making model that emphasizes small incremental steps with a focus on long-term opportunities.

In SMEs risk-taking depends on the circumstances. It can occur in situations where the survival of the enterprise may be under threat, or where a major competitor is undermining the activities of the enterprise. Entrepreneurs may also be taking risks when they have not gathered all the relevant information, and thus have ignored some important facts in the decision-making process.

On the other hand there are, of course, some circumstances in which an SME will be risk-averse. This often occurs when an enterprise has been damaged by previous risk-taking and the entrepreneur is reluctant to take any kind of risk until confidence returns.

Flexibility

Because of the shorter communication lines between the enterprise and its customers, SMEs can react in a quicker and more flexible way to customer enquiries.

Economies of scale and economies of scope

Economies of scale

Accumulated volume in production and sales will result in lower cost price per unit due to 'experience curve effects' and increased efficiency in production, marketing, etc. Building a

EXHIBIT 1.2 Economies of scale with Nintendo Game Boy

Having sold 200 million Game Boys worldwide from 1989 to mid-2009, Nintendo dominates the hand-held game market, even as it is losing market share in console systems to Sony and Microsoft. Over the past 15 years, such companies as Sega, NEC, SNK and most recently cellphone giant Nokia have launched nine competing portable game systems without much success.

The economies of scale primarily relate to the manufacturing of the hardware. In the software, economies of scale were limited. Many different types of game have to be offered and the popularity of most of them was short-lived. This is especially so in the case of software linked to a film: the popularity of the game diminished as the film ceased to be shown in cinemas.

Bildagentur-online/Alamy

Economies of scale
Accumulated volume in production, resulting in lower cost price per unit.

global presence automatically expands a firm's scale of operations, giving it larger production capacity and a larger asset base. However, larger scale will create competitive advantage only if the company systematically converts scale into **economies of scale**. In principle, the benefits of economies of scale can appear in different ways (Gupta and Govindarajan, 2001):

- Reducing operating costs per unit and spreading fixed costs over larger volume due to experience curve effects.
- Pooling global purchasing gives the opportunity to concentrate global purchasing power over suppliers. This generally leads to volume discounts and lower transaction costs.
- A larger scale gives the global player the opportunity to build centres of excellence for development of specific technologies or products. In order to do this a company needs to focus a critical mass of talent in one location.

Because of size (bigger market share) and accumulated experience, the LSEs will normally take advantages of these factors (see Exhibit 1.2 about Nintendo's Game Boy). SMEs tend to concentrate on lucrative, small, market segments. Such market segments are often too insignificant for LSEs to target, but can be substantial and viable in respect of the SME. However, they will only result in a very limited market share of a given industry.

Economies of scope

Synergy effects and global scope can occur when the firm is serving several international markets: global scope is not taking place if an international marketer is serving a customer that operates in just one country. The customer should purchase a bundle of identical products and services across a number of countries. This global customer could source these products and services either from a horde of local suppliers or from a single global supplier (international marketer) that is present in all of its markets. Compared with a horde of local suppliers, a single global supplier (marketer) can provide value for the global customer through greater consistency in the quality and features of products and services across countries, faster and smoother coordination across countries and lower transaction costs.

Economies of scope
Reusing a resource from one business/country in additional businesses/countries.

The challenge in capturing the **economies of scope** at a global level lies in being responsive to the tension between two conflicting needs: the need for central coordination of most marketing mix elements, and the need for local autonomy in the actual delivery of products and services (Gupta and Govindarajan, 2001).

The LSEs often serve many different markets (countries) on more continents and are thereby able to transfer experience acquired in one country to another. Typically, SMEs serve only a very limited number of international markets outside their home market. Sometimes the SME can make use of economies of scope when it goes into an alliance or a joint venture with a partner who has what the particular SME is missing in the international market in question: a complementary product programme or local market knowledge.

Another example of economies of scale and scope can be found in the world car industry. Most car companies use similar engines and gearboxes across their entire product range so that the same engines or gearboxes can go into different models of cars. This generates enormous potential cost savings for companies such as Ford or Volkswagen. It provides both economies of scale (decreased cost per unit of output) by producing a larger absolute volume of engines or gearboxes, and economies of scope (reusing a resource from one business/country in additional businesses/countries). It is not surprising that the car industry has experienced a wave of mergers and acquisitions aimed at creating larger world car companies of sufficient size to benefit from these factors.

Use of information sources

Typically, LSEs rely on commissioned market reports produced by well-reputed (and well-paid!) international consultancy firms as their source of vital global marketing information.

SMEs usually gather information in an informal manner by use of face-to-face communication. The entrepreneur is able to synthesize this information unconsciously and use it to make decisions. The acquired information is mostly incomplete and fragmented, and evaluations are based on intuition and often guesswork. The whole process is dominated by the desire to find a circumstance that is ripe for exploitation.

Furthermore, the demand for complex information grows as the SME selects a more and more explicit orientation towards the international market and as the firm evolves from a production-oriented ('upstream') to a more marketing-oriented ('downstream') firm (Cafferata and Mensi, 1995).

As a reaction to pressures from international markets, both LSEs and SMEs evolve towards a globally integrated but market-responsive strategy. However, the starting points of the two firm types are different (see Figure 1.3 earlier). The huge global companies have traditionally based their strategy on taking advantage of economies of scale by launching standardized products on a worldwide basis. These companies have realized that a higher degree of market responsiveness is necessary to maintain competitiveness in national markets. On the other hand, SMEs have traditionally regarded national markets as independent of each other. However, as international competences evolve they have begun to realize that there is interconnectedness between their different international markets. They recognize the benefits of coordinating the different national marketing strategies in order to utilize economies of scale in research and development (R&D), production and marketing.

1.4   Should the company 'stay at home' or 'go abroad'?

Solberg (1997) discusses the conditions under which the company should 'stay at home' or further 'strengthen the global position' as two extremes (see Figure 1.6). The framework in Figure 1.3 is based on the following two dimensions:

		Industry globalism		
		Local	*Potentially global*	*Global*
Preparedness for internationalization	*Mature*	3. Enter new business	6. Prepare for globalization	9. Strengthen your global position
	Adolescent	2. Consolidate your export markets	5. Consider expansion in international markets	8. Seek global alliances
	Immature	1. Stay at home	4. Seek niches in international markets	7. Prepare for a buyout

Figure 1.6   The nine strategic windows

Source: Solberg (1997, p. 11). Reprinted with kind permission. In the original article Solberg has used the concept 'globality' rather than 'globalism'.

Industry globalism

In principle, the firm cannot influence the degree of industry globalism, as it is mainly determined by the international marketing environment. Here the strategic behaviour of firms depends on the international competitive structure within an industry. In the case of a high degree of industry globalism there are many interdependencies between markets, customers and suppliers, and the industry is dominated by a few large powerful players (*global*), whereas the other end (*local*) represents a multidomestic market environment, where markets exist independently from one another. Examples of very global industries are PCs, IT (software), records (CDs), movies and aircrafts (the two dominant players being Boeing and Airbus). Examples of more local industries are the more culture-bound industries, like hairdressing, foods and dairies (e.g. brown cheese in Norway).

Preparedness for internationalization

This dimension is mainly determined by the firm. The degree of preparedness is dependent on the firm's ability to carry out strategies in the international marketplace, that is the actual skills in international business operations. These skills or organizational capabilities may consist of personal skills (e.g. language, cultural sensitivity, etc.), the managers' international experience or financial resources. The well-prepared company (*mature*) has a good basis for dominating the international markets and consequently it would gain higher market shares.

In the global/international marketing literature the 'staying at home' alternative is not discussed thoroughly. However, Solberg (1997) argues that with limited international experience and a weak position in the home market there is little reason for a firm to engage in international markets. Instead it should try to improve its performance in its home market. This alternative is window number 1 in Figure 1.6.

If the firm finds itself in a global industry as a dwarf among large multinational firms, then Solberg (1997) argues that it may seek ways to increase its net worth so as to attract partners for a future buyout bid. This alternative (window number 7 in Figure 1.6) may be relevant to

SMEs selling advanced high-tech components (as sub-suppliers) to large industrial companies with a global network. In situations with fluctuations in the global demand the SME, with limited financial resources, will often be financially vulnerable. If the firm has already acquired some competence in international business operations it can overcome some of its competitive disadvantages by going into alliances with firms representing complementary competences (window number 8). The other windows in Figure 1.6 are discussed further by Solberg (1997).

1.5 Development of the global marketing concept

Basically global marketing consists of finding and satisfying global customer needs better than the competition, and of coordinating marketing activities within the constraints of the global environment. The form of the firm's response to global market opportunities depends greatly on the management's assumptions or beliefs, both conscious and unconscious, about the nature of doing business around the world. This worldview of a firm's business activities can be described as the EPRG framework (Perlmutter, 1969; Chakravarthy and Perlmutter, 1985). Its four orientations are:

- E*thnocentric*: the home country is superior and the needs of the home country are most relevant. Essentially headquarters extends ways of doing business to its foreign affiliates. Controls are highly centralized and the organization and technology implemented in foreign locations will essentially be the same as in the home country.
- P*olycentric* (multidomestic): each country is unique and therefore should be targeted in a different way. The polycentric enterprise recognizes that there are different conditions of production and marketing in different locations and tries to adapt to those different conditions in order to maximize profits in each location. The control with affiliates is highly decentralized and communication between headquarters and affiliates is limited.
- R*egiocentric*: the world consists of regions (e.g. Europe, Asia, the Middle East). The firm tries to integrate and coordinate its marketing programme within regions, but not across them.
- G*eocentric* (global): the world is getting smaller and smaller. The firm may offer global product concepts but with local adaptation – think global, act local.

The regio- and geocentric firm (in contrast to the ethnocentric and polycentric) seeks to organize and integrate production and marketing on a regional or global scale. Each international unit is an essential part of the overall multinational network, and communications and controls between headquarters and affiliates are less top-down than in the case of the ethnocentric firm.

This leads us to a definition of global marketing:

Global marketing is defined as the firm's commitment to coordinate its marketing activities across national boundaries in order to find and satisfy global customer needs better than the competition. This implies that the firm is able to:

- develop a global marketing strategy, based on similarities and differences between markets;
- exploit the knowledge of the headquarters (home organization) through worldwide diffusion (learning) and adaptations;
- transfer knowledge and 'best practices' from any of its markets and use them in other international markets.

There follows an explanation of some key terms:

- *Coordinate its marketing activities*: coordinating and integrating marketing strategies and implementing them across global markets, which involves centralization, delegation, standardization and local responsiveness.
- *Find global customer needs*: this involves carrying out international marketing research and analysing market segments, as well as seeking to understand similarities and differences in customer groups across countries.
- *Satisfy global customer needs*: adapting products, services and elements of the marketing mix to satisfy different customer needs across countries and regions.
- *Being better than the competition*: assessing, monitoring and responding to global competition by offering better value, low prices, high quality, superior distribution, great advertising strategies or superior brand image.

The second part of the global marketing definition is also illustrated in Figures 1.7 and 1.8. Further comments follow.

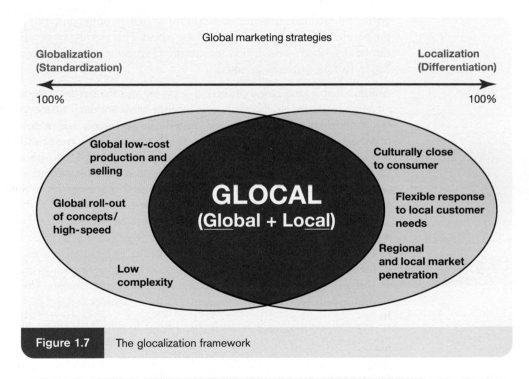

| Figure 1.7 | The glocalization framework |

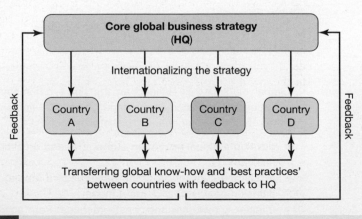

| Figure 1.8 | The principle of transferring knowledge and learning across borders |

Glocalization
The development and selling of products or services intended for the global market, but adapted to suit local culture and behaviour. (Think globally, act locally.)

This global marketing strategy strives to achieve the slogan 'think globally but act locally' (the so-called '**glocalization**' framework), through dynamic interdependence between headquarters and subsidiaries. Organizations following such a strategy coordinate their efforts, to ensure local flexibility while exploiting the benefits of global integration and efficiencies and worldwide diffusion of innovation.

Principally, the value chain function should be carried out where there is the highest competence (and the most cost-effectiveness), and this is not necessarily at head office (Bellin and Pham, 2007).

The two extremes in global marketing, globalization and localization, can be combined into the 'glocalization' framework, as shown in Figure 1.7.

A key element in glocalization is knowledge management, which is continuous learning from experiences. In practical terms, the aim of knowledge management as a learning-focused activity across borders is to keep track of valuable capabilities used in one market that could be used elsewhere (in other geographic markets), so that firms can continually update their knowledge. This is also illustrated in Figure 1.8 with the transfer of knowledge and best practices from market to market. However, knowledge developed and used in one cultural context is not always easily transferred to another. The lack of personal relationships, the absence of trust, and cultural distance all conspire to create resistance, frictions and misunderstandings in cross-cultural knowledge management.

As globalization becomes a centrepiece in the business strategy of many firms – be they engaged in product development or providing services – the ability to manage the 'global knowledge engine' to achieve a competitive edge in today's knowledge-intensive economy is one of the keys to sustainable competitiveness. In the context of global marketing the management of knowledge is de facto a cross-cultural activity, whose key task is to foster and continually upgrade collaborative cross-cultural learning (this will be discussed further in Chapter 19). Of course, the kind and/or type of knowledge that is strategic for an organization and which needs to be managed for competitiveness varies depending on the business context and the value of different types of knowledge associated with it.

1.6   Forces for global integration and market responsiveness

In Figure 1.9 it is assumed that SMEs and LSEs are learning from each other.

The consequence of both movements may be an action-oriented approach, where firms use the strengths of both orientations. The following section will discuss the differences in the starting points of LSEs and SMEs in Figure 1.9. The result of the convergence movement of LSEs and SMEs into the upper-right corner can be illustrated by Figure 1.9.

An example of a LSEs movement from 'left' to 'right' is given in Figure 1.9, where McDonald's has adapted its menus to the local food cultures (see also Exhibit 1.3). SMEs have traditionally been strong on 'high degree of responsiveness', but their tendency to decentralization and local decision-making, has made them more vulnerable with regard to the low degree of coordination across border (which on the contrary is a characteristic of LSEs).

Global integration
Recognizing the similarities between international markets and integrating them into the overall global strategy.

Market responsiveness
Responding to each market's needs and wants.

The terms 'glocal strategy' and 'glocalization' have been introduced to reflect and combine the two dimensions in Figure 1.9: globalization (*y*-axis) and localization (*x*-axis). The glocal strategy approach reflects the aspirations of a global integrated strategy, while recognizing the importance of local adaptations/market responsiveness. In this way glocalization tries to optimize the balance between standardization and adaptation of the firm's international marketing activities (Bellin and Pham, 2007; Svensson, 2001, 2002).

First let us try to explain the underlying forces for global coordination/**global integration** and **market responsiveness** in Figure 1.9.

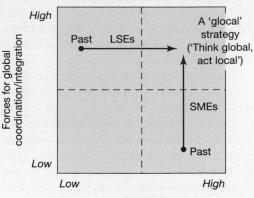

| Figure 1.9 | The global integration/market responsiveness grid: the future orientation of LSEs and SMEs |

Forces for global coordination/integration

In the shift towards integrated global marketing, greater importance will be attached to transnational similarities for target markets across national borders and less on cross-national differences. The major drivers for this shift are (Sheth and Parvatiyar, 2001; Segal-Horn, 2002):

● *Removal of trade barriers (deregulation).* Removal of historic barriers, both tariff (such as import taxes) and non-tariff (such as safety regulations), which have constituted barriers to trade across national boundaries. Deregulation has occurred at all levels: national, regional (within national trading blocs) and international. Thus deregulation has an impact on globalization because it reduces the time, costs and complexity involved in trading across boundaries.

● *Global accounts/customers.* As customers become global and rationalize their procurement activities they demand suppliers provide them with global services to meet their unique global needs. Often this may consist of global delivery of products, assured supply and service systems, uniform characteristics and global pricing. Several LSEs such as IBM, Boeing, IKEA, Siemens and ABB make such global demands of their smaller suppliers, typical SMEs. For these SMEs managing such global accounts requires cross-functional customer teams, in order to deploy quality consistency across all functional units. This issue is further discussed in Chapter 19 (section 19.3).

● *Relationship management/network organization.* As we move towards global markets it is becoming increasingly necessary to rely on a network of relationships with external organizations, for example, customer and supplier relationships, to pre-empt competition. The firm may also have to work with internal units (e.g. sales subsidiaries) located in many and various parts of the world. Business alliances and network relationships help to reduce market uncertainties, particularly in the context of rapidly converging technologies and the need for higher amounts of resources to cover global markets. However, networked organizations need more coordination and communication.

● *Standardized worldwide technology.* Earlier differences in world market demand were due to the fact that advanced technological products were primarily developed for the defence and government sectors before being scaled down for consumer applications. However, today the desire for gaining scale and scope in production is so high that worldwide availability of products and services should escalate. As a consequence we may witness more homogeneity in the demand and usage of consumer electronics across nations.

- *Worldwide markets.* The concept of 'diffusions of innovations' from the home country to the rest of the world tends to be replaced by the concept of worldwide markets. Worldwide markets are likely to develop because they can rely on world demographics. For example, if a marketer targets its products or services to the teenagers of the world, it is relatively easy to develop a worldwide strategy for that segment and draw up operational plans to provide target market coverage on a global basis. This is becoming increasingly evident in soft drinks, clothing and sports shoes, especially in the Internet economy.

- *Global village.* The term 'global village' refers to the phenomenon in which the world's population shares commonly recognized cultural symbols. The business consequence of this is that similar products and similar services can be sold to similar groups of customers in almost any country in the world. Cultural homogenization therefore implies the potential for the worldwide convergence of markets and the emergence of a global marketplace, in which brands such as Google, Coke, Nike and Levi's are universally aspired to.

- *Worldwide communication.* New Internet-based low-cost communication methods (e-mailing, e-commerce, Facebook, LinkedIn, Twitter, etc.) ease communication and trade across different parts of the world. As a result customers within national markets are able to buy similar products and similar services across parts of the world.

- *Global cost drivers.* Categorized as economies of scale and economies of scope, these were discussed in section 1.3.

Forces for market responsiveness

These are as follows:

- *Cultural differences.* Despite the global village cultural diversity clearly continues. Cultural differences often pose major difficulties in international negotiations and marketing management, reflecting differences in personal values and in the assumptions people make about how business is organized. Every culture has its opposing values. Markets are people, not products. There may be global products, but there are not global people.

- *Regionalism/protectionism.* Regionalism is the grouping of countries into regional clusters based on geographic proximity. These regional clusters (such as the European Union or NAFTA, the North American Free Trade Agreement) have formed regional trading blocs which may represent a significant blockage to globalization, because regional trade is often seen as incompatible with global trade. In this case, trade barriers that are removed from individual countries are simply reproduced for a region and a set of countries. Thus all trading blocs create outsiders as well as insiders. Therefore one may argue that regionalism results in a situation where protectionism reappears around regions rather than individual countries.

Deglobalization
Moving away from the globalization trends and regarding each market as special, with its own economy, culture and religion.

- ***Deglobalization*** trend. More than 2,500 years ago the Greek historian Herodotus (based on observations) claimed that everyone believes their native customs and religion are the best. Current movements in Arab countries, or the big demonstrations accompanying conferences such as the World Economic Forum in Davos, or the World Trade Organization (WTO) meetings show that there could be a return to old values, promoting barriers to the further success of globalization. Rhetorical words such as 'McDonaldization' and 'Coca-Colonization' describe in a simple way fears of US cultural imperialism.

Whether or not 11 September 2001 means that globalization will continue is debatable. Quelch (2002) argues that it will, because 11 September is motivating greater cross-border cooperation among national governments on security matters, and this cooperation will reinforce interaction in other areas.

Exhibit 1.3 shows an example of McDonald's movement towards more localization.

EXHIBIT 1.3 McDonald's is moving towards a higher degree of market responsiveness

McDonald's (www.mcdonalds.com) has now expanded to more than 32,000 restaurants in over 100 countries. Executives at the headquarters of the McDonald's Corporation in Oak Brook, Illinois, have learned that despite the cost/savings inherent in standardization, success is often about being able to adapt to the local environment. Here are some examples.

Japan

McDonald's first restaurant in Japan opened during 1971. At that time fast food here was either a bowl of noodles or miso soup.

With its first-mover advantage, McDonald's kept its lead in Japan. By 1997 McDonald's had over 1,000 outlets across that nation, and these sold more food in Japan than any other restaurant company. This includes an annual 500 million burgers.

Among the offerings of McDonald's Co. (Japan) Ltd are chicken tatsuta, teriyaki chicken, and the Teriyaki McBurger. Burgers are garnished with a fried egg. Beverages include iced coffee and corn soup.

McDonald's in Japan imports about 70 per cent of its food needs, including pickles from the United States and beef patties from Australia. High volumes facilitate bargaining with suppliers, in order to guarantee sourcing at a low cost.

Japan Tamagoburger
McDonald's Corporation

India

McDonald's now has over 150 restaurants in India and was launched there in 1996. It has had to deal with a market that is 40 per cent vegetarian with an aversion to either beef or pork among meat eaters; with a hostility to frozen meat and fish; and with the general Indian fondness for spice with everything.

The Big Mac was replaced by the Maharaja Mac, made from mutton, and also on offer were vegetarian rice-patties flavoured with vegetables and spice.

Riceburger
McDonald's Corporation

Other countries

In tropical markets, guava juice was added to the McDonald's product line. In Germany, McDonald's did well selling beer as well as McCroissants. Banana-fruit pies became popular in Latin America and McSpaghetti noodles became a favourite in the Philippines. In Thailand, McDonald's introduced the Samurai Pork Burger with sweet sauce. Meanwhile, McDonald's in New Zealand launched the Kiwiburger served with beetroot sauce and optional apricot pie.

In Singapore, where fries came to be served with chilli sauce, the Kiasuburger chicken breakfast became a best-seller. Singapore was among the first markets in which McDonald's introduced a delivery service.

As indicated, McDonald's has achieved economies of scale and cost savings through standardization and in its packaging. In 2003,

Veggie McCurry Pan
McDonald's Corporation

McDonald's announced that all its restaurants – 30,000 in over 100 countries – would soon be adopting the same brand packaging for menu items. According to a company press release, the new packaging would feature photographs of real people doing things they enjoy, such as listening to music, playing soccer and reading to their children. McDonald's global chief marketing officer was quoted as saying, 'It is the first time in our history that a single set of brand packaging, with a single brand message, will be used concurrently around the world.' Two years later, in 2005, the company had to pull back when it announced plans to *localize* its packages (Frost 2006).

Source: adapted from a variety of public media.

1.7   The value chain as a framework for identifying international competitive advantage

Value chain
A categorization of the firm's activities providing value for the customers and profit for the company.

The **value chain** shown in Figure 1.10 provides a systematic means of displaying and categorizing activities. The activities performed by a firm in any industry can be grouped into the nine generic categories shown.

At each stage of the value chain there exists an opportunity to contribute positively to the firm's competitive strategy by performing some activity or process in a way that is better and/or different than the competitors' offer, and so provide some uniqueness or advantage. If a firm attains such a competitive advantage, which is sustainable, defensible, profitable and valued by the market, then it may earn high rates of return, even though the industry structure may be unfavourable and the average profitability of the industry modest.

In competitive terms, value is the amount that buyers are willing to pay for what a firm provides them with (perceived value). A firm is profitable if the value it commands exceeds the costs involved in creating the product. Creating value for buyers that exceeds the cost of doing so is the goal of any generic strategy. Value, instead of cost, must be used in analysing competitive position, as firms often deliberately raise their costs in order to command a premium price via differentiation. The concept of buyers' perceived value will be discussed further in Chapter 4.

The value chain displays total value and consists of value activities and margin. Value activities are the physically and technologically distinct activities that a firm performs and are the building blocks by which a firm creates a product valuable to its buyers. Margin is the difference between total value (price) and the collective cost of performing the value activities.

The value chain activities are a key link between the fundamental company resources and the strategic position in the global market. The company resources are only valuable when they are transformed into activities, which generate lower cost or higher value than rivals (Sheehan and Foss, 2009). Hence, competitive advantage is a function of either providing comparable buyer value more efficiently than competitors (lower cost), or performing activities at comparable cost but in unique ways that create more customer value than the competitors are able to offer and, hence, command a premium price (differentiation). The firm might be able to identify elements of the value chain that are not worth the costs. These can then be unbundled and produced outside the firm (outsourced) at a lower price.

Value activities can be divided into two broad types: primary activities and support activities. *Primary activities*, listed along the bottom of Figure 1.10, are those involved in the physical creation of the product, its sale and transfer to the buyer, as well as after-sales assistance. In any firm, primary activities can be divided into the five generic categories shown in the figure. *Support activities* support the primary activities and each other by providing purchased inputs, technology, human resources and various firm-wide functions. The dotted lines reflect the fact that procurement, technology development and human

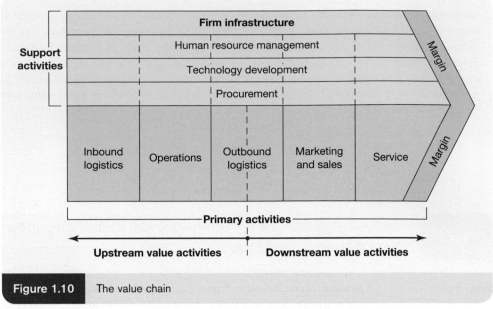

| **Figure 1.10** | The value chain |

Source: reprinted with the permission of The Free Press, a Division of Simon & Schuster, Inc. from *Competitive Advantage: Creating and Sustaining Superior Performance* by Michael E. Porter. Copyright © 1985, 1998 Michael E. Porter. All rights reserved.

resource management can be associated with specific primary activities as well as supporting the entire chain. Firm infrastructure is not associated with particular primary activities, but supports the entire chain.

Primary activities

The primary activities of the organization are grouped into five main areas: inbound logistics, operations, outbound logistics, marketing and sales and service:

1. *Inbound logistics.* The activities concerned with receiving, storing and distributing the inputs to the product/service. These include materials, handling, stock control, transport, etc.
2. *Operations.* The transformation of these various inputs into the final product or service: machining, packaging, assembly, testing, etc.
3. *Outbound logistics.* The collection, storage and distribution of the product to customers. For tangible products this would involve warehousing, material handling, transport, etc.; in the case of services it may be more concerned with arrangements for bringing customers to the service if it is in a fixed location (e.g. sports events).
4. *Marketing and sales.* These provide the means whereby consumers/users are made aware of the product/service and are able to purchase it. This would include sales administration, advertising, selling, etc. In public services, communication networks that help users access a particular service are often important.
5. *Services.* All the activities that enhance or maintain the value of a product/service. Asugman *et al.* (1997) have defined after-sales service as 'those activities in which a firm engages after purchase of its product that minimize potential problems related to product use, and maximize the value of the consumption experience'. After-sales service consists of the following: the installation and start-up of the purchased product, the provision of spare parts for products, the provision of repair services, technical advice regarding the product and the provision and support of warranties.

Each of these groups of primary activities is linked to support activities.

Support activities

These can be divided into four areas:

1. *Procurement.* This refers to the process of acquiring the various resource inputs to the primary activities (not to the resources themselves). As such, it occurs in many parts of the organization.
2. *Technology development.* All value activities have a 'technology', even if it is simply know-how. The key technologies may be concerned directly with the product (e.g. R&D, product design) or with processes (e.g. process development) or with a particular resource (e.g. raw material improvements).
3. *Human resource management.* This is a particularly important area that transcends all primary activities. It is concerned with the activities involved in recruiting, training, developing and rewarding people within the organization.
4. *Infrastructure.* The systems of planning, finance, quality control, etc., are crucially important to an organization's strategic capability in all primary activities. Infrastructure also consists of the structures and routines of the organization that sustain its culture.

As indicated in Figure 1.10, a distinction is also made between the production-oriented 'upstream' activities and the more marketing-oriented 'downstream' activities.

Having looked at Porter's original value chain model, a simplified version will be used in most parts of this book (Figure 1.11). This simplified version is characterized by the fact that it contains only the primary activities of the firm.

Although value activities are the building blocks of competitive advantage, the value chain is not a collection of independent activities, but a system of interdependent activities. Value activity is related by horizontal linkages within the value chain. Linkages are relationships between the way in which one value activity is dependent on the performance of another.

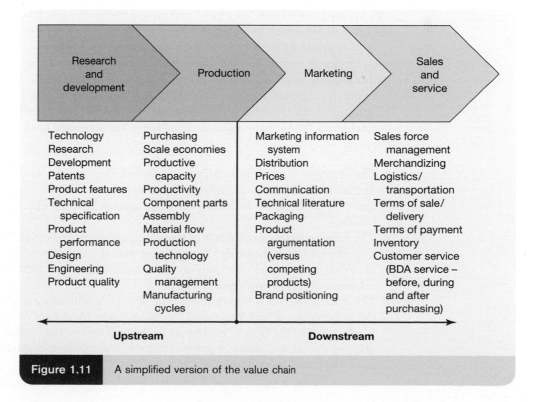

Figure 1.11   A simplified version of the value chain

Furthermore, the chronological order of the activities in the value chain is not always as illustrated in Figure 1.11. In companies where orders are placed before production of the final product (build to order) the sales and marketing function takes place before production.

In understanding the competitive advantage of an organization the strategic importance of the following types of linkage should be analysed in order to assess how they contribute to cost reduction or value added. There are two kinds of linkage:

- *internal linkages* between activities within the same value chain, but perhaps on different planning levels within the firm;
- *external linkages* between different value chains 'owned' by the different actors in the total value system.

Internal linkages

There may be important links between the primary activities. In particular, choices will have been made about these relationships and how they influence value creation and strategic capability. For example, a decision to hold high levels of finished stock might ease production scheduling problems and provide a faster response time to the customer. However, it will probably add to the overall cost of operations. An assessment needs to be made of whether the added value of stocking is greater than the added cost. Suboptimization of the single value chain activities should be avoided. It is easy to miss this point in an analysis if, for example, the marketing activities and operations are assessed separately. The operations may look good because they are geared to high-volume, low-variety, low-unit-cost production. However, at the same time the marketing team may be selling quickness, flexibility and variety to the customers. When put together these two potential strengths are weaknesses because they are not in harmony, which is what a value chain requires. The link between a primary activity and a support activity may be the basis of competitive advantage. For example, an organization may have a unique system for procuring materials. Many international hotels and travel companies use their computer systems to provide immediate real-time quotations and bookings worldwide from local access points.

As a supplement to comments about the linkages between the different activities, it is also relevant to regard the value chain (illustrated in Figure 1.11 in a simplified form) as a thoroughgoing model on all three planning levels in the organization.

In purely conceptual terms, a firm can be described as a pyramid as illustrated in Figure 1.12. It consists of an intricate conglomeration of decision and activity levels, having three distinct levels, but the main value chain activities are connected to all three strategic levels in the firm:

- The *strategic level* is responsible for formulation of the firm's mission statement, determining objectives, identifying the resources that will be required if the firm is to attain its objectives, and selecting the most appropriate corporate strategy for the firm to pursue.
- The *managerial level* has the task of translating corporate objectives into functional and/or unit objectives and ensuring that resources placed at its disposal (e.g. in the marketing department) are used effectively in the pursuit of those activities that will make the achievement of the firm's goals possible.
- The *operational level* is responsible for the effective performance of the tasks that underlie the achievement of unit/functional objectives. The achievement of operational objectives is what enables the firm to achieve its managerial and strategic aims. All three levels are interdependent, and clarity of purpose from the top enables everybody in the firm to work in an integrated fashion towards a common aim.

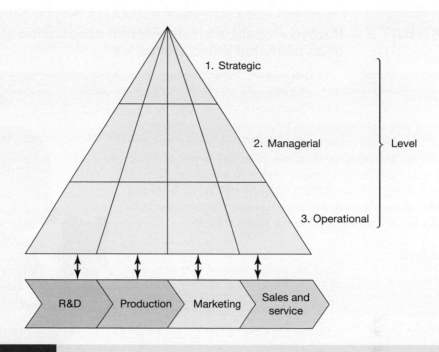

| Figure 1.12 | The value chain in relation to the strategic pyramid |

External linkages

One of the key features of most industries is that a single organization rarely undertakes all value activities from product design to distribution to the final consumer. There is usually a specialization of roles, and any single organization usually participates in the wider value system that creates a product or service. In understanding how value is created it is not enough to look at the firm's internal value chain alone. Much of the value creation will occur in the supply and distribution chains, and this whole process needs to be analysed and understood.

Suppliers have value chains that create and deliver the purchased inputs used in a firm's chain (the upstream part of the value chain). Suppliers not only deliver a product, but can also influence a firm's performance in many other ways. For example Benetton, the Italian fashion company, managed to sustain an elaborate network of suppliers, agents and independent retail outlets as the basis of its rapid and successful international development during the 1970s and 1980s.

In addition, products pass through the value chain channels on their way to the buyer. Channels perform additional activities that affect the buyer and influence the firm's own activities. A firm's product eventually becomes part of its buyer's value chain. The ultimate basis for differentiation is a firm and its product's role in the buyer's value chain, which is determined by buyer needs. Gaining and sustaining competitive advantage depends on understanding not only a firm's value chain, but how the firm fits into the overall value system.

There are often circumstances where the overall cost can be reduced (or the value increased) by collaborative arrangements between different organizations in the value system. It will be seen in Chapter 11 that this is often the rationale behind downstream collaborative arrangements, such as joint ventures, subcontracting and outsourcing between different organizations (e.g. sharing technology in the international motor manufacture and electronics industries).

EXHIBIT 1.4 Pocoyo – upstream–downstream cooperation about globalization of an animated preschool series

One of the most successful TV-programmes for preschool kids, Pocoyo, was created by Zinkia Entertainment and sold woldwide by Granada Ventures. It is now a global brand and has been sold to more than 100 countries since it was launched in late 2005. Produced with bright blocks of colour against a stark white background, Pocoyo has been designed to hold the attention of young children.

Pocoyo Series © Zinkia Entertainment, S.A.

Pocoyo

Pocoyo is a young boy with an array of qualities ready to capture the imagination of children, inspiring them to watch, listen and interact. He is a curious enthusiastic little boy in blue. As he explores his world through each story, Pocoyo gets help and on occasion hindrance from his friends Loula, Pato, Elly and Sleepy Bird.

Pocoyo has at its core a fascinating concept – one of learning through laughter. Clinical studies have shown that laughter not only increases the enjoyment and engagement of children in the programme, but also is proven to increase learning by 15 per cent. By working closely with behavioural psychologists during programme development, Pocoyo uses simple and effective visual jokes that help children to discover magic and humour in the simplest of things. And far from painting an idealized version of childhood, Pocoyo is sometimes moody, noisy and miserable – just like a real preschooler.

The value chain of Pocoyo

As illustrated in Pocoyo's value chain (see Figure 1.13) Zinkia Entertainment is taking care of the development and production of the Pocoyo series (upstream functions) whereas Granada Ventures takes care of global licensing and publishing rights (downstream functions).

Zinkia Entertainment is a company founded in 2001. Located in Madrid, Spain, its main focus is to create animated series for TV and games for mobile devices and for game platforms. The company has more than 100 employees and its series have been sold in more than 100 countries worldwide. It is a creative factory producing audiovisual content, focusing on animation and cinematic documentaries as well as interactive

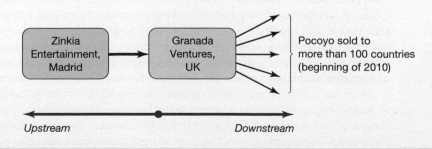

Figure 1.13 The Pocoyo value chain

content for online communities, consoles and multiplayer mobile games. Since the company was established, Zinkia's projects include, among others, Pocoyo (52 × 7 minutes), a 3D animated preschool series. In June 2006, Pocoyo was awarded the Cristal award for the 'Best TV Series in the world' at the 30th International Festival of Annecy.

Zinkia Entertainment's partner in the Pocoyo value chain is Granada Ventures, the merchandise, licensing and publishing division of the UK-based television channel ITV plc. Established in October 2003, following the merger of Granada and Carlton, the company's remit is to drive secondary revenue streams for the corporation by moving brands beyond broadcast by selling them worldwide on a licensing basis, mainly to other TV channels. The company currently owns worldwide licensing and publishing rights of almost 1,000 products and 3,000 DVD titles in television, film and sports. This includes brands such as Pocoyo and Hell's Kitchen as well as established brands such as 'I'm A Celebrity . . . Get Me Out Of Here!'

Cultural issues in the globalization of Pocoyo

Normally global branding is comprehensive and the cultural demands of the market are difficult to define. However it seems that the core themes of Pocoyo – learning, gentle humour, visual stimulus and play – cross all national borders.

Pocoyo was developed in Spain, with a great deal of input from the UK. In the original rushes, Pocoyo was often seen with a dummy in his mouth, which caused a few alarm bells to ring in Britain. The Madrid team had not even begun to consider that this might be the cause of any controversy, but in line with current cultural queries on the parental right and wrongs of using a pacifier in other parts of the globe, the dummy had to go.

Worldwide brand extensions

Brand extensions into merchandise are equally important for ensuring Pocoyo's world success and longevity. Granada Ventures has been able to give Pocoyo a life off-screen with books, bath toys and clothing. Children can play with the character, along with their parents and peers, around the clock. This creates a virtuous brand circle, increasing loyalty and affection.

Sources: Donohoe, G. (2006) 'How to reach children in every nation', *Brand Strategy*, June, p. 10; www.zinkia.com/; www.granadaventures.co.uk/.

Internationalizing the value chain

International configuration and coordination of activities

All internationally oriented firms must consider an eventual internationalization of the value chain's functions. The firm must decide whether the responsibility for the single value chain function is to be moved to the export markets or is best handled centrally from head office. Principally, the value chain function should be carried out where there is the highest competence (and the most cost-effectiveness), and this is not necessarily at head office.

A distinction immediately arises between the activities labelled downstream on Figure 1.11 and those labelled upstream. The location of downstream activities, those more related to the buyer, is usually tied to where the buyer is located. If a firm is going to sell in Australia, for example, it must usually provide service in Australia, and it must have salespeople stationed in Australia. In some industries it is possible to have a single sales force that travels to the buyer's country and back again; other specific downstream activities, such as the production of advertising copy, can sometimes also be performed centrally. More typically, however, the firm must locate the capability to perform downstream activities in each of the countries in which it operates. In contrast, upstream activities and support activities are more independent of where the buyer is located (Figure 1.14). However, if the export markets are culturally close to the home market, it may be relevant to control the entire value chain from head office (home market).

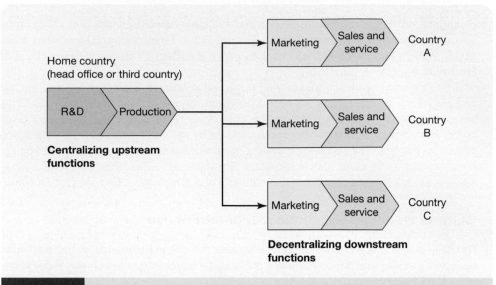

| Figure 1.14 | Centralizing the upstream activities and decentralizing the downstream activities |

Source: Hollensen, S. (2008) *Essentials of Global Marketing*, FT/Prentice Hall.

This distinction carries some interesting implications. First, downstream activities create competitive advantages that are largely country specific: a firm's reputation, brand name and service network in a country grow largely out of its activities and create entry/mobility barriers largely in that country alone. Competitive advantage in upstream and support activities often grows more out of the entire *system* of countries in which a firm competes than from its position in any single country.

Second, in industries where downstream activities or other buyer-tied activities are vital to competitive advantage, there tends to be a more multidomestic pattern of international competition. In many service industries, for example, not only downstream activities but frequently upstream activities are tied to buyer location, and global strategies are comparatively less common. In industries where upstream and support activities such as technology development and operations are crucial to competitive advantage, global competition is more common. For example, there may be a large need in firms to centralize and coordinate the production function worldwide to be able to create rational production units that are able to exploit economies of scale.

Furthermore, as customers increasingly join regional cooperative buying organizations, it is becoming more and more difficult to sustain a price differentiation across markets, which will put pressure on the firm to coordinate a European price policy. This will be discussed further in Chapter 15.

The distinctive issues of international strategies, in contrast to domestic, can be summarized in two key dimensions of how a firm competes internationally. The first is called the *configuration* of a firm's worldwide activities, or the location in the world where each activity in the value chain is performed, including the number of places. For example, a company can locate different parts of its value chain in different places – factories in China, call centres in India and retail shops in Europe. IBM is an example of a company that exploits wage differentials by increasing the number of employees in India from 9,000 in 2004 to 50,000 by mid-2007 and by planning for massive additional growth. Most of these employees are in IBM Global Services, the part of the company that is growing fastest but has the lowest margins – which the Indian employees are supposed to improve, by reducing (wage) costs rather than raising the prices (Ghemawat, 2007).

The second dimension is called *coordination*, which refers to how identical or linked activities performed in different countries are coordinated with each other (Porter, 1986).

1.8   Value shop and the service value chain

Value shops
A model for solving problems in a service environment. Similar to workshops. Value is created by mobilizing resources and deploying them to solve a specific customer problem.

Value networks
The formation of several firms' value chains into a network, where each company contributes a small part to the total value chain.

Michael Porter's value-chain model claims to identify the sequence of key generic activities that businesses perform in order to generate value for customers. Since its introduction in 1985, this model has dominated the thinking of business executives. Yet a growing number of services businesses, including banks, hospitals, insurance companies, business consulting services and telecommunications companies, have found that the traditional value-chain model does not fit the reality of their service industry sectors. Stabell and Fjeldstad (1998) identified two new models of value creation – **value shops** and **value networks**. They argue that the value chain is a model for making products, while the value *shop* is a model for solving customer or client problems in a service environment. The value network is a model for mediating exchanges between customers. Each model utilizes a different set of core activities to create and deliver distinct forms of value to customers.

The main differences between the two types of value chains are illustrated in Table 1.2.

Table 1.2	The traditional value chain versus the service value chain

Traditional value chain model	Service value chain (value shop) model
Value creation through transformation of inputs (raw material and components) to products.	Value creation through customer problem-solving. Value is created by mobilizing resources and activities to resolve a particular and unique customer problem. Customer value is not related to the solution itself but to the value of solving the problem.
Sequential process ('first we develop the product, then we produce it, and finally we sell it').	Cyclical and iterative process.
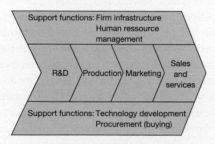	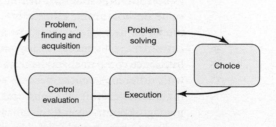
The traditional value chain consists of primary and support activities: primary activities are directly involved in creating and bringing value to customers: upstream (product development and production) and downstream activities (marketing and sales and service). Support activities that enable and improve the performance of the primary activities are procurement, technology development, human resource management and firm infrastructure.	The primary activities of a value shop are: 1. **Problem-finding**: activities associated with the recording, reviewing and formulating of the problem to be solved and choosing the overall approach to solving the problem. 2. **Problem-solving**: activities associated with generating and evaluating alternative solutions. 3. **Choice**: activities associated with choosing among alternative problem solutions. 4. **Execution**: activities associated with communicating, organizing and implementing the chosen solution. 5. **Control and evaluation**: activities associated with measuring and evaluating to what extent implementation has solved the initial statement.
Examples: production and sales of furniture, consumer food products, electronic products and other mass products.	Examples: banks, hospitals, insurance companies, business consulting services and telecommunications companies.

Source: based on Stabell and Fjeldstad (1998).

Value shops (as in workshops, not retail stores) create value by mobilizing resources (e.g. people, knowledge and skills) and deploying them to solve specific problems such as curing an illness, delivering airline services to the passengers or delivering a solution to a business problem. Shops are organized around making and executing decisions – identifying and assessing problems or opportunities, developing alternative solutions or approaches, choosing one, executing it and evaluating the results. This model applies to most service-oriented organizations such as building contractors, consultancies and legal organizations. However, it also applies to organizations that are primarily configured to identify and exploit specific market opportunities, such as developing a new drug, drilling a potential oilfield, or designing a new aircraft.

Different parts of a typical business may exhibit characteristics of different configurations. For example, production and distribution may resemble a value chain; research and development a value shop.

Value shops make use of specialized knowledge-based systems to support the task of creating solutions to problems. However, the challenge is to provide an integrated set of applications that enable seamless execution across the entire problem-solving or opportunity-exploitation process. Several key technologies and applications are emerging in value shops – many focus on utilizing people and knowledge better. Groupware, intranets, desktop videoconferencing and shared electronic workspaces enhance communication and collaboration between people, essential to mobilizing people and knowledge across value shops. Integrating project planning with execution is proving crucial, for example, in pharmaceutical development, where bringing a new drug through the long, complex approval process a few months early can mean millions of dollars in revenue. Technologies such as inference engines and neural networks can help to make knowledge about problems and the process for solving them explicit and accessible.

The term 'value network' is widely used but imprecisely defined. It often refers to a group of companies, each specializing in one piece of the value chain, and linked together in some virtual way to create and deliver products and services. Stabell and Fjelstad (1998) define value networks quite differently – not as networks of affiliated companies, but as a business model for a single company that mediates interactions and exchanges across a network of its customers. This model clearly applies best to telecommunications companies, but also to insurance companies and banks, whose business, essentially, is mediating between customers with different financial needs – some saving, some borrowing, for example. Key activities include operating the customer-connecting infrastructure, promoting the network, managing contracts and relationships and providing services.

Some of the most IT-intensive businesses in the world are value networks – banks, airlines and telecommunications companies, for instance. Most of their technology provides the basic infrastructure of the 'network' to mediate exchanges between customers. However, the competitive landscape is now shifting beyond automation and efficient transaction processing to monitoring and exploiting information about customer behaviour.

The aim is to add more value to customer exchanges through better understanding of usage patterns, exchange opportunities, shared interests and so on. Data mining and visualization tools, for example, can be used to identify both positive and negative connections between customers.

Competitive success often depends on more than simply performing your primary model well. It may also require the delivery of additional kinds of complementary value. Adopting attributes of a second value configuration model can be a powerful way to differentiate your value proposition or defend it against competitors pursuing a value model different to your own. It is essential, however, to pursue another model only in ways that leverage the primary model. For example, Harley-Davidson's primary model is the chain – it makes and sells products. Forming the Harley Owners Group (HOG) – a network of customers – added value to the primary model by reinforcing the brand identity, building loyalty, and providing valuable information and feedback about customers' behaviours and preferences. Amazon.com is a value chain like other book distributors, and initially used technology to make the process vastly more efficient. Now, with its book recommendations and special interest groups, it is adding the characteristics of a value network. Our research suggests that the value network in particular offers opportunities for many existing businesses to add more value to their customers, and for new entrants to capture market share from those who offer less value to their customers.

Combining the product value chain and the service value chain

Blomstermo *et al.* (2006) make a distinction between *hard* and *soft services*. Hard services are those where production and consumption can be decoupled. For example software services can be transferred into a CD, or some other tangible medium, which can be mass-produced, making standardization possible. With soft services, where production and consumption occur simultaneously, the customer acts as a coproducer, and decoupling is not viable. The soft-service provider must be present abroad from its first day of foreign operations. Figure 1.15 is mainly valid for soft services, but at the same time in more and more industries we see that physical products and services are combined.

Most product companies offer services to protect or enhance the value of their product businesses. Cisco, for instance, built its installation, maintenance, and network-design service business to ensure high-quality product support and to strengthen relationships with enterprise and telecom customers. A company may also find itself drawn into services when it realizes that competitors use its products to offer services of value. If it does nothing, it risks not only the commoditization of its own products – something that is occurring in most product markets, irrespective of the services on offer – but also the loss of customer

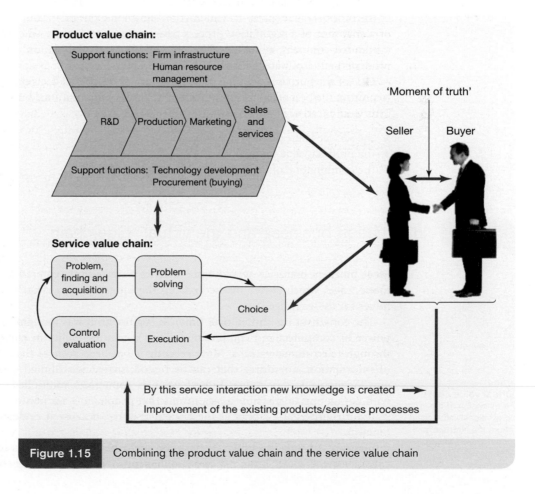

| Figure 1.15 | Combining the product value chain and the service value chain |

relationships. To make existing service groups profitable, or to succeed in launching a new embedded service business, executives of product companies must decide whether the primary focus of service units should be to support existing product businesses or to grow as a new and independent platform.

When a company chooses a business design for delivering embedded *services* to customers, it should remember that its strategic intent affects which elements of the delivery life cycle are most important. If the aim is to protect or enhance the *value* of a product, the company should integrate the system for delivering it and the associated *services* in order to promote the development of product designs that simplify the task of *service* (e.g. by using fewer subsystems or integrating diagnostic software). This approach involves minimizing the footprint of *service* delivery and incorporating support into the product whenever possible. If the company wants the *service* business to be an independent growth platform, however, it should focus most of its delivery efforts on constantly reducing unit costs and making the *services* more productive (Auguste *et al.*, 2006).

In the 'moment of truth' (e.g. in a consultancy service situation), the seller represents all the functions of the focal company's product and service value chain – at the same time. The seller (the product and service provider) and the buyer create a service in an interaction process: 'The service is being created and consumed as it is produced'. Good representatives on the seller's side are vital to service brands' successes, being ultimately responsible for delivering the seller's promise. As such a shared understanding of the service brand's values needs to be anchored in their minds and hearts to encourage brand-supporting behaviour. This internal brand-building process becomes more challenging as service brands expand internationally drawing on workers from different global domains.

Figure 1.15 also shows the cyclic nature of the service interaction (moment of truth) where the post-evaluation of the service value chain gives input for the possible redesign of the product value chain. The interaction shown in Figure 1.15 could also be an illustration or a snapshot of a negotiation process between seller and buyer, where the seller represents a branded company, which is selling its projects as a combination of 'hardware' (physical products) and 'software' (services).

One of the purposes with the learning nature of the overall decision cycle in Figure 1.15 is to pick up the best practices among different kinds of international buyer–seller interactions. This would lead to implications for a better set-up of:

- the service value chain (value shop)
- the product value chain
- the combination of the service and product value chain.

1.9   Information business and the virtual value chain

Most business managers would agree that we have recently entered a new era, 'the information age', which differs markedly from the industrial age. What have been the driving forces for these changes?

The consensus has shifted over time. To begin with it was thought to be the automation power of computers and computation. Then it was the ability to collapse time and space through telecommunications. More recently it has been seen as the value-creating power of information, a resource that can be reused, shared, distributed or exchanged without any inevitable loss of value; indeed value is sometimes multiplied. Today's fascination with competing on invisible assets means that people now see knowledge and its relationship with intellectual capital as the critical resource, because it underpins innovation and renewal.

Virtual value chain
An extension of the conventional value chain, where the information processing itself can create value for customers.

One way of understanding the strategic opportunities and threats of information is to consider the **virtual value chain** as a supplement to the physical value chain (Figure 1.16).

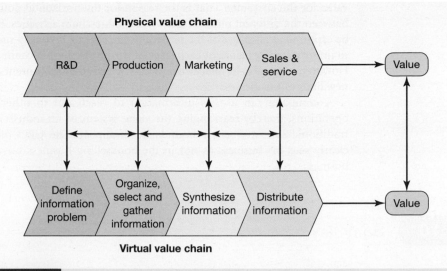

Figure 1.16   The virtual value chain as a supplement to the physical chain

By introducing the virtual value chain Rayport and Sviokla (1996) have made an extension of the conventional value chain model, which treats information as a supporting element in the value-adding process. They show how information in itself can be used to create value.

Fundamentally, there are four ways of using information to create business value (Marchand, 1999):

1. *Managing risks.* In the twentieth century the evolution of risk management stimulated the growth of functions and professions such as finance, accounting, auditing and controlling. These information-intensive functions tend to be major consumers of IT resources and people's time.
2. *Reducing costs.* Here the focus is on using information as efficiently as possible to achieve the outputs required from business processes and transactions. This process view of information management is closely linked with the re-engineering and continuous improvement movements of the 1990s. The common elements are focused on eliminating unnecessary and wasteful steps and activities, especially paperwork and information movements, and then simplifying and, if possible, automating the remaining processes.
3. *Offering products and services.* Here the focus is on knowing one's customers, and sharing information with partners and suppliers to enhance customer satisfaction. Many service and manufacturing companies focus on building relationships with customers and on demand management as ways of using information. Such strategies have led companies to invest in point-of-sale systems, account management, customer profiling and service management systems.
4. *Inventing new products.* Finally, companies can use information to innovate – to invent new products, provide different services and use emerging technologies. Companies such as Intel and Microsoft are learning to operate in 'continuous discovery mode', inventing new products more quickly and using market intelligence to retain a competitive edge. Here, information management is about mobilizing people and collaborative work processes to share information and promote discovery throughout the company.

Every company pursues some combination of the above strategies.

In relation to Figure 1.16 each of the physical value-chain activities might make use of one or all four information-processing stages of the virtual value chain, in order to create extra value for the customer. That is the reason for the horizontal double arrows (in Figure 1.16) between the different physical and virtual value-chain activities. In this way information can be captured at all stages of the physical value chain. Obviously such information can be used to improve performance at each stage of the physical value chain and to coordinate across it. However, it can also be analysed and repackaged to build content-based products or to create new lines of businesses.

A company can use its information to reach out to other companies' customers or operations, thereby rearranging the value system of an industry. The result might be that traditional industry sector boundaries disappear. The CEO of Amazon.com, Jeff Bezos, clearly sees his business as not in the bookselling business but in the information-broker business.

1.10   Summary

Global marketing is defined as the firm's commitment to coordinate its marketing activities across national boundaries in order to find and satisfy global customer needs better than the competition does. This implies that the firm is able to:

- develop a global marketing strategy, based on similarities and differences between markets;
- exploit the knowledge of the headquarters (home organization) through worldwide diffusion (learning) and adaptations;
- transfer knowledge and best practices from any of its markets and use them in other international markets.

SMEs are often characterized by an entrepreneurial and action-oriented decision-making model, where drastic changes in strategy are possible because decision-making is intuitive, sporadic and unstructured. On the other hand SMEs are more flexible than LSEs and are able to react more quickly to sudden changes in the international environment.

However, as a consequence of LSEs often acting as a confederation of SMEs, there seems to be a convergence of the marketing behaviour in SMEs and LSEs towards a market-responsiveness approach.

Porter's original value chain model was introduced as a framework model for major parts of this book. In understanding how value is created it is not enough to look at the firm's internal value chain alone. In most cases the supply and distribution value chains are interconnected, and this whole process needs to be analysed and understood before considering an eventual internationalization of value chain activities. This also involves decisions about configuration and coordination of the worldwide value-chain activities.

As a supplement to the traditional (Porter) value chain, the service value chain (based on the so-called value shop concept) has been introduced. Value shops create value by mobilizing resources (people, knowledge and skills,) and deploying them to solve specific problems. Value shops are organized around making and executing decisions in the specific service interaction situation with a customer – identifying and assessing service problems or opportunities, developing alternative solutions or approaches, choosing one, executing it and evaluating the results. This model applies to most service-oriented organizations.

Many product companies want to succeed with embedded services: as competitive pressures increasingly commoditize product markets, services will become the main differentiator of *value* creation in coming years. However, companies will need a clearer understanding of the strategic rules of this new game – and will have to integrate the rules into their operations – to realize the promise of these fast-growing businesses.

At the end of this chapter the virtual value chain was introduced as a supplement to the physical value chain, thus using information to create further business value.

CASE STUDY 1.1

Build-A-Bear Workshop (BBW): how to manage the global comeback?

In spring 2010 the founder of BBW, Maxine Clark, is enjoying one of the beautiful May days before she will have to pack her luggage for her next trip to Europe, where she will have some further negotiations with some potential master franchisees. The last two years have been difficult for BBW after a financial crisis that hit the whole world in 2008. Maxine still believes 100 per cent in the BBW concept, which takes advantage of the new trend in our experience economy – to let consumers participate in the creation of customer value. However, it seems that the global wave of enthusiasm has been sated, and how can BBW get it back on track again with new international growth as the result?

Background

Build-A-Bear Workshop, Inc. (BBW) – www.buildabear.com – is the leading and only global company that offers a create-your-own animal service in the retailing experience sector.

Founded in 1997, the company currently operates more than 400 Build-A-Bear Workshop stores worldwide, including company-owned stores in the United States, Puerto Rico, Canada, the United Kingdom, Ireland and France, and franchise stores in Europe, Asia, Australia and Africa.

Build-A-Bear Workshop posted total revenue of $468 million in the fiscal year 2008.

Since opening the first store in St. Louis, Missouri in October 1997, BBW have sold over 70 million stuffed animals. BBW have grown their store base from 200 stores at the end of the fiscal year 2005 to 346 as of 3 January 2009 and increased revenue from $362 million in 2005 to $468 million in the fiscal year 2008.

As of January, 2009, BBW employed approximately 1,200 full-time and 4,800 part-time employees.

BBW does not own or operate any manufacturing facilities. Their animal skins, stuffing, clothing and accessories are produced by factories located primarily in China.

The company's motto is *Where Best Friends Are Made*. It is headquartered in Overland, Missouri.

How it started

Maxine Clark left Payless Shoe*Source* in 1996. At that time she was 47 years old and her financial rewards in retailing had been very high. When she left Payless, she could have left retailing or even retired. She had earned enough money to do anything she wanted, even if pay or responsibilities were not comparable. She had the luxury to learn and start up something totally new.

Generally, she was bored by shopping, and she was looking to recreate the excitement and magic that she felt as a child when she visited certain stores. Going shopping was an event. Customers became part of the store, and it was special.

Maxine Clark remembers:

I like to say the lightbulb went off for Build-A-Bear Workshop one day in the summer of 1996. I was out shopping with my friend Katie, who was 10 years old at the time. We were on a mission to find Beanie Babies, but the store that had promised a new shipment had none left. Katie looked at me and said, 'These are so easy – we could make them.' She meant go to my basement and do a craft project, but what I heard was so much bigger and the idea for Build-A-Bear Workshop was born.

Source: http://www.businessweek.com/smallbiz/content/sep 2007/sb20070912_785676.htm?Chan=search.

In the process of developing a retail entertainment concept for children, Clark visited toy factories and children's retail stores, put together a list of ideas, then consulted the experts: children. Clark consulted first with the children of a friend, then formed an advisory board of 20 children, ages 6 to 14, and showed them three of her ideas. The decision to pursue the Build-A-Bear concept emerged from the board's enthusiasm, combined with Clark's personal preference for teddy bears and the high profit margin for stuffed animals.

Clark then hired design consultant Adrienne Weiss Co. of Los Angeles, using 80 per cent of her $750,000 personal savings investment, to develop the Build-A-Bear concept. Clark collaborated with consultants in developing every detail, including artwork, employee costumes, store design and company logo. The logo features a teddy bear being measured, stitched, stuffed and groomed. All lettering is similar to children's printing.

Maxine Clark opened her first Build-A-Bear Workshop concept store in a St. Louis shopping mall (in the USA) in 1997. Sales were near $400,000 in the store in less than four months.

In 1999 the success of the retail concept attracts venture capital for expansion; Build-A-Bear opens ten new stores in United States. The sales in these stores averaged $700 per square foot of retail space, an enormous success in contrast to national mall averages of $350 per square foot. The cost of opening a new store ranged from $500,000 to $700,000, but with annual sales estimated at $2 million per store, Clark easily found capital investment for expansion.

In 2003 BBW's international expansion begins with new locations in Canada and England. Although Clark intended to take the company global from its inception, concrete plans did not begin to take shape until late 2002. In November 2002 Build-A-Bear signed a franchise agreement with Japan, held by Tech R&DS Co. Ltd. The company also began a search for locations in the United Kingdom. These new countries for BBW were chosen in response to requests from customers who had visited stores while in the United States or had visited the company's website. A high number of addresses in the Find-A-Bear ID database for these countries indicated strong interest in the Build-A-Bear concept.

Customers' retailing experience

A Build-A-Bear Workshop store is an average of 3,000 square feet. Every element of the store design was intended to delight children under the age of 12.

Guests who visit Build-A-Bear Workshop stores enter a teddy bear-themed environment. They will be met by store associates, known as master Bear Builder associates, who share the experience with guests at each of the phases of the bear-making process, which consists of eight stuffed animal-making stations: Choose Me, Hear Me, Stuff Me, Stitch Me, Fluff Me, Dress Me, Name Me and Take Me Home. To attract their target guests, BBW has designed their stores to provide a 'theme park'

Build-A-Bear

destination in the mall that is open and inviting with an entryway that spans the majority of their storefront and highly visual and colourful teddy bear themes and displays.

At **Choose Me**, guests are introduced to all the furry characters in the store and then select one, which soon becomes their new friend. There are more than 30 varieties of stuffed animals including teddy bears, bunnies, dogs, kitties and more. Build-A-Bear Workshop stuffed animals are very affordable, ranging in price from $10–25.

At **Hear Me**, guests may select from several sound choices to place inside their stuffed animal to further personalize their new friend. The sound chip is inserted safely inside the new friend during the stuffing process. Guests can record their own 10-second Build-A-Sound message. Pre-recorded sounds include giggles, growls, barks, meows and other animal sounds, as well as messages such as 'I Love You' or songs like 'Take Me Out To The Ballgame'.

At **Stuff Me**, with the help of master Bear Builder associates, guests fill their new friend with stuffing for just the right amount of huggability. A very special step that is unique to Build-A-Bear Workshop also happens at this station. Each guest selects a small satin heart – a Build-A-Bear Workshop trademark, adds to it his or her own love and wishes, and carefully places it inside their new furry friend. This process brings the furry friendship to life (see picture below).

At **Stitch Me**, the last seam is neatly pulled shut, nearly completing each new best friend. Before

Build-A-Bear

date and of course, its name. The furry friend is then entered into the Find-A-Bear ID programme and this information is used to create a personalized birth certificate for the furry friend.

Finally, at the **Take Me Home** station, the guests receive their customized birth certificate and a special Stuff Fur Stuff® club membership, a rewards programme for our guests. Instead of a traditional shopping bag, each new furry friend is then placed in their very own 'Cub Condo' carrying case, which is designed as a handy travel carrier and new home.

The duration of a guest's experience can vary greatly depending on their preferences. Most guests choose to participate in the full animal-making process and all eight stations, a process which BBW believe averages 45 minutes to complete. Because customers are involved with creating their purchase, they remember it vividly and tell lots of other people about it. Almost half of our new customers heard about the store from a friend or family member.

Guests can continue the fun with their bear friends when they get home and sit at their computer. At buildabearville.com, guests can bring their new furry friend to life online for free by using the code found on their birth certificate. They create a unique online character and play games to earn Bear Bills, which can be used to purchase more clothes, furniture for their Cub Condo houses and other items. Guests can also trade items with other citizens in the world. Membership to the site is free and does not expire.

Beyond bringing their new friend to life online for free, guests are rewarded for in-store purchases. When they make a clothing or accessory purchase in store or at www.buildabear.com, they receive a receipt code. The code gives them virtual store credit to use at the Bear Boutique in Build-A-Bearville, which is the only place to find exclusive virtual fashions and furniture items for their virtual furry friends.

To provide the fun of making a furry friend to groups – birthday parties, scout troops, company outings and family reunions – Build-A-Bear Workshop offers a Build-A-Party® programme. This exclusive service allows guests to plan and customize their own party with preselected animals, clothes and accessories.

Overall, BBW believe they are strongly positioned to lead in this retail space with over 70 million stuffed animals sold and over 24 million households in their online database.

On average each customer spends approximately $50 in the BBW store (including web-sales afterwards).

stitching the furry friend, the master Bear Builder associate inserts a barcode, allowing it to hopefully be reunited with its owner if ever lost and returned to Build-A-Bear Workshop. Thousands of furry friends have been reunited through our exclusive Find-A-Bear® ID programme. The barcode also generates a unique code on the birth certificate so guests can bring their new friend to life online for free at buildabearville.com to continue their friendship adventure when they get home.

At **Fluff Me**, the guest brushes the animal to make sure their new friend is well groomed and huggable!

At **Dress Me**, guests may dress their new friend in the beary latest furry fashions. The bear apparel boutique features clothes and accessories for all occasions. Build-A-Bear Workshop® even has its own fashion expert mascot, 'Pawlette Coufur', Fashion Advisor to the Furry Famous. Build-A-Bear Workshop works with a variety of partners, including Hello Kitty, Disney and Harley-Davidson.

At the **Name Me** the guests answer several questions about their new bear friend, including the birth

Customer feedback drives the business

BBW's primary audience is e-mail-savvy; the company relies heavily on electronic communications. So, Maxine Clark's e-mail inbox fills up with 4,000 notes per month, most of them from customers.

Those voices have created most of the company's new products. Some customer suggestions: add a black Labrador as a product. The company did. In its first six months, it sold 100,000 units. The company had already been offering shoes to go with each animal. Why not add socks, a customer suggested. Shortly thereafter, the company did. Another customer suggested party rooms for birthdays and get-togethers, which the company began to offer in selected stores in 2002.

Every e-mail writer receives a personal response from Maxine Clark or one of the company's executive team. Maxine Clark stays close to customers with a 'Cub Advisory Board', a group of 20 boys and girls 8–17 years old who review new products and suggest additional ones. It meets with Clark and her team three or four times per year.

BBW involvement in cause marketing

BBW believes in the teddy bear philosophy of being good people and good bears. Throughout its 11-year history the company has given guests a voice to support causes that are important to them, helping children, families, animals and the environment. Since the company's inception, BBW has donated over $20 million to these causes.

One of these partnership is with the World Wildlife Fund (WWF), offering a series of WWF co-branded plush animals in stores. In 2000 Build-A-Bear Workshop introduced the giant panda, the first in a series of co-branded stuffed animals. Since then, a new furry friend has been launched each year, many representing animals in danger around the world. In addition to the giant panda, Build-A-Bear Workshop has sold the Bengal tiger, leopard, lion, polar bear and the giraffe. Each WWF bear animal comes with a collector's medallion featuring the WWF official panda logo and a numbered Certificate of Authenticity, further enhancing its value to the collector.

In 2006 BBW announced that it had given $1 million to the WWF through the sales of its WWF Collectibear stuffed animal series. For each plush animal sold one dollar goes to WWF to protect and conserve wildlife around the world.

In 2009 Build-A-Bear Workshop® continued its partnership with the WWF by introducing the newest member of the WWF Collectibear® series.

Starting 28 August, make your own WWF Gray Wolf ($25) at Build-A-Bear Workshop stores or buildabear.com®. In the United States and Canada $1 from the sale will be donated to WWF to help protect endangered animals and their habitats.

BBW retail store base, international expansion and franchise strategy

The BBW retail segment includes the operating activities of company-owned stores in the United States, Canada, the United Kingdom, Ireland and France.

The table lists of BBW's **346 company-owned stores** in the United States, Canada, the United Kingdom, Ireland and France as of 3 January 2009.

Company-owned stores	Number of stores (January 2009)
United States	271
Canada	21
United Kingdom:	
England	42
Scotland	6
Wales	1
Northern Ireland	1
Ireland	1
France	3
	346

In 2003, BBW began to expand the Build-A-Bear Workshop brand outside of the United States, opening company-owned stores in Canada and our first franchised location in the United Kingdom. As of 3 January 2009, there were 62 Build-A-Bear Workshop franchised stores located in the following countries:

Country	No. stores
Japan	10
South Africa	9
Denmark	8
Australia	6
Thailand	6
Singapore	5
Germany	4
Russia	4
Norway + Sweden	3
Benelux*	3
Other	4
Total	62

* Benelux includes Belgium, the Netherlands and Luxembourg.

All stores outside of the US, Canada, the United Kingdom, Ireland and France are currently operated by third-party franchisees under separate master franchise agreements covering each country. Master franchise rights are typically granted to a franchisee for an entire country or group of countries for a specified term. The terms of these master franchise agreements vary by country but typically BBW receives an initial, one-time franchise fee and continuing royalties based on a percentage of sales made by the franchisees' stores. The terms of these agreements range up to ten years with a franchisee option to renew for an additional term if certain conditions are met.

Revenue from international franchise fees was $3.6 million for fiscal 2008 – it represents less than 1 per cent of the total revenues.

Competition

Because BBW is mall-based, BBW see their competition as those mall-based retailers that compete for prime mall locations, including various apparel, footwear and specialty retailers. BBW also competes with toy retailers, such as Wal-Mart, Toys Я Us, Target, Kmart and Sears and other discount chains, as well as with a number of companies that sell teddy bears and dolls in the United States and elsewhere, including, but not limited to, Ty, Fisher Price, Mattel, Ganz, Russ Berrie, Applause, Boyd's, Hasbro, Commonwealth, Gund and Vermont Teddy Bear. Since BBW sells a product that integrates merchandise and experience, BBW also view their competition as any company that competes for guests' time and entertainment dollars, such as movie theatres, amusement parks and arcades, other mall-based entertainment venues and online entertainment.

BBW is aware of several small companies that operate 'make your own' teddy bear and stuffed animal stores or kiosks in retail locations, but BBW believes none offer the breadth and depth of the Build-A-Bear Workshop experience or operates as a national or international retail company.

BBW also believes that there is an emerging trend within children's play patterns towards Internet and online play. According to Emarketer.com, kids aged 8 to 11 reported that they spend between one and two hours online each day. In 2007, 24 per cent of US child and teen Internet users will visit virtual worlds. By 2011, an estimated 53 per cent will do so. Therefore, BBW believes they can compete with other companies and Internet sites that vie for children's attention in the online space including webkinz.com, clubpenguin.com and neopets.com.

Until now, Build-A-Bear Workshop is the only virtual world with real world retail stores. A growing number of traditional children's toy and entertainment companies have also developed their own virtual world online, including Barbie.com, be-bratz.com and virtualmagickingdom.com.

BBW's marketing strategy

While BBW offers consumers an interactive and personalized experience, their tangible product is stuffed animals, including our flagship product, the teddy bear, a widely adored stuffed animal for over 100 years. According to data published by the Toy Industry Association and The NPD Group, sales of the traditional toy market were $22.2 billion in the United States (excluding video games) in 2008 with plush and doll sales having a combined 20 per cent share of the traditional toy market. According to further data provided by The NPD Group, worldwide toy sales topped $71.96 billion dollars in 2007. In 2008, *Playthings Magazine* ranked BBW as the tenth largest toy retailer in the United States for 2007 based on sales.

The overall BBW strategy is directly connected to the customer contacts in the BBW store area. In contrary to normal personnel in stores, the BBW shop assistants are trained more to be 'entertainers' (providing an experience to the children) than being traditional shop selling assistants.

BBW's pricing strategy

Unlike other mall-based retailers that frequently use markdowns or sale events to drive sales, BBW uses value-added marketing to raise brand awareness and drive traffic to our stores and makes limited use of markdowns.

BBW's advertising strategy

BBW employs a variety of different marketing tools and programmes to drive traffic to their stores and raise brand awareness. BBW use television advertising that targets both children and adults to keep their experience and BBW products at top of mind. Periodically BBW features specific new product introductions and promotions as a call-to-action to visit their stores. BBW also uses radio, print and online advertising integrating their message across various touch points to maximize their reach to new and existing guests. BBW leverages the database from their Stuff Fur Stuff club loyalty programme with over four million active members in their direct mail

Table 1	BBB financial situation 2006–2008		
BBW	2008 US$ (millions)	2007 US$ (millions)	2006 US$ (millions)
Total revenues	467	474	437
Less costs:			
Variable costs (materials etc.)	270	259	228
Selling, general, administrative	186	177	159
Other costs	6	16	21
Net income (net profits)	**5**	**22**	**29**

Source: BBW's 10K report.

Table 2	Retail sales per gross square foot (only BBW stores in North America)		
	Fiscal 2008 US$	Fiscal 2007 US$	Fiscal 2006 US$
Net retail sales per gross square foot			
Store age >5 years	448	517	577
Store age 3–5 years	455	537	556
Store age <3 years	432	497	592
All comparable stores	**445**	**516**	**573**

Source: BBW's 10K report.

and e-mail programs and provide information and e-commerce on their website, www.buildabear.com.

BBW have developed licensing and strategic relationships with some of the leading retail and cultural organizations in North America and Europe. We believe that our guest base and our position in our industry category makes us an attractive partner and our customer research and insight allows us to focus on strategic relationships with other companies that we believe are appealing to our guests.

BBW financial results

The last three years main financial results of BBW indicate that problems are coming up.

Same-store sales is Wall Street's favourite metric for evaluating retailers. Wall Street will take one look at this trend, punish the stock, and move on in search of the next big thing. But could it be that a business still has value despite the pressure on same store sales that we see above? After all, same-store sales is but one metric.

For example, if costs are dropping faster than sales, there are still profits to be made. Unfortunately,

Build-A-Bear's full-year operating margins as a percentage of sales have actually been in decline for the last three years.

But consider the level of sales a Build-A-Bear store achieves in its first year. If that number is ridiculously high, then there is room to allow for declines in the next several years while still making comfortable profits. For the sake of comparison, here are Build-A-Bear's sales per square foot compared with an assortment of successful American retailers. BBW use net retail sales per gross square foot and comparable store sales as performance measures for our business. The following table details net retail sales per gross square foot by age of store for the periods presented.

As seen in Table 2 the sales problems appear to be biggest in the newest stores – at least the percentage drop in retail sales per gross square foot is biggest in stores <3 years.

Since BBW opened its first store more than 10 years ago, it has expanded to most parts of the world, In the following, the expansion to the Northern European market is further explained.

BBW expands to Scandinavia and Germany

In 2002 the Dane, Søren Nielsen and his daughter experienced the BBW concept for the first time in United States. He was very enthusiastic about the concept and shortly after coming home to Denmark formed a company together with some friends. In 2003 this new company, Choose Holding ApS, bought the franchise rights for Denmark for US$250,000. The first BBW shop opened in Copenhagen in April 2004.

The initial business was to establish five stores in Denmark the first five years, based on the experience in United States, where there is a shop per 1 million inhabitants. However, Choose Holding ApS had established nine stores in Denmark up to August 2009.

In 2005 Choose Holding ApS acquired the franchise rights for Norway and Sweden. The first store in Sweden opened in 2005, and in Norway in 2006.

The group is led by John Kristensen and Soren Nielsen and currently has nine stores in Denmark, two in Sweden and one in Norway.

After the success in Scandinavia, the founders of Choose Holding ApS acquired the franchise rights for Germany for US$750,000. The first two BBW stores opened in Hamburg in 2006 with two further shores in Berlin and Braunschweig. The plan is to open 50 BBW shops in Germany during the next five years. However, the market in Germany is quite different from that in Scandinavia:

- The children using bears are older.
- The parents are more involved in the buying process than the children.

- The dressing in BBW is more relaxed than most Germans are used to – the managers of the German BBW shops are mostly involved with the administrative tasks and not involved with selling and direct contact to customers in the front line – contrary to the traditional BBW way of communicating directly to the customers.
- The slogan '*Where best friends are made*' did not work in Germany. It had to be adapted to '*Beste Freunde zum selbermachen*' (Best friends to make for oneself).

These differences meant at the German BBW shop did not perform as planned, and the four German BBW shops were taken over by one of the founders of Choose Holding ApS in 2008.

QUESTIONS

1. How would you characterize the current global BBW strategy?

2. Is the headquarters of BBW in the USA following the right mixture of own stores and franchised stores?

3. What would you consider as the main reasons for the BBW failure in Germany?

4. How should BBW manage the global comeback?

Sources: www.buildabear.com (Financial Reports, 10K); http://www.businessweek.com/smallbiz/content/sep2007/sb20070912_785676.htm?Chan=search; http://www.funduniverse.com/company-histories/BuildABear-Workshop-Inc-Company-History.html; http://www.fyens.dk/article/948187:Business-Fyn--Bjoerne-eventyr-fik-voksevaerk (28.02.2008); http://borsen.dk/investor/nyhed/122205/.

CASE STUDY 1.2

Arcor: a Latin American confectionery player is globalizing its business

Arcor (www.arcor.com.ar/eng/) was founded in 1951 to produce sweets. However, in order to tell the company's history fully we must go back to 1924, the year Amos Pagani, a young Italian immigrant, decided to start a bakery in the Province of Córdoba. Today Arcor is still a private company owned by the Pagani family.

In the 1970s and 1980s Arcor transformed itself into a vast industrial complex, showing the way for other companies in the country, and continued to grow both in Argentina and in different countries in the region. Arcor started operations in Paraguay in 1976, in Uruguay in 1979, in Brazil in 1981 and in Chile in 1989.

In 1999 in Brazil Arcor opened the most advanced chocolate plant in the region, whose facilities also include the largest product distribution centre in that country. This was a start-up that put the company at the cutting edge of technology and production on the continent. It also permitted Arcor to consolidate its position in the very attractive Latin American market.

In order to continue with its expansion process Arcor established itself in Barcelona in 2002. Arcor's goal has always been to expand beyond the borders of its own country, and the opening of this new office allows the company to create closer bonds with customers from the European Economic Community, the Middle East and Africa.

Today the Arcor Group has 41 plants in the region (30 in Argentina, 5 in Brazil, 4 in Chile, one in Mexico and one in Peru).

ARCOR prepares more than 1,500 products in the four areas that make up its business focus: foods, confectionery, chocolates, cookies and crackers. In all these segments the company has developed a very high degree of know-how that has allowed it to become a true specialist in everything it produces. Arcor has the widest product portfolio in the bakery and confectionery market in all key sectors, except for dairy.

At present Arcor is well established in Latin America, but outside this area it is relatively weak. Of the total sales in 2007 of US$1,850 million less than 5 per cent derived from outside Latin America.

In the coming years, Arcor faces three big challenges within its international expansion framework: becoming the no. 1 Latin American confectionery and chocolate company; continuing to grow and establish itself in high development potential markets outside Latin America, such as the emerging Asian markets; and strengthening product penetration in the most demanding markets in the world: the United States, Japan and the European Union.

The group is an active participant in various strategic alliances (production and/or marketing agreements) with international players, such as Nestlé and Brach's. The most recent example is their partnership with Danone Group (France) in the biscuits and cereal bar business in Argentina, Brazil and Chile. In April 2004 the two companies merged their biscuit manufacturing activities into a single company, Bagley Latinoamérica SA, which resulted in the biggest biscuit company in South America. The joint venture company is owned 49 per cent by Danone SA (France) and 51 per cent by Arcor. This partnership includes highly recognized brands in local markets like Formis, Maná, Saladix, Hogareñas, Sonrisas, Merengadas, Criollitas, Rumba, Opera, Aymoré, Triunfo, Selts and more. Arcor also manufactures private label products and brands for third parties, such as Wal-Mart Stores Inc. and the Sara Lee Corp.

In 2000 the Arcor Group launched www.arcorsales.com, the first food industry website in Latin America devoted to business-to-business (B2B) markets, a new trade channel for its products, to leverage those currently in use.

In 2006, it partnered with the Bimbo Group for the production of sugar and chocolate confectionery in Mexico, in order to serve the Mexican market and also other world markets.

QUESTIONS

1. What would be the major obstacles to Arcor's attempt to penetrate markets outside Latin America?

2. How could Arcor use the concept of the virtual value chain to increase internationalization?

3. Where are Arcor's competitive advantages in the value chain?

VIDEO CASE STUDY 1.3 Nivea

download from www.pearsoned.co.uk/hollensen

Nivea (www.nivea.com) is Beiersdorf's (www.beiersdorf.com) largest brand in terms of sales, product and geographical reach. The brand is a market leader in a number of product areas, including skin care and sun care, especially in Europe.

Nivea and Beiersdorf UK Ltd.

Questions

1. Which degree of market responsiveness and global coordination/integration does Nivea represent?

2. Do you think that the Nivea Vital commercial (shown in the video) is able to cross borders without any adaptation? If not, which elements should be adapted?

3. Which marketing problems does Nivea anticipate when penetrating the US market?

For further exercises and cases, see this book's website at **www.pearsoned.co.uk/hollensen**

Questions for discussion

1. What is the reason for the 'convergence of orientation' in LSEs and SMEs?

2. How can an SME compensate for its lack of resources and expertise in global marketing when trying to enter export markets?

3. What are the main differences between global marketing and marketing in the domestic context?

4. Explain the main advantages of centralizing upstream activities and decentralizing downstream activities.

5. How is the 'virtual value chain' different from the 'conventional value chain'?

References

Asugman, G., Johnson, J.L. and McCullough, J. (1997) 'The role of after-sales service in international marketing', *Journal of International Marketing*, 5(4), pp. 11–28.

Auguste, B.G., Harmon, E.P. and Pandit, V. (2006) 'The right service strategies for product companies', *McKinsey Quarterly*, 1 March, pp. 10–15.

Beinhocker, E., Davis, I. and Mendonca, L. (2009) '10 trends you have to watch', *Harvard Business Review*, July–August 2009, pp. 55–60.

Bellin, J.B. and Pham, C.T. (2007) 'Global expansion: balancing a uniform performance culture with local conditions', *Strategy & Leadership*, 35(6), pp. 44–50.

Blomstermo, A., Sharma, D.D. and Sallis, J. (2006) 'Choice of foreign market entry mode in service firms', *International Marketing Review*, 23(2), pp. 211–229.

Bonaccorsi, A. (1992) 'On the relationship between firm size and export intensity', *Journal of International Business Studies*, fourth quarter, pp. 605–635.

Cafferata, R. and Mensi, R. (1995) 'The role of information in the internationalization of SMEs: a typological approach', *International Small Business Journal*, 13(3), pp. 35–46.

Chakravarthy, B.S., and H.V. Perlmutter (1985) 'Strategic planning for a global business', *Columbia Journal of World Business*, 20(2), pp. 3–10.

Friedman, T. (2005) *The World is Flat*. Farrar, Straus and Giroux, New York.

Frost, R. (2006) 'Global Packaging: What's the difference?', www.Brandchannel.com, 16 January 2006.

Ghemawat, P. (2007) 'Managing differences – the central challenge of global strategy', *Harvard Business Review*, March, pp. 59–68.

Gupta, A.K. and Govindarajan, V. (2001) 'Converting global presence into global competitive advantage', *Academy of Management Executive*, 15(2), pp. 45–56.

Johnson, G. (1988) 'Rethinking incrementalism', *Strategic Management Journal*, 9, pp. 75–91.

Julien, P.E., Joyal, A., Deshaies, L. and Ramangalahy, C. (1997) 'A typology of strategic behaviour among small and medium-sized exporting businesses: a case study', *International Small Business Journal*, 15(2), pp. 33–49.

Knight, G. (2000) 'Entrepreneurship and marketing strategy: the SME under globalization', *Journal of International Marketing*, 8(2), pp. 12–32.

Marchand, D.A. (1999) 'Hard IM choices for senior managers', Part 10 of 'Your guide to mastering information management', *Financial Times*, 5 April.

Mintzberg, H. (1987) 'The strategy concept I: five Ps for strategy', *California Management Review*, 30(1), pp. 11–24.

Mintzberg, H. and Waters, A. (1985) 'Of strategies, deliberate and emergent', *Strategic Management Journal*, 6, pp. 257–272.

Perlmutter, H.V. (1969) 'The tortuous evolution of the multinational corporation', *Columbia Journal of World Business*, 9(January–February), pp. 9–18.

Porter, M.E. (1986) 'Competition in global industries: a conceptual framework', in Porter, M.E. (ed.), *Competition in Global Industries*, Harvard Business School Press, Boston, MA.

Quelch, J.A. (2002) 'Does globalization have staying power?', *Marketing Management*, March/April, pp. 18–23.

Quinn, J.B. (1980) 'Strategies for change: logical incrementalism', *Sloan Management Review*, 20(1), pp. 7–21.

Rayport, J.F. and Sviokla, J.J. (1996) 'Exploiting the virtual value chain', *McKinsey Quarterly*, 1, pp. 21–36.

Sheehan, N. and Foss, N.J. (2009) 'Exploring the roots of Porter's activity-based view', *Journal of Strategy and Management*, 2(3), pp. 240–260.

Segal-Horn, S. (2002) 'Global firms: heroes or villains? How and why companies globalize', *European Business Journal*, 14(1), pp. 8–19.

Sheth, J.N. and Parvatiyar, A. (2001) 'The antecedents and consequences of integrated global marketing', *International Marketing Review*, 18(1), pp. 16–29.

Solberg, C.A. (1997) 'A framework for analysis of strategy development in globalizing markets', *Journal of International Marketing*, 5(1), pp. 9–30.

Stabell, C.B. and Fjeldstad, Ø.B. (1998) 'Configuring value for competetive advantage: on chains, shops, and networks', *Strategic Management* Journal, 19, pp. 413–437.

Svensson, G. (2001) ' "Glocalization" of business activities: a "glocal strategy" approach', *Management Decision*, 39(1), pp. 6–18.

Svensson, G. (2002) 'Beyond global marketing and the globalization of marketing activities', *Management Decision*, 40(6), pp. 574–583.

CHAPTER 2
Initiation of internationalization

Contents

Case studies

Learning objectives

After studying this chapter you should be able to:

- Discuss the reason (motives) why firms go international.
- Explain the difference between proactive and reactive motives.
- Analyse the triggers of export initiation.
- Explain the difference between internal and external triggers of export initiation.
- Describe different factors hindering export initiation.
- Discuss the critical barriers in the process of exporting.

2.1   Introduction

Internationalization occurs when the firm expands its R&D, production, selling and other business activities into international markets. In many larger firms internationalization may occur in a relatively continuous fashion, with the firm undertaking various internationalization stages on various foreign expansion projects simultaneously, in incremental steps, over a period of time. However, for SMEs, internationalization is often a relatively discrete process; that is, one in which management regards each internationalization venture as distinct and individual.

In the pre-internationalization stages SME managers use information to achieve enough relevant knowledge to initiate internationalization (Freeman, 2002). Figure 2.1 illustrates the different stages in pre-internationalization, and the rest of this chapter refers to the stages in Figure 2.1.

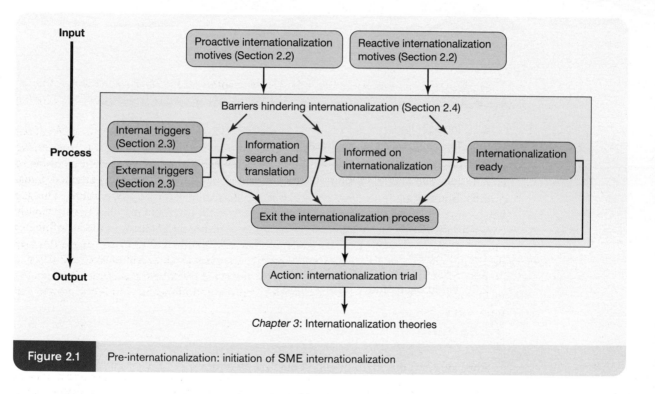

Figure 2.1   Pre-internationalization: initiation of SME internationalization

2.2   Internationalization motives

The fundamental reason for exporting, in most firms, is to make money. However, as in most business activities, one factor alone rarely accounts for any given action. Usually a mixture of factors results in firms taking steps in a given direction.

Internationalization motives
The fundamental reasons – proactive and reactive – for internationalization.

Table 2.1 provides an overview of the major **internationalization motives**. They are differentiated into proactive and reactive motives. *Proactive* motives represent stimuli to attempt strategy change, based on the firm's interest in exploiting unique competences (e.g. a special technological knowledge) or market possibilities. *Reactive* motives indicate that the firm reacts to pressures or threats in its home market or in foreign markets and adjusts passively to them by changing its activities over time.

Let us take a closer look at each export motive.

Table 2.1	Major motives for starting export	
Proactive motives		**Reactive motives**
• Profit and growth goals		• Competitive pressures
• Managerial urge		• Domestic market: small and saturated
• Technology competence/unique product		• Overproduction/excess capacity
• Foreign market opportunities/market information		• Unsolicited foreign orders
• Economies of scale		• Extend sales of seasonal products
• Tax benefits		• Proximity to international customers/psychological distance

Source: adapted from Albaum *et al.* (1994, p. 31).

Proactive motives

Profit and growth goals

The desire for short-term profit is especially important to SMEs if they are at a stage of initial interest in exporting. The motivation for growth may also be of particular importance for the firm's export start.

Over time, the firm's attitude towards growth will be influenced by the type of feedback received from past efforts. For example, the profitability of exporting may determine management's attitude towards it. Of course the perceived profitability, when planning to enter international markets, is often quite different from profitability actually attained. Initial profitability may be quite low, particularly in international start-up operations. The gap between perception and reality may be particularly large when the firm has not previously engaged in international market activities. Despite thorough planning, sudden influences often shift the profit picture substantially. For example, a sudden shift in exchange rates may drastically alter profit forecasts even though they were based on careful market evaluation.

The stronger the firm's motivation to grow, the greater will be the activities it generates, including search activity for new possibilities, in order to find means of fulfilling growth and profit ambitions.

Managerial urge

Managerial urge
Managers' motivation that reflects the desire and enthusiasm to drive internationalization forward.

Managerial urge is a motivation that reflects the desire, drive and enthusiasm of management towards global marketing activities. This enthusiasm can exist simply because managers like to be part of a firm that operates internationally. Further, it can often provide a good reason for international travel. Often, however, the managerial urge to internationalize is simply a reflection of general entrepreneurial motivation – of a desire for continuous growth and market expansion.

Managerial attitudes play a critical role in determining the exporting activities of the firm. In SMEs export decisions may be the province of a single decision-maker; in LSEs they can be made by a decision-making unit. Irrespective of the number of people involved in the export decision-making process, the choice of a foreign market entry strategy is still dependent on the decision-maker's perceptions of foreign markets, expectations concerning these markets and the company's capability of entering them.

The internationalization process may also be encouraged by the cultural socialization of the managers. Managers who either were born or have the experience of living or travelling abroad may be expected to be more internationally minded than other managers. Prior occupation in exporting companies, or membership in trade and professional associations, may also reinforce key decision-makers' perceptions and evaluations of foreign environments.

Technology competence/unique product

A firm may produce goods or services that are not widely available from international competitors or may have made technological advances in a specialized field. Again, real and perceived advantages should be differentiated. Many firms believe that theirs are unique products or services, even though this may not be the case in the international market. If products or technology are unique, however, they can certainly provide a sustainable competitive edge and result in major business success abroad. One issue to consider is how long such a technological or product advantage will continue. Historically, a firm with a competitive edge could count on being the sole supplier to foreign markets for years to come. This type of advantage, however, has shrunk dramatically because of competing technologies and a frequent lack of international patent protection.

However, a firm producing superior products is more likely to receive enquiries from foreign markets because of the perceived competence of its offerings. Several dimensions in the product offering affect the probability that a potential buyer will be exposed to export stimuli. Furthermore, if a company has developed unique competences in its domestic market, the possibilities of spreading unique assets to overseas markets may be very high because the opportunity costs of exploiting these assets in other markets will be very low.

Foreign market opportunities/market information

It is evident that market opportunities act as stimuli only if the firm has or is capable of securing those resources necessary to respond to the opportunities. In general, decision-makers are likely to consider a rather limited number of foreign market opportunities in planning their foreign entry. Moreover, such decision-makers are likely to explore first those overseas market opportunities perceived as having some similarity with the opportunities in their home market.

From time to time certain overseas markets grow spectacularly, providing tempting opportunities for expansion-minded firms. The attraction of the South East Asian markets is based on their economic successes, while the attraction of the Eastern European markets is rooted in their newfound political freedoms and desire to develop trade and economic relationships with countries in western Europe, North America and Japan. Other countries that are likely to increase in market attractiveness as key internal changes occur include the People's Republic of China and South Africa.

Specialized marketing knowledge or access to information can distinguish an exporting firm from its competitors. This includes knowledge about foreign customers, marketplaces or market situations that is not widely shared by other firms. Such special knowledge may result from particular insights based on a firm's international research, special contacts a firm may have, or simply being in the right place at the right time (e.g. recognizing a good business situation during a vacation trip). Past marketing success can be a strong motivator for future marketing behaviour ('logical incrementalism' – see the discussion in section 1.3). Competence in one or more of the major marketing activities will often be a sufficient catalyst for a company to begin or expand exports.

Economies of scale – learning curve

Becoming a participant in global marketing activities may enable the firm to increase its output and therefore climb more rapidly on the learning curve. Ever since the Boston Consulting Group showed that a doubling of output can reduce production costs by up to 30 per cent this effect has been very much sought. Increased production for the international market can therefore also help in reducing the cost of production for domestic sales and make the firm more competitive domestically as well. This effect often results in seeking market share as a primary objective of firms. (See Exhibits 1.2 and 2.1 as examples of this.) At an initial level of internationalization it may mean an increased search for export markets; later on it can result in opening foreign subsidiaries and foreign production facilities.

EXHIBIT 2.1 Global marketing and economics of scale in Japanese firms

Japanese firms exploit foreign market opportunities by using a penetration pricing strategy – a low-entry price to build up market share and establish a long-term dominant market position. They do accept losses in the early years, as they view it as an investment in long-term market development. This can be achieved because much of Japanese industry (especially the *keiretsu* type of organization) is supported or owned by banks or other financial institutions with a much lower cost of capital.

Furthermore, because of the lifetime employment system, labour cost is regarded as a fixed expense, not a variable as it is in the West. Since all marginal labour cost will be at the entry salary level, raising volume is the only way to increase productivity rapidly. As a result market share, not profitability, is the primary concept in Japanese firms, where scale of operation and experience allow economies of scale, which also help to reduce distribution costs. The international trading companies typically take care of international sales and marketing, allowing the Japanese firm to concentrate on economies of scale, resulting in lower cost per unit.

Source: Genestre *et al.* (1995).

Through exporting, fixed costs arising from administration, facilities, equipment, staff work and R&D can be spread over more units. For some companies a condition for exploiting scale effects on foreign markets to the fullest extent is the possibility of standardizing the marketing mix internationally. For others, however, standardized marketing is not necessary for scale economies.

Tax benefits

Tax benefits can also play a major motivating role. In the United States a tax mechanism called the Foreign Sales Corporation (FSC) has been instituted to assist exporters. It is in conformity with international agreements and provides firms with certain tax deferrals. Tax benefits allow the firm either to offer its products at a lower cost in foreign markets or to accumulate a higher profit. This may therefore tie in closely with the profit motivation.

However, anti-dumping laws enforced by WTO (the World Trade Organization) punish foreign producers for selling their products on local markets at very low prices in order to protect local producers. This is the law that every signatory to the WTO agreement (and most countries have signed this agreement) must abide by.

Reactive motives

Competitive pressures

A prime form of reactive motivation is reaction to competitive pressures. A firm may fear losing domestic market share to competing firms that have benefited from economies of scale gained by global marketing activities. Further, it may fear losing foreign markets permanently to domestic competitors that decide to focus on these markets, knowing that market share is most easily retained by the firm that obtains it initially. Quick entry may result in similarly quick withdrawal once the firm recognizes that its preparations have been insufficient. In addition to this, knowing that other firms, particularly competitors, are internationalizing provides a strong incentive to internationalize. Competitors are an important external factor stimulating internationalization. Coca-Cola became international much earlier than Pepsi did, but there is no doubt whatever that Coca-Cola's move into overseas markets influenced Pepsi to move in the same direction.

Domestic market: small and saturated

A company may be pushed into exporting because of a small home market potential. For some firms, domestic markets may be unable to sustain sufficient economies of scale and scope, and these companies automatically include export markets as part of their market-entry strategy. This type of behaviour is likely for industrial products that have few, easily identified customers located throughout the world, or for producers of specialized consumer goods with small national segments in many countries.

A saturated domestic market, whether measured in sales volume or market share, has a similar motivating effect. Products marketed domestically by the firm may be at the declining stage of the product life cycle. Instead of attempting a push-back of the life cycle process, or in addition to such an effort, firms may opt to prolong the product life cycle by expanding the market. In the past such efforts were often met with success as customers in many developing countries only gradually reached a level of need and sophistication already attained by customers in industrialized nations. Some developing nations are still often in need of products for which the demand in the industrialized world is already on the decline. In this way firms can use the international market to prolong the life cycle of their product. (See also section 14.4, The product life cycle, for further discussion.)

Many US appliance and car manufacturers initially entered international markets because of what they viewed as near-saturated domestic markets. US producers of asbestos products found the domestic market legally closed to them, but because some overseas markets had more lenient consumer protection laws they continued to produce for overseas markets.

Another perspective on market saturation is also relevant for understanding why firms may expand overseas. Home market saturation suggests that unused productive resources (such as production and managerial slack) exist within the firm. Production slack is a stimulus for securing new market opportunities, and managerial slack can provide those knowledge resources required for collecting, interpreting and using market information.

Overproduction/excess capacity

If a firm's domestic sales of a product are below expectation the inventory can be above desired levels. This situation can be the trigger for starting export sales via short-term price cuts on inventory products. As soon as the domestic market demand returns to previous levels global marketing activities are curtailed or even terminated. Firms that have used such a strategy may encounter difficulties when trying to employ it again because many foreign customers are not interested in temporary or sporadic business relationships. This reaction from abroad may well lead to a decrease in the importance of this motivation over time.

In some situations, however, excess capacity can be a powerful motivation. If equipment for production is not fully utilized firms may see expansion into the international market as an ideal possibility for achieving broader distribution of fixed costs. Alternatively, if all fixed costs are assigned to domestic production, the firm can penetrate international markets with a pricing scheme that focuses mainly on variable costs. Although such a strategy can be useful in the short term it may result in the offering of products abroad at a lower cost than at home, which in turn may stimulate parallel importing. In the long run, fixed costs have to be recovered to ensure replacement of production equipment. A market penetration strategy based on variable cost alone is therefore not feasible over the long term.

Sometimes excess production capacity arises because of changing demand in the domestic market. As domestic markets switch to new and substitute products companies making older product versions develop excess capacity and look for overseas market opportunities.

Unsolicited foreign orders

Many small companies have become aware of opportunities in export markets because their products generate enquiries from overseas. These enquiries can result from advertising in trade journals that have a worldwide circulation, through exhibitions and by other means. As a result a large percentage of exporting firms' initial orders were unsolicited.

Extend sales of seasonal products

Seasonality in demand conditions may be different in the domestic market from other international markets. This can act as a persistent stimulus for foreign market exploration that may result in a more stable demand over the year.

A producer of agricultural machinery in Europe had demand from its domestic market primarily in the spring months of the year. In an attempt to achieve a more stable demand over the year it directed its market orientation towards the southern hemisphere (e.g. Australia, South Africa), where it will be summer when the northern hemisphere has winter and vice versa.

Proximity to international customers/psychological distance

Physical and psychological closeness to the international market can often play a major role in the export activities of a firm. For example, German firms established near the Austrian border may not even perceive their market activities in Austria as global marketing. Rather, they are simply an extension of domestic activities, without any particular attention being paid to the fact that some of the products go abroad.

Unlike US firms, most European firms automatically become international marketers simply because their neighbours are so close: a European firm operating in Belgium needs to go only 100 km to be in multiple foreign markets.

Shock effects
Managers experience a 'shock' when they realize that they do not know enough about a local market, especially when they perceive it as having a close psychic distance.

However, even for nearby markets managers are exposed to so-called **shock effects** because of unexpected knowledge gaps during the post-entry period. The managers believe that they know everything about the local market, but realize later that they do not. Managers of entrant firms may take more precautions when entering distant markets and may spend more time on planning because they are fully aware of the significant psychic distance; however, they may fail to take these precautions in countries that they perceive as having a close psychic distance (Pedersen and Petersen, 2004).

Consequently, geographic closeness to foreign markets may not necessarily translate into real or perceived closeness to the foreign customer. Sometimes cultural variables, legal factors and other societal norms make a foreign market that is geographically close seem psychologically distant. For example, research has shown that US firms perceive Canada as psychologically much closer than Mexico. Even England, mainly because of similarity in language, is perceived by many US firms as much closer than Mexico or other Latin American countries, despite the geographic distances.

In a study of small UK firms' motives for going abroad, Westhead *et al.* (2002) found the following main reasons for starting exporting of their products/services:

● being contacted by foreign customers that place orders;
● one-off order (no continuous exporting);
● the availability of foreign market information;
● part of growth objective of the firm;
● export markets actively targeted by key founder/owner/manager.

The results in the Westhead *et al.* (2002) study also showed that the bigger the firm the more likely that it would have cited *proactive* stimuli/motives.

The results of Suárez-Ortega and Alamo-Vera (2005) suggest that the main driving forces motivating internationalization are found within the firm, and are therefore based on the management's strengths and weaknesses. They conclude that it is not the external environment that mainly influences the internationalization activities, but the pool of resources and capabilities within the firm that might be appropriately combined to succeed in international markets. Consequently, the speed and intensity of internationalization can be emphasized through programmes aimed at enhancing managers' skills and capabilities. Also export promotion programmes aiming to get more non-exporters to become interested in exporting should emphasize activities that increase managers' awareness of export advantages.

EXHIBIT 2.2 Internationalization of Haier – proactive and reactive motives

The Chinese manufacturer of home appliances (e.g. refrigerators), Haier Group, was near bankruptcy when Mr Zhang Ruimin was appointed plant director in 1984, the fourth one that year. It is Zhang Ruimin who has led the company to grow to the world's fourth largest home appliance manufacturer. In 2008 Haier Group reported sales of over US$17.8 billion.

Kevin Lee/Bloomberg/Getty Images.

Proactive motives

Zhang Ruimin had an internationalization mindset for the initial stage of Haier's development. In 1984, soon after having joined the plant, he introduced technology and equipment from Liebherr, a German company, to produce several popular refrigerator brands in China. At the same time he actively expanded cooperation with Liebherr by manufacturing refrigerators based on its standards which were then sold to Liebherr, as a way of entering the German market. In 1986 the value of Haier's exports reached US$3 million for the first time. Zhang Ruimin later commented on this strategy: 'Exporting to earn foreign exchange was necessary at that time'.

When Haier invested in a plant in the United States, Zhang Ruimin thought it gained location advantage by setting up plants overseas to avoid tariffs and reduce transportation costs. Internalization advantage had been attained through controlling services and marketing/distribution, and ownership advantage had been achieved by developing design and R&D capabilities through utilizing high-quality local human resources.

Reactive motives

The entry of global home appliance manufacturers into the Chinese market forced Haier to seek international expansion. In particular, since China joined the WTO almost every international competitor has invested in China, establishing wholly-owned companies. The best defensive strategy for Haier would be to have a presence in its competitors' home markets.

The saturation of the Chinese home appliance market, with intensifying competition, has been a major motive. After the mid-1990s price wars broke out one after another in various categories of the market. At the end of 2000, Haier's market shares in China of refrigerators, freezers, air conditioners and washing machines had reached 33, 42, 31 and 31 per cent, respectively. The potential for further development in the domestic market was therefore limited.

One of the important external triggers for the internationalization of Haier has been the Chinese government. Being an international player, Haier gained some special conditions that other Chinese companies could not obtain. For instance, Haier had already been approved to establish a financial company, to be the majority shareholder of a regional commercial bank and to form a joint venture with a US insurance company. Without its active pursuit of internationalization as well as a dominant position in home appliance sectors it would normally be impossible for a manufacturer to get approval to enter the financial sector.

Source: adapted from Liu and Li, 2002.

Triggers of export initiation (change agents)

Internationalization triggers
Internal or external events taking place to initiate internationalization.

For internationalization to take place someone or something within or outside the firm (so-called change agents) must initiate the process and carry it through to implementation (see Table 2.2). These are known as **internationalization triggers**. One conclusion from the research done in this area is that it is rare that an isolated factor will trigger the firm's internationalization process. In most cases it is a combination of factors that initiates the internationalization process.

Internal triggers

Perceptive management/personal networks

Perceptive managements gain early awareness of developing opportunities in overseas markets. They make it their business to become knowledgeable about these markets, and maintain a sense of open-mindedness about where and when their companies should expand overseas. Perceptive managements include many cosmopolites in their ranks.

A trigger factor is frequently foreign travel, during which new business opportunities are discovered or information received which makes management believe that such opportunities exist. Managers who have lived abroad, have learned foreign languages or are particularly interested in foreign cultures are likely, sooner rather than later, to investigate whether global marketing opportunities would be appropriate for their firm.

Often managers enter a firm having already had some global marketing experience and personal networks from previous jobs and try to use this experience to further the business activities of their new firm (Vissak *et al.*, 2008). In developing their goals in their new job managers frequently consider an entirely new set of options, one of which may be global marketing activities.

Specific internal event

A significant event can be another major change agent. A new employee who firmly believes that the firm should undertake global marketing may find ways to motivate management. Overproduction or a reduction in domestic market size can serve as such an event, as can the receipt of new information about current product uses. For instance, a company's research activity may develop a by-product suitable for sale overseas, as happened with a food-processing firm that discovered a low-cost protein ideal for helping to relieve food shortages in some parts of Africa.

Research has shown that in SMEs the initial decision to export is usually made by the president, with substantial input provided by the marketing department. The carrying out of the decision – that is, the initiation of actual global marketing activities and the implementation

Table 2.2	Triggers of export initiation	
Internal triggers		**External triggers**
• Perceptive management/personal networks		• Market demand
• Specific internal event		• Network partners
• Importing as inward internationalization		• Competing firms
		• Outside experts

of these activities – is then primarily the responsibility of marketing personnel. Only in the final decision stage of evaluating global marketing activities does the major emphasis rest again with the president of the firm. In order to influence a firm internally, therefore, it appears that the major emphasis should be placed first on convincing the president to enter the international marketplace and then on convincing the marketing department that global marketing is an important activity. Conversely, the marketing department is a good place to be if one wants to become active in international business.

In a recent study of internationalization behaviour in Finnish SMEs, Forsman *et al.* (2002) found that the three most important triggers for starting up operations internationally were:

● management's interest in internationalization;
● foreign enquiries about the company's products/services;
● inadequate demand in the home market.

In this study it is interesting to notice that companies do not regard contacts from Chambers of Commerce or other support organizations as important for getting their international activities going. However, Chambers of Commerce are often used for obtaining further information about a foreign country after an initial trigger has led to the consideration of going international.

Inward/outward internationalization

Internationalization has traditionally been regarded as an outward flow and most internationalization models have not dealt explicitly with how earlier inward activities, and thereby gained knowledge, can influence later outward activities. A natural way of internationalizing would be first to get involved in inward activities (imports) and thereafter in outward activities (exports). Relationships and knowledge gathered from import activities could thus be used when the firm engages in export activities (Welch *et al.*, 2001).

Welch and Loustarinen (1993) claim that **inward internationalization** (importing) may precede and influence **outward internationalization** (international market entry and marketing activities) – see Figure 2.2.

A direct relationship exists between inward and outward internationalization in the way that effective inward activities can determine the success of outward activities, especially in the early stages of internationalization. The inward internationalization may be initiated by one of the following:

● *the buyer*: active international search of different foreign sources (buyer initiative = reverse marketing); or
● *the seller*: initiation by the foreign supplier (traditional seller perspective).

During the process from inward to outward internationalization the buyer's role (in country A) shifts to that of seller, both to domestic customers (in country A) and to foreign customers. Through interaction with the foreign supplier the buyer (importer) gets access to the network of the supplier, so that at some later time there may be an outward export to members of this network.

Inward international operations thus usually cover a variety of different forms used to strengthen a firm's resources. Of course inward flows imply importing products needed for the production process, such as raw materials and machinery, but inward operations can also include finances and technology through different operational forms, such as franchising, direct investments and alliances (Forsman *et al.*, 2002). In some cases inward foreign licensing may be followed by outward technology sales. According to Fletcher (2001) and Freeman (2002), inward and outward activities and the links between them can develop in different ways. The links are most tangible in counter-trade arrangements (where the focal firm initiates exporting to the same market from which importing takes place), but they can

Inward/outward internationalization
Imports as a preceding activity for the later market entries in foreign markets.

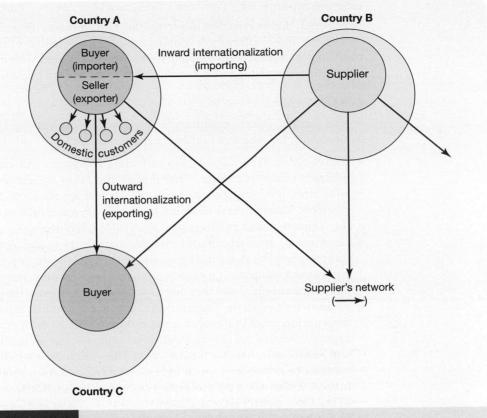

| Figure 2.2 | Inward/outward internationalization: a network example |

also be found in the networks of relationships between subunits within a multinational enterprise and in strategic alliances.

External triggers

Market demand

Growth in international markets also causes the demand for the products of some companies to grow, pushing the makers of these products into internationalization. Many pharmaceutical companies entered international markets when growth in the international demand for their products was first getting under way. The US-based company Squibb entered the Turkish market before it was large enough to be profitable; but the market was growing rapidly, which encouraged Squibb to internationalize further.

Network partners

The firm's network partners can sometimes emerge as a key source of internationalization-enhancing knowledge and function as a key trigger in the process of internationalization (Vissak *et al.*, 2008). Examples of such network partners can be distributors, trade associations, research institutes or universities. An already established contact to a domestic distributor may lead to his foreign distribution network. Formal and informal (often online) meetings among managers from different firms at trade association meetings, conventions or business round tables often serve as a major change agent. It has even been suggested that the decision to export may be made by small firms on the basis of the collective experience of the group of firms to which they belong.

Competing firms

Information that an executive in a competing firm considers certain international markets to be valuable and worthwhile developing captures the attention of management. Such statements not only have source credibility but are also viewed with a certain amount of fear because the competitor may eventually infringe on the firm's business.

Outside experts

Several outside experts encourage internationalization. Among them are export agents, governments, Chambers of Commerce and banks.

- *Export agents* Export agents, export trading companies and export management firms generally qualify as experts in global marketing. They are already dealing internationally with other products, have overseas contacts and are set up to handle other exportable products. Many of these trade intermediaries approach prospective exporters directly if they think that their products have potential markets overseas.
- *Governments* In nearly all countries governments try to stimulate international business through providing global marketing expertise (export assistance programmes). For example, government stimulation measures can have a positive influence not only in terms of any direct financial effects that they may have, but also in relation to the provision of information.
- *Chambers of Commerce* Chambers of Commerce and similar export production organizations are interested in stimulating international business, both exports and imports. These organizations seek to motivate individual companies to get involved in global marketing and provide incentives for them to do so. These incentives include putting the prospective exporter or importer in touch with overseas business, providing overseas market information, and referring the prospective exporter or importer to financial institutions capable of financing global marketing activity.
- *Banks* Banks and other financial institutions are often instrumental in getting companies to internationalize. They alert their domestic clients to international opportunities and help them to capitalize on these opportunities. Of course, they look forward to their services being used more extensively as domestic clients expand internationally.

Information search and translation

Of all resources, information and knowledge are perhaps the most critical factor in the initiation of the internationalization process in the SME (see also Figure 2.1 earlier).

Because each international opportunity constitutes a potential innovation for the SME the management must acquire appropriate information. This is especially important to SMEs, which typically lack the resources to internationalize in the manner of LSEs. Consequently the management launches an *information search* and acquires relevant information from a number of sources, such as internal written reports, government agencies, trade associations, personal contacts or the Internet, relevant to the intended internationalization project. In the *information translation* stage the internationalization information is transformed by managers into knowledge within the firm. It is through the information search and translation into knowledge that management becomes informed on internationalization. At this stage the firm has entered a cycle of continuous search and translation into internationalization knowledge. This cycle continues until management is satisfied that it has sufficiently reduced the uncertainty associated with the internationalization project to ensure a relatively high probability of success. Once sufficient information has been acquired and translated into usable knowledge the firm leaves the cycle, becoming *internationalization ready*. It is here that the firm proceeds to action, that is, an *internationalization trial*. 'Action' refers to behaviours and activities that management executes based on the knowledge that it has acquired. At this stage the firm could be said to have an embedded internationalization culture, where even the most challenging foreign markets can be overcome, leading to further internationalization and 'storage' of actual internationalization knowledge in the heads of the managers.

The above description represents the firm more or less in isolation. However, the network theory recognizes the importance of the firm's membership in a constellation of firms and organizations. By interacting within such a constellation the firm derives advantages well beyond what it could obtain in isolation. At the most fine-grained level, knowledge is created by individuals. Individuals acquire explicit knowledge via specific means and tacit knowledge through hands-on experience (experiential learning).

The nature of the pre-internationalization process (illustrated in Figure 2.1) will be unique in each firm because of several factors at the organization and individual levels within the firm (Knight and Liesch, 2002). For example, for SMEs it seems that the managers' personal networks tend to speed up the pre-internationalization process. These personal networks are used for creating cross-border alliances with suppliers, distributors and other international partners (Freeman *et al.*, 2006).

Throughout the process depicted in Figure 2.1 the firm may exit from the pre-internationalization process at any time, as a result of the barriers hindering internationalization. The manager may decide to do nothing, an outcome that implies exiting from pre-internationalization.

2.4   Internationalization barriers/risks

A wide variety of barriers to successful export operations can be identified. Some problems mainly affect the export start; others are encountered in the process of exporting.

Barriers hindering internationalization initiation

Critical factors hindering *internationalization initiation* include the following (mainly internal) barriers:

- insufficient finances;
- insufficient knowledge;
- lack of foreign market connections;
- lack of export commitment;
- lack of capital to finance expansion into foreign markets;
- lack of productive capacity to dedicate to foreign markets;
- lack of foreign channels of distribution;
- management emphasis on developing domestic markets;
- cost escalation due to high export manufacturing, distribution and financing expenditures.

Inadequate information on potential foreign customers, competition and foreign business practices are key barriers facing active and prospective exporters. Obtaining adequate representation for overseas distribution and service, ensuring payment, import tariffs and quotas and difficulties in communicating with foreign distributors and customers are also major concerns. Serious problems can also arise from production disruptions resulting from a requirement for non-standard export products. This will increase the cost of manufacturing and distribution.

In a study of craft micro-enterprises (less than ten employees) in the United Kingdom and Ireland, Fillis (2002) found that having sufficient business in the domestic market was the major factor in the decision not to export. Other reasons of above-average importance were: lack of export inquiries, relating to the reactive approach to business; complicated exporting procedures; poor levels of exporting assistance; and limited government incentives. Similar results were supported by a study by Westhead *et al.* (2002), who found that for small firms 'focus on local market' was the main reason for not exporting any of their products. The internationalization process can also go in other directions than expected – see Exhibit 2.3.

EXHIBIT 2.3 De-internationalization at British Telecommunications (BT)

BT started its internationalization from the middle of 1990s. Over the the next years BT built a global strategy seeking to position itself as a leading supplier of telecommunication services to multinational companies in different countries. However, the percentage increase in international activities has slowed down over the years. In 1994 less than 1 per cent of total turnover came from international activities. In 2002 this increased to 11 per cent, and in 2007 to 15 per cent of its £20 Bill turnover. So though BT overall has experienced a sharp increase in turnover from international activities it has also experienced some setbacks in the internationalization process, especially in the beginning, as indicated in Figure 2.3.

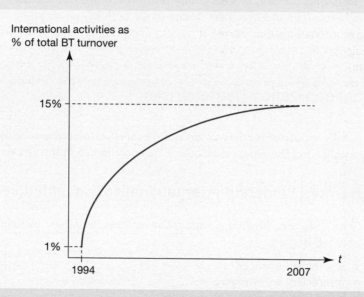

| Figure 2.3 | Illustration of BT's internationalization 1994–2007 |

Source: Hollensen, S. (2008) *Essentials of Global Marketing*, FT/Prentice Hall, p. 47.

In the beginning of the internationalization process BT built its international strategy around three guiding principles:

1. Not over-committing itself by building its own infrastructure based on uncertain traffic flows.
2. Achieving quick and reliable access to targeted marketplaces by entering distribution partnerships and equity joint ventures. This strategy involved relatively low risk and allowed speedy access into marketplaces with partners who had intimate knowledge of local market conditions.
3. Ensuring that the strategy gave them sufficient strategic flexibility to be able to adjust rapidly to changing market conditions

At its height in 1999, BT had 25 equity joint ventures and 44 distribution partnerships. Within the equity joint ventures, BT took a minority stake within the stated intention to gradually upgrade this stake to a controlling investment over time. BT would also often take a stake in its distribution partners as a means of giving them incentives to sell the BT products.

De-internationalization at BT

In 2002, BT launched a new corporate strategy that was considerably more defensive than its predecessor. There were two main problems with the series of joint ventures and partnerships:

1. BT needed different skills and competences for different partners. This made coordination of activities between partners very complex. As a consequence, BT found itself on a steep learning curve with this large number of partners.
2. The strategy of only taking minority stakes in the joint ventures rebounded on BT. Furthermore, there was little imperative by partners to fully support the roll out of BT products especially where they were in competition with their own offering. When BT attempted to increase its financial stake within the partner, it often found that the other shareholders had exactly the same intent.

Subsequently, BT made divestments, both in North America and in Asia.

What can we learn from the BT study?

BT's de-internationalization was driven by financial health, where the high cost of market entry combined with falling prices (driven by excess capacity in the telecommunication sector) led to declining profits throughout the 1990s.

Consequently, the new defensive strategy represented a process of de-internationalization as BT retreated from the USA and Asian market ('Multiple Withdrawal' in Figure 2.4). BT's new international strategy is based on the European market where there are interdependencies with the core UK business. This means that BT tries to own and control all aspects of the delivery mechanism within the European market.

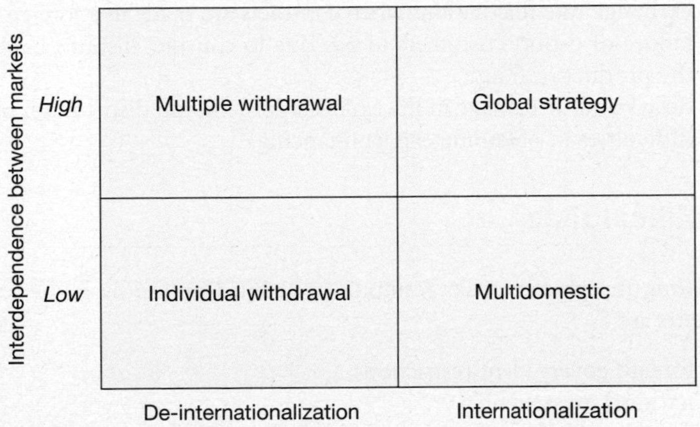

	De-internationalization	Internationalization
High	Multiple withdrawal	Global strategy
Low	Individual withdrawal	Multidomestic

Interdependence between markets

Figure 2.4   Global strategy options

Source: Hollensen, S. (2008) *Essentials of Global Marketing*, FT/Prentice Hall, p. 48.

This BT case study demonstrates that the future development of the global marketing strategy can work in both directions. If the globalization of markets goes well in a company, the interdependence and synergies between markets can be further utilized to strengthen the global strategy (upper right corner in Figure 2.4). However, the case study also shows that divestment in individual locations cannot occur in isolation without damaging the firm's global value proposition. Therefore, BT's de-internationalization also means (because of the high dependence of markets) that BT had to make multiple market withdrawal.

If we talk about SMEs (that is not the case with BT!) we will often experience a low interdependence between markets, and in that case we will talk about a 'multidomestic' strategy, if we increase internationalization (lower right corner in Figure 2.4) and individual withdrawal, if we decrease internationalization (lower left corner in Figure 2.4).

Source: adapted from Turner and Gardiner (2007); BT Financial Report (2007). From Hollensen, S. (2008) *Essentials of Global Marketing*, FT/Prentice Hall.

Barriers hindering the further process of internationalization

Critical barriers in the process of internationalization may generally be divided into three groups: general market risks, commercial risks and political risks.

General market risks

General market risks include:

- comparative market distance;
- competition from other firms in foreign markets;
- differences in product usage in foreign markets;
- language and cultural differences;
- difficulties in finding the right distributor in the foreign market;
- differences in product specifications in foreign markets;
- complexity of shipping services to overseas buyers.

Commercial risks

The following fall into the commercial risks group:

- exchange rate fluctuations when contracts are made in a foreign currency;
- failure of export customers to pay due to contract dispute, bankruptcy, refusal to accept the product or fraud;
- delays and/or damage in the export shipment and distribution process;
- difficulties in obtaining export financing.

Political risks

Among the political risks resulting from intervention by home and host country governments are:

- foreign government restrictions;
- national export policy;
- foreign exchange controls imposed by host governments that limit the opportunities for foreign customers to make payment;
- lack of governmental assistance in overcoming export barriers;
- lack of tax incentives for companies that export;
- high value of the domestic currency relative to those in export markets;
- high foreign tariffs on imported products;
- confusing foreign import regulations and procedures;
- complexity of trade documentation;
- enforcement of national legal codes regulating exports;
- civil strife, revolution and wars disrupting foreign markets.

The importance of these risks must not be overemphasized, and various risk-management strategies are open to exporters. These include:

- Avoid exporting to high-risk markets.
- Diversify overseas markets and ensure that the firm is not overdependent on any single country.
- Insure risks when possible. Government schemes are particularly attractive.
- Structure export business so that the buyer bears most of the risk. For example, price in a hard currency and demand cash in advance.

In Fillis (2002) over one-third of the exporting craft firms indicated that they encountered problems once they entered export markets. The most common problem was connected with the choice of a reliable distributor, followed by difficulties in promoting the product and matching competitors' prices.

2.5   Summary

Water-borne diseases
Caused by the ingestion of water contaminated by human or animal faeces or urine containing pathogenic bacteria or viruses; these include cholera, typhoid, amoebic and bacillary dysentery and other diarrhoeal diseases.

This chapter has provided an overview of the pre-internationalization process. It opened with the major motives for firms to internationalize. These were differentiated into proactive and reactive motives. Proactive motives represent internal stimuli to attempt strategy change, based on the firm's interest in exploiting unique competences or market possibilities. Reactive motives indicate that the firm reacts to pressures or threats in its home market or in foreign markets and adjusts passively to them.

For internationalization to take place someone or something – triggers – inside or outside the firm must initiate it and carry it through. To succeed in global marketing the firm has to overcome export barriers. Some barriers mainly affect the export initiation and others are encountered in the process of exporting.

CASE STUDY 2.1

LifeStraw: Vestergaard-Frandsen transforms dirty water into clean drinking water

Creating products to save people's lives in the developing world is the mission of a company – Vestergaard-Frandsen (VF) – www.vestergaard-frandsen.com – based in Lausanne, Switzerland. The 'Profit for a purpose' approach has turned humanitarian responsibility into VFs core business. The company is offering complex emergency response and disease-control products.

VESTERGAARD FRANDSEN

DISEASE CONTROL TEXTILES

Vestergaard-Frandsen.

Vestergaard Frandsen began life 50 years ago in Denmark as a modest manufacturer of hotel and restaurant uniforms. Today its headquarters are in Lausanne, Switzerland, and the sole focus of the

150 employees is on what the CEO Mikkel Vestergaard Frandsen calls 'humanitarian entrepreneurship'. Originally a textile company that began in Denmark in 1957, they now develop innovative products that prevent the transmission of water-borne and insect-borne diseases in developing countries. For **water-borne diseases** VF has its LifeStraw – see below for a description. For insect-borne diseases VF is one of the world's leading producers of bed nets impregnated with insecticide. The purpose is to prevent malaria, caused by the blood-sucking bites of mosquitoes. Besides mosquito intensive areas, this product is used in refugee camps and disaster areas all over the world.

Vestergard Frandsen, which is family-owned, does not disclose financial data, but over the years it has sold 165 million mosquito nets, and the company makes a profit.

The concept for the LifeStraw began with the work of the Carter Center, founded by Jimmy and Rosalynn Carter. It has been their mission since

1986 to eradicate guinea worm disease (GWD) in Africa and Asia. The most effective way to prevent this disease is to filter drinking water, so the tiny water fleas are not ingested to begin the life cycle of GWD starts. The LifeStraw has played a substantial role in the prevention of this disease, and many other bacterial and viral infections caused by a lack of safe drinking water in many developing countries.

The lack of safe drinking water

Water in drinking form is becoming scarcer in certain places, and its availability is a major social and economic concern. Currently, about a billion people around the world routinely drink unhealthy water.

About 99.7 per cent of the earth's water is contained in undrinkable forms such as oceans, underground, ice caps and glaciers. Due to increased contamination and pollution both above and below the ground, the condition of the remaining 0.3 per cent is now questionable with many countries finding it increasingly difficult to source drinkable water that is of an acceptable quality.

Throughout history clashes between and within countries have occurred over water and its supply. Many people believe that in the future conflicts and even wars will be waged over water supplies; particularly as uncontaminated water becomes increasingly scarce.

More than one billion people in the world do not have access to safe drinking water – i.e. around one-sixth of the world's population. The average distance that women in Africa and Asia walk to collect water is 6 km.

The LifeStraw product

The LifeStraw is a portable water purifier that is easy to use, has no replaceable parts, and needs no electrical power or batteries to work. This lightweight filter removes 99.999 per cent of waterborne bacteria, 99.99 per cent of water-borne viruses and removes particles down to 15 microns in size. This small water purifier will filter a minimum of 700 litres (185 gallons) of water!

The LifeStraw comes in two forms: one is for personal use and the other for the household.

The personal LifeStraw is portable and looks very much like an ordinary straw. It hangs around the neck, and you can drink water from any source without getting sick. It eliminates 99.999 per cent of all bacteria, and it functions, really, as a water treatment plant in a straw.

The household version of the straw is for a family of up to six people and lasts more than three years. It's simple to use. It hangs from a wall, you pour dirty water into the top, it filters down through a hollow fibre and comes out clean. The process is quick, and

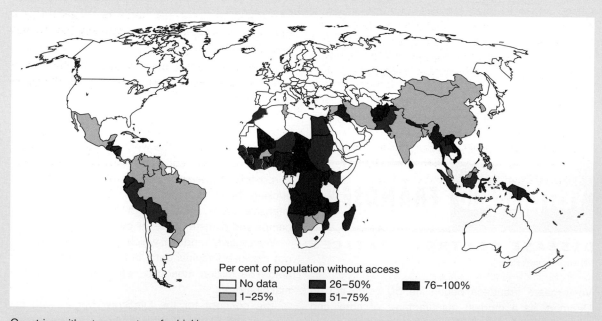

Per cent of population without access

☐ No data   ■ 26–50%   ■ 76–100%
▨ 1–25%   ■ 51–75%

Countries without access to safe drinking water

Source: from *World's Water 1998–1999* by Peter H. Gleick. Copyright © 1998 Island Press. Reproduced by permission of Island Press, Washington, DC.

you can drink the water right away; there's no need to store it for a long period.

Five million people die each year (mainly children) from water-borne diseases. The World Health Organization (WHO) estimates that safe water could prevent 1.4 million child deaths from diarrhoea each year.

A product as simple and inexpensive as the LifeStraw could change these numbers and do it right at the point of consumption. The cost for a personal LifeStraw is about $3: the family size LifeStraw is about $15 and can be used up to two years in the home.

Children drinking water from the LifeStraw in India
Vestergaard-Frandsen.

How does the LifeStraw function?

What first meets the water when sucked up is a pre-filter of PE filter textile with a mesh opening of 100 microns, shortly followed by a second textile filter in polyester with a mesh opening of 15 microns. In this way all big articles are filtered out, even clusters of bacteria are removed. Then the water is led into a chamber of iodine impregnated beads, where bacteria, viruses and parasites are killed. The second chamber is a void space, where the iodine being washed off the beads can maintain their killing effect. The last chamber consists of granulated active carbon, whose role is to remove most of the bad smell of iodine and those parasites that have not been taken by the pre-filter or killed by the iodine. The biggest parasites will be taken by the pre-filter, the weakest killed by the iodine, and the medium range parasites will be picked up by the active carbon.

Customers and distribution of LifeStraw

Customers are mainly foreign governmental aid agencies, international relief and development organizations, foundations, and charities.

The best way for people (end-users) in these risky areas to get a LifeStraw is through a charitable organization, which are funding and sometimes also buying the products. The NGOs then take the product to the rural households where the poorest people live.

QUESTIONS

1. In McNeil (2009) Kevin Starace states: '*Vestergaard is just different from other companies we work with. They think of end users as a consumer rather as a patient or a victim*.' What can be the meaning behind this statement?

2. Which factors are most critical in the further internationalization process of Vestergaard Frandsen?

Sources: www.vestergaard-frandsen.com; Donald G. McNeil Jr (2009) A company prospers by saving poor people's lives. *New York Times – Science Times*, 3 February.

CASE STUDY 2.2

Elvis Presley Enterprises Inc. (EPE): internationalization of a cult icon

More than 25 years after his death Elvis Presley has one of the most lucrative entertainment franchises in the world. Despite the sorry state of his affairs in 1977 the empire of Elvis has thrived due in large part to the efforts of the people who handled his estate after his grandmother died in 1980, including his ex-wife Priscilla Beaulieu Presley, his daughter Lisa Marie and Jack Soden, the CEO of Elvis Presley Enterprises Inc. (www.elvis.com), the company that handles all the official Elvis properties.

Priscilla Presley was involved in the masterstroke decision to open Elvis's mansion, Graceland, to the public in 1982. Graceland gets more than 600,000 visitors per year, according to EPE's website. Over half of Graceland's visitors are under the age of 35. While visitors come from all parts of the world the majority still come from different parts of the United States. The Graceland tour costs US$25, which means that EPE makes US$15 million on those tickets alone, plus what it receives from photographs, hotel guests, meals and souvenirs.

EPE's other revenue streams include a theme restaurant called Elvis Presley's Memphis; a hotel, down at the end of Lonely Street, called Heartbreak Hotel; licensing of Elvis-related products, the development of Elvis-related music, film, video, TV and stage productions, and more.

Ironically, EPE gets very little money from Elvis's actual songs, thanks to a deal Elvis's infamous former manager, Colonel Tom Parker, made with RCA in 1973, whereby Elvis traded the rights for all future royalties from the songs he had recorded up to that point for a measly US$5.4 million – half of which he had to give to Parker.

In 2002, the twenty-fifty anniversary of his death was an international spectacle. A remix of the 1968 Elvis song 'A little less conversation' became a global hit single and the CD 'Elvis: 30 #1 Hits' went triple platinum. In mid-2004, to commemorate the fiftieth anniversary of Presley's first professional recording, 'That's All Right' was re-released, and made the charts around the world, including the top three in the United Kingdom and top 40 in Australia.

In mid-October 2005, *Variety* named the top 100 entertainment icons of the twentieth century, with Presley landing in the top ten, along with the Beatles, Marilyn Monroe, Lucille Ball, Marlon Brando, Humphrey Bogart, Louis Armstrong, Charlie Chaplin, James Dean and Mickey Mouse.

Until 2005 EPE was wholly owned by the Elvis Presley Trust/Lisa Marie Presley. In February 2005, the media and entertainment company CKX Inc. acquired an 85 per cent interest in EPE including its physical and intellectual properties. Lisa Marie Presley retained a 15 per cent ownership in the company and continued to be involved, as did her mother Priscilla. The pre-existing EPE management team remained in place as did the company's operations.

Graceland is the second most visited private residence in the United States, behind the White House. Attendance ranges from a few hundred visitors on a weekday in the dead of winter to 2,000–3,500 visitors per day in the spring and early summer, to over 4,000 per day in July at the height of the travel season. However, EPE's business extends far beyond the Graceland operation. It includes worldwide licensing of Elvis-related products and ventures, the development of Elvis-related music, film, video, television and stage productions, the ongoing development of EPE's Internet presence, the management of significant music publishing assets and more.

Sources: http://www.elvis.com/corporate/elvis_epe.asp; money.cnn.com/2002/08/15/news/elvis.

QUESTIONS

1. What are the main motives for the internationalization of EPE?

2. What can EPE do to maintain a steady income stream from abroad?

3. What are the most obvious assets for further internationalization of EPE?

VIDEO CASE STUDY 2.3 TOMS Shoes

download from www.pearsoned.co.uk/hollensen

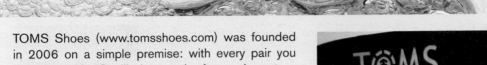

TOMS Shoes (www.tomsshoes.com) was founded in 2006 on a simple premise: with every pair you purchase, TOMS will give a pair of new shoes to a child in need. One for one. Using the purchasing power of individuals to benefit the greater good is what we're all about.

In 2006 Blake Mycoskie, an American traveller, went to Argentina and found that many children there had no shoes to protect their feet. Wanting to help, he created TOMS Shoes, a company that would match every pair of shoes purchased with a pair of new shoes given to a child in need. One for One. Blake returned to Argentina with a group of family, friends and staff later that year with 10,000 pairs of shoes made possible by caring TOMS customers.

In developing countries wearing shoes prevents feet from getting cuts and sores on unsafe roads and from contaminated soil. Not only are these injuries painful, they are also dangerous when wounds become infected. The leading cause of disease in developing countries is soil-transmitted parasites which penetrate the skin through open sores. Wearing shoes can prevent this and ultimately the risk of amputation.

Since the beginning in 2006, TOMS has given over 400,000 pairs of shoes to children in need through the One for One model. Because of your support, in 2008 TOMS plans to give over 300,000 pairs of shoes to children in need around the world.

TOMS is built on the loyalty of customers who choose a better tomorrow with every purchase. TOMS has one of the coolest internship programmes in the country, according to *Inc. Magazine*. Many of those passionate interns stay with TOMS and become hard-working, full-time employees.

Toms Shoes' HQ is in Santa Monica, California.

Tiffany Rose/WireImage/Getty.

Questions

1. What would be the key barriers in the early days of internationalization if TOMS Shoes decided to expand to Europe?
2. What have been the driving forces (motives) for the early internationalization of TOMS Shoes?

For further exercises and cases, see this book's website at **www.pearsoned.co.uk/hollensen**

Questions for discussion

1. Export motives can be classified as reactive or proactive. Give examples of each group of export motives. How would you prioritize these motives? Can you think of motives other than those mentioned in the chapter? What are they?

2. What is meant by 'change agents' in global marketing? Give examples of different types of change agent.

3. Discuss the most critical barriers to the process of exporting.

4. What were the most important change agents in the internationalization of Haier (Exhibit 2.2)?

5. What were the most important export motives in Japanese firms (Exhibit 2.1)?

References

Albaum, G., Strandskov, J., Duerr, E. and Dowd, L. (1994) *International Marketing and Export Management* (2nd edn). Addison-Wesley, Reading, MA.

Fillis, I. (2002) 'Barriers to internationalization: an investigation of the craft microenterprises', *European Journal of Marketing*, (7–8), pp. 912–927.

Fletcher, R. (2001) 'A holistic approach to internationalization', *International Business Review*, 10, pp. 25–49.

Forsman, M., Hinttu, S. and Kock, S. (2002) 'Internationalization from an SME perspective', paper presented at the 18th Annual IMP Conference, September, Lyon, pp. 1–12.

Freeman, S. (2002) 'A comprehensive model of the process of small firm internationalization: a network perspective', paper presented at the 18th Annual IMP Conference, September, Dijon, pp. 1–22.

Freeman, S., Edwards, R. and Schroder, B. (2006) 'How smaller born-global firms use networks and alliances to overcome constraints to rapid internationalization', *Journal of International Marketing*, 14(3), pp. 33–63.

Genestre, A., Herbig, D. and Shao, A.T. (1995) 'What does marketing really mean to the Japanese?', *Marketing Intelligence and Planning*, 13(9), pp. 16–27.

Gleick, P. (1998) *The World's Water: The Biennial Report on Freshwater Resources*. Oakland, California, www.worldwater.org.

Knight, G.A. and Liesch, P.W. (2002) 'Information internalization in internationalizing the firm', *Journal of Business Research*, 55, pp. 981–995.

Liu, H. and Li, K. (2002) 'Strategic implications of emerging Chinese multinationals: the Haier case study', *European Management Journal*, 20(6), pp. 699–706.

Pedersen, T. and Petersen, B. (2004) 'Learning about foreign markets: are entrant firms exposed to a "shock effect?"', *Journal of International Marketing*, 12(1), pp. 103–123.

Suárez-Ortega, S.M. and Àlamo-Vera, F.R. (2005) 'SMES' internationalization: firms and managerial factors', *International Journal of Entrepreneurial Behavior & Research*, 11(4), pp. 258–279.

Turner, C. and Gardiner, P.D. (2007) 'De-internationalisation and global strategy: the case of British Telecommunications (BT)', *Journal of Business & Industrial Marketing*, 22(7), pp. 489–497.

Vissak, T., Ibeh, K. and Paliwoda, S. (2008) 'Internationalising from the European periphery: triggers, processes and trajectories', *Journal of Euromarketing*, 17(1), pp. 35–48.

Welch, L.S., Benito, G.R.G., Silseth, P.R. and Karlsen, T. (2001) 'Exploring inward–outward linkages in firms' internationalization: a knowledge and network perspective', paper presented at the 17th Annual IMP Conference, September, Oslo, pp. 1–26.

Welch, L.S. and Loustarinen, R.K. (1993) 'Inward–outward connections in internationalization', *Journal of International Marketing*, 1(1), pp. 44–56.

Westhead P., Wright, M. and Ucbasaran, D. (2002) 'International market selection strategies selected by "micro" and "small" firms', *Omega – The International Journal of Management Science*, 30, pp. 51–68.

CHAPTER 3
Internationalization theories

Contents

Case studies

Learning objectives

After studying this chapter you should be able to:

- Analyse and compare the three theories explaining a firm's internationalization process:
    (i)   the Uppsala internationalization model,
    (ii) the transaction cost theory, and
    (iii) the network model.
- Explain the most important determinants for the internationalization process of SMEs.
- Discuss the different factors which influence internationalization of services.
- Explain and discuss the relevance of the network model for an SME serving as a subcontractor.
- Explain the term 'born global' and its connection to Internet marketing.

3.1 Introduction

Having discussed the barriers to starting internationalization in Chapter 2, we will begin this chapter by presenting the different theoretical approaches to international marketing and then choose three models for further discussion in sections 3.2, 3.3 and 3.4.

Historical development of internationalization

Much of the early literature on internationalization was inspired by general marketing theories. Later on, internationalization dealt with the choice between exporting and FDI (foreign direct investment). During the past 20 years there has been much focus on internationalization in networks, by which the firm has different relationships not only with customers but also with other actors in the environment.

The traditional marketing approach

The Penrosian tradition (Penrose, 1959; Prahalad and Hamel, 1990) reflects the traditional marketing focus on the firm's core competences combined with opportunities in the foreign environment.

The cost-based view of this tradition suggested that the firm must possess a 'compensating advantage' in order to overcome the 'cost of foreignness' (Kindleberger, 1969; Hymer, 1976). This led to the identification of technological and marketing skills as the key elements in successful foreign entry.

The life cycle concept for international trade

Sequential modes of internationalization were introduced by Vernon's 'product cycle hypothesis' (1966), in which firms go through an exporting phase before switching first to market-seeking FDI, and then to cost-oriented FDI. Technology and marketing factors combine to explain standardization, which drives location decisions.

Vernon's hypothesis is that producers in advanced countries (ACs) are 'closer' to the markets than producers elsewhere; consequently the first production facilities for these products will be in the ACs. As demand expands a certain degree of standardization usually takes place. Economies of scale through mass production become more important. Concern about production cost replaces concern about product adaptations. With standardized products the less developed countries (LDCs) may offer competitive advantages as production locations. One example of this is the movement of production locations for personal computers from ACs to LDCs. The life cycle concept is illustrated in Figure 15.4, later in this book.

The Uppsala internationalization model

Uppsala internationalization model
Additional market commitments are made in small incremental steps: choosing additional geographic markets with small psychic distances, combined with choosing entry modes with few additional risks.

The Scandinavian 'stages' models of entry suggest a sequential pattern of entry into successive foreign markets, coupled with a progressive deepening of commitment to each market. Increasing commitment is particularly important in the thinking of the Uppsala School (Johanson and Wiedersheim-Paul, 1975; Johanson and Vahlne, 1977). The main consequence of this **Uppsala internationalization model** is that firms tend to intensify their commitment towards foreign markets as their experience grows. (See also section 3.2.)

The internationalization/transaction cost approach

In the early 1970s intermediate forms of internationalization such as licensing were not considered interesting. Buckley and Casson (1976) expanded the choice to include licensing as a means of reaching customers abroad, but in their perspective the multinational firm would usually prefer to 'internalize' transactions via direct equity investment rather than license its capability. Joint ventures were not explicitly considered to be in the spectrum of governance choices until the mid-1980s (Contractor and Lorange, 1988; Kogut, 1988).

Buckley and Casson's focus on market-based (externalization) versus firm-based (internalization) solutions highlighted the strategic significance of licensing in market entry. Internationalization involves two interdependent decisions regarding location and mode of control.

The internalization perspective is closely related to the transaction cost (TC) theory (Williamson, 1975). The paradigmatic question in internalization theory is that, upon deciding to enter a foreign market, should a firm do so through internalization within its own boundaries (a subsidiary) or through some form of collaboration with an external partner (externalization)? The internalization and TC perspectives are both concerned with the minimization of TC and the conditions underlying market failure. The intention is to analyse the characteristics of a transaction in order to decide on the most efficient, i.e. TC minimizing, governance mode. The internalization theory can be considered the TC theory of the multinational corporation (Rugman, 1986; Madhok, 1998).

Dunning's eclectic approach

In his eclectic ownership-location-internalization (OLI) framework Dunning (1988) discussed the importance of locational variables in foreign investment decisions. The word 'eclectic' represents the idea that a full explanation of the transnational activities of firms needs to draw on several strands of economic theory. According to Dunning the propensity of a firm to engage itself in international production increases if the following three conditions are being satisfied:

1. *Ownership advantages*: a firm that owns foreign production facilities has bigger ownership advantages compared to firms of other nationalities. These 'advantages' may consist of intangible assets, such as know-how.
2. *Locational advantages*: it must be profitable for the firm to continue these assets with factor endowments (labour, energy, materials, components, transport and communication channels) in the foreign markets. If not, the foreign markets would be served by exports.
3. *Internalization advantages*: it must be more profitable for the firm to use its advantages rather than selling them, or the right to use them, to a foreign firm.

The network approach

The basic assumption in the network approach is that the international firm cannot be analysed as an isolated actor but has to be viewed in relation to other actors in the international environment. Thus the individual firm is dependent on resources controlled by others. The relationships of a firm within a domestic network can be used as connections to other networks in other countries (Johanson and Mattson, 1988).

In the following three sections (sections 3.2 to 3.4) we will concentrate on three of the approaches presented above.

The difference between cultural distance and psychic distance

Cultural distance (discussed in Chapter 7) refers to the (macro) cultural level of a country and is defined as the degree to which (factual) cultural values in one country are different from those in another country, i.e. 'distance' between countries.

Psychic distance
The perceived degree of difference between two markets, in terms of differences in language, culture and political system, which disturbs the flow between the firm and the market.

Psychic distance (discussed in this chapter) can be defined as the individual manager's perception of the differences between the home and the foreign market, and it is a highly subjective interpretation of reality. Therefore, psychic distance cannot be measured with factual indicators, such as publicly available statistics on level of education, religion, language and so forth. The distinction between the two concepts is important for managers. By assessing psychic distance at the individual level, it is possible to take appropriate steps to reduce the manager's psychic distance towards foreign markets (Sousa and Bradley, 2005, 2006).

| 3.2 | The Uppsala internationalization model |

The stage model

During the 1970s a number of Swedish researchers at the University of Uppsala (Johanson and Wiedersheim-Paul, 1975; Johanson and Vahlne, 1977) focused on the internationalization process. Studying the internationalization of Swedish manufacturing firms, they developed a model of the firm's choice of market and form of entry when going abroad. Their work was influenced by Aharoni's (1966) seminal study.

With these basic assumptions in mind, the Uppsala researchers interpreted the patterns in the internationalization process they had observed in Swedish manufacturing firms. They had noted, first of all, that companies appeared to begin their operations abroad in fairly nearby markets and only gradually penetrated more far-flung markets. Second, it appeared that companies entered new markets through exports. It was very rare for companies to enter new markets with sales organizations or manufacturing subsidiaries of their own. Wholly owned or majority-owned operations were established only after several years of exports to the same market.

Johanson and Wiedersheim-Paul (1975) distinguish between four different modes of entering an international market, where the successive stages represent higher degrees of international involvement/market commitment:

Stage 1: no regular export activities (sporadic export).
Stage 2: export via independent representatives (export modes).
Stage 3: establishment of a foreign sales subsidiary.
Stage 4: foreign production/manufacturing units.

The assumption that the internationalization of a firm develops step by step was originally supported by evidence from a case study of four Swedish firms. The sequence of stages was restricted to a specific country market. This market commitment dimension is shown in Figure 3.1.

The concept of market commitment is assumed to contain two factors – the amount of resources committed and the degree of commitment. The amount of resources could be operationalized to the size of investment in the market (marketing, organization, personnel, etc.), while the degree of commitment refers to the difficulty of finding an alternative use for the resources and transferring them to the alternative use.

International activities require both general knowledge and market-specific knowledge. Market-specific knowledge is assumed to be gained mainly through experience in the market, whereas knowledge of the operations can be transferred from one country to another; the latter will thus facilitate the geographic diversification in Figure 3.1. A direct relation between market knowledge and market commitment is postulated: knowledge can be considered as a dimension of human resources. Consequently, the better the knowledge about a market, the more valuable are the resources and the stronger the commitment to the market.

Figure 3.1 implies that additional market commitment as a rule will be made in small incremental steps, both in the market commitment dimension and in the geographical dimension. There are, however, three exceptions. First, firms that have large resources experience small consequences of their commitments and can take larger internationalization steps. Second, when market conditions are stable and homogeneous, relevant market knowledge can be gained in ways other than experience. Third, when the firm has considerable experience from markets with similar conditions, it may be able to generalize this experience to any specific market (Johanson and Vahlne, 1990).

The geographical dimension in Figure 3.1 shows that firms enter new markets with successively greater psychic distance. Psychic distance is defined in terms of factors such as differences in language, culture and political systems, which disturb the flow of information between the firm and the market. Thus firms start internationalization by going to those markets they can most easily understand. There they will see opportunities, and there the perceived market uncertainty is low (Brewer, 2007).

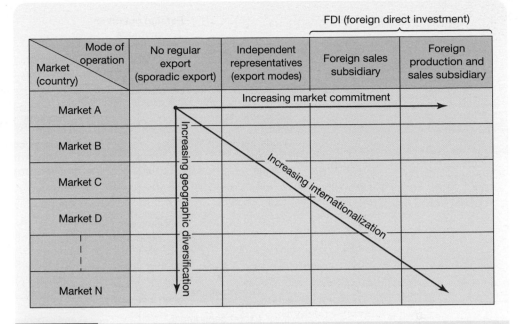

| Figure 3.1 | Internationalization of the firm: an incremental (organic) approach |

Source: adapted from Forsgren and Johanson (1975, p. 16).

The original stage model has been extended by Welch and Loustarinen (1988), who operate with six dimensions of internationalization (see Figure 3.2):

1. *sales objects* (what?): goods, services, know-how and systems;
2. *operations methods* (how?): agents, subsidiaries, licensing, franchising management contracts;
3. *markets* (where?): political/cultural/psychic/physical distance differences between markets;
4. *organizational structure*: export department, international division;
5. *finance*: availability of international finance sources to support the international activities;
6. *personnel*: international skills, experience and training.

Critical views of the original Uppsala model

Various criticisms of the Uppsala model have been put forward: one is that the model is too deterministic (Reid, 1983; Turnbull, 1987).

It has also been argued that the model does not take into account interdependencies between different country markets (Johanson and Mattson, 1986). It seems reasonable to consider a firm more internationalized if it views and handles different country markets as interdependent than if it views them as completely separate entities.

Studies have shown that the internationalization process model is not valid for service industries. In research into the internationalization of Swedish technical consultants – a typical service industry – it has been demonstrated that the cumulative reinforcement of foreign commitments implied by the process model is absent (Sharma and Johanson, 1987).

The criticism has been supported by the fact that the internationalization process of new entrants in certain industries has recently become more spectacular. Firms have lately seemed prone to *leapfrog* stages in the establishment chain, entering 'distant' markets in terms of psychic distance at an early stage, and the pace of the internationalization process generally seems to have speeded up.

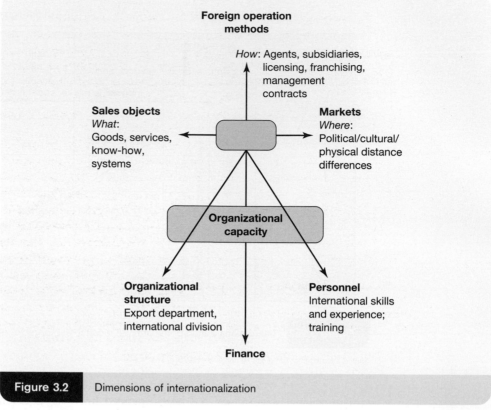

Figure 3.2   Dimensions of internationalization

Source: Welch and Loustarinen (1988). Reproduced with permission from The Braybrooke Press Ltd.

Nordström's preliminary (1990) results seem to confirm this argument. The United Kingdom, Germany and the United States have become a more common target for the very first establishment of sales subsidiaries by Swedish firms than their Scandinavian neighbours.

The leapfrogging tendency not only involves entering distant markets. We can also expect a company to leapfrog some intermediate entry modes (foreign operation methods) in order to move away from the sequentialist pattern and more directly to some kind of foreign investment (Figure 3.3).

In market no. 1 the firm follows the mainstream evolutionary pattern, but in market no. 6 the firm has learned from the use of different operation methods in previous markets, and therefore chooses to leapfrog some stages and go directly to foreign investment.

Others have claimed that the Uppsala model is not valid in situations of highly internationalized firms and industries. In these cases, competitive forces and factors override psychic distance as the principal explanatory factor for the firm's process of internationalization. Furthermore, if knowledge of transactions can be transferred from one country to another, firms with extensive international experience are likely to perceive the psychic distance to a new country as shorter than firms with little international experience.

Nordström (1990) argues that the world has become much more homogeneous and that consequently psychic distance has decreased.

Firms today also have quicker and easier access to knowledge about doing business abroad. It is no longer necessary to build up knowledge in-house in a slow and gradual trial and error process. Several factors contribute to this. For example, universities, business schools and management training centres all over the world are putting more and more emphasis on international business.

Probably even more important, the absolute number of people with experience of doing business abroad has increased. Hence it has become easier to hire people with the experience and knowledge needed, rather than develop it in-house. The number of people with experience

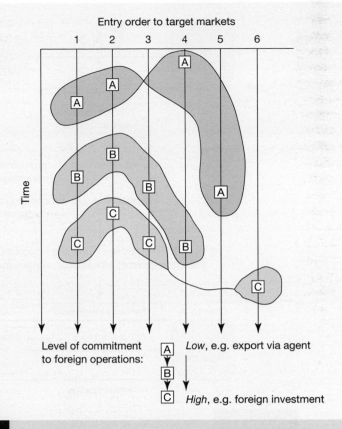

Entry order to target markets

Level of commitment to foreign operations:

A   *Low*, e.g. export via agent

B

C   *High*, e.g. foreign investment

Figure 3.3	Internationalization pattern of the firm as a sum of target country patterns

Source: Welch and Loustarinen (1988). Reproduced with permission from The Braybrooke Press Ltd.

of doing business abroad has increased over time as an effect of continuous growth in world trade and foreign direct investment.

The spectacular development of information technologies, in terms of both absolute performance and diminishing price/performance ratios, has made it easier for a firm to become acquainted with foreign markets, thus making a leapfrog strategy more realistic (see also section 3.6 on Internet-based born globals).

In spite of the criticisms the Uppsala model has gained strong support in studies of a wide spectrum of countries and situations. The empirical research confirms that commitment and experience are important factors explaining international business behaviour (Cumberland, 2006). In particular, the model receives strong support regarding export behaviour, and the relevance of cultural distance has also been confirmed.

3.3   The transaction cost analysis model

The foundation for this model was made by Coase (1937). He argued that 'a firm will tend to expand until the cost of organizing an extra transaction within the firm will become equal to the cost of carrying out the same transaction by means of an exchange on the open market' (p. 395). It is a theory which predicts that a firm will perform internally those activities it can undertake at lower cost through establishing an internal (hierarchical) management control and implementation system while relying on the market for activities in which independent outsiders (such as export intermediaries, agents or distributors) have a cost advantage.

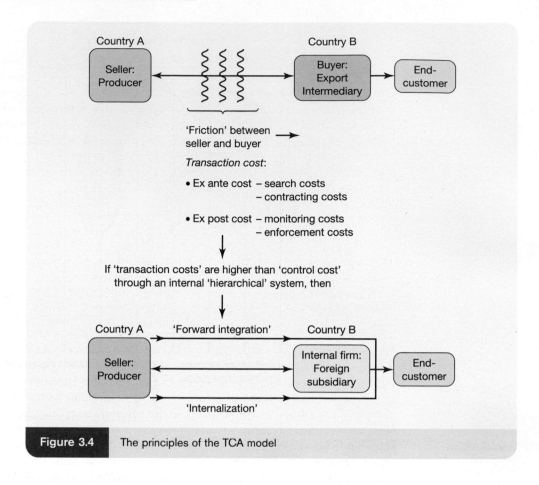

| **Figure 3.4** | The principles of the TCA model |

Transaction costs
The 'friction' between buyer and seller, which is explained by opportunistic behaviour.

Opportunistic behaviour
Self-interest with guile – misleading, distortion, disguise and confusion.

Transaction cost analysis
Transaction cost analysis concludes that if the friction between buyer and seller is higher than through an internal hierarchical system then the firm should internalize.

Internalize
Integrate an external partner into one's own organization.

Transaction costs emerge when markets fail to operate under the requirements of perfect competition (friction-free); the cost of operating in such markets (i.e. the transaction cost) would be zero, and there would be little or no incentive to impose any impediments to free market exchange. However, in the real world there is always some kind of friction between buyer and seller, resulting in transaction costs (see Figure 3.4).

The friction between buyer and seller can often be explained by **opportunistic behaviour**. Williamson (1985) defines it as a 'self-interest seeking with guile'. It includes methods of misleading, distortion, disguise and confusion. To protect against the hazards of opportunism, the parties may employ a variety of safeguards or governance structures. The term 'safeguard' (or alternatively 'governance structure') as used here can be defined as a control mechanism, which has the objective of bringing about the perception of fairness or equity among transactors. The purpose of safeguards is to provide, at minimum cost, the control and trust that is necessary for transactors to believe that engaging in the exchange will make them better off. The most prominent safeguard is the legal contract. A legal contract specifies the obligations of each party and allows a transactor to go to a third party (i.e. a court) to sanction an opportunistic trading partner.

The **transaction cost analysis** (TCA) framework argues that cost minimization explains structural decisions. Firms **internalize**, that is, integrate vertically, to reduce transaction costs. Transaction costs can be divided into *different forms of costs* related to the transactional relationship between buyer and seller. The underlying condition for the following description of the cost elements is this equation:

transaction cost = *ex ante* costs + *ex post* costs = (search costs + contracting costs) + (monitoring costs + enforcement costs)

Ex ante costs

- *Search costs*: these include the cost of gathering information to identify and evaluate potential export intermediaries. Although such costs can be prohibitive to many exporters, knowledge about foreign markets is critical to export success. The search costs for distant, unfamiliar markets, where available (published) market information is lacking and organizational forms are different, can be especially prohibitive (e.g. exports from the United Kingdom to China). In comparison, the search costs for nearby, familiar markets may be more acceptable (e.g. export from United Kingdom to Germany).
- *Contracting costs*: these are the costs associated with negotiating and writing an agreement between seller (producer) and buyer (export intermediary).

Ex post costs

- *Monitoring costs*: the costs associated with monitoring the agreement to ensure that both seller and buyer fulfil the predetermined set of obligations.
- *Enforcement costs*: the costs associated with the sanctioning of a trading partner who does not perform in accordance with the agreement.

A fundamental assumption of transaction cost theory is that firms will attempt to minimize the combination of these costs when undertaking transactions. Thus, when considering the most efficient form of organizing export functions, transaction cost theory suggests that firms will choose the solution that minimizes the sum of *ex ante* and *ex post* costs.

Williamson (1975) based his analysis on the assumption of transaction costs and the different forms of governance structure under which transactions take place. In his original work, he identified two main alternatives of governance markets: externalization and internalization (hierarchies). In the case of **externalization**, market transactions are by definition external to the firm and the price mechanism conveys all the necessary governance information. In the case of **internalization**, the international firm creates a kind of internal market in which the hierarchical governance is defined by a set of internal contracts.

> **Externalization**
> Doing business through an external partner (importer, agent, distributor).
>
> **Internalization**
> Doing business through own internal system (own subsidiaries).

Externalization and internalization of transactions are equated with intermediaries (agents, distributors) and sales subsidiaries (or other governance structures involving ownership control) respectively.

In this way, Williamson's framework provides the basis for a variety of research into the organization of international activity and the choice of international market entry mode. We will return to this issue in Part III of this book.

The conclusion of the transaction cost theory is:

> If the transaction costs (defined above) through externalization (e.g. through an importer or agent) are higher than the control cost through an internal hierarchical system, then the firm should seek internalization of activities, i.e. implementing the global marketing strategy in wholly owned subsidiaries. More simply: if the friction between buyer and seller is too high then the firm should rather internalize, in the form of its own subsidiaries.

Limitations of the TCA framework

Narrow assumptions of human nature

Ghoshal and Moran (1996) have criticized the original work of Williamson as making too narrow an assumption of human nature (opportunism and its equally narrow interpretation of economic objectives). They also wonder why the theory's mainstream development has remained immune to such important contributions as Ouchi's (1980) insight on social control. Ouchi points to the relevance of intermediate forms (between markets and hierarchies), such as the clan, where governance is based on a win–win situation (in contrast to a zero-sum game situation).

Sometimes firms will even build trust with their externalized agents and distributors by turning them into partners. In this way the firms would avoid large investments in subsidiaries around the world.

Excluding 'internal' transaction costs

The TCA framework also seems to ignore the internal transaction cost, assuming zero friction within a multinational firm. One can imagine severe friction (resulting in transaction cost) between the head office of a firm and its sales subsidiaries when internal transfer prices have to be settled.

Relevance of intermediate forms for SMEs

One can also question the relevance of the TCA framework to the internationalization process of SMEs (Christensen and Lindmark, 1993). The lack of resources and knowledge in SMEs is a major force for the externalization of activities, but because the use of markets often raises contractual problems, markets in many instances are not real alternatives to hierarchies for SMEs. Instead, the SMEs have to rely on intermediate forms of governance, such as contractual relations and relations based on clan-like systems created by a mutual orientation of investments, skills and trust-building. Therefore SMEs are often highly dependent on the cooperative environment available. Such an approach will be presented and discussed in the next section.

Importance of production cost is understated

It can be argued that the importance of transaction cost is overstated and that the importance of production cost has not been taken into consideration. Production cost is the cost of performing a particular task/function in the value chain, such as R&D costs, manufacturing costs and marketing costs. According to Williamson (1985), the most efficient choice of internationalization mode is one that will help *minimize the sum of production and transaction costs*.

3.4 The network model

Basic concept

Business networks
Actors are autonomous and linked to each other through relationships, which are flexible and may alter accordingly to rapid changes in the environment.
The 'glue' that keeps the relationships together is based on technical, economic, legal and especially personal ties.

Business networks are a mode of handling activity interdependences between several business actors. As we have seen, other modes of handling or governing interdependences in a business field are markets and hierarchies.

The **network model** differs from the market with regard to relations between actors. In a market model, actors have no specific relations to each other. The interdependences are regulated through the market price mechanism. In contrast, in the business network the actors are linked to each other through exchange relationships, and their needs and capabilities are mediated through the interaction taking place in the relationships.

Network model
The relationships of a firm in a domestic network can be used as bridges to other networks in other countries.

The industrial network differs from the hierarchy in the way that the actors are autonomous and handle their interdependences bilaterally rather than via a coordinating unit on a higher level. Whereas a hierarchy is organized and controlled as one unit from the top, the business network is organized by each actor's willingness to engage in exchange relationships with some of the other actors in the network. The networks are more loosely coupled than are hierarchies; they can change shape more easily. Any actor in the network can engage in new relationships or break off old ones, thereby modifying its structure. Thus business networks can be expected to be more flexible in response to changing conditions in turbulent business fields, such as those where technical change is very rapid.

It can be concluded that business networks will emerge in fields where coordination between specific actors can give strong gains and where conditions are changing rapidly. Thus the network approach implies a move away from the firm as the unit of analysis, towards exchange between firms and between a group of firms and other groups of firms as the main object of study. However, it also implies a move away from transactions towards more lasting exchange relationships constituting a structure within which international business takes place and evolves.

Evidently, business relationships and consequently industrial networks are subtle phenomena, which cannot easily be observed by an outsider: that is, a potential entrant. The actors are tied to each other through a number of different bonds: technical, social, cognitive, administrative, legal, economic, etc.

A basic assumption in the network model is that the individual firm is dependent on resources controlled by other firms. The companies get access to these external resources through their network positions. Because the development of positions takes time and depends on resource accumulations, a firm must establish and develop positions in relation to counterparts in foreign networks.

To enter a network from outside requires that other actors be motivated to engage in interaction, something which is resource-demanding and may require several firms to make adaptations in their ways of performing business. Thus foreign market or network entry of the firm may very well be the result of interaction initiatives taken by other firms that are insiders in the network in the specific country. However, the chances of being the object of such initiatives are much greater for an insider.

The networks in a country may well extend far beyond country borders. In relation to the internationalization of the firm, the network view argues that the internationalizing firm is initially engaged in a network which is primarily domestic.

The relationships of a firm in a domestic network can be used as bridges to other networks in other countries. In some cases the customer demands that the supplier follows it abroad if the supplier wants to keep the business at home. An example of an international network is shown in Figure 3.5. It appears that one of the sub-suppliers established a subsidiary in Country B. Here the production subsidiary is served by the local company of the sub-supplier. Countries E and F, and partly Country C, are sourced from the production subsidiary in Country B. Generally it can be assumed that direct or indirect bridges exist between firms and different country networks. Such bridges can be important both in the initial steps abroad and in the subsequent entry of new markets.

The character of the ties in a network is partly a matter of the firms involved. This is primarily the case with technical, economic and legal ties. To an important extent, however, the ties are formed between the persons engaged in the business relationships. This is the case with social and cognitive ties. Industries as well as countries may differ with regard to the relative importance of firm and personal relationships, but it can be expected that the personal influence on relationships is strongest in the early establishment of relationships. Later in the process routines and systems will become more important.

When entering a network, the internationalization process of the firm will often proceed more quickly. In particular, SMEs in high-tech industries tend to go directly to more distant markets and to set up their own subsidiaries more rapidly. One reason seems to be that the entrepreneurs behind those companies have networks of colleagues dealing with the new technology. Internationalization, in these cases, is an exploitation of the advantage that this network constitutes.

Four cases of internationalization

The Uppsala internationalization model treated internationalization independently of the situation and the competition in the market. In the following we will try to combine these

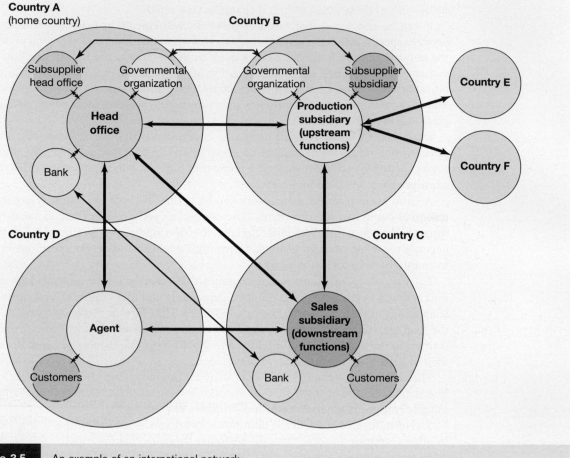

| Figure 3.5 | An example of an international network |

two important aspects. A 'production net' contains relationships between those firms whose activities together produce functions linked to a specific area. The firm's degree of internationalization shows the extent to which the firm has positions in different national nets, how strong those positions are and how integrated they are.

The network model also has consequences for the meaning of internationalization of the market. A production net can be more or less internationalized. A high degree of internationalization of a production net implies that there are many and strong relationships between the different national sections of the global production net. A low degree of internationalization means that the national nets have few relationships with each other.

We will distinguish between four different situations, characterized by on the one hand a low or a high degree of internationalization of the firm and on the other, a low or high degree of internationalization of the market (the production network) (Figure 3.6).

The early starter

In this situation competitors, customers, suppliers and other firms in the domestic market as well as in foreign markets have no important international relationships.

The people behind the Uppsala internationalization model have described this situation and its transition to the lonely international (section 3.2). Gradual and slow involvement in the market via an agent, leading to a sales subsidiary and then a manufacturing subsidiary, is primarily a process by which market knowledge gives the basis for stronger commitments.

		Degree of internationalization of the market	
		Low	High
Degree of internationalization of the firm	Low	The early starter	The late starter
	High	The lonely international	The international among others

| Figure 3.6 | Four cases of internationalization of a firm |

Source: Johanson and Mattson (1988, p. 298). Reprinted by permission of Taylor & Francis.

The lonely international

In this situation the firm has experience of relationships with others in foreign countries. It has acquired knowledge and means to handle environments that differ with respect to culture, institutions and so on. The knowledge situation is also more favourable when establishing the firm in a new national net.

Initiatives to further internationalization do not come from other parties in the production nets, as the firm's suppliers, customers and competitors are less internationalized. On the contrary, the lonely international has the competences to promote internationalization of its production net and, consequently, the firms engaged in it. The firm's relationships with, and in, other national nets may function as a bridge to those nets for its suppliers and customers.

The late starter

In a situation with international customers and competitors, the less internationalized firm can be 'pulled out' of the domestic market by its customers or complementary suppliers to the customers. Sometimes the step abroad can be rather large in the beginning.

How will the firm go abroad in this situation? Here we will differentiate between SMEs and LSEs.

SMEs going abroad in an internationalized world probably have to be highly specialized and adjusted to solutions in specific sections of the production nets. Starting production abroad is probably a question of what bonds are important to the customers, and in this matter SMEs are very flexible.

LSEs that have become large in the domestic market are often less specialized than small firms, and their situation is often more complex than that of the small firm. One possibility is to get established in a foreign production net through acquisition or joint venture.

In general, it is probably more difficult for a firm that has become large at home to find a niche in highly internationalized nets. It cannot, as the small firm can, adjust in the flexible way which may be necessary in such a net.

Compared to the early starter, the late starter often finds it difficult to establish new positions in a tightly structured net. The best distributors are already linked to competitors. Competitors can, more or less legally, make the late newcomer unprofitable by predatory pricing. When we compare early and late starters we can see how important timing is in global marketing.

The international among others

In this situation the firm has the possibility of using positions in one net to bridge over to other nets, with regard to both extensions and penetration. There is a strong need for coordination of the international activities along the value chain (e.g. R&D, production and marketing/ sales). Operations in one market may make it possible to utilize production capacity for sales in other markets. This may lead to production coordination by product specialization and increased intra-firm trade across borders.

Establishment of sales subsidiaries is probably speeded up by high internationalization because the international knowledge level is higher and there is a stronger need to coordinate sales and marketing activities in different markets.

The relevance of the network model for the SME serving as a subcontractor

Until now a network has been connected with development of mutual trust and interests between firms in the network. In the following, domination and control characteristics will form the starting point for the formation of a more power-balanced network.

In the SME context it is clear that where, for example, a small firm derives a significant proportion of its turnover and profits from acting as a subcontractor to another, often larger firm, the small firm becomes dependent on the latter. In turn, the large firm may acquire power over its subcontractor. This power can be measured in terms of the larger company's influence on decision-making within the smaller firm in areas such as pricing and investment.

Exchange networks are based on control, coordination and cooperation. By 'control' is understood quasi-hierarchical relationships allowing one company to dominate another: for example, the relationship that traditionally obtains in the car industry between the major manufacturers and their subcontractors. By 'coordination' is understood a situation in which a 'leading' or 'hub' firm in the network orchestrates the value-adding chain. This allows firms to specialize in those components of the value chain in which they have competitive advantage, abandoning and farming out those activities in which they are disadvantaged to network partners that do have strengths in these areas.

Cooperation is the result of increasing specialization in small market niches, which has tended to encourage interdependency between firms in the value-added chain. Whereas in many subcontracting relationships in the past the subcontractor simply followed instructions of the dominating firm on design and manufacture, the need to adjust to ever-quicker changes in the marketplace can have the effect of making the subcontractor a more equal partner in the whole design to production process. The nature of the relationship between subcontractor and buyer thereby changes. Greater trust is required to make the partnership a success. Greater coordination is also required, creating a role for companies that simply 'manage' the value chain. In order to meet the pressures of these new circumstances the small firm will depend on the nature and number of its links to other firms. As a result the need for and value of networking have increased.

Where the network is dominated by a single firm and relationships are of the traditional subcontracting kind, competition on price (or prices simply being imposed by the dominating firm) is the rule. Also, cooperating firms know that, while optimal networking is an effective strategy to reduce risk, less optimal networking will increase risk by increasing their dependence on, for example, a potentially unreliable supplier. To overcome the danger of dependence, traditional risk-reduction strategies can be implemented, such as the implementation of multiple sourcing by the purchasing company, or client diversification by the selling company.

3.5 Internationalization of SMEs

In the face of globalization threats many SMEs attempt to expand their sales into foreign markets. International expansion provides new and potentially more profitable markets, helps increase the firm's competitiveness and facilitates access to new product ideas, manufacturing innovations and the latest technology.

At the macro environment and industry levels, globalization gives rise to market turbulence, increased competition from (especially) multinational firms, loss of protected markets due to trade liberalization, and the emergence of international marketing opportunities, all of which can affect the operations and performance of the SME. In such an environment possession by management of an entrepreneurial orientation is expected to provide certain benefits.

It may be more appropriate to take a holistic view of the very small, entrepreneurial, or start-up firm's cross-border business activities, rather than to focus on discrete entry mode types. The challenge facing most entrepreneurial firms is to establish and develop a viable, competitive and sustainable business, usually with limited resources, and often by adopting flexible, imaginative and innovative business practices. International business activity for many firms, and particularly high-technology firms, may be an integral part of that process. In that respect too, internationalization is a firm-specific behaviour, in relation to and encompassing its international business activities.

The assumption made here therefore is that internationalization, for entrepreneurial firms, is a growth and development process. It may involve one or a number of value chain activities, some of which may be more internationalized, or more frequently subject to internationalization, than others. Internationalization may be part of the process, but for very small and very young firms internationalization is more likely to occur, in the first instance, through links and transactions with organizations and individuals in the external environment. The process may include both inward and outward links – see Table 3.1 and Figure 2.2 (earlier) – and these are likely to reflect the firms' current areas of competence and expertise, and/or its current level of needs and perceived inadequacies.

Initial international expansion may involve specific combinations of inward/outward value chain activities, which are not necessarily directly reciprocal. Efficiency and synergy in linkage combinations is an important concern for internationalizing firms.

The element of *time* is considered more important here than development stages that, even if specifically determined, would vary considerably between firms.

Table 3.1	SMEs inward–outward cross-border business activities	
	Inward	**Outward**
R&D	Contract-in R&D License-in technology from overseas-based firms	License-out technology to overseas-based firm Contract-out R&D to overseas-based firm
Production	Technical service or consultancy performed in the home country for overseas-based clients Contract-in manufacture for overseas-based firms	Contract-out manufacture to overseas-based firm Technical service or consultancy performed overseas Minority investment in overseas production Majority investment in overseas production
Marketing and distribution	Import from overseas-based supplier Import with distribution in the home country Management or marketing service or consultancy performed in the home country for overseas-based clients	Exporting through home country-based intermediary Exporting through foreign-based agent/distributor Exporting through overseas-based sales representative or branch Management or marketing services or consultancy performed overseas

Source: adapted from Jones (2001, p. 197).

Importance of personal factors

International entrepreneurship argues that the founders of international new ventures are more alert to the possibilities of combing resources from different national markets because of the competences they have developed from their earlier activities.

Research results by Manolova and Brush (2002) indicate that owners/founders are likely to draw on their international experience, skills, or overall competences when internationalizing their own firms. Therefore, for managers with these sets of skills and positive environmental perceptions, the process of internationalization has 'less uncertainty', and hence is more likely to be pursued than it is for managers without comparable skills or perceptions.

Manolova and Bush (2002) clearly indicate that personal factors matter with respect to SME internationalization but, more importantly, 'some personal factors matter more than others'. Owners/founders or managers who have more positive perceptions of the international environment would also be more likely to internationalize their own small businesses.

The most important finding from Manolova and Bush (2002) is that internationalization is not a function of 'demographics', but is instead a function of 'perceptions'. If the owner/founder or manager perceives that there is a lower level of environmental uncertainty in a particular international market, or perceives that there is the requisite skill set to internationalize, then chances are high that the small firm will be pursuing a strategy of internationalization. Additionally, the findings show that public policy directives, as well as education and training programmes, need to recognize that there are significant differences in small firm internationalization that are based upon the technology sector. Knowledge of these differences can be used to guide the development of small firm internationalization initiatives that match sector characteristics.

Entrepreneurial orientation is associated with opportunity seeking, risk-taking, and decision action catalyzed by a strong leader or an organization possessed of a particular value system. SMEs with an entrepreneurial orientation engage in product market innovations, undertake relatively risky ventures and initiate proactive innovations.

Innovativeness refers to a corporate environment that promotes and supports novel ideas, experimentation and creative processes that may lead to new products, techniques or technologies. Risk-taking reflects the propensity to devote resources to projects that entail a substantial possibility of failure, along with chances for high returns. Proactiveness is the opposite of reactiveness and implies taking initiative, aggressively pursuing ventures and being at the forefront of efforts to shape the environment in ways that benefit the firm. Autonomy suggests the independent action of a person or a team in giving birth to an idea or a vision and then carrying it through to fruition. Finally, competitive aggressiveness refers to the firm's tendency to challenge its competitors intensely and directly in order to outperform them in the marketplace.

However, SMEs may lack the resources to compete head to head with larger rivals at home and invasions from abroad. Globalization may pose many challenges and can make the business milieu substantially more hostile for smaller firms, but all in all, given the turbulence posed by globalization, it is expected that SMEs with an entrepreneurial orientation will fare better than those without it.

Technology acquisition is one way of enabling the firm to compete more effectively or launch products that better satisfy customer needs. Innovation arising from acquired technology is a key source of competitive advantage, particularly in turbulent environments, that can enable firms to market new or improved goods faster than competitors. Technology acquisition can give rise to products that are better adapted to the specific needs of foreign markets. Firms can gain additional benefits by responding to the forces of globalization. SMEs that respond by appropriately adapting their marketing and other strategies to globalization demands are likely to perform better than firms that do not. Nature and pace of internationalization are conditioned by product, industry, and other external environmental variables, as well as by firm-specific factors. Therefore, at any given point in time, SMEs will be in a state of internationalization, which will be subject to both backward and forward momentum, instead of progressing through stages, as in the Uppsala model.

The SME's internationalization is unlikely to come off well unless the firm prepares in advance. Advance planning has often been regarded as important to the success of new ventures. Such planning is especially important in international ventures, in which the business environment can be considerably more complex than at home. Thus *internationalization preparation* describes a firm's efforts to prepare in advance as it seeks to expand into foreign markets. Such preparation involves conducting international market research, committing human, financial and other resources to supporting the international venture and adapting products to suit the needs of target foreign markets.

In the next section we will look at a special case of SME internationalization – the so-called 'born globals'.

3.6 Born globals

Introduction

In recent years research has identified an increasing number of firms that certainly do not follow the traditional stages pattern in their internationalization process. In contrast, they aim at international markets or maybe even the global market right from their birth.

Born global
A firm that from its birth globalizes rapidly without any preceding long-term internationalization period.

A **born global** can be defined as a firm that from its inception pursue a vision of becoming global and globalize rapidly without any preceding long term domestic or internationalization period (Oviatt and McDougall, 1994; Gabrielsson and Kirpalani, 2004).

Born globals represent an interesting case of firms operating under time and space compression conditions that have allowed them to assume a global geographic scope since their start up. This 'time–space compression' phenomenon (Harvey, 1996) means that geographical processes can be reduced and compressed into 'here and now' trade and information exchange over the globe – if available infrastructure, communication and IT devices are put in place together with skilled people. The global financial market is a good example of the phenomenon (Törnroos, 2002).

Oviatt and McDougall (1994) grouped born globals (or 'international new ventures' as they call them) into four different categories, dependent on the number of value chain activities performed combined with the number of countries involved. For example, they distinguish the 'export/import start-up' from the 'global start-up', whereby the latter – contrary to the former – involves many activities coordinated across many countries.

Born globals are typically characterized by being SMEs with less than 500 employees and annual sales under $100 million – and reliance on cutting-edge technology in the development of relatively unique product or process innovations. The most distinguishing feature of born global firms is that they tend to be managed by entrepreneurial visionaries, who view the world as a single, borderless marketplace from the time of the firm's founding. Born globals are small, technology-oriented companies that operate in international markets from the earliest days of their establishment. There is growing evidence of the emergence of born globals in numerous countries of the developed world.

More recently the concept of *born-again global firms* has been proposed, i.e. long-established firms that previously focused on their domestic markets but that suddenly embrace rapid and dedicated internationalization (Bell *et al.*, 2001).

The born global phenomenon suggests a new challenge to traditional theories of internationalization.

Born globals are challenging traditional theories

Born globals may be similar to the 'late starter' or the 'international among others' (Johanson and Mattson, 1988). In the latter situation both the environment and the firm are highly internationalized. Johanson and Mattson point out that internationalization processes of firms will be much faster in internationalized market conditions, among other reasons because the need for coordination and integration across borders is high. Since relevant partners/distributors will often be occupied in neighbouring markets, firms do not necessarily follow a 'rings in the water' approach to market selection. In the same vein their 'establishment chain' need not follow the traditional picture because strategic alliances, joint ventures, etc., are much more prevalent; firms seek partners with supplementary skills and resources. In other words internationalization processes of firms will be much more individual and situation-specific in internationalized markets.

Many industries are characterized by *global sourcing activities* and also by networks across borders. The consequence is that innovative products can very quickly spread to new markets all over the world – because the needs and wants of buyers become more homogeneous. Hence the internationalization process of subcontractors may be quite diverse and different from the stages models. In other words, the new market conditions pull the firms into many markets very fast. Finally, financial markets have also become international, which means that an entrepreneur in any country may seek financial sources all over the world.

In the case of born globals we may assume that the background of the decision-maker (founder) has a large influence on the internationalization path followed. Market knowledge, personal networking of the entrepreneur or international contacts and experience transmitted from former occupations, relations and education are examples of such international skills obtained prior to the birth of the firm. Factors such as education, experience from living abroad, experience of other internationally oriented jobs, etc., mould the mind of the founder and decrease the psychic distances to specific product markets significantly; the previous experience and knowledge of the founder extends the network across national borders, opening possibilities for new business ventures (Madsen and Servais, 1997).

Often born globals govern their sales and marketing activities through a specialized network in which they seek partners that complement their own competences; this is necessary because of their limited resources.

In many ways the slow organic Uppsala-model process and the accelerated 'born global' pathways are the opposites of one another, at the two extremes of a spectrum (see Figure 3.7). They also often represent the choice of doing it alone (the organic pathway), while the born global pathway is based on different types of cooperation and partnerships in order to facilitate rapid growth and internationalization.

In spite of the different time frames and prerequisites for the pathways, there are also some common characteristics in all models. Internationalization is seen as a process where knowledge and learning go hand in hand, even in rapid internationalization. Past knowledge contributes to current knowledge of the company. Firms aiming for the born global pathway do not have time to develop these skills in the organic way (inside the firm), they need to possess them beforehand or to be able to acquire them underway, i.e. through collaborating with other firms already possessing these supplementary competences (Melén and Nordman, 2009).

Most often born globals must choose a business area with homogeneous and minimal adaptation of the marketing mix. The argument is that these small firms cannot take a multidomestic approach as can large firms, simply because they do not have sufficient scale in operations worldwide. They are vulnerable because they are dependent on a single product (niche market) that they have to commercialize in lead markets first, no matter where such markets are situated geographically. The reason is that such markets are the key to broad and rapid market access, which is important because these firms often incur relatively high fixed R&D costs, which occur upfront, i.e. before any sales are made. Since this is the key factor influencing the choice of the initial market the importance of psychic distance as a market selection criterion is reduced. In order to survive, firms must quickly catch the growth track to cover the initial expenses. Finally, competition for a typical born global is very intense and its products may become obsolete rather quickly (e.g. in the case of software). If a company is to take full advantage of the market potential during its 'global window of opportunity', it may be forced to penetrate all major markets simultaneously (Âijö *et al.*, 2005).

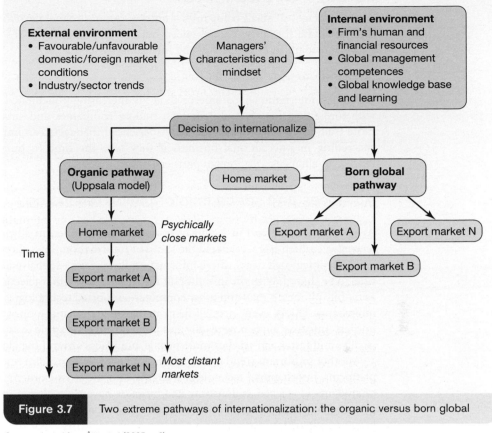

Figure 3.7   Two extreme pathways of internationalization: the organic versus born global

Source: adapted from Âijö *et al.* (2005, p. 6).

Factors giving rise to the emergence of born globals

The number and influence of born-global firms in international trade is likely to increase (Knight *et al.*, 2004). Several trends may explain the increasing importance of born globals and help explain why such companies can successfully enter international markets.

Increasing role of niche markets

There is a growing demand among customers in mature economies for specialized or customized products. With the globalization of markets and increasing worldwide competition from large multinationals, many smaller firms may have no choice but to specialize in the supplying of products that occupy a relatively narrow global niche.

Advances in process/technology production

Improvements in microprocessor-based technology imply that low-scale, batch-type production can be economical. New machine tools now permit the manufacture of complex, non-standard parts and components with relative ease. New technologies allow small companies to achieve comparable footing with large multinationals in the production of sophisticated products for sale around the world. Technology allows small importers to streamline production in ways that make their products highly competitive in the global marketplace. Furthermore, technology is facilitating the production of widely diverse products on an ever-smaller scale. The consequence of this is increasing specialization in many industries – more and more consumer goods will likely be tailor made to fit ever more diverse preferences.

Flexibility of SMEs/born globals

The advantages of small companies – quicker response time, *flexibility*, adaptability, and so on – facilitate the international endeavours of born globals. SMEs are more flexible and quicker to adapt to foreign tastes and international standards.

Global networks

Successful international commerce today is increasingly facilitated through partnerships with foreign businesses – distributors, trading companies and subcontractors, as well as more traditional buyers and sellers. Inexperienced managers can improve their chances for succeeding in international business if they take the time to build mutually beneficial, long-term alliances with foreign partners.

Advances and speed in information technology

A very important trend in favour of born globals is the recent advance in *communications technology*, which has accelerated the speed of information flows. Gone are the days of large, vertically integrated firms where information flows were expensive and took a considerable time to be shared. With the invention of the Internet and other telecommunication aids such as mobile phones, e-mail and other computer-supported technologies such as electronic data interchange (EDI), even in small firms managers can manage operations efficiently across borders. Information is now readily and more quickly accessible to everyone. Everything gets smaller and faster and reaches more people and places around the globe.

Another important trend is the *globalization of technology*. Joint research and development platforms, international technology transfers, and the cross-border education and exchange of students in science, engineering and business have all exploded in recent years. As such, new and better approaches to manufacturing, product innovation and general operations have become much more readily available to smaller firms.

The Internet revolution offers new opportunities for young SMEs to establish a global sales platform by developing e-commerce websites. Today many new and small firms are born globals in that they are 'start-ups' on the Internet and sell to a global audience via a centralized e-commerce website.

Generally, it seems that service- and information-based Internet companies have internationalized more rapidly than electronic retailers or manufacturers selling tangible product. Therefore, internet-based companies tend to serve a greater number of international markets than do the electronic retailers or manufacturers (Kim, 2003).

3.7   Internationalization of services

As goods go through increasingly more complex value chains to increase firms' relative competitive advantage, services will play a more important role in their marketing. Services themselves are also getting more complex as information technology enables unlimited variations for both sales and after-sales support for target markets.

In the literature on international marketing of services an internationalization strategy is often considered more risky for service firms than for manufacturers. The main reason for this is that in many services the producer and the production facilities are part of the service, which requires that the firm has greater control of its resources than would otherwise be the case. In traditional international marketing models focusing on the needs of manufacturing firms, the internationalization process can start on a minor scale using indirect export channels followed by a step-by-step move towards more direct channels. This enables the firm gradually to increase its understanding of quality expectations, personnel requirements, distribution and media structures and buying behaviour peculiarities on the foreign market. For service firms the situation is different. They immediately face all of these and other problems related to entering a foreign market. A service firm has to find an entry mode and a strategy that helps it to cope with this situation as well as possible. The choice, of course, depends on the type of service and market.

First let us look at some characteristics of services.

Characteristics of services

A service is a complicated phenomenon. The word has many meanings, ranging from personal service to service as a product. Services are not things, they are processes or activities, and these activities are intangible in nature. The term can be even broader in scope. A machine, or almost any physical product, can be turned into a service to a customer if the seller makes efforts to tailor the solution to meet the most detailed demands of that customer. A machine is still a physical good, of course, but the way of treating the customer with an appropriately designed machine is a service.

Most often a service involves interactions of some sort with the service provider. However, there are situations where the customer as an individual does not interact with the service firm.

For most services, *three* basic characteristics can be identified.

1. **Services are at least to some extent produced and consumed simultaneously.** Services are produced and consumed simultaneously (this is also called the 'inseparability' characteristic) – it is difficult to manage quality control and to do marketing in the traditional sense, since there is no pre-produced quality to control before the service is sold and consumed.

   One should realize that *it is the visible part of the service process that matters in the customer's mind.* As far as the rest is concerned, a customer can only experience the result; but the visible activities are experienced and evaluated in every detail. Quality control and marketing must therefore take place at the time and place of simultaneous service production and consumption.

   Most definitions of services imply that services do not result in *ownership* of anything. Normally this is true. When we use the services of an airline we are entitled, for example, to be transported from one place to another, but when we arrive at our destination there is nothing left but the remaining part of the ticket and the boarding card.

   Because of this it is not possible to keep services in stock in the same way as goods. If an aeroplane leaves the airport half-full the empty seats cannot be sold the next day; they are lost. Instead, capacity planning becomes a critical issue. Even though services cannot be kept in stock, one can try to *keep customers in stock*. For example, if a restaurant is full, it is always possible to try to keep the customer waiting in the bar until there is a free table.

2. **The customer participates in the service production process, at least to some extent.** The customer is not only a receiver of the service; the customer also participates in the service process as a production resource in an interaction with the firm's personnel. Therefore service to one customer is not exactly the same as the 'same' service to the next customer.

   In many cases what the customer wants and expects is not known in detail at the beginning of the service process (service production process) or, consequently, what resources are needed, to what extent and in what configuration they should be used. A bank customer may only realize what his needs actually are during interactions with a teller or a loan officer. Thus the firm has to adjust its resources and its ways of using its resources accordingly. Customer-perceived value follows from a successful and customer-oriented management of resources relative to customer sacrifice, not from a pre-produced bundle of features.

3. **Services are processes consisting of activities or a series of activities rather than things.** One important characteristic of services is their *process* nature. Services are processes consisting of a series of activities where a number of different types of resources – people as well as other kinds of resources – are used, often in direct interactions with the customer, so that a solution is found to a customer's problem. Because the customer participates in the process, the process, especially the part in which the customer is participating, becomes part of the solution.

In order to understand service management and the marketing of services it is critical that one realises that the consumption of a service is *process consumption* rather than *outcome consumption*. The consumer or user perceives the service process (or service production process) as part of the service consumption, not simply the outcome of that process, as in traditional marketing of physical goods. When consuming a physical product customers make use of the product itself; that is they consume the outcome of the production process. In contrast, when consuming services customers perceive the process of producing the service to a greater or smaller degree, but always to a critical extent, as well as taking part in the process.

Factors to consider in the internationalization of services

Information technologies

Through information technologies service marketers can interact with customers to antici-pate and serve their needs. Improving the service offering, providing alternative service delivery choices and communicating with the customer all foster better relationships with customers. The use of computerized communication allows the service marketer to establish an ongoing relationship with the customer at each stage of the consumption process. Online databases of customers can show consumption patterns and help track demand fluctuations. Automated service-delivery mechanisms can provide a means for varying levels of self-service. In short, international services marketers need to examine information technologies to discover better ways to manage customer relationships.

The proliferation of information technology has made it possible for international service firms to serve customers 24 hours a day and seven days a week (commonly known as 24/7). Information technologies change the scale and the economics of service organizations. Home-based service organizations are now able to serve the needs of clients all over the world with a combination of computers, telephones, fax machines and electronic mail. In future it will be easy for groups of home-based service organizations to form flexible networks that quickly adapt to customer needs. However, even a firm that chooses to internationalize using electronic marketing cannot manage its service operations totally on its own. On foreign markets it has, for example, to rely on at least postal and delivery services, and the possibility of the service firm controlling such network partners may be very limited.

Cultural issues

Cultural issues will necessarily have a significant impact on the acceptability and adoption pattern of services. Since services inherently involve some level of human interaction the likelihood of cultural incompatibility is greater. For example, nations that culturally define the housewife's role as the family caretaker will probably not be very keen on using day-care centres.

However we design our service and whatever means of serving the market we choose there will be a need to adjust to *local cultural preferences*. Some means of internationalization – franchising, for example – provide an easier route to delivering culturally sensitive services by drawing on local management knowledge. Consumer services are likely to require greater cultural adaptation than do business-to-business services.

However, we cannot ignore culture and all firms providing services internationally should consider the provision of appropriate cultural training to staff, the use of local employees and, where needed, changes to the service offering itself. Without these provisions the company runs the risk of losing business to local companies or more culturally aware international service providers. Service businesses may be 'about people', but the technology and systems remain important. Even the best people struggle to deliver when systems are not in place to facilitate delivery.

Services do not necessarily require a physical presence. For established service businesses, confronting the competition from competitors trading via the Internet (or, in some industries, digital television) presents a major challenge, especially for those firms that have extensive investments in property and staff around the globe.

Geographic locations

The strategic issue of location can be divided into two main aspects: where generally to locate a hospitality operation and then the specific issue of selecting suitable sites. In the hospitality industry the key factor in the location decision is demand. In simple terms, operations are located where demand is highest, and sited so that such demand can easily access the provision. Strategic success derives from matching the type and size of the business with the site available.

The factors that influence location in the accommodation and food service sectors are different. Hotels are primarily located near where people are travelling or at destinations that require them to stay away from home.

Standardization versus customization

An important strategic issue in marketing services internationally is the extent to which each service might be standardized. In addition to the necessity for customer contact for many service categories, many host government regulations in numerous services sectors make standardization very difficult. Accounting and financial services markets are governed by very different rules around the world.

With globalization, the impact of cultural adaptation will need to be central to the study of operational topic areas such as joint venturing, materials management, purchasing, new product development, layout and process design, supervision and motivation, training, workforce scheduling, environmental management and labour–management relations. These are all key areas of front-room and back-room management that are likely to require adaptation from country to country as services are globalized.

Local workers will need to be trained in their native language. The globalization of front-room operations with its verbal customer contact still depends heavily on cultural adaptation of the service. The experience of the Walt Disney Company in its opening of Disneyland Paris is an example of the problems of controlling the customer contact experience in a foreign culture. Some concessions to French culture were made, such as adopting both the French and English languages for the park. However, a more troubling problem was training independently minded French nationals to act out the roles of Disney characters and perform their duties in a courteous manner. When the service is defined by the customer contact experience then translating the required human behaviour of service personnel across national boundaries becomes a challenge.

Common customer needs for services vary more widely across nations than is the case for products, and addressing them requires localized solutions.

Retailing provides an excellent example of a service business that is difficult to standardize. Despite much talk about the internationalization of retail trade, local retailing regulations vary considerably, not only across countries (including within the European Union), but also within the provinces of each country.

Implications for international marketing of services

It is possible to distinguish between five main strategies for internationalizing services. These are not mutually exclusive, and in some cases some will also work well for manufactured goods (Grönroos, 1999):

1. direct export
2. systems export/following the large customers abroad
3. direct entry/own subsidiary
4. indirect entry/intermediate mode
5. electronic marketing/Internet.

Direct export of services may basically take place on industrial markets. Consultants and firms repairing and maintaining valuable equipment may have their base in the domestic market and whenever needed move the resources and system required to produce the service to the client abroad. Repair services on valuable equipment are often exported in this way. Some consultants work in a similar fashion. No step-by-step learning can take place as the service has to be produced immediately. Because of this, the risk of making mistakes can be substantial.

Systems export/following the large customers abroad is a joint export by two or more firms whose solutions complement each other. A service firm may support a goods-exporting firm or another company. For example, when a manufacturer delivers equipment or turnkey factories to international buyers a need for engineering services, distribution, cleaning, security and other services often exists. This gives service firms an opportunity to expand their markets abroad. As the literature suggests, systems export is the traditional mode for service export. For example, advertising agencies and banks have extended their accessibility abroad because of their clients' activities in international markets. In systems export the services are mainly marketed in industrial markets abroad. For example, law firms expand into multiple cities in an attempt to align themselves with their corporate accounts, service companies are pushed by their customers to operate in the same countries as their clients. The truly global company wants and demands truly global service of its travel agents, auditors, consultants and others. The weakness of this strategy for a company already committed to overseas operations is that it ignores the possible vast markets where clients are not represented.

Direct entry/own subsidiary means that the service firm establishes a service-producing organization of its own on the foreign market. For manufactured goods in the first stage of a learning process a sales office can be such an organization. For a service firm, a local organization normally has to be able to produce and deliver the service from the beginning. The time for learning becomes short. Almost from day one the firm has to be able to cope with problems with production, human resource management and consumer behaviour. In addition, the national government may consider the new, international service provider a threat to local firms and even to national pride.

Indirect entry/intermediate mode is used when the service firm wants to avoid establishing a local operation that is totally or partly owned by itself but wants to establish a permanent operation in the foreign market.

- Licensing agreements give a local firm exclusive rights to use the professional concept of the firm. This of course requires that exclusive rights can be guaranteed.
- Franchising is a concept often used by restaurant and food service industries for indirect entry into a foreign market. Local service firms get the exclusive right to a marketing concept, which may also include rights to a certain operational mode, and in this way the concept can be replicated as much as existing demand allows throughout the foreign market. The internationalizing firm as the franchisor gets the local knowledge that the franchisees possess, whereas franchisees get an opportunity to grow with a new and perhaps well-established concept. With a reasonably standardized service offering, it would also be possible to franchise a consultancy overseas.
- Another form of indirect entry is *management contracts*, which are often used, for example, in the hotel business. As far as the need for market knowledge is concerned, indirect entry is probably the least risky of the internationalization strategies discussed so far. Conversely, the internationalizing firm's control over the foreign operations is normally more limited when using this entry strategy (own subsidiary).

Electronic marketing/Internet as an internationalizing strategy means that the service firm extends its accessibility through the use of advanced electronic technology. The Internet provides firms with a way of communicating their offerings and putting them up for sale, and a way of collecting data about the buying habits and patterns of customers and using network partners to arrange delivery and payment. The electronic bookstore Amazon.com is a good example of a firm internationalizing its services using electronic marketing. When launching the concept it had to take into account the interest in its services that would automatically develop outside national borders. TV shops (satellite television) are examples of other ways of internationalizing services using advanced technology. When using Internet marketing the firm is not bound to any particular location. The service can be administered from anywhere on the globe and still reach customers throughout a vast international market via the Internet.

3.8   Summary

The main conclusions of this chapter are summarized in Table 3.2.

Table 3.2	Summary of the three models explaining the internationalization process of the firm		
	Uppsala internationalization model	**Transaction cost analysis model**	**Network model**
Unit of analysis	The firm	The transaction or set of transactions	Multiple inter-organizational relationships between firms Relationships between one group of firms and other groups of firms
Basic assumptions about firms' behaviour	The model is based on behavioural theories and an incremental decision-making process with little influence from competitive market factors. A gradual learning-by-doing process	In the real world there is friction/transactional difficulties between buyer and seller. This friction is mainly caused by opportunistic behaviour: the self-conscious attention of the single manager (i.e. seeking of self-interest with guile)	The 'glue' that keeps the network (relationships) together is based on technical, economic, legal and especially personal ties. Managers' personal influence on relationships is strongest in the early phases of the establishment of relationships. Later in the process routines and systems will become more important
Explanatory variables affecting the development process	The firm's knowledge/market commitment Psychic distance between home country and the firm's international markets	Transactional difficulties and transaction costs increase when transactions are characterized by asset specificity, uncertainty, frequency of transaction	The individual firms are autonomous. The individual firm is dependent on resources controlled by other firms Business networks will emerge in fields where there is frequent coordination between specific actors and where conditions are changing rapidly
Normative implications for international marketers	Additional market commitments should be made in small incremental steps: choose new geographic markets with small psychic distances from existing markets Choose an entry mode with few marginal risks	Under the above-mentioned conditions (i.e. prohibitively high transaction costs), firms should seek internalization of activities (i.e. implement the global marketing strategy in wholly owned subsidiaries)	The relationships of a firm in a domestic network can be used as bridges to other networks in other countries. Such direct or indirect bridges to different country networks can be important in the initial steps abroad and in the subsequent entry of new markets. Sometimes an SME can be forced to enter foreign networks: for example, if a customer requires that the sub-supplier (an SME) follows it abroad. As an example see Case Study 13.2 on LM Glasfiber

Born globals represent a relatively new research field in international marketing. Born globals share some fundamental similarities: they possess unique assets, focus on narrow global market segments, are strongly customer oriented and the entrepreneur's vision and competences are of crucial importance. In the end, for these firms, being global does not seem to be an option but a necessity. They are pushed into globalization by global customers and national/regional market segments that are too small. They can sustain their immediate global reach thanks to entrepreneurial vision and competences, and a deep awareness and knowledge of their competitive advantage in foreign markets.

In this chapter, the importance of the personal factors in the internationalization process of SMEs is emphasized.

For internationalization of services the following five main strategies were identified: (1) direct export; (2) systems export/following the large customers abroad; (3) direct entry/own subsidiary; (4) indirect entry/intermediate mode; (5) electronic marketing/Internet.

CASE STUDY 3.1

Cryos: they keep the stork busy around the world

The market for babies stretches across the globe and it is created by a deep and persistent demand from people who have been denied the blessings of reproduction. Recent statistics indicate that 10 per cent of couples are infertile (www.repromedltd.com). Some decide they will live their lives together without children of their own. Others may pursue adoption – a procedure made more difficult because of the number of single women who choose to keep their children. A third option is for the couple to consult with their physician and to undergo artificial insemination using donor semen. It is many couples' deeply felt wish to have children that is the basis for the Danish-based Cryos International Sperm Bank.

Take artificial insemination. Sperm banking is now global; clients are no longer limited to the small donor pools at local sperm banks. For sperm banks technology plays a major role in the globalization drive. Concern about genetic defects and infectious diseases has led to sophisticated and expensive means of testing donations. Storage and transport methods have also grown more complicated. The improvements add to the investment required to operate a sperm bank. That, in turn, promotes consolidation in the industry.

History

Cryos International Sperm Bank was established in 1987 in Aarhus, Denmark, by Ole Schou. 'Cryos' is Greek and means 'ice' (from *crystallos*) and refers to the sperm conservation process. The word is also known from 'cryobiology'. In English a sperm bank is often called a 'cryobank'.

The office and laboratory were initially established as a service both for men who were going to have a vasectomy and for cancer patients who wanted to have their sperm frozen before chemotherapy or radiation, which might make them infertile.

In 1990 the donor programme was established, and the first donor semen was released and delivered after six months' quarantine in May 1991. Demand increased very quickly. Clinics in Denmark started to receive semen from Cryos, quickly followed by clinics in Norway, Finland, Iceland, the United Kingdom, Greece, Germany, Italy, Switzerland, Belgium and other countries. The clinics were particularly satisfied with the good quality of semen, resulting in high pregnancy results (between 20 and 30 per cent per cyclus) and the professional service, with immediate supply from a relatively high selection of different donors.

In 1994 two new departments were opened in the cities of Copenhagen and Odense, and later in Aalborg. In 1995 Cryos started distributing other sperm-related products such as preparation media. The same year Cryos started its own production of the culture media 'SpermWash'.

The 'suppliers'

On average, across all age groups, it can take up to 13 straws to conceive a child. (An amount of sperm enough for one insemination is stored in a sealed

With permission from Cryos International–Denmark ApS.

plastic straw.) In Denmark, there are approximately 500 donors, some who begin donating in their 20s. The cut-off age is 40. The average donor continues in the programme for five years and can provide sperm several times a week. Donors get about €50–80 a straw, dependent on the sperm quality.

If their sperm does not sell, they are removed from the donor pool. On average each donor is responsible for conceiving 20 to 30 babies throughout the world.

Among Cryos' donors, around 20 per cent have chosen not to be anonymous. Their average age is 32, while that of anonymous donors is between 23 and 25 years.

And there is a market for donors who can be traced.

Unlike heterosexuals, lesbians and single women often prefer a donor that can be traced because they know their children will one day want to know who their biological father is.

The Cryos business today

Cryos has become the largest sperm bank in the world, with more than 250 donors and more than 15,000 units of semen distributed each year, resulting in 1,200 pregnancies per year.

Cryos employs a total of 40 people: 10 medical doctors, 5 biologists and 15 authorized laboratory technicians. An additional 10 people are employed in sales and administration.

The freezing of patients' own sperm has continued, involving several hundred patient deposits.

Cryos total sales have risen from two million euros (2.7 million dollars) in 2006 to three million in 2008.

Of the income from donor semen 5 per cent is reserved for scientific and development purposes.

Cryos will continue to offer a high-quality service related to its area of knowledge including donor semen, patient deposits and other semen-related clinical products. Furthermore, Cryos will continue to try to develop new and improved sperm-related knowledge and/or equipment for clinical use.

Using air freight and proprietary freezing techniques, Cryos can deliver to almost any customer in the world within 72 hours. The sperm travels in liquid-nitrogen tanks that, without refilling, can last a week. The quality of the sperm can be validated through laboratory tests.

Cryos | Denmark

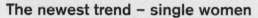

Search

■ HOME ■ PRIVATE ■ CLINICS ■ SEMEN STORAGE ■ ABOUT US

Products

SpermFilter
SpermFilter® is a silane-silica based density gradient medium used in ART for separation and
purification of highly motile human spermatozoa.

SpermWash
SpermWash® culture medium is used for semen preparation by "swim-up" for IUI or IVF, for
washing of spermatozoa and/or for diluting stock solution of density-gradients.

SpermCryo All-round
SpermCryo™ is a highly concentrated cryoprotective medium used for freezing of human semen.

COA Request
Downloads of certificate of analysis for the above media.

IUI catheters
IUI catheters for insemination of purified spermatozoa into the uterine cavity.

Counting Chambers
Counting chambers for clinical or scientific semen analysis.

Incubator
Incubators for incubation of media and for "swim-up" preparation.

CBS high security straws
Accessories that have been developed especially for the freezing of human embryos and semen.

With permission from Cryos International–Denmark ApS.

The newest trend – single women

A phenomenon that has increased demand for Cryos'
products and services in the past four years is the
increasing number of highly educated single women
who prioritized their careers and want to have a child
before it is too late.

Internationalization of the fertility market and Cryos

Today, Cryos exports 85 per cent of its more than
15,000 sperm donations to more than 400 clinics in
60 countries.

However, while the sperm from a Danish Viking
with blond hair and blue eyes may be exactly what
clients are looking for in northern Europe, it is not
always the ideal in other parts of the world. Therefore
Cryos has opened a franchise in New York and
another one in Bombay, in India. In the next five years,
Cryos plans to open up to 10 new offices, expanding
further in Europe, Asia, Africa and Australia to give it
a broad ethnical donor base to meet the demands of
people all around the world.

Laws that prevent anonymous sperm donations
in countries like Sweden, Britain, The Netherlands,
Austria and Germany have also led to a rise in 'fertility
tourism', where women visit clinics in other countries
to be inseminated, for example French women who
go to Belgium and Swedes who go to Denmark.

In addition to selling sperm to clinics, Cryos has
recently begun direct online sales to the public in
order to meet the demands of some clients. It has
set up a online catalogue of 50 donors, including
44 who remain anonymous, on its website, listing
donors' profiles with their IQ, childhood photographs, hobbies, school grades and other personal
information.

Buyers can select the sperm of the donor that
most appeals to them – not an option at clinics,
where sperm quality is the only determining factor –
and buy it online for up to 8,000 euros.

The initiative has been heavily criticised in Denmark
and other countries, where opponents argue that sperm
should not be handled like a supermarket product.

The US market

In 2001 Cryos opened a branch in the United States
(Scandinavian Cryobank) in order to meet the
specific market situation and the growing demand
for Scandinavian donors. The sperm bank market in
the United States is very different from that in other
markets around the world, because it is not the
clinics but the patients who choose a sperm bank
and select the donor. The service includes patient
access to donor lists, extended profiles, a patient
phone service, etc., all of which could not be organized within the 'clinic-only service' concept of Cryos.

Marketing to Americans

About 5 million people in the United States are infertile, and half seek treatment to have a baby. Donor eggs are used by about 10 per cent of couples in treatment. While there are strict guidelines for screening the health of donor sperm, there are no government mechanisms in place to track actual use of the sperm, which can be frozen and stored for decades.

In the United States infertility treatment is a $1 billion a year industry and growing. The US market for donor sperm is estimated at around 100 million a year.

Recently, the CEO of Cryos, Ole Schou, has launched a global franchising system focusing on quality so that the concept of Cryos can be copied in other clinics around the world. The franchising system involves a very comprehensive package of laboratory standards, control systems, training systems, franchising contracts, marketing plans, investment, financing, computer systems, etc.

The following is taken from the Cryos brochure 'Open your own Cryos Sperm Bank':

Cryos International's franchise concept focuses on the establishment of sperm banks worldwide. Our goal is to provide an extensive selection of high quality donor semen as well as a range of clinical sperm related products to patients and clinics all over the world through our network of sperm banks.

Cryos' franchise concept is based on an agreement between two legally independent parties which gives you (the franchisee) the right to market our products and services using our trademark, trade name and operating methods. The franchisee is obliged to pay the franchisor fees for these rights and the franchisor is obliged to provide rights and support to the franchisees. Cryos offers a defined set of guidelines described in our manuals, making it easy and simple to start your own sperm bank. With a Cryos sperm bank concept it is possible to set up and run a successful sperm bank with a good reputation from day one.

Sources: http://www.cryosinternational.com/dk; Agence France-Presse (2009) 'Business booms at world's biggest sperm bank', 15 May 2009, (http://news.id.msn.com/lifestyle/article.aspx?cp-documentid=3317067); Spar, D.L. (2006) 'Where babies come from – supply and demand in an infant marketplace', *Harvard Business Review*, February, pp. 133–42; Talan, J. (2005) 'For prospective parents in the market for a blonde-haired, blue-eyed tot, Danish sperm makes the sale', *Newsday*, 5 June 2005.

QUESTIONS

1. Would you characterize Cryos as a 'born global'? Why/why not?
2. What do you think about Ole Schou's ideas of a 'global franchising system'?
3. What ethical and moral issues are involved for Cryos in selling sperm worldwide?

CASE STUDY 3.2

Classic media: internationalization of Postman Pat

On 14 December 2006, Entertainment Rights announced it would acquire US-based rival Classic Media for $210 million (£107 million). The deal was completed on 11 January 2007.

On 1 April 2009 it was announced that Entertainment Rights would be acquired by Boomerang Media (formed by the founders of subsidiary Classic Media, Eric Ellenbogen and John Engelman). On 11 May 2009, it was announced that the subsidiaries and offices of Entertainment Rights would be absorbed under the name Classic Media (CM).

Entertainment Rights' acquisition of Classic Media, which owns the rights to *Lassie* and *The Lone Ranger*,

for £107m in 2006, helped create the massive debt which brought the company to its knees.

By the acquisition of Entertainment Rights Classic Media also has got access to one of the biggest icons among small kids in the preschool age, Postman Pat.

Postman Pat

Set in the fictional Yorkshire village of Greendale, Postman Pat and his faithful companion, Jess the Cat, began delivering post on BBC1 25 years ago in September 1981. Postman Pat continues to air on the BBC in the United Kingdom with episodes licensed and the broadcast platform secured beyond

2010. The target viewer group for the show is the preschool age (2–6 years).

Postman Pat and the TV shows have now been shown in more than 100 countries around the world. With sales in so many international markets, it is important that the brand awareness created by the TV platform is leveraged through the development of a strong licensing and merchandising line. For example, in the United Kingdom in 2004 Marks & Spencer acquired the rights for using the characters in 70 of its top stores. The programme included a range of nightwear, underwear, slippers, watches and puzzles for children aged 3–6. Postman Pat and Jess the Cat proved to be an irresistible gift buy for parents, grandparents, guardians and others.

In May 2009, CM secured partnership with one of the UK's largest theme parks – Flamingo Land in North Yorkshire – for Postman Pat and other characters from Special Delivery service to take up residence. In October 2009 CM teamed up with Timeless Films to make a 3D animated Postman Pat movie for 2011. It is the first time that Postman Pat will appear on the big screen after almost 30 years on television. Timeless Films will distribute the movie in the UK and internationally.

Source: Sweney, M. (2009) 'Boomerang Media buys Postman Pat owner Entertainment Rights', Guardian.co.uk, 1 April 2009; 'Marks & Spencer takes on Postman Pat', Weekly E-news, Issue 76, 14 September 2004, www.licensmag.com.

© J.F.T.L Images/Alamy.

QUESTIONS

1. List the criteria that you should use for choosing new international markets.

2. If you were to advise CM would you recommend them to use the 'organic' or 'born global' pathway for the internationalization of Postman Pat?

3. What values/benefits can CM transfer to the license partners for consumer products apart from using the Postman Pat characters?

VIDEO CASE STUDY 3.3 Reebok

download from www.pearsoned.co.uk/hollensen

Reebok (www.reebok.com and www.adidas-group.com) specializes in the design, marketing and distribution of sports and fitness products including footwear, apparel and accessories, as well as footwear and apparel for non-athletic use. In August 2005 Adidas bought Reebok for $3.8 billion, giving the company about 20 per cent of the US market and the potential to challenge market leader Nike.

Questions

1. Which of the internationalization theories is best for explaining the Adidas acquisition of Reebok?
2. What could be the motives behind Adidas' acquisition of Reebok?
3. Which of the three internationalization theories is best for explaining whether Reebok follows the establishment of its retailers, for example Foot Locker, in international markets?
4. Is Reebok able to copy its US marketing approach (connecting to the youth segment through famous rappers, like 50 Cent) in other international markets?

For further exercises and cases, see this book's website at **www.pearsoned.co.uk/hollensen**.

Questions for discussion

1. Explain why internationalization is an ongoing process in constant need of evaluation.
2. Explain the main differences between the three theories of internationalization: the Uppsala model, the transaction cost theory and the network model.
3. What is meant by the concept of 'psychological' or 'psychic distance'?

References

Aharoni, Y. (1966) *The Foreign Investment Decision Process*. Harvard Business School Press, Boston, MA.

Âijö, T., Kuivalainen, O., Saarenketo, S., Lindqvist, J. and Hanninen, H. (2005) *Internationalization Handbook for the Software Business*, Centre of Expertise for Software Product Business, Espoo, Finland.

Bell, J., McNaughton, R. and Young S. (2001) 'Born-again global firms: an extension to the born global phenomenon', *Journal of International Management*, 7(3), pp. 173–190.

Brewer, P.A. (2007) 'Operationalzing psychic distance: a revised approach', *Journal of International Marketing*, 15(1), pp. 44–66.

Buckley, P.J. and Casson, M. (1976) *The Future of the Multinational Enterprise*. Holmes & Meier, New York.

Christensen, P.R. and Lindmark, L.L. (1993) 'Location and internationalization of small firms', in Lindquist, L. and Persson, L.O. (eds) *Visions and Strategies in European Integration*, Springer Verlag, Berlin and Heidelberg.

Coase, R.H. (1937) 'The nature of the firm', *Economica*, pp. 386–405.

Contractor, F.J. and Lorange, P. (eds) (1998) *Cooperative Strategies in International Business*. Lexington Books, Lexington, MA.

Cumberland, F. (2006) 'Theory development within international market entry mode – an assessment', *The Marketing Review*, 6, pp. 349–373.

Dunning, J.H. (1988) *Explaining International Production*. Unwin, London.

Forsgren, M. and Johanson, J. (1975) *International företagsekonomi*. Norstedts, Stockholm.

Gabrielsson, M. and Kirpalani, M.V.H. (2004) 'Born globals; how to reach new business space rapidly', *International Business Review*, 13, pp. 555–571.

Ghoshal, S. and Moran, P. (1996) 'Bad for practice: a critique of the transaction cost theory', *Academy of Management Review*, 21(1), pp. 13–47.

Grönroos, Christian (1999) 'Internationalization strategies for services', *Journal of Services Marketing*, 13(4/5), 290–297.

Harvey, D. (1996) *Justice, Nature and the Geography of Difference*. Basil Blackwell, Oxford.

Hymer, S.H. (1976) The International Operations of National Firms: A study of direct foreign investment. Unpublished 1960 Ph.D. thesis, MIT Press, Cambridge, MA.

Johanson, J. and Mattson, L.G. (1986) 'International marketing and internationalization processes: some perspectives on current and future research', in Paliwoda, S. and Turnbull, P. (eds), *Research in Developments in International Marketing*, Croom Helm, Beckenham (UK).

Johanson, J. and Mattson, L.G. (1988) 'Internationalization in industrial systems', in Hood, N. and Vahlne, J.E. (eds), *Strategies in Global Competition*, Croom Helm, Beckenham (UK).

Johanson, J. and Vahlne, J.E. (1977) 'The internationalization process of the firm: a model of knowledge development and increasing foreign market commitment', *Journal of International Business Studies*, 8(1), pp. 23–32.

Johanson, J. and Vahlne, J.E. (1990) 'The mechanism of internationalization', *International Marketing Review*, 7(4), pp. 11–24.

Johanson, J. and Wiedersheim-Paul, F. (1975) 'The internationalization of the firm: four Swedish cases', *Journal of Management Studies*, October, pp. 305–322.

Jones, M.V. (2001) 'First steps in internationalization: concepts and evidence from a sample of small high-technology firms', *Journal of International Management*, 7, pp. 191–210.

Kim, D. (2003) 'The internationalization of US Internet portals: does it fit the process model of internationalization?, *Marketing Intelligence & Planning*, 21(1), pp. 23–36.

Kindleberger, C.P. (1969) *American Business Abroad.* Yale University Press, New Haven, CT.

Knight, G., Madsen, K.M. and Servais, P. (2004) 'An inquiry into born-global firms in Europe and the USA', *International Marketing Review*, 21(6), pp. 645–665.

Kogut, B. (1988) 'Joint ventures: theoretical and empirical perspective', *Strategic Management Journal*, 9, pp. 319–332.

Madhok, A. (1998) 'The nature of multinational firm boundaries: transaction cost, firm capabilities and foreign market entry mode', *International Business Review*, 7, pp. 259–290.

Madsen, T.K. and Servais, P. (1997) 'The internationalization of born globals: an evolutionary process?', *International Business Review*, 6(6), pp. 561–583.

Manolova, T.S. and Brush, C.G. (2002) 'Internationalization of small firms – personal factors re-visited', *International Small Business Journal*, 20(1), pp. 9–31.

Melén, S. and Nordman, E.R. (2009) The internationalization modes of born globals: a longitudinal study, *European Management Journal*, 27, pp. 243–254.

Nordström, K.A. (1990) The internationalization process of the firm: searching for new patterns and explanations, Research paper, Stockholm School of Economics.

Ouchi, W.G. (1980) 'Markets, bureaucracies and clans', *Administrative Science Quarterly*, 25, pp. 129–142.

Oviatt, B. and McDougall, P. (1994) 'Towards a theory of international new ventures', *Journal of International Business Studies*, 25(1), pp. 45–64.

Penrose, E. (1959) *The Theory of the Growth of the Firm.* Blackwell, London.

Prahalad, C.K. and Hamel, G. (1990) 'The core competence and the corporation', *Harvard Business Review*, May, pp. 71–97.

Reid, S.D. (1983) 'Firm internationalization, transaction costs and strategic choice', *International Marketing*, 1(2), p. 44.

Rugman, A.M. (1986) 'New theories of the multinational enterprise: an assessment of internationalization theory', *Bulletin of Economic Research*, 38(2), pp. 101–118.

Sharma, D.D. and Johanson, J. (1987) 'Technical consultancy in internationalization', *International Marketing Review*, Winter, pp. 20–29.

Sousa, C.M.P. and Bradley, F. (2005) 'Global markets: does psychic distance matter?' *Journal of Strategic Marketing*, 13 (March), pp. 43–59.

Sousa, C.M.P. and Bradley, F. (2006) 'Cultural distance and psychic distance: two peas in a pod?', *Journal of International Marketing*, 14(1), pp. 49–70.

Turnbull, P.N. (1987) 'Interaction and international marketing: an investment process', *International Marketing Review*, Winter, pp. 7–19.

Törnroos, J.-Å. (2002) 'Internationalization of the firm: a theoretical review with implications for business network research', Paper presented at the 18th Annual IMP Conference, September, Lyon, pp. 1–21.

Vernon, R. (1966) 'International investment and international trade in the product cycle', *Quarterly Journal of Economics*, 80, pp. 190–207.

Welch, L.S. and Loustarinen, R. (1988) 'Internationalization: evolution of a concept', *Journal of General Management*, 14(2), pp. 36–64.

Williamson, O.E. (1975) *Markets and Hierarchies: Analysis and Antitrust Implications.* The Free Press, New York.

Williamson, O.E. (1985) *The Economic Institutions of Capitalization.* The Free Press, New York.

CHAPTER 4
Development of the firm's international competitiveness

Contents

Case studies

Learning objectives

After studying this chapter you should be able to:

- Define the concept of international competitiveness in a broader perspective from a macro to a micro level.
- Discuss the factors influencing the firm's international competitiveness.
- Explain how Porter's traditional competitive-based five forces model can be extended to a collaborative (five sources) model.
- Explore the idea behind the competitive triangle.
- Analyse the basic sources of competitive advantage.
- Explain the steps in competitive benchmarking.
- Explain how a company can create customer value by the use of Blue Ocean Strategy.

4.1   Introduction

The topic of this chapter is how the firm creates and develops competitive advantages in the international market. Development of a firm's international competitiveness takes place interactively with the environment. The firm must be able to adjust to customers, competitors and public authorities. To be able to participate in the international competitive arena the firm must have established a competitive basis consisting of resources, competences and relations to others in the international arena.

To enable an understanding of the development of a firm's international competitiveness in a broader perspective, a model in three stages (see Figure 4.1) will be presented:

1. analysis of national competitiveness (the Porter diamond) – macro level;
2. competition analysis in an industry (Porter's five forces) – meso level;
3. value chain analysis – micro level:
   (a) competitive triangle;
   (b) benchmarking.

The analysis starts at the macro level and then moves into the firm's competitive arena through Porter's five-forces framework. Based on the firm's value chain, the analysis is concluded with a discussion of which activities/functions in the value chain are the firm's core competences (and must be developed internally in the firm) and which competences must be placed with others through alliances and market relations.

The graphical system used in Figure 4.1 (which will be referred to throughout this chapter) places the models after each other in a hierarchical windows logic, where you get from stage 1 to stage 2 by clicking on the icon box: 'Firm strategy, structure and rivalry'. Here Porter's five-forces model appears. From stage 2 to 3 we click the middle box labelled 'Market competitors/Intensity of rivalry' and the model for a value chain analysis/competitive triangle appears.

Individual competitiveness and time-based competition

In this chapter the analysis ends at the firm level but it is possible to go a step further by analysing individual competitiveness (Veliyath and Zahra, 2000). The factors influencing the capacity of an individual to become competitive would include intrinsic abilities, skills, motivation levels and the amount of effort involved. Traditional decision-making perspectives maintain that uncertainty leads executives to search for more additional information with which to increase certainty. However, Kedia *et al.* (2002) showed that some executives increase competitiveness by using tactics to accelerate analysis of information and alternatives during the decision-making process. For example, these executives examine several alternatives simultaneously. The comparison process speeds their analysis of the strengths and weaknesses of options.

4.2   Analysis of national competitiveness (the Porter diamond)

Analysis of national competitiveness represents the highest level in the entire model (Figure 4.1). Michael E. Porter called his work *The Competitive Advantage of Nations* (1990), but as a starting point it is important to say that it is firms which are competing in the international arena, not nations. Yet the characteristics of the home nation play a central role in a firm's international success. The home base shapes a company's capacity to innovate rapidly in technology and methods, and to do so in the proper directions. It is the place from which competitive advantage ultimately emanates and from which it must be sustained. Competitive

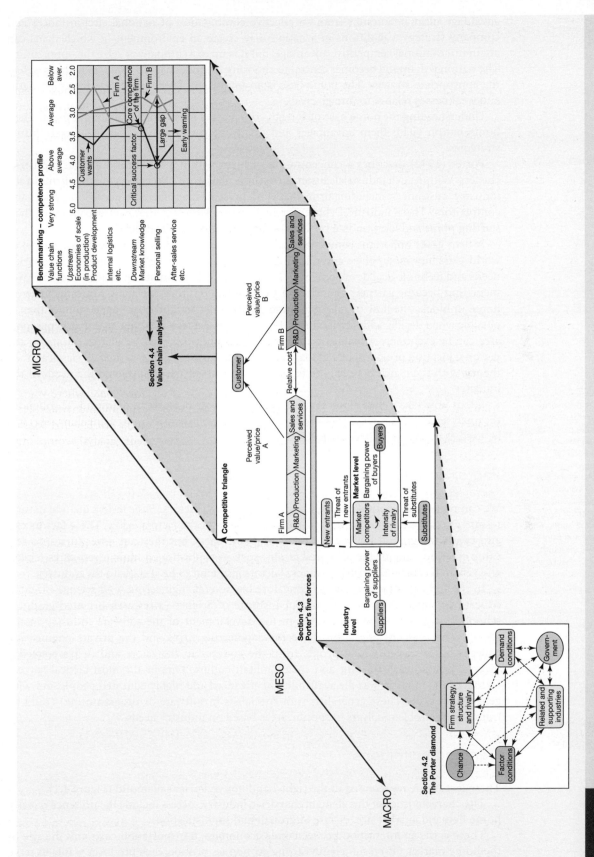

Figure 4.1   Development of a firm's international competitiveness

advantage ultimately results from an effective combination of national circumstances and company strategy. Conditions in a nation may create an environment in which firms can attain international competitive advantage, but it is up to a company to seize the opportunity. The national diamond becomes central to choosing the industries to compete with, as well as the appropriate strategy. The home base is an important determinant of a firm's strengths and weaknesses relative to foreign rivals.

Understanding the home base of foreign competitors is essential in analysing them. Their home nation yields them advantages and disadvantages. It also shapes their likely future strategies.

Porter (1990) describes a concentration of firms within a certain industry as industrial clusters. Within such industrial clusters firms have a network of relations to other firms in the industry: customers (including firms that work on semi-manufactured goods), suppliers and competitors. These industrial clusters may go worldwide, but they will usually have their starting point and location in a certain country or region of a country.

A firm gains important competitive advantages from the presence in its home nation of world-class buyers, suppliers and related industries. They provide insight into future market needs and technological developments. They contribute to a climate for change and improvement, and become partners and allies in the innovation process. Having a strong cluster at home unblocks the flow of information and allows deeper and more open contact than is possible when dealing with foreign firms. Being part of a cluster localized in a small geographic area can be even more valuable, so the central question we can ask is: what accounts for the national location of a particular global industry? The answer begins, as does all classical trade theory, with the match between the factor endowments of the country and the needs of the industry.

Porter's diamond

The characteristics of the home base play a central role in explaining the international competitiveness of the firm – the explaining elements consist of factor conditions, demand conditions, related and supporting industries and firm strategy – structure and rivalry, chance and government.

Let us now take a closer look at the different elements in **Porter's diamond**. Throughout the analysis the Indian IT/software industry (especially illustrated by the Bangalore area) will be used as an example (Nair *et al.* 2007).

Factor conditions

We can make a distinction between basic and advanced factors. *Basic factors* include natural resources (climate, minerals, oil), where the mobility of the factors is low. These factors can also create the ground for international competitiveness, but they can never turn into real value creation without the *advanced factors*, such as sophisticated human resources (skills) and research capabilities. Such advanced factors also tend to be specific to the industry.

In the Indian software industry, Bangalore has several engineering- and science-oriented educational institutions and the Indian Institute of Science (a research-oriented graduate school) can be identified as essential in the development of the software industry in the region. The presence of the public-sector engineering firms and the private engineering colleges has attracted young people from the country to Bangalore and it has created a diverse, multilingual, tolerant and cosmopolitan culture. One of the most critical success factors of the industry was the availability of advanced and highly educated people, but with generalized skills. These generalists (not specialists in software or programming) could be trained into problem-solvers in specific areas based on industry needs.

Demand conditions

These factors are represented in the right-hand box of Porter's diamond (Figure 4.1).

The characteristics of this element that drive industry success include the presence of early home demand, market size, its rate of growth and sophistication.

There exists an interaction between scale economies, transportation costs and the size of the home market. Given sufficiently strong economies of scale, each producer wants to serve a geographically extensive market from a single location. To minimize transportation costs the producer chooses a location with large local demand. When scale economies limit the number of production locations the size of a market will be an important determinant of its attractiveness. Large home markets will also ensure that firms located at that site develop a cost advantage based on scale and often on experience as well.

An interesting pattern is that of an early large home market that has become saturated forces efficient firms to look abroad for new business. For example, the Japanese motorcycle industry with its large home market used its scale advantages in the global marketplace after an early start in Japan. The composition of demand also plays an important role.

A product's fundamental or core design nearly always reflects home market needs. In electrical transmission equipment, for example, Sweden dominates the world in the high-voltage distribution market. In Sweden there is a relatively large demand for transporting high voltage over long distances, as a consequence of the location of population and industry clusters. Here the needs of the home market shaped the industry that was later able to respond to global markets (with ABB as one of the leading producers in the world market).

The sophistication of the buyer is also important. The US government was the first buyer of computer chips and remained the only customer for many years. The price inelasticity of government encouraged firms to develop technically advanced products without worrying too much about costs. Under these conditions the technological frontier was clearly pushed much further and much faster than it would have been had the buyer been either less sophisticated or more price sensitive.

The Indian software industry was kicked off in connection with the Y2K problem (caused due to a coding convention in older systems that assigned only two digits for the year count, thereby creating a potential disruption as the calendar year turned 2000), where US firms contracted with Indian software firms, which had employees who were skilled in older programming languages such as Cobol and Fortran. As their experience with US firms increased and the Y2K problems were solved, India-based software firms began diversifying and offering more value-added products and service. Serving demanding US customers forced the Indian software firms to develop high-quality products and services. This experience later helped to address the needs of IT customers in Germany, Japan and other markets.

Related and supporting industries

The success of an industry is associated with the presence of suppliers and related industries within a region.

In many cases competitive advantages come from being able to use labour that is attracted to an area to serve the core industry, but which is available and skilled for supporting this industry. Coordination of technology is also eased by geographic proximity. Porter argues that Italian world leadership in gold and silver jewellery has been sustained in part by the local presence of manufacturers of jewellery-making machinery. Here the advantage of clustering is not so much transportation cost reductions but technical and marketing cooperation. In the semiconductor industry, the strength of the electronics industry in Japan (which buys the semiconductors) is a strong incentive to the location of semiconductors in the same area. It should be noted that clustering is not independent of scale economies. If there were no scale economies in the production of intermediate inputs, then the small-scale centres of production could rival the large-scale centres. It is the fact that there are scale economies in both semiconductors and electronics, coupled with the technological and marketing connections between the two, that give rise to clustering advantages.

In the beginning, Bangalore's lack of reliable supporting industries, for example tele-communication and power supply, was a problem, but many software firms installed their own generators and satellite communication equipment. Firms that provide venture capital, recruitment assistance, network, hardware maintenance and marketing/accounting support have emerged in the Bangalore area to support the software firms. In addition the presence of consulting firms such as KPMG, PriceWaterhouseCoopers and Ernst & Young can assist incoming multinational companies with entering the Indian market, for example by solving their currency and location problem. Consequently, a whole system of support has now evolved around the software industry.

Firm strategy, structure and rivalry

This fairly broad element includes how companies are organized and managed, their objectives and the nature of domestic rivalry.

One of the most compelling results of Porter's study of successful industries in ten different nations is the powerful and positive effect that domestic competition has on the ability to compete in the global marketplace. In Germany, the fierce domestic rivalry among BASF, Hoechst and Bayer in the pharmaceutical industry is well known. Furthermore, the process of competition weeds out inferior technologies, products and management practices, and leaves only the most efficient firms as survivors. When domestic competition is vigorous firms are forced to become more efficient, adopt new cost-saving technologies, reduce product development time and learn to motivate and control workers more effectively. Domestic rivalry is especially important in stimulating technological developments among global firms.

The small country of Denmark has three producers of hearing-aids (William Demant, Widex and GN Resound/Danavox), which are all among the top ten of the world's largest producers of hearing-aids. In 1996 Oticon (the earlier William Demant) and Widex fought a technological battle to be the first in the world to launch a 100 per cent digitalized hearing-aid. Widex (the smaller of the two producers) won, but forced Oticon at the same time to keep a leading edge in technological development.

In relation to the Indian software industry, most firms in the Bangalore area experience fierce competition. The competition about future customers is not just with local firms, but also with firms outside Bangalore and multinational companies such as IBM and Accenture. It has resulted in a pressure on firms to deliver quality products and services, but also to be cost-effective. This competition has encouraged firms to seek international certifications, with a rating in software development. Today the Bangalore area has the world's highest concentration of companies with the so-called CMM-SEI (Carnegie Mellon University's Software Engineering Institute) Level 5 certification (the highest quality rating).

Government

According to Porter's diamond model, government can influence and be influenced by each of the four main factors. Governments can play a powerful role in encouraging the development of industries within their own borders that will assume global positions. Governments finance and construct infrastructure, providing roads, airports, education and health care, and can support use of alternative energy (e.g. wind turbines) or other environmental systems that affect factors of production.

In relation to the indian software industry, the federal government in Delhi had targeted software as a growth area already in the 1970s, because of its high skill requirements and labour intensity. Though the 1970s and 1980s the industry was mainly dominated by public-sector companies, like CMC. In 1984 the government started liberalizing industrial and investment policies, which gave access to IT companies from abroad, e.g. Texas Instruments. One of the new initiatives was also setting up 'Technology Parks', e.g. the software technology parks (STP) in Bangalore.

Thus Bangalore's success in becoming a software hub can be contributed to the state government's active role in the early and later stages of the industry's evolution.

Chance

According to Porter's diamond, national/regional competitiveness may also be triggered by random events.

When we look at the history of most industries we also see the role played by chance. Perhaps the most important instance of chance involves the question of who comes up with a major new idea first. For reasons having little to do with economics, entrepreneurs will typically start their new operations in their home countries. Once the industry begins in a given country scale and clustering effects can cement the industry's position in that country.

In relation to the development of competitiveness of the Indian software industry (especially in Bangalore) two essential events can be identified:

1. The Y2K problems (described earlier), which created the increased demand for services of Indian software firms.
2. The collapse of the dot-com boom in 2001 in USA and Europe, which created the search for ways to cut costs by outsourcing software-functions to India.

In summary, we have identified six factors that influence the location of global industries: factors of production, home demand, the location of supporting industries, the internal structure of the domestic industry, chance and government. We have also suggested that these factors are interconnected.

In relation to the software industry in India (Bangalore), which we used as our example throughout discussion of the diamond model, the following conclusions can be drawn (Nair *et al.* 2007):

1. The software industry in Bangalore started off by serving not its domestic customers, but demanding North American customers. Also, the rivals for software firms tend not to be local but more global.
2. The support needed for software services is much less sophisticated than for manufacturing. For the manufacturing sector it is also important to have access to a well-functioning physical infrastructure (transport, logistics etc.), which is not necessary for the software industry because most of the logistics can be done over the Internet. That is one of the reasons why Bangalore's software industry created international competitiveness, but the manufacturing sector did not.
3. The software industry is very much dependent on advanced and well-educated human resources as the key factor input.

While the Bangalore-based firms started off at the low end of the value chain (performing coding work for the Y2K problem) they have continuously moved in the direction of delivering more value-added service in emerging areas.

4.3 Competition analysis in an industry

The next step in understanding the firm's competitiveness is to look at the competitive arena in an industry, which is the top box in the diamond model (see Figure 4.1).

One of the most useful frameworks for analysing the competitive structure was developed by Porter (1980). He suggests that competition in an industry is rooted in its underlying economic structure and goes beyond the behaviour of current competitors. The state of competition depends upon five basic competitive forces, as shown in Figure 4.1. Together these factors determine the ultimate profit potential in an industry, where profit is measured in terms of long-run return on invested capital. The profit potential will differ from industry to industry.

To make things clearer we need to define a number of key terms. An *industry* is a group of firms that offer a product or class of products which are close substitutes for each other. Examples are the car industry and the pharmaceutical industry (Kotler, 1997, p. 230). A *market* is a set of actual and potential buyers of a product and sellers. A distinction will be made between industry and market level, as we assume that the industry may contain several different markets. This is why the outer box in Figure 4.1 is designated 'industry level' and the inner box 'market level'.

Thus the *industry level* (**Porter's five-forces model**) consists of all types of actors (new entrants, suppliers, substitutes, buyers and market competitors) that have a potential or current interest in the industry.

The *market level* consists of actors with a current interest in the market: that is, buyers and sellers (market competitors). In section 4.4 (value chain analysis) this market level will be further elaborated on as the buyers' perceived value of different competitor offerings will be discussed.

Although division into the above-mentioned two levels is appropriate for this approach, Levitt (1960) pointed out the danger of 'marketing myopia', where the seller defines the competition field (i.e. the market) too narrowly. For example, European luxury car manufacturers showed this myopia with their focus on each other rather than on the Japanese mass manufacturers, who were new entrants into the luxury car market.

The goal of competition analysis is to find a position in industry where the company can best defend itself against the five forces, or can influence them in its favour. Knowledge of these underlying pressures highlights the critical strengths and weaknesses of the company, shows its position in the industry, and clarifies areas where strategy changes yield the greatest pay-off. Structure analysis is fundamental for formulating competitive strategy.

Each of the five forces in the Porter model comprises a number of elements that combine to determine the strength of each force, and its effect on the degree of competition. Each will now be discussed.

Market competitors

The intensity of rivalry between existing competitors in the market depends on a number of factors:

- *The concentration of the industry.* Numerous competitors of equal size will lead to more intense rivalry. There will be less rivalry when a clear leader (at least 50 per cent larger than the second) exists with a large cost advantage.
- *Rate of market growth.* Slow growth will tend towards greater rivalry.
- *Structure of costs.* High fixed costs encourage price cutting to fill capacity.
- *Degree of differentiation.* Commodity products encourage rivalry, while highly differentiated products, which are hard to copy, are associated with less intense rivalry.
- *Switching costs.* When switching costs are high because the product is specialized, the customer has invested a lot of resources in learning how to use the product or has made tailor-made investments that are worthless with other products and suppliers (high asset-specificity), rivalry is reduced.
- *Exit barriers.* When barriers to leaving a market are high due to such factors as lack of opportunities elsewhere, high vertical integration, emotional barriers or the high cost of closing down plant, rivalry will be more intense than when exit barriers are low.

Firms need to be careful not to spoil a situation of competitive stability. They need to balance their own position against the well-being of the industry as a whole. For example, an intense price or promotional war may gain a few percentage points in market share, but lead to an overall fall in long-run industry profitability as competitors respond to these moves. It is sometimes better to protect industry structure than to follow short-term self-interest.

Suppliers

The cost of raw materials and components can have a major bearing on a firm's profitability. The higher the bargaining power of suppliers, the higher the costs. The bargaining power of suppliers will be higher in the following circumstances:

- Supply is dominated by few companies and they are more concentrated than the industry they sell to.
- Their products are unique or differentiated, or they have built up switching costs.
- They are not obliged to contend with other products for sale to the industry.

- They pose a credible threat of integrating forwards into the industry's business.
- Buyers do not threaten to integrate backwards into supply (i.e. taking over the suppliers' activities).
- The market is not an important customer to the supplier group.

A firm can reduce the bargaining power of suppliers by seeking new sources of supply, threatening to integrate backwards into supply and designing standardized components so that many suppliers are capable of producing them.

Buyers

The bargaining power of buyers is higher in the following circumstances:

- Buyers are concentrated and/or purchase in large volumes.
- Buyers pose a credible threat of integrating backwards to manufacture the industry's product.
- Products they purchase are standard or undifferentiated.
- There are many suppliers (sellers) of the product.
- Buyers earn low profits, which create a great incentive to lower purchasing costs.
- The industry's product is unimportant to the quality of the buyer's products, but price is very important.

Firms in the industry can attempt to lower buyer power by increasing the number of buyers they sell to, threatening to integrate forward into the buyer's industry (i.e. taking over the buyer's activities), or producing highly valued, differentiated products. In supermarket retailing, the brand leader normally achieves the highest profitability, partially because being number one means that supermarkets need to stock the brand, thereby reducing buyer power in price negotiations.

Customers who purchase the product but are not the end user (such as OEMs or distributors) can be analysed in the same way as other buyers. Non end-customers can gain significant bargaining power when they can influence the purchase decision of customers downstream (Porter, 2008). Over the years ingredient supplier DuPont has created enormous clout by advertising its 'Teflon' brand not only to the manufacturers of cooking equipment, but also to downstream end-customers (households). (See the section about ingredient branding in Chapter 11.)

Substitutes

The presence of substitute products can reduce industry attractiveness and profitability because they put a constraint on price levels.

If the industry is successful and earning high profits it is more likely that competitors will enter the market via substitute products in order to obtain a share of the potential profits available. The threat of substitute products depends on:

- the buyer's willingness to substitute
- the relative price and performance of substitutes
- the costs of switching to substitutes.

The threat of substitute products can be lowered by building up switching costs, which may be psychological. Examples are the creation of strong, distinctive brand personalities, and maintaining a price differential commensurate with perceived customer values.

New entrants

New entrants can serve to increase the degree of competition in an industry. In turn, the threat of new entrants is largely a function of the extent to which barriers to entry exist in the market. Some key factors affecting these entry barriers include:

- economies of scale
- product differentiation and brand identity, which give existing firms customer loyalty

- capital requirements in production
- switching costs – the cost of switching from one supplier to another
- access to distribution channels.

Because high barriers to entry can make even a potentially lucrative market unattractive (or even impossible) to enter for new competitors, the marketing planner should not take a passive approach but should actively pursue ways of raising barriers to new competitors.

High promotional and R&D expenditures and clearly communicated retaliatory actions to entry are some methods of raising barriers. Some managerial actions can unwittingly lower barriers. For example, new product designs that dramatically lower manufacturing costs can make entry by newcomers easier.

Strategic groups

Strategic groups can be defined as groups of companies that are likely to respond similarly to environmental changes and that have similar business models or similar combinations of strategies. For example, the restaurant industry can be divided into several strategic groups including fast food and fine dining, based on variables such as preparation time, pricing, and presentation. The number of groups within an industry and their composition depends on the dimensions used to define the groups. An industry could have only one strategic group if all the firms followed essentially the same strategy. At the other extreme, each firm could be a different strategic group.

Strategic group analysis is a technique used to provide management with information in regards to the firm's position in the market and a tool to identify their direct competitors. The five forces industry analysis will form the first step in this process. After having identified the forces, the major competitors in the industry based on competitive variables will also be outlined. Competitors will then be divided into strategic groups based on similarities in strategies and competitive positions. Often a two dimensional grid is made to position firms along an industry's two most important dimensions in order to distinguish direct rivals (those with similar strategies or business models) from indirect rivals. Firms may try to shift to a more favourably situated group, and how hard such a move proves to be will depend on whether entry barriers for the target strategic group are high or low.

The collaborative five-sources model

Porter's original model is based on the hypothesis that the competitive advantage of the firm is best developed in a very competitive market with intense rivalry relations. The five-forces framework thus provides an analysis for considering how to squeeze the maximum competitive gain out of the context in which the business is located – or how to minimize the prospect of being squeezed by it – on the five competitive dimensions that it confronts.

Since the early 1990s, however, an alternative school (e.g. Reve, 1990; Kanter, 1994; Burton, 1995) has emerged which emphasizes the positive role of cooperative (rather than competitive) arrangements between industry participants, and the consequent importance of what Kanter (1994) has termed 'collaborative advantage' as a foundation of superior business performance.

An all-or-nothing choice between a single-minded striving for either competitive or collaborative advantage would, however, be a false one. The real strategic choice problem that all businesses face is where (and how much) to collaborate, and where (and how intensely) to act competitively.

Put another way, the basic questions that firms must deal with in respect of these matters are:

- choosing the combination of competitive and collaborative strategies that are appropriate in the various dimensions of the industry environment of the firm;
- blending the two elements together so that they interact in a mutually consistent and reinforcing, and not counterproductive, manner;
- in this way, optimizing the firm's overall position, drawing upon the foundation and utilization of both collaborative and competitive advantage.

Table 4.1	The five-sources model and the corresponding five forces in the Porter model
Porter's five-forces model	**The five-sources model**
Market competitors	Horizontal collaborations with other enterprises operating at the same stage of the production process/producing the same group of closely related products (e.g. contemporary global partnering arrangements among car manufacturers).
Suppliers	Vertical collaborations with suppliers of components or services to the firm – sometimes termed vertical quasi-integration arrangements (e.g. the *keiretsu* formations between suppliers and assemblers that typify the car, electronics and other industries in Japan).
Buyers	Selective partnering arrangements with specific channels or customers (e.g. lead users) that involve collaboration extending beyond standard, purely transactional relationships.
Substitutes	Related diversification alliances with producers of both complements and substitutes. Producers of substitutes are not 'natural allies', but such alliances are not inconceivable (e.g. collaborations between fixed-wire and mobile telephone firms in order to grow their joint network size).
New entrants	Diversification alliances with firms based in previously unrelated sectors, but between which a blurring of industry borders is potentially occurring, or a process (commonly due to new technological possibilities) that opens up the prospect of cross-industry fertilization of technologies/business that did not exist before (e.g. the collaborations in the emerging multimedia field).

Source: from Burton (1995). Reproduced with permission from The Braybrooke Press Ltd.

This points to the imperative in the contemporary context of complementing the competitive strategy model with a sister framework that focuses on the assessment of collaborative advantage and strategy. Such a complementary analysis, which is called the *five-sources framework* (Burton, 1995), is outlined below.

Corresponding to the array of five competitive forces that surround a company – as elaborated in Porter's treatment – there are also five potential sources for the building of collaborative advantage in the industrial environments of the firm (the **five-sources model**). These sources are listed in Table 4.1.

In order to forge an effective and coherent business strategy, a firm must evaluate and formulate its collaborative and competitive policies side by side. It should do this for two purposes:

Five-sources model
Corresponding to Porter's five competitive forces there are also five potential sources for building collaborative advantages together with the firm's surrounding actors.

- to achieve the appropriate balance between collaboration and competition in each dimension of its industry environment (e.g. relations with suppliers, policies towards customers/channels);
- to integrate them in a way that avoids potential clashes and possibly destructive inconsistencies between them.

This is the terrain of composite strategy, which concerns the bringing together of competitive and collaborative endeavours.

4.4 Value chain analysis

Until now we have discussed the firm's international competitiveness from a strategic point of view. To get closer to the firm's core competences we will now look at the market-level box in Porter's five-forces model, which deals with buyers and sellers (market competitors). Here we will look more closely at what creates a competitive advantage among market competitors towards customers at the same competitive level.

Customer perceived value

Success in the marketplace is dependent not only upon identifying and responding to customer needs, but also upon our ability to ensure that our response is judged by customers to be superior to that of competitors (i.e. high perceived value). Several writers (e.g. Porter, 1980; Day and Wensley, 1988) have argued that causes of difference in performance within a market can be analysed at various levels. The immediate causes of differences in the performance of different firms, these writers argue, can be reduced to two basic factors (D'Aveni, 2007): the *perceived value compared to the customer's perceived sacrifice (costs)*.

Perceived value is the *relation* between the benefits customers realize from using the product/service (the numerator in Figure 4.2) and the costs, direct and indirect, that they incur in finding, acquiring and using it (the denominator in Figure 4.2). The higher this relation is the better the perceived value for the customer and the better competitiveness.

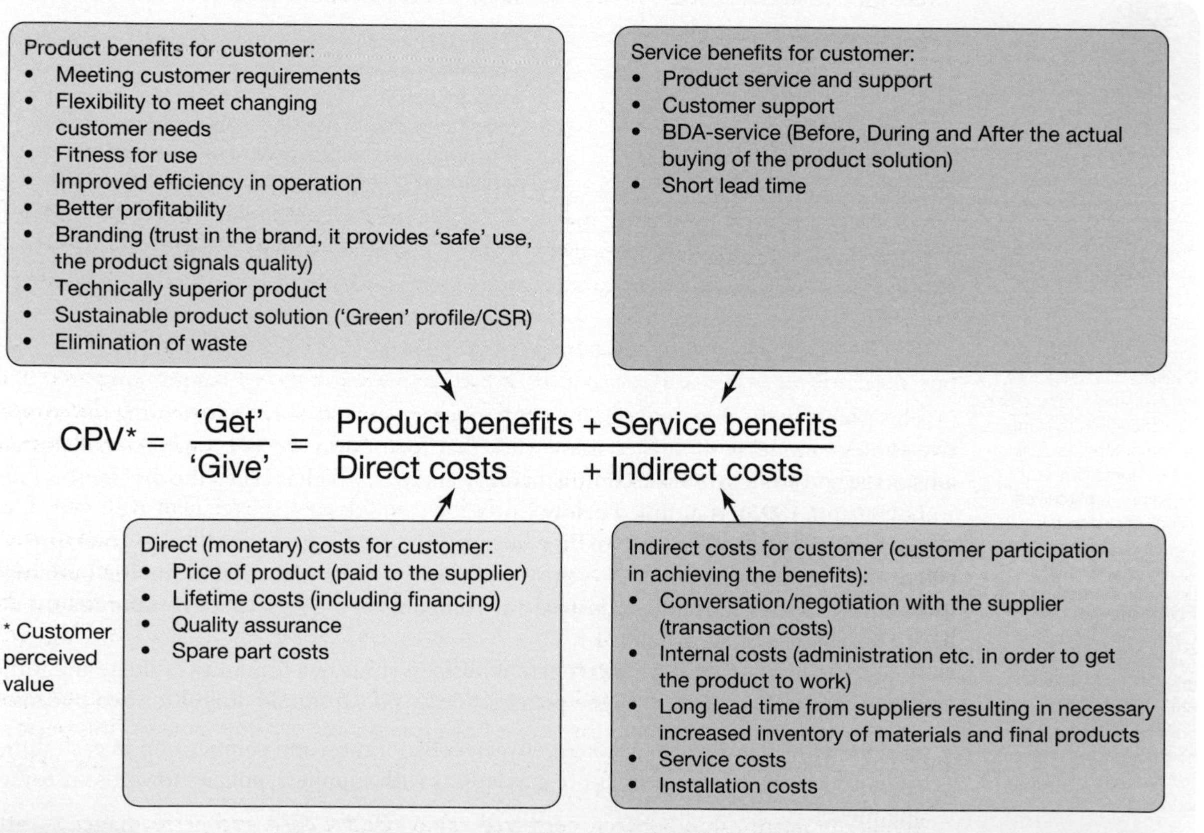

Product benefits for customer:
- Meeting customer requirements
- Flexibility to meet changing customer needs
- Fitness for use
- Improved efficiency in operation
- Better profitability
- Branding (trust in the brand, it provides 'safe' use, the product signals quality)
- Technically superior product
- Sustainable product solution ('Green' profile/CSR)
- Elimination of waste

Service benefits for customer:
- Product service and support
- Customer support
- BDA-service (Before, During and After the actual buying of the product solution)
- Short lead time

$$CPV^* = \frac{\text{'Get'}}{\text{'Give'}} = \frac{\text{Product benefits + Service benefits}}{\text{Direct costs} \quad + \text{Indirect costs}}$$

* Customer perceived value

Direct (monetary) costs for customer:
- Price of product (paid to the supplier)
- Lifetime costs (including financing)
- Quality assurance
- Spare part costs

Indirect costs for customer (customer participation in achieving the benefits):
- Conversation/negotiation with the supplier (transaction costs)
- Internal costs (administration etc. in order to get the product to work)
- Long lead time from suppliers resulting in necessary increased inventory of materials and final products
- Service costs
- Installation costs

Figure 4.2   Illustration of customer value (perceived value)

Source: adapted from Anderson *et al.* (2007, 2008); McGrath and Keil (2007); Smith and Nagle (2005).

Please do not think about Figure 4.2 as a mathematical formula for calculating an exact measure of 'customer perceived value' (CPV). Instead think about what the customer 'gets' compared to the sacrifices that the customer 'gives' in order to be able to use or consume the product/service.

After the product/service has been purchased and is being used or consumed, the level of the customer's satisfaction can be evaluated. If the actual customer satisfaction with both purchase and quality exceeds the initial expectations, then the customer will tend to buy the product/service again, and the customer may become loyal towards the company's product/service (brand loyalty).

The components driving customer benefits include product values service values, technical values and commitment value. The components driving cost fall into two categories: those that relate to the price paid, and those representing the internal costs incurred by the customer. These components can be unbundled into salient attributes. Commitment to value, for example, includes investment in personnel and customer relations. Internal cost might reflect set-up time and expense, maintenance, training and individual physical energy.

If the benefits exceed the costs, then a customer will at least consider purchasing your product. For example, the value to an industrial customer may be represented by the rate of return earned on the purchase of a new piece of equipment. If the cost reductions or revenue enhancements generated by the equipment justify the purchase price and operating costs of the equipment through an acceptable return on investment, then value has been created.

When we talk about customer value we should be aware that the customer value is not only being created by the company itself. Sometimes customer value is created in a co-creation process with customers or suppliers (Grönroos, 2009), or even with complementors and/or competitors. This extended version of 'customer value creation' leads us to the concept of the value net, which is introduced in section 4.7.

The competitive triangle

The more value customers perceive in a market offering relative to competing offerings and the lower the costs in producing the value relative to competing producers, the higher the performance of the business. Hence firms producing offerings with a higher perceived value and/or lower relative costs than competing firms are said to have a competitive advantage in that market.

Competitive triangle
Consists of a customer, the firm and a competitor (the 'triangle'). The firm or competitor 'winning' the customer's favour depends on perceived value offered to the customer compared to the relative costs between the firm and the competitor.

Perceived value
The customer's overall evaluation of the product/service offered by a firm.

This can be illustrated by the **competitive triangle** (see Figure 4.1, earlier). There is no one-dimensional measure of competitive advantage, and **perceived value** (compared to the price) and relative costs have to be assessed simultaneously. Given this two-dimensional nature of competitive advantage it will not always be clear which of the two businesses will have a competitive advantage over the other.

Looking at Figure 4.3, firm A will clearly have an advantage over firm B in case I, and clearly have a disadvantage in case IV, while cases II and III do not immediately allow such a conclusion. Firm B may have an advantage in case II, if customers in the market are highly quality conscious and have differentiated needs and low price elasticity, while firm A may have a similar advantage in case II when customers have homogeneous needs and high price elasticity. The opposite will take place in case III.

Even if firm A has a clear competitive advantage over firm B, this may not necessarily result in a higher return on investment for A, if A has a growth and B a hold policy. Thus performance would have to be measured by a combination of return on investment and capacity expansion, which can be regarded as postponed return on investment.

While the relationship between perceived value, relative costs and performance is rather intricate, we can retain the basic statement that these two variables are the cornerstone of competitive advantage. Let us take a closer look at these two fundamental sources of competitive advantage.

		Perceived value (compared to the purchase price)	
		Higher for A	*Higher for B*
Relative costs	*Lower for A*	I	II
	Lower for B	III	IV

Figure 4.3   Perceived value, relative costs and competitive advantage

Perceived value advantage

We have already observed that customers do not buy products, they buy benefits. Put another way, the product is purchased not for itself but for the promise of what it will 'deliver'. These benefits may be intangible: that is, they may relate not to specific product features but rather to such things as image or reputation. Alternatively, the delivered offering may be seen to outperform its rivals in some functional aspect.

Perceived value is the customer's overall evaluation of the product/service offered. Thus establishing what value the customer is actually seeking from the firm's offering (value chain) is the starting point for being able to deliver the correct mix of value-providing activities. It may be some combination of physical attributes, service attributes and technical support available in relation to the particular use of the product. This also requires an understanding of the activities that constitute the customer's value chain.

Unless the product or service we offer can be distinguished in some way from its competitors there is a strong likelihood that the marketplace will view it as a 'commodity', and the sale will tend to go to the cheapest supplier. Hence the importance of seeking to attach additional values to our offering to mark it out from the competition.

What are the means by which such value differentiation may be gained?

If we start in the value chain perspective (see section 1.7), we can say that each activity in the business system adds perceived value to the product or service. Value, for the customer, is the perceived stream of benefits that accrue from obtaining the product or service. Price is what the customer is willing to pay for that stream of benefits. If the price of a good or service is high it must provide high value, otherwise it is driven out of the market. If the value of a good or service is low its price must be low, otherwise it is also driven out of the market. Hence, in a competitive situation, and over a period of time, the price that customers are willing to pay for a good or service is a good proxy measure of its value.

If we look especially at the downstream functions of the value chain, a differential advantage can be created with any aspect of the traditional 4-P marketing mix: product, distribution, promotion and price are all capable of creating added customer perceived value. The key to whether improving an aspect of marketing is worthwhile is to know if the potential benefit provides value to the customer.

If we extend this model particular emphasis must be placed upon the following (see Booms and Bitner, 1981; Magrath, 1986; Rafiq and Ahmed, 1995):

- *People.* These include both consumers, who must be educated to participate in the service, and employees (personnel), who must be motivated and well trained in order to ensure that high standards of service are maintained. Customers identify and associate the traits of service personnel with the firms they work for.

- *Physical aspects.* These include the appearance of the delivery location and the elements provided to make the service more tangible. For example, visitors experience Disneyland by what they see, but the hidden, below-ground support machinery is essential for the park's fantasy fulfilment.
- *Process.* The service is dependent on a well-designed method of delivery. Process management assures service availability and consistent quality in the face of simultaneous consumption and production of the service offered. Without sound process management balancing service demand with service supply is extremely difficult.

Of these three additional Ps, the firm's *personnel* occupy a key position in influencing customer perception of product quality. As a consequence the *image* of the firm is very much influenced by the personnel. It is therefore important to pay particular attention to the quality of employees and to monitor their performance. Marketing managers need to manage not only the service provider–customer interface but also the actions of other customers; for example, the number, type and behaviour of other people will influence a meal at a restaurant.

Relative cost advantage

Each activity in the value chain is performed at a cost. Getting the stream of benefits that accrue from the good or service to the customer is thus done at a certain 'delivered cost', which sets a lower limit to the price of the good or service if the business system is to remain profitable. Decreasing the price will thus imply that the delivered cost be first decreased by adjusting the business system. As mentioned earlier, the rules of the game may be described as *providing the highest possible perceived value to the final customer, at the lowest possible delivered cost.*

A firm's cost position depends on the configuration of the activities in its value chain versus that of competitors and its relative location on the cost drivers of each activity. A cost advantage is gained when the cumulative cost of performing all the activities is lower than competitors' costs. This evaluation of the relative cost position requires an identification of each important competitor's value chain. In practice, this step is extremely difficult because the firm does not have direct information on the costs of competitors' value activities. However, some costs can be estimated from public data or interviews with suppliers and distributors.

Relative cost advantage
A firm's cost position depends on the configuration of the activities in its value chain versus that of the competitors.

Creating a **relative cost advantage** requires an understanding of the factors that affect costs. It is often said that 'big is beautiful'. This is partly due to economies of scale, which enable fixed costs to be spread over a greater output, but more particularly it is due to the impact of the *experience curve.*

The experience curve is a phenomenon that has its roots in the earlier notion of the learning curve. The effects of learning on costs were seen in the manufacture of fighter planes for the Second World War. The time taken to produce each plane gradually fell as learning took place. The combined effect of economies of scale and learning on cumulative output has been termed the experience curve. The Boston Consulting Group estimated that costs reduced on average by approximately 15–20 per cent each time cumulative output doubled.

Subsequent work by Bruce Henderson, founder of the Boston Consulting Group, extended this concept by demonstrating that all costs, not just production costs, would decline at a given rate as volume increased. In fact, to be precise, the relationship that the experience curve describes is between real unit costs and cumulative volume.

This suggests that firms with greater market share will have a cost advantage through the experience curve effect, assuming that all companies are operating on the same curve. However, a move towards a new manufacturing technology can lower the experience curve for adopting companies, allowing them to leapfrog over more traditional firms and thereby gain a cost advantage even though cumulative output may be lower.

The general form of the experience curve and of leapfrogging to another curve are shown in Figure 4.4.

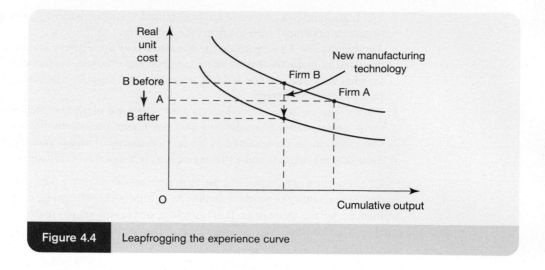

Figure 4.4   Leapfrogging the experience curve

Leapfrogging the experience curve by investing in new technology is a special opportunity for SMEs and newcomers to a market, since they will (as a starting point) have only a small market share and thereby a small cumulative output.

The implications of the experience curve for the pricing strategy will be discussed further in Chapter 16. According to Porter (1980) there are other cost drivers that determine the costs in value chains:

- *Capacity utilization.* Underutilization incurs costs.
- *Linkages.* Costs of activities are affected by how other activities are performed. For example, improving quality assurance can reduce after-sales service costs.
- *Interrelationships.* For example, different strategic business units (SBUs) sharing of R&D, purchasing and marketing will lower costs.
- *Integration.* For example, deintegration (outsourcing) of activities to sub-suppliers can lower costs and raise flexibility.
- *Timing.* For example, first movers in a market can gain cost advantage. It is cheaper to establish a brand name in the minds of the customers if there are no competitors.
- *Policy decisions.* Product width, level of service and channel decisions are examples of policy decisions that affect costs.
- *Location.* Locating near suppliers reduces inbound distribution costs. Locating near customers can lower outbound distribution costs. Some producers locate their production activities in eastern Europe or the Far East to take advantage of low wage costs.
- *Institutional factors.* Government regulations, tariffs, local content rules, etc., will affect costs.

The basic sources of competitive advantage

Resources
Basic units of analysis –
financial, technological,
human and organizational
resources – found in
the firm's different
departments.

Competences
Combination of
different resources into
capabilities and later
competences – being
something that the firm
is really good at.

The perceived value created and the costs incurred will depend on the firm's **resources** and its **competences** (see Figure 4.5).

Resources

Resources are the basic units of analysis. They include all inputs into the business processes – that is, financial, technological, human and organizational resources. Although resources provide the basis for competence building, on their own they are barely productive.

Resources are necessary in order to participate in the market. The competitors in a market will thus not usually be very different with regard to these skills and resources, and the latter will not explain differences in created perceived value, relative costs and the resulting performance. They are failure preventers, but not success producers. They may, however,

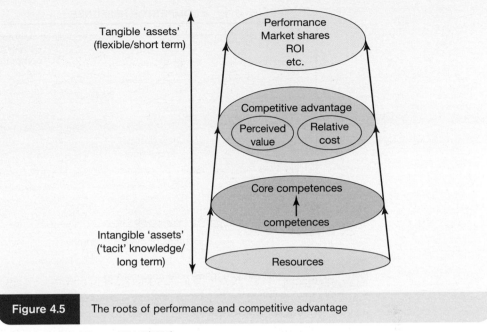

| Figure 4.5 | The roots of performance and competitive advantage |

Source: adapted from Jüttner and Wehrli (1994).

act as barriers to entry for potential new competitors, and hence raise the average level of performance in the market.

Competences

Competences – being components of a higher level – result from a combination of the various resources. Their formation and quality depend on two factors. The first factor is the specific capabilities of the firm in integrating resources. These capabilities are developed and improved in a collective learning process. On the other hand, the basis for the quality of a competence is the resource assortment. This forms a potential for competences, which should be exploited to the maximum extent.

Cardy and Selvarajan (2006) classify competences into two broad categories: *personal* or *corporate*. Personal competences are possessed by individuals and include characteristics such as knowledge, skills, abilities, experience and personality. Corporate competences belong to the organization and are embedded processes and structures that tend to reside within the organization, even when individuals leave. These two categories are not entirely independent. The collection of personal competences can form a way of doing things or a culture that becomes embedded in the organization. In addition, corporate characteristics can determine the type of personal competences that will best work or fit in the organization.

Core competences
Value chain activities in which the firm is regarded as better than its competitors.

A firm can have a lot of competences but only a few of them are **core competences**: that is, a value chain activity in which the firm is regarded as a better performer than any of its competitors (see Figure 4.6).

In Figure 4.6 a core competence is represented by a strategic resource (asset) that competitors cannot easily imitate and which has the potential to earn long-term profit. The objective of the firm will be to place products and services at the top-right corner. The top-left corner also represents profit possibilities, but the competitive advantage is easier to imitate, so the high profit will only be short term. The bottom-left corner represents the position of the price-sensitive commodity supplier. Here the profits are likely to be low because the product is primarily differentiated by place (distribution) and especially price.

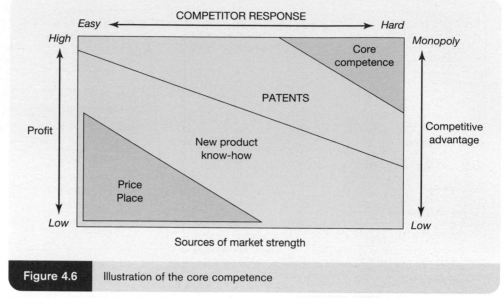

| **Figure 4.6** | Illustration of the core competence |

Source: reprinted from *Long Range Planning*, vol. 27, no. 4, Tampoe, M. (1994) 'Exploiting the core competences of your organization', p. 74, Copyright 1994, with permission from Elsevier.

Competitive benchmarking

The ultimate test of the efficiency of any marketing strategy has to be in terms of profit. Those companies that strive for market share, but measure market share in terms of volume sales, may be deluding themselves to the extent that volume is bought at the expense of profit.

Because market share is an 'after the event' measure, we need to utilize continuing indicators of competitive performance. This will highlight areas where improvements in the marketing mix can be made.

Competitive benchmarking
A technique for assessing relative marketplace performance compared with main competitors.

In recent years a number of companies have developed a technique for assessing relative marketplace performance, which has come to be known as **competitive benchmarking**. Originally the idea of competitive benchmarking was literally to take apart a competitor's product, component by component, and compare its performance in a value engineering sense with your own product. This approach has often been attributed to the Japanese, but many Western companies have also found the value of such detailed comparisons.

The concept of competitive benchmarking is similar to what Porter (1996) calls operational effectiveness (OE), meaning performing similar activities better than competitors perform them. However, Porter also thinks that OE is a necessary but not a sufficient condition for outperforming rivals. Firms also have to consider strategic (or market) positioning, meaning the performance of *different* activities from rivals or performing similar activities in different ways. Only a few firms have competed successfully on the basis of OE over a long period, and the main reason is the rapid diffusion of best practices. Competitors can rapidly imitate management techniques and new technologies with support from consultants.

However, the idea of benchmarking is capable of extension beyond this simple comparison of technology and cost effectiveness. Because the battle in the marketplace is for 'share of mind', it is customers' perceptions that we must measure.

The measures that can be used in this type of benchmarking programme include delivery reliability, ease of ordering, after-sales service, the quality of sales representation and the accuracy of invoices and other documentation. These measures are not chosen at random, but are selected because of their importance to the customer. Market research, often based on in-depth interviews, would typically be employed to identify what these 'key success factors' are. The elements that customers identify as being the most important (see Figure 4.7) then

Examples of value chain functions (mainly downstream functions)	Customer Importance to customer (key success factors)					Own firm (Firm A) How do customers rate performance of our firm?					Key competitor (Firm B) How do customers rate performance of key competitor?				
	High importance			Low importance		Good				Bad	Good				Bad
	5	4	3	2	1	5	4	3	2	1	5	4	3	2	1
Uses new technology															
High technical quality and competence															
Uses proven technology															
Easy to buy from															
Understands what customers want															
Low price															
Delivery on schedule															
Accessible for enquiries															
Takes full responsibility															
Flexible and quick															
Known contact person															
Provides customer training															
Take account of future requirements															
Courteous and helpful															
Specified invoices															
Gives guarantees															
ISO 9000 certified															
Right first time															
Can give references															
Environment conscious															

Figure 4.7   Competitive benchmarking (example with only a few criteria)

form the basis for the benchmark questionnaire. This questionnaire is administered to a sample of customers on a regular basis: for example, German Telecom carries out a daily telephone survey of a random sample of its domestic and business customers to measure customers' perceptions of service. For most companies an annual survey might suffice; in other cases, perhaps a quarterly survey, particularly if market conditions are dynamic. The output of these surveys will typically be presented in the form of a competitive profile, as in the example in Figure 4.7.

Most of the criteria mentioned above relate to downstream functions in the value chain. Concurrently with closer relations between buyers and suppliers, especially in the industrial market, there will be more focus on the supplier's competences in the upstream functions.

Development of a dynamic benchmarking model

On the basis of the value chain's functions, we will suggest a model for the development of a firm's competitiveness in a defined market. The model will be based on a specific market as the market demands are assumed to differ from market to market, and from country to country.

Before presenting the basic model for development of international competitiveness we will first define two key terms:

1. *Critical success factors.* Those value chain functions where the customer demands/expects the supplier (firm X) to have a strong competence.
2. *Core competences.* Those value chain functions where firm X has a strong competitive position.

The strategy process

The model for the strategy process is shown in Figure 4.8.

Stage 1: analysis of situation (identification of competence gaps)

We will not go into detail here about the problems there have been in measuring the value chain functions. The measurements cannot be objective in the traditional way of thinking, but must rely on internal assessments from firm representatives (interviews with relevant managers) supplemented by external experts ('key informants') who are able to judge the market's (customers) demand now and in the future.

The competence profile for firm A in Figure 4.1 (top-right diagram) is an example of how a firm is not in accordance with the market (= customer) demand. The company has its core competences in parts of the value chain's functions where customers place little importance (market knowledge in Figure 4.1).

If there is a generally good match between the critical success factors and firm A's initial position, it is important to concentrate resources and improve this core competence to create sustainable competitive advantages.

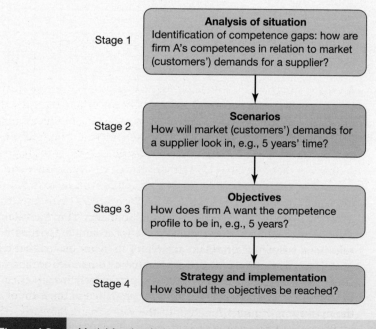

Stage 1	**Analysis of situation** Identification of competence gaps: how are firm A's competences in relation to market (customers') demands for a supplier?
Stage 2	**Scenarios** How will market (customers') demands for a supplier look in, e.g., 5 years' time?
Stage 3	**Objectives** How does firm A want the competence profile to be in, e.g., 5 years?
Stage 4	**Strategy and implementation** How should the objectives be reached?

Figure 4.8   Model for development of core competencies

If, on the other hand, there is a large gap between customers' demands and the firm's initial position in critical success factors in Figure 4.1 (as with the personal selling functions), it may give rise to the following alternatives:

- Improve the position of the critical success factor(s).
- Find business areas where firm A's competence profile better suits the market demand and expectations.

As a new business area involves risk, it is often important to identify an eventual gap in a critical success factor as early as possible. In other words, an early warning system must be established that continuously monitors the critical competitive factors so that it is possible to start initiatives that limit an eventual gap as early as possible.

In Figure 4.1 the competence profile of firm B is also shown.

Stages 2 and 3: scenarios and objectives

To be able to estimate future market demand different scenarios are made of the possible future development. These trends are first described generally, then the effect of the market's future demand/expectations on a supplier's value chain function is concretized.

By this procedure the described 'gap' between market expectations and firm A's initial position becomes more clear. At the same time the biggest gap for firm A may have moved from personal sales to, for example, product development. From knowledge of the market leader's strategy it is possible to complete scenarios of the market leader's future competence profile.

These scenarios may be the foundation for a discussion of objectives and of which competence profile the company wants in, say, five years' time. Objectives must be set realistically and with due consideration of the organization's resources (the scenarios are not shown in Figure 4.1).

Stage 4: strategy and implementation

Depending on which of firm A's value chain functions are to be developed, a strategy is prepared. This results in implementation plans that include the adjustment of the organization's current competence level.

4.5   The sustainable global value chain – CSR

A value chain comprises all activities necessary to 'bring a product from conception to market'. Therefore, it includes product development, different phases of production, extraction of raw materials, semi-finished materials, component production and assembly, distribution, marketing and even recycling. As these activities may be spread over several different firms and countries, the value chain can become global (see also Chapter 1).

In order that the value chain should also be strategic Porter and Kramer (2006) wrote that corporate social responsibility (CSR) should contribute to firm value chain practices and/or improve the context of competitiveness. Porter and Kramer used the example of Nestlé's CSR initiatives, elaborated to illustrate that CSR integrated to the value chain benefited Nestlé, as the activities reinforced the primary activities and support activities of Nestlé's company value chain. Building on this example, it can be advocated that company CSR programmes could be so designed that the CSR activity forms part of the firm value chain by contributing either to the primary activities and/or the support activities. Such CSR initiatives help firms to secure purchased inputs, reduce operational costs, smooth logistics and/or contribute to the marketing and sales function of the value chain. Similarly, CSR activities could also be intelligently planned to contribute to the support activities like procurement, manpower development etc. of the company's value chain.

4.6 CSR and international competitiveness

Porter and Kramer (2006) advocated that when company CSR activities improve the context of competitiveness of the firm, the CSR activity becomes strategic in nature. The reinforcement of context of competitiveness by company CSR initiatives would benefit the whole industry, so firms have to secure and capture the improvement in the context so that the firm benefits. Thus, Porter and Kramer (2006) argue strategic CSR activities should be so designed that they improve the context of competitiveness of a firm/industry and these benefits have to find a way into the company value chain. However, in developing countries this logic of thinking needs to be altered. In the context of a developing country, the firm context of competitiveness is weak. So even if the CSR initiative only betters the context of competitiveness it is of strategic importance for the firms. Thus CSR activities directed towards the competitive context could bring enormous opportunities of strategic significance to the firm. Porter and Kramer wrote that CSR activities could improve the input factors of production, such as skilled labour or necessary physical infrastructure required to compete. Demand conditions of products and services in a given industry could be influenced by CSR activities by setting higher standards for the quality of products and services (in terms of product safety features, environment friendliness and socially responsible performance features). CSR initiatives could also make the local demand conditions more refined and of substantial size. CSR initiatives could be done to influence and frame rules and regulations for healthy competition, better investment climate, protection of intellectual property etc. so as to make inter-firm rivalry situation favourable. Finally, CSR could be designed to build capacity of the weak related and supporting industries concerned or the raw material suppliers.

When companies undertake such a CSR initiative, they can gain both tangible (physical resources such as raw material, human resource, increased profits etc.) and intangible resources (reputation, brand name, goodwill, know-how) which can be of strategic importance to them. If such resources are unique to the firm, valuable to the firm's customers, rare, inimitable or imperfectly substitutable for the competitors then such resources are strategic resources and can provide the firm competitive advantage.

In the following we will analyse some specific condition under which a sustainable global value chain (SGVC) might gain international competitiveness. Here, we use a bottom-line definition of international competitiveness: a global value chain is competitive internationally as long as its products can be profitably sold on export markets. In addition, we define SGVC as the global value chains in which the products and the production process result from environmental, social and/or economical concerns and practices. Considering the growing number of contributions to sustainable development and CSR literature, we recognize that many different types of SGVC could be identified (related to specific social or environmental issues) with different specificities.

Value added from CSR activities can occur if revenues increase or costs decrease due to the CSR involvement of a company (Figure 4.9).

CSR benefits

CSR-induced revenue increases can come from additional sales due to increases in sales quantities, prices or margins. These can be stimulated by cause-related marketing campaigns, CSR-specific product line changes or improved possibilities of winning public tenders, for example due to the use of environmentally friendly technologies. CSR-induced revenue increases can also refer to CSR grants and subsidies. The sales may increase as a result of:

- better branch value
- better customer attraction and retention (higher repurchase rates, higher market shares)
- higher employed attractiveness (more applications per vacancy, better hiring rate)
- higher employee motivation and retention (lower fluctuation rate, absenteeism).

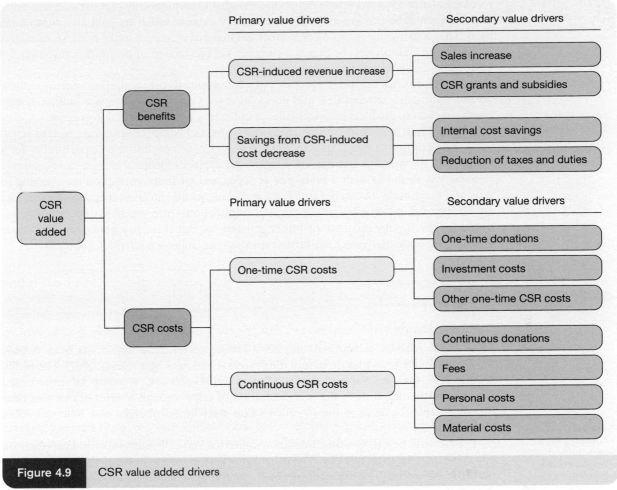

| Figure 4.9 | CSR value added drivers |

Source: adapted from Weber, M. (2008) The business case for corporate social responsibility: a company-level measurement approach for CSR, *European Management Journal*, 26, 4: 247–61. Reproduced with permission from Elsevier.

Savings from CSR-induced cost decreases can result from internal cost savings due to efficiency improvements or triggered by CSR-specific collaborations with, for example NGOs that provide knowledge or contacts to critical stakeholders such as public authorities, reducing the costs for product or market development. Cost savings can also come from tax concessions or reductions of certain duties granted by governments to promote CSR activities, e.g. tax concessions for environmentally friendly technologies.

When evaluating CSR benefits, managers need to carefully consider the time period in scope. As CSR benefits often occur after a time lag, evaluations should focus on longer time periods. As argued above, for some CSR benefits it is difficult to isolate the impact of CSR form other influencing factors. In this context, the evaluation of complementary figures as well as CSR KPIs can be helpful.

CSR costs

One-time CSR costs include one-time donations such as the donations granted to support the Tsunami victims in 2004. One-time CSR costs also include investment costs, for example for the installation of smoke filters that are beyond legal requirements, and other one-time costs caused by the CSR activities in scope.

Continuous CSR costs include donations intended to continuously support a certain cause and fees such as licence fees to use certain labels or patents, which are paid on a continuous basis. They also include recurring personnel and material costs such as the costs for managers coordinating CSR projects or material costs for the production of promotion materials for example in cause-related marketing campaigns.

It is often difficult to assess CSR costs using conventional cost accounting systems as these do not distinguish between CSR and non-CSR costs. Conventional cost accounting assigns overhead costs to products based on volume indicators such as production volume.

While CSR in a company's value chain and context of competitiveness are certain actual activity descriptions, other CSR activities can also provide new business opportunities for a firm and in the next two sections these aspects are explored further.

Society is abundant with a multitude of social and environmental problems varying in type and magnitude. Two major problems and consequently business market opportunities are widespread: poverty and environmental degradation – the 'green' market. Poverty is a threat for the healthy existence of future generations. But these two issues can also create business opportunities, which are further discussed in Hollensen (2010), Chapter 9.

4.7 The value net

Value-chain analysis (section 4.4) implies a linear process, ignoring inputs from outside the chain – many firms may input into the process at various stages (Neves, 2007). The reality is therefore that the value-chain becomes a value network, a group of interrelated entities, which contribute to the overall creation of value through a series of complex relationships, and the result is the so-called **value net** (Brandenburger and Nalebuff, 1996; Teng, 2003).

Value net
A company's value creation in collaboration with suppliers and customers (vertical network partners) and complementors and competitors (horizontal network partners).

The value net reveals two fundamental symmetries. Vertically, customers and suppliers are equal partners in creating value. The other symmetry is on the horizontal for competitors and complementors. The mirror image of competitors is complementors. A complement to one product or service is any other product or service that makes the first one more attractive, i.e., computer hardware and software, hot dogs and mustard, catalogues and overnight delivery service, red wine and dry cleaners. The value net helps you understand your competitors and complementors 'outside in'. Who are the players and what are their roles and the interdependences between them? Re-examine the conventional wisdom of 'Who are your friends and who are your enemies?' The suggestion is to know your business inside out and create a value net with the other players.

With Figure 4.10 in mind, we can also think about how the different actors can add value to the total global value chain. For example, the Swedish furniture giant IKEA provides an example of customer co-creation. The retailer enables customers to pay less for furniture but also encourages them to transport and then assemble the furniture themselves. Compared with a traditional furniture store, IKEA's business model is very much dependent on the value creation on the customer side (Michel *et al.*, 2008).

The concept of a 'value net' is further explained and discussed in Hollensen (2010).

4.8 Blue ocean strategy and value innovation

Kim and Mauborgne (2005a, b, c) use the ocean as a metaphor to describe the competitive space in which an organization chooses to swim. **Red oceans** refer to the frequently accessed marketspaces where the products are well-defined, competitors are known and competition

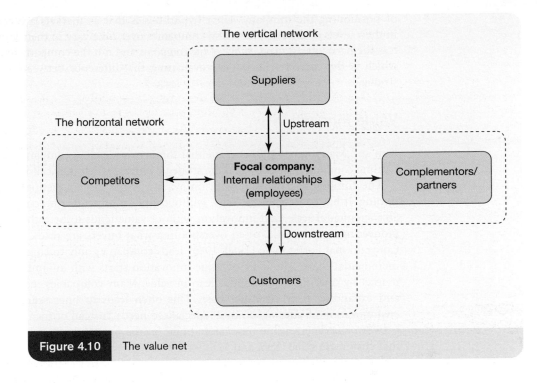

| Figure 4.10 | The value net |

Red oceans
Tough head-to-head competition in mature industries often results in nothing but a bloody red ocean of rivals fighting over a shrinking profit pool.

Blue oceans
The unserved market, where competitors are not yet structured and the market is relatively unknown. Here it is about avoiding head-to-head competition.

is based on price, product quality and service. In other words, red oceans are an old paradigm that represents all the industries in existence today.

In contrast, the **blue oceans** denote an environment where products are not yet well-defined, competitors are not structured and the market is relatively unknown. Companies that sail in the blue oceans are those beating the competition by focusing on developing compelling value innovations that create uncontested marketspace. Adopters of blue ocean strategy believe that it is no longer valid for companies to engage in head-to-head competition in search of sustained, profitable growth.

In Michael Porter's work (1980, 1985) companies are fighting for competitive advantage, battling for market share and struggling for differentiation: blue ocean strategists argue that cut-throat competition results in nothing but a bloody red ocean of rivals fighting over a shrinking profit pool.

Blue ocean is a market space that is created by identifying an unserved set of customers, then delivering a compelling new value proposition to them. This is done by reconfiguring what is on offer to better balance customer needs with the economic costs of doing so. This is as opposed to a red ocean, where the market is well defined and heavily populated by the competition.

Blue-ocean strategy should not be a static process but a dynamic one. Consider The Body Shop. In the 1980s, The Body Shop was highly successful, and rather than compete head on with large cosmetics companies, it invented a whole new market space for natural beauty products. During the 1990s The Body Shop also struggled, but that does not diminish the excellence of its original strategic move. Its genius lay in creating a new market space in an intensely competitive industry that historically competed on glamour (Kim and Mauborgne, 2005b).

Kim and Mauborgne (2005a) is based on a study of 150 strategic moves that spanned more than 100 years (1880–2000) and 30 industries. Their first point in distinguishing this strategy from the traditional strategic frameworks is that in the traditional business literature the company forms the basic unit of analysis, and the industry analysis is the means of positioning the company. Their hypothesis is that as markets are constantly changing in their levels of attractiveness, and companies over time vary in their level of performance, it is the particular *strategic move of the company*, and not the company itself or the industry, which is the correct criterion for evaluating the difference between red and blue ocean strategies.

Value innovation

Kim and Mauborgne (2005a) argue that tomorrow's leading companies will succeed not by battling competitors, but by making strategic moves, which they call *value innovation*.

The combination of value with innovation is not just marketing and taxonomic positioning. It has consequences. Value without innovation tends to focus on value creation on an incremental scale, and innovation without value tends to be technology-driven, market pioneering, or futuristic, often overshooting what buyers are ready to accept and pay for. Conventional Porter logic (1980, 1985) leads companies only to compete at the margin for incremental share. The logic of value innovation starts with an ambition to dominate the market by offering a tremendous leap in value. Many companies seek growth by retaining and expanding their customer base. This often leads to finer segmentation and greater customization of offerings to meet specialized needs. Instead of focusing on the differences between customers, value innovators build on the powerful commonalities in the features that customers value (Kim and Mauborgne, 1997).

Value innovation is intensely customer focused, but not exclusively so. Like value chain analysis it balances costs of delivering the value proposition with what the buyer values are, and then resolves the trade-off dilemma between the value delivered and the costs involved. Instead of compromising the value wanted by the customer because of the high costs associated with delivering it, costs are eliminated or reduced if there is no or less value placed on the offering by the customer. This is a real win–win resolution that creates the compelling proposition. Customers get what they really want for less, and sellers get a higher rate of return on invested capital by reducing start-up and/or operational delivery costs. The combination of these two is the catalyst of blue ocean market creation. Exhibit 4.1 illustrates this by using the case of Formule 1.

The output of the value innovation analysis is the value curves of the different marketers in the industry (also called 'strategy canvas' in Kim and Mauborgne, 2005c – see Exhibit 4.1). These different value curves raise four basic questions for the focal firm:

1. Which factors should be reduced well below the industry standard?
2. Which of the factors that the industry takes for granted should be eliminated?
3. Which factors should be raised well above the industry standard?
4. Which factors should be created that the industry has never offered?

The resulting new value curve should then determine if firm is on its way into the 'blue ocean'.

An example of value creation in action is the plush toy animal market which has been dominated by companies such as Gund, which patented a stuffing technique to increase the animals' softness and 'huggability'. The first competitor to attempt a blue ocean strategy within this market was Build-A-Bear Workshop in 1997 (see also Case Study 1.1). Build-A-Bear developed a unique value proposition by letting the customers co-create the value. This is done by allowing customers (children age 3–10 years) to experience the joy of creating their own bear. This concept has meant that the retail chain has grown very quickly – it sold 55 million bears in its first 12 years (Sheehan and Vaidyanathan, 2009).

EXHIBIT 4.1 Value innovation at Hotel Chain Formule 1

When Accor launched Formule 1 (a line of French budget hotels) in 1985, the budget hotel industry was suffering from stagnation and overcapacity. The top management urged the managers to forget everything they knew of the existing rules, practices and traditions of the industry. There were two distinct market segments in the industry. One segment consisted of no-star and one-star (very cheap, around €20 per room per night) and the other segment was two-star hotels, with an average price €40 per room. These more expensive two-star hotels attracted customers by offering better sleeping facilities than the cheap segment. Accor's management undertook market research and found out what most

Tony Souter © Dorling Kindersley.

customers of all budget hotels wanted: a good night's sleep at a low price. Then they asked themselves (and answered) the four fundamental questions:

1. Which of the factors that the budget hotel industry took for granted should be eliminated? The Accor management eliminated such standard hotel features as costly restaurants and appealing lounges. Accor reckoned that they might lose some customers by this, but they also knew that most customers could live without these features.
2. Which factors should be reduced well below the industry standard? Accor also believed that budget hotels were over-performing along other dimensions. For example, at Formule 1 receptionists are on hand only during peak check-in and checkout hours. At all other times, customers use an automated teller. The rooms at Formule 1 are small and equipped only with a bed and bare necessities – no desks or decorations. Instead of closets there are a few shelves for clothing.
3. Which factors should be raised well above the industry standard? As seen in Formule 1's value curve (Figure 4.11) the following factors:
   ● the bed quality,
   ● hygiene, and
   ● room quietness,
   were raised above the relative level of the low-budget hotels (the one-star and two-star hotels). The price performance was perceived as being at the same level as the average one-star hotels.
4. Which new factors (that the industry had never offered) should be developed? These covered cost-minimizing factors such as the availability of room keys via an automated teller. The rooms themselves are modular blocks manufactured in a factory, a method which may not result in the nicest architectural aesthetics but gives economies of scale in production and considerable cost advantages. Formule 1 has cut the average cost of building a room in half and its staff costs (in relation to total sales) dropped below the industry average (approximately 30 per cent) to between 20 and 23 per cent. These cost savings have allowed Accor to improve the features, that customers value most ('a good night's sleep at a low price').

   Note that in Figure 4.11 if the price is perceived as relatively low, it is regarded as a strong performance.

What has happened with Accor and Formule 1?

Today Accor is owner of several hotel chains (besides Formule 1) – Etap, Mercure, Sofitel, Novotel, Ibis and Motel 6. In 2008 the sales of Accor Group were €7.7 billion with operating profits of €875 million.

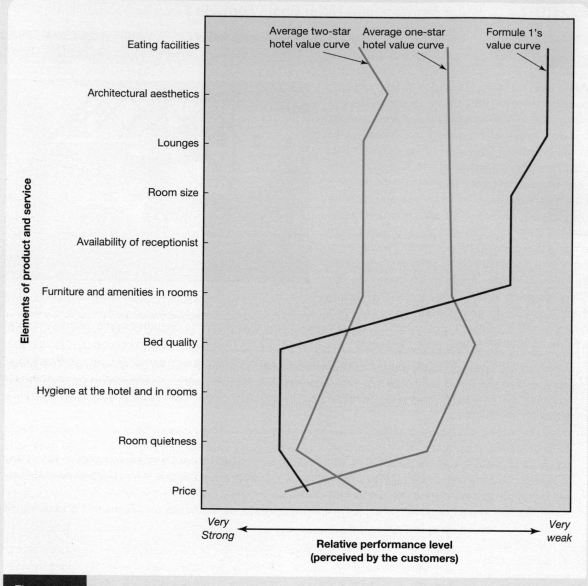

| Figure 4.11 | Formule 1's value curve |

Source: Adapted from Kim and Mauborgne (1997).

In France the Formule 1 has abbreviated its name to Hotel F1. In the rest of Europe the brand name has been incorporated into the Etap hotels. Outside Europe, 55 hotels are operated under the Formule 1 brand in South Africa, Australia, Brazil, Indonesia, Japan and New Zealand. Accor's market share in the European budget hotel segment is approximately 50 per cent.

Source: www.accor.com; www.hotelformule1.com; Kim and Mauborgne (1997).

4.9   Summary

The main issue of this chapter is how the firm creates and develops competitive advantages in the international marketplace. A three-stage model allows us to understand the development of a firm's international competitiveness in a broader perspective:

1. analysis of national competitiveness (the Porter diamond);
2. competition analysis (Porter's five forces);
3. value chain analysis:
    (a) competitive triangle;
    (b) benchmarking.

Analysis of national competitiveness

The analysis starts at the macro level, where the Porter diamond indicates that the characteristics of the home nation play a central role in the firm's international success.

Competition analysis

The next stage is to move to the competitive arena where the firm is the unit of analysis. Porter's five-forces model suggests that competition in an industry is rooted in its underlying economic structure and goes beyond the behaviour of current competitors. The state of competition depends upon five basic competitive forces which determine the profit potential in an industry.

Strategic group analysis helps to identify who the most direct competitors are and on what basis they compete. It also raises the question of how likely or possible it is for another organization to move from one strategic group to another.

Value chain analysis

Here we look at what creates a competitive advantage at the same competitive level (among industry competitors). According to the *competitive triangle*, it can be concluded that firms have a competitive advantage in a market if they offer products with:

- a higher perceived value to the customers;
- lower relative costs than competing firms.

A firm can find out its competitive advantages or core competences by using *competitive benchmarking*, which is a technique where customers measure marketplace performance of the firm compared to a first-class competitor. The measures in the value chain that can be used include delivery reliability, ease of ordering, after-sales service and quality of sales representation. These value chain activities are chosen on the basis of their importance to the customer. As customers' perceptions change over time, it may be relevant to try and estimate customers' future demands on a supplier of particular products.

According to the blue ocean strategy, the red oceans represent all the industries in existence today. This is *known* market space. Blue oceans denote all the industries not in existence today. This is *unknown* market space.

In the red oceans, industry boundaries are defined and accepted, and the competitive rules of the game are known. Here companies try to outperform their rivals to grab a greater share of existing demand. As the market space gets more and more crowded, prospects for profits and growth are reduced. Products become commodities, and cut-throat competition turns the red ocean bloody.

By integrating corporate social responsibility initiatives into the value chain, firms can gain both tangible (physical resources such as raw material, human resource, increased profits etc.) and intangible resources (reputation, brand name, goodwill, know-how) which can be of strategic importance to the firm. If such resources are unique to the firm, valuable to the firm's customers, rare, inimitable or imperfectly substitutable for the competitors then such resources are strategic resources and can provide the firm competitive advantage.

Blue oceans, in contrast, are defined by untapped market space, demand creation and the opportunity for highly profitable growth. While blue oceans are occasionally created well beyond existing industry boundaries, most are created by expanding existing industry boundaries. In blue oceans, competition is irrelevant as the rules of the game are waiting to be set.

Once a company has created a blue ocean, it should prolong its profit and growth sanctuary by swimming as far as possible in the blue ocean, making itself a moving target, distancing itself from potential imitators, and discouraging them in the process. The aim here is to dominate the blue ocean over imitators for as long as possible. However, as other companies' strategies converge on your market, and the blue ocean turns red with intense competition, companies need to reach out to create a new blue ocean to break away from the competition yet again.

CASE STUDY 4.1

Nintendo Wii: Nintendo's Wii takes first place on the world market – can it last?

A few years ago, very few analysts would have predicted that Nintendo Wii would be market leader in the games console market against the established Playstation 3 (PS 3) and Xbox 360 brands. But analysts can be in error: in the week ending 23 August 2007 www.Vgchartz.com data, which is based on sample data from retailers all over the world, indicated that Nintendo's Wii (which was released in November 2006 – one year after the Xbox 360), passed Xbox 360 lifetime units sales, making Nintendo the new world market leader in both the games console businesses.

This will have a large impact on third party publishers and will undoubtedly influence the decisions that the three major players (Microsoft, Sony and Nintendo) will make in the future.

One factor that has no doubt helped Nintendo's Wii to gain so quickly is the console's broad appeal across all age groups, demographics and countries.

Nintendo – key facts and financial data

Nintendo Co. was founded in 1889 as the Marufuku Company to make and sell 'hanafuda', Japanese game cards. It became the Nintendo Playing Card Company in 1951 and began making theme cards under a licensing agreement with Disney in 1959. During the 1980s Nintendo sought new products, releasing Game Boy in 1989 and the Super Family Computer game system (Super NES in the US) in 1991. The company broke with tradition

in 1994 by making design alliances with companies like Silicon Graphics. After creating a 32-bit product in 1995, Nintendo launched the much-touted N64 game system in 1996. It also teamed with Microsoft and Nomura Research Institute on a satellite-delivered Internet system for Japan. Price wars between the top contenders continued in the US and Japan.

In 1998 Nintendo released Pokémon, which involves trading and training virtual monsters (it had been popular in Japan since 1996), in the US. The company also launched the video game 'The Legend of Zelda: Ocarina of Time', which sold 2.5 million units in about six weeks. Nintendo issued 50 new games for 1998, compared to Sony's 131.

Nintendo announced in 1999 that its next-generation game system, Dolphin (later renamed GameCube), would use IBM's PowerPC microprocessor and Matsushita's DVD players.

In September 2001 Nintendo launched the long-awaited GameCube console system (which retailed at $100 less than its console rivals, Sony's PlayStation 2 and Microsoft's XBox); the system debuted in North America in November. In addition, the company came out with Game Boy Advance, its newest hand-held model with a bigger screen and faster chip.

In 2003 Nintendo bought a stake (about 3 per cent) in game developer and toy maker Bandai, a move expected to solidify cooperation between the two companies in marketing game software.

Today Nintendo (www.nintendo.co.jp) is engaged in the creation of interactive entertainment products. It manufactures and markets hardware and software for its home video game systems. The company primarily operates in Japan, Europe and America. It is headquartered in Kyoto, Japan, and employs about 3,400 people.

In the fiscal year 2007 Nintendo's recorded revenues were $8,189.4 million, an increase of 90 per cent over 2006. The operating profit of the company was $1,916.2 million during fiscal year 2007, compared to $773.7 million in 2006. Approximately 67 per cent of the company's revenue is generated from regions outside Japan. The net profit was $1,478.2 million in fiscal year 2007, an increase of 77.2 per cent over 2006.

Nintendo has managed to achieve higher returns on its investments, assets and equity compared to the industry average.

Nintendo has not raised any capital through debt in the past few years. The company's total debt to equity ratio at the beginning of 2007 is zero compared the industry average of 12 per cent. Debt-free status indicates the company's ability to finance its operations efficiently. Additionally, having no debt obligation provides the company with significant liquidity and financial flexibility.

The Nintendo Wii
Bob Riha Jr/WireImage/Getty Images.

The video game console industry

The interactive entertainment software market is characterized by short product life cycles and frequent introductions of new products.

The game consoles are relatively expensive in the beginning of the product life cycle. Hard-core game freaks pay dearly to have a console early, but sales really jump in years two and three, as Moore's law and economies of scale drive prices down and third-party developers release must-have games. By year four the buzz has begun about the next generation, and at that time, the games consoles can be found at the local grocery store at discount prices.

Nintendo has been operating in the video game console market since 1977 with colour television games, and is considered the oldest company in this market. It is one of the largest console manufacturers in the world, and a leader in the hand-held console market. The company had released four generations of consoles over the past two decades, which include Nintendo Entertainment System, Super Nintendo Entertainment System, Nintendo 64 and GameCube.

Nintendo has dominated the hand-held games market since its release of the original Game Boy hand-held system in 1989. In fiscal year 2007, Nintendo sold 79.5 millions units of Game Boy Advance (GBA). Nintendo DS, another hand-held console of Nintendo, sold 40.3 millions units in fiscal 2007.

Nintendo launches Wii

The company's latest console, Wii, was launched in November 2006. Nintendo's arguments for using this brand name were:

- Wii sounds like 'we', which emphasizes this console is for everyone.
- Wii can easily be remembered by people around the world, no matter what language they speak.
- Wii has a distinctive 'ii' spelling that symbolizes both the unique controllers and the image of people gathering to play.

The genius of the Wii is that it has changed the rules and invented a type of gaming with massively enhanced interaction between player and game.

Wii's blue ocean strategy

Nintendo is attempting to create a blue ocean by creating a unique gaming experience and keeping the cost of its system lower than Sony's and Microsoft's.

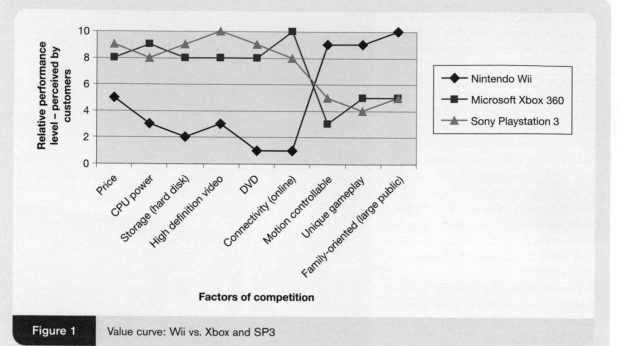

| **Figure 1** | Value curve: Wii vs. Xbox and SP3 |

In a recent Forbes.com interview, Perrin Kaplan, vice president of marketing and corporate affairs for Nintendo of America, discusses its implementation of blue ocean.

Inside Nintendo, we call our strategy 'Blue Ocean.' This is in contrast to a 'Red Ocean.' Seeing a Blue Ocean is the notion of creating a market where there initially was none – going out where nobody has yet gone. Red Ocean is what our competitors do – heated competition where sales are finite and the product is fairly predictable. We're making games that are expanding our base of consumers in Japan and America. Yes, those who've always played games are still playing, but we've got people who've never played to start loving it with titles like Nintendogs, Animal Crossing and Brain Games. These games are Blue Ocean in action.

(Forbes, 2006)

Part of blue ocean strategy involves creating a strategy canvas that depicts the current market space and relative offering level for major attributes that companies compete on. It helps visualize which offerings cost more to compete on. It also helps companies identify which values to eliminate, reduce and/or raise and finally, it helps identify new values that aren't currently competed on.

Here's a strategy canvas for the new Nintendo Wii when compared to Microsoft's Xbox 360 and Sony's PlayStation 3.

The bottom of the graph lists the primary sources of competitive advantages:

Price: Wii is 30–40 per cent cheaper than Xbox 360 and Sony Playstation 3.

CPU power: Wii has comparatively low processor speed, it has no Dolby 5.1 (sound system). Both PS3 and Xbox 360 have processors that are far more powerful than you'll find in most PCs.

Storage (hard disk): in the basic model Wii has no hard disk.

High definition video: Both PS3 and Xbox 360 use high-end graphics chips that support high-definition games and are prepared for high definition TV. Wii's graphics are marginally better than the PS2 and the original Xbox, but Wii pales next to the PS3 and Xbox 360.

DVD: both Sony and Microsoft provide the DVD opportunity. Sony even includes a blu-ray DVD drive.

Connectivity (online): the Xbox especially has positioned itself as the online games console with multiplayer functions.

Motion controllable: with its innovative motion control stick Wii adds new value to game playing. The stick integrates the movements of a player directly into the video game (tennis, golf, sword fights, etc.).

Unique gameplay: the new Wii gaming console senses depth and motion from players, thus adding a whole new element to the play experience.

Table 1	World sales of games consoles (units) and market shares			
	2005 million units (%)	2006 million units (%)	2007 million units (%)	2008 million units (%)
Sony				
PS2	16.8	11.7	8.6	7.4
PS3	–	1.2	7.2	10.3
Total	16.8 (69%)	12.9 (53%)	15.8 (40%)	17.7 (33%)
Microsoft				
Xbox	3.6	0.7	–	–
Xbox 360	1.2	6.8	7.8	11.2
Total	4.8 (20%)	7.5 (31%)	7.8 (20%)	11.2 (21%)
Nintendo				
GameCube	2.7	1.0	–	–
Wii	–	3.0	15.5	24.8
Total	2.7 (11%)	4.0 (16%)	15.5 (40%)	24.8 (46%)
Total	24.3 (100%)	24.4 (100%)	39.1 (100%)	53.7 (100%)

Source: www.vgchartz.com; http://vgchartz.com/hwcomps.php?weekly=1.

Family oriented (large public): with the motion control stick Nintendo opens up the console world to a completely new public of untapped non-gamers from the age of app. 30. Parents to the teens and even grandparents are getting easily into how to have game fun on the Wii

Wii's ´market shares compared to Microsoft (Xbox) and Sony (SP3)

Table 1 shows the worldwide sales of games consoles from 2005 to 2008, together with the corresponding market share.

Current Wii sales are pretty evenly split between the three major markets – 30 per cent have been sold in Japan, the American market (including Canada and South America) accounts for 40 per cent million and other markets (including Europe and Australia and a few niche markets) for 30 per cent million units sold, respectively. The sales of Sony (PS2 and PS3) and Microsoft (Xbox and Xbox 360) has been more unequally distributed: Microsoft sells most Xbox and Xbox 360 in North America, whereas the Sony's biggest markets for PS2 and PS3 are Japan, China and the rest of Asia.

At the retail level games consoles are sold through a variety of electronic and audio/video retailers, super-markets, discount stores, department stores and Internet retail stores.

Nintendo's strategy

Wii has managed to become a market leader by emphasizing its simplicity and lower price (than Sony and Microsoft) to break down barriers for new customers.

Nintendo has attracted non-traditional users, such as women and those over 60 years old, with easy-to-play titles such as Brain Training and Wii Fit (launched in April/May 2008). The Brain Training software is sold among middle-aged people, who seek to stimulate their memories and learning processes. The £70 Wii Fit game comes with a balance board – which links to the Wii console wirelessly. Players can stand, sit or lie on the board and undertake a range of exercises such as yoga and press-ups, as well as simulate to slalom skiing or hula hooping – all with the guidance of an on-screen fitness expert. Experts think that this game can help people lose weight. Playing the Nintendo Wii Fit can also improve balance and help avoid falls among older people. Researchers also ultimately hope to determine the effectiveness of computer games in developing muscle strength and coordination and reducing the risk of falls for people with Parkinson's disease.

Nintendo is highly dependent on sub-suppliers, both for both hardware and software. The company commissions a number of sub-suppliers and contract manufacturers to produce the key components of game consoles or assemble finished products. The company was not able to meet the growing demand for its the new Wii console, which was launched in November 2006, as its suppliers were not able to ramp up their production to meet the demand. A shortage of key components or the finished products had a negative effect on the company's revenues.

Nintendo is also very much dependent on its software suppliers, who are all developing new games based on licensing agreement with Nintendo.

While the hardware (consoles) market is dominated by three players, the software market is more open and fragmented with several regional players and local developers. However, the games software industry is undergoing a period of consolidation. At the end of 2007, French Vivendi Games acquired a 52 per cent stake in Activision and created a new entity, Activision Blizzard, which in size is close to that of the market leader, Electronic Arts. For example, Activision Blizzard launched *Guitar Hero World Tour* for all three platforms in December 2007, at the same time as the announcement of the acquisition of Activision.

The competitors' strategy

Sony Playstation

In 2008, cumulative sales of Playstation2 (PS2) reached 130 million units, making it the world's best selling game platform. However, the 2006–07 launch of Sony's new-generation PS3 did not translate into the immediate success that the company had hoped for. PS3 was not as successful as the Nintendo Wii. Sony suffers from a perception that it is a complex console only to be used in a darkened room by qualified young men. The core age group used to be a tight demographic group of 14- to 30-year-old men.

Microsoft Xbox 360

Microsoft continues to target the 'serious' gamer segment with the Xbox 360. The Xbox graphics, games and Xbox live Internet gaming have been popular with the core user segment, primarily young males. The US market remains the most important so far, accounting for nearly 50 per cent of the overall Xbox sales.

Xbox is the console with the highest 'game attach' rate. This is defined as the average number of games each console owner buys. For the Xbox 360,

Microsoft managed a 'games per console' average of 8 to 1 in 2008, the highest in the industry.

The strength of Microsoft's software distribution network has also kept the company alive in the business, allowing Microsoft to have a presence in more worldwide markets than Nintendo. Microsoft is strongly positioned in countries like China, India, Malaysia and South Africa, all of which are growth markets, and this is promising for future sales of Xbox.

The two competitors, Sony and Microsoft, have now (May 2010) published their plans to overtake the Wii position. At the end of 2010 the following two products are expected in the market:

- Sony's device (controller, which tracks the movement of a 'wand') is similar to Nintendo's controller. A camera sits on top of the TV and detects the motion of a coloured orb attached to the end of a wand held by the player. It will be available in North America, Europe, Japan and other Asian countries. Sony has not confirmed its price.
- Unlike its rivals, Microsoft's Natal does not use a controller. Instead, a series of sensors allow the gamer to control the action using gestures, movement and speech.

QUESTIONS

1. What were Microsoft's motives in entering the games console market with Xbox?
2. What are the competitive advantages of Microsoft Xbox and Sony Playstation 3?
3. What are the competitive advantages in the business model of Wii?
4. What do you think are Nintendo's chances of creating a long-term blue ocean with Wii?

Sources: www.Vgchartz.com.
Smith, G. (2009) 'Seniors may benefit from Wii game system', 16 April, http://www.hpodemo.com/common/news/news_results.asp?task=Headline&id=11597&StoreID=A340488DBE514E6AAAA2480FC2404258.
O'Brian, J.M. (2007) 'Wii will rock you', *Fortune*, 4 June, http://money.cnn.com/magazines/fortune/fortune_archive/2007/06/11/100083454/index.ht. Forbes interview, 7 June 2006. http://www.forbes.com/technology/cionetwork/2006/02/07/xbox-ps3-revolution-cx_rr_0207nintendo.html).
Gamespot (2006) 'Microsoft to ship 13–15 million 360s by June 2007', 21 July; www.gamespot.com.
Financial Times (2000) 'Companies and markets: Microsoft to take on video game leaders', 10 March.
New Media Age (2000) 'Let the games begin', 8 March.
BBC News (2002) 'Works starts on new Xbox', 26 June.
BBC News (2002) 'Price cut boosts Xbox sales', 24 July.
CNN News (2002) 'Console wars: round two', 22 May.

CASE STUDY 4.2

Senseo: creating competitiveness through an international alliance

A brief history of coffee

Coffee was first consumed in the ninth century, when it was discovered in the highlands of Ethiopia. From there, it spread to Egypt and Yemen, and by the fifteenth century had reached Azerbaijan, Persia, Turkey and northern Africa. From the Muslim world coffee spread to Italy, then to the rest of Europe, to Indonesia, and to the Americas.

Coffee has played an important role in many societies throughout modern history. In Africa and Yemen, it was used in religious ceremonies. As a result, the Ethiopian Church banned its secular consumption. It was banned in Ottoman Turkey in the seventeenth century for political reasons, and was associated with rebellious political activities in Europe.

For many decades almost all coffee has been sold as filter coffee in package sizes of one pound (500 grams). However, during the last decade things have changed. New products and package sizes have been introduced. The present case deals with a few of these new innovations. Today coffee has become a popular drink around the world and comes in many variations, both in terms of roasting and of brewing.

Spurred by the strength of coffee bar culture in many developed markets, manufacturers have attempted to increase value sales by introducing a similar 'café experience' at home. The battle among coffee makers for at-home use has intensified, with leading coffee players, such as Procter & Gamble, Kraft Foods and Philips & Sara Lee (Senseo), launching single-service pod machines which can brew a high-quality cup of coffee in less than one minute.

The influence of specialist coffee shops with their speciality coffee products based on the espresso fresh coffee bean has significantly influenced the consumption habits of younger people especially. These consumers increasingly abandoned classic filter coffee and embraced the Italian-American varieties of espresso fresh coffee beans and coffee pods/capsules. The coffee produced by espresso/café crema grinders and pod/capsule machines have two things in common: less caffeine and a milder taste than traditional filter coffee, while providing the 'crema' effect enjoyed by many consumers.

The history and categorization of the coffee maker

Before the coffee maker was invented, coffee was prepared in boiling water. The beans were roasted on an open fire and then added to boiling water for consumption. This process did not bring the desired taste and aroma, and coffee lovers started to devise ways to come up with a machine or a coffee maker that would prepare tasty coffee.

In 1912 Frau Benz invented the Melitta coffee filter, which is an efficient disposal method for coffee. Prior to this, linen or cloth was used for the filtering purpose of coffee.

The coffee maker market can be categorized into roughly three types:

1. Traditional filter machines
2. Espresso machines
3. Pod coffee machines. This is a sector that was actually pioneered by Nespresso, but the market leader now is Senseo. Their growth is driven by their ease of use and affordable pricing – later described in more depth.

These three categories are by no means complete and there are many categories that are not covered here.

A new and innovative filter-type coffee maker was invented in the 1960s and had more advanced features than the earlier varieties. Developed further over time, this new design came to be manufactured by many companies and its demand rose in the market. The leading brands in this market were Melitta and the Mr Coffee brand, which was manufactured with automatic drip process (Joe DiMaggio was its spokesperson from 1974). Today, the Mr Coffee holds a major part of the market share in the world.

An espresso coffee drink gives more energy and it is tastier than the other coffee drinks. The first espresso maker was invented by a manufacturing company owned by Lugia Bezzer in 1901 in Italy. Mr Bezzer was looking for a way to help speed up his employee's coffee breaks and worked out that if pressure was applied in the brewing process, the drink could be made in a lot less time. Nicknamed 'The fast coffee machine', the espresso machine patent was sold in 1905. The new owner, Desidero Pavoni, developed an espresso machine that used a piston pump to force water through a tube and into the coffee.

The commercial espresso machine was invented in 1946. Since then, the espresso maker under different brands has been produced by many companies. Some of the prominent brands include Juda, Mrs Coffee, Kitchenaid and Braun. The modern espresso machine comes in various features, styles, colours and prices.

The world market for coffee machines (coffee makers) looks like this:

Table 1	The global market for coffee machines (2008)
Retail volume (million units)	
Western Europe	17.8
Eastern Europe	0.6
North America	28.4
Latin America and Carribbean	4.1
Asia Pacific (minus Australia and NZ)	2.9
Australia and NZ	0.3
Africa and Middle East	0.7
World total	54.8

Source: adapted from Euromonitor International.

As shown in Table 1, the market volumes vary a lot between the regions. There are also huge differences, within the different world regions. For the Western European market the overall picture for the coffee machine market (divided into the three categories) looks like this:

The number of coffee machines in European kitchens is expected to be 100 million units.

Traditional filter coffee machines have still the highest volume market share (55 per cent). There is a considerable trend towards Espresso full-automatic and an extremely strong trend towards espresso portioned machines. Low-comfort and low-quality machines (hand-operated espresso piston, pad-filters, combis) are losing market share.

Across the western European region, the national markets are very different. Italy, Switzerland and Portugal have a huge market share of espresso machines; over 70 per cent. On the other hand there are countries with a very low market share of espresso machines such as Belgium, Germany or the Netherlands, with less than 20 per cent. In Belgium or the Netherlands pad-filters are quite popular with a market share of about 40 per cent. It is interesting to have a look at the markets in value. Assuming roughly that typical prices are 30 euros for filter machines, 70 euros for pad-filters and 200 euros for espresso machines an opposite picture evolves. Espresso machines are strongly dominating the market in value (see Table 2).

For many decades almost all coffee has been sold as filter coffee in package sizes of one pound (500 grams). However, during the last decade things have changed. New products and package sizes have been introduced. The remaining of this present case deals with one of these new innovations: the single-serve coffee pod system.

The single-serve coffee pod system

While the single serve brewing concept has proved successful in western Europe, particularly the Netherlands and France, the trend is still in its early stages in the US, and is yet to impact most devel-

Table 2	The Western European coffee machine market			
Category	Typical brands	Sold units in millions 2008	Typical price € 2008	Value in millions € 2008
Traditional filter machines	Melitta, Mr Coffee	10.0	30	300
Pod coffee machines	Nespresso, Senseo	3.5	70	245
Espresso machines	De Longhi, Jura, Krups and Rowenta, Rotel	4.3	200	860
Total		**17.8**		**€1,405**

Source: adapted from: Jürg Nipkow and Eric Bush: Coffee machines: recommendations for policy design, Report 7 August 2008, Topten International Group TIG, Paris, www.topten.info.

oping markets, where disposable incomes have not reached levels that would sustain demand. However, manufacturers hope that the concept will take hold with American consumers because it allows coffee to be made quickly, cleanly and in small quantities. That said, product choice remains limited, and with 'closed' systems, consumers must stick to buying coffee pods compatible with their single-serve machine.

As consumers face growing choices of new style coffee makers for home use, one of the deciding factors could be the availability of pods. After consumers have made their machine choice, probably based on price and the physical aspects of each machine, having easy access to the coffee pods themselves will be key. Flexibility may also turn out to be a competitive advantage. In addition to coffee, the Tassimo system allows consumers to make hot chocolate or tea, a feature rival Senseo offers only on upmarket models with specially purchased pods. On the other hand, Melitta One:One decided that the battle for pod control could only be won by revamping its pods to fit both its own system and those machines marketed by competitors.

Coffee pods and capsules largely imitate the benefits of freshly prepared espresso/café crema with the added benefit of convenience. They require less preparation time and offer standard one or two cup sizes, which appeal to single people. This segment has grown a lot to account (in Germany, for example) for 10 per cent of retail value sales of fresh ground coffee in 2008. Due to the much higher unit prices of coffee pods, it accounted for only just over 5 per cent of retail volume sales of fresh ground coffee in the same year.

Senseo

The basis for the success of coffee pods was provided in 2001, when Philips introduced coffee pod machines under the Senseo brand. These machines are geared towards the use of coffee pods produced by Douwe Egberts.

So the Senseo coffee pod system is the result of a partnership between electronics expert Philips (supplier of the Senseo machine) and coffee roaster Douwe Egberts (supplier of the coffee pods) – both world-renowned companies from the Netherlands. Coffee pods are tiny packages weighing 5–10 grams. A traditional bag contains 25 pods – a pod is put into the machine and within 45 seconds or so it transforms into one up of coffee (0.15–0.25 litre).

The two alliance partners

Philips

Royal Philips Electronics of the Netherlands (NYSE: PHG, AEX: PHI) is a diversified health and well-being company, focused on improving people's lives through timely innovations. As a world leader in healthcare, lifestyle and lighting, Philips integrates technologies and design into people-centric solutions, based on fundamental customer insights and the brand promise of 'sense and simplicity'.

Headquartered in the Netherlands, Philips employs more than 118,000 employees in more than 60 countries worldwide. With sales of €26 billion in 2008, the company is a market leader in cardiac care, acute care and home healthcare, energy efficient lighting solutions and new lighting applications, as well as lifestyle products for personal well-being and pleasure with strong leadership positions in flat TV, male shaving and grooming, portable entertainment and oral health care.

Sara Lee/Douwe Egberts (DE)

Douwe Egberts was founded in the middle of the eighteenth century by the Dutch entrepreneur Egbert Douwes and his wife Akke Thysses. The company's activities included coffee, tea and household and body care products. Soon they developed a reputation regionally by also supplying shop owners elsewhere, thereby spreading the Douwe Egberts brand around the country. Gradually, Douwe and his descendants built a company that grew to become the Dutch market leader for its core products, coffee and tea. Since 1978 Douwe Egberts has been owned by the Sara Lee Corporation, which opened new horizons worldwide. Today Douwe Egberts is the second largest coffee roaster in the world and the company employs over 26,000 people worldwide.

The company prospered, and continued to grow throughout The Netherlands, but it was not until the mid-twentieth century that it expanded beyond the borders of its homeland. In 1948, Douwe Egberts began selling coffee, tea and tobacco in Belgium. Over the next 20 years, the company added sales in Belgium, France and Spain. In 1978, the company was acquired by international food corporation Sara Lee. Since then, Sara Lee and Douwe Egberts has become the second largest coffee roaster in the world. Familiarly known as Sara Lee/DE, the company is a subsidiary of Sara Lee and employs over 26,000 people around the world.

The Douwe Egberts brands include Pickwick tea, Douwe Egberts coffee, Piazza d'Oro espresso,

Cafitesse, Pilao coffee and of course, the Senseo system. Sara Lee sells products in nearly 200 countries. The Sara Lee brands include Sara Lee, Earth Grains, Hillshire Farm, Jimmy Dean, Ball Park, Bimbo, Kiwi, Ambi Pur, Sanex and of course, Douwe Egberts.

Sara Lee/DE's part of the partnership is, of course, coffee. Douwe Egberts offers a wide variety of coffee blends to suit most tastes, as well as tea in pods to fit the Senseo machine. The current blends include Sumatra, Brazil, Kenya and Colombia, each of them with the characteristics common to the named region. In addition, there are selected specialty beverages, including espresso, cappuccino and Café Noir, a sweet, dark blend with a chocolate finish. There are also flavoured pods, which include Paris (vanilla caramel), Vienna (hazelnut, vanilla and mocha), and a number of limited edition varieties that are currently only available in select European locations. For tea lovers, Douwe Egberts offers Earl Grey and minty green T-pods for the Senseo.

In 1998, Sara Lee/DE filed a patent in Belgium to protect their use of the coffee pod system. When the Senseo hit the market and competitors realized that the patent prevented them from manufacturing coffee pods the patent was successfully challenged in the Belgian court. As of 2004, the year that the Senseo was introduced in the US, other companies have the legal right to make and sell coffee pods that fit the Senseo system. In addition, several pod-makers on the market allow consumers to make their own coffee pods. This allows flexibility in making the coffee or tea of your choice utilizing the Senseo brewing system.

Philips and Douwe Egberts

Working in tandem, the two companies developed every aspect of Senseo – from its patented coffee machine and the brewing process to its one-of-a-kind coffee pods. The machine uses single portion Senseo coffee pods, containing the finest ground coffee, to guarantee a perfect cup every time it is used. Senseo has now been launched in more than a dozen countries worldwide. The biggest markets are Austria, Australia, Belgium, China, Denmark, France, Germany, the Netherlands, UK and US.

Since Philips and Douwe Egberts introduced the coffee pod machine in spring 2001 it has sold more than 15 million coffee machines and more than 8 billion coffee pods in the first seven years of its life time. It is estimated that over five million coffee pod machines were sold in Germany by mid-2007. As coffee made from coffee pod machines is very expensive when consumed in large quantities, these machines are used as an additional coffee option rather than as a replacement for standard coffee machines. The typical owner of a coffee pod machine is young (40 years old and under), but owners include single people, couples and adults with small children.

When the Senseo coffee pod machine was introduced the end-user price was around €75: the current recommended price is €69, but in spring 2009 it was available for around €58.

It is reported that almost one-third of Dutch households own a Senseo machine, and the figure is expected to climb steadily in the years to come. Although most Dutch households continue to use both conventional filter coffee machines and single-serve coffee systems, unit sales of the latter in recent years have outperformed the former. Nevertheless, industry experts suggest that it will take a long time for conventional filter machines to disappear completely (just as it took a lot of years for colour TV to supersede black and white TV or DVDs to oust VHS). Many Dutch households are expected to continue to use conventional machines when holding a party and the Senseo-type machines for everyday use. The consumption behaviour of Dutch households is suggested to be a rough model of the average household within the EU.

Competitive advantages of Senseo

Low-cost followers from China, used to selling cheaper filter coffee machines, have had problems catching up on this alliance, because they cannot easily copy the tight collaboration between Philips and Sara Lee's Douwe Egberts subsidiary that produces the coffee packets designed especially for the Senseo machine.

When big retail chains like Aldi and Wal-Mart see a product like this, they usually go to China and ask for something similar. In the Senseo-case it is not so easy, because the main profits from the Senseo concept come partly from coffee machines but mainly from coffee pods. This makes life difficult for the Chinese competitors who have to recoup that money from machines alone.

Presently the market price for a traditional cup of filter coffee lies somewhere between 4 and 5 euro cents, whereas the price of a cup of pod coffee (7–10 grams) varies between 16 cents (Senseo) and 30–32 cents (Nespresso and Tchibo). Thus, for obvious reasons, coffee producers are very interested in the 'sky high' profit margins of the pods compared to the ruinous price levels of the traditional coffee package sizes (400 and 500 grams). The strategy of developing mini-packages (where the kilo price is much higher) represents a current retail trend. For instance the German candy producer Haribo has for some time sold a unit package containing 10–25 mini-packages.

Once the pods were introduced, no one had the slightest idea that this market niche would develop so fast and be so successful. While the competition in the ordinary coffee market continues to be as fierce as ever, the price competition in the pod market, while present, appears to exist in a different world. It seems that many consumers do not 'think' in unit or kilo prices.

As an industry executive recently remarked: 'Suddenly it has become possible to earn money by simply selling coffee.' For a generation or so coffee has been a typical discount product. In a lot of European markets, traditional coffee has been used by retailers (supermarkets, discount stores) as a promotional tool for generating store traffic. In TV ads and sales fliers specific brands are often on promotion and the retailer is losing money on the promoted coffee brand. However, once the consumer enters the store to buy the brand they will normally continue shopping in the same retail store and buy a lot of products that are not on promotion, thereby more than compensating for the loss generated by the promoted brand.

In 2004 the German Market of pods was 2,750 tons (30 per cent up from 2003). Senseo alone sold 650 million pods. The same year Nestlé globally sold 1.3 billion pods (34 per cent up from 2003). During 2003 and 2004 Philips sold two million Senseo coffee machines. When Tchibo launched its Cafissimo machine the 60,000 units available were sold within two days! Because the machines are sold below production prices (€69–99), the producers of the machines are being compensated by the coffee producers. For instance, Philips obtains a part of the profit generated by the sales of the Senseo pods.

Instead of bringing in two constituent brands (Philips and Sara Lee) to create a third brand (Senseo), the alliance team introduced a co-branding strategy, leveraging the equity in the Douwe Egberts and Philips brands to give credibility to the new composite brand, Senseo, forming a separate and unique product, thus ensuring single-minded focus.

Creating an overall identity that transparently links the coffee and appliance as part of one lock-and-key system, and building consumer intimacy around this, was a crucial building block to success, something from which our local equivalent can learn.

Not only has this alliance brought an innovation to consumers, Douwe Egberts and Philips have benefited from creating a new segment within coffee and coffee machines.

You have to ensure that both partners are aligned behind the collaboration, that the key people involved in managing the collaboration have the personal skills to make the collaboration a success, and that a sound co-branding strategy exists for the new product. In addition, there must be a commitment in funding that allows the partners to fully exploit the new product to the target market, creating demand and thus ensuring trade support. Creating a new category through shifting consumer behaviour requires a long-term commitment and an investment strategy to match. In the USA alone, for every dollar Procter & Gamble Co. and Sara Lee have reaped selling coffee for their 'revolutionary' single-cup systems, they have spent three on marketing.

Invariably there will always be issues around the area of intellectual property, and financial arrangements. In the case of the Senseo collaboration, it was agreed that Philips would hold the intellectual property for the coffee machine, whilst Douwe Egberts would retain it for the coffee. In order to ensure that Philips were aligned to view Senseo as a longer-term proposition, Douwe Egberts allowed Philips a share of royalties in the Senseo coffee brand.

Senseo.

A new model of the Senseo machine – the Senseo New Generation – was launched in selected markets in 2007. This updated version allows the user to adjust the height of the mechanism to accommodate larger cups or mugs, has an indicator light function which shows when there is insufficient water for two cups (as opposed to the previous model which only showed whether there was sufficient water left for one cup), features a larger water reservoir and has an option which allows the user to adjust the amount of hot water used per cup.

Competition is emerging

Following the success of Senseo, other branded manufacturers and the leading discounters copied Douwe Egberts's coffee pods and introduced their own for Senseo machines. The pod machines were also copied.

The battle among coffee makers for at-home use intensified in 2005. As a result of the growing competition from me-too products, Douwe Egberts started to seek legal protection for its coffee pods and it tried to prohibit the distribution of the me-too coffee pods. However, in 2006, the European patent covering the Senseo pods was completely revoked on appeal by the European Patent Office. Following the success of Senseo, the leading coffee companies jumped on the bandwagon and introduced not only their own coffee pods but also a similar system based on capsules. In 2005, Tchibo introduced a machine and capsules under Cafissimo, Kraft Foods/Braun introduced Tassimo and, in September 2006, Nestlé and the machine manufacturer Krups introduced Dolce Gusto to Germany.

Unlike the Nespresso system, which has been on the market for over ten years and is positioned as a top-end premium product, Dolce Gusto is a mass product and, like most products by Nestlé, it offers extra amounts of milk foam. All of these new systems are 'closed' systems, which means, for example, that consumers can only use capsules manufactured by Tchibo together with the 'Cafissimo' machine. However, most of the leading brands continue to offer coffee pods that can be used in the Senseo and similar machines.

The only temporary loser in this game was Melitta Unternehmensgruppe Bentz KG, which introduced the 'MyCup' coffee pod system in autumn 2004, as its differently shaped pods were not compatible with the coffee machines of other manufacturers. Consumers refused to buy these coffee pods and Melitta temporarily withdrew its coffee pod system. It launched universal coffee pods in the beginning of 2007 but also kept the differently shaped 'MyCup' pods in its range. At the same time, Melitta launched another product: empty pod sachets that can be filled with coffee chosen by the consumer, significantly reducing the cost per cup. However, as these sachets are awkward to handle, it is uncertain if they will catch on with consumers.

Private labelling – for example in Germany

In Europe, private label plays an ever increasing role in coffee pods, especially in Germany. Here the private labels accounted for over a 45 per cent share of retail volume sales in 2008, as many German consumers remain extremely price conscious. In the traditional fresh ground coffee category, private label accounted for a 33 per cent share of retail volume sales in 2008.

The discounter Aldi continues to play a major role in private label in all coffee categories. In 2008, Aldi led in coffee pods (25 per cent share of retail volume sales) and whole coffee beans (18 per cent retail volume share). Only in traditional fresh grounded coffee are the giant branded player Kraft Foods and Tchibo ahead of Aldi in terms of retail volume shares.

The continued success of Aldi is not simply due to low prices. In 2006, Aldi's fresh ground coffee and coffee pods were rated as 'very good' by the leading consumer magazine, *Stiftung Warentest*. In fact, Aldi's coffee pods came out on top, ahead of more premium and more expensive branded products. Quality is very important to German consumers, who are prepared to search for tasty products at low prices.

QUESTIONS

1. What are the key success factors in this industry?

2. Explain how the competences represented in the Senseo concept can create international competitiveness.

3. Which threats is Senseo facing in the future sales of its product concept?

4. Which new markets are relevant for Senseo to enter?

Sources: Senseo (www.senseo.com); Philips (www.philips.com); Euromonitor International (www.euromonitor.com); Nipcow, J. and Bush, E. (2008) Coffee Machines: recommendations for policy design, 7 August, Topten International Group Report (www.topten.info).

VIDEO CASE STUDY 4.3 Nike

download from www.pearsoned.co.uk/hollensen

Nike (www.nike.com) is the largest seller of athletic footwear and athletic apparel in the world. Nike's strategy for growth around the globe is to develop greater reach into diverse market segments. The three main segments are (1) performance athletes, (2) participant athletes, and (3) those that influence the world and the culture of sport. Partnerships are formed with athletes not just because of their status, but also because they are integral in the product development process. For example, to increase market share in Europe, Nike needed to produce a strong soccer product, which it did with the help of star soccer players.

Questions

1. Discuss how Nike's growth can be attributed to its targeting of diverse market global segments.

2. How did Nike penetrate the European soccer footwear market?

3. What are the key driving forces behind Nike's international competitiveness?

For further exercises and cases, see this book's website at **www.pearsoned.co.uk/hollensen**

Questions for discussion

1. How can analysis of national competitiveness explain the competitive advantage of the single firm?

2. Identify the major dimensions used to analyse a competitor's strengths and weaknesses profile. Do local, regional and global competitors need to be analysed separately?

3. How can a country with high labour costs improve its national competitiveness?

4. As the global marketing manager for Coca-Cola, how would you monitor reactions around the world to a major competitor such as Pepsi?

References

Anderson, J.C., Kumar, N. and Narus, J.A. (2007) 'Value merchants', *Marketing Management*, March/April, pp. 31–35.

Anderson, J.C., Kumar, N. and Narus, J.A. (2008) 'Certified value sellers', *Business Strategy Review*, Spring, pp. 48–53.

Booms, B.H. and Bitner, M.J. (1981) 'Marketing strategies and organization structures for service firms', in Donnelly, J.H. and George, W.R. (eds), *Marketing of Services*, American Marketing Association, Chicago, IL.

Brandenburger, A.M. and B.J. Nalebuff (1996) *Co-operation and Co-ompetition*, Doubleday, New York.

Burton, J. (1995) 'Composite strategy: the combination of collaboration and competition', *Journal of General Management*, 21(1), pp. 1–23.

Cardy, R.L. and Selvarajan, T.T. (2006) 'Competencies: alternative frameworks for competitive advantage', *Business Horizons*, 49, pp. 235–245.

Day, G.S. and Wensley, R. (1988) 'Assessing advantage: a framework for diagnosing competitive super-iority', *Journal of Marketing*, 52(2), pp. 1–20.

D'Aveni, R.A. (2007) 'Mapping your competitive position', *Harvard Business Review*, November, pp. 111–120.

Grönroos, C. (2009) 'Marketing as promise management: regaining customer management for marketing', *Journal of Business & Industrial Marketing*, 24(5/6), pp. 351–359.

Hollensen, S. (2010) *Marketing Management – A Relationship Approach*, 2nd edn. Pearson Education, Harlow.

Holmberg, S.R. and Cummings, J.L. (2009) 'Building successful strategic alliances', *Long Range Planning*, 42, pp. 164–193.

Jüttner, U. and Wehrli, H.P. (1994) 'Competitive advantage: merging marketing and the competence-based perspective', *Journal of Business and Industrial Marketing*, 9(4), pp. 42–53.

Kanter, R.M. (1994) 'Collaborative advantage: the art of alliances', *Harvard Business Review*, July–August, pp. 96–108.

Karnani, A. (2007) 'The mirage of marketing to the bottom of the pyramid: how the private sector can help alleviate poverty', *California Management Review*, 49(4), pp. 90–111.

Kedia, B.L., Nordtvedt, R. and Perez, L.M. (2002) 'International business strategies, decision-making theories, and leadership styles: an integrated framework', *CR*, 12(1), pp. 38–52.

Kim, W.C. and Mauborgne, R. (1997) 'Value innovation: the strategic logic of high growth', *Harvard Business Review*, 75(1), pp. 102–112.

Kim, W.C. and Mauborgne, R. (2005a) *Blue Ocean Strategy: How to Create Market Space and Make the Competition Irrelevant*. Harvard Business School Publishing Corporation, Boston, MA.

Kim, W.C. and Mauborgne, R. (2005b) 'Value innovation: a leap into the blue ocean', *Journal of Business Strategy*, 26(4), pp. 22–28.

Kim, W.C. and Mauborgne, R. (2005c) 'Blue ocean strategy – from theory to practice', *California Review*, 47(3), pp. 105–121.

Kotler, P. (1997) *Marketing Management: Analysis, Planning, Implementation, and Control*, 9th edn. Prentice-Hall, Englewood Cliffs, NJ.

Levitt, T. (1960) 'Marketing myopia', *Harvard Business Review*, July–August, pp. 45–56.

Lorenzoni, G. and Ferriani, S. (2008) 'Searching for new units of analysis: firms, dyads and networks', *European Management Review*, 5(2), pp. 125–133.

Magrath, A.J. (1986) 'When marketing service's 4 Ps are not enough', *Business Horizons*, May–June, pp. 44–50.

McGrath, R.G. and Keil, T. (2007) 'The value captor's process – getting the most out of your new business ventures', *Harvard Business Review*, May, pp. 128–136.

Michel, S., Brown, S.W. and Gallan, A.S. (2008) 'Service-logic innovations: how to innovate customers, not products', *California Management Review*, 50(3) pp. 49–65.

Nair, A., Ahlstrom, D. and Filer, L. (2007) 'Localized advantage in a global economy: the case of Bangalore', *Thunderbird International Business Review*, 49(5), September–October, pp. 591–618.

Neves, M.F. (2007) 'Strategic marketing plans and collaborative networks', *Marketing Intelligence & Planning*, 25(2), pp. 175–192.

Porter, M.E. (1980) *Competitive Strategy*. The Free Press, New York.

Porter, M.E. (1985) *Competitive Advantage: Creating and Sustaining Superior Performance*. The Free Press, New York.

Porter, M.E. (1990) *The Competitive Advantage of Nations*. The Free Press, New York.

Porter, M.E. (1996) 'What is strategy?', *Harvard Business Review*, November–December, pp. 61–78.

Porter, M.E. (2008) 'The competitive forces that shape strategy', *Harvard Business Review*, January, pp. 78–93.

Porter, M.E. and Kramer, M.R. (2006) 'Strategy and society: the link between competitive advantage and corporate social responsibility', *Harvard Business Review*, 84(12), pp. 56–68.

Rafiq, M. and Ahmed, P.K. (1995) 'Using the 7Ps as a generic marketing mix', *Marketing Intelligence and Planning*, 13(9), pp. 4–15.

Ravald, A. and Grönroos, C. (1996) 'The value concept and relationship marketing', *European Journal of Marketing*, 30(2), pp. 19–30.

Reve, T. (1990) 'The firm as a nexus of internal and external contracts', in Aoki, M., Gustafsson, M. and Williamson, O.E. (eds), *The Firm as a Nexus of Treaties*. Sage, London.

Sheehan, N.T. and Vaidyanathan, G. (2009) 'Using a value creation compass to discover "Blue Oceans"', *Strategy & Leadership*, 37(2), pp. 13–20.

Smith, G.E. and Nagle, T.T. (2005) A Question of Value, *Marketing Management*, July/August, pp. 38–43.

Tampoe, M. (1994) 'Exploiting the core competences of your organization', *Long Range Planning*, 27(4), pp. 66–77.

Teng, B.-S. (2003) 'Collaborative advantage of strategic alliances: value creation in the value net', *Journal of General Management*, 29(2), pp. 1–22.

Veliyath, R. and Zahra, S.A. (2000) 'Competitiveness in the 21st century: reflections on the growing debate about globalization', *ACR*, 8(1), pp. 14–33.

Weber, M. (2008) 'The business case for corporate social responsibility: a company-level measurement approach for CSR', *European Management Journal*, 26, pp. 247–261.

CASE STUDY I.1

Zara: a Spanish retailer goes to the top of world fashion

Zara (www.inditex.com) is a fashion retail chain of Inditex Group owned by the Spanish businessman, Amancio Ortega, who also owns brands such as Massimo Dutti, Pull and Bear, Oysho, Uterqüe, Stradivarius and Bershka. The Inditex group (which Zara belongs to) is headquartered in La Coruña, North West Spain, where the first Zara store opened in 1975. It is claimed that Zara needs just two weeks to develop a new product and get it to stores, compared with a two-month industry average. Zara has resisted the industry-wide trend towards outsourcing fast fashion production to low-cost countries. Its most unusual strategy is its policy of zero advertising; the company prefers to invest a percentage of revenues in opening new stores instead.

Main shareholder of Inditex, Amancio Ortega
Copyright © Inditex.

Zara's business model

Zara is a vertically integrated retailer. Unlike similar apparel retailers, Zara controls most of the steps on the supply chain: it designs, produces and distributes itself.

Zara is a fashion imitator and focuses its attention on understanding the current fashion trend, which is what customers want, and then delivering it, rather than promoting predicted season's trends via fashion shows and similar channels of influence, which the fashion industry traditionally used.

Of the products Zara sells 50 per cent are manufactured in Spain, 26 per cent in the rest of Europe and 24 per cent in Asian and African countries and the rest of the world. So while some competitors (e.g. Gap, Inc.) outsource all production to Asia, Zara makes its most fashionable items – half of all its merchandise – at a dozen company-owned factories in Spain and Portugal, particularly in Galicia and northern Portugal where labour is cheaper than most of western Europe. Clothes with a longer shelf life, such as basic T-shirts, are outsourced to low-cost suppliers, mainly in Asia and Turkey.

The store acts as a point of sale and also influences the design and speed of production. It is the end and starting point of the business system. Zara's business cycle starts with customers' judgements on the new designs of clothes and the information collected by staff members who travel to fashion cities, observing people on the streets, browsing publications and visiting the venues that are frequented by their potential customers.

What distinguishes Zara from its competitors is the feedback that Zara's managers get from the customers at the point of sale in the stores about new clothing that they are interested in. Store managers report the demands of customers and the sales trends to the headquarters on a daily basis. The design group (over 300 designers for Inditex – 200 for Zara alone) will use the feedback to create new articles or modifications to the existing goods and then deliver the items to the stores. All stores receive goods twice a week and each shipment contains new products. These frequent shipments also avoid large inventories. In the stores around 60 per cent of Zara products are permanent and the remaining 40 per cent vary continually.

Zara can offer considerably more products than similar companies. It launches about 30,000 model items annually compared with 10,000 items for its key competitors. The company can design a new product and have finished goods in its stores in four to five weeks; it can modify existing items in as little as two weeks. Shortening the product life cycle means greater success in meeting consumer preferences. If a design doesn't sell well within a week it is withdrawn from shops, further orders are cancelled and a new design is pursued. No design stays on the shop floor for more than four weeks, which encourages Zara fans to make repeat visits. An average high-street store in Spain

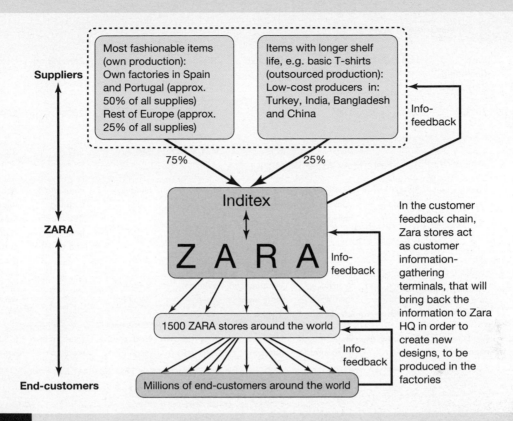

Figure 1	Zara's business model

expects customers to visit 3 times a year, but that figure will be up to 17 times for Zara.

Zara's core competence lies in the ability to recognize and assimilate the continuous changes in fashion, rapidly designing new models that respond to customer needs and wants. Zara uses its flexible business model to adapt to changes occurring during a season, reacting to them by bringing new products to the stores in a short time. For Zara the keys to global competitiveness are the time factor and the ability to adapt the offer precisely and quickly to the customer desires. The logistics system, based on software designed by the company's own teams, means that the time between receiving an order at the distribution centres (in Spain only) to the delivery of the goods in the store is on average 24 hours for European stores and a maximum of 48 hours for American or Asian stores.

Zara's (Inditex's) store brand portfolio

Over the past 30 years, Inditex has built a portfolio of brands (see Table 1 for details) through brand acquisition – Massimo Dutti in 1991 and Stradivarius in 1999 – and brand development by using a multi-brand strategy and an extension strategy. In line with the multi-brand development strategy, Zara was created in 1975, Pull & Bear in 1991, Bershka in 1998 and Oysho in 2001 and Uterqüe in 2008. The extension strategy was applied to Zara Home. Inditex used the name of the existing Zara brand to take advantage of the transfer of associations between the parent brand and the extended one, Zara Home.

Zara store in Moscow, Russia

| Table 1 | Inditex's brand store portfolio |

	Zara (including Zara Kids)	Pull & Bear	Massimo Dutti	Bershka	Stradivarius	Oysho	Zara Home	Uterqüe
Year of foundation	1975	1991	1991	1998	1999	2001	2003	2008
Number of stores	1,314 + 230 = 1,544	593	481	609	471	381	247	33
Product	Fast fashion clothing	Casual clothes	Quality and conventional fashion	Avant-garde clothing	Trendy clothing	Lingerie	Household clothing (textiles for bed, bath and table)	Accessories (handbags, footwear, leather goods and costume jewellery)
Target end customer	Women, men and children, ages 0–45	Women, and men, ages 13–23	Women, and men, ages 25–45	Women, and men, ages 13–23	Women, ages 15–25	Youths (Women)	–	Mainly women, ages 15–45
Price/quality	Medium-low/ medium	Medium-low/ medium	Medium-high/ medium-high	Medium-low/ medium	Medium-low/ medium	Medium-low/ medium	Medium-low/ medium	Medium-high/ high

Source: based on Lopez and Fan (2009).

- Zara is the flagship chain (66 per cent of total Inditex turnover). It encompasses many different styles, from daily clothes, more informal, to the more serious or formal, through dresses and suits for festival events. Fashion for women, men and children.
- Pull and Bear focuses on youth fashion, with a very urban style. Aimed primarily at teens and pre-teens, both for girls and boys.
- Massimo Dutti highlights are designs that are more elegant, classic and studied, for daily and formal clothes. It is more expensive than the rest of stores of the group. Fashion for women, men and, recently, for children.
- Bershka began distributing fashion for girls, and, more recently, for boys too. It also has a youthful style, although not as urban as Pull & Bear.
- Stradivarius aimed at the young woman. A mix between Pull & Bear and Bershka, but more similar to the last.
- Oysho lingerie and women's underwear (but also includes pyjamas, accessories, bathing suits in the summer and more) also includes collections for little girls and babies.
- Zara Home interiors, utensils for household furnishings, accessories, kitchenware, Zara Home Kids (for children).
- Uterqüe the latest addition to Inditex. Accessories including shoes, handbags, jewellery, sunglasses.

Intends to present a sober image, inspired by the English clubs, but at the same time clear and modern. More costly than the group's other brands, except Massimo Dutti, it still aims to be price competitive with the big brands in the market.

All these brands were built within the domestic market and then launched for international markets. This multi-brand portfolio has allowed Inditex to target different segments more effectively. However, the cost of maintaining several brands and the risk of cannibalization are the major drawbacks of this strategy. Inditex tries to tackle cannibalization by differentiating the brands mainly through the product, target markets (customer groups and countries), store presentation and retail image.

Zara has attractive pricing with an average selling price €15–20. The company's market share is below 1 per cent of the general clothing market in most countries.

Human Resource policy and training

At the beginning of 2009 Zara (Inditex) had 89,000 employees. During 2008, 573 establishments were opened around the world, including five new markets (Ukraine, South Korea, Montenegro, Honduras and Egypt) and a new commercial format, Uterqüe, was created which represents a challenge in the selection, training and internal promotion of employees to occupy new management responsibilities.

The stores continue to be the main motor of employment in the company, representing 89 per cent of the total number of employees in the Group. The fact that Inditex's particular business model is designed at constantly adapting to customers' needs means that management considers training and internal promotion of its professionals as key elements of its activity.

Training of the staff is also a huge investment each year. The internal training plans are adapted to the needs of the Group professionals according to their activity and are of a diverse nature:

- entry training for new employees
- management and administration of teams
- languages
- information systems
- new technologies
- individual training plans
- store management systems
- presentation of collections
- training in products, raw materials and CSR.

In the linguistic sphere, the Spanish and English language are priorities. The materials taught on each course vary according to the nature of the activity of each professional and the specific vocabulary required.

Competition

Zara's major global competitors in terms of market share are Gap Inc. and H&M. The following presents some information of the two companies (see also Table 2 for a direct comparison of these three global competitors).

Gap Inc.

Gap, Inc. is an American clothing and accessories retailer based in San Francisco, California, and founded in 1969 by Donald Fisher and Doris F. Fisher. The company has five primary brands: the namesake Gap banner, Banana Republic, Old Navy, Piperlime and Athleta. As of September 2008, Gap Inc. has approximately 150,000 employees and over 3,100 stores worldwide. Gap Inc. remains the largest speciality apparel retailer in the US, though it has recently been surpassed by the Spanish-based Inditex Group as the world's largest apparel retailer. Despite its publicly-traded status, the founding Fisher family remains deeply involved in Gap Inc.'s business. Donald Fisher served as Chairman of the Board until 2004; when he stepped down, he was succeeded by his son, Robert J. Fisher.

H&M

The company was established in Västerås, Sweden, in 1947 by Erling Persson though at the time it only sold women's clothing and was called Hennes, Swedish for 'hers'. In 1968, Persson acquired the premises and inventory of a Stockholm hunting equipment store named Mauritz Widforss. Included in the inventory was a supply of men's clothing, prompting Persson to expand into menswear. Accordingly, he renamed the store Hennes & Mauritz, later abbreviated to H&M.

Today the majority of H&M's clothing is outsourced and manufactured in Turkey and Bangladesh.

H&M describes its mission as 'Fashion and quality at the best price'. H&M's goals for 2008 have been to intensify the sales in the existing stores, as well as to increase the number of new stores by 10 to 15 per cent per year. In 2008 129 new stores opened their doors and 9 closed. Expansion and maintaining of financial stability are H&M's strategic goals. In the last five years revenues (excluding VAT) increased by 65 per cent, and the operating profits increased by 88 per cent. Today H&M is not the largest, but the most profitable in the world – see Table 2.

H&M has an extensive network throughout much of Europe but its main markets are in northern Europe. The biggest markets are Germany, UK and Sweden. H&M opened its first US store in New York (Manhattan) in March 2000. As of January 2009, H&M has at least 169 individual stores in the United States and their first store was opened in mainland China in 2007.

Internationalization strategy

Zara opened its first store in 1975 in La Coruña, northwest Spain. During the 1980s, Zara focused on and expanded within the domestic market, opening stores in all Spanish cities with a population greater than 100,000 inhabitants. The maturity of the Spanish market led Zara to search for international opportunities in 1988. Portugal was an attractive and familiar market due to its geographical and cultural proximity to Spain and international expansion of Zara started with the opening of a store in Oporto. Through establishment in Portugal Zara acquired international market experience and knowledge and realized that it would have to adjust its business model to suit the new international markets.

During the next stages of internationalization Zara expanded into international markets with a minimum level of psychic (cultural) distance from Spain, adding one or two countries per year to its market portfolio. In 1990 Zara started operating in France (Paris) a geographically contiguous country, a fashion capital and a starting point for the later expansion in northern Europe.

Table 2	The three main global competitors in fashion retailing (end of 2008)		
2008 – figures	**Inditex-Zara (Spain)**	**Gap, Inc. (United States)**	**H&M (Sweden)**
Net sales (million €)	10,410	10,150	8,680
Net profits (million €)	1,250	677	1,500
Growth in sales (%) compared to 2007	+9%	−10%	+13%
% International sales (outside home country)	Inditex 66% Zara 70%	19%	93%
Number of employees	90,000	150,000	53,500
Number of stores and Global reach	Inditex 4,359 stores in 73 countries Zara 1,520 stores in 72 countries	3,100 stores in 24 countries	1,740 stores in 34 countries
Business model and production	High degree of vertical integration – mainly own production facilities	Partial vertical integration – control over design, distribution and sales – production is outsourced	Partial vertical integration – control over design, distribution and sales – production is outsourced
Promotion and advertising	Only 0.3 per cent of turnover. The store is the main promotional tool	3–3.5 per cent of turnover spent on advertising	4 per cent of turnover spent on advertising
Brand portfolio	8 brand stores: Zara, Pull and Bear, Massimo Dutti, Bershka, Stradivarius, Oysho, Zara Home and Uterqüe	5 brand stores: Gap, Banana Republic, Old Navy, Piperlime and Athleta	1 brand store: single format

Mexico was added in 1992. This market, though geographically distant, is culturally (language etc.) close to the home country Spain, and provided reference to the later expansion to the South American market. The experience gained in the international environment made Zara more determined and intent on a rapid global expansion, regardless of cultural or geographical proximity. They began this stage by opening a store in Israel in 1997. One year later, 1998, Zara entered eight countries, consolidating its presence in the Middle East with Kuwait, Lebanon and the United Arab Emirates. Between 2000 and 2003 Zara consolidated its position in the European market as opposed to gaining a foothold in new countries (the enlargement of the European Union in 2004 justifies the considerable number of European countries that were incorporated that year). Between 2003 and 2009 a lot of new store openings were made in new countries, and Zara (Inditex) now has over 4,000 in 73 countries (September 2009).

At the early stages of internationalization, the management at Zara was following an ethnocentric orientation whereby the stores in foreign countries had to be a replication of the Spanish stores. However, this approach encountered unexpected difficulties in some countries due to cultural differences. Therefore, Zara decided to move towards a geocentric orientation, allowing some stores abroad to adopt local solutions rather than merely replicate the home market. The company sells a largely homogeneous product for a global market, but some adjustments have to be made to its product offerings, for example as a consequence of customers' size differences in Asian and European countries.

Once the entry decision is made for a particular country, Zara follows a pattern of expansion strategy known as 'oil stain' (dominate strongly in one place, then spread across the surface of the country, like an oil stain on water). Zara opens its first store, the so-called flagship store, in a strategic area with the purpose of getting information about the market and acquiring expertise. The experience guides Zara in the later phases of expansion in that country.

Entry mode strategy

Over time Zara has mainly used the hierarchical and intermediate mode.

Hierarchical modes

Zara has adopted the hierarchical modes (direct investment) in most European and southern European countries, resulting in full ownership of the stores. Those markets where the hierarchical model is used are characterized by high growth potential and relatively low sociocultural distance (low country risk) between Spain and target market.

The intermediate modes (joint venture and franchising) are mainly used in countries where the sociocultural distance is high.

Joint ventures

This is a co-operative strategy in which facilities and know-how of the local company are combined with the international fashion expertise of Zara. This mode is especially used in large, competitive markets where it is difficult to acquire property to set up retail outlets or where there are other kinds of obstacles that require co-operation with a local company. For example, in 1999 Zara entered into a 50-50 joint venture with the German firm Otto Versand, which had experience in the distribution sector and market knowledge in one of Europe's largest markets, Germany. Zara also has entered a joint venture in Japan.

Recently, Zara (Inditex) and the Tata Group have signed an agreement to form a joint venture to develop Zara stores in India. Zara will control 51 per cent of the venture, while Trent Limited, a Tata Group company, will control the remaining 49 per cent. The partnership plans to open its first stores starting in 2010 in New Delhi, Mumbai and other major cities of India.

Tata is one of the largest conglomerates in India, with a corporate history dating back more than 140 years and operations spanning seven industries: information systems and communications, engineering, materials, services, energy, consumer products and chemicals. In many of these industries, Tata Group companies are among the largest in the world. The group estimates that its 2007/2008 revenues totalled US$62.5 billion. Tata employs more than 350,000 people worldwide.

Zara views their entry into the Indian market as one of significant strategic importance. India is one of the most important countries in the world by GDP, growing by around 9 per cent p.a. in the last four years and is also the second most populated country, with a population of more than 1.1 billion. Ten areas have a population of more than three million, e.g., Mumbai, Delhi, Bangalore or Kolkata.

Franchising

Zara is choosing this mode for high-risk countries which are socioculturally distant or have small markets with low sales forecasts like Kuwait, Andorra, Puerto Rico, Panama or the Philippines. At beginning of 2009, there were 543 franchised stores, out of a total of 4,000 stores (Inditex).

Zara's franchisees follow the same business model as its own stores regarding the product, store location, interior design, logistic and human resources strategy. However, franchisees are responsible for investing in fixed assets and recruiting the staff. Zara gives franchisees the opportunity of exclusivity in their geographic area, although Zara has the right to open its own stores in the same location after a fixed number of years.

QUESTIONS

1. Which theory is the best representative of Zara's (Inditex's) internationalization?

2. Please evaluate the competitive strategy of the three world market leaders. Which of the three will be the future winner of global retailing in the fashion world?

3. What are the advantages and disadvantages of Zara's (Inditex's) multi-brand store strategy?

4. How successful do you think Zara has been by meeting the 'risk of cannibalization' as a consequence of the multi-brand strategy?

5. What are the advantages and disadvantages of going into a joint venture with Tata in India?

Sources: Lopez, C. and Fan, Y. (2009) 'Case study: Internationalisation of the Spanish fashion brand Zara', *Journal of Fashion Marketing and Management*, 13(2), pp. 279–296; www.inditex.com; Zara press release: Inditex and Trent of the Tata Group agree to open stores in India beginning 2010, 5 February 2009, http://www.inditex.com/en/press/press_releases/extend/00000689; Datamonitor: www.datamonitor.com.

CASE STUDY I.2

Manchester United: still trying to establish a global brand

Manchester United (abbreviated as ManUtd, www.manutd.com) has developed into one of the most famous and financially successful football clubs in the world, being recognized in virtually every country, even those with little interest in the sport. Real Madrid has displaced ManUtd from the pole position in Deloitte's football money league. The list, which has been running for the last 9 years, identifies the top 20 clubs in terms of revenue.

The top five in 2008 were: Real Madrid with €365.8 million, Manchester United (€324.8 million), FC Barcelona (€308.8 million), Bayern Munich (€295.3 million) and Chelsea (€268.9 million) (Deloitte, 2009). Having won the Premier League and Champions League in 2007/08, United would have overtaken Real Madrid at the top of the Deloitte Football Money League had it not been for the depreciation of the pound. The top 20 clubs now generate more than three times the combined revenue of the clubs in the first Money League publication in 1996/97.

The most valuable US sport teams, the National Football League's Washington Redskins and baseball's New York Yankees, are both worth somewhat more but more than any US sports team, ManUtd has built a global brand.

Since the mass commercialization of football in 1992, Manchester United has unquestionably been the team to beat. In the past 16 seasons, it has collected 10 Premier League titles, four FA Cups and two Champion League trophies. Old Trafford regularly attracts more than 75,000 fans paying above and beyond £45 a ticket, 30 or so times a season.

The intangible assets of ManUtd

ManUtd has developed a huge fanbase. In 2009, its global fan base reached 100 million. Europe had 35 million, Asia (including Australia) had 50 million, Southern Africa had 8 million, and the Americas had 7 million. Expanding this base and developing life-long allegiances is critical to ManUtd's long-term growth, and providing international fans with a taste of the excitement at a game, through TV and Internet coverage, is key to maintaining and building the brand.

Manchester United Ltd.

Brand assets

ManUtd's brand assets includes (1) the physical aspects of logos, colours, names and facilities, and (2) the intangible aspects of reputation, image and perception. The official mascot of the team is the Red Devil. Although centrally featured in ManUtd's logo, the mascot doesn't play a prominent role in promotions. The team's nickname is the Reds, which seems logical enough, given the dominant colour of its home jerseys, but unfortunately, Liverpool, another top team in the Premier League, is also referred to as the Reds.

International brand evolution

For British fans of ManUtd, passions run deep. Although the brand is solidly entrenched in British soccer fans' psyches, it is in transition. ManUtd is no longer simply a British brand; it is a world brand. It boasts incredible number of fans in China. A survey of China's 12 largest markets shows that 42 per cent of fans are between 15 and 24, and that 26 per cent are between 25 and 34. The team is positioned to take advantage of China's growing middle class, with members who are anxious to enjoy the good life and associate themselves with successful Western brands. As an early entrant, ManUtd has the chance to establish itself as one of Asia's dominant brands (Olson *et al.*, 2006).

Although the absolute numbers are much smaller, the United States also represents fertile ground. Of course, international soccer must compete with established groups such as the Major League Baseball, National Football League, the National Basketball Association and the National Hockey League, but soccer has become a staple at schools across the country. A recent, unprompted awareness study of European soccer teams revealed that among North American fans, the most frequently mentioned team was ManUtd, at 10 per cent; Liverpool, Real Madrid and Barcelona each generated 3 per cent, and Arsenal generated 2 per cent. The study also showed that awareness of ManUtd is strongest in the north-eastern and western parts of the United States.

In order to be successful in foreign markets, ManUtd must generate memberships, sell kits and other merchandise, have access to media markets (including TV, Internet, mobile phones and publishing), set up soccer schools, form licensing agreements with strong local sponsors and embark on tours to create halo effects.

The challenge ManUtd faces is accomplishing this transition without destroying what made it distinctly British and highly successful. Today's team is composed of players from around the globe. (Although ManUtd still has British players, the Premier League is no longer dominated by them.) This raises another concern: strong teams employ strong players who become brands themselves. Most notable for ManUtd was the rise of David Beckham to the ranks of superstar, on the pitch and in the media, through his marriage to Victoria, previously one of the Spice Girls. ManUtd considered that Beckham's market value was greater than they could afford, so they sold him to Real Madrid one year before his contract expired. Now the brand building of ManUtd depends on new and upcoming stars such as Wayne Rooney, Cristiano Ronaldo and Rio Ferdinand. At the same time as they are ManUtd brand-builders, they are also able to build their own personal brand.

Brand challenges

ManUtd is in the enviable position of market leader during a time of dramatic media growth in the world's most popular game. However, leaders can stumble and the team is not immune to the sensitive nature of sports fans. To address this concern, ManUtd has developed a customer relationship management (CRM) database of more than 2.5 million fans. Many of these database members are game-day customers.

A substantial group of US ManUtd fans are not loyal. They climb on the bandwagon of the team when it has success, only to climb off the instant it stumbles. With the number of US soccer players holding steady at 18 million, the market is relatively small.

Chinese fans don't possess the same level of experience with professional teams as US fans and might not be as fickle. Nevertheless, cultural and physical barriers exist between British and Chinese fans. To develop deeper loyalties in Chinese markets, ManUtd established a Mandarin website, started a soccer school in Hong Kong, and is constantly planning Asian tours while looking to add Asian players to the roster. Although these are sound moves to build brand loyalty, well-funded competitors such as Chelsea or Liverpool can copy ManUtd.

Even in England, ManUtd faces significant challenges. Especially after the Glazer invasion (see below) it generates a love-them-or-hate-them mentality. Fans of opposing teams were thrilled to see Chelsea, Arsenal and Liverpool secure the three major championships – leaving ManUtd without a major trophy in the last two years.

Then Glazer came . . .

In the late 1990s and early part of the 2000s, an increasing source of concern for many United supporters was the possibility of the club being taken over. The supporters' group IMUSA (Independent Manchester United Supporters' Association) were extremely active in opposing a proposed takeover by Rupert Murdoch in 1998. However, they could do nothing in May 2005 when the US sports tycoon Malcolm Glazer (who also owns the American Football team Tampa Bay Buccaneers) paid $1.4 billion for a 98 per cent stake in ManUtd, following a nearly year-long takeover battle. So is the ManUtd brand worth $1.5 billion? Glazer seemed to think so, as he paid roughly $200 million more than the team's open-market stock valuation.

It was a hostile takeover which plunged the club into massive debt as his bid was heavily funded by borrowing on the assets owned already by ManUtd, and the takeover was fiercely opposed by many fans of the club. Many supporters were outraged and some formed a new club called F.C. United of Manchester.

After the takeover the Glazer family (Malcolm Glazer and his three sons) took big steps to shore up the club's finances. They cut more than 20 staff members, including some executives. They also raised ticket prices and were lending 23 players to other clubs, saving ManUtd more than $20 million in fees and salaries. In general, they have been cutting expenses everywhere they can.

ManUtd in recent seasons

Both 2007–08 and 2008–09 were very successful for Manchester United.

In 2007–08 they won both Premier League and the Champions League.

The 2008–09 season was Manchester United's seventeenth in the Premier League, and their thirty-fourth consecutive season in the top division of English football. After winning a third consecutive Premier League title for the second time to equal Liverpool's record of 18 league titles, the team aimed to become the first team to retain the Champions League since Milan in 1990. However, they were beaten 2–0 by Barcelona in the final at the Stadio Olimpico in Rome on 27 May 2009.

In December 2008, the club became the first English side to win the FIFA Club World Cup when they beat LDU Quito (Ecuador) 1–0 in the final. Two months later, on 1 March 2009, the club added the 2008–09 League Cup to their trophy cabinet. United secured a third consecutive Premier League with a goalless draw at home to Arsenal on 16 May 2009. This made them the first team ever to win three consecutive English top titles on two separate occasions, having previously done so between 1999 and 2001.

Sponsorships

On 23 November 2005 Vodafone ended their £36 million, four-year shirt sponsorship deal with ManUtd. On 6 April 2006, ManUtd announced AIG (US-based financial services giant) as its new shirt sponsors for the team in a British record shirt sponsorship deal worth £56.5 million to be paid over four years (£14.1 million a year). The four-year agreement has been heralded as the largest sponsorship deal in British history, eclipsing Chelsea's deal with Samsung.

AIG's sponsorship with ManUtd runs through to May 2010 and AIG have no plans to renew it. In the wake of the global credit crunch in 2009, AIG needed a $150 billion bailout from the US government to avoid bankruptcy.

The 13-year deal with American sportswear manufacturer, Nike, assures the English club a guaranteed annual fee of about £23 million as well as a share of revenue over an agreed level.

Financial situation

The last two years for Manchester United Ltd look like this:

	2008	2007
Revenues (£m)	257	308
Profit after tax (£m)	66	60

The biggest cost element are the wages for the players: in 2008 they accounted for approximately £80 million. On the surface the financial figures look very good, but the financial figures from the Red Football Ltd (Manchester United Ltd's parent company = the owner), are somewhat surprising. Red Football Ltd recorded a pre-tax loss of £44.8m in 2008, while its debts increased from £604m to £649m. As a result, United needs to spend more than £70 million a year in financing costs, just to service the debt. Manchester United's debt is far more than any other club in the Premier League. Liverpool has about £350m and West Ham has about £230m.

Sources: Deloitte (2009) *Football Money League report*, 12 February; Kemp, E. (2009) Manchester United, *Marketing*, 29 April; Cohn, L. and Holmes, S. (2005) 'ManU gets kicked in the head – Again', *Business Week*, 12 December, pp. 34–35; *Accountancy* (2006) 'Manchester United loses top spot in Deloitte football league', March, 137(1351), p. 16; Olson, E.M., Slater, S.F., Cooper R.D. and Reddy V. (2006) 'Good sport: Manchester United is no longer just a British brand', *Marketing Management*, 15(1), pp. 14–16.

QUESTIONS

1. How do you evaluate the international competitiveness of ManUtd after the takeover by Malcolm Glazer?

2. Discuss and explain how the different alliances can increase the international competitiveness of ManUtd.

3. What are the main threats to retaining 'Manchester United' as a global brand?

It is a lovely spring morning in central Tokyo in 2010. Although the city is just awakening, with all its noise and stress, that does not bother the chairman of Bridgestone Corporation, Shoshi Arakawa, as he is on his way to work.

Some basic data about Bridgestone

Bridgestone Corporation (Bridgestone) is one of the world's largest manufacturers of tyres and other rubber products. The company is primarily engaged in the production of tyres and tubes for passenger cars, trucks and buses, construction and mining vehicles, industrial machinery, agricultural machinery, aircraft, motorcycles and scooters. The company has operations in Japan, the United States and Europe. It is headquartered in Tokyo, Japan and employs about 113,700 people.

The company reached revenues of $32 billion during the fiscal year ended December 2008, a decrease of 4.5 per cent over 2007. The operating profit of the company during the fiscal year 2008 was $1.3 billion, a decrease of 47 per cent over the 2007 fiscal year. As the tyres segment accounts for nearly 75 per cent of the company's total revenues, its strong market position in the tyre segment ensures a stable top line for the company.

The prospects look good. On his way into his office Shoshi Arakawa asks his assistant to give him a copy of the different manufacturers' 2008 market shares in the world market (see Table 1), plus Bridgestone's 2008 market shares in the most important tyre markets in the world. Arakawa has a meeting with the board of directors the next day, when they will discuss Bridgestone's strategies in Europe, Asia and North America.

As Table 1 demonstrates together with Goodyear and Michelin, Bridgestone is among the world's largest manufacturers of tyres. Bridgestone has a 20 per cent worldwide market share (see Table 2).

However, Bridgestone still has a comparatively low market share (10 per cent) and low brand awareness in Europe. The question for Shoshi Arakawa is How can Bridgestone increase its market share in Europe?

Welcome to Bridgestone, one of the world's largest manufacturers of tires and other rubber products.
Well known brands, including the Bridgestone and Firestone names, herald the company's strong presence in tire markets worldwide.
Bridgestone's diversified operations include business in automotive parts, industrial goods, chemical products and sporting goods.

Table 1	Market share for tyres in the world market, 2008
Manufacturer	**Market share (%)**
Michelin	20
Bridgestone	20
Goodyear	17
Continental	7
Pirelli	5
Sumitomo	4
Yokohama	3
Cooper	2
Toyo	2
Others	20

Table 2	Bridgestone's market share for tyres in the most important markets, 2008
Market area	**Bridgestone market share (%)**
Asia	29
Europe	10
US	22
World total	19

The following is a condensed report on the market conditions for tyres in Europe.

The European tyre market

The European market for car tyres (including commercial vehicles) has been fairly stable from 2000 to 2008. Competition among tyre producers is fierce and tyre prices in real terms have fallen over the past few years.

In 2008 the total western European market for tyres was 229.8 million. A breakdown of the total market is shown in Table 3. This table shows sales of new tyres for new cars (new sales) and replacements of worn tyres (replacement sales). Table 4 shows the total European tyre market broken down into countries, together with the market shares of the most important producers in the individual markets. On the basis of Table 4 the Boston Consulting Group (BCG) charts for the individual producers have been prepared (see Figure 1). Note that the areas of the circles show total sales in the respective countries and not the sales of the individual companies in the markets in question, which is normally the case in BCG charts.

Retreaded tyres

So far the markets have been described on the assumption that only the production and sale of new tyres was involved. For many years consumers have considered the retreaded tyre one of low price and low quality. In consequence, European consumers have been somewhat reluctant to buy retreaded tyres. Tyres can be recycled. The main problem is economic: recycling costs more than dumping, so many tyres end up in landfills or on illegal dumps, adding to those already polluting the landscape. Tyre dumps are potentially dangerous: they can catch fire and, when they do, toxic chemicals are released, leaving an oily residue that can contaminate groundwater.

Currently only about 15 per cent of the European Union's scrap tyres are retreaded and reused. The percentage has been decreasing over the last few years because new tyres are now so price competitive that many consumers prefer to buy them. However retreaded tyres are still recommended by the European Commission, primarily for two reasons:

1. Waste problems connected to the accumulation of used tyres have made retreaded tyres an environmentally correct recycling solution.

Table 3	The European tyre market, 2008		
Million units	Car tyres	Truck tyres	Total
New sales	65.4	9.3	74.7
Replacement sales	131.8	23.3	155.1
Total	**197.2**	**32.6**	**229.8**

Table 4	The tyre market in main European markets (cars and trucks), 2008						
	France	Germany	Italy	Spain	UK	Other markets	Total
Sales (million units)							
New sales	13.2	22.7	7.0	9.1	8.7	14.0	74.7
Replacement sales	24.2	36.7	15.8	8.9	22.0	47.5	155.1
Total	**37.4**	**59.4**	**22.8**	**18.0**	**30.7**	**61.5**	**229.8**
Producers' market shares (%)							
Michelin	55	24	31	44	30	–	32.0
Continental	4	26	8	7	13	–	14.4
Goodyear	7	16	11	4	16	–	11.3
Pirelli	5	6	23	13	11	–	10.4
SP (Dunlop)	10	10	4	4	14	–	8.9
Bridgestone/Firestone	7	5	8	18	7	–	10.0
Others	12	13	15	10	9	–	13.0
Total	**100**	**100**	**100**	**100**	**100**	**–**	**100.0**

Note: 'Other markets' include Eastern Europe and Scandinavia, for which market shares are not available.

Table 5	Sales of retreaded tyres in main European markets, 2008 (million units)				
	France	Germany	Italy	Spain	UK
Cars	2.30	3.50	2.70	0.03	4.80
Trucks	0.85	1.40	0.95	0.44	0.95
Total	3.15	4.90	3.65	0.47	5.75

Table 6	Producers' nationality and different brand names	
Producer	Nationality (ownership)	Brands
Michelin	France	Michelin, Kléber, Tyremaster
Continental	Germany	Continental, Uniroyal, Semperit, Barum, Viking, Gislaved, Mabor, Sava
Bridgestone/ Firestone	Japan	Bridgestone, Firestone, Dayton, Europa, First Stop
Pirelli	Italy	Pirelli, Curier
Goodyear	US	Goodyear, Dunlop, Kelly, Fulda
Others		Stomil, Tigar, Komho, Lassa, Marshal, Toyo

2. The use of retreaded tyres reduces consumption of natural rubber, natural minerals, metal wire, oil and other chemicals that are normally used in the production of new tyres.

In 2008 sales of retreaded tyres were distributed as shown in Table 5. The European Commission encourages and recommends the increased use of retreaded tyres (rising to approximately 20 per cent of total sales).

One threat against such a development is, however, that the price of new imported tyres from the Far East is sometimes lower than that of retreaded tyres.

Characteristics of the leading producers

Some market players such as Goodyear operate primarily in tyres. However, other companies, such as Bridgestone and Continental, operate in a diverse range of markets. Additionally, economic crisis and shrinking revenues of the competitive automotive industry environment are causing pricing pressures, which further intensify rivalry. Players are facing increasing pressure from automobile manufacturers to absorb more costs related to product design, engineering and tooling, as well as other items. Such pressures could reduce profit margins for the players. However, there are regions where demand for tyres is rising – i.e. Asia, and is partially driven by a shift to radial technology and strong economic growth in countries such as India and China. Overall, the degree of rivalry is strong.

In many western European countries the producers use several different brands to appeal to a larger clientele who have different preferences for different brands of tyres. A list of brand names is given in Table 6.

Europe's leading tyre suppliers may be briefly characterized as follows.

Michelin

Michelin is currently the largest tyre manufacturer in the world together with Bridgestone.

Compagnie Generale des Etablissements Michelin (Michelin) manufactures a wide range of tyres, publishes maps and guides and operates digital services such as wireless application protocol (WAP) and mobile Internet

services. The company has a presence in 170 countries worldwide. It is headquartered in France and employs about 113,000 people.

The company recorded revenues of US$24.7 billion during the fiscal year ended December 2008. The increase was primarily attributable to increased revenues from passenger car, light truck and truck segments. The net profit was $1,000 million during fiscal year 2008.

The French-based company organizes its operations into the following business units:

- passenger car and light truck tyres
- truck tyres
- earthmover tyres
- agricultural tyres
- aircraft tyres
- two-wheel tyres
- components (rubber and elastomers, reinforcement materials)
- suspension systems
- tourism services (maps, guidebooks).

In contrast to its traditional single-brand strategy Michelin now has a long list of associate brands such as BF Goodrich, Kléber, Riken, Kormoran, Taurus, Laurent, Wolber, Tyremaster, Siamtyre, and Uniroyal (North America only). The company produces 3,500 different types of tyre, which are made in 65 factories in 13 countries.

As part of the group's strategy to expand its share outside Europe, particularly in Asia and Latin America, Michelin has acquired MRF in the Philippines and the Colombian manufacturer Icollantas. In Europe, meanwhile, Michelin has announced plans to improve productivity by 20 per cent within three years. It expects to achieve

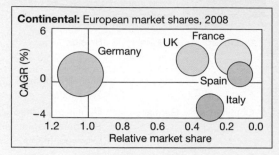

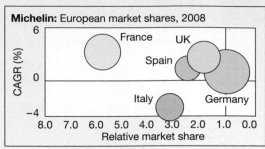

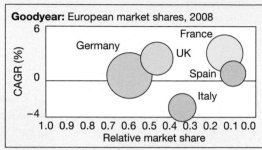

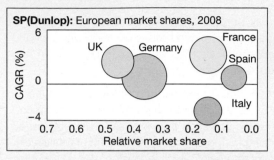

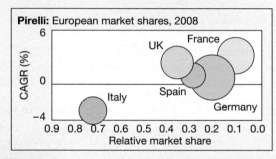

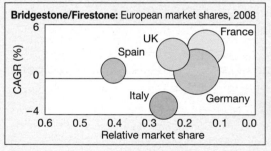

| **Figure 1** | BCG charts for leading tyre producers |

Notes:
CAGR = compound annual growth rate.
Relative market share = the market share of the individual producer in relation to the largest producer on the market.
Source: MarketLine.

this through developing its products, services and multibrand policy while restructuring all its European activities, possibly by closing plants or terminating technical activities and services.

In Europe Michelin is the clear market leader, with a market share of 32 per cent, well ahead of Continental and Goodyear. Michelin's largest market is North America, which takes about 45 per cent of its tyre production, followed by Europe with 40 per cent and Asia with 5 per cent.

In the 1990s Michelin registered huge financial losses which led to widespread rationalization: for example, staff numbers were reduced. Since then, there has been considerable fluctuation in Michelin's results.

Bridgestone/Firestone

Bridgestone was founded by Shojiro Ishibashi in 1931. (The English translation of the surname Ishibashi is 'stone bridge'.) Firestone was acquired by the Japanese-owned Bridgestone Corporation in 1988. Traditionally, Bridgestone has targeted the upper 'price-quality' segment, while Firestone appeals more to the 'mid-range' segment. Firestone has in particular contributed to strengthening the group's sales to car producers (new sales) in Europe (primarily Ford, Opel/Vauxhall, VW/Audi and Fiat).

Of the total turnover, around 25 per cent comes from non-tyre products, including conveyor belts, rubber crawlers, construction materials and vibration isolation parts (for vehicles). In Europe, Brussels-based Bridgestone/Firestone Europe SA oversees local production and R&D at the European facilities. There are five European tyre plants: one in France, one in Italy and three in Spain. Bridgestone's European sales subsidiaries are located in Austria, Benelux, Denmark, Finland, France, Germany, Italy, Poland, Portugal, Russia, Spain, Sweden, Switzerland and the United Kingdom.

Table 7	Brand awareness in the major European markets: spontaneous (unaided) awareness (%)					
Brand	UK	Germany	France	Italy	Spain	Total
Michelin	73	78	98	92	90	85
Pirelli	51	45	40	91	66	57
Goodyear	52	48	56	70	41	54
Dunlop	60	53	48	25	25	44
Firestone	32	25	40	37	69	38
Continental	12	65	15	26	20	31
Bridgestone	10	26	7	17	9	15
Population (million)	58	81	58	57	39	223

Source: compiled by the author from different sources.

However, brand awareness is still lower for Bridgestone than some of its competitors, as shown in Table 7 (the situation in 2008). As a consequence Bridgestone began supplying Bridgestone tyres to Formula One teams in 1996.

The company's status as tyre supplier to the Formula One World Championship is an important part of its promotional strategy and has helped increase awareness of the Bridgestone brand substantially in recent years, particularly in Europe.

Bridgestone users took five Drivers' championship titles and five Constructors' championship titles (1998, 2001–2004) for the period in competition with Goodyear (1997–1998) and Michelin (2001–2006). Cooperation with Scuderia Ferrari and Michael Schumacher worked particularly well in this period.

From 2008 to 2010 Bridgestone has been the sole tyre supplier to the FIA Formula One World Championship. Michelin chose to conclude its Formula One tyre programme at the end of the 2006 season, and since the start of the 2008 season all teams have used Bridgestone tyres.

Bridgestone is looking to increase its global market share to 25 per cent from 20 per cent and its European market share to around 15 per cent from its current 10 per cent. To achieve this the company admits that it needs to gain a much stronger presence in Europe and North America, even though its share in North America has been increasing during the last 15 years.

The company's main focus is on its Bridgestone and Firestone brands, although its multibrand approach to business extends to a range of budget and private brands such as Europa and First Stop in Europe or Dayton, Gillette and Peerless in North America.

Continental

Continental is Germany's largest manufacturer of tyres for commercial vehicles.

The company also manufactures power transmission systems, engine and suspension mounts, vehicle interiors and electronic brake and traction control systems. The company operates in the Americas, Europe, Asia and Africa. It is headquartered in Hanover, Germany and employs about 69,000 people. The company recorded revenues of $24 billion during the fiscal year ended December 2008. The net income was $1,000 million during fiscal year 2008.

Continental produces tyres for all forms of vehicles: cars, trucks, heavy vehicles, agricultural machinery, bicycles, motor cycles, etc. and bought the rights to use the Uniroyal brand all over Europe from Michelin.

Continental is the fourth-largest tyre manufacturer in the world as well as being a world leader in the braking segment following the 1998 acquisition of ITT's Brake and Chassis Division. The Group's operations are split into five different sectors:

1. the Passenger Tyre Group (controlling the controlled distribution chains)
2. the Commercial Vehicle Tyre Group
3. the Automotive Systems Group (includes Continental Teves)
4. Continental General Tyre (the group's US subsidiary)
5. ContiTech (industrial rubber products).

Continental was the first manufacturer to actively develop a multibrand strategy due to the uneven strength of its key brands across Europe. Today the company has eight main brands – Continental, Uniroyal (in Europe only), Semperit, General, Viking, Gislaved, Barum and Mabor. Part of its global strategy is to increase its strength in markets where it is underrepresented, considered by the company to be the United States, France, Italy, Spain and Asia.

Continental's main strategy is to develop a position as a complete systems supplier to the automotive industry. It has been developing wheel assembly facilities in conjunction with vehicle manufacturers worldwide for some time and the company's Automotive Systems Group has also focused on high-tech automotive developments.

Continental is very dependent on the German market, which accounts for 33 per cent of its worldwide sales.

Goodyear

The Goodyear Tyre and Rubber Company (Goodyear) develops, manufactures, distributes and sells tyres and rubber products. The company has operations across the world. It is headquartered in Ohio, USA and employs about 72,000 people; 20 per cent of them are working in Europe. The company recorded revenues of $20 billion in fiscal 2008. Net income reached $600 million in 2008.

Goodyear has 86 factories in 26 different countries. Some 55 per cent of the Group's sales relate to the US market, where Goodyear is the market leader. Besides tyres, the company makes several lines of belt, hose and other rubber products, rubber-related chemicals and owns retail stores worldwide. It is split into six business units:

1. Goodyear Asia
2. Goodyear European Union
3. Goodyear Latin America
4. North American Tire
5. Engineered and Chemical Products
6. Goodyear Eastern Europe, Africa and Middle East.

Its tyres are sold under various brand names besides Goodyear, including Dunlop, Kelly, Fulda, Lee, Sava, Pneumant, India and Debica.

The Group's main aims are to maintain its current status by holding a number one or number two position in specific markets, keeping up a fast and profitable growth in all core businesses and gaining strategic acquisitions and expansions while being the lowest cost producer of the top three companies.

The alliance with Sumitomo Rubber Industries/Dunlop was announced in January 1999 and covered the establishment of four joint venture sales companies, one in North America, two in Japan and one in Europe. Following this alliance, Sumitomo (owner of the Dunlop brand) gave effective control of its US and European operations to Goodyear.

Pirelli

The Italian Pirelli Group has Three main activities: tyres, cables and broadband networking, and employs 31,000 employees worldwide.

Pirelli is the sixth-largest tyre manufacturer in the world. The company has a presence in all areas of the tyre market but its particular strengths lie in the high-performance end of the passenger tyre market, where it can justifiably claim market leadership within Europe. The Pirelli brand is an out-and-out premium brand. However, the Group also owns a number of subsidiary brands including Courier, Ceat, Armstrong and the Metzeler brand of motorcycle tyres.

Within Europe Pirelli has key manufacturing plants in Italy, Germany, Spain and the United Kingdom.

Pirelli has the best market position in Italy, where it is second to Michelin, and tried in vain in 1992 to acquire its German competitor, Continental. In 2008 the turnover reached $6.6 billion with $60 million in net profits.

Innovation in the European tyre industry

The global tyres and rubber market benefits from significant scale economies. Tyres are usually mass-produced and mass-marketed, requiring significant capital outlay. Moreover, intellectual property is required, including a large number of patents, trademarks and copyrights. Large expenditure will be required for research, development and certain engineering activities relating to the design and development of products and services as well as to the formulation and design of manufacturing processes and equipment. Innovation is important to get customers' attention.

One example of such innovation is Pirelli's 2008 innovation: 'chipped' tyres. Sensors have been integrated into the tyres and implemented the TPMS (tyre pressure monitoring systems), but Pirelli has taken it a step further, putting a sensor package on the tyre carcass itself. One implementation of the 'Cyber Tyre', which harnesses power from the vibrations of the vehicle and beams information including tyre pressure, temperature, and load to the vehicle's computer. The high-tech rubber will be more sophisticated and capable of communicating directly with stability control and antilock brakes to improve the effectiveness of dynamic safety systems. Cyber Tyre will also carry a three-axis accelerometer that will facilitate real-time calculations of friction coefficients, contact force and load.

The distribution of tyres in Europe

The majority of replacement sales (replacement of tyres) take place through specialized tyre distributors:

- independent chains (tyre specialists)
- producer-owned chains (e.g. in Germany Continental owns the Vergös chain and Michelin owns the Euromaster chain)
- vehicle dealerships (the replacement tyres provided by these companies are more expensive and end users are often willing to pay more for the brand name of the vehicle manufacturer, e.g. Mercedes-Benz)
- franchise-based chains.

In addition, service stations, garages and auto-centres have a certain share of replacement sales. This share is highest in newly developed Eastern European markets, while it is decreasing in western Europe.

QUESTIONS

As a consultant for Chairman Shoshi Arakawa you are required to answer the following questions.

1. Make an assessment of the competitive strategies that Michelin, Continental and Goodyear respectively may pursue to strengthen their European market positions.

2. Make an assessment of the alternative competitive strategies that Bridgestone can pursue to strengthen its European market position (you can also include central and Eastern Europe).

3. Give a well-reasoned proposal for criteria to be used by Bridgestone when choosing a market (country) that requires a larger marketing effort (you can also include central and Eastern Europe).

4. Give a well-reasoned proposal for Bridgestone's distribution and communication strategies in a market chosen by you.

On a lovely spring morning in April 2007, while giving her kids some Cheerios, the CEO of Cereal Partners Worldwide S.A. (CPW), Carol Smith thinks about how CPW might expand international sales and/or capture further market shares in the saturated breakfast cereals market. Right now, CPW is the no. 2 in the world market for breakfast cereals, but it is a tough competition, primarily with the Kellogg Company, which is the world market leader.

Maybe there would be other ways of gaining new sales in this competitive market? Carol has just read the business best-seller *Blue Ocean Strategy* and she is fascinated by the thought of moving competition in the cereals breakfast market from the red to the blue ocean. The question is how?

Maybe it would be better just to take the head-on battle with Kellogg Company. After all, CPW has managed to beat Kellogg in several minor international markets (e.g. in the Middle and Far East).

The children have finished their Cheerios and it is time to drive them to the kindergarten in Lausanne, Switzerland where CPW has its HQ. Later that day, Carol has to present the long-term global strategy for CPW, so she hurries to her office, and starts preparing the presentation. One of her marketing managers has prepared a background report about CPW and its position in the world breakfast cereals market. The following shows some important parts of the report.

History of breakfast cereals

Ready-to-eat cereals first appeared during the late 1800s. According to one account, John Kellogg, a doctor who belonged to a vegetarian group, developed wheat and corn flakes to extend the group's dietary choices. John's brother, Will Kellogg, saw potential in the innovative grain products and initiated commercial production and marketing. Patients at a Battle Creek, Michigan, sanitarium were among Kellogg's first customers.

Another cereal producer with roots in the nineteenth century was the Quaker Oats Company. In 1873, the North Star Oatmeal Mill built an oatmeal plant in Cedar Rapids, Iowa. North Star reorganized with other enterprises and together they formed Quaker Oats in 1901.

The Washburn Crosby Company, a predecessor to General Mills, entered the market during the 1920s. The company's first ready-to-eat cereal, Wheaties, was introduced to the American public in 1924. According to General Mills, Wheaties was developed when a Minneapolis clinician spilled a mixture of gruel that he was making for his patients on a hot stove.

Cereal Partners Worldwide

Cereal Partners Worldwide (CPW) was formed in 1990 as a 50:50 joint venture between Nestlé and General Mills (see Figure 1), in order to produce and sell ready-to-eat breakfast cereals worldwide outside United States and Canada. CPW has a portfolio of over 50 brands, including Cheerios, Nesquik and Shedded Wheat.

General Mills

General Mills, a leading global manufacturer of consumer food products, operates in more than 30 global markets and exports to over 100 countries. It has 66 production facilities: 34 are located in the United States; 15 in the Asia/Pacific region; six in Canada; five in Europe; five in Latin America and Mexico; and one in South Africa. The company is headquartered in Minneapolis, Minnesota. In financial year 2009 the total net sales were US$15.9 of which 15 per cent came

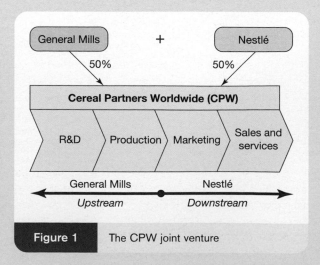

Figure 1 The CPW joint venture

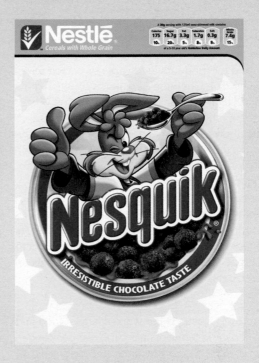

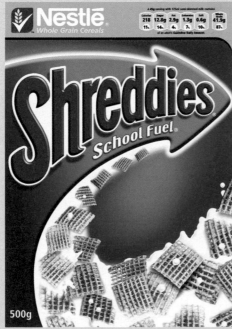

Société des Produits Nestlé SA. The Nestlé name and image is reproduced with kind permission of Société des Produits Nestlé SA.

from outside the United States. The company has 30,000 employees.

In October 2001 General Mills completed the largest acquisition in its history when it purchased the Pillsbury Company from Diageo. The US$10.4 billion deal almost doubled the size of the company, and consequently boosted General Mills' worldwide ranking, making it one of the world's largest food companies. However, the company is heavily debt-laden following its Pillsbury acquisition, which will continue to eat into operating and net profits for the next few years.

The company now has more than 100 US consumer brands, including Betty Crocker, Cheerios, Yoplait, Pillsbury Doughboy, Green Giant and Old El Paso.

Integral to the successes of General Mills has been its ability to build and sustain huge brand names and maintain continued net growth. Betty Crocker, originally a pen name invented in 1921 by an employee in the consumer response department, has become an umbrella brand for products as diverse as cookie mixes to ready meals. The Cheerios cereal brand, which grew rapidly in the US post-war generation, remains one of the top cereal brands worldwide.

However, heavy domestic dependence leaves the company vulnerable to variations in that market, such as supermarket price-cutting or sluggish sales in prominent product types such as breakfast cereals.

Internationally, General Mills uses its 50 per cent stake in Cereal Partners Worldwide (CPW) to sell its breakfast cereals outside North America. Cereal sales have faced tough competition recently leading to significant drops in sales, particularly tough competition from private labels.

Nestlé

Founded in 1866, Nestlé is the world's largest food and beverage company in terms of sales. The company began in the field of dairy-based products and diversified to food and beverages in the 1930s. Nestlé is headquartered in Vevey, Switzerland and the company has 500 factories in 83 countries. It has about 406 subsidiaries located across the world. The company employs 247,000 people around the world, of which 131,000 employees work in factories, the remainder work in administration and sales.

Nestlé's businesses are classified into six divisions based on product groups, which include beverages; milk products, nutrition and ice cream; prepared dishes and cooking aids; chocolate, confectionery and biscuits; pet care; and pharmaceutical products. Nestlé's global brands include Nescafé, Taster's Choice, Nestlé Pure Life, Perrier, Nestea, Nesquik, Milo, Carnation, Nido, Nestlé, Milkmaid, Sveltesse, Yoco, Mövenpick, Lactogen, Beba, Nestogen, Cerelac, Nestum, PowerBar, Pria, Nutren, Maggi, Buitoni, Toll House, Crunch, Kit-Kat, Polo, Chef, Purina, Alcon and L'Oréal (in which it has an equity stake).

Nestlé reported net sales of $110 billion for the fiscal year 2009.

CPW

CPW markets cereals in more than 130 countries, except for the United States and Canada, where the two companies market themselves separately. The joint venture was established in 1990 and the agreement also extends to the production of private label cereals in the UK. Volume growth for CPW was 4 per cent in 2005. The company's cereals are sold under the Nestlé brand, although many originated from General Mills.

Brand names manufactured (primarily by General Mills) under the Nestlé name under this agreement include Corn Flakes, Crunch, Fitness, Cheerios and Nesquik. Shredded Wheat and Shreddies were once made by Nabisco (before their acquisition by General Mills), but are now mamufactured by General Mills and marketed by CPW.

The CPW turnover in 2008 was a little less than US$3 billion. CPW has 14 factories and employs nearly 4,000 people all over the world.

When CPW was established in 1990 each partner was bringing distinctive competences into the joint venture.

General Mills

- proven cereal marketing expertise
- technical excellence in products and production processes (upstream competences)
- broad portfolio of successful brand.

Nestlé

- world's largest food company
- strong worldwide organization
- deep marketing and distribution knowledge (downstream competences).

CPW is number 2 in most international markets, but it is also market leader in some of the smaller breakfast cereal markets like China (70 per cent), Poland (60 per cent), Turkey (60 per cent), East/Central Europe (50 per cent) and South East Asia (50 per cent).

The world market for breakfast cereals

In the early 2000s breakfast cereal makers were facing stagnant, if not declining, sales. Gone are the days of the family breakfast, of which a bowl of cereal was standard fare. The fast-paced American lifestyle has more and more consumers eating breakfast on the go. Quick-serve restaurants like McDonald's, ready-to-eat breakfast bars, bagels and muffins offer consumers less labour-intensive alternatives to cereal. Although the value of product shipped by cereal manufacturers has grown in absolute figures, increased revenues came primarily from price hikes rather than market growth.

English-speaking nations represented the largest cereal markets. Consumption in non-English markets was estimated at only one-fourth the amount consumed by English speakers (see Table 1), where the breakfast cereal consumption per capita is 6 kg in the UK, but only 1.5 kg in south-west Europe (France, Spain and Portugal). On the European continent, consumption per capita averaged 1.5 kg per year.

Growth in the cereal industry has been slow to non-existent in this century. The question at hand for the industry is how to remake cereal's image in light of the new culture. Tinkering with flavourings and offerings, such as the recent trend toward the addition of dried fresh fruit, provides some relief, but with over 150 different choices on store shelves and 20 new offerings added annually, variety has done more to overwhelm than excite consumers. In addition, cereal companies are committing fewer dollars to their marketing budgets.

Table 1	Breakfast cereal consumption per capita per year – 2008
Region	**Per capita consumption per year (kg)**
Sweden	9.0
Canada	7.0
UK	6.0
Australia	6.0
USA	5.0
South-west Europe (France, Spain)	1.5
South East Asia	0.1
Russia	0.1
China	0.1

Table 2	World market for breakfast cereals by region – 2008	
Region	**Billion US$**	**%**
North America	10	45
Europe (west + east)	7	30
Rest of the World	6	25
Total	**23**	**100**

Development in geographical regions

As seen in Table 2, the United States is by far the largest breakfast cereals market in the world. In total North America accounts for 45 per cent of the global sales of $23 billion in 2008. The United States accounts for about 90 per cent of the North American market.

The European region accounts for 30 per cent of global sales, at $7 billion in 2005. By far the largest market is the UK, contributing nearly 40 per cent of the regional total, with France and Germany other key, if notably smaller, players. Eastern Europe is a minor breakfast cereal market, reflecting the product's generally new status in the region. However, the market is vibrant as new lifestyles born from growing urbanization and Westernization – key themes in emerging

market development – have fuelled steady sales growth. Despite its low level of per capita spending, Russia is the largest market in Eastern Europe, accounting for over 40 per cent of regional sales in 2008. The continued steady growth of this market underpinned overall regional development over the review period. Cereals remain a niche market in Russia, as they do across the region, with the product benefiting from a perception of novelty. A key target for manufacturers has been children and young women, at which advertising has been aimed.

The Australasian breakfast cereals sector, like western Europe and North America, is dominated by a single nation, Australia, is becoming increasingly polarized. In common with the key US and UK markets, breakfast cereals in Australia are suffering from a high degree of maturity, with annual growth at a low single-digit level.

The Latin American breakfast cereals sector is the third largest in the world, but at US$2 billion in 2008, it is notably overshadowed by the vastly larger North American and western European markets. However, in common with these developed regions, one country plays a dominant role in the regional make-up: Mexico, accounting for nearly 60 per cent of the overall breakfast cereal markets in Latin America.

In common with Eastern Europe, breakfast cereal sales, whilst small in Africa and the Middle East, have displayed marked growth in recent years as a direct result of greater urbanization and a growing trend (in some areas) towards Westernization. Given the overriding influence of this factor on market development, sales are largely concentrated in the more developed regional markets, such as Israel and South Africa, where the investment by multinationals has been at its highest.

In Asia the concept of breakfast cereals is relatively new, with the growing influence of Western culture fostering a notable increase in consumption in major urban cities. Market development has been rapid in China, reflecting the overall rate of industry expansion in the country, with breakfast cereals sales rising by 15 per cent per year. In the region's developed markets, in particular Japan, market performance is broadly similar, although the key growth driver is different, in that it is health. Overall, in both developed and developing markets, breakfast cereals are in their infancy. Per capita consumption rates (Table 1) are still very low, leaving considerable scope for future growth.

CPW penetrates emerging markets, like Russia and China

Cereal Partners Worldwide has performed best in developing markets such as Russia and China, where market leader Kellogg has not yet established a strong presence. Although the Russian and Chinese markets are still relatively small in global terms (with $260 million and $71 million of sales in a $23 billion global industry), they are growing rapidly. Moreover, per capita consumption rates are still very low (particularly in China), leaving considerable scope for future growth.

The Nestlé brand has had a presence in the Chinese packaged food market since 1990, providing an excellent springboard for the launch of Cereal Partners Worldwide in the country. CPW itself entered the Chinese breakfast cereals market in 2004, when it opened a manufacturing facility in the city of Tianjin, and it has relied on a combination of strong branding and intensive marketing to gain market share, particularly in children's cereals, where its market share stood at 60 per cent in 2008.

All of CPW's breakfast cereals are marketed under the name 'Que Cao', which means bird's nest in Mandarin. This name, together with a universal visual identity/logo and the tagline 'Choose Quality, Choose Nestlé' are the cornerstones of its Chinese marketing strategy, appearing on packaging, point-of-sale materials and media advertising. In-store promotions and sampling are also utilized. Moreover, unlike many of its indigenous rivals, CPW can afford to spend heavily on television advertising.

Thus the marketing of these breakfast cereals is integrated into a wider portfolio of products. However, this approach is not without its dangers, as demonstrated in 2005 when Nestlé's reputation in China took a hit after its baby formula was found to be contaminated with iodine. In this case, the fallout from the scandal does not seem to have had a serious impact on the Chinese operations of Cereal Partners Worldwide.

In addition, CPW's marketing strategy in China is predicated on segmenting the market into two groups: urban and rural customers. It targets its latest and most innovative products at the wealthier urban population, which is forecast to become the majority in around 2010, emphasizing issues relating to health and wellness. In terms of China's diminishing rural population, who have significantly less disposable income than their urban counterparts, it takes a lower-cost approach, adapting existing product lines and highlighting such issues as basic nutrition and affordability, as well as quality and safety.

In China there are two contradictory forces at play. Although the country's birth rate fell significantly, mainly due to the government's One Child Policy, disposable income is rising rapidly, so families now have much more money to spend on each child. As a result, the current generation, dubbed China's 'Little Emperors' by some marketers, would appear to be a ripe market for

premium and value-added products, which Cereal Partners Worldwide will have to exploit if its leadership of this category is not to be overtaken. None of CPW's three children's breakfast cereals brands in China, Trix, Star and Koko Krunch, are particularly healthy, which may make the company vulnerable to competitors with stronger health and wellness plays as issues such as childhood obesity come more to the fore in China.

Another risk for Cereal Partners Worldwide is that it is relatively weak in hot cereals, which accounted for more than 50 per cent of the total Chinese breakfast cereals sales in 2008.

Health trend

With regard to health, breakfast cereals have been hurt by the rise of fad diets such as Atkins and South Beach, which have heaped much scorn on carbohydrate-based products. The influence of these diets is on the wane but their footprint remains highly visible on national eating trends. In addition, the high sugar content of children's cereals has come under intense scrutiny, which caused a downturn in this sector, although the industry is now coming back with a range of 'better for you' variants.

Regarding convenience, this trend, once a growth driver for breakfast cereals, has now become a threat, with an increasing number of consumers opting to skip breakfast. Portability has become a key facet of convenience, a development that has fed the emergence and expansion of breakfast bars at the expense of traditional foods, such as breakfast cereals. In an increasingly cash-rich, time-poor society, consumers are opting to abandon a formal breakfast meal and instead are relying on an 'on-the-go' solution, such as breakfast bars or pastries. These latter products, in particular breakfast bars, are taking a share from cereals, a trend that looks set to gather pace in the short term.

Trends in product development

The market for breakfast products will continue to be impacted by factors such as the speeding up of society, the entry of more women into the workforce and the further growth of single- and two-person households as people delay marriage and have fewer children. These trends will fuel demand for products that are portable and/or easy to prepare as an increasing number of consumers grab breakfast on the way to work or school.

Consumer awareness of health and nutrition has also played a major part in shaping the industry in recent years. Cereal manufacturers began to tout the benefits of eating breakfast cereal right on the package – vitamin-fortified, low in fat and a good source of fibre.

Another trend, begun in the 1990s and picking up steam in the 2000s, is adding dehydrated whole fruits to cereal, which provides colour, flavour and nutritional value. Yet touting health benefits to adults and marketing film characters to children have not been sufficient to reinvigorate this mature industry.

Under the difficult market conditions, cereal packaging is receiving new attention. Packaging was a secondary consideration, other than throwing in special offers to tempt kids. These days, with meal occasions boiled down to their bare essentials, packaging and delivery have emerged as key weapons in the cereal marketer's arsenal. New ideas circulating in the industry usually include doing away with the traditional cereal box, which has undergone little change in its lifetime. Alternatives range from clear plastic containers to a return of the small variety six-packs.

Trends in distribution

The ways in which breakfast products are brought to market in the developed world are not expected to change a great deal. The distribution of breakfast foods is already characterized by a high percentage of sales through supermarkets/hypermarkets, for reasons of convenience and economy. However, supermarkets/hypermarkets will face more intense competition from hard discounters such as Aldi and Lidl, which have been increasing their penetration, notably in Europe. Hard discounters appeal to price-conscious consumers, and continued economic uncertainty in key markets such as France and Germany has fuelled growth in this segment.

Discounters are also widening their reach in emerging market regions, such as Eastern Europe, where price sensitivity is high, and are stepping up their private label development with premium breakfast products that compete effectively with established brands. As a result of the fierce competition between supermarkets/hypermarkets and hard discounters, independent food stores are likely to lose out further in the future, as they will find it increasingly difficult to compete in times of tighter margins and heavy promotion.

In an increasingly time-poor, cash-rich culture, consumers are also proving ever more willing to frequent convenience or impulse stores for the purchase of 'on-the-go' breakfast solutions such as cereals in pots complete with milk, in-cup porridge, cereal bars and artisanal rolls and pastries. Successful formats include outlets such as service station forecourts and urban supermarket formats, which are well placed to allow consumers to pop in on their way to work, college or school. This trend is expected to become more pronounced in the future, as people have less time to eat at home.

While e-commerce is not generally suited to breakfast products, due to their fresh and perishable nature, manufacturers will likely make greater use of their websites to inform consumers about nutritional issues and new products, as well as to suggest recipes or generally increase brand visibility. In developing markets, the growing use of the Internet will serve to make consumers increasingly aware of Western brands.

Independent food stores (where breakfast cereals are traditionally sold) have suffered a decline during the past years. They have been at a competitive disadvantage compared to their larger and better resourced chained competitors.

Table 3	The world market for breakfast cereals, by company – 2005			
Manufacturer	Germany % market share	UK % market share	USA % market share	World % market share
Kellogg Company	27	30	30	30
CPW (General Mills + Nestlé)	12	15	30	20
PepsiCo (Quaker)	–	6	14	10
Weetabix	–	10	–	5
Private label	35	15	10	15
Others	26	24	16	20
Total	100	100	100	100

In the United States General Mills and Nestlé market each of their breakfast cereal products independently, because the CPW only covers international markets outside the United States.

Trends in advertising

Advertising expenditures of most cereal companies were down in recent years due to decreases in consumer spending. However, there are still a lot of marketing activities going on.

Celebrity endorsements continue to play a critical part of for example General Mills's marketing strategies, in particular its association with sporting personalities dating back to the 1930s with baseball sponsorship. One of the main lines of celebrity endorsement involves Wheaties boxes and a long line of sports people have appeared on the box since the 1930s. In 2001, Tiger Woods, spokesman for the Wheaties brand, appeared on special edition packaging for Wheaties to commemorate his victory of four Grand Slam golf titles.

Private label competition intensifies

Across many categories, rising costs have led to price increases in branded products which have not been matched by any pricing actions taken in private labels. As a result, the price gaps between branded and private label products have increased dramatically and in some cases can be as much as 30 per cent.

This creates intense competitive environments for branded products, particularly in categories such as cereals e.g. for Kellogg's and CPW, as consumers have started to focus more on price than brand identity. This shift in focus is partly the result of private labels' increased quality as they compete for consumer loyalty and confidence in their label products.

Competitors

The competitive situation in three main markets (Germany, UK and USA) is shown in Table 3.

Kellogg's

The company that makes breakfast foods and snacks for millions began with only 25 employees in Battle Creek in 1906. Today, Kellogg Company employs more than 25,000 people, manufactures in 17 countries and sells its products in more than 180 countries.

Kellogg was the first American company to enter the foreign market for ready-to-eat breakfast cereals. Company founder Will Keith (W.K.) Kellogg was an early believer in the potential of international growth and began establishing Kellogg's as a global brand with the introduction of *Kellogg's Corn Flakes*® in Canada in 1914. As success followed and demand grew, Kellogg Company continued to build manufacturing facilities around the world, including Sydney, Australia (1924), Manchester, England (1938), Queretaro, Mexico (1951), Takasaki, Japan (1963), Bombay, India (1994) and Toluca, Mexico (2004).

Kellogg Company is the leader among global breakfast cereal manufacturers with 2008 sales revenue of $12.8 billion (net earnings were $1,148 million). Wal-Mart Stores, Inc. and its affiliates accounted for approximately 17 per cent of consolidated net sales during 2008.

Established in 1906, Kellogg Company was the world's market leader in ready-to-eat cereals throughout most of the twentieth century. In 2005, Kellogg had 30 per cent of the world market share for breakfast cereals (see Table 3). Canada, the United Kingdom and Australia represented Kellogg's three largest overseas markets.

A few well-known Kellogg products are Corn Flakes, Frosted Mini-Wheats, Corn Pops and Fruit Loops.

PepsiCo

In August 2001, PepsiCo merged with Quaker Foods, thereby expanding its existing portfolio. Quaker's family of brands includes Quaker Oatmeal, Cap'n Crunch and Life cereals, Rice-A-Roni and Near East side dishes, and Aunt Jemima pancake mixes and syrups.

The Quaker Food's first puffed product, 'Puffed Rice', was introduced in 1905. In 1992, Quaker Oats held an 8.9 per cent share of the ready-to-eat cereal market, and its principal product was Cap'n Crunch. Within the smaller hot cereal segment, however, the company held approximately 60 per cent of the market. In addition to cereal products, Quaker Oats produced Aunt Jemima Pancake mix and Gatorade sports drinks.

The PepsiCo brands in the breakfast cereal sector include Cap'n Crunch, Puffed Wheat, Crunchy Bran, Frosted Mini Wheats and Quaker.

Despite recent moves to extend its presence into new markets, PepsiCo tends to focus on its North American operations.

Weetabix

Weetabix is a UK manufacturer, with a relatively high market share (10 per cent) in the United Kingdom. The company is owned by a private investment group – Lion Capital. It sells its cereals in over 80 countries and has a product line that includes Weetabix, Weetos and Alpen. Weetabix is headquartered in Northamptonshire, UK. In 2008 Weetabix has an estimated turnover of US$1 billion.

Sources: www.cerealpartners.co.uk; www.generalmills.com; www.nestle.com; www.euromonitor.com; www.datamonitor.com; www.marketwatch.com; Bowery, J. (2006) 'Kellogg broadens healthy cereals portfolio', *Marketing*, 8 February, p. 5; Sanders, T. (2006) 'Cereals spark debate', *Food Manufacture*, August, 81(8), p. 4; Reyes, S. (2006) 'Saving private label', *Brandweek*, 5 August, 47(19), pp. 30–34; Hanson, P. (2005) 'Market focus breakfast cereals', *Brand Strategy*, March, 190, p. 50; Pehanich, M. (2003) 'Cereals run sweet and healthy', *Prepared Foods*, March, pp. 75–76; Vignali, C. (2001) 'Kellogg's – internationalisation versus globalisation of the marketing mix', *British Food Journal*, 103(2), pp. 112–130.

QUESTIONS

Carol has heard that you are the new global marketing specialist so you are called in as a last-minute consultant before the presentation to the board of directors. You are confronted with the following questions, which you are supposed to answer as best you can.

1. How can General Mills and Nestlé create international competitiveness by joining forces in CPW?

2. Evaluate the international competitiveness of CPW compared to the Kellogg Company.

3. Suggest how CPW can create a blue ocean strategy.

4. Where and how can CPW create further international sales growth?

PART I
The decision whether to internationalize
Chs 1–4

PART II
Deciding which markets to enter
Chs 5–8

PART III
Market entry strategies
Chs 9–13

PART IV
Designing the global marketing programme
Chs 14–17

PART V
Implementing and coordinating the global marketing programme
Chs 18–19

Part II Contents

Part II Case studies

PART II

Deciding which markets to enter

Introduction to Part II

After considering the initial phase in Part I, The decision whether to internationalize, the structure of this part follows the process of selecting the 'right' international market. First, Chapter 5 presents the most important international marketing research tools for analysing the internal and external environment. Then the political and economic environment (Chapter 6) and the sociocultural environment (Chapter 7) are used as inputs to the process from which the output is the target market(s) that the firm should select as a basis for development of the international marketing mix (see Part IV). The structure of Part II is shown in Figure II.1.

As Figure II.1 shows, the research tools presented in Chapter 5, and the forces in Chapters 6 and 7, provide the environmental framework that is necessary for:

● the selection of the right market(s) (Chapter 8)
● the subsequent development of the global marketing mix.

The discussion following Chapters 6 and 7 will be limited to the major macroenvironmental dimensions affecting market and buyer behaviour and thus the global marketing mix of the firm.

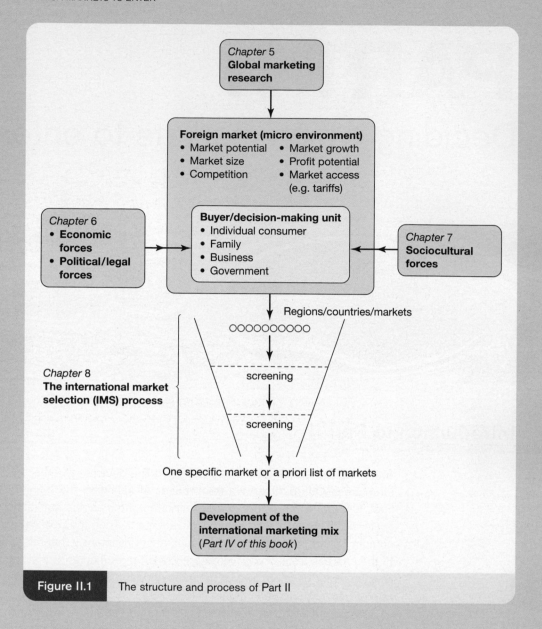

Figure II.1   The structure and process of Part II

CHAPTER 5
Global marketing research

Contents

Learning objectives

After studying this chapter you should be able to:

- Explain the importance of having a carefully designed international information system.
- Link global marketing research to the decision-making process.
- Discuss the key problems in gathering and using international market data.
- Distinguish between different research approaches, data sources and data types.
- Discuss opportunities and problems with qualitative market research methods.
- Understand how online surveys are carried out.
- Understand the relevance of the World Wide Web as an important data source in global marketing research.

5.1 Introduction

Information is a key ingredient in the development of successful international marketing strategies. Lack of familiarity with customers, competitors and the market environment in other countries, coupled with the growing complexity and diversity of international markets makes it increasingly critical to collect information in relation to these markets.

In contrast to a researcher concerned with only one country, an international market researcher has to deal with a number of countries that may differ considerably in a number of important ways. Therefore many international marketing decisions are concerned with priorities and allocation of resources between countries.

The prime function of global marketing is to make and sell what international buyers want, rather than simply selling whatever can be most easily made. Therefore what customers require must be assessed through marketing research and/or through establishing a decision support system, so that the firm can direct its marketing activities more effectively by fulfilling the requirements of the customers.

The term 'marketing research' refers to gathering, analysing and presenting information related to a well-defined problem. Hence the focus of marketing research is a specific problem or project with a beginning and an end.

Marketing research differs from a decision support system (DSS) or marketing information system (MIS), which is information gathered and analysed on a continual basis. In practice, marketing research and DSS/MIS are often hard to differentiate, so they will be used interchangeably in this context.

At the end of this chapter a proposal for setting up an international MIS will be presented.

5.2 The changing role of the international researcher

The role of international market research is primarily to act as an aid to the decision-maker. It is a tool that can help to reduce the risk in decision-making caused by the environmental uncertainties and lack of knowledge in international markets. It ensures that the manager bases a decision on the solid foundation of knowledge and focuses strategic thinking on the needs of the marketplace rather than the product.

Earlier marketing research was regarded as a staff function and not a line function. Marketing researchers had little interaction with marketing managers and did not participate in marketing decision-making. Likewise, external providers of marketing research had little interaction with marketing managers. However, as we have moved into the new millennium this line of demarcation between marketing research and marketing, and thus the distinction between marketing researchers and marketing managers, is becoming thinner and thinner.

As the line and staff boundary blurs marketing managers are becoming increasingly involved in marketing research. This trend towards making marketing research more of a line function, rather than a staff function, is likely to continue and even accelerate in the near future where 'sense and respond' will increasingly characterize firms' approach to business. Thus the traditional marketing researcher in a commercial firm narrowly focused on the production of presentations and reports for management will become a rare breed. The transition of marketing researchers to researchers-cum-decision-makers has already begun. Indeed some of the most effective-researchers of customer satisfaction are not only participating in decision-making but are also deployed as part of the team to implement organizational changes in response to customer satisfaction surveys.

The availability of better decision tools and decision support systems is facilitating the transition of research managers to decision-makers. Senior managers can now directly access internal and external secondary data from computers and internet sites around the world.

In this millennium good marketing researchers will be good marketing managers, and vice versa.

5.3   Linking global marketing research to the decision-making process

Global marketing research should be linked to the decision-making process within the firm. The recognition that a situation requires action is the initiating factor in the decision-making process.

Even though most firms recognize the need for domestic marketing research this need is not fully understood for global marketing activities. Most SMEs conduct no international market research before they enter a foreign market. Often decisions concerning entry into and expansion in overseas markets and the selection and appointment of distributors are made after a subjective assessment of the situation. The research done is usually less rigorous, less formal and less quantitative than in LSEs. Furthermore, once an SME has entered a foreign market, it is likely to discontinue any research of that market. Many business executives therefore appear to view foreign market research as relatively unimportant.

A major reason that firms are reluctant to engage in global marketing research is a lack of sensitivity to cross-cultural customer tastes and preferences. What information should the global marketing research/DSS provide?

Table 5.1 summarizes the principal tasks of global marketing research, according to the major decision phases of the global marketing process. As can be seen, both internal

Table 5.1	Information for the major global marketing decisions
Global marketing decision phase	**Information needed**
1. Deciding whether to internationalise	Assessment of global market opportunities (global demand) for the firm's products
	Commitment of the management to internationalize
	Competitiveness of the firm compared to local and international competitors
	Domestic versus international market opportunities
2. Deciding which markets to enter	Ranking of world markets according to market potential of countries/regions
	Local competition
	Political risks
	Trade barriers
	Cultural/psychic distance to potential market
3. Deciding how to enter foreign markets	Nature of the product (standard versus complex product)
	Size of markets/segments
	Behaviour of potential intermediaries
	Behaviour of local competition
	Transport costs
	Government requirements
4. Designing the global marketing programme	Buyer behaviour
	Competitive practice
	Available distribution channels
	Media and promotional channels
5. Implementing and controlling the global marketing programme	Negotiation styles in different cultures
	Sales by product line, sales force customer type and country/region
	Contribution margins
	Marketing expenses per market

(firm-specific) and external (market) data are needed. The role of a firm's internal information system in providing data for marketing decisions is often forgotten.

How the different types of information affect the major decisions is thoroughly discussed in the different parts and chapters of this book. Besides the split between internal and external data, the two major sources of information are **primary data** and **secondary data**:

Primary data
Information that is collected first-hand, generated by original research tailor-made to answer specific research questions.

Secondary data
Information that has already been collected for other purposes and thus is readily available.

1. *Primary data.* These can be defined as information that is collected first-hand, generated by original research tailor-made to answer specific current research questions. The major advantage of primary data is that the information is specific (fine-grained), relevant and up to date. The disadvantages of primary data are, however, the high costs and amount of time associated with its collection.
2. *Secondary data.* These can be defined as information that has already been collected for other purposes and is thus readily available. The major disadvantage is that the data are often more general and coarse-grained in nature. The advantages of secondary data are the low costs and amount of time associated with its collection. For those who are unclear on the terminology, secondary research is frequently referred to as desk research.

The two basic forms of research (primary and secondary) will be discussed in further detail later in this chapter.

If we combine the split of internal/external data with primary/secondary data, it is possible to place data in four categories. In Figure 5.1 this approach is used to categorize indicator variables for answering the following marketing questions. Is there a market for the firm's product A in country B? If yes, how large is it and what is the possible market share for the

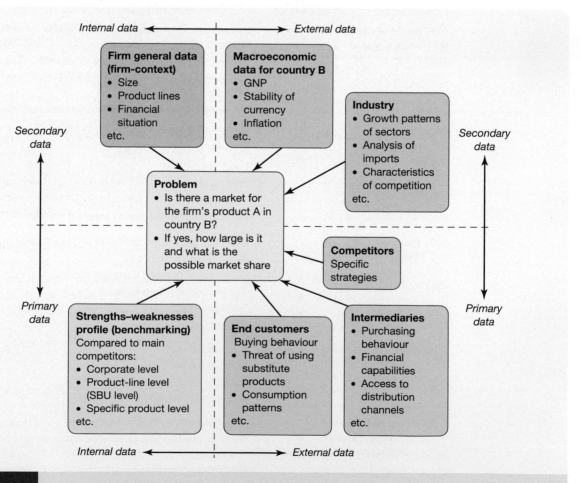

Figure 5.1   Categorization of data for assessment of market potential in a country

firm? Note that in Figure 5.1 only a limited number of indicator variables are shown. Of course the one-market perspective in Figure 5.1 could be expanded, to cover not only country B (as in Figure 5.1) but a range of countries, e.g. the EU.

As a rule, no primary research should be done without first searching for relevant secondary information, and secondary data should be used whenever available and appropriate. Secondary data often help to define problems and research objectives. In most cases, however, secondary sources cannot provide all the information needed and the company must collect primary data.

In Figure 5.1 the most difficult and costly kind of data to obtain is probably the strengths–weaknesses profile of the firm (internal and primary data). However, because it compares the profile of the firm with those of its main competitors, this quadrant is a very important indicator of the firm's international competitiveness. The next two sections discuss different forms of secondary and primary research.

With many international markets to consider it is essential that firms begin their market research by seeking and utilizing secondary data.

5.4   Secondary research

Advantages of secondary research in foreign markets

Secondary research conducted from the home base is less expensive and less time-consuming than research conducted abroad. No contacts have to be made outside the home country, thus keeping commitment to possible future projects at a low level. Research undertaken in the home country about the foreign environment also has the benefit of objectivity. The researcher is not constrained by overseas customs. As a preliminary stage of a market-screening process secondary research can quickly generate background information to eliminate many countries from the scope of enquiries.

Disadvantages of secondary research in foreign markets

Problems with secondary research in foreign countries are:

- *Non-availability of data.* In many developing countries secondary data are very scarce. These weak economies have poor statistical services – many do not even carry out a population census. Information on retail and wholesale trade is especially difficult to obtain. In such cases primary data collection becomes vital.
- *Reliability of data.* Sometimes political considerations may affect the reliability of data. In some developing countries governments may enhance the information to paint a rosy picture of the economic life in the country. In addition, due to the data collection procedures used, or the personnel who gathered the data, many data lack statistical accuracy. As a practical matter, the following questions should be asked to judge effectively the reliability of data sources (Cateora, 1993, p. 346):
  - Who collected the data? Would there be any reason for purposely misrepresenting the facts?
  - For what purpose was the data collected?
  - How was the data collected (methodology)?
  - Are the data internally consistent and logical in the light of known data sources or market factors?
- *Data classification.* In many countries the data reported are too broadly classified for use at the micro level.
- *Comparability of data.* International marketers often like to compare data from different countries. Unfortunately the secondary data obtainable from different countries are not readily comparable because national definitions of statistical phenomena differ from one country to another. The term 'supermarket', for example, has a variety of meanings around

the world. In Japan a supermarket is quite different from its UK counterpart. Japanese 'supermarkets' usually occupy two- or three-storey structures; they sell daily necessities such as foodstuff, but also clothing, furniture, electrical home appliances and sporting goods, and they have a restaurant.

In general the availability and accuracy of recorded secondary data increases as the level of economic development increases. However, there are many exceptions: India is at a lower level of economic development than other countries but has accurate and complete development of government-collected data.

Although the possibility of obtaining secondary data has increased dramatically the international community has grown increasingly sensitive to the issue of data privacy. Readily accessible large-scale databases contain information valuable to marketers but considered privileged by the individuals who have provided the data. The international marketer must therefore also pay careful attention to the privacy laws in different nations and to the possible consumer response to using such data. Neglecting these concerns may result in research backfiring and the corporate position being weakened.

In doing secondary research or building a decision support system there are many information sources available. Generally these secondary data sources can be divided into internal and external sources (Figure 5.1). The latter can be classified as either international/global or regional/country-based sources.

Internal data sources

Internal company data can be a most fruitful source of information. However, it is often not utilized as fully as it should be.

The global marketing and sales departments are the main points of commercial interaction between an organization and its foreign customers. Consequently a great deal of information should be available, including:

- *Total sales.* Every company keeps a record of its total sales over a defined time period: for example, weekly records, monthly records and so on.
- *Sales by country.* Sales statistics should be split up by countries. This is partly to measure the progress and competence of the export manager or the salesperson (sometimes to influence earnings because commission may be paid on sales) and partly to measure the degree of market penetration in a particular country.
- *Sales by products.* Very few companies sell only one product. Most companies sell a range of products and keep records for each kind of product or, if the range is large, each product group.
- *Sales volume by market segment.* Such segmentation may be geographical or by type of industry. This will give an indication of segment trends in terms of whether they are static, declining or expanding.
- *Sales volume by type of channel distribution.* Where a company uses several different distribution channels it is possible to calculate the effectiveness and profitability of each type of channel. Such information allows marketing management to identify and develop promising channel opportunities, and results in more effective channel marketing.
- *Pricing information.* Historical information relating to price adjustments by product allows the organization to establish the effect of price changes on demand.
- *Communication mix information.* This includes historical data on the effects of advertising campaigns, sponsorship and direct mail on sales. Such information can act as a guide to the likely effectiveness of future communication expenditure plans.
- *Sales representatives' records and reports.* Sales representatives should keep a visit card or file on every 'live' customer. In addition, sales representatives often send reports to the sales office on such matters as orders lost to competitors and possible reasons why, as well as on firms that are planning future purchasing decisions. Such information could help to bring improvements in marketing strategy.

External data sources

One very basic method of finding international business information is to begin with a public library or a university library. The Internet can also help in the search for data sources. The Internet has made thousands of databases for intelligence research available (i.e. research on competitors). In addition, electronic databases carry marketing information ranging from the latest news on product development to new thoughts in the academic and trade press and updates in international trade statistics. However, the Internet will not totally replace other sources of secondary data. Cost compared to data quality will still be a factor influencing a company's choice of secondary data sources.

Secondary data used for estimation of foreign market potential

Secondary data are often used to estimate the size of potential foreign markets. In assessing current product demand and forecasting future demand reliable historical data are required. As previously mentioned, the quality and availability of secondary data are frequently inadequate. Nevertheless estimates of market size must be attempted in order to plan effectively. Despite limitations there are approaches to forecasting future demand in a market with a minimum of information. A number of techniques are available (see Craig and Douglas, 2000). Here four are examined in some detail: proxy indicators, chain ratio method, lead–lag analysis and estimation by analogy.

Proxy indicators

Proxy indicators are useful in situations where a direct measure is difficult to obtain. Indirect variables serve as surrogate or proxy.

Ownership of durables by households has also been suggested as a proxy for a country's economic development. For example, consumption of refrigerators or any other household appliance can be a good proxy for washing machines. Even television consumption can be used as a proxy. Another proxy could be total number of households connected with resident telephone lines. In developing countries, relatively privileged people have a telephone in their homes. The assumption is that the households with resident telephones have the potential to buy a washing machine.

The method can provide robust estimation and is relatively inexpensive and convenient to implement, but the use of proxy variables can also cause validity problems. The degree of precision depends on the choice of proxy variable (Waheeduzzaman, 2008). In Chapter 6 (Table 6.1) the Big Mac Index (the relative Big Mac prices in different countries) is used as a proxy variable for the likely future currency development against the US$.

Chain ratio method

The chain ratio method is a simple arithmetic technique where ratios are used to reduce a base population. The purpose of the reduction technique is to derive a realistic demand. It can provide reasonably precise estimates if the ratios are logical and make practical sense. For example, the market potential for household air conditioners in a country is dependent on the rate of urbanization (percentage of people living in cities), total number of households, percentage of population having access to electricity and percentage of population who can afford the product. Multiplying these metrics would provide a rough estimate for the potential air conditioners market in a country. If the market researcher should estimate the total market potential for washing machines in Thailand, he would like this: Thailand has 17.6 million households, 82 per cent of these households have electricity and 50 per cent have a running water supply. Multiplying these variables $17.6 \times 0.82 \times 0.50$, the total market potential comes out at 7.2 million.

Though robust, the method can offer estimates that are close to real data. It is relatively inexpensive and convenient to implement (Waheeduzzaman, 2008).

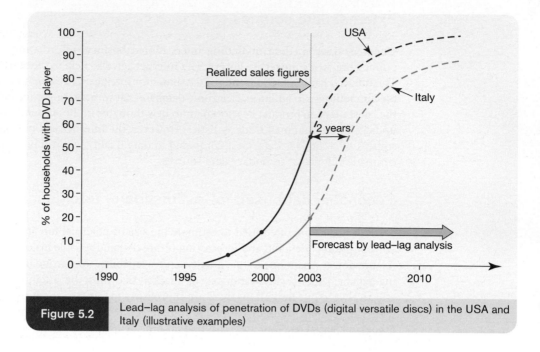

| Figure 5.2 | Lead–lag analysis of penetration of DVDs (digital versatile discs) in the USA and Italy (illustrative examples) |

Lead–lag analysis

This technique is based on the use of time-series data from one country to project sales in other countries. It assumes that the determinants of demand in the two countries are the same, and that only time separates them. This requires that the diffusion process and specifically the rate of diffusion is the same in all countries. Of course this is not always the case, and it seems that products introduced more recently diffuse more quickly (Craig and Douglas, 2000).

Lead–lag analysis
Determinants of demand and the rate of diffusion are the same in two countries, but time separates the two.

Figure 5.2 shows the principle behind the **lead–lag analysis** with an illustrative example in the DVD market. By the end of 2003 it is assumed that 55 per cent of US households will have at least one DVD in their home, whereas it is assumed that 'only' 20 per cent of Italian households will have a DVD. We define the time-lag between the American and the Italian DVD market as two years. So if we were to estimate the future penetration of DVDs in Italian households (and as a consequence also demand) we could make a parallel displacement of the S-formed US penetration curve by two years, as illustrated in Figure 5.2. This also shows how rapidly new products today are diffused from market to market. The difficulty in using the lead–lag analysis includes the problem of identifying the relevant time lag and the range of factors that impact future demand. However, the technique has considerable intuitive appeal to managers and is likely to guide some of their thinking.

When data are not available for a regular lead–lag analysis, estimation by analogy can be used.

Estimation by analogy

Estimation by analogy
A correlation value (between a factor and the demand for the product) for one market is used in another international market.

Estimation by analogy is essentially a single-factor index with a correlation value (between a factor and demand for a product) obtained in one country applied to a target international market. First a relationship (correlation) must be established between the demand to be estimated and the factor, which is to serve as the basis for the analogy. Once the known relationship is established the correlation value then attempts to draw an analogy between the known situation and the market demand in question.

Example

We want to estimate the market demand for refrigerators in Germany. We know the market size in the United Kingdom but we do not know it in Germany.

As nearly all households in the two countries already have a refrigerator, a good correlation could be number of households or population size in the two countries. In this situation we choose to use population size as the basis for the analogy:

Population size in the United Kingdom: 60 million
Population size in Germany: 82 million
Furthermore we know that the number of refrigerators sold in the United Kingdom in 2002 was 1.1 million units.

Then by analogy we estimate the sales to be the following in Germany:

$(82/60) \times 1.1$ million units = 1.5 million units

A note of caution

Generally caution must be used with estimation by analogy because the method assumes that factors other than the correlation factor used (in this example population size) are similar in both countries, such as the same culture, buying power of consumers, tastes, taxes, prices, selling methods, availability of products, consumption patterns and so forth. Despite the apparent drawbacks it is still useful where international data are limited.

5.5 Primary research

Qualitative and quantitative research

If a marketer's research questions are not adequately answered by secondary research it may be necessary to search for additional information in primary data. These data can be collected by **qualitative research** and **quantitative research**. Quantitative and qualitative techniques can be distinguished by the fact that quantitative techniques involve getting data from a large, representative group of respondents.

The objective of qualitative research techniques is to give a holistic view of the research problem, therefore these techniques must have a large number of variables and few respondents (illustrated in Figure 5.3). Choosing between quantitative and qualitative techniques is a question of trading off breadth and depth in the results of the analysis.

Qualitative research
Data analysis based on questionnaires from a large group of respondents.

Quantitative research
Provides a holistic view of a research problem by integrating a larger number of variables, but asking only a few respondents.

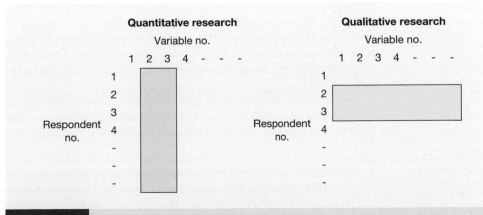

| Figure 5.3 | The trade-off in the choice between quantitative and qualitative research |

Table 5.2	Quantitative versus qualitative research	
Comparison dimension	Quantitative research (e.g. a postal questionnaire)	Qualitative research (e.g. a focus group interview or the case method)
Objective	To quantify the data and generalize the results from the sample to the population of interest	To gain an initial and qualitative understanding of the underlying reasons and motives
Type of research	Descriptive and/or casual	Exploratory
Flexibility in research design	Low (as a result of a standardized and structured questionnaire: one-way communication)	High (as a result of the personal interview, where the interviewer can change questions during the interview: two-way communication)
Sample size	Large	Small
Choice of respondents	Representative sample of the population	Persons with considerable knowledge of the problem (key informants)
Information per respondent	Low	High
Data analysis	Statistical summary	Subjective, interpretative
Ability to replicate with same result	High	Low
Interviewer requirements	No special skills required	Special skills required (an understanding of the interaction between interviewer and respondent)
Time consumption during the research	*Design phase*: high (formulation of questions must be correct). *Analysis phase*: low (the answers to the questions can be coded)	*Design phase*: low (no 'exact' questions are required before the interview). *Analysis phase*: high (as a result of many 'soft' data)

Other differences between the two research methodologies are summarized in Table 5.2. Data retrieval and analysis of quantitative respondent data are based on a comparison of data between all respondents. This places heavy demands on the measuring instrument (the questionnaire), which must be well structured (with different answering categories) and tested before the survey takes place. All respondents are given identical stimuli: that is, the same questions. This approach will not usually give any problems, as long as the respondent group is homogeneous. However, if it is a heterogeneous group of respondents it is possible that the same question will be understood in different ways. This problem is intensified in cross-cultural surveys.

Data retrieval and analysis of qualitative data, however, are characterized by a high degree of flexibility and adaptation to the individual respondent and their special background. Another considerable difference between qualitative and quantitative surveys is the source of data:

● Quantitative techniques are characterized by a certain degree of distance as the construction of the questionnaire, data retrieval and data analysis take place in separate phases. Data retrieval is often done by people who have not had anything to do with the construction of the questionnaire. Here the measuring instrument (the questionnaire) is the critical element in the research process.

- Qualitative techniques are characterized by proximity to the source of data, where data retrieval and analysis are done by the same person, namely, the interviewer. Data retrieval is characterized by interaction between the interviewer and the respondent, where each new question is to a certain degree dependent on the previous question. Here it is the interviewer and their competence (or lack of the same) which is the critical element in the research process.

Qualitative techniques imply a less sharp separation between data retrieval and analysis/interpretation, since data retrieval (e.g. the next question in a personal interview) will be dependent on the interviewer's interpretation of the previous answer. The researcher's personal experience from fieldwork (data retrieval) is generally a considerable input into the analysis phase. In the following section the two most important qualitative research methods are presented.

Triangulation: mixing qualitative and quantitative research methods

Quantitative and qualitative research methods often complement each other. Combined use of quantitative and qualitative research methods in the study of the same phenomenon is termed triangulation (Denzin, 1978; Jick, 1979). The triangulation metaphor is from navigation and military strategy, which use multiple reference points to locate an object's exact position. Similarly, market researchers can improve the accuracy and validity of their judgements by collecting both quantitative and qualitative data. Sometimes qualitative research methods explain or reinforce quantitative findings and even reveal new information.

Sometimes it is relevant to use qualitative data collected by, for example, in-depth interview of a few key informants as exploratory input to the construction of the best possible questionnaire for the collection of quantitative data. In this way triangulation can enrich our understanding of a research question before a structured and formalized questionnaire is designed.

Research design

Figure 5.4 shows that designing research for primary data collection calls for a number of decisions on research approaches, contact methods, sampling plan and research instruments. The following pages will look at the various elements of Figure 5.4 in further detail.

Research problem/objectives

Companies are increasingly recognizing the need for primary international research. As the extent of a firm's international involvement increases, so does the importance and complexity of its international research. The primary research process should begin with a definition of the research problem and the establishment of specific objectives. The major difficulty here is translating the business problem into a research problem with a set of specific researchable objectives. In this initial stage researchers often embark on the research process with only a vague grasp of the total problem. Symptoms are often mistaken for causes, and action determined by symptoms may be oriented in the wrong direction.

Research objectives may include obtaining detailed information for better penetrating the market, for designing and fine-tuning the marketing mix, or for monitoring the political climate of a country so that the firm can expand its operations successfully. The better defined the research objective is, the better the researcher will be able to determine the information requirement.

Research approaches

In Figure 5.4 three possible research approaches are indicated: observation, surveys and experiments.

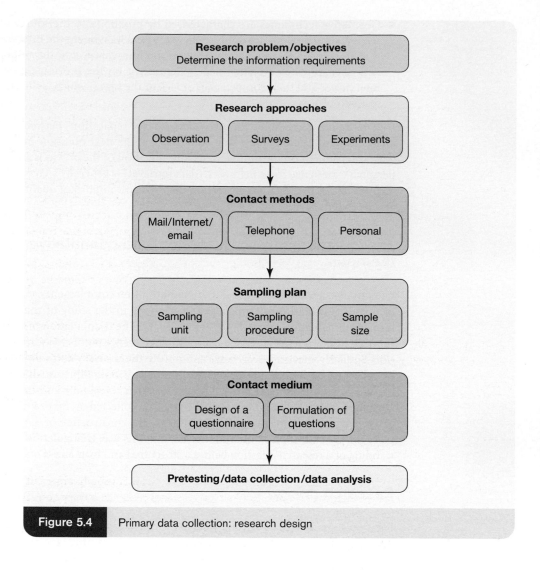

Figure 5.4   Primary data collection: research design

Observation

This approach to the generation of primary data is based on watching and sometimes recording market-related behaviour. Observational techniques are more suited to investigating what people do than why they do it. Here are some examples of this approach:

● Store checks: a food products manufacturer sends researchers into supermarkets to find out the prices of competing brands or how much shelf space and display support retailers give its brands. To conduct in-store research in Europe, for example, store checks, photo audits of shelves and store interviews must be scheduled well in advance and need to be preceded by a full round of introductions of the researchers to store management and personnel.
● Mechanical observations are often used to measure TV viewership.
● Cash register scanners can be used to keep track of customer purchases and inventories.

Observational research can obtain information that people are unwilling or unable to provide. In some countries individuals may be reluctant to discuss personal habits or consumption. In such cases observation is the only way to obtain the necessary information. In contrast, some things are simply not observable, such as feelings, attitudes and motives, or private behaviour. Long-term or infrequent behaviour is also difficult to observe. Because of these limitations, researchers often use observation along with other data collection methods.

Experiments

Experiments gather casual information. They involve selecting matched groups of subjects, giving them different treatments, controlling unrelated factors and checking for differences in group responses. Thus experimental research tries to explain cause and effect relationships.

The most used marketing research application of experiments is in test marketing. This is a research technique in which a product under study is placed on sale in one or more selected localities or areas, and its reception by consumers and the trade is observed, recorded and analysed. In order to isolate, for example, the sales effects of advertising campaigns, it is necessary to use relatively self-contained marketing areas as test markets.

Performance in these test markets gives some indication of the performance to be expected when the product goes into general distribution. However, experiments are difficult to implement in global marketing research. The researcher faces the task of designing an experiment in which most variables are held constant or are comparable across cultures. To do so represents a major challenge. For example, an experiment that intends to determine a casual effect within the distribution system of one country may be difficult to transfer to another country where the distribution system is different. As a result experiments are used only rarely, even though their potential value to the international market researcher is recognized.

Surveys

The survey research method is based on the questioning of respondents and represents, both in volume and in value terms, perhaps the most important method of collecting data. Typically the questioning is structured: a formal questionnaire is prepared and the questions are asked in a prearranged order. The questions may be asked verbally, in writing or via a computer.

Survey research is used for a variety of marketing issues, including:

- customer attitudes
- customer buying habits
- potential market size
- market trends.

Unlike experimental research, survey research is usually aimed at generating descriptive rather than casual data. Unlike observational research, survey research usually involves the respondent.

Because of the importance and diversity of survey research in global marketing, it is on this particular aspect that we now concentrate.

Contact methods

The method of contact chosen is usually a balance between speed, degree of accuracy and costs. In principle there are four possibilities when choosing a contact method: mail surveys, Internet/e-mail, telephone interviews and personal (face-to-face) interviews. Each method has its own strengths and weaknesses. Table 5.3 gives an overview of these.

Mail

Mail surveys are among the least expensive. The questionnaire can include pictures – something that is not possible over the phone. Mail surveys allow the respondent to answer at their leisure, rather than at the often inconvenient moment they are contacted for a phone or personal interview. For this reason, they are not considered as intrusive as other kinds of interviews. However, mail surveys take longer than other kinds. You will need to wait several weeks after mailing out questionnaires before you can be sure that you have obtained most of the responses. In countries of lower educational and literacy levels, response rates to mail surveys are often too small to be useful.

Internet/e-mail surveys (online surveys)

These can collect a large amount of data that can be quantified and coded into a computer. A low research budget combined with a widely dispersed population may mean that there is no alternative to the e-mail/Internet survey. E-mail surveys are both very economical and

Table 5.3	Strengths and weaknesses of the four contact methods			
Questions/questionnaire	Mail	Internet/e-mail	Telephone	Personal
Flexibility (ability to clarify problems)	Poor	Fair	Good	Excellent
Possibility of in-depth information (use of open-ended questions)	Fair	Poor	Fair	Excellent
Use of visual aids	Good	Excellent	Poor	Good
Possibility of a widely dispersed sample	Excellent	Excellent	Excellent	Fair
Response rates	Poor	Fair	Good	Fair
Asking sensitive questions	Good	Poor	Poor	Fair
Control of interviewer effects (no interviewer bias)	Excellent	Fair	Fair	Poor
Speed of data collection	Poor	Excellent	Excellent	Good
Costs	Good	Excellent	Excellent	Poor

very fast. It is possible to attach pictures and sound files. However, many people dislike unsolicited e-mail even more than unsolicited regular mail.

One of the advantages with online surveys in international market research is the saving on travelling costs. Often researchers have to travel to countries in which research is conducted, especially in the case of face-to-face interviews (Adiham *et al.*, 2009). This leads to high travelling costs and increases the time needed to execute the fieldwork. In online research the respondents can be recruited and interviewed from any computer anywhere in the world. Most of the people who are connected to the Internet know how to use chat rooms and speak English.

Online surveys can be conducted through e-mail or they can be posted on the Web. When a wide audience is targeted the survey can be designed as a pop-up survey, which would appear as a web-based questionnaire in a browser window while users are browsing the respective websites. Such a web-based survey is appropriate for a wide audience, where all the visitors to certain websites have an equal chance to enter the survey. However, the researcher's control over respondents entering the web-based surveys is lower than for e-mail surveys.

Telephone interviews

In some ways these are somewhere between personal and mail surveys. They generally have a response rate higher than mail questionnaires but lower than face-to-face interviews, their cost is usually less than with personal interviews, and they allow a degree of flexibility when interviewing. However, the use of visual aids is not possible and there are limits to the number of questions that can be asked before respondents either terminate the interview or give quick (invalid) answers to speed up the process. With computer-aided telephone interviewing (CATI), centrally located interviewers read questions from a computer monitor and input answers via the keyboard. Routing through the questionnaire is computer controlled, helping the process of interviewing. Some research firms set up terminals in shopping centres, where respondents sit down at a terminal, read questions from a screen and type their answers into the computer.

Personal interviews

Personal interviews take two forms – individual and group interviewing. *Individual interviewing* involves talking with people in their homes or offices, in the street or in shopping arcades. The interviewer must gain the cooperation of the respondents. *Group interviewing* (*focus-group interviewing*) consists of inviting six to ten people to gather for a few hours with a trained moderator to talk about a product, service or organization. The moderator needs objectivity, knowledge of the subject and industry and some understanding of group and consumer behaviour. The participants are normally paid a small sum for attending.

Personal interviewing is quite flexible and can collect large amounts of information. Trained interviewers can hold a respondent's attention for a long time and can explain difficult questions. They can guide interviews, explore issues and probe as the situation requires. Interviewers can show subjects actual products, advertisements or packages and observe reactions and behaviour.

The main drawbacks of personal interviewing are the high costs and sampling problems. Group interview studies usually employ small sample sizes to keep time and costs down, but it may be hard to generalize from the results. Because interviewers have more freedom in personal interviews the problem of interviewer bias is greater.

Thus there is no 'best' contact method – it all depends on the situation. Sometimes it may even be appropriate to combine the methods.

Sampling plan

Sampling plan

A scheme outlining the group (or groups) to be surveyed in a marketing research study, how many individuals are to be chosen for the survey, and on what basis this choice is made.

Except in very restricted markets it is both impractical and too expensive for a researcher to contact all the people who could have some relevance to the research problem. This total number is known statistically as the 'universe' or 'population'. In marketing terms, it comprises the total number of actual and potential users/customers of a particular product or service.

The population can also be defined in terms of elements and sampling units. Suppose that a lipstick manufacturer wants to assess consumer response to a new line of lipsticks and wants to sample females over 15 years of age. It may be possible to sample females of this age directly, in which case a sampling unit would be the same as an element. Alternatively, households might be sampled and all females over 15 in each selected household interviewed. Here the sampling unit is the household, and the element is a female over 15 years old.

What is usually done in practice is to contact a selected group of consumers/customers to be representative of the entire population. The total number of consumers who could be interviewed is known as the 'sample frame', while the number of people who are actually interviewed is known as the 'sample'.

Sampling procedure

There are several kinds of sampling procedure, with probability and non-probability sampling being the two major categories:

- *Probability sampling.* Here it is possible to specify in advance the chance that each element in the population will have of being included in a sample, although there is not necessarily an equal probability for each element. Examples are simple random sampling, systematic sampling, stratified sampling and cluster sampling (see Malhotra 1993 for more information).
- *Non-probability sampling.* Here it is not possible to determine the above-mentioned probability or to estimate the sampling error. These procedures rely on the personal judgement of the researcher. Examples are convenience sampling, quota sampling and snowball sampling (see Malhotra 1993 for more information).

Given the disadvantages of non-probability samples (results are not projectable to the total population, and sampling error cannot be computed) one may wonder why they are used so frequently by marketing researchers. The reasons relate to the inherent advantages of non-probability sampling:

- Non-probability samples cost less than probability samples.
- If accuracy is not critical non-probability sampling may have considerable appeal.
- Non-probability sampling can be conducted more quickly than probability sampling.
- Non-probability sampling, if executed properly, can produce samples of the population that are reasonably representative (e.g. by use of quota sampling) (Malhotra, 1993, p. 359).

Sample size

Once we have chosen the sampling procedure the next step is to determine the appropriate sample size. Determining the sample size is a complex decision and involves financial, statistical and managerial considerations. Other things being equal the larger the sample, the less the sampling error. However, larger samples cost more money, and the resources (money and time) available for a particular research project are always limited.

In addition the cost of larger samples tends to increase on a linear basis, whereas the level of sampling error decreases at a rate only equal to the square root of the relative increase in sample size. For example, if sample size is quadrupled data collection costs will be quadrupled too, but the level of sampling error will be reduced by only one-half. Among the methods for determining the sample size are:

- *Traditional statistical techniques* (assuming the standard normal distribution).
- *Budget available*. Although seemingly unscientific this is a fact of life in a business environment, based on the budgeting of financial resources. This approach forces the researcher to consider carefully the value of information in relation to its cost.
- *Rules of thumb*. The justification for a specified sample size may boil down to a 'gut feeling' that this is an appropriate sample size, or it may be a result of common practice in the particular industry.
- *Number of subgroups to be analysed*. Generally speaking the more subgroups that need to be analysed, the larger the required total sample size.

In transnational market research, sampling procedures become a rather complicated matter. Ideally a researcher wants to use the same sampling method for all countries in order to maintain consistency. Sampling desirability, however, often gives way to practicality and flexibility. Sampling procedures may have to vary across countries in order to ensure reasonable comparability of national groups. Thus the relevance of a sampling method depends on whether it will yield a sample that is representative of a target group in a certain country, and on whether comparable samples can be obtained from similar groups in different countries.

Contact medium/measurement instrument

Designing the questionnaire

A good questionnaire cannot be designed until the precise information requirements are known. It is the vehicle whereby the research objectives are translated into specific questions. The type of information sought, and the type of respondents to be researched, will have a bearing upon the contact method to be used, and this in turn will influence whether the questionnaire is relatively unstructured (with open-ended questions), aimed at depth interviewing, or relatively structured (with closed-ended questions) for 'on the street' interviews.

In cross-cultural studies open-ended questions appear useful because they may help to identify the frame of reference of the respondents. Another issue is the choice between direct and indirect questions. Societies have different degrees of sensitivity to certain questions. Questions related to the income or age of the respondent may be accepted differently in different countries. Thus the researcher must be sure that the questions are culturally acceptable. This may mean that questions which can be asked directly in some societies will have to be asked indirectly in others.

Formulation (wording) of questions

Once the researcher has decided on specific types of questions the next task is the actual writing of the questions. Four general guidelines are useful to bear in mind during the wording and sequencing of each question:

- *The wording must be clear*. For example, try to avoid two questions in one.
- *Select words so as to avoid biasing the respondent*. For example, try to avoid leading questions.
- *Consider the ability of the respondent to answer the question*. For example, asking respondents about a brand or store that they have never encountered creates a problem. Since respondents may be forgetful, time periods should be relatively short. For example: 'Did you purchase one or more cola(s) within the last week?'
- *Consider the willingness of the respondent to answer the question*. 'Embarrassing' topics that deal with things such as borrowing money, sexual activities and criminal records must be

dealt with carefully. One technique is to ask the question in the third person or to state that the behaviour or attitude is not unusual prior to asking the question. For example: 'Millions of people suffer from haemorrhoids. Do you or does any member of your family suffer from this problem?' It is also a feasible solution to ask about embarrassing topics at the end of the interview.

The impact of language and culture is of particular importance when wording questions. The goal for the global marketing researcher should be to ensure that the potential for misunderstandings and misinterpretations of spoken or written words is minimized. Both language and cultural differences make this issue an extremely sensitive one in the global marketing research process.

In many countries different languages are spoken in different areas – in Switzerland German is used in some areas and French and Italian in others – and the meaning of words often differs from country to country. For example, in the United States the concept of 'family' generally refers only to the parents and children. In the southern part of Europe, the Middle East and many Latin countries it may also include grandparents, uncles, aunts, cousins and so forth.

When finally evaluating the questionnaire, the following items should be considered:

- Is a certain question necessary? The phrase 'It would be nice to know' is often heard, but each question should either serve a purpose or be omitted.
- Is the questionnaire too long?
- Will the questions achieve the survey objectives?

Pretesting

No matter how comfortable and experienced the researcher is in international research activities, an instrument should always be pretested. Ideally such a pretest is carried out with a subset of the population under study, but a pretest should at least be conducted with knowledgeable experts and/or individuals. The pretest should also be conducted in the same mode as the final interview. If the study is to be on the street or in the shopping arcade, then the pretest should be the same. Even though a pretest may mean time delays and additional cost the risks of poor research are simply too great for this process to be omitted.

Data collection

The global marketing researcher must check that the data are gathered correctly, efficiently and at a reasonable cost. The market researcher has to establish the parameters under which the research is conducted. Without clear instructions the interviews may be conducted in different ways by different interviewers. Therefore the interviewers have to be instructed about the nature of the study, start and completion time and sampling methodology. Sometimes a sample interview is included with detailed information on probing and quotas. Spot checks on these administration procedures are vital to ensure reasonable data quality.

Data analysis and interpretation

Once data have been collected the final steps are the analysis and interpretation of findings in the light of the stated problem. Analysing data from cross-country studies calls for substantial creativity as well as scepticism. Not only are data often limited, but frequently results are significantly influenced by cultural differences. This suggests that there is a need for properly trained local personnel to function as supervisors and interviewers; alternatively international market researchers require substantial advice from knowledgeable local research firms that can also take care of the actual collection of data. Although data in cross-country analyses are often of a qualitative nature the researcher should, of course, use the best and most appropriate tools available for analysis. On the other hand, international researchers should be cautioned against using overly sophisticated tools for unsophisticated data. Even the best of tools will not improve data quality. The quality of data must be matched with the quality of the research tools.

EXHIBIT 5.1 Market research in India is challenging

Today India is on every multinational's radar and there is an increasing trend towards formulating an India-specific strategy. The trillion dollar plus Indian GDP in purchasing-power parity terms (PPP) is now ranked fourth place and with 40 per cent of the population under the age of 15 years, the future is increasingly looking more promising for India.

One uniform strategy cannot be adopted for the Indian market. India is more of a continent than a country with its numerous religions, languages, dialects, customs and traditions. Spread across 29 states and 6 union territories, this market of a billion people is something that needs to be well researched and understood before making the entry strategy. Here some of the most important challenges when doing market research in India:

- One of the largest drawbacks in India is the availability of secondary data in the public domain. Certainly countries like China are better documented. Whatever is available is either outdated or is highly fragmented, with no single authoritative source. For example, the latest government census data available is for 2001.

- Company data may be maintained in hard copy, but the digitization process is only a recent phenomenon and progress is slow. This can be prominently seen in dealings with the Registrar of Companies (RoC). Individual RoC offices have different levels of digitization, making it extremely difficult to get similar data for companies across India.

- Although English is the most prevalent business language, consumer insights may well not be covered in English alone. There are 10 major languages that are spoken and have to be considered whilst covering the market. There are also challenges in the translation of questionnaires, as well as their responses.

- Culturally, too, there is a challenge in the interviewing process. For example, when there's a group discussion scheduled, there are bound to be drop-outs or delays at the last minute. Therefore, the sample size of respondents to be taken should be almost double that of the successful numbers intended. In case of high net-worth individuals or senior personnel, additional gestures like personally escorting them have to be provided to ensure that there is participation and cooperation.

- There is a difference between attracting respondents in large cities versus smaller ones. The respondents in smaller cities tend to be more cooperative and willing compared to those from larger ones, where incentives are almost a must for participation.

- Use of technology enablers to streamline the research process. Computer-aided telephonic interviewing (CATI), which is pretty popular internationally for fast turnaround and cost minimization, has its limitations in an Indian context. This could be attributed to the lack of penetration of phone lines across the strata of society and also to the cultural lack of interest in answering the phone. So, CATI is seen to be effective only in the more affluent areas, which constitute around 10 per cent of the country.

- Business respondents (business customers, channel members, suppliers, business partners) have an inherent tendency to be suspicious of giving interviews and sharing information. They tend to respond either vaguely or provide responses that do not necessarily reflect reality in the market. Therefore it is imperative that cross-checks are done.

In conclusion, there are a few golden rules to succeed with market research in India:

- Use multiple data collection sources to validate and strengthen hypothesis about market characteristics

- Hire locally experienced personnel or choose a local partner for the practical reseach tasks.

Source: based on Ramamurthy and Naikare (2009).

Problems with using primary research

Most problems in collecting primary data in international marketing research stem from cultural differences among countries, and range from the inability of respondents to communicate their opinions to inadequacies in questionnaire translation (Cateora *et al.*, 2000).

Sampling in field surveys

The greatest problem of sampling stems from the lack of adequate demographic data and available lists from which to draw meaningful samples. For example, in many South American and Asian cities street maps are unavailable, and streets are neither identified nor houses numbered. In Saudi Arabia, the difficulties with probability sampling are so acute that non-probabilistic sampling becomes a necessary evil. Some of the problems in drawing a random sample include:

- no officially recognized census of population
- incomplete and out-of-date telephone directories
- no accurate maps of population centres, therefore no area samples can be made.

Furthermore, door-to-door interviewing in Saudi Arabia is illegal.

Non-response

Non-response is the inability to reach selected elements in the sample frame. As a result opinions of some sample elements are not obtained or properly represented. A good sampling method can only identify elements that should be selected; there is no guarantee that such elements will ever be included.

The two main reasons for non-response errors are:

1. *Not being at home.* In countries where males are still dominant in the labour force it may be difficult to contact a head of household at home during working hours. Frequently only housewives or servants are at home during the day.
2. *Refusal to respond.* Cultural habits in many countries virtually prohibit communication with a stranger, particularly for women. This is the case in the Middle East, much of the Mediterranean area and throughout most of South East Asia – in fact wherever strong traditional societies persist. Moreover, in many societies such matters as preferences for hygienic products and food products are too personal to be shared with an outsider. For example, in many Latin American countries a woman may feel ashamed to talk with a researcher about her choice of brand of sanitary towel, or even hair shampoo or perfume. Respondents may also suspect that the interviewers are agents of the government, seeking information for the imposition of additional taxes. Finally, privacy is becoming a big issue in many countries: for example, in Japan the middle class is showing increasing concern about the protection of personal information.

Language barriers

This problem area includes the difficulty of exact translation that creates problems in eliciting the specific information desired and in interpreting the respondents' answers.

In some developing countries with low literacy rates written questionnaires are completely useless. Within some countries the problem of dialects and different languages can make a national questionnaire survey impractical – this is the case in India, which has 25 official languages.

The obvious solution of having questionnaires prepared or reviewed by someone fluent in the language of the country is frequently overlooked. In order to find possible translation errors marketers can use the technique of *back translation*, where the questionnaire is translated from one language to another, and then back again into the original language. For example, if a questionnaire survey is going to be made in France, the English version is translated into French and then translated back to English by a different translator. The two English versions are then compared and, where there are differences, the translation is checked thoroughly.

Measurement

The best research design is useless without proper measurements. A measurement method that works satisfactorily in one culture may fail to achieve the intended purpose in another country. Special care must therefore be taken to ensure the **reliability** and **validity** of the measurement method.

In general, 'how' you measure refers to reliability and 'what' you measure refers to validity.

If we measure the same phenomenon over and over again with the same measurement device and we get similar results then the method is reliable. There are three types of validity: construct, internal and external.

- *Construct validity* establishes correct operational measures for the concepts being studied. If a measurement method lacks construct validity it is not measuring what it is supposed to.
- *Internal validity* establishes a causal relationship, whereby certain conditions are shown to lead to other conditions.
- *External validity* is concerned with the possible generalization of research results to other populations. For example, high external validity exists if research results obtained for a marketing problem in one country will be applicable to a similar marketing problem in another country. If such a relationship exists it may be relevant to use the analogy method for estimating market demand in different countries. Estimating by analogy assumes, for example, that the demand for a product develops in much the same way in countries that are similar.

The concepts of reliability and validity are illustrated in Figure 5.5. In the figure, the bull's eye is what the measurement device is supposed to 'hit'.

Situation 1 shows holes all over the target, which could be due to the use of a bad measurement device. If a measurement instrument is not reliable there are no circumstances under which it can be valid. However, just because an instrument is reliable, the instrument is not automatically valid. We see this in *situation 2*, where the instrument is reliable but is not measuring what it is supposed to measure. The shooter has a steady eye, but the sights are not adjusted properly. *Situation 3* is the ideal situation for the researcher to be in. The measurement method is both reliable and valid.

An instrument proven to be reliable and valid in one country may not be so in another culture. The same measurement scales may have different reliabilities in different cultures because of various levels of consumers' product knowledge. Therefore it may be dangerous simply to compare results in cross-country research. One way to minimize the problem is to adapt measurement scales to local cultures by pretesting measures in each market of interest until they show similar and satisfactory levels of reliability.

Reliability
If the same phenomenon is measured repeatedly with the same measurement device and the results are similar then the method is reliable (the 'how' dimension).

Validity
If the measurement method measures what it is supposed to measure, then it has high validity (the 'what' dimension). There are three types of validity: construct, internal and external.

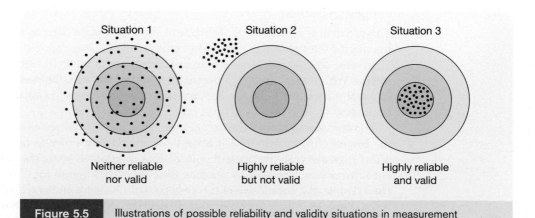

Situation 1	Situation 2	Situation 3
Neither reliable nor valid	Highly reliable but not valid	Highly reliable and valid

Figure 5.5   Illustrations of possible reliability and validity situations in measurement

Source: McDaniel and Gates, (2007, p. 283).

However, as different methods may have varying reliabilities in different countries, it is essential that these differences can be taken into account in the design of a multicultural survey. Thus, a mail survey could be most appropriate to use in country A and personal interviews in country B. In collecting data from different countries it is more important to use techniques with equivalent levels of reliability than to use the same techniques across countries.

5.6   Other types of marketing research

A distinction is made between ad hoc and continuous research.

Ad hoc research

An ad hoc study focuses on a specific marketing problem and collects data at one point in time from one sample of respondents. Examples of ad hoc studies are usage and attitude surveys, and product and concept tests via custom-designed or multi-client studies. More general marketing problems (e.g. total market estimates for product groups) may be examined by using Delphi studies (see below).

Custom-designed studies

These are based on the specific needs of the client. The research design is based on the research brief given to the marketing research agency or internal marketing researcher. Because they are tailor-made such surveys can be expensive.

Multi-client studies

These are a relatively low-cost way for a company to answer specific questions without embarking on its own primary research. There are two types of multi-client study:

1. *Independent research studies.* These are carried out totally independently by research companies (e.g. Frost and Sullivan Inc.) and then offered for sale.
2. *Omnibus studies.* Here a research agency will target specified segments in a particular foreign market and companies will buy questions in the survey. Consequently interviews (usually face-to-face or by telephone) may cover many topics. Clients will then receive an analysis of the questions purchased. For omnibus studies to be of use the researcher must have clearly defined research needs and a corresponding target segment in order to obtain meaningful information.

Delphi studies

This type of research approach clearly aims at qualitative rather than quantitative measures by aggregating the information of a group of experts. It seeks to obtain answers from those who possess particular in-depth expertise instead of seeking the average responses of many with only limited knowledge.

The area of concern may be future developments in the international trading environment or long-term forecasts for market penetration of new products. Typically 10–30 key informants are selected and asked to identify the major issues in the area of concern. They are also requested to rank their statements according to importance and explain the rationale behind the ranking. Next the aggregated information is returned to all participants, who are encouraged to state clearly their agreements or disagreements with the various rank orders and comments. Statements can be challenged and then, in another round, participants can respond to the challenges. After several rounds of challenge and response a reasonably coherent consensus is developed.

One drawback of the technique is that it requires several steps, and therefore months may elapse before the information is obtained. However, the emergence of e-mail may accelerate the process. If done properly the Delphi method can provide insightful forecast data for the international information system of the firm.

Continuous research (longitudinal designs)

A longitudinal design differs from ad hoc research in that the sample or panel remains the same over time. In this way a longitudinal study provides a series of pictures that give an in-depth view of developments taking place. The panel consists of a sample of respondents who have agreed to provide information at specified intervals over an extended period.

There are two major types of panel:

1. *Consumer panels.* These provide information on their purchases over time. For example, a grocery panel would record the brands, pack sizes, prices and stores used for a wide range of supermarket brands. By using the same households over a period of time measures of brand loyalty and switching can be achieved, together with a demographic profile of the type of person or household who buys particular brands.
2. *Retailer panels.* By gaining the cooperation of retail outlets (e.g. supermarkets) sales of brands can be measured by laser scanning the barcodes on goods as they pass through the checkout. Although brand loyalty and switching cannot be measured in this way retail audits can provide accurate assessments of sales achieved by store. The A.C. Nielsen Company is a major provider of retail data.

Sales forecasting

A company can forecast its sales either by forecasting the market sales (called *market forecasting*) and then determining what share of this will accrue to the company or by forecasting the company's sales directly. Techniques for doing this are dealt with later in the chapter. The point is that planners are only interested in forecasts when the forecast comes down to individual products in the company.

We will now examine the applicability and usefulness of the short-, medium- and long-term forecasts in so far as company planners are concerned and then look at each from individual company departmental viewpoints.

- *Short-term forecasts.* These are usually for periods up to three months ahead, and as such are really of use for tactical matters such as production planning. The general trend of sales is less important here than short-term fluctuations.
- *Medium-term forecasts.* These have direct implications for planners. They are of most importance in the area of business budgeting, the starting point for which is the sales forecast. Thus if the sales forecast is incorrect the entire budget is incorrect. If the forecast is over-optimistic then the company will have unsold stocks, which must be financed out of working capital. If the forecast is pessimistic then the firm may miss out on marketing opportunities because it is not geared up to produce the extra goods required by the market. More to the point is that when forecasting is left to accountants they will tend to err on the conservative side and will produce a forecast that is less than actual sales, the implications of which have just been described. This serves to re-emphasize the point that sales forecasting is the responsibility of the sales manager. Such medium-term forecasts are normally for one year ahead.
- *Long-term forecasts.* These are usually for periods of three years or more depending on the type of industry being considered. In industries such as computers three years is considered long term, whereas for steel manufacture ten years is a long-term horizon. Long-term forecasts are worked out from macroenvironmental factors such as government policy,

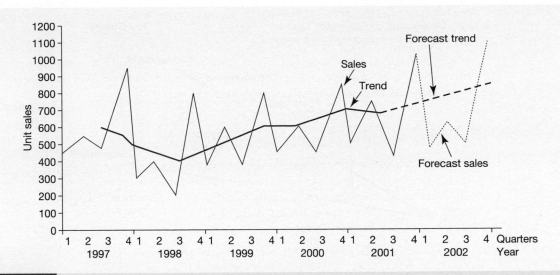

| Figure 5.6 | An example of trend forecasting |

economic trends, etc. Such forecasts are needed mainly by financial accountants for long-term resource implications, but such matters of course are boards of directors' concerns. The board must decide what its policy is to be in establishing the levels of production needed to meet the forecast demand; such decisions might mean the construction of a new factory and the training of a workforce. Forecasts can be produced for different horizons, starting at an international level and then ranging down to national levels, by industry and then by company levels until we reach individual product-by-product forecasts. This is then broken down seasonally over the time span of the forecasting period, and geographically right down to individual salesperson areas. It is these latter levels that are of specific interest to sales management, or it is from this level of forecasting that the sales budgeting and remuneration system stems.

Figure 5.6 shows an example of trend forecasting.

The unit sales and trend are drawn in as in Figure 5.6. The trend line is extended by sight (and it is here that the forecaster's skill and intuition must come in). The deviations from trend are then applied to the trend line, and this provides the sales forecast.

In this particular example it can be seen that the trend line has been extended slowly upwards, similar to previous years. The technique, as with many similar techniques, suffers from the fact that downturns and upturns cannot be predicted, and such data must be subjectively entered by the forecaster through manipulation of the extension to the trend line.

Scenario planning

Scenarios
Stories about plausible alternative futures.

Convergent
Factors driving developments in the same direction.

Divergent forces
Forces driving developments apart from each other.

Scenarios are stories about plausible alternative futures (Wright, 2005). They differ from forecasts in that they explore possible futures rather than predict a single point future. Figure 5.7 shows two different scenarios – A and B – where the outcome – measured on two dimensions – is influenced by both **convergent** and **divergent forces**.

Figure 5.7 shows that the diverging and converging factors have to be balanced. Time flows from the left to the right and the courses of the scenarios pass through a number of time windows, each made up of the key dimensions the scenario writers want to highlight. In Figure 5.7 two 'time windows' are shown: one in two years from now and another one in five years from now. The two dimensions could be e.g. 'worldwide market share' and 'worldwide market growth' for one of the company's main products. The 'convergent forces' would mean that Scenario A and B would come nearer to each other over time. The 'divergent forces' would have the opposite effect.

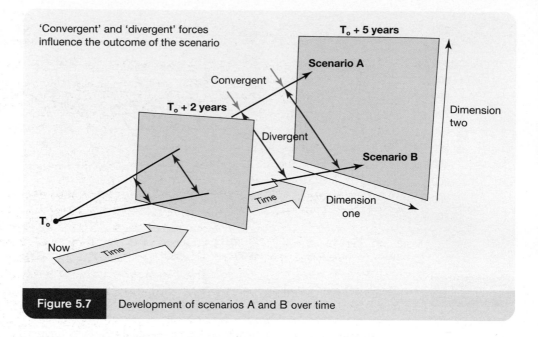

| **Figure 5.7** | Development of scenarios A and B over time |

Examples of *convergent* forces would be:

- high degree of macroeconomic stability in key international markets
- increasing standardization of products across borders.

An example of a *divergent* force would be cultural diversity among target markets.

Scenario planning allows us to consider a range of alternative futures, each of which is dramatically different from the other and from the current operating environment. Rather than rely on a single 'most likely' forecast it is possible to compare and contrast alternative opinions on how your industry may evolve.

Because it is externally oriented scenario planning is very effective at identifying growth strategies for the company as well as potential threats to its market position. Scenarios can also help to identify the specific external industry changes that are causing falling market share or margins.

Guidelines for scenario planning

- *Establish a core planning team.* Analysing the strategic implications of scenarios is best done in teams. The creative dynamics of an effective group are likely to provide the types of breakthrough that will make the scenario process worthwhile. What seems obvious to one person will be surprising to another. A good rule of thumb is to have five to eight people in the planning group.
- *Get a cross-section of expertise.* Include the heads of all functional areas – sales, marketing, operations, purchasing, information technology, personnel, etc. We also recommend including individuals beyond the top executives. This injects new perspectives on your company or your line of trade. This is a great time to involve the rising stars and innovative thinkers in the organization.
- *Include outside information and outside people.* Focus on injecting interesting and challenging perspectives into the discussion. In a group composed solely of insiders it will be hard to achieve breakthrough insights. Outsiders may be customers, suppliers or consultants. If possible, involve an executive from another line of trade or even from outside wholesale distribution. However, many executives feel uncomfortable letting outsiders participate in the planning process of their companies.

| 5.7 | Setting up an international MIS |

Once research has been conducted and the data collected and analysed, the next step is to incorporate this information into management decision-making. More and more businesses are now concerned with increasing the productivity of their marketing efforts, especially in their marketing research departments.

A massive amount of data is available from a wide variety of sources. The trick is to transform that data, ranging from statistics and facts to opinions and predictions, into information that is useful to the organization's marketing decision-makers. The importance of a timely and comprehensive information system is becoming more evident with the increased need to develop closer customer relationships, the increasing costs of making wrong marketing decisions, the greater complexity of the marketplace, and the elevated level of competitor aggressiveness. The need for current and relevant knowledge may result in the development and implementation of information systems that incorporate data management procedures involving generating new data or gathering existing data, storing and retrieving data, processing data into useful information, and disseminating information to those individuals who need it. The **international marketing information system** is an interacting organization of people, systems and processes devised to create a regular, continuous and orderly flow of information essential to the marketer's problem-solving and decision-making activities. As a planned, sequential flow of information tailored to the needs of a particular marketing manager, the international MIS can be conceptualized as a four-stage process consisting of locating, gathering, processing and utilizing information. Figure 5.8 illustrates the central issues to be addressed in each of the four international MIS-stages.

In this holistic international MIS model, input data flow into the system from three major sources: the microenvironment, the macroenvironment and from functional areas of the

International marketing information system
An interacting organization of people, systems and processes devised to create a regular, continuous flow in information essential to the international marketer's problem-solving and decision-making activities around the world.

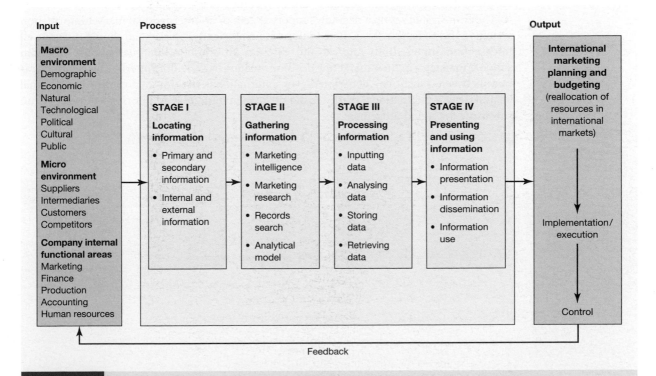

Figure 5.8   International marketing information system

Source: Schmidt and Hollensen (2006), p. 587.

firm. The output information will then be made available to management for analysis, planning, implementation and control purposes. The proposed model meets the exigencies of the ever-expanding role of the MIS professional that has to provide timely, accurate and objective information for management to be able to navigate its way through the complex and fast-changing world of business globalization. Against the backdrop of a dynamic business environment, companies are increasingly developing their marketing information systems to provide managers with real-time market information. Likewise, they are expanding from local to national to global operations while consumers are becoming ever more selective in their product choices.

5.8 Summary

The basic objective of the global marketing research function is to provide management with relevant information for more accurate decision-making. The objective is the same for both domestic and global marketing. However, global marketing is more complex because of the difficulty of gathering information about multiple and different foreign environments.

In this chapter, special attention has been given to the information collection process and the use of marketing information. This coverage is far from being exhaustive, and the reader should consult marketing research textbooks for specific details related to particular research topics.

An international marketer should initiate research by searching first for any relevant secondary data. Typically a great deal of information is already available, and the researcher needs to know how to identify and locate the international sources of secondary data.

If it is necessary to gather primary data the international marketer should be aware that it is simply not possible to replicate elsewhere the methodology used in one country. Some adaptation of the research method to different countries is usually necessary.

The firm should set up a decision support system or an international market information system (MIS) to handle the gathered information efficiently. This system should integrate all information inputs, both internal and external. In addition, an international MIS can support managers in their marketing decision-making by providing interlinkage and integration between functional departments or international divisions. However, in the final analysis, every international marketer should keep in mind that an information system is no substitute for sound judgement.

CASE STUDY 5.1

Teepack Spezialmaschinen GmbH: organizing a global survey of customer satisfaction

Teepack (www.teepack.com) is a specialized manufacturer of tea bag machines for the world's best-known brands of tea and herbs and fruit teas, such as Lipton, Pickwick, Twinings and Lyons/Tetley.

Teepack is a sister company of Teekanne, the leading tea, herb and fruit tea packing company in Germany, with the Teefix, Pompadour and Teekanne brands. The Teekanne Group has production and sales subsidiaries in several countries. There are about 1,300 employees in the Group and a turnover of €177 million (2007). In Teepack there are 200 employees, who generate a turnover of €30 million (2008). Teepack is the only manufacturer of tea bag machines that also has an ownership relation to a major tea bag brand manufacturer (Teekanne).

The invention of the automatic tea bag-packaging machine by Teepack in 1949 revolutionized the tea market with the double-chamber tea bag. It meant that production volumes could be increased dramatically. Today the latest generation of these machines is capable of production speeds of almost 400 tea bags per minute, i.e. some 4 billion a year.

The tea bag produced on Teepack machines is the most sold double-chamber tea bag in the world. Important benefits are that it has considerably larger space between the two bag chambers and offers maximum tea bag stability and durability without adding glue or heat sealing.

The popularity of this practical tea bag has continued to grow. For example, in Germany 82 per cent of tea sales are in double-chamber tea bags; in the United States the figure is about 90 per cent and in Europe, if you omit the United Kingdom, the figure is close to 100 per cent. Even in the former UK colony, Australia, the double-chamber tea bag has almost convinced the consumers. 'Down under', sales of UK tea bags and the double-chamber tea bag more or less balance themselves out.

Since 1950 Teepack GmbH has been the number one producer of double-chamber tea bag packaging machines in the world and has sold more than 2,000 of its packaging machine 'Constanta'. Thanks to Teepack's packaging machines Lipton is the market leader of the international tea market. Up to 1957 Teepack had sold more than 100 tea bag-packaging machines in the United States.

Technical innovation resulted in Teepack engineers developing a new, even more efficient machine – 'Perfecta'. Since 1990 more than 200 Perfecta machines have been sold worldwide.

Today Teepack has a market share of about 70 per cent of the global double-chamber tea bag machine market. Their product range contains more than 200 machines.

QUESTIONS

Please visit www.teepack.com before you answer the questions.

1. How would you forecast worldwide demand for tea bag machines?

2. How can Teepack and Teekanne use the relationships to each other in regard to collecting relevant market research data for both companies?

3. Argue the case for the market analysis method you would choose if you had to evaluate the competitiveness of Teepack Spezialmaschinen on the global tea bag packaging machine market.

4. In order to achieve better customer feedback, the top management of Teepack is interested in learning how to measure customer satisfaction. Propose a questionnaire design that contains some of the themes which it would be relevant to include in the questionnaire.

CASE STUDY 5.2

Tchibo: expanding the coffee shops' business system In Eastern Europe

Tchibo Frisch-Röst-Kaffee GmbH (Hamburg, Germany) was founded in 1949 by Max Herz. Tchibo was originally set up as a mail order company and at that time sent coffee by post. The original mail-order coffee company has grown into a multinational enterprise, active in many more sectors than just traditional coffee retailing. For example, at the end of 2003 Tchibo was one of the top two online shops in Germany.

The first Tchibo specialist coffee shop with coffee counter service opened in Hamburg in 1955. The idea was that customers would have the chance to try the coffee before they bought a whole packet. This idea has been consistently developed ever since.

The retailing concept typical of Tchibo combines sales of roasted coffee with counter sales of coffee specialities, surrounded by attractive merchandise that changes every week.

Table 1 shows the Tchibo coffee shops in Europe. Tchibo is market leader in the German, Austrian, Czech, Hungarian and Polish household roasted coffee market with its coffee brands Tchibo, Gala von Eduscho and local brands. This success is partly based on the systematic development of a business 'system',

Tchibo.

which combines Tchibo roasted coffee and coffee bar sales with a rich variety of innovative consumer merchandise and services. The number of Tchibo Coffee shops is now around 1,000 (see Table 1). In comparison, Starbucks has around 9,000 own company-operated coffee shops in 47 countries. The product range in the Tchibo coffee business system is being developed on a continual basis and expanded by offering innovative weekly changing new products. Tchibo's uniqueness is emphasized by the fact that not all products are offered at the same time but that the assortment changes 52 times a year. The motto 'A new experience every week' enables Tchibo to surprise its customers every Wednesday with introduction of a new theme, made of around 25 products.

In 2007 Tchibo decided to withdraw from France and Netherlands.

In the United Kingdom, Tchibo had successfully opened about 100 coffee shops mainly in the southern part of England, as stand-alone coffee shops in the British supermarket chains Somerfields and Sainsbury. However, in late 2008, following a consultation period, Tchibo was considering closing half of its existing retail stores (100 stores) and restructuring the head office and field teams. The UK business had been burdened by sluggish demand and a drop in British consumers' confidence had aggravated the situation. The company has also

Table 1	Tchibo coffee shops in Europe in 2008
Country	**Number of coffee shops**
Germany	around 600
United Kingdom	around 70
Switzerland	around 100
Austria	around 200
Poland	around 50
Czech Republic	around 25
Turkey	around 25
Total	**around 1070**

Source: Tchibo and other public sources.

announced the closure of a series of coffee shops in its core German market, where it has suffered intense competition from discount supermarkets.

Tchibo is owned by some members of the Herz family, which also hold a majority stake in Beiersdorf, the maker of Nivea personal care products.

QUESTIONS

Tchibo is planning to expand its business system in Eastern Europe. The company plans to open over 400 coffee shops in Russia, Ukraine and Romania.

However, in order to develop the right promotion to the right customer group, Tchibo asks you as an international marketing consultant to answer the following questions.

1. Which market analysis should be made in Eastern Europe in order to target the right promotion campaign to the right customer group?

2. How would you estimate the potential market for coffee shops (in general) in Europe?

3. How will you use market analysis methods for estimating the possible European market share of Tchibo coffee shops?

Sources: www.tchibo.com; Reuters: German coffee firm Tchibo scales down the UK business, 26 November 2008; http://www.reuters.com/article/rbssConsumerGoodsAndRetailNews/idUSLQ26922220081126; Germany's Tchibo mulls exit from Britain, *Business News for the Food Industry* (Flexnews), 26 November 2008, http://www.flex-news-food.com/pages/20678/Coffee/Germany/germanys-tchibo-mulls-exit-britain.html.

VIDEO CASE STUDY 5.3 Ziba

download from www.pearsoned.co.uk/hollensen

Ziba (www.ziba.com) is an internationally recognized design consultancy that helps companies create meaningful ideas and designs based on understanding consumer behaviour in a deep way. Ziba's current client list includes Fortune 100 heavyweights like Microsoft, Whirlpool and P&G, as well as technology start-ups, service organizations and consumer electronic companies.

Currently there are approximately 100 employees in the company.

Questions

1. Describe some of the market research methodologies that Ziba make use of.

2. Generally, why is 'defining the research problem' a crucial part of the research process?

3. How is Ziba transforming knowledge about consumer behaviour into meaningful insights that can help its customers?

4. Generally, how is marketing research done in an international environment different from national marketing research?

For further exercises and cases, see this book's website at **www.pearsoned.co.uk/hollensen**

Questions for discussion

1. Explore the reasons for using a marketing information system in the international market. What are the main types of information you would expect to use?

2. What are some of the problems that a global marketing manager can expect to encounter when creating a centralized marketing information system? How can these problems be solved?

3. What are the dangers of translating questionnaires (which have been designed for one country) for use in a multi-country study? How would you avoid these dangers?

4. Identify and classify the major groups of factors that must be taken into account when conducting a foreign market assessment.

5. A US manufacturer of shoes is interested in estimating the potential attractiveness of China for its products. Identify and discuss the sources and the types of data that the company will need in order to obtain a preliminary estimate.

6. Identify and discuss the major considerations in deciding whether research should be centralized or decentralized.

7. Distinguish between internal and external validity. What are the implications of external validity for international marketers?

8. Would Tokyo be a good test market for a new brand planned to be marketed worldwide? Why or why not?

9. If you had a contract to conduct marketing research in Saudi Arabia what problems would you expect in obtaining primary data?

10. Do demographic variables have universal meanings? Is there a chance that they may be interpreted differently in different cultures?

11. In forecasting sales in international markets, to what extent can the past be used to predict the future?

12. How should the firm decide whether to gather its own intelligence or to buy it from outside?

References

Adiham, P.T., Gajre, S. and Kejriwal, S. (2009) 'Cross-cultural competitive intelligence strategies', *Marketing Intelligence & Planning*, 27(5), pp. 666–680.

Cateora, P.R. (1993) *International Marketing*, 8th edn. Irwin, Homewood, IL.

Cateora, P.R., Graham, J.L. and Ghauri, P.N. (2000) *International Marketing*. European edition, McGraw-Hill Publishing, Maidenhead.

Craig, S.C. and Douglas, S.P. (2000) *International Marketing Research*, 2nd edn. John Wiley & Sons, Chichester.

Denzin, N.K. (1978) *The Research Act*, 2nd edn. McGraw-Hill, New York.

Jick, T.D. (1979) 'Mixing qualitative and quantitive methods: triangulation in action', *Administrative Science Quarterly*, 24, December, pp. 602–611.

Malhotra, N.K. (1993) *Marketing Research: An Applied Orientation*. Prentice-Hall, Englewood Cliffs, NJ.

McDaniel, C. Jr. and Gates, R. (2007) *Marketing Research*, 7th edn. John Wiley & Sons, Inc.

Ramamurthy, K. and Naikare, A. (2009) 'Analysing the Indian market', *Business India in Practice*, Spring, pp. 28–31.

Schmidt, M. and Hollensen, S. (2006) *Marketing Research – An International Approach*. FT/Prentice Hall, Harlow (UK).

Waheeduzzaman, A.N.M. (2008) 'Market potential estimation in international markets: a comparison of methods', *Journal of Global Marketing*, 21(4), pp. 307–320.

Wright, A. (2005) 'Using scenarios to challenge and change management thinking', *Total Quality Management*, 16(1), pp. 87–103.

CHAPTER 6
The political and economic environment

Contents

Case studies

Learning objectives

After studying this chapter you should be able to:

- Discuss how the political/legal environment will affect the attractiveness of a potential foreign market.
- Distinguish between political factors in the home country environment and the host country environment.
- Explain the steps in a political risk-analysis procedure.
- Distinguish between tariff barriers and non-tariff barriers.
- Describe the major trading blocs.
- Explore why the structure of consumption is different from country to country.
- Explain how managers can influence local politics.
- Define regional economic integration and identify different levels of integration.
- Discuss the benefits and drawbacks associated with regional economic integration.
- Evaluate consequences of the EMU and the euro on European business.

6.1 Introduction

This chapter is devoted to macroenvironmental factors that explain the many forces to which a firm is exposed. The marketer has to adapt to a more or less uncontrollable environment within which they plan to operate. In this chapter the environmental factors in the foreign environment are limited to the political/legal forces and the economic forces.

6.2 The political/legal environment

This section will concentrate mainly on political issues. The political/legal environment comprises primarily two dimensions:

1. the home country environment;
2. the host country environment.
   Besides these two dimensions there is also a third.
3. The general international environment (see Figure 6.1).

Home country environment

A firm's home country political environment can constrain its international operations as well as its domestic operations. It can limit the countries that the international firm may enter.

The best-known example of the home country political environment affecting international operations was South Africa. Home country political pressure induced some firms to leave the country altogether. After US companies left South Africa the Germans and the Japanese remained as the major foreign presence. German firms did not face the same political pressure at home that US firms had. However, the Japanese government was embarrassed when Japan became South Africa's leading trading partner, and as a result some Japanese companies reduced their South African activity.

One challenge facing multinationals is the triple-threat political environment. Even if the home country and the host country do not present problems, they may face threats in third markets. Firms that did not have problems with their home government or the South African government, for example, could be troubled or boycotted about their South African operations in third countries, such as the United States. Today European firms face problems in the United States if they do business in Cuba. Nestlé's problems with its infant formula controversy were most serious, not at home in Switzerland, or in African host countries, but in a third market – the United States.

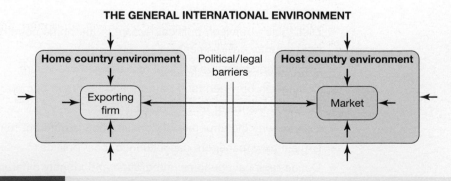

Figure 6.1   Barriers in the political/legal environment

A third area in which some governments regulate global marketing concerns bribery and corruption. In many countries payments or favours are a way of life, and an 'oiling of the wheels' is expected in return for government services. In the past many companies doing business internationally routinely paid bribes or did favours for foreign officials in order to gain contracts.

Many business managers argue that their home country should not apply its moral principles to other societies and cultures in which bribery and corruption are endemic. If they are to compete globally, these managers argue, they must be free to use the most common methods of competition in the host country. Particularly in industries that face limited or even shrinking markets, such stiff competition forces firms to find any edge possible to obtain a contract.

On the other hand, applying different standards to management and firms, depending on whether they do business abroad or domestically, is difficult to envisage. Also, bribes may open the way for shoddy performance and loose moral standards among managers and employees, and may result in a concentration on how best to bribe rather than on how best to produce and market products.

The global marketer must distinguish carefully between reasonable ways of doing business internationally – including compliance with foreign expectations – and outright bribery and corruption.

Promotional activities (sponsored by governmental organizations)

The programmes adopted by governmental organizations to promote exporting are an increasingly important force in the international environment. Many of the activities involve implementation and sponsorship by government alone, while others are the results of the joint efforts of government and business.

Furthermore, so-called regulatory supportive activities are direct government attempts to make its country's products more competitive in world markets. Also, there are attempts to encourage greater participation in exporting, particularly by smaller companies.

The granting of subsidies is of special interest: export subsidies are to the export industries what tariffs are to domestic industries. In both cases the aim is to ensure the profitability of industries and individual firms that might well succumb if exposed to the full force of competition. For export industries, revenue is supplemented by subsidies, or costs are reduced by subsidies to certain input factors. Subsidies can be given through lower taxes on profits attributable to export sales, refunding of various indirect taxes, etc. Furthermore, a subsidy may take the form of a direct grant, which enables the recipient to compete against companies from other countries that enjoy cost advantages, or may be used for special promotion by recipient companies.

In a broader sense, government export promotion programmes, and programmes for global marketing activities in general, are designed to deal with the following internal barriers (Albaum *et al.*, 2002):

- lack of motivation, as global marketing is viewed as more time consuming, costly and risky, and less profitable, than domestic business;
- lack of adequate information;
- operational/resource-based limitations.

Some of these programmes are quite popular in developing countries, especially if they enjoy the support of the business community.

Financial activities

Through the membership of international financial organizations such as the International Monetary Fund (IMF) and the World Bank the national government can assume its role as an international banker. The granting of subsidies is another financially based promotional activity of national governments.

One of the most vital determinants of the results of a company's export marketing programme is its credit policy. The supplier that can offer better payment terms and financing conditions may make a sale, even though its price may be higher or the quality of its product inferior to that of its competitors.

If the credit terms are extended the risks of non-payment increase, and many exporters are reluctant to assume the risks. Consequently, it may be necessary to offer exporters the opportunity of transferring some of the risk to governmental organizations through credit insurance. *Export credit insurance* and guarantees cover certain commercial and political risks that might be associated with any given export transaction.

Information services

Many large companies can collect the information they need themselves. Other firms, even if they do not possess the expertise to do their own research, can afford to hire outside research agencies to do it. However, a large number of companies are not in a position to take either of these approaches. For these firms, generally smaller companies or newcomers to global marketing, their national government is the major source of basic marketing information.

Although the information relevant for international/export marketers varies from country to country, the following kinds are typically available (Albaum *et al.*, 2002, pp. 119–120):

- economic, social and political data on individual countries, including their infrastructure;
- summary and detailed information on aggregate global marketing transactions;
- individual reports on foreign firms;
- specific export opportunities;
- lists of potential overseas buyers, distributors and agents for various products in different countries;
- information on relevant government regulations both at home and abroad;
- sources of various kinds of information not always available from the government: for example, foreign credit information;
- information that will help the company manage its operation: for example, information on export procedures and techniques.

Most types of information are made available to firms through published reports or through the Internet. In addition, government officials often participate in seminars and workshops aimed at helping the international marketer.

Export-facilitating activities

A number of national government activities can stimulate export. These include (Albaum *et al.*, 2002, pp. 119–120):

- Trade development offices abroad, either as a separate entity or as part of the normal operations of an embassy or consulate.
- Government-sponsored trade fairs and exhibitions. A trade fair is a convenient marketplace in which buyers and sellers can meet, and in which an exporter can display products.
- Sponsoring trade missions of business people who go abroad for the purpose of making sales and/or establishing agencies and other foreign representation.
- Operating permanent trade centres in foreign market areas, which run trade shows often concentrating on a single industry.

From the national government's point of view, each of these activities represents a different approach to stimulating the growth of exports. From the point of view of an individual company, these activities provide relatively low-cost ways of making direct contact with potential buyers in overseas markets.

Promotion by private organizations

Various non-governmental organizations play a role in the promotion of global marketing. These include (Albaum *et al.*, 2002, p. 120):

- industry and trade associations, national, regional and sectoral industry associations, associations of trading houses, mixed associations of manufacturers and traders and other bodies;
- chambers of commerce: local chambers of commerce, national chambers, national and international associations of chambers, national chambers abroad and binational chambers;
- other organizations concerned with trade promotion: organizations carrying out export research, regional export promotion organizations, world trade centres, geographically oriented trade promotion organizations, export associations and clubs, international business associations, world trade clubs and organizations concerned with commercial arbitration;
- export service organizations, banks, transport companies, freight forwarders, export merchants and trading companies.

The type of assistance available to firms includes information and publications, education and assistance in technical details and promotion in foreign countries.

State trading

Many of the former communist countries are now allowing some private trading activities, either through joint ventures or as a result of privatization of state-owned enterprises. However, there are still countries with active state trading, such as Cuba and to some extent China.

Private businesses are concerned about state trading for two reasons. First, the establishment of import monopolies means that exporters have to make substantial adjustments in their export marketing programmes. Second, if state traders wish to utilize the monopolistic power they possess, private international marketers will have a difficult time.

Host country environment

Managers must continually monitor the government, its policies and its stability to determine the potential for political change that could adversely affect operations of the firm.

Political risks

There is political risk in every nation, but the range of risks varies widely from country to country. In general, political risk is lowest in countries that have a history of stability and consistency. Three major types of political risk can be encountered:

1. *ownership risk*, which exposes property and life
2. *operating risk*, which refers to interference with the ongoing operations of a firm
3. *transfer risk*, which is mainly encountered when companies want to transfer capital between countries.

Political risk can be the result of government action, but it can also be outside the control of government. The types of action and their effects can be classified as follows:

- *Import restrictions.* Selective restrictions on the import of raw materials, machines and spare parts are fairly common strategies to force foreign industry to purchase more supplies within the host country and thereby create markets for local industry. Although this is done in an attempt to support the development of domestic industry, the result is often to hamstring and sometimes interrupt the operations of established industries. The problem then becomes critical when there are no adequately developed sources of supply within the country.

- *Local-content laws.* In addition to restricting imports of essential supplies to force local purchase, countries often require a portion of any product sold within the country to have local content: that is, to contain locally made parts. This requirement is often imposed on foreign companies that assemble products from foreign-made components. Local-content requirements are not restricted to developing countries. The European Union (EU) has a 45 per cent local-content requirement for foreign-owned assemblers. This requirement has been important for Far East car producers.

- *Exchange controls.* Exchange controls stem from shortages of foreign exchange held by a country. When a nation faces shortages of foreign exchange, controls may be levied over all movements of capital or, selectively, against the most politically vulnerable companies to conserve the supply of foreign exchange for the most essential uses. A problem for the foreign investor is getting profits and investments into the currency of the home country (transfer risks).

- *Market control.* The government of a country sometimes imposes control to prevent foreign companies from competing in certain markets. Some years ago the US government threatened to boycott foreign firms trading with Cuba. The EU countries have protested against this threat.

- *Price controls.* Essential products that command considerable public interest, such as pharmaceuticals, food, petrol and cars, are often subjected to price controls. Such controls can be used by a government during inflationary periods to control the environmental behaviour of consumers or the cost of living.

- *Tax controls.* Taxes must be classified as a political risk when used as a means of controlling foreign investments. In many cases they are raised without warning and in violation of formal agreements. In underdeveloped countries, where the economy is constantly threatened with a shortage of funds, unreasonable taxation of successful foreign investments appeals to some governments as the most convenient and quickest way of finding operating funds.

- *Labour restrictions.* In many nations labour unions are very strong and have great political influence. Using their strength, unions may be able to persuade the government to pass very restrictive laws that support labour at heavy cost to business. Traditionally labour unions in Latin America have been able to prevent lay-offs and plant shutdowns. Labour unions are gradually becoming strong in western Europe as well. For example, Germany and a number of other European nations require labour representation on boards of directors.

- *Change of government party.* A new government may not honour an agreement that the previous government has made with the company. This is a particular issue in the developing countries, where the governing party changes quite often.

- *Nationalization (expropriation).* Defined as official seizure of foreign property, **nationalization** is the ultimate government tool for controlling foreign firms. This most drastic action against foreign firms is fortunately occurring less often as developing countries begin to see foreign direct investment as desirable.

Nationalization
Takeover of foreign companies by the host government.

- *Domestication.* This can be thought of as creeping expropriation and is a process by which controls and restrictions placed on the foreign firm gradually reduce the control of the owners. The firm continues to operate in the country while the host government is able to maintain leverage on the foreign firm through imposing different controls. These controls include: greater decision-making powers accorded to nationals; more products produced locally rather than imported for assembly; gradual transfer of ownership to nationals (demand for local participation in joint ventures); and promotion of a large number of nationals to higher levels of management. Domestication provides the host country with enough control to regulate the activities of the foreign firm carefully. In this way, any truly negative effects of the firm's operations in the country are discovered and prompt corrective action may be taken.

Trade barriers from home country to host country

Free trade between nations permits international specialization. It also enables efficient firms to increase output to levels far greater than would be possible if sales were limited to their own domestic markets, thus permitting significant economies of scale. Competition increases, prices of goods in importing countries fall, while profits increase in the exporting country.

While countries have many reasons for wishing to trade with each other, it is also true to say that all too frequently an importing nation will take steps to inhibit the inward flow of goods and services by effecting **trade barriers**.

Trade barriers
Trade laws (often tariffs) that favour local firms and discriminate against foreign ones.

One of the reasons why international trade is different from domestic trade is that it is carried on between different political units, each one a sovereign nation exercising control over its own trade. Although all nations control their foreign trade, they vary in the degree of control. Each nation or trading bloc invariably establishes trade laws that favour its indigenous companies and discriminate against foreign ones.

There are two main reasons why countries levy tariffs:

1. *To protect domestic producers.* First, tariffs are a way of protecting domestic producers of a product. Because import tariffs raise the effective cost of an imported good, domestically produced goods can appear more attractive to buyers. In this way domestic producers gain a protective barrier against imports. Although producers receiving tariff protection can gain a price advantage, protection can keep them from increasing efficiency in the long run. A protected industry can be destroyed if protection encourages complacency and inefficiency when it is later thrown into the lion's den of international competition.
2. *To generate revenue.* Second, tariffs are a source of government revenue. Using tariffs to generate government revenue is most common among relatively less-developed nations. The main reason is that less-developed nations tend to have less formal domestic economies that presently lack the capability to record domestic transactions accurately. The lack of accurate record keeping makes the collection of sales taxes within the country extremely difficult. Nations solve the problem by simply raising their needed revenue through import and export tariffs. Those nations obtaining a greater portion of their total revenue from taxes on international trade are mainly the poorer nations.

Trade distortion practices can be grouped into two basic categories: tariff and non-tariff barriers.

Tariff barriers

Tariffs
A tool that is used by governments to protect local companies from outside competition. The most common forms are quotas, *ad valorem* and discriminatory.

Tariffs are direct taxes and charges imposed on imports. They are generally simple, straightforward and easy for the country to administer. While they are a barrier to trade they are a visible and known quantity and so can be accounted for by companies when developing their marketing strategies.

Tariffs are used by poorer nations as the easiest means of collecting revenue and protecting certain home industries. They are a useful tool for politicians to show indigenous manufacturers that they are actively trying to protect their home markets.

The most common forms of tariffs are:

- *Specific.* Charges are imposed on particular products, by either weight or volume, and usually stated in the local currency.
- *Ad valorem.* The charge is a straight percentage of the value of the goods (the import price).
- *Discriminatory.* In this case the tariff is charged against goods coming from a particular country, either where there is a trade imbalance or for political purposes.

Non-tariff barriers

In the past 40 years the world has seen a gradual reduction in tariff barriers in most developed nations. However, in parallel to this, non-tariff barriers have substantially increased. Non-tariff barriers are much more elusive and can be more easily disguised. Their effect can be more devastating because they are an unknown quantity and are much less predictable.

Among non-tariff barriers the most important (not mentioned earlier) are as follows.

Quotas

A restriction on the amount (measured in units or weight) of a good that can enter or leave a country during a certain period of time is called a *quota*. After tariffs, a quota is the second most common type of trade barrier. Governments typically administer their quota systems by granting quota licences to the companies or governments of other nations (in the case of import quotas), and domestic producers (in the case of export quotas). Governments normally grant such licences on a year-by-year basis.

There are two reasons why a government imposes *import quotas*:

1. It may wish to protect its domestic producers by placing a limit on the amount of goods allowed to enter the country. This helps domestic producers maintain their market shares and prices because competitive forces are restrained. In this case, domestic producers win because of the protection of their markets. Consumers lose because of higher prices and less selection due to lower competition. Other losers include domestic producers whose own production requires the import to be slapped with a quota. Companies relying on the importation of so-called 'intermediate' goods will find the final cost of their own products increases.
2. It may impose import quotas to force the companies of other nations to compete against one another for the limited amount of imports allowed. Thus those wishing to get a piece of the action will likely lower the price that they are asking for their goods. In this case, consumers win from the resulting lower prices. Domestic producers of competing goods win if external producers do not undercut their prices, but lose if they do.

Likewise, there are at least two reasons why a country imposes *export quotas* on its domestic producers:

1. It may wish to maintain adequate supplies of a product in the home market. This motive is most common among countries exporting natural resources that are essential to domestic business or the long-term survival of a nation.
2. It may restrict exports to restrict supply on world markets, thereby increasing the international price of the good. This is the motive behind the formation and activities of the Organization of Petroleum Exporting Countries (OPEC). This group of nations from the Middle East and Latin America attempts to restrict the world's supply of crude oil to earn greater profits.

A unique version of the export quota is called a *voluntary export restraint* (VER) – a quota that a nation imposes on its exports usually at the request of another nation. Countries normally self-impose a voluntary export restraint in response to the threat of an import quota or total ban on the product by an importing nation. The classic example of the use of a voluntary export restraint is the automobile industry in the 1980s. Japanese carmakers were making significant market share gains in the US market. The closing of US carmakers' production facilities in the United States was creating a volatile anti-Japan sentiment among the population and the US Congress. Fearing punitive legislation in Congress if Japan did not limit its auto exports to the United States, the Japanese government and its carmakers self-imposed a voluntary export restraint on cars headed for the United States.

Consumers in the country that imposes an export quota benefit from greater supply and the resulting lower prices if domestic producers do not curtail production. Producers in an importing country benefit because the goods of producers from the exporting country are restrained, which may allow them to increase prices. Export quotas hurt consumers in the importing nation because of reduced selection and perhaps higher prices. However, export quotas might allow these same consumers to retain their jobs if imports were threatening to put domestic producers out of business. Again, detailed economic studies are needed to determine the winners and losers in any particular export quota case.

Embargoes

A complete ban on trade (imports and exports) in one or more products with a particular country is called an *embargo*. An embargo may be placed on one or a few goods or completely ban trade in all goods. It is the most restrictive non-tariff trade barrier available and is typically applied to accomplish political goals. Embargoes can be decreed by individual nations or by supranational organizations such as the United Nations. Because they can be very difficult to enforce, embargoes are used less today than in the past. One example of a total ban on trade with another country has been the United States' embargo on trade with Cuba.

Administrative delays

Regulatory controls or bureaucratic rules designed to impair the rapid flow of imports into a country are called *administrative delays*. This non-tariff barrier includes a wide range of government actions such as requiring international air carriers to land at inconvenient airports; requiring product inspections that damage the product itself; purposely understaffing customs offices to cause unusual time delays; and requiring special licences that take a long time to obtain. The objective of such administrative delays for a country is to discriminate against imported products – in a word, it is protectionism.

Although Japan has removed some of its trade barriers many subtle obstacles to imports remain. Products ranging from cold pills and vitamins to farm products and building materials find it hard to penetrate the Japanese market.

Local-content requirements

Laws stipulating that a specified amount of a good or service be supplied by producers in the domestic market are called local-content requirements. These requirements can state that a certain portion of the end product consist of domestically produced goods, or that a certain portion of the final cost of a product have domestic sources.

The purpose of local-content requirements is to force companies from other nations to employ local resources in their production processes – particularly labour. Similar to other restraints on imports, such requirements help protect domestic producers from the price advantage of companies based in other, low-wage countries. Today companies can circumvent local-content requirements by locating production facilities inside the nation stipulating such restrictions.

Historical development of barriers

Non-tariff barriers become much more prevalent in times of recession. The United States and Europe have witnessed the mobilization of quite strong political lobby groups as indigenous industries, which have come under threat, lobby their governments to take measures to protect them from international competition. The last major era of protectionism was in the 1930s. During that decade, under the impact of the most disastrous trade depression in history, most countries of the world adopted high tariffs.

After the Second World War there was a reaction against the high tariff policy of the 1930s and significant efforts were made to move the world back to free trade. World organizations, such as General Agreement on Tariffs and Trade (GATT) and its successor WTO, have been developed to foster international trade and provide a trade climate in which such barriers can be reduced.

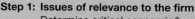

> **Step 1: Issues of relevance to the firm**
> Determine critical economic/business issues relevant to the firm. Assess the relative importance of these issues.

> **Step 2: Potential political events**
> Determine the relevant political events.
> Determine their probability of occurring.
> Determine the cause and effect relationships.
> Determine the government's ability and willingness to respond.

> **Step 3: Probable impacts and responses**
> Determine the initial impact of probable scenarios.
> Determine possible responses to initial impacts.
> Determine initial and ultimate political risk.

Figure 6.2 Three-step process of political risk analysis

The political risk-analysis procedure

The goal of this procedure is to help firms make informed decisions based on the ratio of the return to risk, so that firms can enter or stay in a country when the ratio is favourable and avoid or leave a country when the ratio for them is poor.

Generally political risks are addressed through the building of relationships with the various stakeholders of the company (Erevelles *et al.*, 2005):

- the government
- customers
- employees
- the local community.

Building relationships with government

Managers must be able to deal with the political risks, rules and regulations that apply in each national business environment. Moreover, laws in many nations are susceptible to frequent change, with new laws continually being enacted and existing ones modified. To influence local politics in their favour, managers can propose changes that positively affect their local activities:

- *Lobbying.* Influencing local politics always involves dealing with local lawmakers and politicians, either directly or through lobbyists. Lobbying is the policy of hiring people to represent a company's views on political matters. Lobbyists meet with local public officials and try to influence their position on issues relevant to the company. They describe the benefits that a company brings to the local economy, natural environment, infrastructure and workforce. Their ultimate goal is getting favourable legislation passed and unfavourable legislation rejected.
- *Corruption/bribery.* Though illegal in most countries bribes are common for gaining political influence and building relationships to political decision-makers. This issue is further discussed in section 18.6: Transnational bribery in cross-cultural negotiations.

Building relationships with customers

Local customers support companies that have provided them with desirable products and services. For example, in the case of expropriation the firm that has excelled in relationship building with its customers will have considerable support from them, as they will fear losing the benefits that the firm provides.

Building relationships with employees

Local employees can be very protective of a company, even in times of instability, especially if they perceive that their jobs could be affected by government interference. Therefore, well-treated employees will usually be interested in the company's survival, because they perceive it to be key to their own survival.

Building relationships with the local community

The local community may be concerned that the foreign company will extract materials and labour and make a profit, but fail to give back something to the local environment and the local people. Therefore the company needs to be a good 'local citizen' and reinvest in the local community.

6.3 The economic environment

Market size and growth are influenced by many forces, but the total buying power in the country and the availability or non-availability of electricity, telephone systems, modern roads and other types of infrastructure will influence the direction of that spending.

Economic development results from one of three types of economic activity:

1. *Primary*. These activities are concerned with agriculture and extractive processes (e.g. coal, iron ore, gold, fishing).
2. *Secondary*. These are manufacturing activities. There are several evolutions. Typically countries will start manufacturing through processing the output of primary products.
3. *Tertiary*. These activities are based upon *services* – for example, tourism, insurance and health care. As the average family income in a country rises the percentage of income spent on food declines, the percentage spent on housing and household activities remains constant, and the percentage spent on service activities (e.g. education, transport and leisure) will increase.

How exchange rates influence business activities

Times of crisis are not the only occasions during which companies are affected by exchange rates. In fact movement in a currency's exchange rate affects the activities of both domestic and international companies. Let us now examine how exchange rate changes affect the business decisions of companies, and why stable and predictable rates are desirable.

Exchange rates affect demand for a company's products in the global marketplace. When a country's currency is *weak* (valued low relative to other currencies), the price of its exports on world markets declines and the price of imports increases. Lower prices make the country's exports more appealing on world markets. They also give companies the opportunity to take market share away from companies whose products are highly priced in comparison.

Furthermore, a company selling in a country with a *strong* currency (one that is valued high relative to other currencies) while paying workers in a country with a weak currency improves its profits.

The international lowering of the value of a currency by the nation's government is called devaluation. The reverse, the intentional raising of its value by the nation's government, is called revaluation. These concepts are not to be confused with the terms *weak* and *strong* currencies, although their effects are similar.

Devaluation lowers the price of a country's exports on world markets and increases the price of imports because the country's currency is now worth less on world markets. Thus a government might devalue its currency to give its domestic companies an edge over competition from other countries. It might also devalue to boost exports so that a trade deficit can be eliminated. However, such a policy is not wise because devaluation reduces consumers' buying power. It also allows inefficiencies to persist in domestic companies because there is now less pressure to be concerned with production costs. In such a case, increasing inflation may be the result. *Revaluation* has the opposite effect: it increases the price of exports and reduces the price of imports.

As we have seen, unfavourable movements in exchange rates can be costly for both domestic and international companies. Therefore, managers prefer that exchange rates be *stable*. Stable exchange rates improve the accuracy of financial planning, including cash flow forecasts. Although methods do exist for insuring against potentially adverse exchange rate movements, most of these are too expensive for small- and medium-sized businesses. Moreover, as the unpredictability of exchange rates increases, so too does the cost of insuring against the accompanying risk.

Law of one price

An exchange rate tells us how much of one currency we must pay to receive a certain amount of another, but it does not tell us whether a specific product will actually cost us more or less in a particular country (as measured in our own currency). When we travel to another country we discover that our own currency buys more or less than it does at home. In other words, we quickly learn that exchange rates do not guarantee or stabilize the buying power of our currency. Thus we can lose purchasing power in some countries while gaining it in others.

The law of one price stipulates that an identical product must have an identical price in all countries when price is expressed in a common-denominator currency. For this principle to apply products must be identical in quality and content in all countries, and must be entirely produced within each particular country.

Big Mac Index/Big MacCurrencies

The usefulness of the law of one price is that it helps us determine whether a currency is over-valued or undervalued. Each year *The Economist* magazine publishes what it calls its 'Big MacCurrencies' exchange-rate index (see Table 6.1).

The index is based on the theory of purchasing-power parity (PPP), the notion that a dollar should buy the same amount in all countries. The theory naturally relies on certain assumptions, such as negligible transportation costs, that goods and services must be 'trad-able', and that a good in one country does not differ substantially from the same good in another country. Thus, in the long run, the exchange rate between two currencies should move towards the rate that equalizes the prices of an identical basket of goods and services in each country. In this case the 'basket' is a McDonald's Big Mac, which is produced in about 120 countries. The Big Mac PPP is the exchange rate that would mean hamburgers cost the same in the United States as abroad. Comparing actual exchange rates with PPP indicates whether a currency is under- or overvalued.

This index uses the law of one price to determine the exchange rate that should exist between the US dollar and other major currencies. It employs the McDonald's Big Mac as its single product to test the law of one price. Why the Big Mac? Because each Big Mac is fairly identical in quality and content across national markets and almost entirely produced within the nation in which it is sold. The underlying assumption is that the price of a Big Mac in any world currency should, after being converted to dollars, equal the price of a Big Mac in the United States. A country's currency would be overvalued if the Big Mac price (converted to

Table 6.1	The hamburger standard (based on 4 February 2009 Big Mac prices)				
Country	Big Mac price in local currency	In US dollars	Implied PPP of the US$ (local price divided by price in US)	Actual exchange rate 1 USD =	Over(+)/ Under(−) valuation against the dollar, %
United States	$3.54	3.54	–	1.00	–
Argentina	Peso 11.50	3.30	3.25	3.49	−7
Australia	A$3.45	2.19	0.97	1.57	−38
Brazil	Real 8.02	3.45	2.27	2.32	−2
Britain	£2.29	3.30	1.55*	1.44*	−7
Canada	C$4.16	3.36	1.18	1.24	−5
Chile	Peso 1,550	2.51	438	617	−29
China	Yuan 12.50	1.83	3.53	6.84	−48
Czech Republic	Koruna 65.94	3.02	18.6	21.9	−15
Denmark	DK29.50	5.07	8.33	5.82	43
Egypt	Pound 13.0	2.34	3.67	5.57	−34
Euro area	€3.42	4.38	1.04	1.28	24
Hong Kong	HK$13.30	1.72	3.76	7.75	−52
Hungary	Forint 680	2.92	192	233	−18
Indonesia	Rupiah 19,800	1.74	5,593	11,380	−51
Israel	Shekel 15.0	3.69	4.24	4.07	4
Japan	¥250	3.23	81.9	89.8	−9
Malaysia	Ringgit 5.50	1.52	1.55	3.61	−57
Mexico	Peso 33.0	2.30	9.32	14.40	−35
New Zealand	NZ$4.90	2.48	1.38	1.97	−30
Norway	Kroner 40.0	5.79	11.3	6.91	−63
Peru	Sol 8.06	2.54	2.28	3.18	−28
Philippines	Peso 98.0	2.07	27.7	47.4	−42
Poland	Zloty 7.00	2.01	1.98	3.48	−43
Russia	Rouble 62.00	1.73	17.5	35.70	−51
Saudi Arabia	Riyal 10.0	2.66	2.82	3.75	−25
Singapore	S$3.95	2.61	1.12	1.51	−26
South Africa	Rand 16.95	1.66	4.79	10.02	−53
South Korea	Won 3,300	2.39	932	1,380	−32
Sweden	Skr 38.0	4.58	10.7	8.30	29
Switzerland	SFr 6.50	5.60	1.84	1.16	58
Taiwan	NT$75.00	2.23	21.2	33.60	−37
Thailand	Baht 62.0	1.77	17.50	35.0	−50
Turkey	Lire 5.15	3.13	1.45	1.64	−12

* Dollars per pound.
Source: *The Economist*, 4 February 2009 © The Economist Newspaper Limited, London (4.2.09).

dollars) is higher than the US price. Conversely, a country's currency would be undervalued if the converted Big Mac price was lower than the US price.

Such large discrepancies between a currency's exchange rate on currency markets and the rate predicted by the Big Mac Index are not surprising, for several reasons. For one thing, the selling price of food is affected by subsidies for agricultural products in most countries. Also, the Big Mac is not a 'traded' product in the sense that one can buy Big Macs in low-priced countries and sell them in high-priced countries. Prices can also be affected because Big Macs are subject to different marketing strategies in different countries. Finally, countries impose different levels of sales tax on restaurant meals.

The drawbacks of the Big Mac Index reflect the fact that applying the law of one price to a single product is too simplistic a method for estimation of exchange rates. Nonetheless, a recent study finds that currency values in 8 out of 12 industrial countries do tend to change in the direction suggested by the Big Mac Index. And for six out of seven currencies that change more than 10 per cent the Big Mac Index was as good a predictor as more sophisticated methods.

Table 6.1 also uses the concept of purchasing-power parity (PPP), which economists use when adjusting national income data (gross national product [GNP], etc.) to improve comparability. PPPs are the rates of currency conversion that equalize the purchasing power of different currencies by eliminating the differences in price levels between countries. In their simplest form PPPs are simply price relatives that show the ratio of the prices in national currencies of the same good or service in different countries.

A way to see how a PPP is calculated is to consider Table 6.1 for a product that is identical in several countries. For example, a Big Mac costs Peso 11.50 in Argentina. If we divide 11.50 with the price in the United States, $3.54, the result will be the PPP of the dollar = 3.25 (the 'theoretical' exchange rate of the Peso). Then if we divide 3.25 with the actual exchange rate, 3.49, we find that the Argentina Peso is undervalued by $1 - (3.25/3.49) \times 100 = 7$ per cent.

However, the easiest way to calculate the over- or undervaluation of the local currency against the US$ is to divide the local Big Mac price (in US$) with the US Big Mac Price. So, for example, the Indonesian Rupiah is undervalued with $1 - (1.74/3.54) \times 100 = 51$ per cent.

PPPs are not only calculated for individual products; they are calculated for a 'basket' of products, and PPP is meaningful only when applied to such a basket.

Classification by income

Gross national product (GNP)
Gross national product is the value of all goods and services produced by the domestic economy over a one-year period, including income generated by the country's international activities.

GNP per capita
Total GNP divided by its population.

Countries can be classified in a variety of ways. Most classifications are based on national income (GDP or GNP per capita) and the degree of industrialization. The broadcast measure of economic development is **gross national product (GNP)** – the value of all goods and services produced by a country during a one-year period. This figure includes income generated both by domestic production and by the country's international activities. *Gross domestic product* (GDP) is the value of all goods and services produced by the domestic economy over a one-year period. In other words, when we add to GDP the income generated from exports, imports and the international operations of a nation's companies, we get GNP. A country's **GNP per capita** is simply its GNP divided by its population. GDP per capita is calculated similarly.

Both GNP per capita and GDP per capita measure a nation's income per person. In this regard GNI (gross national income) can be regarded as the same as GNP.

Less developed countries (LDCs)

This group includes underdeveloped countries and developing countries. The main features are a low GDP per capita (less than $3,000), limited amount of manufacturing activity and a very poor and fragmented infrastructure. Typical infrastructure weaknesses are in transport, communications, education and health care. In addition, the public sector is often slow-moving and bureaucratic.

It is common to find that LDCs are heavily reliant on one product and often on one trading partner. The typical pattern for single-product dependence is the reliance on one agricultural crop or on mining. Colombia (coffee) and Cuba (sugar) are examples of extreme dependence upon agriculture. The risks posed to the LDC by changing patterns of supply and demand are great. Falling commodity prices can result in large decreases in earnings for the whole country. The resultant economic and political adjustments may affect exporters to that country through possible changes in tariff and non-tariff barriers.

A wide range of economic circumstances influences the development of the LDCs in the world. Without real prospects for rapid economic development private sources of capital are reluctant to invest in such countries. This is particularly the case for long-term infrastructure projects. As a result, important capital spending projects rely heavily on world aid programmes.

The quality of distribution channels varies considerably between countries. There are often great differences between the small-scale, under-capitalized distribution intermediaries in LDCs and the distributors in more advanced countries. Retailers, for example, are more likely to be market traders. The incidence of large-scale self-service outlets will be comparatively low.

Newly industrialized countries (NICs)

NICs are countries with an emerging industrial base: one that is capable of exporting. Examples of NICs are the 'tigers' of South East Asia: Hong Kong, Singapore, South Korea and Taiwan. Brazil and Mexico are examples of NICs in South America. In NICs, although the infrastructure shows considerable development, high growth in the economy results in difficulties with producing what is demanded by domestic and foreign customers.

Advanced industrialized countries

These countries have considerable GDP per capita, a wide industrial base, considerable development in the services sector and substantial investment in the infrastructure of the country.

This attempt to classify the economies of the world into neat divisions is not completely successful. For example, some of the advanced industrialized countries (e.g. the United States and France) have important agricultural sectors.

Regional economic integration

Economic integration has been one of the main economic developments affecting world markets since the Second World War. Countries have wanted to engage in economic cooperation to use their respective resources more effectively and to provide large markets for member-country producers.

Some integration efforts have had quite ambitious goals, such as political integration; some have failed as a result of perceptions of unequal benefits from the arrangement or a parting of the ways politically. Figure 6.3, a summary of the major forms of economic cooperation in regional markets, shows the varying degrees of formality with which integration can take place. These economic integration efforts are dividing the world into trading blocs.

The levels of economic integration will now be described.

Free trade area

The free trade area is the least restrictive and loosest form of economic integration among nations. In a free trade area all barriers to trade among member countries are removed. Each member country maintains its own trade barriers vis-à-vis non-members.

The European Free Trade Area (EFTA) was formed in 1960 with an agreement by eight European countries. Since that time EFTA has lost much of its original significance due to its members joining the European Union. All EFTA countries have cooperated with the European Union through bilateral free trade agreements, and since 1994 through the European Economic Area (EEA) arrangement that allows for free movement of people, products, services and capital within the combined area of the European Union and EFTA. Of the EFTA countries, Iceland and Liechtenstein have decided not to apply for membership of the European Union and Norway turned down membership after a referendum in 1994. Switzerland has also decided to stay out of the European Union.

After three failed tries during the last century the United States and Canada signed a free trade agreement that went into effect in 1989. North American free trade expanded in 1994 with the inclusion of Mexico in the North American Free Trade Agreement (NAFTA).

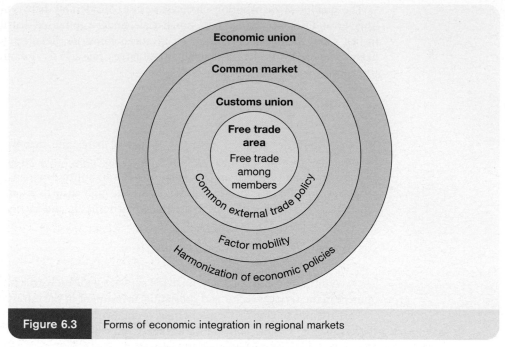

| **Figure 6.3** | Forms of economic integration in regional markets |

Customs union

The customs union is one step further along the spectrum of economic integration. As in the free trade area, goods and services are freely traded among members. In addition, however, the customs union establishes a common trade policy with respect to non-members. Typically this takes the form of a common external tariff, whereby imports from non-members are subject to the same tariff when sold to any member country. The Benelux countries formed a customs union in 1921 that later became part of wider European economic integration.

Common market

The common market has the same features as a customs union. In addition, factors of production (labour, capital and technology) are mobile among members. Restrictions on immigration and cross-border investment are abolished. When factors of production are mobile capital, labour and technology may be employed in their most productive uses.

The removal of barriers to the free movement of goods, services, capital and people in Europe was ratified by the passing of the Single European Act in 1987 with the target date of 31 December 1992 to complete the internal market. In December 1991 the EEC agreed in Maastricht that the so-called 1992 process would be a step towards cooperation beyond the economic dimension. While many of the directives aimed at opening borders and markets were completed on schedule some sectors, such as cars, will take longer to open up.

Economic union

The creation of true economic union requires integration of economic policies in addition to the free movement of goods, services and factors of production across borders. Under an economic union members harmonize monetary policies, taxation and government spending. In addition, a common currency is used by members and this could involve a system of fixed exchange rates. The ratification of the Maastricht Treaty in late 1993 resulted in the European

Union being effective from 1 January 1994. Clearly the formation of a full economic union requires the surrender of a large measure of national sovereignty to a supranational body. Such a union is only a short step away from political unification, but many countries in the European Union (especially in the northern part of Europe) are sceptical about this development because they fear a loss of national identity.

Enlargement of EU

The EU can already look back on a history of successful enlargements. The Treaties of Paris (1951), establishing the European Coal and Steel Community (ECSC), and Rome (1957), establishing the European Economic Community (EEC) and EURATOM (European Atomic Energy Community), were signed by six founding members: Belgium, France, Germany, Italy, Luxembourg and the Netherlands. The EU then underwent four successive enlargements: 1973, Denmark, Ireland and the United Kingdom; 1981, Greece; 1986, Portugal and Spain; 1995, Austria, Finland and Sweden.

After growing from 6 to 15 members, the European Union prepared for its biggest enlargement ever in terms of scope and diversity. Thirteen countries had applied to become new members and ten of these – Cyprus, the Czech Republic, Estonia, Hungary, Latvia, Lithuania, Malta, Poland, the Slovak Republic and Slovenia – joined on 1 May 2004. Bulgaria and Romania joined on 1 January 2007, while Turkey is not currently negotiating its membership. However, Turkey wants to be a member of the EU and the issue will be taken up again in the future.

The current 27 member states of the European Union as on 1 January 2010 are: Austria, Belgium, Bulgaria, Cyprus, Czech Republic, Denmark, Estonia, Finland, France, Germany, Greece, Hungary, Ireland, Italy, Latvia, Lithuania, Luxembourg, Malta, Netherlands, Poland, Portugal, Romania, Spain, Slovakia, Slovenia, Sweden and the United Kingdom.

New countries wanting to join the EU need to fulfil the economic and political conditions known as the 'Copenhagen criteria', according to which a prospective member must (http://europa.eu.int/comm/enlargement): be a stable democracy, respecting human rights, the rule of law and the protection of minorities; have a functioning market economy; and adopt the common rules, standards and policies that make up the body of EU law.

6.4 The European economic and monetary union and the euro

The Maastricht Treaty resulted in the European Economic and Monetary Union (EMU), which also included the new common European currency, the euro (introduced on 1 January 1999). The euro involves the extension of the 'law of one price' across a market comprising more than 320 million consumers, representing one-fifth of the world economy, which should promote increased trade and stimulate greater competition. Consequently the development of this 'new' Europe has an importance beyond the relatively small group of nations currently involved in its creation.

Today, the euro is one of the world's most powerful currencies, used by more than 320 million Europeans in twenty-two countries. As at 1 January 2010, the 16 Eurozone countries that officially use the Euro are:

- Belgium, Germany, Ireland, Spain, France, Italy, Luxembourg, the Netherlands, Austria, Portugal and Finland (joined 1999)
- Greece (joined 2001)
- Slovenia (joined 2007)
- Cyprus, Malta (joined 2008)
- Slovakia (joined 2009)

Notably, the United Kingdom, Denmark, and Sweden have thus far decided not to convert to the euro. Other new EU member countries are working towards becoming part of the Eurozone.

On the other hand, Andorra, Kosovo, Montenegro, Monaco, San Marino and the Vatican City are not EU members but do officially use the euro as their currencies. A total of $16 + 6 = 22$ countries are using the euro as at 1 January 2010.

The consequences of European economic integration will not be restricted to so-called 'European' business. Most obviously the developments associated with the EMU will have a direct impact upon all foreign subsidiaries located within the new euro market. These companies will be forced to adapt their accounting, personnel and financial processes to accommodate the new currency.

The EMU will also affect the international competitiveness of European companies. Reductions in transaction costs, exchange rate risk, intensified domestic competition and the possibilities of gleaning additional economies of scale should all facilitate reductions in the cost structures of European firms, with inevitable consequences upon their external competitors. However, this may be negated by the impact of demands for wage equalization and restrictions imposed by regulations.

With so many important issues in the EMU there is no single economic consensus concerning the likely development of the European economy.

Supporters of EMU claim that the greater nominal exchange rate stability, lower transaction costs (by the introduction of the euro) and price transparency (across European borders) resulting in reduction of information costs will increase the international competitiveness of European business, raising consumer welfare together with the demand for cheaper products. The establishment of an independent European Central Bank (ECB) is anticipated to ensure a low level of inflation, reduce real interest rates and thereby stimulate investment, output and employment.

Opponents of the EMU claim the following:

- The loss of national economic policy tools will have a destabilizing impact.
- The lack of 'real' convergence of participating economies is likely to increase the problem of asymmetric shocks.
- The ECB's attempts at stabilization by the use of a single instrument, a common interest rate, are likely to prove insufficient because the common monetary policy affects EU members differently due to differences in factors, including the concentration of owner-occupation and variable interest borrowing.

Benefits of regional integration

Nations engage in specialization and trade because of the gains in output and consumption, and higher standards of living for all should result from higher levels of trade between nations.

Trade creation

As we have seen, economic integration removes barriers to trade and/or investment for nations belonging to a trading bloc. The increase in the level of trade between nations that results from regional economic integration is called trade creation. One result of trade creation is that consumers and industrial buyers in member nations are faced with a wider selection of goods and services.

Another result of trade creation is that buyers can acquire goods and services at less cost following the lowering of trade barriers such as tariffs. Furthermore, lower costs tend to lead to higher demand for goods because people have more money left over after a purchase to buy other products.

Greater consensus

The WTO works to lower barriers on a global scale. Efforts at regional economic integration differ in that they comprise smaller groups of nations – ranging anywhere from several countries to as many as 30 or more nations. The benefit of trying to eliminate trade barriers in smaller groups of countries is that it can be easier to gain consensus from fewer members as opposed to, say, the 133 countries that comprise the WTO.

Political cooperation

There can also be political benefits from efforts at regional integration. A group of nations can have significantly greater political weight in the world than the nations have individually. Thus nations can have more say when negotiating with other countries. Moreover, integration involving political cooperation can reduce the potential for military conflict between member nations.

Drawbacks of regional integration

Although trade tends to benefit countries, it can also have substantial negative effects. Let us now examine the more important of these.

Trade diversion

The flip side of trade creation is trade diversion – the diversion of trade away from nations not belonging to a trading bloc towards member nations. Trade diversion can occur after formation of a trading bloc because of the lower tariffs charged between member nations. It can actually result in reduced trade with a more efficient non-member producer and increased trade with a less efficient producer within the trading bloc. In this sense economic integration can unintentionally reward a less efficient producer within the trading bloc. Unless there is other internal competition for the producer's good or service buyers will be paying more after trade diversion due to the inefficient production methods of the producer.

Shifts in employment

Perhaps the most controversial aspect of regional economic integration is how people's jobs are affected. Industries requiring mostly unskilled labour, for example, will tend to shift production to low-wage nations within a trading bloc.

Thus trade agreements do cause dislocations in labour markets – some jobs are lost while others are gained.

It is highly likely that countries protecting low-wage domestic industries from competition will see these jobs move to the country where wages are lower once trade and investment barriers are removed. But this is also an opportunity for workers to upgrade their skills and gain more advanced job training. This can help nations increase their competitiveness because a better educated and more skilled workforce attracts higher-paying jobs than does a less skilled workforce. However, an opportunity for a nation to improve some abstract 'factors of production' is little consolation to people finding themselves suddenly without work.

Loss of national sovereignty

Successive levels of integration require that nations surrender more of their national sovereignty. A certain amount of sovereignty has to be surrendered to the trading bloc.

Major trading blocs

Gross domestic product
Plus/minus net income from assets (e.g. subsidiaries abroad) is GNI (= GNP).

Table 6.2 shows the major trading blocs together with their population, GNI (gross national income) and GNI per capita. GNI (= GNP) is the current income indicator used by the World Bank. Previously the World Bank used **gross domestic product** (GDP) which is the total value of all goods and services produced by capital and workers in a country. GNI is GDP plus net income from assets abroad (e.g. subsidiaries). This means that GNI is the total value of all goods and services produced by a country's residents or corporations, regardless of their location (World Bank, 2005).

The size and economic importance of the EU, USA and Japan stand out. The affluence of Luxembourg and Denmark – both small countries – is marked by high values of GNI per capita.

Besides the major trading blocs mentioned in Table 6.2 the most important global market will be the 'triad'.

The triad of Europe, North America and Japan

The global economic size of these three, Europe, the United States and Japan, is disproportionate to their actual number or physical size. Ohmae (1985) cites Japan and the United States alone as accounting for 30 per cent of the free world total, and that with the addition of the United Kingdom, Germany, France and Italy this increases to 45 per cent. Aside from economic wealth these countries share other similarities: mature, stagnant economies; ageing populations; dynamic technological developments and constantly escalating costs of research and development and production facilities. This is all part of the new reality as Ohmae sees it.

This triad creates a market of 600 million with marked demographic similarities and levels of purchasing power as a result of the following:

● growth of capital-intensive manufacturing
● accelerated tempo of new technology
● concentrated pattern of consumption.

A reaction to any of those forces above is protectionism. Ohmae shows that industries critical to wealth generation in the 1980s were all concentrated in Japan, the United States and Europe, constituting more than 80 per cent of global production and consumption. The implication of the triad is that these 600 million consumers share the same desire for the same goods: Gucci bags, Sony Walkmans, McDonald's hamburgers, etc. While there is an international youth market for denims, CDs and tapes, tastes are not the same, nor is purchasing power equal. Psychographic segmentation based on values and attitudes that may also be shared across national boundaries is what is important.

The answer to market entry in each of the triad regions comes through consortia and joint ventures that pose a new challenge for the corporation, as Ohmae points out, of learning how to communicate institutionally with the very different corporate cultures and languages of other companies.

Per capita income

The statistic most frequently used to describe a country economically is its per capita income. This figure is used as a shorthand expression for a country's level of economic development as well as its degree of modernization and progress in health, education and welfare. Partial justification for using this figure in evaluating a foreign economy lies in the fact that it is commonly available and widely accepted. A more pertinent justification is that it is, in fact, a good indicator of the size or quality of a market.

Table 6.2	Major trading blocs as of 1 January 2008				
Organization	Type	Members	Population (million)	GNI (US$bn)	GNI per capita (US$)
European Union	Political and economic union	Belgium	10.7	374.5	44,330
		Luxembourg	0.5	41.4	84,890
		Denmark	5.5	325.1	59,130
		France	62.0	2,702.2	42,250
		Germany	82.1	3,485.7	42,440
		Ireland	4.5	221.2	49,590
		Italy	59.9	2,109.9	35,240
		UK	61.4	2,787.2	45,390
		Netherlands	16.4	824.6	50,150
		Greece	11.2	322.0	28,650
		Portugal	10.6	218.4	20,560
		Spain	45.6	1,456.5	31,960
		Sweden	9.2	469.7	50,940
		Austria	8.3	386.0	46,260
		Finland	5.3	255.7	48,120
		Bulgaria	7.6	41.8	5,490
		Cyprus	0.9	19.6	22,950
		Czech Republic	10.4	173.2	16,600
		Estonia	1.3	19.1	14,270
		Latvia	2.3	26.9	11,860
		Lithuania	3.4	39.9	11,870
		Hungary	10.0	128.6	12,810
		Malta	0.4	6.8	16,680
		Poland	38.1	453.0	11,880
		Romania	21.5	170.6	7,930
		Slovakia	5.4	78.6	14,540
		Slovenia	2.0	49.0	24,010
		Total	**496.5**	**17,187.2**	**34,617**
Association of South East Asian Nations (ASEAN)	Limited trade and cooperation agreement	Indonesia	228.2	458.2	2,010
		Brunei	0.4	10.2	26,740
		Vietnam	86.3	77.0	890
		Malaysia	27.0	188.1	6,970
		Singapore	4.8	168.2	34,760
		Philippines	90.3	170.4	1,890
		Thailand	67.4	191.7	2,840
		Laos	6.2	4.7	750
		Myanmar	49.2	n.a.	n.a.
		Cambodia	14.7	8.9	600
		Total	**574.5**	**1,277.4**	**2,223**
Asia Pacific Economic Cooperation (APEC, excl. ASEAN, USA and Canada)	Formal institution	China	1,325.6	3,678.5	2,770
		Japan	127.7	4,879.2	38,210
		South Korea	48.6	1,046.3	21,530
		Taiwan*	23.0	724.5	31,500
		Australia	21.4	862.5	40,350
		New Zealand	4.3	119.2	27,940
		Total	**1,550.6**	**11,310.2**	**7,294**
North American Free Trade Area (NAFTA)	Free trade area	US	304.1	14,466.1	47,580
		Canada	33.3	1,390.0	41,730
		Mexico	106.4	1,061.4	9,980
		Total	**443.8**	**16,917.5**	**39,119**

* According to the *CIA World Factbook* as Taiwan is not in the World Bank Statistics.
Source: based on *World Bank* (2008).

The per capita income figures vary widely among the countries of the world. The World Bank finds over half the world's population living in countries with an average per capita income of only $330.

However, some criticism can also be made of per capita income figures:

- *Uneven income distribution.* Per capita figures are less meaningful if there is great unevenness of income distribution in the country. This has already been discussed. Per capita income figures are averages and are meaningful if most people in the country are near the average. Frequently, however, this is not the case. Among world nations the Scandinavian countries have a relatively equal distribution of income among people. Even here, however, marketers are very attentive to differences in income levels when studying potential for their product if the product is at all income-sensitive. Many countries have a relatively uneven distribution of income. An extreme example is Brazil, where the lowest 20 per cent of the population receive less than 3 per cent of the national income, whereas the highest 20 per cent receive 63 per cent of that income. This may directly impact the size of the market, especially number of potential customers for certain products.
- *Purchasing power is not reflected.* Per capita income comparisons are expressed in a common currency – usually US dollars – through an exchange rate conversion. The impact of speculation can pull a currency away from its 'true' value.
- *Lack of comparability.* A large part of a European's budget, for example, goes on food, clothing and shelter. In many less developed nations these items may be largely self-provided, i.e. self-sufficient, and are therefore not reflected in national income totals.

Structure of consumption

While it is important to measure the volume of consumption among various cultures, nations and societies, the characteristics of that consumption reveal its structure. Consumption in most advanced countries is characterized by a higher proportion of expenditure devoted to capital goods than in poor countries, where substantially more is spent on consumer goods.

The structural differences with regard to expenditure among nations can be explained by a theory propounded by the German statistician Engel. The law of consumption (Engel's law) states that poorer families and societies spend a greater proportion of their income on food than well-to-do people. Housing, in particular, receives a much smaller share of income in underdeveloped countries than in the advanced nations.

The structure of consumption can also vary among developed countries. While the average person in England eats 13 pounds of cereal a year, per capita consumption in France is just 1 pound, and in Japan less than one-quarter of a pound. Americans eat about 10 pounds of cereal each per year (Jain, 1996, p. 193).

6.5 Poverty as a market opportunity

Poverty is a widespread reality in the modern world. The poor people's market has been seen as a gold mine for reaping business profits and it has been called the 'bottom of the pyramid' (BOP) market (Prahalad, 2004). According to Prahalad focus on the BOP market should be a part of core business and should not be just CSR initiatives: catering to the BOP market (by satisfying unmet social needs and new consumer preferences) business organizations can create market opportunities of substantial value. The development of the business of micro finance is an example of such nature.

According to Prahalad (2004), marketers who believe that the BOP is a valuable unserved market also believe that even the poor can be good customers. Despite their low level of income, they are discerning consumers who want value and are well aware of the value brands favoured by more affluent consumers. This school for thoughts recognizes the obstacle that low income creates. It postulates that if companies take the correct steps and devote sufficient resources to satisfying the needs of the BOP, they can overcome barriers to consumption.

Prahalad recognizes that serving the low-income sector requires a commercial strategy in response to the needs of those people; to succeed, other players have to get involved – mainly local and central government, financial institutions and non-governmental organizations (NGOs). He proposes four key elements to thrive in the low-income market:

1. creating buying power;
2. shaping aspirations through products innovation and consumer education;
3. improving access through better distribution and communication systems; and
4. tailoring local solutions.

In the following we will focus on the BOP-market in relation to 'the poor as consumers'.

The poor as consumers

Poverty is a matter of degrees and involves subjective judgements. Prahalad (2004) uses the criterion of $2 per day at purchasing power parity (PPP) rates in 1990 prices (equivalent to $3.50 in 2008 prices). At this level of poverty, the basic needs of survival are met, but just barely.

Prahalad claims that the BOP potential market is $13 trillion at PPP. According to Karnani (2007) this grossly over-estimates the BOP market size. The *average* consumption of poor people is $1.25 per day. Assuming there are 2.7 billion poor people, this implies a BOP market size off $1.2 trillion at PPP in 2002. Karnani suggests this may also be an overestimated figure and he thinks that the global BOP can be as little as US$0.3 trillion compared to the US$11 trillion economy in the USA alone.

According to Hammond *et al.* (2007), the BOP is concentrated in four regional areas: Africa, Asia, Eastern Europe and Latin America and the Caribbean: 12.3 per cent of the BOP lives in Africa, 72.2 per cent in Asia, 6.4 per cent in Eastern Europe and the remaining 9.1 per cent in Latin America and the Caribbean. Rural areas dominate most BOP markets in Africa and Asia while urban areas dominate most in Eastern Europe and Latin America and the Caribbean.

Some researchers have been very critical of Prahalad's (2004) BOP concept (e.g. Karnani, 2007; Pitta *et al.*, 2008). This group dismisses the published calculations about the size of the BOP and its wealth. They describe the economy size of the BOP as considerably smaller than Prahalad's estimate and cite the inherent subsistence problem: the poor spend 80 per cent of their income on food, clothing and fuel.

The critics of Prahalad also argue that it is very unlikely that companies will be able to attend the BOP market profitably. In fact, the costs of serving this segment can be very high. BOP customers are usually much dispersed geographically; they are very heterogeneous, which reduces the opportunities for obtaining significant economies of scale: and their individual transactions usually represent a low amount of money. In addition, consumers at the BOP are very price sensitive, which, again, makes profitability a difficult goal to achieve.

According to Maslow, there are five core human motives that are satisfied in a hierarchical manner:

1. physiological;
2. safety and security;
3. belonging;
4. self-esteem; and
5. self-actualization.

According to this theory, unless lower order needs are satisfied, higher-level ones remain dormant. However, BOP consumes more than mere survival needs. Indeed the highest increase in the last decade has been in the category of communications and technology; a higher order need. The need to communicate, improve social bonds, get more knowledge and self-esteem are important too. So, while the Maslow framework is a useful way to categorize basic needs, motivation and priorities for BOP's higher order needs might perhaps be explained by other concepts such as social capital and family systems, cultural differences and compensatory consumption (Subrahmanyan and Gomez-Arias, 2008).

BOP like all other consumers also look for goods and services to provide entertainment, sports, cultural and spiritual outlets. Traditional forms of entertainment such as religious festivals and fairs continue to be popular. For example, many poor Indian families spend beyond their means on weddings to save face and to conform to social norms (Subrahmanyan and Gomez-Arias, 2008). Western firms attempt to reap profits from the BOP using current marketing techniques will probably fail. Failure will result because the products are too expensive or complicated, are not available in small enough quantities or sizes, or are simply not what the poor want. The BOP is not low-hanging fruit. It is a market with potential, and achieving that potential will require costly effort and innovative strategies.

Rather than viewing the poor primarily as consumers, this chapter suggests a focus on the segment of producers and marketers of products and services, i.e. potential entrepreneurs that can improve their economic situation by increasing their income level.

The poor as marketers of products and services

In order for the BOP to develop successful entrepreneurs, there are three critical aspects that should be fulfilled in order to serve the BOP market (Pitta *et al.*, 2008)

- access to credit (micro finance)
- the establishment of alliances
- adaptation of the marketing mix.

Access to credit (micro finance)

The concept that a poor consumer could gain a small loan and become a producer contributing to family income and independence is tantalizing. There is evidence that microloans have succeeded in aiding the bottom of the pyramid. There is also evidence that many of the would-be entrepreneurs failed to capitalize on such credit (Karnani, 2007).

Formal commercial credit has been unavailable to this market and the cost of accessing and getting financial services in the informal financial market is enormous.

The decision to award the 2006 Nobel Peace Prize to Muhammad Yunus and the Grameen Bank in Bangladesh has underlined the potential of micro finance in developing countries. Micro finance banks have been set up in most African countries over the past decade but the sheer scale of the Grameen operations is staggering. Providing individuals or very small businesses with access to what are often very small sums of money may seem like a marginal contribution to economic growth but it can widen a nation's economic base and promote the kind of growth that leads to real increases in living standards.

Grameen Bank has now provided credit to over 7 million people, 97 per cent of them women. Most loans are very small and rarely exceed $100. In Bangladesh, the bank usually operates in local temples or village halls. Loans are often used to improve irrigation or to buy new tools to improve efficiency. As part of the Nobel Prize, Yunus was awarded 10 million Swedish Krona ($1.35m), which will be used to find new ways of helping poor people set up their own businesses.

EXHIBIT 6.1 Grameen Danone Foods opens plant in Bangladesh

Grameen Danone Foods Ltd, a joint venture between four Grameen companies and the French company Danone has been set up to provide nutrition-rich yogurts for children in Bangladesh.

The company was inaugurated by French football star Zinedine Zidane at a function in Dhaka, marketing the start of production at the company's first plant in Bogra, Bangladesh.

The yogurt, Shakti Doi, will be made from full cream milk and contain protein, vitamins, iron, calcium and zinc to fulfil the nutritional need of the children. The initial price has been set with a view to being affordable to low-income groups.

Professor Muhammad Yunus, chairman of the Grameen Group, says: 'This represents a unique initiative in creating a social business enterprise with a declared mission to maximize benefits to the people served'.

Over 1,000 women will sell the products locally, generating additional income for their families, and by sourcing raw materials and marketing of products locally business opportunities will be created for local people.

It will also aim to reduce its ecological imprint by selling the yogurt in special biodegradable cups and partly powering the plant by biogas and solar power.

The main objective of the company is profit maximization but creating job opportunities for the poor and it has been agreed no profits will be taken from the company.

Source: based on DII (www.dairyindustries.com), December 2006.

The establishment of alliances

BOP requires the involvement of multiple players including private companies, governments, non-governmental organizations, financial institutions and other organizations – e.g. communities.

By infusing the profit motive into value creation, the hope is that private companies will take the leading role in serving the BOP and, thus, the purpose of alleviating poverty will more likely succeed.

Lastly, the public sector has an important role in developing the BOP proposition. The focus is changing from traditional governmental assistance delivery to different ways of creating a sustainable environment for aiding the BOP. For example, the provision of funding and training to entrepreneurs is a way governments can support consumers and producers at the BOP.

Alliances in the health care sector are also very important. For example, the cost of a ten-day supply of a life-saving antibiotic cannot be reduced realistically using the 'smaller package size' option. The implication would be either reduced daily doses or fewer full strength doses. Both are likely to breed drug-resistant organisms and thereby threaten the life of the patient and society. To remedy this situation, other players like governments and NGOs will be important and marketers must realize that collaborating with them is important.

6.6   Summary

In this chapter we have concentrated on analysing the political/legal and the economic environment as it affects the firm in international markets. Most companies are unable to influence the environment of their markets directly, but their opportunities for successful business conduct depend largely on the structure and content of that environment. A marketer serving international markets or planning to do so, therefore, has to assess carefully the political and legal environments of the markets served or under consideration to draw the appropriate managerial consequences.

Political environment

The international marketer's political environment is complex because of the interaction among domestic, foreign and international politics. When investing in a foreign country firms have to be sensitive to that country's political concerns. The firm should prepare a monitoring system that allows it to evaluate the political risks – such as expropriation, nationalization and restrictions against exports and/or imports – systematically. Through skilful adaptation and control political risks can be reduced or neutralized.

Tariffs have traditionally been used as barriers to international trade. International trade liberalization during the last decade of the twentieth century led to a significant reduction of tariff barriers. Therefore governments have been increasingly using non-tariff barriers to protect those of their countries' industries that they think are unable to sustain free international competition. A government may also support or deter international business through its investment policy, that is, the general rules governing legislation concerning domestic as well as foreign participation in the equity or ownership of businesses and other organizations of the country.

There are various trade barriers that can inhibit global marketing. Although nations have used the WTO to lessen many of the restrictions several of these barriers will undoubtedly remain.

The political risk perspective of a nation can be studied using factors such as:

- a change in government policy
- the stability of the government
- the quality of the host government's economic management
- the host country's attitude towards foreign investment
- the host country's relationship with the rest of the world
- the host country's relationship with the parent company's home government
- the attitude towards the assignment of foreign personnel
- the closeness between the government and people
- the fairness and honesty of administrative procedures.

The importance of these factors varies from country to country and from firm to firm. Nevertheless, it is desirable to consider them all to ensure a complete knowledge of the political outlook for doing business in a particular country.

Economic environment

The economic environment is a major determinant of market potential and opportunity. Significant variations in national markets originate in economic differences. Population characteristics, of course, represent one major dimension. The income and wealth of the nation's people are also extremely important because these key figures determine people's purchasing power. Countries and markets may be at different stages of economic development, each stage having different characteristics.

The Maastricht Treaty resulted in the European Economic and Monetary Union. Consequently the development of this 'new' Europe has an importance beyond the relatively small group of nations currently involved in its creation.

Formal methods for gauging economic development in other nations include: (a) national production, such measures as gross national product and gross domestic product; (b) purchasing-power parity, or the relative ability of two countries' currencies to buy the same 'basket' of goods in those two countries. This index is used to correct comparisons that are made.

CASE STUDY 6.1

G-20 and the economic and financial crises: what on earth is globalization about?
Massive protests during a meeting in London in 2009

The Group of Twenty (G-20) finance ministers and central bank governors was established in 1999 to bring together important industrialized and developing economies to discuss key issues in the global economy on a regular basis. The G-20 was created as a response both to the financial crises of the late 1990s and to a growing recognition that key emerging-market countries (represented in the G-8) were not adequately included in the core of global economic discussion and governance. The inaugural meeting of the G-20 took place in Berlin, on 15–16 December 1999, hosted by German and Canadian finance ministers. The G-20 is made up of the finance ministers and central bank governors of 19 countries: Argentina, Australia, Brazil, Canada, China, France, Germany, India, Indonesia, Italy, Japan, Mexico, Russia, Saudi Arabia, South Africa, South Korea, Turkey, United Kingdom, the USA and the European Union (the twentieth member of the G-20).

On 2 April 2009, the world leaders from the G-20 countries – representing 85 per cent of the world's output – met in London. They met against the backdrop of the worst international banking crisis in generations.

The London summit took place at a time when the world confronts the worst economic crisis since the Second World War and was chaired by UK Prime Minister Gordon Brown (the UK currently has the Chair for the G-20 Finance Ministers meeting).

Building on the outcome of the Washington Summit in November 2008, the aims of the London summit were to bring together leaders of the world's major economies and key international institutions to take the collective action necessary to stabilize the world economy and secure recovery and jobs.

Real action was agreed at the London summit including detailed commitments to strengthen the financial system and additional resources amounting to 1.1 trillion dollars to support jobs and growth across the world.

Like at other World Bank or G-8 meetings there were also massive protests and demonstrations in London. There were an estimated 5,000 people taking part in these demonstrations. The motives were multifaceted: the protesters were as varied as anti-war campaigners, environmentalists (wanting the G-20 to consider moving away from fossil fuel) and anti-globalization activists. The arguments for and against globalization are:

For globalization

For consumers and avowed capitalists globalization is largely a good thing. The fall of protectionist barriers has stimulated free movement of capital and paved the way for companies to set up several bases around the world. The rise of the Internet and recent advances in telecommunications have spurred on the already surging train. Vigorous trade has made for more choice in the high street, greater spending, rising living standards and a growth in international travel. Supporters of globalization say it has promoted information exchange, led to a greater understanding of other cultures and allowed democracy to triumph in most countries.

Against globalization

As the street protests indicate there is a growing opposition to the forces of globalization. The anti-globalization movement developed in the late twentieth century to combat the globalization of corporate economic activity and the free trade with developing nations that might result from such activity.

Critics say the West's gain has been at the expense of developing countries. Demonstrators say rich countries should forgive the debts of the poorest nations. Generally speaking, protesters believe that these global institutions and agreements (WTO, World Bank/IMF, G-8, G-20) undermine local decision-making methods. Many governments and free trade institutions are seen as acting for the good of transnational (or multinational) corporations (e.g. Microsoft, Unilever).

Rock star Bono of U2, who has attended several of these meetings to press for debt relief, said that people's concerns needed to be heard and addressed. He urged ministers to go further to provide debt relief and has lately achieved some results in this area.

SAUL LOEB/AFP/Getty Images.

The already low share of the global income of the poorest people in the world has dropped even more in the past decade, but in the developed world not everyone has been a winner. The freedoms granted by globalization are leading to increased insecurity in the workplace. Manual workers in particular are under threat as companies shift their production lines overseas to low-wage economies.

Developing countries are demanding that the EU and the United States cut back their agricultural subsidy programmes and provide market access for products like Central American sugar or Brazilian orange juice. However, as agribusiness is focal in several EU countries and in the United States, and with thousands of agricultural jobs being at stake in these areas, it is unlikely the US or the EU adminis-

tration will negotiate seriously on these issues in the near future.

At the heart of the demonstrators' concerns is the fact that huge transnational companies are becoming more powerful and influential than democratically elected governments, putting shareholder interests above those of communities and even customers. Ecological campaigners say corporations are disregarding the environment in the stampede for worldwide megaprofits. Human rights groups say corporate power is restricting individual freedom. Even business people behind small firms have sympathy for the movement, afraid as they are that global economies of scale will put them out of work.

The mere fact that the debate can take place simultaneously across countries and continents, however, may well show that the celebrated global village is already here.

Source: based on http://news.bbc.co.uk/2/hi/in_depth/business/2009/g20/default.stm.

QUESTIONS

1. What were the key arguments of the anti-globalization groups?

2. How could these protests affect the operations of multinational companies?

3. How could the G-20 do a better marketing job in communicating its views to the global audience?

CASE STUDY 6.2

Sauer-Danfoss: which political/economic factors would affect a manufacturer of hydraulic components?

Sauer-Danfoss (www.sauer-danfoss.com) is a comprehensive sub-supplier of mobile hydraulic solutions as either components or integrated systems to manufacturers of mobile equipment in

agriculture, construction, material handling and road building, as well as specialty vehicles in forestry and on-highway. With more than 6,000 employees and around 20 factories in North America, Europe and

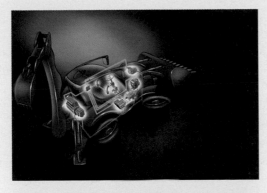

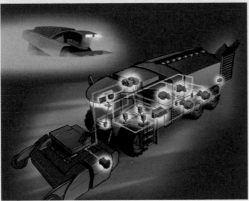

East Asia, Sauer-Danfoss is among the largest manufacturers and suppliers of mobile hydraulics in the world today. It has its principal business centres in Ames, Iowa (US), Neumünster (Germany) and Nordborg (Denmark).

QUESTIONS

1. Which political and economic factors in the global environment would have the biggest effect on the future global sales of Sauer-Danfoss hydraulic components/systems to:

   (a) manufacturers of construction and mining equipment (e.g. Caterpillar)?

   (b) manufacturers of agricultural machinery (e.g. John Deere)?

2. What are the biggest problems in forecasting future demand for a sub-supplier such as Sauer-Danfoss?

The two blue images represent the agricultural market (combine harvester) and construction market (excavator)
Source: © Blue Graphics Concept Sauer-Danfoss.

VIDEO CASE STUDY 6.3 Debate on globalization

download from www.pearsoned.co.uk/hollensen

Globalization seems inevitable, but it is not without controversy. The debate on globalization will continue as people try to make sure that the benefits of global trade outweigh the costs for all countries, not just a select few. Despite the pervasive influence of globalization, it is hard to pin down one definition that will suit everybody. For our purposes, globalization refers to an interdependent world economy – in which people in one part of the world interact with people in another part as buyers, sellers or intermediaries.

Questions

1. In your opinion, is globalization inevitable? Are the overall benefits of globalization positive? What are the gains and losses from globalization?

2. What external influences does a company encounter when determining how and where to conduct business globally?

3. How do the stages that a company goes through evolve as its operations become more globalized?

For further exercises and cases, see this book's website at **www.pearsoned.co.uk/hollensen**

Questions for discussion

1. Identify different types of barrier to the free movement of goods and services.

2. Explain the importance of a common European currency to firms selling goods to the European market.

3. How useful is GNP when undertaking a comparative analysis of world markets? What other approaches would you recommend?

4. Discuss the limitations of per capita income in evaluating market potential.

5. Distinguish between: (a) free trade area, (b) customs union, (c) common market, (d) economic and monetary union and (e) political union.

6. Why is the international marketer interested in the age distribution of the population in a market?

7. Describe the ways in which foreign exchange fluctuations affect: (a) trade, (b) investments, (c) tourism.

8. Why is political stability so important for international marketers? Find some recent examples from the press to underline your points.

9. How can the change of major political goals in a country have an impact on the potential for success of an international marketer?

10. A country's natural environment influences its attractiveness to an international marketer of industrial products. Discuss.

11. Explain why a country's balance of trade may be of interest to an international marketer.

References

Albaum, G., Strandskov, J. and Duerr, E. (2002) *International Marketing and Export Management*, 4th edn. Financial Times/Pearson Education, Harlow.

Erevelles, M.S., Horton, V. and Marinova, A. (2005) 'The triadic model: a comprehensive framework for managing country risk', *The Marketing Journal*, 15(2), pp. 1–17.

Hammond, A., Kramer, W.J., Tran, J., Katz, R. and Walker, C. (2007) *The Next 4 Billion*. World Resource Institute, Washington.

Jain, S.C. (1996) *International Marketing Managment*. South-Western College Publishing, Cincinnati, OH.

Karnani, A. (2007) 'The mirage of marketing to the bottom of the pyramid: how the private sector can help alleviate poverty', *California Management Review*, 49, pp. 90–111.

Ohmae, K. (1985) *Triad Power: The Coming Shape of Global Competition*. The Free Press, New York.

Pitta, D.A., Guesalaga, R. and Marshall, P. (2008) 'The quest for the fortune and the bottom of the pyramid: potential and challenges', *Journal of Consumer Marketing*, 25(7), 393–401.

Prahalad, C.K. (2004) *Fortune at the Bottom of the Pyramid: Eradicating Poverty through Profits*. Upper Saddle River, NJ: Wharton School Publishing.

Sabrahmanyan, S. and Gomez-Arias (2008) 'Integrated approach to understand consumer behavior of bottom of pyramid', *Journal of Consumer Marketing*, 25/7, pp. 402–412.

Whyman, P. (2002) 'Living with the euro: the consequences for world business', *Journal of World Business*, 37(3), pp. 208–215.

World Bank (2005) *Data & Statistics – Quick Reference Tables*. World Bank, Washington, DC, http://web.worldbank.org/.

World Bank (2008) *World Development Indicators Database*, www.worldbank.org.

CHAPTER 7
The sociocultural environment

Contents

Learning objectives

After studying this chapter you should be able to:

- Discuss how the sociocultural environment will affect the attractiveness of a potential market.
- Define culture and name some of its elements.
- Explain the '4 + 1' dimensions in Hofstede's model.
- Discuss the strengths and weaknesses of Hofstede's model.
- Discuss whether the world's cultures are converging or diverging.

7.1   Introduction

Culture as a concept is very difficult to define. Every author who has dealt with culture has given a different definition. Hofstede's (1980) definition is perhaps the best known to management scholars and is used here: 'Culture is the collective programming of the mind which distinguishes the members of one human group from another . . . Culture, in this sense, includes systems of values; and values are among the building blocks of culture' (p. 21).

The importance of culture to the international marketer is profound. It is an obvious source of difference and some cultural differences are easier to manage than others. In tackling markets in which buyers speak different languages or follow other religions, for instance, the international marketer can plan in advance to manage specific points of difference. Often a greater problem is to understand the underlying attitudes and values of buyers in different countries.

The concept of culture is broad and extremely complex. It encompasses virtually every part of a person's life. The way in which people live together in a society is influenced by religion, education, family and reference groups. It is also influenced by legal, economic, political and technological forces. There are various interactions between these influences. We can look for cultural differences in the ways different societies communicate: different spoken languages are used, and the importance of spoken and other methods of communication (e.g. the use of space between people) will vary. The importance of work, the use of leisure and the types of reward and recognition that people value vary from culture to culture. In some countries people are highly motivated by monetary rewards, while in other countries and cultures social position and recognition are more important.

Culture develops through recurrent social relationships which form patterns that are eventually internalized by members of the entire group. In other words, a culture does not stand still, but changes slowly over time. Finally, cultural differences are not necessarily visible but can be quite subtle, and can surface in situations where one would never notice them.

It is commonly agreed that a culture must have these three characteristics:

1. *It is learned*: that is, acquired by people over time through their membership of a group that transmits culture from generation to generation. In the case of a national culture, you learn most intensively in the early years of life. By the age of five you are already an expert in using your language. You have internalized values associated with such functions as:
   - interacting with other members of your family
   - eliciting rewards and avoiding punishments
   - negotiating for what you wanted
   - causing and avoiding conflict.
2. *It is interrelated*: that is, one part of the culture is deeply connected with another part such as religion and marriage, business and social status.
3. *It is shared*: that is, tenets of a culture extend to other members of the group. The cultural values are passed on to an individual by other members of the culture group. These include parents, other adults, family, institutions such as schools, and friends.

Culture can be thought of as having three other levels (Figure 7.1). The tangible aspects of a culture – things you can see, hear, smell, taste or touch – are artefacts or manifestations of underlying values and assumptions that a group of people share. The structure of these elements is like that of an iceberg.

The part of the iceberg that you see above the water is only a small fraction of what is there. What you cannot see are the values and assumptions that can sink your ship if you mistakenly run into them. Daily behaviour is influenced by values and social morals that work closer to the surface than the basic cultural assumptions. The values and social norms help people to make adjustments to their short-term daily behaviour; these standards change over shorter periods of time (ten or twenty years), whereas the basic cultural assumptions are probably formed over centuries.

Culture
The learned ways in which a society understands, decides and communicates.

For the purposes of this book we will define **culture** as the learned ways in which a society understands, decides and communicates.

The visible daily behaviour
e.g. – body language
     – clothing
     – lifestyle
     – drinking and eating habits

Values and social morals
e.g. – family values
     – sex roles
     – friendship patterns

Basic cultural assumptions
e.g. – national identity
     – ethnic culture
     – religion

Figure 7.1	The visible and invisible parts of culture

One way to approach the analysis of cultural influences is to examine cultures by means of a high-context/low-context analysis. Because languages are an important component of culture and an important means of communication we will look at both spoken languages and silent languages.

The differences between some cultures may be large. Language and value differences between the Swiss and Chinese cultures, for instance, are considerable. There are also differences between the Spanish and Italian cultures, but they are much fewer. Both have languages based on Latin – they use the same written form of communication and they have similar, although not identical, values and norms.

EXHIBIT 7.1 Scotch whisky crossing international borders

Scotch whisky is consumed globally but bought for many different reasons. The right image has to be communicated for each culture, without of course losing any of the product's core brand values. The key value for Scotch generally is status.

In the United Kingdom this tends to be underplayed, and is never brash or 'in-your-face'. In Italy the image is more tied to machismo and any Scotch ad would have to show a man with a woman on his arm, flaunting the status the drink confers. In Japan, however, the status value is all about going with the majority. It is not aspirational to be individualistic in Japan.

Thus the understated drinker image that might work in the United Kingdom is inappropriate in other countries.

Source: MacKenzie (1998).

The use of communication techniques varies in different cultures. In some languages communication is based strictly on the words that are said or written; in others the more ambiguous elements such as surroundings or the social status of the message giver are important variables in the transmission of understanding. Hall (1960a) used this finding to make a generalized division between what he referred to as 'low-context cultures' and 'high-context cultures'.

7.2   Layers of culture

The norms of behaviour accepted by the members of the company organization become increasingly important with the company's internationalization. When people with increasingly diverse national cultural backgrounds are hired by international firms the layers of culture can provide a common framework to understand the various individuals' behaviour and their decision-making process of how to do business.

The behaviour of the individual person is influenced by different layers of culture. The national culture determines the values that influence business/industry culture, which then determines the culture of the individual company.

Figure 7.2 illustrates a typical negotiation situation between a seller in one country and a buyer in another country. The behaviour of the individual buyer or seller is influenced by cultural aspects on different levels, which are interrelated in a complex way. Each of the different levels influences the individual's probable behaviour.

In Figure 7.2 the different levels are looked at from a 'nesting' perspective, where the different culture levels are nested into each other in order to grasp the cultural interplay between the levels. The total nest consists of several levels:

- *National culture.* This gives the overall framework of cultural concepts and legislation for business activities.
- *Business/industry culture.* Every business is conducted within a certain competitive framework and within a specific industry (or service sector). Sometimes these may overlap but, in general, a firm should be able to articulate quite clearly what business it is in. This level has its own cultural roots and history, and the players within this level know the rules of the game. Industry culture is very much related to a branch of industry, and this culture of business behaviour and ethics is similar across borders. For example, shipping, the oil business, international trading and electronics have similar characteristics across national borders.

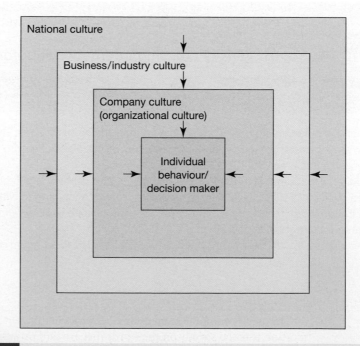

Figure 7.2   The different layers of culture

- *Company culture (organizational culture).* The total organization often contains sub-cultures of various functions. Functional culture is expressed through the shared values, beliefs, meanings and behaviours of the members of a function within an organization (e.g. marketing, finance, shipping, purchasing, top management and blue-collar workers).
- *Individual behaviour.* The individual is affected by the other cultural levels. In the inter-action environment the individual becomes the core person who 'interacts' with the other actors in industrial marketing settings. The individual is seen as important because there are individual differences in perceiving the world. Culture is learned; it is not innate. The learning process creates individuals due to different environments in learning and different individual characteristics.

Further to these levels a 'global culture'-level could be added as the outer boundary of the layer model. Examples from this level could be worldwide enterprises, global brands or organizations, occupation on a global scale and industry on a global scale. Organizational forms operating within multiple national boundaries on two or more continents are global, and their shared belief patterns comprise a global culture. An example is the World Trade Organization, which provides policies for business organizations on a global scale (Wilhelms *et al.*, 2009).

7.3   High- and low-context cultures

Edward T. Hall (1960a) introduced the concept of high and low contexts as a way of under-standing different cultural orientation. Table 7.1 summarizes some of the ways in which high- and low-context cultures differ.

Low-context cultures
Rely only on spoken and written language ('get everything down in the written contract'). Low degree of complexity in communication.

High-context cultures
Use more elements surrounding the message. The cultural context in where the message is communicated has a lot to say. High degree of complexity in communication.

- **Low-context cultures** rely on spoken and written language for meaning. Senders of messages encode their messages, expecting that the receivers will accurately decode the words used to gain a good understanding of the intended message.
- **High-context cultures** use and interpret more of the elements surrounding the message to develop their understanding of the message. In high-context cultures the social import-ance and knowledge of the person and the social setting add extra information, and will be perceived by the message receiver.

Figure 7.3 shows the contextual differences in the cultures around the world. At one extreme are the low-context cultures of northern Europe. At the other extreme are the high-context cultures. The Japanese and Arabs have a complex way of communicating with people according to their sociodemographic background.

In an analysis of industrial buyer behaviour in Arab countries Solberg (2002) found that building trust with partners willing to endorse one's products takes more time in Arab coun-tries than is customary in the West. Networking – using the power of other partners – seems to play a far greater role for Arab buyers. In Arab countries the position of the agent and his network with prominent families may be critical for success. 'Falling in love' with the wrong agent may therefore spoil the exporter's chances of spending a long time in the market.

The greater the context difference between those trying to communicate, the greater the difficulty in achieving accurate communication.

7.4   Elements of culture

There are varying definitions of the elements of culture, including one (Murdoch, 1945) that counts 73 'cultural universals'.

The following elements are usually included in the concept of culture.

Table 7.1	General comparative characteristics of cultures	
Characteristic	**Low-context/individualistic (e.g. western Europe, US)**	**High-context/collectivistic (e.g. Japan, China, Saudi Arabia)**
Communication and language	Explicit, direct	Implicit, indirect
Sense of self and space	Informal handshakes	Formal hugs, bows and handshakes
Dress and appearance	Dress for individual success, wide variety	Indication of position in society, religious rule
Food and eating habits	Eating is a necessity, fast food	Eating is a social event
Time consciousness	Linear, exact, promptness is valued, time = money	Elastic, relative, time spent on enjoyment, time = relationships
Family and friends	Nuclear family, self-oriented, value youth	Extended family, other-oriented, loyalty and responsibility, respect for old age
Values and norms	Independence, confrontation of conflict	Group conformity, harmony
Beliefs and attitudes	Egalitarian, challenge authority, individuals control destiny, gender equity	Hierarchical, respect for authority, individuals accept destiny, gender roles
Mental process and learning	Lateral, holistic, simultaneous, accepting life's difficulties	Linear, logical, sequential, problem-solving
Business/work habits	Deal oriented ('quickly getting down to business'), rewards based on achievement, work has value	Relationship oriented ('first you make a friend, then you make a deal'), rewards based on seniority, work is a necessity

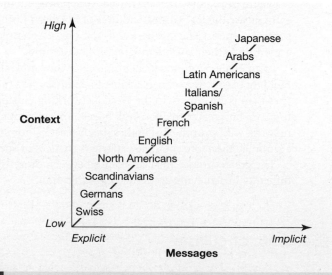

Figure 7.3	The contextual continuum of differing cultures

Source: Usunier, J.-C. (2000). *International Marketing*, Pearson Education Limited.

Language

A country's language is the key to its culture and can be described as the mirror of the culture. Thus, if one is to work extensively with any one culture, it is imperative to learn the language. Learning a language well means learning the culture because the words of the language are merely concepts reflecting the culture from which it derives.

Language can be divided into two major elements. The verbal language of vocal sounds in patterns that have meaning is the obvious element. Non-verbal language is less obvious, but it is a powerful communicator through body language, silences and social distance.

Verbal language

Verbal language is an important means of communication. In various forms, such as plays and poetry, the written word is regarded as part of the culture of a group of people. In the spoken form, the actual words spoken and the ways in which the words are pronounced provide clues to the receiver about the type of person who is speaking.

Language capability plays four distinct roles in global marketing:

1. Language is important in information-gathering and evaluation efforts. Rather than rely completely on the opinions of others, the manager is able to see and hear personally what is going on. People are far more comfortable speaking their own language, and this should be treated as an advantage. The best intelligence is gathered on a market by becoming part of the market rather than observing it from the outside. For example, local managers of a global corporation should be the firm's primary source of political information to assess potential risk. But take care, they may also be biased.
2. Language provides access to local society. Although English may be widely spoken, and may even be the official company language, speaking the local language may make a dramatic difference. For example, firms that translate promotional materials and information are seen as being serious about doing business in the country.
3. Language capability is increasingly important in company communications, whether within the corporate family or with channel members. Imagine the difficulties encountered by a country manager who must communicate with employees through an interpreter.
4. Language provides more than the ability to communicate; it extends beyond mechanics to the interpretation of contexts.

A very important dimension of the language that can vary by culture is the extent to which communication is explicit or implicit. In explicit-language cultures managers are taught that to communicate effectively you should 'say what you mean, and mean what you say'. Vague directives and instructions are seen as a sign of poor communication abilities. The assumption in explicit-language cultures is that the burden of effective communication is on the speaker. In contrast, in implicit-language cultures (mostly high context) the assumption is that the speaker and listener both share the burden of effective communication. Implicit communication also helps avoid unpleasant and direct confrontations and disagreements.

Estimates of the main spoken languages around the world are given in Table 7.2.

Chinese is spoken as the mother tongue (or first language) by three times more people than the next largest language, English. However, Chinese is overtaken by English when spoken business-language population numbers are taken into account.

It should be noted that official languages are not always spoken by the whole population of a country. For example, French is an official language in Canada, but many Canadians have little or no fluency in French.

Hence English is often, but by no means always, the common language between business people of different nationalities.

Table 7.2	Official languages and spoken languages in the world

Mother tongue (first language)	No. of speakers (million)
Chinese	1,000
English	350
Spanish	250
Hindi	200
Arabic	150
Bengali	150
Russian	150
Portuguese	135
Japanese	120
German	100
French	70
Punjabi	70

Note: Chinese is composed of a number of dialects of which Mandarin is the largest.
Source: adapted from Phillips *et al.* (1994, p. 97).

Non-verbal language

Non-verbal language
More important in high-context cultures: time, space (conversational distance between people), material possessions, friendship patterns and business agreements.

Non-verbal language is a powerful means of communication, according to Hall (1960a). The importance of non-verbal communication is greater in high-context countries. In these cultures people are more sensitive to a variety of different message systems, while in the low-context Anglo-Germanic cultures many of these non-verbal language messages would not be noticed.

Non-verbal language messages, according to Hall (1960b), communicate up to 90 per cent of the meaning in high-context cultures. Table 7.3 describes some of the main non-verbal languages.

EXHIBIT 7.2 Sensuality and touch culture in Saudi Arabian versus European advertising

Although Saudi Arabia has a population of only about 9 million people (including 2 million immigrants) the country is the sixth-biggest fragrance market in the world behind the United States, Japan, Germany, France and Italy. Saudi Arabia also has the world's highest per capita consumption of fragrance, leaving all other countries far behind.

In promoting perfumes the big importers generally use the same advertising materials used by marketers in Europe. What is specifically Arabian in the campaigns is often dictated by Arabian morals.

Normally Saudi Arabia is a high-touch culture, but inappropriate use of touch in advertising messages may cause problems. The Drakkar Noir pictures show two advertisements for the men's perfume, in which Guy Laroche (via the advertising agency Mirabelle) tones down the sensuality for the Arab version. The European ad (left) shows a man's hand clutching the perfume bottle and a woman's hand seizing his bare forearm. In the Saudi version (right), the man's arm is clothed in a dark jacket sleeve, and the woman is touching the man's hand only with her fingertip.

Drakkar Noir: Sensuality and touch culture in Europe and Saudi Arabia
Source: Field (1986).

Table 7.3	The main non-verbal languages in international business
Non-verbal language	**Implications for global marketing and business**
Time	The importance of being 'on time'. In the high-context cultures (Middle East, Latin America), time is flexible and not seen as a limited commodity.
Space	Conversational distance between people.
	Example: individuals vary in the amount of space they want separating them from others. Arabs and Latin Americans like to stand close to people they are talking with. If an American, who may not be comfortable with such close range, backs away from an Arab, this might be taken incorrectly as a negative reaction.
Material possessions	The relevance of material possessions and interest in the latest technology. This can have a certain importance in both low-context and high-context countries.
Friendship patterns	The significance of trusted friends as a social insurance in times of stress and emergency.
	Example: in high-context countries extended social acquaintance and the establishment of appropriate personal relations are essential to conducting business. The feeling is that one should often know one's business partner on a personal level before transactions occur.
Business agreements	Rules of negotiations based on laws, moral practices or informal customs.
	Example: rushing straight to business will not be rewarded in high-context cultures because deals are made not only on the basis of the best product or price, but also on the entity or person deemed most trustworthy. Contracts may be bound by handshakes, not complex agreements – a fact that makes some, especially Western, business people uneasy.

Manners and customs

Changes occurring in manners and customs must be carefully monitored, especially in cases that seem to indicate a narrowing of cultural differences between peoples. Phenomena such as McDonald's and Coca-Cola have met with success around the world.

Understanding manners and customs is especially important in negotiations because interpretations based on one's own frame of reference may lead to incorrect conclusion. To negotiate effectively abroad one needs to read all types of communication correctly.

In many cultures certain basic customs must be observed by the foreign business person. One of them concerns the use of the right and left hands. In so-called right-hand societies the left hand is the 'toilet hand' and using it to eat, for example, is considered impolite.

Technology and material culture

Material culture results from technology and is directly related to how a society organizes its economic activity. It is manifested in the availability and adequacy of the basic economic, social, financial and marketing infrastructures.

With technological advancement comes cultural convergence. Black-and-white television sets penetrated the US market extensively more than a decade before they reached similar levels in Europe and Japan. With colour television, the lag was reduced to five years. With videocassette recorders, the difference was only three years, but this time the Europeans and the Japanese led the way, while Americans concentrated on cable systems. With the compact disc, penetration rates were even after only one year. Today, with the Internet or MTV available by satellite across Europe, no lag exists.

Social institutions

Social institutions – business, political, family or class-related – influence the behaviour of people and the ways in which people relate to each other. In some countries, for example, the family is the most important social group, and family relationships sometimes influence the work environment and employment practices.

In Latin America and the Arab world a manager who gives special treatment to a relative is considered to be fulfilling an obligation. From the Latin point of view, it makes sense only to hire someone you can trust. In the United States and Europe, however, it is considered favouritism and nepotism. In India there is a fair amount of nepotism, but there too it is consistent with the norms of the culture. By knowing the importance of family relationships in the workplace and in business transactions embarrassing questions about nepotism can be avoided.

An important part of the socialization process of consumers worldwide is *reference groups*. These groups provide the values and attitudes that become influential in shaping behaviour. Primary reference groups include the family, co-workers and other intimate groupings, whereas secondary groups are social organizations in which less continuous interaction takes place, such as professional associations and trade organizations.

Social organizations also determine the roles of managers and subordinates and how they relate to one another. In some cultures managers and subordinates are separated. In other cultures they are on a more common level, and work together in teams.

Education

Education includes the process of transmitting skills, ideas and attitudes, as well as training in particular disciplines. Even primitive peoples have been educated in this broader sense. For example, the bushmen of South Africa are well educated for the culture in which they live.

One function of education is the transmission of the existing culture and traditions to the new generation. However, education can also be used for cultural change. The promotion of a communist culture in the People's Republic of China is a notable example, but this, too, is an aspect of education in most nations. Educational levels will have an impact on various business functions. Training programmes for a production facility will have to take the educational backgrounds of trainees into account.

The global marketing manager may also have to be prepared to overcome obstacles in recruiting a suitable sales force or support personnel. For example, Japanese culture places a premium on loyalty, and employees consider themselves to be members of the corporate family. If a foreign firm decides to leave Japan employees may find themselves stranded in mid-career, unable to find a place in the Japanese business system. University graduates are therefore reluctant to join all but the largest and most well-known of foreign firms.

If technology is marketed the level of sophistication of the product will depend on the educational level of future users. Product adaptation decisions are often influenced by the extent to which targeted customers are able to use the product or service properly.

Values and attitudes

Our attitudes and values help determine what we think is right or appropriate, what is important, and what is desirable. Some relate to marketing, and these are the ones we will look at here.

The more rooted values and attitudes are in central beliefs (such as religion), the more cautiously the global marketing manager has to move. Attitude towards change is basically positive in industrialized countries, whereas in more tradition-bound societies change is viewed with great suspicion, especially when it comes from a foreign entity.

In a conservative society there is generally a greater reluctance to take such risks. Therefore the marketer must also seek to reduce the risk involved in trying a new product as perceived by customers or distributors. In part this can be accomplished through education; guarantees, consignment selling or other marketing techniques can also be used.

Aesthetics

Aesthetics
What is meant by good taste in art, music, folklore and drama may vary a lot from culture to culture.

Aesthetics refers to attitudes towards beauty and good taste in the art, music, folklore and drama of a culture. The aesthetics of a particular culture can be important in the interpretation of symbolic meanings of various artistic expressions. What is and what is not acceptable may vary dramatically even in otherwise highly similar markets. Sex in advertising is an example.

It is important for companies to evaluate in depth such aesthetic factors as product and package design, colour, brand name and symbols. For instance, some conventional brand names that communicate positive messages in the United States have a totally different meaning in another country, which may substantially damage corporate image and marketing effectiveness (see Table 7.4).

Religion

The major religions are shared by a number of national cultures:

- Christianity is the most widely practised. The majority of Christians live in Europe and the Americas, and numbers are growing rapidly in Africa.
- Islam is practised mainly in Africa, the Arab countries and around the Mediterranean and in Indonesia. There has been a recent rise in Islamic fundamentalism in Iran, Pakistan, Algeria and elsewhere.

Table 7.4	US brand names and slogans with offensive foreign translations			
Company	**Product**	**Brand name or slogan**	**Country**	**Meaning**
ENCO	Petroleum	Former name of EXXON	Japan	'Stalled car'
American Motors	Automobile	Matador	Spain	'Killer'
Ford	Truck	Fiera	Spain	'Ugly old woman'
Pepsi	Soft drink	'Come alive with Pepsi'	Germany	'Come out of the grave'

Source: Copeland and Griggs (1985, p. 62).

- Hinduism is most common in India. Beliefs emphasize the spiritual progress of each person's soul rather than hard work and wealth creation.
- Buddhism has adherents in central and South East Asia, China, Korea and Japan. Like Hinduism it stresses spiritual achievement rather than wealth, although the continuing development of these regions shows that it does not necessarily impede economic activity.
- Confucianism has adherents mainly in China, Korea and Japan. The emphasis on loyalty and obligation between superiors and subordinates has influenced the development of family companies in these regions.

Religion can provide the basis for transcultural similarities under shared beliefs in Islam, Buddhism or Christianity, for example. Religion is of the utmost importance in many countries. In the United States and Europe substantial efforts are made to keep government and church matters separate; nevertheless there remains a healthy respect for individual religious differences. In some countries, such as Lebanon and Iran, religion may be the very foundation of the government and a dominant factor in business, political and educational decisions.

Religion may affect the global marketing strategy directly in the following ways:

- Religious holidays vary greatly among countries, not only from Christian to Muslim, but even from one Christian country to another. In general, Sundays are a religious holiday in all nations where Christianity is an important religion. In the Muslim world, however, the entire month of Ramadan is a religious holiday for all practical purposes.

    In Saudi Arabia, for example, during the month of Ramadan, Muslims fast from sunrise to sunset. As a consequence worker production drops. Many Muslims rise earlier in the morning to eat before sunrise and may eat what they perceive to be enough to last until sunset. This affects their strength and stamina during the working day. An effort by management to maintain normal productivity levels will probably be rejected, so managers must learn to be sensitive to this and similar customs.
- Consumption patterns may be affected by religious requirements or taboos. Fish on Friday for Catholics used to be the classic example. Taboos against beef for Hindus and pork for Muslims and Jews are other examples. The pork restriction exists in Israel as well as in Islamic countries in the Middle East such as Saudi Arabia, Iraq and Iran and South East Asian countries such as Indonesia and Malaysia.
- Islamic worshippers pray facing the holy city of Mecca five times each day. Visiting Westerners must be aware of this religious ritual. In Saudi Arabia and Iran it is not unusual for managers and workers to place carpets on the floor and kneel to pray several times during the day.
- The economic role of women varies from culture to culture, and religious beliefs are an important cause. In the Middle East women may be restricted in their capacity as consumers, as workers or as respondents in a marketing study. These differences can require major adjustments in the approach of a management conditioned to Western markets. Women are, among other things, required to dress in such a way that their arms, legs, torso and faces are concealed. An American female would be expected to honour this dress code while in the host country.

EXHIBIT 7.3 **Polaroid's success in Muslim markets**

During the past 30 years Polaroid's instant photography (though the original camera cannot be bought today) has been largely responsible for breaking down taboos against picture-taking in the Arab world, especially those concerning women revealing their faces.

When Polaroid entered the market in the mid-1960s it discovered that instant photography had a special appeal. Because of religious constraints there were only a few photo-processing laboratories, but with Polaroid's instant cameras Arab men were able to photograph their wives and daughters without fear of a stranger in a film laboratory seeing the women unveiled and without the risk of someone making duplicates.

ROBYN BECK/AFP/Getty Images.

Source: Harper (1986).

7.5 Hofstede's original work on national cultures (the '4 + 1' dimensions model)

While an international manager may have neither the time nor the resources to obtain a comprehensive knowledge of a particular culture, a familiarity with the most pervasive cultural 'differentiators' can provide useful guidance for corporate strategy development. One approach to identifying these pervasive fundamental differences of national cultures is provided by Hofstede (1983). Hofstede tried to find an explanation for the fact that some concepts of motivation did not work in the same way in all countries. He based his research on an extensive IBM database from which – between 1967 and 1973 – 116,000 questionnaires (from IBM employees) were used in 72 countries and in 20 languages.

According to Hofstede, the way people in different countries perceive and interpret their world varies along four dimensions: power distance, uncertainty avoidance, individualism and masculinity.

1. *Power distance* refers to the degree of inequality between people in physical and educational terms (i.e. from relatively equal to extremely unequal). In high power distance societies power is concentrated among a few people at the top who make all the decisions. People at the other end simply carry these decisions out. They accept differences in power and wealth more readily. In low power distance societies, on the other hand, power is widely dispersed and relations among people are more egalitarian. The lower the power distance the more individuals will expect to participate in the organizational decision-making process. A high power-distance score was observed in Japan. The United States and Canada record a middle-level rating on power distance, but countries such as Denmark, Austria and Israel exhibit much lower ratings.

2. *Uncertainty avoidance* concerns the degree to which people in a country prefer formal rules and fixed patterns of life, such as career structures and laws, as means of enhancing security. Another important dimension of uncertainty avoidance is risk-taking. High

uncertainty avoidance is probably associated with risk aversion. Organization personnel in low uncertainty-avoidance societies face the future as it takes shape without experiencing undue stress. In high uncertainty-avoidance cultures managers engage in activities such as long-range planning to establish protective barriers to minimize the anxiety associated with future events. On uncertainty avoidance the United States and Canada score quite low, indicating an ability to be more responsive in coping with future changes. Japan, Greece, Portugal and Belgium score high, indicating their desire to meet the future in a more structured and planned fashion.

3. *Individualism* denotes the degree to which people in a country learn to act as individuals rather than as members of groups. In individualistic societies people are self-centred and feel little need for dependency on others. They seek fulfilment of their own goals over the group's. In collectivistic societies members have a group mentality. They are inter-dependent on each other and seek mutual accommodation to maintain group harmony. Collectivistic managers have high loyalty to their organizations, and subscribe to joint decision-making. The United Kingdom, Australia, Canada and the United States show very similar high ratings on individualism, while Japan, Brazil, Colombia, Chile and Venezuela exhibit very low ratings.

4. *Masculinity* relates to the degree to which 'masculine' values, such as achievement, performance, success, money and competition, prevail over 'feminine' values, such as quality of life, maintaining warm personal relationships, service, care for the weak, preserving the environment and solidarity. Masculine cultures exhibit different roles for men and women, and perceive anything big as important. The feminine cultures value 'small as beautiful', and stress quality of life and environment over materialistic ends. A relatively high masculinity index was observed for the United States, Italy and Japan. In low-masculinity societies such as Denmark and Sweden people are basically motivated by a more qualitative goal set as a means to job enrichment. Differences on masculinity scores are also reflected in the types of career opportunity available in organizations and associ-ated job mobility.

EXHIBIT 7.4 Marriott International fights against 'high power distance' in Asia

Marriott International operates hotels in 60 countries, and the company is planning further expansion abroad, especially in Asia. Marriott emphasizes its 'care of associates' mindset in every hotel and region it enters. The focus of this can vary depending on the needs of the region. In Eastern Europe where employees are gener-ally sceptical of management, Mariott aims to gain associates' trust and emotional attachment; whereas in Asia, where notions of employee empowerment are not widespread (i.e. a high 'power distance'), the company makes an effort to train and empower associates to make independent decisions and take initiative.

Thomas J. Peterson/Alamy.

Source: based on Bellin and Pham (2007).

5. *Time perspective.* In a 23-country study, some years after Hofstede's original work, Hofstede and Bond (1988) identified a fifth dimension that they first termed Confucian dynamism and then renamed 'time orientation'. This time orientation is defined as the way members in an organization exhibit a pragmatic future-oriented perspective rather than a conventional history or short-term point of view. The consequences of a high score on the long-term orientation (LTO) index are: persistence, ordering relationships by status and observing this order. The opposite is short-term orientation, which includes personal steadiness and stability.

Most South East Asian markets, such as China, Hong Kong, Taiwan and South Korea, score high on the LTO index. This tendency has something to do with the Confucian traditions prevalent there. On the other hand many European countries are short-term oriented.

7.6 The strengths and weaknesses of Hofstede's model

The model's strengths are:

- Though the data are 30 years old no study since then has been based on such a large sample (116,000 respondents).
- The *information population* (IBM employees) is *controlled* across countries, which means comparisons can be made. This is a strength despite the difficulties of generalizing to other occupational groups within the same national culture.
- The *four dimensions* tap into deep cultural values and make significant comparisons between national cultures.
- The connotations of each dimension are highly *relevant*. The questions asked of the respondents relate to issues of importance to international managers.
- No other study compares so many other national cultures in so much detail. Simply, this is *the best there is.*

The model's weaknesses are:

- As with all national cultural studies, this one assumes that *national territory* and the limits of the culture correspond. However, cultural homogeneity cannot be taken for granted in countries that include a range of culture groups or with socially dominant and inferior culture groups, such as the United States, Italy (the north/south debate), Belgium (French and Flemish cultures) and Spain (Basque, Catalan and Castillian). The break-up of Yugoslavia during the 1990s demonstrates the futility of trying to create tight political units from disparate national cultures.
- Hofstede's respondents worked within a *single industry* (the computer industry) and a single multinational. This is misleading for two reasons. In any one country the values of IBM employees are typical only to a small group (educated, generally middle class, city-dwelling); other social groups, for instance unskilled manual workers, public sector employees, family entrepreneurs, etc., are more or less unrepresented. This problem of representation would occur whichever single company provided respondents.
- There may be technical difficulties in Hofstede's research due to an overlap between the four dimensions, e.g. small power distance/feminine and large power distance/masculine.
- Likewise the definition of the dimensions may be different from culture to culture, for example, collectivist behaviour in one context might have different connotations elsewhere. For instance, Japanese collectivism is organization based but Chinese collectivism is family based. In Japanese terms, a Taiwanese employee who places his family interests above the interests of the Japanese-owned multinational is disloyal and cannot be fully trusted.

EXHIBIT 7.5 Pocari Sweat – a Japanese soft drink expands sales in Asia

Pocari Sweat is a popular Japanese soft and sports drink, manufactured by Otsuka Pharmaceutical Co., Ltd. The brand started selling in Japan in 1980 and has secured a good foothold for international expansion. The drink is now distributed in 16 countries and regions such as China, South Korea, Taiwan, Thailand, Indonesia, Egypt and the United Arab Emirates. In addition it can be obtained in the Chinatown areas of many cities around the world.

Pocari Sweat's slogan is:

'Pocari Sweat – A drink that smoothly supplies the lost water and electrolytes during perspiration.' 'About 60 per cent of the human body is made up of body fluids and which contains a critical balance of sodium and other ions' is also included in advertising.

www.pocarisweat.info

Contrary to the odd name and its translucent-grey colour, Pocari Sweat does not taste like sweat; it is a mild-tasting, relatively light, sweet drink.

● What do you think about the brand name (Pocari Sweat) and its slogan?

Sources: Otsuka Pharmaceutical Co., Ltd. www.pocarisweat.infopocarisweat.info (website of Pocari Sweat).

7.7   Managing cultural differences

Having identified the most important factors of influence from the cultural environment on the firm's business and analysed those factors, the international marketer is able to take decisions about how to react to the results of the analysis.

In accordance with Chapter 8 (The international market selection process) less attractive markets will not be considered further. On the other hand, in the more attractive markets, marketing management must decide to what extent adaptions to the given cultural specifics are needed.

For example, consider *punctuality*. In the most low-context cultures – the Germans, Swiss and Austrians, for example – punctuality is considered extremely important. If you have a meeting scheduled for 9.00 a.m. and you arrive at 9.07 a.m. you are considered 'late'. Punctuality is highly valued within these cultures, and to arrive late for a meeting (thus 'wasting' the time of those forced to wait for you) is not appreciated.

By contrast, in some southern European nations, and within Latin America, a somewhat looser approach to time may pertain. This does not imply that one group is 'wrong' and the other 'right'. It simply illustrates that different approaches to the concept of time have evolved for a variety of reasons, over many centuries, within different cultural groups. Culture can and does influence the business sector in different parts of the world to function in distinct ways.

Another example of how cultural differences influence the business sector concerns the presentation of business cards. Within the United States – which has a very informal culture – business cards are typically presented in a very casual manner. Cards are often handed out quickly and are just as quickly placed into the recipient's pocket or wallet for future reference.

In Japan, however – which has a comparatively formal culture – the presentation of a business card is a more carefully orchestrated event. There, business cards are presented by holding the card up with two hands while the recipient carefully scrutinizes the information it contains. This procedure ensures that one's title is clearly understood: an important factor for the Japanese, where one's official position within one's organizational hierarchy is of great significance.

To simply take the card of a Japanese and immediately place it in one's card holder could well be viewed (from a Japanese perspective) in a negative light. However, within the United States, to take several moments to carefully and deliberately scrutinize an American's business card might also be taken in a negative way, perhaps suggesting that the giver's credibility is in doubt.

These examples – the sense of time/punctuality and the presentation of the business card – illustrate just two of the many ways in which cultural factors can influence business relationships.

In attempting to understand another culture we inevitably interpret our new cultural surroundings on the basis of our existing knowledge of our own culture.

In global marketing it is particularly important to understand new markets in the same terms as buyers or potential buyers in that marketplace. For the marketing concept to be truly operational the international marketer needs to understand buyers in each marketplace and be able to use marketing research in an effective way.

Lee (1966) used the term *self-reference criterion* (SRC) to characterize our unconscious reference to our own cultural values. He suggested a four-step approach to eliminate SRC:

1. Define the problem or goal in terms of home country culture, traits, habits and norms.
2. Define the problems or goals in terms of the foreign culture, traits, habits and norms.
3. Isolate the SRC influence in the problem and examine it carefully to see how it complicates the problem.
4. Redefine the problem without the SRC influence and solve for the foreign market situation.

It is therefore of crucial importance that the culture of the country is seen in the context of that country. It is better to regard the culture as different from, rather than better or worse than, the home culture. In this way differences and similarities can be explored and the reasons for differences can be sought and explained.

7.8 Convergence or divergence of the world's cultures

As we saw earlier in this book, the right mix between local knowledge of different cultures and globalization/integration of national marketing strategies is the key to success in global marketing.

There seems to be a great difference in attitude towards the globalization of cultures among different age groups, youth culture being more international/global than other age groups (Smith, 2000).

Youth culture

Countries may be at different stages in the evolution of particular product and service categories, but in most cases youth is becoming more homogeneous across national markets. Youth cultures are more international than national. There are still some strong national characteristics and beliefs, but they are being eroded. The McDonald's culture is spreading into southern Europe, and at the same time we can see satellite TV taking the values of MTV, *The Simpsons*, and Ricky Lake all over the world, with English language culture in their wake.

Differences between youth and adult markets are changing in several key respects, the professionals agree. Younger consumers differ from adults in emphasizing quality and being both discerning and technically literate. Younger consumers are now much more self-reliant and take responsibility far earlier. They are sensible, sophisticated and grown-up at an early age.

Generational barriers are now very blurred. The style leaders for many young people – musicians, sports stars and so on – are often in their 30s and 40s. Cultural and family influences remain very strong throughout Europe and the rest of the world. Few young people have 'role models', but they respect achievers in music and sport – and their parents, particularly if their parents have succeeded from humble beginnings.

The lack of clarity in age-group targeting has to be weighed against a growth in cross-border consistencies. However, marketers should beware of strategies aimed too blatantly at younger consumers. Young people tend to reject marketing and promotions that are obviously targeted at 'youth'. They perceive these to be false and hypocritical (Smith, 1998).

Today's young people have greater freedom than previous generations. They are more culturally aware and are reluctant to take anything – or anyone – at face value. Pasco (2000) argues that getting youngsters to relate to celebrities is increasingly difficult. Celebrities often fail or disappoint young people, and again they 'sell out', giving up the integrity for which they were admired in the first place.

Disillusion with celebrities has led young people to look elsewhere for inspiration. They select values from a range of individuals rather than buy wholesale into one. Despite their mistrust of corporations the young increasingly aspire to, and engage with, brands. It appears safer to invest emotionally in brands than in celebrities.

7.9 The effects of cultural dimensions on ethical decision-making

As more and more firms operate globally an understanding of the effects of cultural differences on ethical decision-making becomes increasingly important for avoiding potential business pitfalls and for designing effective *international marketing* management programmes.

Culture is a fundamental determinant of ethical decision-making. It directly affects how an individual perceives ethical problems, alternatives and consequences. In order to succeed in today's international markets managers must recognize and understand how ideas, values and moral standards differ across cultures, and how these in turn influence marketing decision-making.

Some countries, such as India, are well known for 'requiring' small payments if customs officials are to allow goods to enter the country. While this may be a bribe and illegal, the ethics of that country seem to allow it (at least to a certain extent). The company is then left with a problem: does it bribe the official, or does it wait for normal clearance and let its products sit in the customs warehouse for a considerably longer time?

Fees and commissions paid to a firm's foreign intermediate or to consultant firms for their services are a particular problem – when does the legal fee become a bribe? One reason for employing a foreign representative or consultants is to benefit from their contacts with decision-makers, especially in a foreign administration. If the export intermediary uses part of the fee to bribe administrators there is little that the firm can do.

Thus every culture – national, industry, organizational or professional – establishes a set of moral standards for business behaviour, that is, a code of business ethics. This set of standards influences all decisions and actions in a company, including, for example, what and how to manufacture (or not), what wages are appropriate to pay, how many hours personnel should work under what conditions, how to compete and what communication guidelines to follow. Which actions are considered right or wrong, fair or unfair, in the conduct of business and which are particularly susceptible to ethical norms is heavily influenced by the culture in which they take place (bribery is discussed further in Chapter 19).

The ethical commitment of an international company is illustrated in Figure 7.4 as a continuum from unacceptable ethical behaviour to most ethical decision-making.

The adherence only to the letter of the law reflects minimally acceptable ethical behaviour. A classification of a company as 'most ethical' requires that the firm's code of ethics should address the following six major issues:

1. *Organizational relations*, including competition, strategic alliances and local sourcing.
2. *Economic relations*, including financing, taxation, transfer prices, local reinvestment, equity participation.

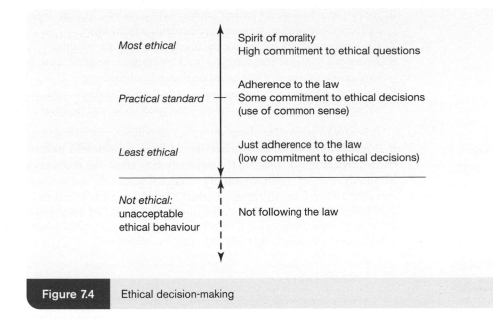

Most ethical — Spirit of morality
High commitment to ethical questions

Practical standard — Adherence to the law
Some commitment to ethical decisions
(use of common sense)

Least ethical — Just adherence to the law
(low commitment to ethical decisions)

Not ethical:
unacceptable
ethical behaviour — Not following the law

| Figure 7.4 | Ethical decision-making |

EXHIBIT 7.6 Google decides to stop censoring of its Chinese website

China has the world's largest internet population. China has 384 million internet users, according to government data, more than the total population of the US. The number may grow to 840 million, or 61 per cent of the population, by 2013.

Google, Inc., the world's biggest search engine company, first entered the Chinese market in early 2000 by creating a Chinese language version of its home page. Google's approach was to maintain a Chinese-language version of Google.com that was housed in the United States but could handle search requests originating within China. In this way, the technology was not subject to Chinese censorship laws as the facilities were not within China's physical boundaries, and Google did not need a licence from the Chinese government to operate its business.

In 2004, Google realized that its approach in China was not sustainable. Google was losing market share to Baidu, and others (for example, Microsoft and Yahoo) were gaining ground through their local presence. In January 2006, Google announced the creation of Google.cn, which was located in China and subject to Chinese filtering. With Google.cn, the company did exclude material and links from sources the government deemed subversive or harmful in order to comply with local Chinese laws and regulations. The Chinese government in Beijing has tight control over online content in a vast system, removing information it considers harmful, such as pornography and violent content, but also politically sensitive material.

On 12 January 2010, Google announced that it was no longer willing to continue censoring results on Google.cn, citing a breach of the Gmail accounts of Chinese human rights activists. On the 22 March 2010 Google repeated this message, which points to a de facto withdrawal from China, putting the ball in the court of a Chinese regime that virtually everyone expects will begin censoring search results on the Google.cn site.

Google has only a third of the search-engine market in China, which is dominated by the Chinese giant Baidu. Although its revenues have continued to rise, many analysts believe that Google would have a hard time in China, and after leaving China, it would be even harder for Google to make a comeback there.

● Is it a wise decision for Google to withdraw from the Chinese market instead of abiding by the China's censorship laws?

Sources: various public media.

3. *Employee relations*, including compensation, safety, human rights, non-discrimination, collective bargaining, training and sexual harassment.
4. *Customer relations*, including pricing, quality and advertising.
5. *Industrial relations*, including technology transfer, research and development, infrastructure development and organizational stability/longevity.
6. *Political relations*, including legal compliance, bribery and other corrupt activities, subsidies, tax incentives, environmental protection and political involvement.

It is easy to generalize about the ethics of political pay-offs and other types of payments; it is much more difficult to make the decision to withhold payment of money when the consequences of not making the payment may affect the company's ability to do business profitably or at all. With the variety of ethical standards and levels of morality that exist in different cultures, the dilemma of ethics and pragmatism which faces international business cannot be resolved until more countries decide to deal effectively with the issue.

7.10 Social marketing

Social marketing
Planning, execution and evaluation of programmes to influence the voluntary behaviour of target audiences in order to improve their personal welfare (e.g. encouraging people to give up smoking).

Social marketing can be understood as the application of commercial marketing technologies to the analysis, planning, execution and evaluation of programmes designed to influence the voluntary behaviour of target audiences in order to improve their personal welfare and that of their society (Hastings, 2003).

Social marketing is about changing behaviour: encouraging people to give up smoking, take exercise, or visit a sexual health clinic. These changes do not, for the most part, occur overnight. They involve a series of steps from initial contemplation through to reinforcement after the fact, a process that is both dynamic and precarious: the individual can regress or change heart at any point.

Social marketing is founded on trust, and therefore we have to start thinking in terms of long-term relationship building.

Social marketing has clear relations to commercial marketing. However, social marketing is distinct from commercial marketing in that it focuses on resolving social problems, whereas commercial marketing focuses on producing various goods or services for a profit. The 'customer' of social marketing is normally not expected to pay a price equal to the cost of providing the service, whereas the customer of commercial marketing is expected to do so. Furthermore, social marketing should not be confused with socially responsible marketing, something in which all marketers should be engaged. Socially responsible marketing is commercial marketing that appropriately takes into account its social responsibilities in marketing ordinary products and services.

As such, social marketing focuses on influencing people's behaviour away from ways of acting or lifestyles that are designated as leading or contributing to a social problem and towards other ways of acting and lifestyles that will improve these people's well-being (or the well-being of others). This attempt to change people's behaviour may also involve modifications in their attitudes, values, norms and ideas. It may also require behavioural and value changes in the communities or groups of people with whom they live and/or associate.

The well-being of the individuals and/or society is not simply subjectively identified by the individuals involved but is subject to determination through processes of social argumentation and justification. This does not mean that everyone will agree with these processes.

Social marketers target people who may not believe, at least at the outset, that they suffer from a problem or any deficiency in their welfare. As such, social problems are identified independently of what any particular person or people may or may not believe. It is compatible with social marketing that the people social marketers address strongly believe that they do not have a problem. This might be the case of teenagers who abuse alcohol or drugs, fathers of Muslim girls in Bangladesh who do not really believe that their daughters should receive an education, or men in parts of Africa who wish to have their future wives undergo female circumcision. Case II.2 (Female Health Company) illustrates some aspects of social marketing by attempting to change sexual behaviour, especially among women in developing countries.

7.11 Summary

For international marketers it is important to understand customers' personal values and accepted norms of behaviour in order to market to them properly. At the same time marketers must search for groups with shared cognitions that result in shared views of the marketer's offerings and in similar product-related behaviour to simplify their task. Such groups may even exist across country borders.

How we perceive other cultures stems from our own cultural mindset, and it is very difficult not to take the ethnocentric point of view when classifying other cultures. Classification of cultures is necessary to develop marketing and advertising strategies in the global marketplace. Classifying cultures on dimensions has proved to be the most constructive method. It helps in vocalizing and labelling cultural differences and similarities. Many of the cultural differences are reflected in the type of communication culture used. In this chapter different models for classification have been discussed.

High/low-context cultures

The difference between high- and low-context communication cultures helps us understand why, for example, Asian (high-context) and Western (low-context) styles are so different, and why Asians prefer indirect verbal communication and symbolism over the direct assertive communication approaches used by Western people. Other dimensions, such as different concepts of time, can also explain major differences between East and West.

Hofstede's model

In order to construct a more refined classification system, Hofstede developed a model of '4 +1' dimensions for comparing work-related values, based on data collected in an extensive study. This model also proves useful for comparing cultures with respect to consumption-related values. As a result it can explain the variety of values and motivations used in marketing and advertising across cultures.

It can also explain differences in actual consumption behaviour and product use and can thus assist in predicting consumer behaviour or effectiveness of marketing strategies for cultures other than one's own. This will be particularly useful for companies that want to develop global marketing and advertising strategies.

The problem of business ethics is infinitely more complex in the international marketplace because value judgements differ widely among culturally diverse groups. What is commonly accepted as right in one country may be completely unacceptable in another. Giving business gifts of high value, for example, is generally condemned in Western countries, but in many countries of the world gifts are not only accepted but expected.

Social marketing can be defined as the planning and implementation of programmes designed to generate social change (e.g. stopping smoking is a lifestyle change). It is a system that can be used to change the way people think or behave. Social marketing is still based on concepts of commercial marketing and, like commercial marketing, it utilizes research to tailor messages to a particular target audience. The goal of social marketing is to get people to think differently about old ideas and focus on new concepts that will add values to their lives. Social marketing is especially prevalent among non-profit-making organizations, government agencies, community-based organizations, private foundations, social/health issue coalitions and indeed any entity that wants to effect social change.

CASE STUDY 7.1

Lifan: a Chinese sub-supplier and brand manufacturer of motorcycles is aiming at the global market

In 1992 Yin Mingshan established the Lifan Group (www.lifan.com.cn) in Chongqing together with nine employees. Yin Mingshan was then 54 years old and came from a job as an editor in the Chongqing Publishing Agency. Lifan started out as a supplier of motorcycle parts to original equipment manufacturers (OEMs) of complete motorcycles and later became a supplier of complete motorcycle engines. Today it is a producer of its own branded Lifan motorcycle.

In ten years Lifan has developed into a state-level, large private enterprise – Chongqing Lifan Industrial (Group) Co. Ltd. There are more than 3,800 employees in the Group, which includes eight companies, three marketing companies and one city-level technical centre. Lifan was the first private company to establish a Party Committee within the company to help in its development.

In September 2001 Lifan motorcycles were first sold to Japan, thus overwriting the established pattern of no motorcycles being exported to Japan from China. In Vietnam Lifan motorcycles have absolute predominance. The commercial counsellor of the Vietnamese Embassy in China said: 'In Vietnam, the Lifan brand is more famous than Honda.'

In order to make the best use of its brand, Lifan is manufacturing as an outsourcer household electrical goods, wine, anti-theft doors, mineral water, garniture, sports shoes, etc. and building a 'Lifan Pyramid' with motorcycles, engines, automobile electrics, agricultural machines and media.

In 2002 the Lifan Group achieved the following sales:

- 714,000 branded motorcycles, placing it fourth in the Chinese motorcycle industry;
- 1,840,000 motorcycle engines, which made it number one in the Chinese motorcycle industry.

More than 1 million motorcycle engines were exported to foreign markets. In 2002 Lifan had total

www.lifan.com.cn

sales of $478 million, of which $117 million came from export. Its motorcycles were exported to over 70 countries.

World market for motorcycles

The Japanese company Yamaha has published a market survey result, which shows the demand for motorcycles in the world will reach 27.5 million units, 60 per cent higher than in 2001. The survey indicated that due to the continuous expansion of the Vietnamese and Indian motorcycle markets, the demand in 2002 in the Asian market (excluding China) is expected to reach 10.2 million units, 10 per cent higher than in 2001. The demand in China will reach 11.7 million units, 5 per cent higher than in 2001. The demand in Japan is expected to be 810,000 units in 2002, 3.8 per cent higher than in 2001 and in North America demand will be around 800,000 units, about 3 per cent higher than in 2001.

Since 1995 Chinese motorcycle production has ranked first in the world. In 2001 28.8 million units were exported from China which made China the number one motorcycle export country. However, there is still a gap between the motorcycle great powers such as Japan in areas such as sales income, brand, R&D and quality.

The management philosophy of Yin Mingshan, CEO of Lifan

Here are some statements, taken directly from the Lifan website:

Fellows, our burden is heavy, but we have confidence. Honda and Yamaha are all over, what shall we Lifan people do? I believe, with our plan of 'Big Lifan', 'New Lifan', with enterprise culture integration, the Lifan people will work together. When the civil industry is in the most dangerous situation, Lifan people are forced to shout out: 'innovation, innovation, innovation'. Then the ideal of 'Long live Lifan' will come true

Finally, I wish all staff a Happy New Year and a Happy Family.

Yin Mingshan at the Spring Festival
(Chinese New Year), March 2003.

The penetration of Lifan motorcycles in the world market has caused concern in the Japanese motorcycle manufacturing industry. This is the main reason the Japanese press showed an interest in the Lifan Group, but Japanese journalists also think 90 per cent of Chinese motorcycles are copying Japanese models.

Lifan invests in automobiles

Lifan has long held the ambition to enter the automobile industry. In January 2005 it made its debut into the car market with the introduction of the Lifan 520 sedan, assembled in the company's new plant in China. The US$9,700 price tag on the car includes leather seats, dual airbags, a huge boot and a DVD system with a video screen facing the front passenger – a combination that could cost twice as much in a comparably equipped mid-size sedan in the United States.

Wages of less than $100 a month have helped control the cost. The assembly plant is better organized than many Chinese factories, although it still maintains large inventories of parts and materials awaiting assembly, incurring interest charges to finance these supplies.

President of the Lifan Group, Yin Mingshan, has no doubts that China can also compete with the United States. 'Americans work five days a week, we in China work "seven days",' he says. 'Americans work 8 hours a day, and we work 16 hours' (www.lifan.cn/en/shownews).

Lifan has started exports of its Lifan 520 sedan to developing countries in Asia, the Middle East and the Caribbean, but several more years of work are needed before the company is ready to compete in industrialized countries.

As Yin Mingshan concludes: 'Chairman Mao taught us: if you can win then fight the war, if you cannot win, then run away. I want to train my army in these smaller markets, and when we are ready, we will move on to bigger markets.'

Chongqing motorcycle manufacturers turn to automobiles

As Lifan aggressively enters automobile manufacturing two more motorcycle manufacturers in Chongqing, Loncin and Zongshen, are also targeting the automobile industry. Loncin and Chendu Shanlu Automobile Co. Ltd established the Loncin Chendu Automobile Co. Ltd and plan to reach an annual output of 30 million automobiles in three years.

Data shows that the domestic motorcycle market capacity has reached 12 million units, and will reach 15 million units within five years. This is its saturated capacity. Meanwhile, owing to tough market competition, the profit of each motorcycle manufacturer is reducing rapidly.

Honda has pushed forward a cheap style to the South East Asia market, only US$700+ against the price advantage of Chongqing motorcycles. This is a great threat to Chongqing motorcycle manufacturers and their overseas markets. Though they have been exploring new bases and seeking new markets in the Middle East, South Asia, South America and Africa, they know the motorcycle industry is at the top of the growth curve.

Compared to the sad state of affairs in the motorcycle industry, the automobile manufacturing industry has a wonderful future. In recent years the bus market has been increasing at better than 20 per cent. Under the push of expanding financial policies, highways are being laid out all over the country, which has brought senior-grade buses a broad market space. Existing urban buses are old, but with the development of cities they will be updated. A survey by Lifan shows that in the next ten years, market capacity for buses will be still over 20 per cent. The huge market demands ensures profit. The profit on automobiles is about 10 per cent, with a net profit of 8 per cent, twice that of motorcycles. In the coming five years this figure won't be changing much (Lifan News, 6 March 2003).

Source: adapted from the Lifan website.

QUESTIONS

1. Based on the information in the case, how is the international marketing management philosophy in Lifan different from a typical company in western Europe?

2. How can the difference in marketing management philosophy be explained by the differences in culture between western Europe and China?

3. How should Lifan overcome the cultural differences if they decide to enter the western European market?

CASE STUDY 7.2

IKEA catalogue: are there any cultural differences?

IKEA was founded in Älmhult, Sweden in 1943 by Ingvar Kamprad. The company name is a composite of the first letters in his name in addition to the first letters of the names of the property and the village in which he grew up: Ingvar Kamprad Elmtaryd Agunnaryd – IKEA.

The IKEA business philosophy is: 'We shall offer a wide range of well-designed, functional home furnishing products at prices so low that as many people as possible will be able to afford them.'

In the late 1940s, the first IKEA advertisements appeared in local newspapers. Demand for IKEA

Illustration of the same product in the IKEA Catalogue in Denmark and Shanghai
Inter IKEA Systems BV.

products soared, and Ingvar Kamprad quickly outgrew his ability to make individual sales calls. As a result, he began operating a mail order catalogue and distributed his products via the county milk van. This resourceful solution to a difficult problem led to the annual IKEA catalogue.

First published in Swedish in 1951, the IKEA catalogue was, in 2009, published each summer in 56 different editions, in 27 languages for 35 countries, and is considered to be the main marketing tool of the retail giant, consuming 70 per cent of the company's annual marketing budget. In terms of publishing quantity, the catalogue has surpassed the Bible as the world's most published work – at an estimated 199 million copies (in 2009) worldwide – triple that of its less materialistic counterpart. (However, since the catalogue is free of charge, the Bible continues to be the most purchased non-fiction work.)

In Europe alone the catalogue reaches more than 220 million people annually. Containing over 300 pages and about 12,000 products, it is distributed free of charge both in stores and by mail. The annual catalogue is distributed in August/September of each year and is valid for a full year. Prices in the catalogue are guaranteed not to increase while the catalogue is valid. Most of the catalogue is produced by IKEA Catalogue Services AB in IKEA's home town of Älmhult, Sweden.

At the beginning of 2009 there were 280 IKEA stores operating under a franchise from Inter IKEA Systems BV. Total IKEA turnover in 2005 was €22.7 billion.

IKEA accounts for just 5 to 10 per cent of the furniture market in each country in which it operates. More important is that the awareness of the IKEA brand is much bigger than the size of the company. That is because IKEA is far more than a furniture merchant. It sells a Scandinavian lifestyle that customers around the world embrace.

Cultural difference

There are about 12,000 products in the total IKEA product range. Each store carries a selection of these 12,000 products depending on store size. The core range is the same worldwide, but there are differences in how the IKEA catalogue displays its products in the different national editions. Here we have two different illustrations featuring the same product. Our two illustrations for the same product are taken from the Danish and Chinese catalogues.

Source: www.ikea.com.

QUESTIONS

1. Discuss the advantages and disadvantages of having the same product range shown in all IKEA catalogues around the world?

2. The catalogue is the most important element in IKEA's global marketing planning. Discuss if there could be some cultural differences in the effectiveness of the catalogue as a marketing tool.

3. Explain some cultural differences which are illustrated by the two different illustrations of the same product (from the Danish and Chinese IKEA catalogues).

VIDEO CASE STUDY 7.3 Communicating in the global world

Download from www.pearsoned.co.uk/hollensen

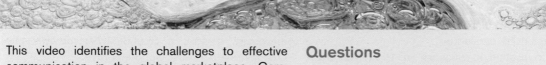

This video identifies the challenges to effective communication in the global marketplace. Communication across language, cultural, time and technology barriers can be challenging. A significant amount of research needs to be conducted before a company can engage in successful global business ventures. It is necessary to examine thoroughly differences in gestures, expressions and dialect when communicating across cultures so as not to offend anyone. Understanding time zones is also important, as they force organizations to plan carefully in advance in order to develop, translate and deliver information in a timely manner.

Questions

1. Language can be a barrier to effective communication. What steps can a company take to minimize language barriers across borders?

2. Cultural differences need to be considered when communicating across borders. What characteristics of a country's culture need to be researched to ensure business success across borders?

3. This video mentions that some companies have trusted contacts in a country they wish to do business with, while other companies rely on a significant amount of research to learn more about cultural characteristics, etc. What method do you feel is most effective for gathering useful, accurate and up-to-date information regarding cultural issues?

For further exercises and cases, see this book's website at **www.pearsoned.co.uk/hollensen**

Questions for discussion

1. As English is the world language of business, is it necessary for UK managers to learn a foreign language?

2. According to Hofstede and Hall, Asians are (a) more group-oriented, (b) more family-oriented and (c) more concerned with social status. How might such orientations affect the way you market your product to Asian consumers?

3. Do you think that cultural differences between nations are more or less important than cultural variations within nations? Under what circumstances is each important?

4. Identify some constraints in marketing to a traditional Muslim society. Use some of the examples in the chapter.

5. What layers of culture have the strongest influence on business people's behaviour?

6. The focus of this chapter has mainly been the influence of culture on international marketing strategies. Try also to discuss the potential influences of marketing on cultures.

7. What role does the self-reference criterion play in international business ethics?

8. Compare the role of women in your country to their role in other cultures. How do the different roles affect women's behaviour as consumers and as business people?

References

Bellin, J.B. and Pham, C.T. (2007) 'Global expansion: balancing a uniform performance culture with local conditions', *Strategy & Leadership*, 35(6), pp. 44–50.

Copeland, L. and Griggs, L. (1985) *Going International*. Random House, New York.

Field, M. (1986) 'Fragrance marketers sniff out rich aroma', *Advertising Age* (special report on Marketing to the Arab world), 30 January, p. 10.

Hall, E.T. (1960a) *The Silent Language*. Garden City, NY, Doubleday.

Hall, E.T. (1960b) 'The silent language in overseas business', *Harvard Business Review*, May–June, pp. 87–97.

Harper, T. (1986) 'Polaroid clicks instantly in Moslem market', *Advertising Age* (special report on Marketing to the Arab world), 30 January, p. 12.

Hastings, G. (2003) 'Relational paradigms in social marketing', *Journal of Macromarketing*, 23(1), pp. 6–15.

Hofstede, G. (1980) *Culture's Consequences: International Differences in Work-related Values*, Sage, Beverly Hills, CA, and London.

Hofstede, G. (1983) 'The cultural relativity of organizational practices and theories', *Journal of International Business Studies*, Fall, pp. 75–89.

Hofstede, G. and Bond, M.R. (1988) 'The Confucius connection: from cultural roots to economic growth', *Organizational Dynamics*, 16(4), pp. 4–21.

Lee, J. (1966) 'Cultural analysis in overseas operations', *Harvard Business Review*, March–April, pp. 106–114.

MacKenzie, S. (1998) 'Boundary commission', *Marketing Week*, 29 January.

Murdoch, G.P. (1945) 'The common denominator of cultures', in Linton, R. (ed.), *The Science of Man in the World Crises*. Columbia University Press, New York.

Pasco, M. (2000) 'Brands are replacing celebrities as role models for today's youth', *Kids Marketing Report*, 27 January.

Phillips, C., Doole, I. and Lowe, R. (1994) *International Marketing Strategy: Analysis, Development and Implementation*. Routledge, London.

Smith, D.S. (1998) 'Europe's youth is our future', *Marketing*, 22 January.

Smith, K.V. (2000) 'Why SFA is a tough sell in Latin America', *Marketing News*, 3 January.

Solberg, C.A. (2002) 'Culture and industrial buyer behaviour: the Arab experience', Paper presented at the 18th IMP Conference.

Usunier, J.C. (2000) *International Marketing*. Pearson Education, Harlow.

Wilhelms, R.W., Shaki, M.K. and Hsiao, C.-F. (2009) 'How we communicate about cultures', *Competitiveness Review: An International Business Journal*, 19(2), pp. 96–105.

CHAPTER 8
The international market selection process

Contents

Learning objectives

After studying this chapter you should be able to:

- Define international market selection and identify the problems in achieving it.
- Explore how international marketers screen potential markets/countries using secondary and primary data (criteria).
- Distinguish between preliminary and fine-grained screening.
- Realize the importance of segmentation in the formulation of the global marketing strategy.
- Choose among alternative market expansion strategies.
- Distinguish between concentration and diversification in market expansion.

8.1   Introduction

Identifying the 'right' market(s) to enter is important for a number of reasons:

- It can be a major determinant of success or failure, especially in the early stages of internationalization.
- This decision influences the nature of foreign marketing programmes in the selected countries.
- The nature of geographic location of selected markets affects the firm's ability to coordinate foreign operations.

In this chapter a systematic approach to international market selection (IMS) is presented. A study of recently internationalized US firms showed that on average firms do not follow a highly systematic approach. However, those firms using a systematic sequence of steps in IMS showed a better performance (Yip *et al.*, 2000; Brouthers and Nakos, 2005).

8.2   International market selection: SMEs versus LSEs

The international market selection process is different in small and medium-sized enterprises (SMEs) and large-scale enterprises (LSEs).

In the SME, the IMS is often simply a reaction to a stimulus provided by a change agent. This agent can appear in the form of an unsolicited order. Government agencies, chambers of commerce and other change agents may also bring foreign opportunities to the firm's attention. Such cases constitute an externally driven decision in which the exporter simply responds to an opportunity in a given market.

In other cases, the IMS of SMEs is based on the following criteria (Johanson and Vahlne, 1977):

- Low psychic distance: low uncertainty about foreign markets and low perceived difficulty of acquiring information about them. Psychic distance has been defined as differences in language, culture, political system, level of education or level of industrial development.
- Low cultural distance: low perceived differences between the home and destination cultures (cultural distance is normally regarded as part of psychic distance).
- Low geographic distance.

Using any one of these criteria often results in firms entering new markets with successively greater psychic distance. The choice is often limited to the SMEs' immediate neighbours, since geographic proximity is likely to reflect cultural similarity, more knowledge about foreign markets and greater ease in obtaining information. When using this model the decision-maker will focus on decision-making based on incrementalism where the firm is predicted to start the internationalization by moving into those markets they can most easily understand. It is generally believed that SMEs and firms which are early in their internationalization process are more likely to use a psychic distance or other rule of thumb procedures than LSEs with international experience (Andersen and Buvik, 2002).

By limiting their consideration to a nearby country, SMEs effectively narrow the IMS into one decision: to go or not to go to a nearby country. The reason for this behaviour can be that SME executives, usually being short of human and financial resources, find it hard to resist the temptation of selecting target markets intuitively.

In a study of internationalization in Danish SMEs Sylvest and Lindholm (1997) found that the IMS process was very different in 'old' SMEs (established before 1960) from that in 'young' SMEs (established in 1989 or later). The young SMEs entered more distant markets much earlier than the older SMEs, who followed the more traditional step-by-step IMS process. The reason for the more rapid internationalization of young SMEs may be their status as sub-suppliers to larger firms, where they are 'pulled out' to international markets by their large customers and their international networks.

While SMEs must make first entry decisions by selecting targets among largely unknown markets, LSEs with existing operations in many countries have to decide in which of them to introduce new products. By drawing on existing operations, LSEs have easier access to product-specific data in the form of primary information that is more accurate than any secondary database. As a result of this the LSEs can be more proactive. Although selecting markets based on intuition and pragmatism can be a satisfying way for SMEs, the following will be based on a more proactive IMS process, organized in a systematic and step-by-step analysis.

However, in real life the IMS process will not always be a logical and gradual sequence of activities, but an iterative process involving multiple feedback loops (Andersen and Strandskov, 1998). Furthermore, in many small subcontracting firms exporting firms do not actively select their foreign markets. The decision about IMS is made by the partner obtaining the main contract (main contractor), thus pulling the SME into international markets (Brewer, 2001; Westhead *et al.*, 2002). SMEs are often selling to global customers (so-called global accounts) who have a global scope of operation and they expect delivery of the SME's product and services at multiple country sites. SMEs with already established global distribution networks and production sites in more business hubs are often better positioned to supply these global account customers, for example in the automotive sector (Meyer, 2009).

8.3   Building a model for international market selection

Research from the Uppsala school on the internationalization process of the firm has suggested several potential determinants of the firm's choice of foreign markets. These can be classified into two groups: (1) environmental and (2) firm characteristics (see Figure 8.1).

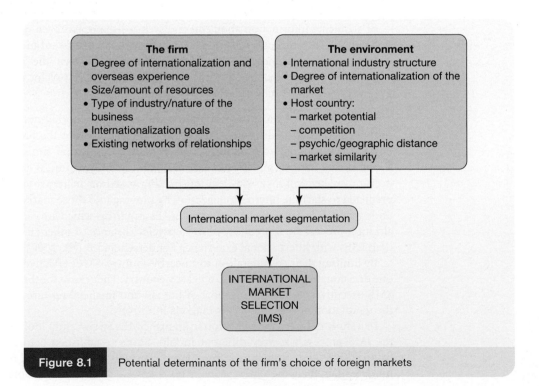

| Figure 8.1 | Potential determinants of the firm's choice of foreign markets |

Let us look first at the environment. How do we define 'international markets'? The following approach suggests two dimensions:

1. The international market as a country or a group of countries.
2. The international market as a group of customers with nearly the same characteristics. According to this latter definition a market can consist of customers from several countries.

Most books and studies in global marketing have attempted to segment the world market into the different countries or groups of countries. This has been done for two principal reasons:

1. International data are more easily (and sometimes exclusively) available on a nation by nation basis. It is very difficult to acquire accurate cross-national statistical data.
2. Distribution management and media have also been organized on a nation by nation basis. Most agents/distributors still represent their manufacturers only in one single country. Few agents sell their products on a cross-national basis.

However, country markets or multi-country markets are not quite adequate. In many cases boundary lines are the result of political agreement or war and do not reflect a similar separation in buyer characteristics among people on either side of the border.

Presentation of a market-screening model

In Figure 8.1 an outline model for IMS was presented. In the following we will look in more detail at the box labelled 'international market segmentation'. The elements of IMS are shown in Figure 8.2.

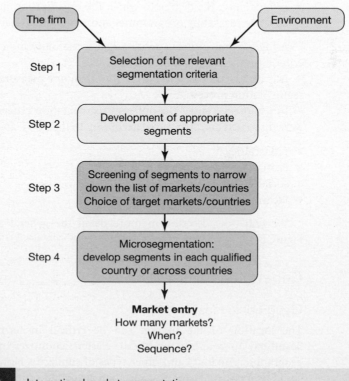

| **Figure 8.2** | International market segmentation |

General characteristics
Geographic
Language
Political factors
Demography
Economy
Industrial structure
Technology
Social organization
Religion
Education

High degree of measurability, accessibility and actionability

Specific characteristics
Cultural characteristics
Lifestyle
Personality
Attitudes and tastes

Low degree of measurability, accessibility and actionability (however, high degree of relevance in specific situations)

Figure 8.3	The basis of international market segmentation

Steps 1 and 2: defining criteria

In general, the criteria for effective segmentation are:

- *measurability*: the degree to which the size and purchasing power of resulting segments can be measured;
- *accessibility*: the degree to which the resulting segments can be effectively reached and served;
- *substantiality/profitability*: the degree to which segments are sufficiently large and/or profitable;
- *actionability*: the degree to which the organization has sufficient resources to formulate effective marketing programmes and 'make things happen'.

A high degree of measurability and accessibility indicates more general characteristics as criteria (at the top of Figure 8.3) and vice versa.

It is important to realize that more than one measure can be used simultaneously in the segmentation process.

In Chapters 6 and 7 the different segmentation criteria in the international environment were discussed and structured according to the PEST approach:

- political/legal
- economic
- social/cultural
- technological.

We will now describe in more detail the general and specific criteria mentioned in Figure 8.3.

General characteristics

Geographic location

The location of the market can be critical in terms of segmenting world markets. Scandinavian countries or Middle Eastern countries may be clustered according to their geographic proximity and other types of similarity. However, the geographic location alone could be a critical factor. For instance, air conditioning needs in some of the Arab countries could make a manufacturer consider these countries as specific clusters.

Language

Language has been described as the mirror of the culture. On one level its implications for the international marketer are self-evident: advertising must be translated; brand names must be vetted for international acceptability; business negotiations must often be conducted through expensive interpreters or through the yet more expensive acquisition of a foreign translator. In the latter case genuine fluency is essential; persuasion and contract negotiation present enough difficulties even in a mother tongue.

Less obvious is the fact that foreign language may imply different patterns of thought and different customer motivations. In such cases a knowledge – again, a good knowledge – of the language will do more than facilitate communication; it provides automatic insight into the relevant culture.

Political factors

Countries may be grouped and world markets segmented according to broad political characteristics. Until recently the Iron Curtain was the basis of one such division. In general terms, the degree of power that the central government has may be the general criterion for segmentation. It is possible, for instance, that a company is producing certain chemicals but that, due to government regulations, many of the world markets may be considered too difficult to enter.

Demography

Demographics is a critical basis for segmentation. For instance, it is often necessary to analyse population characteristics in terms of the proportion of elderly people or children in the total population.

If the country's population is getting older and the number of infants per thousand is declining, which is the case in some European countries, a baby food company would not consider entering that country. In Europe birth rates are tumbling and lifespans lengthening. Baby-based industries from toys to foods and nappies face sharp competition. Consumer electronics and housing may also be affected.

Economy

As the earlier studies have indicated, economic development level could be a critical variable for international market segmentation. Electric dishwashers or washer–dryers require a certain level of economic development and the market for these products in India is not good. However, in western European countries these products are becoming almost a basic necessity. On the basis of the level of economic development certain specific consumption patterns emerge. Societies with high personal income spend more time and money on services, education and recreation. Thus it may be possible to arrange certain income groups from different countries into clusters.

Industrial structure

A country's industrial structure is depicted by the characteristics of its business population. One country may have many small retailers; another may rely on a large number of department stores for retail distribution. One country may be thriving on small manufacturers; another may have very concentrated and large-scale manufacturing activity. The type of competition that exists at the wholesale level may be the critical specific factor for clustering international markets. The international marketer may wish to work with a series of strong wholesalers.

Technology

The degree of technological advancement or the degree of agricultural technology may easily be the basis for segmentation. A software company planning to enter international markets may wish to segment them on the basis of the number of PCs per thousand of the population and it may not be worthwhile for this company to enter markets below a certain number of PCs per thousand of the population. For example, it may find Pakistan, Iran and most Arab countries, all of Africa and all of eastern Europe less than satisfactory for entry.

Social organization

The family is an important purchasing group in any society. In Europe marketers are accustomed to either the so-called nuclear family, with father, mother and children all living together under one roof, or, increasingly as society changes, the single-parent family. In other countries the key unit is the extended family, with three or four generations all in the same house.

In the United States, for instance, socio-economic groupings have been used extensively as segmentation tools. A six-category classification is used: upper upper class, lower upper, upper middle, lower middle, upper lower and lower lower. The US high-income professionals are relegated to the lower upper class, described as those 'who have earned their position rather than inherited it', the nouveaux riches.

In contrast, it would have been hard to find useful socio-economic groupings in Russia beyond white-collar worker, blue-collar worker and farm worker.

Religion

Religious customs are a major factor in marketing. The most obvious example, perhaps, is the Christian tradition of present giving at Christmas, yet even in this simple matter pitfalls lie in wait for the international marketer: in some Christian countries the traditional exchange of presents takes place not on Christmas Day but on other days in December or early January.

The impact of religion on marketing becomes most evident in the case of Islam. Islamic laws, based on the Koran, provide guidance for a whole range of human activities, including economic activity.

Education

Educational levels are of importance to the international marketer from two main standpoints: the economic potential of the youth market and, in developing countries, the level of literacy.

Educational systems vary a lot from country to country. The compensation for on-the-job training also varies a great deal. As a result the economic potential of the youth market is very different from country to country.

In most industrialized countries literacy levels are close to 100 per cent and the whole range of communications media is open to the marketer. In developing countries literacy rates can be as low as 25 per cent, and in one or two 15 per cent or less, although at such low levels the figures can be no more than estimates. In those same countries television sets and even radios are economically beyond the reach of most of the population, although communal television sets are sometimes available. The consumer marketer faces a real challenge in deciding on promotional policies in these countries, and the use of visual material is more relevant.

Specific characteristics

Cultural characteristics

Cultural characteristics may play a significant role in segmenting world markets. To take advantage of global markets or global segments firms require a thorough understanding of what drives customer behaviour in different markets. They must learn to detect the extent to which similarities exist or can be achieved through marketing activities. The cultural behaviour of the members of a given society is constantly shaped by a set of dynamic variables that can also be used as segmentation criteria: language, religion, values and attitudes, material elements and technology, aesthetics, education and social institutions. These different elements were dealt with more extensively in Chapters 6 and 7.

Lifestyles

Typically activity, interest and opinion research is used as the tool for analysing lifestyles. However, such a research tool has not been developed for international purposes. Perhaps certain consumption habits or practices may be used as an indication of the lifestyle that is being studied. Food consumption habits can be used as one such general indicator. Types of food eaten can easily indicate lifestyles that an international food company should be ready to consider. For example, Indian-style hot curries are not likely to be very popular in Germany given its rather bland cooking. Very hot Arab dishes are not likely to be very popular in western Europe.

Personality

Personality is reflected in certain types of behaviour. A general characteristic may be temper, so that segmentation may be based on the general temper of people. Latin Americans or Mediterranean people are known to have certain personality traits, and perhaps those traits are a suitable basis for the segmentation of world markets. One example is the tendency to haggle. In pricing, for instance, the international firm will have to use a substantial degree of flexibility where haggling is widespread. Haggling in a country such as Turkey is almost a national pastime. In the underground bazaars of Istanbul the vendor would be almost offended if the customer accepted the first asking price.

Attitudes, tastes or predispositions

These are all complex concepts, but it is reasonable to say that they can be utilized for segmentation. Status symbols can be used as indicators of what some people in a culture consider would enhance their own self-concept as well as their perception among other people.

Step 3: screening of markets/countries

This screening process can be divided in two:

- *Preliminary screening.* This is where markets/countries are screened primarily according to external screening criteria (the state of the market). In the case of SMEs the limited internal resources (e.g. financial resources) must also be taken into account. There will be a number of countries that can be excluded in advance as potential markets.
- *Fine-grained screening.* This is where the firm's competitive power (and special competences) in the different markets can be taken into account.

Preliminary screening

The number of markets is reduced by coarse-grained, macro-oriented screening methods based on criteria such as:

- restrictions in the export of goods from one country to another
- gross national product per capita
- cars owned per 1,000 of the population
- government spending as a percentage of GNP
- population per hospital bed.

Business Environment Risk Index
A useful tool in the coarse-grained, macro-oriented screening of international markets.

When screening countries it is particularly important to assess the political risk of entering a country. Over recent years marketers have developed various indices to help assess the risk factors in the evaluation of potential market opportunities, one of which is the Business Environment Risk Index (**BERI**). An alternative for BERI is e.g. BMI (Business Monitor International) – www.businessmonitor.com. Other organizations such as the Economist Intelligence Unit also have a Country Risk Service (www.eiu.com). Or you can follow

Table 8.1	Criteria included in the overall BERI index		
Criteria	**Weights**	**Multiplied with the score (rating) on a scale of 0–4***	**Overall BERI index[†]**
Political stability	3		
Economic growth	2.5		
Currency convertibility	2.5		
Labour cost/productivity	2		
Short-term credit	2		
Long-term loans/venture capital	2		
Attitude towards the foreign investor and profits	1.5		
Nationalization	1.5		
Monetary inflation	1.5		
Balance of payments	1.5		
Enforceability of contracts	1.5		
Bureaucratic delays	1		
Communications: phone, fax, Internet access	1		
Local management and partner	1		
Professional services and contractors	0.5		
Total	**25**	× 4 (max.)	= max. 100

* 0 = unacceptable; 1 = poor; 2 = average conditions; 3 = above average conditions; 4 = superior conditions.
[†] Total points: >80 favourable environment for investors, advanced economy; 70–79 not so favourable, but still an advanced economy; 55–69 an immature economy with investment potential, probably an NIC; 40–54 a high-risk country, probably an LDC. Quality of management has to be superior to realize potential. <40 very high risk. Would only commit capital if there were some extraordinary justification.

Euromoney's country risk index: their Country Risk Survey, published twice a year, monitors the political and economic stability of 185 sovereign countries. Results focus foremost on economics, specifically sovereign default risk and/or payment default risk for exporters. Users of these country risk analysis normally have to pay for these subscription services.

BMI, Euromoney, BERI and other services measure the general quality of a country's business climate. They assess countries several times a year on different economic, political and financial factors on a scale from 0 to 4. The overall index ranges from 0 to 100 (see Table 8.1). The BERI index has been questioned as a general management decision tool and should therefore be supplemented by in-depth country reports before final market entry decisions are made.

Among other macro-oriented screening methods is the *shift-share approach* (Green and Allaway, 1985; Papadopoulos *et al.*, 2002). This approach is based upon the identification of relative changes in international import shares among various countries. The average growth rate of imports for a particular product for a 'basket' of countries is calculated and then each country's actual growth rate is compared with the average growth rate. The difference, called the 'net shift', identifies growing or declining markets. This procedure has the advantage that it takes into account both the absolute level of a country's imports and their relative growth rate. On the other hand, it examines only those criteria and does not take into account other macro-oriented criteria.

Fine-grained screening

As the BERI index focuses only on the political risk of entering new markets, a broader approach that includes the competences of the firm is often needed.

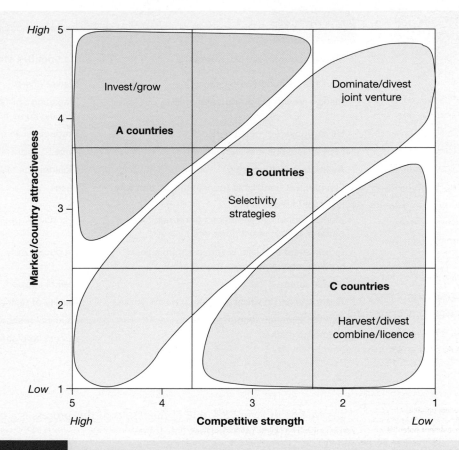

| **Figure 8.4** | The market attractiveness/competitive strength matrix |

For this purpose a powerful aid to the identification of the 'best opportunity' target countries is the application of the market attractiveness/competitive strength matrix (Figure 8.4). This market portfolio model replaces the two single dimensions in the Boston Consulting Group (BCG) growth–share matrix with two composite dimensions applied to global marketing issues. Measures on these two dimensions are built up from a large number of possible variables, as listed in Table 8.2. In the following, one of the important dimensions will be described and commented upon.

Market size

The total market volume per year for a certain country/market can be calculated as:

Production (of a product in a country)
+ import
− <u>export</u>
= theoretical market size
+/− <u>changes in stock size</u>
= effective market size

Production, import and export figures can usually be found in the specific country's statistics, if it is a standardized product with an identifiable customs position.

A more precise location of a particular country (in Figure 8.4) may be determined by using the questionnaire in Figure 8.5.

Table 8.2	Dimensions of market/country attractiveness and competitive strength	
Market/country attractiveness	**Competitive strength**	
Market size (total and segments)	Market share	
Market growth (total and segments)	Marketing ability and capacity (country-specific know-how)	
Buying power of customers	Products fit to market demands	
Market seasons and fluctuations	Price	
Average industry margin	Contribution margin	
Competitive conditions (concentration, intensity, entry barriers, etc.)	Image	
Market prohibitive conditions (tariff/non-tariff barriers, import restrictions, etc.)	Technology position	
Government regulations (price controls, local content, compensatory exports, etc.)	Product quality	
Infrastructure	Market support	
Economic and political stability	Quality of distributors and service	
Psychic distance (from home base to foreign market)	Financial resources	
	Access to distribution channels	

As we saw in Figure 8.4, one of the results of this process is a prioritzied classification of countries/markets into distinct categories:

- *A countries.* These are the primary markets (i.e. the key markets), which offer the best opportunities for long-term strategic development. Here companies may want to establish a permanent presence and should therefore embark on a thorough research programme.
- *B countries.* These are the secondary markets, where opportunities are identified but political or economic risk is perceived as being too high to make long-term irrevocable commitments. These markets would be handled in a more pragmatic way due to the potential risks identified. A comprehensive marketing information system would be needed.
- *C countries.* These are the tertiary or 'catch what you can' markets. They will be perceived as high risk, and so the allocation of resources will be minimal. Objectives in such countries would be short term and opportunistic; companies would give no real commitment. No significant research would be carried out.

Step 4: develop subsegments in each qualified country and across countries

Once the prime markets have been identified firms then use standard techniques to segment markets within countries, using variables such as:

- demographic/economic factors
- lifestyles
- consumer motivations
- geography
- buyer behaviour
- psychographics, etc.

Time of analysis:
Analysis of product area:
In country:

A. Market attractiveness

	1 Very poor	2 Poor	3 Medium	4 Good	5 Very good	% Weight factor	Result (grading × weight)
Market size							
Market growth							
Buying structure							
Prices							
Buying power							
Market access							
Competitive intensity							
Political/economic risks							
etc.							
Total						100	

Market attractiveness = Result : 100 = ...

B. Relative competitive strength
with regard to the strongest competitor = ...

	1 Very poor	2 Poor	3 Medium	4 Good	5 Very good	% Weight factor	Result (grading × weight)
Products fit to market demands							
Prices and conditions							
Market presence							
Marketing							
Communication							
Obtainable market share							
Financial results							
etc.							
Total						100	

Relative competitive strength = Result : 100 = ...

Figure 8.5 Underlying questionnaire for locating countries on a market attractiveness/ competitive strength matrix

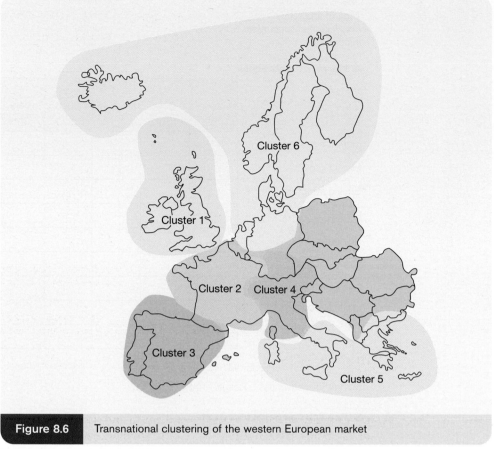

| Figure 8.6 | Transnational clustering of the western European market |

Source: Welford and Prescott (1996). *European Business: An Issue-Based Approach*, 3rd edition. Reprinted by permission of Pearson Education Ltd.

Thus the prime segmentation basis is geographic (by country) and the secondary is within countries. The problem here is that depending on the information basis, it may be difficult to formulate fully secondary segmentation bases. Furthermore, such an approach can run the risk of leading to a differentiated marketing approach, which may leave the company with a very fragmented international strategy.

The drawback of traditional approaches lies in the difficulty of applying them consistently across markets. If a company is to try to achieve a consistent and controlled marketing strategy across all its markets it needs a transnational approach to its segmentation strategy.

It can be argued that companies competing internationally should segment markets on the basis of consumers, not countries. Segmentation by purely geographical factors leads to national stereotyping. It ignores the differences between customers within a nation and ignores similarities across boundaries.

Cluster analysis can be used to identify meaningful cross-national segments, each of which is expected to evoke a similar response to any marketing mix strategy. Figure 8.6 shows an attempt to segment the western European market into six clusters.

Once the firm has chosen a certain country as a target market the next stage in the micro-segmentation process is to decide with which products or services the company wishes to become active in the individual countries. Here it is necessary to make a careful market segmentation, especially in the larger and more important foreign markets, in order to be in a position to exhaust the market potential in a differentiated manner (Figure 8.7).

In this context it is necessary to draw attention to a specific strategic procedure, which is oriented worldwide towards similar market segments. Here it is not the country-specific market attractiveness that influences the decision on specific markets, but the recognition of

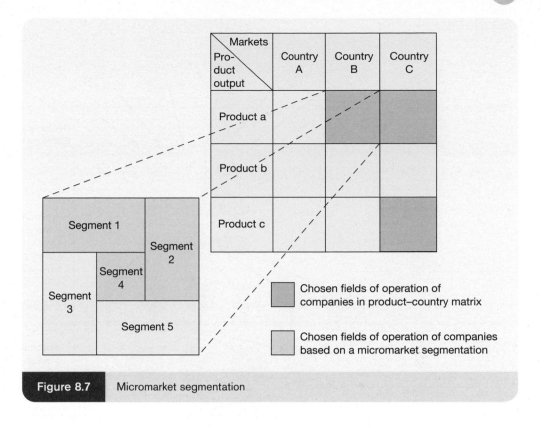

Figure 8.7	Micromarket segmentation

the existence of similar structures of demand and similar consumer habits in segments (and perhaps only in small segments) of different markets.

An illustration of the whole international market segmentation/screening process (steps 1–4 in Figure 8.2) is seen in Figure 8.8.

The model in Figure 8.8 begins by regarding the world market as the potential market for a firm's product. However, if the firm only regards western Europe as a possible market, then the firm may start the screening process at this lower level. The six western European clusters are based on the transnational clustering in Figure 8.6. The further down in the model, the greater the use of primary data (personal interviews, field research, etc.), as well as screening from internal criteria. Furthermore, the firm may discover a *high market potential* in some geographic segments. However, this is not the same as a *high sales potential* for the firm's product. There may be some restrictions (e.g. trade barriers) on the exporting of products to a particular country. Also the management of the company may have a policy of selecting only markets that are culturally similar to the home market. This may exclude far distant countries from being selected as target markets, though they may have a high market potential. Furthermore, to be able to transform a high market potential into a high sales potential, there must be a harmony between the firm's competences (internal criteria) and the value-chain functions that customers rate as important to them. Only in this situation will a customer regard the firm as a possible supplier, equal to other possible suppliers. In other words, in making the IMS, the firm must seek synergy between the possible new target market and its own strengths, objectives and strategy. The firm's choice of new international markets is very much influenced by the existence of complementary markets and marketing skills gained in these markets.

In general, Figure 8.8 is based on proactive and systematic decision-making behaviour by the firm. This is not always a realistic condition, especially not in SMEs, where a *pragmatic approach* is required. Often firms are not able to segment from their own criteria but must expect to be evaluated and chosen (as sub-suppliers) by much larger firms. The pragmatic approach to IMS can also give rise to the firm choosing customers and markets with a background similar to the managers' own personal network and cultural background.

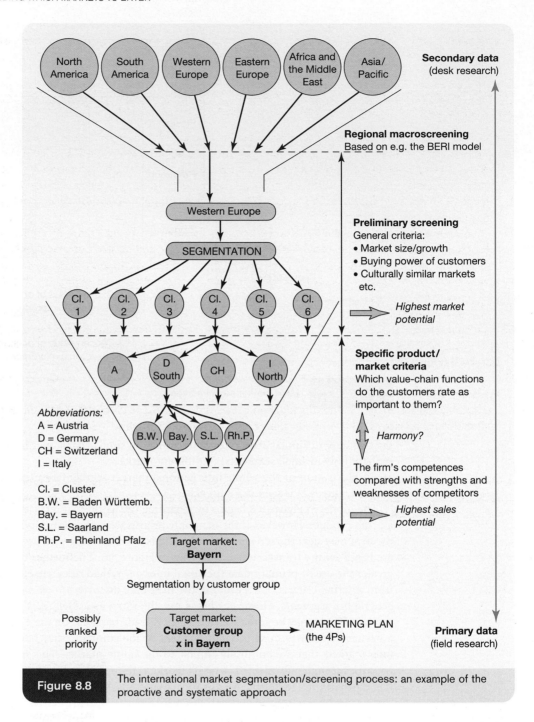

| Figure 8.8 | The international market segmentation/screening process: an example of the proactive and systematic approach |

Contingencies, serendipity and 'management feel' play an important role in both early and late phases of IMS. In a qualitative study of Australian firms Rahman (2003) found that an important factor that firms take into consideration at the final stage of evaluating the attractiveness of foreign markets is 'management feel'. One of the companies said:

> At the end of the day much of the decision depends on the management's feel about the market. There will always be some uncertainties in the market, particularly when you are deciding about the future, and international markets are no exception in this regard. So, we managers will have to make the decision within the limited information available to us, and 'gut feel' plays a big role in that. Rahman (2003, p. 124)

EXHIBIT 8.1 Konica Minolta Solutions Europe B.V. makes an international market screening for its laser printers[1]

The Konica Minolta Group in Europe (www.konicaminolta.eu) has operations in 23 countries throughout Europe and their total number of employees woldwide is approximately 34,000. These companies directly market Konica Minolta products, primarily image information and optical products but also industrial instruments. They offer rapid-response services in line with customer needs. Konica Minolta's marketing network has subsequently grown to include 33 subsidiaries around the world. Around 80 per cent of sales are generated outside Japan.

Konica Minolta Printing Solutions Europe B.V. is a wholly owned subsidiary of Konica Minolta Holding, Inc. in Tokyo, Japan. It is an innovative developer, manufacturer and supplier of document printing solutions. The product line includes colour and monochrome laser printers (see Figure 8.9), associated supplies and accessories. These products can be applied for general office, electronic publishing, graphic design, advanced imaging and home office applications.

Konica Minolta Printing Solutions Europe B.V. is located in Nieuwegein, The Netherlands. It was established in 1977 and currently has 350 employees. It distributes products through a worldwide network of e-commerce, reseller, retail and distribution partners and is responsible for the so-called EMEA area – Europe, Middle East and Africa.

The most important competitors in laser printers are Hewlett Packard (the market leader), Lexmark, Oki, Epson, Canon, Samsung, Dell and Xerox.

Screening filters were used to identify the right export area. The IMS model shows the screening process with the filters numbered at the side to the right. Each filter is described individually.

Filter 1: regional macro screening

Konica Minolta Printing Solution in Nieuwegein focuses its business exclusively on Europe, Middle East and Africa (EMEA). The company has the knowledge to export to these continents and within these areas it is knowledgable about marketing across different cultures, norms and values.

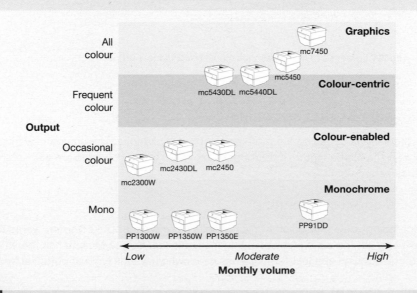

| Figure 8.9 | The laser printer range of Konica Minolta |

---

[1] The exhibit does not necessarily reflect the current strategy of Konica Minolta Printing Solutions Europe B.V.

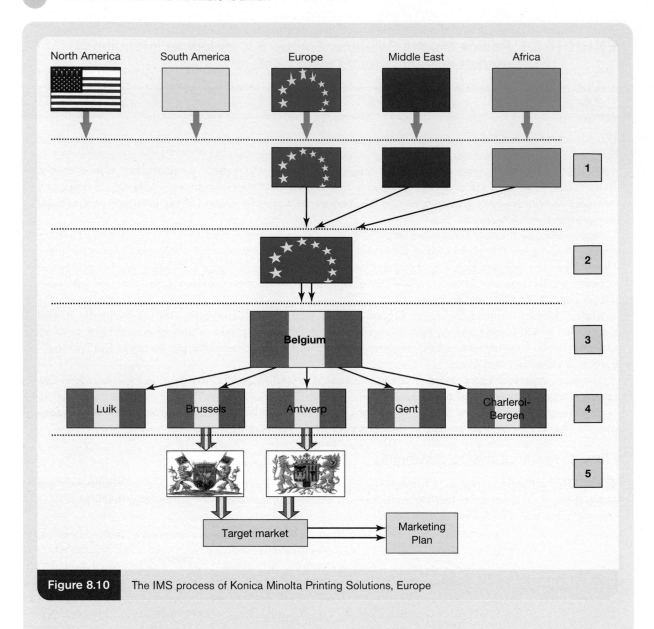

North America   South America   Europe   Middle East   Africa

Figure 8.10   The IMS process of Konica Minolta Printing Solutions, Europe

Filter 2: preliminary market screening

This part of the screening is based on the preference of Konica Minolta. The company wants to concentrate on the countries near the Netherlands, i.e. European countries. These countries are also interesting because of high potential markets.

Filter 3: specific country screening

This part of the screening is also based on Konica Minolta's preference. The company wants to invest its time and money in Belgium, but the main problem in this market is that Konica Minolta has too little knowledge of the most important distribution channel, the business users who have the highest potential for Konica Minolta.

Filter 4: specific market screening

Konica Minolta selected the largest industrial areas in Belgium – Antwerp, Brussels, Charleroi-Bergen, Gent, Luik – because of their huge profit potential.

Filter 5: city market screening

The city regions Antwerp and Brussels have the most activity in comparison to the other industrial areas in Belgium. Therefore these two city regions have the largest concentration of market potential for the Konica Minolta printers. Despite the fact that competition in these two city regions is also very tough, Antwerp and Brussels are chosen as the top priorities for the further specific marketing planning.

Conclusion

The conclusion of the IMS above is that the Brussels and Antwerp region has the highest potential as an export area for Konica Minolta. These two cities have a lot of activities and they complement each other. Antwerp has a lot of education institutions and wholesalers and Brussels is an international city. As the decision-making heart of Europe, Brussels has become an international capital, where worldwide opinion leaders meet to influence and do business.

Sources: (and special thanks to): Fontys University Eindhoven – Department of Marketing Management; BA Project, 'From Sales to Customer Relation Management', prepared by Roderick Akihary, Jan van Raamsdonk, Kim van Oostwaard, Sylwia Wróblewska, Martijn Hassouna and Natascha Ramautar, Tutor, Geert Timmers, Docent, Fontys University Eindhoven, College Year 2005/2006. A special thanks to Konica Minolta Printing Solutions Europe for contributing the photos.

The company also has to consider the competitors' current positions in the potential market. Even in situations where the potential market is very large and apparently attractive, the competitors may be so strong that it would be too resource-demanding for the company to enter the market in an attempt to gain market shares from the competitors.

8.4 Market expansion strategies

The choice of a market expansion strategy is a key decision in export marketing. First, different patterns are likely to cause development of different competitive conditions in different markets over time. For example, a fast rate of growth into new markets characterized by short product life cycles can create entry barriers towards competitors and give rise to higher profitability. On the other hand, a purposeful selection of relatively few markets for more intensive development can create higher market shares, implying stronger competitive positions.

In designing their strategy firms have to answer two underlying questions:

1. Will they enter markets incrementally (the waterfall approach = trickle-down) or simultaneously (the shower approach)? (See Figure 8.11.)
2. Will entry be concentrated or diversified across international markets?

Incremental versus simultaneous entry

The waterfall approach is based on the assumption that initially a product or a technology may be so new or expensive that only the advanced (wealthy) countries can use it or afford it. Over time, however, the price will fall until it is inexpensive enough for developing and less developed countries to buy it. Consequently, following this approach, a firm may decide to enter international markets on an incremental or experimental basis, entering first a single key market in order to build up experience in international operations, and then subsequently entering other markets one after the other. Alternatively, a firm may decide to enter

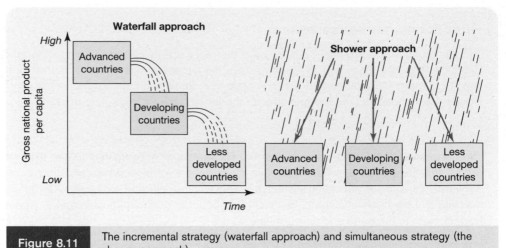

| Figure 8.11 | The incremental strategy (waterfall approach) and simultaneous strategy (the shower approach) |

Source: Keegan, Warren J.; Green, Mark, *Global Marketing*, 2nd, © 2000. Electronically reproduced by permission of Pearson Education, Inc., Upper Saddle River, New Jersey.

a number of markets simultaneously in order to leverage its core competence and resources rapidly across a broader market base. (Read about Sanex's shower approach in Exhibit 8.2.)

For the big global company the two strategies can be translated into the concept of the *international product life cycle* (Vernon, 1966), as illustrated in Figure 8.9. (See also Figure 15.6).

EXHIBIT 8.2 Sanex's aggressive search for cross-border niches: an example of the shower approach

Sanex was developed as a liquid personal soap in 1984. Its success was established quickly – within a year it had gained market leadership in Spain. Soon afterwards it was bought by the US consumer giant Sara Lee, which has four main product sectors:

1. packaged meats and bakery products
2. personal products
3. coffee and groceries
4. household and personal care products.

Source: © Sanex Global Brand.

The market basis for Sanex was the growing shower gel market in Europe. Consumers were moving from the ritual of bathing to the more hygienic routine of showering. The Sanex concept of healthy skin fitted perfectly with this trend. The word 'Sanex' is derived from sano, which is Spanish for 'healthy'. The idea behind the positioning was to build up a cross-border (European) concept of health in consumers' minds. This positioning strategy was in contrast to the positioning of the established players such as Procter & Gamble, Unilever, Colgate-Palmolive and Henkel. They were marketing their products under the cosmetic umbrella with strong perfume and colours and high levels of detergents, supported by the sort of advertising familiar in the cosmetic industry, using beautiful women and exotic surroundings.

The market expansion strategy of Sanex was to launch the product simultaneously on a number of European markets (the 'shower approach' in Figure 8.11). The idea behind this strategy was that Sanex should obtain a 'first-mover advantage', which meant that the big competitors did not have time to copy the product concept before Sanex had product extensions ready for international market launching. The concept of Sanex's shower gel was well understood in most countries, but the potential for the brand would be different. If the habit of showering was well established, the opportunity for Sanex would be better. In the United Kingdom, for example, baths are still very important, although the frequency of showering has increased. In another big potential market, the United States, people use bars of soap, although they have begun to switch to liquid soap.

In a relatively short time Sanex succeeded in developing and launching a broad range of products, including deodorants, colognes and body milk. Sanex is now marketed throughout Europe and the Far East.

Source: Mazur and Lannon (1993, p. 23).

Entry on an incremental basis, especially into small markets, may be preferred where a firm lacks experience in foreign markets and wishes to edge gradually into international operations. Information about, and familiarity with, operating in foreign markets is thus acquired step by step. This strategy may be preferable if a company is entering international markets late and faces entrenched local competition. Equally, if a firm is small and has limited resources, or is highly risk averse, it may prefer to enter a single or a limited number of markets and gradually expand in a series of incremental moves rather than making a major commitment to international expansion immediately.

EXHIBIT 8.3 An example of the 'trickle-up' strategy

According to the waterfall approach (trickle-down), multinational corporations have stripped away features of new products or technologies, originally for advanced countries, to offer them at lower prices to people in developing countries, often adding details based on local research on user habits and needs. Now the opposite process, called 'trickle-up strategy' is happening. This is where multinationals are taking low-cost products initially developed for emerging markets and adapting them for bargain-hungry audiences in North America, Europe, Japan and Australia. Let us look at trickle-up in action.

XO laptop computer

One Laptop per Child.

Nicholas Negroponte founded 'One Laptop per Child' in 2005, with the purpose of distributing small and simple laptops (with internet access) to children who have no access to formal education. This concept was then developed into the simple 'XO Laptop', released in 2007 and distributed (by international organizations) to many developing countries.

In 2008 major PC makers such as Dell began rolling out their own versions of netbooks, intended not for developing markets but for mainstream audiences in developed nations. The smaller form factor was inspired by machines such as the XO, and their lower prices – often as low as US$300 – appeal to budget-conscious consumers.

Source: based on http://images.businessweek.com/ss/09/04/0401_pg_trickleup/11.htm.

Some companies prefer a rapid entry into world markets in order to seize an emerging opportunity or forestall competition. Rapid entry facilitates early market penetration across a number of markets and enables the firm to build up experience rapidly. It also enables a firm to achieve economies of scale in production and marketing by integrating and consolidating operations across these markets. This may be especially desirable if the product or service involved is innovative or represents a significant technological advance, in order to forestall pre-emption or limitation by other competitors. While increasingly feasible due to developments in global information technology, simultaneous entry into multiple markets typically requires substantial financial and management resources and entails higher operating risk.

The appropriate expansion strategy for the SME

The SME often exploits domestic market opportunities to build up company resources which later may be used in international markets (Figure 8.12). The company strategy for market expansion should be concentrated on the product-market segment where the core competences of the company give it a competitive advantage (here product A, B, C and market 1, 2).

The process might evolve step by step, taking one market at a time, market 1, niche 1, learning from it, and then using it as a bridgehead to transfer that competence to the same niche in the next market (market 2, niche 1). The company may develop its international operations by continuing to develop new markets in a step by step process, ensuring consolidation and profitability before moving on.

Concentration versus diversification

The firm must also decide whether to concentrate resources on a limited number of similar markets, or alternatively to diversify across a number of different markets. A company may concentrate its efforts by entering countries that are highly similar in terms of market characteristics and infrastructure to the domestic market. Management could also focus on a

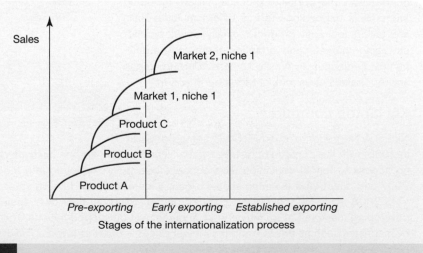

| Figure 8.12 | Appropriate global marketing strategies for SMEs |

Source: Bradley (1995). *International Marketing Strategy*, 2nd edition. Reproduced by permission of Pearson Education Ltd.

group of proximate countries. Alternatively, a company may prefer to diversify risk by entering countries that differ in terms of environmental or market characteristics. An economic recession in one country could be counterbalanced by growth in another market. The strength of competition also often varies from one market to another, and profits in a relatively protected or less competitive market may be funnelled into more fiercely competitive markets. Spreading out operations over a broader geographic base, and investing in different regions throughout the world, may also diversify risk, since in some industries markets in different regions are not interdependent (i.e. trends in one region will not spill over into another).

The question of concentrating or diversifying on the country level can be combined with concentration or diversification on the customer (segment) level. The resulting matrix (Figure 8.13) illustrates the four possible strategies.

From Figure 8.13 four expansion alternatives can be identified:

1. few customer groups/segments in few countries
2. many customer groups/segments in few countries
3. few customer groups/segments in many countries
4. many customer groups/segments in many countries.

A company can calculate its degree of export concentration and compare it over time or with other firms, using the Herfindahl index. This index is defined as the sum of the squares of the percentage of sales in each foreign country.

$$C = \sum S_i^2 \quad i = 1, 2, 3, 4 \ldots n \text{ countries}$$

where C = the export concentration index of the firm
      S_i = exports to country i as a percentage (measured in decimal numbers from 0 to 1)
        of the firm's total exports

$$\sum S_i = 1$$

	Market/customer target group	
	Concentration	*Diversification*
Country *Concentration*	1	2
Country *Diversification*	3	4

Figure 8.13   The market expansion matrix

Source: Ayal and Zif (1979, p. 84).

Maximum concentration ($C = 1$) occurs when all the export is made to one country only, and minimum concentration ($C = 1/n$) exists when exports are equally distributed over a large number of countries.

The factors favouring country diversification versus concentration are shown in Table 8.3.

Table 8.3	International market diversification versus market concentration	
Factors favouring country diversification	**Factors favouring country concentration**	
Company factors		
High management risk consciousness (accept risk)	Low management risk consciousness (risk-averse)	
Objective of growth through market development	Objective of growth through market penetration	
Little market knowledge	Ability to pick 'best' markets	
Product factors		
Limited specialist uses	General uses	
Low volume	High volume	
Non-repeat	Repeat-purchase product	
Early or late in product life cycle	Middle of product life cycle	
Standard product saleable in many markets	Product requires adaptation to different markets	
Radical innovation can trigger new global customer solutions	Incremental innovation – narrow market scope	
Market factors		
Small markets – specialized segments	Large markets – high-volume segments	
Unstable markets	Stable markets	
Many similar markets	Limited number of markets	
New or declining markets	Mature markets	
Low growth rate in each market	High growth rate in each market	
Large markets are very competitive	Large markets are not excessively competitive	
Established competitors have large share of key markets	Key markets are divided among many competitors	
Low customer loyalty	High customer loyalty	
High synergy effects between countries	Low synergy effect between countries	
Learning can be transferred across markets	Lack of awareness of global opportunities and threats	
Short competitive lead time	Long competitive lead time	
Marketing factors		
Low communication costs for additional markets	High communication costs for additional markets	
Low order-handling costs for additional markets	High order-handling costs for additional markets	
Low physical distribution costs for additional markets	High physical distribution costs for additional markets	
Standardized communication in many markets	Communication requires adaptation to different markets	

Source: adapted from Ayal and Zif (1979); Piercy (1981); Katsikea *et al.* (2005).

EXHIBIT 8.4 **Bajaj is selecting new international markets ignored by global leaders**

Mining the markets ignored by global leaders – like Indian motorcycle maker Bajaj Auto, which expanded into 50 countries by focusing on small motorcycles (with engines of 200cc or less) that offer exceptional value for money; Bajaj's huge line-up of simple motor bikes targets different preferences at a wide range of price points.

In 2008-09 Bajaj sold approximately 1.9 million motorcycles, of which one third were exported. While the world's three largest motorcycle companies (Honda, Yamaha and Suzuki) focus on developed markets like United States and western Europe, the world's fourth-largest motorcycle manufacturer, Bajaj, has chosen to focus on developing countries.

Bajaj Auto.

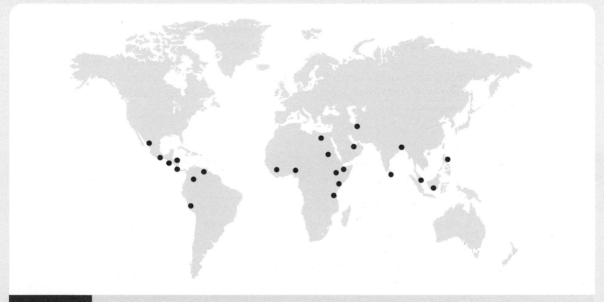

| Figure 8.14 | Location of Bajaj's international dealers |

www.bajajauto.com.

Bajaj has a distribution network covers 50 countries. It has a dominant presence in Sri Lanka, Colombia, Bangladesh, Central America, Peru and Egypt and is also gaining an increasing foothold in Africa. As a consequence, the company has commissioned an assembly unit in Nigeria with the help of its distributor to cater to the growing demand in the African markets.

As a part of the company's policy to be closer to the markets in which it operates, Bajaj Auto has its own sales offices in Monterrey (Mexico), Dubai and Colombo (Sri Lanka) in addition to its subsidiary PT BAI in Indonesia.

Source: adapted from Sirkin *et al.* (2008) and www.bajajauto.com.

8.5 The global product/market portfolio

The corporate portfolio analysis provides an important tool to assess how to allocate resources, not only across geographic areas but also across different product business (Douglas and Craig, 1995). The global corporate portfolio represents the most aggregate level of analysis and it might consist of operations by product businesses or by geographic areas.

As illustrated in Figure 8.15 (based on the market attractiveness/competitive strength matrix of Figure 8.4), Unilever's most aggregate level of analysis is its different product businesses. With this global corporate portfolio as a starting point, the further analysis of single corporate product business can go in a product or geographic dimension or a combination of the two.

It appears from the global corporate portfolio in Figure 8.15 that Unilever's foods business is characterized by high market attractiveness and high competitive strengths. However, a more distinct picture of the situation is obtained by analysing underlying levels. This more detailed analysis is often required to give an operational input to specific market-planning decisions.

By combining the product and geographic dimensions it is possible to analyse the global corporate portfolio at the following levels (indicated by the arrows in the example of Figure 8.15):

1. product categories by regions (or vice versa)
2. product categories by countries (or vice versa)
3. regions by brands (or vice versa)
4. countries by brands (or vice versa).

Of course, it is possible to make further detailed analysis of, for example, the country level by analysing different customer groups (e.g. food retailers) in certain countries.

Thus it may be important to assess the interconnectedness of various portfolio units across countries or regions. A customer (e.g. a large food retail chain) may have outlets in other countries, or the large retailers may have formed cross-border alliances in retailing with central purchasing from suppliers (e.g. Unilever) – see also section 16.7 on international retailing.

8.6 Summary

Especially in SMEs international market selection is simply a reaction to a stimulus provided by a change agent, in the form of an unsolicited order.

A more proactive and systematic approach to IMS entails:

1. selection of relevant segmentation criteria
2. development of appropriate segments
3. screening of segments to narrow down the list of appropriate countries (choice of target)
4. micro segmentation: development of subsegments in each qualified country or across countries.

However, the *pragmatic approach* to IMS is often used successfully by firms. Coincidences and the personal network of top managers play an important role in the 'selection' of the firm's first export market. In making the IMS, the firm must seek the synergy between the possible new target market and its own strengths, objectives and strategy. The firm's choice of new international markets is very much influenced by the existence of complementary markets and marketing skills gained in these markets.

After the four steps described above the market expansion strategy of the chosen market is a key decision. In designing this strategy the firm has to answer two underlying questions:

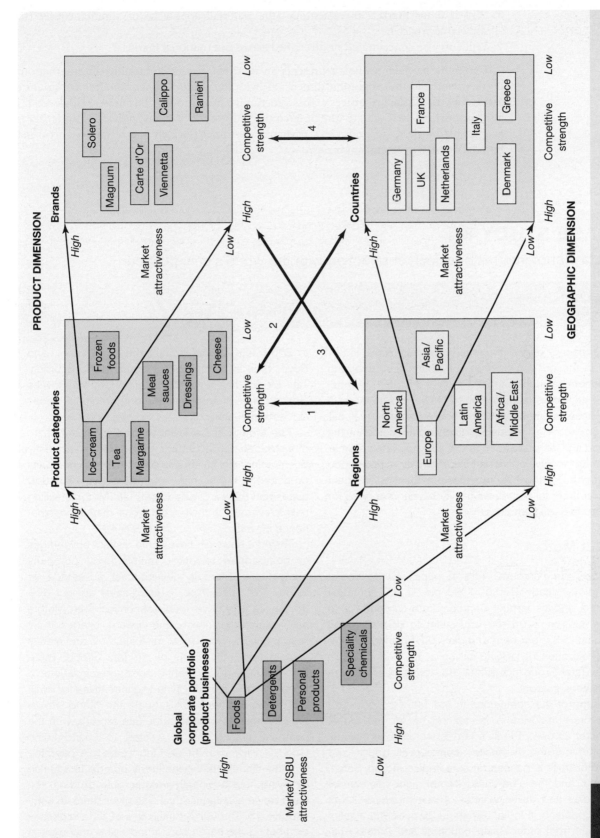

PRODUCT DIMENSION

Brands

Solero
Magnum
Carte d'Or
Viennetta
Calippo
Ranieri

Market attractiveness — High / Low

Competitive strength — High / Low

Product categories

Ice-cream
Frozen foods
Tea
Meal sauces
Margarine
Dressings
Cheese

Market attractiveness — High / Low

Competitive strength — High / Low

Global corporate portfolio (product businesses)

Foods
Detergents
Personal products
Speciality chemicals

Market/SBU attractiveness — High / Low

Competitive strength — High / Low

GEOGRAPHIC DIMENSION

Countries

Germany
UK
Netherlands
France
Italy
Denmark
Greece

Market attractiveness — High / Low

Competitive strength — High / Low

Regions

North America
Europe
Asia/ Pacific
Latin America
Africa/ Middle East

Market attractiveness — High / Low

Competitive strength — High / Low

1
2
3
4

Figure 8.15   Unilever's global portfolio

1. Will it enter markets incrementally (the waterfall approach) or simultaneously (the shower approach)?
2. Will entry be concentrated or diversified across international markets?

Corporate portfolio analysis represents an excellent way of combining the international market selection (the geographic dimension) with the product dimension. It is important to assess how to allocate resources across geographic areas/product businesses. However, it is also important to evaluate the interconnectedness of various portfolio units across geographic borders. For example, a particular customer (located in a certain country) may have businesses in several countries.

CASE STUDY 8.1

Tata Nano: international market selection with the world's cheapest car

The majority of growth in the global automobile industry in the coming decade will come from emerging economies such as India, China and Eastern Europe, and the largest contribution to growth of auto markets in these countries will be the fast-growing small car segment. The increasing disposable income of the middle-class population is the key driver of small car markets in developing nations. However, in developed regions like the US and western Europe, stringent environmental standards are increasing the need for more fuel-efficient cars.

Tata Motors

Indian conglomerate Tata Group (www.tata.com) employs nearly 300,000 people in 85 countries and is India's largest conglomerate company, with revenues in 2006–07 equivalent to US$28 billion (equal to 3.2 per cent of India's GDP), and a market capitalization of US$73 billion at the end of 2007. The Tata Group comprises 98 companies in seven business sectors.

One of the companies in the Tata Group is Tata Motors. Tata Motors is gearing up for the global market as one of India's largest automobile makers, manufacturers of buses, commercial trucks and tractor-trailers, passenger cars (Indica, Indigo, Safari, Sumo and the ultra-cheap Nano), light commercial vehicles and utility vehicles. The company sells its cars primarily in India, but about 20 per cent of sales comes from other Asian countries and Africa, Australia, Europe, the Middle East and South America.

In 2008 Tata Motors bought the Jaguar and Land Rover brands from Ford for about US$2.3 billion. Tata Motors has a workforce of 22,000 employees working in its three plants and other regional offices across the country.

Tata Motors has a lower than 20 per cent share of the Indian passenger car market and has recently been suffering a sales slump. In 2007 the company produced 237,343 cars and more than 300,000 buses and trucks. Outside India Tata Motor is selling only a few cars so their international marketing experience is weak.

They do, however, have some distinct advantages in comparison to other multinational company competitors. There is definite cost advantage as labour cost is 8–9 per cent of sales against 30–35 per cent in developed economies. Tata Motors have extensive backward and forward linkages and it is strongly interwoven with machine tools and metals sectors from other parts of the Tata Group. There are favourable government polices and regulations to boost the auto industry including incentives for R&D.

The acquisitions of Jaguar and Land Rover created financial pressure for Tata Motors, with the company stating that it wanted to spend some US$1.5 billion over the next four years to expand the facilities manufacturing the luxury brands. In addition to giving Tata a globally recognizable product, the Land Rover and Jaguar deal also gives them an entry into the US. Through a deal with Fiat, Tata is already distributing the Italian cars in India and may expand the offering into South America, a Fiat stronghold.

The alternative for Tata Nano
© david pearson/Alamy.

Development of Tata Nano

In 2008 Tata unveiled the Nano, the cheapest car in the world, at the Auto Expo in New Delhi. The car seats up to five people, gets up to 55 miles to the gallon, and sells for about US$2,230. At first the Nano will be sold only in India, but Tata hopes to export them after a few initial years of production; the Nano might be exported to Europe as early as 2012. First shipments to Indian customers are expected in mid-2009.

Tata Nano started with the vision of Ratan Tata, chairman of Tata Motors' parent, Tata Group, to create an ultra low-cost car for a new category of Indian consumer: someone who couldn't afford the US$5,000 sticker price of what was then the cheapest car on the market and instead drove his family around on a US$1,000 motorcycle. Many drivers in India can only afford motorcycles and it is fairly common to see an Indian family of four using a motorcycle to get around (see Photo 1).

In India alone there are 50 to 100 million people caught in that automotive chasm. Until now none of the Indian automakers have focused on that segment, and in this respect the Nano is a great example of the blue ocean strategy.

The customer was ever-present in the development of the Nano. Tata didn't set the price of the Nano by calculating the cost of production and then adding a margin. Rather it set US$2,500 as the price that it thought customers could pay and then worked back, with the help of partners willing to take on a challenge, to build a US$2,500 car that would reward all involved with a small profit.

The Nano engineers and partners didn't simply strip features out of an existing car – the tack Renault took with its Dacia Logan, which sells in India for roughly US$10,000. Instead, they looked at their target customers' lives for cost-cutting ideas. So, for instance, the Nano has a smaller engine than other cars because more horsepower would be wasted in India's jam-packed cities, where the average speed is 10 to 20 miles per hour.

The Nano aims to bring the joys of motoring to millions of Indians, doing for the subcontinent what the Volkswagen Beetle did for Germany and the Mini for Britain. But the plan has horrified environmentalists who fear that the demand from India's aspirational and increasingly middle-class population – now numbering 50 million in a country with a total 1.1 billion people – for more cars will add to pollution and global warming.

The global automotive industry and the current crises

In 2007, a total of 71.9 million new automobiles were sold worldwide: 22.9 million in Europe, 21.4 million in Asia-Pacific, 19.4 million in USA and Canada, 4.4 million in Latin America, 2.4 million in the Middle East and 1.4 million in Africa. The markets in North America and Japan were stagnant, while those in South America and Asia grew strongly. Of the major

Tata Nano
© P Cox/Alamy.

markets, Russia, Brazil, India and China saw the most rapid growth.

Since mid-2008 the sales from the world automotive industry have been developing negatively as a result of the current financial crises.

Segmentation of the global low-cost car (LCC) market

There is no doubt that the competitive landscape for the global car market has been altered dramatically and permanently. Oxyer *et al.* (2008) forecast that the global low-cost market (defined as ultra-low-cost + regular low-cost car market in Figure 1) is expected to grow from 2 million cars in 2008 to 17.5 million cars in 2020.

Moreover, the huge potential of this market is attracting the attention of manufacturers and vendors

worldwide, with a number of global players recently entering the low-cost car sector. There is no doubt that first movers will have the opportunity to capture market share and build consumer loyalty. The dynamic and powerful ultra-low-cost car (ULCC) market is forcing car manufacturers to rethink their strategies. It is indisputable that using traditional design, manufacturing and distribution approaches to achieve ultra low-cost car entry prices below US$3,500 will be a difficult task. A low price point and low profit margins – estimated at around 3 per cent at the base model levels – will provide tough competition in the ULCC market.

Two of the most promising markets for Tata Nano are characterized in India and China, who are expected to account for about 60 to 70 per cent of the future ULCC production and demand.

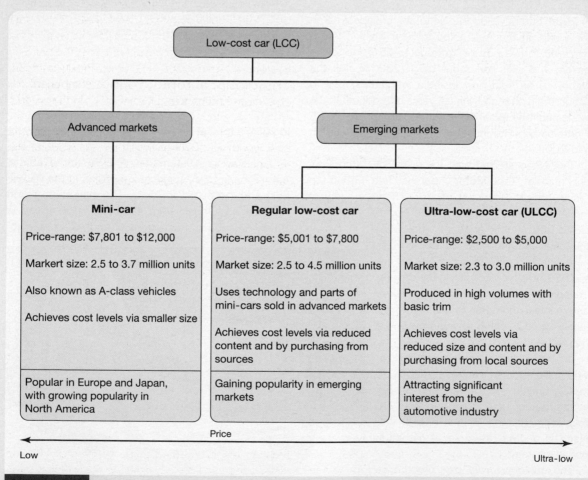

Figure 1   Segmentation of the low-cost car market

Source: based on Oxyer *et al.* (2008).

India

India is likely to evolve into a global hub for small car manufacturing. Currently it is one of the largest producers of small cars with the small car segment accounting for about three-quarters of the Indian car market. The fast-growing small car market has encouraged several global auto companies (Renault Nissan, Toyota, Hyundai) to announce plans for the launch of small cars in India. With the launch of Tata Nano, the stage is set for around a dozen new small and compact cars to be launched in India in the next two years.

Currently, Maruti Suzuki India, the largest passenger car manufacturer in India, has more than a 60 per cent share of the domestic small car segment.

The implication of the impending advent of an inexpensive passenger car such as the Nano on urban transport in India has to be seen in the context of overall trends in motorization in the country. Auto sales (passenger and commercial vehicles, three-wheelers and two-wheelers) in India almost doubled in five years from about 5.23 million units in 2001–02 to 10.11 million units in 2006–07. During 2006–07 alone, sales of passenger cars grew at a scorching rate of 22 per cent. Over the same period, sales of two-wheelers went up by about 11.5 per cent. Thus, merits of the case aside, it is evident that the country is rapidly motorizing. And with incomes rising in an economy growing at a rate of 8 per cent or more annually, there is no sign of this abating. However, it is also true that the vast majority of vehicles sold in India are two-wheelers (motorcycles), which currently comprise 77 per cent of market share – close to eight million two-wheelers were sold in 2006–07.

China

Small car demand in China is expected to increase in the long term. However, the narrow price gap between the small car and medium car segment has made medium segment cars a more attractive choice for consumers.

Mini-cars account for more than one-third of the total volume sales in the Japanese auto market. Suzuki and Daihatsu are the market leaders in the small car market in Japan. A large number of Japanese consumers are moving from luxury cars to mini-cars due to environmental standards and increasing gas prices.

The Tata Nano business model

Tata began the development process with 600 closely integrated suppliers, only 100 of which remain. Independent suppliers provide 80 per cent of the Nano's components, and 97 per cent of the vehicle is sourced in India. Suppliers such as Bosch worked with Tata and employed Indian engineers with motorcycle, rather than automobile, design experience to craft innovative low-cost components.

Reduce the number and complexity of parts

By focusing on the essentials and encouraging creativity in making components smaller, lighter and cheaper, Tata avoided engineering non-functional, non-essential parts. Bosch, for example, adapted a smaller and lighter motorcycle starter for use in the Nano.

European suppliers with production capacity in India had a big advantage over rivals when Tata Motors started to look for partners for its Nano. One reason the Nano is the cheapest car in the world is because 97 per cent of its parts are locally sourced. It is impossible to deliver a low-cost component out of western Europe to a different place in the world.

Half of the 100 vendors for the project are locating with Tata in a 142-hectare vendor park in Singur next to the new plant that will produce the Nano. Singur is a suburb of Calcutta in eastern India. Here are some of European suppliers with key parts on the Nano:

Seat belts	Autoliv
HVAC	Behr
Starter motor, engine-control module, injectors, sensors	Bosch
Transmission speed sensors, fuel-level sensor, fuel pump	Continental
Fuel filter, air cleaner	Mahle
Glazings	Saint-Gobain
Speed sensors	TT Electronics
Clutches	Valeo

Most of these suppliers can only be profitable on Nano parts because they produce high-volume parts in a low-wage country like India, where they also conduct some research and development.

Standardize at every stage of the value chain

Similar to Henry Ford's 'any colour so long as it's black' approach, the Nano offers consumers few options, and only a few have any impact on the manufacturing process.

The Nano's distribution model for India is also new. The company plans to mobilize large numbers of third parties to reach remote rural consumers, tailor the products and services to serve their needs, and add value to the core product or service through ancillary services. For example, one plant will produce vehicle modules that are then sent to a number of strategically positioned satellite mini-factories, where the Nano will be assembled and delivered to the buyer. A central warehouse will stock spare parts and accessories.

Export of Tata Nano to Europe and/or North America

There are two clear barriers for Tata Nano when considering these two regions:

- **Emission standards.** Western Europe, Japan and North America established emissions standards more than a decade ago. Emerging markets such as China and India are adopting European standards, but with a five- to seven-year lag. Autos in the lightweight low-cost car segment, with their small engines and modest fuel consumption, will meet current emissions standards.
- **Safety regulations.** North America and Europe have similar government-developed safety regulations with respect to seat belts, rollover and rear-, side- and frontal-protection standards.

In developing countries, the standards are lower, and ultra low-cost cars will encounter few, if any difficulties, in meeting those standards. As European and North American governments continue to establish higher standards, there will be compliance issues.

As a consequence of these and other barriers (tariffs), the US$2,500 target base price of Nano for the Indian market can jump to nearly double the price in a European country:

Tata Nano	US$
Base price	2,500
+ Conversion (cost for fitting to emission standard and safety regulations)	500
+ Logistics costs	375
+ Marketing	125
+ Manufacturer profit	105
+ Dealership profit	108
+ Import tariffs	93
Expected MSRP (manufacturer's suggested retail price)	3,806
+ Sales tax	400
Total costs	**4,206**

The actual price that the private car buyer pays could be substantially higher in heavily taxed countries such as Denmark.

Competition

The five cheapest cars in the world at the beginning of 2009 are:

No.	Model	Producer	Price US$/€
1	Nano	Tata Motors in India	2,500/1,688
2	QQ3	Chery Automobiles in China	5,000/1,726
3	M800	Suzuki-Maruti in India	5,200/3,451
4	Merrie Star	Geely Automobiles in China	5,500/3,796
5	S-RV mini SUV	Geely Automobiles in China	5,780/3,989

Source: based on www.timesonline.co.uk.

There are now several competitors on their way into the ULLC market:

Renault-Dacia Logan

Renault has already sold 450,000 of the bare bones US$7,200 (€4,969) Logan sedan since its launch in 2004. The price tag of this stripped-down family car is almost half the cost of competing sedans.

The Bajaj Auto and Renault joint venture

Bajaj Auto and Renault's plans of launching an ultra small car to take on Tata Motors' Nano may get delayed once again as a new set of differences over branding crops up between the two partners. This delay is likely to postpone the introduction of the car until 2011–12.

Hyundai

According to the UK media, Hyundai Motors is working on development of an ultra-cheap car that will compete against the Nano. Hyundai is the second-largest car manufacturer in India. Currently, Hyundai is the biggest rival of Indian car market leader Maruti Suzuki India.

VW

VW also plans to launch a low-cost car called Up! in both India and Russia. The low-cost car, which will share some of the components of VW's compact Polo, is designed to be an affordable car for developing countries.

Toyota

Toyota has also plans for entering the Indian low-cost car market. Their 35 billion yen (US$343 million) new production facility, to be located on the outskirts of the southern city of Bangalore, will start output in 2010 with initial capacity of 100,000 units a year. Analysts expect the new cars to have a price tag of around 700,000 to 800,000 yen (US$6,900–US$7,850). That will not immediately compete with Tata Motor's US$2,500 People's cars, though in the future Toyota may jump into the LCC market using Daihatsu's know-how.

Toyota holds a 16 per cent share in the US car market, but its sales in emerging markets remain small. For example, its market share in India is 3 per cent.

QUESTIONS

1. What could be the main reasons for Tata Motors to enter the global ultra-low-cost car market?

2. What are the competitive advantages that Tato Motors would enjoy with their Nano in emerging markets?

3. Which screening criteria would you suggest for Tata Nano's IMS process?

4. Which world regions and specific countries would you suggest Tata Nano should enter after India and China?

Sources: www.tatamotors; http://tatanano.inservices.tatamotors.com/tatamotors/; Thottan, J. (2009) 'Nano power – India's Ratan Tata kept his promise to produce the world's cheapest car. Is this the start of an auto-industry revolution?', *Time*, 6 April, pp. 43–45; *Economic Times of India* (2009) 'In India, a setback for small car rival to Tata's Nano', 22 May, 2009; Van den Waeyenberg, S. and Hens, L. (2008) 'Crossing the bridge to poverty with low-cost cars', *Journal of Consumer Marketing*, 25(7), pp. 439–445; Oxyer, D., Deans, G., Shivaraman, S., Ghosh, S. and Pleines, R. (2008) 'A Nano car in every driveway? How to succeed in the ultra-low-cost car market', *A.T. Kearney Business Journal – Executive Agenda*, XI(2), pp. 55–62; general public information.

CASE STUDY 8.2

Philips Lighting: screening markets in the Middle East

Royal Philips Electronics of the Netherlands is one of the world's biggest electronics companies, as well as the largest in Europe, with 161,500 employees in over 60 countries and sales in 2005 of €30.395 billion.

In 1891 the Dutch mechanical engineer Gerard Philips starts the production of carbon-filament lamps in a former buckskin factory in Eindhoven. Among his first major clients were early electricity companies who include the provision of lamps in their power supply contracts.

Today Philips is number one in the world market for lighting. Their lighting products (light bulbs and lamps) are found all around the world: not only everywhere in the home, but also in a multitude of professional applications, for example, in 30 per cent of offices, 65 per cent of the world's top airports, 30 per cent of hospitals, 35 per cent of cars and 55 per cent of major football stadiums.

Competition

Philips Lighting is world leader in lighting products manufacturing. Its market shares are 50 per cent in Europe, 36 per cent in North America and 14 per cent in the rest of the world. Since the 1980s, Philips has participated intensively in the concentration of this industrial sector by purchasing smaller national companies such as Companie des Lampes (France), AEG (Germany) and Polam Pila (Poland). It has also developed joint ventures with Westinghouse Lamps, Kono Sylvania and EBT China.

GE

General Electric Lighting (GEL) holds a 50 per cent share of the US market but had only a 2 per cent market share in Europe in 1988. In order to reach a 30 per cent market share in 2010, GEL has acquired several European national companies as Tungsram (Czechoslovakia), Thorn Emi (UK), Sivi (Italy) and Linder Licht (Germany). In 1994 GEL built a logistic unit in France to supply France, Germany, Benelux, Switzerland, Italy and Austria. It now intends to reduce prices in connection with supermarket chains.

OSRAM

A 100 per cent subsidiary of the giant German holding Siemens, Osram achieves an 86 per cent share of its turnover by exporting (46 per cent in North America, 41 per cent in the EU, 6 per cent in South America and 6 per cent in Asia). Strategy for the coming years is to increase Asian market shares by doubling its turnover in Asia.

Other significant manufacturers are Sylvania Lighting International and Panasonic.

Philips Lighting market screening in the Middle East

At the beginning of the twenty-first century Philips needed a coherent marketing strategy for the whole Middle East region. The first task was to select the most attractive markets in the region. Over the years Philips has developed a model which shows a correlation between a country's demand for lighting and its GDP per capita. During discussions with

Outdoor advertising for Philips Lighting in Iraq (Bagdad)
Royal Philips Electronics of the Netherlands.

agents/distributors in many countries, Philips was completely dependent on its information about market size. If Philips underestimated market size, it missed market opportunities. That was the main reason why this model was developed, so that the company could cross-check market estimations of its agents/distributors.

Figure 1 shows that lighting (demand for lamps and bulbs) is a basic need for a country and as soon as a country starts developing this basic need increases. However, as the country's wealth increases the growth in the demand slows down, because at later stages of economic development basic lighting needs are covered, as we can see in the case of Israel.

Basically, in order to find the most attractive markets Philips Lighting used the model (shown in Figure 1 and Table 1) in combination. The demand

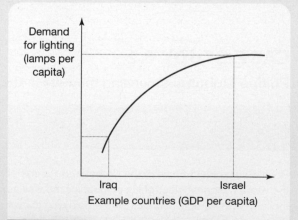

| **Figure 1** | The relationship between the wealth of a country and the demand for lighting |

Table 1	Basic demographic data in the Middle East (2007)		
Markets	Population (million)	GNP 2007 (% growth)	GNP per cap (US$)
Bahrain	0.6	3.0	8,620
Egypt	61.9	5.0	1,232
Iran	66.0	3.0	1,670
Iraq	19.7	−5.0	758
Israel	5.5	7.1	15,700
Jordan	4.6	5.0	2,359
Kuwait	2.2	3.5	15,970
Lebanon	3.2	4.0	4,250
Libya	5.5	3.5	4,982
Oman	2.4	4.3	6,268
Palestine	2.1	−5.0	630
Qatar	0.6	2.0	13,520
Saudi Ababia	20.6	3.5	5,943
Syria	17.0	6.0	982
UAE	2.5	0.5	17,840
Yemen	15.0	3.0	793
Middle East	229.4	–	–

Source: Wim Wils, Eindhoven, Fontys Export Day, 13 October 2004, update via www.worldbank.org.

for lighting per capita has to be multiplied by the number of inhabitants in a country. Israel and Kuwait have the highest GDP/capita but their population size is small. On the other hand Iraq and Iran were (and still are) large markets for lighting, but they are very tough to enter because of their politically chaotic situations.

However, the Philips Lighting Middle East managers did not use market size as the only market selection criterion for priority; instead the models were used as a starting point for discussions with agents and distributors in the countries. If the Philips sales in large lighting markets were very low, this would indicate a low Philips market share (unless the market size was also low). This would lead to a

discussion with the local agents and distributors about how to increase the local Philips market shares in cooperation with the local distributor.

Sources: PowerPoint presentation from Wim Wils, Eindhoven, Fontys Export Day, 13 October 2004; www.philips.com; www.worldbank.org.

QUESTIONS

1. Discuss the appropriateness of the screening model used in this case.

2. Suggest another screening model that could be relevant for Philips Lighting to use in the Middle East.

VIDEO CASE STUDY 8.3 **Hasbro**
download from www.pearsoned.co.uk/hollensen

Hasbro (www.hasbro.com) is a worldwide leader in entertainment products and services, such as GI Joe, the Easy Bake Oven and Monopoly. Hasbro is a US$3 billion company with brands in 100 countries, launching 1,000 new products each year. Although the company distributes primarily through big-box retailers such as Wal-Mart and Toys 'Я' Us, it also uses alternate distribution channels such as pharmacies and smaller toy stores. In these channels, Hasbro knows that it needs to provide a different product or different packaging to compete.

Questions

1. What are the foundations of Hasbro's global success?
2. What demographic changes and social issues might influence the future global market for toys and games?
3. What are the most important screening criteria for Hasbro in the IMS?

For further exercises and cases, see this book's website at **www.pearsoned.co.uk/hollensen**

Questions for discussion

1. Why is screening of foreign markets important? Outline the reasons why many firms do not systematically screen countries/markets.
2. Explore the factors which influence the international market selection process.
3. Discuss the advantages and disadvantages of using only secondary data as screening criteria in the IMS process.
4. What are the advantages and disadvantages of an opportunistic selection of international markets?
5. What are the differences between a global market segment and a national market segment? What are the marketing implications of these differences for a firm serving segments on a worldwide basis?
6. Discuss the possible implications that the firm's choice of geographic expansion strategy may have on the ability of a local marketing manager of a foreign subsidiary to develop and implement marketing programmes.

References

Andersen, O. and Buvik, A. (2002) 'Firms' internationalization and alternative approaches to the international customer/market selection', *International Business Review*, 11, pp. 347–363.

Andersen, P.H. and Strandskov, J. (1998) 'International market selection', *Journal of Global Marketing*, 11(3), pp. 65–84.

Ayal, I. and Zif, J. (1979) 'Market expansion strategies in multinational marketing', *Journal of Marketing*, 43 (Spring), pp. 84–94.

Brewer, P. (2001) 'International market selection: developing a model from Australian case studies', *International Business Review*, 10, pp. 155–174.

Brouthers, L.E. and Nakos, G. (2005) 'The role of systematic international market selection on small firms' export performance', *Journal of Small Business Management*, 43(4), pp. 363–381.

Douglas, S. and Craig, C.A. (1995) *Global Marketing Strategy*. McGraw-Hill, New York.

Green, R.T. and Allaway, A.W. (1985) 'Identification of export opportunities: a shift-share approach', *Journal of Marketing*, 49 (Winter), pp. 83–88.

Johanson, J. and Vahlne, J.E. (1977) 'The internationalization process of the firm: a model of knowledge development and increasing foreign market commitment', *Journal of International Business Studies*, 8(1), pp. 23–32.

Katsikea, E.S., Theodosiou, M., Morgan, R.E. and Papavassiliou, N. (2005) 'Export market expansion strategies of direct-selling small and medium-sized firms: implications for export activities', *Journal of International Marketing*, 13(2), pp. 57–92.

Mazur, L. and Lannon, J. (1993) 'Crossborder marketing lessons from 25 European success stories', *EIU Research Report*, The Economist Intelligence Unit Limited, London, pp. 17–19.

Meyer, K.E. (2009) 'Global focusing: corporate strategies under pressure', *Strategic Change*, 18, pp. 195–207.

Papadopoulos, N., Chen, H. and Thomas, D.R. (2002) 'Toward a tradeoff model for international market selection', *International Business Review*, 11, pp. 165–192.

Piercy, N. (1981) 'Company internationalization: active and reactive exporting', *European Journal of Marketing*, 15(3), pp. 26–40.

Rahman, S.H. (2003) 'Modelling of international market selection process: a qualitative study of successful Australian international businesses', *Qualitative Market Research: An International Journal*, 6(2), pp. 119–132.

Sirkin, H.L., Hemerling, J.W. and Bhattacharya, A.K. (2008) 'Globality: challenger companies are drastically redefining the competitive landscape', *Strategy and Leadership*, 36(6), pp. 36–41.

Sylvest, J. and Lindholm, C. (1997) 'Små globale virksomheder', *Ledelse & Erhvervsøkonomi*, 61 (April), pp. 131–143.

Vernon, R. (1966) 'International investment and international trade in product cycle', *Quarterly Journal of Economics*, 80, pp. 190–208.

Welford, R. and Prescott, K. (1996) *European Business: An Issue-based Approach*. Pitman, London.

Westhead, P., Wright, M., Ucbasaran, D. (2002) 'International market selection strategies selected by "micro" and small firms', *Omega*, 30, pp. 51–68.

Yip, G.S., Biscarri, J.G. and Monti, J.A. (2000) 'The role of the internationalization process in the performance of newly internationalizing firms', *Journal of International Marketing*, 8(3), pp. 10–35.

CASE STUDY II.1

Bajaj Auto: The Indian motorcycle manufacturer internationalizes its business

The Bajaj Group is amongst the top 10 business houses in India. Its footprint stretches over a wide range of industries, spanning automobiles (two-wheelers and three-wheelers), home appliances, lighting, iron and steel, insurance, travel and finance.

The group's flagship company, Bajaj Auto Ltd (www.bajajauto.com), is ranked as the world's fourth-largest two- and three-wheeler manufacturer and the Bajaj brand is well-known across several countries in Latin America, Africa, the Middle East, South and South East Asia.

Bajaj Auto.

Company history

1945 Bajaj Auto is founded.
1960 Rahul Bajaj becomes the Indian licensee for Vespa scooters.
1977 Technical collaboration with Piaggio ends.
1984 Work begins on a second plant.
1998 Bajaj plans to build its third plant to meet demand.
2000 Thousands of workers are laid off to cut costs.

Founded in 1926, at the height of India's movement for independence from the British, the group has an illustrious history. The integrity, dedication, resourcefulness and determination to succeed which are characteristic of the group today, are often traced back to its birth during those days of relentless devotion to a common cause. The Bajaj Group was formed in the first days of India's independence from Britain. Its founder,

Jamnalal Bajaj, had been a follower of Mahatma Gandhi, who reportedly referred to him as a fifth son. This close relationship and his deep involvement in the independence movement did not leave Jamnalal Bajaj with much time to spend on his newly launched business venture.

His son, Kamalnayan Bajaj, then 27, took over the reins of business in 1942. He too was close to Gandhi and it was only after Independence in 1947 that he was able to give his full attention to the business. Kamalnayan Bajaj not only consolidated the group, but also diversified into various manufacturing activities.

In 1959, Bajaj obtained license from the Government of India to manufacture two- and three-wheelers and it went public in 1960.

Rahul Bajaj reportedly adored the famous Vespa scooters made by Piaggio of Italy. In 1960, at the age of 22, he became the Indian licensee for the make; Bajaj Auto began producing its first two-wheelers the next year.

Rahul Bajaj became the group's chief executive officer in 1968 after first picking up an MBA at Harvard. He lived next to the factory in Pune, an industrial city three hours' drive from Bombay. The company had an annual turnover of Rs 72 million (approximately €1 million) at the time. By 1970, the company had produced 100,000 vehicles. The oil crisis soon drove cars off the roads in favour of two-wheelers, which were much cheaper to buy and many times more fuel-efficient.

The technical collaboration agreement with Piaggio of Italy expired in 1977. Afterward, Piaggio, maker of the Vespa brand of scooters, filed patent infringement suits to block Bajaj scooter sales in the United States, United Kingdom, West Germany and Hong Kong. Bajaj's scooter exports plummeted from Rs 133.2 million (€1.9 million) in 1980–81 to Rs 52 million (€0.7 million) in 1981–82. Pretax profits were cut in half, to Rs 63 million (€0.9 million).

New competition in the 1980s

Japanese and Italian scooter companies began entering the Indian market in the early 1980s. Although some boasted superior technology and flashier brands, Bajaj Auto had built up several advantages in the previous decades. Its customers liked the durability of the product and the ready availability of maintenance; the company's distributors permeated the country.

The Bajaj M-50 debuted in 1981. The new fuel-efficient, 50cc motorcycle was immediately successful, and the company aimed to be able to make 60,000 of them a year by 1985. Capacity was the most important constraint for the Indian motorcycle industry.

The 1986–87 fiscal year saw the introduction of the Bajaj M-80 and the Kawasaki Bajaj KB100 motorcycles (under license from Kawasaki). The company was making 500,000 vehicles a year at this point.

Bajaj Auto.

A possible joint venture with Piaggio was discussed in 1993 but aborted. Rahul Bajaj told the *Financial Times* that his company was too large to be considered a potential collaborator by Japanese firms. It was hoping to increase its exports, which then amounted to just 5 per cent of sales. The company began by shipping a few thousand vehicles a year to neighbouring Sri Lanka and Bangladesh, but soon was reaching markets in Europe, Latin America, Africa and West Asia. Its domestic market share, barely less than 50 per cent, was slowly slipping.

Bajaj Auto produced one million vehicles in the 1994–95 fiscal year. The company was the world's fourth-largest manufacturer of two-wheelers, behind Japan's Honda, Suzuki and Kawasaki. New models included the Bajaj Classic and the Bajaj Super Excel. Bajaj also signed development agreements with two Japanese engineering firms, Kubota and Tokyo R&D. Bajaj's most popular models cost about Rs 20,000 (€286). 'You just can't beat a Bajaj,' stated the company's marketing slogan.

Although its domestic market share continued to slip, falling to 40.5 per cent, Bajaj Auto's profits increased slightly at the end of the 1997–98 fiscal year. Bajaj's competitors were doing well, but their net profit were still more than the next four biggest companies combined and Hero Honda Motors was the most serious local threat.

The present Chairman of the group, Rahul Bajaj, took charge of the business in 1965. Under his leadership, the turnover of the Bajaj Auto Ltd has gone up from Rs 72 million to Rs 89 billion (€1,270 million) in 2008–09. Its product portfolio has expanded from one model to a complete range of motorcycle models at the 'light' end of the market.

The world market for motorcycles

After the Second World War, the BSA Group became the largest producer of motorbikes in the world, producing up to 75,000 bikes per year in the 1950s. The German company NSU Motorenwerke AG held the position of largest manufacturer from 1955 until the 1970s. From 1960 to the 1990s the small two-stroke motorbikes became very popular throughout the world.

Motorcycles are the most affordable form of motorized transport in many parts of the world, and for most of the world's population, they are also the most common type of motor vehicle. There are around 300 million motorcycles in use worldwide. About 45 million of those are in India, the region's second-biggest fleet after China, with more than 100 million. Worldwide there are about 33 motorcycles per 1,000 people. This compares to around 590 million cars, or about 91 per 1,000 people. Most of the motorcycles, 70 per cent, are in the developing countries of Asia, while 33 per cent of the cars (195 million) are concentrated in the US and Japan.

Thus two separate motorcycle markets exist. The first is centred in the industrialized triad (i.e., the US, Japan and western Europe), where motorcycles are seen as pleasure vehicles by consumers who already have one or more automobiles. These motorcycles on average tend to be larger, more powerful machines which cost on average about €5,000 to €6,000 (in the US and Europe), and somewhat less in Japan.

The other, much larger market in volume terms is found in the emerging economies of the Asia Pacific, Latin America and Africa/Middle East regions, where motorcycles are seen as primary family and work

Table 1	World market for motorcycles (largest manufacturers and countries)	
Largest motorcycle manufacturers	**Millions of motorcycles sold worldwide (2008)**	**% world market share (2008)**
1. Honda (Japan)	9	20
2. Yamaha (Japan)	5	10
3. Suzuki (Japan)	4	8
4. Bajaj (India)	2	4
5. Kawasaki (Japan)	1	2
Others	26	56
Total	**47**	**100**
Largest markets (countries)	**Millions of motorcycles sold worldwide (2008)**	**% world market share (2008)**
1. China	15	32
2. India	8	17
Other countries	24	51
Total	**47**	**100**

Source: based on various sources.

vehicles. These vehicles are cheaper, smaller and less powerful than triad motorcycles.

Today, the motorcycle industry is mainly dominated by Japanese companies such as Honda, Kawasaki, Suzuki, and Yamaha (see Table 1), although Harley-Davidson, BMW and Triumph continue to be popular in the heavy weight motorcycle segment.

Overall Honda is the world's biggest with manufacturing sites located in India (3 million units), China (2 million units) and Brazil (1 million units). The biggest part of Honda's 9 million units is in the category 100–150cc.

Indian market for motorcycles

India is the world's largest market for motorcycles behind China, but it is overwhelmingly dominated by smaller, inexpensive bikes used primarily for transportation. It is also a market dominated by several well-entrenched Japanese and Indian manufacturers.

In India, the 'license raj' that existed between the 1940s to 1980s did not allow foreign companies to enter the market and imports were tightly controlled. This regulatory maze, before economic liberalization, made business easier for local players to have a seller's market. Customers in India were forced to wait up to 12 years to buy a scooter from Bajaj. The CEO of Bajaj commented that he did not need a marketing department, only a dispatch department. By the year 1990, Bajaj had a waiting list that was 26 times its annual

output for scooters. In the mid-1980s, Indian government regulations changed and permitted foreign companies to enter the Indian market through minority joint ventures. The two-wheeler market changed with Indo-Japanese joint ventures such as the Hero Honda and TVS Suzuki. With a larger selection of two-wheelers on the Indian market, consumers started to gain influence over the products they bought and raised customer expectations. India's growing middle class was tired of the inadequate public transport system and in search of economical and reliable personal transport. As a response to this the motorcycle industry produced more models, styling options, prices and different fuel efficiencies. The foreign companies new technologies helped make the products more reliable and of better quality. Indian companies had to change to keep up with their global counterparts.

Overall, Hero Honda Motor is the market leader with approximately 42 per cent of the Indian motorcycle market (2008), followed by Bajaj Auto Ltd with approximately 25 per cent and TVS Motor Co. (Suzuki) with 19 per cent.

Currently Bajaj Auto's market share in the 'entry level' 100cc segment (which accounts for 70 per cent of the total Indian motorcycle market) stands at 10 per cent, while that of Hero Honda is at 80 per cent. In the 125cc segment (and above) Bajaj's market share is much higher, but this market segment accounts for only 30 per cent of the total market.

Competitor in India: Hero Honda Motors Ltd

In 1984, the Hero Group, then the world's largest manufacturers of bicycles, entered into a joint venture with Honda Motors of Japan to create Hero Honda Motors Ltd, which has gone on to become the world's largest manufacturer of two-wheelers. Hero Honda's success and market leading position relied on its ability to create a motorcycle that required little maintenance and had enormous fuel efficiency. It was not inexpensive, but it had a reputation of lasting the distance over years without requiring any serious repairs. Spare parts were easy to get and inexpensive.

Bajaj's results and internationalization until now

In 2008–09 Bajaj sold approximately 1.9 million motorcycles, of which 634,000 motorcycles (a growth of 25 per cent compared to 2007–08) were exported to the areas listed in Table 2:

Table 2	International sales of Bajaj motorcycles (2008–09)
	1000 units (2008–09)
Total sales of motorcycles (domestic + export)	1,910
Of which for exports	634 (33%)
Geographical spread of export markets	
South Asia (mainly Bangladesh and Sri Lanka)	32%
South East Asia (mainly Thailand, Indonesia, Philippines)	13%
Africa and Middle East (mainly Nigeria, Iran)	30%
Latin America (mainly Central America and Columbia)	25%
Total	100%

Source: based on various sources.

Bajaj now has a distribution network that covers 50 countries. It has a dominant presence in Sri Lanka, Colombia, Bangladesh, Central America, Peru and Egypt and an increasing foothold in Africa. As a consequence, the company has commissioned an assembly unit in Nigeria with the help of its distributor to cater to the growing demand in the African markets.

As part of the company's policy to be closer to the markets in which it operates, Bajaj Auto has its own sales offices in Monterrey (Mexico), Dubai and Colombo (Sri Lanka) in addition to its subsidiary PT BAI in Indonesia.

The outcome of all these efforts can be found in Bajaj's financial results (Table 3):

Table 3	Bajaj's financial results 2007–09	
1 eur = 70 IMD (Rs)	2008–09 million €	2007–08 million €
Net sales	1,276	1,310
Profit before taxation	137	162

Source: based on www.bajajauto.com

In 2008–09 the average number of employees was 10,500.

QUESTIONS

1. Which theory is the most representative of Bajaj's internationalization process?
2. What are the advantages and disadvantages of Bajaj's international focus market strategy?
3. Would it be relevant for Bajaj to enter the North American or western European motor cycle market?

Source: www.bajajauto.com.

CASE STUDY II.2

The Female Health Company (FHC): the female condom is seeking a foothold in the world market for contraceptive products

It's time to take control. Give your vagina a choice.
Toronto Public Health Department Female Condom Campaign Slogan

Source: FHC 2001 Annual Report.

On one of her few days off in Autumn 2009, Senior Strategic Advisor Mary Ann Leeper, is thinking about the great opportunities for the female condom. The potential market for the product of her company, the female condom, is huge, but FCH has still not been making positive net profits during the last few years. Mary Ann is thinking about how to reach FHC's long-term goal: 3 per cent of the 12 billion unit male condom market (US$3–4 billion in value). She accepts that the product is still relatively young in the world market for contraceptives, but she thinks it must be possible to produce better positive financial results with such a high-quality product. The big question is how . . .

Background to the contraceptive market

The market for contraceptives has long been heavily influenced by social and political considerations. From the early days of the pill, the growing numbers of abortions and the decision to make the pill freely available in the early 1970s to the emergence of the AIDS threat in the 1980s, this sector has always been more than a mere product category.

Of the 44 million people infected with HIV worldwide an estimated 29 million (or about 70 per cent) are African. In some countries (such as Botswana) more than 20 per cent of the population are infected by HIV. The number of African AIDS orphans was expected to reach 15 million in 2003. Over 30 million people have already died from AIDS – more than the number of deaths from all African wars – and 11,000 new cases are diagnosed every day. The deadly disease is decimating Africa's labour force and seriously impeding the continent's economic recovery and development.

The increase in the pandemic has been linked to such cultural practices as polygamy, female genital mutilation, widow inheritance and sexual practices and behaviour that are culturally imposed in some societies.

Image courtesy of the Female Health Company and Mayer Laboratories, Inc. (www.mayerlabs.com), US distributor of the Female condom.

In Swaziland, for example, the local culture celebrates virility or the *ingwanwa* – a man who engages in multiple sexual encounters, while the female equivalent, *igwandla* is shunned. The AIDS disease is also fuelled by a popular myth that sex with a virgin cures AIDS.

The total market consists of a very broad range of products, with oral contraceptives (the pill) and male condoms the most popular. Other, 'natural' forms of contraception are also practised, such as withdrawal and the safe period. Men and women may also be surgically sterilized.

Contraceptive products are available in pharmacies or general retail outlets, over the counter (OTC), or via prescription. Contraceptive products are also widely distributed in public clinics. In terms of the two leading forms of contraception, the contraceptive pill is available only on prescription, while condoms are widely available in chemists, supermarkets and vending machines, etc. Growth in distribution channels has been a feature of the condom market since the second half of the 1980s in response to the AIDS crisis.

Condom usage has risen substantially over the past six years, while use of the pill has remained broadly stable. The pill remains a popular contraceptive (based upon surveys of women – surveys of men and women show use of condom and pill as about equal).

The product

The female condom is made of polyurethane – a thin but strong material that is resistant to tearing. It consists of a soft, loose-fitting sheath and two flexible O-rings. One of the rings is used to insert the device and helps to hold it in place. The other ring remains outside the vagina after insertion. The female condom lines the vagina, preventing skin from touching skin during intercourse. The female condom is prelubricated and disposable and is intended for use only once. The product offers an additional benefit to the 10–15 per cent of the population that are allergic to latex and who, as a result, may be irritated by latex male condoms.

In 2005, FHC announced that it had completed development of its second generation female condom, FC2. FC2 is made of a nitrile polymer which allows for a more rapid and economical manufacturing process. It has the same physical design, specifications, safety and efficacy profile as the female condom the company presently sells. FC2 has been approved by the European Union and has received the CE mark; it is currently under review by the World Health Organization (WHO). FHC is in discussions with the US Food and Drug Administration (FDA) regarding requirements for US distribution.

Because of the modified manufacturing procedure, it is expected that having FC2 available will result in a meaningful reduction in costs which will ultimately reduce the cost to customers based on the purchase of sufficient volume. It is FHC's objective to use this opportunity to accelerate market penetration.

FHC and the female condom

The female condom was invented by a Danish physician who obtained a US patent for the product in 1988, and subsequently sold certain rights to the female condom to a US company. The first female condom became available in 1992, since which time more than 50 million have been sold around the world. It is marketed under the name FC female condom in the United States, Femidom in the United Kingdom and Myfemy in other markets, such as Japan.

The Female Health Company manufactures, markets and sells the female condom, which is a product under a woman's control, unlike the male condom. FHC is based in Chicago, but has production in London. FHC's UK manufacturing subsidiary received a Queen's Award for enterprise in April 2002, in recognition of international trade achievements. FHC owns worldwide rights to the female condom, including patents that have been issued in a number of countries. The problem in many less developed countries (such as many in Africa) is that most men do not want to use condoms and, when it comes to sexual relationships, women do not have power to negotiate. In many cultures it is accepted that men can do what they like: the female condom is a way of empowering and protecting women in those countries.

The female condom can prevent unintended pregnancy and sexually transmitted diseases (STDs), including HIV/AIDS. It is the only HIV/AIDS product specifically developed and approved by regulatory agencies in the United States, the European Union, Japan and the People's Republic of China, among others, since the epidemic began about 20 years ago, for the prevention of the transmission of HIV/AIDS through sexual contact.

The product is currently sold or available in various venues including commercial (private sector) outlets, public sector clinics and research programmes in over 75 countries. It is commercially marketed in 21 countries, including the United States, the United Kingdom, Canada, France and Japan. However, the female condom is mainly sold to the global public sector. In the United States it is marketed to city and state public health clinics as well as not-for-profit organizations. Following several years of testing the efficacy and acceptability of the female condom, in 1996 FHC entered into a three-year agreement with the Joint United Nations Programme on AIDS (UNAIDS), which has subsequently been extended. Under the agreement UNAIDS facilitates the availability and distribution of the female condom in the developing world and the FHC will sell the product to developing countries at a reduced price based on the total number of units purchased. The current price per unit is approximately £0.43, or €0.52. Pursuant to this agreement, the product is currently available in over 80 countries with major UN health programmes in about ten countries including Zimbabwe, Tanzania, Brazil, Uganda, South Africa, Namibia, Ghana and Haiti.

Studies have shown that female condoms are reused up to five times. WHO has explained the procedure that should be used regarding the washing and preparation of the female condom, if it is going to be reused, on its website. WHO, UNAIDS and FHC all state that the female condom should only be reused when a new one is not available.

Global market potential and FHC sales

It is estimated the global annual market for male condoms is 12 billion units. The major segments are in the global public sector, the United States, Japan, India and the People's Republic of China. However, the majority of all acts of sexual intercourse, excluding those intended to result in pregnancy, are completed without protection. As a result it is estimated that the potential market for barrier contraceptives is much larger than the identified male condom market.

Currently it is estimated that more than 8 billion male condoms are distributed worldwide by the public sector each year. The rest, 4 billion male condoms, is estimated to go through the traditional retailing systems. The female condom is seen as an important addition to prevention strategies by the public sector because studies show that its availability decreases the amount of unprotected sex by as much as one-third over offering only a male condom.

FHC expects to derive the vast majority, if not all, of its future revenue from the female condom, its sole current product. While management believe the global potential for the female condom is significant, the product is in the early stages of commercialization.

The competitive situation

FHC's female condom participates in the same market as male condoms but is not seen as directly competing with male condoms. Rather, the FHC believes that providing female condoms is additional in terms of prevention and choice. Latex male condoms cost less and have brand names that are more widely recognized than the female condom. In addition, male condoms are generally manufactured and marketed by companies with significantly greater financial resources than FHC.

A new direct competitor has arrived at the scene: Medtech Products Ltd (MP), a male latex condom company with a manufacturing facility in Chennai, India, has developed a natural latex female condom. MP's female condom has been marketed under various names including V-Amour, VA Feminine Condom and L'Amour.

The United States Agency for International Development (USAID) and Family Health International (FHI) are currently evaluating the MP female condom for consideration along with the FC2 to qualify for an in-depth phase 3 clinical study evaluation. The MP product's manufacturing process has a CE mark for distribution in Europe and is available in German stores. MP received Indian Drug Controller approval in January 2003.

Another competitor is also in operation: PATH, an international, non-profit organization based in the United States, has a female condom product in early stage development.

Neither the MP female condom nor the PATH woman's condom have received FDA approval or been listed as essential products for procurement by WHO.

The Indian case

In July 2006 FHC announced the first purchase of the FC female condom by the Indian government for use in its HIV/AIDS prevention programmes. The number of HIV/AIDS victims in India is the largest of any nation and is growing rapidly. While still being less than 1 per cent of its 1 billion plus population, the government is aggressively developing prevention programmes to preclude what has occurred in Sub-Saharan Africa where HIV/AIDS victims exceed 20 per cent of the population in some countries. As a consequence of the growing Indian market, in July 2006 FHC made an agreement with Hindustan Latex Limited (HLL) to manufacture FHC's second generation female condom (FC2) in India. HLL is an Indian government company (www.hindlatex.com) with an annual male condom manufacturing capacity of 1 billion units.

FHC today

FHC's total net revenue in 2008 was approximately $25.5 million, and with net income of $4.8 million. In 2008 FHC sold nearly 35 million female condoms, up 34 per cent from 2007 and nearly triple the number sold 5 years ago. In 2008, female condoms were shipped to 93 countries. To meet demand FHC expanded manufacturing capacity in Malaysia and together with the Indian partner Hindustan Latex Limited, a new FC2 manufacturing facility was brought on line in Kochi, India.

The new generation female condoms, FC2 (made of nitrile polymer) and the 'old' generation FC1 are functionally equivalent, but FC2 is simpler and less costly to produce, particularly for high-volume production. The new FC2 needs separate approval by government authorities, and this has already happened in a number of countries. In 2008 FC2 accounted for 40 per cent of the total FHC sales.

QUESTIONS

1. How would you explain FHC's internationalization process up to now?

2. What are the main cultural barriers for expanding global sales of the female condom?

3. Which screening criteria would you use if FHC had plans to expand into new developing markets?

4. Besides having distribution to the public sector particularly in Africa, Latin America and recently India, FHC is also trying to commercialize the female condom in consumer markets around the world. Where and how should FHC attack consumer markets?

CASE STUDY II.3

Tipperary Mineral Water Company: market selection inside/outside Europe

The Irish firm Tipperary Mineral Water Company (TMWC) was founded in 1986 by Patrick and Nicholas Cooney. It has since developed into a major national brand in the £40 million Irish mineral water market, with about 15 per cent market share there. The market share outside Ireland is very small.

In 2005 the 60 employees in the company generated a total turnover of about £7 million. The net profit was £0.3 million.

TMWC is a part of the Gleeson Group, which has a solid base in the Irish drinks market and ranks among the top 200 companies in Ireland. As a consequence TMWC has a solid and sound financial background.

Tipperary mineral water (sparkling and still) is available in a range of packaging options including 200ml, 500ml, 1-litre, 1.5-litre and 2-litre bottles. All bottles are recyclable and all labels bear the recyclable symbol. The product range has been extended into the office and leisure market, with 19 litre Tipperary Cooler Dispensers for offices. You can see the product range at www.tipperary-water.ie/tippindex.html.

Mineral water in Ireland

General acceptance of bottled water as an alternative to alcohol when socializing is a relatively recent phenomenon in Ireland and Britain. However, it has long been a way of life in continental Europe and the United States. This has as much to do with historical traditions as the quality of tap water. France has a tradition of drinking bottled water going back to Roman times. French consumers today use different brands on different occasions and have a highly developed palate for water, which could be said for most continental countries.

Ireland is therefore at an early stage of development as regards the consumption of bottled water. Few consumers can distinguish between alternative brands and sales of sparkling water are greater than still water. In Europe and the United States bottled water is part of the way of life and sales of still water greatly outweigh sales of sparkling water, with much substitution of bottled for tap water.

Consumption per capita of bottled water in Ireland is perhaps 8 litres per capita per annum, with the United

Part of you

Gleeson Group.

Kingdom consuming 14 litres. However, consumption per capita in France is 118 litres per capita per annum, with Germany averaging 75, and the United States about 30.

Tipperary as a brand name abroad gains instant recognition from the song 'It's a long way from Tipperary', which is one of the most international of songs. It was particularly popular during the First and Second World Wars as a marching song and was broadcast to a worldwide cinema audience through Movietone news reports.

The location of Ireland to source bottled water is a good idea in that Ireland is generally perceived as green, unspoiled and lacking in industrialization or pollution.

The European market for mineral water

The following examines the retail market for mineral water in six major markets: France, Italy, the United Kingdom, Germany, Spain and Benelux (Belgium, the Netherlands and Luxembourg). Sales through 'horeca' (hotels, restaurants and catering establishments) are for the main part excluded.

Mineral water originates from a pure earth source and contains healthy constituents such as minerals and trace elements. It must be bottled at source and must not undergo any form of treatment except that of separating the iron from sulphur to avoid any discolouration or smell. Nothing may be added or taken away from the water, except carbon dioxide to make sparkling water. Mineral water has benefited from the shift away from alcohol consumption due to stricter drink-drive laws and health awareness generally. Greater concern over the quality of municipal tap water supplies has also underpinned rising demand for mineral water.

Table 1 shows the total market values of mineral water in the major European markets. The mineral water market is broken down into:

- still
- sparkling
- flavoured.

Table 1	Value sales of mineral waters in US dollars by country, 1999
Country	**US$ (millions)**
Germany	3,491
Italy	2,421
France	2,087
UK	657
Spain	415
Benelux	354

Source: based on data from *Euromonitor*.

Still water is the dominant sector in the mineral water market, offering a direct, healthy alternative to tap water. Sparkling water demand is more meal/occasion-specific, and the digestive properties on offer mean that sparkling water tends to attract a higher margin. Flavoured water remains a negligible influence on most markets, but is the most dynamic sector where sales exist.

An increased spread of distribution outlets and wider availability have exposed mineral water to a greater audience: it has established a commodity status in several countries and this is increasingly affecting trends apparent in the market. As a consequence the mineral water market is characterized by high levels of private label penetration.

Competitive situation in the European mineral water market

The global bottled water market underwent dramatic changes in terms of brand ownership in 1992, when the Swiss food giant Nestlé bought all Perrier's mineral water brands except Volvic, which was sold to BSN (now known as Groupe Danone). Today Nestlé (with brands such as Perrier and Vittel) and Danone (with brands including Evian and Volvic) are the leading mineral water producers, both in Europe and throughout the world. The market shares of the manufacturers in the major markets are shown in Table 2.

Domestic producers continue to have a significant presence, despite increasing consolidation, in France (Groupe Neptune with Castel), Italy (San Benedetto), Spain (Vichy Catlan) and Benelux (Spadel from Belgium is the market leader with 29 per cent of total value sales in 1999).

As an international marketing consultant you are contacted by the management group of TMWC. They want you to prepare a report in which you give well-founded solutions to the following tasks.

Table 2   Characteristics of four major mineral water markets (sales in hotels, restaurants and catering are not included), 1999

	UK		France		Germany		US	
Market sectors (millions litres)	*Type*		*Type*		*Type*		*Type*	
	Flavoured	33	Flavoured	125	Flavoured	63	Flavoured	139
	Still	518	Still	5,750	Still	2,308	Still	4,709
	Carbonated	290	Carbonated	1,120	Carbonated	3,758	Carbonated	2,315
	Total	**841**	**Total**	**6,995**	**Total**	**6,129**	**Total**	**7,163**
Market shares (per cent)	Companies (brands)		Companies (brands)		Companies (brands)		Companies (brands)	
	Premier Waters Ltd	17	Group Danone (Evian)	40	Gerolsteiner Brunnen GmbH & Co	11	Nestlé SA (Perrier, Poland Spring)	19
	Perrier Vittel (UK) Ltd	9	Perrier Vittel SA	26	Die Blauen Quelien Mineralund Heilbrune AG	6	Group Danone SA (Evian)	10
	Eden Valley Mineral Water Co. Ltd	5	Groupe Neptune SA	12	Mineralbrunnen berkingen-Teinach AG	4	PepsiCo	5
	Highland Ltd	5	St Amand	2	Visla Brunnen	3	McKesson BHOC	4
	Strathmore Ltd	2	Private label	8	Apollinaris Schweppes GmbH & Co.	3	Suntory Ltd	3
	Spadel (UK) Ltd	1	Other	12	Coca-Cola Schweppes Beverages Ltd	3	Private label	26
	Coca-Cola Schweppes Beverages Ltd	1	**Total**	**100**	Frankenbrunnen	2	Other	34
	Ballygowan Ltd	45			Rheinfelsquell	2	**Total**	**100**
	Private label	14			Richard Haringer Getränke	2		
	Other				Private label	3		
	Total	**100**			Other	61		
					Total	**100**		

Distribution of mineral water and comments (per cent)

Channels		Channels		Channels		Channels	
Supermarkets/hypermarkets	69	Supermarkets/hypermarkets	75	Supermarkets/hypermarkets	39	Supermarkets/hypermarkets	43
Other stores	13	General merchandiser	15	Specialist bulk stores	32	Small food outlets/superettes	21
Small food outlets	9	Small food outlets	5	Traditional food retailers	17	Vending machine	15
General merchandisers	4	Other stores	2	Discount stores	8	General merchandisers	11
Outdoor	3	Outdoor	2	Other	4	Other stores	8
Vending machine	1	Vending machine	1	**Total**	**100**	Outdoor	2
Other	1	**Total**	**100**			**Total**	**100**
Total	**100**						

In the supermarkets/hypermarkets J. Sainsbury and Tesco are the two leading mineral water retailers. As demand grows, mineral water is starting to be delivered to British homes by milkmen.

The three giants of the hypermarket operators are Carrefour, Leclerc and Intermarché, the latter being mainly large supermarkets. Wholesalers are under threat as large supermarkets and hypermarkets are increasingly dealing directly with manufacturers. Very hot summer weather will drive impulse sales through local outlets.

Unlike other food markets, traditional retailers hold a comparatively high share of the distribution breakdown (17 per cent) because mineral water is seen as an everyday essential item.

Discount stores are of particular importance for the distribution of carbonated mineral water, predominantly selling private label products.

Private label sales accounted for over 26 per cent of volume sales distribution in 1999, reflecting the strength of major supermarket/hypermarket retailers. Vending is a convenient, clean way for consumers to obtain water.

Comments on consumer profiles

Private label products have benefited from the fact that mineral water is a fairly homogenous product, making pricing the most important consideration for many consumers. Mineral water is consumed more by women than by men in the UK.

This is particularly noticeable with sparkling water where consumption by females is almost twice the level of male consumption.

Consumers in higher income socio-economic groups drink much more mineral water than lower earners.

According to a study carried out by Credoc (a consumer research body) in 1998, 35.6 per cent of French households refused to drink tap water. The low share of the carbonated type is due to the fact that most French people continue to drink still water with meals. Flavoured waters, particularly the sparking variety, can compete more directly with soft drinks and therefore appeal to a younger market.

The emergence and popularity of the five litre bottles demonstrates that more and more people are using mineral water not only for drinking, but also for preparation of tea, coffee and in cooling.

The Germans are the fourth largest group of mineral water consumers in Europe behind the Italians, French and Belgians with a per capita consumption of 97 litres in 1999.

The trend towards a healthy lifestyle is responsible for the recent surge in the number of teenagers who drink mineral water.

Climate also plays an important role in the consumption of mineral water with 85 per cent of Bavarians drinking it regularly, compared to 72 per cent of their northern counterparts.

Mineral water consumption is higher among women than it is among men, as the former tend to be more conscious about their eating habits and the latest health trends.

Consumers between the ages of 35 and 44 consume mineral water more frequently than consumers in other age groups.

Consumption is related to household income, as usage is higher in wealthier households.

Consumption is lowest among consumers aged 65 and over, a group that has not accepted the concept of paying for water, when tap water is free.

QUESTIONS

1. Which country or countries in Europe (outside Ireland) would you recommend TMWC to concentrate on?

2. Which country or countries outside Europe would you recommend TMWC to concentrate on (use Table 3)?

Table 3	Volume and value of all mineral waters by country			
	Per capita volume 1999 (litres)	Total value 1999 (US$ million)	% change 1993–1999 (US$ value)	Per capita value 1999 (US$)
Argentina	13.1	300	46.6	8.40
Australia	8.4	133	48.6	7.20
Brazil	8.9	1,244	219.9	7.78
Canada	18.6	436	44.6	14.39
Chile	5.2	46	33.3	3.13
China	0.4	447	48.9	0.36
Colombia	14.2	755	92.5	20.87
Hong Kong, China	7.1	47	40.5	7.21
India	0.0	12	923.6	0.01
Indonesia	4.1	270	52.9	1.34
Israel	22.8	117	71.0	20.13
Japan	5.4	757	60.3	6.01
Malaysia	1.2	28	28.0	1.30
Mexico	4.6	365	39.3	3.79
New Zealand	2.3	9	53.7	2.46
Philippines	3.3	136	170.8	1.85
Singapore	7.0	47	97.1	15.16
South Africa	0.3	17	165.6	0.38
South Korea	11.5	408	48.5	8.87
Taiwan	7.6	149	83.7	6.95
Thailand	0.0	1	54.1	0.01
Turkey	2.6	165	56.0	2.59
USA	34.7	8,567	48.8	31.98
Venezuela	5.7	86	88.2	3.72
Vietnam	0.5	26	991.9	0.33

Source: based on data from *Consumer International*, 1999.

Towards the end of 2006 Charlotte and Henrik Jorst can look back at 15 hectic but successful years. Their company was founded in an apartment in New York, from where its first marketing efforts took place. The two entrepreneurs started selling relatively expensive watches bearing a logo that American companies might use as company presents. During the Gulf Crisis however it was very difficult to sell watches in that price range. In 1990 Charlotte and Henrik visited a watch fair in Basel in order to find a manufacturer who was able to produce the watches at a lower cost price. They found a Danish-owned company, Comtech Watches, with headquarters in Aarhus and a clock and watch factory in Hong Kong.

In 1992 Charlotte and Henrik had an annual turnover of US$800,000, primarily through an advertisement on the back page of a big mail-order catalogue for Father's Day. Since then events followed each other in quick succession. In 1995 the chain store Bloomingdale's included the Skagen Design watches in its assortment and other retail chains like Macy's, Nordstrom and Watch World have followed. In addition, the watches are sold in big gift and design shops.

In 1998 Skagen Designs had an annual turnover of almost US$30 million; in 2005 turnover had increased to approximately US$70 million.

Charlotte and Henrik Jorst
Skagen Designs.

Skagen designs – the story in brief

1986 Party at Carlsberg. Even if Henrik Jorst has brought his girlfriend, he manages to make Charlotte Kjølbye his neighbour at dinner, and they fall head over heels in love. Shortly after the party Carlsberg sends Henrik to New York. From New York Henrik manages Carlsberg's USA sales. Charlotte stays on for a year and a half in Denmark keeping in close contact with Henrik on the phone.

1986 Charlotte joins Henrik in the United States and reigns as Miss Carlsberg for the summer and fall months. After a Danish colleague sends them a few of his sample corporate watches to sell in the United States, Charlotte and Henrik embark on their dream of starting their own business and begin working in the world of watches. They are married in May.

1990 Henrik quits his job at Carlsberg. Charlotte walks New York trying to sell the Danish Jacob Jensen watches to watchmakers. They have hardly any money. Charlotte gives birth to their daughter Christine.

1991 The Jorsts design a few sample corporate watches and exhibit them at the New York Premium and Incentive Show in the Spring. At this fair, several retailers notice the watches and wonder why the two Danes present them as corporate watches and not branded goods. The retailers state that if the watches were available without the corporate logos they would purchase them for their stores. During the summer they produce 800 copies of four different watches with the name *Skagen Denmark*. A few months later all watches are sold out and an additional amount was produced.

1992 Sitting at the dinner table Henrik and Charlotte design 30 different models, all labelled 'Skagen

Denmark'. In a New York street Charlotte meets one of the managers from the mail order giant 'The Sharper Image'. She takes a chance, and yes, he features the Skagen watches on the back page of the Father's Day catalogue. Everything is sold out. From the apartment in New York Henrik and Charlotte have a turnover of US$800,000.

1993 There are not many states in the United States where business taxes are almost equal to zero. In Florida and Nevada this is, however, the case. One day they fly to Incline Village at Lake Tahoe – one of the world's best ski resorts. They lose their hearts and buy a house that is much too expensive, but big. The company moves into every room from kitchen cupboards to garage. They still do it all by themselves. Charlotte gives birth to their daughter Camilla.

1995 Five years after starting the company. Now, it becomes *really* big. Bloomingdale's takes the watches on trial. Sold out – on one single day. They engage employees in a small, rented office not far from their home at the lake. After a year the office is too small, and after another year the same happens again.

1998 The magazine *Inc.* puts Skagen Designs on the list of the 250 fastest growing, privately owned companies. During five years the turnover has increased by almost 1,200 per cent. Finally, the rest of the company moves out of the villa at Lake Tahoe. New headquarters are opened in Reno, Nevada. An office is opened in Denmark to handle European distribution and an additional 80 stores throughout Denmark begin selling the Skagen Denmark line.

1999 The number of employees is approaching 100. *Inc.* magazine's 'Inc. 500' lists the company as one of the fastest-growing companies in the United States. Henrik gives Charlotte a horse as present for their ten-year wedding anniversary. The family moves from Lake Tahoe to a large house of 650 square metres on the outskirts of Reno. It is situated on the top of a hill with a beautiful view of the Sierra Nevada Mountains. Skagen begins its ongoing presence in major magazines such as *InStyle* and *GQ*. Distribution begins in the United Kingdom.

2000 Distribution begins in Germany and the Netherlands.

2001 Skagen Designs exhibits for the first time at BaselWorld – The Watch and Jewellery Show in Basel, Switzerland.

2002 Distribution begins in additional countries including Finland, Iceland, Ukraine and Kuwait.

2003 More countries join the Skagen Designs team and distribution begins in Belgium, Serbia, Montenegro, United Arab Emirates, Norway, France and Italy.

2004 To handle increasing growth, the European HQ office in Copenhagen moves to a larger facility. The European HQ targets large department stores in Germany and France.

2005 The former Director of Sales and Product Development, Scott Szybala is appointed as President. Scott's responsibilities are to oversee the daily operations as well as the strategic direction for Skagen Designs, reporting directly to Charlotte and Henrik, who continue to be closely involved in the company's product development and sales.

2006 Skagen Designs becomes an official sponsor of Team CSC, one of the best teams in professional cycling, with a record-breaking number of victories. Today, Henrik and Charlotte still approve all products that Skagen designs.

2009 Skagen continues its expansion into product (jewellery and sunglasses) and geographical markets, for example in Eastern Europe and the Far East.

Internal policies

Skagen Designs has its name from the Danish fishing village of Skagen; a popular retreat for artists from around the world. Many say this place has the perfect source of natural light and those who visit find its unique charm to be a mix between nature-given and man-made romanticism. This region has inspired not only the brand name, but also the Jorst design philosophy. The colours, shapes and simplicity inspire the design team. The design team is on the pulse of current fashions, with regular visits to design centres around the world including Switzerland, Italy, France, New York and Hong Kong. Skagen Designs tries to stay true to its classic design philosophy and is never content to follow established trends.

The Skagen Designs' logo symbolizes the meeting of the Skagerak and the Kattegat seas that surround the village of Skagen.

Charlotte and Henrik have divided the work between them. Charlotte is primarily in charge of sales and marketing, while Henrik is in charge of the company's finance and administration.

In the United States the watches are sold at very competitive prices compared with other design watches: typically at a level of US$100–120.

The core competences of Skagen Designs are assessed as follows:

- Development of new watch concepts following the fashion trend with 'the finger on the pulse'.
- Human resource policy – both Charlotte and Henrik spend a lot of time walking around and communicating with employees and to let them feel that Skagen Designs is one big team with the same family-oriented values in all parts of the worldwide organization.

The Skagen Royal Nights watch
Skagen Designs.

- Quick and flexible management decisions.
- New products are introduced five times a year (November, January, March, May and August) providing retailers with seasonal updates and giving consumers the opportunity to update the style for each season.
- Well-developed partnerships with the 'upstream' specialists in the Far East who are in charge of the production at competitive prices.

Marketing the watches

In the United States Skagen Design products are launched through fashion papers like *Vogue*, *InStyle* and *Accessories*. TV shows like *Jeopardy* and *Wheel of Fortune* have been sponsored as well as actors in the series *Ally McBeal* and *The Practice*.

The company's national advertising is also placed in major industry publications as well as out-of-home advertising opportunities including billboards, buses and phone kiosks to support peak selling periods such as spring fashion, Mother's Day, Father's day, autumn fashion and Christmas.

In 2006 Skagen Designs became an official sponsor of the professional cycling team CSC. Skagen Denmark's Team CSC watch collection was comprised of six new styles of performance-inspired, Swiss-made watches featuring ultra lightweight and durable titanium cases and water-resistant leather straps. The Skagen sponsorship of the CSC team ended after the 2006 season.

Competitors

As a fashion company Skagen Designs is competing with all the major international companies designing watches – for example, Calvin Klein, Coach, Guess, Gucci, Swatch, Alfex and Jacob Jensen. Most of these companies possess a financial strength many times larger than Skagen Designs.

QUESTIONS

As an expert in international marketing Charlotte and Henrik have called you in to get valuable input in connection with the international expansion of Skagen Designs. Therefore, you need to answer the following questions. If necessary, make your own conditions and remember to state the reasons for your answers.

1. What screening criteria should Skagen Designs use in connection with its choice of new markets for its watch collection?
2. Make a specific choice of new markets for Skagen Designs. Table 1 and Table 2 can be used to support your argument.
3. Which 'market entry mode' should Skagen Designs use on the chosen markets?
4. Skagen Designs has launched other product lines (e.g. sunglasses, branded items for the home) with varying success. What should be the guidelines for including other product lines in the Skagen Designs collection?
5. Which criteria should Skagen Designs use for its selection of future sponsor partners?
6. Skagen Designs is considering online sale of its watches. What problems and possibilities do you see for the company in this area? On this basis what are your conclusions?

Table 1		Volume of different watch markets, 2008				
	2003	2004	2005	2006	2007	2008
Retail volume in thousands of units						
Belgium	624.98	515.02	714.37	739.44	778.06	819.53
France	5,035.20	4,913.47	4,987.27	4,837.80	4,827.73	4,825.53
Germany	7,501.72	7,452.94	8,217.55	10,284.34	10,918.50	9,859.88
Italy	5,712.08	5,482.23	5,366.33	5,874.31	6,525.52	6,893.24
Netherlands	5,613.00	5,850.00	5,931.00	6,073.00	6,200.00	6,414.00
Spain	12,299.70	12,018.98	11,810.19	11,533.47	11,308.69	10,989.01
Sweden	2,491.00	2,565.00	2,641.00	2,719.50	2,800.00	2,884.00
United Kingdom	17,800.00	17,900.00	18,100.00	18,400.00	16,000.00	15,500.00
Hungary	1,106.19	1,113.93	1,126.19	1,134.07	1,140.87	1,150.00
USA	63,954.47	55,441.04	50,370.68	48,500.85	51,593.56	53,037.50
Mexico	35,690.68	38,721.57	34,946.59	47,598.71	46,780.14	47,851.56
China	57,500.00	60,000.00	61,000.00	61,900.00	59,725.00	64,000.00
India	33,469.00	35,876.98	38,829.72	41,778.67	47,232.00	52,324.80
Japan	9,864.95	9,751.41	9,615.49	9,530.93	9,431.18	9,333.77
Australia	3,189.74	3,505.84	3,604.25	3,817.23	3,920.20	4,001.79
South Africa	23,117.73	21,081.80	26,000.23	15,925.30	18,117.89	16,348.31
Number of watches per 1,000 people						
Belgium	61.04	50.18	69.29	71.41	74.86	78.62
France	85.71	83.22	84.04	81.09	80.49	80.04
Germany	91.30	90.60	99.68	124.59	132.13	119.21
Italy	99.03	94.78	92.51	101.03	112.03	118.17
Netherlands	353.82	365.92	368.26	375.06	380.97	392.24
Spain	309.56	299.56	292.26	284.13	277.52	268.82
Sweden	281.11	288.76	296.44	304.19	312.12	320.36
United Kingdom	303.53	303.13	305.59	309.62	268.40	259.19
Hungary	108.22	109.21	110.68	111.82	112.85	114.08
USA	232.45	199.78	180.02	171.95	181.46	185.06
Mexico	363.59	388.41	345.29	463.43	448.98	452.90
China	45.69	47.31	47.79	48.15	46.11	49.07
India	33.19	35.00	37.28	39.51	44.00	48.05
Japan	77.72	76.61	75.45	74.70	73.83	73.00
Australia	166.54	180.59	183.30	192.60	195.87	198.05
South Africa	527.18	470.37	569.51	343.00	381.02	336.62

Source: adapted from Euromonitor and trade sources/national statistics.

Table 2 Value of different watch markets, 2008 (US$ million)

	2003	2004	2005	2006	2007	2008
Belgium	23.91	17.06	20.50	26.20	29.51	30.34
France	934.22	910.42	945.84	1,097.25	1,205.66	1,205.42
Germany	1,429.95	1,519.96	1,762.75	2,699.99	2,846.60	2,954.50
Italy	951.62	918.02	934.11	1,103.06	1,215.72	1,311.61
Netherlands	189.50	191.64	204.00	250.15	275.03	284.86
Spain	804.77	792.48	849.75	1,027.89	1,141.35	1,155.92
Sweden	214.69	198.02	218.48	273.54	312.97	318.41
United Kingdom	960.77	942.91	1,064.11	1,225.10	1,328.51	1,359.78
Hungary	19.56	19.50	21.98	25.40	28.33	29.09
USA	7,477.65	6,486.85	6,321.98	6,426.05	7,118.52	7,206.49
Mexico	200.44	246.59	274.57	303.69	353.17	434.30
China	405.27	500.66	518.67	544.28	604.10	655.09
India	191.37	232.18	288.58	416.40	675.55	975.02
Japan	4,560.11	4,109.99	4,077.30	4,493.29	4,916.32	4,901.23
Australia	171.92	168.72	181.51	226.99	264.75	281.81
South Africa	245.67	221.85	235.62	228.68	323.93	451.58
US$ per capita						
Belgium	2.34	1.66	1.99	2.53	2.84	2.91
France	15.90	15.42	15.94	18.39	20.10	19.99
Germany	17.40	18.48	21.38	32.71	34.45	35.72
Italy	16.50	15.87	16.10	18.97	20.87	22.49
Netherlands	11.95	11.99	12.67	15.45	16.90	17.42
Spain	20.25	19.75	21.03	25.32	28.01	28.28
Sweden	24.23	22.29	24.52	30.60	34.89	35.37
United Kingdom	16.38	15.97	17.97	20.62	22.29	22.74
Hungary	1.91	1.91	2.16	2.50	2.80	2.89
USA	27.18	23.38	22.59	22.78	25.04	25.15
Mexico	2.04	2.47	2.71	2.96	3.39	4.11
China	0.32	0.39	0.41	0.42	0.47	0.50
India	0.19	0.23	0.28	0.39	0.63	0.90
Japan	35.93	32.29	32.00	35.22	38.49	38.33
Australia	8.98	8.69	9.23	11.45	13.23	13.95
South Africa	5.60	4.95	5.16	4.93	6.81	9.30

Source: adapted from Euromonitor and trade sources/national statistics.

PART I
The decision whether to internationalize
Chs 1–4

PART II
Deciding which markets to enter
Chs 5–8

PART III
Market entry strategies
Chs 9–13

PART IV
Designing the global marketing programme
Chs 14–17

PART V
Implementing and coordinating the global marketing programme
Chs 18–19

Part III Contents

Part III Case studies

PART III
Market entry strategies

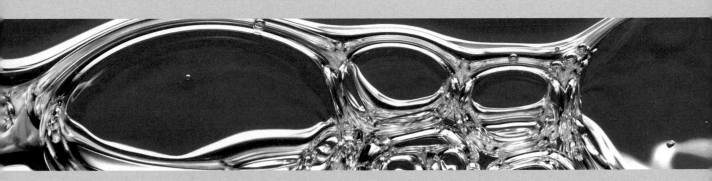

Introduction to Part III

Once the firm has chosen target markets abroad (see Part II) the question arises as to the best way to enter those markets. In Part III we will consider the major market entry modes and criteria for selecting them. An international market entry mode is an institutional arrangement necessary for the entry of a company's products, technology and human capital into a foreign country or market.

To separate Part III from later chapters, look at Figure III.1, which shows the classical distribution systems in a national consumer market.

In this context the chosen market entry mode (here, own sales subsidiary) can be regarded as the first decision level in the vertical chain that will provide marketing and distribution to the next actors in the vertical chain. In Chapter 17 we will take a closer look at the choice between alternative distribution systems at the single national level.

Some firms have discovered that an ill-judged market entry selection in the initial stages of its internationalization can threaten its future market entry and expansion activities. Since it is common for firms to have their initial mode choice institutionalized over time, as new products are sold through the same established channels and new markets are entered using the same entry method, a problematic initial entry mode choice can survive through the institutionalization of this mode. Inertia in the shift process of entry modes delays the transition to a new entry mode. The reluctance of firms to change entry modes once they are in place, and the difficulty involved in so doing, makes the mode of entry decision a key strategic issue for firms operating in today's rapidly internationalizing marketplace (Hollensen, 1991).

For most SMEs the market entry represents a critical first step, but for established companies the problem is not how to enter new emerging markets, rather how to exploit opportunities more effectively within the context of their existing network of international operations.

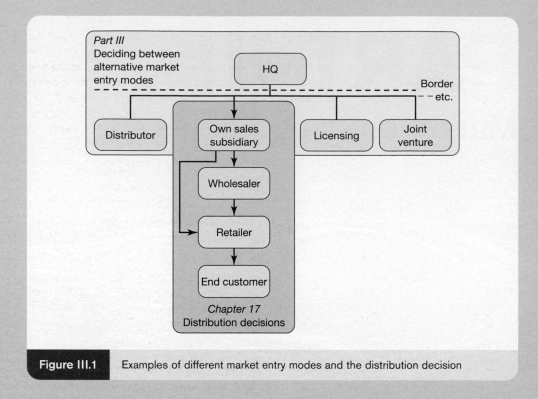

Figure III.1   Examples of different market entry modes and the distribution decision

There is, however, no ideal market entry strategy, and different market entry methods might be adopted by different firms entering the same market and/or by the same firm in different markets. Petersen and Welch (2002) found that a firm often combines modes to enter or develop a specific foreign market. Such 'mode packages' may take the form of concerted use of several operation modes in an integrated, complementary way. In some cases a firm uses a combination of modes that compete with each other. Sometimes this occurs when a firm attempts a hostile takeover of an export market. The existing local distributor might be able to resist giving up the market, depending on the nature of existing obligations, but the exporter nevertheless may establish a wholly owned sales subsidiary.

As shown in Figure III.2, three broad groupings emerge when one looks at the assortment of entry modes available to the firm when entering international markets. There are different degrees of control, risk and flexibility associated with each of these different market entry modes. For example, the use of hierarchical modes (investment modes) gives the firm ownership and thereby high control, but committing heavy resources to foreign markets also represents a higher potential risk. At the same time heavy resource commitment creates exit barriers, which diminish the firm's ability to change the chosen entry mode in a quick and easy way. So the entry mode decision involves trade-offs, as the firm cannot have both high control and high flexibility.

Figure III.3 shows three examples representing the main types of market entry mode. By using hierarchical modes, transactions between independent actors are substituted by intra-firm transactions, and market prices are substituted by internal transfer prices.

Many factors should be considered in deciding on the appropriate market entry mode. These factors (criteria) vary with the market situation and the firm in question.

Chapter 9 will examine the different decision criteria and how they influence the choice among the three main groupings of market entry modes. Chapter 10 (Export modes), Chapter 11 (Intermediate modes) and Chapter 12 (Hierarchical modes) will discuss in more detail the three main types of entry mode. A special issue for SMEs is

CHAPTER 9
Some approaches to the choice of entry mode

Contents

Learning objectives

After studying this chapter you should be able to:

- Identify and classify different market entry modes.

- Explore different approaches to the choice of entry mode.

- Explain how opportunistic behaviour affects the manufacturer/intermediary relationship.

- Identify the factors to consider when choosing a market entry strategy.

9.1 Introduction

Entry mode
An institutional arrangement for the entry of a company's products and services into a new foreign market. The main types are export, intermediate and hierarchical modes.

We have seen the main groupings of **entry modes** available to companies that wish to take advantage of foreign market opportunities. At this point we are concerned with the question: what kind of strategy should be used for the entry mode selection?

According to Root (1994) there are three different rules:

1. *Naive rule.* The decision-maker uses the same entry mode for all foreign markets. This rule ignores the heterogeneity of the individual foreign markets.
2. *Pragmatic rule.* The decision-maker uses a workable entry mode for each foreign market. In the early stages of exporting the firm typically starts doing business with a low-risk entry mode. Only if the particular initial mode is not feasible or profitable will the firm look for another workable entry mode. In this case not all potential alternatives are investigated, and the workable entry may not be the 'best' entry mode.
3. *Strategy rules.* This approach requires that all alternative entry modes are systematically compared and evaluated before any choice is made. An application of this decision rule would be to choose the entry mode that maximizes the profit contribution over the strategic planning period subject to (a) the availability of company resources, (b) risk and (c) non-profit objectives.

Although many SMEs probably use the pragmatic or even the naive rule, this chapter is inspired mainly by an analytical approach, which is the main principle behind the strategy rule.

9.2 The transaction cost approach

The principles of transaction cost analysis have already been presented in Chapter 3 (section 3.3). This chapter will go into further details about 'friction' and opportunism.

The unit of analysis is the transaction rather than the firm. The basic idea behind this approach is that in the real world there is always some friction between the buyer and seller in connection with market transactions. This friction is mainly caused by opportunistic behaviour in the relation between a producer and an export intermediary.

In the case of an agent, the producer specifies sales-promoting tasks that the export intermediary is to solve in order to receive a reward in the shape of commission.

In the case of an importer, the export intermediary has a higher degree of freedom as the intermediary itself, to a certain extent, can fix sales prices and thus base its earnings on the profit between the producer's sales price (the importer's buying price) and the importer's sales price.

No matter who the export intermediary may be, there will be some recurrent elements that may result in conflicts and opportunistic actions:

- stock size of the export intermediary;
- extent of technical and commercial service that the export intermediary is to carry out for its customers;
- division of marketing costs (advertising, exhibition activities, etc.) between producer and export intermediary;
- fixing of prices: from producer to export intermediary, and from the export intermediary to its customers;
- fixing of commission to agents.

Opportunistic behaviour from the export intermediary

In this connection the export intermediary's opportunistic behaviour may be reflected in two activities:

1. In most producer–export intermediary relations a split of the sales promoting costs has been fixed. Thus statements by the export intermediary of too high sales promotion activities (e.g. by manipulating invoices) may form the basis of a higher payment from producer to export intermediary.
2. The export intermediary may manipulate information on market size and competitor prices in order to obtain lower ex-works prices from the producer. Of course, this kind of opportunism can be avoided if the export intermediary is paid a commission of realized turnover (the agency case).

Opportunistic behaviour from the producer

In this chapter we have so far presumed that the export intermediary is the one who has behaved opportunistically. The producer may, however, also behave in an opportunistic way, as the export intermediary must also use resources (time and money) on building up the market for the producer's product programme. This is especially the case if the producer wants to sell expensive and technically complicated products.

Thus the export intermediary carries a great part of the economic risk, and will always have the threat of the producer's change of entry mode hanging over its head. If the export intermediary does not live up to the producer's expectations it risks being replaced by another export intermediary, or the producer may change to its own export organization (sales subsidiary), as the increased transaction frequency (market size) can obviously bear the increased costs.

The last case may also be part of a deliberate strategy from the producer: namely, to tap the export intermediary for market knowledge and customer contacts in order to establish a sales organization itself.

What can the export intermediary do to meet this situation?

Heide and John (1988) suggest that the agent should make a number of further 'offsetting' investments in order to counterbalance the relationship between the two parties. These investments create bonds that make it costly for the producer to leave the relationship: that is, the agent creates 'exit barriers' for the producer (the principal). Examples of such investments are as follows:

- Establish personal relations with the producer's key employees.
- Create an independent identity (image) in connection with selling the producer's products.
- Add further value to the product, such as a BDA (before–during–after) service, which creates bonds in the agent's customer relations.

If it is impossible to make such offsetting investments Heide and John (1988) suggest that the agent reduces its risk by representing more producers.

These are the conditions that the producer is up against, and when several of these factors appear at the same time the theory recommends that the company (the producer) internalizes rather than externalizes.

9.3   Factors influencing the choice of entry mode

A firm's choice of its entry mode for a given product/target country is the net result of several, often conflicting forces. The need to anticipate the strength and direction of these forces makes the entry mode decision a complex process with numerous trade-offs among alternative entry modes.

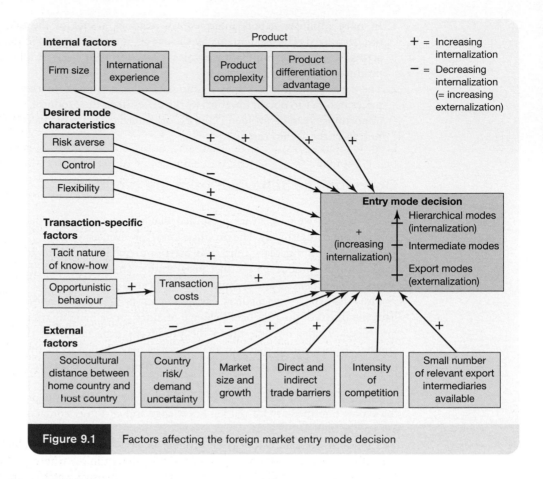

Figure 9.1   Factors affecting the foreign market entry mode decision

Generally speaking the choice of entry mode should be based on the expected contribution to profit. This may be easier said than done, particularly for those foreign markets where relevant data are lacking. Most of the selection criteria are qualitative in nature, and quantification is very difficult.

As shown in Figure 9.1, four groups of factors are believed to influence the entry mode decision:

1. internal factors
2. external factors
3. desired mode characteristics
4. transaction-specific behaviour.

In what follows a proposition is formulated for each factor: how is each factor supposed to affect the choice of foreign entry mode? The direction of influence is also indicated both in the text and in Figure 9.1. Because of the complexity of the entry mode decision the propositions are made under the condition of other factors being equal.

Internal factors

Firm size

Size is an indicator of the firm's resource availability; increasing resource availability provides the basis for increased international involvement over time. Although SMEs may desire a high level of control over international operations and wish to make heavy resource commitments to foreign markets, they are more likely to enter foreign markets using export modes because they do not have the resources necessary to achieve a high degree of control or to make these resource commitments. Export entry modes (market modes), with their lower resource commitment, may therefore be more suitable for SMEs. As the firm grows it will increasingly use the hierarchical model.

International experience

Another firm-specific factor influencing mode choice is the international experience of managers and thus of the firm. Experience, which refers to the extent to which a firm has been involved in operating internationally, can be gained from operating either in a particular country or in the general international environment. International experience reduces the cost and uncertainty of serving a market, and in turn increases the probability of firms committing resources to foreign markets, which favours direct investment in form of wholly owned subsidiaries (hierarchical modes).

Dow and Larimo (2009) conclude from their survey that practitioners should be aware that not all forms of experience are equal. International experience from similar countries (with low perceived psychic distance) is positively associated with the choice of a high-control entry mode (i.e. entry by wholly owned subsidiary). This indicates that exploiting each geographic region in succession may be advisable, instead of 'jumping' from region to region. This would maximize the benefits of within-cluster experience.

In developing their theory of internationalization Johanson and Vahlne (1977) assert that uncertainty in international markets is reduced through actual operations in foreign markets (experiential knowledge) rather than through the acquisition of objective knowledge. They suggest that it is direct experience with international markets that increases the likelihood of committing extra resources to foreign markets.

Product/service

The physical characteristics of the product or service, such as its value/weight ratio, perishability and composition, are important in determining where production is located. Products with high value/weight ratios, such as expensive watches, are typically used for direct exporting, especially where there are significant production economies of scale, or if management wishes to retain control over production. Conversely, in the soft drinks and beer industry, companies typically establish licensing agreements, or invest in local bottling or production facilities, because shipment costs, particularly to distant markets, are prohibitive.

The nature of the product affects channel selection because products vary so widely in their characteristics and use, and because the selling job may also vary markedly. For instance, the technical nature of a product (high complexity) may require service both before and after sale. In many foreign market areas marketing intermediaries may not be able to handle such work. Instead firms will use one of the hierarchical modes.

Blomstermo *et al.* (2006) distinguish between *hard* and *soft services*. Hard services are those where production and consumption can be decoupled. For example software services can be transferred into a CD, or some other tangible medium, which can be mass-produced, making standardization possible. With soft services, where production and consumption occur simultaneously, the customer acts as a co-producer and decoupling is not viable. The soft-service provider must be present abroad from their first day of foreign operations. Blomstermo *et al.* (2006) conclude that there are significant differences between hard- and soft-service suppliers regarding choice of foreign market entry mode. Managers in soft services are much more likely to choose a high control entry mode (hierarchical mode) than hard services. It is important for soft-service suppliers to interact with their foreign customers, thus they should opt for a high degree of control, enabling them to monitor the co-production of the services.

Products distinguished by physical variations, brand name, advertising and after-sales service (e.g. warranties, repair and replacement policies) that promote preference for one product over another may allow a firm to absorb the higher costs of being in a foreign market. Product differentiation advantages give firms a certain amount of impulse in raising prices to exceed costs by more than normal profits (quasi rent). They also allow firms to limit competition through the development of entry barriers, which are fundamental in the competitive strategy of the firm, as well as serving customer needs better and thereby strengthening the competitive position of the firm compared to other firms. Because these product differentiation advantages represent a 'natural monopoly' firms seek to protect their competitive advantages from dissemination through the use of hierarchical modes of entry.

External factors

Sociocultural distance between home country and host country

Socioculturally similar countries are those that have similar business and industrial practices, a common or similar language, and comparable educational levels and cultural characteristics. Sociocultural differences between a firm's home country and its host country can create internal uncertainty for the firm, which influences the mode of entry desired by that firm.

The greater the perceived distance between the home and host country in terms of culture, economic systems and business practices, the more likely it is that the firm will shy away from direct investment in favour of joint venture agreements or even low-risk entry modes like agents or an importer. This is because the latter institutional modes enhance firms' flexibility to withdraw from the host market, if they should be unable to acclimatize themselves comfortably to the unfamiliar setting. To summarize, other things being equal, when the perceived distance between the home and host country is great, firms will favour entry modes that involve relatively low resource commitments and high flexibility. Dow and Larimo (2009) found that the perceived cultural distance (psychic distance) is much more than Hofstede's cultural dimensions. In particular, language difference seems to be one of the least important factors. Other issues, such as differences in religion, degree of democracy, industrial development and so on, have a much greater impact on entry mode choice.

Country risk/demand uncertainty

Foreign markets are usually perceived as riskier than the domestic market. The amount of risk the firm faces is a function not only of the market itself but also of its method of involvement there. In addition to its investment the firm risks inventories and receivables. When planning its method of entry the firm must do a risk analysis of both the market and its method of entry. Exchange rate risk is another variable. Moreover, risks are not only economic; there are also political risks.

When country risk is high a firm would do well to limit its exposure to such risk by restricting its resource commitments in that particular national domain. That is, other things being equal, when country risk is high, firms will favour entry modes that involve relatively low resource commitments (export modes).

Unpredictability in the political and economic environment of the host market increases the perceived risk and demand uncertainty experienced by the firm. This in turn disinclines firms to enter the market with entry modes requiring heavy resource commitments; on the other hand, flexibility is highly desired.

Market size and growth

Country size and rate of market growth are key parameters in determining the mode of entry. The larger the country and the size of its market, and the higher the growth rate, the more likely management will be to commit resources to its development, and to consider establishing a wholly owned sales subsidiary or to participate in a majority-owned joint venture. Retaining control over operations provides management with direct contact and allows it to plan and direct market development more effectively.

Small markets, on the other hand, especially if they are geographically isolated and cannot be serviced efficiently from a neighbouring country, may not warrant significant attention or resources. Consequently they may be best supplied via exporting or a licensing agreement.

While unlikely to stimulate market development or maximize market penetration this approach enables the firm to enter the market with minimal resource commitment, and frees resources for potentially more lucrative markets.

Direct and indirect trade barriers

Tariffs or quotas on the import of foreign goods and components favour the establishment of local production or assembly operations (hierarchical modes).

Product or trade regulations and standards, as well as preferences for local suppliers, also have an impact on mode of entry and operation decisions. Preferences for local suppliers, or tendencies to 'buy national', often encourage a company to consider a joint venture or other contractual arrangements with a local company (intermediate modes). The local partner helps in developing local contacts, negotiating sales and establishing distribution channels, as well as in diffusing the foreign image.

Product and trade regulations and customs formalities similarly encourage modes involving local companies, which can provide information about and contacts in local markets and can ease access. In some instances, where product regulations and standards necessitate significant adaptation and modification, the firm may establish local production, assembly or finishing facilities (hierarchical modes).

The net impact of both direct and indirect trade barriers is thus likely to be a shift towards performing various functions such as sourcing, production and developing marketing tactics in the local market.

Intensity of competition

When the intensity of competition is high in a host market firms will do well to avoid internalization, as such markets tend to be less profitable and therefore do not justify heavy resource commitments. Hence, other things being equal, the greater the intensity of competition in the host market the more the firm will favour entry modes that involve low resource commitments (export modes).

Small number of relevant intermediaries available

In such a case the market field is subject to the opportunistic behaviour of the few export intermediaries, and this will favour the use of hierarchical modes in order to reduce the scope for opportunistic behaviour.

EXHIBIT 9.1 Zara is modifying their preferred choice of entry mode, depending on the psychic distance to new markets

Zara (www.inditex.com) is a fashion retail chain of Inditex Group owned by Spanish tycoon Amancio Ortega. Zara's preferred entry mode is the hierarchical mode (direct investment), which is used in most European countries, resulting in full ownership of the stores. In 2008, 87 per cent of the Zara stores were own managed. Those markets where the hierarchical model is used, are characterized by high growth potential and relative low sociocultural distance (low country risk) between Spain and target market.

The intermediate modes (usually joint venture and franchising) are mainly used in countries where the sociocultural distance is relatively high.

Joint ventures

This is a cooperative strategy in which facilities and know-how of the local company are combined with the international fashion expertise of Zara. This particular mode is used in large, competitive markets where it is difficult to acquire property to set up retail outlets or where there are other kinds of obstacles that require cooperation with a local company. For example, in 1999 Zara entered into a 50-50 joint venture with the German firm Otto Versand, which had experience in the distribution sector and market knowledge in one of Europe's largest markets, Germany.

Franchising

Zara is choosing this mode for high-risk countries which are socioculturally distant or have small markets with a low sales forecast such as Kuwait, Andorra, Puerto Rico, Panama or the Philippines.

Whatever entry mode Zara is using, the main characteristic of their franchise model is the total integration of franchised stores with own-managed stores in terms of product, human resources, training, window-dressing, interior design, logistical optimization and so on. This ensures uniformity in store management criteria and a global image in the eyes of customer around the world.

Source: adapted from the Zara case study and different public media.

Desired mode characteristics

Risk-averse

If the decision-maker is risk-averse they will prefer export modes (e.g. indirect and direct exporting) or licensing (an intermediate mode) because they typically entail low levels of financial and management resource commitment. A joint venture provides a way of sharing risk, financial exposure and the cost of establishing local distribution networks and hiring local personnel, although negotiating and managing joint ventures often absorbs considerable management time and effort. However, modes of entry that entail minimal levels of resource commitment and hence minimal risks are unlikely to foster the development of international operations and may result in significant loss of opportunity.

Control

Mode of entry decisions also need to consider the degree of control that management requires over operations in international markets. Control is often closely linked to the level of resource commitment. Modes of entry with minimal resource commitment, such as indirect exporting, provide little or no control over the conditions under which the product or service is marketed abroad. In the case of licensing and contract manufacturing management needs to ensure that production meets its quality standards. Joint ventures also limit the degree of management control over international operations and can be a source of considerable conflict where the goals and objectives of partners diverge. Wholly owned subsidiaries (hierarchical mode) provide the most control, but also require a substantial commitment of resources.

Flexibility

Equity
Some investment of a defined financial value.

Management must also weigh up the flexibility associated with a given mode of entry. The hierarchical modes (involving substantial **equity** investment) are typically the most costly but the least flexible and most difficult to change in the short run. Intermediate modes (contractual agreements and joint ventures) limit the firm's ability to adapt or change strategy when market conditions are changing rapidly.

Transaction-specific factors

The transaction cost analysis approach was discussed in Chapter 3 (section 3.3) and earlier in this chapter. We will therefore refer to only one of the factors here.

Tacit nature of know-how

Tacit
Difficult to articulate and express in words – tacit knowledge has often to do with complex products and services, where functionality is very hard to express.

When the nature of the firm-specific know-how transferred is **tacit** it is by definition difficult to articulate. This makes the drafting of a contract (to transfer such complex know-how) very problematic. The difficulties and costs involved in transferring tacit know-how provide an incentive for firms to use hierarchical modes. Investment modes are better able to facilitate the intra-organizational transfer of tacit know-how. By using a hierarchical mode the firm can utilize human capital, drawing upon its organizational routines to structure the transfer problem. Hence, the greater the tacit component of firm-specific know-how, the more a firm will favour hierarchical modes.

9.4   Summary

Seen from the perspective of the manufacturer (international marketer), market entry modes can be classified into three groups:

1. export modes: low control, low risk, high flexibility
2. **intermediate modes** (contractual modes): shared control and risk, split ownership
3. hierarchical modes (investment modes): high control, high risk, low flexibility.

Intermediate modes
Somewhere between using export modes (external partners) and hierarchical modes (internal modes).

It cannot be stated categorically which alternative is the best. There are many internal and external conditions which affect this choice and it should be emphasized that a manufacturer wanting to engage in global marketing may use more than one of these methods at the same time. There may be different product lines, each requiring a different entry mode.

CASE STUDY 9.1

Jarlsberg: the king of Norwegian cheeses is deciding about entry modes in new markets

Jarlsberg cheese (www.jarlsberg.com) has been well received in the US market. Nearly 50 years after entering the United States it is now the imported cheese with the biggest market share of its category in the competitive US supermarkets.

However, following the quota which the WTO has set up between Norway and the United States, Jarlsberg can only sell a limited amount of cheese from Norway to the US. The quota on Jarlsberg to the US is approximately 7,000 tons. To increase sales, a licenced production was set up in Ohio in 2000, with an annual production of approximately 5,000 tons. Quality control is maintained by using a cheese culture produced in Norway (based on a secret recipe from 1956), premium quality milk only, tailor-made production lines and key people educated within dairy technology/science.

The total export of Norwegian cheese to the United States in 2008 was approximately 8,000 tonnes, of which the majority was Jarlsberg. This means that the quota which the WTO set up between Norway and the United States was full: Jarlsberg had to find other ways of selling cheese in the United States.

The story

Professor Ole M. Ystgaard and his employees at the Norwegian Agricultural School developed Jarlsberg in the 1950s. The cheese is based on traditions from Swiss cheese makers, who developed cheese with holes in the 1830s.

Jarlsberg cheese arrived in the United States in 1963. In the beginning, the Jarlsberg management team travelled around the country to demonstrate how the cheese could be used for everyday meals and at parties. After just two years Jarlsberg had a sales volume of 450,000 kg in the market, and the managers understood they had a 'hot' product.

Jarlsberg has become a high-status product, served by celebrities at high-society parties.

Tine.

Norseland Inc.

Norseland Inc. was founded in 1978. The purpose of the company was to market and distribute Jarlsberg and other Norwegian cheese in the United States. The company is a wholly owned subsidiary of TINE Norwegian Dairies, which has the main responsibility for the production and marketing of Jarlsberg cheese. In 2002 Norseland had net sales of US$130 million, about half of this derived from imported Norwegian Jarlsberg, 25 per cent from Jarlsberg produced in Ohio and the remainder from sales of products from other companies, among them French Unilever Boursin. Norseland's strategy is to sell exclusive cheeses only, and the company commands respect in the US retail trade where a 90 per cent distribution coverage has been achieved. Norseland has a regional office in Montreal, Canada, where an additional 1,350 tonnes of Jarlsberg were sold in 2008.

The US cheese market

The total US market for hard cheese is approximately 400,000 tons, but the market also consumes a lot of soft cheese. Though Jarlsberg only has a small market share in the total hard cheese market (in 2008 Jarlsberg sold 12,600 tons to the US market) this represents the largest market share in the Swiss-like cheese category.

The largest producer of cheese for the US market is Philip Morris, including the company Nabisco which Philip Morris bought in December 2000. The most well-known brands from Philip Morris come from Kraft, which markets the popular soft cheese,

Philadelphia. The second-largest cheese producer for the US market is ConAgra Foods, which had total sales of US$13 billion in 2008.

In general, the tendency to consume cheese is higher in the eastern part of the United States, whereas 'healthy' food products are focused on more in the western part of the country. There is a tendency to eat more imported cheese as personal income increases.

Jarlsberg's customers and marketing

Jarlsberg cheese has some snob appeal. Customers want to show they have good taste and they accept the higher price of Jarlsberg compared to other competitive products without complaining. The mild and creamy taste appeals to Americans, and many think that the taste of the traditional Swiss cheese, Emmenthal, is too sharp.

Characteristics of the typical Jarlsberg buyer are:

- female
- earning more than US$90,000 per year
- over 40 years old.

It is important to buyers that it is an imported cheese. The fact that it is a Norwegian cheese plays a minor role and Norseland does not use this in its marketing.

Norseland's objective is to attract new and younger consumers for its Jarlsberg cheese. To achieve this objective it wants to make contracts and deals with retail chains like 7-Eleven, which also sells sandwiches, etc.

Besides its own sales force of about 25 sales people, Norseland uses nearly 500 'cheese brokers' (distributors), who sell all over the United States. These are external sales representatives who visit shops, retail chains and restaurants in order to sell and market products, among them Jarlsberg.

Five years from now Jarlsberg aims to be present in at least five new countries, either sourced through the existing production units (e.g. in USA or Ireland) or supplied from Norway.

QUESTIONS

1. Which kind of market entry mode would you generally suggest for Jarlsberg

   (a) in Scandinavia?

   (b) in Asia?

2. What are the general motives for choosing a hierarchical mode (own subsidiary) in the United States?

CASE STUDY 9.2

Ansell condoms: is acquisition the right way to gain market shares in the European condom market?

Ansell Limited is the new name of the company formerly known as Pacific Dunlop Limited.

The company's name was changed in April 2002 as a result of its strategic repositioning to concentrate on its core business, protective products and services in a broad health care context, and following the disposition of a series of other business units that did not fit within the strategy. Ansell Limited is an Australian publicly listed company with its corporate head office located in Richmond, Australia.

In 1905 Eric Ansell, a former Dunlop employee, took the machinery and set up his own company, The Ansell Rubber Company, in Melbourne, Australia, manufacturing toy balloons and condoms. The rest is history: Ansell made strategic acquisitions and expansions and invested in the research and development necessary to bring a number of products to the world market.

Today Ansell Limited is a global leader in barrier protective products. With operations in the Americas, Europe and Asia, Ansell employs more than 11,000 people worldwide and holds leading positions in the natural latex and synthetic polymer glove and condom markets.

Ansell Condom brands are marketed globally through the Personal Healthcare division of Ansell Healthcare, and their main office in Red Bank, NJ, USA. This 100-year-old company has fostered some innovations in latex condoms and gloves. It manufactures and markets a variety of condoms with flavours, colours, spermicide, studded and ribbed features. Ansell markets branded condoms worldwide, each

with its own unique marketing strategy that has been tailored to the particular country or region. A quick list of their brands around the globe includes: *LifeStyles* (for the US market), *Mates* (for the UK market), *KamaSutra* (for the Indian market), *Contempo*, *Manix*, *Primex*, *Pleasure* and *Chekmate*.

Additionally, the company participates in the public sector market where condoms are supplied through health and social welfare programmes and agencies, mainly in developing countries around the world. Ansell also participates in a broad range of studies and educational activities and continues to expand their market presence with the introduction of new products. Lifestyle Ultra Sensitive condoms with spermicide, for instance, were developed to meet demand for a thinner condom that includes a spermicide to maximize protection from sexually transmitted diseases (STDs).

Global manufacturing

Estimated worldwide condom production is around 15 billion pieces annually (2008). Currently there are about 100 manufacturing plants operating globally. The majority of these plants manufacture only condoms made from natural rubber latex, and some also produce other latex products such as gloves, finger cots and catheters. The majority of the plants are therefore in locations where natural rubber latex plantations reside, and where labour costs are competitive.

The production of condoms is much more labour-intensive than that of glove manufacturing, because of more stringent testing needs, more complicated packaging and significant product differentiation.

An estimate of condom production per country in 2008 is shown in Table 1.

World market for male condoms

Condoms offer protection against both unwanted pregnancies (contraception) and STDs (prophylaxis). The latter property is unique to condoms. Although there is considerable superficial variation in the types of condoms available (e.g. ribbed, thin and thick)

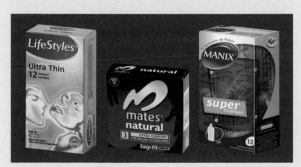

Ansell Healthcare.

Table 1	Estimated 2008 condom production by country
Country	Annual production in billions of pieces
India	3.3
Thailand	2.8
China	2.5
Japan	2.0
Malaysia	1.5
USA	1.0
Europe	1.0
South Korea	0.5
Indonesia	0.3
South America	0.2
Vietnam	0.2
Other	0.1
Total	15.4

there has been little fundamental change in the latex condom over the years.

Organizations that comprise the global public health sector currently distribute approximately 10 billion male condoms, generally free of charge or at a nominal cost, to sexually active people throughout the world, mostly in developing nations. It is estimated that another 5 billion male condoms are distributed through commercial channels, mostly in developed countries such as the United States, Japan and European nations. The size of the world market for male condoms and how it is made up is shown in Table 2.

In 2008, 35 per cent of condoms were purchased by the United Nations Population Fund. The World Health Organization (WHO) is also a buyer.

Besides the direct competitors, described in Table 3, it is essential to emphasize the role of the indirect competitors, which are those with a product of substitution. According to the Durex Sex

Survey, the male condom is globally the most popular form of contraception (41 per cent of people use it). Among the 59 per cent non-condom users, 19 per cent of the population uses the pill, 8 per cent natural methods and the rest (75 per cent) use no contraception.

With 14 per cent of the global market share for condoms, Ansell is the second largest manufacturer of condoms. The company has 50 per cent of the Polish market, 8 per cent in Germany, 20 per cent in Brazil (third largest), number 1 in Australia, and is the fastest-growing brand in Canada.

In the distribution of male condoms in the commercial sector, there has been a movement from the pharmacies toward the retail chains (supermarkets). For example, in the early 1990s supermarkets accounted for around 25 per cent of the UK retail sales of condoms while pharmacies accounted for over a half. Today, the supermarkets account for around 40 per cent of retail sales, a share mostly drawn from the pharmacies, which have seen their share fall to 30 per cent. Therefore, national retailing chains (supermarkets, Boots and Superdrug) now account for at least 65 per cent of condom sales in the United Kingdom.

Key competitors (manufacturers) in the world male condom market

SSL International

In 1929 the London Rubber Company (LRC) registered the DUREX condom trademark, whose name was derived from **Du**rability, **R**eliability and **Ex**cellence. The next important steps as a global condom's provider were in 1951 with the introduction of the first fully automated production process and two years later with the development of the first electronic testing machines.

In the UK home market, during the 1980s, Durex condoms began to be sold in public areas (e.g. supermarkets, pubs), due to the AIDS fear. That decade showed a sharp development in marketing

Table 2	World market for male condoms (2008)	
		Per year (billions)
Global public health sector (UN, WHO and local governments)		10
Commercial channels (mainly in the US, Japan and European nations)		5
World market		15

Source: adapted from different public sources.

Table 3	Company shares on the world market for male condoms (2008)			
Company	Nationality	Major brands	Key strategies (MS = market share)	Market share (%)
Seton Scholl London (SSL)	UK	Durex, Durex Avanti, Durex Pleasure, Durex Fetherlite, Durex Extra Sensitive, etc.	A true global brand with strong positions in all main markets, except US (15 per cent MS) and Japan (5 per cent MS). In UK the Durex MS is 85 per cent	25
Ansell Limited	Australia/US	LifeStyles, Mates, Contempo, Manix, Primex, KamaSutra, Pleasure and Chekmate	Semi-global company with relatively strong market positions in US, UK, Asian and AUS/NZ markets. Local/regional brands, e.g. LifeStyles for US and Mates for UK	14
Church & Dwight Co	US	Trojan, Trojan Magnum, Trojan Pleasure, Trojan Enz	Market leader in US market, minor position in UK	8
Okamoto Industries	Japan	Beyond Seven, Skinless Skin	Home market-oriented: 60 per cent MS of the Japanese market, but with little exports, mainly to US	10
Others: Sagami Rubber Industries (JP), Fuji Latex Co (JP), DKT Indonesia (Indonesia), Mayer Laboratories (JP) and about 70 other manufacturers around the world			Domestic-and regional-oriented companies with strong positions in local markets	43
Total				100

Source: estimations based on different public sources.

with the first Durex poster campaign in 1982, as well as the first condom advertising on television (1987).

Finally, in the 1990s, Durex has followed a marketing policy aimed at increasing the awareness of the brand with the installation of free-standing outdoor Durex vending machines (1992); the sponsorship of MTV's events (1995); the first Durex Sex Survey (1995); the launch of the first selection of coloured, flavoured and ribbed condoms in the same pack (1996); and in 1997 the launch of the first non-latex protection called Avanti.

At the beginning of the twenty-first century, Durex launched www.Durex.com over 30 countries. These websites, featuring localized pages, in particular the use of local language, provide sexual information, allow people to question specialists, give details of Durex condoms and any sponsored events.

Durex is nowadays part of SSL International Plc, which was formed in 1999 from the merger of the Seton-Scholl Group and London International, the former owner of LRC. It is a worldwide company producing a range of branded products such a Scholl and Marigold gloves, sold to medical and consumer health care markets.

With a market share of approximately 25 per cent, Durex's position can be defined as the world market leader of the sector. Obviously, at different national levels, rankings can be slightly different with, for example, 80–85 per cent of market share in the United

Kingdom, 55–60 per cent in Italy, 10–15 per cent in the United States and around 5 per cent in Japan.

Durex condoms are manufactured in 17 factories worldwide.

Church & Dwight Company Inc

Armkel, LLC, Church & Dwight's 50/50 joint venture with the private equity group, Kelso & Company, acquired in 2001 the remainder of the Carter-Wallace consumer products businesses, including Trojan Condoms.

The Trojan brand accounts for the largest proportion of condom supplies in the United States with around 60–70 per cent market share.

The company markets condoms under the Trojan brand name in Canada, Mexico and recently, in limited distribution, in the United Kingdom. In Canada, the Trojan brand has a leading market share. It entered the UK condom market in 2003, but at present has only a small share. The company markets its condoms through distribution channels similar to those of its domestic condom business.

Okamoto

Okamoto has been in existence since 1934. It holds a remarkable 60 per cent market share in Japan, where condoms are the preferred method of birth control.

In late 1988, Okamoto introduced it condoms to the US market, but without great success until recently.

Latest development – possible acquisition of an European key condom player

Following financial problems at some European condom manufacturers with relatively strong local brands, Ansell is now considering acquiring one of these manufacturers.

Sources: www.ansell.com; www.durex.com; http://www.churchdwight.com/conprods/personal/; http://www.okamoto-condoms.com/; 'Polish condom producer acquires condomi', *Polish News Bulletin*, 21 January 2005; Office of Fair Trading (2006) *Condoms – Review of the undertakings given by LRC Products Limited*, OFT837, HMSO; http://www.wikinvest.com/stock/Ansell_(ANN-AU).

QUESTIONS

1. What are the differences between the global strategies of Ansell and the other three competitors?

2. Which entry mode would you recommend for Ansell's sourcing (purchasing or production) of condoms?

3. What are the pros and cons for Ansell acquiring a European competitor? In your opinion, is it a good idea?

VIDEO CASE STUDY 9.3 Understanding entry modes into the Chinese market

download from www.pearsoned.co.uk/hollensen

China became a member of the World Trade Organization (WTO) on 11 December, 2001 and, overall, the Chinese economy has shown exceptional economic growth over the last five years, closely associated with China's increased integration with the global economy. With a population exceeding 1.3 billion, continued economic growth and a large supply of inexpensive and productive labour, China lures businesses from around the world. Most global firms agree that companies can not be globally successful if they ignore this huge emerging market.

Questions

1. What factors do companies consider when determining the best form of operation to use when entering the Chinese market?

2. What have been the challenges and opportunities for foreign companies in establishing collaborative arrangements in China?

3. How have Chinese government policies and attitudes towards foreign businesses evolved? How have these changes affected foreign companies' forms of operations in China?

For further exercises and cases, see this book's website at **www.pearsoned.co.uk/hollensen**

Questions for discussion

1. Why is choosing the most appropriate market entry and development strategy one of the most difficult decisions for the international marketer?

2. Do you agree with the view that LSEs use a rational analytic approach (strategy rule) to the entry mode decision, while SMEs use a more pragmatic/opportunistic approach?

3. Use Figure 9.1 to identify the most important factors affecting the choice of foreign entry mode. Prioritize the factors.

References

Blomstermo, A., Sharma, D.D. and Sallis, J. (2006) 'Choice of foreign market entry mode in service firms', *International Marketing Review*, 23(2), pp. 211–229.

Dow, D. and Larimo, J. (2009) 'Challenging the conceptualization and measurement of distance and international experience in entry mode choice research', *Journal of International Marketing*, 17(2), pp. 74–98.

Heide, J.B. and John, G. (1988) 'The role of dependence balancing in safeguarding transaction-specific assets in conventional channels', *Journal of Marketing*, 52(January), pp. 20–35.

Johanson, J. and Vahlne, J.E. (1977) 'The internationalization process of the firm – a model of knowledge', *Journal of International Business Studies*, 8(1), pp. 23–32.

Root, F.R. (1994) *Entry Strategies for International Markets*, revised and expanded edition. The New Lexington Press, Lexington, MA.

CHAPTER 10
Export modes

Learning objectives

After studying this chapter you should be able to:

- Distinguish between indirect, direct and cooperative export modes.
- Describe and understand the five main entry modes of indirect exporting:
  - export buying agent;
  - broker;
  - export management company/export house;
  - trading company; and
  - piggyback.
- Describe the two main entry modes of direct exporting:
  - distributor;
  - agent.
- Discuss the advantages and disadvantages of the main export modes.
- Discuss how manufacturers can influence intermediaries to be effective marketing partners.

10.1   Introduction

With export entry modes a firm's products are manufactured in the domestic market or a third country and then transferred either directly or indirectly to the host market. Export is the most common mode for initial entry into international markets. Sometimes an unsolicited order is received from a buyer in a foreign country, or a domestic customer expands internationally and places an order for its international operations. This prompts the firm to consider international markets and to investigate their growth potential.

Exporting is thus typically used in initial entry and gradually evolves towards foreign-based operations. In some cases where there are substantial scale economies or a limited number of buyers in the market worldwide (e.g. for aerospace), production may be concentrated in a single or a limited number of locations, and the goods then exported to other markets.

Exporting can be organized in a variety of ways, depending on the number and type of intermediaries. As in the case of wholesaling, export and import agents vary considerably in the range of functions performed. Some, such as export management companies, are the equivalent of full-service wholesalers and perform all functions relating to export. Others are highly specialized and handle only freight forwarding, billing or clearing goods through customs.

In establishing export channels a firm has to decide which functions will be the responsibility of external agents and which will be handled by the firm itself. While export channels may take many different forms, for the purposes of simplicity three major types may be identified: indirect, direct and cooperative export marketing groups.

1. *Indirect export.* This is when the manufacturing firm does not take direct care of exporting activities. Instead another domestic company, such as an export house or trading company, performs these activities, often without the manufacturing firm's involvement in the foreign sales of its products.
2. *Direct export.* This usually occurs when the producing firm takes care of exporting activities and is in direct contact with the first intermediary in the foreign target market. The firm is typically involved in handling documentation, physical delivery and pricing policies, with the product being sold to agents and distributors.
3. *Cooperative export.* This involves collaborative agreements with other firms (export marketing groups) concerning the performance of exporting functions.

In Figure 10.1 the different export modes are illustrated in a value chain perspective.

Partner mindshare

Partner mindshare
The level of mindshare that the manufacturer's product occupies in the mind of the export partner (e.g. agent or distributor).

No matter which of the three export modes the manufacturer uses in a market, it is important to think about what level of 'mindshare' the manufacturer occupies in the mind of the export-partner. **Partner mindshare** is a measurement of the strength of a relationship in terms of trust, commitment and cooperation. There is a strong and proven correlation between mindshare levels and how willing an export intermediary is to place one company brand in front of another, or how likely the intermediary is to defect. Mindshare also expresses itself very clearly in sales performance. Intermediaries who have high mindshare will, typically, sell more than those with low mindshare.

Mindshare can be broken down into three drivers (Gibbs, 2005):

1. commitment and trust
2. collaboration
3. mutuality of interest and common purpose.

Good mindshare is going to depend upon scoring well across the board. For example, there are manufacturers who are good communicators but are not trusted.

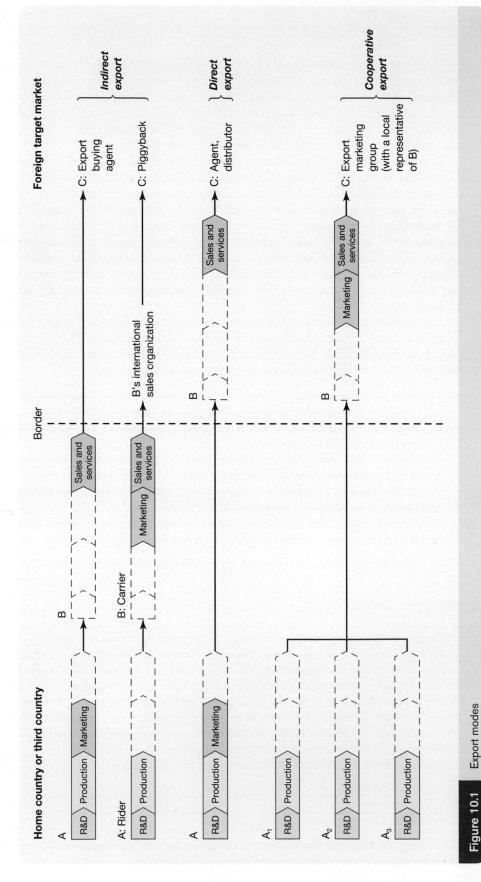

Figure 10.1 Export modes

Note: A, A_1, A_2 and A_3 are manufacturers of products/services.
B is an independent intermediary (agent).
C is the customer.

As well as these three mindshare drivers there is a fourth group we need to measure – product, brand and profit. This group measures the perceived attractiveness of the supplier's product offering to the intermediary. The manufacturer can think of this as a hygiene driver. Broadly speaking, the performance of the manufacturer needs to be as good as the competition for him to garner the full benefit from strong mindshare.

Many manufacturers with excellent products and strong brands which offer good profits struggle precisely because they are seen by the export partner as arrogant, untrustworthy and unhelpful. In other words, they have low mindshare at the export partner.

Each of the three drivers can be broken down further. For instance, collaboration is based partly on a measure of how good the manufacturer is at cooperating on sales. Another constituent of collaboration measures its ability to cooperate on marketing. Other constituents measure whether it is perceived as communicating relevant information in a timely way, how much real joint planning takes place and how valuable the export intermediary finds this process.

Mindshare is severely damaged when suppliers refuse to share resources with partners. Partners may feel excluded – not part of the family. If the intermediary has no long-term stake in manufacturer, and has more mindshare with a competitor, they could choose to simply wind down activities with that intermediary. Alternatively, the manufacturer can fight back by integrating its products and campaigns into the intermediary's business plan and going out of its way to show commitment to the intermediaries. At the multinational US computer technology corporation Oracle they are doing this by saying: 'Our approach is to give marketing materials to our partners. Give them the things they would get if they were internal employees' (Hotopf, 2005).

Manufacturers need to understand the partners' business models, goals, their value to the manufacturer and what it would cost to replace them. However, the manufacturer also needs to look at the long-term value of the relationship (life time value = year-on-year value multiplied by the number of years that the manufacturer typically does business with export intermediaries). This can be used to justify investments in the relationship.

10.2   Indirect export modes

Indirect export modes
A manufacturer uses independent export organizations located in its own country (or third country).

Indirect export occurs when the exporting manufacturer uses independent organizations *located in the producer's country*. In indirect exporting the sale is like a domestic sale, in fact the firm is not really engaging in global marketing, because its products are carried abroad by others. Such an approach to exporting is most likely to be appropriate for a firm with limited international expansion objectives. If international sales are viewed primarily as a means of disposing of surplus production, or as a marginal, use of **indirect export modes** may be appropriate. This method may also be adopted by a firm with minimal resources to devote to international expansion which wants to enter international markets gradually, testing out markets before committing major resources and effort to developing an export organization.

It is important for a firm to recognize, however, that the use of agents or export management companies carries a number of risks. In the first place the firm has little or no control over the way the product or service is marketed in other countries. Products may be sold through inappropriate channels, with poor servicing or sales support and inadequate promotion, or be under- or overpriced. This can damage the reputation or image of the product or service in foreign markets. Limited effort may be devoted to developing the market, resulting in lost potential opportunities.

Particularly significant for the firm interested in gradually edging into international markets is that, with indirect exporting, the firm establishes little or no contact with markets abroad. Consequently the firm has limited information about foreign market potential, and obtains little input to develop a plan for international expansion. The firm will have no means to identify potential sales agents or distributors for its products.

While exporting has the advantage of the least cost and risk of any entry method it allows the firm little control over how, when, where and by whom the products are sold. In some cases the domestic company may even be unaware that its products are being exported.

Moreover, an SME that is already experienced in traditional exporting may have resources that are too limited to open up a great number of export markets by itself. Thus, through indirect export modes the SME is able to utilize the resources of other experienced exporters and to expand its business to many countries.

There are five main entry modes of indirect exporting:

1. export buying agent
2. broker
3. export management company/export house
4. trading company
5. piggyback (shown as a special case of indirect exporting in Figure 10.1).

Export buying agent (export commission house)

Some firms or individuals do not realize that their products or services have potential export value until they are approached by a buyer from a foreign organization, who might make the initial approach, purchase the product at the factory gate and take on the task of exporting, marketing and distributing the product in one or more overseas markets.

Export buying agent
A representative of foreign buyers who is located in the exporter's home country. The agent offers services to the foreign buyers, such as identifying potential sellers and negotiating prices.

The **export buying agent** is a representative of foreign buyers who resides in the exporter's home country. As such, this type of agent is essentially the overseas customer's hired purchasing agent in the exporter's domestic market, operating on the basis of orders received from these buyers. Since the export buying agent acts in the interests of the buyer, it is the buyer that pays a commission. The exporting manufacturer is not directly involved in determining the terms of purchase; these are worked out between the export buying agent and the overseas buyer.

The export commission house essentially becomes a domestic buyer. It scans the market for the particular merchandise it has been requested to buy and sends out specifications to manufacturers inviting bids. Other conditions being equal, the lowest bidder gets the order and there is no sentimentality, friendship or sales talk involved.

From the exporter's point of view, selling to export commission houses represents an easy way to export. Prompt payment is usually guaranteed in the exporter's home country, and the problems of physical movement of the goods are generally taken completely out of its hands. There is very little credit risk and the exporter has only to fulfil the order according to specifications. A major problem is that the exporter has little direct control over the global marketing of products.

Small firms find that this is the easiest method of obtaining foreign sales but, being totally dependent on the purchaser, they are unlikely to be aware of a change in consumer behaviour and competitor activity, or of the purchasing firm's intention to terminate the arrangement. If a company is intent upon seeking longer-term liability for its export business it must adopt a more proactive approach, which will inevitably involve obtaining a greater understanding of the markets in which its products are sold.

Broker

Another type of agent based in the home country is the export/import broker. The chief function of a broker is to bring a buyer and a seller together. Thus the broker is a specialist in performing the contractual function, and does not actually handle the products sold or bought. For its services the broker is paid a commission (about 5 per cent) by the principal. The broker commonly specializes in particular products or classes of product. Being a commodity specialist there is a tendency for the broker to concentrate on just one or two products. Because the broker deals primarily in basic commodities, for many potential export marketers this type of agent does not represent a practical alternative channel of distribution. The distinguishing characteristic of export brokers is that they may act as the agent for either the seller or the buyer.

Export management company/export house

Export houses or export management companies (EMCs) are specialist companies set up to act as the 'export department' for a range of non-competing companies (Rosenbloom and Andras, 2008). As such the EMC conducts business in the name of each manufacturer it represents. All correspondence with buyers and contracts are negotiated in the name of the manufacturer, and all quotations and orders are subject to confirmation by the manufacturer.

By carrying a large range EMCs can spread their selling and administration costs over more products and companies, as well as reducing transport costs because of the economies involved in making large shipments of goods from a number of companies.

EMCs deal with the necessary documentation, and their knowledge of local purchasing practices and government regulations is particularly useful in markets that might prove difficult to penetrate. The use of EMCs, therefore, allows individual companies to gain far wider exposure of their products in foreign markets at much lower overall costs than they could achieve on their own, but there are a number of disadvantages, too:

- The export house may specialize by geographical area, product or customer type (retail, industrial or institutional), and this may not coincide with the supplier's objectives. So the selection of markets may be made on the basis of what is best for the EMC rather than for the manufacturer.
- As EMCs are paid by commission they might be tempted to concentrate upon products with immediate sales potential, rather than those that might require greater customer education and sustained marketing effort to achieve success in the longer term.
- EMCs may be tempted to carry too many product ranges and as a result the manufacturer's products may not be given the necessary attention from sales people.
- EMCs may carry competitive products that they may promote to the disadvantage of a particular firm.

Manufacturers should therefore take care in selecting a suitable EMC and be prepared to devote resources to managing the relationship and monitoring its performance.

As sales increase the manufacturer may feel that it could benefit from increased involvement in international markets by exporting itself. However, the transition may not be very easy. First, the firm is likely to have become very dependent on the export house and, unless steps have been taken to build contacts with foreign customers and to build up the firm's knowledge of its markets, moving away from using an EMC could prove difficult. Second, the firm could find it difficult to withdraw from its contractual commitments to the export house. Third, the EMC may be able to substitute products from an alternative manufacturer and so use its existing customer contacts as a basis for competing against the original manufacturer.

Trading company

Trading companies are part of the historical legacy from colonial days and, although different in nature now, they are still important trading forces in Africa and the Far East. Although international trading companies have been active throughout the world, it is in Japan that the trading company concept has been applied most effectively. There are thousands of trading companies in Japan involved in exporting and importing, and the largest firms (varying in number from 9 to 17 depending upon source of estimate) are referred to as general trading companies or *Soge Shosha*. This group of companies, which includes C. Itoh, Mitsui and Company and Mitsubishi Shoji Kaisha, handle 50 per cent of Japan's exports and 67 per cent of its imports. While the smaller trading companies usually limit their activities to foreign trade, the larger general trading companies are also heavily involved in domestic distribution and other activities.

Trading companies play a central role in such diverse areas as shipping, warehousing, finance, technology transfer, planning resource development, construction and regional development (e.g. turnkey projects), insurance, consulting, real estate and deal-making in general (including facilitating investment and joint ventures). In fact it is the range of financial services offered that is a major factor distinguishing general trading companies from others. These services include the guaranteeing of loans, the financing of both accounts receivable and payable, the issuing of promissory notes, major foreign exchange transactions, equity investment and even direct loans.

Another aspect of their operations is to manage counter-trade activities (barter), in which sales into one market are paid for by taking other products from that market in exchange. The essential role of the trading company is to find a buyer quickly for the products that have been taken in exchange. Sometimes this can be a very resource-demanding process.

Counter-trade is still a very widespread trading form in Eastern Europe and developing countries because of their lack of 'hard' currency. One of the motivations for Western firms to go into counter-trade is the low-cost sources of production and raw materials for use in the firm's own production (Okoroafo, 1994).

Piggyback

In piggybacking the export-inexperienced SME, the 'rider', deals with a larger company (the carrier) which already operates in certain foreign markets and is willing to act on behalf of the rider that wishes to export to those markets. This enables the carrier to utilize fully its established export facilities (sales subsidiaries) and foreign distribution. The carrier is either paid by commission and so acts as an agent or, alternatively, buys the product outright and so acts as an independent distributor. **Piggyback** marketing is typically used for products from unrelated companies that are non-competitive (but related) and complementary (allied).

Piggyback
An abbreviation of 'pick-a-back': i.e. choosing a back to ride on. It is about the rider's use of the carrier's international distribution organization.

Sometimes the carrier will insist that the rider's products are somewhat similar to its own, in view of the need to deal with technical queries and after-sales service 'in the field'. Branding and promotional policies are variable in piggybacking. In some instances the carrier may buy the products, put its own brand on them and market them as its own products (private labels). More commonly the carrier retains the brand name of the producer and the two work out promotional arrangements between them. The choice of branding and promotional strategy is a function of the importance of brand to the product and of the degree to which the brand is well established.

Piggybacking has the following advantages/disadvantages for the carrier and the rider.

Carrier

Advantages

A firm that has a gap in its product line or excess capacity in its export operation has two options. One is to develop internally the products necessary to round out its line and fill up its exporting capacity. The other option is to acquire the necessary products outside by piggy-backing (or acquisition). Piggybacking may be attractive because the firm can get the product quickly (someone already has it). It is also a low-cost way to get the product because the carrier firm does not have to invest in R&D, production facilities or market testing for the new product. It can just pick up the product from another firm. In this way the firm can broaden its product range without having to develop and manufacture extra products.

Disadvantages

Piggybacking can be extremely attractive for the carrier, but some concerns exist about quality control and warranty. Will the rider maintain the quality of the products sold by another firm? This depends in part on whose brand name is on the product. If the rider's name is on the product the quality incentive might be stronger. A second concern is continuity of supply. If the carrier develops a substantial market abroad, will the rider firm develop its production capacity, if necessary? Each of these items should be a subject in the agreement between the two parties. If the piggybacking arrangement works out well there is another potential advantage for the carrier. It might find that the rider is a good acquisition candidate or joint-venture partner for a stronger relationship.

Rider

Advantages

Riders can export conveniently without having to establish their own distribution systems. They can observe carefully how the carrier handles the goods and hence learn from the carrier's experience – perhaps to the point of eventually being able to take over its own export transactions.

Disadvantages

For the smaller company this type of agreement means giving up control over the marketing of its products – something that many firms dislike doing, at least in the long run. Lack of commitment on the part of the carrier and the loss of lucrative sales opportunities in regions not covered by the carrier are further disadvantages.

In summary, piggyback marketing provides an easy, low-risk way for a company to begin export marketing operations. It is especially well suited to manufacturers that are either too small to go directly into exports or do not want to invest heavily in foreign marketing.

10.3 Direct export modes

Direct exporting occurs when a manufacturer or exporter sells directly to an importer or buyer located in a foreign market area. In our discussion of indirect exporting we examined ways of reaching foreign markets without working very hard. Indeed, in the indirect approaches, foreign sales are handled in the same way as domestic sales: the producer does the global marketing only by proxy (that is, through the firm that carries its products overseas). However, both the global marketing know-how and the sales achieved by these indirect approaches are limited.

As exporters grow more confident they may decide to undertake their own exporting task. This will involve building up overseas contacts, undertaking marketing research, handling documentation and transportation, and designing marketing mix strategies. **Direct export modes** include export through foreign-based agents and distributors (independent intermediaries).

The terms 'distributor' and 'agent' are often used synonymously. This is unfortunate because there are distinct differences: distributors, unlike agents, take title to the goods, finance the inventories and bear the risk of their operations, whereas agents do not. Distributors are paid according to the difference between the buying and selling prices rather than by commission (agents). Distributors are often appointed when after-sales service is required, as they are more likely than agents to possess the necessary resources.

Distributors

Exporting firms may work through **distributors (importers)**, which are the exclusive representatives of the company and are generally the sole importers of the company's product in

Direct export modes
The manufacturer sells directly to an importer, agent or distributor located in the foreign target market.

Distributors (importers)
Independent company that stocks the manufacturer's product. It will have substantial freedom to choose own customers and price. It profits from the difference between its selling price and its buying price from the manufacturer.

their markets. As independent merchants, distributors buy on their own accounts and have substantial freedom to choose their own customers and to set the conditions of sale. For each country exporters deal with one distributor, take one credit risk and ship to one destination. In many cases distributors own and operate wholesale and retail establishments, warehouses and repair and service facilities. Once distributors have negotiated with their exporters on price, service, distribution and so on their efforts focus on working their own suboperations and dealers.

The distributor category is broad and includes more variations, but distributors usually seek exclusive rights for a specific sales territory and generally represent the manufacturer in all aspects of sales and servicing in that area. The exclusivity is in return for the substantial capital investment that may be required on the part of the distributor in handling and selling products.

Agents

Agents
Independent company that sells on to customers on behalf of the manufacturer (exporter). Usually it will not see or stock the product. It profits from a commission (typically 5–10 per cent) paid by the manufacturer on a pre-agreed basis.

Agents may be exclusive, where the agent has exclusive rights to specified sales territories; semi-exclusive, where the agent handles the exporter's goods along with other non-competing goods from other companies; or non-exclusive, where the agent handles a variety of goods, including some that may compete with the exporter's products.

An agent represents an exporting company and sells to wholesalers and retailers in the importing country. The exporter ships the merchandise directly to the customers, and all arrangements on financing, credit, promotion, etc., are made between the exporter and the buyers. Exclusive agents are widely used for entering international markets. They cover rare geographic areas and have subagents assisting them. Agents and subagents share commissions (paid by the exporter) on a pre-agreed basis. Some agents furnish financial and market information, and a few also guarantee the payment of customers' accounts. The commissions that agents receive vary substantially, depending upon services performed, the market's size and importance and competition among exporters and agents.

The advantages of both agents and distributors are that they are familiar with the local market, customs and conventions, have existing business contacts and employ foreign nationals. They have a direct incentive to sell through either commission or profit margin, but since their remuneration is tied to sales they may be reluctant to devote much time and effort towards developing a market for a new product. Also, the amount of market feedback may be limited as the agent or distributor may see itself as a purchasing agent for its customers rather than as a selling agent for the exporter. If the agent or distributor is performing well and develops the market it risks being replaced by a subsidiary of the principal. Therefore a long-term strategy is needed whereby it might be useful to include the agent in any new entry-mode decision (e.g. advent of a subsidiary) to avoid the disincentive of being replaced.

Choice of an intermediary

The selection of a suitable intermediary can be a problematic process, but the following sources may help a firm to find such an intermediary:

- asking potential customers to suggest a suitable agent;
- obtaining recommendations from institutions such as trade associations, chambers of commerce and government trade departments;
- using commercial agencies;
- poaching a competitor's agent;
- advertising in suitable trade papers.

In selecting a particular intermediary the exporter needs to examine each candidate firm's knowledge of the product and local markets, experience and expertise, required margins,

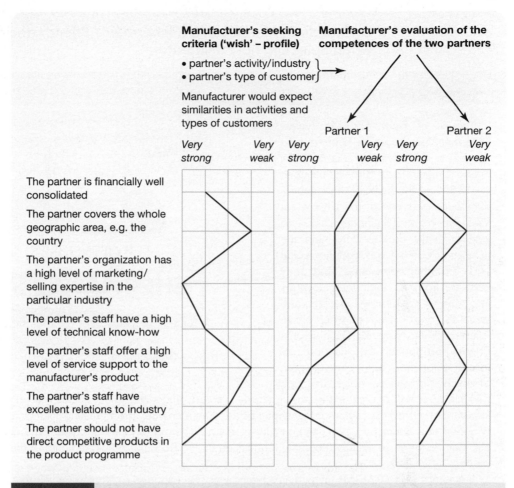

| Figure 10.2 | An example of matchmaking between a manufacturer and two potential distribution partners |

credit ratings, customer care facilities and ability to promote the exporter's products in an effective and attractive manner.

Figure 10.2 shows the matchmaking of a manufacturer and its 'wish'-profile, and two potential intermediaries and their performance profiles in a particular market.

If Partners 1 and 2 were the only potential candidates for the manufacturer, Partner 2 would probably be chosen because of the better match of profiles between what the manufacturer wants on the market (wish-profile) and the performance profile of Partner 2.

The criteria listed in Figure 10.2 would probably not be the only criteria in a selection process. Some other specific desirable characteristics of an intermediary (to be included in the decision-making process) are (Root, 1998):

- size of firm
- physical facilities
- willingness to carry inventories
- knowledge/use of promotion
- reputation with suppliers, customers and banks
- record of sales performance
- cost of operations
- overall experience
- knowledge of English or other relevant languages
- knowledge of business methods in manufacturer's country.

EXHIBIT 10.1 Lofthouse of Fleetwood's (Fisherman's Friend) decision criteria when selecting new distributors

Lofthouse of Fleetwood Ltd (www. fishermansfriend.com), a family-owned company, first created Fisherman's Friend Original Extra Strong Lozenges in 1865 in Fleetwood, Lancashire. Fleetwood was one of the UK's great fishing ports and Fisherman's Friend was originally produced to help the fishermen combat the coughs, colds and bronchial problems that they suffered from on their long voyages into the inhospitable waters and freezing conditions of the North Atlantic fishing grounds. Fisherman's Friend produces 13 flavours of lozenges for the global market, seven of which are available in the UK (sugar

Fisherman's Friend is a registered trademark of Lofthouse of Fleetwood Ltd.

free blackcurrant, original extra strong, aniseed, cherry, sugar free mint, sugar free original and sugar free lemon). The core proposition of Fisherman's Friend as a unique, strong-tasting medicinal sweet, that comes wrapped in a paper bag, remains constant globally. Fisherman's Friend Original Extra Strong Lozenges are still manufactured to exactly the same formulation as in 1865, but other elements of the marketing mix vary country by country.

It was not until 1974 that Fisherman's Friend was first exported to Norway, which remains the highest per capita consuming market in the world today. Today the lozenges are available in 120 countries worldwide, and have grown to become a major international brand: 80 per cent of sales remain in Europe with the UK currently accounting for 4 per cent of total production. Germany is the largest market. Asia follows with around 15 per cent, then North America and other global regions take up the rest. Fisherman's Friend sees the most growth in Russia, China and India because their brand has a global taste. Generally the taste of Fisherman's Friend is accepted worldwide, except in Japan – the Japanese the brand too strong and prefer very sweet things such as Turkish delight.

Lofthouse of Fleetwood contracts (outsources) its marketing activities to an independent company, Impex Management, so that it can focus on R&D and manufacturing. In new international markets Impex Management selects and interviews up to six candidate distributors, undertaking detailed SWOT (strengths, weaknesses, opportunities, threats) analysis on their potential. After the interviews Impex and Lofthouse meet to choose the ideal partner for a particular market.

Among the criteria for selecting a distributor, Lofthouse and Impex have agreed on using the following:

- Size: Lofthouse wants a distributor to be small enough for Fisherman's Friend to have an important role and an adequate share of the distributor's total turnover and attention. Lofthouse prefers to be a big fish in a smaller pool. This needs to be balanced against the need to have a distributor big enough to have the right contacts to the retailers.
- Products: a distributor should be selling complementary product lines and have experience and suitable contacts in relevant product markets. They should not be handling direct competitors' products – Lofthouse wants exclusivity.
- Organizational structure for sales: the number of sales representatives and their coverage of the market (which geographical regions and types of retail channels are covered? How often?)

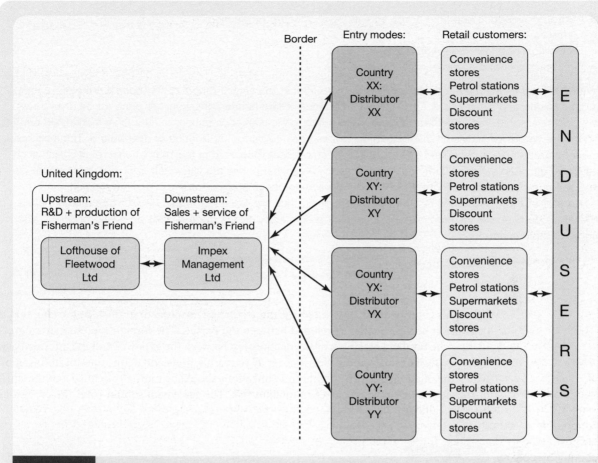

Figure 10.3   International distribution system of Fisherman's Friend

- Financial status: Lofthouse wants the distributor to be financially stable and secure.
- Culture and values: Lofthouse is looking for long-term relationships. Therefore it is important that the distributor has similar culture and values as Lofthouse.
- Family business: as Lofthouse is a family-owned business, they are looking primarily for distributors that are also family businesses.

One distributor that has had a long-term and successful relationship with Lofthouse and Fisherman's Friend is its Dutch distributor, Concorp Brands (earlier Nedean Zoetwaren BV). Its profile fits most of the criteria above. The company distributes confectionery in the Dutch market. Fisherman's Friend was taken into the portfolio in 1974. The company employs approximately 40 people, of whom half are involved on a day-to-day basis in sales for the Dutch market. The sales force is divided in two:

1. impulse outlets: convenience stores, petrol stations and tobacconists
2. grocery channels: supermarkets, discount stores etc.

Around 40 per cent of Fisherman's Friends are sold through impulse outlets, the rest (60 per cent) through grocery channels.

Currently (November 2009) Concorp Brands acts as a distributor in the Netherlands representing following brands:

- Freedent (chewing gum from Wrigley/Mars, USA)
- Skittles (sweets from Wrigley/Mars, USA)

- Autodrop (liquorice and acid drops from its own Concorp production)
- Oldtimes (liquorice from NL)
- Ricola (lozenge from Switzerland)
- Fisherman's Friend (lozenge from England)

When selling in the Netherlands and other international markets through distributors, Lofthouse cannot dictate resale and retail prices for Fisherman's Friends. There is one consistant list price for all distributors, but distributors are free to set resale prices, according to the market conditions in their local market, although Lofthouse/Impex will advise a distributor if its prices seem to be too far from other distributors. The euro has meant a greater price transparency across European borders. Buyers from the international retail chains such as Carrefour, Ahold, Tesco, Lidl and Aldi know very well what prices are like in different European countries and will buy in countries with low prices, if the price differences across borders are relatively high.

As part of the distributor's contract with Lofthouse, they are expected to carry about one month's stock. Generally demand for Fisherman's Friend is fairly predictable, unless there is a flu epidemic or some other unpredictable event.

Sources: www.fishermansfriend.com; Brassington and Pettitt (2006); http://www.lz-blog.de/spotlight/2009/08/27/talk-with-fishermans-friend/.

When an intermediary is selected by the exporting manufacturer it is important that a contract is negotiated and developed between the parties. The foreign representative agreement is the fundamental basis of the relationship between the exporter and the intermediary, therefore the contract should clearly cover all relevant aspects and define the conditions upon which the relationship rests. Rights and obligations should be mutually defined and the spirit of the agreement must be one of mutual interest. The agreement should cover the provisions listed in Table 10.1.

Table 10.1	Contracts with intermediaries	

1. General provisions

Identification of parties to the contract	Definition of territory or territories
Duration of the contract	Sole and exclusive rights*
Definition of covered goods	Arbitration of disputes

2. Rights and obligations of manufacturer

Conditions of termination	Inspection of distributor's books
Protection of sole and exclusive rights	Trademarks/patents
Sales and technical support	Information to be supplied to the distributor
Tax liabilities	Advertising/promotion
Conditions of sale	Responsibility for claims/warranties
Delivery of goods	Inventory requirements
Prices	Termination and cancellation*
Order refusal	

3. Rights and obligations of distributor

Safeguarding manufacturer's interests	Customs clearance
Payment arrangements	Observance of conditions of sale
Contract assignment	After-sales service
Competitive lines*	Information to be supplied to the manufacturer

* Most important and contentious issues.
Source: Root, F. R. (1998) *Entry Strategies for International Markets: Second Revised and Expanded Edition*, pp. 90–91. Copyright © Jossey-Bass 1998. Reprinted with permission of John Wiley & Sons, Inc.

For most exporters the three most important aspects of their agreement with foreign representatives are sole or exclusive rights, competitive lines and termination of the agreement. The issue of agreeing territories is becoming increasingly important, as in many markets distributors are becoming fewer in number, larger in size and sometimes more specialized in their activity. The trend to regionalization is leading distributors increasingly to extend their territories through organic growth, mergers and acquisitions, making it more difficult for firms to appoint different distributors in individual neighbouring markets.

In general there are some principles that apply to the law of agency in all nations:

● An agent cannot take delivery of the principal's goods at an agreed price and resell them for a higher amount without the principal's knowledge and permission.
● Agents must maintain strict confidentiality regarding their principal's affairs and must pass on all relevant information.
● The principal is liable for damages to third parties for wrongs committed by an agent 'in the course of his or her authority' (e.g. if the agent fraudulently misrepresents the principal's firm).

During the contract period the support and motivation of intermediaries is important. Usually this means financial rewards for volume sold, but there can also be other means:

● significant local advertising and brand awareness development by the supplying firm;
● participation in local exhibitions and trade fairs, perhaps in cooperation with the local intermediary;
● regular field visits and telephone calls to the agent or distributor;
● regular meetings of agents and distributors arranged and paid for by the supplying company in the latter's country;
● competitions with cash prizes, free holidays, etc., for intermediaries with the highest sales;
● provision of technical training to intermediaries;
● suggestion schemes to gather feedback from agents and distributors;
● circulation of briefings about the supplying firm's current activities, changes in personnel, new product developments, marketing plans, etc.

Evaluating international distribution partners

Even if the firm has been very careful in selecting intermediaries a need can arise to extricate oneself quickly from a relationship that appears to be going nowhere.

In the process of evaluating international distribution partners Figure 10.4 can be used.

		Low	Medium	High
Country (market) attractiveness	High	7. Get new partner	8. Grow partner	9. Consider integration
	Medium	4. Get new partner	5. Grow partner / Maintain	6. Maintain position
	Low	1. Consider exit	2. Maintain position	3. Consider alternative mode

Partner performance

Figure 10.4   International partner matrix

According to Figure 10.4 the two most important criteria for evaluation international distributor partners are:

1. the performance of the distributor partner;
2. the general attractiveness of the market where the partner operates.

Performance can be evaluated by using criteria like achieved turnover and market share, profits generated for the manufacturer, established network to potential customers, etc. The country (market) attractiveness can be evaluated by using criteria like those discussed in Chapter 8 (Table 8.2 and Figure 8.5), for example, market size and market growth.

If the partner performance is low combined with a low attractiveness of the country (Cell 1), then the company should consider an exit from that country, especially if the low attractiveness seems to be a long-term phenomenon.

If the partner performance is high, but the country attractiveness is low (Cell 3), then the company could consider a shift to another entry mode (e.g. a joint venture). In this way the company can prevent dissatisfaction on the partner's side by rewarding it with a bigger part of the created profit pool in such a difficult market (low attractiveness).

If the partner is doing badly on a very attractive market (Cell 7), the partner should be switched with another (and better) one.

If the market is very attractive and the partner is doing a good job (Cell 9), then the company could consider forward integration, by turning the existing entry mode (distributor) into a subsidiary and promoting the distributor as the new CEO of the subsidiary, provided they have the necessary competences for such a position and are endowed with sufficient management talent.

The other cells of Figure 10.4 are mainly concerned with maintaining current position or 'growing' the existing partner. This can be done by offering training in the company's product/service solutions at HQ, or visiting the partner in the local market in order to show it that you are committed to its selling efforts in that local market.

Termination of contracts with distribution partners

Cancellation clauses in distribution partner agreements usually involve rights under local legislation and it is best that a contract is scrutinized by a local lawyer before signature, rather than after a relationship has ended and a compensation case is being fought in the courts.

Termination laws differ from country to country, but the European Union situation has been largely reconciled by a Directive regarding agents that has been effective in all EU member states since 1994. Under the Directive, an agent whose agreement is terminated is entitled to:

- full payment for any deal resulting from its work (even if concluded after the end of the agency);
- a lump sum of up to one year's past average commission;
- compensation (where appropriate) for damages to the agent's commercial reputation caused by unwarranted termination.

Outside western Europe some countries regard agents as basically employees of client organizations, while others see agents as self-contained and independent businesses. It is essential to ascertain the legal position of agency agreements in each country in which a firm is considering doing business. For example, laws in Saudi Arabia are extremely strong in protecting agents.

10.4 Cooperative export modes/export marketing groups

Export marketing groups are frequently found among SMEs attempting to enter export markets for the first time. Many such firms do not achieve sufficient scale economies in manufacturing and marketing because of the size of the local market or the inadequacy of the management and marketing resources available. These characteristics are typical of traditional, mature, highly fragmented industries such as furniture and clothing. Frequently the same characteristics are to be found among small, recently established high-technology firms.

Figure 10.1 shows an export marketing group with manufacturers A_1, A_2 and A_3, each having separate upstream functions but cooperating on the downstream functions through a common, foreign-based agent.

One of the most important motives for SMEs to join with others is the opportunity of effectively marketing a complementary product programme to larger buyers. The following example is from the furniture industry.

Manufacturers A_1, A_2 and A_3 have their core competences in the upstream functions of the following complementary product lines:

A_1 Living room furniture
A_2 Dining room furniture
A_3 Bedroom furniture.

Together they form a broader product concept that could be more attractive to a buyer in a furniture retail chain, especially if the total product concept targets end customers with a certain lifestyle.

The cooperation between the manufacturers can be tight or loose. In a loose cooperation the separate firms in a group sell their own brands through the same agent, whereas a tight cooperation often results in the creation of a new export association. Such an association can act as the exporting arm of all member companies, presenting a united front to world markets and gaining significant economies of scale. Its major functions are:

- exporting in the name of the association
- consolidating freight, negotiating rates and chartering ships
- performing market research
- appointing selling agents abroad
- obtaining credit information and collecting debts
- setting prices for export
- allowing uniform contracts and terms of sale
- allowing cooperative bids and sales negotiation.

Firms in an association can research foreign markets more effectively together, and obtain better representation in them. By establishing one organization to replace several sellers they may realize more stable prices, and selling costs can be reduced. Through consolidating shipments and avoiding duplicated effort firms realize transportation savings, and a group can achieve standardization of product grading and create a stronger brand name, just as the California fruit growers did with Sunkist products.

Considering all the advantages for an SME in joining an export marketing group, it is surprising that so few groups are actually running. One of the reasons for this could be that the firms have conflicting views as to what the group should do. In many SMEs there are strong feelings of independence inspired by their founders and entrepreneurs, which may be contrary, for example, to the common goal setting of export marketing groups. One of the major tasks of the export group is to balance the interests of the different stakeholders in the group.

10.5   Summary

The advantages and disadvantages of the three main types of export mode are summarized in Table 10.2.

Table 10.2	Advantages and disadvantages of the different export modes for the manufacturer	
Export mode	**Advantages**	**Disadvantages**
Indirect exporting (e.g. export buying agent, broker or export management company)	Limited commitment and investment required. High degree of market diversification is possible as the firm utilizes the internationalization of an experienced exporter. Minimal risk (market and political). No export experience required.	No control over marketing mix elements other than the product. An additional domestic member in the distribution chain may add costs, leaving smaller profit to the producer. Lack of contact with the market (no market knowledge acquired). Limited product experience (based on commercial selling).
Direct exporting (e.g. distributor or agent)	Access to local market experience and contacts with potential customers. Shorter distribution chain (compared to indirect exporting). Market knowledge acquired. More control over marketing mix (especially with agents). Local selling support and services available.	Little control over market price because of tariffs and lack of distribution control (especially with distributors). Some investment in sales organization required (contact from home base with distributors or agents). Cultural differences, providing communication problems and information filtering (transaction costs occur). Possible trade restrictions.
Export marketing groups	Shared costs and risks of internationalization. Provide a complete product line or system sales to the customer.	Risk of unbalanced relationships (different objectives). Participating firms are reluctant to give up their complete independence.

CASE STUDY 10.1

Lysholm Linie Aquavit: international marketing of the Norwegian Aquavit brand

Lysholm Linie Aquavit is marketed by the Norwegian spirits manufacturer Arcus Group (www.arcus.no), which has approximately 1.3 billion Norwegian Kroner (€150 million) sales (2008) and 480 employees. Around half of the Arcus sales is generated outside Norway.

Aquavit, which translates as 'water of life', a slightly yellow or colourless alcoholic liquor, is produced in the Scandinavian countries by redistilling neutral spirits such as grain or potatoes and flavouring them with caraway seeds. It is often consumed as an aperitif.

The alcohol content in the various aquavits varies somewhat, but starts at 37.5 per cent. Most brands contain about 40 per cent alcohol but Lysholm Linie Aquavit has an alcohol content of 41.5 per cent. (Lysholm is the name of the distillery in Trondheim where the aquavit is made, and from this point on the name 'Linie Aquavit' is used.)

The history of Aquavit

Aquavit was originally used for medicinal purposes, but from the 1700s stills became commonplace in Scandinavian homes.

The definition of aquavit becomes complicated when you try to distinguish it and other spirits popular in the northern climate. The term 'schnapps', for instance, is widely used in Germany, Switzerland and Scandinavia (the Danish say 'snaps') to mean any sort of neutral spirits, flavoured or otherwise. Then there's 'brannvin' a term used similarly in Sweden. (Like the Dutch word 'brandewijn' from which we derive the word 'brandy': it means burnt wine.) The famous Swedish vodka Absolut began life in 1879 as a product called 'Absolut Renat Brannvin' which might be translated as 'absolutely pure schnapps', said to have been distilled ten times. However, the Swedish government's alcohol monopoly launched Absolut's as an international brand in 1979, and labelled it vodka.

Making Linie Aquavit

Caraway is the most important herb in aquavit, but the mixture of herbs varies from brand to brand. Linie Aquavit is derived from Norwegian potato alcohol blended with spices and herbal infusions, and caraway and aniseed predominate. After the alcohol and the herbs have been mixed the aquavit is poured into 500-litre oak barrels. Norwegian specialists travel to Spain for the express purpose of selecting the best barrels from those used in the production of Oloroso sherry for several years. Sherry casks are used because they remove the raw, more volatile aspects of the liquor; the aquavit takes on a golden hue, and the residual sherry imparts a gentle sweetness.

Many theories have been put forward to explain how the man behind Linie Aquavit, Jørgen B. Lysholm, came up with the idea of sending aquavit around the world on sailboats in sherry casks in order to produce the special flavour. In the early 1800s the family tried to export aquavit to the West Indies, but the ship, *Trondheim's Prøve*, returned with its cargo unsold. This is when they discovered the beneficial effects of the long ocean voyage and the special storage had on the aquavit: the length of the journey, the constant gentle rocking of the boat and the variation in temperature on deck all helped give Linie Aquavit its characteristic taste. Lysholm subsequently commercialized his maturation method and this is still how things are done today.

Linie Aquavit has one of Norway's long-established shipping companies as its steady travel partner. The first Wilhelmsen liner vessel carrying Linie Aquavit set sail in 1927. Since that time, Wilhelmsen has been the sole carrier of this distinguished product. The barrels are tightly secured in specially designed cribs before being loaded onto containers, which remain on deck during the entire journey. The journey from Norway to Australia and back again takes four-and-a-half months and crosses the equator (or the line, as sailors prefer to call it) twice. In fact, this is where Linie Aquavit gets its name. On the back of each bottle is the name of the ship and the date that it first crossed the equator.

International sales of Linie Aquavit and Vikingfjord vodka

Arcus AS is Norway's sole manufacturer of hard liquor and it is this company which produces Linie Aquavit. The company also taps (i.e. bottles) wine from wine producers all over the world and imports a select range of bottled wines. With a market share of about 30 per cent, Arcus AS is the leading player in the Norwegian wine and spirits market.

The international aquavit markets (primarily Sweden, Norway, Denmark, Germany and the United States) are dominated (except the last) by local aquavit brands. At present Linie Aquavit is the market

Arcus Gruppen AS (www.arcus.no).

leader in Norway with a 20 per cent market share. In Denmark and Sweden the market share is 5 per cent. Germany is the most important export market and Linie Aqavit holds 10 per cent of the aquavit market in competition with brands like Malteserkreutz and Bommerlunde.

Arcus has established a subsidiary in Sweden, but elsewhere is only using export modes (foreign-based intermediaries).

Until 2009 Linie Aquavit was distributed by the Berentzen Group in Germany. From April 2009 Arcus has transferred its German distribution to Racke Eggers & Franke (located in Bremen/Germany), which is a subsidiary of Racke GmbH + Co. KG, Mainz. Racke offers a broad assortment of spirit brands, especially for retailers and the restaurant, hotel and catering industry, not only for Germany, but also for the rest of Europe. The volume for Linie Aquavit in Germany is expected to reach 750,000 bottles in 2009 and the ambition is to sell 1 million bottles within 3 years. With Racke as its distribution partner, Arcus hopes that Linie Aquavit can strengthen its market position in the southern part of Germany, and in the general on-trade segment (bars, restaurants and hotels), where Linie Aquavit has until now been relatively weak.

Linie Aquavit has long been the national spirit of Norway and among the flagships in the portfolio of Arcus. However, with more than 80 years of experience as supplier and producer of spirits and wine, Arcus has a widely diverse portfolio including international premium brands such Vikingfjord Vodka. Vikingfjord Vodka has – despite the fact that the US market is usually described as the toughest vodka market in the world – become one of the eight-largest imported vodka brands in the space of a few years with a volume growth of approximately 30 per cent in 2008.

Sources: www.arcus.no, Arcus Financial Report 2008.

QUESTIONS

1. What are the main advantages and disadvantages for Arcus of using export modes, compared to other entry modes, for its Linie Aquavit?

2. What should be Arcus' main criteria for selecting new distributors, or cooperation partners, for Linie Aquavit in new markets?

3. Would it be possible to pursue an international branding strategy for Linie Aquavit?

4. Which brand should be the major brand for the US market: Linie Aquavit or Vikingfjord Vodka?

CASE STUDY 10.2

Parle Products: an Indian biscuit manufacturer is seeking agents and cooperation partners in new export markets

A long time ago, when the British ruled India, a small factory was set up in the suburbs of Mumbai city to manufacture sweets and toffees. The year was 1929 and the market was dominated by famous international brands that were freely imported. Despite the odds and unequal competition the company, called Parle Products (www.parleproducts.com), survived and succeeded by adhering to high quality and improvising from time to time.

Today, Parle enjoys a 40 per cent share of the total Indian biscuit market and a 15 per cent share of the total confectionery market in India. The Parle Biscuit brands, Parle-G, Monaco and Krackjack, and confectionery brands, such as Melody, Poppins, Mangobite and Kismi, enjoy a strong image and appeal among consumers.

If you thought that a typical family-run Indian company could not top the worldwide charts, think again. The home-grown biscuit brand, Parle G, has proved the belief wrong by becoming the largest selling biscuit brand in the world. However, in most European markets Parle Products has to fight against a particular competitor, United Biscuits (producer of McVitie's). In all European markets the market share of Parle Products is very small.

Parle Products Pvt. Ltd.

United Biscuits (UB)

United Biscuits was founded in 1948 following the merger of two Scottish family businesses – McVitie & Price and McFarlane Lang. In 1960 UB added to its portfolio with the acquisition of Crawford's Biscuits and MacDonald's Biscuits.

In 2000 UB was bought by Finalrealm, a consortium of investors, and reverted to private limited company status.

Brand muscle

UB's brands rank number one or two in seven countries, they have five of the top ten biscuit brands in the United Kingdom, France and Spain, and four out of the top ten leading snack brands in the United Kingdom. More than 89 per cent of UK households bought McVitie's products in 2001. Anyone would agree that it has brand muscle.

Consumer insight

UB's unique position as the largest UK snack food player, with a balanced portfolio of both sweet and savoury brands, gives it a unique understanding of how to respond effectively to changing consumer needs and wants.

Parle Products

Parle Products is the leader in the glucose and salty biscuit category but does not have a strong presence in the premium segment, with Hide-n-Seek being its only brand.

An extensive distribution network, built over the years, is a major strength for Parle Products. Its biscuits and sweets are available to consumers even in the most remote places and in the smallest of villages in India, some with a population of just 500.

Parle has nearly 1,500 wholesalers, catering to 425,000 retail outlets directly or indirectly. A 200-strong dedicated field force services these wholesalers and retailers. Additionally, there are 31 depots and customs and freight agents supplying goods to the wide distribution network.

The Parle marketing philosophy emphasizes catering to the masses. The company constantly endeavours to design products that provide nutrition and fun for everyone and most Parle offerings are in the low- and mid-range price segments based on understanding the Indian consumer psyche. This value-for-money positioning helps generate large sales volumes for the products.

The other global biscuit brands include Oreo from Nabisco and McVitie's from UK-based United Biscuits. According to market reports Parle Products commands (with Parle G as the market leader) a 40 per cent market share in the RS 3,500 core biscuit market in India. In the confectionery segment the company enjoys a mere 15 per cent market share and faces competition from Britannia's Tiger brand of biscuits, amongst others.

The company's flagship brand, Parle G, contributes more than 50 per cent to the company's total turnover. The other biscuits in the Parle Products' basket include Marie, Cheeslings, Jeffs, Sixer and Fun Centre.

Source: adapted from Jain and Zachariah (2002); http://www.bsstrategist.com/archives/2002/mar/.

QUESTIONS

1. Which region of the world would you recommend Parle Products to penetrate as its first choice?

2. What kind of export mode would be most relevant for Parle Products?

3. How could Parle Products conduct a systematic screening of potential distributors or agents in foreign markets?

4. What would be the most important issues for Parle Products to discuss with a potential distributor/agent before final preparation of a contract?

VIDEO CASE STUDY 10.3 Honest Tea

download from www.pearsoned.co.uk/hollensen

Honest Tea is a tea company based in Maryland, USA, and was founded in 1998 to sell 'bottled iced tea that tastes like tea'. They are best known for their line of bottled organic tea products, but they also produce tea bags and other bottled drinks. Honest Tea has a strong focus on social responsibility and has become a role model of philanthropic business practices. The CEO believes a social mission is not only socially responsible but also financially sustainable because it enhances customer loyalty. The hope is that Honest Tea will become a well-known national brand and will have impact around the world.

Questions

1. Discuss how its policies regarding social responsibility helps Honest Tea in its exporting efforts.

2. What research method would you recommend for selecting the most suitable agent in Germany?

For further exercises and cases, see this book's website at **www.pearsoned.co.uk/hollensen**

Questions for discussion

1. Why is exporting frequently considered the simplest way of entering foreign markets and thus favoured by SMEs?

2. What procedures should a firm follow in selecting a distributor?

3. Why is it difficult – financially and legally – to terminate a relationship with overseas intermediaries? What should be done to prevent or minimize such difficulties?

4. Identify the ways to reach foreign markets by making a domestic sale.

5. What is the difference between direct and indirect exporting?

6. Discuss the financial and pricing techniques for motivating foreign distributors.

7. Which marketing tasks should be handled by the exporter and which ones by its intermediaries in foreign markets?

8. How can the carrier and the rider both benefit from a piggyback arrangement?

9. When a firm begins direct exporting, what tasks must it perform?

10. Discuss the various ways of communicating with foreign distributors.

11. 'When exporting to a market, you're only as good as your intermediary there.' Discuss.

12. The international marketer and the intermediary will have different expectations concerning the relationship. Why should these expectations be spelled out and clarified in the contract?

References

Brassington, F. and Pettitt, S. (2006) *Principles of Marketing*. Pearson, Harlow.

Gibbs, R. (2005) 'How to measure and master mindshare', *The Routes to Market – Journal*, (www.viaint.com), June, pp. 2–5.

Hotopf, M. (2005) 'Winning partner mindshare', *The Routes to Market – Journal*, (www.viaint.com), February, pp. 13–16.

Jain, S. and Zachariah, R. (2002) 'Parle G largest – selling biscuit brand in world', *Business Standard* (Mumbai) 14 March.

Okoroafo, S.C. (1994) 'Implementing international countertrade: a dyadic approach', *Industrial Marketing Management*, 23, pp. 229–234.

Root, F.R. (1998) *Entry Strategies for International Markets*, revised and expanded edition. The New Lexington Press, Lexington, MA.

Rosenbloom, B. and Andras, T.L. (2008) 'Wholesalers as global marketers', *Journal of Marketing Channels*, 15(4), pp. 235–252.

CHAPTER 11
Intermediate entry modes

Contents

Learning objectives

After studying this chapter you should be able to:

- Describe and understand the main intermediate entry modes:
  - contract manufacturing;
  - licensing;
  - franchising; and
  - joint venture/strategic alliances.
- Discuss the advantages and disadvantages of the main intermediate entry modes.
- Explain the different stages in joint-venture formation.
- Explore the reasons for the 'divorce' of the two parents in a joint-venture constellation.
- Explore different ways of managing a joint venture/strategic alliance.

11.1   Introduction

So far we have assumed that the firm entering foreign markets is supplying them from domestic or third country plants. This is implicit in any form of exporting. However, sometimes the firm may find it either impossible or undesirable to supply all foreign markets from domestic or third country production. Intermediate entry modes are distinguished from export modes because they are primarily vehicles for the transfer of knowledge and skills between partners, in order to create foreign sales. They are distinguished from the hierarchical entry modes in that there is no full ownership (by the parent firm) involved, but ownership and control can be shared between the parent firm and a local partner. This is the case with the (equity) joint venture.

Intermediate entry modes include a variety of arrangements, such as licensing, franchising, management contracts, turnkey contracts, joint ventures and technical know-how or coproduction arrangements. In Figure 11.1 the most relevant intermediate modes are shown in the usual value chain perspective.

Generally speaking, contractual arrangements take place when firms possessing some sort of competitive advantage are unable to exploit this advantage because of resource constraints, for instance, but are able to transfer the advantage to another party. The arrangements often entail long-term relationships between partner firms and are typically designed to transfer intermediate goods such as knowledge and/or skills between firms in different countries.

11.2   Contract manufacturing

Several factors may encourage the firm to produce in foreign markets:

- Desirability of being close to foreign customers. Local production allows better interaction with local customer needs concerning product design, delivery and service.
- Foreign production costs (e.g. labour) are low.
- Transportation costs may render heavy or bulky products non-competitive.
- Tariffs or quotas can prevent entry of an exporter's products.
- In some countries there is government preference for national suppliers.

Contract manufacturing
Manufacturing is outsourced to an external partner, specialized in production and production technology.

Contract manufacturing enables the firm to have foreign sourcing (production) without making a final commitment. Management may lack resources or be unwilling to invest equity to establish and complete manufacturing and selling operations, but contract manufacturing keeps the way open for implementing a long-term foreign development policy when the time is right. These considerations are perhaps most important to the company with limited resources. Contract manufacturing enables the firm to develop and control R&D, marketing, distribution, sales and servicing of its products in international markets, while handing over responsibility for production to a local firm (see Figure 11.1).

Payment by the contractor to the contracted party is generally on a per unit basis, and quality and specification requirements are extremely important. The product can be sold by the contractor in the country of manufacture, its home country, or some other foreign market.

This form of business organization is quite common in particular industries. For example, Benetton and IKEA rely heavily on a contractual network of small overseas manufacturers.

Contract manufacturing also offers substantial flexibility. Depending on the duration of the contract, if the firm is dissatisfied with product quality or reliability of delivery it can shift to another manufacturer. In addition, if management decides to exit the market it does not have to sustain possible losses from divesting production facilities. On the other hand, it is necessary to control product quality to meet company standards. The firm may encounter problems with delivery, product warranties or fulfilling additional orders. The manufacturer

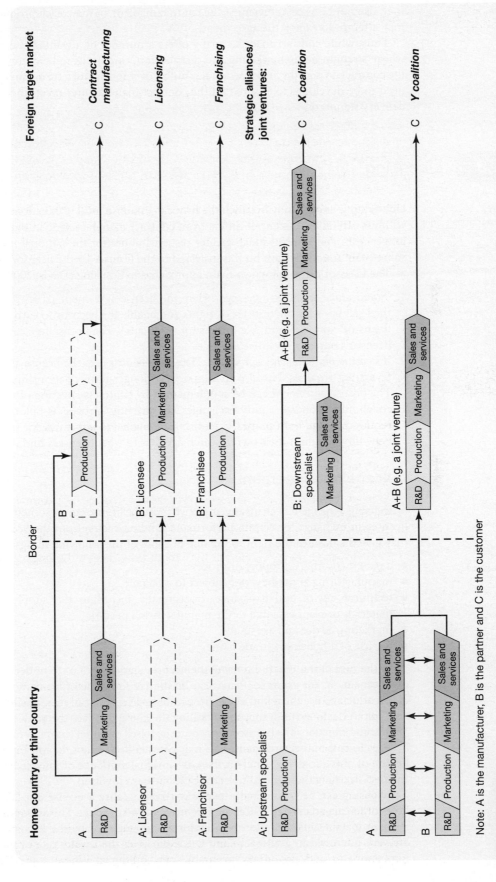

Figure 11.1   Intermediate modes

Note: A is the manufacturer, B is the partner and C is the customer

may also not be as cost efficient as the contracting firm, or may reach production capacity, or may attempt to exploit the agreement.

Thus, while contract manufacturing offers a number of advantages, especially to a firm whose strength lies in marketing and distribution, care needs to be exercised in negotiating the contract. Where the firm loses direct control over the manufacturing function mechanisms need to be developed to ensure that the contract manufacturer meets the firm's quality and delivery standards.

11.3 Licensing

Licensing
The licensor gives a right to the licensee against payment, e.g. a right to manufacture a certain product based on a patent against some agreed royalty.

Licensing is another way in which the firm can establish local production in foreign markets without capital investment. It differs from contract manufacturing in that it is usually for a longer term and involves much greater responsibilities for the national firm, because more value chain functions have been transferred to the licensee by the licensor (see Figure 11.1).

The licensor can employ two main approaches to licensing (Davis, 2008):

1. *'Stand-alone' licensing agreement.* Here the license agreement serves primarily to specify the legal basis for the transfer of rights and enable the licensor to earn royalties (or other forms of compensation like lump sum payments). The license fees can then finance the licensor's ongoing inventive activities.
2. *'Licensing plus' licensing agreement.* Here the licensor uses the license as a means not only to extract royalties, but also to support the longer-term relationship with the licensee. The license agreement can be supplemented by contracts covering other aspects of R&D collaboration and/or equity exchange. The inventive process is tailored to the evolving requirements of both parties. Scientists and engineers who work for such licensors must be willing to adjust their own research agendas to what licensees find important.

A licensing agreement

A licensing agreement is an arrangement wherein the licensor gives something of value to the licensee in exchange for certain performance and payments from the licensee. The licensor may give the licensee the right to use one or more of the following things:

- a patent covering a product or process;
- manufacturing know-how not subject to a patent;
- technical advice and assistance, occasionally including the supply of components, materials or plant essential to the manufacturing process;
- marketing advice and assistance;
- the use of a trademark/trade name.

In the case of trademark licensing the licensor should try not to undermine a product by overlicensing it. For example, Pierre Cardin diluted the value of his name by allowing some 800 products to use the name under license. Over-licensing can increase income in the short run, but in the long run it may mean killing the goose that laid the golden egg.

In some situations the licensor may continue to sell essential components or services to the licensee as part of the agreement. This may be extended so that the total agreement may also be one of cross-licensing, wherein there is a mutual exchange of knowledge and/or patents. In cross-licensing there might not be a cash payment involved.

Licensing can be considered a two-way street because a license also allows the original licensor to gain access to the licensee's technology and product. This is important because the licensee may be able to build on the information supplied by the licensor. Some licensors are very interested in grantbacks and will even lower the royalty rate in return for product improvements and potentially profitable new products. Where a product or service is involved the licensee is responsible for production and marketing in a defined market area. This responsibility is followed by all the profits and risks associated with the venture. In exchange the licensee pays the licensor royalties or fees, which are the licensor's main source of income from its licensing operations and that usually involve some combination of:

- A lump sum not related to output. This can include a sum paid at the beginning of an agreement for the initial transfer of special machinery, parts, blueprints, knowledge and so on.
- A minimum royalty – a guarantee that at least some annual income will be received by the licensor.
- A running royalty – normally expressed as a percentage of normal selling price or as a fixed sum of money for units of output.

Other methods of payment include conversions of royalties into equity, management and technical fees and complex systems of counter-purchase, typically found in licensing arrangements with eastern European countries.

If the foreign market carries high political risk then it would be wise for the licensor to seek high initial payments and perhaps compress the timescale of the agreement. Alternatively, if the market is relatively free of risk and the licensee is well placed to develop a strong market share, then payment terms will be somewhat relaxed and probably influenced by other licensors competing for the agreement.

The licensing agreement or contract should always be formalized in a written document. The details of the contract will probably be the subject of detailed negotiation and hard bargaining between the parties, and there can be no such thing as a standard contract.

In the following we see licensing from the viewpoint of a *licensor* (licensing out) and a *licensee* (licensing in). This section is written primarily from the licensor's viewpoint, but licensing in may be an important element in smaller firms' growth strategies, and therefore some consideration is given to this issue too.

Licensing out

Generally there is a wide range of strategic reasons for using licensing. The most important motives for licensing out are:

- The licensor firm will remain technologically superior in its product development. It wants to concentrate on its core competences (product development activities) and then outsource production and downstream activities to other firms.
- The licensor is too small to have financial, managerial or marketing expertise for overseas investment (own subsidiaries).
- The product is at the end of its product life cycle in the advanced countries because of obsolescent technology or model change. A stretching of the total product life cycle is possible through licensing agreements in less developed countries.
- Even if direct royalty income is not high margins on key components to the licensee (produced by the licensor) can be quite handsome.
- If government regulations restrict foreign direct investment or if political risks are high licensing may be the only realistic entry mode.
- There may be constraints on imports into the licensee country (tariff or non-tariff barriers).

When setting the price for the agreement the costs of licensing should not be underestimated. Table 11.1 presents a breakdown of costs of licensing out by Australian firms.

Licensing in

Empirical evidence shows (Young *et al.*, 1989, p. 143) that many licensing agreements actually stem from approaches by licensees. This would suggest that the licensee is at an

Table 11.1	Relative costs of licensing overseas (%)
Breakdown of total costs of licensing overseas	
Protection of industrial property	24.4
Establishment of licensing agreement	46.6
Maintenance of licensing agreement	29.0
	100.0
Breakdown of establishment costs	
Search for suitable licensee	22.8
Communication between involved parties	44.7
Adoption and testing of equipment for licensee	9.9
Training personnel for licensee	19.9
Other (additional marketing activity and legal expenses)	2.7
	100.0
Breakdown of maintenance costs	
Audit of licensee	9.7
Ongoing market research in market of licensee	7.2
Back-up services for licensee	65.0
Defence of industrial property rights in licensee's territory	11.0
Other	7.1
	100.0

Sources: based on Carstairs and Welch (1981) and Young *et al.* (1989, p. 132).

immediate disadvantage in negotiations and general relations with the licensor. In other cases licensing in is used as the easy option, with the license being renewed regularly and the licensee becoming heavily dependent on the technology supplier (the licensor).

As Figure 11.2 shows, licensing in can improve the net cash flow position of the licensee, but mean lower profits in the longer term. Because technology licensing allows the firms to

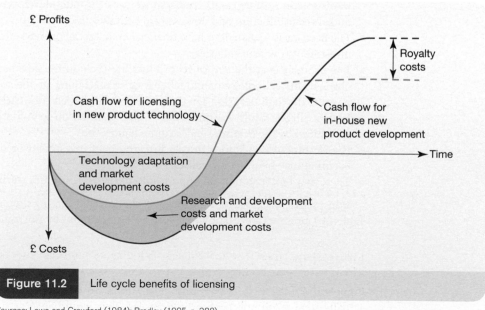

Figure 11.2	Life cycle benefits of licensing

Sources: Lowe and Crawford (1984); Bradley (1995, p. 388).

have products on the market sooner than otherwise, the firm benefits from an earlier positive cash flow. In addition, licensing means lower development costs. The immediate benefits of quick access to new technology, lower development costs and a relatively early cash flow are attractive benefits of licensing.

Table 11.5 (see section 11.6) summarizes the advantages and disadvantages of licensing for the licensor.

11.4 Franchising

Franchising
The franchisor gives a right to the franchisee against payment, e.g. a right to use a total business concept/system, including use of trade marks (brands), against some agreed royalty.

The term **franchising** is derived from the French, meaning 'to be free from servitude'. Franchise activity was almost unknown in Europe until the beginning of the 1970s. The concept was popularized in the United States, where over one-third of retail sales are derived from franchising, in comparison with about 11 per cent in Europe (Young *et al.*, 1989, p. 111).

A number of factors have contributed to the rapid growth rate of franchising. First, the general worldwide decline of traditional manufacturing industry and its replacement by service-sector activities has encouraged franchising. It is especially well suited to service and people-intensive economic activities, particularly where these require a large number of geographically dispersed outlets serving local markets. Second, the growth in popularity of self-employment is a contributory factor to the growth of franchising. Government policies in many countries have improved the whole climate for small businesses as a means of stimulating employment.

A good example of the value of franchising is the Swedish furniture manufacturer IKEA, which franchises its ideas throughout the Western world, especially in Europe and North America. In terms of retail surface area and the number of visitors to retail stores, this company has experienced very significant growth through franchising in recent years.

Franchising is a marketing-oriented method of selling a business service, often to small independent investors who have working capital but little or no prior business experience. However, it is something of an umbrella term that is used to mean anything from the right to use a name to the total business concept. Thus there are two major types of franchising:

1. *Product and trade name franchising.* This is very similar to trademark licensing. Typically it is a distribution system in which suppliers make contracts with dealers to buy or sell products or product lines. Dealers use the trade name, trademark and product line. Examples of this type of franchising are soft drink bottlers such as Coca-Cola and Pepsi.
2. *Business format* 'package' franchising.

The latter is the focus of this section.

International business format franchising is a market entry mode that involves a relationship between the entrant (the franchisor) and a host country entity, in which the former transfers, under contract, a business package (or format) that it has developed and owns, to the latter. This host country entity can be either a franchisee or a master franchisee (subfranchisor). The franchise system can be set up as a direct or indirect system – see Figure 11.3.

In the direct system the franchisor is controlling and coordinating the activities of the franchisees directly. In the indirect system a master franchisee (subfranchisor) is appointed to establish and service its own subsystem of franchisees within its territory.

The advantages of the direct system include access to local resources and knowledge, more adaptation, and the possibility of developing a successful master franchisee (subfranchisor) as a tool for selling the concept to other prospective franchisees within the country. The indirect system also has disadvantages, including monitoring issues because of loss of control. There have been examples of a master franchisee holding the subfranchisees hostage to compete against the franchisor. Ultimately, the success of the indirect system will be determined by the capabilities and commitment of the master franchisee (Welsh *et al.*, 2006).

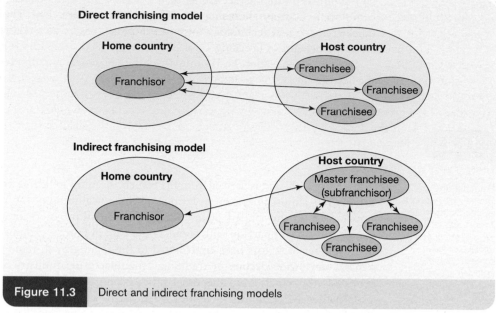

Figure 11.3 Direct and indirect franchising models

Sources: based on Welsh *et al.* (2006) in Hollensen, S. (2008) *Essentials of Global Marketing*, FT/Prentice Hall, p. 233.

EXHIBIT 11.1 Build-A-Bear Workshop's use of the indirect franchising model

Build-A-Bear Workshop, Inc. (BBW) – www.buildabear.com – is the leading and only global company that offers a create-your-own animal service in the retailing experience sector (see also Case study 1.1 in Chapter 1).

Founded in 1997 in the United States, the company currently operates more than 400 Build-A-Bear Workshop stores worldwide, mainly based on a franchising concept. Build-A-Bear Workshop posted total revenue of US$468 million in the fiscal year 2008.

The indirect franchising model the the BBW case looks like this:

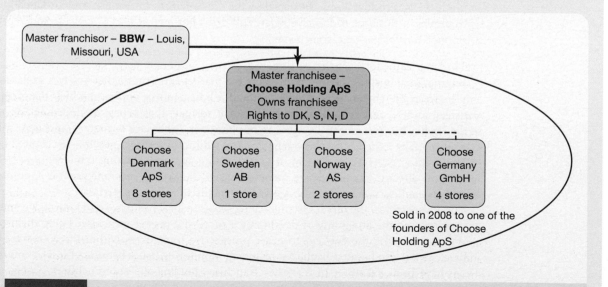

Figure 11.4 The BBW indirect franchising model for Scandinavia and Germany

In 2003 this new company, Choose Holding ApS, bought the franchise rights for Denmark for USD 250,000. The first BBW shop opens in Copenhagen in April 2004. In 2005 Choose Holding ApS acquires the franchise rights for Norway and Sweden. The first store in Sweden opens in 2005, and in Norway in 2006.

After the success in Scandinavia, the founders of Choose Holding ApS acquired the franchise rights for Germany for US$750,000. The first two BBW stores open in Hamburg in 2006. However, Choose Holding found that the German market was quite different from the Scandinavian market. Due to these problems the German company was sold off to one of founders of Choose Holding (read Case Study 1.1 for more details).

Source: Case study 1.1. (Chapter 1) in this book.

The package transferred by the franchisor contains most elements necessary for the local entity to establish a business and run it profitably in the host country in a prescribed manner, regulated and controlled by the franchisor. The package can contain:

- trademarks/trade names
- copyright
- designs
- patents
- trade secrets
- business know-how
- geographic exclusivity
- design of the store
- market research for the area
- location selection.

In addition to this package the franchisor also typically provides local entities with managerial assistance in setting up and running local operations. All locally owned franchisees can also receive sub-supplies from the franchisor or the master franchisees (subfranchisor) and benefit from centrally coordinated advertising. In return for this business package the franchisor receives from the franchisee (or subfranchisor) an initial fee up front and/or continuing franchise fees, based typically on a percentage of annual turnover as a mark-up on goods supplied directly by the franchisor.

There is still a lively debate about the differences between licensing and franchising, but if we define franchising in the broader 'business format' (as here), we see the differences presented in Table 11.2.

Types of business format franchise include business and personal services, convenience stores, car repairs and fast food. US fast-food franchises are some of the best-known global franchise businesses and include McDonald's, Burger King and Pizza Hut.

The fast-food business is taken as an example of franchising in the value chain approach of Figure 9.1. The production (e.g. assembly of burgers) and sales and service functions are transferred to the local outlets (e.g. McDonald's restaurants), whereas the central R&D and marketing functions are still controlled by the franchisor (e.g. McDonald's head office in the United States). The franchisor will develop the general marketing plan (with the general advertising messages), which will be adapted to local conditions and cultures.

As indicated earlier, business format franchising is an ongoing relationship that includes not only a product or a service but also a business concept. The business concept usually includes a strategic plan for growth and marketing, instruction on the operation of the business, elaboration of standards and quality control, continuing guidance for the franchisee, and some means of control of the franchisee by the franchisor. Franchisors provide a wide variety of assistance for franchisees, but not all franchisors provide the same level of support. Some examples of assistance and support provided by franchisors are in the areas of finance, site selection, lease negotiation, cooperative advertising, training and assistance with store opening. The extent of ongoing support to franchisees also varies among franchisors. Support

Table 11.2	How licensing and franchising differ
Licensing	**Franchising**
The term 'royalties' is normally used.	'Management fees' is regarded as the appropriate term.
Products, or even a single product, are the common element.	Covers the total business, including know-how, intellectual rights, goodwill, trademarks and business contacts. (Franchising is all-encompassing, whereas licensing concerns just one part of the business.)
Licences are usually taken by well-established businesses.	Tends to be a start-up situation, certainly as regards the franchisee.
Terms of 16–20 years are common, particularly where they relate to technical know-how, copyright and trade marks. The terms are similar for patents.	The franchise agreement is normally for 5 years, sometimes extending to 11 years. Franchises are frequently renewable.
Licensees tend to be self-selecting. They are often established businesses and can demonstrate that they are in a strong position to operate the licence in question. A licensee can often pass its licence on to an associate or sometimes unconnected company with little or no reference back to the original licensor.	The franchisee is very definitely selected by the franchisor, and its eventual replacement is controlled by the franchisor.
Usually concerns specific existing products with very little benefit from ongoing research being passed on by the licensor to its licensee.	The franchisor is expected to pass on to its franchisees the benefits of its ongoing research programme as part of the agreement.
There is no goodwill attached to the licence as it is totally retained by the licensor.	Although the franchisor does retain the main goodwill, the franchisee picks up an element of localized goodwill.
Licensees enjoy a substantial measure of free negotiation. As bargaining tools they can use their trade muscle and their established position in the marketplace.	There is a standard fee structure and any variation within an individual franchise system would cause confusion and mayhem.

Sources: based on Perkins (1987, pp. 22, 157) and Young *et al.* (1989, p. 148).

areas include central data processing, central purchasing, field training, field operation evaluation, newsletters, regional and national meetings, a hotline for advice and franchisor–franchisee advisory councils. The availability of these services is often a critical factor in the decision to purchase a franchise, and may be crucial to the long-term success of marginal locations or marginally prepared owners.

International expansion of franchising

Franchisors, as other businesses, must consider the relevant success factors in making the decision to expand their franchising system globally. The objective is to search for an environment that promotes cooperation and reduces conflict. Given the long-term nature of a franchise agreement country stability is an important factor.

Where should the international expansion start? The franchising development often begins as a response to a perceived local opportunity, perhaps as an adaptation of a franchising concept already operating in another foreign market. In this case the market focus is clearly local to begin with. In addition, the local market provides a better environment for testing and developing the franchising format. Feedback from the marketplace and franchisees can be obtained more readily because of the ease of communication. Adjustments can be made more quickly because of the close local contact. A whole variety of minor changes in the format may be necessary as a result of early experience in areas such as training, franchisee choice, site selection, organization of suppliers, promotion and outlet decoration. The early stages of franchise development represent a critical learning process for the franchisor, not just about how to adapt the total package to the market requirements but also regarding the nature of the franchising method itself. Ultimately, with a proven package and a better understanding of its operation, the franchisor is in a better position to attack foreign markets, and is more confident about doing so with a background of domestic success.

Developing and managing franchisor–franchisee relationships

Franchising provides a unique organizational relationship in which the franchisor and franchisee each bring important qualities to the business. The franchise system combines the advantages of economy of scale offered by the franchisor with the local knowledge and entrepreneurial talents of the franchisee. Their joint contribution may result in success. The franchisor depends on franchisees for fast growth, an infusion of capital from the franchise purchase fee, and an income stream from the royalty fee paid by franchisees each year. Franchisors also benefit from franchisee goodwill in the community and, increasingly, from franchisee suggestions for innovation. The most important factor, however, is the franchisee's motivation to operate a successful independent business. The franchisee depends on the franchisor for the strength of the trademark, technical advice, support services, marketing resources and national advertising that provides instant customer recognition.

There are two additional key success factors, which rest on the interdependence of the franchisee and the franchisor:

1. integrity of the whole business system;
2. capacity for renewal of the business system.

Integrity of the business system

The business will be a success in a viable market to the extent that the franchisor provides a well-developed, proven business concept to the franchisee and the franchisee is motivated to follow the system as it is designed, thereby preserving the integrity of the system. Standardization is the cornerstone of franchising: customers expect the same product or service at every location. Deviations from the franchising business concept by individual franchisees adversely affect the franchisor's reputation. The need for the integrity of the system requires that the franchisor exerts control over key operations at the franchise sites (Doherty and Alexander, 2006).

Capacity for renewal of the business system

Although most franchisors conduct research and development within the parent company, the highest proportion of innovation originates from franchisees in the field. Franchisees are most familiar with customers' preferences. They sense new trends and the opportunity to introduce a new product and service. The issue is getting the franchisee to share new ideas with the parent company. Not all franchisees are willing to share ideas with the franchisor, for a number of reasons. The most common is failure of the franchisor to keep in close contact with the franchisees; the most troubling is a lack of trust in the franchisor. The franchisor needs to promote a climate of trust and cooperation for mutual benefit.

Handling possible conflicts

Conflict is inherent in the franchisor–franchisee relationship, since all aspects that are good for the franchisor may not be good for the franchisee. One of the most basic conflicts is failure of either the franchisor or the franchisee to live up to the terms of the legal agreement.

Disagreement over objectives may be the result of poor communication on the part of the franchisor, or failure on the part of the franchisee to understand the franchisor's objectives. Both franchisor and franchisee agree on the need for profits in the business, not only to provide a living but to stay competitive. However, the two parties may disagree on the means of achieving profits. The number of conflicts between franchisors and franchisees may be reduced by establishing extensive monitoring of the franchisee (e.g. computer-based accounting, purchasing and inventory systems). Another way of reducing the number of conflicts is to view franchisors and franchisees as partners in running a business; both objectives and operating procedures have to be in harmony. This view requires a strong common culture with shared values established by the use of intensive communication between franchisor and franchisees in different countries (e.g. cross-national/regional meetings, cross-national/regional advisory councils).

11.5 Joint ventures/strategic alliances

Joint venture
An equity partnership typically between two partners. It involves two 'parents' creating the 'child' (the joint venture acting in the market).

A **joint venture** (JV) or a strategic alliance is a partnership between two or more parties. In international joint ventures these parties will be based in different countries, and this obviously complicates the management of such an arrangement.

A number of reasons are given for setting up joint ventures:

- Complementary technology or management skills provided by the partners can lead to new opportunities in existing sectors (e.g. multimedia, in which information processing, communications and the media are merging).
- Many firms find that partners in the host country can increase the speed of market entry.
- Many less developed countries, such as China and South Korea, try to restrict foreign ownership.
- Global operations in R&D and production are prohibitively expensive, but are necessary to achieve competitive advantage.

The formal difference between a joint venture and a strategic alliance is that a strategic alliance is typically a non-equity cooperation, meaning that the partners do not commit equity into or invest in the alliance. The joint venture can be either a contractual non-equity joint venture or an equity joint venture.

In a contractual joint venture no joint enterprise with a separate personality is formed. Two or more companies form a partnership to share the cost of investment, the risks and the long-term profits. An equity joint venture involves the creation of a new company in which foreign and local investors share ownership and control. Thus, according to these definitions, strategic alliances and non-equity joint ventures are more or less the same (Figure 11.5).

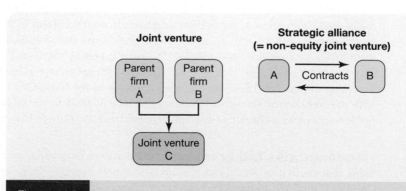

| **Figure 11.5** | Joint ventures and strategic alliances |

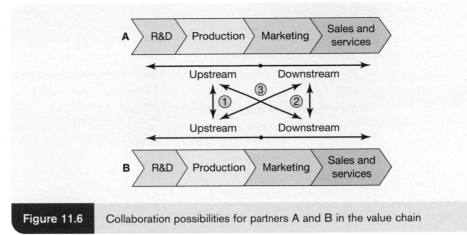

Figure 11.6 Collaboration possibilities for partners A and B in the value chain

Source: adapted from Lorange and Roos (1995, p. 16).

The question of whether to use an equity or a non-equity joint venture is a matter of how to formalize the cooperation. Much more interesting is to consider the roles that partners are supposed to play in the collaboration.

In Figure 11.6 two different types of coalition are shown in the value chain perspective. These are based on the possible collaboration pattern along the value chain. In Figure 11.4 we see two partners, A and B, each having its own value chain. Three different types of value chain partnership appear:

1. *Upstream-based collaboration*. A and B collaborate on R&D and/or production.
2. *Downstream-based collaboration*. A and B collaborate on marketing, distribution, sales and/or service.
3. *Upstream/downstream-based collaboration*. A and B have different but complementary competences at each end of the value chain.

Types 1 and 2 represent the so-called **Y coalition** and type 3 represents the so-called **X coalition** (Porter and Fuller, 1986, pp. 336–7):

- *Y coalitions*. Partners share the actual performance of one or more value chain activities: for example, joint production of models or components enables the attainment of scale economies that can provide lower production costs per unit. Another example is a joint marketing agreement where complementary product lines of two firms are sold together through existing or new distribution channels, and thus broaden the market coverage of both firms.
- *X coalitions*. Partners divide the value chain activities between themselves: for example, one partner develops and manufactures a product while letting the other partner market it. Forming X coalitions involves identifying the value chain activities where the firm is well positioned and has its core competences. Take the case where A has its core competences in upstream functions but is weak in downstream functions. A wants to enter a foreign market but lacks local market knowledge and does not know how to get access to foreign distribution channels for its products. Therefore A seeks and finds a partner, B, which has its core competences in the downstream functions but is weak in the upstream functions. In this way A and B can form a coalition where B can help A with distribution and selling in a foreign market, and A can help B with R&D or production.

In summary, X coalitions imply that the partners have asymmetric competences in the value chain activities: where one is strong the other is weak and vice versa. In Y coalitions, on the other hand, partners tend to be more similar in the strengths and weaknesses of their value chain activities.

Y coalition
Each partner in the alliance/JV contributes with complementary product lines or services. Each partner takes care of all value chain activities within their product line.

X coalition
The partners in the value chain divide the value chain activities between them, e.g. the manufacturer (exporter) specializes in upstream activities, whereas the local partner takes care of the downstream activities.

Table 11.3	Stages in joint-venture formation

1. Joint venture objectives

Establish strategic objectives of the joint venture and specify time period for achieving objectives.

2. Cost–benefit analysis

Evaluate advantages and disadvantages of joint venture compared with alternative strategies for achieving objectives (e.g. licensing) in terms of:

(a) financial commitment

(b) synergy

(c) management commitment

(d) risk reduction

(e) control

(f) long-run market penetration and

(g) other advantages/disadvantages.

3. Selecting partner(s)

(a) profile of desired features of candidates

(b) identifying joint-venture candidates and drawing up shortlist

(c) screening and evaluating possible joint-venture partners

(d) initial contact/discussions and

(e) choice of partner.

4. Develop business plan

Achieve broad agreement on different issues.

5. Negotiation of joint-venture agreement

Final agreement on business plan.

6. Contract writing

Incorporation of agreement in legally binding contract, allowing for subsequent modifications to the agreement.

7. Performance evaluation

Establish control systems for measuring venture performance.

Source: adapted from Young *et al.* (1989, p. 233).

Stages in joint-venture formation

The various stages in the formation of a joint venture are shown in Table 11.3.

Step 1: joint-venture objectives

Joint ventures are formed for a variety of reasons: entering new markets, reducing manufacturing costs and developing and diffusing new technologies rapidly. Joint ventures are also used to accelerate product introduction and overcome legal and trade barriers expeditiously. In this period of advanced technology and global markets implementing strategies quickly is essential. Forming alliances is often the fastest, most effective method of achieving objectives. Companies must be sure that the goal of the alliance is compatible with their existing businesses, so their expertise is transferable to the alliance. Firms often enter into alliances based on opportunity rather than linkage with their overall goals. This risk is greatest when a company has a surplus of cash.

There are three principal objectives in forming a joint venture:

1. *Entering new markets.* Many companies recognize that they lack the necessary marketing expertise when they enter new markets. Rather than trying to develop this expertise internally the company may identify another organization that possesses those desired marketing skills. By capitalizing on the product development skills of one company and the marketing skills of the other, the resulting alliance can serve the market quickly and effectively. Alliances may be particularly helpful when entering a foreign market for the first time because of the extensive cultural differences that may abound. They may also be effective domestically when entering regional or ethnic markets.

2. *Reducing manufacturing costs.* Joint ventures may allow companies to pool capital or existing facilities to gain economies of scale or increase the use of facilities, thereby reducing manufacturing costs.

3. *Developing and diffusing technology.* Joint ventures may also be used to build jointly on the technical expertise of two or more companies in developing products that are technologically beyond the capability of the companies acting independently.

Step 2: cost–benefit analysis

A joint venture/strategic alliance may not be the best way of achieving objectives. Therefore this entry mode should be evaluated against other entry modes. Such an analysis could be based on the factors influencing the choice of entry mode (see section 9.3).

Step 3: selecting partner(s)

If it is accepted that a joint venture is the best entry mode for achieving the firm's objectives, the next stage is the selection of the joint-venture partner. This normally involves five stages.

Establishing a desired partner profile

Companies frequently search for one or more of the following resources in a partner:

- development know-how
- sales and service expertise
- low-cost production facilities
- strategically critical manufacturing capabilities
- reputation and brand equity
- market access and knowledge
- cash.

Identifying joint-venture candidates

Often this part of partner selection is not performed thoroughly. The first candidate, generally discovered through contacts established by mail, arranged by a banker or a business colleague already established in the country, is often the one with whom the company undertakes discussions. Little or no screening is done, nor is there an in-depth investigation of the motives and capabilities of the candidate. At other times the personal network that executives maintain with senior managers from other firms shapes the set of prospective joint-venture partners that companies will generally consider. All too often, however, alliances are agreed upon informally by these top managers without careful attention to how appropriate the partner match may be. Instead of taking this reactive approach the firm should proactively search for joint-venture candidates. Possible candidates can be found among competitors, suppliers, customers, related industries and trade association members.

Screening and evaluating possible joint-venture partners

Relationships get off to a good start if partners know each other. Table 11.4 gives some criteria that may be used to judge a prospective partner's effectiveness. These suggestions only

Table 11.4	Analysis of prospective partners: examples of criteria that may be used to judge a prospective partner's effectiveness by assessing existing business ventures and commercial attitudes

1. **Finance**

   Financial history and overall financial standing (all the usual ratios).

   Possible reasons for successful business areas.

   Possible reasons for unsuccessful business areas.

2. **Organization**

   Structure of organization.

   Quality and turnover of senior managers.

   Workforce conditions/labour relations.

   Information and reporting systems; evidence of planning.

   Effective owner's working relationship with business.

3. **Market**

   Reputation in marketplace and with competitors.

   Evidence of research/interest in service and quality.

   Sales methods; quality of sales force.

   Evidence of handling weakening market conditions.

   Results of new business started.

4. **Production**

   Condition of existing premises/works.

   Production efficiencies/layouts.

   Capital investments and improvements.

   Quality control procedures.

   Evidence of research (internal/external); introduction of new technology.

   Relationship with main suppliers.

5. **Institutional**

   Government and business contacts (influence).

   Successful negotiations with banks, licensing authorities, etc.

   Main contacts with non-national organizations and companies.

   Geographical influence.

6. **Possible negotiating attitudes**

   Flexible or hard line.

   Reasonably open or closed and secretive.

   Short-term or long-term orientation.

   Wheeler-dealer or objective negotiator.

   Positive, quick decision-making or tentative.

   Negotiating experience and strength of team support.

Sources: Walmsley (1982); Paliwoda (1993).

form an outline sketch of the type of information that can be used to grade partners. They cover areas where there is a reasonable chance of forming a view by the appraisal of published information and by sensible observation and questioning.

Initial contacts/discussions

Since relationships between companies are relationships between people it is important that the top managers of the firm meet personally with top managers from the remaining two or three possible partners. It is important to highlight the personal side of a business relationship. This includes discussion of personal and social interests to see if there is a good chemistry between the prospective partners.

Choice of partner

The chosen partner should bring the desired complementary strength to the partnership. Ideally the strengths contributed by the partners will be unique, for only these strengths can be sustained and defended over the long term. The goal is to develop synergies between the contributions of the partners, resulting in a win–win situation for both. Moreover, the partners must be compatible and willing to trust one another.

It is important that neither partner has the desire to acquire the other partner's strength, or the necessary mutual trust will be destroyed. Dow Chemical Company, a frequent and successful alliance practitioner, uses the negotiation process to judge other corporate cultures and, consequently, their compatibility and trustworthiness.

Commitment to the joint venture is essential. This commitment must be both financial and psychological. Unless there is senior management endorsement and enthusiasm at the operating level an alliance will struggle, particularly when tough issues arise.

Step 4: develop a business plan

Issues that have to be negotiated and determined prior to the establishment of the joint venture include:

- ownership split (majority, minority, 50–50);
- management (composition of board of directors, organization, etc.);
- production (installation of machinery, training, etc.);
- marketing (the 4-Ps, organization).

Step 5: negotiation of joint-venture agreement

As Figure 11.7 shows, the final agreement is determined by the relative bargaining power of both prospective partners.

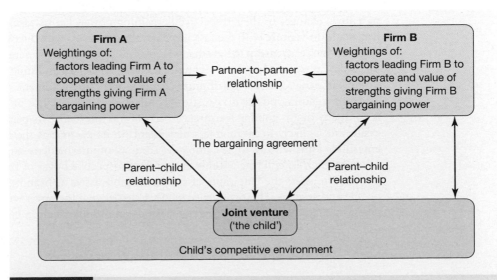

| **Figure 11.7** | Partner-to-partner relationships creating a joint venture |

Source: Harrigan (1985, p. 50).

Step 6: contract writing

Once the joint-venture agreement has been negotiated it needs to be written into a legally binding contract. Of course, the contract should cover the 'marriage' conditions of the partners, but it should also cover the 'divorce' situation, such as what happens with 'the child' (the joint venture).

Step 7: performance evaluation

Evaluating joint-venture performance is a difficult issue. Managers often fall into the trap of assessing partnerships as if they were internal corporate divisions with unambiguous goals operating in low-risk, stable environments. Bottom-line profits, cash flow, market share and other traditional financially oriented output measures become standard indicators of performance. These measures may be inappropriate for two reasons. First, they reflect a short-term orientation, and maximization of initial output too soon can jeopardize the prospects for alliances positioned for the long term. Second, the goals of many alliances may not be readily quantifiable. For instance, a partnership's objectives may involve obtaining access to a market or blocking a competitor.

Many alliances need considerable time before they are ready to be judged on conventional output measures. Only after partnerships mature (i.e. when the operations of the alliance are well established and well understood) can managers gradually shift to measure output, such as profits and cash flows.

Expecting too much too soon in terms of profit and cash flows from an alliance working under risky conditions can endanger its future success.

Managing the joint venture

In recent years we have seen an increasing number of cross-border joint ventures. However, it is dangerous to ignore the fact that the average lifespan for alliances is only about seven years, and nearly 80 per cent of joint ventures ultimately end in a sale by one of the partners.

Harrigan's model (Figure 11.8) can be used as a framework for explaining this high 'divorce rate'.

Changes in bargaining power

According to Bleeke and Ernst (1994), the key to understanding the 'divorce' of the two parents is changes in their respective bargaining power. Let us assume that we have established a joint venture with the task of penetrating markets with a new product. In the initial stages of the relationship the product and technology provider generally has the most power, but unless those products and technologies are proprietary and unique power usually shifts to the party that controls distribution channels and thus customers.

The bargaining power is also strongly affected by the balance of learning and teaching. A company that is good at learning can access and internalize its partner's capabilities more easily, and is likely to become less dependent on its partner as the alliance evolves. Before entering a joint venture some companies see it as an intermediate stage before acquiring the other partner. By entering a joint venture the prospective buyer of the partner is in a better position to assess the true value of such intangible assets as brands, distribution networks, people and systems. This experience reduces the risk that the buyer will make an uninformed decision and buy an expensive 'lemon' (Nanda and Williamson, 1995).

Other change stimuli and potential conflicts

Diverging goals

As the joint venture progresses the goals of the two partners may diverge. For example, unacceptable positions can develop in the local market when the self-interest of one partner

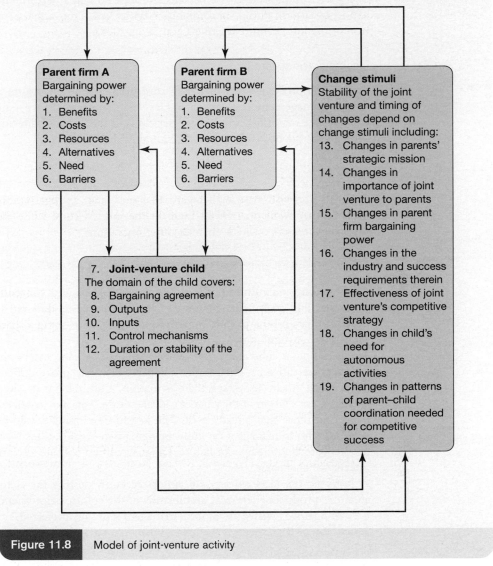

| **Figure 11.8** | Model of joint-venture activity |

Source: Harrigan (1985, p. 52).

conflicts with the interest of the joint venture as a whole, as in the pricing of a single-source input or raw material.

Diverging goals typically arise in the local market entry joint ventures. These joint ventures are created when multinational enterprises (MNEs) take local partners to enter foreign markets. The MNE is usually interested in maximizing its global income, that is, the net income of all of its affiliates, and this means that it is quite willing to run losses on some affiliates if this leads to higher net income for the whole network. The local partner, however, wants to maximize the profits of the specific affiliate of which it is part owner. Conflicts then flare up whenever the two goals are incompatible, as global income maximization is not necessarily compatible with the maximization of the separate profits of each affiliate. For example, conflicts may arise concerning the role given to the joint venture within the MNE network (and particularly on its allocation of export markets). This was the case when General Motors (GM) set up with Daewoo to manufacture subcompact cars for the Korean market and for export to the United States under GM's Pontiac badge. Since GM's Opel subsidiary was selling similar subcompacts in Europe, GM limited the joint venture's export to its US Pontiac subsidiary. Dissatisfied with Pontiac's performance, Daewoo decided to export to Eastern Europe in competition with Opel, a move that contributed to the dissolution of the joint venture (Hennert and Zeng, 2005).

Double management

A potential problem is the matter of control. By definition, a joint venture must deal with double management. If a partner has less than 50 per cent ownership that partner must in effect let the majority partner make decisions. If the board of directors has a 50–50 split it is difficult for the board to make a decision quickly if at all.

Repatriation of profits

Conflicts can also arise with regard to issues such as repatriation of profits, where the local partner wants to reinvest them in the joint venture while the other partner wishes to repatriate them or invest them in other operations.

Mixing different cultures

An organization's culture is the set of values, beliefs and conventions that influence the behaviour and goals of its employees. This is often quite different from the culture of the host country and the partner organization. Thus, developing a shared culture is central to the success of the alliance.

Partnering is inherently very people-oriented. To the extent that the cultures of the partners are different, making the alliance work may prove difficult. Cultural differences often result in an 'us versus them' situation. Cultural norms should be consistent with management's vision of the alliance's ideal culture. This may entail creating norms as well as nurturing those that already exist. The key to developing a culture is to acknowledge its existence and to manage it carefully. Bringing two organizations together and letting nature take its course is a recipe for failure. Language differences are also an obvious hurdle for an international alliance.

Ignoring the local culture will almost certainly destroy the chances of it accepting the alliance's product or service. Careful study of the culture prior to embarking on the venture is vital. Again, extensive use of local managers is usually preferred.

Shared equity

Shared equity may also involve an unequal sharing of the burden. Occasionally, international companies with 50–50 joint ventures believe that they are giving more than 50 per cent of the technology, management skill and other factors that contribute to the success of the operation, but are receiving only half the profits. Of course, the national partner contributes local knowledge and other intangibles that may be underestimated. Nevertheless, some international companies believe that the local partner gets too much of a 'free ride'.

Developing trust in joint ventures

Developing trust takes time. The first times that companies work together their chances of succeeding are very slight, but once they find ways to work together all sorts of opportunities appear. Working together on relatively small projects initially helps develop trust and determine compatibility while minimizing economic risk. Each partner has a chance to gauge the skills and contributions of the other, and further investment can then be considered. Of course, winning together in the marketplace on a project of any scale is a great way to build trust and overcome differences. It usually serves as a precursor to more ambitious joint efforts.

Providing an exit strategy

As indicated earlier, there is a significant probability that a newly formed joint venture will fail, even if the previously mentioned key principles are followed. The anticipated market may not develop, one of the partner's capabilities may have been overestimated, the corporate strategy of one of the partners may have changed, or the partners may simply be incompatible. Whatever the reason for the failure, the parties should prepare for such an outcome by addressing the issue in the partnership contract. The contract should provide for the liquidation or distribution of partnership assets, including any technology developed by the alliance.

Control mechanisms

Control mechanisms may be positive, which parents employ in order to promote certain behaviours, or negative, which are used by a parent to stop or prevent the JV from implementing certain activities or decisions. Positive controls tend to be exercised through informal mechanisms, including staffing, reporting relationships and participation in the planning process. On the other hand, the more bureaucratic negative control includes reliance on such mechanisms as formal agreements, approval or veto by parents and the use of the venture's board of directors.

Control-related failures are likely to occur if control practices are not re-evaluated and modified in response to changing circumstances. This is the job of both partners in the JV. Responding to problems on an ad hoc basis will result in control-related failures (Vaidya, 2009).

Split control (50–50) or dominant control structure

Finally, a question that often causes discussion between the joint venture (JV) parents is the question if the joint venture should be based on a split (50–50) or on a dominant control structure (e.g. 60-40). Some researchers (Anderson and Gatignon, 1986) believe that dominant control structures often make JVs easier to manage and may be more successfully executed than when the decision-making control is shared by the parents. Other researchers (e.g. Geringer and Hebert, 1991) disagree and state that a split control structure, where each parent or the joint venture managers exerts dominant control (and have responsibility) over different value chain activities of the JV, is also as beneficial to both the parties.

11.6 Other intermediate entry modes

Management contracting emphasizes the growing importance of services and management know-how. The typical case of management contracting is where one firm (contractor) supplies management know-how to another company that provides the capital and takes care of the operating value chain functions in the foreign country. Normally the contracts undertaken are concerned with management operating/control systems and training local staff to take over when the contracts are completed. It is usually not the intention of the contractor to continue operating after the contract expires. Normally it is the philosophy to operate, transfer know-how to the local staff and then depart. This will usually create a strong competitive position from which to pick up other management contracts in the area.

Management contracts typically arise in situations where one company seeks the management know-how of another company with established experience in the field. The lack of management capability is most evident for developing countries. Normally the financial compensation to the contractor for the management services provided is a management fee, which may be fixed irrespective of the financial performance or may be a percentage of the profit (Luostarinen and Welch, 1990). The advantages and disadvantages of management contracting and different intermediate entry modes are listed in Table 11.5.

Table 11.5	Advantages and disadvantages of the different intermediate modes	
Intermediate entry mode	**Advantages**	**Disadvantages**
Contract manufacturing (seen from the contractor's viewpoint)	Permits low-risk market entry. No local investment (cash, time and executive talent) with no risk of nationalization or expropriation. Retention of control over R&D, marketing and sales/after-sales service. Avoids currency risks and financing problems. A locally made image, which may assist in sales, especially to government or official bodies. Entry into markets otherwise protected by tariffs or other barriers. Possible cost advantage if local costs (primarily labour costs) are lower. Avoids intra-corporate transfer-pricing problems that can arise with a subsidiary.	Transfer of production know-how is difficult. Contract manufacture is only possible when a satisfactory and reliable manufacturer can be found – not always an easy task. Extensive technical training will often have to be given to the local manufacturer's staff. As a result, at the end of the contract, the subcontractor could become a formidable competitor. Control over manufacturing quality is difficult to achieve despite the ultimate sanction of refusal to accept substandard goods. Possible supply limitation if the production is taking place in developing countries.
Licensing (seen from the licensor's viewpoint)	Increases the income on products already developed as a result of expensive research. Permits entry into markets that are otherwise closed on account of high rates of duty, import quotas and so on. A viable option where manufacture is near the customer's base. Requires little capital investment and should provide a higher rate of return on capital employed. There may be valuable spin-off if the licensor can sell other products or components to the licensee. If these parts are for products being manufactured locally or machinery, there may also be some tariff concessions on their import. The licensor is not exposed to the danger of nationalization or expropriation of assets. Because of the limited capital requirements, new products can be exploited rapidly, on a worldwide basis, before competition develops. The licensor can take immediate advantage of the licensee's local marketing and distribution organization and of existing customer contacts. Protects patents, especially in countries that give weak protection for products not produced locally. Local manufacture may also be an advantage in securing government contracts.	The licensor is ceding certain sales territories to the licensee for the duration of the contract; should it fail to live up to expectations, renegotiation may be expensive. When the licensing agreement finally expires, the licensor may find they have established a competitor in the former licensee. The licensee may prove less competent than expected at marketing or other management activities. Costs may even grow faster than income. The licensee, even if it reaches an agreed minimum turnover, may not fully exploit the market, leaving it open to the entry of competitors, so that the licensor loses control of the marketing operation. Danger of the licensee running short of funds, especially if considerable plant expansion is involved or an injection of capital is required to sustain the project. This danger can be turned to advantage if the licensor has funds available by a general expansion of the business through a partnership. License fees are normally a small percentage of turnover, about 5 per cent, and will often compare unfavourably with what might be obtained from a company's own manufacturing operation. Lack of control over licensee operations. Quality control of the product is difficult – and the product will often be sold under the licensor's brand name. Negotiations with the licensee, and sometimes with local government, are costly. Governments often impose conditions on transferral of royalties or on component supply.

Intermediate entry mode	Advantages	Disadvantages
Franchising (seen from franchisor's viewpoint)	Greater degree of control compared to licensing. Low-risk, low-cost entry mode (the franchisees are the ones investing in the necessary equipment and know-how). Using highly motivated business contacts with money, local market knowledge and experience. Ability to develop new and distant international markets, relatively quickly and on a larger scale than otherwise possible. Generating economies of scale in marketing to international customers. Precursor to possible future direct investment in foreign market.	The search for competent franchisees can be expensive and time-consuming. Lack of full control over franchisee's operations, resulting in problems with cooperation, communications, quality control, etc. Costs of creating and marketing a unique package of products and services recognized internationally. Costs of protecting goodwill and brand name. Problems with local legislation, including transfers of money, payments of franchise fees and government-imposed restrictions on franchise agreements. Opening up internal business knowledge may create potential future competitor. Risk to the company's international profile and reputation if some franchisees underperform ('free riding' on valuable brand names).
Joint venture (seen from parent's viewpoint)	Access to expertise and contacts in local markets. Each partner agrees to a joint venture to gain access to the other partner's skills and resources. Typically, the international partner contributes financial resources, technology or products. The local partner provides the skills and knowledge required for managing a business in its country. Each partner can concentrate on that part of the value chain where the firm has its core competence. Reduced market and political risk. Shared knowledge and resources: compared to wholly owned subsidiary, less capital and fewer management resources are required. Economies of scale by pooling skills and resources (resulting in e.g. lower marketing costs). Overcomes host government restrictions. May avoid local tariffs and non-tariff barriers. Shared risk of failure. Less costly than acquisitions. Possibly better relations with national governments through having a local partner (meets host country pressure for local participation).	Objectives of the respective partners may be incompatible, resulting in conflicts. Contributions to joint venture can become disproportionate. Loss of control over foreign operations. Large investments of financial, technical or managerial resources favour greater control than is possible in a joint venture. Completion might overburden a company's staff. Partners may become locked into long-term investments from which it is difficult to withdraw. Transfer pricing problems as goods pass between partners. The importance of the venture to each partner might change over time. Cultural differences may result in possible differences in management culture among participating firms. Loss of flexibility and confidentiality. Problems of management structures and dual parent staffing of joint ventures. Nepotism perhaps the established norm.
Management contracting (seen from contractor's viewpoint)	If direct investment or export is considered too risky – for commercial or political reasons – this alternative might be relevant. As with other intermediate entry modes, management contracts may be linked together with other forms of operation in foreign markets. Allows a company to maintain market involvement, so puts it in a better position to exploit any opportunity that may arise. Organizational learning: if a company is in its early development stages of internationalization, a management contract may offer an efficient way of learning about foreign markets and international business.	Training future competitors: the management transfer package may in the end create a competitor for the contractor. Creates a great demand for key personnel. Such staff are not always available, especially in SMEs. Considerable effort needs to be put into building lines of communication at local level as well as back to contractor. Potential conflict between the contractor and the local government as regards the policy of the contract venture. Little control, which also limits the ability of a contractor to develop the capacity of the venture.

Other management contracts may be part of a deal to sell a processing plant as a project or a turnkey operation. This issue will be dealt with more intensively in section 13.8.

EXHIBIT 11.2 McDonald's + Coca-Cola + Disney = a powerful alliance

Today business is being driven by two fashionable ideas: globalization and core competences. The first compels companies to look for ways to sell their product in as many different places as possible, which often requires other people to help them. The second, the fashion for a firm sticking to what it does best, means that they must often let outsiders help them with everything else.

The ties binding Coca-Cola, McDonald's and Disney vary enormously.

McDonald's ↔ Disney

In 1997 McDonald's and Disney began a formal ten-year alliance. The first specific outcome was a Disney film, *Flubber*, whose box-office returns were helped by tie-ins at McDonald's. In July 1998 a promotion started of *Armageddon*, an US$111 million film starring Bruce Willis, with McDonald's selling tickets and special 'Astromeals' at each of its 23,500 restaurants worldwide. This time the target was not children but young adults – a market in which McDonald's is weaker.

McDonald's ↔ Coca-Cola

This alliance has no formal agreement – no piece of paper to fall back on. Although Coca-Cola sells drinks to other restaurants, its relationship with McDonald's goes far beyond that of a mere supplier. It has helped its partner to set up new operations around the world. Coca-Cola is sold in almost twice as many countries as McDonald's.

Coca-Cola ↔ Disney

Coca-Cola's ties to Disney are probably the weakest of the three – but they are still considerable. Coca-Cola has been the sole provider of soft drinks at Disney parks since 1955, and it has had a marketing alliance in place since 1985. Coca-Cola has also helped Disney overseas.

QUESTIONS

1. What is it that makes the Coca-Cola–Disney–McDonald's triumvirate so powerful in the globalization process?

2. What factors could make the alliance of Coca-Cola–Disney–McDonald's break up?

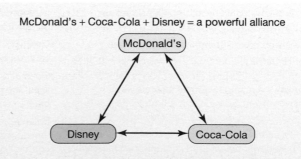

McDonald's + Coca-Cola + Disney = a powerful alliance

Figure 11.9 McDonald's + Coca-Cola + Disney = a powerful alliance

11.7 | Summary

Intermediate entry modes are distinguished from export modes because they are primarily vehicles for the transfer of knowledge and skills between partners, in order to create foreign sales. They are distinguished from hierarchical entry modes in that there is no full ownership (by parent firm) involved. Ownership and control can be shared between the parent firm and the local partner. This is, for example, the case with the (equity) joint venture.

The advantages and disadvantages of the different intermediate entry modes are summarized in Table 11.5.

CASE STUDY 11.1

Hello Kitty: can the cartoon cat survive the buzz across the world?

When, in 1974, employees at the Japanese design company Sanrio created Hello Kitty (www.sanrio.com/characters/HelloKitty/), the small, rounded cartoon cat with a red bow between her ears and no mouth, they could never have dreamt that she would become the global megastar she is today. Sales of Hello Kitty merchandise now account for approximately one third of Saniro's app. €650 million annual turnover and her face adorns 50,000 products, sold in more than 60 countries.

© 1976, 2010 SANRIO CO., LTD.

History

Hello Kitty was created with the focus of being a small gift, whatever the product is. The unique selling proposition (USP) has always been 'small gift, big smile'.

Hello Kitty's creator started out as the Japanese equivalent of Hallmark cards. Sanrio was founded by Shintaro Tsuji in 1960; Tsuji, a qualified chemist, lost his mother when he was 13 and spent an unhappy childhood with reluctant relatives. He attended a kindergarten run by a Canadian missionary and saw for the first time the custom of birthdays, which were not traditionally celebrated in Japan. He decided he would use his company to foster the culture of gift-giving.

The little half-Japanese, half-English cat has become so globally recognizable that it is, perhaps, inevitable that the Japanese board of tourism has appointed her their official tourism ambassador to China and Hong Kong. This is not the first time the world has looked to Hello Kitty to perform an ambassadorial role; she has been United States children's ambassador for UNICEF since 1983.

As an experiment in 1971, in the wake of student riots, the company began printing rounded, cutesy images on previously blank writing stationery and in 1974, Hello Kitty was drawn. She was drawn without a mouth, which later made her the perfect cross-cultural representative. She wasn't given a mouth, because she speaks from the heart. She's Sanrio's ambassador to the world and isn't bound to any particular language.

Hello Kitty was made partly English because when she was first drawn, foreign, especially English, associations, were particularly popular. The Hello Kitty stationery (pencils, pencil cases, ballpoints pens, paper) and diaries were a hit among schoolgirls during the 1980s and the company soon branched out in to other fancy goods.

In the 1990s, Hello Kitty had a second level at fame as it was was re-marketed as a 'retro' brand. Shops, run by the outlet label Vivitix, marketed Hello Kitty to teens and adults, appealing to their sense of nostalgia.

As eight-year-olds they would have used Hello Kitty pencils and pencil cases in the classroom; in their late teens and early twenties, they reached for Hello Kitty satchels and make-up mirrors. Hello Kitty stands for the innocence and sincerity of childhood and the simplicity of the world. Women and girls all over the world are happy to buy in to the image of the trusting, loving childhood in a safe neighbourhood that Hello Kitty represents. They don't want to let go of that image, so as they grow up, they hang onto Hello Kitty out of nostalgic longing – as if by keeping a symbolic object, they can somehow keep hold of a fragment of their childhood self.

Now, although originally conceived as a character that would appeal to pre-teen girls, Hello Kitty is no longer regarded as being for children only. Along with the likes of Coca-Cola and Nike, she has become a brand phenomenon.

Hello Kitty is technically just one character who inhabits an entire, fictional world dreamt up by Sanrio. She lives in cyberspace (on the fondant-coloured Sanriotown website, www.sanrio.com/characters/HelloKitty/). Hello Kitty has her own birthday, 1 November (which makes her a Scorpio) and, as her English heritage befits, she lives in London with her parents and twin sister, Mimmy. Her many hobbies include travelling, music, reading and 'eating yummy cookies her sister Mimmy bakes'.

Other characters who share Hello Kitty's world include Dear Daniel, Kathy, Tippy and Thomas.

Sanrio's theme park, Puroland, opened in 1990; it features Sanrio's most popular characters, with Hello Kitty as its star draw, and with yearly figures of 1.5 million visitors from around the world, it is one of Japan's most popular visitor attractions.

Hello Kitty even became an animated character. She first appeared on the American-animated Hello Kitty's Furry Tale Theater, which was shown on US television throughout 1987. Another series ran in 1991.

When Hello Kitty was first marketed to the US, the cultural differences meant that changes to the Japanese version had to be made. Sanrio's market research showed American consumers responded best to pink and purple kitties and worst to anything blue, yellow or red. The American audience also took against one of Hello Kitty's friends, a little snail, which had to be eliminated from the merchandise.

However, Sanrio got it right in the end and now there are no differences in the American and Japanese lines of merchandise. Indeed, when Sanrio tried to customise Hello Kitty for its Taiwanese and Hong Kong markets, putting her in local dress and in local surroundings, the products did not sell. Her mixed English-Japanese heritage was part of her charm.

Hello Kitty business today

Its primary business is making and marketing what it calls social communication gifts. The company also operates restaurants and two theme parks in Japan, produces movies and publishes books and magazines – all based on its multitude of cute characters. Sanrio licenses or sells thousands of items – including Hello Kitty stationery, school and desk accessories, clothing, cosmetics, and room decor – that turn up for sale around the world. Over 4,000 stores sell the products in the Americas alone, including some 200 Sanrio boutiques.

There are more than 50,000 licensed Hello Kitty products total available in 60 countries worldwide. There are 500 new Hello Kitty products launched around the world each month and 500 products are discontinued. The idea is to change the product range in order to match different and emerging marketing, business and cultural trends across the world. In China Sanrio operates about 100 shops. Sanrio also partners with artists to make speciality products, such as nail artist Eriko Kurosaki's 2007 Hello Kitty collection.

Some time ago Sanrio signed a deal with Sony Ericsson for their mobile phone. Just recently Sanrio signed a licensing deal with iPod manufacturer, Apple, which has launched a range of Hello Kitty branded products. Mobile phones are attractive products for the Hello Kitty brand: children are now using mobiles as much as teenagers and adults. Mobiles or smartphones are objects that everybody has in their pocket and it is always seen.

In May 2008 Sanrio announced the formation of the Global Consumer Products division to build on the company's efforts in licensing, new product development, and co-branding partnerships. To that end, it has formed a partnership to open a theme park in Taiwan. Sanrio already operates a pair of 'Hello Kitty' theme parks in Japan and hopes to cut similar deals.

© 1976, 2010 SANRIO CO., LTD.

Marketing and advertising

While the licensing partners may advertise the Hello Kitty products, Sanrio relies purely on its partners' marketing and word of mouth. Hello Kitty don't rely on animations, films or film shows to be promoted and is probably one of the only brands in the world that rely solely on the partners' advertising and word of mouth.

Licensing

Normally licensing is done as a very technical and commercial deal. However, Sanrio is very involved with the creative side and its decisions to work with certain licensee partners are more about their ability to create Hello Kitty products which appeal to the loyal consumer and protect what the brand stands for.

Competition

Sanrio does not tend to worry much about competition, as the Hello Kitty has been out there as a brand for more than 30 years. However, Sanrio has respect for a newcomer such as Don Ed Harry, who is an American tattoo artist born and raised in Southern California. Hardy is recognized for incorporating Japanese tattoo aesthetic and technique into his work. For example, in 2004, French fashion designer Christian Audigier licensed the rights to produce the high-end Ed Hardy clothing line, which is based on Hardy's imagery (Varley, 2009).

Sales figures

The company's sales in Japan and United States have been declining, while the products have continued to grow in popularity in Europe, Asia and Brazil. In 2008 the sales in Japan fell 28 per cent to approximately €180 million. However, in Europe sales rose 62 per cent to approximately €35 million. Sanrio blamed falling birth rates, unseasonable weather and a saturated market for its dip domestically. Sales in North America were also down in the fiscal year 2008 due to the softening economy and financial crises and a flawed product strategy for Christmas. Traffic at its two theme parks is down despite the addition of new attractions. The company blamed a reduction of group discounts for this decline.

Despite the current problems, Sanrio is confident that the Hello Kitty phenomenon is not over yet. Only the future will tell whether the speechless but iconic cat will be heard for the coming decades, but currently its brand equity serves as a solid business platform for Sanrio.

QUESTIONS

1. Do you think that Hello Kitty will continue to rule the world? What are the pros and cons?

2. What are the reasons that Hello Kitty is licensed to so many different product manufacturers?

3. Suggest the future licensing strategy for Hello Kitty.

Sources: information from www.sanrio.com/characters/HelloKitty/; Varley, M. (2009) 'Can Hello Kitty continue to rule the world?', *Brand Strategy*, February, pp. 32–36; adapted from Walker, E. (2008) 'Top cat – how "Hello Kitty" conquered the world – Japan's new tourism ambassador', *The Independent* (London), 21 May copyright The Independent, www.independent.co.uk.

CASE STUDY 11.2

Ka-Boo-Ki: licensing in the LEGO brand

The Danish toy manufacturer LEGO is known worldwide for its LEGO bricks. LEGO is a strong and well-known brand. In the 1990s LEGO management received (among others) the results of three consumer surveys:

1. 'Image power' is a measure of brands' impact, where consumers' awareness of the world's leading brands is combined with their judgement of the brands' quality. In the United States and Japan LEGO was not placed among the top ten, but the results from Europe were impressive. Here LEGO was placed at number five after four car brands: Mercedes-Benz, Rolls-Royce, Porsche and BMW. LEGO was in front of brands such as Nestlé, Rolex, Jaguar and Ferrari.
2. A US survey, conducted in Europe, the United States and Japan, showed that LEGO is number 13 in the list of most appreciated brands.
3. A survey by a German market analysis institute showed that LEGO is one of the most well-known brands in toys in the new German Federal Republic, with an awareness share of 67 per cent. Matchbox is number 2 with 41 per cent.

The LEGO management has decided to exploit this strong brand image and a managing director for the new business area LEGO Licensing A/S has been appointed. The company's objective is to generate income from licensing suitable partners, which will use the LEGO brand in marketing their own products.

The LEGO management has noticed that Coca-Cola has an income of Danish Kr3 billion from licensing alone. Coca-Cola's strategy can be characterized as 'brand milking', where a brand is sold to the highest bidder in each product area.

Ideas become viable

In 1993 the idea of licensing the LEGO brand became viable for the Danish textile firm Ka-Boo-Ki, as it was given the rights to use the LEGO brand in connection with the production and sale of children's clothes. Ka-Boo-Ki's Managing Director, Torben Klausen, was earlier employed in LEGO's

Children in Ka-Boo-Ki clothes (LEGO licence)
© 2010 the Lego Group. Used with permission.

international marketing department, where he was in charge of coordinating the European marketing of LEGO bricks. From this position he was able to follow the development of the licensing concept. Since 1993 things have been developing very fast. In mid-1997 Ka-Boo-Ki, which has invested a considerable amount of money in the R&D of LEGO children's clothes, was selling to approximately 900 shops, primarily in Scandinavia and England.

Torben Klausen says:

We received a strong international brand from the first day. But in selling LEGO children's comes an obligation to live up to the LEGO company's unique quality demands. LEGO must approve all new models that are put on the market, and that is between 350 and 400 a year.

LEGO children's clothes distinguish themselves from other brands by being functional and having strong colours and an uncompromising quality. This means a relatively high price for the clothes, and that the products are not sold in discount shops. The clothes are sold on the basis of a shop-in-shop concept, where merchandising and display facilities are very important.

QUESTIONS

You have just been employed by LEGO Licensing A/S in connection with the development of the licensing data. You are given the following assignments.

1. What are the most important factors determining future market demand for LEGO children's clothes from Ka-Boo-Ki?

2. Which other products could be considered for licensing out the LEGO brand?

3. List some criteria for choosing suitable licensees and future products for the LEGO brand (licensing out).

4. What values/benefits can LEGO transfer to the licensee (e.g. Ka-Boo-Ki) apart from the use of the LEGO brand?

5. What values/benefits can the licensee transfer to the licensor?

VIDEO CASE STUDY 11.3 Marriott

download from www.pearsoned.co.uk/hollensen

Marriott (www.marriott.com) is a worldwide operator and franchisor of 2,741 hotels and related facilities in 67 countries. Quality and consistent service is Marriott's main focus and keeps the company in the top position in its industry. The company is responsible for pioneering segmentation in the hospitality industry. With a wide array of hotels, Marriott meets the needs of various customer segments. Before developing any additional hotel chains and their respective brands, the company always tests properties first. Marriott is active in soliciting feedback from its customer base and focuses on really understanding its customer targets.

Questions

1. What could be the main motives for Marriott in using franchising, compared to other entry modes and operation forms?

2. Identify several major categories of segmentation used by Marriott. For each relate specific examples of hotel services tailored to various target markets; www.marriott.com offers a brief description of 13 brands of various Marriott hotels catering to different types of customers.

For further exercises and cases, see this book's website at **www.pearsoned.co.uk/hollensen**

Questions for discussion

1. Why are joint ventures preferred by host countries as an entry strategy for foreign firms?

2. Why are strategic alliances used in new product development?

3. Under what circumstances should franchising be considered? How do these circumstances vary from those leading to licensing?

4. Do you believe that licensing in represents a feasible long-term product development strategy for a company? Discuss in relation to in-house product development.

5. Why would a firm consider forming partnerships with competitors?

6. Apart from the management fees involved, what benefits might a firm derive from entering into management contracts overseas?

References

Anderson, E. and Gatignon, H. (1986) 'Modes of foreign entry: a transaction cost and analysis and propositions', *Journal of International Business Studies*, Fall, pp. 1–26.

Bleeke, J. and Ernst, D. (1994) *Collaborating to Compete: Using Strategic Alliances and Acquisitions in the Global Marketplace*. John Wiley, New York.

Bradley, F. (1995) *International Marketing Strategy*, 2nd edn. Prentice Hall, Hemel Hempstead.

Carstairs, R.T. and Welch, L.S. (1981) *A Study of Outward Foreign Licensing of Technology by Australian Companies*. Licensing Executives Society of Australia, Canberra.

Davis, L. (2008) 'Licensing strategies of the new intellectual property vendors', *California Management Review*, 50(2), pp. 6–30.

Doherty, A.M. and Alexander, N. (2006) 'Power and control in international retail franchising', *European Journal of Management*, 40(11/12), pp. 1292–1316.

Geringer, J.M. and Hebert, L. (1991), 'Measuring performance of international joint ventures', *Journal of International Business Studies*, 22, pp. 249–263.

Harrigan, K.R. (1985) *Strategies for Joint Ventures*. Lexington Books and D.C. Heath, Lexington, MA.

Hennert, J.-F., Zeng, M. (2005) 'Structural determinants of joint venture performance', *European Management Review*, 2, pp. 105–115.

Lorange, P. and Roos, J. (1995) *Strategiske allianser i globale strategier*. Norges Eksportråd, Oslo.

Lowe, J. and Crawford, N. (1984) *Technology Licensing and the Small Firm*. Gower, Aldershot.

Luostarinen, R. and Welch, L. (1990) *International Business Operations*. Helsinki School of Economics, Helsinki.

Nanda, A. and Williamson, P.J. (1995) 'Use joint ventures to ease the pain of restructuring', *Harvard Business Review*, November–December, pp. 119–128.

Paliwoda, S. (1993) *International Marketing*. Heinemann, Oxford.

Perkins, J.S. (1987) 'How licensing and franchising differ', *Les Nouvelles*, 22(4), pp. 155–158.

Porter, M.E. and Fuller, M.B. (1986) 'Coalition and global strategy', in Porter, M.E. (ed.), *Competition in Global Strategies*, Harvard Business School Press, Boston, MA, pp. 315–344.

Vaidya, S. (2009) 'International joint ventures: an integrated framework', *Competitiveness Review: An International Business Journal*, 19(1), pp. 8–16.

Walmsley, J. (1982) *Handbook of International Joint Ventures*. Graham & Trotman Ltd, London.

Welsh, D.H.B., Alon, I. and Falbe, C.M. (2006) 'An examination of international retail franchising in emerging markets', *Journal of Small Business Management*, 44(1), pp. 130–149.

Young, S., Hamill, J., Wheeler, S. and Davies, J.R. (1989) *International Market Entry and Development*. Harvester Wheatsheaf/Prentice Hall, Hemel Hempstead.

CHAPTER 12
Hierarchical modes

Contents

Case studies

Learning objectives

After studying this chapter you should be able to:

- Describe the main hierarchical modes:
  - domestic-based representatives
  - resident sales representatives
  - foreign sales subsidiary
  - sales and production subsidiary and
  - region centres.
- Compare and contrast the two investment alternatives: acquisition versus greenfield.
- Explain the different determinants that influence the decision to withdraw investments from a foreign market.

12.1 Introduction

Hierarchical mode
The firm owns and controls the foreign entry mode/organization.

The final group of entry modes is the **hierarchical mode**, where the firm completely owns and controls the foreign entry mode. Here it is a question of where the control in the firm lies. The degree of control that head office can exert on the subsidiary will depend on how many and which value chain functions can be transferred to the market. This again depends on the allocation of responsibility and competence between head office and the subsidiary, and how the firm wants to develop this on an international level. An organization that is not wholly owned (i.e. 100 per cent) will here be viewed as an export mode or an intermediate mode. The following example, though, may suggest some of the problems involved in this sharp division: a majority-owned (e.g. 75 per cent) joint venture is, according to definition, an intermediate mode, but in practice a firm with 75 per cent will generally have nearly full control, similar to a hierarchical mode.

If a producer wants greater influence and control over local marketing than export modes can give it is natural to consider creating their own companies in the foreign markets. However, this shift involves an investment, except in the case of the firm having its own sales force, which is considered an operating cost (see Figure 12.1).

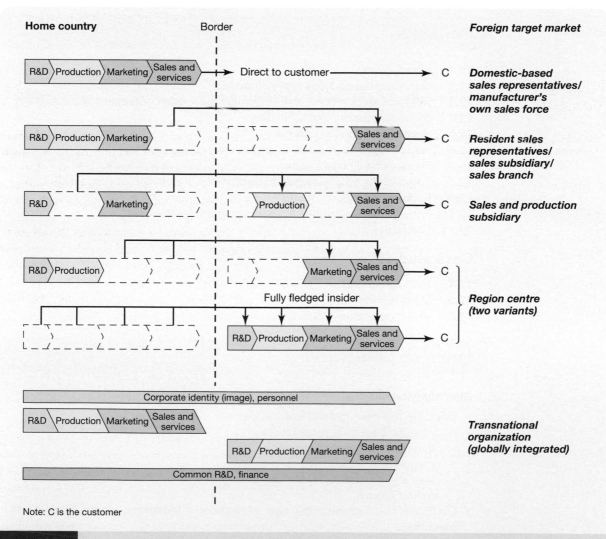

Note: C is the customer

| Figure 12.1 | Hierarchical modes in a value chain perspective |

As a firm goes through Figure 12.1 it chooses to decentralize more and more of its activities to the main foreign markets. In other words, it transfers the responsibility of performing the value chain functions to the local management in the different countries. While moving through Figure 12.1 the firm also goes from one internationalization stage to another (Perlmutter, 1969):

- *Ethnocentric orientation*, represented by the domestic-based sales representatives. This orientation represents an extension of the marketing methods used in the home country to foreign markets.
- *Polycentric orientation*, represented by country subsidiaries. This orientation is based on the assumption that markets/countries around the world are so different that the only way to succeed internationally is to manage each country as a separate market with its own subsidiary and adapted marketing mix.
- *Regiocentric orientation*, represented by a region of the world (section 12.6).
- *Geocentric orientation*, represented by the transnational organization. This orientation is based on the assumption that the markets around the world consist of similarities and differences and that it is possible to create a transnational strategy which takes advantage of the similarities between the markets by using synergy effects to leverage learning on a worldwide basis.

The following description and discussion concerning hierarchical modes takes Figure 12.1 as its starting point.

12.2 Domestic-based sales representatives

Domestic-based sales representative
The sales representative resides in the home country of the manufacturer and travels abroad to perform the sales function.

A **domestic-based sales representative** is one who resides in one country, often the home country of the employer, and travels abroad to perform the sales function. As the sales representative is a company employee better control of sales activities can be achieved than with independent intermediaries. Whereas a company has no control over the attention that an agent or distributor gives to its products or the amount of market feedback provided, it can insist that various activities be performed by its sales representatives.

The use of company employees also shows a commitment to the customer that the use of agents or distributors may lack. Consequently they are often used in industrial markets, where there are only a few large customers that require close contact with suppliers, and where the size of orders justifies the expense of foreign travel. This method of market entry is also found when selling to government buyers and retail chains, for similar reasons.

12.3 Resident sales representatives/foreign sales branch/foreign sales subsidiary

In all these cases the actual performance of the sales function is transferred to the foreign market. These three options all display a greater customer commitment than using domestic-based sales representatives. In making the decision whether to use travelling domestic-based representatives or resident sales representatives in any particular foreign market a firm should consider the following:

- *Order making or order taking*. If the firm finds that the type of sales job it needs done in a foreign market tends towards order taking it will probably choose a travelling domestic-based sales representative, and vice versa.

- *The nature of the product.* If the product is technical and complex in nature and a lot of servicing/supply of parts is required the travelling salesperson is not an efficient entry method. A more permanent foreign base is needed.

Sometimes firms find it relevant to establish a formal branch office, to which a resident salesperson is assigned. A **foreign branch** is an extension and a legal part of the firm. A foreign branch also often employs nationals of the country in which it is located as salespeople. If foreign market sales develop in a positive direction the firm (at a certain point) may consider establishing a wholly owned sales subsidiary. A foreign **subsidiary** is a local company owned and operated by a foreign company under the laws of the host country.

The sales subsidiary provides complete control of the sales function. The firm will often keep a central marketing function at its home base, but sometimes a local marketing function can be included in the sales subsidiary. When the sales function is organized as a sales subsidiary (or when sales activities are performed) all foreign orders are channelled through the subsidiary, which then sells to foreign buyers at normal wholesale or retail prices. The foreign sales subsidiary purchases the products to be sold from the parent company at a price. This, of course, creates the problem of intra-company transfer pricing. In Chapter 16 this problem will be discussed in further detail.

One of the major reasons for choosing sales subsidiaries is the possibility of transferring greater autonomy and responsibility to these subunits, being close to the customer. However, another reason for establishing sales subsidiaries may be the tax advantage. This is particularly important for companies headquartered in high-tax countries. With proper planning companies can establish subsidiaries in countries with low business income taxes and gain an advantage by not paying taxes in their home country on the foreign-generated income until such income is actually repatriated to them. Of course the precise tax advantages that are possible with such subsidiaries depend upon the tax laws in the home country compared to the host country.

One of the most interesting things to determine for a firm doing business in a foreign market is when to switch from an agent to having its own sales subsidiary and own sales force (Ross *et al.*, 2005). Figure 12.2 shows the total sales and marketing costs associated with using two different entry modes:

Foreign branch
An extension of and a legal part of the manufacturer (often called a sales office). Taxation of profits takes place in the manufacturer's country.

Subsidiary
A local company owned and operated by a foreign company under the laws and taxation of the host country.

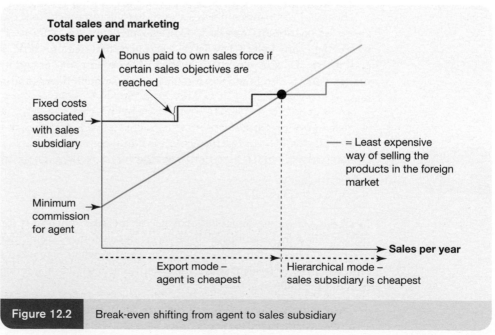

| **Figure 12.2** | Break-even shifting from agent to sales subsidiary |

Source: Hollensen, S. (2008) *Essentials of Global Marketing*, FT/Prentice Hall, p. 245.

1. *Agent*: this curve is based on a contract where the agents get a minimum annual commission independent of annual sales. The agents will get the same percentage in commission independent of how much they generate in annual sales.
2. *Sales subsidiary*: this curve is based on the assumption that the sales force in the sales subsidiary will have a fixed salary per annum (independent of the annual sales), but will be paid an extra bonus if they fulfil certain sales objectives.

Under these circumstances there will be a certain break-even point where it is more advantageous (from a financial standpoint) to switch from an agent to own sales subsidiary. Of course other issues, such as control, flexibility and level of investment must be considered before making such a switch.

<table>
<tr><td>**12.4**</td><td>## Sales and production subsidiary</td></tr>
</table>

Sales subsidiaries may be perceived as taking money out of the country and contributing nothing of value to the host country in which they are based, especially in developing countries. In those countries a sales subsidiary will generally not be in existence long before there are local demands for a manufacturing or production base.

Generally, if the company believes that its products have long-term market potential in a country that is relatively stable politically, then only full ownership of sales and production will provide the level of control necessary to meet the firm's strategic objectives fully. However, this entry mode requires great investment in terms of management time, commitment and money. There are considerable risks, too, as subsequent withdrawal from the market can be extremely costly – not simply in terms of financial outlay but also in terms of reputation in the international and domestic market, particularly with customers and staff.

Japanese companies have used this strategy to build a powerful presence in international markets over a long period of time. Their patience has been rewarded with high market shares and substantial profits, but this has not been achieved overnight. They have sometimes spent more than five years gaining an understanding of markets, customers and competition, as well as selecting locations for manufacturing, before making a significant move.

The main reasons for establishing some kind of local production are:

- *To defend existing business.* Japanese car imports to Europe were subject to restrictions, and as their sales increased so they became more vulnerable. With the development of the single European market Nissan and Toyota set up operations in the UK.
- *To gain new business.* Local production demonstrates strong commitment and is the best way to persuade customers to change suppliers, particularly in the industrial markets where service and reliability are often the main factors when making purchasing decisions.
- *To save costs.* By locating production facilities overseas costs can be saved in a variety of areas such as labour, raw materials and transport.
- *To avoid government restrictions* that might be in force to restrict imports of certain goods.

Assembly operations

An assembly operation is a variation of the production subsidiary. Here a foreign production plant might be set up simply to assemble components manufactured in the domestic market or elsewhere. The firm may try to retain key component manufacture in the domestic plant, allowing development, production skills and investment to be concentrated, and maintaining the benefit from economies of scale. Some parts or components may be produced in various countries (multi-sourcing) in order to gain each country's comparative advantage. Capital-intensive parts may be produced in advanced nations, and labour-intensive assemblies may be produced in a less developed country, where labour is abundant and labour costs are low.

This strategy is common among manufacturers of consumer electronics. When a product becomes mature and faces intense price competition it may be necessary to shift all of the labour-intensive operations to LDCs. This is the principle behind the international product life cycle (IPLC): see also Chapter 14 (Figure 14.8).

12.5 Subsidiary growth strategies

As multinational corporations (MNCs) face ever greater competition, their subsidiaries located in developed countries are increasingly vulnerable to being closed and having their operations relocated to low-cost Eastern bloc and Asian nations. To cope with this cost differential, subsidiary managers are constantly urged to contribute beyond their core mandate, to move their subsidiary's activities up the value chain and to be innovative and entrepreneurial.

Scott and Gibbons (2009) suggest that the subsidiaries are employing four mutually reinforcing strategies to enhance their position:

1. *Seizing the initiative and growing the subsidiary autonomy*: many subsidiaries are restrained from extending their original charter and must act within well-defined limits laid down by headquarters. Headquarters management is the ultimate decision-maker on the subsidiary's future and the role of subsidiary management is to work within the system to influence their decisions. The key to growing a subsidiary's autonomy is to actively manage its relationship with headquarters and to ensure the 'right' impression of the subsidiary is given. The subsidiary management can develop this HQ confidence in a subsidiary's management skills by proactively involving headquarters in non-routine events, demonstrating the subsidiary's openness and alignment with organizational goals. Greater headquarters confidence in subsidiary management's judgements leads to greater autonomy, allowing a subsidiary freedom to act on opportunities. Subsidiary management should also be able to identify key decision-makers at all levels in HQ and in this way develop a network of relationships with these HQ personnel, which then can endorse the subsidiary's credibility within the organization, and provide support when the subsidiary is seeking additional investment for further expansion.

2. *Building information networks to external partners*: many production subsidiaries are operating within a small indigenous market selling all of their products/services within their MNC organizational structure, often at artificial transfer prices. This removes the subsidiary from the final customer, resulting in a vacuum – artificially sheltering subsidiary management and staff from the direct relationship between costs and bottom line profitability. It also leads to an absence of real market response, and inhibits market initiative and innovation, cutting off the potential to develop and drive the next generation of products. To protect itself from this state of vacuum the subsidiary should recognize the need to build external links to customers, suppliers, industry members and third-level institutions. This would enable the subsidiary to know its local markets and to anticipate not just the requirements of lead users but also to seek new perspectives on the future. In addition, they need to exploit their membership of a common community of subsidiaries within the MNC. Communicating and interacting with dispersed subsidiaries provides access to a network of knowledge and opportunities denied to indigenous competitors. For example developing an external customer base drives down costs, increases subsidiary agility and reduces isolation from market dynamics. If the local market is too small, a strategy would be to develop new international markets for the subsidiary's product by identifying markets and market segments not currently addressed by the parent organization and then modify the product offering to address these market needs.

3. *Creating a climate for entrepreneurship*: subsidiaries should create a climate which encourages risk-taking. This is critical if employees are to act entrepreneurially. Accept that taking risks increases the risk of failure and that punishing failure inhibits risk-taking.

There is a need to celebrate the value of well-considered subsidiary innovations. The subsidiary management could define a structure of mentors and champions of innovation that will support individual entrepreneurial efforts. This would send a clear message of the subsidiary's commitment to risk-taking and innovation. Management rewards and sanctions traditionally focus on measures of short-term, largely financial, performance. This can shift management attention from achieving long-term strategic performance to avoiding short-term risk-taking. Integrating measures of longer term objectives within short-term goals and including non-financial measures of performance will promote management efforts at building a sustainable future, such as directing resources at identified market opportunities.

4. *Promoting subsidiary strategy development*: the traditional perspective that subsidiaries just accept their assigned role from headquarters has shifted and most subsidiaries now actively engage in subsidiary strategy development, in addition to their involvement in overall MNC strategy. The subsidiary strategy development processes comprises of setting targets and identifying ways of increasing headquarters investment in their operation. A subsidiary needs to be constantly seeking an edge, an advantage that will secure its place within the group so that its existence will not rely on being the low-cost producer. Subsidiary strategy development encompasses anticipating the MNCs future expansion needs and initiating campaigns to win future investment in advance of the 'competing' sister subsidiaries. Often, investment decisions are made off stage before the issue arrives at board level, so there is a need to position for the investment in advance by utilizing a network of relationships at headquarters, particularly the identified key decision-makers. The subsidiary CEO must be the driver of the subsidiary's strategy development process, with ultimate responsibility for both the subsidiary's survival and for achieving its role as defined by the MNC.

Due to continuing globalization of systems and processes, there are increasing restrictions (from the HQ) on the ability of subsidiaries to develop a unique position to ensure their survival and growth. In this process the subsidiary must clearly define its boundaries, as there are activities that it may not be cost-effective or strategically beneficial to pursue. However, the subsidiary CEO must identify the value-added business that will generate strong returns and then bring the problem and its solution to HQ rather than waiting for it to take the initiative. As suggested above there are many ways that a subsidiary can make itself more valued by its parent company (HQ).

12.6   Region centres (regional headquarters)

Until now choice of foreign entry mode has mainly been discussed in relation to one particular country. If we suspend this condition, we consider option 3 in Figure 12.3, where 'geographically focused start-up' is an attempt to serve the specialized needs of a particular region of the world. It is very difficult for competitors to imitate a successful coordination of value chain activities in a particular region, as it involves tacit knowledge and is socially complex.

The world is increasingly being regionalized through the formation of such groupings as the European Union, the North American Free Trade Area (NAFTA) and the Association of South East Asian Nations (ASEAN).

Region centres
The regional HQ ('lead country') will usually play the role of coordinating and stimulating sales in the whole region.

In Figure 12.1 two examples of **region centres** are shown. The first variant shows that the downstream functions have been transferred to the region. In the second variant even greater commitment is shown to the region because here all the value chain activities are moved to the region, whereby the firm has become a fully fledged insider in the region. At this stage the firm has all the necessary functions in the region to compete effectively against local and regional competitors. At the same time, the firm can respond to regional customer needs. This situation is also illustrated in the lower part of Figure 12.3, where many activities are coordinated across countries.

		Number of countries involved	
		Few	*Many*
Coordination of value chain activities	*Few activities coordinated across countries (primarily logistics)*	New international market makers	
		Export/import start-up ①	Multinational trader ②
	Many activities coordinated across countries	Geographically focused start-up	Global start-up

<small>③ ④</small>

Figure 12.3 Types of international new venture

Source: reprinted by permission from Macmillan Publishers Ltd: *Journal of International Business Studies*, Vol. 25, No. 1, pp. 45–64, Toward a theory of international new ventures, by Oviatt, B. M. and McDougall, P. P., copyright 1994, published by Palgrave Macmillan.

Formation of region centres implies creation of a regional headquarters or appointment of a 'lead country', which will usually play the role of coordinator and stimulator with reference to a single homogeneous product group (see Figure 12.4).

The coordination role consists of ensuring three things:

1. Country and business strategies are mutually coherent.
2. One subsidiary does not harm another.
3. Adequate synergies are fully identified and exploited across business and countries.

The stimulator role consists of two functions:

1. facilitating the translation of 'global' products into local country strategies
2. supporting local subsidiaries in their development (Lasserre, 1996).

Figure 12.4 (an example of a multinational company having its head office in Germany) shows that different countries/subsidiaries can have a leading function for different product groups. In the diagram there is a world market such that for products A and E only one country/subsidiary has the coordination function on a global basis (France and the United Kingdom, respectively). For product D there are three regions with a lead country in each region.

The choice of a lead country is influenced by several factors:

- the marketing competences of the foreign subsidiaries
- the quality of human resources in the countries represented
- the strategic importance of the countries represented
- location of production
- legal restrictions of host countries.

The country with the best 'leading' competences should be chosen for the job as lead country.

12.7 Transnational organization

In this final stage of internationalization companies attempt to coordinate and integrate operations across national boundaries so as to achieve potential synergies on a global scale. Management views the world as a series of interrelated markets. At this stage the employees tend to identify more strongly with their company than with the country in which they operate.

	Product A	Product B	Product C	Product D	Product E
Head office Germany	○	LC	○	○	○
Subsidiary France	LC	○	○	LC	○
Subsidiary UK	○	□	○	○	LC
Subsidiary Italy	○	○	LC	○	○
Subsidiary US	○	○	LC	LC	□
Subsidiary Canada	○	LC	○	□	○
Subsidiary Brazil	□	□	○	○	○
Subsidiary Japan	○	○	○	LC	○
Subsidiary Singapore	○	□	○	○	○

LC Lead country   Area of lead function
○ Product introduced
▨ Product not yet introduced
□ Execution of a country-oriented approach

| **Figure 12.4** | The lead country concept |

Source: Raffée and Kreutzer (1989). Published with permission of Emerald Publishing Ltd; www.emeraldinsight.com.

Transnational organization
Integration and coordination of operations (R&D, production, marketing, and sales and services) across national boundaries in order to achieve synergies on a global scale.

Common R&D and frequent geographical exchange of human resources across borders are among the characteristics of a **transnational organization**. Its overall goal will be to achieve global competitiveness through recognizing cross-border market similarities and differences, and linking the capabilities of the organization across national boundaries. One of the relatively few international companies that have reached this stage is Unilever – see also section 8.5.

In summary, managing a transnational organization requires the sensitivity to understand:

- when a global brand makes sense or when local requirements should take precedence;
- when to transfer innovation and expertise from one market to another;
- when a local idea has global potential;
- when to bring international teams together fast to focus on key opportunities.

12.8 Establishing wholly owned subsidiaries – acquisition or greenfield

All the hierarchical modes presented in this chapter (except domestic-based sales representatives) involve investment in foreign-based facilities. In deciding to establish wholly owned operations in a country a firm can either acquire an existing company or build its own operations from scratch (greenfield investment).

Acquisition

Acquisition enables rapid entry and often provides access to distribution channels, an existing customer base and, in some cases, established brand names or corporate reputations. In some cases, too, existing management remains, providing a bridge to entry into the market and allowing the firm to acquire experience in dealing with the local market environment. This may be particularly advantageous for a firm with limited international management expertise, or little familiarity with the local market.

In saturated markets the industry is highly competitive or there are substantial entry barriers, and therefore there is little room for a new entrant. In these circumstances acquisitions may be the only feasible way of establishing a base in the host country.

Acquisitions take many forms. According to Root (1987) acquisition may be horizontal (the product lines and markets of the acquired and acquiring firms are similar), vertical (the acquired firm becomes supplier or customer of the acquiring firm), concentric (the acquired firm has the same market but different technology, or the same technology but different markets) or conglomerate (the acquired firm is in a different industry from that of the acquiring firm). No matter what form the acquisition takes, coordination and styles of management between the foreign investor and the local management team may cause problems.

Greenfield investment

The difficulties encountered with acquisitions may lead firms to prefer to establish operations from the ground up, especially where production logistics is a key industry success factor, and where no appropriate acquisition targets are available or they are too costly.

The ability to integrate operations across countries, and to determine the direction of future international expansion, is often a key motivation to establish wholly owned operations, even though it takes longer to build plants than to acquire them. Further motives for greenfield investment can also include incentives offered by the host country.

Furthermore, if the firm builds a new plant, it can not only incorporate the latest technology and equipment, but also avoid the problems of trying to change the traditional practices of an established concern. A new facility means a fresh start and an opportunity for the international company to shape the local firm into its own image and requirements.

12.9 Location/relocation of HQ

The starting point is to consider the traditional checklist of HQ site selection criteria (Baaij *et al.* 2005):

- corporate tax advantages
- investment incentives
- investment climate
- company law (internal restriction – the owners' wishes have to be followed)
- operational costs
- quality, availability and costs of the workforce
- quality of living (major hotels and restaurants, proximity of quality housing, cultural life and recreation, quality of schools, cultural diversity, safety, crime and health factors, personal taxes, cost of living, etc.)
- level of infrastructure (in particular transportation, communication and IT)
- extent of high-level business services (e.g. accounting, legal and management consulting)
- sufficient representative office space
- the presence of other major corporations.

The main benefit of using this checklist is not to find suitable sites, but to eliminate unsuitable ones. Once these factors have been assessed, more strategic criteria for the right HQ location can be considered.

There are three strategic motives that can affect the HQ location decision:

1. mergers and acquisitions
2. internationalization of leadership and ownership
3. strategic renewal.

Mergers and acquisitions

When companies of equal size merge, they need to find a neutral location for the headquarters of the merged corporation. In 1987, ASEA from Västerås in Sweden and BBC Brown Boveri of Baden, Switzerland merged to create ABB Asea Brown Boveri. The new headquarters were not situated in either original location, but in Zurich.

Internationalization of leadership and ownership

In the case of acquisitions, the obvious solution is the most effective – the new headquarters is that of the acquirer, and the acquired corporation relocates (e.g. DaimlerChrysler). The second motive – internationalization of leadership and ownership – makes corporations less sensitive to national sentiments or ties to a specific country. Foreign board executives and shareholders will be less attached to the traditional home country, and less likely to resist a cross-border relocation of the headquarters.

Strategic renewal

The final reason for relocating headquarters is strategic renewal. This was a key reason for Philips Electronics' relocation to Amsterdam after 106 years of emotional ties to Eindhoven, the town where Philips was founded. Relocation can be a mechanism of change because it symbolizes a fresh start and a break with the past.

12.10   Foreign divestment: withdrawing from a foreign market

While a vast theoretical and empirical literature has examined the determinants of entering into foreign direct investments, considerably less attention has been given to the decision to exit from a foreign market.

Most of the studies undertaken show a considerable 'loss' of foreign subsidiaries over time:

- Between 1967 and 1975 the 180 largest US-based multinationals added some 4,700 subsidiaries to their networks, but more than 2,400 affiliates were divested during the same period (Boddewyn, 1979).
- Out of 225 FDIs undertaken by large Dutch multinationals in the period 1966–88, only just over half were still in existence in 1988 (Barkema et al., 1996).

Closing down a foreign subsidiary or selling it off to another firm is a strategic decision, and the consequence may be a change of foreign entry mode (e.g. from a local sales and production subsidiary to an export mode or a joint venture), or a complete withdrawal from a host country.

The most obvious incentive to exit is profits that are too low, which in turn may be due to high costs, permanent decreases in local market demand or the entry into the industry of more efficient competitors. Besides being voluntary, the divestment may also be a result of expropriation or nationalization in the foreign country.

In order to investigate further the question of why foreign divestments take place it is necessary to look at the specific factors that may influence incentives and barriers to exit, and

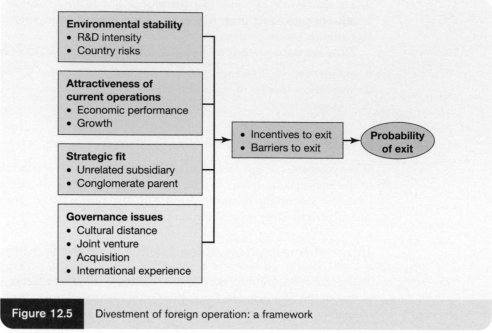

Figure 12.5 Divestment of foreign operation: a framework

Source: Benito (1996, Figure 2).

thereby the probability of exiting from a foreign subsidiary. Benito (1996) classifies the specific factors into four main groups (Figure 12.5).

Environmental stability

This is a question of the predictability of the environment – competitively and politically – in which the foreign subsidiary operates:

- *R&D intensity.* Perceived barriers to exit are likely to increase due to large market-specific investments made in R&D and the marketing of the products.
- *Country risks.* These risks are typically outside the firm's scope of control. Political risks may often lead to forced divestment, with the result that expropriation takes place.

Attractiveness of current operations

- *Economic performance.* Unsatisfactory economic performance (i.e. inability to produce a net contribution to overall profits) is the most obvious reason why particular subsidiaries are sold off or shut down. On the other hand, if the subsidiary is a good economic performer, the owners may see an opportunity to obtain a good price for the unit while it is performing well.
- *Growth.* Economic growth in the host country would normally make FDI even more attractive, thereby increasing the barriers to exit from such a country. However, the attractiveness of the location would make such operations more likely targets for takeovers by other investors.

Strategic fit

Unrelated expansion (i.e. diversification) increases the governance cost of the business, and economies of scale and scope are also rarely achieved by unrelated subsidiaries. Hence these factors increase the incentives to exit.

The same arguments apply to a conglomerate parent.

EXHIBIT 12.1 Wal-Mart's withdrawal from the German market

Wal-Mart (www.walmartstores.com) was founded by Sam Walton in 1962, with the opening of the first Wal-Mart discount store. Today there are more than 8,100 retail stores under 55 different store brands in 16 countries (Argentina, Brazil, Canada, Chile, China, Costa Rica, El Salvador, Guatemala, Honduras, India, Japan, Mexico, Nicaragua, Puerto Rico, United Kingdom and the United States). With fiscal year 2009 sales of US$401 billion (only 20 per cent outside USA), Wal-Mart employs more than 2.1 million associates world-wide. Wal-Mart had high hopes for Germany (the world's third-largest retail market after the US and Japan) when it entered the market in 1997 by acquiring Wertkauf GmbH with its 21 hypermarkets. One year later Wal-Mart aquired a further 74 Interspar stores of Spar AG.

However, nine years later Wal-Mart had to withdraw from the German market. What happened? There are several explanation for this withdrawal:

1. Wal-Mart appointed a CEO for Germany who spoke no German. Not only that, he insisted that his managers work in English. The next CEO, an Englishman, tried to run the show from England. The men at the top misunderstood both the employees and the customers. Other surprises for Wal-Mart were Germany's short shopping hours, including almost no Sunday trading. Wal-Mart Germany felt frustration with German shopping regulations – the feared *Ladenschlussgesetz* which regulates store opening times – and restrictions on discounting.

2. Wal-Mart's American managers pressured German executives to enforce American-style management practices in the workplace. Employees were forbidden, for instance, from dating colleagues in positions of influence. Workers were also told not to flirt with one another.

3. The German Wal-Mart management threatened to close certain stores if staff did not agree to work longer hours than their contracts foresaw and did not permit video surveillance of their work. As a consequence Wal-Mart Germany had several conflicts with the trade union.

4. Some cultural misunderstandings: German Wal-Mart shoppers didn't like having their purchases bagged by others and German shoppers like to hunt for bargains on their own, without smiling assistants at their elbows.

5. Some of the American products did not fit into the German homes: for example, American pillowcases are a different size than German. As a consequence Wal-Mart Germany ended up with a huge stock of pillow-cases that they could not sell to German customers.

6. Wal Mart did not reach 'critical mass' in Germany. Its infrastructure in Germany, which involved two head-quarters (for a while) and three logistics centres, piled up costs without achieving economies of scale. With its relatively low number of stores it reached only 2 per cent of the German food market. It was up against fierce competition from Aldi and Lidl, two German discount chains. For example, Aldi had a network of 4,000 stores, compared to Wal-Mart's approximately 100 stores.

After nine years of trying to make a go of it, in July 2006 Wal-Mart sold its 85 stores to German rival Metro.

Wal-Mart's attempt to apply the company's proven US success formula in an unmodified manner to the German market turned out to be a fiasco. This case shows how important is is to address cultural differences when setting up international operations.

Sources: *The Economist* 'After struggling for years, Wal-Mart withdraws from Germany', US Edition, 5 August, 2006; *The Independent* 'Mighty Wal-Mart admits defeat in Germany', 29 July 2006, London; www.walmartstores.com.

Governance issues

● *Cultural distance.* Closeness between home country and host countries results in easier monitoring and coordination of production and marketing activities in the various locations. Thus culturally close countries increase the barriers to exit and vice versa.

- *Joint venture and acquisition.* A joint venture with a local partner can certainly reduce barriers to the penetration of a foreign market by giving rapid access to knowledge about the local market. On the other hand, whenever a joint venture is set up with a foreign partner, both different national and corporate cultures may have an impact on its success. Joint ventures and acquisitions are put in a difficult situation in the often critical initial phases of the integration process. Thus a lack of commitment in the parent company or companies may increase the incentive to exit.
- *Experience.* Firms learn from experience how to operate in the foreign environment, and how to search for solutions to problems that emerge. As experience is accumulated it becomes easier to avoid many of the problems involved in running foreign subsidiaries and to find workable solutions if problems should arise. This also includes the unpleasant decision to close down a subsidiary.

12.11 Summary

The advantages and disadvantages of the different hierarchical entry modes are summarized in Table 12.1.

Furthermore, this chapter discussed under what circumstances foreign divestment is likely to take place. The most obvious reason to exit from a market seems to be low profits earned in the market.

Table 12.1	Advantages and disadvantages of different hierarchical entry modes	
Hierarchical entry mode	**Advantages**	**Disadvantages**
Domestic-based sales representatives	Better control of sales activities compared to independent intermediaries. Close contact with large customers in foreign markets close to home country.	High travel expenses. Too expensive in foreign markets, far away from home country.
Foreign sales, branch/sales and production subsidiary	Full control of operation. Eliminates the possibility that a national partner gets a 'free ride'. Market access (sales subsidiary). Acquire market knowledge directly (sales subsidiary). Reduce transport costs (production subsidiary). Elimination of duties (production subsidiary). Access to raw materials and labour (production subsidiary).	High initial capital investment required (subsidiary). Loss of flexibility. High-risk (market, political and economic). Taxation problems.
Region centres/ transnational organization	Achieves potential synergies on a regional/global scale. Regional/global scale efficiency. Leverage learning on a cross-national basis. Resources and people are flexible and can be put into operating units around the world	Possible threats: ● increasing bureaucracy ● limited national-level responsiveness and flexibility. A national manager can feel they have no influence. Missing communication between head office and region centres.

Table 12.1	*Continued*	
Hierarchical entry mode	**Advantages**	**Disadvantages**
Acquisition	Rapid entry to new markets. Gaining quick access to: • distribution channels • a qualified labour force • existing management experience • local knowledge • contacts with local market and government • established brand names/reputation.	Usually an expensive option. High-risk (taking over companies that are regarded as part of a country's heritage can raise considerable national resentment if it seems that they are being taken over by foreign interests). Possible threats: • lack of integration with existing operation; • communication and coordination problems between acquired firm and acquirer.
Greenfield investment	Possible to build in an 'optimum' format, i.e. in a way that fits the interests of the firm (e.g. integrating production with home base production). Possible to integrate state-of-the-art technology (resulting in increased operational efficiency).	High investment cost. Slow entry of new markets (time-consuming process).

CASE STUDY 12.1

Polo Ralph Lauren: Polo moves distribution for South East Asia in-house

Polo Ralph Lauren Corporation, founded in 1967 by Ralph Lauren, is a leader in the design, marketing and distribution of premium lifestyle products, including men's, women's and children's apparel, accessories, fragrances and home furnishings.

Total net revenue in 2009 was US$5 billion and net profits were US$595 million.

From 2007–09 the net revenues have developed as shown in Table 1.

Table 1	Polo Ralph Lauren's net revenues in different regions 2007–9		
Net revenues	**2009 (millions US$)**	**2008 (millions US$)**	**2007 (millions US$)**
USA and Canada	3,589	3,653	3,452
Europe	1,028	945	768
Japan	393	272	65
Other regions (including South East Asia)	9	10	11
Total	**5,019**	**4,880**	**4,295**

Polo Ralph Lauren operates in three distinct but integrated segments:

1. **Wholesale**. The wholesale business (representing approximately 57 per cent of 2009 net revenues) consists of wholesale-channel sales made principally to major department stores, specialty stores and golf and pro shops located throughout the US, Europe and Asia. The number of shops, where Polo Ralph Lauren is represented by wholesalers, is approximately 6,097.

2. **Retail.** The retail business (representing approximately 39 per cent of 2009 net revenues) consists of retail-channel sales directly to consumers through full-price and factory retail stores located throughout the US, Canada, Europe, South America and Asia, and through the retail internet sites located at www.RalphLauren.com and www.Rugby.com. Polo Ralph Lauren has 163 own full-price retail stores and 163 own factory stores worldwide, totalling approximately 2.5 million square feet.

3. **Licensing**. Licensing business (representing approximately 4 per cent of 2009 net revenues) consists of royalty-based arrangements under which they license the right to third parties to use the various trademarks in connection with the manufacture and sale of designated products, such as apparel, eyewear and fragrances, in specified geographical areas for specified periods.

RalphLauren.com offers the customers access to the full breadth of Ralph Lauren apparel, accessories and home products, allows them to reach retail customers on a multi-channel basis and reinforces the luxury image of the brands. RalphLauren.com averaged 2.9 million unique visitors a month and acquired approximately 350,000 new customers, resulting in 1.7 million total customers in 2009.

In August 2008 the company launched Rugby.com, its second e-commerce website. Rugby.com offers clothing and accessories for purchase – previously only available at Rugby stores – along with style tips, unique videos and blog-based content. Rugby.com offers an extensive array of Rugby products for young men and women.

The business is typically affected by seasonal trends, with higher levels of sales resulting primarily from key vacation travel, back-to-school and holiday shopping periods (e.g. Christmas) in the retail segment.

By the end of March, 2009, Polo Ralph Lauren had approximately 17,000 employees, both full and part-time, consisting of approximately 12,000 in the US and approximately 5,000 in foreign countries.

Ralph Lauren Fragrances

Since 1967, the distinctive brand image has been consistently developed across an expanding number of products, price tiers and markets. Reflecting a distinctive American lifestyle under the direction of internationally renowned designer Ralph Lauren, they have a considerable influence on the way people dress and the way that fashion is advertised throughout the world.

Currently the product portfolio consists of four product lines:

1. *Apparel:* products include extensive collections of men's, women's and children's clothing.
2. *Accessories:* products encompass a broad range, including footwear, eyewear, watches, jewellery, hats, belts and leather goods, including handbags and luggage.
3. *Home:* Coordinated products for the home include bedding and bath products, furniture, fabric and wallpaper, paint, tabletop and giftware.
4. *Fragrance*: Fragrance products are sold under our Romance, Polo, Lauren, Safari, Ralph and Black Label brands, among others.

Use of licensing in far distance markets

Polo Ralph Lauren grants their license right to sell at wholesale specified categories of products in far distance markets. These geographic area licensees source products from product licensing partners and independent sources.

Each licensing partner pays Polo Ralph Lauren royalties based upon its sales of their products, generally subject to a minimum royalty requirement for the right to use the company's trademarks and design services. In addition, licensing partners may be required to allocate a portion of their revenues to advertise the products and share in the creative costs associated with these products. Larger allocations are required in connection with launches of new products or in new territories. The licenses generally have three to five-year terms and may grant the licensee conditional renewal options.

Polo Ralph Lauren works closely with their licensing partners to ensure that their products are developed, marketed and distributed so as to reach the intended market opportunity and to present consistently to consumers worldwide the distinctive perspective and lifestyle associated with their brands. Many aspects of the packaging, merchandising, distribution, advertising and promotion of the products are subject to continuing oversight by Polo

Ralph Lauren. The result is hopefully a consistent identity for Ralph Lauren products across product categories and international markets.

At the moment Polo Ralph Lauren has four licensing partners, covering the following geographical areas:

1. Oroton Group/PRL Australia: Australia and New Zealand
2. Doosan Corporation: Korea
3. P.R.L. Enterprises, S.A.: Panama, Aruba, Curacao, The Cayman Islands, Costa Rica, Nicaragua, Honduras, El Salvador, Guatemala, Belize, Colombia, Ecuador, Bolivia, Peru, Antigua, Barbados, Bonaire, Dominican Republic, St Lucia, St Martin, Trinidad and Tobago
4. Dickson Concepts: Hong Kong, China, Philippines, Malaysia, Singapore, Taiwan, Thailand and Indonesia

Typically, the international licensing partners acquire the right to sell, promote, market and/or distribute various categories of the Polo Ralph Lauren products in a given geographic area.

Shift from licensing to hierarchical mode in South East Asia

In February 2009, Polo Ralph Lauren entered into an agreement with Dickson Concepts (based in Hong Kong) to assume direct control of its Polo-branded licensed apparel businesses in South East Asia effective 1 January 2010 in exchange for a payment of US$20 million and certain other consideration. Until 1 January 2010 Dickson had the company's licensee for Polo-branded apparel in the South East Asia region, which is comprised of China, Hong Kong, Indonesia, Malaysia, the Philippines, Singapore, Taiwan and Thailand. In South East Asia, Dickson Concepts sold Polo merchandise through approximately 40 free-standing stores and nearly 100 shop-in-shops.

QUESTIONS

1. What may be the main motives for Polo Ralph Lauren to shift the entry mode from licensing to hierarchical mode in South East Asia?

2. Would you recommend them to take all geographical licenses back in-house, and turn them into hierarchical modes? If not, why?

Sources: Karmizadeh, M. (2009) 'Polo will move distribution for Southeast Asia in-house', *Women's Wear Daily*, 17 February 2009, 197(35), p. 10; www.ralphlauren.com, especially Annual Report 2009.

CASE STUDY 12.2

Durex condoms: SSL will sell Durex condoms in the Japanese market through its own organization

Durex condoms will go on sale in Japan for the first time after SSL International, the manufacturer and distributor of health care products, announced it is to expand its operation in the country. SSL International was formed in June 1999 by the merger of Seton Scholl Health Care with LIG (London International Group). Durex is the most sold condom brand in the world, available in more than 140 countries, and with approximately 22 per cent of the global branded condom market. The Durex brand name was registered in 1929, with the name Durex derived from Durability, Reliability and Excellence.

Generally the SSL managers run a brand-oriented strategy: 'We want Durex to be the Coca-Cola of the condom world.' The move into Japan was made possible by the 1999 merger. Seton Scholl has its own presence in Japan, with marketing and distribution networks set up, whereas LIG did not. Through Seton Scholl Japan it already distributes Scholl products such as shoes and other footwear products throughout the country as well as surgical gloves, which are manufactured by the old LIG company.

SSL has terminated a long-term contract with Okamoto, the largest supplier of condoms in Japan, freeing it to vie for a share of the country's 200 million condom market. The Chief Executive, said, 'It now makes sense for us to take control of our own destiny in Japan.' SSL aims to have won 5 per cent of the market within five years, generating £10 million worth of new revenue. SSL has bought out its partner in Seton Scholl Japan, giving it full control. Iain Carter again: 'We saw more prospect of generating value for shareholders by going it alone in Japan.' He added that Durex was already well known as an international brand in the country.

The Japanese market for condoms is said to be the world's largest, with annual turnover worth about £200 million. It is dominated by Okamoto (42 per cent market share) and other locally produced products. The Japanese market is as large because until June 1999 the contraceptive pill was banned and most people had to rely on condoms for birth control. Experts say that it will still take one or two generations before the pill is widely used in Japan.

One reason it took 40 years for the contraceptive pill to be legalized in Japan was lobbying by condom-makers against its introduction. Japanese health officials said they were concerned that use of the pill, instead of condoms, would spread sexually transmitted diseases. It was even claimed, by other opponents, that the urine of women on the pill would pollute rivers and deform fish.

Sources: Adapted from: *Financial Times* (2000) 'SSL goes it alone in Japan with Durex', 3 February; *New Media Age* (1997) 'Condom brand goes global on web', 1 May.

QUESTIONS

1. What were the main motives for SSL establishing its own distribution channels for condoms in Japan?

2. What are the major barriers to SSL reaching a higher market share for condoms in Japan?

VIDEO CASE STUDY 12.3 Starbucks
download from www.pearsoned.co.uk/hollensen

Starbucks Corporation (www.starbucks.com) is named after the first mate in Herman Melville's *Moby Dick*. It was founded in 1971 in Seattle. The original name of the company was Starbucks Coffee, Tea and Spices, later changed to Starbucks Coffee Company. Starbucks sells more than coffee; it sells the Starbucks experience. Leveraging a strong brand, the company is expanding into new markets at home and abroad. The challenge is to grow while maintaining a consistent, high-quality customer experience.

Questions

1. What could be the main motives for Starbucks in owning most of its coffee houses compared to other entry modes and operation forms?

2. How does Starbucks' entry into the grocery market affect the company's relationships with its retail customers?

3. How did Starbucks make the successful transition from a niche to a mainstream marketer? What can the company do to maintain its 'small company feel' as it expands globally?

For further exercises and cases, see this book's website at **www.pearsoned.co.uk/hollensen**

Questions for discussion

1. By what criteria would you judge a particular foreign direct investment activity to have succeeded or failed?

2. What are a firm's major motives in deciding to establish manufacturing facilities in a foreign country?

3. Is the establishment of wholly owned subsidiaries abroad an appropriate international market development mode for SMEs?

4. What is the idea behind appointing a 'lead country' in a region?

5. Why is acquisition often the preferred way to establish wholly owned operations abroad? What are the limitations of acquisition as an entry method?

6. What are the key problems associated with profit repatriation from subsidiaries?

References

Baaij, J.M., Berghe, D.V.D., Den Bosch, F.A.J. and Volberda, B.W. (2005) 'Rotterdam or anywhere: relocating corporate HQ', *Business Strategy Review*, Summer, pp. 45–48.

Barkema, H.G., Bell, J. and Pennings, J.M. (1996) 'Foreign entry, cultural barriers and learning', *Strategic Management Journal*, 17, pp. 151–166.

Benito, G. (1996) *Why are Subsidiaries Divested? A Conceptual Framework.* Working Paper No. 3–93, Institute of International Economics and Management, Copenhagen Business School.

Boddewyn, J.J. (1979) 'Foreign divestment: magnitude and factors', *Journal of International Business Studies*, 10, pp. 21–27.

Lasserre, P. (1996) 'Regional headquarters: the spearhead for Asian Pacific markets', *Long Range Planning*, 29(1), pp. 30–37.

Oviatt, B.M. and McDougall, P.P. (1994) 'Toward a theory of international new ventures', *Journal of International Business Studies*, 25(1), pp. 45–64.

Perlmutter, H. (1969) 'The torturous evolution of multinational corporations', *Columbia Journal of World Business*, January–February, pp. 9–18.

Raffée, H. and Kreutzer, R. (1989) 'Organizational dimensions of global marketing', *European Journal of Marketing*, 23(5), pp. 43–57.

Ross, W.T., Dalsace, F. and Anderson, E. (2005) 'Should you set up your own sales force or should you outsource it? Pitfalls in the standard analysis, *Business Horizons*, 48, pp. 23–36.

Root, F.R. (1987) *Entry Strategies for International Markets.* Lexington Books, Lexington, MA.

Scott, P.S. and Gibbons, P.T. (2009) 'How subsidiaries are battling to survive and grow', *Strategy and Leadership*, 37(4), pp. 43–47.

CHAPTER 13
International sourcing decisions and the role of the sub-supplier

Contents

Learning objectives

After studying this chapter you should be able to:

- Describe the role of subcontractors in the vertical chain.
- Explore the reasons for international outsourcing.
- Explain the development of a buyer–seller relationship.
- Discuss alternative routes of subcontractor internationalization.
- Explain how turnkey contracts differ from conventional subcontracting.

13.1   Introduction

Recent studies of subcontracting and competitiveness have emphasized the importance of outsourcing: moving functions or activities out of an organization. Outsourcing is often more efficient, except in the case of the firm's core competences, which are considered central to its success. Thus the issue is whether an organization should perform certain functions itself ('make') or source ('buy') these activities from outside. If LSEs outsource an increasing number of value chain functions this provides business opportunities for SMEs as subcontractors to LSEs (main contractors).

A subcontractor can be defined as a person or a firm that agrees to provide semi-finished products or services needed by another party (main contractor) to perform another contract to which the subcontractor is not a party. According to this definition, the characteristics of subcontractors that distinguish them from other SMEs are:

- Subcontractors' products are usually part of the end product, not the complete end product itself.
- Subcontractors do not have direct contact with the end customers, because the main contractor is usually responsible to the customer.

The position of subcontractors in the vertical production chain is shown in Figure 13.1.

OEM
(original equipment manufacturer) the customer of a sub-supplier (e.g. Autoliv in Case study III.3 is a sub-supplier of airbags for their OEMs, the auto manufacturers such as VW or BMW).

In the **OEM** contract (OEM stands for original equipment manufacturer), the contractor is called the OEM or 'sourcer', whereas the parts suppliers are regarded as 'manufacturers' of OEM products (= subcontractors = sub-suppliers). Typically the OEM contracts are different from other buyer–seller relationships because the OEMs (contractors) often have much stronger bargaining power than the subcontractors. However, in a partner-based buyer–seller relationship the power balance will be more equal. There are cases where a subcontractor improved its bargaining position and went on to become a major force in the market (Cho and Chu, 1994).

The structure of the remainder of this chapter is shown in Figure 13.2.

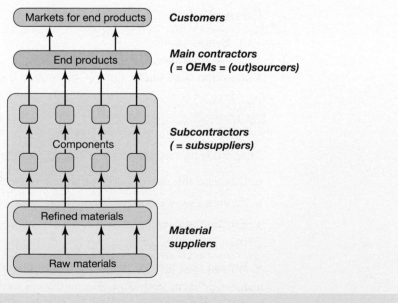

| Figure 13.1 | Subcontractor's position in the vertical chain |

Source: adapted from Lehtinen (1991, p. 22).

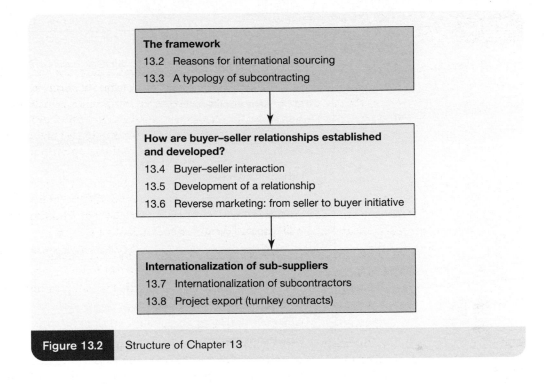

Figure 13.2   Structure of Chapter 13

13.2   Reasons for international sourcing

More and more international firms are buying their parts, semi-finished components and other supplies from international subcontractors. Creating competitiveness through the subcontractor is based on the understanding that the supplier can be essential to the buyer (contractor) for a number of reasons.

Concentration on in-house core competences

A contractor wishes to concentrate management time and effort on those core business activities that make the best use of in-house skills and resources. There may also be special difficulties in obtaining suitably skilled labour in-house.

Lower product/production costs

In this respect there are two underlying reasons for outsourcing:

1. *Economies of scale.* In many cases the subcontractor produces similar components for other customers, and by use of the experience curve the subcontractor can obtain lower production costs per unit.
2. *Lower wage costs.* The labour costs involved in the domestic country can make the in-house operation uneconomic and motivate international sourcing. For example, 80 per cent of the labour cost of clothing manufacture is in the sewing stage. Short production runs of different sizes of clothes permit only a low degree of mechanization. Moreover, adjusting the tooling for each run is relatively labour-intensive (Hibbert, 1993). Therefore a large part of labour-intensive clothing production is moved to low-wage countries in eastern Europe and the Far East.

Ultimate customer cost/value	Strategic business factors
Marketability	Intermediate customer factors
Downstream channel costs	
Product improvement	
Supplier cost commitment	Tactical input factors
Supplier R&D	
Transaction overhead costs	
Payment terms	Indirect financial costs
Logistics chain costs	
Production costs	
Lot-size costs	Operational/logistics costs
Receive/make-ready costs	
Quality costs	
Warranty terms	Quality costs/factors
Transportation terms	Landed costs
Transportation costs	
Initiating/maintaining a supply relationship	Supply relational costs
FOB terms	Direct transaction costs
Cost of transaction method	
Basic price of materials	Traditional basic input costs

Figure 13.3	The total cost/value hierarchy model

Source: Cavinato (1992).

General cost efficiency

If a firm plans to be more cost efficient than its competitors it has to minimize the total costs towards the end (ultimate) customer. Figure 13.3 shows a model of the different cost elements, from the basic price of materials to the ultimate customer cost.

Each element of the supply chain is a potential candidate for outsourcing. Quality costs, inventory costs (not explicitly mentioned in Figure 13.3) and buyer–supplier transaction costs are examples of costs that should be included in every calculation. However, some of these costs are difficult to estimate and consequently are easily overlooked when evaluating a subcontractor.

For example, the quality of a subcontractor's product or service is essential to the buyer's quality. However, it is not only a question of the quality of the product or service. The quality of the delivery processes also has a major impact on the buyer's performance. Uncertainties, as far as lead times are concerned, have an impact on the buyer's inventory investments and cost efficiency, and they may cause delays in the buyer's own delivery processes. Thus the buyer's own delivery times towards the end customers are determined by the subcontractors and their delivery. Another important fact is that the cost of components and parts is to a large extent already determined at the design stage. Thus, close cooperation between buyer and seller at this stage can give rise to considerable cost advantages in production and distribution.

Increased potential for innovation

Ideas for innovation can be generated by the subcontractor due to its more in-depth understanding of the component. New ideas can also be transferred from other customers of the subcontractor.

Fluctuating demand

If the main contractor is confronted with fluctuating demand levels, external uncertainty and short product life cycles, it may transfer some risk and stock management to the subcontractor, leading to better cost and budget control.

Finally, it should be mentioned that when buying from international sources, fluctuations in exchange rates become particularly important, especially when there is a lag from the time the contract is signed to when payment is made. When the currency in the country of the main contractor is very strong against a particular country this can be an incentive for the main contractor to buy from this country.

In summary, price is a very important reason for (international) outsourcing, but the main contractors increasingly regard cooperation with critical subcontractors as advantageous to the buying firm's competitiveness and profitability.

13.3 A typology of subcontracting

Traditionally, a subcontractor has been defined as a firm carrying out day-to-day production based on the specifications of another firm (the main contractor). The variety of subcontracting relationships that are appearing indicates a need for a more differentiated typology.

Figure 13.4 displays a typology of subcontractors based on differences in the contractor–subcontractor relationship. The typology displays the interplay between the degree of coordination needed and the complexity of the tasks to be solved.

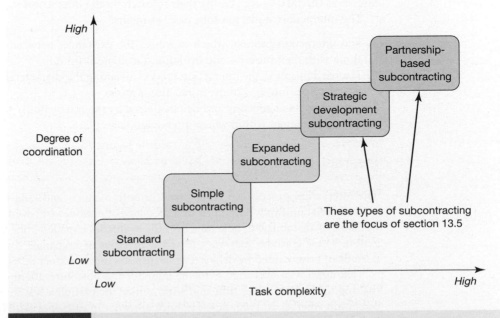

| **Figure 13.4** | Typology of subcontracting |

Source: adapted from Blenker and Christensen (1994).

- *Standard subcontracting.* Economies of scale often operate in the global market with standardized products, in which case no adaptation to specific customers is needed.
- *Simple subcontracting.* Information exchange is simple because the contractor specifies criteria for contribution. The contractor's in-house capacity is often a major competitor.
- *Expanded subcontracting.* There is some mutual specialization between the two parties and exit costs are higher for both parties. Therefore single sourcing (one supplier for a product/component) may replace multisourcing (more suppliers for a product/component).
- *Strategic development subcontracting.* This is very important to the contractor. Subcontractors possess a critical competence of value to the contractor. They are involved in the contractor's long-term planning, and activities are coordinated by dialogue.
- *Partnership-based subcontracting.* This is a relationship based on a strong mutual strategic value and dependency. The subcontractor is highly involved in the R&D activities of the contractor.

There is a certain overlap between the different types of subcontractor and in a specific relationship it can be very difficult to place a subcontractor in a certain typology. Depending primarily on the task complexity, a main contractor may have both standard subcontractors and partnership-based subcontractors. Also a subcontractor may play more than one of the roles in Figure 13.4, but only one at a time.

13.4 Buyer–seller interaction

Traditionally, subcontracting has been defined as the production activities that one firm carries out on the day-to-day specification of another firm. Outsourced activities increasingly include R&D, design and other functions in the value chain. Thus what starts with simple transactions (so-called episodes) may, if repeated over time, evolve into a relationship between buyer and seller.

Interaction theory was developed by the Swedes but spread into France, the United Kingdom, Italy and Germany when a group of like-minded researchers formed what became known as the IMP Group, basing their research on the interaction model (Figure 13.5).

The interaction model has four basic elements:

1. The interaction process, which expresses the exchanges between the two organizations along with their progress and evolution throughout time.
2. The participants in the interaction process, meaning the characteristics of the supplier and the customer involved in the interaction process.
3. The atmosphere affecting and being affected by the interaction.
4. The environment within which interaction takes place.

Interaction process

The interaction process can be analysed in both a short- and long-term perspective. Over time the relationship is developed by a sequence of episodes and events that tends to institutionalize or destabilize it, depending on the evaluations made by the two firms in the interaction. These episodes may vary in terms of types of exchange: commercial transactions, periods of crisis caused by delivery, price disputes, new product development stages, etc.

Through social exchange with the supplier the customer attempts to reduce decision-making uncertainty. Over time and with mutual adaptation a relationship-specific mode of operation emerges and may act as a shock absorber in case of crisis. This mode of operation can take the form of special procedures, mutual developments, communication style between individuals and more or less implicit rules. These rules are modified through past exchanges and form the framework for future exchanges.

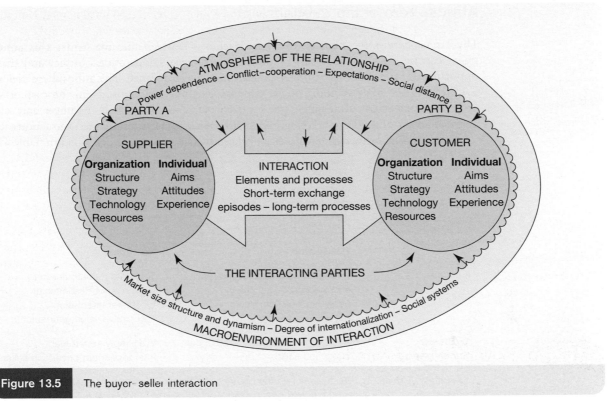

| **Figure 13.5** | The buyer–seller interaction |

Source: Turnbull and Valla (1986). Reprinted by permission of Taylor & Francis.

Interacting parties

The participants' characteristics strongly influence the way they interact. Three analytical perspectives of buyer and seller, at different levels, may be taken into account.

The social system perspective

Dimensions such as culture – languages, values and practices – and the operating modes of the firm influence the distance between actors that will limit or encourage collaboration.

The organizational perspective

The relationship between buyer and seller is influenced by three organizational dimensions:

1. The characteristics of each firm's technology (i.e. products and production technology) strongly influence the nature of the interaction between the two organizations.
2. The complexity of products sold, for example, conditions the very nature and the density of the interaction between supplier and customer.
3. Relationship characteristics: a supplier can choose to develop a stable relationship with a customer, or the supplier can regard the relationship as a pure transaction-based exchange where the supplier typically makes 'one-shot' business with a customer purely to increase sales volume and with no further involvement.

The individual perspective

The individuals' characteristics, their objectives and their experience will influence the way social exchanges and social contacts take place, and subsequently the development of supplier–customer interaction.

Atmosphere of the relationship

The atmosphere is the 'climate' that has developed between the two firms. This atmosphere can be described in terms of power–dependence, cooperation–conflict and trust–opportunism, and in terms of understanding and social distance. The atmosphere concept is central to the understanding of the supplier–customer relationship. In the case of key account management, atmosphere plays a particularly important role. As buyer and seller approach each other the marketing exchanges are changing from single transactions to a relationship. The further characteristics of these two situations are described in Table 13.1 and Figure 13.6.

Table 13.1	Marketing exchange understanding	
	Transaction	Relationship
Objective	To make a sale (sale is end result and measure of success). Customer needs satisfaction (customer buys values).	To create a customer (sale is beginning of relationship). Customer integration (interactive value generation).
Customer understanding	Anonymous customer. Independent buyer and seller.	Well-known customer. Interdependent buyer and seller.
Marketers' task and performance criteria	Assessment on the basis of products and prices. Focus on gaining new customers.	Assessment on the basis of problem-solving competence. Focus on value enhancing of existing customers.
Core aspects of exchange	Focus on products. Sale as a conquest. Discrete event. Monologue to aggregated broad customer segments.	Focus on service. Sale as an agreement. Continuing process. Individualized dialogue.

Source: Jüttner and Wehrli (1994). Published with permission of Emerald Publishing Ltd. www.emeraldinsight.com.

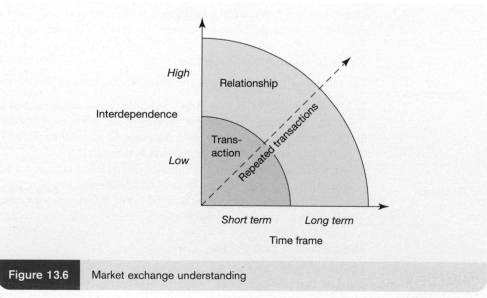

| Figure 13.6 | Market exchange understanding |

Source: Jüttner and Wehrli (1994). Published with permission of Emerald Publishing Ltd; www.emeraldinsight.com.

Interaction environment

Supplier–customer relationships evolve in a general macroenvironment that can influence their very nature. The following analytical dimensions are traditionally considered: political and economic context, cultural and social context, market structure, market internationalization and market dynamism (growth, innovation rate).

13.5 Development of a relationship

A relationship between two firms begins, grows and develops – or fails – in ways similar to relationships between people. The development of a relationship has been mapped out in a five-phase model: awareness, exploration, expansion, commitment and dissolution, and these are shown in Figure 13.7.

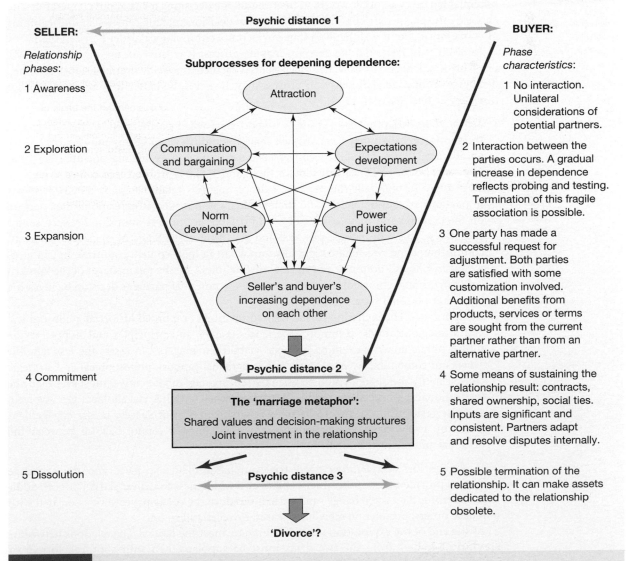

Figure 13.7   The five-phase relationship model

Figure 13.7 shows the initial psychic *distance 1* between a buyer and a seller (both from different countries and cultures) which is influenced by the psychological characteristics of the buyer and the seller, the firm's organizational culture and the national and industry culture to which the firm belongs. For example, a firm entering a psychically distant market is likely to perceive large differences between the two countries, resulting in high uncertainty (Magnusson and Boyle, 2009). The apparent lack of understanding serves as a motivation to spend more resources on research and planning, leading to a reduction of the psychic distance. Figure 13.7 also shows that the initial psychic distance 1 at the beginning of the relationship is reduced to *psychic distance 2* through the interaction process of the two partners. However, relationships do not always last forever. The partners may 'move from each other' and the position may increase to *distance 3*. If the problems in the relationship are not solved, it may result in a 'divorce'.

The marriage metaphor
The process of reducing the psychic distance + increasing dependence between buyer and seller = shared values and joint investments in the relationship.

Within such a framework one might easily characterize a marketing relationship as a marriage between a seller and a buyer (the dissolution phase being a 'divorce'). The use of **the marriage metaphor** indicates that business relationships involve interorganizational relationships, but certainly also interpersonal relationships (Mouzas *et al.*, 2007). Dwyer *et al.* (1987) call the first phase in a relationship *awareness*, which means that the partners recognize each other as potential partners. In other words, in their model the decisions made about cooperating and choosing the partner are combined. Both types of decision-making can exist at the beginning of cooperation, but it is difficult to state any definite chronological order between them.

In SMEs it is likely that the decision-making process is reactive, in the way that the SME probably first realizes the existence of a potential partner (maybe 'love at first sight') and then decides to cooperate. The selection process may, however, be better if companies look for three key criteria (Kanter, 1994):

1. *Self-analysis.* Relationships get off to a good start when partners know themselves and their industry, when they have assessed changing industry conditions and decided to seek an alliance. It also helps if executives have experience in evaluating potential partners. They will not be easily attracted by the first good-looking prospect that comes along.

2. *Chemistry.* To highlight the personal side of business relationships is not to deny the importance of sound financial and strategic analysis. But successful relations often depend on the creation and maintenance of a comfortable personal relationship between senior executives. This will include personal and social interests. Signs of managers' interests, commitment and respect are especially important in high-context countries. In China, as well as in Chinese-dominated businesses throughout Asia, the top manager of the Western company should show honour and respect to the potential partner's decision by investing his or her personal time.

3. *Compatibility.* The courtship period tests compatibility on broad historical, philosophical and strategic grounds: common experiences, values and principles and hopes for the future. While analysts examine financial viability, managers can assess the less tangible aspects of compatibility. What starts out as personal rapport, philosophical and strategic compatibility and shared vision between two companies' top executives must eventually be institutionalized and made public ('getting engaged'). Other stakeholders get involved, and the relationship begins to become depersonalized. But success in the engagement phase of a new alliance still depends on maintaining a careful balance between the personal and the institutional.

In Figure 13.7's *exploration phase* trial purchases may take place and the exchange outcomes provide a test of the other's ability and willingness to deliver satisfaction. In addition, electronic data interchange can be used to reduce the costly paperwork associated with purchase orders, production schedule releases, invoices and so on.

At the end of the exploration phase it is time to 'meet the family'. The relations between a handful of leaders from the two firms must be supplemented with approval, formal or informal, by other people in the firms and by stakeholders. Each partner has other outside relationships that may need to approve the new relationship.

When a party (as is the case in the *expansion phase*) fulfils perceived exchange obligations in an exemplary fashion, the party's attractiveness to the other increases. Hence motivation to maintain the relationship increases, especially because high-level outcomes reduce the number of alternatives that an exchange partner might use as a replacement.

The romance of courtship quickly gives way to day-to-day reality as the partners begin to live together ('setting up house'). In the *commitment phase* the two partners can achieve a level of satisfaction from the exchange process that actually precludes other primary exchange partners (suppliers) that could provide similar benefits. The buyer has not ceased attending other alternative suppliers, but maintains awareness of alternatives without constant and frequent testing.

During the description of the relationship development, the possibility of a withdrawal has been implicit. The **dissolution phase** may be caused by the following problems:

Dissolution phase
'Divorce': termination of the relationship. It can make the assets dedicated to the relationship obsolete.

● Operational and cultural differences emerge after collaboration is under way. They often come as a surprise to those who created the alliance. Differences in authority, reporting and decision-making styles become noticeable at this stage.

● People in other positions may not experience the same attraction as the chief executives. The executives spend a lot of time together both informally and formally. Other employees have not been in touch with one another, however, and in some cases have to be pushed to work with their overseas counterparts.

● Employees at other levels in the organization may be less visionary and cosmopolitan than top managers and less experienced in working with people from different cultures. They may lack knowledge of the strategic context in which the relationship makes sense and see only the operational ways in which it does not.

● People just one or two tiers from the top might oppose the relationship and fight to undermine it. This is especially true in organizations that have strong independent business units.

● Termination of personal relationships, because managers leave their positions in the companies, is a potential danger to the partnership.

Firms have to be aware of these potential problems before they go into a relationship, because only in that way can they take action to prevent the dissolution phase. By jointly analysing the extent and importance of the attenuating factors, the partners will become more aware of the reasons for continuing the relationship, in spite of the trouble they are already in. Moreover, this awareness increases the parties' willingness to engage in restorative actions, thus trying to save the relationship from dissolution (Tähtinen and Vaaland, 2006). Consequently, many organizations allow their alliances to continue in their initial form for too long, while the original conditions change in unforeseen ways, sometimes favouring a new structure. For instance, a 2004 McKinsey study found that more than 70 per cent of companies were part of major alliances in need of restructuring. McKinsey's results further indicate that alliances that change their scope have a 79 per cent success rate versus 33 per cent for the ventures that remain essentially unchanged (Gulati *et al.*, 2008).

13.6 Reverse marketing: from seller to buyer initiative

Reverse marketing
The buyer (and not the seller as in traditional marketing) takes the initiative in searching for a supplier that is able to fulfil their needs.

Reverse marketing describes how purchasing actively identifies potential subcontractors and offers suitable partners a proposal for long-term cooperation. Similar terms are proactive procurement and buyer initiative (Ottesen, 1995). In recent years the buyer–seller relationship has changed considerably. The traditional relationship, in which a seller takes the initiative by offering a product, is increasingly being replaced by one in which the buyer actively searches for a supplier that is able to fulfil its needs.

	Current activities	New activities
Existing suppliers	Intensify current activities	Develop and add new activities
New potential suppliers	Replace existing suppliers Add suppliers: secure deliveries	Develop new activities not covered by existing suppliers

Figure 13.8 Supplier development strategies

Today, many changes are taking place in the utilization of the purchasing function:

- Reduction in the number of subcontractors.
- Shorter product life cycles, which increase the pressure to reduce the time to market (just in time).
- Upgraded demands on subcontractors (zero defects). In addition, firms are demanding that their suppliers become certified. Those that do not comply may be removed from the approved supplier list.
- Purchasing that no longer just serves the purpose of getting lower prices. The traditional arm's-length relationships are increasingly being replaced by long-term partnerships with mutual trust, interdependence and mutual benefits.

Implementing a reverse marketing strategy starts with fundamental market research and with an evaluation of reverse marketing options (i.e. possible suppliers). Before choosing suppliers the firm may include both present and potential suppliers in the analysis as well as current and desired activities (Figure 13.8).

Based on this analysis the firm may select a number of suitable partners as suppliers and rank them in order of preference.

13.7 Internationalization of subcontractors

In Chapter 3 the internationalization process was described as a learning process (the Uppsala school). Generally speaking it is something that can be described as a gradual internationalization. According to this view the international development of the firm is accompanied by an accumulation of knowledge in the hands of management and by growing capabilities and propensities to manage international affairs. The main consequence of this way of thinking is that firms tend to increase their commitment towards foreign markets as their experience grows. The number of adherents to this theory has grown, but there has also been much criticism of it.

The main problem with the model is that it seems to suggest the presence of a deterministic and mechanistic path that firms implementing their internationalization strategy must follow. Sometimes it happens that firms leapfrog one or more stages in the establishment chain; at other times firms stop their internationalization altogether (Welch and Luostarinen, 1988).

Concerning internationalization among contractors and subcontractors, there is a central difference. The internationalization of subcontractors is closely related to their customers.

The concept of subcontractor indicates that the strategies of such a firm, including its internationalization strategy, cannot be seen in isolation from the strategies of its partner, the contractor. Therefore the internationalization of subcontractors may show irregular paths, such as leapfrogging.

Andersen *et al.* (1995) introduce four basic routes of internationalization (note that sometimes there is an overlap between the different routes, e.g. between routes 2 and 3).

Route 1: following domestic customers

If a contractor is internationalizing and establishing a production unit in a foreign market some subcontractors (standard or simple in Figure 13.4) may be replaced with local suppliers, because they might be able to offer the standard components at cheaper prices. However, subcontractors in the upper part of Figure 13.4 and with a strategic value to the contractor will be maintained if they commit themselves to foreign direct investment: claims for direct delivery to the foreign production unit or claims for after-sales service on delivered components may result in the establishment of a local sales and/or production subsidiary by the subcontractor. In most cases such a direct foreign investment related directly to a specific contractor is based on a guarantee of procurement over some years (until the payback period has passed).

When the furniture chain IKEA established itself in the North American market it took along some strategically important Scandinavian subcontractors, some of which also established subsidiaries in North America. Other examples are the Japanese car manufacturers that established production units in the United States and pulled along a lot of Japanese subcontractors to establish subsidiaries there. This route is similar to the 'late starters' in the model of Johanson and Mattson (1988) in Figure 3.6.

Route 2: internationalization through the supply chain of an multinational corporation

Deliveries to one division of a multinational corporation may lead to deliveries to other divisions, or to parts of its network. One case is when mergers and acquisitions take place between firms, and create new business opportunities for dynamic subcontractors.

The strategic alliance between the French car manufacturer Renault and the Swedish Volvo is one example, where Swedish subcontractors have become involved in the subcontracting system of Renault, and French subcontractors have opportunities to get into the subcontracting system of Volvo (Christensen and Lindmark, 1993).

Route 3: internationalization in cooperation with domestic or foreign system suppliers

In collaboration with other specialized subcontractors, system suppliers may be involved in international system supplies by taking over the management of whole supplies of subsystems (see Figure 13.9).

Systems supplies result in the development of a new layer of subcontractors (second-tier subcontractors). Through the interaction between a system supplier and a domestic main contractor the system supplier can get access to the network of a global contractor (the dotted line in Figure 13.9) because of the network/contract between the contractor and the global contractor. For example, a Japanese car seat supplier supplies the Japanese Toyota factory (domestic main contractor). This can eventually give the supplier access to other Toyota factories around the world (global contractors) and their global networks.

In many cases the collaboration between the subcontractors will be characterized by exchange of tacit, not easily transferable, knowledge. The reason for this is that the complete subsystem is frequently based on several fields of competence, which have to be coordinated

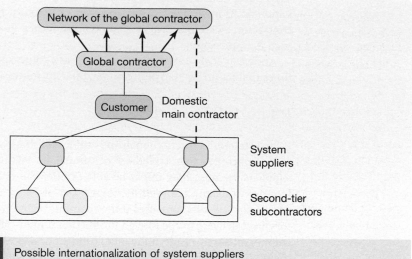

| Figure 13.9 | Possible internationalization of system suppliers |

by use of tacit knowledge and communication. In the case of the Japanese car seat supplier, the system supplier should have a tight relationship with the subcontractors (suppliers of leather head rests, etc.) in order to adapt the car seat to the individual car models. (See also Exhibit 13.1.)

Route 4: independent internationalization

The need to gain economies of scale in production forces the standard contractor, in particular, to use the route of independent internationalization. In other cases it cannot be recommended that small subcontractors follow the independent route. The barriers of independent internationalization are too high for small firms with limited resources. For these firms, route 3 (collaboration with other subcontractors) seems to be a more realistic way to internationalize.

EXHIBIT 13.1 An example of Japanese network sourcing: the Mazda seat-sourcing case

Mazda adopts a policy of splitting its seat purchases between two suppliers, Delta Kogyo and the Toyo Seat Company. The present division is approximately 60 per cent to Delta and 40 per cent to Toyo. Each of these companies is responsible for different models of seats. Note that each individual item, such as a seat for the Mazda 626, is single sourced for the product life cycle of typically three to five years, but seat production in general is, in effect, dual sourced.

Both Delta Kogyo and the Toyo Seat Company are informally assured of a certain percentage of the Mazda seat business at any one time. This percentage is approximately one-third of the total Mazda seat purchases. Thus each firm has an assured long-term share of Mazda's seat business. When asked about the length of relationship that Mazda has with its suppliers, Mr Nakamichi of Mazda's marketing division said that relationships with all suppliers, whether they are affiliates, subcontractors or common part suppliers, were established for an 'indefinite' period of time. In addition, the last third of the seat business was available to whichever of the suppliers had performed the best over the life cycle of previous car models.

The two seat makers rely on Mazda for a very high percentage of their business. In the case of Delta Kogyo, Mazda business represents around two-thirds of its total sales. In addition, both suppliers are members of Mazda's *keiretsu* (network) and hence come into direct contact with each other on a regular basis. Additionally, since they are direct competitors for only a third of Mazda's seat business, there is a significant degree of openness between the two firms. This openness in some instances takes the form of cooperation in solving mutual or individual problems, because the other seat supplier is often in a better position to give advice than Mazda itself.

However, competition for the remaining third of the Mazda seat business is very intense, since both firms know that they have only one chance to gain the orders for a new car model every three to five years. The most interesting aspect of this competition is that it is based primarily on performance since the last contract was awarded. The areas of competition include design abilities, management strength, cost-reduction progress, quality record and, perhaps surprisingly, the amount of assistance that the supplier has given to its direct competitor either within the auspices of the *keiretsu* or on separate occasions. Thus either firm can obtain new business as long as the other does not fall below 33 per cent of Mazda's total seat purchases. A situation has been created in which there is creative tension between cooperation and competition.

Indeed, when one of the suppliers approaches the lower limit of its 33 per cent supply Mazda typically uses its own engineers, and possibly those of the supply competitor, to help the weaker supplier in terms of a joint value analysis/value engineering programme. Because neither supplier wants to be forced into this situation both will work diligently to avoid this fate – and at the same time to enhance their own competitiveness.

Mazda is careful to ensure that neither supplier is forced into a situation of unprofitability, since this would obviously mean that Mazda would suffer in the long term. This is not to say that either supplier is allowed to make excessive profits. Indeed profit as a percentage of sales is roughly equalized throughout the supply network, including the Mazda organization itself. During recessionary periods Mazda and its network of suppliers would make no more than about 2 per cent profit on sales. Thus members of the supply network stand or fall together, increasing the shared bonds and the willingness to help any member of the network.

Source: Reproduced with permission from the publisher, John Wiley & Sons, Inc., 'Network sourcing: a hybrid approach', *Journal of Supply Chain Management* (formerly *The International Journal of Purchasing and Materials Management*), by Peter Hines 5 April 2006, pp. 17–24.

13.8   Project export (turnkey contracts)

This chapter has dealt mainly with sourcing (subcontracting) in the industrial market. Although marketing of subsupplies to international projects has a number of similarities with subsupplies in the industrial market in general, it also has the characteristics of the special marketing situation in the project market: for example, the long and often very bureaucratic selection of sub-suppliers for ad hoc supplies.

The sub-supplier market in project export, however, is also very internationalized, and the main part of marketing should be conducted in those centres or countries where the main contractor is domiciled. For example, London is the domicile of a number of building contracting businesses, which work in those countries that used to be in the British Empire.

Project export

Combination of hardware (e.g. buildings and infrastructure) and software (technology and project know-how), e.g. in the form of a factory for ice cream production.

Project export is a very complex international activity, involving many market players. The preconditions for project export are a technology gap between the exporting and importing countries and that the exporter possesses the specific product and technology know-how that is being demanded in the importing country.

Project export involves supplies or deliveries that contain a combination of hardware and software. When the delivery is concluded it will constitute an integrated system that is able to produce the products and/or the services, which the buyer requires. An example of this type of project is the construction of a dairy in a developing country.

Hardware is the blanket term for the tangible, material or physical contribution of the project supply. Hardware is composed of buildings, machines, inventory, transport equipment, etc., and is specified in the quotation and contract between buyer and seller in the form of drawings, unit lists, descriptions and so on.

Software is the blanket term for the intangible contributions in a project supply. Software includes know-how and service. There are three types of know-how:

1. *technology know-how*, comprising product, process and hardware know-how;
2. *project know-how*, comprising project management, assembly and environmental know-how;
3. *management know-how*, which in general terms involves tactical and operational management, and specifically includes marketing and administrative systems.

Service includes advisory services and assistance in connection with various applications and approvals (environmental approval, financing of the project, planning permission, etc.).

The marketing of projects is different from the marketing of products in the following respects:

- Decision of purchase, apart from local business interests, often involves decision processes in national and international development organizations. This implies the participation of a large number of people and a heavily bureaucratic system.
- The product is designed and created during the negotiation process, where the requirements are put forward.
- It often takes years from the disclosure of needs to the purchase decision being taken. Therefore total marketing costs are very large.
- When the project is taken over by the project buyer, the buyer–seller relations cease. However, by cultivating these relations before, during and after the project, a 'sleeping' relationship can be woken again in connection with a new project (Hadjikhani, 1996).

Financing a project is a key problem for the seller as well as the buyer. The project's size and the time used for planning and implementation result in financial demands that make it necessary to use external sources of finance. In this connection the following main segments can be distinguished. The segments arise from differences in the source of financing for the projects:

- Projects where *multilateral organizations*, such as the World Bank or regional development banks, are a primary source of finance.
- Projects where *bilateral organizations* are a primary or essential source of finance.
- Projects where a *government institution* acts as buyer. This was normal in the command economies, where government companies acted as buyers. However, it can also be found in liberal economies: for example, in connection with the development of social infrastructure or the building of a bridge.
- Projects where a *private person or firm* acts as buyer, as when Unilever builds a factory in Vietnam for the production of ice cream.

For large-scale projects, like a new airport, there may be many partners forming a consortium, where we will have the concept of a 'leader firm', but each partner would undertake financing, organization, supervision and/or construction etc., of a part of the project on the basis of their specific expertise.

Organizing export projects involves establishing an interaction between different firms from the West on the one side, and firms and authorities typically from developing countries on the other. Creating or adapting an organization that is able to function under these conditions is a precondition of project marketing.

13.9 Summary

This chapter has analysed the buyer–seller relationship from different angles in the internationalized environment. The advantages and disadvantages for the contractor and subcontractor of going into a relationship are summarized in Table 13.2.

Table 13.2	Advantages and disadvantages of buyer–seller relationships for contractor and subcontractor	
	Advantages	**Disadvantages**
Contractor (buyer)	The contractor is flexible by not investing in manufacturing facilities.	The availability of suitable manufacturers (subcontractors) cannot be assumed. Outsourcing tends to be relatively less stable than in-house operations.
	The subcontractor can source the products more cheaply (because of e.g. cheaper labour costs) than by own production.	The contractor has less control over the activities of the subcontractor.
	The contractor can concentrate on in-house core competences.	Subcontractors can develop into competitors.
	Complement of the contractor's product range.	Quality problems of outsourced products can harm the business of the contractor.
	New ideas for product innovation can be carried over from the subcontractor.	Assistance to the subcontractor may increase the costs of the whole operation.
Subcontractor (seller)	Access to new export markets because of the internationalization of the contractor (especially relevant for the so-called late starters).	Risk of becoming dependent on the contractor because of expanding production capacity and concurrent overseas expansion of sales and marketing activities in order to meet the demands of the contractor.
	Exploits scale economies (lower cost per unit) through better capacity utilization.	
	Learns product technology of the contractor.	
	Learns marketing practices of the contractor.	

The project export situation differs from the 'normal' buyer–seller relationship in the following ways:

- The buying decision process often involves national and international development organizations. This often results in very bureaucratic selection of subcontractors.
- Financing of the project is a key problem.

CASE STUDY 13.1

Syngenta AG: a world market leader in crop protection is defending its position

The world's growing population (over 7 billion people, growing to more than 8 billion within the next 25 years) and unresolved food problems, with the expected farm land to be constant at 1.5 billion hectares, indicates a long-term growing demand for crops and higher yields. The main crops to be protected are wheat, rice, corn, soy, grapes and vegetables. Crop protection means protection from insects (by insecticides), fungus (by fungicides) and weeds (by herbicides). There is also a growing market for genetically treated crops. This market falls under 'seed treatment' or 'seeds business'.

Crops and the crop protection methods vary a lot from continent to continent, and even from country to country. It depends very much on the single country's culture and history. Certain countries favour certain crops. For example, France is a wine-producing country, whereas Germany is more a beer-drinking nation, and therefore grows more hops. In Asia soy and rice play a major role, and in South America, most bananas are produced. The country-specific legal restrictions may be different in different countries. For example, allowed levels for crop protection in bananas are five times higher in US than in the EU which means, that the crop protection methods for bananas sent to the EU have to be different compared to the US.

Syngenta AG was formed in 2000 through a merger between Novartis AG and AstraZeneca.

Both the Novartis and AstraZeneca agribusinesses had existed since the 1930s.

Syngenta is a world leading agribusiness operating in the two main business:

1. crop protection
2. seeds businesses.

Syngenta's major production sites are located in Switzerland, USA, UK, China and India.

Syngenta manages its supply chain globally and on a product-by-product basis, from raw materials through delivery to the customer, in order to maximize both cost and capital efficiency and responsiveness. While individual active substances are normally produced at one manufacturing site, formulations are produced and packaged at several different strategically located plants, close to the principal markets in which those products are sold. Syngenta operates major formulation and packing plants in Belgium, Brazil, China, France, India, South Korea, Switzerland, the United Kingdom and the United States. Syngenta outsources the manufacture of a wide range of raw materials, from commodities through fine chemicals to dedicated intermediates and active ingredients. Sourcing decisions are based on a combination of logistical, geographical and commercial factors. Syngenta has a strategy of maintaining, when available, multiple sources of supply. Most purchases of supply chain materials are directly or indirectly influenced by commodity price volatility, due to price dependence on gas and oil. Total raw material spending is approximately 30 per cent of sales.

The total sales in 2008 was €11.6 billion (26 per cent increase compared to 2006), with income before taxes of €1.7 billion. The total sales show the following product and geographical split (Table 1):

Table 1	Total sales 2008 – product and geographical split		
Product split of total sales – billion €		**Geographical split of total sales – billion €**	
Crop protection	9.2	Europe, Africa and Middle East	4.3
Seeds	2.4	NAFTA	3.6
		Latin America	2.2
		Asia Pacific	1.5
Total	**11.6**	**Total**	**11.6**

Crop spraying
Courtesy of Syngenta.

Crop protection

Syngenta is active in herbicides, especially for corn, cereals, soybean and rice; fungicides mainly for corn, cereals, fruits, grapes, rice, soybean and vegetables; insecticides for fruits, vegetables and field crops; seed care, primarily in corn, soybean, cereals and cotton; and professional products, such as products for public health and products for turf and ornamentals.

Herbicides are products that prevent or reduce weeds that compete with the crop for nutrients, light and water. Herbicides can be subdivided into (i) selective herbicides, which are crop-specific and control weeds without harming the crop and (ii) non-selective herbicides, which reduce or halt the growth of all vegetation with which they come in contact.

Fungicides are products that prevent and cure fungal plant diseases that affect crop yield and quality. Insecticides are products that control chewing pests such as caterpillars and sucking pests such as aphids, which reduce crop yields and quality.

Seed care products are insecticides and fungicides used to protect growth during the early stages. Professional products are herbicides, insecticides and fungicides used in markets beyond commercial agriculture, and include a broad range of premium growing media mixes for professional flower growers.

Syngenta has a broad product range, making Syngenta number one or two in all of its target segments, underpinned by strong worldwide market coverage. Syngenta focuses on all major crops – in particular, corn, cereals, soybean, fruits and vegetables, and applies its technologies to other crops, such as oilseeds, sugar beets, rice and cotton, and to turf and ornamentals.

The use of seed care products is an effective, efficient and targeted method to protect the seedling and the young plant against diseases and insects during the period when they are most vulnerable. Syngenta's broad range of fungicides and insecticides allows us to provide a modern portfolio of safe and highly effective products. As seeds increase in value, seed protection becomes more important.

Seeds

Syngenta develops, produces and markets seeds and plants that have been developed using advanced genetics and related technologies and sells seed products in all major territories. The end customers are livestock feeders, grain processors, food processors and other partners in the food chain.

As there are large synergies between Syngenta's two main product segments. For example, distribution channels and competitors are very similar.

Crop protection

From treated corn seeds to finished corncob
Courtesy of Syngenta.

Syngenta's international marketing, sales organization and communication strategy

Syngenta has its own sales subsidiaries (and marketing organizations) in all major markets with dedicated sales forces that provide customer and technical service, product promotion and market support. Products are sold to the end user through independent distributors and dealers, most of whom also handle other manufacturers' products. The products are normally sold through a two-step or three-step distribution chain. In the two-step chain Syngenta sells its products to cooperatives or independent distributors, which then sell to the grower as the end user. In the three-step system, Syngenta sells to distributors or cooperative unions who act as wholesalers and sell the product to independent dealers or primary cooperatives before on-selling to growers. Syngenta also sells directly to large growers in some countries.

The international marketing activities are directed towards the distributors, agricultural consultants and growers. They consist of a broad range of advertising and promotional tools, such as meetings with growers and distributors, field demonstrations, advertisements in specialized publications, direct marketing activities, or information via the Internet. Syngenta is also in constant contact with the food and feed chain to evaluate current and future needs and expectations.

The crop protection industry is subject to environmental risks in three main areas: manufacturing, distribution and use of product. Syngenta aims to minimize or eliminate environmental risks by using appropriate equipment, adopting best industry practice and providing grower training and education. The entire value chain of business activities, from research and development to end use, operates according to the principles of product stewardship. Syngenta is strongly committed to the responsible and ethical management of our products from invention through ultimate use, and a key element of our marketing is grower support and education. This is particularly important with respect to small growers in developing countries. For many years, Syngenta has held numerous courses around the world for growers as a result of which tens of thousands of people have been trained in the safe and sustainable use of crop protection products. Syngenta also trains agricultural extension workers and distributors so that they can further disseminate good practice and reach an even wider audience.

Syngenta also employs environmental scientists around the world who study all aspects of a product's environmental behaviour.

Competition in the crop protection industry

The leading companies in the crop protection industry are mainly dedicated agribusinesses or large chemical companies based in Western Europe and North America. These companies compete on the basis of strength and breadth of product range, product development and differentiation, geographical coverage, price and customer service. Market pressures and the need to achieve a high level of research and development capability, particularly with the advent of biotechnology, have led to consolidation in the industry.

The total world market for crop protection in 2008 was approximately €50 billion. The top six world companies account for about 80 per cent of the worldwide market. Syngenta's key competitors include BASF, Bayer, Dow, DuPont and Monsanto. In

Table 2	Major players in the global crop protection market	
Company	Country (HQ)	World market share (%) in 2008
Syngenta	Switzerland	20
Monsanto	USA	20
Bayer	Germany	15
BASF	Germany	10
Dupont	USA	10
Dow	USA	5
Others	China, India	20
Total		**100** (total world market in 2008 is approximately €50 billion)

many countries, generic producers of off-patent compounds are additional competitors to the research-based companies in the commodity segment of the market.

In certain business areas, product features are basically the same because patents ran out many years ago. In 'blind tests' the products would be impossible to differentiate by the end-customers (the farmers). Thus, innovative sales, branding and marketing concepts play a very important role in the crop protection business.

Due to:

- Lower crop prices
- Farmers' lower prices for their end products (milk prices etc.)
- The general financial crises in 2009

the world market has decreased by approximately 10–20 per cent during 2009–2010.

QUESTIONS

1. Try to illustrate the total supply chain (value chain) of Syngenta.

2. Explain the role of main actors in the value chain.

3. How should Syngenta interrelate and interact with these actors in order to maximize total added value of the supply chain?

Source: adapted from www.syngenta.com.

CASE STUDY 13.2

LM Glasfiber A/S: following its customers' international expansion in the wind turbine industry

LM Glasfiber A/S is the world's leading supplier of rotor blades for wind turbines. Its headquarters are located in Lunderskov, Denmark and it has 14 manufacturing bases in ten Danish towns, with more than 1,700 employees in modern production areas covering some 100,000 m².

The company is internationally represented, with manufacturing facilities and sales offices in Germany, the Netherlands, Spain, the United States, India and China. Its customers are thus guaranteed prompt and punctual delivery with a high level of service worldwide.

LM Glasfiber's establishment in India is explained and illustrated in Figure 1. Typically, rotor blades represent approximately 20 per cent of a wind turbine's value (excluding mounting, installation etc.).

Figure 1 shows the phases that LM Glasfiber (as sub-supplier) went through in order to globalize via the buyers'/wind turbine manufacturers' network, especially Micon's network.

The 1 in the figure indicates that LM Glasfiber has very large deliveries of rotor blades to the Danish network of wind turbine manufacturers ('domestic contracts'), the largest being NEG Micon (in 1999), Vestas (wind systems), Bonus (energy) and Nordex. Even though the total Danish network covers more than 50 per cent of the world market for wind turbines it should be remembered that competition between the companies in the international market is very keen. Having close relations with the Danish Wind Turbine Manufacturers' Association, LM Glasfiber also cooperates very closely with the research environment within wind turbine technology by way of relations with the Ris National Laboratory.

This example is based on LM Glasfiber's relations with Micon in the mid 1990s – at the time the

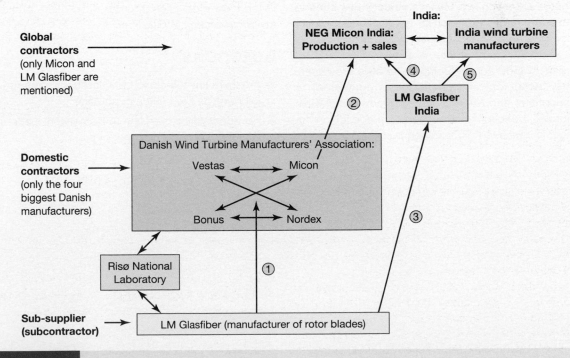

| Figure 1 | LM Glasfiber's globalization through the network of the customer |

www.lmglasfiber.com. Copyright LM Glasfiber A/S.

second-biggest wind turbine manufacturer in the world (Micon merged with Vestas in May, 2004). As regards sub-suppliers Micon's strategy has been to outsource the biggest part of its rotor blade production. However, Micon has always aimed at having an adequate share of internal sub-suppliers of rotor blades in order for the company to have the necessary technological preparedness compared to competitors and external sub-suppliers. This flexible sourcing concept is an essential precondition for Micon's continued globalization process.

The 2 in the figure shows Micon's establishment of a sales and manufacturing company in India at the beginning of the 1990s. India is an attractive market for wind turbines, as power supply is poor, especially in the countryside. The Indian government has therefore supported the mounting of wind turbines that can contribute to stabilizing the power supply (often in cooperation with foreign development aid organizations).

LM Glasfiber realized that it had to start manufacturing rotor blades in India to continue being one of India's sub-suppliers. Three in the figure shows the 1994 establishment of LM Glasfiber India Ltd – a joint venture between LM Glasfiber A/S, the Industrialization Fund for Developing Countries, and the Indian wind turbine manufacturer NEPC. The 4 therefore shows the local deliveries of rotor blades and the back-up service that LM Glasfiber India can provide by being a local company. As a consequence of the partnership with NEPC, LM Glasfiber has now (via the local joint venture) gained access to NEPC's network, which includes several markets in Asia. Finally the 5 shows that LM Glasfiber has been able to use its relationship with NEPC as a springboard to other markets in Asia.

At the start of 2007 LM Glasfiber has convinced three or four of its major suppliers to follow it to India. Consequently, these sub-suppliers have also established local production in order to be close to their major customer, LM Glasfiber.

QUESTIONS

1. Are there any threats to LM Glasfiber's strategy in following its key customer abroad?

2. How does this case relate to the network model in Chapter 3?

VIDEO CASE STUDY 13.3 Eaton Corporation

download from www.pearsoned.co.uk/hollensen

Eaton Corporation (www.eaton.com) is a diversified industrial manufacturer with a range of products from car valves to circuit breakers. The company operates primarily in the US and Europe. Its headquarters are in Cleveland, Ohio and it employs 59,000 people. Eaton operates through four business divisions: automotive, electrical, fluid power and truck, but it is facing stiff competition across its market segments. As the US market makes up two-thirds of its total revenues one of Eaton's future tasks is to focus more on non-US growth markets.

Questions

1. What are Eaton's key challenges in establishing long-term relationships with its new global OEM customers?
2. Why is the fast-changing marketing environment so crucial to Eaton's international marketing plan?
3. What makes Eaton's channel management challenging? Why does the company continue to sell through multiple global channels?

For further exercises and cases, see this book's website at **www.pearsoned.co.uk/hollensen.**

Questions for discussion

1. What are the reasons for the increasing level of outsourcing to international subcontractors?
2. Describe the typology of subcontractors based on the differences in the contractor/subcontractor relationship.
3. Explain the shift from seller to buyer initiative in subcontracting.
4. Explain the main differences between the US and the Japanese sub-supplier systems.
5. How are project exports/turnkey projects different from general subcontracting in the industrial market?
6. Project export is often characterized by a complex and time-consuming decision-making process. What are the marketing implications of this for the potential subcontractor?

References

Andersen, P.H., Blenker, P. and Christensen, P.R. (1995) *Internationalization of Subcontractors: In Search of a Theoretical Framework.* The Southern Denmark Business School, Kolding.

Blenker, P. and Christensen, P.R. (1994) 'Interactive strategies in supply chains: a double-edged portfolio approach to SME', Subcontractors Positioning Paper presented at the 8th Nordic Conference on Small Business Research.

Cavinato, J.L. (1992) 'A total cost/value model for supply chain competitiveness', *Journal of Business Logistics*, 13(2), pp. 285–301.

Cho, Dong-Sung and Chu, Wujin (1994) 'Determinants of bargaining power in OEM negotiations', *Industrial Marketing Management*, 23, pp. 342–355.

Christensen, P.R. and Lindmark, L. (1993) 'Location and internationalization of small firms', in Lindquist, L. and Persson, L.O. (eds), *Visions and Strategies in European Integration*, Springer Verlag, Berlin/Heidelberg.

Dwyer, R.F., Schurr, P.H. and Oh, S. (1987) 'Developing buyer–seller relationships', *Journal of Marketing*, 51 (April), pp. 11–27.

Gulati, R., Sytch, M. and Mehrotra, P. (2008) 'Breaking up is never easy: planning for exit in a strategic alliance', *California Management Review*, 50(4), pp. 147–163.

Hadjikhani, A. (1996) 'Project marketing and the management of discontinuity', *International Business Review*, 5(3), pp. 319–336.

Hibbert, E.P. (1993) 'Global make or buy decisions', *Industrial Marketing Management*, 22, pp. 67–77.

Hines, P. (1995) 'Network sourcing: a hybrid approach', *International Journal of Purchasing and Materials Management*, 13(2), pp. 18–24.

Johanson, J. and Mattson, L.G. (1988) 'Internationalization in industrial systems', in Hood, N. and Vahlne, J.E. (eds), *Strategies in Global Competition*, Croom Helm, Beckenham, pp. 287–314.

Jüttner, U. and Wehrli, H.P. (1994) 'Relationship marketing from a value system perspective', *International Journal of Service Industry Management*, 5, pp. 54–73.

Kanter, R.M. (1994) 'Collaborative advantage', *Harvard Business Review*, July–August, pp. 96–107.

Lehtinen, U. (1991) 'Alihankintajarjestelma 1990-luvulla [Subcontracting system in the 1990s]', *Publications of SITRA*, 114, Helsinki.

Magnusson, P. and Boyle, B.A. (2009) 'A contingency perspective on psychic distance in international channel relationships', *Journal of Marketing Channels*, 16(1), pp. 77–99.

Mouzas, S., Henneberg, S. and Naudé, P. (2007) 'Trust and reliance in business relationships', *European Journal of Marketing*, 41(9/10), pp. 1016–1032.

Ottesen, O. (1995) *Buyer Initiative: Ignored, but Imperative for Marketing Theory.* Working Paper, Department of Business Administration, Stavanger College, Norway.

Tähtinen, J. and Vaaland, T. (2006) 'Business relationships facing the end: why restore them?', *Journal of Business & Industrial Marketing*, 21(1), pp. 14–23.

Turnbull, P.W. and Valla, J.P. (1986) *Strategies for International Industrial Marketing.* Croom Helm, London.

Welch, L.S. and Luostarinen, R. (1988) 'Internationalization: evolution of a concept', *Journal of General Management*, 14(2), pp. 36–64.

CASE STUDY III.1

Raleigh bicycles: does the iconic bicycle brand still have a chance on the world market?

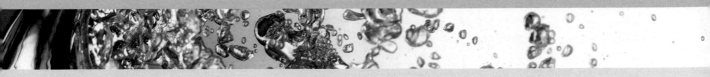

The name Raleigh (www.raleigh.co.uk) has been synonymous with bikes since the company was founded in a small workshop on Raleigh Street by three men in 1886. Frank Bowden, a successful lawyer and convert to cycling, bought the firm in 1887 and in December 1888 founded The Raleigh Cycle Company as a limited liability private company. It grew rapidly and within a few years was a large public company capitalized at £100,000 (equivalent to about £6m today).

Raleigh survived the Great Depression well with the introduction of value-for-money products. It acquired Humber cycles in 1932 and the following year started producing a three-wheeler car. In 1934 Raleigh reverted to public company status, as Raleigh Cycle Holdings Ltd, with a share issue of more than £2m (about £70m today). By 1938, its production of bicycles had grown to nearly 500,000 units per annum and the company had stopped making motorcycles and cars, and focused on the production of small arms munitions in the Second World War. The three-wheeler car business became one of the first management buy-outs in 1935, being re-formed as the Reliant car business.

After the war, despite shortages of fuel and steel, Raleigh's cycle production rose rapidly. By 1949, it had reached about 750,000, the majority of which was exported.

Raleigh International Ltd.

In 1951, Raleigh produced more than a million cycles, but between 1950 and 1962, as increasingly prosperous consumers abandoned the cycle in favour of the car, cycle sales in the UK halved. This led Raleigh in 1958 to resume moped production and later to launch a motor scooter (they ceased this production again in 1970 and from there they concentrated on bicycle sales). More significantly, during this period Raleigh acquired two major rival groups: Triumph and Three Spires in 1954, and BSA (including New Hudson and Sunbeam) in 1957. Raleigh itself was then taken over by Tube Investments (TI) which already owned the Phillips and Hercules names, although the new operation was run by Raleigh management. The effect of these mergers was that Raleigh's sales figures showed a slight upward trend during most of the 1950s. The TI takeover followed a collaborative venture with Raleigh in South Africa.

During the 1960s Raleigh's sales growth closely mirrored that of the UK cycle industry, enabling the company to hold its market share at around 60 per cent.

In the late 1960s, Schwinn and other US cycle makers had discovered a grassroots Californian trend towards high-rise cycles for adolescents and were now capitalizing on it. Responding to this, in 1969 Raleigh launched the Chopper in the USA. It was too expensive and too late for the American market but the following year it was released in the UK, where it was hugely successful. In its ten-year production, about 1.5 million were sold in the UK alone. With the Chopper, Raleigh had created a new market in the UK and other developed countries for expensive toy cycles with features which appealed to children rather than simply selling scaled-down adult bicycles, which it continued to exploit. Moreover, in contrast to toys such as the Chopper, it offered fine Carlton lightweights to the discerning enthusiast. Thus, in 1975 Raleigh enjoyed record sales of 599,000 units in the UK, although market share was beginning to decline slightly.

Overseas, Raleigh was also doing quite well. In the Netherlands, it was selling 50,000 cycles a year under its own name and Gazelle, the leading Dutch manufacturer (at that time owned by Raleigh), was selling a further 250,000. Raleigh's Canadian factory had recently doubled in size to produce 150,000 units a year. In the USA, there was a new factory in Oklahoma, supported by a network of large, modern warehouses in New Jersey, Massachusetts, Illinois and California.

Importantly, Raleigh still benefited from Britain's imperial heritage, with huge sales of black, 28-inch wheel roadsters in former colonial territories, particularly in Africa and Iran. The company had recently opened a new factory in Nigeria, where Raleigh was selling some 200,000 cycles a year. Producing large numbers of traditional roadsters was what Raleigh did most profitably.

Around the late 1970s and early 1980s Raleigh sponsored a European-based road-racing team. It enjoyed great success, including team wins in the Tour de France in 1977 and 1983. Raleigh also built the bike ridden to victory in the Tour by Joop Zoetemelk who rode for TI-Raleigh Creda in 1980 – the only British-built Tour de France winner in the race's history.

In the early 1980s export sales to USA, Nigeria and Iran collapsed through a perfect storm of currency exchange rate, oil price moves and revolution, but this was compensated by the introduction of the BMX bicycle, a market which Raleigh captured and owned with the Raleigh Burner.

By 1985 Raleigh was suffering badly as the BMX hype rapidly died. By 1986, sales were 38 per cent down on the 1983 peak. This dip in sales was matched by the industry as a whole, but Tube Investments now lost patience with Raleigh. TI decided to sell the company and, on 1 April 1987, it was bought by Derby International. Derby was a private company whose founder was Edward Gottesman, an Anglo-American tax lawyer, resident in London for many years. Gottesman, like Frank Bowden, was both entrepreneurial and interested in bicycles. He had heard that TI was keen to dispose of Raleigh and appreciated the value of the Raleigh brand, especially in America. Being a tax lawyer, he registered the Derby company in Luxembourg and installed Alan Finden-Crofts, a former BTR Plc Executive, as CEO.

Derby initially acquired the Nottingham operation including Sturmey-Archer and Raleigh's operations in the Netherlands (including Gazelle), South Africa, Canada, Australia, France, Germany and the Irish Republic. Initially the Raleigh sales increased. The move to profitability surprised many and confounded the sceptical view of some that Derby was only interested in asset stripping.

By 1992, Derby was the largest cycle group in the world, with a sales turnover of US$477 million. In 1998, this was US$465 million. The company was recapitalized in 1998 as a result of which Gottesman

and Finden-Crofts realized most of their investment and became The Derby Cycle Corporation, based at Kent in the state of Washington, USA. It remained a private company, 65 per cent owned by Thayer Capital Partners and 13 per cent owned by Perseus Capital, a group of US-based private equity investors, financed by a public issue of bonds on the US market.

The turnaround gave Derby the wherewithal to acquire two US bicycle manufacturers/distributors, Raleigh Cycle Company of America, and its US licensee owned by rival bicycle manufacturer Huffy Corporation and West Coast Cycles.

In 2000, The Derby Cycle Corporation controlled Raleigh USA, Raleigh UK, Raleigh Canada and Raleigh Ireland. In the latter three markets, Raleigh was the number one manufacturer of bicycles. Derby began a series of divestitures, selling Sturmey-Archer which is now owned by SunRace of Taiwan, and attempted to sell Brooks, which is now owned by Selle Royal of Italy. Raleigh sold its Triumph road site to the university of Nottingham in 2000 in a sale and buyback deal, closing its factory in 2002. In 2001, following financial problems, there was a management buy-out of all the remaining Raleigh companies led by Alan Finden-Crofts.

On 26 October 2001, a management group led by Alan Finden-Crofts acquired the operations of Derby Cycle Corporation in a deal worth about $73 million, including more than $50 million in assumed debt. At the same time, Germany's Wiener Bike Parts and Derby South Africa were sold off. Finden-Crofts then owned 42 per cent of Derby Cycle, which was reorganized under a new holding company renamed Raleigh Cycle Limited.

After four years of losses, Raleigh UK managed a small profit on sales of £35 million in 2003. It then had about 200 employees. Raleigh America had sales of about US$75 million. Nostalgically, Raleigh brought back its 1970s-era Chopper in the spring of 2004.

Around 2005 the new Raleigh had six major subsidiaries: Derby Cycle Werke (Germany, formally Khalkoff); Raleigh America (USA); Raleigh Canada; Raleigh Taiwan; Raleigh UK Limited and Raleigh International.

In October 2005 Derby Cycle Werke was sold for US$40 million to the investment firm Finatem II Beteiligungsgesellschaft, which specializes in investing in medium-sized German companies. Derby Cycle Werke holds the licenses for Diamondback in continental Europe, and Raleigh for Austria, Germany and Switzerland. It also owns the Univega and Focus brands.

In 2004 Raleigh UK started its Cyclelife initiative. The Cyclelife concept is based on franchising and was created to compete effectively with chain stores in the UK by giving all Cyclelife participants a national identity. In April 2009 there were 100 Cyclelife stores in the UK. In September 2009 the first Cyclelife dealership started in Ireland.

The bicycle world market

Currently only 18 per cent of the world population sometimes uses a bicycle. This means that there is still a huge potential number of customers out there: 82 per cent of the world population.

According to Table 1 the global bicycle market, including bicycles, parts and accessories, is estimated to have total retail sales of about €36 billion. In 2008, worldwide demand of bicycles is approximately 90 million units, of which approximately 60 per cent are produced (but not bought) in China (with Taiwan as the core bicycle production centre). In comparison roughly 40 million cars were produced worldwide.

During the 1980s Taiwan took over Japan's role as the world's leading supply nation. The world bicycle market is highly fragmented. The world's biggest bicycle producer, Giant in Taiwan, produces almost 2 million bicycles, securing them a market share of 2.2 per cent. Taiwanese firms have opened their own overseas production centres. Meanwhile Japan retains its prime role in the supply of cycle components, again drawing on cheap labour in other parts of the Far East. Japanese Shimano is one example of a huge component supplier.

The world electric bicycle (e-bike) market

The modern electric bicycle (e-bike) is true to the concept of a pedal bicycle with assisting propulsion, being ridable without power. Batteries have finite capacity, which means that the hybrid human/electric power mix is much more likely to be emphasized than is the case with a combustion engine. Electric bicycles are gaining acceptance, especially in Europe and Asia, in response to increasing traffic congestion, an ageing population and concern about the environment.

Electric motorized bicycles can be *power-on-demand*, where the motor is activated by a handlebar mounted throttle, and/or a *pedelec* (from **ped**al **elec**tric), also known as *electric assist*, where the electric motor is regulated by pedalling. These have a sensor to detect the pedalling speed, the pedalling force, or both. An electronic controller provides assistance as a

Raleigh website
Raleigh International Ltd. (www.raleigh.com).

function of the sensor inputs, the vehicle speed and the required force. Most controllers also provide for manual adjustment.

Range is a key consideration with electric bikes, and is affected by factors such as motor efficiency, battery capacity, efficiency of the driving electronics, aerodynamics, hills and weight of the bike and rider. The range of an electric bike is usually stated as somewhere between 7 km (uphill on electric power only) to 70 km (minimum assistance) and is highly dependent on whether or not the bike is tested on flat roads or hills.

There have been some interesting advances in materials science and battery technology that now make electric bicycles more practical than in previous years. Much of this has come from the computer industry. For example, battery technology has advanced a great deal. The battery systems to choose from include lead-acid, NiCd, NiMH and Lithium-ion batteries.

Three factors are important when choosing the right battery: weight, how long the battery lasts, and how long it takes to recharge.

Lithium-ion batteries are very common in consumer electronic devices, especially the portable type. The qualities that make them ideal in consumer electronics also make them ideal for bicycles. For example, they have one of the best energy-to-weight ratios of any battery type and recharging them is straightforward. Additionally, they do not suffer from 'memory effect' – which is when a battery that is only partially discharged is subsequently recharged but never regains its full capacity again. Furthermore, the charge lost over time when not in use is negligible.

However, lithium-ion batteries do have certain drawbacks. For one, the shelf life is limited in comparison to nickel cadmium batteries. From time of manufacturing, regardless of the number of charge and discharge

| Table 1 | Total European and world bicycle market + e-bikes (2008) |

Market volume (1,000 units of bicycles – consumption)	Germany	France	UK	Italy	NL	Rest of EU	Total EU	Japan	China (incl. Taiwan)	USA	Total world (incl ROW.)
Total market (1,000)	4,500	3,500	3,400	2,000	1,400	13,200	28,000	10,000	28,000	18,000	90,000
Most important manufacturers /brands	MIFA Derby Cycle Werke	Eddy Merckx Peugeot	Raleigh Universal	Bianchi Alan Cinelli	Gzzelle	??	Raleigh Derby	??	Giant Co Tianjin Xinri Shandong	Connondale Merlin	Giant Man Ltd (Taiwan) Trek
Raleigh brand market shares %	??	??	20%	??	??	??	??	??	??	??	??
% volume – e-biFkes	2.6	1.5	2.1	1.5	7.0	1.0	1.8	3.0	54.0	1.7	20.0
Total e-bikes market (1,000)	117	52	71	30	98	132	500	300	15,000	300	18,000
Market value (mill. €)											
Total value (mill. €) – all bicycles including parts and accessories (average price: €400 per unit – unless for China)	1,800	1,400	1,360	800	560	5,280	11,200	4,000	5,600 (average price: €200 per unit)	7,200	36,000
Total value – e-bikes (mill. €) (average price: €1,500 per unit – unless for China)	175	78	96	45	147	198	750	450	4,500 (average price: €300 per unit)	450	9,000
% value – e-bikes	9.7	5.5	7.1	5.6	26.0	3.8	6.7	11.3	80.4	6.3	25.0

Source: www.bike-eu.com (market reports), China Sourcing Reports (bicycles).

cycles, the battery's capacity will decline. This means that the battery has to be exchanged every second or third year.

Worldwide, the total e-bike (which in Table 1 is regarded as a part of the total world bicycle market), is estimated to 18 million unit, which represents a value of approximately €9 billion. Most of the worldwide demand for e-bikes is found in China, where consumers are buying 54 per cent of all e-bikes sold worldwide.

The share of e-bikes (of the total bicycle market) varies a lot from market to market. In Europe (apart from the Netherlands) the percentage is still relatively low, whereas in Asia the percentage is as high as 50 per cent (e.g. in China).

In April 2009 the EN 15194 standard for 'Electronically Power-assisted Cycles' (EPAC) was officially announced by the National Standards Boards (NSBs') of 30 countries (27 EU member states and Iceland, Norway and Switzerland of the European Free Trade Association).

Current Raleigh international marketing strategy

By the 1930s Raleigh was already exporting from Nottingham all over the world. This was not done by just sending a single model of bicycle to all these countries, but by gathering information about each market and adapting the design of bicycles to the local market. The policy of adaptation was continued until the 1960s when Raleigh had 60,000 different models of bicycle in its range, each of which had a demand to fill. After the 1960s takeover of Raleigh by TI, the Raleigh product range was gradually rationalized and standardized. However, the consequence was that Raleigh lost market share in many countries, mainly to local competition as customers would not accept the 'standardized' changes being made.

Today Raleigh has five group companies, the first three directly supplying the United Kingdom, the USA and Canada; the fourth selling to all other countries around the world; and the last a trading company based in Taiwan inspecting the quality of shipments from far Eastern supplies for both Raleigh group companies and third party companies.

As indicated earlier, in the UK, Raleigh builds their business model mainly on the franchise-based Cyclelife store concept.

In international markets Raleigh has cancelled their bicycle manufacturing units (the bicycles are now sourced from Far East). Instead they mainly rely on a licensing concept: revenue is generated by finding partners around the world who are willing to pay a royalty fee for having the exclusive right to sell under the Raleigh brand, or one of the other Raleigh companies' brands in their chosen market. By taking this approach Raleigh can choose the international partners that they want to work with and refuse to work with partners wishing to sell inferior quality bicycles with the Raleigh name. Raleigh can keep the control of its brand by having the contractual right to veto any bicycle that is not appropriate for the Raleigh brand.

When the partners have been chosen, Raleigh is quite flexible in how the licensing contracts are drawn up, by allowing licensees a relatively free reign on how they market the Raleigh name locally. Through this strategy Raleigh is becoming a stronger brand in a lot of countries, for example in Finland where Raleigh bicycles had not been sold before. The licensee spent a lot of time and effort promoting Raleigh and the licensee reports it is now the third biggest brand in the country.

The licensing strategy also has had the consequence that the Raleigh brand is perceived in different ways in different countries. Here are some examples:

- Holland: the Raleigh bicycle is the Managing Directors' bicycle; it is seen as exclusive and has a very high price to match the image.
- Ireland: a Raleigh bicycle is seen as a family bicycle which cannot command any more money per bicycle than other internationally branded competitor's bicycles.
- Germany: the Raleigh bicycle is used mainly for leisure and exercise.
- Kuwait: the rise in income has meant the bicycle is perceived as a poor man's transport so the majority of bicycles sold there are for the immigrant workforce to get to work cheaply.

R09 Power Elegance (e-bike)
Raleigh International Ltd.

- Africa: in South Africa, Raleigh has sponsored a successful national cycling team and based all of their marketing around this team, thus suggesting Raleigh is 'setting the pace' in South Africa.

Team Raleigh
Raleigh International Ltd.

Today Raleigh's market share of the UK bicycle market is 20 per cent (2007) – in the heydays it used to be 60 per cent.

The strategy to license the Raleigh name to partners has minimized the fixed costs and the financial situation today is much better than it used to be: the Raleigh UK Group's latest financials (2008) show the company with a profit of £1.4m on turnover of £31m. In 2002 the business lost nearly £6m.

QUESTIONS

1. Characterize the internationalization 'balance' between standardization and adaptation over the history of Raleigh.

2. Does the iconic bicycle brand still have a chance on the world market?

3. Please compare and evaluate Raleigh's current entry modes (business models): franchising and licensing with other alternatives.

4. E-bike sales are increasing across Europe. Electric bicycles are being seen as a commuting alternative to the car, allowing customers to arrive at work on their bicycle without having to shower and change. This is an area where Raleigh already has a product. Should Raleigh sell a standardized e-bike concept, or should it adapt its marketing mix to each local market depending on the culture and potential future e-bike sales?

Sources: www.bike-eu.com market reports; Global bicycle stats http://quickrelease.tv/?p=279; http://www.bikebiz.com/news/29247/ Guardian-profiles-Gouldthorp; http://www.guardian.co.uk/business/ 2007/nov/23/cycling; http://tectrends.com/tectrends/article/ 00169044.html; special thanks to Gerry Appleton and John Macnaughtan from Raleigh.

At the beginning of 2010 Ingvar Kamprad, founder of the Swedish furniture retailing giant IKEA, is concerned 'his' firm may be growing too quickly. He used to be in favour of rapid expansion, but he has now become worried that the firm may be forced to close stores in the event of a sustained economic downturn.

Although IKEA is one of Sweden's best-known exports, it has not in a strict legal sense been Swedish since the early 1980s. The store has made its name by supplying Scandinavian designs at Asian prices. It has managed its international expansion without stumbling. Indeed, its brand – which stands for clean, green and attractive design and value for money – is as potent today as it has been at any time in more than 60 years in business.

The parent of all IKEA companies – the operator of 253 of the 287 worldwide IKEA stores – is Ingka Holding, a private Dutch-registered company. Ingka Holding (which is named after the first and last name of the founder) belongs entirely to the Stichting Ingka Foundation. This is a Dutch-registered, tax-exempt, non-profit-making legal entity, which was given the shares of Ingvar Kamprad in 1982. *Stichtingen*, or foundations, are the most common form of not-for-profit organization in the Netherlands; tens of thousands of them are registered.

Most Dutch *stichtingen* are tiny, but if Stichting Ingka Foundation were listed it would be one of the Netherlands' ten largest companies by market value. Its main asset is the Ingka Holding group, which is conservatively financed and highly profitable.

Valuing the Ingka Holding Group is awkward, because IKEA has no direct competitors that operate globally. Shares in Target, a large, successful chain of stores in the United States that makes a fifth of its sales from home furnishings, are priced at 20 times the store's latest full-year earnings. Using that price/earnings ratio, the Ingka Holding Group is worth €35 billion.

Now Ingvar Kamprad has heard that the top management of the IKEA Group plans to make a further international expansion, into South America, because of

www.ikea.com

the growth opportunities there. Kamprad is very sceptical about these plans and his personal assistant has asked you, as an international marketing specialist, to get an expert opinion about the plans . . .

IKEA – the story

IKEA Svenska AB, founded in 1943, is the world's largest furniture retailer and specializes in stylish but inexpensive Scandinavian designed furniture. In 1943 the founder of IKEA, Ingvar Kamprad from Agunnaryd, Sweden, registered the name IKEA, which was formed from the founder's initials (IK) plus the first letters of Elmtaryd and Agunnaryd, the farm and village where he grew up.

The first IKEA store opens in Älmhult, Sweden in 1958. Then the internationalization process started.

About corporate IKEA

IKEA has grown into the world's largest furniture retailer, with 237 stores in 35 countries (2007) and a workforce of some 90,000 people since its first outlet opened in Älmhult in 1958. The firm is noted for its rapid international expansion and has recently set up stores in Eastern Europe and Russia.

IKEA's success in the retail industry can be attributed to its vast experience in the retail market, product differentiation and cost leadership. The company is one of the world's most successful multinational retailing firms, operating as a global organization, with its unique concept that its furniture is sold in kits that are assembled by the customer at home.

The firm, which remains in private ownership, racked up sales of nearly €23 billion in 2002.

There are about 12,000 products in the total IKEA product range. Each store carries a selection of these 12,000 products depending on store size and the core range is the same worldwide.

IKEA accounts for just 5 to 10 per cent of the furniture market in each country in which it operates. More important is that the awareness of the IKEA brand is much bigger than the size of the company because IKEA is far more than a furniture merchant. It sells a Scandinavian lifestyle that customers around the world embrace.

The IKEA business idea is to offer a wide range of home furnishing items of good design and function, excellent quality and durability, at prices so low that the majority of people can afford them. The company targets the customer who is looking for value and is willing to do a little bit of work serving themselves, transporting the items home and assembling the furniture. The typical IKEA customer is a young low- to middle-income family.

As mentioned, IKEA's retailing is based on a franchise system. Inter IKEA Systems B.V., located in Delft (the Netherlands), is the owner and franchisor of the IKEA concept. The IKEA Group is a private group of companies owned by a charitable foundation in the Netherlands. It is active in developing, purchasing, distributing and selling IKEA products. The IKEA experience is more than just products, however, it is a retail concept. For the concept to work all aspects must be in place. IKEA products are therefore sold only in IKEA stores franchised by Inter IKEA Systems B.V. However, most of the global product policy (including product development) and the global marketing is centralized to the Swedish part of the company, IKEA of Sweden.

IKEA performs some of the value chain activities internally, while it uses its relationships with suppliers to combine its internal and their external resources for the sake of both efficiency and development. For instance, products are developed in close interaction with suppliers while taking into consideration the impact of the raw materials, components and facilities involved, since all these resources entail costs and have an impact on quality, design and function. In fact, next to low costs, reasonable quality, appealing designs and adequate product functionality are major goals for IKEA. These goals induce the company to promote a *constant* product and technical development, which

contributes to its image as an innovative and fashion-oriented firm, but which depends heavily on the contribution of its entire network of suppliers.

To cope with such tasks, IKEA needs advanced skills in marketing, retailing, logistics, purchasing, product development and technologies. This need of competence is reflected by IKEA's complex organization. However, the complexity of IKEA's organization is overshadowed by that of its industrial network – internal and external (see Figure 1). This network includes 1,380 direct suppliers and about 10,000 sub-suppliers, spread over 60 countries: 287 IKEA stores (253 own stores plus 34 franchised stores), are located in 30 countries including Europe, Australia, the US and China.

Between IKEA's stores and suppliers stands a vital, but less visible part of IKEA's network: its wholesale and logistic operations, comprising 27 distribution centres and 11 customer distribution centres in 16 countries. Since IKEA does not own any transport facilities, this network is physically connected via another group of external actors, about 500 logistic partners.

A pivotal role in this network is played by 'IKEA of Sweden', (located in Âlmhult, Sweden) a leading business unit that not only manages IKEA's product range, but also *supervises* the entire IKEA universe and develops long-term marketing, logistics and purchasing strategies. IKEA of Sweden has both an overall responsibility and a coordinating role in the development, purchase, distribution and marketing of each single product (Baraldi, 2008).

Product development and production

The team behind each product consists of designers, product developers and purchasers who get together to discuss design, materials and suitable suppliers. Everyone contributes with their specialist knowledge. Purchasers, for example, use their contacts with suppliers all over the world via IKEA Trading Service Offices. Who can make this product of the best quality for the right price at the right time? Products are often developed in close cooperation with suppliers and often only one supplier is appointed to supply all the stores around the world.

IKEA does have its own manufacturing facilities. In 1991 it acquired its own sawmills and production plants and establishes the industrial group Swedwood to produce wood-based furniture and wooden components. The primary motive behind this acquisition was to ensure production capacity for IKEA. However, most of the production takes place at subcontractors all over the world.

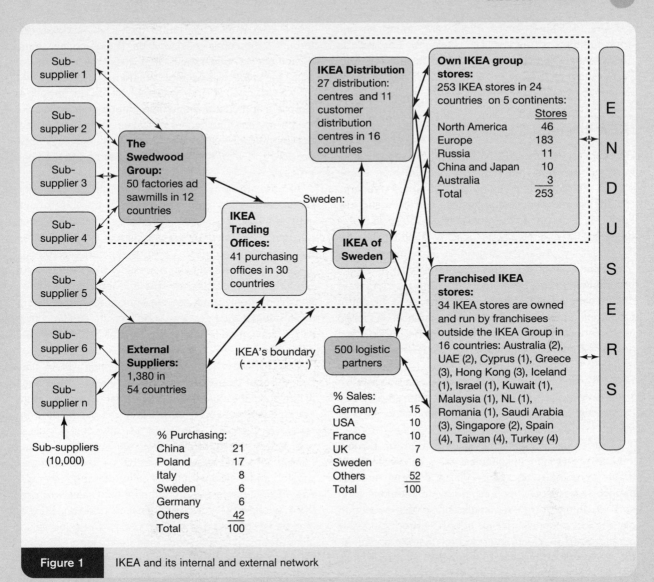

Figure 1   IKEA and its internal and external network

End-consumers

In order to keep costs low, IKEA shoppers are pro-sumers – half producers and half consumers. In other words, they have to assemble the products themselves. To facilitate shopping, IKEA provides catalogues, tape measures, shopping lists and an Internet website to help the consumer with fitting the furniture into the room. Car roof racks are available for purchase at cost and IKEA pick-up vans/mini-trucks are available to rent. IKEA's success is based on the relatively simple idea of keeping the cost between manufacturers and customers down. Costs are kept under control starting at the design level of the value-added chain. IKEA also keeps costs down by packing items compactly in flat standardized packaging and stacking them as high as

possible to reduce storage space during and after distribution.

Effective marketing through catalogues is what usually attracts the customer first; what keeps customers coming back is good service. IKEA believes that a strong in-stock position, in which the most popular style and design trends are correctly anticipated, is crucial to keep customers satisfied. For that IKEA depends on leading-edge technology and the company has developed its own global distribution network. By utilizing control points in the distribution cycle the firm is able to insure timely delivery of products to retail stores all over the world.

IKEA thinks that consumer tastes are merging globally. To take one example, they have been exporting the 'streamlined and contemporary Scandinavian style' to the United States since 1985, and found several opportunities to export US style to Europe, as Europeans picked up on some US furnishing concepts. To respond to this new demand IKEA now markets 'American-style' furnishings in Europe.

IKEA strategy

Bureaucracy is fought at all levels in the organization. Kamprad believes that simplicity and common sense should characterize planning and strategic direction. In addition, the culture emphasizes efficiency and low cost, which is not to be achieved at the expense of quality or service. Symbolic policies, such as only flying economy class and staying at economical hotels, employing young executives and sponsoring university programmes, have been integrated into the corporate culture and have further inspired the spirit of entrepreneurship in the organization. For instance, all design teams enjoy complete autonomy in their work, but are expected to design new and appealing products regularly.

IKEA has improved its value chain by a cooperative focus on suppliers and customers. The firm emphasizes centralized control and standardization of the product mix.

In order to maintain cost leadership in the market, internal production efficiencies must be greater than those of competitors. Under IKEA's global strategy suppliers are usually located in low-cost nations, with close proximity to raw materials and reliable access to distribution channels. These suppliers produce highly standardized products intended for the global market, the size of which provides the firm with the opportunity to take advantage of economies of scale. IKEA's role is not only to integrate operations globally and design products centrally, but also to find an effective combination of low cost, standardization, technology and quality.

In the case of IKEA, a standardized product strategy does not mean complete cultural insensitivity. The company is, rather, responding to globally emerging consumer tastes and preferences. Retail outlets all over the world carry the basic product range, which is universally accepted, but also place great emphasis on the product lines that appeal to local customer preferences.

IKEA has modified the value chain approach by integrating the customer into the process and introducing a two-way value system between customers, suppliers and IKEA's headquarters. In this global sourcing strategy the customer is a supplier of time, labour, information, knowledge and transport. On the other hand, the suppliers are customers, receiving technical assis-

tance from IKEA's corporate technical headquarters through various business services. The company wants customers to understand that their role is not to consume value, but rather to create it.

IKEA's role in the value chain is to mobilize suppliers and customers to help them further add value to the system. Customers are clearly informed in the catalogues of what the firm's business systems provide, and what they are expected to add to the final process.

In order to furnish the customer with good quality products at a low cost, the firm must be able to find suppliers that can deliver high-quality items at low cost per unit. The company's headquarters provides carefully selected suppliers with technical assistance, leased equipment and the necessary skills needed to produce high-quality items. This long-term supplier relationship not only produces superior products, but also adds internal value to the suppliers. In addition, this value chain modification differentiates IKEA from its competitors.

Directly linked to its mission statement, IKEA has built its cost leadership position on these processes. It furnishes the customer with a quality product with components derived from all over the world utilizing multilevel competitive advantages, low cost logistics and large simple retail outlets in suburban areas. Furthermore, cost leadership has been effectively incorporated into the organization's culture through symbols and efficient processes. In return for high sales volumes IKEA accepts low profit margins. In addition, IKEA's marketing emphasis on budget prices and good value clearly communicates cost leadership to customers. IKEA's strategy demonstrates that the perception that cost leadership equals poor quality in products and services is incorrect. High quality is associated with input and process variables. Cost reduction, on the other hand, does not mean reducing the quality of these variables, but rather doing things better, and more efficiently. Cost leadership is a part of the management process and culture.

From this discussion it is possible to conclude that IKEA effectively aligns its cost leadership platform, focusing on the needs of its target market segment. Differentiation, as indicated in the modification of the value chain, also focuses on this particular segment.

The internationalization of IKEA

IKEA has applied a conservative policy to internationalization. As a general rule, the firm does not enter a new potential market by opening a retail outlet. Instead, a supplier link with the host nation is established. This is a strategic, risk-reducing approach in which local suppliers can provide valuable input on political and legal, cultural, financial and other issues that provide opportunities and/or threats to the IKEA concept. In the 1970s and 1980s IKEA concentrated its international expansion in Europe and in North America, mainly through company-owned subsidiaries and stores.

Expansion by franchising

IKEA mostly approaches unknown, relatively small and high-risk markets by franchising. At the beginning of 2010 there are 34 franchised stores (see Figure 1) are granted by Inter IKEA Systems B.V. as part of a detailed international expansion plan. Serious applicants are carefully researched and evaluated and franchises are granted only to companies and/or individuals with strong financial backing and a proven record in retail. Franchisees have to carry basic items, but have the freedom to design the rest of the product mix to fit local market needs. The basic core items number approximately 12,000 simple and functional products. The centralized head office is actively involved in the selection processes and provides advice. In addition, all products have to be purchased from IKEA's product lines. In order to maintain service, quality and logistic standards, individual franchisees are periodically audited and compared to overall corporate performance. Extensive training and operational support is provided from headquarters. All franchisees pay franchise fees to IKEA Holdings. All catalogues and promotional advertising is the responsibility of headquarters. Franchising has been used as a vehicle for the company's generic focus strategy.

Balance of autonomy and strategic direction

As IKEA continues to expand overseas the significance of centralized strategic direction will increase. Naturally rapid internationalization will trigger a range of challenges imposed on the headquarters, such as:

- The complexity of the logistics system will increase.
- It will be more difficult to respond to national needs and cultural sensitivity issues.
- Emerging demographic trends will force the organization to broaden its focus strategy to respond to varying nation-level consumer groups.

With all these challenges emerging it might be very difficult to maintain a central organizational structure. The best way to meet these challenges is to find the proper balance between country-level autonomy and centralized intervention. With reference to IKEA's long-term relationship and control over its suppliers in exchange for quality assurance, technology transfers and economies of scale factors may trigger potential suppliers to integrate forward and produce competitive products for IKEA's local competitors. With logistics complications and long lead times IKEA is forced to maintain high control levels over its suppliers. For instance, if the supplier responsible for the screws component to a table cannot deliver on time, the supplier of the table-top has to adapt its production to the new scenario. Without IKEA's centralized logistics system this example could lead to severe store shortages, leading to losses in sales.

The Brazilian market for furniture

According to the Brazilian Association of Furniture Manufacturers (ABIMOVEL), the Brazilian furniture market was estimated at approximately US$4.5 billion in 2008, of which about US$150 million were imports. The market can be broken down into three main categories: residential (60 per cent), office (25 per cent), and institutional organizations, such as schools, hospitals and hotels (15 per cent).

Brazil has 4.6 million hectares of planted forests, almost all of which is located in the south of the country. Wood from such forests is mainly used in the production of furniture, pulp and paper. The main furniture production centres, as well as the most important markets, are also located in southern Brazil.

As the Brazilian furniture market continues to reap more and more of its profits from exports, production is increasingly tailored to satisfy market niches that demand differentiated products. To meet this need the Brazilian industry is investing more in design and development, although investments are smaller in comparison to investments made in the United States, Italy and Germany. Brazil is also importing state-of-the-art equipment to address quality issues mandated by foreign markets, e.g. the US, Italian and German ones. Today the segment requires import of equipment such as wood-drying machinery, finishing machinery and tools.

According to the Brazilian Furniture Association there are approximately 14,500 Brazilian furniture manufacturers, most of which are small. These firms are typically family-owned companies whose capital is exclusively Brazilian. Historically, the greater proportion of Brazilian manufacturers have been concentrated in areas of large population density in southern Brazil.

The process of trade liberalization initiated in 1990 introduced significant changes in Brazil's trade regime, resulting in a more open and competitive economy.

The Brazilian economy was deeply affected by the crises in the Asian and Russian markets. As a consequence the currency suffered deeply from the devaluation in January 1999. Brazilian imports of furniture were also seriously affected by this devaluation, and the industry is currently suffering from the unfavourable (for Brazilians) *real*–dollar exchange rate.

US exports of furniture to Brazil reached $50 million in 2008 (35 per cent of total Brazilian furniture imports). US exports to Brazil were particularly strong in the area of seats, new-design office furniture, and high-end, high-value-added residential furniture. Market analysts estimate that in the next three to four years imports of institutional furniture, such as that used in hospitals and hotels, will increase considerably, mainly imports from the United States.

Imports

Brazilian furniture imports totalled US$150 million in 2008. This represents 3 per cent of the total furniture market in Brazil. The USA holds 35 per cent of the imported furniture market, followed by Germany with 30 per cent, Italy with 20 per cent, and other countries with 15 per cent.

End-user analysis

The different industry segments – residential, commercial and institutional – make up the Brazilian market. Each of those areas has its own purchasing approach. For example, the public institutions may import directly from its headquarters and, in the case of the furniture industry, the end-user might be an importer or a store chain.

It is important to mention that there are no major distributor chains in Brazil. Most furniture imports are made through direct importers and, in a smaller proportion, local manufacturers wishing to complement their product line.

High-end furniture and mattresses are commonly imported into Brazil by direct importers or furniture stores. Interior decorators and architects are also considered decision-makers, since they are the ones who recommend brands and styles to their final clients.

Import climate

Brazil has a tariff-based import system and has simplified the process for obtaining import licences. Import tariffs are levied *ad valorem* on the cost, insurance and freight (CIF) value of the imports. Import tax (IPI – see below) for furniture varies from 5–10 per cent.

The industrial products tax (IPI) is a federal tax levied on most domestic and imported manufactured products. It is assessed at the point of sale by the manufacturer or processor in the case of domestically produced goods, and at the point of customs clearance in the case of imports. The tax rate varies by product and is based on the product's CIF value plus duties.

Interest rates in Brazil have decreased from 2008 to 2010 (estimated at 8.0 per cent per year in June 2010), but it is still at a relatively high level and this discour-

ages demand for bank loans. The few sources of funds available for long-term financing are provided by the National Bank for Economic and Social Development (BNDES), through leasing operations and by foreign government export agencies.

Distribution and business practices

Major end-users of furniture will only purchase from well-known and reliable suppliers. Although large end-users may import directly from foreign suppliers, they are always concerned with after-sales service. Technical assistance and availability of replacement parts are considered important factors in the purchasing decision. In some segments, such as commercial and institutional, this factor may determine from whom the end-user will purchase. A physical presence in the market, either through an agent or a manufacturing plant, increases the end-user's trust in the supplier's commitment to this market and facilitates the sale.

The retail scene in Brazil

For many years the popular wisdom in Brazil was that shopping malls were only for rich people. The 1984 opening of Center Norte mall in São Paulo changed all that. It is strategically placed next to a subway and a bus terminal: proximity to mass transit is essential, since many low-income consumers do not own cars. Center Norte was followed by other shopping malls in other cities, such as Rio de Janeiro and Belo Horizonte.

Economic instability, difficulties in obtaining financing at reasonable interest rates and customs barriers for certain imports have slowed down the entry of foreign retailers to Brazil. Among the international chains that have been attracted by Brazil's 80 million consumers are JC Penney, Zara and the Dutch chain C&A, that leads the fashion sector in Brazil. International franchisors such as Benetton, Lacoste, Hugo Boss, Polo Ralph Lauren and McDonald's operate in Brazilian shopping centres, some on a large scale.

Those who have set up shops in Brazil have varied results directly related to their ability to adapt to local conditions. Sears, for example, had extremely negative results, due to the centralization of decision-making in Chicago. Similarly, Zara tried to bring its European management policy and market approach to Brazil and faced poor financial results in the beginning. The contrast is the excellent performance of C&A, whose policies and procedures were defined in Brazil for the local market. JC Penney acquired a local chain (Renner) and accelerated its expansion with good results (ICSC Worldwide Commission, 2000).

QUESTIONS

1. Until now IKEA's international marketing strategy has been tightly and centrally controlled by corporate headquarters. However, high local pressures emerging due to demographic and cultural differences might force the local IKEA shops to take strategic initiatives to respond to local market needs. In this connection discuss the regional headquarters and transnational organization (presented in Chapter 12) as hierarchical entry mode alternatives to the very centralized strategy emanating from IKEA's headquarters.

2. IKEA has not yet explored joint venture and strategic alliances strategies. Evaluate the pros and cons regarding these two entry strategies versus the traditional IKEA entry mode – own stores and franchising.

3. Should IKEA penetrate the South American market by establishing a shop in Brazil?

4. In the light of the political and economic situation in South America, outline the sourcing concept that should be implemented in the South American market.

Sources: IKEA Annual Report 2008 Baraldi, E. (2008) 'Strategy in industrial networks: experiences from IKEA', *California Management Review*, 50(4) pp. 99–126; www.ikea.com; BBC News (2003) news.bbc.co.uk, 'IKEA founder worried over growth', 3 January; ICSC Worldwide Commission (2000) 'Shopping centres: a world of opportunities', www.icsc.org.

CASE STUDY III.3

Autoliv airbags: transforming Autoliv into a global company

Chief executive officer of Autoliv Inc., Jan Carlson, is in the middle of a board of directors' meeting in Stockholm in December 2010, discussing how it is possible to further globalize Autoliv. He takes out a situation report for the business area of airbags. As there are a couple of new members on the board Jan takes the opportunity to give a broader introduction to the business area than he usually does. The following is his status report.

Situation report for the business area of airbags

Business concept

Autoliv Inc., which is a Fortune 500 company, is the world's largest automotive safety supplier with sales to all the leading car manufacturers in the world. Autoliv's shares are listed on the New York Stock Exchange and on the Stockholm Stock Exchange. The company develops, markets and manufactures airbags, seat belts, safety electronics, steering wheels, anti-whiplash systems, seat components and child seats. Autoliv has 80 subsidiaries (production plants) and joint ventures in 30 vehicle-producing countries, with around 34,000 employees. In addition, Autoliv has technical centres in 9 countries with 20 crash test tracks – more than any other automotive safety supplier.

Autoliv aims to develop, manufacture and market systems and components worldwide for personal safety in automobiles. This includes the mitigation of injuries to autombile occupants and pedestrians and the avoidance of accidents. Autoliv wants to be the systems supplier and the development partner to car producers that satisfy all the needs in the area of personal safety. To fulfil its business concept Autoliv has strong product lines:

- frontal and side-impact airbags (including all key components such as inflators with initiators, textile cushions, electronics with sensors and software, steel and plastic parts);
- seat belts (including all key components such as webbing, retractors and buckles);
- seat belt features (including pretensioners, load limiters, height adjusters and belt grabbers);
- seat subsystems (including anti-whiplash systems);
- steering wheels (including integrated driver airbags);
- roll-over protection (including sensors, pretensioners and airbag curtains).
- Night-vision system with pedestrian detection and warning (this product was introduced in BMW cars in 2008).

Autoliv's short- and medium-range radar system provides all-weather object detection and tracking to improve safety and to provide assistance to the driver. The radar can be used for blind spot detection, lane change assist, adaptive cruise control, collision mitigation by braking and for back-up and park assist functions. The radar could also provide front and side pre-crash sensing that scans up to 30 metres around the vehicle to provide an advanced warning of an imminent collision. This additional time could be used to prime airbags and active seatbelts. (An active seatbelt has an electrically driven pretensioner that tightens the belt as a precaution in hazardous situations.) Autoliv already delivers active seatbelts to four premium brand vehicle models for three different customers.

In 2008 the penetration rate of frontal and side airbags in Europe was nearly 100 per cent. For curtain airbags in new cars the penetration rate was 70 per cent in Europe, 50 per cent in North America, 30 per cent in Japan and 20 per cent in the rest of the world.

The following concentrates on the business area of airbags.

Production strategy

Autoliv has final assembly of restraint systems, located close to major customers' plants for just-in-time supply (see Figure 1). Most of the component production (textiles and stamped metal components, etc.) has been outsourced during the past five years.

Since major automobile manufacturers are continually expanding production into more countries, it is also Autoliv's strategy to have manufacturing capacity where the major vehicle manufacturers have or are likely to set up production facilities. As a consequence Autoliv has more plants for automotive safety products in more countries than any other supplier.

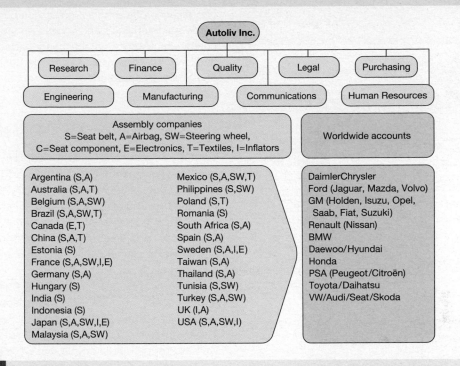

Figure 1   Autoliv's corporate structure

The product: the airbag

Even the best belt designs cannot prevent all head and chest injuries in serious head-on crashes. This is where airbags help, by creating an energy-absorbing cushion between an occupant's upper body and the steering wheel, instrument panel or windshield. Independent research has shown that driver deaths in head-on crashes are about 20 per cent lower in cars with frontal airbags than in similar cars with belts only. In all kinds of crash deaths are down by about 15 per cent over and above lives already being saved by belts.

Although airbags may seem complicated they are in fact relatively simple. In moderate and severe head-on crashes sensors signal inflators to fill the bags with harmless gas. The bags fill in a fraction of a second and begin deflating the instant they cushion people, but in the United States a few occupants have died of broken necks. Peak inflation is in less than one-twentieth of a second, faster than the blink of an eye. The speed and force of airbag inflation may occasionally cause injuries, mostly minor abrasions or bruises, but in the United States some occupants have died of broken necks caused by airbags that inflated with great force. Those at the greatest risk of injury caused by an airbag are those who drive or ride unbelted, small children, short or obese adults, and certain disabled people.

Injury risk from the bag itself can be reduced by choosing a driving or passenger position that does not put your face or chest close to the steering wheel or instrument panel. The combination of seat belt and airbag provides maximum protection in all kinds of crash.

Together with Volvo Autoliv has also developed the first side airbags to protect drivers and front-seat passengers in side-impact crashes. These bags are typically smaller than frontal airbags and they inflate more quickly. Volvo was the first manufacturer to offer side airbags in its 850 model in 1994. Volvo's bag is mounted on the outside of driver and front-seat passenger seat backs. Since 1996 side bags have been standard in all Volvo models.

The history of airbags goes back to the early 1950s. The product idea was patented in 1951 by Walter Linderer from Munich. It was in the United States, however, that the concept came into existence, driven by the North Americans' reluctance to use seat belts and hindered by the car manufacturers, who initially ridiculed the idea. In 1981 only 2,636 airbag systems were produced.

However, in late 1989 automatic restraint systems became compulsory in all passenger cars in the United States on the driver's side and, while this included automatically fastening seat belts, it seemed that the airbag had at last arrived. By 1992, 10 million airbag-equipped cars had been delivered to the United States. In 1993 came the requirement that all new light vehicles of model year 1999 produced in the United States had to be

Source: www.autoliv.com

coordination offices this organization contributes to low corporate overheads and short response times for the customers. (Autoliv's global headquarters in Stockholm has only 40 employees.) Autoliv's business directors and their organizations coordinate all activities with major customers on a global basis.

The world market for safety content

With its successful growth strategy, Autoliv has become the global leader in the US$18 billion automobile occupant restraint market (includes airbags, seatbelts and related electronics). Frontal and side airbags account for 55 per cent of that market, seat belts for 25 per cent and electronics for 20 per cent.

The world market for airbags was an area of spectacular growth during the 1990s.

In the United States frontal airbags – both on the driver and the passenger side – are compulsory under federal law in all new light vehicles sold after 1 September 1998. The US market for frontal airbags therefore fluctuates with the car production cycle, but sales of side airbags are now about to take off. Their penetration rate was less than 20 per cent among new US light vehicles in 2001. Both Ford and General Motors have announced aggressive plans for curtain side airbags such as Autoliv's Inflatable Curtain. In addition, new regulations in the United States will require vehicle manufacturers to phase in more valuable 'advanced airbags' during a three-year period starting on 1 September 2003.

In Europe, Autoliv estimates that more or less all new vehicles have dual airbags. Installations of side impact airbags began in 1994, but in 2001 two-thirds of all new vehicles in Europe had such systems for chest protection. In addition, 25 per cent had a separate side-impact airbag for head protection (such as the inflatable curtain). In 2009 the European penetration rate for both frontal and side airbags is nearly 100 per cent for new cars.

In Japan, where development started later than in Europe, penetration rates for frontal airbags are nearly as high as in Europe, while the penetration rate for side airbags is below the level in Europe.

In the rest of the world, penetration rates vary greatly from country to country, but the average is still less than 50 per cent for both driver and passenger airbags.

In Table 1 the total new car production (light vehicles) is split up into the different regions, and the total safety value per vehicle is mentioned.

Although the safety content in mature markets is expected to increase, it is estimated that the global average safety content per vehicle will remain almost unchanged at approximately US$272 (see Table 1) during the next three-year period 2009-11, because of the downward price pressure in the industry. China, for

fitted with frontal airbags for the driver and the front-seat occupant. The next stage will be the compulsory fitting of airbags to both the driver and front passenger sides.

Autoliv introduced its first airbag system in 1990. It was designed to meet US requirements, where not all states have laws on wearing seat belts. The airbag therefore had to be relatively large. Autoliv has developed a special system (the Eurobag system) for markets where wearing a seat belt is compulsory. In this system the airbags have less volume (but they are still effective) and therefore the price can be kept at a lower level than some of the competitors. In the Eurobag system the airbags are 30–45 litres on the driver's side and 60–100 litres on the passenger's side. Furthermore, the Eurobag system is lighter and less bulky.

An airbag system consists of an electronic control unit and an airbag module. The electronic control unit contains (among other things) a sensor, while the module essentially consists of a gas generator, a nylon bag and a cover for the steering wheel centre or the instrument panel, depending on where the airbag module is placed. Autoliv typically supplies entire systems adapted to individual car models.

Organization

In France, Germany, Spain, Sweden, the United Kingdom and the United States, local management is regionally responsible for Autoliv's operations in countries around them. As a result the main customers have the advantage of dealing with Autoliv both in their home market and when they have or are going to establish production in other markets. Together with two regional

Table 1	The world market for vehicle safety (airbags, seat belts and electronics) and Autoliv market share per major region (2008)				
	Production of light vehicles millions (%)	**Safety value per vehicle (US$ per vehicle)**	**Total market for vehicle safety (billion US$)**	**Autoliv market shares by region (%)**	**Autoliv total sales by region (billions US$)**
Europe	21 million (32)	350	7.4	43	3.2
North America	13 million (19)	330	4.3	39	1.7
Japan	11 million (16)	290	3.2	18	0.6
Rest of the world (ROW)	22 million (33)	150	3.3	28	0.9
Total	67 million (100)	272	18.2	35	6.4

Source: Autoliv Financial Report 2008; Autoliv PowerPoint presentations.

instance, introduced a crash-test rating programme in 2006, similar to the European programme and Brazil has plans to make frontal airbags mandatory. However, the safety market is only expected to grow by a small percentage in the next years due to the effect of an increasing number of low-end vehicles with low safety content, primarily for emerging markets in Eastern Europe and Asia. For instance, the safety content in India is, presently, less than one-fifth of the average safety value per vehicle in North America or western Europe.

For side airbags, which were invented by Autoliv and introduced in 1994, Autoliv's global market share is still 40 per cent (see also Table 2). For other recent safety improvements, such as seat belt pre-tensioners and load limiters, Autoliv's global market position is strong.

In North America, Autoliv estimates that in 2001 it accounted for a little less than one-third of the airbag products market and the same for the seat belt market compared with just over 10 per cent in 1999. (Autoliv did not sell seat belts in the United States until 1993.) Autoliv made its big entry into the North American market in 1996 when it acquired Morton Automotive Safety Products, which at that time was North America's largest airbag producer. The airbag business has given Autoliv an opportunity to expand its seat belt business now as complete systems sourcing takes place. In 2000 Autoliv acquired the North American seat belt business of NSK. Autoliv's market share for seat belts also increased as a result of new contracts, and the increasing number of new United States vehicles with seat belt pre-tensioners.

In Europe, Autoliv estimates its market share to be about 43 per cent with a somewhat higher market share for seat belts than for airbags. In Japan, Autoliv has a strong position in the airbag inflator market, but its market share is still behind the European market share. Local assembly of airbag modules began in 1998. In 2000 Autoliv acquired the second largest

Table 2	Autoliv's customer mix, 2008	
Car manufacturer	**Share of total global vehicle production (67 million vehicles) (%)**	**Share of Autoliv's total sales (US$6.4 billion) (%)**
General Motors	11	10
Renault/Nissan	9	13
Ford (Ford + Volvo)	7	12 (8 + 4)
Daimler	3	5
Chrysler	1	4
PSA (Citroën and Peugeot)	5	8
VW	11	11
Toyota	14	6
BMW	2	6
Hyundai/Kia	6	4
Honda	7	6
Others	24	15
Total	100	100

Japanese steering wheel company with a market share exceeding 20 per cent, and 40 per cent of NSK's Asian seat belt operations with the option to acquire the remaining shares in two steps in 2002 and 2003. Including NSK's sales, Autoliv accounts for approximately a fifth of the Japanese seat belt market.

In other countries, such as Argentina, Australia, China, India, Malaysia, New Zealand, South Africa and Turkey, where Autoliv established production early, the company has achieved strong market positions in several places.

Competitors

In the late 1990s the number of major suppliers of occupant restraint systems was reduced from nine to four. As a result of the consolidation among producers of light vehicles the new entities that have been formed require suppliers to be cost efficient and have the capability to deliver the same products to all the companies' plants worldwide.

The four leading car occupant restraint suppliers now account for approximately 80 per cent of the world market (worth US$18.2 billion) as opposed to 50 per cent 10 years ago. During this period Autoliv has increased its share to slightly more than 35 per cent and has replaced TRW (a US publically traded company) as the market leader. Another important auto safety supplier is Takata (a privately owned Japanese company). Both TRW and Takata have about 25 per cent market share. Delphi (the world's largest automotive components supplier) and KSS (Key Safety Systems), have less than 5 per cent each.

In Japan, Korea and China there are a number of local manufacturers that often have close ties with the domestic vehicle manufacturers in these countries. Toyota, for instance, has in-house suppliers for seatbelts, airbags and steering wheels that receive the majority of the Toyota business in Japan for these products. Consequently, these safety product suppliers are often the toughest competitors in these markets.

Customers

Several of the world's largest car producers are among Autoliv's customers (see Table 2). Autoliv typically accounts for between 25 and 75 per cent of customers' purchases of seat belts and airbags and supplies all major car makers in the world and most car brands. In the development of a new car model, a process that takes several years, Autoliv in many cases functions as a development partner for the car manufacturer. This typically means that Autoliv gives advice on new safety-enhancing products and assists in adaptation and conduct testing (including full-scale crash tests with the vehicle) of the safety systems.

Autoliv's earlier relatively high dependence on Ford, General Motors and Chrysler has declined, particularly in North America. These customers accounted globally for 26 per cent of their consolidated sales in 2008 (and for 22 per cent excluding Volvo) compared to 42 per cent in 1997. This evolution is partly a reflection of the fact that their share of the global light vehicle production has declined from 33 per cent in 1997 to 21 per cent in 2008.

In Table 3, the category 'Others' represents Autoliv's growing order intake from Chinese manufacturers

Table 3	Three years of economic development at Autoliv Inc.		
Key figures	2008	2007	2006
Sales (US$ million)	6,473	6,769	6,188
Pre-tax profit (US$ million)	249	446	481

Source: based on www.autoliv.com

like Chery, Great Wall and other local Chinese vehicle manufacturers. The same trend goes for other Asian OEMs. As a result, the Asian vehicle manufacturers now account for 29 per cent of Autoliv's sales globally compared to 20 per cent in 1997. Honda and Hyundai-KIA have become their fastest-growing customers.

The fact that premium vehicles are especially important for Autoliv is evidenced by Volvo and BMW which account for 0.6 and 2.2 per cent respectively of the global vehicle production but for 4 and 6 per cent respectively of the Autoliv sales.

No customer accounts for more than 13 per cent of Autoliv's sales (Table 2). Most of these car makers can be characterized as Autoliv's global accounts (GAs) – see also Chapter 19. Traditional customers are also increasingly turning to global contracts rather than regional contracts as before. Consequently, Autoliv believes these trends in the vehicle industry tend to strengthen Autoliv's competitive position in the long term.

The contracts are generally divided among a car maker's different car models, with each contract usually running for the life of the car model. No contract accounts for more than 5 per cent of consolidated sales. Of the 2005 total sales in Table 3, Europe accounts for 54 per cent, North America 26 per cent, Japan 9 per cent and the rest of the world 11 per cent.

The total number of employees (whole Autoliv Group, including subsidiaries) in December 2008 was about 34,000.

With this positive news Jan Carlson finishes his presentation of Autoliv's position in the global automotive safety market. He would like a discussion of the following, to which you are asked to contribute.

QUESTIONS

1. Describe Autoliv's role as a sub-supplier for large auto manufacturers in a market that is characterized by consolidation.

2. Which car manufacturer should Autoliv target to strengthen its global competitive position?

3. What strategic alternative does Autoliv have to strengthen its competitive position outside Europe?

CASE STUDY III.4

IMAX Corporation: globalization of the film business

Back in 1997 the CEO of IMAX, Richard L. Gelfond, was sceptical about building a story with Hollywood movie stars into the big screen format. At that time his answer to the criticism of IMAX® films' missing story was: 'It is too expensive and risky for us to put all our eggs in one basket and hire a major movie star.'

However, in 2003 new technological achievements have made it possible to show, for example, *Matrix Reloaded* on the huge screen format. This is not just the projection of the standard theatrical print on an IMAX screen – the film will undergo the patented IMAX DMR (digital remastering) process, which enhances the quality of the image and soundtrack to the huge IMAX 15/70 format. The same has happened to *Apollo 13*, featuring Oscar®-winning actor Tom Hanks.

So though IMAX have been through financial tough times the company now seems to be looking towards a brighter future.

The IMAX Corporation

The IMAX Corporation is involved in a wide variety of out-of-home entertainment business activities. It designs and manufactures projection and sound systems for giant-screen theatres based on a patented technology. The IMAX Corporation is the world's largest producer and distributor of films for giant-screen theatres.

The IMAX Corporation, together with its wholly owned subsidiaries, is one of the world's leading entertainment technology companies whose principal activities are:

- the design, manufacture, marketing and leasing of proprietary projection and sound systems for Imax theatres principally owned and operated by institutional and commercial customers in more than 36 countries (1 September 2003);
- the development, production, digital remastering, post-production and distribution of certain films shown in the IMAX theatre network;
- the operation of certain IMAX theatres located primarily in the United States and Canada; and
- the provision of other services to the IMAX theatre network including designing and manufacturing IMAX camera equipment for rental to film-makers

and providing ongoing maintenance services for the IMAX projection and sound systems.

The IMAX theatre network is the most extensive large-format network in the world, with 239 theatres operating in more than 36 countries. Of these, 115 are in institutional locations and 102 in commercial locations. While IMAX's roots are in the institutional market, it believes that the commercial market is potentially larger. To increase the demand for IMAX theatre systems, it is currently working to position the network as a new window for Hollywood event films. To this end IMAX has both developed a technology that allows standard 35mm movies to be converted to its format and is also working to build strong relationships with Hollywood studios and commercial exhibition companies.

IMAX theatre systems combine advanced, high-resolution projection systems, sound systems and screens as much as eight storeys high (approximately 80 feet) that extend to the edge of a viewer's peripheral vision to create the audiovisual experience. As a result audiences feel as if they are a part of the on-screen action in a way that is more intense and exciting than in traditional theatres. In addition, IMAX's 3D theatre systems combine the same projection and sound systems and up to eight storey screens with 3D images that further increase the audience's feeling of immersion in the film. IMAX believes that its network of 3D theatres is the largest out-of-home, 3D distribution network in the world.

History

The IMAX system has its roots in EXPO '67 in Montreal, Canada, where multi-screen films were the hit at the fair. A small group of Canadian film-makers/entrepreneurs (Graeme Ferguson, Roman Kroitor and Robert Kerr), who had made some of those popular films, decided to design a new system using a single powerful projector rather than the cumbersome multiple projectors used at that time. The result was the IMAX motion picture projection system, which would revolutionize giant-screen theatre. As the IMAX screen is about ten times the size of a conventional movie screen picture quality has to be very good. The camera required is also much bigger than a conventional movie camera, but for anyone with film experience it is not hard to learn to use.

The much acclaimed *Fires of Kuwait* was nominated for an Academy Award in the Feature Documentary category in 1993. Since the premiere in 1970 more than 700 million people have enjoyed the IMAX® Experience™.

In 1977, IMAX was awarded the sole Oscar® for Scientific and Technical Achievement by the Academy of Motion Picture Arts and Sciences. The award recognized IMAX's innovation in creating the world's best film capture and projection system as well as IMAX's acceptance as part of the entertainment mainstream.

IMAX Ridefilm: entry and departure

Historically, another part of the corporation was the IMAX® Simulation Ride System, which combined giant-screen technology with aspects of an amusement park ride.

One of Ridefilm Corporation's new state-of-the-art projects became reality in 1993. *Back to the Future – The Ride*, directed by Douglas Trumbull, premiered in June at Universal Studios, Hollywood. This high-tech attraction was considered by entertainment industry experts to be the paradigm for the film experience of the future. The Ridefilm concept consisted of 18-person projection rooms in which the seats are equipped with seat belts and move with the action on the screen. The film is projected on a 180-degree screen, with digital surround sound.

IMAX never succeeded in becoming profitable in the Ridefilm business. One of the reasons for that might be that it never reached the critical mass of about 100 cinemas needed in order to support the three or four Ridefilms that must be made each year to make the business profitable. In the fiscal year 1999 IMAX was forced to write off Ridefilm's assets, resulting in a charge of US$13.6 million.

IMAX's business today

Generally speaking IMAX does not own its theatres, but leases its projection and sound systems and licenses the use of its trademarks. IMAX derives revenue principally from theatre system lease agreements, maintenance agreements, film production agreements and distribution of films.

In 2002, IMAX introduced a technology that can convert live-action 35mm films to its 15/70-format at a modest incremental cost, while meeting IMAX's high standards of image and sound quality. IMAX believes that this proprietary system, known as IMAX DMR (Digital Re-Mastering), has positioned IMAX theatres as a new release window or distribution platform, for Hollywood biggest event films. As of 31 December 2005, IMAX, along with its studio partners, had released 11 IMAX DMR films. In 2005, IMAX released

four films converted through the IMAX DMR process contemporaneous with the releases of the films to conventional 35mm theatres, rereleased one IMAX DMR film that had previously been released in 2004, and released one film made specifically for IMAX theatres. In March 2003, IMAX introduced IMAX MPX, a new theatre projection system designed specifically for use by commercial multiplex operators. The IMAX MPX system, which is highly automated, was designed to reduce the capital and operating costs required to run an IMAX theatre while still offering consumers the image and sound quality of the trademarked experience viewers derive from IMAX theatres known as 'The IMAX Experience'. During 2005, IMAX signed agreements for 31 MPX theatre systems from North American and international commercial theatre exhibitors.

Theatre system leases

IMAX's system leases generally have 10–20-year initial terms and are typically renewable by the customer for one or more additional ten-year terms. As part of the lease agreement IMAX advises the customer on theatre design and custom assemblies and supervises the installation of the system; provides training in using the equipment to theatre personnel; and for a separate fee provides ongoing maintenance of the system. Prospective theatre owners are responsible for providing the location, the design and construction of the building, the installation of the system and any other necessary improvements. Under the terms of the typical lease agreement the title to all theatre system equipment (including the projection screen, the projector and the sound system) remains IMAX's. IMAX has the right to remove the equipment for non-payment or other defaults by the customer. The contracts are generally not cancellable by the customer unless IMAX fails to perform its obligations. The contracts are generally denominated in US dollars, except in Canada and Japan, where contracts are generally denominated in Canadian dollars and Japanese yen, respectively.

The typical lease agreement provides for three major sources of revenue: (i) initial rental fees, (ii) ongoing additional rental payments and (iii) ongoing maintenance fees. Rental payments and maintenance fees are generally received over the life of the contract and are usually adjusted annually based on changes in the local consumer price index. The terms of each lease agreement vary according to the system technology provided and the geographic location of the customer.

IMAX films

IMAX produces films that are financed internally and through third parties. With respect to the latter, IMAX generally receives a film production fee in exchange for producing the films and is appointed the exclusive distributor of the film. When IMAX produces films it typically hires production talent and specialists on a project-by-project basis, allowing IMAX to retain creative and quality control without the burden of significant ongoing overhead expenses. Typically the ownership rights to films produced for third parties are held by the film sponsors, the film investors and IMAX.

IMAX is a significant distributor of 15/70 format films, with distribution rights to more of these films than any competing distributor and generally distributes films that it produces and it has acquired distribution rights to films produced by independent producers. As a distributor, IMAX generally receives a percentage of box office receipts.

International marketing

IMAX markets its theatre systems through a direct sales force and marketing staff located in offices in Canada, the United States, Europe, China and Japan. In addition, IMAX has agreements with consultants, business brokers and real estate professionals to find potential customers and theatre sites for IMAX on a commission basis.

IMAX has experienced an increase in the number of commercial theatre and international signings since 1995. The commercial theatre segment of IMAX's network is now its largest. As at 31 December 2008, 38.0 per cent of all theatres are outside North America. IMAX's institutional customers include science and natural history museums, zoos, aquaria and other educational and cultural centres. IMAX also leases its systems to theme parks, tourist destination sites, fairs and expositions. See Table 1 for an outline of IMAX's operations by area.

Table 1	IMAX Breakdown of installations by geographic segment as at 31 December 2008	
	2008 installed base	**2007 installed base**
Canada	23	23
United States	192	150
Mexico	17	17
Europe	49	46
Japan	10	11
China	18	14
Rest of World	42	38
Total	**351**	**299**

Source: based on www.imax.com

Table 2	IMAX revenue by geographic area		
Revenue and net income (US$1,000)	**2008**	**2007**	**2006**
Canada	5,162	5,866	9,585
United States	67,867	69,381	71,535
Europe	14,460	13,645	18,468
Asia (excluding China)	5,628	7,361	7,828
China	3,263	11,497	6,235
Mexico	5,000	2,750	8,418
Rest of world	4,846	5,332	5,639
Total	**106,226**	**115,832**	**127,708**
Net income (million US$)	−33.6	−26.9	−16.8

Source: based on www.imax.com

For information on revenue breakdown by geographic area see Table 2 (revenue by geographic area is based on the location of the theatre). Table 2 also shows that IMAX has been in a clearly negative financial development during the last three years. During the last three years IMAX has lost US$77.3 million.

No one customer represents more than 5 per cent of IMAX's installed base of theatres. IMAX has no dependence upon a single customer, or a few customers, the loss of any one or more of which would have a material adverse effect on IMAX.

As of 31 December 2008 IMAX had 326 employees, excluding hourly employees at company-owned and operated theatres.

IMAX enters the Chinese market

The first IMAX projection system in a theatre in China was installed in December 2001 and 13 additional IMAX theatre systems are scheduled to be installed in China by 2008. China is now IMAX's second-largest market (after the United States) and fastest-growing market. However, the geopolitical instability of the region comprising China, Taiwan, North Korea and South Korea could result in some economic risks.

There are currently 81 IMAX theatres scheduled to be operating in Asia by 2014, including more than 40 scheduled to be open in China by 2012. For example in September 2009, IMAX Corporation and Guangzhou Jinyi Film & Television Group, Co., Ltd, a leading entertainment developer and exhibitor in China, announced an agreement to open four IMAX theatres in China. The first three installations were scheduled to be completed during the second half of 2011 in the cities of Chongqing, Tianjin and Shenyang. A fourth installation is scheduled for 2012 in a yet-to-be determined location. Each IMAX theatre will be part of a newly constructed multiplex, and each will utilize IMAX's digital projection technology. Established in 2004, Guangzhou Jinyi Film owns 19 multiplexes with 150 screens in Guangzhou, Beijing, Tianjin, Xiamen, Fuzhou, Wuhan, Suzhou, Shenzhen and Chongqing, in addition to other affiliated cinemas. Guangzhou Jinyi Film will show both Hollywood movies and mainstream Chinese films.

The four-theatre deal is the second multi-theatre announcement between IMAX and a Greater China area exhibition company in three months, following the June agreement between IMAX and Chinese film studio Huayi Bros to release mainstream Chinese films to IMAX theatres in China and other parts of Asia.

Competition in the industry

The out-of-home entertainment industry is very competitive, and IMAX faces a number of challenges. IMAX competes with other large-format film projection system manufacturers as well as, indirectly, conventional motion picture exhibitors.

Audience watching *Apollo 13* in an IMAX theatre
IMAX Corporation.

IMAX competes with a number of manufacturers of large-format film projection systems, most of which utilize smaller film formats, including eight-perforation film frame, 70mm and ten-perforation film frame and 70mm formats, which IMAX believes deliver an image that is inferior to the IMAX experience. As already mentioned, the IMAX theatre network and the number of 15/70 format films to which IMAX has distribution rights are substantially larger than those of its competitors, and IMAX DMR films are available exclusively to the IMAX network. IMAX's customers generally consider a number of criteria when selecting a large-format theatre, including quality, reputation, brand name recognition, type of system, features, price and service. IMAX believes that its competitive strengths include the value of the IMAX® brand name, the quality and historic up-time of IMAX cinema systems, the number and quality of 15/70 format films that it distributes, the quality of the sound system in the IMAX theatre, the potential availability of Hollywood event films to IMAX cinemas through IMAX DMR technology and the level of IMAX's service and maintenance efforts. Nearly all of the best performing large-format theatres in the world are IMAX's.

In addition to existing competitors, IMAX may also face competition in the future from companies in the entertainment industry with new technologies and/or

substantially greater capital resources. IMAX faces competition from a number of alternative motion picture distribution channels such as home video, pay-per-view, video-on-demand, DVD, and syndicated and broadcast television. IMAX competes for the public's leisure time and disposable income with other forms of entertainment, including sporting events, concerts, live theatre and restaurants.

Furthermore, the out-of-home entertainment industry in general is undergoing significant changes. Primarily due to technological developments and changing consumer tastes, numerous companies are developing, and are expected to continue to develop, new entertainment products for the out-of-home entertainment industry, which may compete directly with IMAX's products.

The motion picture exhibition industry is in the early stages of conversion from film-based to electronic-based media. IMAX is similarly in the early stages of developing a digital projection system that can be utilized in IMAX theatres.

In recent years, a number of companies have introduced digital 3D projection technology. According to the National Association of Theater Owners there are approximately 1,700 conventional-sized screens in US multiplexes equipped with digital 3D systems. However IMAX believes that its IMAX brand name and its IMAX

DMR technology, including its patented theatre geometry, differentiate it significantly from other 3D presentations. Until now the IMAX theatres have outperformed the conventional theatres on a per-screen revenue basis.

However, the competitive risks could include the need for IMAX to raise additional capital to finance remanufacturing of theatre systems and associated conversion costs, capital that may not be available to IMAX on attractive terms.

The commercial success of IMAX's products is ultimately dependent on consumer preferences. The out-of-home entertainment industry in general continues to go through significant changes, primarily due to technological developments and changing consumer tastes. Numerous companies are developing new entertainment products for the out-of-home entertainment industry and there are no guarantees that some of these new products will not be competitive with, superior to or more cost-effective than IMAX's products.

Newest development

At the end of September 2009, IMAX Corporation and Sony Pictures announced that the highly anticipated motion picture Michael Jackson's *THIS IS IT* would be released for a special run in select digital IMAX(R) theatres worldwide during the film's limited two-week engagement in thousands of theatres globally starting on 28 October 2009. *THIS IS IT* will be digitally remastered by the use of IMAX DMR technology. The crystal-clear images coupled with IMAX's customized theatre geometry and powerful digital audio create a unique environment that will make audiences feel as if they are in the movie. Chronicling the months from March through to June 2009, the film is produced with the full support of the estate of Michael Jackson and drawn from more than one hundred hours of behind-the-scenes footage, featuring Jackson rehearsing a number of his songs for the show, that never took place because of his death on 25 June 2009.

Sources: Imax press releases; www.imax.com.

QUESTIONS

1. Discuss the statement back in 1997: 'It is too expensive and risky for us to put all our eggs in one basket and hire a major movie star.'

2. What are the main reasons for the failure of Imax Ridefilm?

3. Can IMAX's core competences be transferred to the marketing of high-volume commercial products? Which types of product could these be?

4. What are possibilities of growing the IMAX business with the new IMAX MPX system combined with their new IMAX DMR technology, which enables Hollywood studios to digitally remaster their films into IMAX's 15/70?

5. What should IMAX do to turn around its negative financial development?

PART I
The decision whether to internationalize
Chs 1–4

PART II
Deciding which markets to enter
Chs 5–8

PART III
Market entry strategies
Chs 9–13

PART IV
Designing the global marketing programme
Chs 14–17

PART V
Implementing and coordinating the global marketing programme
Chs 18–19

Part IV Contents

Part IV Case studies

PART IV
Designing the global marketing programme

Introduction to Part IV

Once the firm has decided how it will enter the international market(s) (see Part III), the next issue is how to design the global marketing mix.

Part IV is mainly based on the traditional 4P marketing mix:

- Chapter 14: Product
- Chapter 15: Price
- Chapter 16: Place (Distribution)
- Chapter 17: Promotion.

The original 4P marketing mix was primarily derived from research on manufacturing business to consumer (B2C) companies, where the the essence of the marketing mix concept is the idea of a set of controllable variables or a 'toolkit' (the 4Ps) at the disposal of marketing management which can be used to influence customers. However, especially in business to business (B2B) marketing, the marketing mix is also influenced by the interaction process itself between buyer and seller, so that the influence process is negotiation and not persuasion as implied by the traditional 4P mix. Furthermore there has been concern that the classic 4Ps do not incorporate the characteristics of services – namely inherent intangibility, perishability, heterogeneity (variability), inseparability and ownership.

The most influential of the alternative frameworks is, however, Booms and Bitner's (1981) *7Ps mix* where they suggest that the traditional 4Ps need to be extended to include an additional three Ps: *participants, physical evidence* and *process*. Their framework is discussed below.

Participants

Any person coming into contact with customers can have an impact on overall satisfaction. Participants are all human actors who play a part in service delivery, namely the firm's personnel and other customers. Because of the simultaneity of production and consumption, the firm's personnel occupy a key position in influencing customer perceptions of product quality. This is especially the case in 'high-contact' services, such as restaurants, airlines and professional consulting services. In fact, the firm's employees are part of the product and hence product quality is inseparable from the quality of the service provider. It is important, therefore, to pay particular attention to the quality of employees and to monitor their performance. This is especially important in services because employees tend to be variable in their performance, which can lead to variable quality.

The participants' concept also includes the customer who buys the service and other customers in the service environment. Marketing managers therefore need to manage not only the service provider–customer interface but also the actions of other customers. For example, the number, type and behaviour of people will partly determine the enjoyment of a meal at a restaurant.

Process

This is the process involved in providing a service to the customers. It is the procedures, mechanisms and flow of activities by which the service is acquired and delivered. The process of obtaining a meal at a self-service, fast-food outlet such as McDonald's, is clearly different from that at a full-service restaurant. Furthermore, in a service situation customers are likely to have to queue before they can be served and the service delivery itself is likely to take a certain length of time. Marketers have to ensure that customers understand the process of acquiring a service and that the queuing and delivery times are acceptable to customers.

Physical evidence

Unlike a product, a service cannot be experienced before it is delivered, which makes it intangible. This means that potential customers perceive greater risk when deciding whether or not to use a service. To reduce the feeling of risk, thus improving success, it is often vital to offer customers some tangible clues to assess the quality of the service provided. This is done by providing physical evidence, such as case studies or testimonials. The physical environment itself (i.e. the buildings, furnishings, layout, etc.) is instrumental in customers' assessment of the quality and level of service they can expect, for example in restaurants, hotels, retailing and many other services. In fact, the physical environment is part of the product itself.

It can be argued that there is no need to amend or extend the 4Ps, as the extensions suggested by Booms and Bitner can be incorporated into the existing framework. The argument is that consumers experience a bundle of satisfactions and dissatisfactions that derive from all dimensions of the product whether tangible or intangible. The process can be incorporated in the distribution. Buttle (1989), for example, argues that the product and/or promotion elements may incorporate participants (in the Booms and Bitner framework) and that physical evidence and processes may be thought of as being part of the product. In fact, Booms and Bitner (1981) themselves argue that product decisions should involve the three extended elements in their proposed mix.

Therefore Part IV of this text still uses the structure of the 4Ps, but at the same time the three extended Ps will be incorporated in Chapters 15 to 18.

Globalization

Since the beginning of the 1980s the term 'globalization' has increasingly become a matter of debate. In his article 'The globalization of markets' (1983) Levitt provoked much controversy concerning the most appropriate way for companies to become international. Levitt's support of the globalization strategy received both support and criticism. Essentially the two sides of this debate represented local marketing versus global marketing and focused on the central question of whether a standardized, global marketing approach or a country-specific, differentiated marketing approach has the most merits. In Part IV we learn that there are different forces in the international environment that may favour either increasing globalization or increasing adaptation of a firm. The starting point is illustrated by the existing balance point on the scale illustrated in Figure IV.1. Which force will win not only depends on the environmental forces but also on the specific international marketing strategy that the firm might favour. Figure IV.2 shows the extremes of these two strategies.

Hence, a fundamental decision that managers have to make regarding their global marketing strategy is the degree to which they should standardize or adapt their global marketing mix. The following three factors provide vast opportunities for marketing standardization (Meffert and Bolz, 1993):

1. *Globalization of markets.* Customers are increasingly operating on a worldwide basis and are characterized by an intensively coordinated and centralized purchasing process. As a countermeasure, manufacturers establish a global key account management in order to avoid individual country subsidiaries being played off against each other in separate negotiations with, for example, global retailers.
2. *Globalization of industries.* Many firms can no longer depend on home markets for sufficient scale economies and experience curve effects. Many industries, such as computers, pharmaceuticals and automobiles, are characterized by high R&D costs that can be recouped only via worldwide, high-volume sales.
3. *Globalization of competition.* As a consequence of the worldwide homogenization of demand, the different markets are interrelated. Therefore firms can plan their activities on a worldwide scale and attempt to establish a superior profile vis-à-vis other global competitors. Hence, country subsidiaries no longer operate as profit centres, but are viewed as parts of a global portfolio.

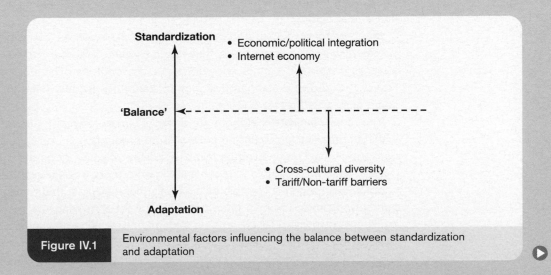

Figure IV.1   Environmental factors influencing the balance between standardization and adaptation

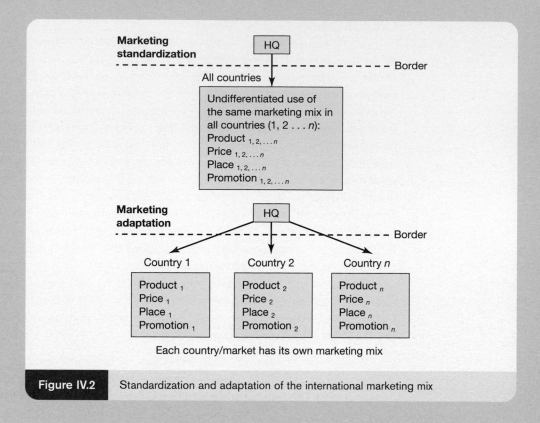

| Figure IV.2 | Standardization and adaptation of the international marketing mix |

The standardized marketing concept can be characterized by two features:

1. Standardization of marketing processes is mainly concerned with a standardized decision-making process for cross-country marketing planning. By standardizing the launch of new products, controlling activities, etc., rationalization of the general marketing process is sought.
2. Standardization of marketing programmes and the marketing mix is concerned with the extent to which individual elements of the 4Ps can be unified into a common approach for different national markets.

These two characteristics of standardization are often interrelated: for many strategic business units process-oriented standardization is the precondition for the implementation of standardized marketing programmes.

Many writers discuss standardization and adaptation as two distinct options. The commercial reality, however, is that few marketing mixes are totally standardized or adapted. Instead it is more relevant to discuss *degrees* of standardization. Therefore Figure IV.3 shows a standardization-potential profile for two different products by the same company (Procter & Gamble).

The results indicate that there are different ways of realizing a standardized concept within the marketing mix. In the case of both products it is possible to standardize the package at least on an average level. Difficulties arise as far as the price policy is concerned. Here it is possible to reach a standardized price positioning only for disposable nappies. So Procter & Gamble selects only those markets that possess the necessary purchasing power to pay a price within the target price range. In the case of alcoholic drinks it is nearly impossible to gain a standardized price positioning due to legal constraints. In Denmark, for example, consumers have to pay twice as much for the same Johnny Walker whisky as they do in Germany because of tax regulations. In many cases

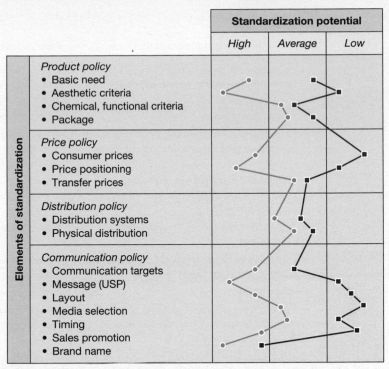

	Standardization potential		
	High	Average	Low
Product policy • Basic need • Aesthetic criteria • Chemical, functional criteria • Package			
Price policy • Consumer prices • Price positioning • Transfer prices			
Distribution policy • Distribution systems • Physical distribution			
Communication policy • Communication targets • Message (USP) • Layout • Media selection • Timing • Sales promotion • Brand name			

Elements of standardization

● Standardization profile of a special disposable nappy (e.g. Pampers)
■ Standardization profile of a special drink (e.g. Johnny Walker)

Figure IV.3 Analysis of a company's standardization potential

Source: adapted from Kreutzer (1988). Reproduced with kind permission from Emerald Group Publishing Ltd; www.emeraldinsight.com.

it is possible to use one brand name on a worldwide basis. There are negative effects connected with particular names in only a few cases; you have to change brand names to avoid these unintentional images.

We end this introduction to Part IV by listing in Table 1 the main factors favouring standardization versus adaptation of the global marketing programme.

Supporters of *standardization* view markets as increasingly homogeneous and global in scope and scale and believe that the key for survival and growth is the ability to standardize goods, services and processes. The overall conceptual argument is that the world is becoming increasingly similar in terms of environmental factors and customer requirements and irrespective of geographical locations, consumers have the same demands.

Supporters of *adaptation* indicate difficulties in using a standardized approach and therefore support adaptation to fit the unique dimensions of different international markets. Proponents of adaptation claim that there are substantial differences between countries and even between regions in the same country.

Since competitive advantages play a critical role in the global marketing strategy, similarity in the nature of competitive advantages across international markets would favour the use of similar strategies across markets, facilitating a standardization of the strategy. Competitive advantages arise from core competences (see also Chapter 4), so firms possessing core competences would be in a better position to standardize their marketing strategies than firms that do not possess core competences (Viswanathan and Dickson, 2007).

Companies operating internationally should not make a one-time choice between the poles of absolute standardization or adaptation. Multinational companies operating

Table 1	Main factors favouring standardization versus adaptation
Factors favouring standardization	**Factors favouring adaptation**
• Economies of scale in R&D, production and marketing (experience curve effects)	• Local environment-induced adaptation: sociocultural, economic and political differences (no experience curve effects)
• Global competition	• Local competition
• Convergence of tastes and consumer needs (consumer preferences are homogeneous)	• Variation in consumer needs (consumer needs are heterogeneous because of cultural differences)
• Centralized management of international operations (possible to transfer experience across borders)	• Fragmented and decentralized management with independent country subsidiaries
• A standardized concept is used by competitors	• An adapted concept is used by competitors
• *High* degree of transferability of competitive advantages from market to market	• *Low* degree of transferability by competitive advantages from market to market
Further issues:	*Further issues:*
• Easier communication, planning and control (through Internet and mobile technology)	• Legal issues – differences in technical standards
• Stock cost reduction	

Source: Hollensen, S. (2008) *Essentials of Global Marketing*, FT/Prentice Hall, p. 299, Table 1.

in several countries using diverse entry modes, must integrate different international marketing approaches. They should focus attention on aspects of the business (value chain activities) that require global standardization and aspects that demand local adaptation (Vrontis *et al.*, 2009).

References

Booms, B.H. and Bitner, M.J. (1981) 'Marketing strategies and organization structures for service firms', in Donnelly, J.H. and George, W.R. (eds), *Marketing of Services*, American Marketing Association, Chicago, IL, pp. 47–51.

Buttle, F. (1989) 'Marketing services', in Jones, P. (eds), *Management in Service Industries*, Pitman, London, pp. 235–259.

Kreutzer, R. (1988) 'Standardization: an integrated approach in global marketing', *European Journal of Marketing*, 22(10), pp. 19–30.

Levitt, T. (1983) 'The globalization of markets', *Harvard Business Review*, May–June, pp. 92–102.

Meffert, H. and Bolz, J. (1993) 'Standardization of marketing in Europe', in Halliburton, C. and Hünerberg, R. (eds), *European Marketing: Readings and cases*, Addison–Wesley, Wokingham, England, pp. 45–62.

Viswanathan, N.K. and Dickson, P.R. (2007) 'The fundamentals of standardizing global marketing strategy', *International Marketing Review*, 24(1), pp. 46–63.

Vrontis, D., Thrassou, A. and Lamprianou, I. (2009) 'International marketing adaptation versus standardization of multinational companies', *International Marketing Review*, 26(4/5), pp. 477–500.

Further reading

Berman, B. (2002) 'Should your firm adopt a mass customization strategy?', *Business Horizons*, July–August, pp. 51–60.

Biemans, W. (2001) 'Designing a dual marketing program', *European Management Journal*, 19(6), December, pp. 670–677.

Solberg, C.A. (2000) 'Educator insights: standardization or adaptation of the international marketing mix: the role of the local subsidiary/representative', *Journal of International Marketing*, 8(1), pp. 78–98.

CHAPTER 14
Product decisions

Contents

Case studies

Learning objectives

After studying this chapter you should be able to:
- Discuss the influences that lead a firm to standardize or adapt its products.
- Explore how international service strategies are developed.
- Distinguish between the product life cycle and the international product life cycle.
- Discuss the challenge of developing new products for foreign markets.
- Explain and illustrate the alternatives in the product communication mix.
- Define and explain the different branding alternatives.
- Discuss brand piracy and the possible anti-counterfeiting strategies.
- Explain what is meant by a 'green' product.
- Discuss alternative environmental management strategies.

14.1 Introduction

The product decision is among the first decisions that a marketing manager makes in order to develop a global marketing mix. This chapter examines product-related issues and suggests conceptual approaches for handling them. Also discussed are international brand (labelling) strategies and service policies.

14.2 The dimensions of the international product offer

In creating an acceptable product offer for international markets it is necessary to first examine what contributes to the 'total' product offer. Kotler (1997) suggests five levels of the product offer that should be considered by marketers in order to make the product attractive to international markets. In the product dimensions of Figure 14.1 we include not just the core physical properties, but also additional elements such as packaging, branding and after-sales service that make up the total package for the purchaser.

We can also see from Figure 14.1 that it is much easier to standardize the core product benefits (functional features, performance, etc.) than it is to standardize the support services, which often have to be tailored to the business culture and sometimes to individual customers.

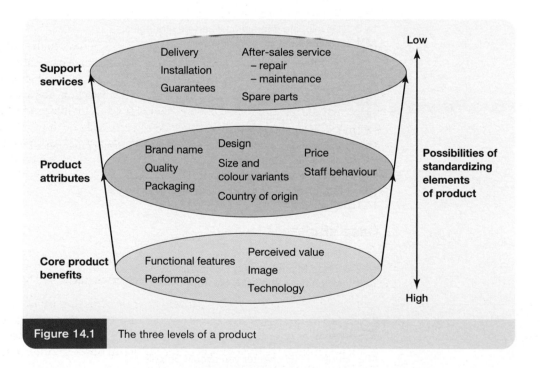

| Figure 14.1 | The three levels of a product |

14.3 Developing international service strategies

We have seen from the definition of a product that services often accompany products, but products are also an increasingly important part of our international economy in their own right. As Figure 14.2 shows, the mix of product and service elements may vary substantially. Figure 14.2 assumes that the customer is more or less passive in the buying and consuming process. That is, of course, not always realistic. More and more, offerings cannot be represented

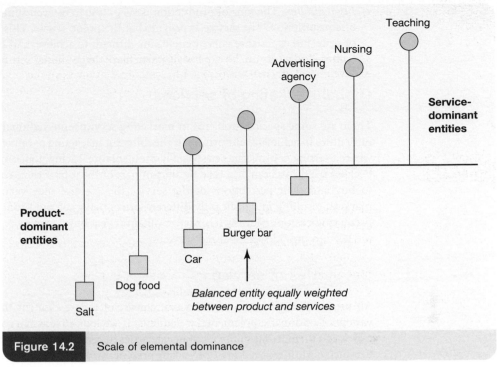

| Figure 14.2 | Scale of elemental dominance |

Source: Czinkota and Ronkainen (1995, p. 526).

accurately by points on either end of a tangibility continuum. Rather, offerings are complex mixes of concrete objects, rendered services and customer participation. Customers do not seek products; they seek satisfaction. Products thus represent vehicles for service, because they enable customers to pursue their individualized satisfaction. For instance, when customers purchase new software for their computer, they may get a tangible product (CDs) to take home and install on their computer. However, what they are truly buying is the ability to perform a new task or an existing task in a new way. The installation CDs are filled up with knowledge, encrypted with the capabilities of various service providers, which then require that the customer demonstrate the competence and willingness to liberate this stored knowledge (Michel *et al.*, 2008).

Characteristics of services

Before considering possible international service strategies it is important to consider the special nature of global service marketing. Services are characterized by the following features:

- *Intangibility*. As services such as air transport or education cannot be touched or tested, the buyers of services cannot claim ownership or anything tangible in the traditional sense. Payment is for use or performance. Tangible elements of the service, such as food or drink on airlines, are used as part of the service in order to confirm the benefit provided and to enhance its perceived value.
- *Perishability*. Services cannot be stored for future use – for example, unfilled airline seats are lost once the aircraft takes off. This characteristic causes considerable problems in planning and promotion in order to match supply and demand. To maintain service capacity constantly at levels necessary to satisfy peak demand will be very expensive. The marketer must therefore attempt to estimate demand levels in order to optimize the use of capacity.
- *Heterogeneity*. Services are rarely the same because they involve interactions between people. Furthermore, there is high customer involvement in the production of services. This can cause problems of maintaining quality, particularly in international markets where there are quite different attitudes towards customer service.

- *Inseparability*. The time of production is very close to or even simultaneous with the time of consumption. The service is provided at the point of sale. This means that economies of scale and experience curve benefits are difficult to achieve, and supplying the service to scattered markets can be expensive, particularly in the initial setting-up phase.

Global marketing of services

There are some specific problems in marketing services internationally. There are particular difficulties in achieving uniformity of the different marketing parameters in remote locations where exerting control can be especially problematic. Pricing, too, can be extremely difficult, because fixed costs can be a very significant part of the total service costs. Consumers' ability to buy and their perceptions of the service they receive may vary considerably between markets, resulting in significantly different prices being set and profits generated. Moreover, preserving customer loyalty in order to obtain repeat business may prove difficult because of the need to provide personalized services.

Categories of service

All products, both goods and services, consist of a core element that is surrounded by a variety of optional supplementary elements. If we look first at the core service products we can assign them to one of three broad categories depending on their tangibility and the extent to which customers need to be physically present during service production. These categories are presented in Table 14.1.

Categories of supplementary service

The core service provider, whether a bed for the night or a bank account, is typically accompanied by a variety of supplementary elements, which can be grouped into eight categories (Lovelock and Yip, 1996):

1. *Information*. To obtain full value from any good or service, customers need relevant information about it, ranging from schedules to operating instructions and from user warnings to prices. Globalization affects the nature of that information (including the languages and format in which it is provided). New customers and prospects are especially information hungry and may need training in how to use an unfamiliar service.
2. *Consultation and advice*. Consultation and advice involve a dialogue to probe customer requirements and then develop a tailored solution. Customers' need for advice may vary widely around the world, reflecting such factors as level of economic development, nature of the local infrastructure, topography and climate, technical standards and educational levels.
3. *Order taking*. Once customers are ready to buy suppliers need to make it easy for them to place orders or reservations in the language of their choice, through telecommunications and other channels, at times and in locations that are convenient to them.
4. *Hospitality: taking care of the customer*. Well-managed businesses try, at least in small ways, to treat customers as guests when they have to visit the supplier's facilities (especially when, as is true for many people-processing operations, the period extends over several hours or more). Cultural definitions of appropriate hospitality may differ widely from one country to another, such as the tolerable length of waiting time (much longer in Brazil than in Germany) and the degree of personal service expected (not much in Scandinavia, but lavish in Indonesia).
5. *Safekeeping: looking after the customer's possessions*. When visiting a service site customers often want assistance with their personal possessions, ranging from car parking to packaging and delivery of new purchases. Expectations may vary by country, reflecting culture and levels of affluence.
6. *Exceptions*. Exceptions fall outside the routine of normal service delivery. They include special requests, problem-solving, handling of complaints/suggestions/compliments

Table 14.1	Three categories of service		
Categories of service	Characteristics	Examples (service provider)	Possibilities of worldwide standardization (hence utilizing economies of scale, experience effects, lower costs)
People processing	Customers become part of the production process. The service firm needs to maintain local geographic presence.	Education (schools, universities). Passenger transport (airlines, car rental). Health care (hospitals). Food service (fast-food, restaurants). Lodging service (hotel).	No good possibilities: because of 'customer involvement in production' many local sites will be needed, making this type of service very difficult to operate globally.
Possession processing	Involves tangible actions to physical objects to improve their value to customers. The object needs to be involved in the production process, but the owner of the object (the customer) does not. A local geographic presence is required.	Car repair (garages). Freight transport (forwarding agent). Equipment installation (e.g. electrician). Laundry service (launderette).	Better possibilities: compared to people-processing services, this involves a lower degree of contact between the customer and the service personnel. This type of service is not so culture-sensitive.
Information-based services	Collecting, manipulating, interpreting and transmitting data to create value. Minimal tangibility. Minimal customer involvement in the production process.	Telecommunication services (telephone companies). Banking. News. Market analysis. Internet services (producers of homepages on the WWW, database providers).	Very good possibilities: of worldwide standardization from one central location (single sourcing) because of the 'virtual' nature of these services.

and restitution (compensating customers for performance failures). Special requests are particularly common in people-processing services, such as in the travel and lodging industries, and may be complicated by differing cultural norms. International airlines, for example, find it necessary to respond to an array of medical and dietary needs, sometimes reflecting religious and cultural values. Problem-solving is often more difficult for people who are travelling overseas than it would be in the familiar environment of their native country.

7. *Billing.* Customers need clear, timely bills that explain how charges are computed. With abolition of currency exchange restrictions in many countries bills can be converted to the customer's home currency. Hence currencies and conversion rates need to be clarified on billing statements. In some instances prices may be displayed in several currencies, even though this policy may require frequent adjustments in the light of currency fluctuations.

8. *Payment.* Ease and convenience of payment (including credit) are increasingly expected by customers when purchasing a broad array of services.

Source: Copyright © 1996, by The Regents of the University of California. Reprinted from *The California Management Review*, Vol. 38, No. 2. By permission of The Regents.

Heating contracting serves as a good example. Traditionally, owners of office buildings would buy a heating system and maintain it over its lifetime. However, with service contracting innovation, the heating company does not sell the heating equipment to the owner but instead offers a guaranteed temperature all year around for a predefined rate. In the tourism industry, all inclusive vacation resorts target customers who prefer to pay a fixed price for their entire stay instead of being charged for individual purchases (Michel *et al.*, 2008).

Not every core service is surrounded by all eight supplementary elements. In practice the nature of the product, customer requirements and competitive pressures help to determine which supplementary service must be offered. In many cases the provider of the supplementary services can be located in one part of the world and the services delivered electronically to another. For example, order-taking/reservations and payment can be handled through tele-communication channels, ranging from voice telephone to the Web. As long as appropriate languages are available many such service elements could be delivered from almost anywhere.

In summary, the information-based services offer the best opportunities of global standardization. The two other types of service (people processing and possession processing) both suffer from their inability to transfer competitive advantages across borders. For example, when Euro Disneyland in Paris opened Disney suffered from not being able to transfer the highly motivated staff of its US parks to Europe.

The accelerating development within information technology (the Internet/the Web) has resulted in the appearance of new types of information service (e.g. information on inter-national flight schedules), which offer great opportunities for standardization.

Service in the business-to-business market

Business-to-business markets differ from customer markets in many ways:

● fewer and larger buyers, often geographically concentrated
● a derived, fluctuating and relatively inelastic demand
● many participants in the buying process
● professional buyers
● a closer relationship
● absence of intermediaries
● technological links.

For services in consumer markets an alternative for dissatisfied consumers is always to exit from the supplier–consumer relationship, as the number of firms offering the same kind of products is usually high, making it is easy to switch between products and firms.

In the business-to-business market, however, bonds between the buyer and seller make the firms more unwilling to break the relationship. Of course the exit opportunity also exists to some extent in the business-to-business market, but the loss of investment in bonds and commitment tends to create exit barriers, because the costs of changing supplier are high. Furthermore, it can be difficult to find a new supplier.

Professional service firms, such as consulting engineering firms, have similarities with typical business-to-business service firms, but they involve a high degree of customization and have a strong component of face-to-face interaction. The service frequently takes the form of a hundred-million-dollar project and is characterized by the development of long-term relationships between firms, but also the management of day-to-day relationships during the project. When a pro-fessional service firm (whether it be an accountant, architect, engineer or management consultant) sells to its clients it is less the services of the firm than the services of specific individuals that it is selling. As a consequence professional service firms require highly skilled individuals.

Filiatrault and Lapierre (1997) made a study of the cultural differences in consulting engineering projects between Europe (France) and North America (Canada). In North America the consulting engineering firms are generally smaller and they work in an economic environment closer (than in Europe) to pure competition. The contracts in Europe are very large and often awarded by governments. The French consultants recognized that there is more flexibility in managing in North America than in Europe. Subcontracting also appears to be more popular in North America.

14.4   The product life cycle

PLC
Product life cycle concerns the life of a product in the market with respect to business/commercial costs and sales measures. Simply explained, it is a theory in which products or brands follow a sequence of stages including introduction, growth, maturity and sales decline.

Time to market
The time it takes from the idea for a product being conceived until it is available for sale. TTM is important in those industries where products are outmoded quickly.

The concept of the product life cycle (**PLC**) provides useful inputs into making product decisions and formulating product strategies.

Products, like individuals, pass through a series of stages. Each stage is identified by its sales performance and characterized by different levels of profitability, various degrees of competition and distinctive marketing programmes. The four stages of the PLC are introduction, growth, maturity and decline. The basic model of the PLC is shown in Figure 14.3, where also the stages prior to the actual sales are included. In total these stages represent the so-called time to market (TTM).

Time to market (TTM) is the length of time it takes from a product being conceived until its being available for sale. TTM is important in industries where products are outdated quickly, for example in the IT industry.

Rapid time-to-market is important for the competitive success of many companies for the following reasons:

● competitive advantage of getting to market sooner
● premium prices early in life cycle
● faster break-even on development investment and lower financial risk
● greater overall profits and higher return on investment.

The key process requirements for rapid time to market are:

● clear understanding of customer needs at the start of the project and stability in product requirements or specifications;
● a characterized, optimized product development process;
● a realistic project plan based on this process;
● availability of needed resources to support the project and use of full-time, dedicated personnel;
● early involvement and rapid staffing build-up to support the parallel design of product and process;

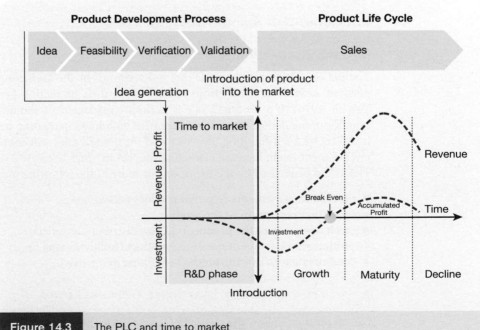

| **Figure 14.3** | The PLC and time to market |

Source: Hollensen, S. (2010) *Marketing Management*, 2nd edition, FT/Prentice Hall, Fig. 11.7.

- virtual product development including digital assembly modelling and early analysis and simulation to minimize time-consuming physical mock-ups and testing; and
- design re-use and standardization to minimize the design content of a project.

Pure speed, that is, bringing the product to market as quickly as possible is valuable in fast-moving industries, is not always the best objective. Many managers calculate that the shorter the product development project. the less it will cost, so they attempt to use TTM as a means of cutting expenses. Unfortunately, a primary means of reducing TTM is to staff the project more heavily, so a faster project may actually be more expensive.

The PLC emphasizes the need to review marketing objectives and strategies as products pass through various stages. It is helpful to think of marketing decisions during the lifetime of a product. However, sometimes it is hard to know when a product is leaving one stage and entering the next. The life-cycle concept helps managers think about their product line as a portfolio of investments.

Most organizations offer more than one product or service, and many operate in several markets. The advantage here is that the various products – the product portfolio – can be managed so that they are not all in the same phase in their life cycles. Having products evenly spread out across life cycles allows for the most efficient use of both cash and human resources. Figure 14.4 shows an example of such life-cycle management and some of the corresponding strategies that follow the different stages of the product life cycle.

The current investment in C, which is in the growth phase, is covered by the profits being generated by the earlier product B, which is at maturity. This product had earlier been funded by A, the decline of which is now being balanced by the newer products. An organization looking for growth can introduce new goods or services that it hopes will be bigger sellers than those that they succeed. However, if this expansion is undertaken too rapidly, many of these brands will demand investment at the beginning of their life cycles, and even the earliest of them will be unlikely to generate profits fast enough to support the numbers of later launches. Therefore, the producer will have to find another source of funds until the investments pay off.

However, managers also need to be aware of the limitations of the PLC so they are not misled by its prescriptions.

Limitations of the product life cycle

Misleading strategy prescriptions

The PLC is a dependent variable that is determined by the marketing mix; it is not an independent variable to which firms should adapt their marketing programmes (Dhalla and Yuspeh, 1976). If a product's sale is declining management should not conclude that the brand is in the decline stage. If management withdraws marketing resources from the brand it will create a self-fulfilling prophecy and the brand's sales will continue to decline. Instead management might increase marketing support in order to create a recycle (see Figure 14.5). This could be realized by the use of one or more of the following measures:

- product improvements (e.g. new product packaging)
- reposition perception of the product
- reach new users of the product (via new distribution outlets)
- promote more frequent use of the product (fulfilling same need)
- promote new uses of the product (fulfilling new needs).

Fads

Not all products follow the classic PLC curve. Fads are fashions that are adopted very quickly by the public, peak early and decline very fast. It is difficult to predict whether something will be only a fad, or how long it will last. The amount of mass-media attention together with other factors will influence the fad's duration.

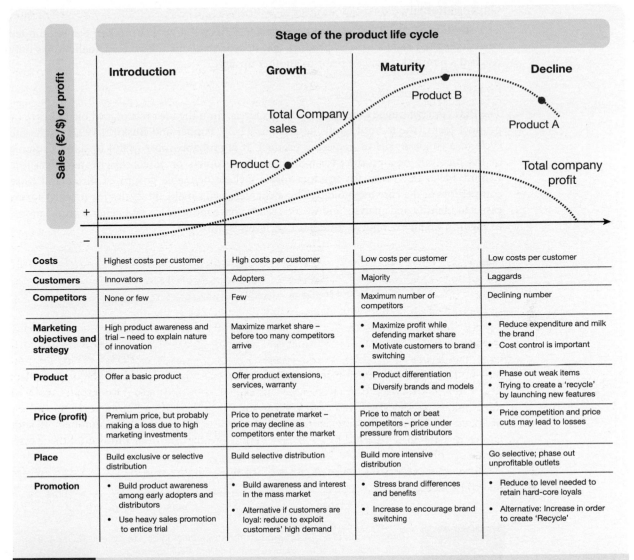

| Stage of the product life cycle | | | |
Introduction	Growth	Maturity	Decline
Costs			
Highest costs per customer	High costs per customer	Low costs per customer	Low costs per customer
Customers			
Innovators	Adopters	Majority	Laggards
Competitors			
None or few	Few	Maximum number of competitors	Declining number
Marketing objectives and strategy			
High product awareness and trial – need to explain nature of innovation	Maximize market share – before too many competitors arrive	• Maximize profit while defending market share • Motivate customers to brand switching	• Reduce expenditure and milk the brand • Cost control is important
Product			
Offer a basic product	Offer product extensions, services, warranty	• Product differentiation • Diversify brands and models	• Phase out weak items • Trying to create a 'recycle' by launching new features
Price (profit)			
Premium price, but probably making a loss due to high marketing investments	Price to penetrate market – price may decline as competitors enter the market	Price to match or beat competitors – price under pressure from distributors	• Price competition and price cuts may lead to losses
Place			
Build exclusive or selective distribution	Build selective distribution	Build more intensive distribution	Go selective; phase out unprofitable outlets
Promotion			
• Build product awareness among early adopters and distributors • Use heavy sales promotion to entice trial	• Build awareness and interest in the mass market • Alternative if customers are loyal: reduce to exploit customers' high demand	• Stress brand differences and benefits • Increase to encourage brand switching	• Reduce to level needed to retain hard-core loyals • Alternative: Increase in order to create 'Recycle'

Figure 14.4   The product life cycle and its strategic marketing implications

Source: Hollensen, S. (2010) *Marketing Management*, 2nd edition, FT/Prentice Hall, Fig. 7.5.

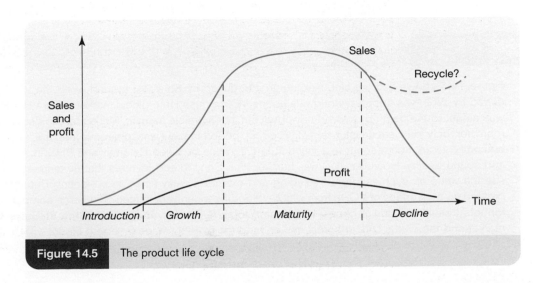

Figure 14.5   The product life cycle

Unpredictability

The duration of the PLC stages is unpredictable. Critics charge that markets can seldom tell what stage the product is in. A product may appear to be mature when actually it has only reached a temporary plateau prior to another upsurge.

Levels of product life cycle

The PLC concept can be examined at various levels, from the life cycle of a whole industry or product form (the technological life cycle or TLC) (Popper and Buskirk, 1992) to the life cycle of a single model of a specific product. It is probably most useful to think in terms of the life cycle of a product form such as photocopiers or video cassette recorders (see Exhibit 14.1). Life cycles for product forms include definable groups of direct and close competitors and a core technology. These characteristics make life cycles for product forms easier to identify and analyse, and would seem to have more stable and general implications. In Figure 14.6 an example of different PLC levels is shown.

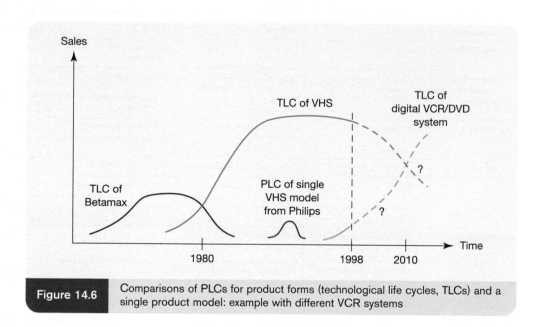

Figure 14.6 Comparisons of PLCs for product forms (technological life cycles, TLCs) and a single product model: example with different VCR systems

EXHIBIT 14.1 The global VHS/Betamax contest in the VCR business

Figure 14.6 shows that the Betamax format introduced by Sony lost ground when the VHS standard (introduced by JVC) was adopted worldwide as the VCR diffused into global markets. The VHS/Betamax contest was a fight to the death by two virtually equal but incompatible formats. Market forces decided that there was room for only one successful format. Product performance was apparently not the crucial factor in the outcome, as an independent test found little difference between Betamax and VHS in, for example, picture and sound quality. However, JVC was quicker than Sony to add features that consumers could immediately see the value of, such as longer recording and extended delay times. In promoting Betamax Sony evidently created an awareness of VCRs from which VHS subsequently benefited. The fierce competition between the formats (resulting in lower prices) accelerated total VCR sales. Today (2010) the VHS system is out of the market and the digital DVD recorder has entered the maturity stage (see also Figure 14.4).

Another example of a TLC shift happened when the compact disc (CD) format was introduced as a result of a joint development between Philips and Sony. A key factor in the success of the CD format displacing the old LP record format was the ownership by Sony of CBS in the United States, and by Philips of Polygram in Europe, two of the biggest music software companies in the world. This contributed to the new CD format establishing itself as the industry standard. However, there were also a number of barriers to the adoption of the new format. The potential users had already invested in LP record collections and the prices of discs and players were relatively high at the beginning of the TLC.

Product life cycles for different products of the firm

So far in this chapter we have treated products as separate, distinct entities. However, many firms are multiproduct, serving multimarkets. Some of these products are 'young' and some are 'older'. Young products will require investment to finance their growth, others will generate more cash than they need. Somehow firms have to decide how to spread their limited resources among the competing needs of products so as to achieve the best performance of the firm as a whole. Figure 14.7 shows an example of a company (British Leyland)

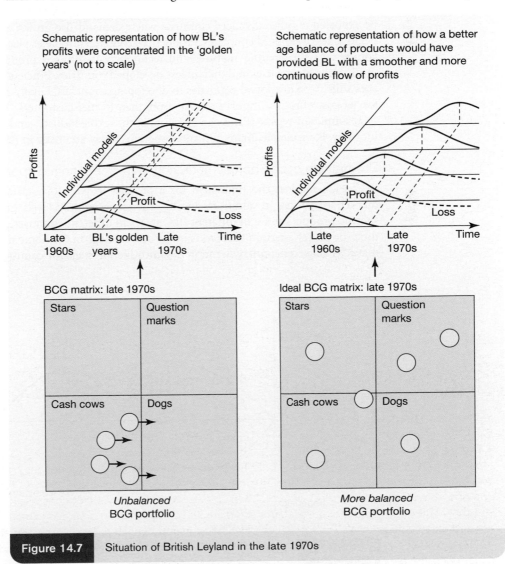

| **Figure 14.7** | Situation of British Leyland in the late 1970s |

Source: partly reprinted from *Long Range Planning*, 17(3), McNamee, P. (1984) 'Competitive analysis using matrix displays', pp. 98–114, copyright 1984, with permission from Elsevier.

that did not succeed in achieving a balanced product portfolio (note that the PLC curves are represented by profit and not sales).

Product life cycles for different countries

When expanding the concept of the PLC to international markets two different approaches appear:

1. international product life cycle (IPLC) – a macroeconomic approach;
2. PLCs across countries – a microeconomic approach.

The international product life cycle

The IPLC theory (originally Vernon, 1966) describes the diffusion process of an innovation across national boundaries (Figure 14.8). For each curve net export results when the curve is above the horizontal line; if the curve is below the horizontal line net import results for a particular country.

Typically, demand first grows in the innovating country (here the United States). In the beginning excess production in the innovating country (greater than domestic demand) will be exported to other advanced countries where demand also grows. Only later does demand begin in less developed countries. Production, consequently, takes place first in the innovating country. As the product matures and technology is diffused production occurs in other industrialized countries and then in less developed countries. Efficiency/comparative advantages shift from developed countries to developing countries. Finally, advanced countries, no longer cost-effective, import products from their former customers.

Examples of typical IPLCs can be found in the textile industry and the computer/software industry. For example, many software programs today are made in Bangalore, India.

Product life cycles across countries: a microeconomic approach

In foreign markets the time span for a product to pass through a stage may vary from market to market. In addition, due to different economic levels in different countries, a specific product can be in different PLC stages in different countries. Figure 14.9 shows that the product (at a certain time, t_1) is in the decline stage in the home market, while it is in the maturity stage for country A and in the introduction stage for country B (Majaro, 1982).

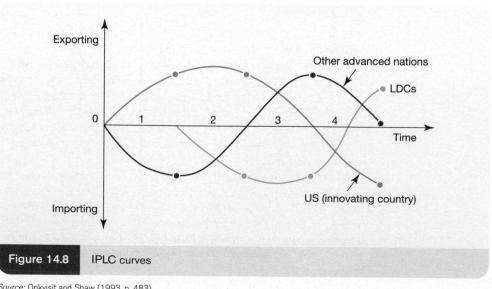

Figure 14.8	IPLC curves

Source: Onkvisit and Shaw (1993, p. 483).

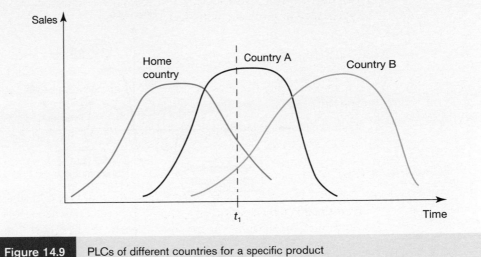

Figure 14.9   PLCs of different countries for a specific product

New products for the international market

Customer needs are the starting point for product development, whether for domestic or global markets. In addition to customer needs conditions of use and ability to buy the product form a framework for decisions on new product development for international markets.

Developing new products/cutting the time to market

As a consequence of increasing international competition, time is becoming a key success factor for an increasing number of companies that manufacture technologically sophisticated products. This time competition and the level of technological development mean that product life cycles are getting shorter and shorter.

In parallel to shorter PLCs, the product development times for new products are being greatly reduced. This applies not only to technical products in the field of office communication equipment, but also to cars and consumer electronics. In some cases there have been reductions in development times of more than half.

Similarly, the time for marketing/selling, and hence also for R&D cost to pay off, has gone down from about four years to only two years. This new situation is illustrated in Figure 14.10.

For all types of technological product it holds true that the manufactured product must have as good a quality as required by the customer (i.e. as good as necessary), but not as good as technically feasible. Too frequently technological products are over-optimized and therefore too expensive from the customer's point of view (a good analysis of 'quality' is to be found in Guiltinan *et al.*, 1997).

As we have indicated in earlier chapters, Japanese and European suppliers to the car industry have different approaches to the product development process. Figure 14.11 shows an example with suppliers of dashboard instruments for cars. The two Japanese manufacturers start the engineering design phase two years later than the European manufacturer. This enables the Japanese to develop a product fully in a shorter time using the newest technology and to launch it almost simultaneously with their competitors.

The reason for the better time competition of the Japanese manufacturers is the intensive use of the following measures:

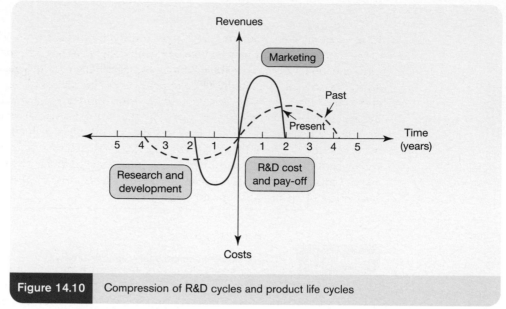

Figure 14.10 Compression of R&D cycles and product life cycles

Source: reprinted from *Long Range Planning*, 28(2), Töpfer, A. (1995) 'New products: cutting the time to market', p. 64, Copyright 1995, with permission from Elsevier.

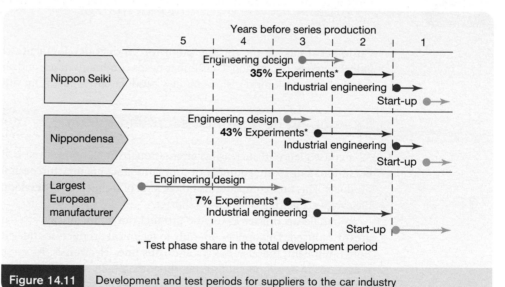

Figure 14.11 Development and test periods for suppliers to the car industry

Source: reprinted from *Long Range Planning*, 28(2), Töpfer, A. (1995) 'New products: cutting the time to market', p. 72, Copyright 1995, with permission from Elsevier.

- early integration of customers and suppliers
- multiskilled project teams
- interlinking of R&D, production and marketing activities
- total quality management
- parallel planning of new products and the required production facilities (simultaneous engineering)
- high degree of outsourcing (reduction of internal manufacturing content).

Today product quality is not enough to reach and to satisfy the customer. Quality of design and appearance play an increasingly important role. A highly qualified product support and customer service is also required.

Quality deployment function (QDF)

QDF is considered a main tool for 'listen to the voice of the customer' in the new product development process. It may be used to identify opportunities for product improvement or differentiation. QDF is a useful technique for translating customer needs into new product attributes and for responding to requirements of the successful development process. It encourages communication between engineering, production and marketing. Besides the involvement of customer requirements in the new product development process QDF permits the reduction of design time and design cost while maintaining or enhancing the quality of the design. QDF originated in 1972 at Mitsubishi's Kobe shipyard and is used widely both in Japan and the United States. It has reduced design time and cost at Toyota by 40 per cent. The time- and cost-reducing effect arises because more effort is allocated in the early stages of the product innovation process.

Degrees of product newness

A new product can have several degrees of newness. It may be an entirely new invention (new to the world) or it may be a slight modification of an existing product. In Figure 14.12 newness has two dimensions: newness to the market (consumers, channels and public policy) and newness to the company. The risk of market failure also increases with the newness of the product. Hence the greater the newness of the product, the greater the need for a thorough internal company and external environment analysis, in order to reduce the risk involved.

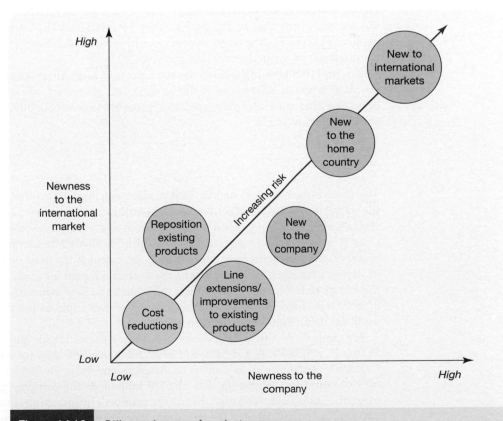

Figure 14.12   Different degrees of product newness

		Product		
		Standard	*Adapt*	*New*
Promotion	*Standard*	Straight extension	Product adaptation	Product invention
	Adapt	Promotion adaptation	Dual adaptation	

Figure 14.13	Product/communication mode

Source: based on Keegan (1995), pp. 489–94, p. 498, Table 13–1.

The product communication mix

Having decided upon the optimum standardization/adaptation route and the newness of the product, the next most important (and culturally sensitive) factor to be considered is that of international promotion.

Product and promotion go hand in hand in foreign markets and together are able to create or destroy markets in very short order. We have considered above the factors that may drive an organization to standardize or adapt its product range for foreign markets. Equally important are the promotion or the performance promises that the organization makes for its product or service in the target market. As with product decisions, promotion can be either standardized or adapted for foreign markets.

Keegan (1995) has highlighted the key aspects of marketing strategy as a combination of standardization or adaptation of the product and promotion of elements of the mix, and offers five alternative and more specific approaches to product policy. These approaches are shown in Figure 14.13.

Straight extension

This involves introducing a standardized product with the same promotion strategy throughout the world market (one product, one message worldwide). By applying this strategy successfully major savings can be made on market research and product development. Since the 1920s Coca-Cola has adopted a global approach, which has allowed the company to make enormous cost savings and benefits from continual reinforcement of the same message. While a number of writers have argued that this will be the strategy adopted for many products in the future, in practice only a handful of products might claim to have achieved this already. A number of firms have tried and failed. Campbell's soups, for example, found that consumers' taste in soup was by no means international.

An example of successful extension is Unilever's worldwide introduction of Organics Shampoo, which was first launched in Thailand in late 1993 after joint development work by Unilever's Hair Innovation Centres in Bangkok and Paris. By 1995 the brand was sold in over 40 countries, generating sales of £170 million. In the two-page advertisement from a magazine shown here and used during the product's introduction into Argentina, the basic advertising concept all over the world (including Argentina) has been 'Organics – the first ever root-nourishing shampoo'.

'Straight extension' of Organics shampoo to Argentina

Promotion adaptation

Use of this strategy involves leaving a product unchanged but fine-tuning promotional activity to take into account cultural differences between markets. It is a relatively cost-effective strategy as changing promotion messages is not as expensive as adapting products. An example of this strategy is illustrated by Lux.

LUX soap (Unilever): the United Kingdom versus India

The UK version of the LUX advertisement is based on the classic transborder advertising campaign, 'the beauty soap of film stars', which has been standardized to a high degree. In India the LUX campaign has been given a special local touch.

The Indian version is one of three advertisements that trace LUX's association with film stars from the past era to the current stars of today and the potential film stars of tomorrow. The advertisement focuses on three past legendary beauties of Indian cinema who have endorsed the brand. The creative statement is in a cinema poster style, keeping the brand image in mind, and in a sepia tone to give it a nostalgic feel.

Product adaptation

By modifying only the product a manufacturer intends to maintain the core product function in the different markets. For example, electrical appliances have to be modified to cope with different electrical voltages in different countries. A product can also be adapted to function under different physical environmental conditions. Exxon changed the chemical composition of petrol to cope with the extremes of climate, but still used the 'Put a tiger in your tank' campaign unchanged around the world.

Dual adaptation

By adapting both product and promotion for each market the firm is adopting a totally differentiated approach. This strategy is often adopted by firms when one of the previous

Advertisements for Lux in the UK and India

three strategies has failed, but particularly if the firm is not in a leadership position and is therefore reacting to the market or following competitors. It applies to the majority of products in the world market. The modification of both product and promotion is an expensive but often necessary strategy.

An example of dual adaptation is shown opposite, with the launch of Kellogg's Basmati Flakes in the nascent breakfast cereal market in India. This product was specially created to

Kellogg's dual adaption for the Indian market

suit Indian tastes, India being a large rice-eating country, and the advertising campaign was a locally adapted concept based on international positioning. Note that the product is available only in the Bombay area.

Product invention

Product invention is adopted by firms, usually from advanced nations, that are supplying products to less developed countries. Products are specifically developed to meet the needs of the individual markets. Existing products may be too technologically sophisticated to operate in less developed countries, where power supplies may be intermittent and local skills limited. Keegan (1995) uses a hand-powered washing machine as a product example.

EXHIBIT 14.2 Product invention – solar-powered portable charging systems for India

By developing a solar-powered portable charging system for its digital cameras and photo printers, Hewlett-Packard has been able to make successful inroads into the vast Indian rural market. This incremental innovation has enabled HP to successfully sell digital cameras and printers to consumers living in villages in India that have not yet benefited from the national rural electrification programme. The business model employed by HP to tap into the potential of the rural market is innovative. Unlike in urban markets where the camera and printer are sold outright to customers, the village entrepreneurs lease the equipment and purchase consumables from HP. Another major contributing factor to HP's success in penetrating the rural market in India was knowledge about rural communities that it was able acquire through the stay of a team of HP employees in the homes of local families for a couple of days, and from attending community meetings.

Source: adapted from Varadarajan (2009).

14.6   Product positioning

Product positioning is a key element in the successful marketing of any organization in any market. The product or company that does not have a clear position in the customer's mind consequently stands for nothing and is rarely able to command more than a simple commodity or utility price. Premium pricing and competitive advantage are largely dependent upon the customer's perception that the product or service on offer is markedly different in some way from competitive offers (Devaney and Brown, 2008). How can we achieve a credible market position in international markets?

Since it is the buyer/user perception of benefit-generating attributes that is important, product positioning is the activity by which a desirable 'position' in the mind of the customer is created for the product. Positioning a product for international markets begins with describing specific products as comprising different attributes that are capable of generating a flow of benefits to buyers and users.

The global marketing planner puts these attributes into bundles so that the benefits generated match the special requirements of specific market segments. This product design problem involves not only the basic product components (physical, package, service and country of origin) but also brand name, styling and similar features.

Viewed in a multidimensional space (commonly denoted as 'perceptual mapping'), a product can be graphically represented at a point specified by its attributes. The location of a product's point in perceptual space is its 'position'. Competitors' products are similarly located (see also Johansson and Thorelli, 1985). If points representing other products are close to the point of the prototype then these other products are close competitors of the prototype. If the prototype is positioned away from its closest competitors in some international markets and its positioning implies important features for customers, then it is likely to have a significant competitive advantage.

Country-of-origin effects

The country of origin of a product, typically communicated by the phrase 'made in [country]', has a considerable influence on the quality perception of that product. Some countries have a good reputation and others a poor reputation for certain products. For example, Japan and Germany have good reputations for producing cars. The country-of-origin effects are especially critical among eastern European consumers. A study by Ettensén (1993) examined the brand decision for televisions among Russian, Polish and Hungarian consumers. These consumers evaluated domestically produced television products much lower than Western-made products, regardless of brand name. There was a general preference for televisions manufactured in Japan, Germany and the United States.

EXHIBIT 14.3 **Chinese piano manufacturers are experiencing the 'Country Of Origin' (COO) effect**

The Chinese piano industry is a useful example to show the opportunities and challenges facing Chinese brands. China has overtaken Japan and South Korea to become the world's largest piano-producing nation. One of the brand manufacturers, Pearl River, has become the world's largest piano manufacturer with annual sales of about 100,000 units. As piano making is still a labour-intensive industry, Chinese manufacturers enjoy a big cost and price advantage. This also motivates international dealers to stock Chinese pianos, because of a larger profit margin. However, the biggest branding dilemma facing Chinese piano manufacturers is negative perceptions of 'made in China' as a label. It is difficult for individual firms to change this perception and requires the country to change its image in general, which may take a generation. It has taken Japanese Yamaha more than 30 years to change its image from a cheap 'me-too' product to a leading global brand. An important buying influence also comes from music teachers, and many of them advise their students not to buy Chinese-made instruments.

To overcome this difficulty, Chinese manufacturers could try to link their brands to Western-oriented values and names. For example, Longfeng Piano could emphasize that its Kingsburg model is designed by the world-renowned German designer Klaus Fenner.

Source: adapted from Fan (2007). From Hollensen, S. (2008) *Essentials of Global Marketing*, FT/Prentice Hall, p. 311, Exhibit 11.1.

The country of origin is more important than the brand name, and this can be good news for Western firms that are attempting to penetrate the eastern European region with imports whose brand name is not yet familiar. Another study (Johansson *et al.*, 1994) showed that some products from eastern Europe have done well in the West, despite negative country-of-origin perceptions. For example, Belarus tractors have sold well in Europe and the United States not only because of their reasonable price but also because of their ruggedness. Only the lack of an effective distribution network has hindered the firm's ability to penetrate Western markets to a greater degree.

When considering the implications of product positioning it is important to realize that positioning can vary from market to market, because the target customers for the product differ from country to country. In confirming the positioning of a product or service in a specific market or region it is therefore necessary to establish in the consumer's perception exactly what the product stands for and how it differs from existing and potential competition. In developing a market-specific product positioning the firm can focus upon one or more elements of the total product offer, so the differentiation might be based upon price and quality, one or more attributes, a specific application, a target consumer or direct comparison with one competitor.

EXHIBIT 14.4 Madame Tussauds – a brand which brings people closer to celebrities on a global basis

The attraction's history is a rich and fascinating one with roots dating back to the Paris of 1770. It was here that Madame Tussaud learnt to model wax likenesses under the tutelage of her mentor, Dr Philippe Curtius. Her skills were put to the test during the French Revolution when she was forced to prove her allegiance by making the death masks of executed aristocrats. It was in the early nineteenth century that she came to Britain, bringing with her a travelling exhibition of revolutionary relics and effigies of public heroes and rogues.

In March 2007, the Tussauds Group was sold to the Blackstone Group in a £1 billion deal. The company has been merged with the Merlin Entertainments Group. In 2009 Merlin attracted around 30 million visitors to all its attractions, which makes them the world's second-largest visitor attraction operator after Disney. The Merlin Entertainments Group operates in 12 countries and has more than 13,000 employees.

Brand experience

The future for brands is about building memorable consumer experiences. Experience-oriented companies like Madame Tussauds need to have something that goes beyond the product. Madame Tussauds' selling point is not about waxworks, it is about bringing people closer to celebrities and what they do in life.

Barack Obama (London) and the local Chinese popstars (Twins) (Shanghai)
Madame Tussauds London (left) and Madame Tussauds Shanghai (right).

Choice of new location

The choice of a new location is based on many different criteria. Madame Tussauds has a product development team that investigates how many tourists visit a city, whether they fit the profile of the attraction's visitors and whether there's enough space. Detailed research is vital to take a concept into a new market. After opening in Hong Kong Madame Tussauds recently opened its second Asian branch in Shanghai. As China's largest and wealthiest city with over 13 million residents and nearly 40 million tourists a year, Shanghai represents a good opportunity for the company.

Interactivity with the waxwork figures

The new Shanghai branch has the most interactivity of all the attractions, with fewer waxwork figures and more to do around them. The Tiger Woods exhibit allows visitors to putt on the green and see their scores come up. The latest guest to have a hole-in-one is recorded on the leaderboard. Visitors can also go into a karaoke booth with models of some famous Chinese popstars, called Twins (see the photo), sing with them and view themselves on video. People can also dress up like Charlie Chaplin and see themselves on a movie screen in black and white.

Balancing local and global branding

The research of Madame Tussauds shows a 98 per cent brand recognition in the UK market. However, in Asia, the term 'madame' sometimes implies a bar or club to many consumers, and saying that the brand is a 'wax attraction' does not mean anything in the Asian market as there is no tradition of that type of museum there.

For Madame Tussauds it is important to make sure the brand maintains a good mix of local and global content. This is a delicate balance: too much local content does not fit with the idea of a global brand, while too little emphasis on global figures can disappoint international customers. The new Chinese venue overwhelmingly features local faces, such as actor Ge You, kung fu king Jackie Chan, the pop-group Twins and basketball superstar Yao Ming; it also has global figures such as David Beckham, Michael Jackson and Brad Pitt. The London attraction has a wide range of global figures such as Angelina Jolie, Beyonce Knowles and Barack Obama (see the photo), but international tourists also love Margaret Thatcher, Princess Diana, Winston Churchill and the Queen. The photo illustrates the Madame Tussauds mixture of global content (like Barack Obama) and local content (like the Twins).

Expanding the Madame Tussauds brand on a global scale is a challenge, but when it comes down to the essentials, Madame Tussauds is not about waxworks – it is about consumer experiences and bringing people into interaction with the celebrities.

Sources: with kind permission from Madame Tussauds Group, especially Global Marketing Director Nicky Marsh from London (www.madame-tussauds.com) and Cathy Wong, External Affairs Consultant from Shanghai (www.madame-tussauds.com.cn); Marsh, N. (2006) 'Translating experiences across the world', *Brand Strategy*, June, p. 11; Macalister, T. (2005) 'Madame Tussauds to open in Shanghai', *The Guardian* (London), 19 September, p. 20.

14.7 Brand equity

Brands have become omnipresent in all parts of the global culture (Cayla and Arnould, 2008). A study by Citibank and Interbrand in 1997 found that companies basing their business on brands had outperformed the stock market for 15 years. The same study does, however, note the risky tendency of some brand owners to reduce investments in brands in the mid-1990s, with negative impacts on their performance (Hooley *et al.*, 1998, p. 120).

The following two examples show that brands add value for customers:

- The classic example is that in blind test 51 per cent of consumers prefer Pepsi to Coca-Cola, but in open tests 65 per cent prefer Coca-Cola to Pepsi: soft drink preferences are based on brand image, not taste (Hooley *et al.*, 1998, p. 119).

- Skoda cars have been best known in the United Kingdom as the butt of bad jokes, reflecting a widespread belief that the cars are of very low quality. In 1995 Skoda was preparing to launch a new model in the United Kingdom, and did 'blind and seen' tests of the consumers' judgement of the vehicle. The vehicle was rated as better designed and worth more by those who did not know the make. With the Skoda name revealed perceptions of the design were less favourable and estimated value was substantially lower. This leads us from the reputation of the company to branding (Hooley *et al.*, 1998, p. 117).

Definitions of brand equity

Brand equity
A set of brand assets and liabilities which can be clustered into five categories: brand loyalty, brand awareness, perceived quality, brand associations and other proprietary brand assets. Brand equity is the premium a customer/consumer would pay for the branded product or service compared to an identical unbranded version of the same product/service.

Although the definition of **brand equity** is often debated, the term deals with the brand value, beyond the physical assets associated with its manufacture.

David Aaker of the University of California at Berkeley, one of the leading authorities on brand equity, has defined the term as 'a set of *brand assets and liabilities* linked to the brand, its name and symbol, that add to or subtract from the value provided by a product or service to a firm or to the firm's customers' (Aaker, 1991, p. 15).

Aaker has clustered those assets and liabilities into five categories:

1. *Brand loyalty*. Encourages customers to buy a particular brand time after time and remain insensitive to competitors' offerings.
2. *Brand awareness*. Brand names attract attention and convey images of familarity. May be translated as how big a percentage of the customers know the brand name.
3. *Perceived quality*. 'Perceived' means that the customers decide upon the level of quality, not the company.
4. *Brand associations*. The values and the personality linked to the brand.
5. *Other proprietary brand assets*. Include trademarks, patents and marketing channel relationships.

Brand equity can be thought of as the additional cash flow achieved by associating a brand with the underlying values of the product or service. In this connection it is useful (although incomplete) to think of a brand's equity as *the premium a customer/consumer would pay for the branded product or service compared to an identical unbranded version of the same product/service.*

Hence brand equity refers to the strength, depth and character of the consumer–brand relationship. A strong equity implies a positive force that keeps the consumer and the brand together, in the face of resistance and tension. The strength, depth and character of the customer–brand relationship is referred to as the *brand relationship quality* (Marketing Science Institute, 1995).

14.8   Branding decisions

Closely linked to product positioning is the question of branding. The basic purposes of branding are the same everywhere in the world. In general, the functions of branding are:

- to distinguish a company's offering and differentiate one particular product from its competitors
- to create identification and brand awareness
- to guarantee a certain level of quality and satisfaction
- to help with promotion of the product.

All of these purposes have the same ultimate goals: to create new sales (market shares taken from competitors) or induce repeat sales (keep customers loyal).

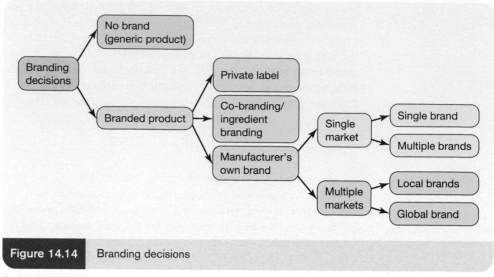

Figure 14.14	Branding decisions

Source: adapted from Onkvisit and Shaw (1993, p. 534).

Figure 14.14 demonstrates the four levels of branding decisions. Each alternative at the four levels has a number of advantages and disadvantages, which are presented in Table 14.2. We will discuss these options in more detail below.

EXHIBIT 14.5 Unilever's Snuggle fabric softener – an example of local brands in multiple markets

An effective example of promotion adaptation is illustrated by Unilever's Snuggle Fabric softener. The product was initially launched in Germany as an economy brand in a category dominated by Procter & Gamble. In order to counteract the negative quality inferences associated with low price, Unilever emphasized softness as the product's key point of difference. The softness association was communicated through the name, 'Kuschelweich', which means 'enfolded in softness', and this was illustrated through a picture of a teddy bear on the package. When the product was launched in France, Unilever kept the brand positioning of economy and softness but changed the name to 'Cajoline', meaning softness in French. In addition, the teddy bear that had been inactive in Germany now took the centre stage in the French advertising as the brand symbol for softness and quality. Success in France led to global expansion and in each case the brand name was changed to connote softness in the local language while the advertising featuring the teddy bear remained virtually identical across global markets. By the 1990s, Unilever was marketing the fabric softener around the globe with over a dozen brand names, all with the same product positioning and advertising support. More importantly, the fabric softener was generally the number 1 or number 2 brand in each market.

Source: adapted from Keller and Sood (2001).

Brand versus no brand

Branding is associated with added costs in the form of marketing, labelling, packaging and promotion. Commodities are 'unbranded' or undifferentiated products. Examples of products with no brand are cement, metals, salt, beef and other agricultural products.

Table 14.2	Advantages and disadvantages of branding alternatives	
	Advantages	**Disadvantages**
No brand	Lower production cost. Lower marketing cost. Lower legal cost. Flexible quality control.	Severe price competition. Lack of market identity.
Branding	Better identification and awareness. Better chance for production differentiation. Possible brand loyalty. Possible premium pricing.	Higher production cost. Higher marketing cost. Higher legal cost.
Private label	Possibility of larger market share. No promotional problems.	Severe price competition. Lack of market identity.
Co-branding/ ingredient branding	Adds more value to the brand. Sharing of production and promotion costs. Increases manufacturer's power in gaining access to retailers' shelves. Can develop into long-lasting relationships based on mutual commitment.	Consumers may become confused. Ingredient supplier is very dependent on the success of the final product. Promotion cost for ingredient supplier.
Manufacturer's own brand	Better price due to higher price inelasticity. Retention of brand loyalty. Better bargaining power. Better control of distribution.	Difficult for small manufacturer with unknown brand. Requires brand promotion.
Single market, single brand	Marketing efficiency. Permits more focused marketing. Eliminates brand confusion. Good for product with good reputation (halo effect).	Assumes market homogeneity. Existing brand's image harmed when trading up/down. Limited shelf space.
Single market, multiple brands	Market segmented for varying needs. Creates competitive spirit. Avoids negative connotation of existing brand. Gains more retail shelf space. Does not harm existing brand's image.	Higher marketing cost. Higher inventory cost. Loss of economies of scale.
Multiple markets, local brands (see also Exhibit 14.5)	Meaningful names. Local identification. Avoidance of taxation on international brand. Allows variations of quantity and quality across markets.	Higher marketing cost. Higher inventory cost. Loss of economies of scale. Diffused image.
Multiple markets, global brand	Maximum marketing efficiency. Reduction of advertising costs. Elimination of brand confusion. Good for culture-free product. Good for prestigious product. Easy identification/recognition for international travellers. Uniform worldwide image.	Assumes market homogeneity. Problems with black and grey markets. Possibility of negative connotation. Requires quality and quantity consistency. LDCs' opposition and resentment. Legal complications.

Source: adapted from Onkvisit and Shaw (1989). Published with permission from Emerald Publishing Ltd. www.emeraldinsight.com.

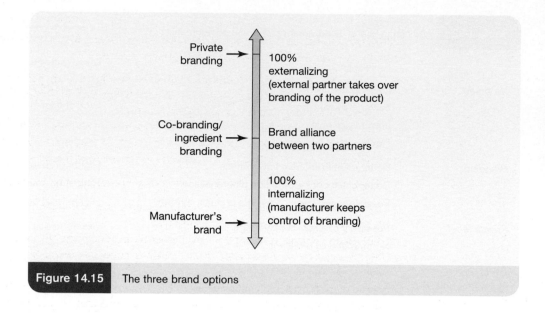

| Figure 14.15 | The three brand options |

Private label versus co-branding versus manufacturer's own brand

These three options can be graded as shown in Figure 14.15.

The question of consumers having brand loyalty or shop loyalty is a crucial one. The competitive struggle between the manufacturer and the retailer actualizes the need for a better understanding of shopping behaviour. Both actors need to be aware of determinants of shop choice, shopping frequency and in-store behaviour. Where manufacturers pay little attention to the shopping behaviour of their consumers, this helps to anticipate the increasing power of certain retail chains.

Private label

Private label
Retailer's own brand, e.g. Sainsbury's Taste the difference.

Private labelling is most developed in the United Kingdom, where Marks & Spencer, for instance, mostly sell own-label (**private label**) products. At Sainsbury's own labels account for 60 per cent of the sales. Compared with the high share of private labelling in northern Europe, the share in southern Europe (e.g. Spain and Portugal) is no higher than 10 per cent.

The retailer's perspective

For the retailer there are two main advantages connected with own-label business:

1. *Own labels provide better profit margins.* The cost of goods typically makes up 70–85 per cent of a retailer's total cost. So if the retailer can buy a quality product from the manufacturer at a lower price this will provide a better profit margin for the retailer. In fact private labels have helped UK food retailers to achieve profit margins averaging 8 per cent of sales, which is high by international standards. The typical figure in France and the United States is 1–2 per cent (Steenkamp and Kumar, 2009).
2. *Own labels strengthen the retailer's image with its customers.* Many retail chains try to establish loyalty to their particular chain of shops by offering their own quality products. In fact premium private-label products (e.g. Sainsbury's Taste the difference) that compete in quality with manufacturers' top brands have seen a growth in market share, whereas the share of cheap generics is declining.

The manufacturer's perspective

Although private brands are normally regarded as threats for manufacturers there may be situations where private branding is a preferable option:

● Because there are no promotional expenses associated with private branding for the producer, the strategy is especially suitable for SMEs with limited financial resources and limited competences in the downstream functions.
● The private brand manufacturer gains access to the shelves of the retail chains. With increasing internationalization of the big retail chains this may also result in export business for the SME that has never been in international markets.

There are also a number of reasons why private branding is bad for the manufacturer:

● By not having its own identity, the manufacturer must compete mainly on price, because the retail chain can always switch supplier.
● The manufacturer loses control over how its products should be promoted. This may become critical if the retailer does not do a good job in pushing the product to the consumer.
● If the manufacturer is producing both its own brands and private brands there is a danger that the private brands will cannibalise the manufacturer's brand-name products.

Exhibit 14.6 shows an example with Kellogg, which has moved from a brand strategy to a private brand strategy.

EXHIBIT 14.6 Kellogg is under pressure to produce under Aldi's own label

In February 2000 Kellogg (the cereal giant) made an own-label deal with German supermarket chain Aldi. It is the first time that Kellogg has supplied own label.

A slogan on Kellogg's cereal packets claims: 'If you don't see Kellogg's on the box . . . it isn't Kellogg's in the box.' But now Kellogg has negotiated a deal with Aldi to supply products in Germany bearing a different brand name. Reports in Germany say that the deal was made after Aldi announced it would no longer pay brand suppliers' prices and threatened to cut top brands from its shelves.

Source: adapted from various public media.

Quelch and Harding (1996) argue that many manufacturers have over-reacted to the threat of private brands. Increasing numbers of manufacturers are beginning to make private-label products to take up excess production capacity. According to Quelch and Harding more than 50 per cent of US manufacturers of branded consumer packaged goods already make private-label goods as well.

Managers typically examine private-label production opportunities on an incremental marginal cost basis. The fixed overhead costs associated with the excess capacity used to make the private-label products would be incurred anyway, but if private-label manufacturing were evaluated on a full-cost basis rather than on an incremental basis it would, in many cases, appear much less profitable. The more private-label production grows as a percentage of total production, the more an analysis based on full costs becomes relevant (Quelch and Harding, 1996).

Manufacturer's own brand

From the Second World War until the 1960s brand manufacturers managed to build a bridge over the heads of the retailers to the consumers. They created consumer loyalty for their particular brand by using sophisticated advertising (culminating in TV advertising) and other promotional techniques.

Since the 1960s various sociological changes (notably the car) have encouraged the rise of large, efficient retailers. Nowadays the distribution system is being turned upside down. The traditional supply chain, powered by manufacturer 'push', is becoming a demand chain, driven by consumer 'pull'. Retailers have won control over distribution not just because they decide the price at which goods are sold, but also because both individual shops and retail companies have become much bigger and more efficient. They are able to buy in bulk and to reap economies of scale, mainly due to advances in transport and, more recently, in information technology. Most retail chains have not only set up computer links between each store and distribution warehouses, they are also hooked up with the computers of the firm's main suppliers, through an electronic data interchange system.

After some decades of absence private labels reappeared in the 1970s as generic products pioneered by Carrefour in France, but were soon adopted by UK and US retailers. Ten years ago there was a distinct gap in the level of quality between private-label and brand-name products. Today the gap has narrowed: private-label quality levels are higher than ever before and they are more consistent, especially in categories historically characterized by little product innovation.

Co-branding/ingredient branding

Despite the similarities between co-branding and ingredient branding there is also an important difference, as we shall see below.

Co-branding

Co-branding
Form of cooperation between two or more brands, which can create synergies that create value for both participants, above the value they would expect to generate on their own.

Co-branding is a form of cooperation between two or more brands with significant customer recognition, in which all the participants' brand names are retained. It is of medium- to long-term duration and its net value creation potential is too small to justify setting up a new brand and/or legal joint venture. The motive for co-branding is the expectation of synergies that create value for both participants, above the value they would expect to generate on their own (Bengtsson and Servais, 2005).

In the case of co-branding, the products are often complementary, in the way that one product can be used or consumed independently of the other (e.g. Bacardi Rum and Coca-Cola). Hence co-branding may be an efficient alternative to traditional brand extension strategies (Figure 14.16).

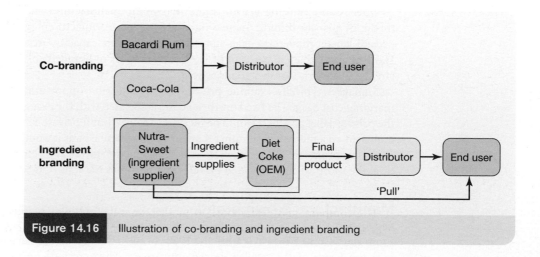

Figure 14.16   Illustration of co-branding and ingredient branding

EXHIBIT 14.7 Shell's co-branding with Ferrari and LEGO

In 1999–2000 Shell ran a £50 million co-branding campaign with Ferrari and LEGO. Some people might have thought that this was an attempt to persuade people, mainly in the West, that Shell's controversial attempt to dump the Brent Spar oil platform in the North Sea was not a true reflection of the company.

However, it may be more accurate to say that Shell was seeking a 'brand image transfer'. In the petrol retailer market traditionally driven by price and more price promotions, Shell wanted both Ferrari's sexy, sporty image and the family values of LEGO. Furthermore Shell was and is no longer only in the petroleum and oils business, where price promotions are the main focus of marketing activity. The company is also involved in food retailing, where loyalty programmes are important.

What were the benefits for Ferrari and LEGO? Ferrari gained sponsorship and royalty income from model car sales, while LEGO got improved global distribution. The co-branding strategy involved the use of ten exclusive small boxed toys and a big Ferrari LEGO car carrying a Shell logo. Shell wanted to sell between 20 and 40 million units of LEGO globally, and the deal made Shell one of the world's largest toy distributors.

Source: adapted from various public media.

Ingredient branding

Normally the marketer of the final product (OEM) creates all of the value in the consumer's eyes. In the case of Intel and NutraSweet the ingredient supplier is seeking to build value in its products by branding and promoting the key component of an end product. When promotion ('pull' strategy: see Figure 14.16) of the key component brand is initiated by the ingredient supplier the goal is to build awareness and preference among consumers for that ingredient brand. Simultaneously, it may be the manufacturer (OEM) that seeks to benefit from a recognized ingredient brand, for example some computer manufacturers are benefiting from the quality image of using an Intel chip.

However, **ingredient branding** is not suitable for every supplier of components. An ingredient supplier should fulfil the following requirements:

Ingredient branding
The supplier delivers an important key component to the final OEM-product, e.g. Intel delivers its processor to the major PC manufacturers.

- The ingredient supplier should be offering a product that has a substantial advantage over existing products. DuPont's Teflon, NutraSweet, Intel chips and the Dolby noise reduction system are all examples of major technological innovations, the result of large investments in R&D.
- The ingredient should be critical to the success of the final product. NutraSweet is not only a low-calorie sweetener, but has a taste that is nearly identical to that of sugar.

Single brand versus multiple brands (single market)

A single brand or family brand (for a number of products) may be helpful in convincing consumers that each product is of the same quality or meets certain standards. In other words, when a single brand in a single market is marketed by the manufacturer, the brand is assured of receiving full attention for maximum impact.

The company may also choose to market several (multiple) brands in a single market. This is based on the assumption that the market is heterogeneous and consists of several segments.

EXHIBIT 14.8 Roundup – a global brand for multiple markets

Roundup is the brand name of a broad-spectrum herbicide produced by the US company Monsanto: it contains the active ingredient glyphosate, Roundup is referred to as a non-selective herbicide, meaning it removes most weeds. Monsanto developed and patented glyphosate herbicide in the 1970s. The original Roundup was introduced in 1974 in the US. The brand is registered in more than 130 countries. Glyphosate is the most used herbicide in the world, and Roundup is the number one-selling herbicide worldwide since at least 1980.

In the late 1990s, Roundup became the best-selling agricultural chemical of all times and a profitable product for Monsanto. This success was the result of several factors. One was a conscious strategy to reduce price in the US, where patent protection gave it a strong market position until September 2000. Prices were lower outside the US, where patents expired earlier, and between 1995 and 2000, Monsanto reduced the price by an average of 9 per cent a year.

The Roundup line of products represents about half of Monsanto's revenue in 2008 of US$11.4 billion.

It retained exclusive rights in the US until its US patent expired in 2000, and maintained a predominant market share in countries where the patent expired earlier. Monsanto also produces seeds which grow into plants genetically engineered to be tolerant to glyphosate, which are known as Roundup Ready crops. The glyphosate tolerance-imparting gene contained in these seeds is patented. Such crops allow

Monsanto Company.

farmers to use glyphosate as a post-emergence herbicide against most broadleaf and narrowleaf weeds.

Today more than 30 companies worldwide make glyphosate, and many of them are in China. The growing number of producers has in 2009–2010 resulted in oversupply of generic glyphosate to the world market, and a downward pressure on the world market price.

However, in the post-patent world markets, Roundup has maintained its market leadership and a premium position. In consumers' mind Roundup has become identical with a whole product category.

Sources: www.monsanto.com plus additional sources. With permission from Monsanto Europe S.A.

Local brands versus a global brand (multiple markets)

A company has the option of using the same brand in most or all of its foreign markets or of using individual, local brands.

A single, global brand is also known as an international or universal brand (see also Exhibit 14.8 regarding the Monsanta's Round-up brand). A Eurobrand is a slight modification of this approach, as it is a single product for a single market of 15 or more European countries, with an emphasis on the search for intermarket similarities rather than differences.

A global brand is an appropriate approach when a product has a good reputation or is known for quality. In such a case a company would be wise to extend the brand name to other products in the product line. Examples of global brands are Coca-Cola, Shell and the Visa credit card. Although it is possible to find examples of global brands, local brands are probably more common among big multinational companies than people realize. Boze and Patton (1995) have studied branding practices of six multinational companies in 67 countries:

EXHIBIT 14.9 Maggi – local brands for multiple markets through acquisitions

Today Maggi is a Nestlé brand of instant soups and other instant food products. The original company came into existence in 1872 in Switzerland, when Julius Maggi took over his father's mill. It quickly became a pioneer of industrial food production, aiming at the improvement of the nutrition of workers families. It was the first to bring a protein-rich legume meal to the market, which was followed by ready-made soup based on a legume meal in 1886. In 1897, Julius Maggi founded the company Maggi GmbH in the German town of Singen where it is still established today. Maggi cubes are used as part of the local cuisine. Throughout many countries, Maggi products, especially bouillon cubes, are widely sold with some repackaging to reflect local terminology. Many multinational companies, such as Nestlé, follow such a 'multi-local' strategy, preferring to follow specific trends. Thus Nestlé's ready-made soups were launched in the following ways, in these different markets:

Société des Produits Nestlé SA. The Nestlé name and image is reproduced with kind permission of Société des Produits Nestlé SA.

Germany: Under the name 'Maggi, 5 Minuten Terrine' and positioned as a practical nutritious food for men and women between 30 and 40.
France: Under its own name 'Bolino' (with Maggi in small print) and positioned as an instant snack for the young single person.
United Kingdom and Switzerland: Under the name 'Quick Lunch', and positioned as a quick meal approved by mothers.
Poland: Under the name 'Flaki – Danie to 5 minut'. Here Nestlé had to adjust the taste of the soup to the Polish soup recipes. At the time of the launch of the Maggi brand there was already an existing strong Polish brand. However, Nestlé acquired this competitor and the Maggi products were launched under the umbrella brand 'Wineary' (under which Flaki was also introduced).

Generally, Nestlé's international brand strategy within ready-to-made soups is that it wants to behave as a local, and if they can not do this with Maggi, they acquire a local brand.

Source: Adapted from various public sources.

1. Colgate-Palmolive – headquartered in the United States.
2. Kraft General Foods (now part of Philip Morris) – headquartered in the United States.
3. Nestlé – headquartered in Switzerland.
4. Procter & Gamble – headquartered in the United States.
5. Quaker Oats – headquartered in the United States.
6. Unilever – headquartered in the United Kingdom and the Netherlands.

The findings of the research are summarized in Table 14.3. Of the 1,792 brands found in the 67 countries, 44 per cent were only marketed in one country. Only 68 brands (4 per cent) could be found in more than half of the countries. Of these 68 brands, only the following six were found in all 67 countries: Colgate, Lipton, Lux, Maggi, Nescafé and Palmolive. Hence these were the only true world brands.

Surprisingly, each of the six multinationl corporations (MNCs) seems to follow the practice of multiple brands in a single market. No official explanation was offered for this strategy, but a Nestlé manager explained 'that he believed it is a very important marketing advantage to provide a brand name not found in any other country, especially those adjacent to the nation or bigger than it' (Boze and Patton, 1995, p. 24).

Table 14.3	Brands of six multinational companies in 67 countries				
Company	Total no. of brands	Brands found in 50% or more countries		Brands in only one country	
		Number	% of total	Number	% of total
Colgate	163	6	4	59	36
Kraft GF	238	6	3	104	44
Nestlé	560	19	4	250	45
P&G	217	18	8	80	37
Quaker	143	2	1	55	38
Unilever	471	17	4	236	50
Total	**1,792**	**68**	**4**	**784**	**44**

Source: Boze and Patton (1995, p. 22). Reproduced with kind permission from the *Journal of Consumer Marketing*, Emerald Group Publishing Ltd.

The use of umbrella brands varies a lot among the MNCs examined. Of the six MNCs Colgate is the most intensive user of its two company names:

1. *Colgate.* Mostly dental products: toothpaste, tooth powder, toothbrushes, dental floss, mouthwash and shaving cream.
2. *Palmolive.* Hair products, shaving products, hand lotion, talc, deodorant, sun screen, toilet soap, bath products, liquid detergent (dishes and fine fabrics) and automatic dishwasher detergent.

It should be emphasized that the big MNCs prefer to acquire some local brands instead of using a global brand.

The results in Table 14.4 are also confirmed by a 2008 survey, sponsored by Millward Brown. Here the conclusion is that there are relatively few truly global brands and fewer still that manage to create a really strong connection with consumers in many countries (Hollis, 2009).

14.9 Sensory branding

Branding is essentially about building emotional ties between consumer and product. Nearly all the brand communication we experience encompasses just two senses – sight and hearing (print advertising, TV commercials, etc.). Yet the way in which we engage with the world around us uses all five senses: sight, sound, smell, touch and taste. Almost our entire understanding of the world is experienced through our senses. Our senses are our link to memory and can tap right into emotion. In the following the aspects of **sensory branding** are explained by some examples.

Sensory branding
Normally brand communication involves just two senses – sight and hearing. Sensory branding involves all five senses: sight, hearing (sound), smell, touch and taste.

Sight

In some sectors the revolution in sight is already underway. Drinks companies have become expert at using colour to revitalize ageing brands and catch the interest of younger consumers. Gordon's Gin is a classic example. In 2004, the company took its Sloe Gin out of its trademark emerald green bottle (still used for the Original Gin) and repackaged it in clear glass to reveal the rich sloe purple of its ingredients. The move was followed by high-profile advertising, focusing on the 'colourful flavours' and aromas imparted by the herbs in Gordon's three different formulations (Original, Distiller's Cut and Sloe), and positioning the brand as the 'Colorful Gin'.

Drinks companies (perhaps with an eye to the day when alcohol advertising might eventually be banned) are also adept at building sensory cues into brand communications. For an example look no further than Smirnoff Ice, which builds TV, web-based, and experiential marketing campaigns (featuring public snowball fights) around Uri – a fictitious Smirnoff Ice drinker who lives in the frozen wastes of Eastern Europe – aimed, one might guess, at forging a mental link between Smirnoff's fantasy world of ice and the generic pleasure of drinking ice-cold spirits.

Sound

In the automotive industry, for example, advances in acoustic design enable manufacturers to engineer, with great precision, how a door will sound as it closes.

Mercedes-Benz has 12 engineers dedicated to the sound of opening and closing doors. The sound is artificially generated and even the vibrations in the door are generated by electric impulses. Neglected sound details have even become powerful tools. Take the simple ring of a Nokia mobile phone. The Nokia tune has created awareness similar to the 'Intel Inside' tune.

Kellogg's trademarked crunchy sound and feel of eating cornflakes was created in sound labs and patented in the same way that the company owns its recipe and logo.

Smell

Incorporating smell into branding has already begun. As far back as 1973 Singapore Airlines broke through the barriers of traditional branding with their Singapore girl, a move which proved to be successful. Since then Singapore Airlines has focused on the emotional experience of air travel which includes a high sensory element (see Exhibit 14.10).

When Rolls-Royce started getting complaints about its new models not quite living up to the predecessors, it found out that the only difference was the smell. The interiors of older Rolls-Royce cars smelt of natural substances like wood, leather, hessian and wool. Modern safety regulations mean that most of these materials are no longer used, and have been replaced by foams and plastics. Using a 1965 Silver Cloud as a reference the Rolls-Royce team spent a considerable amount of time recreating the 'original' smell of Rolls-Royce. Today, before each new Rolls-Royce leaves the factory, the unique smell of Rolls-Royce is added to the underside of the car's seats to recreate the 'classic' Rolls-Royce.

Early in 2000 Crayola needed to protect its brand from the many unauthorized competitors in Asia. It is difficult to protect a colour pen which draws generic colours, and even harder to differentiate the product when the logo is barely recognizable. Crayola decided to leverage the smell. By analysing the scent of the original pen, Crayola artificially manufactured the smell and patented it, making it impossible to imitate. Today the smell of Crayola colour pens takes adults back to their childhood. The very characteristic smell is an essential component of the Crayola product with the aim of stimulating the memory of generations of kids in years to come.

Touch

One brand that epitomizes sensory stimulation is Lush, the hand-made cosmetics company. Pass the entrance of a Lush store and you are hit by a rush of fragrance. Lush co-founder Mark Constantine says: 'Packaging is so boring. Smelling and touching is just more fun for the senses.' What is more, he adds, 'If you don't use packaging you can use higher quality ingredients' (Lindstrom, 2004).

Taste

Taste is an obvious sense for companies that deal with food and beverages, for example Hennessy Cognac, KFC Fried Chicken and Coca-Cola. Every brand in these industries want to create a unique and specific taste to associate with their brand.

Of all the senses, taste most relies on the others. In fact, nearly 80 per cent of taste is derived from your sense of smell. In order to get a full sensory experience with taste, all other senses must be appealed to:

- sight: appearance, attractiveness, colour, shape
- smell: aroma
- touch: texture, temperature
- sound: consistency, texture.

EXHIBIT 14.10 Sensory branding at SIA (Singapore Airlines)

By the end of the 1990s a new set of brand tools were invented at SIA. With a brand platform that emphasizes smoothness and relaxation, the strategy was to move away from portraying itself as merely an airline and to present itself as an entertainment company.

In short, SIA is not just a means of transport; it provides access to a world of experiences. The aircraft cabin provides the ambience lighting, in-flight entertainment system, movies, music, newspapers, amenities and other mechanical provisions, but the 'Singapore Girl' is the human being who mediates between the airline and its passengers. She answers the needs of the passengers by being able to communicate in the language the passenger speaks even if it is not English, she brings the food, water, blankets and answers questions as to how to use the in-flight systems. She is a personification of the airline.

SIA synergizes appeals to the senses of sight, smell and sound to strongly link each 'sensory touch point' to the other. As explained below, each sensory channel is optimized to consistently reflect and communicate the brand's core values:

- **Sight:** the cabin crew uniforms are based on colours and patterns that decorate the cabin interior. Each stewardess is assessed as either *cool* or *warm*. Those assessed *cool* wear blue eye shadow and rosy blush; those assessed *warm* wear brown eye shadows and peach blush. In addition, as the details on their training procedures reveal, the stewardess not only has to look the brand, she has to act the brand.
- Smell is another aspect of the sensory experience that SIA has leveraged with a consistency that equals that of the colour scheme used in matching make up and uniforms. In the late 1990s, SIA introduced Stefan Floridian Waters, an aroma which has been specifically designed as part of the company. Stefan Floridian Waters formed the scent in the flight attendants' perfume, was blended into the hot towels served before take off and generally permeated the entire fleet of the company's planes. The patented aroma has since become a unique and very distinct positioning of SIA.
- **Sound:** The same Asian style music is played on commercials, in the airport lounges as well as in the cabin prior to take-off. Although not well documented, the Singapore Girl also has her own *Singapore Girl* jingle that used to be played in TV commercials. The primary message in the ad '*Singapore Airlines – A Great Way to Fly*' is consistently conveyed in exclusive print media and voiced in TV-commercials featuring the Singapore Girl in different themes and settings. These repeated communications through song, word and music are ingrained in memory and call to attention the core aspirations that shape the SIA brand.

SIA has built into its leverage of sight, smell and sound its unique Asian heritage, symbolized and personified by the Singapore Girl.

Source: adapted from Lindstrom (2004) and Heracleous *et al.* (2004); www.brandchannel.com, 6 March 2006.

By its nature, the use of taste is limited primarily to food and beverage products. Kellogg's has spent years experimenting with taste and synergy between sound (crunch) and the taste. When Kellogg's introduced their unique crunch to the market, the brand moved up the ladder.

There are some non-food or beverage products that have been able to incorporate this sense, such as dental products. It is important to remember that everyone is different in which sense(s) they rely on to validate their experience.

In summary, the general rule of thumb is that the more senses a brand appeals to, the stronger the message will be perceived. Interestingly, stronger bonding directly translates to higher prices that consumers will be prepared to pay.

14.10   Celebrity branding

Celebrity branding
Type of advertising in which a celebrity uses their status in society to promote a product, service, charity or cause.

Celebrity branding is a type of advertising in which celebrities uses their status in society to promote a product, service or charity. Celebrity branding can take several different forms, from a celebrity simply appearing in advertisements for a product, service or charity, to a celebrity attending public relations (PR) events, creating their own line of products or services, and/or using their name as a brand. The most popular forms of celebrity brand lines are for clothing and perfume. Many singers, models and film stars now have at least one licensed product or service which bears their name.

The power of a celebrity to draw consumers' attention to their products is not a new phenomenon. However, the number of ways celebrities can now reach consumers (for a vast array of products and services) explains the growth of celebrity licensing. The practice of name-dropping by using celebrities to advertise or market a product appears to have increased markedly in the past few years in many industries. Accordingly, if your product appeals to a specific target group, a celebrity can help people in that target group immediately identify with the licensed product. For example, several celebrity brands in the fragrance industry have become top-selling products in what has otherwise been described in the industry as a 'dismal market'.

A cornerstone of many recent celebrity brands has been a fashion line, which offers another opportunity for an artist to convey an image and a message to the consumer (and profit economically from the relationship).

The phenomenon started slowly, with Michael Jordan's Air Jordan Nikes taking the nation by storm in 1985. The previous year, the Babe Ruth estate (he was an American baseball player and a national icon) became one of the first to trademark a deceased celebrity's name and litigate against its misuse, clearing the way for other (living and dead) public figures to protect their names and likenesses as intellectual property. Since then, building deceased-celebrity brands such as those of Marilyn Monroe, Elvis Presley, James Dean and Albert Einstein has become a business in itself.

During recent years, the line between person and brand has blurred, and celebrities have begun applying techniques from the corporate world to their careers: marketing and protecting a brand identity, trademarking and licensing their names, launching their own product lines and embracing product endorsements to boost their perceived value to consumers.

However, the marriage of branding and celebrity can have its problems. If not positioned correctly, a successful brand can become a boomerang. If an endorsement does not fit a star's perceived identity, then it can work against the star.

Implementing a celebrity branding strategy

When it comes to adding to brand recognition, using a celebrity could be a tremendous asset. However, it is no surprise that such licensing decisions must be weighed carefully. Aligning a product with a licensed property does not necessarily mean that the product (or the licensed property) will assist each other from a marketing or branding perspective. It is clear that many companies have found a suitable balance between the risks of licensing and the rewards of licensing.

In the entertainment industry, the term 'Q score' is used to rate a celebrity's overall fame or popularity. The higher the Q score, the more well known a celebrity is. The celebrity branding that makes sense involves a celebrity who has built a brand themselves that can continue to be leveraged through additional products and services. The actual value of a celebrity licence will depend on four things:

1. How famous the celebrity is (the Q score).
2. What product the celebrity is promoting.
3. What the quality of the licensed product is.
4. The amount of design input the celebrity has in either the marketing or the product itself.

Treating the celebrity as part of a brand means setting up and positioning the licence for when the brand will be marketed. While this timing is not necessarily essential for celebrities who have been around for years (think Paul Newman and Elizabeth Taylor), it may be very important for a celebrity who is competing with several others for recognition. Of course, if a celebrity is a trendsetter (think David Beckham and Oprah Winfrey), the affiliation itself may add instant credibility to the licensing of the name without respect to any other timing.

As important as the timing is the product itself, and the quality of the product. These factors are also essential to ensure the success (and continued success) of a brand. A consumer may purchase a product initially because of a celebrity name, but the consumer will only continue to purchase the product if it is perceived as good quality.

The final consideration is the involvement of the celebrity with the brand. Generally, celebrities today are very involved in the products, their design and their marketing. This involvement will lend credibility to the product and further improve the chances of a successful licence.

Steps involved with international celebrity licensing

Celebrity licensing involves a grant to a licensee that permits the use of the name, signature, voice, image, likeness or other identifiable attribute of a celebrity under certain circumstances. For the most part, celebrity licensing is very similar to other licensing situations, and a licence can be as broad or as narrow as the parties mutually desire. The three basic elements to negotiate in a celebrity licence are (Hoosear, 2006):

1. identifying and clearing the rights involved
2. negotiating the terms and scope of the licence
3. determining the payment and other terms of the licence.

Identify the rights involved

The most important component in celebrity licensing is to state precisely the scope of the grant the licensee is receiving. Celebrities possess a variety of identifiable, and therefore licensable, elements. For example, Elvis Presley as a celebrity would have a variety of licensable elements, from his name or signature alone to his distinctive clothes and music, and the multitude of images and photographs from his numerous movies and TV shows. Likewise, not all of these elements may be owned by the celebrity herself. For example, the affiliated television or movie producers, or studios, would clearly have rights in the films and recordings. Accordingly, the licensor may need to clear certain rights with other entities besides the celebrity.

Celebrity licensing can involve many intellectual property rights: the right of publicity, trademark rights and copyrights. Therefore, it is essential to the successful negotiation of the licence to understand the differences between these rights and how they are licensed. While trademark and copyright law are not exclusive to celebrity licensing, the right of publicity – a state law right – primarily pertains only to celebrity licensing. Accordingly, a celebrity will probably rely on a combination of trademarks, copyrights and the right of publicity to protect and promote their persona in licensing, whether it be for an advertising company, for a product or for the actual branding of a product itself.

Negotiating the terms and scope of the licence

In the context of a licence for the use of a celebrity's name, image, likeness or other attribute such as voice, there are several criteria that are determinants in the licence terms.

Another material criterion in a licence for the use of a celebrity is the duration of the advertising or merchandising campaign. A campaign that has a one-year term will be more expensive than a campaign that lasts one month. In addition, the how, when and where of the campaign using the celebrity is important. For example, in advertising campaigns, the medium used will determine the cost. A use restricted to radio will not be as expensive as a use involving television. It must also be determined whether the use is to be single run or in a prime time slot, and whether the campaign is of a local, regional, national or international nature.

Determining the payment and other terms of the licence

On the most basic level, there is a difference between a licence for a merchandise campaign compared to a licence for an advertising campaign. An advertising use may involve a flat fee for promoting a product, whereas a merchandising use would involve some type of royalty payment based on a relationship between the product and the celebrity. The celebrity would often get a guaranteed royalty as well. This effectively ensures that the celebrity is not sharing all the risk with the licensee, generally a proper division given that it is the licensee's duty to know its market and the risks associated with the introduction of the product. Finally, a licensee should expect to pay a premium for exclusive use of the celebrity in either a certain product category or for exclusive use of the celebrity for a certain period of time.

It is of course the celebrity's right to decide initially whether they will be involved in a licence. As such, the celebrity may set the terms and royalty for participation in the licence, and the licensee has the right to negotiate those terms or find a different celebrity (if one fits the needed requirements) to use if the celebrity's terms are more than the licensee can afford.

There are clearly risks involved with celebrity licensing, which a licensee must consider in selecting a celebrity to advertise or label its product. The criminal trial of, for example, Martha Stewart in the United States, is a clear indication to the risks that can come from a celebrity spokesperson. An interesting alternative is licences using deceased celebrities. A deceased celebrity offers certain advantages in that they generally cannot act in a manner that would embarrass or hurt the image of the licensor's product.

A growth industry

Celebrity licensing is an emerging growth industry. As licensees continue to realize the effectiveness of celebrity association with their products, the trend will continue to broaden to include all types of celebrities (living and deceased). Despite potential risks, there can be no question that the connection between a product and a celebrity creates an image in the consumer's mind that translates into product recognition (and finally sales). This connection should be attractive to licensees seeking to distance their products from the competition. A carefully chosen celebrity can therefore bring additional success to an advertising or merchandising campaign.

14.11 Implications of the Internet for collaboration with customers on product decisions

Firms are realizing the importance of collaboration for creating and sustaining competitive advantage. Collaboration with partners and even competitors has become a strategic imperative for firms in the networked world of business. More recently, scholars in strategy and marketing have focused on collaboration with customers to cocreate value (Prahalad and Ramaswamy, 2004).

The Internet is an open, cost-effective and ubiquitous network. These attributes make it a global medium with unprecedented reach, contributing to reduced constraints of geography and distance. The Internet enhances the ability of firms to engage customers in collaborative innovation in several ways. It allows firms to transform episodic and one-way customer interactions into a persistent dialogue with customers. Internet-based virtual environments allow the firm to engage in interaction with a much larger number of customers without significant compromises on the richness of the interaction (Evans and Wuster, 2000).

Customization and closer relationships

The new business platform recognizes the increased importance of customization of products and services. Increased commoditization of standard features can only be countered through customization, which is most powerful when backed up by sophisticated analysis of customer data.

Mass-marketing experts such as Nike are experimenting with ways of using digital technology to enable customization. Websites that can display three-dimensional images, for example, will certainly boost the attractiveness of custom tailoring.

EXHIBIT 14.11 Business models of Dell and HP

In the personal computer industry Dell and HP are worldwide market leaders. However, the business models of the two companies differs, as the following table demonstrates.

HP has business systems of the type traditionally associated with branded products. It has high R&D expenditure, low-cost, low-variety, large-run manufacturing systems and a one-month finished products inventory.

	Dell	HP
Target customer	Knowledgeable customer buying multiple units	Multiple customer segments with varied needs
Value proposition	Customized PC at competitive price	'Brand' with quality image
Value capture	Through pushing latest components upgrades and low-cost distribution system	Through premium for the 'brand' and reseller push
Buiness system R&D	Limited	Considerable
Manufacturing	Flexible assembly, cost advantage	High-speed, low-variety, low-cost manufacturing system
Supply chain	Made to order; inventory: one week, mainly component	Made to stock; delivery; inventory: one-month finished product
Marketing	Moderate advertising	Expensive brand advertising
Sales and distribution	Primarily through sales force, telemarketing and the Internet	Primarily through third-party resellers

Dell primarily targets corporate accounts but with built-to-order, customized PCs at reasonable prices. Dell has minimal R&D expenditure, a made-to-order, flexible manufacturing system (which puts Dell at a slight disadvantage compared to HP), one-week parts inventory and an efficient distribution system. Dell has been a pioneer in PC sales through the Internet. After a decrease in profits, Dell decided in 2009/2010 to change their business model towards a more standardized mass-production model, with focus on cost reductions, in order to stay price-competitive in relation to their main competitor, HP.

Source: adapted from Kumar (1999) and other public media.

The challenge is clear: to use IT to get closer to customers. There are already many examples of this. Dell is building a closer relationship with its end customer by letting them design their own PCs on the Internet. Customers who have ordered their computers from Dell can then follow their computers along the various stages of the production process in real time on their personalized website. Such experimentation is advisable because the success of 'build-to-order' models such as Dell's represents a challenge to current 'build-to-stock' business platforms, which Compaq generally uses. In Exhibit 14.11 there is a comparison of the business models of Dell and HP. Dell's basic business principle is the close relationship between the PC manufacturer and the end customer, without further intermediaries in the distribution channel. This allows Dell to individualize the computers more to customers' specific needs.

Computers can also be remotely diagnosed and fixed over the Internet today; this may soon be true of many other appliances. Airlines now communicate special fares to preferred customers through e-mails and special websites. Cars will soon have Internet protocol addresses, which will make possible a range of personal, in-vehicle information services.

Customers can also be involved in the early stages of product development so that their inputs can shape product features and functionality. Pharmaceutical companies are experimenting with the possibility of analysing patients' genes to determine precisely what drugs should be administered in what dosages.

The transformation in the business platform can be seen in university textbook publishing. This industry – which has seen little innovation since the advent of the printing press – is now in the midst of major changes. Publishers are creating supplementary website links to provide additional ways for students and lecturers to be connected during courses (e.g. www.pearsoned.co.uk and www.wiley.com). The publisher's role, which traditionally was selling textbooks at the beginning of term, is becoming that of an educational consultant or value-adding partner throughout the term.

EXHIBIT 14.12   Ducati motorcycles – product development through web communities

Founded in 1926, Italian Ducati builds racing-inspired motorcycles characterized by unique engine features, innovative design, advanced engineering and overall technical excellence. The company produces motorcycles in six market segments which vary in their technical and design features and intended customers: Superbike, Supersport, Monster, Sport Touring, Multistrada and the new SportClassic. The company's motorcycles are sold in more than 60 countries worldwide, with a primary focus in western European, Japanese and North American markets. Ducati has won 13 of the last 15 World Superbike Championship titles and more individual victories than the competition put together.

Ducati was quick to realize the potential of using the Internet to engage customers in its new product development efforts. The company set up a web division and a dedicated website, www.ducati.com, in early 2000, inspired by the Internet sales of the MH900 evolution, a limited-production motorcycle. Within 30 minutes, the entire year's production was sold out, making Ducati a leading international e-commerce player. Since then, Ducati has evolved its site to create a robust virtual customer community that had 160,000 registered

Ducati.

users as of July 2004. Community management has become so central at Ducati that management has replaced the words 'marketing' and 'customer' with the words 'community' and 'fan'. Ducati considers the community of fans to be a major asset of the company and it strives to use the Internet to enhance the 'fan experience'. Ducati involves its fans on a systematic basis to reinforce the places, the events and the people that express the Ducati lifestyle and Ducati's desired brand image. The community function is tightly connected with product development and the fan involvement in the community directly influences product development.

Ducati.

Virtual communities play a key role in helping Ducati to explore new product concepts. Ducati has promoted and managed ad hoc online forums and chat rooms for over three years to harness a strong sense of community among Ducati fans.

Ducati also realized that a significant number of its fans spend their leisure time not only riding their bikes, but also maintaining and personalizing them. As a result, fans have deep technical knowledge that they are eager to share with other fans. To support such knowledge sharing, the company has created the 'Tech Café', a forum for exchanging technical knowledge. In this virtual environment, fans can share their projects for customizing motorcycles, provide suggestions to improve Ducati's next generation products, and even post their own mechanical and technical designs, with suggestions for innovations in aesthetic attributes as well as mechanical functions.

While not all fans participate in the online forums, those who do participate provide rich inputs for exploring new product concepts and technical solutions. These forums also help Ducati to enhance customer loyalty, because its fans are more motivated to buy products they helped to create.

Ducati managers also monitor vertical portals created for bikers, including Motorcyclist.com and Motoride.com; and Ducati monitors other virtual communities that have lifestyle associations with the Ducati brand. For instance, Ducati has entered into a partnership with the fashion company DKNY to tap into its community and interact with its members.

To validate its insights, Ducati uses online customer surveys to test product concepts and to quantify customer preferences. As a testimony to the ability of Ducati to create an ongoing customer dialogue and create a sense of engagement with its fans, Ducati gets extraordinary response rates – often in excess of 25 per cent – when it surveys its customers. Ducati uses customer feedback for activities that go beyond product development.

Ducati also pursues Internet-based customer collaboration at the back end of its new product development (NPD) process. Virtual communities play an important role at the product design and market testing stages. For instance, in early 2001, the community managers of Ducati.com identified a group of customers on its website that had particularly strong relationships with the company. They decided to transform such customers into active partners, involving them in virtual teams that cooperate with Ducati professionals from R&D, product management and design. These virtual teams of customers work with the company's engineers to define attributes and technical features for the 'next bike'.

Within the virtual community, current and future Ducati bike owners discuss and review proposed product modifications that can be tested online in the form of virtual prototypes. They can even vote to reject proposed modifications, personalize products to their preferences, and can ask Ducati technicians for suggestions on personalizing their bikes to individual taste.

Sources: adapted from www.ducati.com and Sawhney *et al.* (2005).

Dynamic customization of product and services

The second stage of the customer interaction vector focuses on the opportunities and challenges in dynamically customizing products and services. Competitive markets are rapidly eroding margins due to price-based competition, and companies are seeking to enhance margins through customized offerings. Dynamic customization is based on three principles: modularity, intelligence and organization.

1. *Modularity*: an approach for organizing complex products and processes efficiently. Product or service modularity requires the partitioning of a task into independent modules that function as a whole within overall architecture.
2. *Intelligence*: continuous information exchange with consumers allows companies to create products and processes using the best possible modules. Website operators can match buyer and seller profiles and make recommendations based on their shared interests. The result is intelligent sites that learn their visitors' (potential buyers') tastes and deliver dynamic, personalized information about products and services.
3. *Organization*: Dynamic customization of products and services requires a customer-oriented and flexible approach that is fundamentally committed to operating in this new way.

How can the Internet be integrated in future product innovation?

Figure 14.17 shows some of the implications of the Internet on future product innovation. The Internet is seen as the medium through which each 'box' communicates with the R&D function in the company.

- *Design*. Data is gathered directly from the product and is part of designing and developing the product. New product features (such as new versions of software programs) may be built into the product directly from the Internet.

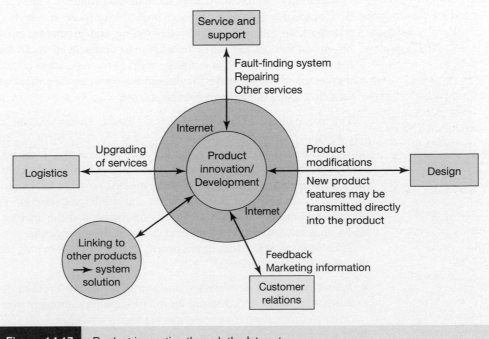

Figure 14.17   Product innovation through the Internet

- *Service and support.* The service department can perform troubleshooting and correction directly through the Internet set-up; for example a Mercedes car driving on the highway may be directly connected to the Mercedes service department. It will monitor the main functions of the car and if necessary make online repairs of, for example, the software of the car.
- *Customer relations.* Data gathered from the product may form part of statistics, comparisons between customers, etc. In this way the customer can compare the performance of their product (e.g. a car) with other customers' product, a kind of benchmarking. This may also strengthen an existing customer relationship.
- *Logistics.* Concurrently with increasing demands for just-in-time deliveries, the Internet will automatically find the distribution and transport that will take the goods from the sub-supplier to the producer and then to the customers in the cheapest and most efficient way (and on time).

A fundamental shift in thinking is to replace the term 'supply chain' with 'demand chain'. The critical difference is that demand-chain thinking starts with the customers and works backwards. This breaks away from parochial approaches that focus solely on reducing transport costs. It supports a 'mass customization' viewpoint, in which bundles of goods and services are offered in ways that support customers' individual objectives.

This does not necessarily imply product differentiation. In fact the service aspects often require differentiation. For example, a company such as Unilever will provide the same margarine to both Tesco and Sainsbury's. However, the ways in which the product is delivered, transactions are processed and other parts of the relationship are managed, can and should be different, since these two competing supermarket chains each have their own ways of evaluating performance. The information systems required to coordinate companies along the demand chain require a new and different approach to that required within individual companies. Some managers believe that if they and their suppliers choose the same standard software package, such as SAP, they will be able to integrate their information systems.

- *Link to other products.* Sometimes a product is used as a subcomponent in other products. Through links in the Internet such subcomponents may be essential inputs for more complex product solutions. The car industry is an example of an industry that already makes a targeted effort in this direction. New cars may be linked together by the Internet in order to communicate, e.g. about technical problems while driving. In the wake of this development a new industry is created, the purpose of which is to provide integrated transport. In this new industry developing and producing cars is only one of several important services. Instead systems are to be developed that can diagnose cars (and correct the error) while the car is running, systems for regulation of traffic, interactive systems that enable drivers to have the desired transport at their disposal when and where they want it without tiresome rental agreements, etc.

The music industry is also undergoing a change. Today you can buy portable players that can download music from the Internet using the MP3 format, and subsequently play the music that is stored in the player. The CD is skipped – and so is the whole distribution facility. The music industry will become completely altered through these different economic conditions. The struggle will be about creating the best portal to the Internet, where the consumer can find the best information on music and the largest selection of music. The problems regarding rights are, however, still being discussed, and the lawyers and politicians have to find a final solution before the market can increase significantly.

Thus innovative product development of the future demands that a company possesses the following characteristics:

- *Innovative product development and strategic thinking.* Product development will contain much technology and demand an interdisciplinary, strategic overview and knowledge in order to find out what new services are worth aiming at.
- *Management of alliances.* Few companies have all the necessary qualifications themselves – innovative product development and the resulting services demand that companies enter into alliances dynamically and in a structured way.

- *New customer relations.* The car industry example above clearly shows that the customers are not car buyers any longer but *buyers of transport services*, and that is quite another matter. This means that companies have to focus on understanding the customers' needs in a quite different way.

Developing brands on the Internet

Clearly consumer product companies such as Procter & Gamble, Colgate, Kraft Foods and consumer durables and business-to-business companies such as General Motors, General Electric, Allied Signal and Caterpillar have crafted their business strategies by leveraging physical assets and developing powerful global brands supported by mass advertising and mass distribution. Remote links with customers apply equally well to these companies. Remote and continuous links with customers become critical as the concepts of brand identity and brand equity are redefined by the Internet.

Kraft Interactive Kitchen (www.kraftfoods.com) is an example of a consumer products company keeping in touch with its consumers by providing information-based services such as meal planners, recipes, tips and cooking techniques. Kraft's intention is to have remote connections and interactions with consumers in new ways.

However, some companies find it difficult to translate a strong offline brand (such as Nike and Levi's) to the Internet, because many of the well-known brands are based on an extensive 'physical' retail distribution system, and many of the retailers are reluctant to support online brands because of the fear of disintermediation (see section 14.6 for more discussion of this issue).

In fact many sites that are run by top brands register minimal online traffic, according to a report by Forrester Research. Forrester studied brand awareness and web-surfing behaviour among 16–22-year-olds, whom advertisers consider to be strongly brand conscious.

Companies are taking a broad approach to branding, integrating it with an overall advertising and marketing strategy. On the net branding is more than logos and colour schemes; it is about creating experiences and understanding customers. Consequently web brand building is not cheap. Building a brand requires a persistent online presence. For some brands that entails a mass-appeal site; for others brand building requires a combination of initiatives, from banner ads to sponsorships.

14.12   'Long tail' strategies

Long tail
Long tail refers to a graph showing fewer products selling in large quantities versus many more products that sell in low quantities. The low-quantity items (the very broad product range) stretch out on the x-axis of the graph, creating a very long tail that generates more revenue overall. Even though a smaller quantity of each item is sold, there is a much greater variety of these items to sell and these 'rare' items are very easy to find via today's online search tools.

Anderson's (2006) '**long tail**' is basically a theory of selling that suggests that in the Internet era, selling fewer copies to more people is a new strategy that can be successfully pursued. In the past, all the interesting business was around a few hits, and many businesses focused entirely on producing the next hit. The group of persons that buy the hard-to-find or 'non-hit' items is the customer demographic called the long tail. Given a large enough availability of choice, a large population of customers, efficient search engines, and negligible stocking and distribution costs, it becomes possible to profitably target the long tail in Chris Anderson's view.

Chris Anderson (2006) advances two distinct but related ideas:

1. Merchandise assortments are growing because when goods don't have to be displayed on store shelves, physical and cost constraints on selection disappear. Search and recommendation tools can keep a selection's vastness from overwhelming customers. In the diagram below, all possible offerings in an imagined product sector are ranked by their sales volume, with the 'green' part (in Figure 14.18) representing products that are unprofitable through brick-and-mortar channels. The long tail, in other words, reveals a previously untapped demand.

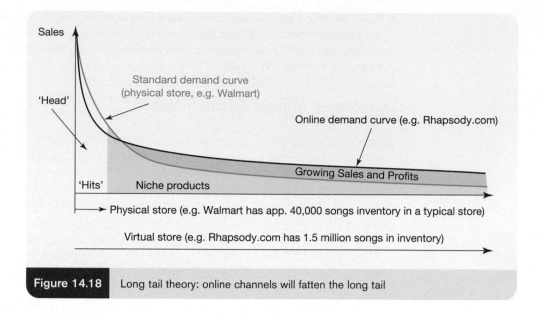

Figure 14.18 Long tail theory: online channels will fatten the long tail

2. Online channels actually change the shape of the demand curve, because consumers value niche products geared to their particular interests more than they value products designed for mass appeal. As Internet retailing enables them to find more of the former, their purchasing will change accordingly. In other words, the tail will steadily grow not only longer, as more obscure products are made available, but also *fatter* (including the red part in Figure 14.18), as consumers discover products better suited to their tastes.

In Figure 14.18 the power of the long tail is illustrated by an example: the online Rhapsody.com download music company, which has an inventory of some 1.5 million tracks, receives 40 per cent of its revenue from songs that are simply not available in retail stores. In contrast, a typical Walmart store has a maximum of approximately 40,000 songs on their CDs on the shelves, and their top 200 CD albums account for 90 per cent of Wal-Mart's sales because they do not have the space to inventory songs that might sell only once a month. For online stores that use technology to cut their cost of inventory, the amount of total business for objects in the tail increases.

Elberse (2008) tries to prove that Anderson's 'Long tail' concept is problematic, and says that consumers are not finding 'hidden gems' out in the long tail: in fact that they are not even venturing into the tail that much. She gives evidence that the activity in the head is even more unusual. What happened? Elberse (2008) research implies that anything good out on the long tail will quickly be elevated to the head if it has any broad appeal at all because of the way the Internet works. It will only be those products of an extremely limited appeal that do not make that jump. Suddenly, a perfectly legitimate long tail buying process has resulted in the 'discovery' of a blockbuster and in the process has ignored the fact that it started out in the long tail.

14.13 Green marketing strategies

As understanding grows about the impact of human activity on the earth's ecosystems, consumer concern about the environment and its links to health and safety will intensify. At the same time, humankind's passion for consumption will persist. The challenge for companies will be to devise business practices and products that are friendly to the environment while also meeting the needs of consumers.

Environmentalists were once considered the only people concerned about the depletion of natural resources, waste accumulation and pollution. Environmentalists around the world are now becoming global in their scope and scale of operations. Their aim is to increase people's awareness of the importance of environmental preservation on a global scale and how the lack of it will have a harmful effect on our planet.

Because ecological grass-root campaigns gain widespread recognition and support, and global media networks such as CNN continue to report on environmental issues and disasters, today's consumer is becoming more environmentally conscious. Various polls and surveys reveal that many consumers are taking environmental issues into consideration as they buy, consume and dispose of products. Consequently there is a direct connection between a company's ability to attract and keep consumers and its ability to develop and execute environmentally sound strategies.

As consumer preferences and government policies increasingly favour a balanced business approach to the environment, managers are paying more attention to the strategic importance of their environmental decisions. Irresponsible behaviour by some firms has led to consumer boycotts, lengthy lawsuits and large fines. Such actions may have harmed firms in less direct ways, such as negative public relations, diversion of management attention and difficulty in hiring top employees.

In Europe particularly the green consumer movement is large and growing, and certain countries can be considered leaders and standard setters in green awareness. Of German consumers, for instance, 80 per cent are willing to pay premiums for household goods that are recycled, recyclable and non-damaging to the environment; in France 50 per cent of consumers will pay more at the supermarket for products they perceive as being environmentally friendly. This trend is growing elsewhere too: according to a European study, consumers throughout the Organization for Economic Cooperation and Development (OECD) area are willing to pay more for green goods (Vandermerwe and Oliff, 1991).

Several retailers have also committed themselves to marketing green products (**green marketing**). Clearly, failing to consider the environmental impact of strategic decisions may affect the financial stability of the firm and the ability of that firm to compete with others in the industry.

Green marketing
Integrating business practices and products that are friendly to the environment while also meeting the needs of the consumer.

Strategic options

Businesses realize that they must be prepared to provide their customers with information on the environmental impact of their products and manufacturing processes.

Figure 14.19 presents four strategic options that are available for the firm with environmental concerns. The choice of strategic environmental posture will depend on how an organization wants to create value for its green customers and how change oriented its approach is.

As we can seen from Figure 14.19, if a firm is more oriented to cost reduction than to benefit enhancement for customers, pollution prevention strategies (options 3 and 4) would probably be chosen in preference to the development of green products: for example by using natural or recycled materials. If a firm is more proactive than accommodative, it tends to be more innovative than otherwise (options 1 and 3).

Although going beyond compliance (i.e. doing more than required according to environmental legislation) is generally perceived as highly desirable, SMEs may not have the resources to act proactively, and hence need to focus on compliance and minor product modification (options 2 and 4).

Environmental management in the value chain perspective

Management cannot afford to be myopic in looking at the finished product without considering the manufacturing and R&D phases as they relate to consumers' perceptions of what constitutes a green product. Nor can a company use traditional marketing principles to gain

		Value creation approach	
		Benefit enhancement for customers	*Cost reduction*
Change orientation	*Proactive*	Green product Innovation (major modification) ①	Pollution prevention Beyond compliance ③
	Accommodative	② Green product Differentiation (minor modification)	④ Pollution prevention Compliance

Figure 14.19 Types of environmental strategic posture

Source: adapted from Starik *et al.* (1996, p. 17).

product acceptance. Put differently, both the input and output activities associated with the design, manufacture and delivery of products must be considered, and each step within the value-creating process must be assessed in the light of its overall environmental impact and consequences.

Figure 14.20 illustrates the resource conversion and pollutant generation relationships. As resources are used to create desired utilities, pollutants are implicitly produced as by-products during each step of the integrated supply chain process. For example, packaging is used to protect the products from damage and is an undesired item once they are consumed. Proper management and awareness of the environmental implications of logistical activities can significantly reduce their negative impact.

Integrative environmental management means that every element in the corporate value chain is involved in the minimization of the firm's total environmental impact from start to finish of the supply chain, and also from beginning to end of the product life cycle.

Reverse logistics in Figure 14.20 results in the shipment of packaging waste, recyclable packages and consumer returns in the logistics system.

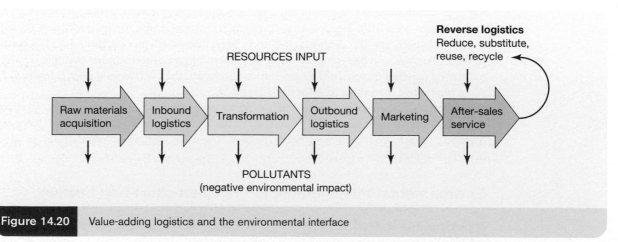

Figure 14.20 Value-adding logistics and the environmental interface

Source: adapted from Wu and Dunn (1995, p. 23) with permission from *International Journal of Physical Distribution and Logistics Management*, Emerald Group Publishing Ltd.

Germany and other European countries state that consumers have the right to leave packaging materials at retail stores and that stores must dispose of them properly. Denmark has for many years also required beer bottles to be reusable. The shipment of these packaging materials back to original sites creates demand for logistical capacity and adds no direct value to the goods.

Management has to consider how to reduce the reverse flows. In relation to Figure 14.20, reverse logistics emphasizes source reduction and substitution over reuse and recycling. Source reduction refers to doing the same things with less resources. The practice reduces total waste in the system. Substitution means using more environmentally friendly materials instead of regular ones that end up as pollutants. Reuse is employing the same item many times in its original form so that little is discarded. Recycling gives discarded materials a new life after some chemical or physical processes.

Consumer preferences and competitive green marketing

A precondition for a successful external green marketing strategy is that managers should cultivate this corporate culture internally. The organization and its people must support a truly green marketing strategy in order for it to succeed. Managers should encourage the increased participation of all employees in order to generate ideas and increase enthusiasm. They should also keep in mind that most customers and employees get satisfaction from being part of an organization that is committed to operating in a socially responsible manner.

It is also important to educate consumers. Labels and displays can play an important role in making an environmental statement about a brand. More than half of all Americans say they have purchased a product because the advertising or label indicated that it was environmentally safe or biodegradable. Explaining how or why a product is environmentally sound can also make a big difference. Product packaging or in-store displays can be a major source of information about environmental action. Point-of-sale demonstrations and knowledgeable salespeople can help to educate consumers. Giving out free samples might be a good way to ease customers' initial reluctance to try a new product.

Another key element of green marketing strategy is credibility. Having a good reputation to begin with can go a long way in helping to ease customer scepticism. Companies with socially responsible corporate values will appear more credible to target audiences, but it is critical that they also back up environmental claims. Customers are still worried about 'greenwashing', that is, false or misleading environmental claims that were prevalent in the 1980s and early 1990s. Now new standards and certifications allow customers to identify green products easily. By following those guidelines, marketers can avoid overstating environmental claims. The use of ecolabels such as 'Blue Angel' in Germany and 'Energy Star' in the United States can help assure customers that the products they are purchasing are in fact green.

In addition to studying consumer responsiveness, it is also crucial to gain an understanding of how competitors are perceived by consumers on greenness compared with the company's brand. At the same time, gathering information about the reality of how competitors are performing on greenness is also necessary. A critical eye must also be focused on the company's own green processes and its upper management commitment to greenness. It must be determined whether consumers perceive the greenness of the company and its competitors accurately or whether misperceptions are creating differentiation in the markets. If a marketer feels that it is possible to truly differentiate a brand in a way that will be honest, credible and long-lasting, then a proactive green strategy will be viable. However, if competitors are really better and are capable of maintaining this edge – or if the cost of becoming greener than competitors does not seem worth the effort, given the prospects for additional revenue – then a more passive strategy will make more sense.

Finally, because consumers buy products and services primarily to fulfil individual needs and wants, companies should continue to highlight the direct benefits of their products. They should not forget to emphasize the traditional product attributes of price, quality, convenience and availability and make only a secondary appeal to consumers on the basis of environmental attributes (Ginsberg and Bloom, 2004).

Green alliances between business and environmental organizations

Strategic alliances with environmental groups (e.g. Greenpeace) can provide five benefits to marketers of consumer goods (Mendleson and Polonsky, 1995):

1. *They increase consumer confidence in green products and their claims.* It can be assumed that if an environmental group supports a firm, product or service, consumers are more likely to believe the product's environmental claims.

2. *They provide firms with access to environmental information.* It is in their role as an information clearing house that environmental groups may be of immense benefit to organizations with which they form strategic alliances. Manufacturers facing environmental problems may turn to their strategic partners for advice and information. In some cases environmental partners may actually have technical staff who can be used to assist in solving organizational problems or implementing existing solutions.

3. *They give the marketer access to new markets.* Most environmental groups have an extensive support base, which in many cases receives newsletters or other group mailings. Their members receive catalogues marketing a variety of licensed products, all of which are less environmentally harmful than other commercial alternatives. Environmental group members represent a potential market that can be utilized by producers, even if these groups do not produce specialized catalogues. An environmental group's newsletter may discuss how a firm has formed a strategic alliance with the group, as well as the firm's less environmentally harmful products. Inclusion of this information in a newsletter is a useful form of publicity.

4. *They provide positive publicity and reduce public criticism.* Forming strategic alliances with environmental groups may also stimulate increased publicity. When the Sydney Olympic Bid Committee announced that Greenpeace was the successful designer for the year 2000 Olympic Village the story appeared in all major newspapers and on the national news. It is highly unlikely that this publicity would have been generated if a more conventional architect had been named as the designer of the village. Once again the publicity associated with the alliance was positive and credible.

5. *They educate consumers about key environmental issues for the firm and its product(s).* Environmental groups are valuable sources of educational information and materials. They educate consumers and the general public about environmental problems and also inform them about potential solutions. In many cases the public views these groups as credible sources of information, without a vested interest. Marketers can also play an important role as providers of environmental information through their marketing activities. In doing so they create environmental awareness of specific issues, their products and their organizations. For example, Kellogg's in Norway educated consumers and promoted its environmental concern by placing environmental information on the packaging of its cereals relating to various regional environmental problems (World Wide Fund for Nature, 1993).

Choosing the correct alliance partner is not a simple task, as environmental groups have different objectives and images. Some groups may be willing to form exclusive alliances, where they partner only one product in a given product category. Other groups may be willing to form alliances with all products that comply with their specific criteria.

The marketer must determine what capabilities and characteristics an alliance partner can bring to the alliance. As with any symbiotic relationship, each partner must contribute to the success of the activity. Poor definition of these characteristics may result in the firm searching out the wrong partner.

McDonald's offers an example of a company that gained credibility through collaboration. The company's collaboration with EDF (Environmental Defense Fund) in the early 1990s over its decision to move from styrofoam to paper packaging similarly allowed the company to increase its credibility on environmental issues with consumers (Argenti, 2004).

14.14   Brand piracy and anti-counterfeiting strategies

Until the 1980s, counterfeiting was a relatively small-scale business, restricted mainly to copying luxury fashion items, such as watches and leather goods, in limited quantities. Since the 1990s it has been transformed into a much bigger, broader industry, with large-scale production and distribution of false versions of different brands (see Exhibit 14.13).

A firm which finds itself exposed to brand piracy has a number of strategic options. These range from identifying and punishing retail outlets to destroying the production facilities of the pirates. The brand manufacturer can also try to convert the pirates into legitimate business.

However, piracy is not only connected to negative issues for the brand manufacturer, if the fake brand and the original brand can be distinguished from each other. In fact, decisions to purchase counterfeits usually reaffirm the brand's values because the recipient buys the product to project the very image that the company tries to portray through its advertising and promotions. Brand piracy can be seen as a positive element for a brand's value as it is a good indicator of a brand's strengths. If the company's product is copied, it is doing the right thing. Some brands embrace the counterfeit market rather than seeing it as a threat. When Georgio Armani was on a trip to Shanghai in 2004, he purchased a fake Armani watch for US$22 instead of the US$710 price tag on his authentic watches. He said: 'It was an identical copy of an Emporio Armani watch . . . it is flattering to be copied. If you are copied, you are doing the thing right' (Whitwell, 2006). Although this was a publicity stunt, it does highlight the fact that consumers of fake brands are the opposite of consumers of the authentic product and so pose no significant threat to the brand owner.

Another element of counterfeiting is that is closes off the competition, as the competitors are 'stuck-in-the-middle'. High-priced branded goods encourage the competition to enter the market at a slightly lower price point. Counterfeiters produce branded goods and sell significantly below the cost of competition. This means the competition is squeezed out as it has nowhere to go: it is priced out of the top market by the original brand and cannot compete with the counterfeit whose prices are too low.

EXHIBIT 14.13 The next stage in pirating: faking an entire company, NEC

After two years' investigation, in 2006 NEC discovered a piracy network in China where the pirates were faking the entire company – the Japanese NEC. The counterfeiters had set up a parallel NEC brand with links to a network of more than 50 electronics factories in China, Hong Hong and Taiwan. In the name of NEC, the pirates copied NEC products and went as far as developing their own range of consumer electronic products – everything from home entertainment centres to MP3 players. They even coordinated manufacturing in the way that they required factories to pay royalties for 'licensed' products and issued official-looking warranty and service documents. The products were shipped and packaged in authentic-looking boxes and display cases.

The investigation records showed that the counterfeiters even carried NEC business cards, commissioned product research and development in the company's name and signed production and supply orders.

Many multinational companies (like NEC) are now facing similar challenges as piracy expands and becomes better organized.

Source: adapted from 'Next step in pirating: faking a company – for NEC an identity crisis in China', *Herald Tribune*, 28 April 2006.

14.15   Summary

In deciding the product policy abroad, it is important to decide what parts (product levels) should be standardized and what parts should be adapted to the local environment. This chapter has discussed the variety of factors that are relevant to this decision.

One very important issue is the question of branding. Different branding alternatives have been discussed. For example, because large (often transnational) retail chains have won control over distribution, they try to develop their own labels. For the retailer, private labels provide better profit margins and strengthen the retailer's image with its customers. Because of the power shift to the retailers the percentage of retail grocery sales derived from private brands has increased in recent years.

The basic purposes of branding are the same everywhere in the world. In general, the functions of branding are:

1. to distinguish a company's offering and differentiate one particular product from its competitors
2. to create identification and brand awareness
3. to guarantee a certain level of quality and satisfaction
4. to help with promotion of the product.

The products sold over electronic markets and the Internet can be grouped into two categories: physical products and purely digital goods and services.

The 'long tail' is a theory of selling that suggests that in the Internet era, selling fewer copies to more people is a new strategy that can be pursued successfully.

This chapter has also discussed issues that are of increasing interest: green marketing strategies, including the need for product adaptation in a 'green' direction. Consumers, shareholders and society at large all stand to benefit when a company integrates environmental friendliness into its marketing strategy. If properly implemented, green marketing can help to increase the emotional connection between consumers and brands. Being branded a green company can generate a more positive public image, which can, in turn, enhance sales and increase stock prices. A green image may also lead consumers to have increased affinity for a company or a specific product, causing brand loyalty to grow.

CASE STUDY 14.1

Danish Klassic: launch of a cream cheese in Saudi Arabia

In the spring of 1987 the product manager of Danish Cheese Overseas, KA, was pleased to note that after some decline (e.g. in Iran) feta sales were improving in the Middle East. However, the company was a little concerned that the feta, according to several expert opinions, could lose ground to the cream cheese that was apparently becoming more and more popular among Arabs in both the cities and provincial areas.

Saudi Arabia in general

Because of its immense income from oil, Saudi Arabia has developed fantastically over the past 30 years. With Islamic tradition as its basis, the country has become more modern.

In 1987 the population was 11.5 million, more than 50 per cent of whom were under 15 years of age, which makes Saudi Arabia a 'young' nation. According

Table 1	Development in population in the three biggest cities in Saudi Arabia	
	Population (million) 1974	Population (million) 2000
Riyadh	0.7	2.4
Jeddah	0.6	2.1
Dammam	0.2	0.8

Source: *Demographic Yearbook 1985*, p. 270, and prognosis from the Saudi Arabian Ministry of Agriculture.

Table 2	Total import of cheese in 1986 (tons)
	Total import
Processed cheese (including cream cheese)	29,500
Feta	18,400
Other types of cheese	2,400
Total	50,300

Source: Saudi Arabian import statistic.

to the Saudi Arabian Ministry of Agriculture, the population was forecast to rise to 19 million in 2000. The expected development in population in the three biggest cities is shown in Table 1.

The cheese market in Saudi Arabia

Traditionally Danish Cheese Overseas has had a strong position in Saudi Arabia, having been the market leader for several years, especially as regards feta and some other types of cheese. However, Danish Cheese Overseas has had some difficulties in the cream cheese market. The market has risen, but to date two globally large exporters of cheese have dominated the market – France and Australia.

The total import of cheese into Saudi Arabia (there is very little local production) is shown in Table 2. So far the share of cheese from Denmark has been about 25 per cent (£10 million). On the basis of this Danish Cheese decided to develop a new cream cheese in order to compete with the big exporters of cheese within the cream/processed segment. The product was to be targeted at the Middle East, where Saudi Arabia is the main market, but was also to form the basis for an international brand: Danish Klassic.

In order to plan the specific details of the product parameter Danish Cheese contacted an international market research bureau that specialized in the Middle East. The objective was to analyse the cream cheese consumption among typical Middle East families living in cities. The final result showed that between 85 and 100 per cent of all family members eat cream cheese on a regular basis (mostly in the middle of the day), and that consumption is especially high among children. Different product concepts were tested among typical families,

and the outcome was a 200g cream cheese in brick cartons. This is a new type of packaging – until then cream cheese had mostly been sold in glass packaging.

Marketing plan for Danish Klassic

The following describes the launch actually made by Danish Cheese Overseas in 1987.

An introduction was held in October 1987, in the form of three trade seminars in the largest cities – Riyadh, Jeddah and Dammam. Here the product concept and the advertising campaign were presented to a large number of distributors and wholesalers (see photos (a)–(e)).

TV commercials

In Saudi Arabia television is considered the most effective medium for mass communication. It therefore became the foundation of the company's marketing. In total, 128 commercial spots were planned for the first year (photo b).

(a) product information
Arla foods.

(b) TV advertising information

(c) print advertising information　(d) point-of-sale equipment　(e) packaging system

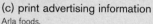
Arla foods.

Print advertisements

- *Consumer-oriented*: the most popular newspapers and family magazines in the big cities, especially directed at women as the decisive buyer unit; (photo c);
- *Distributor-oriented*: trade magazines.
- *In-store promotion*: displays, taste sample demonstrations etc. (photo d).

The campaign material was introduced in both Arabic and English.

The campaign was influenced by a high degree of pull strategy (consumer influence). In this way distributors were induced to build up stocks in order to meet the expected end-user demand. The risk the distributors would face when buying large quantities was limited because the cheese could be kept for a year without being refrigerated.

Photo (a) can be translated as follows:

Product information

- Danish Klassic – a cream cheese spread for the whole family.
- Created from fresh cow's milk from the vigorous fields of Denmark.

Product facts

- It takes 1.5 litres of fresh cow's milk to produce a single box of 200g cheese.
- Danish Klassic is packed in a practical, unbreakable box.
- This cream cheese spread will remain healthy and delicious for a whole year after production – even if not kept under refrigeration.
- Danish Klassic, a combination of high nutrition value and a delicious taste.

This enclosure was also used as an advertisement for many consumer-oriented newspapers and magazines.

Photo (d) can be translated as follows:

Shop demonstrations

- To let your customers know Danish Klassic is in town we plan shop demonstrations in a number of supermarkets all over the country.
- The selected shops will be decorated with giant Danish Klassic boxes.
  - Your customers are bound to notice this cream cheese.
  - Samples will be distributed.
  - Taste it. It's delicious. It's healthy, and full of energy.

What happened to Danish Klassic?

About six months after the introduction in Saudi Arabia, in *Jyllands-Posten* (the Jutland Post), a Danish newspaper published an article on the new product (24 October 1988):

So far MD Foods has shipped 700–800 tons of the new, long-life cheese from the harbour of Esbjerg, but sales are expected to rise to 5,000 tons per year during the next few years ... According to the plan, 'Danish Klassic' is to be marketed in Denmark and in other parts of the world such as South America, where it has scored top marks in recent taste tests.

The new long-life cheese that comes in completely sealed 200g packages is marketed massively through TV spots, the company's own sales representatives, shop promotions and print advertisements. About half of the total investment of DKr30–35 million is allocated to marketing. In this way MD Foods is challenging the multinational food concern, Kraft Food, which, through its various types of cheese in glass packaging, controls the majority of the markets in the Middle East.

However, at the beginning of 1993 MD Foods realised that Danish Klassic could not meet its international sales budgets: later that year MD Foods withdrew the product from the market.

Today MD Foods sells cheese to the Middle East through its sales company, Chesco Cheese Ltd. The cream cheese and other types of cheese are now sold under the brand 'Puck' (photo e) in glass packaging (the 140g and 240g round containers). Its market share of cream cheese is increasing again and today the total sales are very close to those of the market leader Kraft Food.

QUESTIONS

1. What could be the reasons for Danish Klassic not being able to meet expectations? Comment on the following:
   (a) the change of packaging – from glass to plastic brick carton;
   (b) the consumer-oriented advertisement (photo a) – is it targeted at the Saudi Arabian market?
2. What do you think of the brand name Danish Klassic?

Postscript

On 30 September 2005, the *Jyllands-Posten* published an article titled 'Muhammeds ansigt' ('The face of Muhammad'). The article consisted of 12 cartoons, some of which depicted Muhammad.

In late 2005, the Muhammad cartoons controversy received only minor media attention outside of Denmark. Six of the cartoons were reprinted in the Egyptian newspaper *El Fagr* in October 2005, along with a highly critical article, but publication was not considered noteworthy. January 2006 saw some of the pictures reprinted in Scandinavia, then in major newspapers of Denmark's southern neighbours Germany, Belgium and France. Soon after this as protests grew, there were republications around the globe, but mostly in continental Europe. Several editors in the Middle East were fired for their decision, or even their intention, to republish the cartoons. Critics of the cartoons argue that they are blasphemous to people of the Muslim faith.

Organized boycotts of Danish goods began in several Islamic countries. In Saudi Arabia people called for a boycott on Danish products on 20 January 2006 and carried it out from 26 January. The boycott

primarily targeted dairy products produced by Arla Foods, but has also hit other products such as Bang & Olufsen and LEGO. The Foreign Minister of Denmark, Per Stig Møller, stated that the boycott has not been initiated by the Saudi Arabian government. The dairy company Arla Foods launched a massive ad campaign in Saudi Arabia, trying to improve its reputation and stop the boycott. This happened after sales in Saudi Arabia almost came to a complete stop. Arla exports to Saudi Arabia are almost €380 million a year. Arla halted production in the Saudi capital Riyadh and sent home 170 employees. Denmark was concerned about the potential loss of 11,000 jobs resulting from boycotts against Danish products in the Islamic world.

However, during 2008 and 2009 the situation eased and by the end of 2009 the sales of Arla products were above the level for the Middle East region (before the Muhammad cartoons), except for Saudi Arabia where the level is still lower, compared to the situation before the cartoons were published. In Saudi Arabia 30 per cent of the population is boycotting Arla products, and in certain parts of the country the resistance is so strong that the products are considered as off-limits as pork and alcohol.

Hassan Amar/AFP/Getty Images.

Sources: Adapted from The Copenhagen Post Online (2009): 'Arla back on shelves in Mid-East', Tuesday 20 October, http://www.cphpost.dk/news/international/89-international/47250-arla-back-on-shelves-in-the-mid-east.html; Simmons, J. (2006), 'A war of ideas', 10 February, www.BaghdadMuseum.org; www.arla.com.

CASE STUDY 14.2

Zippo Manufacturing Company: has product diversification beyond the lighter gone too far?

History

Zippo (www.zippo.com) was founded in Bradford, Pennsylvania in 1932 when George G. Blaisdell decided to create a lighter that would look good and be easy to use. Blaisdell obtained the rights for an Austrian windproof lighter with a removable top, and redesigned it to his own requirements. He made the case rectangular, attached the lid to the bottom with a welded hinge and surrounded the wick with a windhood. Fascinated by the sound of the name of another recent invention, the zipper, Blaisdell called his new lighter 'Zippo', and backed it with a lifetime guarantee. The 70-year old brand's fame took off during the Second World War, when Zippo's entire production was distributed through commercial outlets run by the US military.

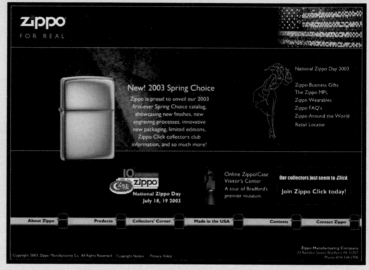

zippo.com.

Today

Zippo has produced over 375 million windproof lighters since its founding in 1932. Except for improvements in the flint wheel and modifications in case finishes, Blaisdell's original design remains virtually unchanged. The lifetime guarantee that accompanies every Zippo lighter still guarantees that 'It works or we fix it free™'.

Although the windproof lighter is the most popular Zippo product, Zippo has been hurt by anti-smoking campaigns. Its business is fundamentally tied to smokers, and it has suffered from US tobacco regulations. Cigarette makers order thousands of Zippos to promote their brands, distributing them to smokers in exchange for coupons. One of the company's recent advertising campaigns suggested 101 ways to use your Zippo. Warming your hands and de-icing car locks were on the list; lighting a cigarette was not.

The success of this product led Zippo to expand the line to its current product family of tape measures, pocket knives, money clips, writing instruments, key holders and its newest product, the multi-purpose lighter. All of these items can be imprinted with company logos or trademarks.

In 1993 Zippo licensed its name to Itochu Fashion System Co., a large clothing manufacturer in Japan. Zippo leather jackets, Zippo jeans and Zippo gloves are now available in Tokyo, and Zippo may license clothes in the United States too. Today Japan is still the biggest export market for Zippo.

Zippo has expanded its sales operations nationally and internationally through a wide network of sales representatives. In more than 120 countries throughout the world Zippo is synonymous with US-made quality and craftsmanship.

Zippo windproof lighters enjoy a widespread and enviable reputation as valuable collectibles. The company produces the *Zippo Lighter Collectors' Guide*, containing illustrations of the lighters and descriptions of the series, as well as an explanation of the date code found on the bottom of every Zippo lighter. Clubs for lighter collectors have been organized in the United Kingdom, Italy, Switzerland, Germany, Japan and the United States. Zippo also sponsors it own collectors club, Zippo Click.

QUESTIONS

1. What are the pros and cons of the product diversification strategy that Zippo has been following recently?

Photo courtesy of Zippo.com

2. On http://swansonrussell.com/experience/outdoorrecreation/casestudy_3.php you will find a case study in which Zippo was repositioned in the late 1990s as an essential tool for avid outdoorsmen. Individual tin and sleeve packaging was developed that reflected the 'tool' position of the lighter. For continuity, similar packaging and graphics were developed for the cans of Zippo lighter fluid, and the lighters and fluid were delivered to retailers in handy self-shipping countertop displays. To support the national roll-out, the advertising company (Swanson Russell) developed a communications programme that included direct mail to major outdoor product distributors, as well as advertising at both the trade and consumer level (pictured here).

   However the outdoor market was entirely new to the Zippo salesforce, who were accustomed to calling on tobacconists and convenience stores. How would you use the PLC concept for this case story?

3. What obstacles would Zippo Manufacturing Company face if it repeated the outdoor campaign in other countries?

VIDEO CASE STUDY 14.3 Swiss Army

download from www.pearsoned.co.uk/hollensen

Swiss Army Brands, Inc. (**www.swissarmy.com**) (SABI) is the only marketer in the US, Canada and the Caribbean of the world-famous Victorinox Original Swiss Army Knife. Swiss Army Inc. is an example of a company that has grown by basing its product expansion on established brand equity. Leveraging the success of the knife, the company expanded into watches, sunglasses, apparel, travel gear and other product categories. The launch of the Swiss watch was an overnight success. Today one out of five watches under US$500 in the United States is Swiss. The company enjoyed similar success with its travel gear and expects to do the same with apparel.

Questions

1. Which factors are attributable to the strong global brand equity of Swiss Army?
2. What are the main motives behind the product line extension from Swiss Army knives into other product areas?
3. Are there any problems for channels of distribution associated with the prospect of Swiss Army stores?
4. How might Swiss Army use 'non-traditional advertising' to promote its brands and new products?

For further exercises and cases, see this book's website at **www.pearsoned.co.uk/hollensen**

Questions for discussion

1. How would you distinguish between services and products? What are the main implications of this difference for the global marketing of services?

2. What implications does the product life cycle theory have for international product development strategy?

3. To what degree should international markets be offered standardized service and warranty policies that do not differ significantly from market to market?

4. Why is the international product policy likely to be given higher priority in most firms than other elements of the global marketing mix?

5. Describe briefly the IPLC theory and its marketing implications.

6. What are the requirements that must be met so that a commodity can effectively be transformed into a branded product?

7. Discuss the factors that need to be taken into account when making packaging decisions for international product lines.

8. When is it appropriate to use multiple brands in (a) a single market and (b) several markets/countries?

9. What is the importance of 'country of origin' in international product marketing?

10. What are the distinguishing characteristics of services? Explain why these characteristics make it difficult to sell services in foreign markets.

11. Identify the major barriers to developing international brands.

12. Discuss the decision to add or drop products to or from the product line in international markets.

13. Why should customer-service levels differ internationally? Is it, for example, ethical to offer a lower customer-service level in developing countries than in industrialized countries?

14. What are the characteristics of a good international brand name?

References

Aaker, D. (1991) *Managing the Brand Equity: Capitalizing on the Value of the Brand Name*. The Free Press, New York.

Anderson, C. (2006) *The Long Tail: Why the Future of Business is Selling less of more*. Hyperion, New York.

Argenti, P.A. (2004) 'Collaborating with activists: how Starbucks works with NGOs', *California Management Review*, 47(1), pp. 91–116.

Bengtsson, A. and Servais, P. (2005) 'Co-branding on industrial markets', *Industrial Marketing Management*, 34, pp. 706–713.

Boze, B.V. and Patton, C.R. (1995) 'The future of consumer branding as seen from the picture today', *Journal of Consumer Marketing*, 12(4), pp. 20–41.

Cayla, J. and Arnould, E.J. (2008) 'A cultural approach to branding in the global marketplace', *Journal of International Marketing*, 16(4), pp. 86–112.

Czinkota, M.R. and Ronkainen, I.A. (1995) *International Marketing*, 4th edn. Dryden Press, Fort Worth, TX.

Devaney, T. and Brown, J. (2008) 'The new brand landscape', *Marketing Health Services*, 28(1), pp. 14–17.

Dhalla, N.K. and Yuspeh, S. (1976) 'Forget the product life concept', *Harvard Business Review*, January–February, pp. 102–112.

Eberse, A. (2008) 'Should you invest in the longtail', *Harvard Business Review*, July, pp. 88–96.

Ettensén, R. (1993) 'Brand name and country of origin: effects in the emerging market economies of Russia, Poland and Hungary', *International Marketing Review*, 5, pp. 14–36.

Evans, P.B. and Wuster, T.S. (2000) *Blown to Bits: How the New Economics of Information Transforms Strategy*. Harvard Business School Press, Boston.

Fan, Y. (2007) 'Marque in the making', *Brand Strategy*, June, pp. 52–54.

Filiatrault, P. and Lapierre, J. (1997) 'Managing business-to-business marketing relationships in consulting engineering firms', *Industrial Marketing Management*, 26, pp. 213–222.

Ginsberg, J.M. and Bloom, P.N. (2004) 'Choosing the right green marketing strategy', *MIT Sloan Management Review*, Fall, pp. 79–84.

Guiltinan, J.P., Paul, G.W. and Madden, T.J. (1997) *Marketing Management: Strategies and Programs*, 6th edn. McGraw-Hill Companies, Inc., New York.

Heracleous, L., Wirtz, J. and Johnston, R. (2004) 'Cost-effective service excellence: lessons from Singapore Airlines', *Business Strategy Review*, 15(1), pp. 33–38.

Hollis, N. (2009) 'Rethinking globalization', *Marketing Research*, Spring, pp. 12–18.

Hooley, G.J., Saunders, J.A. and Piercy, N. (1998) *Marketing Strategy and Competitive Positioning*, 2nd edn. Prentice Hall, Hemel Hempstead.

Hoosear, J.V. (2006) 'Fame and fortune', *Brand Management*, Focus 2006 edition, pp. 41–43.

Johansson, J.K. and Thorelli, H.B. (1985) 'International product positioning', *Journal of International Business Studies*, 16(Fall), pp. 57–75.

Johansson, J.K., Ronkainen, I.A. and Czinkota, M.R. (1994) 'Negative country-of-origin effects: the case of the new Russia', *Journal of International Business Studies*, 25(first quarter), pp. 1–21.

Keegan, W.J. (1995) *Global Marketing Management*, 5th edn. Prentice-Hall, Englewood Cliffs, NJ.

Keller, K.L. and Sood, S. (2001) 'The ten commandments of global branding', 8(2), pp. 1–12.

Kotler, P. (1997) *Marketing Management: Analysis, Planning, Implementation and Control*, 9th edn. Prentice-Hall, Englewood Cliffs, NJ.

Kumar, N. (1999) 'Internet distribution strategies: dilemmas for the incumbent', Mastering Information Management Part 7, Electronic Commerce, *Financial Times*, 15 March.

Lindstrom, M. (2004) *Brand Sense: Build Powerful Brands through Touch, Taste, Smell, Sight, and Sound*. Free Press, New York.

Lovelock, C.H. and Yip, G.S. (1996) 'Developing global strategies for service business', *California Management Review*, 38(2), pp. 64–86.

Majaro, S. (1982) *International Marketing: A Strategic Approach to World Markets*, revised edn. George Allen & Unwin, London.

Marketing Science Institute (1995) *Brand Equity and Marketing Mix: Creating Customer Value*, Conference Summary, Report no. 95–111, September, p. 14. Cambridge, MA: MSI.

McNamee, P. (1984) 'Competitive analysis using matrix displays', *Long Range Planning*, 17(3), pp. 98–114.

Mendleson, N. and Polonsky, M.J. (1995) 'Using strategic alliances to develop credible green marketing', *Journal of Consumer Marketing*, 12(2), pp. 4–18.

Michel, S., Brown, S.W. and Gallan, A.S. (2008) 'Service-logic innovations: how to innovate customers, not products', *California Management Review*, 50(3), pp. 49–65.

Onkvisit, S. and Shaw, J.J. (1989) 'The international dimension of branding: strategic considerations and decisions', *International Marketing Review*, 6(3), pp. 22–34.

Onkvisit, S. and Shaw, J.J. (1993) *International Marketing: Analysis and strategy*, 2nd edn. Macmillan, London.

Popper, E.T. and Buskirk, B.D. (1992) 'Technology life cycles in industrial markets', *Industrial Marketing Management*, 21, pp. 23–31.

Prahalad, C.K. and Ramaswamy, V. (2004) *The Future of Competition: Co-creating Unique Value with Customers*. Harvard Business School Press, Boston.

Quelch, J.A. and Harding, D. (1996) 'Brands versus private labels: fighting to win', *Harvard Business Review*, January–February, pp. 99–109.

Saudi Arabian Ministry of Agriculture (1985) *Demographic Yearbook*. Jedda: Saudi Arabian Ministry of Agriculture.

Sawhney, M., Verona, G. and Prandelli, E. (2005) 'Collaborating to create: the Internet as a platform for customer engagement in product innovation', *Journal of Interactive Marketing*, 19(4), pp. 4–17.

Starik, M., Throop, G.M., Doody, J.M. and Joyce, M.E. (1996) 'Growing on environmental strategy', *Business Strategy and the Environment*, 5, pp. 12–21.

Steenkamp, J.-B. and Kumar, N. (2009) 'Don't be undersold', *Harvard Business Review*, 87(12), pp. 90–95.

Stiff, P. (2005) 'Orgasmic chocolate innovation', Confectionerynews.com, 8 November.

Töpfer, A. (1995) 'New products: cutting the time to market', *Long Range Planning*, 28(2), pp. 61–78.

Vandermerwe, J. and Oliff, M.D. (1991) 'Corporate challenges for an age of reconsumption', *Columbia Journal of World Business*, 26(3), pp. 6–25.

Varadarajan, R. (2009) 'Fortune at the bottom of the innovation pyramid: the strategic logic of incremental innovations', *Business Horizons*, 52, pp. 21–29.

Vernon, R. (1966) 'International investment and international trade in the product life cycle', *Quarterly Journal of Economics*, May, pp. 190–207.

Whitwell, S. (2006) 'Faking it can be good', *Brand Strategy*, May, pp. 30–31.

World Wide Fund for Nature (1993) *Corporate Relationships*. World Wide Fund for Nature, Sydney.

Wu, H.J. and Dunn, S.C. (1995) 'Environmentally responsible logistics systems', *International Journal of Physical Distribution and Logistics Management*, 25(2), pp. 20–38.

CHAPTER 15
Pricing decisions and terms of doing business

Contents

Case studies

Learning objectives

After studying this chapter you should be able to:

- Explain how internal and external variables influence international pricing decisions.
- Explain why and how prices escalate in export selling.
- Discuss the strategic options in determining the price level for a new product.
- Explain the necessary sales volume increase as a consequence of a price decrease.
- Explain what is meant by experience curve pricing.
- Explore the special roles and problems of transfer pricing in global marketing.
- Discuss how varying currency conditions challenge the international marketer.
- Identify and explain the different terms of sale (price quotations).
- Discuss the conditions that affect terms of payment.
- Discuss the role of export credit and financing for successful export marketing.

15.1 Introduction

Pricing is part of the marketing mix, therefore pricing decisions must be integrated with the other three Ps of the marketing mix. Price is the only area of the global marketing mix where policy can be changed rapidly without large direct cost implications. This characteristic, plus the fact that overseas consumers are often sensitive to price changes, results in the danger that pricing action may be resorted to as a quick fix instead of changes being made in other areas of the firm's marketing programme. It is important that management realizes that constant fine-tuning of prices in overseas markets should be avoided and that many problems are not best addressed by pricing action.

Generally, pricing policy is one of the most important yet often least recognized of all the elements of the marketing mix. The other elements of the marketing mix all lead to costs. The only source of profit to the firm comes from revenue, which in turn is dictated by pricing policy. In this chapter we focus on a number of pricing issues of special interest to international marketers.

15.2 International pricing strategies compared with domestic pricing strategies

For many SMEs operating in domestic markets pricing decisions are based on the relatively straightforward process of allocating the total estimated cost of producing, managing and marketing a product or service and adding an appropriate profit margin. Problems for these firms arise when costs increase and sales do not materialize or when competitors undercut them. In international markets, however, pricing decisions are much more complex, because they are affected by a number of additional external factors, such as fluctuations in exchange rates, accelerating inflation in certain countries and the use of alternative payment methods such as leasing, barter and counter-trade.

Of special concern to the global marketing manager are pricing decisions on products made or marketed locally, but with some centralized influence from outside the country in which the products are made or marketed. Broadly speaking, pricing decisions include setting the initial price as well as changing the established price of products from time to time.

15.3 Factors influencing international pricing decisions

An SME exporting for the first time, with little knowledge of the market environment that it is entering, is likely to set a price that will ensure that the sales revenue generated at least covers the costs incurred. It is important that firms recognize that the cost structures of products are very significant, but they should not be regarded as sole determinants when setting prices.

Pricing policy is an important strategic and tactical competitive weapon that, in contrast to the other elements of the global marketing mix, is highly controllable and inexpensive to change and implement. Therefore pricing strategies and action should be integrated with the other elements of the global marketing mix.

Figure 15.1 presents a general framework for international pricing decisions. According to this model, factors affecting international pricing can be broken down into two main groups (internal and external factors) and four subgroups, which we will now consider in more detail.

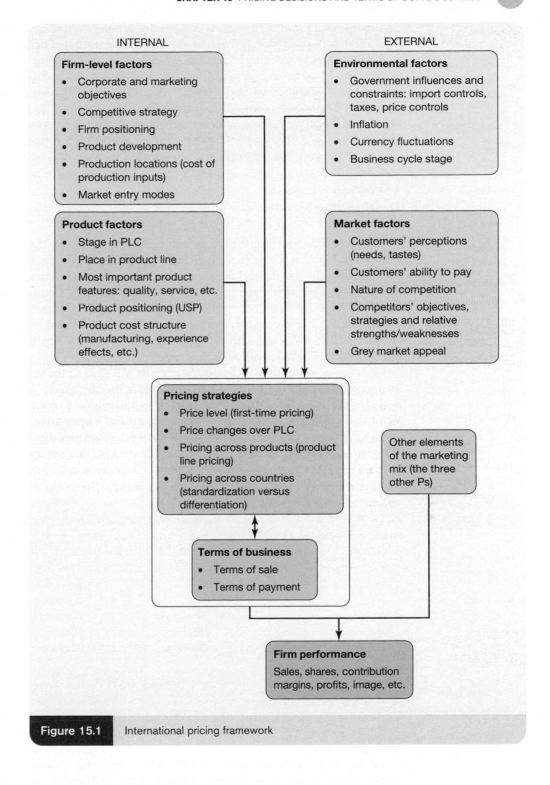

Figure 15.1 International pricing framework

Firm-level factors

International pricing is influenced by past and current corporate philosophy, organization and managerial policies. The short-term tactical use of pricing in the form of discounts, product offers and reductions is often emphasized by managers at the expense of its strategic role, yet in recent years pricing has played a very significant part in the restructuring of many industries, resulting in the growth of some businesses and the decline of others. In particular, Japanese firms have approached new markets with the intention of building market share over a period of years by reducing price levels, establishing the brand name and setting up effective distribution and servicing networks. The market share objectives of these Japanese firms have usually been accomplished at the expense of short-term profits, as international Japanese firms have consistently taken a long-term perspective on profit. They are usually prepared to wait much longer for returns on investments than some of their Western counterparts.

The choice of foreign market entry mode also affects the pricing policy. A manufacturer with a subsidiary in a foreign country has a high level of control over the pricing policy in that country.

Product factors

Key product factors include the unique and innovative features of the product and the availability of substitutes. These factors will have a major impact on the stage of the product life cycle, which will also depend on the market environment in target markets. Whether the product is a service or a manufactured or commodity good sold into consumer or industrial markets is also significant.

Price escalation
All cost factors (e.g. firms' net ex-works price, shipping costs, tariffs, distributor mark-up) in the distribution channel add up and lead to price escalation. The longer the distribution channel, the higher the final price in the foreign market.

The extent to which the organization has had to adapt or modify the product or service, and the level to which the market requires service around the core product, will also affect cost and thereby have some influence on pricing.

Costs are also helpful in estimating how rivals will react to the setting of a specific price, assuming that knowledge of one's own costs helps in the assessment of competitors' reactions. Added to the above is the intermediary cost, which depends on channel length, intermediary factors and logistical costs. All these factors add up and lead to **price escalation**.

The example in Table 15.1 shows that due to additional shipping, insurance and distribution charges, the exported product costs some 21 per cent more in the export market than at

Table 15.1	Examples of price escalation		
	Domestic channel (a)	Foreign marketing channel (b)	(c)
	Firm ↓ Wholesaler Retailer ↓ Consumer	Firm ↓ Border ↓ Wholesaler Retailer ↓ Consumer	Firm ↓ Border ↓ Importer Wholesaler Retailer ↓ Consumer
	£	£	£
Firm's net price	100	100	100
Insurance and shipping costs	–	10	10
Landed cost	–	110	110
Tariff (10 per cent of landed cost)	–	11	11
Importer pays (cost)	–	–	121
Importer's margin/mark-up (15 per cent of cost)	–	–	18
Wholesaler pays (cost)	100	121	139
Wholesaler's/mark-up (20 per cent of cost)	20	24	28
Retailer pays (cost)	120	145	167
Retail margin/mark-up (40 per cent of cost)	48	58	67
Consumer pays (price) (exclusive of VAT)	168	203	234
per cent price escalation over domestic channel	–	21	39

home. If an additional distribution link (an importer) is used, the product costs 39 per cent more abroad than at home.

Many exporters are not aware of rapid price escalation; they are preoccupied with the price they charge to the importer. However, the final consumer price should be of vital concern because it is on this level that the consumer can compare prices of different competitive products and it is this price that plays a major role in determining the foreign demand.

Price escalation is not a problem for exporters alone. It affects all firms involved in cross-border transactions. Companies that undertake substantial intra-company shipment of goods and materials across national borders are exposed to many of the additional charges that cause price escalation.

The following management options are available to counter price escalation:

- *Rationalizing the distribution process.* One option is to reduce the number of links in the distribution process, either by doing more in-house or by circumventing some channel members.
- *Lowering the export price from the factory* (firm's net price), thus reducing the multiplier effect of all the mark-ups.
- *Establishing local production of the product* within the export market to eliminate some of the cost.
- *Pressurizing channel members to accept lower profit margins.* This may be appropriate if these intermediaries are dependent on the manufacturer for much of their turnover.

It may be dangerous to overlook traditional channel members. In Japan, for example, the complex nature of the distribution system, which often involves many different channel members, makes it tempting to consider radical change. However, existing intermediaries do not like to be overlooked, and their possible network with other channel members and the government may make it dangerous for a foreign firm to attempt to cut them out.

Environmental factors

The environmental factors are external to the firm and thus uncontrollable variables in the foreign market. The national government control of exports and imports is usually based on political and strategic considerations.

Generally speaking, import controls are designed to limit imports in order to protect domestic producers or reduce the outflow of foreign exchange. Direct restrictions commonly take the form of tariffs, quotas and various non-tariff barriers. Tariffs directly increase the price of imports unless the exporter or importer is willing to absorb the tax and accept lower profit margins. Quotas have an indirect impact on prices. They restrict supply, thus causing the price of the import to increase.

Since tariff levels vary from country to country there is an incentive for exporters to vary the price somewhat from country to country. In some countries with high customs duties and high price elasticity the base price may have to be lower than in other countries if the product is to achieve satisfactory volume in these markets. If demand is quite inelastic the price may be set at a high level, with little loss of volume, unless competitors are selling at lower prices.

Government regulations on pricing can also affect the firm's pricing strategy. Many governments tend to have price controls on specific products related to health, education, food and other essential items. Another major environmental factor is fluctuation in the exchange rate. An increase (revaluation) or decrease (devaluation) in the relative value of a currency can affect the firm's pricing structure and profitability.

Market factors

One of the critical factors in the foreign market is the purchasing power of the customer – the customers' ability to pay. The pressure of competitors may also affect international pricing. The firm has to offer a more competitive price if there are other sellers in the market. Thus the nature of competition (e.g. oligopoly or monopoly) can influence the firm's pricing strategy.

Under conditions approximating pure competition price is set in the marketplace. Price tends to be just enough above costs to keep marginal producers in business. Thus, from the point of view of the price-setter, the most important factor is cost. The closer the substitutability of products, the more nearly identical the prices must be, and the greater the influence of costs in determining prices (assuming a large enough number of buyers and sellers).

Under conditions of monopolistic or imperfect competition the seller has some discretion to vary the product quality, promotional efforts and channel policies in order to adapt the price of the total product to serve preselected market segments. Nevertheless the freedom to set prices is still limited by what competitors charge, and any price differentials from competitors must be justified in the minds of customers on the basis of differential utility: that is, perceived value.

When considering how customers will respond to a given price strategy, Nagle (1987) has suggested nine factors that influence the sensitivity of customers to prices:

1. More distinctive product.
2. Greater perceived quality of products.
3. Consumers are less aware of substitutes in the market.
4. Difficulty in making comparisons (e.g. in the quality of services such as consultancy or accountancy).
5. The price of a product represents a small proportion of total expenditure of the customer.
6. The perceived benefit for the customer increases.
7. The product is used in association with a product bought previously, so that, for example, components and replacements are usually extremely highly priced.
8. Costs are shared with other parties.
9. The product or service cannot be stored.

Price sensitivity is reduced in all these nine cases.

In the following sections we discuss the different available pricing strategies.

15.4 International pricing strategies

In determining the price level for a new product the general alternatives are as shown in Figure 15.2.

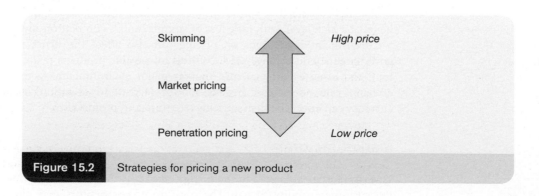

| Figure 15.2 | Strategies for pricing a new product |

Skimming

In this strategy a high price is charged to 'skim the cream' from the top end of the market, with the objective of achieving the highest possible contribution in a short time. For a marketer to use this approach the product has to be unique, and some segments of the market must be willing to pay the high price. As more segments are targeted and more of the product is made available the price is gradually lowered. The success of skimming depends on the ability and speed of competitive reaction.

Products should be designed to appeal to affluent and demanding consumers, offering extra features, greater comfort, variability or ease of operation. With skimming the firm trades off a low market share against a high margin.

Problems with skimming are:

- Having a small market share makes the firm vulnerable to aggressive local competition.
- Maintenance of a high-quality product requires a lot of resources (promotion, after-sales service) and a visible local presence, which may be difficult in distant markets.
- If the product is sold more cheaply at home or in another country grey marketing (parallel importing) is likely.

Market pricing

If similar products already exist in the target market, market pricing may be used. The final customer price is based on competitive prices. This approach requires the exporter to have a thorough knowledge of product costs, as well as confidence that the product life cycle is long enough to warrant entry into the market. It is a reactive approach and may lead to problems if sales volumes never rise to sufficient levels to produce a satisfactory return. Although firms typically use pricing as a differentiation tool the global marketing manager may have no choice but to accept the prevailing world market price.

From the price that customers are willing to pay it is possible to make a so-called retrograde calculation where the firm uses a 'reversed' price escalation to calculate backwards (from market price) to the necessary (ex factory) net price. If this net price can create a satisfactory contribution margin then the firm can go ahead.

Penetration pricing

A penetration pricing policy is used to stimulate market growth and capture market shares by deliberately offering products at low prices. This approach requires mass markets, price-sensitive customers and reduction in unit costs through economies of scale and experience curve effects. The basic assumption that lower prices will increase sales will fail if the main competitors reduce their prices to a correspondingly low level. Another danger is that prices might be set so low that they are not credible to consumers. There are confidence levels for prices below which consumers lose faith in the product's quality.

Motives for pricing at low levels in certain foreign markets might include:

- Intensive local competition from rival companies.
- Lower income levels of local consumers.
- Some firms argue that, since their R&D and other overhead costs are covered by home sales, exporting represents a marginal activity intended merely to bring in as much additional revenue as possible by offering a low selling price.

Japanese companies have used penetration pricing intensively to gain market share leadership in a number of markets, such as cars, home entertainment products and electronic components.

Price changes

Price changes on existing products are called for when a new product has been launched or when changes occur in overall market conditions (such as fluctuating foreign exchange rates).

Table 15.2 shows the percentage sales volume increase or decrease required to maintain the level of profit. An example (the figure in bold type in Table 15.2) shows how the table functions. A firm has a product with a contribution margin of 20 per cent. The firm would like to know how much the sales volume should be increased as a consequence of a price reduction of 5 per cent, if it wishes to keep the same total profit contribution. The calculation is as follows:

Before price reduction

Per product	sales price	£100
	variable cost per unit	£80
	contribution margin	£20
Total contribution margin: 100 units @ £20 =		£2,000

After price reduction (5 per cent)

Per product	sales price	£95
	variable cost per unit	£80
	contribution margin	£15
Total contribution margin: 133 units @ £15 =		£1,995

As a consequence of a price reduction of 5 per cent, a 33 per cent increase in sales is required.

Table 15.2	Sales volume increase or decrease (%) required to maintain total profit contribution								
	Profit contribution margin (price – variable cost per unit as % of the price)								
Price reduction	**5**	**10**	**15**	**20**	**25**	**30**	**35**	**40**	**50**
(%)	Sales volume increase (%) required to maintain total profit contribution								
2.0	67	25	15	11	9	7	7	5	4
3.0	150	43	25	18	14	11	9	8	6
4.0	400	67	36	25	19	15	13	11	9
5.0		100	50	**33**	25	20	17	14	11
7.5		300	100	60	43	33	27	23	18
10.0			200	100	67	50	40	33	25
15.0				300	150	100	75	60	43
	Profit contribution margin (price – variable cost per unit as % of the price)								
Price increase	**5**	**10**	**15**	**20**	**25**	**30**	**35**	**40**	**50**
(%)	Maximum sales volume reduction (%) required to maintain total profit contribution								
2.0	29	17	12	9	7	6	5	5	4
3.0	37	23	17	13	11	9	8	7	6
4.0	44	29	21	17	14	12	10	9	7
5.0	50	33	25	20	17	14	12	11	9
7.5	60	43	33	27	23	20	18	16	13
10.0	67	50	40	33	29	25	22	20	17
15.0	75	60	50	43	37	33	30	27	23

If a decision is made to change prices, related changes must also be considered. For example, if an increase in price is required it may be accompanied, at least initially, by increased promotional efforts.

When reducing prices the degree of flexibility enjoyed by decision-makers will tend to be less for existing products than for new products. This follows from the high probability that the existing product is now less unique, faces stronger competition and is aimed at a broader segment of the market. In this situation the decision-maker will be forced to pay more attention to competitive and cost factors in the pricing process.

The timing of price changes can be nearly as important as the changes themselves. For example, a simple tactic of time lagging competitors in announcing price increases can produce the perception among customers that you are the most customer-responsive supplier. The extent of the time lag can also be important.

In one company an independent survey of customers (Garda, 1995) showed that the perception of being the most customer-responsive supplier was generated just as effectively by a six-week lag in following a competitor's price increase as by a six-month lag. A considerable amount of money would have been lost during the unnecessary four-and-a-half-month delay in announcing a price increase.

<table>
<tr><td>

Experience curve pricing

Combination of the experience curve (lowering costs per unit with accumulated production of the product) with typical market price development within an industry.

</td><td>

Experience curve pricing

Price changes usually follow changes in the product's stage in the life cycle. As the product matures more pressure will be put on the price to keep the product competitive because of increased competition and less possibility of differentiation.

Let us also integrate the cost aspect into the discussion. The experience curve has its roots in a commonly observed phenomenon called the learning curve, which states that as people repeat a task they learn to do it better and faster. The learning curve applies to the labour portion of manufacturing cost. The Boston Consulting Group extended the learning effect to cover all the value-added costs related to a product – manufacturing plus marketing, sales, administration and so on.

The resulting experience curves, covering all value chain activities (see Figure 15.3), indicate that the total unit costs of a product in real terms can be reduced by a certain percentage with each doubling of cumulative production. The typical decline in cost is 30 per cent (termed a 70 per cent curve), although greater and lesser declines are observed (Czepiel, 1992, p. 149).

</td></tr>
</table>

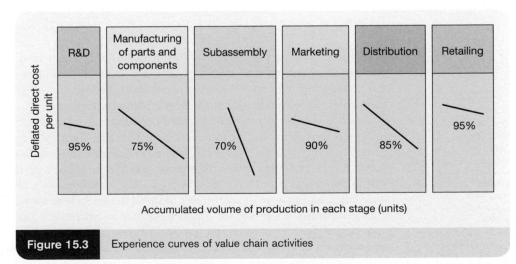

Figure 15.3   Experience curves of value chain activities

Source: Hax, Arnoldo C.; Majluf, Nicholas S., *Strategic Management: An Integrative Perspective, 1st,* © 1984. Electronically reproduced by permission of Pearson Education, Inc., Upper Saddle River, New Jersey

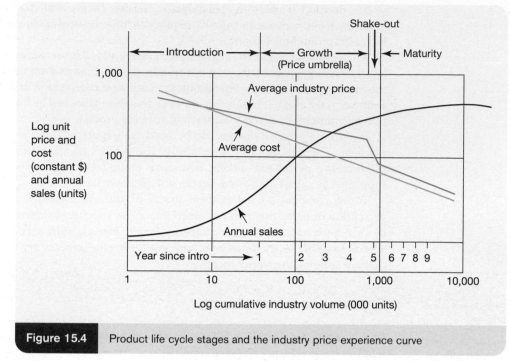

Source: Kotler, Philip, *Marketing Management: Analysis, Planning, Implementation and Control, 7th*, © 1991. Electronically reproduced by permission of Pearson Education, Inc., Upper Saddle River, New Jersey

Figure 15.4	Product life cycle stages and the industry price experience curve

If we combine the experience curve (average unit cost) with the typical market price develop ment within an industry we will have a relationship similar to that shown in Figure 15.4.

Figure 15.4 shows that after the introduction stage (during part of which the price is below the total unit cost), profits begin to flow. Because supply is less than demand prices do not fall as quickly as costs. Consequently the gap between costs and prices widens, in effect creating a price umbrella, attracting new competitors. However, the competitive situation is not a stable one. At some point the umbrella will be folded by one or more competitors reducing the prices in an attempt to gain or retain market share. The result is that a shake-out phase will begin: inefficient producers will be shaken out by rapidly falling market prices, and only those with a competitive price/cost relationship will remain.

Pricing across products (product line pricing)

With across-product pricing the various items in the line may be differentiated by pricing them appropriately to indicate, for example, an economy version, a standard version and a top-of-the-range version. One of the products in the line may be priced to protect against competitors or to gain market share from existing competitors.

Buy in–follow on strategy
Typically the case where two products are linked together: The original product item is priced very low, in order to get customers 'in' and try the product. The follow-on product is then sold at a significantly higher price. The classic case is the Gillette razor (buy in) + blades (follow on).

Products with less competition may be priced higher to subsidize other parts of the product line, so as to make up for the lost contribution of such 'fighting brands'. Another strategy is price bundling (total 'package' price), where a certain price is set for customers who simultan-eously buy several items within the product line (one price for a personal computer package with software and printer). In all such cases a key consideration is how much consumers in different countries want to save money, to spend time searching for the best buy and so forth. Furthermore, some items in the product line may be priced very low to serve as loss leaders and induce customers to try the product. A special variant of this is the so-called **buy in–follow on strategy** (Weigand, 1991). A classic example of this strategy is the razor blade link where Gillette, for example, uses a penetration price on its razor (buy in) but a skimming pricing (a relatively high price) on its razor blades (follow on). Thus the linked product or service – the follow on – is sold at a significant contribution margin. This inevitably attracts hitchhikers who try to sell follow-on products without incurring the cost of the buy in.

The buy in–follow on strategy is different from a low introductory price, which is based on the hope that the customer (of habit) will return again and again at higher prices. With the buy in–follow on strategy sales of two products or services are powerfully linked by factors such as legal contracts, patents, trade secrets, experience curve advantages and technological links.

Other examples of the strategy are:

- The price of a Polaroid instant camera is very low, but Polaroid hopes that this will generate sales of far more profitable films for many years.
- The telephone companies sell mobile (cellular) telephones at a near give-away price, hoping that the customer will be a heavy user of the profitable mobile telephone network.

EXHIBIT 15.1 The Gillette price premium strategy

An incrementally innovative new product can enable a firm to command a higher price as well as realize higher margins than the product it replaces in the marketplace. For example, in 1971 the Gillette Safety Razor Company (acquired by Procter & Gamble in 2005) introduced the Gillette Trac II brand, a razor with two blades fitted in a shaving cartridge. In 2006, it introduced the Gillette Fusion brand, fitted with five blades in a cartridge for shaving plus a sixth blade for trimming. The history of the price per replacement cartridge for Gillette brand razors, spanning the 35-year period from 1971 to 2006, summarized in Table 1, is instructive in this regard.

Table 1	Gillette's price per replacement cartridge (2006 prices, adjusted for inflation)
Gillette product version	**Price per replacement cartridge (2006 prices)**
Gillette II (1971, two-bladed cartridge) 'Two blades are better than one'	$1.00
Gillette Sensor (1990, spring-mounted blades), 'Can sense and adjust to the contours of your face'	$1.22
Gillette Mach3 (1998, three blades), 'You take one stroke, it takes three'	$2.02
Gillette Fusion (2006, five blades plus a trimmer), 'The comfort of five blades, the precision of one'	$3.00

The price per replacement cartridge adjusted for inflation has increased by 200 per cent.

Source: based on Varadarajan (2009).

Product–service bundle pricing
Bundling product and services together in a system-solution product. If the customer thinks that entry price is a key barrier, service contracts can be priced higher, which allows for lower entry product pricing – the practice in many software businesses.

Product–service bundle pricing

The structure and level of pricing is perhaps the most crucial design choice in embedded *services*. To get pricing right, a company needs a clear grasp of its strategic intent and its sources of competitive advantage and must often make trade-offs between product penetration and the growth and margins of its *service* business.

A company's strategic intent largely determines the appropriate extent of product–service bundling and the *value* attributed to services in such bundles. Companies that focus on enhancing or protecting core products should price their services to improve their product penetration. The pricing strategy to achieve such product pull-through varies according to customer purchasing decisions. Companies can raise the *value* of the product in use and increase its pull-through by bundling products and services into a higher-value solution. If the entry price is a key factor, service contracts can be priced higher, which allows for lower product pricing – the practice in many software businesses. In some cases, companies can raise the price of maintenance service contracts to accelerate the rate of product upgrades. The strategic goal of product pull-through also means that sales and field agents should have some flexibility and authority in the pricing of services. However, companies must still actively manage pricing discipline by ensuring that these salespeople are accountable for the total profitability of the bundles they sell.

By contrast, companies aiming to create an independent, growth-oriented service business should price their offerings to achieve profitable growth and set pricing targets as close to the service's value to customers as competitive alternatives permit. These companies should set pricing guidelines and delegate authority centrally, with relatively limited freedom for sales and field personnel and clear rules for discounting. Bundling prices for services and products is usually a bad idea for a growth platform in services, because within any given customer's organization, the person who buys the service might not be the one who buys the product. It is also difficult to bundle prices while holding both product and service business units accountable for their independent sales and margin targets.

The source of competitive advantage – scale or skill – mainly affects pricing structures. If economies of scale drive a business, its pricing should be based on standard units (such as terabytes of storage managed) and it should offer volume discounts to encourage growth in usage. Such companies ought to make the price of any customized variation from their standard service offerings extremely high, since these exceptions push up costs throughout the business.

By contrast, if a service business relies mostly on special skills, it should base its prices on the costs its customers avoid by using its services or on the cost of the next-best alternative. Such value-based pricing requires a sophisticated analysis of a customer segment's total cost of ownership and a deep understanding of the cost structure of the service business. Competitive benchmarks and the cost of deploying the skills should determine the respective upper and lower bounds for these price levels. In the best case, companies can package this intelligence into pricing tools that allow sales and field agents to estimate customer value more accurately and thus improve field-level pricing decisions (Auguste *et al.*, 2006).

Pricing across countries (standardization versus differentiation)

A major problem for companies is how to coordinate prices between countries. There are two essential opposing forces: first, to achieve similar positioning in different markets by adopting largely standardized pricing; and second, to maximize profitability by adapting pricing to different market conditions. In determining to what extent prices should be standardized across borders two basic approaches appear:

1. *Price standardization.* This is based on setting a price for the product as it leaves the factory. At its simplest it involves setting a fixed world price at the headquarters of the firm. This fixed world price is then applied in all markets after taking account of factors such as foreign exchange rates and variance in the regulatory context. For the firm this is a low-risk strategy, but no attempt is made to respond to local conditions and so no effort is made to maximize profits. However, this pricing strategy might be appropriate if the firm sells to very large customers, who have companies in several countries. In such a situation the firm might be under pressure from the customer only to deliver at the same price to every country subsidiary, throughout the customer's multinational organization. In Figure 15.5 this is exemplified, for example, by the international activities of large retail organizations. Another advantage of price standardization is the potential for rapid introduction of new products in international markets and the presentation of a consistent (price) image across markets.

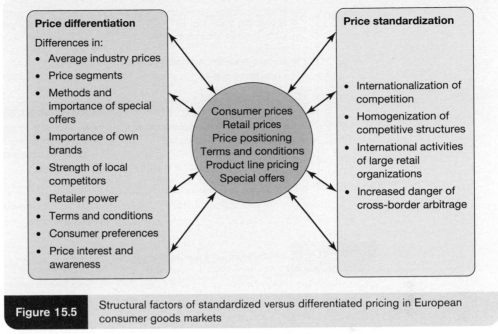

| Figure 15.5 | Structural factors of standardized versus differentiated pricing in European consumer goods markets |

Source: reprinted from *European Management Journal*, vol. 12, no. 2, Diller, H. and Bukhari, I. (1994) 'Pricing conditions in the European Common Market', p. 168, Copyright 1994, with permission from Elsevier.

2. *Price differentiation.* This allows each local subsidiary or partner (agent, distributor, etc.) to set a price that is considered to be the most appropriate for local conditions, and no attempt is made to coordinate prices from country to country. Cross-cultural empirical research has found significant differences in customer characteristics, preference and purchasing behaviour in different countries (Theodosiou and Katsikeas, 2001). The weakness with 'price differentiation' is the lack of control that the headquarters has over the prices set by the subsidiary operations or external partner. Significantly different prices may be set in adjacent markets, and this can reflect badly on the image of multinational firms. It also encourages the creation of parallel importing/grey markets (which are dealt with in greater detail in Chapter 16), whereby products can be purchased in one market and sold in another, undercutting the established market prices in the process.

The underlying forces favouring standardization or differentiation are shown in Figure 15.5.

An international pricing taxonomy

As we discussed previously, pricing decisions in the international environment tend to be a function of the interplay between the external, market-related complexities that shape firm operations and the capabilities of the firm to respond effectively to these contingencies. Solberg's (1997) framework captures this interface in a meaningful way and leads to sufficiently important consequences for the export pricing behaviour of firms in foreign markets. Solberg suggests that firms' international strategic behaviour is shaped primarily by two dimensions: (a) the degree of globalism of the firm's industry (a measure of the market related factors) and (b) its degree of preparedness for internationalization (a measure of the firm's abilities to respond to these factors). These two dimensions are discussed in Chapter 1 (Figure 1.1) with the purpose of suggesting under which circumstances the firm should stay at home, strengthen the global position or something in between. In Figure 15.6 an international pricing taxonomy is proposed along these two dimensions (Solberg *et al.*, 2006).

| **Figure 15.6** | A taxonomy of international pricing practices |

Source: adapted from Solberg *et al.* (2006, p. 31). In the original article Solberg has used the concept 'globality' rather than 'globalism'.

A global industry is dominated by a few, large major competitors that 'rule' their categories in world markets within their product category. Thus the degree of globalism along the industry globalism dimension is considered to vary between two extremes: a monopoly at one end (the right) and atomistic competition at the other (the left). The strategic implication of this perspective is that the monopolistic and oligopolistic global player would be the price-setter, whereas the firm in the atomistic (multilocal) market setting would be exposed to local market forces, finding itself needing to follow market prices in every case. Although most firms fall into intermediate positions along this continuum, we believe that the leverage of the individual international firm in setting its pricing strategy will be greatly influenced by the globalism of the competitive environment in which it will operate.

On the other dimension, *preparedness for internationalization*, experienced firms find international pricing to be a more complicated matter, even though they devote additional resources to collecting and processing greater amounts of information. These firms are found to have the international preparedness that is necessary to offset the effects of reduced prices when they penetrate new markets or respond to competitive attacks, to be more self-confident in setting pricing strategies and, in general, to enjoy higher market shares in the export market. In contrast, smaller and more inexperienced firms seem to be too weak both in relation to their local counterparts and in terms of generating local market insight to be able to determine effective price levels for their products in foreign markets. Therefore, they tend to possess smaller shares in their markets and to follow the pricing practices of their competitors or segment leaders.

Looking through the lens of this framework we assume that large, internationally experienced exporters will be likely to centralize their pricing decisions and will prefer higher degrees of control over those decisions, whereas smaller, often new to export and internationally inexperienced firms will be likely to experiment with decentralized and often opportunistic modes of price-setting behaviour in their market.

The following discusses the characteristics of each of the four strategic prototypes in Figure 15.6.

Prototype 1: the local price follower firm

In this cell the firm (manufacturer) will only have limited international experience, and consequently, the firm's local export intermediate (agent or distributor) will serve as the key informant for the firm. This information asymmetry bears the danger that the export inter-mediate might mislead the exporter by exercising opportunism or by pursuing goals that are in conflict with those of the exporter. That may cause further transaction costs, and lead to internalization (see section 3.3 on transaction cost analysis). Because of limited market knowledge the exporter is prone to calculate its prices crudely and most likely on the basis of cost and the (sometimes insufficient or biased) information from its local export inter-mediary. In the extreme case such an exporter would respond only to unsolicited offers from abroad, and will tend following a pricing procedure based on internal cost information, thus missing potential international business opportunities.

Prototype 2: the global price follower firm

Firms that fall into the global price follower cell have limited preparedness for internationalization. In contrast, however, global price follower firms are often more motivated in expanding their international market involvement, as they are 'pushed' by the global market. Firms in this cell are expected to charge a standardized price in all countries because the interconnected international markets have more or less the same price level.

Given their marginal position in global markets, such firms have limited bargaining leverage and may be compelled to adopt the price level set by global market leaders, often very large global customers (see also the discussion about global account management [GAM] in Chapter 19). The Prototype 2 firms are typically under constant pressure from their more efficient distribution and globally branded counterparts to adjust their prices.

Prototype 3: the multilocal price setter firm

Firms in this cell are well-prepared international marketers with well-entrenched positions in local markets. Typically they are capable of assessing local market conditions through in-depth analyses and evaluation of market information, established market intelligence systems and/or deeply rooted market knowledge. They tend to have a tight control of their local market distribution networks through information and feedback systems. Prototype 3 firms adapt their prices from one market to the next in light of the differentiated requirements of each local market and manage the different market and pricing structures they cope with in their many (multidomestic) markets with relatively high sophistication.

In contrast to their local price follower counterparts (Prototype 1), however, these firms are often the pricing leaders in their local markets and base their pricing strategy primarily on local market conditions in each market. Given their multidomestic orientation, these firms tend to shift pricing decision-making authority to local subsidiary managers, even though their headquarters personnel closely monitors sales trends in each local market. Firms in this cell face challenges from grey market imports in their local markets that are motivated by the opportunity for cheaper producers to exploit price differences across markets (see also section 16.8 on grey marketing).

Prototype 4: the global price leader firm

Firms in this cell hold strong positions in key world markets. They manage smoothly functioning marketing networks, operating mainly through hierarchical entry modes or in combination with intermediate modes like joint ventures or alliances in major world markets. Prototype 4 firms compete against a limited number of competitors in each major market, similar to a global (or a regional) oligopoly. Typical of oligopoly players, they tend to be challenged by the cross-border transparency of the price mechanism; manage global (or regional) constraints, such as demand patterns and market regulation mechanisms; and set prices pan-regionally (i.e. across the EU). Global price leaders tend to maintain relatively high price levels in their markets, though possibly not as effectively as their multilocal counterparts. Compared with the global price leader firm, the multilocal price-setter more effectively erects local entry barriers, such as brand leadership, has closer relationships with its local distributors and a deeper understanding of local conditions in each local market, thus protecting itself from the downside of international price competition (Solberg *et al.*, 2006).

Establishing global-pricing contracts

Global-pricing contract
A customer requiring one global price (per product) from the supplier for all its foreign SBUs and subsidiaries.

As globalization increases the following is heard frequently among global suppliers and global customers: 'Give me a **global-pricing contract** (GPC) and I'll consolidate my worldwide purchase with you.' Increasingly, global customers are demanding such contracts from suppliers. For example, in 1998 General Motor's Powertrain Group told suppliers of components used in GM's engines, transmissions and subassemblies to charge GM the same for parts from one region as they did for parts from another region.

Suppliers do not need to lose out when customers globalize. The most attractive global-pricing opportunities are those that involve suppliers and customers working together to identify and eliminate inefficiencies that harm both. Sometimes, however, suppliers do not have a choice – they cannot afford to shut themselves out of business with their largest and fastest-growing customers.

Suppliers and customers have different advantages and disadvantages with global-pricing contracts, and Table 15.3 illustrates some of these.

One chemicals manufacturer concentrated on relationships with a few select customers. It had decided that its strength lay in value-added services but that potential customers in

Table 15.3	Global pricing contracts: advantages and disadvantages	
	Customers	**Suppliers**
Advantages	Lower prices worldwide coupled with higher levels of service.	Easily gain access to new markets and grow the business.
	Standardization of products and services offered across markets.	Consolidate operations and achieve economies of scale.
	Efficiencies in all processes, including new product development, manufacturing, inventory, logistics and customer service.	Work with industry leaders and influence market development by using them as showcase accounts.
		Collaborate with customers and develop strong relationships that are difficult for potential competitors to break into.
	Faster diffusion of innovations globally.	Rectify price and service anomalies in a customer relationship across country markets.
Disadvantages	Customer might be less adaptable to local market variance and changes over time.	Local managers sometimes resist change, and supplier may get caught in the crossfire between customer's HQ and country managers.
	Supplier might not have capabilities to provide consistent quality and performance across markets.	Supplier might lose the ability to serve other attractive customers.
	Supplier might use customer's over-dependence to extract higher prices.	Customer might not be able to deliver on promises.
		Customer might take advantage of cost information shared in the relationship.
	Local managers might resist global contracts and prefer dealing with local suppliers.	Supplier might become over-dependent on one customer, even when there are other more attractive customers to serve.
	Costs of monitoring global contracts might outstrip the benefits.	Supplier might have a conflict with existing channels of distribution in the new markets.

Source: adapted from Narayandas, Quelch and Swartz (2000, pp. 61–70).

emerging markets were fixated on price. The select customers, however, were interested in money-saving supply and inventory management initiatives developed jointly with the supplier.

Global customers' demands for detailed cost information can also put suppliers at risk. Toyota, Honda, Xerox and others force suppliers to open their books for inspection. Their stated objectives: to help suppliers identify ways to improve processes and quality while reducing costs – and to build trust. However, in an economic downturn the global customer might seek price reductions and supplementary services.

European pricing strategy

In 1991 price differentials for identical consumer goods across Europe were around 20 per cent on average, but much greater differences were apparent in certain products (Simon and Kucher, 1993). In another study by Diller and Bukhari (1994) there were also considerable price differences for identical take-home ice-cream products.

The causes of price differentials are differences in regulations, competition, distribution structures and consumer behaviour, such as willingness to pay. Currency fluctuations can also influence short-term price differences. The pressures of regionalization are accelerating the move to uniform pricing, but Simon and Kucher (1993) warn that this is a potential time bomb, as the pressure is for uniform pricing to be at the lowest pricing levels.

Europe was a price differentiation paradise as long as markets were separated, but it is becoming increasingly difficult to retain the old price differentials. There are primarily two developments that may force companies to standardize prices across European countries:

1. International buying power of cross-European retail groups.
2. Parallel imports/grey markets. Because of differentiated prices across countries, buyers in one country are able to purchase at a lower price than in another country. As a result there will be an incentive for customers in lower-price markets to sell goods to higher-price markets in order to make a profit. Grey marketing will be examined further in section 17.8.

Simon and Kucher (1993) suggest a price 'corridor' (Figure 15.7). The prices in the individual countries may only vary within that range. Figure 15.7 is also interesting in light of the euro, which was implemented fully by January 2002. However, price differences that can

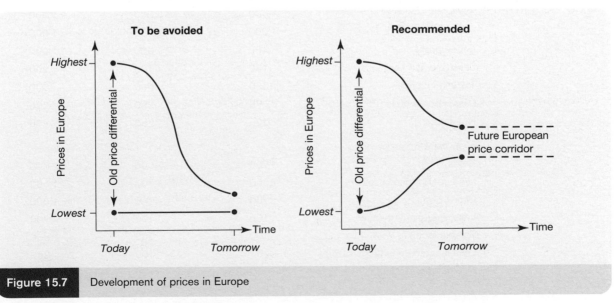

| **Figure 15.7** | Development of prices in Europe |

Source: Simon and Kucher (1993, p. 26). Copyright ESOMAR.

be justified by transportation costs and short-term competitive conditions, etc., may still be maintained. They recommend that business in smaller countries should be sacrificed, if necessary, in order to retain acceptable pricing levels in the big markets such as France, Germany, the United Kingdom and Italy. For example, for a pharmaceutical manufacturer it is more profitable not to sell in the Portuguese pharmaceutical market than to accept a price reduction of 10 per cent in the German market due to parallel imports from Portugal.

Transfer pricing

Prices charged for intra-company movement of goods and services. While transfer prices are internal to the company, they are important externally for cross-border taxation purposes.

Transfer pricing

Transfer prices are those charged for intra-company movement of goods and services. Many purely domestic firms need to make transfer-pricing decisions when goods are *transferred* from one domestic unit to another. While these transfer prices are internal to the company they are important externally because goods being transferred from country to country must have a value for cross-border taxation purposes.

The objective of the corporation in this situation is to ensure that the transfer price paid optimizes corporate rather than divisional objectives. This can prove difficult when a company is organized internationally into profit centres. For profit centres to work effectively a price must be set for everything that is transferred, be it working materials, components, finished goods or services. A high transfer price – for example, from the manufacturing division to a foreign subsidiary – is reflected in an apparently poor performance by the foreign subsidiary (see the high mark-up policy in Table 15.4), whereas a low price would not be acceptable to the domestic division providing the goods (see the low mark-up policy in Table 15.4). This issue alone can be the cause of much mistrust between subsidiaries.

The 'best' of Table 15.4's two mark-up policies seen from the consolidated point of view is to use a high mark-up policy, since it generates a net income of US$550, against US$475 from

Table 15.4	Tax effect of low versus high transfer price on net income (US$)		
	Manufacturing affiliate (division)	Distribution/selling affiliate (subsidiary)	Consolidated company total
Low mark-up policy			
Sales	1,400	2,000	2,000
Less cost of goods sold	1,000	1,400	1,000
Gross profit	400	600	1,000
Less operating expenses	100	100	200
Taxable income	300	500	800
Less income taxes (25%/50%)	75	250	325
Net income	225	250	475
High mark-up policy			
Sales	1,700	2,000	2,000
Less cost of goods sold	1,000	1,700	1,000
Gross profit	700	300	1,000
Less operating expenses	100	100	200
Taxable income	600	200	800
Less income taxes (25%/50%)	150	100	250
Net income	450	100	550

Note: Manufacturing affiliate pays income taxes at 25%. Distribution affiliate pays income taxes at 50%.
Source: based on Eiteman and Stonehill (1986).

using a low mark-up policy. The 'best' solution depends on the tax rates in the countries of the manufacturing and distribution affiliates (subsidiaries).

There are three basic approaches to transfer pricing:

1. *Transfer at cost.* The transfer price is set at the level of the production cost and the international division is credited with the entire profit that the firm makes. This means that the production centre is evaluated on efficiency parameters rather than profitability. The production division normally dislikes selling at production cost because it believes it is subsidizing the selling subsidiary. When the production division is unhappy the selling subsidiary may get sluggish service, because the production division is serving more attractive opportunities first.

2. *Transfer at arm's length.* Here the international division is charged the same as any buyer outside the firm. Problems occur if the overseas division is allowed to buy elsewhere when the price is uncompetitive or the product quality is inferior, and further problems arise if there are no external buyers, making it difficult to establish a relevant price. Nevertheless the arm's-length principle has now been accepted worldwide as the preferred (not required) standard by which transfer prices should be set (Fraedrich and Bateman, 1996).

3. *Transfer at cost plus.* This is the usual compromise, where profits are split between the production and international divisions. The actual formula used for assessing the transfer price can vary, but usually it is this method that has the greatest chance of minimizing executive time spent on transfer-price disagreements, optimizing corporate profits and motivating the home and international divisions. A senior executive is often appointed to rule on disputes.

A good transfer-pricing method should consider total corporate profile and encourage divisional cooperation. It should also minimize executive time spent on transfer-price disagreements and keep the accounting burden to a minimum.

Currency issues

A difficult aspect of export pricing is the decision about what currency the price should be quoted in. The exporter has the following options:

- the foreign currency of the buyer's country (local currency);
- the currency of the exporter's country (domestic currency);
- the currency of a third country (usually US dollars);
- a currency unit such as the euro.

If the exporter quotes in the domestic currency then not only is it administratively much easier, but also the risks associated with changes in the exchange rate are borne by the customer, whereas by quoting prices in the foreign currency the exporter bears the exchange rate risk. However, there are benefits to the exporter in quoting in foreign currency:

- Quoting in foreign currency could be a condition of the contract.
- It could provide access to finance abroad at lower interest rates.
- Good currency management may be a means of gaining additional profits.
- Customers normally prefer to be quoted in their own currency in order to be able to make competitive comparisons and know exactly what the eventual price will be.

Another difficult problem that exporters face is caused by fluctuating exchange rates. A company in a country with a devalued currency can (all other things being equal) strengthen its international competitive position. It can choose to reduce prices in foreign currencies or it can leave prices unchanged and instead increase profit margins.

When the Italian lira dropped by 15–20 per cent in value against the German mark it gave the Italian car producer Fiat a competitive advantage in pricing. The German car exporters, such as Volkswagen, were adversely affected and had to lower their list prices. In this respect the geographic pattern of a firm's manufacturing and sales subsidiaries compared with those of its main competitors becomes very important, because a local subsidiary can absorb most of the negative effects of a devaluation.

15.5   Implications of the Internet for pricing across borders

Europe's single currency, the euro (http://europa.eu.int/euro/) has finally become a reality after more than a decade of planning and preparation. In one stroke the single currency has created the largest single economy in the world, with a larger share of global trade and a greater number of consumers than in the United States.

The implication is that Europe suddenly became a single market by the end of 2000, and people can purchase from another country as easily as they can from a shop across the road. The same currency will be used; only the language issue remains. Opinion in Europe is that as more of the population goes online, and as Europe starts using its new single currency, online shopping will experience a tremendous growth.

Most of this growth has been fuelled by aggressive price cutting from Internet service providers (ISPs). A number of UK companies, for example, are now offering free Internet access or pay-as-you-go models, which have encouraged new sections of the population to try the Internet for the first time.

A European single currency was a long-held ambition for members of the European Union. The idea was first considered in the 1970s, but knocked off-course by oil price rises. It re-emerged in the early 1980s and was finally agreed in the 1992 Maastricht Treaty. There were many accounting criteria to be met by each country, such as the control of the rate of inflation and the debt/GDP ratio. Most countries have met these criteria and were permitted to join the European Monetary Union.

The euro is the currency of 16 European Union member states: Belgium, Germany, Greece, Spain, France, Ireland, Italy, Luxembourg, the Netherlands, Austria, Portugal, Finland, Slovenia, Cyprus, Malta and Slovakia. These countries comprise the 'Eurozone', with some 326 million people.

The United Kingdom is outside the euro region, which will be inconvenient for many US companies who trade heavily with UK companies or have UK subsidiaries.

The main detailed implications of the euro are that it will:

- lower prices for consumers by making prices transparent across Europe;
- create a real single market by reducing 'friction' to trade caused by high transaction costs and fluctuating currencies;
- enhance competition by forcing companies to concentrate on price, quality and production instead of hiding behind weak currencies;
- benefit SMEs and consumers by making it easier for the former to enter foreign markets and allowing the latter, increasingly via the Internet, to shop in the lowest-priced markets;
- establish inflation and interest rate stability via the new European Central Bank; and
- lower the costs of doing business through lower prices, lower interest rates, no transaction costs or loss through exchanging currencies and the absence of exchange rate fluctuations.

In short, the single currency will significantly increase competition, lower transaction costs and bring about greater certainty. These new forces will bring about structural reforms in Europe. Almost every aspect of Europe's business and political environment will be affected.

Perhaps most importantly, marketing and pricing strategies need rethinking. Because the euro will allow easy price comparison across Europe (especially via the Internet), it will reveal the differences between higher- and lower-priced markets.

For those selling via the Internet the euro will make it easier to do business and give encouragement to companies selling to European customers. Since Europeans will now be able to shop and compare prices at the click of a mouse they will also be more favourably inclined towards e-commerce.

In any single European country there is not usually much competition for a given product, because purchasing habits have always been local (in one's own country). Now that Europeans will be able to shop internationally via the Internet they will become aware of other choices and prices for the same product that were not previously known. Competition will heat up for the buyer's euro, and this should put a downward pressure on prices.

However, recent research has also shown that the Internet is not creating a state of perfect competition with decreasing prices as a result. In fact, in some cases, online prices are higher than those of conventional retail outlets. Research has also shown that online consumers are not as price-sensitive as had previously been thought. Consumers become less price-sensitive and more loyal as the level of quality information on a site increases (Kung and Monroe, 2002).

15.6   Terms of sale and delivery

The price quotation describes a specific product, states the price for the product and a specified delivery location, sets the time of shipment and specifies payment terms. The responsibilities of the buyer and the seller should be spelled out as they relate to what is and what is not included in the price quotation and when ownership of goods passes from seller to buyer. Incoterms are the internationally accepted standard definitions for terms of sale set by the International Chamber of Commerce. They have been fully revised for the new millennium in line with developments in commercial practice. Published in September 1999, *Incoterms 2000* may be used to define the responsibilities of buyer and seller in contracts effective from 1 January 2000.

The 13 terms contained in *Incoterms 2000* are:

EXW   *Ex-works* (. . . named place)
FCA   *Free carrier* (. . . named place)
FAS   *Free alongside ship* (. . . named port of shipment)
FOB   *Free on board* (. . . named port of shipment)
CFR   *Cost and freight* (. . . named port of destination)
CIF   *Cost, insurance and freight* (. . . named port of destination)
CPT   *Carriage paid to* (. . . named place of destination)
CIP   *Carriage and insurance paid to* (. . . named place of destination)
DAF   *Delivered at frontier* (. . . named place)
DES   *Delivered ex-ship* (. . . named port of destination)
DEQ   *Delivered ex-quay* (. . . named port of destination)
DDU   *Delivered duty unpaid* (. . . named place of destination)
DDP   *Delivered duty paid* (. . . named place of destination)

Table 15.5 describes the point of delivery and risk shift for some terms of sale.

The following is a description of some of the most popular terms of sale:

- *Ex-works (EXW).* The term 'Ex' means that the price quoted by the seller applies at a specified point of origin, usually the factory, warehouse, mine or plantation, and the buyer is responsible for all charges from this point. This term represents the minimum obligation for the exporter.
- *Free alongside ship (FAS).* Under this term the seller must provide for delivery of the goods free alongside, but not on board, the transportation carrier (usually an ocean vessel) at the point of shipment and export. This term differs from that of FOB, since the time and cost of loading are not included in the FAS term. The buyer has to pay for loading the goods onto the ship.

Table 15.5	Point of delivery and where risk shifts from seller to buyer						
	EXW	**FAS**	**FOB**	**CFR**	**CIF**	**DEQ**	**DDP**
Supplier's factory/warehouse	×						
Dock at port of shipment (export dock)		×					
Port of shipment (on board vessel)			×	×	×		
Port of destination (import dock)					×*	×	
Buyer's warehouse (destination)							×
Main transit risk on	Buyer	Buyer	Buyer	Buyer	Seller	Seller	Seller

* The seller transfers the risk to its insurance company.
Source: adapted from Onkvisit and Shaw (1993, p. 799). Courtesy of Sak Onkvisit.

- *Free on board (FOB)*. The exporter's price quote includes coverage of all charges up to the point when goods have been loaded on to the designated transport vehicle. The designated loading point may be a named inland shipping point, but is usually the port of export. The buyer assumes responsibility for the goods the moment they pass over the ship's rail.
- *Cost and freight (CFR)*. The seller's liability ends when the goods are loaded on board a carrier or are in the custody of the carrier at the export dock. The seller pays all the transport charges (excluding insurance, which is the customer's obligation) required to deliver goods by sea to a named destination.
- *Cost, insurance and freight (CIF)*. This trade term is identical with CFR except that the seller must also provide the necessary insurance. The seller's obligations still end at the same stage (i.e. when goods are loaded or aboard), but the seller's insurance company assumes responsibility once the goods are loaded.
- *Delivered ex-quay (DEQ)*. Ex-quay means from the import dock. The term goes one step beyond CIF and requires the seller to be responsible for the cost of the goods and all other costs necessary to place the goods on the dock at the named overseas port, with the appropriate import duty paid.
- *Delivered duty paid (DDP)*. The export price quote includes the costs of delivery to the importer's premises. The exporter is thus responsible for paying any import duties and costs of unloading and inland transport in the importing country, as well as all costs involved in insuring and shipping the goods to that country. These terms imply maximum exporter obligations. The seller also assumes all the risks involved in delivering to the buyer. DDP used to be known as 'Franco domicile' pricing.

Export price quotations are important because they spell out the legal and cost responsibilities of the buyer and seller. Sellers favour a quote that gives them the least liability and responsibility, such as ex-works, which means the exporter's liability finishes when the goods are loaded on to the buyer's carrier at the seller's factory. Buyers, on the other hand, would prefer either DDP, where responsibility is borne by the supplier all the way to the customer's warehouse, or CIF port of discharge, which means that the buyer's responsibility begins only when the goods are in its own country.

Generally, the more market-oriented pricing policies are based on CIF, which indicates a strong commitment to the market. By pricing ex-works an exporter is not taking any steps to build a relationship with the market and so may be indicating only short-term commitment.

15.7 Terms of payment

The exporter will consider the following factors in negotiating terms of payment for goods to be shipped:

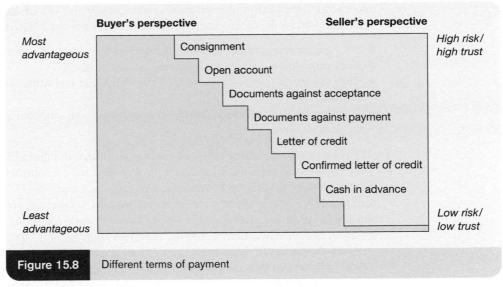

Figure 15.8   Different terms of payment

Source: Chase Manhattan Bank (1984, p. 5).

- practices in the industry
- terms offered by competitors
- relative strength of the buyer and the seller.

If the exporter is well established in the market with a unique product and accompanying service, price and terms of trade can be set to fit the exporter's desires. If, on the other hand, the exporter is breaking into a new market or if competitive pressures call for action, pricing and selling terms should be used as major competitive tools.

The basic methods of payment for exports vary in terms of their attractiveness to the buyer and the seller, from cash in advance to open account or consignment selling. Neither of the extremes will be feasible for longer-term relationships, but they do have their uses in certain situations. The most common payment methods are presented in Figure 15.8.

The most favourable term to the exporter is cash in advance because it relieves the exporter of all risk and allows for immediate use of the money. On the other hand, the most advantageous option seen from the buyer's perspective would be consignment or open account.

The most common arrangements, in decreasing order of attractiveness to the exporter, will now be described.

Cash in advance

The exporter receives payment before shipment of the goods. This minimizes the exporter's risk and financial costs, since there is no collection risk and no interest cost on receivables. However, importers will rarely agree to these terms, since it ties up their capital and the goods may not be received. Consequently such terms are not widely used. They are most likely either when the exporter lacks confidence in the importer's ability to pay (often the case in initial export transactions) or where economic and political instability in the importing country may result in foreign exchange not being made available for importers.

Letter of credit

Worldwide letters of credit are very important and very common. A letter of credit is an instrument whereby a bank agrees to pay a specified amount of money on presentation of documents stipulated in the letter of credit, usually the bill of lading, an invoice and a description of the goods. In general, letters of credit have the following characteristics:

- They are an arrangement by banks for settling international commercial transactions.
- They provide a form of security for the parties involved.
- They ensure payment, provided that the terms and conditions of the credit have been fulfilled.
- Payment by such means is based on documents only and not on the merchandise or services involved.

The process for handling letters of credit is illustrated in Figure 15.9.

In the process the customer agrees to payment by a confirmed letter of credit. The customer begins the process by sending an enquiry for the goods (1). The price and terms are confirmed by a pro forma invoice (2) by the supplier, so that the customer knows for what amount (3) to instruct its bank (the issuing bank) to open a letter of credit (4). The letter of credit is confirmed by a bank (5) in the supplier's country.

When the goods are shipped (6) the shipping documents are submitted by the supplier to its bank (7), so that shipment is confirmed by their presentation (8) together with the letter of credit and all other stipulated documents and certificates for payment (9). The money is automatically transmitted from the customer's account via the issuing bank. The customer may collect the goods (10) only when all the documents have been delivered to it by its bank – the issuing bank (adapted from Phillips *et al.*, 1994, p. 453).

The letter of credit (L/C) has three forms:

1. *Revocable L/C.* Now a rare form, this gives the buyer maximum flexibility as it can be cancelled without notice to the seller up to the moment of payment by the bank.
2. *Irrevocable but unconfirmed L/C.* This is as good as the credit status of the establishing bank and the willingness of the buyer's country to allow the required use of foreign exchange. An unconfirmed L/C should not necessarily be viewed with suspicion. The reason for the lack of confirmation may be that the customer has been unwilling to pay the additional fee for confirmation.
3. *Confirmed irrevocable L/C.* This means that a bank in the seller's country has added its own undertaking to that of the issuing bank, confirming that the necessary sum of money is available for payment, awaiting only the presentation of shipping documents. While it guarantees the seller its money it is much more costly to the buyer. Generally the buyer pays a fixed fee plus a percentage of the value, but where the letter of credit is confirmed the confirming bank will also charge a fee. On the other hand, the confirmation of an irrevocable letter of credit by a bank gives the shipper the most satisfactory assurance that payment will be made for the shipment. It also means that the exporter does not have to seek payment under any conditions from the issuing bank – invariably located in some foreign country – but has a direct claim on the confirming bank in the exporter's home country. Thus the exporter need not be concerned about the ability or willingness of the foreign bank to pay.

Documents against payment and acceptance

In the following two 'documents against' situations the seller ships the goods and the shipping documents, and the draft (bill of exchange) demanding payment is presented to the importer through banks acting as the seller's agent. There are two principal types of bill of exchange: sight draft (documents against payment) and time draft (documents against acceptance).

1. *Documents against payment.* Here the buyer must make payment for the face value of the draft before receiving the documents conveying title to the merchandise. This occurs when the buyer first sees the draft (*sight draft*).

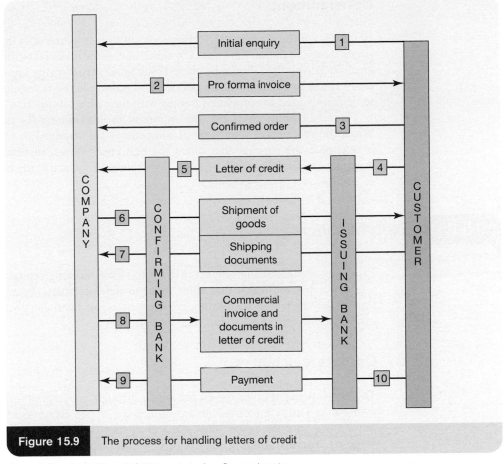

Figure 15.9	The process for handling letters of credit

Source: Phillips *et al.* (1994, p. 454). With permission from Cengage Learning.

2. *Documents against acceptance.* When a draft is drawn 'documents against acceptance' credit is extended to the buyer on the basis of the buyer's acceptance of the draft calling for payment within a specified time and usually at a specified place. Acceptance means that the buyer formally agrees to pay the amount specified by the draft on the due date. The specified time may be expressed as a certain number of days after sight (*time draft*). A time draft offers less security for the seller than a sight draft, because the sight draft demands payment prior to the release of shipping documents. The time draft, on the other hand, allows the buyer a delay of 30, 60 or 90 days in payment.

Open account

The exporter ships the goods without documents calling for payment, other than the invoice. The buyer can pick up the goods without having to make payment first. The advantage of the open account is its simplicity and the assistance it gives to the buyer, which does not have to pay credit charges to banks. The seller in return expects that the invoice will be paid at the agreed time. A major weakness of the method is that there are no safeguards for payment. Exporters should sell on open account only to importers they know very well or that have excellent credit ratings, and to markets with no foreign exchange problems. Open account sales are less complex and expensive than drafts, since there are no documentation requirements or bank charges.

Consignment

Here the exporter retains title of the goods until the importer sells them. Exporters own the goods longer in this method than any other, and so the financial burden and risks are at their greatest. The method should be offered only to very trustworthy importers with an excellent credit rating in countries where political and economic risk is very low. Consignments tend to be mainly used by companies trading with their own subsidiaries.

The credit terms given are also important in determining the final price to the buyer. When the products of international competitors are perceived to be similar the purchaser may choose the supplier that offers the best credit terms, in order to achieve a greater discount. In effect the supplier is offering a source of finance to the buyer.

15.8 Export financing

Exporters need financing support in order to obtain working capital and because importers will often demand terms that allow them to defer payment. Principal sources of export finance include commercial banks, government export financing programmes, export credit insurance, factoring houses and counter-trade.

Commercial banks

The simplest way of financing export sales is through an overdraft facility with the exporter's own bank. This is a convenient way to finance all the elements of the contract, such as purchasing, manufacturing, shipping and credit. The bank is generally more favourably disposed towards granting an overdraft if the exporter has obtained an export credit insurance policy.

Export credit insurance

Export credit insurance is available to most exporters through governmental export credit agencies or through private insurers. Such insurances usually cover the following:

- *political risks* and non-convertibility of currency;
- *commercial risks* associated with non-payment by buyers.

Exporters may be able to use credit insurance to enable them to grant more liberal credit terms or to encourage their banks to grant them financing against their export receivables. The costs of such insurance are often quite low in many markets, ranging from 1–2 per cent of the value of the transaction. Specialized insurance brokers handle such insurance.

Factoring

Factoring means selling export debts for immediate cash. In this way the exporter shifts the problems of collecting payment for completed orders over to organizations or factors that specialize in export credit management and finance.

Ideally the exporter should go to the factor before any contract is signed or shipment made, and secure its willingness to buy the receivable. The factor will check out the credit rating and so forth of the prospective buyer(s), typically by having a correspondent in the importer's country do the necessary checking. Thus the factor acts as a credit approval agency as well as a facilitator and guarantor of payment.

The factor does not usually purchase export debts on terms exceeding 120 days. Factors normally charge a service fee of between 0.75 and 2.5 per cent of the sales value, depending on the workload and the risk carried by the factor.

Forfeiting

This is a finance method developed in Switzerland in the 1950s. It is an arrangement whereby exporters of capital goods can obtain medium-term finance (between one and seven years). The system can briefly be explained as follows.

An exporter of capital goods has a buyer that wishes to have medium-term credit to finance the purchase. The buyer pays some of the cost at once and pays the balance in regular instalments for, say, the next five years. The principal benefit is that there is immediate cash for the exporter and, along with the first cash payment by the buyer, forfeiting can finance up to 100 per cent of the contract value.

Bonding

In some countries (e.g. in the Middle East) contracts are cash or short term. Whereas this is an ideal situation for suppliers, it means that the buyer loses some of its leverage over the supplier as it cannot withhold payment. In this situation a bond or guarantee is a written instrument issued to an overseas buyer by an acceptable third party, either a bank or an insurance company. It guarantees compliance of its obligations by an exporter or contractor, or the overseas buyer will be indemnified for a stated amount against the failure of the exporter/contractor to fulfil its obligations under the contract.

Leasing

Exporters of capital equipment may use leasing in one of two ways:

1. to arrange cross-border leases directly from a bank or leasing company to the foreign buyer;
2. to obtain local leasing facilities either through overseas branches or subdivisions of international banks or through international leasing associations.

With leasing the exporter receives prompt payment for goods directly from the leasing company. A leasing facility is best set up at the earliest opportunity, preferably when the exporter receives the order.

Counter-trade

Counter-trade is a generic term used to describe a variety of trade agreements in which a seller provides a buyer with products (commodities, goods, services, technology) and agrees to a reciprocal purchasing obligation with the buyer in terms of an agreed percentage (full or partial) of the original sales value.

Barter

This is a straightforward exchange of goods for goods without any money transfer. Bilateral barter, where only two parties are involved, is relatively uncommon. The bartering process can, however, be facilitated when a third (trilateral barter) or even more countries (multilateral barter) become involved in a trading chain.

Compensation deal

This involves the export of goods in one direction. The 'payment' of the goods is split into two parts:

1. Part payment in cash by the importer.
2. For the rest of the 'payment' the original exporter makes an obligation to purchase some of the buyer's goods. These products can be used in the exporter's internal production or they may be sold on in the wider market.

Buy-back agreement

The sale of machinery, equipment or a turnkey plant to the buyer's production is financed at least in part by the exporter's purchase of some of the resultant output. Whereas barter and compensation deals are short-term arrangements, buy-back agreements are long-term agreements. The contract may last for a considerable period of time, such as five to ten years. The two-way transactions are clearly linked, but are kept financially separate.

Counter-trade has arisen because of shortages of both foreign exchange and international lines of credit. Some have estimated that the size of counter-trade is as high as 10–15 per cent of world trade.

15.9 Summary

The major issues covered in this chapter include the determinants of price, pricing strategy, how foreign prices are related to domestic prices, price escalation, the elements of price quotation and transfer pricing.

Several factors must be taken into consideration in setting price, including cost, competitors' prices, product image, market share/volume, stage in product life cycle and number of products involved. The optimum mix of these ingredients varies by product, market and corporate objectives. Price-setting in the international context is further complicated by such factors as foreign exchange rates, different competitive situations in each export market, different labour costs and different inflation rates in various countries. Local and regional regulations and laws in setting prices have also to be considered.

The international marketer must quote a meaningful price by using proper international trade terms. When there is doubt about how to prepare a quotation freight forwarders may be consulted (see section 16.5). These specialists can provide valuable information with regard to documentation (e.g. invoice, bill of lading) and the costs relevant to the movement of goods. Financial documents, such as letters of credit, require a bank's assistance. International banks have international departments that can facilitate payment and advise clients regarding pitfalls in preparing and accepting documents.

Ann Heisenfelt/AP/EMPICS.

The Harley-Davidson (HD) Corporation has been dominating the motorcycle industry for many decades. Today, it continues to have a strong presence in the world market for heavyweight cruisers. In the financial year 2005, the net revenues of HD were US$5.3 billion. In 2005 HD had 1,300 dealers selling 329,000 HD motorcycles worldwide and employs about 9,000 people worldwide. In the heavyweight section (651 + cc) HD is a clear market leader in North America with a 48 per cent market share. Their market share in Europe is 9 per cent. The mission statement of the company is to fulfil dreams through the experience of motorcycling, by providing to the motorcyclists and the general public an expanding line of motorcycles, and branded products and services, in selected market segments. HD offers a complete range of motorcycles, parts, accessories, apparel and general merchandise. Strategic licensing of the HD brand helps create future generations of Harley-Davidson enthusiasts.

HD celebrated its 100-year anniversary in 2003. Over the previous century the company managed to create a strong brand image and a loyal customer base within the marketplace. Much of the value of a Harley resides in its tradition – the look, sound and heritage that has made it an all-American symbol. The bikes represent something very basic – a desire for freedom, adventure and individualism.

HD maintains a close relationship with its customers through a variety of programmes (Harley Owners' Group), product offerings and events such as the Daytona bike week, motor shows and rallies, etc. However, the company is facing rigorous competition from Japanese manufacturers, specifically Honda and Yamaha. Harley-Davidson's strength is its brand image within the marketplace, but its weakness is related to production capacity and unfulfilled demand for its products. HD tries to continue to strengthen its positioning strategy by building on the 'Own an American Icon' slogan.

As its average customer's age rises, and sales go down, Harley-Davidson faces the task of attracting younger customers. Part of retooling its image includes releasing a new motorcycle, the Buell, designed for young professionals.

According to the Motorcycle Industry Council (www.mic.org), an industry trade group based in Irvine, California the women's market accounts for about 11 per cent of the total motorcycling population.

Pricing

The international price competition is getting tougher. Compared to similar models from Honda, Harley-Davidson has still has a 30 per cent price premium; even though Harley bikers still wear T-shirts saying 'I'd rather push a Harley than drive a Honda'.

Today, Harley's overseas sales of motorcycles outside the United States is around 25 per cent of its annual total. Europeans like cruiser bikes, but not so much Harley prices. In 2005, the European market share of HD in the heavyweight segment (over 650 cc) was around 9 per cent. The 2004 market leaders in Europe were Honda, Yamaha, Suzuki and BMW, each with around 15 per cent market share.

On 15 October 2009, Harley-Davidson Inc. announced the end of production of Buell Motorcycles to focus more on the Harley-Davidson brand.

Sources: www.harley-davidson.com/; www.mic.org/; www.motorcycle newswire.com/; www.neobike.net/industry.

QUESTIONS

1. Describe HD's general pricing strategy. What does the company's positioning have to do with its pricing strategy?

2. Should Harley alter its price, given strong price pressures from rivals?

3. What should HD do to improve its market share in Europe?

CASE STUDY 15.2

Gillette Co.: is price standardization possible for razor blades?

In the battle to out-blade the competition, Gillette's latest creation, a five-bladed razor called Fusion, leapfrogs the Schick Quattro by one blade and aims to provide an even closer shave to the millions of men who apparently are having trouble with only three or four blades.

Fusion (launched in September 2005) is the first entirely new men's razor system from Gillette since Mach 3, which was launched in 1998. Gillette's previous flagship razor, the Mach 3, has three blades while the Schick Quattro has four, but Gillette president James Kilts insists this latest 'innovation' has nothing to do with the competition: 'The Schick launch has nothing to do with this, it's like comparing a Ferrari to a Volkswagen as far as we're concerned ... There was never a plan to go to four.'

Fusion has one more blade than the Quattro sold by rival Schick, a unit of Energizer Holdings Inc., plus a trimming blade on the back of the pivoting cartridge for shaping facial hair, trimming sideburns and shaving under the nose.

Gillette: courtesy of Procter & Gamble UK.

QUESTIONS

1. Evaluate the price level of Gillette's Fusion.
2. Discuss whether it is possible for Gillette to standardize pricing across borders for its new five-blade, Fusion. Which factors would favour price standardization and which factors would favour price differentiation?

VIDEO CASE STUDY 15.3 Vaseline pricing strategy

download from www.pearsoned.co.uk/hollensen

The Vaseline® journey started in 1859, when a 22-year-old chemist from Brooklyn, New York named Robert A. Chesebrough, went to Pennsylvania to investigate an oil well. The oil industry was in its infancy, and Chesebrough, like many, was hoping to profit from it.

While Chesebrough was there, he discovered a gooey substance known as 'rod wax' that was causing the oil rig workers problems, as it stuck to the drilling rigs, causing them to seize up.

Chesebrough noticed that oil workers would smear their skin with the residue from their drills, as it appeared to aid the healing of cuts and burns. His curiosity led him to take some rod wax home with him and start experimenting with it. After months of testing, he managed to successfully extract usable petroleum jelly.

By 1870, Chesebrough was marketing his petroleum jelly product by the name of Vaseline®, and within ten years, the product's increased exposure and popularity meant that almost every household in America had a jar of Vaseline®.

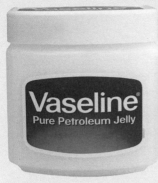

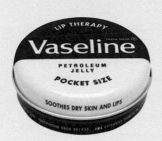

Courtesy of Unilever Danmark A/S

Chesebrough expanded his business to Canada, the United Kingdom and British colonies all over the world. New mothers used it as an absorbent shield for nappy rash. Professionals working in extreme cold weather used it to relieve their dry chapped skin. Even Commander Robert Peary took Vaseline with him when he became (as is generally accepted) the first man to reach the North Pole, because it wouldn't freeze.

By the late 1880s, Chesebrough was selling Vaseline petroleum jelly nationwide at the rate of one jar per minute and most medical professionals recognized it as the standard remedy for skin complaints.

By 1911, the company began opening operation plants and factories in Europe, Canada and Africa in order to facilitate the manufacture and distribution of the product. In 1955, Chesebrough Manufacturing Co. merged with Pond's Extract Company to form Chesebrough-Ponds, Inc. Like Chesebrough, Pond's had a passion and curiosity about skin.

During the 1960s, the company continued to expand to locales such as Argentina, Australia, Brazil, and India.

Vaseline's 100th Anniversary was in 1970, and to mark the occasion a major new product, Vaseline Intensive Care Lotion, was launched with huge success. The brand was later extended to include hand and nail moisturisers and deodorants for men and women.

In 1987, Unilever purchased Chesebrough-Pond's, acquiring successful, internationally known brands such as Pond's and Vaseline®.

Today, Vaseline products are available in over 60 countries around the world. Its rich heritage, healing qualities and efficacy have been passed on from generation to generation for over 130 years.

One way of expanding revenues is through established product categories in which a firm currently does not have a market presence. In 1985 Chesebrough-Pond's entered the market for lip care, a product category in which it did not have a market presence, by launching Vaseline brand petroleum jelly packaged in a 0.35-ounce plastic tube, and directly applicable on the lip, under the brand name Vaseline Lip Therapy. Applying Vaseline petroleum jelly on dry or cracked lips, particularly during the winter season, is one of the many uses for which the product has long been promoted.

Table 1	Vaseline pricing: pure petroleum jelly versus Lip Therapy	
Vaseline product	**List price in United States (US$)**	**Price per ounce of jelly (US$)**
Vaseline Pure Petroleum Jelly (13 ounces in a plastic jar)	2.99	0.23 per ounce of jelly
Vaseline Lip Therapy (0.35-ounce in a tube)	1.99	5.69 per ounce of jelly

Source: based on various sources.

Besides facilitating entry into a new product-market, it is conceivable that the Vaseline profit margins associated with the incremental innovation are considerably higher. While Vaseline brand petroleum jelly in a 13-ounce plastic jar retails for about $2.99 ($0.23 per ounce of jelly), the same product packaged in a 0.35 ounce tube retails for US$1.99 (US$5.69 per ounce of jelly).

Questions

Watch the following YouTube videos:

http://www.youtube.com/watch?v=yptILH36Mkw&feature=related (old commercial – all-purpose Vaseline)
http://www.youtube.com/watch?v=_V9hDR8XDDw&feature=related (Corporate Vaseline commercial)
http://www.youtube.com/watch?v=B4bqv1eVHXs&feature=related (Vaseline Intensive Care Lotion – the Phillippines)

1. If you were a representative of the Vaseline (Unilever) management, how would you justify the price difference? What extra customer value do you create by selling the jelly as Lip Therapy in small tubes?

2. How would you price the Vaseline Intensive care lotion in the Phillippines compared to UK?

Sources: adapted from: Varadarajan (2009); History of Vaseline, www.vaseline.co.uk, with the kind permission of Unilever.

For further exercises and cases, see this book's website at **www.pearsoned.co.uk/hollensen**

Questions for discussion

1. What are the major causes of international price escalation? Suggest possible courses of action to deal with this problem.

2. Explain how exchange rates and inflation affect the way you price your product.

3. In order to protect themselves, how should marketers price their product in a country with high inflation?

4. International buyers and sellers of technology frequently disagree on the appropriate price for knowledge. Why?

5. What methods can be used to compute a transfer price (for transactions between affiliated companies)?

6. What relevance has the international product life cycle theory for pricing strategy in international firms?

7. Why is it often difficult to compute fair arm's-length transfer prices?

8. Explain these terms of sale: EXW, FAS, FOB, CFR, CIF, DEQ and DDP. Which factors will determine the terms of sale?

9. Explain these types of letter of credit: revocable/irrevocable, confirmed/unconfirmed. Under what sets of circumstances would exporters use the following methods of payment:
   (a) revocable letter of credit;
   (b) confirmed letter of credit;
   (c) confirmed irrevocable letter of credit;
   (d) time draft (i.e. bill of exchange)?

10. Name some of the financing sources for exporters.

11. How does inflation affect a country's currency value? Is it a good idea to borrow or obtain finance in a country with high inflation?

12. How and why are export credit financing terms and conditions relevant to international pricing?

13. What is counter-trade? Why should firms be willing to consider counter-trade arrangements in their global marketing efforts?

References

Auguste, B.G., Harmon, E.P. and Pandit, V. (2006) 'The right service strategies for product companies', *McKinsey Quarterly*, 1, March, pp. 10–15.

Chase Manhattan Bank (1984) *Dynamics of Trade Finance.* New York.

Czepiel, J.A. (1992) *Competitive Marketing Strategy.* Prentice-Hall, Englewood Cliffs, NJ.

Diller, H. and Bukhari, I. (1994) 'Pricing conditions in the European Common Market', *European Management Journal*, 12(2), pp. 163–170.

Eiteman, D.K. and Stonehill, A.I. (1986) *Multinational Business Finance*, 4th edn. Addison-Wesley, Reading, MA.

Fraedrich, J.P. and Bateman, C.R. (1996) 'Transfer pricing by multinational marketers: risky business', *Business Horizons*, 39(1), pp. 17–22.

Garda, R.A. (1995) 'Tactical pricing', in Paliwoda, S.J. and Ryans, J.K. (eds), *International Marketing Reader.* Routledge, London, pp. 257–265.

Kung, M. and Monroe, K.B. (2002) 'Pricing on the Internet', *Journal of Product & Brand Management*, 11(5), pp. 274–287.

Nagle, T.T. (1987) *The Strategies and Tactics of Pricing.* Prentice-Hall, Englewood Cliffs, NJ.

Narayandas, D., Quelch, J. and Swartz, G. (2000) 'Prepare your company for global pricing', *Sloan Management Review*, Fall, pp. 61–70.

Onkvisit, S. and Shaw, J.J. (1993) *International Marketing Analysis and Strategy*, 2nd edn. Macmillan, London.

Phillips, C., Doole, I. and Lowe, R. (1994) *International Marketing Strategy: Analysis, Development and Implementation.* Routledge, London.

Simon, H. and Kucher, E. (1993) 'The European pricing bomb – and how to cope with it', *Marketing and Research Today*, February, pp. 25–36.

Solberg, C.A. (1997) 'A framework for analysis of strategy development in globalizing markets', *Journal of International Marketing*, 5(1), pp. 9–30.

Solberg, C.A., Stöttinger, B. and Yaprak, A. (2006) 'A taxonomy of the pricing practices of exporting firms: evidence from Austria, Norway and the United States', *Journal of International Marketing*, 14(1), pp. 23–48.

Theodosiou, M. and Katsikeas, C.S. (2001) 'Factors influencing the degree of international pricing strategy standardization of multinational corporations', *Journal of International Marketing*, 9(3), pp. 1–18.

Varadarajan, R. (2009) 'Fortune at the bottom of the innovation pyramid: the strategic logic of incremental innovations', *Business Horizons*, 52, pp. 21–29.

Weigand, R.E. (1991) 'Buy in–follow on strategies for profit', *Sloan Management Review*, Spring, pp. 29–38.

CHAPTER 16
Distribution decisions

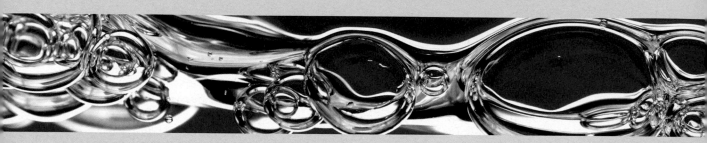

Learning objectives

After studying this chapter you should be able to:

- Explore the determinants of channel decisions.
- Discuss the key points in putting together and managing global marketing channels.
- Discuss the factors influencing channel width (intensive, selective or exclusive coverage).
- Explain what is meant by integration of the marketing channel.
- Describe the most common export documents.
- Define and explain the main modes of transportation.
- Explain how the internationalization of retailing affects the manufacturer.
- Define grey markets and explain how to deal with them.

16.1   Introduction

Access to international markets is a key decision area facing firms into the 2000s. In Part III we considered the firm's choice of an appropriate market entry mode that could assure the entry of a firm's products and services into a foreign market. After the firm has chosen a strategy to get its products into foreign markets the next challenge (and the topic of this chapter: see Figure 16.1) is the distribution of the products within those foreign markets. The first part of this chapter concerns the structure and management of foreign distribution. The second part is concerned with the management of international logistics.

Distribution channels typically account for 15–40 per cent of the retail price of goods and services in an industry.

Over the next few years the challenges and opportunities for channel management will multiply, as technological developments accelerate channel evolution. Data networks are increasingly enabling end-users to bypass traditional channels and deal directly with manufacturers and service providers.

The following presents a systematic approach to the major decisions in international distribution. The main channel decisions and their determinants are illustrated in Figure 16.1. Distribution channels are the links between producers and final customers. In general terms, an international marketer distributes either directly or indirectly. As we saw in Chapter 10, direct distribution amounts to dealing with a foreign firm, while the indirect method means dealing with another home country firm that serves as an intermediary. Figure 16.1 shows that the choice of a particular channel link will be strongly influenced by various characteristics of the host markets. We will now consider these in more detail.

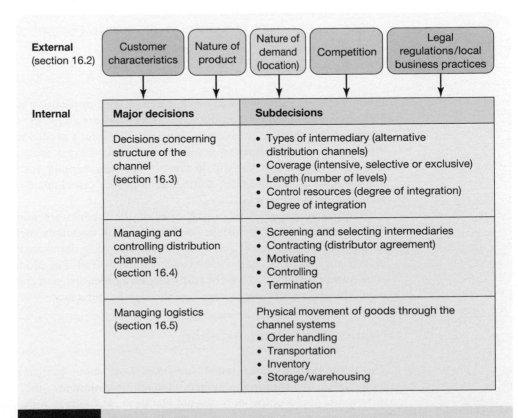

Figure 16.1   Channel decisions

Communication is the fourth and final decision to be made about the global marketing programme. The role of communication in global marketing is similar to that in domestic operations: to communicate with customers so as to provide information that buyers need to make purchasing decisions. Although the communication mix carries information of interest to the customer, in the end it is designed to persuade the customer to buy a product – at the present or in the future.

To communicate with and influence customers, several tools are available. Advertising is usually the most visible component of the promotion mix, but personal selling, exhibitions, sales promotions, publicity (public relations) and direct marketing (including the Internet) are also part of a viable international promotion mix.

One important strategic consideration is whether to standardize worldwide or to adapt the promotion mix to the environment of each country. Another consideration is the availability of media, which varies around the world.

16.2 External determinants of channel decisions

Customer characteristics

The customer, or final consumer, is the keystone in any channel design. Thus the size, geographic distribution, shopping habits, outlet preferences and usage patterns of customer groups must be taken into account when making distribution decisions.

Consumer product channels tend to be longer than industrial product channels because the number of customers is greater, the customers are more geographically dispersed and they buy in smaller quantities. Shopping habits, outlet preferences and usage patterns vary considerably from country to country and are strongly influenced by sociocultural factors.

Nature of product

Product characteristics play a key role in determining distribution strategy. For low-priced, high-turnover convenience products, the requirement is an intensive distribution network. On the other hand it is not necessary or even desirable for a prestigious product to have wide distribution. In this situation a manufacturer can shorten and narrow its distribution channel. Consumers are likely to do some comparison shopping and will actively seek information about all brands under consideration. In such cases limited product exposure is not an impediment to market success.

Transportation and warehousing costs of the product are also critical issues in the distribution and sale of industrial goods such as bulk chemicals, metals and cement. Direct selling, servicing and repair and spare parts warehousing dominate the distribution of such industrial products as computers, machinery and aircraft. The product's durability, ease of adulteration, amount and type of customer service required, unit costs and special handling requirements (such as cold storage) are also significant factors.

Nature of demand/location

The perceptions that the target customers hold about particular products can force modification of distribution channels. Product perceptions are influenced by the customer's income and product experience, the product's end use, its life cycle position and the country's stage of economic development. The geography of a country and the development of its transportation infrastructure can also affect the channel decision.

Competition

The channels used by competing products and close substitutes are important because channel arrangements that seek to serve the same market often compete with one another. Consumers generally expect to find particular products in particular outlets (e.g. speciality stores), or they have become accustomed to buying particular products from particular sources. In addition, local and global competitors may have agreements with the major wholesalers in a foreign country that effectively create barriers and exclude the company from key channels.

Sometimes the alternative is to use a distribution approach totally different from that of the competition and hope to develop a competitive advantage.

Legal regulations/local business practices (Japan)

A country may have specific laws that rule out the use of particular channels or inter-mediaries. For example, until recently all alcoholic beverages in Sweden and Finland had to be distributed through state-owned outlets. Other countries prohibit the use of door-to-door selling. Channel coverage can also be affected by law. In general, exclusive representation may be viewed as a restraint of trade, especially if the product has a dominant market position. EU anti-trust authorities have increased their scrutiny of exclusive sales agreements. The Treaty of Rome prohibits distribution agreements (e.g. grants of exclusivity) that affect trade or restrict competition.

Furthermore, local business practices can interfere with efficiency and productivity and may force a manufacturer to employ a channel of distribution that is longer and wider than desired. Because of Japan's multi-tiered distribution system, which relies on numerous layers of intermediaries, foreign companies have long considered the complex Japanese distribution system as the most effective non-tariff barrier to the Japanese market.

Figure 16.2 shows how the complex Japanese distribution system escalates prices with a factor 5 through both vertical transactions and horizontal transactions (e.g. from one whole-saler to another wholesaler).

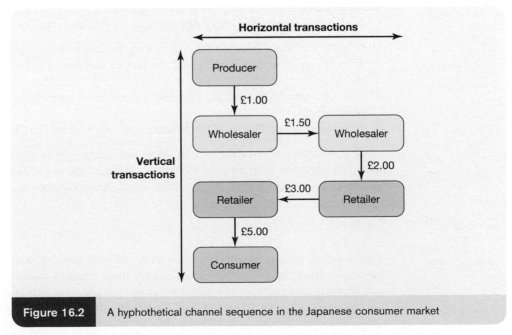

| **Figure 16.2** | A hyphothetical channel sequence in the Japanese consumer market |

Source: Lewison (1996, p. 271).

Keiretsu
A network of businesses that own stakes in one another as a means of mutual security, especially in Japan, and usually including large manufacturers and their suppliers of raw materials and components. The original *keiretsu* were each centred around one bank, which lent money to the *keiretsu*'s member companies and held equity positions in the companies.

While Western firms understand integration as ownership of other suppliers and/or buyers, Japanese firms forge tight collaborations, known as **keiretsu** instead of buying channel members. These alliances are not contractual, but consist of strong links among channel members that originate from personal exchanges and trust to giving long-term supply agreements and technology, sharing vital information and managing resources into developing new products and processes. Accordingly, wholesalers and retailers push the products of one manufacturer, and share information extensively.

These collaborative companies behave as if they were one company in which it becomes very difficult for channel firms to refuse to buy from *keiretsu* members, even when the price is far from being competitive.

The tight-knit *keiretsu* and intimate grouping among affiliated Japanese producers, wholesalers and retailers attempt to form one company by buying high-priced goods and services of group members, rather than acquiring them competitively from non-group members. For example, Matsushita, a leading manufacturer in Japan, formed a *keiretsu* with hundreds of wholesalers and thousands of retailers nationwide. By buying goods and services only from group members, Matsushita *keiretsu* tries to avoid competition among its member firms that helps keep prices high, since they are able to securely control the price and distribution of goods and services from the supplier to the consumer (Rawwas *et al.*, 2008).

Let us now return to the major decisions concerning the structure of the distribution channel (Figure 16.1).

16.3   The structure of the channel

Market coverage

Market coverage
Coverage can relate to geographical areas or number of retail outlets. Three approaches are available: intensive, selective or exclusive coverage.

The amount of **market coverage** that a channel member provides is important. Coverage is a flexible term. It can refer to geographical areas of a country (such as cities and major towns) or the number of retail outlets (as a percentage of all retail outlets). Regardless of the market coverage measure(s) used the company has to create a distribution network (dealers, distributors and retailers) to meet its coverage goals.

As shown in Figure 16.3, three different approaches are available:

1. *Intensive coverage.* This calls for distributing the product through the largest number of different types of intermediary and the largest number of individual intermediaries of each type.
2. *Selective coverage.* This entails choosing a number of intermediaries for each area to be penetrated.
3. *Exclusive coverage.* This involves choosing only one intermediary in a market.

Channel coverage (width) can be identified along a continuum ranging from wide channels (intensive distribution) to narrow channels (exclusive distribution). Figure 16.4 illustrates some factors favouring intensive, selective and exclusive distribution.

Channel length
Number of levels (middlemen) in the distribution channel.

Channel length

This is determined by the number of levels or different types of intermediaries. A country's economic development provides the need for more efficient channels, first lengthening as more intermediaries enter the distribution system, but later shortening as the number of channel layers decreases, as a result of efficiencies such as vertical integration (Jaffe and Yi, 2007). Longer channels, those with several intermediaries, tend to be associated with convenience goods and mass distribution. Japan and China have longer channels for convenience

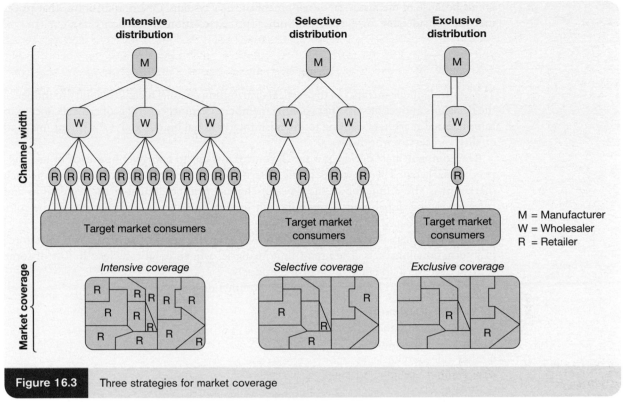

| **Figure 16.3** | Three strategies for market coverage |

Source: Lewison (1996, p. 271).

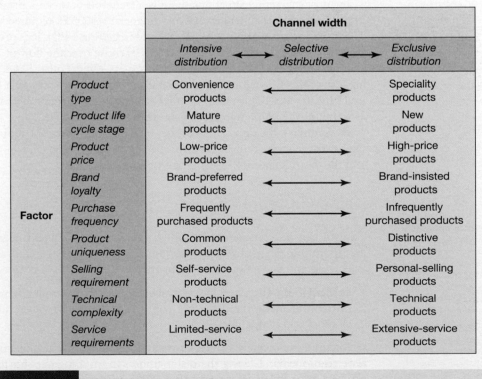

| **Figure 16.4** | Factors influencing channel width |

Source: adapted from Lewison (1996, p. 279).

goods because of the historical development of their systems. One implication is that prices increase considerably for the final consumer (price escalation: see section 15.3).

Control/cost

The 'control' of one member in the vertical distribution channel means its ability to influence the decisions and actions of other channel members. Channel control is of critical concern to international marketers wanting to establish international brands and a consistent image of quality and service worldwide.

The company must decide how much control it wants to have over how each of its products is marketed. The answer is partly determined by the strategic role assigned to each market. It is also a function of the types of channel member available, the regulations and rules governing distribution activity in each foreign market and, to some extent, the roles traditionally assigned to channel members.

Normally a high degree of control is provided by the use of the firm's own sales force in international markets. The use of intermediaries will automatically lead to loss of some control over the marketing of the firm's products.

An intermediary typically performs certain functions:

- carrying of inventory
- demand generation, or selling
- physical distribution
- after-sales service
- extending credit to customers.

In getting its products to end user markets a manufacturer must either assume all of these functions or shift some or all of them to intermediaries. As the old saying goes, 'You can eliminate the intermediary, but not the functions of the intermediary.'

In most marketing situations there is a trade-off between a producer's ability to control important channel functions and the financial resources required to exercise that control. The more intermediaries there are involved in getting a supplier's product to user customers, the less control the supplier can generally exercise over the flow of its product through the channel and the way it is presented to customers. On the other hand, reducing the length and breadth of the distribution channel usually requires that the supplier perform more functions itself. In turn this requires the supplier to allocate more financial resources to activities such as warehousing, shipping, credit, field selling or field service.

In summary, the decision to use an intermediary or to distribute via a company-owned sales force requires a major trade-off between the desire to control global marketing efforts and the desire to minimize resource commitment costs.

Degree of integration

Vertical integration
Seeking control of channel members at different levels of the channel, e.g. the manufacturer's acquisition of the distributor.

Horizontal integration
Seeking control of channel members at the same level of the channel, e.g. the manufacturer's acquisition of the competitor.

Control can also be exercised through integration. Channel integration is the process of incorporating all channel members into one channel system and uniting them under one leadership and one set of goals. There are two different types of integration:

1. **vertical integration**: seeking control of channel members at different levels of the channel;
2. **horizontal integration**: seeking control of channel members at the same level of the channel (i.e. competitors).

Integration is achieved either through acquisitions (ownership) or through tight cooperative relationships. Getting channel members to work together for their own mutual benefit can be a difficult task. However, today cooperative relationships are essential for efficient and effective channel operation.

Figure 16.5 shows an example of vertical integration.

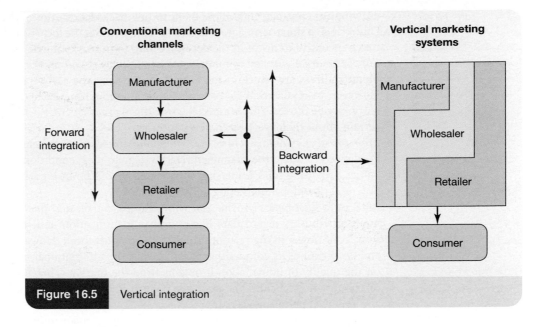

Figure 16.5   Vertical integration

The starting point in Figure 16.5 is the conventional marketing channels, where the channel composition consists of isolated and autonomous participating channel members. Channel coordination is here achieved through arm's-length bargaining. At this point, the vertical integration can take two forms – forward and backward.

- The manufacturer can make forward integration when it seeks control of businesses of the wholesale and retail levels of the channel.
- The retailer can make backward integration, seeking control of businesses at wholesale and manufacturer levels of the channel.
- The wholesaler has two possibilities: both forward and backward integration.

The result of these manoeuvres is the vertical marketing system (Figure 16.5). Here the channel composition consists of integrated participating members, where channel stability is high due to assured member loyalty and long-term commitments.

16.4 Managing and controlling distribution channels

In the beginning of a market entry, partnerships with local distributors make good sense: Distributors know the distinctive characteristics of their market, and most customers prefer to do business with local partners. Arnold (2000) proposes the following guidelines to the international marketer (manufacturer) in order to anticipate and correct potential problems with international distributors:

- *Select distributors – do not let them select you*: typically, manufacturers are approached by potential distributors at international fairs and exhibitions, but the most eager potential distributors are often the wrong people to partner with.
- *Look for distributors capable of developing markets, rather than those with a few obvious contacts*: this means sometimes bypassing the most obvious choice – the distributor who has the right customers and can generate quick sales – in favour of a partner with a greater willingness to make long-term investments and an acceptance of an open relationship.
- *Treat the local distributors as long-term partners, not temporary market-entry vehicles*: many companies actively signal to distributors that their intentions are only for the short term,

drawing up contracts that allow them to buy back distribution rights after a few years. Under such a short-term agreement the problem is that the local distributor does not have much incentive to invest in the necessary long-term marketing development.

- *Support market entry by committing money, managers and proven marketing ideas*: many manufacturers are reluctant to commit resources at the early stages of a market entry. However, to retain strategic control, the international marketer must commit adequate corporate resources. This is especially true during market entry, when companies are least certain about their prospect in new countries.

- *From the start, maintain control over marketing strategy*: an independent distributor should be allowed to adapt the manufacturer's strategy to local conditions. However, only companies providing solid leadership for marketing will be in a position to exploit the full potential of a global marketing network.

- *Make sure distributors provide you with detailed market and financial performance data*: most distributors regard data like customer identification and local price levels as key sources of power in the relationship with the manufacturer. However, the manufacturer's ability to exploit its competitive advantages in the international market depends heavily on the quality of information it obtains from the market. Therefore a contract with the distributor must include the exchange of such information, for example detailed market and financial performance data.

- *Build links among national distributors at the earliest opportunity*: the links may take the form of creating an independent national distributor council or a regional corporate office. The transfer of ideas within local markets can improve performance and result in greater consistency in the execution of international marketing strategies because links to other national distributor networks could be established. This could lead to a cross-national transfer of efficient marketing tools.

Once the basic design of the channel has been determined the international marketer must begin to fill it with the best available candidates, and must secure their cooperation.

Screening and selecting intermediaries

Figure 16.6 shows the most important criteria (qualifications) for selecting foreign distributors, grouped in five categories.

After listing all important criteria (as in Figure 16.6), some of these must then be chosen for a more specific evaluation, where the potential candidates are compared and contrasted against determining criteria.

The example in Table 16.1 uses the first two criteria in each of Figure 16.6's five categories for screening potential channel members, in total ten criteria. The specific criteria to be used depend on the nature of a firm's business and its distribution objectives in given markets. The list of criteria should correspond closely to the marketer's own determinants of success – all the things that are important to beating the competition.

The hypothetical manufacturer (a consumer packaged goods company) used in Table 16.1 considered the distributor's marketing management expertise and financial soundness to be of greatest importance. These indicators will show whether the distributor is making money and is able to perform some of the necessary marketing functions such as extension of credit to customers and risk absorption. Financial reports are not always complete or reliable, or may lend themselves to differences of interpretation, pointing to the need for a third-party opinion. In order to make the weighting and grading in Table 16.1, the manufacturer must have had some personal interviews with the management of each potential distributor. In the example of Table 16.1, Distributor 1 would be selected by the manufacturer.

Alternatively, an industrial goods company may consider the distributor's product compatibility, technical know-how and technical facilities and service support of high importance, and the distributor's infrastructure, client performance and attitude towards its products of low importance. Quite often global marketers find that the most desirable distributors in a given market are already handling competitive products and are therefore unavailable.

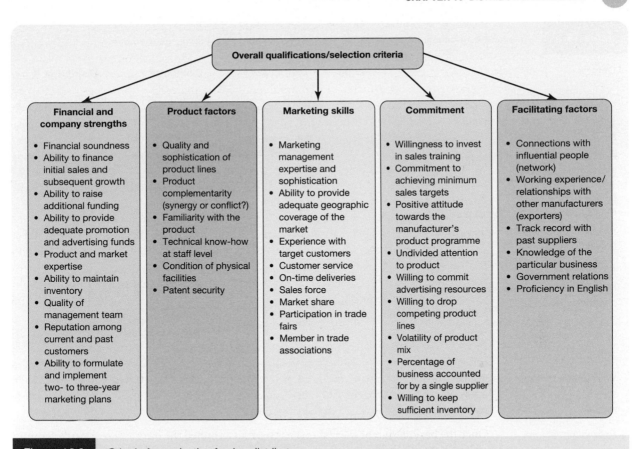

Figure 16.6 Criteria for evaluating foreign distributors

Source: adapted from Cavusgil *et al.* (1995).

A high-tech consumer goods company, on the other hand, may favour financial soundness, marketing management expertise, reputation, technical know-how, technical facilities, service support and government relations. In some countries religious or ethnic differences might make an agent suitable for one part of the market coverage but unsuitable for another. This can result in more channel members being required in order to give adequate market coverage.

Contracting (distributor agreements)

When the international marketer has found a suitable intermediary a foreign sales agreement is drawn up. Before final contractual arrangements are made it is wise to make personal visits to the prospective channel member. The agreement itself can be relatively simple but, given the numerous differences in the market environments, certain elements are essential. These are:

● Names and addresses of both parties.
● Date when the agreement goes into effect.
● Duration of the agreement.
● Provisions for extending or terminating the agreement.
● Description of sales territory.
● Establishment of discount and/or commission schedules and determination of when and how paid.
● Provisions for revising the commission or discount schedules.
● Establishment of a policy governing resale prices.

Table 16.1	An example of distributor evaluation by the use of selection criteria from Figure 16.6						
Criteria (no ranking implied)	**Weight**	**Distributor 1**		**Distributor 2**		**Distributor 3**	
		Rating	Score	Rating	Score	Rating	Score
Financial and company strengths:							
Financial soundness	4	5	20	4	16	3	12
Ability to finance initial sales and subsequent growth	3	4	12	4	12	3	9
Product factors:							
Quality and sophistication of product lines	3	5	15	4	12	3	9
Product complementarity (synergy or conflict?)	3	3	9	4	12	2	6
Marketing skills:							
Marketing management expertise and sophistication	5	4	20	3	15	2	10
Ability to provide adequate geographic coverage of the market	4	5	20	4	16	3	12
Commitment:							
Willingness to invest in sales training	4	3	12	3	12	3	12
Commitment to achieving minimum sales targets	3	4	12	3	9	3	9
Facilitating factors:							
Connections with influential people (network)	3	5	15	4	12	4	12
Working experience/relationships with other manufacturers (exporters)	2	4	8	3	6	3	6
Score			**143**		**122**		**97**

Scales:

Rating	*Weighting*
5 Outstanding	5 Critical success factor
4 Above average	4 Prerequisite success factor
3 Average	3 Important success factor
2 Below average	2 Of some importance
1 Unsatisfactory	1 Standard

- Maintenance of appropriate service facilities.
- Restrictions to prohibit the manufacture and sale of similar and competitive products.
- Designation of responsibility for patent and trade mark negotiations and/or pricing.
- The assignability or non-assignability of the agreement and any limiting factors.
- Designation of the country and state (if applicable) of contract jurisdiction in the case of dispute.

Source: from *International Marketing Management 5th Edition* by Jain. 1996. Reprinted with permission of Professor Subhash C. Jain.

The long-term commitments involved in distribution channels can become particularly difficult if the contract between the company and the channel member is not carefully drafted. It is normal to prescribe a time limit and a minimum sales level to be achieved, in addition to the particular responsibilities of each party. If this is not carried out satisfactorily the company may be stuck with a weak performer that either cannot be removed or is very costly to buy out from the contract.

Contract duration is important, especially when an agreement is signed with a new distributor. In general, distribution agreements should be for a specified, relatively short period (one or two years). The initial contract with a new distributor should stipulate a trial period of either three or six months, possibly with minimum purchase requirements. Duration is also dependent on the local laws and their stipulations on distributor agreements.

Geographic boundaries for the distributor should be determined with care, especially by smaller firms. Future expansion of the product market might be complicated if a distributor claims rights to certain territories. The marketer should retain the right to distribute products independently, reserving the right to certain customers.

The *payment section* of the contract should stipulate the methods of payment as well as how the distributor or agent is to draw compensation. Distributors derive compensation from various discounts, such as the functional discount, whereas agents earn a specific commission percentage of net sales (typically 10–20 per cent). Given the volatility of currency markets the agreement should also state the currency to be used.

Product and conditions of sale need to be agreed on. The products or product lines included should be stipulated, as well as the functions and responsibilities of the intermediary in terms of carrying the goods in inventory, providing service in conjunction with them, and promoting them. Conditions of sale determine which party is to be responsible for some of the expenses (e.g. marketing expenses) involved, which will in turn have an effect on the price to the distributor. These conditions include credit and shipment terms.

Means of communication between the parties must be stipulated in the agreement if a marketer–distributor relationship is to succeed. The marketer should have access to all information concerning the marketing of its products in the distributor's territory, including past records, present situation assessments and marketing research.

Motivating

Geographic and cultural distance make the process of motivating channel members difficult. Motivating is also difficult because intermediaries are not owned by the company. Since intermediaries are independent firms they will seek to achieve their own objectives, which will not always match the objective of the manufacturer. The international marketer may offer both monetary and psychological rewards and intermediaries will be strongly influenced by the earnings potential of the product. If the trade margin is poor and sales are difficult to achieve intermediaries will lose interest in the product and concentrate on products with a more rewarding response to selling efforts, because they make their sales and profits from their own assortment of products and services from different companies.

It is important to keep in regular contact with agents and distributors. A consistent flow of all relevant types of communication will stimulate interest and sales performance. The international marketer may place one person in charge of distributor-related communications and put into effect an exchange of personnel so that both organizations gain further insight into the workings of the other.

Controlling

Control problems are reduced substantially if intermediaries are selected carefully. However, control should be sought through the common development of written performance objectives. These performance objectives might include some of the following: sales turnover per year, market share growth rate, introduction of new products, price charged and marketing communications support. Control should be exercised through periodic personal meetings.

Evaluation of performance has to be done against the changing environment. In some situations economic recession or fierce competition activity prevents the possibility of objectives being met. However, if poor performance is established, the contract between the company and the channel member will have to be reconsidered and perhaps terminated.

Termination

Typical reasons for the termination of a channel relationship are:

- The international marketer has established a sales subsidiary in the country.
- The international marketer is unsatisfied with the performance of the intermediary.

Open communication is always needed to make the transition smooth. For example, the intermediary can be compensated for investments made, and major customers can be visited jointly to assure them that service will be uninterrupted.

Termination conditions are among the most important considerations in the distribution agreement. The causes of termination vary and the penalties for the international marketer may be substantial. It is especially important to find out what local laws say about termination and to check what type of experience other firms have had in the particular country.

In some countries terminating an ineffective intermediary can be time-consuming and expensive. In the European Union one year's average commissions are typical for termination without justification. A notice of termination has to be given three to six months in advance. If the cause for termination is the manufacturer's establishment of a local sales subsidiary, then the international marketer may consider engaging good employees from the intermediary as, for example, managers in the new sales subsidiary. This can prevent a loss of product know-how that has been created at the intermediary's firm. The international marketer could also consider an acquisition of this firm if the intermediary is willing to sell.

16.5　Managing logistics

Logistics
A term used to describe the movement of goods and services between suppliers and end users.

Logistics is the term used to describe the movement of goods and services between supplier(s) and end-users.

Two major phases in the movement of materials are of logistical importance. The first phase is *materials management*, or the timely movement of raw materials, parts and supplies into and through the firm. The second phase is *physical distribution*, or the movement of the firm's finished product to its customers. The basic goal of logistics management is the effective coordination of both phases and their various components to result in maximum cost-effectiveness while maintaining service goals and requirements.

The primary area of concern in this section is the second phase: that is, order handling, transportation, inventory and storage/warehousing.

Order handling

The general procedure for order handling, shipment and payment is shown in Figure 16.7:

1. The sale:
   (a) Importer makes enquiry of potential supplier.
   (b) Exporter sends catalogues and price list.
   (c) Importer requests pro forma invoice (price quote).
   (d) Exporter sends pro forma invoice.
   (e) Importer sends purchase order.
   (f) Exporter receives purchase order.
2. Importer arranges financing through its bank (issuing bank).
3. Importer's bank sends letter of credit (most frequently used form of payment) to exporters bank (advising bank).
4. Exporter's bank notifies exporter that letter of credit is received.
5. Exporter produces or acquires goods.

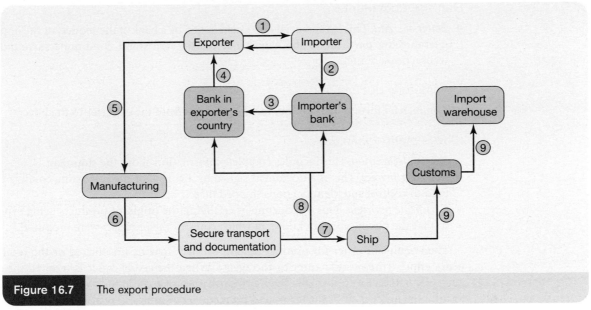

Figure 16.7	The export procedure

Source: Albaum *et al.* (1994, p. 419).

6. Exporter arranges transportation and documentation (obtained by exporter or through freight forwarding company).
   (a) Space reserved on ship or aircraft.
   (b) Documents acquired or produced, as required:
   (c) exporter's licence;
   (d) shipper's export declaration;
   (e) commercial invoice;
   (f) bills of lading;
   (g) marine insurance certificate;
   (h) consular invoice;
   (i) certificate of origin;
   (j) inspection certificates;
   (k) dock receipts.
7. Exporter ships goods to importer.
8. Exporter presents documents to one of the banks for payment.
9. Importer has goods cleared through customs and delivered to its warehouse.

Source: Albaum *et al.* (1994, p. 419).

Most common export documents

This section is drawn from Albaum *et al.* (1994), p. 440.

Transportation documents

- *Bill of lading.* This is a receipt for the cargo and a contract for transportation between a shipper and a transport carrier. It may also be used as an instrument of ownership.
- *Dock receipt.* This is the document acknowledging receipt of the cargo by an ocean carrier.
- *Insurance certificate.* This is evidence that insurance is provided to cover loss or damage to the cargo while in transit.

Banking documents

- *Letter of credit.* This is a financial document issued by a bank at the request of the importer, guaranteeing payment to the exporter if certain terms and conditions surrounding a transaction are met.

Commercial documents

- *Commercial invoice.* This is a bill for the products from the exporter to the buyer.

Government documents

- *Export declaration.* This includes complete information about the shipment.
- *Consular invoice.* This is a document signed by a consul of the importing country that is used to control and identify goods shipped there.
- *Certificate of origin.* This is a document certifying the origin of products being exported, so that the buying country knows in which country the products were produced.

The enquiry or order for products and/or services may be unsolicited or the result of a firm's efforts (the manufacturer or the agent). When the actual order is received the international marketer will normally send a confirmation of receipt, followed by a commitment to fulfil the order if all of the terms and payment arrangements are acceptable for the international marketer.

A pro forma invoice may be prepared by the exporter to indicate the terms that have been agreed upon (or are proposed). The pro forma invoice normally shows the type and amount of merchandise, unit costs and extensions, expected weights and measures, and often other terms (including payment terms). If accepted by the prospective buyer it may serve as a contract.

Order cycles are shortened by rapid processing of orders, and the role of communications technology (such as electronic data interchange) is critical in reducing the time factor. Few countries have efficient and reliable communication systems; however, possessing an efficient international order-processing system would give a firm a competitive advantage.

Transportation

This deals primarily with the mode of transport, which usually constitutes 10–15 per cent of the retail costs of imported goods. There are four main modes of transport: road, water, air and rail.

Road

Roads are very efficient for short hauls of high-value goods, being very flexible in route and time. Goods can be delivered direct to customers' premises. However, restrictions at border controls can be time-consuming, and long distances and the need for sea crossings reduce the attractiveness of freight transport by road. In some parts of the world, particularly in LDCs, road surfaces are poor.

Water

Water transportation is a key mode for international freight movements because it provides a very low-cost way to transport bulky products such as coal and oil. However, water transport is slow and is subject to difficulties caused by the weather – for example, some ports are iced over for part of the winter. Water transport usually needs to be combined with other modes of transport to achieve door-to-door delivery.

Increasingly nations have begun to recognize the importance of appropriate port structures and are developing such facilities in spite of the heavy investment necessary. If such investments are accompanied by concurrent changes in the overall infrastructure transportation efficiency should, in the long run, more than recoup the original investment.

Air

Air freight is available to and from most countries. There has been a tremendous growth in international air freight over recent decades. Air freight is considerably more expensive per tonne/kilometre than the other modes of transport. It accounts for less than 1 per cent of the total volume of international transport, but represents more than 20 per cent of the value shipped by industrialized countries (Sletmo and Picard, 1984). High-value items are more likely to be shipped by air, particularly if they have a high weight-to-volume ratio.

Rail

Rail services provide a very good method of transporting bulky goods over long distances. The increasing use of containers provides a flexible means to use rail and road modes, with minimal load transfer times and costs. High-speed trains are also emerging in Europe and the United States as attractive alternatives. For example, in Europe trains travelling at 190 miles per hour have cut the travel time between major European cities.

The decision about which transportation mode to use is affected by a number of factors:

- cost of different transport alternatives
- distance to the location
- nature of the product
- frequency of the shipment
- value of the shipment
- availability of transport.

The level of economic development is a major determinant of the availability of transportation – in some markets air freight is highly developed compared to rail transportation.

Freight forwarders

Freight forwarders provide an important service to exporters. The full-service foreign freight forwarder can relieve the producer of most of the burdens of distribution across national borders. This is particularly so for small- and medium-sized companies and those that are inexperienced in exporting. Freight forwarders provide a wide range of services, but the general activities and services are:

- coordination of transport services
- preparation and processing of international transport documents
- provision of warehousing
- expert advice.

The traditional view of the freight forwarder is that of a provider of services, a company that does not own transport facilities but which buys from the most appropriate transport provider, and a company that acts as the agent of the exporter. Various changes have taken place that have impacted upon freight forwarders. There has been a tendency for transport companies to extend their activities to include an in-house forwarding function. In addition, larger and more experienced exporters have developed their own in-house transport and documentation expertise. Both these trends have threatened the freight forwarder.

Inventory (at the factory base)

The purpose of establishing inventory – to maintain product movement in the delivery pipeline, in order to satisfy demand – is the same for domestic and international inventory systems.

There are many different cost elements involved in managing an inventory: storage, interest on capital tied up, taxes, lost sales, etc. Since these costs may sometimes be sizeable management must be concerned about inventory control. This involves determining the proper level of inventory to hold so that a balance is maintained between customer service and inventory cost.

In deciding the level of inventory to be maintained the international marketer must consider two factors:

1. *Order cycle time*: the total time that passes between the placement of an order by a customer and the receipt of the goods. Depending on the choice of transportation mode, delivery times may vary considerably. As a result the marketer has to keep larger safety stock in order to be able to satisfy demand in any circumstance. However, the marketer could attempt to reduce order cycle time, thereby reducing costs, by altering transportation method, changing inventory locations or shifting order placement to direct computer-order entry: electronic data interchange (EDI).

2. *Customer service levels*: the ability to fulfil customer orders within a certain time. For example, if within three days 80 per cent of the orders can be fulfilled, the customer service level is 80 per cent. The choice of customer service level for the firm has a major impact on the inventories needed. Because high customer service levels are costly (inventory constitutes tied-up capital) the goal should not be the highest level possible but rather an acceptable level, based on customer expectations. For some products customers may not demand or expect quick delivery. In addition, if higher customer service levels result in higher prices, this may reduce the competitiveness of a firm's product.

Besides these two factors, international inventories can also be used as a strategic tool in dealing with currency valuation changes or hedging against inflation.

Storage/warehousing (in foreign markets)

Sometimes goods and materials need to be stored in the export markets. However, this activity involves more than just storage. In addition to storing products in anticipation of consumer demand warehousing encompasses a broad range of other activities, such as assembling, breaking bulk shipments into smaller sizes to meet customer needs and preparing products for reshipment.

Warehousing decisions focus on three main issues:

1. where the firm's customers are geographically located
2. the pattern of existing and future demands
3. the customer service level required (i.e. how quickly a customer's order should be fulfilled).

The following general observations can be made about warehousing facilities:

- If products need to be delivered quickly storage facilities will be required near the customer.
- For high-value products (e.g. computer software) the location of the warehouse will be of minimal importance as these lightweight products can be air freighted.

EXHIBIT 16.1 How Bosch-Siemens improved customer service and reduced costs by closing warehouses

Bosch-Siemens (BS) is a leading European manufacturer of consumer white goods, with handsome market shares in Germany, Scandinavia, Spain and Greece. Recently the company decided to reduce the number of its European warehouses from 36 to 10. BS aimed to cut costs and reduce the amount of stock it held. The company also wanted to improve its distribution, enhance customer service and reform its logistics structure to boost its share in other markets, particularly the United Kingdom and France.

| Figure 16.8 | Bosch-Siemens' European distribution centres |

Source: Albaum *et al.* (1994, p. 419).

The process of continent-wide rationalization took three years to plan. BS fixed on ten sites as its current optimum, based on effective delivery criteria. It wanted to be able to reach customers within 24–48 hours. On the other hand, the optimum size of a warehouse in terms of cost is 20,000–30,000m^2. Hence BS arrived at ten as its optimum number of warehouses in Europe. These are shown in Figure 16.8.

BS seeks to serve several territories from each warehouse. Thus, for example, it has a warehouse in Sweden that also covers Norway and Finland; and its south-German warehouse supplies Luxembourg, Austria and parts of France.

By cutting warehouses it has reduced total distribution and warehousing costs, brought down staff numbers, holds fewer items of stock, provides greater access to regional markets, makes better use of transport networks and has improved service to customers.

The financial benefit is a saving of €15 million a year, or a reduction of 21 per cent in total logistics costs. BS has also achieved greater flexibility in the use of transport systems such as rail and waterways. It has brought stock numbers down from 1 million items to 700,000.

Source: EIU (1995).

Packaging

A good balance needs to be achieved between the high costs of the substantial export packing required to eliminate all damage and the price and profit implications that this has for the customer and the exporter.

Export packing has been modified over the years from wooden crates. Different countries have different regulations about what materials are acceptable. One example of this is the recycling of containers for reuse, which requires a system for deposits and returns into the distribution channels. In addition, export packing influences customer satisfaction through its appearance and its appropriateness to minimize handling costs for the customer.

During recent years packaging has been simplified by palletization. Computer software is now available from packaging suppliers that can design individual product packaging to maximize the number of units per pallet, and thus per container load. Palletization with shrink-wrap protection, together with containerization, has served both to protect goods against damage and to diminish losses through theft.

Third-party logistics (contract logistics)

A growing preference among international firms is to employ outside logistical expertise. The main thrust behind the idea is that individual firms are experts in their industry and should therefore concentrate only on their operations. Third-party logistics providers, on the other hand, are experts solely at logistics, with the knowledge and means to perform efficient and innovative services for those companies in need. The goal is improved service at equal or lower cost.

One of the greatest benefits of contracting out the logistics function in a foreign market is the ability to take advantage of an in-place network complete with resources and experience. The local expertise and image are crucial when a business is just starting up.

One of the main arguments levelled against contract logistics is the loss of the firm's control in the supply chain. Yet contract logistics does not and should not require the handing over of control. Rather, it offers concentration on one's core competence, a division of labour. The control and responsibility towards the customer remain with the firm, even though operations may move to a highly trained outside organization.

16.6　Implications of the Internet for distribution decisions

The Internet has the power to change drastically the balance of power among consumers, retailers, distributors, manufacturers and service providers. Some participants in the distribution chain may experience an increase in their power and profitability. Others will experience the reverse; some may even find that they have been bypassed and have lost their market share.

Physical distributors and dealers of goods and services that are more conveniently ordered and/or delivered online are indeed subject to increasing pressure from e-commerce. This *disintermediation* process, with increasing direct sales through the Internet, leads manufacturers to compete with their resellers, which results in *channel conflict*. The extent to which these effects are salient depends upon which of the following four Internet distribution strategies are adopted by the manufacturer.

Present only product information on the Internet

As less than 10 per cent of retail sales (in both Europe and the United States) presently occur over the Internet, only a few manufacturers would be willing to endanger their relationships with their distributors for that volume. The risk of conflicts with the existing distributors would be too great. So manufacturers may decide not to sell their products through the Internet and also prohibit their resellers from using the Internet for sales. Only product information is provided on the Internet, with any customer queries being passed on to the appropriate channel member. In industries such as aircraft manufacturing, where sales are large, complex and customized, this may be an appropriate strategy.

Leave Internet business to resellers

Some companies prefer distributors to leave the Internet business for resales and not to sell directly through the Internet. How effective this strategy is depends on the existing distribution structure. It can be effective when manufacturers assign exclusive territories to resellers, since resellers can be restricted to either delivering only to customers within their assigned territory or they can be compensated through profit pass-over agreements if they are adversely affected. Any leads generated by the manufacturer's website are passed on to the appropriate regional reseller.

By contrast, for intensively distributed products where resellers have no assigned territories, resellers simply compete with each other as they would do in the normal, physical marketplace. The global nature of the Internet creates price transparency, which may conflict with differential prices charged by the manufacturer in various markets. Another limitation of this approach is that most consumers search for manufacturers' websites rather than resellers' websites. Inability to purchase from the manufacturer's website can be frustrating for the consumer and can result in lost sales for the manufacturer.

Leave Internet business to the manufacturer only

A third strategy for the manufacturer is to restrict Internet sales exclusively to itself. This strategy is only profitable if the manufacturer has a business model that is aligned with sales through the Internet. The business system of most manufacturers (such as consumer packaged goods companies) is not set up for sales to end-users who place numerous small orders. Alternatively, by selling through the Internet a manufacturer may aim not to generate profits, but rather to learn about this new channel of distribution, collect information on consumers or build its brand. However, regardless of a manufacturer's objectives resellers dislike having to yield the market space to manufacturers.

If the manufacturer uses this strategy it also risks channel conflicts, i.e. creating competition with its own customers (distributors). The PC manufacturer Compaq realized this when it struggled to exploit the Internet, because to do so properly would mean bypassing its distributors. For Compaq it was difficult to remit sales through the Internet without upsetting their distributors and jeopardizing their historically strong relationships with them. In order to limit the direct competition with its customers Compaq introduced a differentiated product line of PCs, Prosignia, for sales through the Internet (Kumar, 1999).

Open Internet business to everybody

The fourth strategy is to let the market decide the winners and open the Internet to everybody – for direct sales and resellers. Manufacturers who have ventured online, either through the third or the fourth strategy, usually sell at retail prices and/or provide only a limited line because of their desire not to compete with their resales. However, this limits the attractiveness of the Internet's value proposition.

Conclusion

The fear of cannibalizing existing distribution channels and potential channel conflict requires manufacturers to trade off existing sales through the traditional distribution network and potential future sales through the Internet. Unfortunately, history suggests that most companies tend to stay with declining distribution networks for too long.

16.7   Special issue 1: international retailing

In the continuing integration of the world economy, internationalization not only concerns advertising, banking and manufacturing industries, it also affects the retailing business. The trend in all industrialized countries is towards larger units and more self-service. The number of retail outlets is dwindling, but the average size is increasing.

However, retailing still shows great differences between countries, reflecting their different histories, geography, culture and economic development. The cultural importance attached to food in Italy provides an opportunity for small specialist food retailers to survive and prosper. In other developed countries, such as the United States, the trend is towards very large superstores that incorporate a wide range of speciality foods. The Italian approach relies on small-scale production by the retail proprietor. The US approach encourages mass production, branding and sophisticated distribution systems to handle inventory and freshness issues.

A consequence of the greater economies of scale and efficiency in US retailing is that the United States tends to have larger retail outlets and a smaller number per capita than other developed countries. Some industrialized countries do not have an extensive modern retail sector. Among them are Japan, France and Italy. Japan has more retail outlets than the United States with only half the population (Jain, 1996, p. 536).

Legislation

A major reason for the lack of growth of large-scale retailing in these countries is legislation. Compared to the United States, retailing in Europe and to some extent Japan is subject to rather stringent legislation. In order to protect the independent retailer in town centres legislation primarily targets competition, new shops and days and hours of opening.

Legislative conditions differ across Europe. In the United Kingdom legislation is liberal, which explains the rapid development of large supermarkets in the 1980s and large specialized stores in the 1990s. In Italy, where legislation is much stricter, the opening of department stores and hypermarkets has been limited.

Legislation can hamper the development of some forms of retailing. Though France was one of the creators of the hypermarket (a giant market), the country passed a law regulating the establishment or expansion of retail stores in 1973. The effect of this law and similar laws in Italy is to allow existing retailers to protest against the establishment of any new, large-scale retailers in their area.

Internationalization of retailing

Both US and European retailers are internationalizing their business. Among large international US retailers are: 7-eleven, McDonald's, Pizza Hut, Blockbuster Video and Toys 'Я' Us. Among the large international European retailers are IKEA, Benetton, The Body Shop and Carrefour.

The Japanese are relative newcomers to this internationalization of retailing, but they are getting deeply involved. One of the Japanese food retailers, Jusco, has supermarkets in Hong Kong, Thailand and Malaysia. South East Asia seems to be the natural zone of influence for Japanese retailers, and they have spread throughout the region.

Despite the trend towards internationalization in retailing a prospective international retailer also faces some serious challenges and problems. The problems begin with the consumers. Retailers' performance in local markets is highly sensitive to variations in consumer behaviour. These are differences in consumer tastes, buying habits and spending patterns from country to country. Such differences have implications for a more differentiated merchandise offering along dimensions such as colour, fabric and site for clothing, and flavour for confectionery and snack foods.

Other problems that retailers will encounter when operating internationally include shortages of key resources such as land and labour, unfavourable tax and tariff structures, restrictions on trading hours and foreign ownership and impenetrable established supplier relationships.

A case study of one US speciality retailer (Barth *et al.*, 1996) has pinpointed the problems of establishing a retail business in Europe. The reasons for the relatively bad financial performance in European retailing can be sought in the following factors:

- higher costs of acquiring real estate in Europe
- more expensive labour in Europe
- the complex legislation for establishing large retail stores in Europe.

EXHIBIT 16.2 Ferrari – the venerable Italian sports maker is going into retailing

Ferrari is working on capitalizing more value from its brand. Currently it has retail sales of €1.8 billion. In 2002 the first Ferrari shop was launched in Ferrari's hometown Maranello (Italy), followed by 29 shops in key locations such as Rome, London, San Francisco, Macau and Barcelona. With the exception of the unit here, all stores are licensed.

© Justin Kase z02z/Alamy

The product range includes baseball caps, sporty sunglasses and T-shirts alongside finely crafted leather bomber jackets, V-neck cashmere sweaters and cotton pique polo shirts. Spring women's looks include white cotton shirts, tan leather jackets, fitted polo shirts and skinny jeans. Branded merchandise allows Ferrari to make contact with consumers in a way that would not otherwise be possible. Someone buying Ferrari apparel can form an emotional tie to the brand without buying a car or even entering a showroom. Trading on people's perceptions of a brand is the key to a successful product.

Approximately 40 per cent of the product range in the typical Ferrari store is developed and produced by Ferrari, whereas the rest (60 per cent) comes from Ferrari's licensees, among which are Puma, Lego, Acer and Mattel. For example, the Ferrari laptop PC from Acer was the first carbon-fibre laptop on the market. A jewellery line licensed to Damiani was launched in 2010, and there are also chessboards, bikes, skis, crash helmets, ashtrays and desk sets forged from used car components.

The Ferrari store concept was created and will be managed in future by the ARP Group. There are plans to grow the number of Ferrari stores from 30 to 50 by 2011, with a focus on the Far East.

The first Ferrari theme park is to open in Abu Dhabi, United Arab Emirates in 2011. Designed to offer a multisensory experience, the park covers more than 4.9 million square feet. It will house over 20 attractions, including what is billed as the world's fastest roller coaster. The largest Ferrari store, at 10,800 square feet, opened in October in Dubai despite the emirate's recent financial problems.

Sources: adapted from www.businessweek.com/globalbiz/content/nov2006/gb20061128_902772.htm; www.theautochannel.com/news/2009/05/19/461591.html; www.ferrari.com.

Stages of internationalization

The 'stages' concept (the Uppsala school: see section 3.2) has been applied to depict the typical movement by retailers towards internationalization. Given the considerable risks and costs involved in expansion outside home markets, most have viewed the prospect with a degree of reluctance. Retail companies will typically move from reluctance to cautious expansion abroad, starting with the closest markets.

The internationalization of retailing has produced different styles of international operation, ranging from multinational to global. Global retailers such as Toys 'Я' Us vary their format very little across national boundaries, achieving the greatest economies of scale but showing the least local responsiveness. Multinational retailers, on the other hand, operate as autonomous entities within each country. A middle course is termed 'transnational' retailing, whereby the company seeks to achieve global efficiency while responding to national opportunities and constraints.

Trade marketing

For too long manufacturers have viewed vertical marketing channels as closed systems, operating as separate, static entities. The most important factors creating long-term, integrated strategic plans and fostering productive channel relationships were largely ignored. Fortunately a new philosophy about channel management has emerged, but to understand its potential we must first understand how power has developed at the retailer level.

Channel power
The ability of a channel member to control marketing variables of any other member in a channel at a different level of distribution.

Power in channel relationships can be defined as the ability of a channel member to control marketing decision variables of any other member in a channel at a different level of distribution. A classic example of this **channel power** is the amount of power wielded by retailers against the food and grocery manufacturers. One result of this may be found in the Exhibit 16.3, where the 'Banana Split' shows that the increasing retailing power has resulted in a retail share of the total value chain in the banana business of 40 per cent. As the balance of power has shifted, more merchandise is controlled by fewer and fewer retailers.

EXHIBIT 16.3 The 'Banana Split' model

At the level of production, bananas tend to be produced either on very small land holdings or on very large plantations. It is estimated that 80 per cent of global exports originate from large-scale plantations and the rest from smaller farms. There is considerable diversity of production systems both within and between banana exporting countries. There is considerably less diversity in the chain after the farm gate. The process of transporting, ripening and distributing bananas is highly concentrated with five very large corporations controlling as much as 80 per cent of banana exports. The remaining 20 per cent of exports is nonetheless very fragmented: a large number of smaller exporting companies are involved in sourcing and marketing of bananas.

The five large transnational banana exporters – Dole, Del Monte, Chiquita, Fyffes and Noboa – are vertically integrated to varying degrees into production, transportation, ripening and distribution. Of the five large transnationals, only Fyffes is not directly involved in producing bananas on company-owned farms. The other large companies own plantations in Latin America, Africa and Asia. The large banana exporters own, or have owned, the infrastructure for shipping and transport.

Once the bananas are offloaded at ports in Europe, the United States and Asia they are transported to ripening facilities so that the fruit can be prepared for distribution. All of the transnational banana exporters own their own ripening and distribution facilities in the markets they supply. In Europe, investment by these companies in ripening and distribution infrastructure increased in the period after 1993 with the shift to a single European market for bananas.

The five transnationals are:

- *Chiquita* controls 25 per cent of the global banana market. Bananas generate 67 per cent of Chiquita's revenues; other interests are in fresh fruit, juices and canned vegetables.
- *Dole* claims to be the world's largest producer of bananas, with approximately 30 per cent of the global banana market. Dole has been 100 per cent owned by CEO David Murdock and family since late 2002.
- *Del Monte Fresh Produce* (completely separate from Del Monte Foods since the break up of RJR Nabisco in 1989) has around 15 per cent of the banana market, and also sells pineapples, melons and other tropical fruit and speciality vegetables.

- **Fyffes** is the largest fresh produce distributor in Europe. Has about 20 per cent of the global banana market. Headquartered in Ireland.
- **Noboa** *(Exportadora Bananera Noboa)* is part of a conglomerate of 110 companies (Grupo Noboa) privately owned by Alvaro Noboa, Ecuador's richest man and twice presidential candidate. It has 10 per cent of the global banana market.

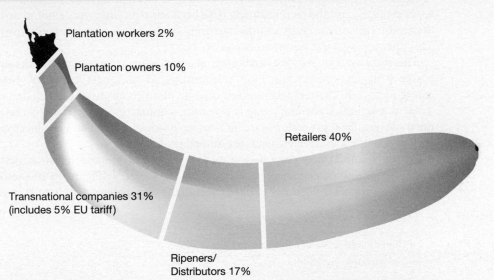

Plantation workers 2%

Plantation owners 10%

Retailers 40%

Transnational companies 31%
(includes 5% EU tariff)

Ripeners/
Distributors 17%

There is a high degree of overlap between the transnational companies and the ripeners/distributors:
Four of the five transnationals are also involved with ripening: Chiquita, Dole, Del Monte and Fyffes.

Figure 16.9   The 'Banana Split' model. How much (in percentages of the retail value in the UK) stays with each chain actor to cover costs and margin

Source: adapted from Vorley, B. (2003), Fig. 7.2, p. 52.

Only around 12 per cent (10 per cent + 2 per cent) of revenues from banana retail sales (see Figure 16.9) remain in producing countries, despite the very limited amount of product transformation outside of the farm or plantation. Forty per cent of retail value may stay with the supermarket even though this is the least demanding part of the chain. The dominance of retailers has had an increasing influence over the structure and distribution of value along the banana chain. The shift of profits towards the downstream end of the chain has been dramatic over the last decade, and the transnationals' margins on bananas are decreasing, whereas the retailers' share of the value chain is increasing. The banana value chain has shifted from being producer-driven to one that is increasingly buyer-driven. A structural over-supply of bananas has also led to lower prices and intense competition. Since the mid-1990s the supermarket chains have consolidated (fewer but more powerful retail chains) and exercised their growing market power over banana transnationals by demanding higher product quality and service, and by passing value functions 'up the chain'. As a response the transnationals are increasingly integrating vertically into ripening, shipping, packing and distribution, but also moving away from direct ownership of production. The transnationals are also trying to provide a wider range of fruit and more value added products in order to increase profits and improve their chances of becoming a preferred supplier of a supermarket chain.

Source: adapted from Vorley (2003) and Marther (2008).

International retailing
Worldwide tendency towards concentration in retailing, creating huge buying power in the big international retail chains.

There is a worldwide tendency towards concentration in retailing resulting in **international retailing**. The concentration in the European food sector is most evident in the northern part of Europe. Since the mid 1990s new players have arrived on the European grocery market, for example, the German discount-chain, Lidl, which is now second in the German discount-sector after Aldi. Lidl is also expanding to the remaining European area (e.g. to Scandinavia, UK and France). In the United Kingdom Tesco is now number 1 and Sainsbury number 2.

A consequence of this development is that there has been a worldwide shift from manufacturer to retailer dominance. Power has become concentrated in the hands of fewer and fewer retailers, and the manufacturers have been left with little choice but to accede to their demands. This often results in manufacturing of the retailers' own brands (private labels). This phenomenon was discussed in section 14.8.

Therefore we can see that traditional channel management, with its characteristics of power struggles, conflict and loose relationships, is no longer beneficial. New ideas are emerging to help channel relationships become more cooperative. This is what is known as 'trade marketing'. Trade marketing is when the manufacturer (supplier) markets directly to the trade (retailers) to create a better fit between product and outlet. The objective is to create joint marketing and strategic plans for mutual profitability.

For the manufacturer (supplier), it means creating twin marketing strategies: one to the consumer and another to the trade (retailers). However, as Figure 16.10 shows, potential channel conflicts exist because of differences in the objectives of the channel members.

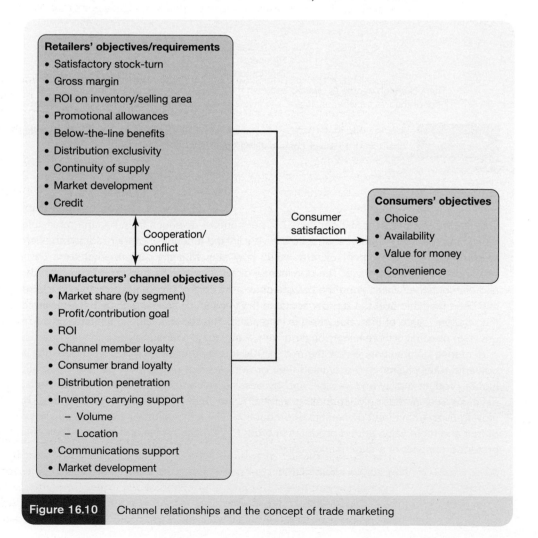

| Figure 16.10 | Channel relationships and the concept of trade marketing |

Despite potential channel conflicts what both parties share, but often forget, is their common goal of consumer satisfaction. If the desired end result is to create joint marketing plans a prerequisite must be an improved understanding of the other's perspective and objectives.

Retailers are looking for potential sales, profitability, exclusivity in promotions and volume. They are currently in the enviable position of being able to choose brands that fulfil those aims.

A private label manufacturer has to create different packages for different retailers. By carefully designing individual packages the manufacturer gains a better chance of striking up a relationship with the best-matched retailer.

Manufacturers can offer retailers a total 'support package' by stressing their own strengths. These include marketing knowledge and experience, market position, proven new product success, media support and exposure and a high return on investment in shelf space.

If a joint strategy is going to be successful manufacturers and retailers must work together at every level, perhaps by matching counterparts in each organization. As a consequence of the increasing importance of the individual customer the concept of the key account (key customer) was introduced. Key accounts are often large retail chains with a large turnover (in total as well as of the supplier's products), which are able to decide quantity and price on behalf of different outlets.

Segmentation of customers is therefore no longer based only on size and geographic position but also on customers' (retailers) structure of decision-making. This results in a gradual restructuring of sales from a geographic division to a customer division. This reorganization is made visible by creating key account managers (managers responsible for customers).

Cross-border alliances in retailing

The focus of this section is alliances between retailers that are both horizontal (i.e. retailer to retailer) and also international, in that they cross the boundaries of nation states. Cross-border retailer alliances are emerging predominantly between Western European retailers and can, in many cases, be interpreted as explicit responses to the perceived threats and opportunities of the EU internal market.

Grey marketing or parallel importing
Importing and selling of products through market distribution channels that are not authorized by the manufacturer. It occurs when the manufacturer uses significantly different market prices for the same product in different countries and mainly exists for high-priced, high-end products, like fashion and luxury apparel.

None of the cross-border alliances in Europe can be described as 'equity participating alliances', which include a cross-shareholding between members. None of the alliances involves the sharing of equity, but they all have a central secretariat with the function of coordinating operational activities – buying, branding, expertise exchange and product marketing.

Until now the range of activities performed by the secretariats of the alliances has been limited and excludes actual processing and central payments. The present advantage for an individual retail member in a cross-border alliance lies primarily in central purchasing from suppliers, where price advantages flow to all members, suggesting that the alliance is attempting to countervail the power of the manufacturer (supplier). Cross-border central buying can be a relevant starting point for both manufacturers and retailers attempting to move towards a pan-European supply network.

16.8 Special issue 2: grey marketing (parallel importing)

Grey marketing or **parallel importing** can be defined as the importing and selling of products through market distribution channels that are not authorized by the manufacturer. It occurs when manufacturers use significantly different market prices for the same product in different countries. This allows an unauthorized dealer (in Figure 16.11, a wholesaler) to buy branded goods intended for one market at a low price and then sell them in another, higher-priced market, at a higher profit than could have been achieved in the 'low-price'

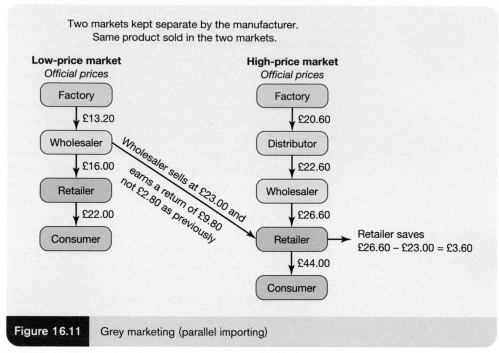

Figure 16.11 Grey marketing (parallel importing)

Source: Paliwoda (1993, p. 300). Reprinted with permission from Butterworth-Heinemann Publishers, a division of Reed Educational & Professional Publishing Ltd.

market. Grey markets mainly exist for high-priced, high-end products, like fashion and luxury fashion apparel, watches, perfume etc.

Grey marketing often occurs because of the fluctuating value of currencies between different countries, which makes it attractive for the 'grey' marketer to buy products in markets with weak currencies and sell them in markets with strong currencies.

Grey markets can also be the result of a distributor in one country having an unexpected over-supply of a product. This distributor may be willing to sell its excess supply for less than the normal margin to recover its investment. Other reasons for lower prices in some countries (which can result in grey marketing) might be lower transport costs, fiercer competition and higher product taxes (high product taxes put pressure on the ex-works price to keep the end-consumer price at an acceptable level).

The particular problem with grey marketing for the manufacturer is that it results in authorized intermediaries losing motivation. The grey marketer usually competes only on price and pays little attention to providing marketing support and after-sales service.

Grey markets are fed by many sources in the e-business. Perhaps the most common are authorized dealers who can make a profit, or at least minimize a loss, by selling to unauthorized dealers. The Internet makes it easier for firms operating in grey territory to reach a wide range of customers. Companies can buy in bulk and resell to unauthorized distributors, a situation that has characterized the market for computer parts for some time. Sometimes a manufacturer itself will sell into the grey market as salespeople struggle to meet quotas or managers attempt to cover costs or make year-end sales goals (Antia *et al.*, 2004).

Possible strategies to reduce grey marketing

Sometimes companies hope that it is a short-term problem and that it will disappear, and it might be if the price difference is the result of the fluctuating value of currencies. At other times a more proactive approach to the problem is needed:

● *Seek legal redress.* Although the legal option can be time consuming and expensive, some companies (e.g. Seiko) have chosen to prosecute grey marketers.

- *Change the marketing mix.* This involves three elements:
  1. *Product strategy.* This strategy is about moving away from the standardization concept (same product for all markets), and introducing a differentiated concept with a different product for each main market.
  2. *Pricing strategy.* The manufacturer can change the ex-works prices to the channel members to minimize price differentials between markets. The manufacturer can also narrow the discount schedules it offers for large orders. This will reduce the incentive for intermediaries to over-order to get lower prices and later sell unsold stock on the grey market, still at a profit.
  3. *Warranty strategy.* The manufacturer may reduce or cancel the warranty period for grey market products. This will require that the products can be identified through the channel system.

16.9   Summary

In this chapter we have examined the management of international distribution channels and logistics. The main structure of this chapter was given in Figure 16.1, and from the discussion it is evident that the international marketer has a broad range of alternatives for selecting and developing an economical, efficient and high-volume international distribution channel.

In many instances the channel structure is affected by external factors and it may vary from nation to nation. Physical distribution (external logistics) concerns the flow of goods from the manufacturer to the customer. This is one area where cost savings through efficiency are feasible, provided the decision is made systematically. The changing nature of international retailing influences distribution planning. During the last decade the balance of power (between manufacturers and retailers) has shifted in favour of the retailers. The manufacturer often has no other choice than to cooperate with large and increasingly concentrated retailers in terms of the 'trade marketing' concept.

A phenomenon of growing importance in international markets is the grey market, which consists of unauthorized traders buying and selling a company's product in different countries. Companies confronted with a grey market situation can react in many ways. They may decide to ignore the problem, take legal action or modify elements of their marketing mix. The option chosen is strongly influenced by the nature of the situation and its expected duration.

CASE STUDY 16.1

De Beers: forward integration into the diamond industry value chain

Since the late 1800s the South African multinational De Beers (www.debeers.com) has regulated both the industrial and gemstone diamond markets and effectively maintained an illusion of diamond scarcity. It has developed and nurtured the belief that diamonds are precious, invaluable symbols of romance. Every attitude consumers hold today about diamonds exists – at least in part – because of the persistent efforts of De Beers.

Moreover, by monitoring the supply and distribution of diamonds throughout the world, De Beers has introduced and maintained an unprecedented degree of price stability for a surprisingly common mineral: compressed carbon. Such unique price stability lies within the cartel's tight control over the distribution of diamonds. De Beers' operating strategy has been pure and simple: to restrict the number of diamonds released into the market in any

⬤

given year and to perpetuate the myth that they are scarce and should therefore command high prices.

De Beers spends about US$200 million a year to promote diamonds and diamond jewellery – 'A diamond is forever' – and the firm controls nearly 70 per cent of the rough diamond market.

De Beers controls a producer's cartel that operates as a quantity-fixing entity by setting production quotas for each member (as does OPEC). De Beers has successfully convinced the producers that the diamond supply must be regulated in order to maintain favourably high prices and profits.

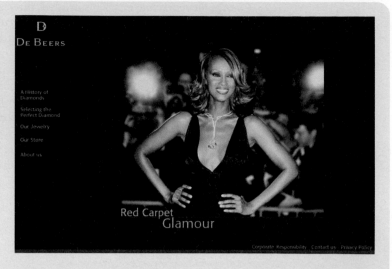

During the early part of the last century much of the diamond cartel's strength rested with De Beers' control of the South African mines. Today the source of power no longer comes from rough diamond production alone, but from a sophisticated network of production, marketing sales and promotion arrangements, all administered by De Beers.

It is interesting to note that diamond prices have little or no relation to the cost of extraction (production).

Table 1 shows average or 'normal' price mark-ups on gemstones along the channel of distribution.

A diamond that may cost US$100 to mine can end up costing a consumer US$920 at a local jewellery store. Business cycles and individual commercial practices may positively or negatively influence these figures, together with the gemstone quality. Diamond sales, known in the trade as 'sights', are held ten times a year in London, in Lucerne, Switzerland and in Kimberley, South Africa. The sales are limited to approximately 160 privileged 'sightholders', primarily owners of diamond-cutting factories in New York, Tel Aviv, Mumbai and Antwerp, who then sell to the rest of the diamond trade.

Diamond output from De Beers' self-owned and self-operated mines constitutes only 43 per cent of the total world value of rough diamonds. Because it is not the sole producer of rough stones in the world De Beers has had to join forces with other major diamond-producing organizations, forming the international diamond cartel that controls nearly three-quarters of the world market.

De Beers has constructed a controlled supply and distribution chain whereby all cartel producers are contracted to sell the majority of their entire output to a single marketing entity: the De Beers-controlled Central Selling Organization (CSO) (see Figure 1).

The total rough diamond supply controlled by the CSO comes from three sources: DeBeers/Centenary-owned mines, outside suppliers contracted to the CSO (cartel members) and open market purchases via buying offices in Africa, Antwerp and Tel Aviv (rough output purchased from countries that have not signed an agreement with De Beers). De Beers functions as the sole diamond distributor. In any given year approximately 75 per cent of the world's diamonds pass through the CSO to cutters and brokers.

The economic success of the cartel depends highly on strict adherence to their rules, written or unwritten. Clients who follow the rules are rewarded with consistent upgrades in the quality and quantity of rough stones in their boxes, while those who

Table 1	Mark-ups on diamonds	
Stage of distribution	Mark-up (%)	Average value of 0.5 carat gem (US$/carat)
Cost of mining	–	100
Mine sales	67	167
Dealers of rough gems	20	200
Cutting units	100	400
Wholesaler dealers	15	460
Retail	100	920

Source: adapted from Ariovich (1985) and Bergenstock and Maskulka (2001).

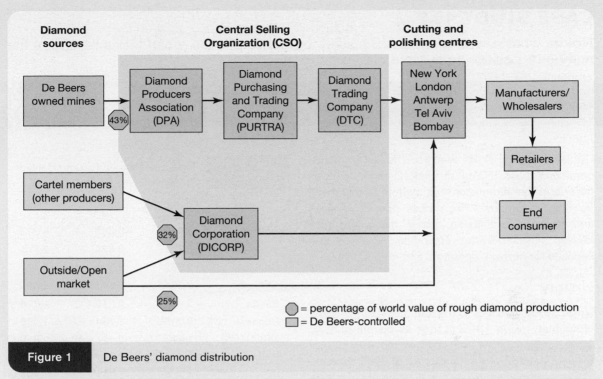

Figure 1 De Beers' diamond distribution

Sources: adapted from De Beers Annual Report and Bergenstock and Maskukla (2001).

circumvent them find progressively worse allocations and risk not being invited back to future sights.

De Beers' 'forward integration' decision

Until 2001 De Beers concentrated on supplying its diamonds to brand manufacturers, such as Cartier. The core business of the De Beers Group remains the mining and marketing of rough diamonds. However, in January 2001 the De Beers Group, the world's premier diamond group, and LVMH Moet Hennessy Louis Vuitton, the world's leading luxury products group, agreed to establish an independently managed joint venture, De Beers LV, to develop the global consumer brand potential of the De Beers name.

LVMH is the home of premier brands in the categories of fashion and leather goods, watches and jewellery, wine and spirits, cosmetics and perfumes. LVMH will contribute with its extensive experience in both developing luxury brands and rolling out premium retail concepts.

The 'mother' company, De Beers SA, contributes to the joint venture with its over 100 years of experience in the form of technology and individual experts to allow for the selection of the most beautiful diamonds.

As part of the joint venture agreement De Beers SA has transferred to De Beers LV the worldwide rights to use the De Beers brand name for luxury goods in consumer markets. From now on, De Beers will design, manufacture and sell premium diamond jewellery under its own brand name. The diamonds bearing De Beers brand name will be sold exclusively through De Beers stores. De Beers has opened a flagship store in London (Oxford Street) and has plans for further openings in New York and Paris.

Source: information and news on www.diamonds.net.

QUESTIONS

1. What could be De Beers' motives for making this 'forward integration' into the retail and consumer market?

2. Is it a wise decision?

3. How should De Beers develop its Internet strategy following this forward integration strategy?

4. Would it be possible for De Beers, with its branded diamonds, to standardize the international marketing strategy across borders?

CASE STUDY 16.2

Nokia: what is wrong in the US market for mobile phones – can Nokia recapture the number 1 position from Motorola?

Finnish company Nokia is a world leader in mobile communications. Nokia connects people to each other and the information that matters to them with easy-to-use products like mobile phones, devices and solutions for imaging, games, media and businesses. Nokia provides equipment, solutions and services for network operators and corporations.

History

Nokia's roots go back to the foundation of the Nokia wood-pulp mill in 1865. It took its current form as a corporation under the laws of the Republic of Finland in 1967, upon the merger of three separate Finnish companies involved in a range of industries. In the 1980s, Nokia strengthened its position in the telecommunications, consumer electronics and personal computer markets. In 1982, it introduced the first fully digital local telephone exchange in Europe and the world's first car phone for the Nordic Mobile Telephone analogue standard. In the early 1990s, Nokia decided to make telecommunications its core business. As a result, it divested a number of other businesses, including paper, rubber, footwear, chemicals, cables, aluminium and television.

Nokia today

Nokia's principal activity is to provide mobile phones, broadband, IP network infrastructure and related services. It also develops mobile Internet applications and solutions for operators and Internet service providers. Nokia is organized into four business groups: mobile phones, network, multimedia and enterprise solutions. As mobile phones account for the largest percentage of the total sales (70 per cent in 2008), this case will concentrate on that business group.

For the fiscal year ended December 2008 the Nokia Corporation generated total revenues of €50,710 million. Profit before tax was €4,966 million for the year. At 31 December 2008, Nokia employed 125,829 people and operated fourteen manufacturing facilities in eight countries around the world for the production of mobile devices and network infrastructure.

Table 1	Nokia's ten largest markets (€ million in net sales) 2006–08		
	2008	**2007**	**2006**
China	5,916	5,898	4,913
India	3,719	3,684	2,713
UK	2,382	2,574	2,425
Germany	2,294	2,641	2,060
Russia	2,083	2,012	1,518
Indonesia	2,046	1,754	1,069
USA	1,907	2,124	2,815
Brazil	1,902	1,257	1,044
Italy	1,774	1,792	1,394
Spain	1,497	1,830	1,139

Source: based on www.nokia.com.

Turnover by region and country

Of the total turnover in 2008 Europe accounts for 37 per cent, Asia-Pacific 22 per cent, Middle East and Africa 14 per cent, China 13 per cent, Latin America 10 per cent and North America 4 per cent. The ten largest markets are shown in Table 1, together with the development in sales from 2006 to 2008.

From Table 1 it appears that the largest increase in net sales among the largest markets is found in India (37 per cent), whereas the largest decline in net sales from 2006 to 2008 is found in the United States (32 per cent).

Nokia's position in the world market for mobile phones

In 2008 worldwide mobile phone shipments totalled 1210 million units, a 46 per cent increase over the 825 million shipments in 2004.

As shown in Table 2, in 2008 Nokia ruled the world mobile handset market with a 38 per cent share, followed by Samsung (18 per cent), Motorola (9 per cent), LG (8 per cent), Sony Ericsson (8 per cent) and others (21 per cent).

Table 2	The world market for mobile handsets (2008)			
Company	HQ country	Number of sold units (million)	World market share (%)	USA market share (%)
Nokia	Finland	460	38	9
Motorola	USA	109	9	23
Samsung	South Korea	193	16	22
LG Electronics Co.	South Korea	97	8	15
Sony Ericsson	Japan/Sweden	97	8	1
Others (e.g. RIM (BlackBerry), Apple (iPhone), Sanyo	Misc.	254	21	30
Total		1210	100	100

Approximately 160 million mobile phones were sold in the USA in 2008.
Source: based on www.idc.com.

Worldwide Nokia's crown is being challenged, by Samsung, for example.

US market for mobile phones and Nokia's position there

The US is not a saturated mobile economy. Around 80 per cent of people have a handset there rather than in the UK where the ratio is more than 100 per cent (some people have two or more devices).

In 2004 Nokia was a market leader in the US mobile phone market, with a share of around 30 per cent, and Motorola was number 2 with a market share of 20 per cent. Since then the roles have been switched and Nokia's market share has decreased to 9 per cent.

In 2008 Motorola led the US market with around 23 per cent market share, followed by Samsung Electronics Co. Ltd and LG Electronics Co. Ltd. RIM, Apple (iPhone), Sanyo, Kyocera Wireless Corp., Sanyo Electric Co. Ltd and UT Starcom Inc. have the remaining 30 per cent.

Nokia is certainly not satisfied with its US market position and is aiming to improve at targeting specific segments as it angles for a bigger slice of the North American market. In 2008, it conducted a worldwide segmentation study, trying to determine what various market niches wanted. The study included more than 50,000 hours of interviews conducted in 18 different countries (including the United States), leading analysts to expect more niche products from Nokia in coming years. The general perception by the US consumer was that Motorola had more features while Nokia was known as cheaper and reliable.

Distribution of mobile phones in the United States

In Europe and Asia, consumers usually buy phones and telephone service separately, so Nokia needs to please only the end-user. In the US, where phones and service are sold together, carriers want control over the way the phones look and perform. Another challenge for Nokia is that the dominant wireless standard in North America is CDMA (code division multiple access); while most Nokia phones are designed to operate on the global standard, GSM (global system for mobile communications) (Hempel, 2009).

In the United States there are two routes in the distribution of mobile phones: (1) from the manufacturer to the telecommunications retailer via a wholesaler; and (2) from the manufacturer via the carrier (i.e. wireless network operator) and its outlets. In recent years, the second route has become dominant.

In the US most handsets, some 63 per cent, are sold from stores owned by the respective carriers. AT&T sold 29 per cent of devices and Verizon 26 per cent with 11 per cent each for T-Mobile and Sprint.

Nokia's performance against Motorola in the US market is probably due to at least two important factors:

1. Differentiation is the key in a market where nearly 80 per cent of consumers already own cell phones and many want distinctive features before being induced to switch. Motorola is clearly reacting to a lifestyle market opportunity. The thin phone by Motorola was designed to hit Nokia where it hurts (Nokia has long excelled at making candy bar-style phones).

2. More than 60 per cent of US mobile phone buyers selected a carrier first, and then chose their new phones from among the phones offered by that carrier. It seems that Motorola's surge in the US market could also be attributed to its extensive carrier agreements and relationships with the most important carriers, e.g. Sprint and Nextel Communications Inc. Some of Motorola's business goes through Verizon, the industry's second-largest carrier, but most of its business goes through many small carriers, scattered around the US market.

In some ways, the importance of the US market is increasing, especially in the high-end market (smart phones). The US is the world's biggest market for smart phones. With the iPhone's success, Apple has transformed the US mobile phone market into a small computer experimental market. Apple users are concentrated in the United States market, and it launched the first mobile phone software Shop.

Nokia is facing tough competition at this top-end of the market (smart phones) from models like Apple's iPhone and Research In Motion's (RIM) BlackBerry.

At a Nokia Conference in January 2006 the Finnish CEO Jorma Ollila was keen to change the status quo in the US market. At the conference he said that Nokia aims to achieve the number 1 position in North America: 'Being above 20 per cent market share is a good first step,' Ollila said. 'Next is establishing ourselves as the strong contender for the No. 1 position' (Kharif, 2006). Thus for Nokia has failed to achieve Ollila's goals, but since Nokia introduced the smart phone, e71x (see picture) to the US market things are going somewhat better, and it seems that Nokia can regain some of its lost ground in the United States in 2009.

Nokia E71
Nokia UK.

Sources: Hempel, J. (2009) Nokia's North America problem – to stay No. 1 in high-end cellphones, the Finnish phonemaker has to take on Apple and RIM on their home turf. So far it hasn't got a foothold, money.cnn.com/2009/01/12/technology/hempel_nokia. fortune/, 1 December; Sourcejuice (2009) 'Nokia's market share in United States only 10 per cent decline', www.sourcejuice.com/ 1156907/2009/04/02/Nokia-market-share-United-States-only-10-decline/, 4 February; Kharif, O. (2006) 'Nokia: Dialing North America', *Business Week Online*, 2nd August; www.nokia.com.

QUESTIONS

1. Prepare illustrations of the distribution channels of mobile phones from Nokia to its end consumers in the United States.

2. What are the reasons for the global leadership of Nokia in mobile phones?

3. Why is Nokia the market leader in mobile phones on the world basis, but not in the US market?

4. What can Nokia do to recapture the number 1 position in the US market?

VIDEO CASE STUDY 16.3 DHL
download from www.pearsoned.co.uk/hollensen

DHL International (www.dhl.com) specializes in cross-border express deliveries. DHL is the global market leader in international express, overland transport and airfreight. It is also the world's number 1 in ocean freight and contract logistics. DHL offers a full range of customized solutions – from express document shipping to supply chain management. DHL links about 120,000 destinations in more than 220 countries and territories and operates cargo airlines. The company provides Internet tracking and order fulfilment services.

Questions

1. What are the macroeconomic drivers for the growth of the logistics business?
2. What are the most important issues in keeping DHL's international competitiveness?
3. How can DHL be perceived as a local company in most countries of the world?

For further exercises and cases, see this book's website at **www.pearsoned.co.uk/hollensen**

Questions for discussion

1. Discuss current distribution trends in world markets.
2. What are the factors that affect the length, width and number of marketing channels?
3. In attempting to optimize global marketing channel performance, which of the following should an international marketer emphasize: training, motivation or compensation? Why?
4. When would it be feasible and advisable for a global company to centralize the co-ordination of its foreign market distribution systems? When would decentralization be more appropriate?
5. Do grey marketers serve useful marketing functions – for consumers and manufacturers?
6. Why is physical distribution important to the success of global marketing?
7. Discuss the reasons why many exporters make extensive use of the services of freight forwarders.
8. Discuss the implications for the international marketer of the trend towards cross-border retailing.
9. Many markets have relatively large numbers of small retailers. How does this constrain the international marketer?
10. How is retailing know-how transferred internationally?
11. What services would the manufacturer like to receive from the retailer?

References

Albaum, G., Strandskov, J., Duerr, E. and Dowd, L. (1994) *International Marketing and Export Management*. Addison-Wesley, Reading, MA.

Antia, K.D., Bergen, M. and Dutta, S. (2004) 'Competing with gray markets', *MIT Sloan Management Review*, Fall, pp. 63–69.

Ariovich, G. (1985) 'The economics of diamond price movements', *Managerial Decision Economics*, 6(4), pp. 234–240.

Arnold, D. (2000) 'Seven rules of international distribution', *Harvard Business Review*, November–December, pp. 131–137.

Barth, K., Karch, N.J., Mclaughlin, K. and Shi, C.S. (1996) 'Global retailing: tempting trouble', *The McKinsey Quarterly*, 1, pp. 117–125.

Bergenstock, D.J. and Maskulka, J.M. (2001) 'The De Beers story: are diamonds forever?', *Business Horizons*, 44(3), pp. 37–44.

Cateora, P.R. (1993) *International Marketing*, 8th edn. Irwin, Homewood, IL.

Cavusgil, S.T., Yeoh, P.-L. and Mitri, M. (1995) 'Selecting foreign distributors – an expert systems approach', *Industrial Marketing Management*, 24, pp. 297–304.

EIU (1995) *The EU50: Corporate Case Studies in Single Market Success*, Research Report, pp. 77–78. London: Economist Intelligence Unit.

Jaffe, E.D. and Yi, L. (2007) 'What are the drivers of channel length? Distribution reform in The People's Republic of China', *International Business Review*, 16, pp. 474–493.

Jain, S. (1996) *International Marketing Management*, 5th edn. South-Western College Publishing, Cincinnati, OH.

Kumar, N. (1999) 'Internet distribution strategies: dilemmas for the incumbent', Mastering Information Management, Part 7, Electronic Commerce, *Financial Times*, 15 March.

Lewison, D.M. (1996) *Marketing Management: An Overview*. Fort Worth, TX, The Dryden Press/Harcourt Brace College Publishers.

Marther, C. (2008) 'Value chains and tropical products in a changing global regime', ICTSD, Issue Paper No. 13, Switzerland (www.ictsd.org).

Onkvisit, S. and Shaw, J.J. (1993) *International Marketing: Analysis and Strategy*, 2nd edn. Macmillan, London.

Paliwoda, S. (1993) *International Marketing*. Heinemann, Oxford.

Rawwas, M.Y.A., Konishi, K., Kamise, S. and Al-Khatib, J. (2008) 'Japanese distribution system: the impact of newly designed collaborations on wholesalers' performance', *Industrial Marketing Management*, 37, 104–115.

Sletmo, G.K. and Picard, J. (1984) 'International distribution policies and the role of air freight', *Journal of Business Logistics*, 6, pp. 35–52.

Vorley, B. (2003) *Food, Inc. – Corporate Concentration from Farm to Consumer*. UK Food Group, London.

CHAPTER 17
Communication decisions (promotion strategies)

Contents

Learning objectives

After studying this chapter you should be able to:

- Define and classify the different types of communication tool.

- Describe and explain the major steps in advertising decisions.

- Describe the techniques available and appropriate for setting the advertising budget in foreign markets.

- Discuss the possibilities of marketing via the Internet.

- Explain how important personal selling and sales force management are in the international marketplace.

- Define and explain the concept of viral marketing.

- Discuss how standardized international advertising has both benefits and drawbacks.

17.1 Introduction

Communication is the fourth and final decision to be made about the global marketing programme. The role of communication in global marketing is similar to that in domestic operations: to communicate with customers so as to provide information that buyers need to make purchasing decisions. Although the communication mix carries information of interest to the customer, in the end it is designed to persuade the customer to buy a product – at present or in the future.

To communicate with and influence customers, several tools are available. Advertising is usually the most visible component of the promotion mix, but personal selling, exhibitions, sales promotions, publicity (public relations) and direct marketing (including the Internet) are also part of a viable international promotion mix.

One important strategic consideration is whether to standardize worldwide or to adapt the promotion mix to the environment of each country. Another consideration is the availability of media, which varies around the world.

17.2 The communication process

In considering the communication process we normally think about a manufacturer (sender) transmitting a message through any form of media to an identifiable target segment audience. Here the seller is the initiator of the communication process. However, if the seller and the buyer have already established a relationship it is likely that the initiative in the communication process will come from the buyer. If the buyer has a positive post-purchase experience with a given offering in one period of time this may dispose the buyer to rebuy on later occasions: that is, take initiatives in the form of making enquiries or placing orders (so-called reverse marketing).

The likely development of the split between total sales volume attributable to buyer and seller initiatives is shown in Figure 17.1. The relative share of sales volume attributable to buyer initiative will tend to increase over time. Present and future buyer initiatives are a function of all aspects of a firm's past market performance: that is, the extent, nature and timing of seller initiative, the competitiveness of offerings, post-purchase experience, the relationships developed with buyers as well as the way in which buyer initiative has been dealt with (Ottesen, 1995).

Key attributes of effective communication

The rest of the chapter will be devoted to the communication process and communicative tools based on seller initiatives. All effective marketing communication has four elements: a sender, a message, a communication channel and a receiver (audience). The communication process in Figure 17.2 highlights the key attributes of effective communication.

To communicate in an effective way the sender needs to have a clear understanding of the purpose of the message, the audience to be reached and how this audience will interpret and respond to the message. However, sometimes the audience cannot hear clearly what the sender is trying to say about its product because of the 'noise' of rival manufacturers making similar and often contradictory claims about their products.

Another important point to consider in the model of Figure 17.2 is the degree of 'fit' between medium and message. For example, a complex and wordy message would be better for the press than for a visual medium such as television or cinema.

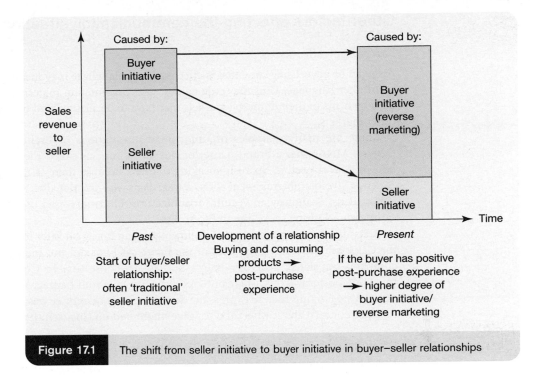

| Figure 17.1 | The shift from seller initiative to buyer initiative in buyer–seller relationships |

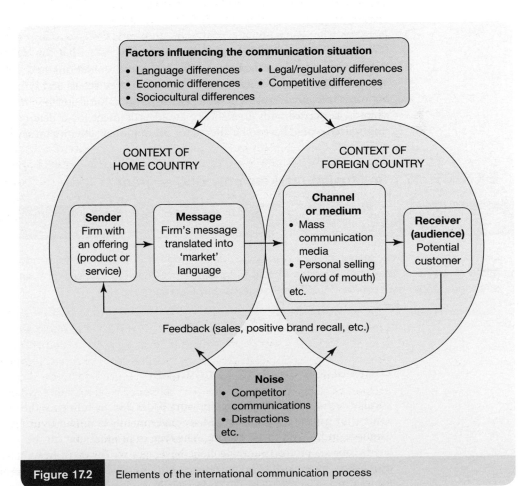

| Figure 17.2 | Elements of the international communication process |

Other factors affecting the communication situation

Language differences

A slogan or advertising copy that is effective in one language may mean something different in another language. Thus the trade names, sales presentation materials and advertisements used by firms in their domestic markets may have to be adapted and translated when used in other markets.

There are many examples of unfortunate translations of brand names and slogans. General Motors has a brand name for one of its models called the Vauxhall Nova – this does not work well in Spanish-speaking markets because there it means 'no go'. In Latin America 'Avoid embarrassment – Use Parker Pens' was translated as 'Avoid pregnancy – Use Parker Pens'. Scandinavian vacuum manufacturer Electrolux used the following in a US ad campaign: 'Nothing sucks like an Electrolux.'

A Danish company made up the following slogan for its cat litter in the UK market: 'Sand for Cat Piss'. Unsurprisingly, sales of the firm's cat litter did not increase! Another Danish company translated 'Teats for baby's bottles' as 'Loose tits'. In Copenhagen airport the following poster was on display until recently: 'We take your baggage and send it in all directions.' A slogan thus used to express the desire to give good service was sufficiently ambiguous to cause concern about where the baggage might end up (Joensen, 1997).

Economic differences

In contrast to industrialized countries, developing countries may have radios but not television sets. In countries with low levels of literacy written communication may not be as effective as visual or oral communication.

Sociocultural differences

Dimensions of culture (religion, attitudes, social conditions and education) affect how individuals perceive their environment and interpret signals and symbols. For example, the use of colour in advertising must be sensitive to cultural norms. In many Asian countries white is associated with grief; hence an advertisement for a detergent where whiteness is emphasized would have to be altered for promotional activities in, say, India.

EXHIBIT 17.1 In Muslim markets only God is great

One of the major car manufacturers was using Muhammad Ali in one of its Arab advertising campaigns. Muhammad Ali is very popular in the Middle East, but the theme was him saying 'I am the greatest': this offended people because the Muslim faith regards only God as great.

Source: Harper (1986).

Legal and regulatory conditions

Local advertising regulations and industry codes directly influence the selection of media and content of promotion materials. Many governments maintain tight regulations on content, language and sexism in advertising. The type of product that can be advertised is also regulated. Tobacco products and alcoholic beverages are the most heavily regulated in terms of promotion. However, the manufacturers of these products have not abandoned their promotional efforts. Camel engages in corporate-image advertising using its Joe Camel. Regulations are found more in industrialized economies than in developing economies, where the advertising industry is not yet as highly developed.

Competitive differences

As competitors vary from country to country in terms of number, size, type and promotional strategies used, a firm may have to adapt its promotional strategy and the timing of its efforts to the local environment.

17.3 Communication tools

Earlier in this chapter we mentioned the major forms of promotion. In this section the different communication tools, listed in Table 17.1, will be further examined.

Table 17.1	Typical communication tools (media)				
	One-way communication			Two-way communication	
Advertising	Public relations	Sales promotion		Direct marketing	Personal selling
Newspapers	Annual reports	Rebates and price discounts		Direct mail/database marketing	Sales presentations
Magazines	Corporate image	Catalogues and brochures		Internet marketing (WWW)	Sales force management
Journals	House magazines	Samples, coupons and gifts		Telemarketing	Trade fairs and exhibitions
Directories	Press relations	Competitions		Viral marketing	
Radio	Public relations			Social networking	
Television	Events				
Cinema	Lobbying				
Outdoor	Sponsorship (product placement)				

Advertising

Advertising is one of the most visible forms of communication. Because of its wide use and its limitations as a one-way method of communication advertising in international markets is subject to a number of difficulties. Advertising is often the most important part of the communications mix for consumer goods, where there are a large number of small-volume customers who can be reached through mass media. For most business-to-business markets advertising is less important than the personal selling function.

The major decisions in advertising are shown in Figure 17.3. We will now discuss these different phases.

Objectives setting

Although advertising methods may vary from country to country the major advertising objectives remain the same. Major advertising objectives (and means) might include some of the following:

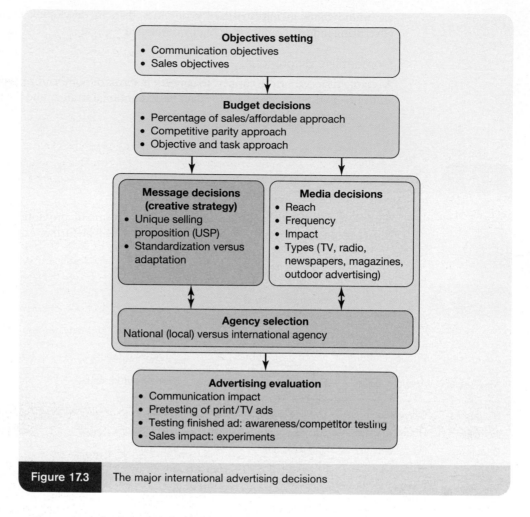

Figure 17.3	The major international advertising decisions

- *Increasing sales from existing customers* by encouraging them to increase the frequency of their purchases; maintaining brand loyalty via a strategy that reminds customers of the key advantages of the product; and stimulating impulse purchases.
- *Obtaining new customers* by increasing consumer awareness of the firm's products and improving the firm's corporate image among a new target customer group.

Budget decisions

Controversial aspects of advertising include determining a proper method for deciding the size of the promotional budget and its allocation across markets and over time.

In theory the firm (in each of its markets) should continue to put more money into advertising, as an amount of money spent on advertising returns more than an amount of money spent on anything else. In practice it is not possible to set an optimum advertising budget, therefore firms have developed more practical guidelines. The manager must also remember that the advertising budget cannot be regarded in isolation, but has to be seen as one element of the overall marketing mix.

Affordable approach/percentage of sales

Percentage of sales method
The firm will automatically allocate a fixed percentage of sales to the advertising budget.

These budgeting techniques link advertising expenditures directly to some measure of profits or, more commonly, to sales. The most popular of these methods is the **percentage of sales method**, whereby the firm automatically allocates a fixed percentage of sales to the advertising budget.

Advantages of this method are:

- For firms selling in many countries this simple method appears to guarantee equality among the markets. Each market seems to get the advertising it deserves.
- It is easy to justify in budget meetings.
- It guarantees that the firm only spends on advertising as much as it can afford. The method prevents 'good money being thrown after bad'.

Disadvantages of this method are:

- It uses historical performance rather than future performance.
- It ignores the possibility that extra spending on advertising may be necessary when sales are declining, in order to reverse the sales trend by establishing a 'recycle' on the product life cycle curve (see section 14.4).
- It does not take into account variations in the firm's marketing goals across countries.
- The 'percentage of sales' method encourages local management to maximize sales by using the easiest and most flexible marketing tool: price (that is, lowering the price).
- The method's convenience and simplicity encourage management not to bother investigating the relationships between advertising and sales or analysing critically the overall effectiveness of its advertising campaigns.
- The method cannot be used to launch new products or enter new markets (zero sales = zero advertising).

EXHIBIT 17.2 Product placement escalates

Product placement is a form of advertisement, where branded products or services are placed in a context usually without ads, such as movies, the storyline of television shows, or news programmes.

Product placement is common practice on reality television, for example *American Idol*. As the costs of making such shows accelerate, the television networks are looking for partners who want to finance programmes in return for some screen time for their products.

Another example of a company which has decided to focus more on product placement is Harley-Davidson. Only 3 per cent of US consumers own a motorcycle (mainly males aged

Copyright © 20th Century Fox/Everett/Rex Features.

35+), but there are another 15 to 20 million individuals in the US (outside the core target group) who have a desire to buy one. The motorcycle brand announced in November 2009 that it had teamed up with an entertainment consulting agency for a major product placement push in film, TV, music and video games.

Source: information from www.harley-davidson.com.

Competitive parity approach
Duplicating the amounts spent on advertising by major rivals.

Competitive parity approach

The **competitive parity approach** involves estimating and duplicating the amounts spent on advertising by major rivals. Unfortunately, determining the marketing expenditures of foreign-based competitors is far more difficult than monitoring home country businesses, whose financial accounts (if they are limited companies) are open to public inspection and whose promotional activities are obvious the moment they occur. Another danger in following the practice of competitors is that they are not necessarily right.

Furthermore, the method does not recognize that the firm is in different situations in different markets. If the firm is new to a market its relationships with customers are different from those of existing domestic companies. This should also be reflected in its promotion budget.

Objective and task approach

Objective and task approach
Determining the advertising objectives and then ascertaining the tasks needed to attain these objectives.

The weaknesses of the above approaches have led some firms to follow the **objective and task approach**, which begins by determining the advertising objectives and then ascertaining the tasks needed to attain these objectives. This approach also includes a cost–benefit analysis, relating objectives to the costs of achieving them. To use this method the firm must have good knowledge of the local market.

A research study (Hung and West, 1991) showed that only 20 per cent of companies in the United States, Canada and the United Kingdom used the objective and task approach. Although it is the 'theoretically correct' way of determining the promotion budget it is sometimes more important to be operational and to use a 'percentage of sales' approach. This is not necessarily a bad method if company experience shows it to be reasonably successful. If the percentage is flexible it allows different percentages in different markets.

Message decisions (creative strategy)

USP
Unique selling proposition is the decisive sales argument for customers to buy the product.

This concerns decisions about what unique selling proposition (**USP**) needs to be communicated, and what the communication is intended to achieve in terms of consumer behaviour in the country concerned. These decisions have important implications for the choice of advertising medium, since certain media can better accommodate specific creative requirements (use of colour, written description, high definition, demonstration of the product, etc.) than others.

An important decision area for international marketers is whether an advertising campaign developed in the domestic market can be transferred to foreign markets with only minor modifications, such as translation into the appropriate languages. Complete standardization of all aspects of a campaign over several foreign markets is rarely attainable. Standardization implies a common message, creative idea, media and strategy, but it also requires that the firm's product has a USP that is clearly understood by customers in a cross-cultural environment.

Standardizing international advertising can lead to a number of advantages for the firm. For example, advertising costs will be reduced by centralizing the advertising campaign in the head office and transferring the same campaign from market to market, as opposed to running campaigns from different local offices.

However, executing an advertising campaign in multiple markets requires a balance between conveying the message and allowing for local nuances. The adaptation of global ideas can be achieved by various tactics, such as adopting a modular approach, adapting international symbols and using international advertising agencies.

Media decisions

The selection of the media to be used for advertising campaigns needs to be done simultaneously with the development of the message theme. A key question in media selection is whether to use a mass or target approach. The mass media (television, radio and newsprint) are effective when a significant percentage of the general public are potential customers. This percentage varies considerably by country for most products, depending on, for example, the distribution of incomes in different countries.

The selection of the media to be used in a particular campaign typically starts with some idea of the target market's demographic and psychological characteristics, regional strengths of the product, seasonality of sales and so on. The media selected should be the result of a careful fit of local advertising objectives, media attributes and target market characteristics. Furthermore, media selection can be based on the following criteria:

- **Reach.** This is the total number of people in a target market exposed to at least one advertisement in a given time period ('opportunity to see', or **OTS**).
- **Frequency.** This is the average number of times within a given time period that each potential customer is exposed to the same advertisement.
- **Impact.** This depends on compatibility between the medium used and the message. *Penthouse* magazine continues to attract advertisers for high-value-added consumer durables, such as cars, hi-fi equipment and clothes, which are geared primarily to a high-income male segment.

High reach is necessary when the firm enters a new market or introduces a new product so that information about, for example, the new product's availability is spread to the widest possible audience. A high level of frequency is appropriate when brand awareness already exists and the message is about informing the consumer that a campaign is under way. Sometimes a campaign should have both a high frequency and extensive reach, but limits on the advertising budget often create the need to trade off frequency against reach.

A media's gross rating points (**GRPs**) are the result of multiplying its reach by the frequency with which an advertisement appears within the media over a certain period. Hence it contains duplicated exposure, but indicates the critical mass of a media effort. GRPs may be estimated for individual vehicles, for entire classes of media or for a total campaign.

The cost of running a media campaign also has to be taken into consideration. Traditionally media planning is based on a single measure, such as 'cost per thousand GRPs'. When dealing with two or more national markets the selection of media also has to take into account:

- differences in the firm's market objectives across countries
- differences in media effectiveness across countries.

Since media availability and relative importance will not be the same in all countries, plans may require adjustment in cross-border campaigns. As a way of distributing advertising messages through new communication channels, co-promotion has a strong foothold. Let us now take a closer look at the main media types.

Television

Television is an expensive but commonly used medium in attempting to reach broad national markets. In most developed countries coverage is no problem. However, television is one of the most regulated of communications media. Many countries have prohibited the advertising of cigarettes and alcohol other than beer. In other countries (e.g. in Scandinavia) there are limits on the number of minutes that TV advertising is permitted. Some countries also prohibit commercial breaks in TV programmes.

Radio

Radio is a lower-cost broadcasting activity than television. Commercial radio started several decades before commercial television in many countries. Radio is often transmitted on a local basis and therefore national campaigns have to be built up on an area-by-area basis.

Newspapers (print)

In virtually all urban areas of the world the population has access to daily newspapers. In fact the problem for the advertiser is not having too few newspapers, but rather having too many of them. Most countries have one or more newspapers that can be said to have a truly national circulation. However, in many countries newspapers tend to be predominantly local or regional and, as such, serve as the primary medium for local advertisers. Attempting to use a series of local papers to reach a national market is considerably more complex and costly.

OTS
Opportunity to see – total number of people in the target market exposed to at least one ad in a given time period ('reach').

Frequency
Average number of times within a given time frame that each potential customer is exposed to the same ad.

Impact
Depends on the compatibility between the medium used and the message (the 'impact' on the consumer's brain).

GRPs
Gross rating points – Reach multiplied by frequency. GRPs may be estimated for individual media vehicles. Media planning is often based on 'cost per 1,000 GRPs'.

EXHIBIT 17.3 Mercedes uses Janis Joplin's hit to market its cars in the United States

Some 30 years ago rock singer Janis Joplin begged the Lord for a Mercedes Benz. The vocal version of a poor woman's evening prayer was a hit then and is still played frequently on radio stations all over the world.

Buying power of the generation of 1968

The generation of 1968 have now reached an age with purchasing power, and the German car company has decided to let the prayer be heard as part of a huge advertising campaign. Mercedes Benz has bought the rights to use the song in its advertisements in coming years. The campaign has already been launched on US TV, where Joplin's 'whisky' voice accompanies the delicate pictures of two of Mercedes' newest luxury models. Many classic rock hits from the 1950s and 1960s have been used commercially in advertisements during recent years, but Joplin's hit is different in two ways. First, it mentions the product directly. Second, the song was originally a satire of the poor's dream that happiness was found in one of the day's most materialistic status symbols.

'It was never meant to be taken seriously,' songwriter Bob Neuwirth recollects, who back in 1970 helped Joplin fabricate the song in a break between two concerts. He has nothing to do with the song today and has not been asked for advice. 'But I am surprised that it took them so long to think of the idea,' he says, and maintains that Joplin had no desperate personal need for an expensive status symbol.

In those days, Joplin owned a Porsche. Mercedes Benz has chosen Joplin as part of an attempt to reach a younger audience through advertisements that, according to the director for Mercedes' North American department Andrew Goldberg, create an instant emotional and physical connection to the product.

The reactions of a test audience have documented that the song produced warm, nostalgic feelings and created a more positive attitude towards Mercedes. 'What she meant by the song 25 years ago can be freely interpreted by anyone. But when a customer sees the advertisement it is solely about emotions and not sociology,' says Goldberg.

Janis Joplin became a world name with the group Big Brother and the Holding Co. at the end of the 1960s, but died from an overdose of heroin on 4 October 1970. Six months later her solo LP *Pearl* was released. It contained among others the Mercedes song, which a chuckling Joplin finishes with the words 'That's it,' after the famous refrain: 'So Lord won't you buy me a Mercedes Benz.' Exactly as she is doing now a quarter of a century later in the advertisement.

Source: translated from an article by Jan Lund in the Danish newspaper *Jyllands-posten*, 24 March 1995.

Many countries have English-language newspapers in addition to local-language newspapers. For example, the aim of the *Asian Wall Street Journal* is to supply economic information in English to influential Asian business people, politicians, top government officials and intellectuals.

Magazines (print)

In general, magazines have a narrower readership than newspapers. In most countries magazines serve to reach specific segments of the population, and for technical and industrial products magazines can be quite effective. Technical business publications tend to be international in their coverage. These range from individual businesses (e.g. beverages, construction, textiles) to worldwide industrial magazines covering many industries.

Marketers of international products have the option of using international magazines that have regional editions (e.g. *Newsweek*, *Time* and *Business Week*). In the case of *Reader's Digest*, local-language editions are distributed.

Cinema

In countries where it is common to subsidize the cost of showing films by running advertising commercials prior to the feature film, cinema advertising has become an important medium. India, for example, has a relatively high level of cinema attendance per capita (few have television at home). Therefore cinema advertisements play a much greater role in India than in, for example, the United States.

Cinema advertising has other advantages, one of the most important being that it has a truly captive audience (no channel hopping!). The problem, of course, is that people know that commercials will be shown before the film. So they will not turn up until the main feature begins.

Outdoor advertising

Outdoor advertising includes posters/billboards, shop signs and transit advertising. This medium shows the creative way in which space can be sold to customers. In the case of transit advertising, for example, a bus can be sold as an advertising medium. In Romania transit advertising is very effective. According to a survey by Mueller (1996), in Bucharest 91 per cent of all consumers surveyed said they remembered the content of transit advertisements, compared with 82 per cent who remembered the content of print adverts. The use of transit media is expanding rapidly in China as well. Outdoor posters/billboards can be used to develop the visual impact of advertising. France is a country associated with the effective use of poster/billboard advertising. In some countries legal restrictions limit the poster space available.

Agency selection

Confronted with the many complex problems that international advertising involves, many businesses instinctively turn to an advertising agency for advice and practical assistance. Agencies employ or have instant access to expert copywriters, translators, photographers, film makers, package designers and media planners who are skilled and experienced in the international field. Only the largest of big businesses can afford to carry such people in-house.

If the international marketer decides to outsource the international advertising functions they have a variety of options:

- Use different national (local) agencies in the international markets where the firm is present.
- Use the services of a big international agency with domestic overseas offices.

In Table 17.2 the different factors favouring a national or an international agency are listed. The single European (pan-European) market is used as an example of an international agency.

Table 17.2	European agency selection: national (local) or pan-European (international)
National (local)	**Pan-European (international)**
Supports national subsidiary.	Reflects new European reality and trends.
Investment in existing brand best handled nationally.	Economies of scale in new product development and branding.
Closer to marketplace.	Uniformity of treatment across Europe.
Smaller size more conducive to personalized service and greater creativity.	Resources and skills of major European or global agency.
Diversity of ideas.	Easier to manage one agency group.

Source: adapted from Lynch (1994, Table 11.4).

The criteria relevant to the choice of a national or an international agency include:

- *Policy of the company*. Has the company got any realistic plans for a more standardized advertising approach?
- *Nature of the advertising to be undertaken*. Corporate image advertising might be best undertaken by a single large multinational agency that operates throughout the world via its own subsidiaries. For niche marketing in specialist country sectors a local agency might be preferred.
- *Type of product*. The campaign for an item that is to be presented in a standardized format, using the same advertising layouts and messages in all countries, might be handled more conveniently by a single multinational agency.

Advertising evaluation

Advertising evaluation and testing is the final stage in the advertising decision process shown in Figure 17.3. Testing advertising effectiveness is normally more difficult in international markets than in domestic markets. An important reason for this is the distance and communication gap between domestic and foreign markets. Thus it can be very difficult to transfer testing methods used in domestic ones to foreign ones. For example, the conditions for interviewing people can vary from country to country. Consequently, many firms try to use sales results as a measure of advertising effectiveness, but awareness testing is also relevant in many cases, e.g. is brand awareness of crucial importance during the early stages of a new product launch.

Testing the impact of advertising on sales is very difficult because it is difficult to isolate the advertising effect. One way to solve this problem is to use a kind of *experiment*, where the markets of the firm are grouped according to similar characteristics. In each group of countries, one or two are used as test markets. Independent variables to be tested against the sales (dependent variable) might include the amount of advertising, the media mix, the unique selling proposition and the frequency of placement.

This kind of experiment is also relevant for testing other types of communication tool mentioned in Table 17.1.

EXHIBIT 17.4 Baileys Irish Cream liqueur: sales expansion with market and product development

In 1993 R&A Bailey and Co. decided to increase sales of its brand in Europe by expanding usage of the drink. A cross-border television advertising campaign, 'Baileys with ice', was developed to reinforce the contemporary all-year-round image of the drink and to distinguish it from the 'stuffy' image of traditional liqueurs with their mainly after-dinner role. The appeal was to younger consumers to drink Bailey's on a greater number of occasions. Special promotional packs were also developed, consisting of a one-litre bottle together with two free liqueur glasses.

In early 1993 Baileys was also launched on the Japanese market after a period of test marketing. The regular brand was offered in addition to a specially developed brand for the Japanese called Baileys Gold, which was developed with ten-year-old malt whiskey to appeal to the Japanese taste for premium-quality spirits. Baileys Gold was also priced at double the price of the regular brand.

Source: MacNamee and McDonnell (1995).

Diageo plc

Table 17.3	Target groups for public relations	
Publics or target groups: domestic markets	**Extra international dimensions: international markets**	
Directly connected with the organization Employees Shareholders	Wider range of cultural issues The degree of remoteness of the corporate headquarters	
Suppliers of raw materials and components Providers of financial services Providers of marketing services (e.g. marketing research, advertising, media)	Is this to be handled on a country-by-country basis, or is some overall standardization desirable?	
Customers of the organization Existing customers Past customers Those capable of becoming customers	May have less knowledge of the company The country-of-origin effect will influence communications	
Environment The general public Government: local, regional, national Financial markets generally	Wide range of general publics Host governments Regional grouping (e.g. EU), world groupings	

Source: Phillips *et al.* (1994, p. 362). Reprinted by permission of Cengage Learning.

Public relations

Word-of-mouth advertising is not only cheap, it is very effective. Public relations (PR) seeks to enhance corporate image building and influence favourable media treatment. PR (or publicity) is the marketing communications function that carries out programmes designed to earn public understanding and acceptance. It should be viewed as an integral part of the global marketing effort.

PR activities involve both internal and external communication. Internal communication is important to create an appropriate corporate culture. The target groups for public relations are shown in Table 17.3.

The range of target groups is far wider in public relations than it is for the other communications tools. Target groups are likely to include the main stakeholder groups of employees, customers, distribution channel members and shareholders. For companies operating in international markets this gives a very wide range of communication tasks. Internal communications in different country subsidiaries, employing people from a number of different countries, with different cultural values, will be particularly challenging.

In a more market-oriented sense, the PR activity is directed towards an influential, though relatively small, target audience of editors and journalists who work for newspapers/magazines, or towards broadcasting aimed at the firm's customers and stakeholders.

Since the target audience is small it is relatively inexpensive to reach. Several methods can be used to gain PR:

- Contribution of prizes at different events.
- Sponsorship of events (sporting, cultural, etc.). According to Meenaghan (1996), the worldwide sponsorship market grew from US$2 billion in 1984 to US$13.02 billion in 1994. In 1994 Europe and the United States together accounted for 32.6 per cent of worldwide sponsorship expenditure.
- Press releases of news about the firm's products, plant and personnel.
- Announcements of the firm's promotional campaigns.
- Lobbying (government).

The degree of control of the PR messages is quite different. Journalists can use PR material to craft an article of so many words, or an interview of so many seconds. How material is used will depend on the journalist and the desired story line. On occasions a thoroughly negative story can result from a press release that was designed to enhance the company image.

Hence PR activity includes anticipating criticism. Criticisms may range from general ones against all multinational corporations to more specific ones. They may also be based on a market: for example, doing business with prison factories in China.

EXHIBIT 17.5 Mixing it with Sports Sponsorship: MMA – mixed martial arts, or marketing-made athletes?

Jay Benjamin runs an agency where he represents the interests of approximately 100 athletes, engaged in MMA (mixed martial arts) and cage fighting. Originally hailing from a background in music contract law, Jay was able to put his legal knowledge to great use; whilst also marrying it with his passion for martial arts. The jewel in Jay's crown is Joachim 'Hellboy' Hansen, the first Dream World Lightweight Champion – a title which he defended over 2008–09; attracting viewing figures of 20 million in Asia alone, per fight.

Sports icons like David Beckham and Andy Murray have spearheaded a trend of athletes choosing to align themselves with entertainment agencies; as opposed to just dedicated sports agencies. Both are currently represented by Simon Fuller's 19 Entertainment Ltd, with Fuller's agency also boasting rights and representation of such legends such as Elvis and Muhammad Ali. This move appears to suggest both a desire and an appetite for sports to take centre stage – across a variety of platforms and industry sectors. In much the same way, Jay has found that the lion's share of his work involves exploiting the market potential of his athletes – through sponsorship marketing and negotiating a mine field of contractual obligations.

Joachim 'Hellboy' Hansen
Courtesy of J. Benjamin, The Network Agency.

Market potential

Sports Sponsorship is moving into new dimensions, aligning itself closely with brand theory. This has meant that an agent's job is becoming more heavily influenced by an ability to both respond to and dictate marketing-driven activities. These developments have encouraged Jay to increase his marketing knowledge and seek the assistance of marketing communications consultants. Following this, the four critical success factors which appear to have emerged for an agent are having:

1. access to a network of industry contacts
2. a strong knowledge of contract law
3. an ability to demonstrate that their client has a following, or is able to attract interest
4. strategic marketing approach.

Off the back of the successes of Hellboy Hansen, Jay has sought to secure lucrative sponsorship deals with interested parties. The key to Jay's approach has been to treat Hansen as a cross-platform marketing proposition in his own right – allowing Jay to apply complex segmentation criteria to his activities. By looking outside of the field of martial arts, Jay has attempted to study the wider habits and lifestyle profiles of potentially interested stakeholders. Most recently this has seen Hellboy Hansen transformed into the virtual world. Hansen is set to be a character in a forthcoming EA video game, available on the Xbox360 and Playstation3 called 'EA Sports MMA'. Hansen's video character will also have clothing which carries paid-for sponsorship branding. Such sponsorship opportunities have now opened the door to additional parties who showed no interest previously towards Hansen's exploits in the 'real world'.

The games world allows exposure to a captive audience for much longer than afforded by traditional advertising methods and real life fight bouts. Gamers' views suggest that they do not express the same irritation within their virtual world – as expressed in connection with such advertising and branding intrusions in the 'real world'. Instead branding and advertising, if carefully placed, can afford added credibility to the game. In addition, athletes are immortalized in a way that overtakes their actual sporting lifetime – with their performances now being in the hands of the gamer. The blurring of reality with fantasy has the effect of a mutual and reciprocal benefit to both parties – and in doing so increases their respective equities and market potential. Further evidence of this has seen Manchester United's Ji Sung Park turned into a Japanese anime-style promotional trailer and manga comic strip, produced by Nike.

So lucrative is this phenomena that athletes and agents may curtail their active sporting life-cycle in the future in pursuit of protecting and capturing brand potential. Rather than simply supporting an athlete's brand image through platforms like games, film, cosmetics, fashion and music videos, a decision may be taken for an athlete to change careers in preference for one of these – in order to seek higher financial rewards. In doing so, these desires may in fact overtake those of achieving sporting excellence. Furthermore agents may feel that they are well positioned to also represent clients in other industry sectors. With marketing in the ascendent, the following appear to have become of more significance within the MMA world:

- Athletes having a striking image and a catchy name allows them to be transformed into brand icons and credible sponsorship offerings which also exist across platforms outside of the field of sports.
- Athletes viewing themselves as having a universal appeal – which gives sponsors an opportunity to not only enter new global markets; but also engage in the denationalization and deterritorization of their brands, in the interests of wealth creation.
- Winning not being enough, but now more importantly how bouts are won. In Hansen's case, his varied flash and fancy moves have ensured that people wish to emulate him – which has now been made that bit easier, through him appearing in a video game. His moves translate well into interesting gaming and make him a firm gamers' favourite.

These trends seem to suggest that a good fighter is judged, by consumers and sponsors alike, not just from their performance but also by their attractiveness as a brand icon.

Marketing challenges

These activities have not been without their problems. Jay lists a few that he has encountered along the way:

- This is largely uncharted water within his field, making it difficult to evaluate and calculate the actual market and brand potential of an athlete. This has especially been made difficult as other agents and associated parties are reluctant to reveal the full nature of their agreements to others – with there seldom being any transparency of sponsorship pricing offered, or an official framework/code of practice.
- There are generally several restrictive contracts to contend with at any one time. Existing agreements – associated with venues, competitions and broadcast rights – have seen innovative attempts to gain further sponsorship for fighters thwarted. For example attempts to use henna body tattoos in the design of a corporate sponsor were blocked, due to venue and broadcast restrictions. To this end, athletes are often forced into last place when it comes to securing sponsorship deals; or at best, agents have to weave their way through a myriad of terms and conditions.

- The precarious nature of fighting means that losses can affect an athlete's market potential much quicker than in other sports – which makes time of the essence, and reduces the rates and length of contract that sponsors wish to agree to.
- The fact that fighters wear little clothing offers limited sponsorship sites. This has driven fighters to adapt their clothing in order to capture more sponsorship, unlike in other sports – where such a wardrobe change may more likely be to enhance sporting performance. In addition, fighters often quickly don other clothing, such as caps after fights – in an attempt to fulfil more sponsorship agreements.

Exhibit written (including interviews conducted) by: Jonathan A. J. Wilson, Senior Lecturer 'Advertising and Marketing Communications', University of Greenwich, London.
Acknowledgements of support: Jay Benjamin, EA Games.
Relevant websites: www.ea.com/games/mma; mma.easports.com/home.action; www.19entertainment.com/; nikelegend.co.kr/; en.wikipedia.org/wiki/Jaochim_Hansen.

Sales promotion

Sales promotion is defined as those selling activities that do not fall directly into the advertising or personal selling category. Sales promotion also relates to so-called below-the-line activities such as point-of-sale displays and demonstrations, leaflets, free trials, contests and premiums such as 'two for the price of one'. Unlike media advertising, which is 'above the line' and earns a commission, below-the-line sales promotion does not. To an advertising agency above the line means traditional media for which they are recognized by the media owners, entitling them to commission.

Sales promotion is a short-term effort directed primarily to the consumer and/or retailer, in order to achieve specific objectives:

- consumer product trial and/or immediate purchase
- consumer introduction to the shop
- encouraging retailers to use point-of-purchase displays for the product
- encouraging shops to stock the product.

In the United States especially, the sales promotion budgets for fast-moving consumer goods (FMCG) manufacturers are larger than the advertising budgets. Factors contributing to the expansion of sales promotion activities include:

- greater competition among retailers, combined with increasingly sophisticated retailing methods;
- higher levels of brand awareness among consumers, leading to the need for manufacturers to defend brand shares;
- improved retail technology (e.g. electronic scanning devices that enable coupon redemptions, etc., to be monitored instantly);
- greater integration of sales promotion, public relations and conventional media campaigns.

In markets where the consumer is hard to reach because of media limitations the percentage of the total communication budget allocated to sales promotions is also relatively high. Different types of sales promotion include:

- *Price discounts.* These are very widely used. A variety of different price reduction techniques is available, such as cash-back deals.
- *Catalogues/brochures.* The buyer in a foreign market may be located at quite a distance from the closest sales office. In this situation a foreign catalogue can be very effective. It must be able to close the gap between buyer and seller in the way that the potential buyer is supplied with all the necessary information, from prices, sizes, colours and quantities

to packing, shipping time and acceptable form of payment. In addition to catalogues, brochures of various types are useful for salespersons, distributors and agents. Translations should be done in cooperation with overseas agents and/or distributors.

- *Coupons.* Coupons are a classic tool for FMCG brands, especially in the United States. A variety of coupon distribution methods exists: door-to-door, on pack, in newspapers. Coupons are not allowed in all European countries.
- *Samples.* A sample gives the potential foreign buyer an idea of the firm and quality of product that cannot be attained by even the best graphic picture. Samples may prevent misunderstandings over style, sizes, models and so on.
- *Gifts.* Most European countries have a limit on the value of the premium or gift given. Furthermore, in some countries it is illegal to offer premiums that are conditional on the purchase of another product. The United States does not allow alcoholic beer to be offered as a free sample.
- *Competitions.* This type of sales promotion needs to be communicated to the potential customers. This can be done on the pack, in stores via leaflets or through media advertising.

The success of sales promotion depends on local adaptation. Major constraints are imposed by local laws, which may not permit premiums or free gifts to be given. Some countries' laws control the amount of discount given at retail level; others require permits for all sales promotions. Since it is impossible to know the specific laws of each country, international marketers should consult local lawyers and authorities before launching a promotional campaign.

Direct marketing

According to Onkvisit and Shaw (1993, p. 717), direct marketing is the total of activities by which products and services are offered to market segments in one or more media for informational purposes or to solicit a direct response from a present or prospective customer or contributor by mail, telephone or personal visit.

Direct marketing covers direct mail (marketing database), telephone selling and marketing via the Internet. A number of factors have encouraged the rapid expansion of the international direct marketing industry (Bennett, 1995, p. 318):

- developments in mailing technology, which have reduced the costs of distributing direct-mail literature;
- escalating costs of other forms of advertising and sales promotion;
- the increasing availability of good-quality lists of prospective customers;
- developments in information technology (especially database technology and desktop publishing) that enable smaller companies to produce high-quality direct marketing materials in-house;
- the increasing availability throughout the developed world of interactive television facilities, whereby consumers may order goods through a teletext system.

Direct mail

Direct mail is a viable medium in many countries. It is especially important when other media are not available. Direct mail offers a flexible, selective and potentially highly cost-effective means of reaching foreign consumers. Messages can be addressed exclusively to the target market, advertising budgets may be concentrated on the most promising market segments, and it will be some time before competitors realize that the firm has launched a campaign. In addition, the size, content, timing and geographical coverage of mailshots can be varied at will: the firm can spend as much or as little as necessary to achieve its objectives. There are no media space or airtime restrictions, and no copy or insertion deadlines to be met. All aspects of the direct-mail process are subject to the firm's immediate control, and it can experiment by varying the approach used in different countries. Direct mail can take many forms – letters, catalogues, technical literature – and it can serve as a vehicle for the distribution of samples. A major problem in the effective use of direct mail is the preparation of a suitable mailing list (marketing database).

European marketers are still far behind the United States in exploiting the medium and also with regard to the response to direct mail in the form of mail orders. Per capita mail-order sales in the United States are more than double those of any European country (Desmet and Xardel, 1996, p. 58). The use of direct mail in Japan is also below that in the United States. One reason for this discrepancy is that the Japanese feel printed material is too impersonal and insufficiently sincere.

Direct mail is not only relevant for the consumer market. However, effective use of direct mail for business-to-business purposes requires the preparation of an accurate customer profile (marketing database), including industry classification, size of target company (measured, for example, by turnover, number of employees or market share), the people to approach in each business (purchasing officer, project development engineer, product manager, etc.), industry purchasing procedures and (where known) supplier selection criteria and the buying motives of prospective customers.

Telemarketing is used today for both consumer and business-to-business campaigns throughout the industrialized world. The telephone can be used both to obtain orders and to conduct fast, low-cost market research. Telemarketing covers cold calling (unsolicited calls) by salespeople, market surveys conducted by telephone, calls designed to compile databases of possible sales prospects and follow-ups to customer requests for further information, resulting from print and broadcast advertisements. Currently, the majority of cross-border telemarketing campaigns focus on business-to-business contacts, essentially because of the combined telephone/fax/database facilities that an increasing number of companies possess and, in consequence, the greater reliability of business-to-business communications.

The administration of international telemarketing normally requires the use of a commercial telemarketing agency. Language skills are required, plus considerable skills and experience in identifying decision-makers in target firms.

In some European countries cold calling of consumers is under close scrutiny in the name of consumer protection and respect for privacy. For example, Germany has prohibited calls on the grounds of privacy invasion, and this ban even applies to an insurance salesperson's announcement of a visit.

In the light of the development in Internet technologies it is very relevant to consider the World Wide Web as a direct marketing tool. This issue was discussed in Chapter 14.

Personal selling

The differences between advertising and personal selling were indicated in Table 17.1. Advertising is a one-way communication process that has relatively more 'noise', whereas personal selling is a two-way communication process with immediate feedback and relatively less 'noise'. Personal selling is an effective way to sell products, but it is expensive. It is used mainly to sell to distribution channel members and in business-to-business markets. However, personal selling is also used in some consumer markets – for example, for cars and for consumer durable products. In some countries labour costs are very low and here personal selling will be used to a greater extent than in high-cost countries.

If personal selling costs on business-to-business markets are relatively high it is relevant to economize with personal selling resources, and use personal selling only at the end of the potential customer's buying process (Figure 17.4). Computerized database marketing (direct mail, etc.) is used in a customer screening process, to point out possible customers, who will then be 'taken over' by salespersons. Their job is to turn 'hot' and 'very hot' customer candidates into real customers.

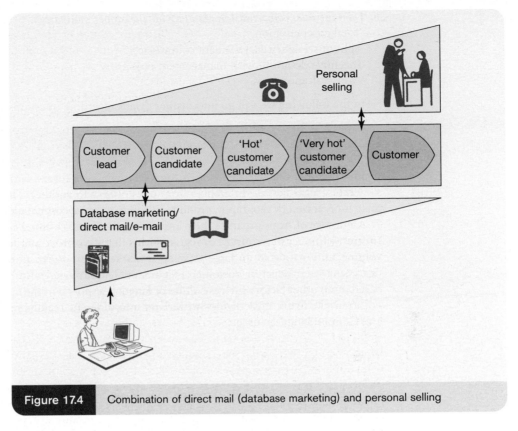

| **Figure 17.4** | Combination of direct mail (database marketing) and personal selling |

Assessing sales force effectiveness

There are five essential questions to ask in assessing sales force effectiveness:

1. *Is the selling effort structured for effective market coverage?*
   Organization
   Size of sales force
   Territory deployment
2. *Is the sales force staffed with the right people?*
   Type of international sales force: expatriates/host country/third country
   Age/tenure/education profile
   Interpersonal skills
   Technical capabilities
   Selling technique
3. *Is strong guidance provided?*
   Written guidelines
   Key tasks/mission definition
   Call frequency
   Time allocation
   People to be seen
   Market/account focus
   Territory planning and control tools
   On-the-job coaching
4. *Is adequate sales support in place?*
   Training
   Technical back-up
   Inside sales staff
   Product and applications literature

5. *Does the sales compensation plan provide the proper motivation?*
Total compensation
Split of straight salary/straight commission
Incentive design/fit with management objectives
Non-cash incentives.

In the following we will go into further details regarding questions 1 and 2.

International sales force organization

In international markets firms often organize their sales forces similarly to their domestic structures, regardless of differences from one country to another. This means that the sales force is organized by geography, product, customer or some combination of these (Table 17.4).

A number of firms organize their international sales force along simple geographical territories within a given country or region. Firms that have broad product lines and large sales volume, and/or operate in large, developed markets may prefer more specialized organizations, such as product or customer assignment. The firm may also organize the sales force based upon other factors such as culture or languages spoken in the targeted foreign markets. For example, firms often divide Switzerland into different regions reflecting French, Italian and German language usage.

Type of international sales force

Management should consider three options when determining the most appropriate international sales force. The salespeople hired for sales positions could be expatriates, host country nationals or third-country nationals. For example, a German working for a German company in the United States is an expatriate. The same German working for a US company in Germany is a host country national. They are a third-country national if assigned to France.

- *Expatriate salespersons.* These are viewed favourably because they are already familiar with the firm's products, technology, history and policies. Thus the 'only' kind of preparation

Table 17.4	Sales force organizational structure		
Structure	**Factors favouring choice of organizational structure**	**Advantages**	**Disadvantages**
Geographic	Distinct languages/cultures Single product line Underdeveloped markets	Clear, simple Incentive to cultivate local business and personal ties Travel expenses	Breadth of customers Breadth of products
Product	Established market Broad product lines	Product knowledge	Travel expenses Overlapping territories/customers Local business and personal ties
Customer*	Broad product lines	Market/customer knowledge	Overlapping territories/products Local business and personal ties Travel expenses
Combination	Large sales volume Large/developed markets Distinct language/cultures	Maximum flexibility Travel expenses	Complexity Sales management Product/market/geography overlap

* By type of industry, size of account, channel of distribution, individual company.

they would need is a knowledge of the foreign market. Yet this may be a great problem for the expatriate salesperson. Whereas some may enjoy the challenge and adjustment, other expatriate personnel find it difficult to come to terms with a new and unfamiliar business environment. The failure to understand a foreign culture and its customers will hinder the effectiveness of an expatriate sales force. The family of the expatriate may also face adaptation problems. However, very expensive items often require selling directly from the head office, which usually involves expatriates.

● *Host country nationals.* These are personnel who are based in their home country. As native personnel they have extensive market and cultural knowledge, language skills and familiarity with local business traditions. Since the government and local community undoubtedly prefer that their own nationals be hired instead of outsiders, the firm can avoid charges of exploitation while gaining goodwill at the same time. Using local sales representatives also permits the firm to become active more quickly in a new market because the adjustment period is minimized.

● *Third-country nationals.* These are employees transferred from one country to another. They tend to be born in one country, employed by a firm based in another country and working in a third country.

The advantages and disadvantages of the three types of international sales force are summarized in Table 17.5.

Expatriates and third-country nationals are seldom used in sales capacities for long periods of time. They are used for three main reasons: to upgrade a subsidiary's selling performance, to fill management positions and to transfer sales policies, procedures and techniques. However, most companies use local nationals as their sales personnel. They are familiar with local business practices and can be managed accordingly.

Trade fairs and exhibitions

A trade fair (TF) or exhibition is a concentrated event at which manufacturers, distributors and other vendors display their products and/or describe their services to current and

Table 17.5	Advantages and disadvantages of sales force types	
Category	**Advantages**	**Disadvantages**
Expatriates	Product knowledge High service levels Train for promotion Greater home control	Highest costs High turnover High training cost
Host country	Economical High market knowledge Language skills Best cultural knowledge Implement actions sooner	Needs product training May be held in low esteem Importance of language skills declining Difficult to ensure loyalty
Third country	Cultural sensitivity Language skills Economical Allows regional sales coverage May allow sales to country in conflict with the home country	Face identity problems Blocked promotions Income gaps Needs product/company training Loyalty assurance

Source: reprinted from *Industrial Marketing Management*, Vol. 24, Honeycutt, E.D. and Ford, J.B. (1995) 'Guidelines for managing an international sales force', p. 138, Copyright 1995, with permission from Elsevier.

prospective customers, suppliers, other business associates and the press. Trade fairs are multi-purpose events involving many interactions between the TF exhibitor and numerous parties.

TFs can enable a company to reach in a few days a concentrated group of interested prospects that might otherwise take several months to contact. Potential buyers can examine and compare the outputs of competing firms in a short period at the same place. They can see the latest developments and establish immediate contact with supplying businesses.

Traditionally TFs have been regarded as a personal selling tool, but Sharland and Balogh (1996) conclude that TFs are an excellent environment for non-selling activities such as information exchange, relationship building and channel partner assessment. TFs offer international firms the opportunity to gather vital information quickly, easily and cheaply. For example, within a short period a firm can learn a considerable amount about its competitive environment, which would take much longer and cost much more to get through other sources (e.g. secondary information).

Whether a marketer should participate in a trade fair depends largely on the type of business relationship it wants to develop with a particular country. A company looking only for one-off or short-term sales might find the TF expense prohibitive, but a firm looking for long-term involvement may find the investment worthwhile.

17.4 International advertising strategies in practice

In the introduction to Part IV the question of standardization or adaptation of the whole marketing mix was discussed. Standardization allows the realization of economies of scale in the production of advertising materials, reducing advertising costs and increasing profitability. On the other hand, because advertising is based largely on language and images, it is mostly influenced by the sociocultural behaviour of consumers in different countries.

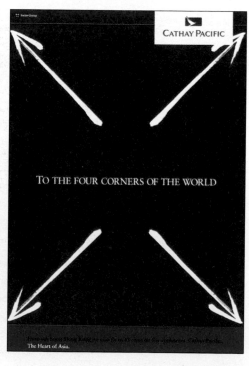

Standardized advertisements from Cathay Pacific

In reality it is not a question of either/or. For the internationally oriented firm it is more a question of the degree of standardization/localization. A study by Hite and Frazer (1988) showed that a majority (54 per cent) of internationally oriented firms were using a combination strategy (localizing advertising for some markets and standardizing advertising for others). Only 9 per cent of the firms were using totally standardized advertising for all foreign markets, much lower than in previous studies (Sorenson and Weichman, 1975; Boddewyn et al., 1986). This could indicate a trend towards less standardization. A total of 37 per cent of the firms reported that they were using only localized advertising. Many of the global companies using standardized advertising are well known (e.g. Coca-Cola, Intel, Philip Morris/Marlboro).

The Cathay Pacific advertisements show that the company uses a standardized strategy in the South East Asian area. The only element of adaptation is the translation of the English text into Japanese.

Examples of adaptation (localization) strategies

Courvoisier Cognac: Hong Kong/China versus Europe

The Chinese love affair with Western alcohol goes back a long way. The first imported brandy arrived in Shanghai in 1859 when Hennessy unloaded its first cargo. Then in 1949 the favourite drink of 'the Paris of the East' suddenly became a symbol of Western capitalist decadence; alcohol shipments came to an abrupt halt and did not resume for the next 30 years. However, when foreign liquor once again became available in the late 1970s, cognac quickly resumed its place as a guest at the Chinese banquet table.

Today cognac and brandy still account for about 80 per cent of all imported spirits in China. Most of the imported brandy goes through Hong Kong via grey markets (see also section 16.8). Chinese awareness of brand and category of cognac is particularly high in the south, where the drinking habits of visiting Hong Kong businessmen set a strong example. This impact is reinforced by alcohol advertising on Hong Kong television, available to millions of viewers in Guangdong province.

Habits of cognac drinking in western Europe and Asia

The key to Chinese consumption patterns lies in the importance of 'face'. Whatever the occasion, be it the father of the bride toasting his son-in-law's family in Beijing or a Shenzhen entrepreneur's night out on the town, brandy is of paramount importance. Unlike their Western counterparts, who like to curl up on the couch with a snifter of brandy, the Chinese consider cognac drinking an extremely social – and conspicuous – pastime.

Two different Courvoisier advertisements are shown: the one for the Western European market shows couples drinking cognac with their coffee; the Asian advertisement shows people drinking cognac from beer glasses during the meal.

Folklore as much as marketing has propelled the growth of cognac sales. Cognac has long had the inestimable commercial benefit of being widely regarded by the Chinese as enhancing a man's sexual prowess. And much to the delight of the liquor companies, the Chinese believe that the older (and pricier) the cognac, the more potent its effect.

Source: adapted from *Business Week* (1984); Balfour (1993).

Prince cigarettes: UK versus Germany

The Danish cigarette company House of Prince has high market share (50–90 per cent) in Scandinavian countries, but outside this area its market share is very low, typically 1–2 per cent.

The House of Prince cigarettes images show advertisements used in the UK and Germany. The UK version is based on an invitation to try the product ('I go for Prince'). The target group is also above average in education and income. The German advertisement is somewhat different. Prince is promoted as an 'original import from Denmark'. Apparently there is no 'buy German' mentality working against the use of this slogan. In the German consumer's mind Danish cigarettes are strongly positioned compared to light German cigarettes. Therefore the product's position is emphasized as 'men's business', with Viking associations and ideas of freedom. Incidentally, the two products Prince and Prince Denmark are not identical. The German Prince Denmark has a milder taste than does Prince.

Advertisements for Prince cigarettes in the UK and Germany

Advertisements for Gamel Dansk in Denmark and Germany

Gammel Dansk (Danish Distillers/Danisco): Denmark versus Germany

The Danish bitter Gammel Dansk has a 75 per cent share of the bitter market in Denmark. Thus the product has a high degree of recognition there (nearly all Danish adults know the label). The objective of the Danish advertisement has therefore primarily been to maintain Gammel Dansk's high degree of recognition.

Although the market share in Denmark is very high, Gammel Dansk does not have any position worth mentioning outside Denmark. In Germany the situation is totally different. Here the knowledge (and trial share) is at a minimum. The Germans have their own Jägermeister and competition is tough. The strategy behind the German campaign has therefore been to make people try Gammel Dansk by letting them fill out a coupon. By sending it in they receive a little bottle of Gammel Dansk and two original Gammel Dansk glasses.

LEGO FreeStyle: Europe versus the Far East

The LEGO images show European and Far Eastern versions of an advertisement for LEGO FreeStyle. The Asian version, 'Build your child's mind', appeals to Asian parents' desire for their children to do well in school.

The Asian educational system is very competitive and only those with the highest grades are admitted to university. In many places in Asia it is a defeat for parents if their child does

Advertisement for LEGO® Freestyle in the Far East

EXHIBIT 17.6 Jarlsberg cheese – cross-border communication

As an input for the company – please read Case Study 9.1.

Until now Jarlsberg's different agents and partners in the different countries have been responsible for the local ads. In the following there are some examples of this localized advertising approach:

Russia
Tine.

UK
Tine.

USA
Tine.

Australia
Tine.

Questions

1. Explain the different cultural characteristics behind the different ads.
2. Would it be a good idea for Jarlsberg to standardize the international advertising.

not do well in school. The Asian version has been run in Hong Kong, Taiwan and Korea (preferably in the local languages because the majority of consumers do not understand English). In Hong Kong the advertisements are run in English or Chinese (depending on the language of the magazine).

The European version implies creativity when playing with the different FreeStyle bricks: 'What will your child make of it?'

Advertisement for LEGO® Freestyle in Europe
© 2010 the Lego Group. Used with permission.

<table>
<tr><td>**17.6**</td><td>## Online communication decisions: viral marketing and social networking</td></tr>
</table>

In the physical marketplace different communication tools are used in the buying process of customers (see Figure 17.5). Traditional mass communication tools (print advertising, TV and radio) can create awareness and this can result in consumers' identification of new needs. From then on other elements of the communication mix take over, such as direct marketing (direct marketing, personal selling) and in-store promotion. Unlike marketing in the physical marketplace the Internet/e-commerce encompasses the entire 'buying' process. Of course, the online markets also make use of traditional mass advertising in order to get potential customers into the online buying process (from the left in Figure 17.5).

Market communication strategies change dramatically in the online world. On the Internet it is easier than ever to actually *communicate* a message to large numbers of people. However, in many cases, it is much harder for your message to be heard above the noise by your target audience. Various strategies for conducting online marketing have been developed in the past several years – from the most common (website linking) to the most

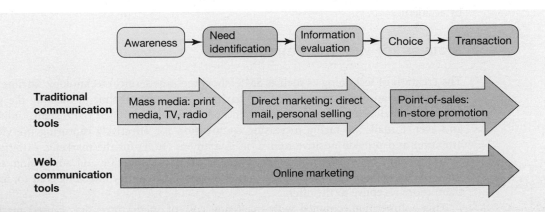

| **Figure 17.5** | The role of Internet communication in the buying process of customers |

expensive (banner advertising) to the most offensive (e-mail spamming), and everything in between. It is almost certain that a continual stream of new market communication strategies will emerge as the Internet medium evolves.

How, then, can a web audience be created? One of the new possibilities in this field is viral marketing.

Viral marketing

Global selling and buying is part of a social process. It involves not only a one-to-one interaction between the company and the customer but also many exchanges of information and influence among the people who surround the customer.

For example, diffusion occurs when an innovation is communicated through certain channels among members of a social system. An innovation is an idea, practice, or object that an individual or unit of adoption perceives as new (Rogers, 1995). According to Rogers, mass media channels are relatively more important for learning about an innovation, whereas interpersonal communication is especially important for persuasion. Thus, consumers communicating via e-mail may be persuaded more readily than those via mass media advertising.

Passing along e-mail is even easier than writing comments. Beyond this, pass-along e-mail seems particularly well suited for the spread of images and/or verbal content that is too detailed to be disseminated via word of mouth.

Viral marketing
Online word-of-mouth is a marketing technique that seeks to exploits existing social networks to produce exponential increases in brand awareness.

The Internet has radically changed the concept of word-of-mouth, so much so that the term **viral marketing** was coined by venture capitalist Steve Jurvetson in 1997. The term was used to describe Hotmail's e-mail practice of appending advertising for itself to outgoing mail from its users. In the Hotmail case each e-mail sent arrived with the appended message '*Get your private, free e-mail from Hotmail at* http://www.hotmail.com'.

The assumption is that if such an advertisement reaches a 'susceptible' user, that user will become 'infected' (i.e. sign up for an account) and can then go on to infect other susceptible users.

Definition

Viral marketing can be defined as a marketing technique that seeks to exploit pre-existing social networks to produce exponential increases in brand awareness, through viral processes similar to the spread of an epidemic. It is word-of-mouth delivered and enhanced online; it harnesses the network effect of the Internet and can be very useful in reaching a large number of people rapidly. From a marketing perspective, it is the process of encouraging individuals to pass along favourable or compelling marketing information they receive in a hypermedia environment: information that is favourable or compelling either by design or by accident.

Motives for viral marketing

The creation of technologies such as SMS (short message service) technology, satellite radio and Internet ad-blocking software are driving a fundamental shift in the way the public consumes media and the advertising often tied to it. Television ads, radio spots, online ads and even e-mails are facing increasing competition for effectively capturing the viewer's attention and provide positive return on investment (ROI) for the marketer. Additionally, consumers are becoming increasingly immune to mass marketing and advertising, so this form of marketing offers something that does not feel like they are being sold to, making them more receptive to the offer.

This competition, coupled with the rising cost of media buys, has caused marketers to search for an alternative means to reach the customer. Viral marketing is an attractive solution because it utilizes the free endorsement of the individual rather than purchasing mass media to spread the word. Because the distribution model is free, viral can potentially be lower cost and more effective than traditional media.

Advantages of viral marketing

- It incurs very little expense since the individual passing on the referral carries the cost of forwarding the brand message. Viral marketing offers SMEs the opportunity to target a whole new set of customers while keeping distribution costs to a minimum.
- Unlike traditional advertising viral is not an interruptive technique. Instead, viral campaigns work the Internet to deliver exposure via peer-to-peer endorsement. Viral campaigns, whether ultimately liked or disliked, are often welcomed by the receiver. The act of forwarding electronic messages containing advertising is voluntary rather than a paid testimonial or a mass ad campaign and thus may be viewed more favourably by the recipient. The focus is on campaigns containing material that consumers want to spend time interacting with and spreading proactively.
- Those forwarding the messages will be more likely to know which of their friends, family members and work colleagues have similar interests and are thus more likely to read the message: hence, more effective targeting. Here, the term 'interests' refers not only to the narrow sense of just the product or service but also includes the way the message is presented, such as the humour, the artwork, or the medium itself.

Disadvantages of viral marketing

Viral marketing, like all marketing, is hit or miss. However, viral marketing by nature is often more risky or controversial than traditional marketing. If done improperly viral marketing can backfire and create negative buzz:

- If particular software is needed that is not widely used, then people will not be able to open or view the message.
- Many people receive viral marketing messages while at the office, and company anti-virus software or firewalls can prevent people from receiving or viewing such attachments.
- For a viral marketing campaign to be successful, it must be easy to use. For example, if the promotion is some sort of game or contest, then asking for referrals should be an option immediately after the game, not as a condition to play.

Developing a viral marketing campaign

Viral marketing is by no means a substitute for a comprehensive and diversified marketing strategy. In employing viral marketing to generate peer-to-peer endorsement, the technique should not be considered as a stand-alone miracle worker.

While the messaging and strategy ranges radically from campaign to campaign, most successful campaigns contain some commonly used approaches. These approaches are often used in combination to maximize the viral effect of a campaign.

Successful viral campaigns are easily spread. The key is to get your customers to do the hard work for you by recommending your company or its promotional offers to friends and colleagues, who in turn will recommend it to their friends and so on. An effective viral marketing campaign can get your marketing message out to thousands of potential customers at phenomenal speeds.

When creating a campaign marketers should evaluate how people will communicate the message or campaign to others.

Creating compelling content

Creating quality content can often be more expensive than simply offering a free product, but the results are often better. Fun is often a vital part of any viral marketing campaign. The general rule of thumb is that the content must be compelling, it must evoke a response on an emotional level from the person viewing it. This fact alone has allowed many smaller brands to capitalize on content-based viral campaigns. Traditionally, larger brands are more reserved and risk adverse to the possibility of negative reaction. Central to the success of these campaigns is one or more of the following: their entry timing (early), their visibility or the simplicity of the idea.

Targeting the right audience

If a campaign is skewed towards a certain audience or certain regions (countries), marketers should make sure they seed towards that audience. Failure to due so may kill a campaign before it ever gets off the ground. The influence and, in some cases, the power of reference groups or opinion leaders in individual decision-making is significant.

Campaign seeding

'Seeding' the original message is a key component of a viral campaign. Seeding is the act of planting the campaign with the initial group who will then go on to spread the campaign to others. The Internet provides a wide array of options for seeding, including:

- e-mail/SMS
- online forums (Google groups)
- social networks (Facebook.com, MySpace.com)
- chatroom environment (MSN Messenger)
- blogs
- podcasts.

When determining where to seed it is important that marketers consider the audience they are aiming for. Is the target audience using the above-mentioned media (technologies) and to what degree?

Companies often use a combination of technologies to 'spread the virus'. Many use SMS. An example of an SMS campaign is that of Heineken, which linked an SMS promotion with the British pub tradition of playing quiz games. Heineken combined both online and offline promotions through point-of-sale signs in pubs, inviting customers to call from their mobile phones, type in the wordplay and receive a series of multiple-choice questions to answer. Food and beverage prizes were awarded for correct answers. From a promotional perspective, the idea was successful as customers told others what they were doing, prompting them to call in too.

Control/measuring results

The goal of a viral campaign is explosive reach and participation. To measure the success of a viral marketing campaign, establish specific and obtainable goals within a time frame. For example, you would like to see a 20 per cent increase in traffic to a website within three months or to double your subscriber rate to an e-mail newsletter in one year.

Marketers should also be adequately prepared to meet the needs of participants in the event that the campaign is successful. Server space, bandwidth, support staff, fulfilment and stocking should be taken into consideration well in advance of campaign launch. The marketer should have the ability to capitalize on the full success of the campaign.

EXHIBIT 17.7 Philips 'Quintippio' viral ad campaign (created by advertising agency Tribal DDB)

In November 2005 a viral website with a fictional 15-bladed razor was developed in order to create some buzz and make fun of the real-life introduction of the four-bladed Schick Quattro and the five-bladed Fusion by Gillette in October 2005 (http://www.quintippio.co.uk/ – the website was removed).

On the website it was possible to download an ad that had run also on TV. The script of the commercial proclaimed: 'Looking for a close shave? Then you're looking for the new Quintippio Mega Shave, now with 15 extra large blades!' A new product, 'Quintippio Multi-Shave' opens the spot and we find out that it has 15 blades. Then a puzzled man looks at it, wondering how he is going to shave his face with it. A voiceover says, 'Everyone's talking more blades – we're talking less irritation.' The selling point is an electric shaver that has a pump for dispensing Nivea skin cream as a shaving lubricant and moisturizer. The spot ends with the claim, 'As close as a blade with less irritation.'

The commercial is genuinely funny – it uses humour to serve the advertising strategy and reinforce the brand positioning. Philips makes fun of both Gillette and Schick for their multi-blade obsession.

Here is what works:

- *Norelco makes the category leader look out of touch* – although the end-benefit of 'multi-blade' is supposed to be 'close shave', it is not clear that either Gillette or Schick remembers this. Gillette's macho, tech-oriented advertising is so obsessed with the product that it seems to forget the consumer in the process.
- *Cool Shave focuses on a relevant, ownable end-benefit* – 'We're talking about less irritation' which presumably is a secondary benefit for many users but not owned by any male shaving system. This spot does a good job of using humour, voiceover, visuals and co-branding (with Nivea) to reinforce this end-benefit. The humour is used to reinforce the brand positioning.
- *Humour reinforces the brand positioning* – showing that Gillette and Schick don't 'get it' with their blade-spawning razors and focusing on a different benefit is worlds more effective than trying to argue that rotary shavers have more blades than multi-blade razors, for example.

That the issue raised in the commercial is relevant is underlined by the 'serious' magazine *The Economist*, which took up the 'Blade running' issue (The Economist, 2006).

The article discusses whether Moore's law (which describes a long-term trend in the history of computing hardware, in which the number of transistors that can be placed on an integrated circuit has doubled approximately every two years) be transferred from computer chips to number of razor blades.

The first Gillette one-blade safety razors using a disposable blade were introduced around 1902. Trac II was the world's first two-blade razor, debuted in 1971. The first three-blade razor, Mach 3, was introduced in 1998. Wilkinson responded to the Mach 3 with the Quattro, the first four-blade razor, introduced in 2003. Gillette Fusion, the first five-bladed razor, was released in 2006.

The article concludes that there are many similarities between Moore's law and the increase in number of razor blades. And as we have seen, the fictional Philips 15-blade razor is already here, and so are the discussions in the media and among internet users – so Philips has reached its goals for its viral marketing campaign.

Sources: adapted from WorldNetDaily.com (2005) 'Razor wars: 15-blade fever', 26 November; *The Economist* (2006) 'The cutting edge – A Moore's law for razor blades', 16 March.

Social networking

Social media encompasses a wide range of online, word-of-mouth forums including social networking websites, blogs, company sponsored discussion boards and chat rooms, consumer-to-consumer e-mail, consumer product or service ratings websites and forums, Internet discussion boards and forums, and sites containing digital audio, images, movies, or photographs, to name a few.

In September 2009 the 10 biggest social media networks in United States (measured by unique users) were:

1. Facebook   122.6 million
2. YouTube   85.1 million
3. MySpace   53.9 million
4. Digg   39.7 million
5. Blogger   29.8 million
6. Flickr   26.9 million
7. Twitter   23.3 million
8. LinkedIn   13.1 million
9. Windows Live   7.3 million
10. Yahoo Buzz   7.1 million

Source: adapted from Damon Segal, www.damonsegal.co.uk and www.compete.com.

While Facebook, YouTube, MySpace, and Twitter continue to dominate social media in the US and some other countries, the global scene tells a different story. In Germany, Russia, China and Japan, the most visited social networking site is not Facebook but home-grown rivals. For example, with 35 million users, Russia's most popular social network, VKontakte – Russian for 'in touch' – has become so ubiquitous that local companies often send job offers through the site. StudiVZ is the most visited social networking site in Germany, where Facebook lags at number 4.

Not all of Facebook's rivals were born overseas: some have migrated from the US. The most famous example is San Francisco-based Friendster, which was a social networking pioneer in the US when it launched in 2002 but then wilted as MySpace and Facebook took off. Far from disappearing, Friendster found new markets abroad and now draws 90 per cent of its traffic from Asia.

Source: http://www.businessweek.com/globalbiz/content/jul2009/gb20090715_921142.htm.

Integrated marketing communications (IMC) have traditionally been considered to be largely one-way in nature. In the old paradigm, the organization and its agents developed the message and transmitted it to potential consumers, who may or may not have been willing participants in the communication process. The control over the dissemination of information was in the hands of the marketing organization. The traditional elements of the promotion mix (advertising, personal selling, public relations and publicity, direct marketing and sales promotion) were the tools through which control was asserted.

The twenty-first century is witnessing an explosion of Internet-based messages transmitted through these media. They have become a major factor in influencing various aspects of consumer behaviour including awareness, information acquisition, opinions, attitudes, purchase behaviour and post-purchase communication and evaluation. Unfortunately, the popular business press and academic literature offers marketing managers very little guidance for incorporating social media into their IMC strategies.

Social networking as communication tools has two interrelated promotional roles (Mangold and Faulds, 2009):

1. Social networking should be consistent with the use of traditional IMC tools. That is, companies should use social media to talk to their customers through such platforms as blogs, as well as Facebook and MySpace groups. These media may either be company-sponsored or sponsored by other individuals or organizations.

2. Social networking is enabling customers to talk to one another. This is an extension of traditional word-of-mouth communication. While companies cannot directly control such consumer-to-consumer (C2C) messages, they do have the ability to influence the conversations that consumers have with one another. However, consumers' ability to communicate with one another limits the amount of control companies have over the content and dissemination of information. Consumers are in control; they have greater access to information and greater command over media consumption than ever before.

Marketing managers are seeking ways to incorporate social media into their IMC strategies. The traditional communications paradigm, which relied on the classic promotional mix to craft IMC strategies, must give way to a new paradigm that includes all forms of social media as potential tools in designing and implementing IMC strategies. Contemporary marketers cannot ignore the phenomenon of social media, where available market information is based on the experiences of individual consumers and is channelled through the traditional promotion mix. However, various social media platforms, many of which are completely independent of the producing/sponsoring organization or its agents, enhance consumers' ability to communicate with one another.

EXHIBIT 17.8 Cadbury and Nestlé are experimenting with social networking in their global IMC

Cadbury's promotion of its new Creme Egg 'Twisted' bar via YouTube

When British confectionery giant Cadbury wanted to promote its new Creme Egg Twisted bar recently, it turned to social media. Dubbed 'Goo on the Loose' the initiative invited British consumers to become CIA agents (Cadbury Intelligence Agents), of which there were around 10,000). Their mission was to track down Twisted bars across Britain, via clues sent on micro-blogging site Twitter.

The Super Agent competition began on Friday 12 June 2009 with Cadbury drafting 10 winners of the Phase One competition as their new Super Agents. Supplied with Flip cameras by Cadbury, the agents then filmed their exploits throughout Britain, uploaded them on YouTube, and won points for generating the most social media exposure via tweets and videos. The aim was to receive the most exposure across all platforms of social media (YouTube, Facebook, MySpace, Bebo and their own personal blog, all linked together with Twitter) in an attempt to win £20,000. On 15 July 2009 it was announced that 'Super Agent' Dean Stokes had won the £20,000.

Courtesy of Cadbury plc.

Nestlé promoted Juicy Juice children fruit drink through Twitter

Switzerland's Nestlé was the first global brand in 2009 to launch a campaign that allows Twitter users to post tweets into an ad unit that can appear anywhere on the web. Nestlé was testing Twitter Pulse (developed by SocialMedia.com) which lets companies capture the stream of Twitter conversations related to their brand

and publicize them across the Web. To promote its *Juicy Juice* children's fruit drink in the US, Nestlé ran a banner ad on a range of parenting sites asking questions such as 'How do you stimulate your child's mind?' and 'How important are vitamin-enhanced foods to you?' Users tweet their responses, which are fed live into a Juicy Juice banner ad on the site. Users who are already logged in to Twitter can answer the questions by posting tweets directly into the ad, while those not logged in are directed to Twitter to enter their username and password.

Société des Produits Nestlé SA. The Nestlé name and image is reproduced with kind permission of Société des Produits Nestlé SA.

Companies such as Cadbury and Nestlé are finding that social media like Twitter, YouTube, and Facebook are inexpensive and effective ways to advertise. By creating a fun online environment that meshes various social media applications, companies are attempting to attract a powerful army of brand ambassadors whose online tweets and videos are more effective than any 30-second television commercial.

Source: based on www.cadbury.com and www.nestle.com.

International marketing managers should recognize the power and critical nature of the discussions being carried on by consumers using social media. The impact of the interactions among consumers in the social media space on the development and execution of IMC strategies is illustrated by the following points (Mangold and Faulds, 2009):

- The Internet has become a mass media vehicle for consumer-sponsored communications. It now represents the number one source of media for consumers at work and the number two source of media at home.
- Consumers are turning away from the traditional sources of advertising: radio, television, magazines and newspapers. Consumers also consistently demand more control over their media consumption. They require on-demand and immediate access to information at their own convenience.
- Consumers are turning more frequently to various types of social media to conduct their information searches and to make their purchasing decisions.
- Social media is perceived by consumers as a more trustworthy source of information regarding products and services than corporate-sponsored communications transmitted via the traditional elements of the promotion mix.

17.6   Summary

Six ingredients of international communication have been presented in this chapter:

1. advertising
2. public relations
3. sales promotion
4. direct marketing
5. personal selling
6. viral marketing/social networking.

As international marketers manage the various elements of the promotions mix in differing environmental conditions decisions must be made about what channels are to be used in the communication, the message, who is to execute or help execute the programme and how the results of the communication plan are to be measured. The trend is towards greater harmonization of strategy, at the same time allowing for flexibility at the local level and early incorporation of local needs into the communication plans.

Hence an important decision for international marketers is whether the different elements of the communication should be standardized worldwide or localized. The main reasons for seeking standardization are:

- customers do not conform to national boundaries
- the company is seeking to build an international brand image
- economies of scale can be achieved
- the few high-quality creative ideas can be exploited as widely as possible
- special expertise can be developed and exploited.

However, some communication tools, especially personal selling, have to be localized to fit the conditions of individual markets. Another reason for the localization of the personal selling tool is that distribution channel members are normally located firmly within a country. Consequently decisions concerning recruitment, training, motivation and evaluation of salespeople have to be made at the local level.

The process of selecting agencies has also been considered. The requisite blend of local knowledge, cultural understanding and management expertise across international markets is elusive. Too much centralization and standardization results in inappropriate marketing communications.

A very important communication tool for the future is the Internet. Any company eager to take advantage of the Internet on a global scale must select a business model for its Internet ventures and estimate how information and transactions delivered through this new direct marketing medium will influence its existing distribution and communication system.

Viral marketing is by no means a substitute for a comprehensive and diversified marketing strategy. It is a credible marketing tactic that can deliver positive ROI when properly executed as a component of an overarching strategic plan. Marketers should utilize viral marketing when the messaging can coincide with and support a measurable business goal.

Social networking and social media (like Facebook and Twitter) are hybrid elements of the promotion mix because they combine characteristics of traditional IMC tools (companies talking to customers) with a highly enhanced form of word-of-mouth (customers talking to one another) whereby marketing managers cannot control the content and frequency of such information. By including social media in the promotion mix, these new communication formats are given a home in standard marketing management practices and theories. This new-found home for social media provides managers with a better understanding of social media and a framework for incorporating it into their IMC strategies, thus communicating more effectively with their target markets.

CASE STUDY 17.1

Helly Hansen: sponsoring fashion clothes in the US market

On a warm autumn day in 1997 Johnny Austad, President of the Norwegian clothing manufacturer Helly Hansen Co. (HH), arrives at the company's US subsidiary. Johnny can still not quite understand the incredible development that HH has seen in the US market. During the last couple of years Helly Hansen

USA has had an increase in turnover of 10 per cent per year, but in 1996 turnover doubled, amounting to one-third of HH's worldwide sales.

How it all started

Helly Hansen Co. was founded in 1877 by the Norwegian captain Helly Juell Hansen. During the era of the sailing ship he felt the forces of nature when he had to stand at the helm in all kinds of weather. Many hours were spent oiling clothes so they would become waterproof before rough weather set in. However, the clothes became stiff and sticky, so when Hansen finally went ashore he decided to develop better rain clothes for Norwegian sailors. Today HH sells its products in more than 20 countries. Production takes place in the company's own factories in Norway and Portugal, as well as in the Far East and via contract manufacturing. Design of the new collections takes place at the company's headquarters in Norway.

American rap group Bad Boys in Helly Hansen clothes
A/S Helly Hansen.

From a producer of functionalistic clothes to a supplier of fashion clothes to the US 'underground'

The honourable 100-year-old Norwegian producer of functionalistic clothes for sailors has by chance become the supplier of fashion clothes to black hip-hoppers in New York's underground. The label, which for generations has been connected with wind and waterproof leisure wear, and work clothes for the quality-conscious consumer who likes to be dressed 'sensibly', has now become a symbol of the avant-garde and the different. The young think the clothes are smart and don't care if they have taped seams or that it might be difficult to breathe through four layers of waterproof coating.

In earlier days, the first and last thing that HH thought of when making jackets was functionalism. The result was a very large collection of jackets with small specialized differences that only real enthusiasts could appreciate. HH's prices, on the other hand, became unreasonably high. By gathering several of the functions in the same jacket HH is able to make allowances for its choosy customers, as well as producing at a price that a larger part of the market is able to pay. Where HH used to direct its collections toward alpine skiers, fishermen, sea sportspeople and snowboarders, it is now beginning to look more at current fashion trends. HH is trying to link its look to street fashion and hopes that in this way its core customers will feel smarter, while new customers will be encouraged to buy because of the look of the clothes.

Before Johnny Austad gets on the plane back to Norway, the US subsidiary receives an enquiry about sponsorship from one of the most well-known rap groups in the United States. The manager of the rap group in question is seeking US$200,000 from HH for Bad Boys to perform in HH clothes at all their concerts in the next six months as well as in their forthcoming music video.

QUESTIONS

As a newly employed marketing assistant in the US HH subsidiary, you are asked to take care of this enquiry. You are specifically asked the following questions.

1. Would you recommend that HH sponsors Bad Boys? Give reasons for your answer.

2. How can an eventual sponsorship be integrated into the total marketing plan for HH clothes in the US market?

CASE STUDY 17.2

Morgan Motor Company: can the British retro sports car brand still be successful after 100 years?

The once-proud British car industry has all but vanished. However, there is one famous producer left in the UK: the Morgan Motor Company. It is the oldest privately held car company in the world and today the company is still 100 per cent family owned.

The company was founded in 1909 by H.F.S. Morgan and was run by him until 1959. Peter Morgan, son of H.F.S., ran the company until a few years before his death in 2003. The company is currently run by Charles Morgan, Peter's son.

Morgan is based in Malvern Link, an area of Malvern, Worcestershire and employs 163 people. All the cars are assembled by hand and the waiting list is one to two years, although it has been as high as 10 years in the past.

Business is strong, despite the economic slow-down. In 1997 Morgan made 480 cars; eleven years later in 2008 the figure was just under 700, and could be 800 in 2009. One day, it may make as many as 1000 cars a year, they say, but only if that can be done Morgan's way. And what a totally unique and utterly inimitable way to make sports cars theirs is.

In 2008 the estimated revenue was around £20 million. The operating profits were £207,000 in 2008, compared to £476,000 in 2007. The company employs 160 people of which 133 are production floor employees.

Morgan Motor Company

Morgan history

The first Morgan design was of course the famous Threewheeler. H.F.S. Morgan designed a fun car, the Morgan Runabout, for people with little money but a sense of adventure. The car was a great success and in the 1920s the Morgan factory in Malvern was making 2,500–3,000 cars a year with a smaller number being built under license in France under the Darmont Morgan brand. Nevertheless each year production always sold out in advance as customers were desperate for small cars in this period.

Morgan Threewheeler sales declined and by 1935 there were only 300 new orders for the threewheeler cars. The reason for this was the arrival of mass-produced popular cars from Ford, Morris and Austin costing a similar price but offering more features for the money.

H.F.S. Morgan had to come up with a new design. He did this in 1936 and announced the Morgan Four Four, a light sports car with four wheels and a four cylinder Coventry Climax engine. From the start the Morgan Four Four was making its name in competition and finished well at Le Mans in 1938 and 1939.

In 1962 Morgan won the two-litre class at Le Mans. A production Morgan beat the specially modified Porsche and Lotus racing cars and then drove home: the car averaged 98 m.p.h. for 24 hours. Following the race the Morgan Plus Four Supersports was launched as a factory model so that customers could buy a Le Mans class winner.

Examples of the car became regular winners in production sports car races across the USA.

The Morgan Motor Company at this time was one of the first companies to benefit from celebrity endorsement – Ralph Lauren, Brigitte Bardot and David Bailey all drove Morgans in the 1960s.

In 1989 a visit was made by Sir John Harvey Jones and the BBC programme *Troubleshooter*.

Sir John criticized the company's strategy of a long waiting list and making everything by hand in such a labour-intensive way. Morgan is probably the only car company which still makes cars the way they were made in the early 1900s – by building them on a wooden frame and crafting them mainly by hand.

Sir John did not really understand Morgan's market. Coachbuilding (by wood) and waiting list were strengths, not weaknesses of the business. Coach-building the cockpit area produced a light, strong cabin that is durable and the waiting list maintained second-hand prices. There was much humour over the 'Sir John Hardly Knows' t-shirts that appeared at Morgan Sports Car Club meetings.

There were also some very beneficial commercial effects of Sir John Harvey Jones's visit. Morgan experienced a big increase in orders and the long waiting list encouraged a price increase, which led to the company making significant profits that could be reinvested.

In April 2009, Princess Anne officially opened the brand new Morgan Visitor Centre, a modern museum bedecked with memorabilia, photos, films and the inevitable gift shop, housing a remarkable range of merchandise for 'Moggie' enthusiasts young and old.

The Morgan philosophy and product range

The company's whole business model is based on longevity and brand reinforcement. This is not a get rich quick business. Among many other distinctions Morgan enjoys is that of being one of just a few family dynasties left in the auto industry. The traditional family influence has engendered a long-time dedication to craft as well as a determination not to grow the company too large for fear of increasing costs and jeopardizing quality. The sense of family ties isn't lost on customers, either. Eager buyers often visit their unborn vehicles in the company's factory as the cars are being built. It is a kind of Build-a-Bear transferred to the car industry. All Morgan cars have a customer's name on them before they begin production. Customers can choose from myriad variants of body, engine size, paint colour, dashboard and leather trim. However, component supply and storage has been complicated by the Morgan customization model, but this has been simplified where possible to make it easier for the business to deliver product.

Morgan's speedy roadsters are entirely hand-crafted, which is perhaps fitting for the oldest privately held sports car manufacturer in the world. As a result, each car takes 130 hours to build and the waiting list is at least 12 months. By comparison, the average US-made Nissan takes just over 28 hours to build and can be had pretty much when you want it. Unlike commonplace vehicles, Morgans feature ash wood frames, hand-moulded body panels and hand-stitched leathers.

Such craftsmanship doesn't come cheap. For the US market, a basic two-seat roadster starts at nearly US$50,000 and the top-of-the-line Aero 8 two-seat road rocket starts around US$140,000 – before adding custom cosmetic, luxury, or performance upgrades. Aero 8 (launched in 2000) was the first completely new Morgan for 30 years and customers wanting to buy one must wait nine months. The two-door Morgan roadsters may look old-fashioned, but they perform as well as the best of today's technologically advanced sports cars.

The Aero 8 is Europe's first AIV (aluminium intensive vehicle) and is 20 per cent lighter than comparable vehicles. It is equipped with a BMW-sourced 4.4 litre V8 engine that gets the car from 0 to 60 in just 4.5 seconds.

As part of the centenary celebrations (100 years in 2009) Morgan announced a truly special model. The brand new Aero Super Sport was launched at Geneva car show in 2009 and the first models were finished at the factory for the first customers in January 2010. The two Aero models, intended for a production run of 100 units, were launched from rendered drawings, with up-front deposits of £25,000 per car required 12 months before build. They quickly sold 100 on plan.

Morgan Aero Supersport (2010 model) including interior
Morgan Motor Company.

Designed and engineered in-house, the Morgan Aero SuperSports is a lightweight aluminium sports car with a luxurious specification. The interior features a comfortable combination of polished hardwoods, hand-stitched leather and electronic technology to create a driving environment that is efficient and ergonomic. In spite of all this opulence the overall weight of the car is still relatively low so the car is responsive to driver inputs and economical to run. Morgan can achieve this due to their unique use of aircraft-style superformed aluminium outer panels and the skills of their craftsmen to hand finish the assembly of each car.

This technology debuted in the 100 AeroMax coupes built by the factory in 2008 and 2009. There has been such was demand for the new Aero SuperSport model, that Morgan have taken the decision to produce the new model in more numbers.

Customer target groups

Morgans are not cars that deliberately target the recession-proof super-rich, but the cars' name and caché has made the marque resilient. Morgan's business model has been robust. First, the cars have great residual value – an AeroMax that sells for £110,000 new can go on sale in Germany for €160,000 within a year. Today, 98 per cent of Morgans ever made are still in existence.

Of growing importance is the number of women who are wealthy in their own right and potential customers. In North America where the number of Morgan distributors has doubled over the past few years, women represent nearly 40 per cent of the top wealth holders with gross assets of more than US$625,000 and in the UK there are now as many woman millionaires as men in the age group 18–44. However, Morgan buyers are not necessarily terribly wealthy, especially not owners of the 1.6 base model costing around £30,000 in the UK. The BMW-engined Aero 8 cost nearly eight times this amount.

Over the years a lot of celebrities have joined the Morgan spirit: Mick Jagger has joined Catherine Deneuve and Jean-Paul Belmondo. Even Miss Piggy has been among an elite alumni of Morgan owners. Morgan cars have appeared in a host of films and TV programmes, including *Moonraker*, *Monty Python's Flying Circus*, *My Girl* and *The Trip*. Several books have been published about Morgan cars.

The Morgan Community

A Morgan community is in place for their huge network of enthusiasts, including:

- Cars can be ordered online or through the global dealer network (26 in the UK, 28 in Europe, 8 in the USA and 6 in the rest of the world).
- The Morgan Sports Car Club: this owners' club, which represents owners in many countries, provides a sense of identity and community for many of the buyers. It has strong links and influences with the factory, and the Morgan community is often consulted on product and brand development. The Club is a powerful, though informal, symbol and promoter of the Morgan core brand proposition. There is an active agenda of meetings and social gatherings. For example, during the celebration in 2009 of the factory's 100 years of existence, many Morgan owners met with the Morgan family at the factory in Malvern Link, UK.
- The Worcester-based Morgan Works racing team. The racing events also create a strong relational bond between owners and the factory.

All these activities represent classic examples of customer relationship marketing.

International marketing

Morgan builds about 700 cars per year, around 30 per cent of which are sold in UK. Besides the UK and US, Morgan cars are sold throughout most of western Europe, as well as in Australia, Japan, New Zealand and South Africa.

For part of the 1950s and 1960s, the USA provided the company with its largest market worldwide, taking up to 85 per cent of all production. This ended with the first wave of US safety and emission regulations in 1971. For many years (1974 to 1992), all Morgans imported into the United States were converted to run on propane as fuel to pass the US emissions regulations. However, this conversion, along with bringing the cars into compliance with US vehicle safety leglislation, was carried out by the dealership and not by the factory, making the cars grey market vehicles.

Comeback in the USA

In 2003 Morgan sold 100 cars in the US, and it has already pre-sold the same number of the Aero 8 which replaces its Plus 8 model. Sales are then expected to rise to 200–250 per year. The Aero 8 was the first Morgan model sold in the US since the 1950s and 1960s.

QUESTIONS

1. How is the Morgan's international communication strategy different from mainstream mass-produced cars?

2. How can Morgan use celebrities in the communication strategy?

3. How can Morgan make use of the new social media?

4. Prepare a global communication plan for the new Aero SuperSport.

Sources: http://www.morgan-motor.co.uk; *The Manufacturer* (2009) 'Morgan Motor Company, 100 not out', August, http://www.themanufacturer.com/uk/profile/9493/Morgan_Motor_Company?PHPSESSID=8a965626552f15dc0f04fdf53a4d9836.

VIDEO CASE STUDY 17.3 BMW Motorcycles

download from www.pearsoned.co.uk/hollensen

Bayerische Motoren Werke (BMW) (www.bmw.com) is one of the leading manufacturers of premium passenger cars and motorcycles in Europe. Although car buyers are extremely familiar with the BMW brand, the brand has a much lower profile among motorcycle buyers. This is a major challenge for BMW Motorcycles, which has been producing high-end motorcycles for more than 80 years. The company's main promotional goal is to attract serious riders who are looking for an exceptional riding experience. To do this, its marketers carefully coordinate every promotional detail to convey a unified brand message positioning the BMW motorcycle as 'the ultimate riding machine', as its advertising slogan states.

Questions

1. What are the advantages of using more personal advertising copy and encouraging customers to become missionaries for BMW motorcycles?

2. Should BMW use standardization or adaptation in promoting the motorcycles outside the United States and Germany?

3. Why is BMW using its website as a virtual showroom rather than also selling online directly to consumers?

4. Should BMW develop and promote a new motorcycle brand to differentiate its motorcycles from competing motorcycle brands (i.e. selling to new target groups) as well as differentiating them from BMW cars?

For further exercises and cases, see this book's website at **www.pearsoned.co.uk/hollensen**

Questions for discussion

1. Identify and discuss problems associated with assessing advertising effectiveness in foreign markets.

2. Compare domestic communication with international communication. Explain why 'noise' is more likely to occur in the case of international communication processes.

3. Why don't more companies standardize advertising messages worldwide? Identify the environmental constraints that act as barriers to the development and implementation of standardized global advertising campaigns.

4. Explain how personal selling may differ overseas from how it is used in the home market.

5. What is meant by saying that advertising regulations vary around the world?

6. Evaluate the 'percentage of sales' approach to setting advertising budgets in foreign markets.

7. Explain how the multinational firm may have an advantage over local firms in training the sales force and evaluating its performance.

8. Identify and discuss problems associated with allocating the company's promotion budget across several foreign markets.

References

Balfour, F. (1993) 'Alcohol industry: companies in high spirits', *China Trade Report*, June, pp. 4–5.

Bennett, R. (1995) *International Marketing: Strategy, Planning, Market Entry and Implementation*. Kogan Page, London.

Boddewyn, J.J., Soehl, R. and Picard, J. (1986) 'Standardization in international marketing: is Ted Levitt in fact right?', *Business Horizons*, 29, pp. 69–75.

Business Week (1984) 'Advertising Europe's new Common Market', July, pp. 62–65.

Business Wire (2006) 'Nearly 90 per cent of Internet users share content via e-mail according to Sharpe Partners' study on viral marketing', 25 January.

Desmet, P. and Xardel, D. (1996) 'Challenges and pitfalls for direct mail across borders: the European example', *Journal of Direct Marketing*, 10(3), pp. 48–60.

The Economist (2006) 'The cutting edge – a Moore's law for razor blades', 16 March.

Harper, T. (1986) 'Polaroid clicks instantly in Moslem markets', *Advertising Age* (special report 'Marketing to the Arab world'), 30 January, p. 12.

Hite, R.E. and Frazer, C. (1988) 'International advertising strategies of multinational corporations', *Journal of Advertising Research*, 28 (August–September), pp. 9–17.

Honeycutt, E.D. and Ford, J.B. (1995) 'Guidelines for managing an international sales force', *Industrial Marketing Management*, 24, pp. 135–144.

Hung, C.L. and West, D.C. (1991) 'Advertising budgeting methods in Canada, the UK and the USA', *International Journal of Advertising*, 10, pp. 239–250.

Joensen, S. (1997) 'What hedder it now on engelsk?', *Politikken* (Danish newspaper), 24 April.

Lynch, R. (1994) *European Marketing*. Irwin, Homewood, IL.

Mangold, W.G. and Faulds, D.J. (2009) 'Social media: The new hybrid element of the promotion mix', *Business Horizons*, 52, pp. 357–365.

MacNamee, B. and McDonnell, R. (1995) *The Marketing Casebook*. Routledge, London.

Meenaghan, T. (1996) 'Ambush marketing: a threat to corporate sponsorship', *Sloan Management Review*, Fall, pp. 103–113.

Mueller, B. (1996) *International Advertising: Communicating Across Cultures*. Wadsworth, Belmont, CA.

Nørmark, P. (1994) 'Co-promotion in growth', *Markedsføring* (Danish marketing magazine), 14, p. 14.

Onkvisit, S. and Shaw, J.J. (1993) *International Marketing: Analysis and Strategy*, 2nd edn. Macmillan, London.

Ottesen, O. (1995) 'Buyer initiative: ignored, but imperative for marketing management – towards a new view of market communication', *Tidsvise Skrifter*, 15, avdeling for Økonomi, Kultur og Samfunnsfag ved Høgskolen i Stavanger.

Phelps, J.E., Lewis, R., Mobilio, L., Perry, D. and Raman, N. (2004) 'Viral marketing or electronic word-of-mouth advertising: examining consumer responses and motivations to pass along e-mail', *Journal of Advertising Research*, 44(4), pp. 333–348.

Phillips, C., Poole, I. and Lowe, R. (1994) *International Marketing Strategy: Analysis, Development and Implementation*. Routledge, London/New York.

Rogers, Everett M. (1995) *Diffusion of Innovations*, 4th edn. New York: The Free Press.

Rosson, J.R. and Seringhaus, F.H.R. (1996) Trade fairs as international marketing venues: a case study. Paper presented at the 12th IMP Conference, University of Karlsruhe.

Sharland, A. and Balogh, D. (1996) 'The value of non-selling activities at international trade shows', *Industrial Marketing Management*, 25, pp. 59–66.

Sorenson, R.Z. and Weichman, V.E. (1975) 'How multinationals view marketing standardization', *Harvard Business Review*, May–June, pp. 38–56.

WorldNetDaily.com (2005) 'Razor wars: 15-blade fever', 26 November.

CASE STUDY IV.1

Absolut Vodka: defending and attacking for a better position in the global vodka market

On a lovely day in March 2009 the CEO of V&S Absolut Spirits, Ketil Eriksen, packs his suitcase for the third time in the month for a business trip to the subsidiary in New York.

In March 2008 France's Pernod Ricard won the battle to buy the maker of Absolut vodka in a costly €5.63 billion (US$8.9 billion) deal that brings it nearly level in sales with global spirits leader Diageo. Pernod's Richard's main gain with the acquisition of V&S Absolut Spirits was V&S's Absolut Vodka. It is the world's second-largest vodka brand, and the world's leading premium vodka. Before the acquisition Penod Richard had a limited vodka portfolio and was only among the world's leading 20 vodka manufacturers. After the acquisition Pernod Ricard becomes the second-largest vodka producer, behind Diageo. Now Pernod has also a total annual volume of 91 million 9-litre cases of spirits (in 2009), up from 75 million before, putting it just behind Diageo's total of 93 million.

While packing he thinks of how hard the company must fight to keep and increase its market share for Absolut Vodka in the United States and other markets. In the last five years Absolut Vodka has increased its world market share, but can it continue?

Absolut accounts for more than half of all imported vodka sales in the United States: it is the third-largest international premium spirit and is available in 130 markets. Among premium vodkas Absolut Vodka is no. 2 worldwide, after Smirnoff.

When Ketil gets on the plane at Stockholm's airport bound for New York, there are two things that worry him:

- Apparently the market share of Absolut Vodka in the United States has reached saturation point. Has V&S Absolut Spirits reached its maximum market share in that country or is it time for a frontal attack on the number one brand, Smirnoff?
- Until now, the market share for Absolut Vodka in Europe (especially in Eastern Europe) has been a lot smaller. This can be a problem, as 80 per cent of the world's vodka is consumed in Russia and the other countries of Eastern Europe (see Table 1).

Marketing of Pernod's Absolut Vodka is primarily dealt with from the (subsidiary) head office in Stockholm and via the subsidiary company The Absolut Spirits Company, Inc. in the United States. Worldwide marketing control is heavily centralized to guarantee consistency and focus, as well as responsibility for the content. In agreements with co-owned and independent distribution organizations, V&S has ensured that responsibility for marketing lies with V&S.

On his way over the Atlantic Ketil thinks back on the story and adventure of Absolut Vodka.

The history of Absolut Vodka

The Swedish state-owned Vin & Sprit AB can justly call the launch of its Absolut Vodka an absolute success. Absolut Vodka is probably the biggest success story in the world of spirits. It has become an icon.

The shape of the bottle

The shape of the bottle dates back to the mid-eighteenth century, but is based on a traditional design: in the sixteenth century, Swedish pharmacies sold a clear, distilled liquid as a cure for ailments such as colic or even the plague. The custom was to ingest it by the spoonful, not by the shot glass.

Rediscovered in an antique store in Stockholm by Gunnar Broman, of the now defunct advertising agency Carlsson & Broman, the clear medicine bottle has since been fine-tuned by Absolut's team of shrewd marketers. The neck was lengthened, curves were adjusted and labels were replaced by printed typeface. To top it off, a medallion bearing the portrait of Lars Olsson Smith, known as 'The King of Vodka', was stamped on each bottle. In 1879, Smith successfully broke Stockholm's spirit monopoly by distilling and marketing Absolut Rent Bränvin (that is, Absolute Pure Vodka). His tipple was the beginning of a dynasty.

The current Absolut family consists (November 2008) of the following variants/flavours:

- *Absolut Vodka* has a rich taste, and is smooth and mellow with a distinct character of grain. Introduced in 1979.
- *Absolut Peppar* is aromatic, complex and spicy. The peppery flavour is a combination of the spicy components in the capsicum pepper family and the fresh green jalapeño pepper. Introduced in 1986.

- *Absolut Citron* is flavoured with citrus fruits. Lemon is dominant, but other citrus flavours are added to give a fuller body. Absolut Citron has a distinctive character made up of lemon and lime with a hint of sweetness. Introduced in 1988.
- *Absolut Kurant* is flavoured with blackcurrant, a distant cousin to the grape. This is a fragrant dark berry that grows on shrubs up to six feet in height. Absolut Kurant has a distinct character, with a hint of tartness and sweetness. Introduced in 1992.
- *Absolut Mandrin* is flavoured with citrus fruits. Mandarin and orange are dominant, but other citrus flavours are added to give a fuller body. Absolut Mandrin has a distinctive character with a hint of sweetness. Introduced in 1999.

The Absolut Company.

- *Absolut Vanilia* has a rich, robust and complex taste of vanilla with notes of butterscotch and hints of dark chocolate. Introduced in 2003.
- *Absolut Raspberri* is rich and intense, revealing the fresh and fruity character of ripened raspberries. Introduced in 2004.
- *Absolut Apeach* is smooth and mellow, with a sophisticated and fruity character of peach. Introduced in 2005.
- *Absolut Ruby Red* is smooth and fruity with a crisp and refreshing character of zesty grapefruit. Introduced in 2006.
- *Absolut Pears* has the fresh and clear aroma of mellow pears with a slight touch of sweet almonds. It's fruity, smooth and full-bodied with a long and slightly dry aftertaste. Introduced in 2007.
- *Absolut Disco*, launched in December 2007.
- *Absolut New Orleans* (mango and black pepper flavour launched in August 2007). This is a special edition in an annual city-themed series: 100 per cent of the profits go toward various Gulf Coast charities after the flood damage from Hurricane Katrina.
- *Absolut 100* 100 proof, black bottle, flavour launched in 2007.
- *Absolut Los Angeles* (blueberry flavour mix launched in July 2008). This is the second in the city-themed series. Absolut is donating US$250,000 from the sale of Absolut Los Angeles to 'Green Way'. 'Green Way' is a Los Angeles-based non-profit organization dedicated to improving urban way of life by restoring nature's services in Los Angeles and other cities. One of their projects is to transform a street in west Los Angeles into a 'Green Street' by planting appropriate trees and other vegetation so that rainwater and other polluted water is naturally cleaned before flowing into the Pacific Ocean.
- *Absolut Boston* (black tea and elderflower flavour with clear bottle, green label launched August 2009).

Introduction to the US market

Independent market research in the United States concluded, in 1979, that no one would buy Swedish vodka. Nevertheless the first shipment of Absolut Vodka was sent off to that country in April 1979; its destination was Boston. Some 90,000 litres were sold worldwide in 1979; and in 2005 worldwide sales were 82.9 million litres, of which about 50 per cent was exported to the United States. Apart from the United States, the most important markets are (in decreasing order of importance): Canada, Greece, Spain, Germany, Mexico, Poland, the United Kingdom, Israel and Sweden.

The Absolut Company.

The marketing of the bottle

For more than 25 years advertisements for Absolut Vodka have been based on the same fundamental concept, with the focus being on the product. The very first advertisement, 'Absolut Perfection', was created in 1980 and today it is the one which is used most often.

Since Andy Warhol, patron saint of pop art, created his first Absolut painting in 1985 ('Absolut Warhol'), artists around the world have been asked to render their interpretation of the bottle. Distinctive advertising campaigns such as 'Absolut London', in which the door of 10 Downing Street resembles an Absolut bottle, have made the vodka brand nearly as famous as Coca-Cola or Nike. In the advertisement 'Absolut Essence' magazine readers were able to fold back the cover and smell the scent of Absolut Kurant. Most countries maintain strict rules concerning alcohol advertisements to consumers, but Absolut's PR machine has milked the free publicity that its advertising generates.

The Absolut Vodka CEOs thoughts have become dream-like on the plane to New York, but he wakes with a start when passengers are asked to buckle their seat belts. To use his time sensibly before landing, Ketil takes a report out of his suitcase describing conditions in the US and world markets. The following is the essence of the report, which also describes recent Absolut Vodka initiatives in this market.

The world market for vodka

Table 1 shows that Eastern European countries account for 86 per cent of the world's total vodka sales, and the area's average consumption per capita per year is also high (five litres). In Poland the average vodka consumption per capita per year is about 10 litres, while the average in the Confederation of Independent States is 5 litres. By comparison, average consumption in the United States is 1.3 litres and in the United Kingdom 0.6 litres. It should be noted that all these figures are based on registered sales and don't include home-made products which are distilled in quite a large part of Eastern Europe as well as in Sweden and Finland.

The markets of Eastern Europe are distinguished not only by their high vodka consumption but also by how much consumers know about alcoholic beverages and their appreciation of quality. However, political uncertainty and the lack of a well-functioning infrastructure in several Eastern European countries make short-term developments difficult to predict. The biggest vodka market in Eastern Europe is Russia, followed by Ukraine.

For several years Absolut Vodka has been exported to most Eastern European countries, and in 1995 the brand was introduced into Poland. Ten years later (in 2005) Poland was the seventh-largest Absolut Vodka market. Thus Absolut Vodka is now represented in all the major vodka markets of the world.

The US market for vodka

In the last 20 years the consumption of alcohol in the United States has decreased by 20 per cent. There are several reasons for this. One of the main reasons is the 'health trend' in the country, which has led to a greater awareness of the harmful effects of alcohol. At the same time a tendency has developed for drinking 'less but better'; thus many people now drink cleaner and more pure alcohol. This has meant that the sale of

	Volume: million litres % of total	Value: US$ million % of total	The Absolut Company % of total	Absolut market share %
Table 1 Distribution of world vodka sales by volume and value. V&S Absolut Spirits' market share 2008				
World				
Eastern Europe	85.9	63.8	6.0	1.3
North America	8.7	20.7	50.0	10.3
Western Europe	3.3	11.7	18.0	6.3
Latin America	0.8	1.5	9.0	7.0
Africa and the Middle East	0.8	1.2	5.0	2.4
Asia-Pacific	0.4	0.9	6.0	10.9
Australasia	0.1	0.2	6.0	3.8
Total World	100.0 (= 4,100 million litres)	100.0 (= 20 billion US$)	100.0 (= 98 million litres)	2.4 (= 98/4,100)

Source: adapted from Impact International and *Euromonitor*.

'super-premium' (high-quality) brands has not fallen but has been stable in the last five years. Nearly all imported brands are in the super-premium segment and this is the main reason that vodka imports have not fallen. Although the vodka importers' share of the total market is only 12–15 per cent, the gross margin on imported vodka represents about 40 per cent of the total gross margin of all vodka sales in the United States.

Historically vodka has not been a differentiated product, but more and more flavoured brands have gradually been introduced to the market, including Absolut Citron, Absolut Peppar and Absolut Kurant. However, it is risky introducing new brands into the American market, as consumers' tastes there are so volatile. A producer can introduce a flavour that is popular one year and unpopular the next.

Product segments

The different product segments are as follows:

- *Platinum*. The most expensive category, with prices around US$25 per bottle or more. Brands in this category include Stolichnaya Cristall. This segment accounts for less than 1 per cent of total US vodka consumption.
- *Super-premium*. Nearly all brands are imported, the leaders being Swedish Absolut, Russian Stolichnaya, Finnish Finlandia and French Grey Goose. The price level is US$15–20 per bottle. This category's share of the total vodka consumption in the United States is about 10 per cent.
- *Premium*. Here we find the world's most popular vodka, American Smirnoff, sold for US$10–12 a bottle. This group's share of the United State's total vodka consumption is 22 per cent.
- *Standard priced*. Here are the two English labels Gilbey's and Gordon's which are sold for US$7–8 a bottle. This category's share is 14 per cent.
- *Popular priced*. This is the largest group. Its share of total US vodka consumption is about 54 per cent, and the group consists of a number of local labels at about US$6 a bottle.

Worldwide, the three largest imported brands are Absolut (number two), Stolichnaya (number six) and Finlandia (number fifteen). Absolut's main competitors are Smirnoff, Finlandia and Stolichnaya, which may be characterized as follows:

- *Stolichnaya* (brand owner: Sojuzplodimport). The pioneer among imported vodka brands, this was the first vodka into be introduced in the United States, in 1972. Stolichnaya was at the time a good alternative to the USA-produced vodka brands as it tasted milder due to a more refined distilling process, but its popularity has been dependent on the political climate between the United States and the former USSR. Today, Stolichnaya is distributed by Absolut Vodka's former importer, Carillon Importers.
- *Finlandia* (brand owner: Alko Group). This brand was introduced into the United States in 1976. Despite many marketing campaigns, Finlandia has never been able to get a grip on the vodka market. In the trade it is estimated that Finlandia has the most exposed position, as all new importers go for the esteemed third place (which seems to be a realistic goal for a new brand). In 2002, Findlandia celebrated its thirtieth anniversary in style by forming a partnership with MGM Pictures for their James Bond film, *Die Another Day*. Bond still likes his martinis shaken, not stirred, but his vodka in that particular film was Finlandia, not Smirnoff.
- *Smirnoff* (brand owner: Diageo Plc) Diageo was created in December 1997, following the merger of Guinness plc and Grand Metropolitan plc. Among the wine and spirits companies included in the merger were Carillon Importers Ltd, The Paddington Corporation, UDV, Glenmore, Schieffelin & Somerset, Heublein Inc., and International Distillers & Vintners North America. Guinness/UDV's primary US division is United Distillers & Vintners North America (UDVNA). In 2008, UDVNA was the second-largest spirits company in the US market, with a 13.5 per cent volume share. Three of the top ten US spirits brands in 2008 were UDVNA brands: Smirnoff vodka, José Cuervo tequila and Gordon's gin and vodka. After a four-year interruption, Smirnoff was confirmed itself as the 'vodka of choice' for James Bond in *Casino Royale*. The renewed strategic alliance between Smirnoff and Bond involved a fully integrated multi-million dollar global media campaign. In several countries, the campaign included on-pack promotions offering two-for-the-price-of-one cinema tickets to *Casino Royale* and a fully interactive *Casino Royale* microsite.

One of the newcomers to the super-premium segment is Grey Goose. It is distilled in Cognac, France from French wheat, then imported by the Sidney Frank Importing Company based in New York. In 1997, it quickly gained a reputation for quality and has won several prestigious awards in distilled spirit competitions. In 2004, Sidney Frank sold the manufacturing rights to Bacardi for US$2.2 billion.

The distribution system for vodka in the United States

Generally, the sale of spirits goes through the distribution system shown in Figure 1. For US producers, the roles of producer/supplier and importer/agent coincide.

The retail ('off-premise') sale of wine, spirits and beer takes place through two different distribution systems. In 'open states' (licensed states) the market is free, and spirits are distributed via liquor stores, supermarkets or other grocery stores where the owner has a license to sell spirits. In 'controlled states' spirits can only be sold in liquor stores owned by the state, similar to the Nordic monopoly system.

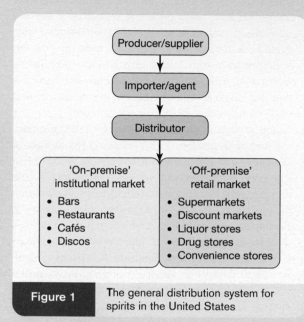

| Figure 1 | The general distribution system for spirits in the United States |

The importer/agent usually has only a small sales force, which concentrates on selling to and servicing a distributor. An importer/agent usually cooperates with one distributor in each state (although one distributor can handle several states), and in large states a distributor can have up to 500 salespeople geographically divided. Generally these salespeople pay for their own car and receive a low basic wage, plus commission. The salesperson in the area concerned visits both the wholesale and the retail market, often once a week, taking orders and in exceptional cases delivering goods and collecting payment.

Absolut Vodka – advertising campaign in 2006

A new range of superpremium brands such as Grey Goose has nibbled into Absolut's image of 'coolness in a bottle'. To fight back, V&S rolled out a new marketing campaign in January 2006 to raise the brand's profile with a new generation of vodka drinkers. The multi-million dollar push in the US was Absolut's first all-new campaign in 25 years – and it also marked the first time the brand was advertised on TV. The ads from Absolut's global agency, TBWA/Chiat/Day in New York, positioned the liquor as 'The Absolute Vodka', while highlighting other classics that are 'absolutes' in

pop culture. One spot featured footage from the Apollo moon landing under the banner 'Absolute Road Trip'. Another showed Marilyn Monroe entertaining troops with the tag line 'Absolute Morale Booster'. The 30-second spots were shown on cable channels such as Comedy Central, Fox Sports Net, and E! Absolut will also continue its iconic print ads starring the Absolut bottle dressed up by fashion designers, famous photographers and artists, with a two-word tag line.

As part of the new marketing push in the US, Absolut also commissioned rock musician Lenny Kravitz to come up with his own interpretation of the Absolut brand. The result is a dance track. Kravitz recorded a new song entitled 'Breathe', which will be featured in the campaign. The result is a track that is a transition from Kravitz's traditional rock and roll to a distinctly dance music sound, with minimal lyrics (no mention of Absolut of vodka anywhere in the lyrics), a memorable melody and pulsating beat.

World market shares for top vodka brands – retail channels

If we include vodka sales through all distribution channels (retail + HORECA (HOtel, REstaurant, CAtering) and duty free) brands such as Stolichnaya and Moskovskaya would be very highly ranked. But in reality these brands do not really exist as discrete products: in Russia, Stolichnaya for instance, is produced by 800 distilleries and in various bottle and case sizes. Moreover, products differ widely between distilleries. Thus, brands such as Stolichnaya are only 'brands' when exported, when control is under a single organisation, Sojuzplodimport.

The leader of the world retail market for vodka is Kristal, with around 7 per cent share of the world market. Kristal is a local Russian brand but it is only being sold on the world's biggest vodka market – Russia. Diageo's Smirnoff is the leading international brand of vodka. These are the only two brands of vodka worldwide commanding more than 5 per cent of global sales.

Western Europe

Smirnoff, with a regional market share of 16 per cent, was the brand leader in western Europe in 2008. Its nearest rival brand, Gorbatschow, held just over 8 per cent of regional sales. Only three brands in western Europe – Smirnoff, Gorbatschow and Absolut – account for more than 5 per cent of regional vodka sales in 2008.

Eastern Europe

The vodka market in Eastern Europe is large and diverse, with hundreds of brands on the market. Consequently regional leader Kristal controlled 'only' 7 per cent of regional sales in 2008, with its nearest rival brand, Smirnov, holding 4 per cent of sales. Diageo's Smirnoff was the largest international brand on the market.

North and Latin America
Diageo's Smirnoff brand was the leader of the North American vodka market in 2008, accounting for 18 per cent of regional sales. Its main rival was the premium Absolut brand. Smirnoff was also the largest vodka brand in Latin America, where it controlled over 24 per cent of the regional market. Smirnoff has few serious rivals in Latin America. Its closest competitor, Oso Negro from José Cuervo, held only 8 per cent of regional sales in 2008.

Rest of the world
In the rest of the world Smirnoff is the dominant brand of vodka. In 2008, it led the market in Asia-Pacific, Australasia, Africa and the Middle East.

Absolut Vodka enters the FAB market

The market for RTD (ready to drink) pre-mixed alcoholic beverages or FAB (flavoured alcoholic beverages) has developed at a rapid pace in the last few years. It is also a market that Absolut Vodka entered in 2004.

The international FAB market
Demand for FAB has grown sharply in the United Kingdom with spirit-based beverages Bacardi Breezer and Smirnoff Ice being the key brands driving the market.

A significant proportion of FABs are consumed on licensed premises, with modern town bars and nightclubs being the most popular venues for consuming these products. They are perceived as trendy, desirable products and are particularly popular among image-conscious consumers within the 18–30 age group who drink directly from the bottle. To a large extent, it is through strong branding that the industry has managed the transition from alcopops, with its connotation of under-age drinking, to the positive, premium image FABs currently enjoy. The use of energy drinks in combination with alcohol has become a popular trend in nightclubs and bars.

Consumption of FABs generally declines steadily with age (particularly after the age of 35), although this category is beginning to attract a wider audience: consumer research, for instance, shows that brands such as Smirnoff Ice are popular with consumers right up to the age of 65! It is clear that there is scope to push the category further among consumers of all ages and backgrounds. Although women continue to consume more than men, the difference in consumption levels according to gender is narrowing.

'Opinion leaders' form the segment of the consumer base that is socially influential in terms of fashions, and the product is taken to places where opinion leaders congregate in an attempt to secure acceptance by these trend-setters. Consequently, this expands the appeal of the product to consumers who are driven by more peer-led drinking. In the designer alcoholic drinks market opinion leaders tend to be young professional adults who frequent city-centre bars. In the international FAB market the club scene (on-premise) is also very important – allying a product with the nightclubbing market increases brand exposure and means that the product acquires acceptance from the socially influential nightclub audience. Both of these are integral to the development of designer alcoholic drinks. The trend for going to stylish bars and drinking expensive cocktails mixed at the bar is another affirmation of wealth and style and it has experienced a resurgence due to rising disposable incomes. 'Cocktail culture' has influenced flavour trends, especially in the premixed spirits market.

The 'cult of the individual' is also a major aspect of culture and is a growing trend across all markets. This term refers to the trend for individuality in consumption. For instance, rather than drinking the same brand as one's peers, consumers drink something that is particular to their own consumption habits in order to assert their own character and individuality. This trend is manifesting itself in both an assertion of individuality and a rejection of blanket marketing. This is a strong driver for sales of designer alcoholic drinks, even though brands have targeted opinion leaders in an attempt to capture more peer-led consumption. Ultimately, the brands' contribution to the consumers' perception of their own individuality is key to the success of designer alcoholic drinks, despite the inherent contradictions in this.

Consumers are becoming more adept at discerning which products are qualitatively better than others; they are also becoming quicker to abandon those that do not appeal to them. This is increasing the pressure on producers to create products that are obviously better than others. Despite the importance of image, poor quality in the premium market is less tolerated among consumers now.

Absolut Vodka entered and disappeared from the international FAB market
As consumer preferences evolve, Absolut Vodka sees an opportunity for launching a more sophisticated product into the international FAB market.

In 2004, V&S entered the international FAB market by starting to sell Absolut Vodka in Canada. Here the 7 per cent abv (alcohol by volume) vodka drink was aimed at the more mature drinker – rather than the younger generation traditionally targeted by RTDs – offering the ease of a pre-mix but with a less sugary taste.

V&S intend to take a more mature approach in its advertising, moving away from the image-based campaigns of other brands, so frequently criticized for glamorizing alcohol consumption and tempting under-age drinkers. The 'product' is to be the centrepiece of any advertising rather than the 'image'.

The Absolut Company.

By the end of 2006 the Absolut Cut had been launched in three flavours:

• *Absolut Cut*, containing a fresh citrus flavour
• *Absolut Clear Cut*, containing a mandarin flavour enhanced by kiwi
• *Absolut Crisp Cut*, containing a crisp apple flavour and a fresh finish of lime.

Absolut Cut has the same distinctive bottle shape as its parent brand and was rolled out to both the on- and off-trade FAB markets in Canada, Australia and UK. However, in July 2007 management concluded that Absolut Cut had failed to deliver sufficient volume in Canada, Australia and the UK, prompting it to be taken off the production line in all three markets.

Having read the above report, the CEO of V&S Absolut Spirits, Ketil Eriksen, acknowledges that it is necessary to get external input on some essential strategic questions. When he lands in New York he has written down the following questions, which he asks you to answer.

QUESTIONS

1. What was the main motive for Richard Pernod's acquisition of V&S (including Absolute Vodka) in 2008?

2. Which alternative marketing strategies does V&S Absolut Spirits have to increase its market share for:
   (a) Absolut Vodka in the USA?
   (b) Absolut Vodka in Europe (including Eastern Europe)?
   (c) Absolut Vodka in other parts of the world?

3. In which region (country) of the world would you recommend V&S Absolut Spirits to allocate more marketing resources?

4. Did Absolut Vodka have the right competences for achieving international success for its Absolut Cut?

5. Should Absolut Vodka relaunch a mixer product in the global FAB market?

Source: Adapted from Euromonitor and public sources.
Sources: Absolut London, Absolut Squeeze, Absolut Perfection, Absolut Berlin and screenshot from absolut.com by permission of Vin & Sprit AB (publ). Absolut® Vodka, Absolut Country of Sweden Vodka and logo, Absolut, Absolut Bottle Design and Absolut Calligraphy are trademarks owned by Vin & Sprit AB (publ). © 2009 Vin & Sprit AB (publ).

CASE STUDY IV.2

Guinness: how can the iconic Irish beer brand compensate for declining sales in the home market?

Beer is an alcoholic beverage made by brewing and fermenting cereals, especially malted barley, usually with the addition of hops as a flavouring agent and stabilizer. One of the oldest of alcoholic beverages (there is archaeological evidence dating to c.3000 BC), beer was well known in ancient Egypt, where it may have been made from bread. At first brewed chiefly in the household and monastery, it became a commercial product in late medieval times and is now made by large-scale manufacture in almost every industrialized country. Although British, European and American beers can differ markedly in flavour and content, brewing processes are similar. A mash, prepared from crushed malt (usually barley), water, and, often, cereal adjuncts such as rice and corn, is heated and rotated in the mash tun to dissolve the solids and permit the malt enzymes to convert the starch into sugar. The solution, called wort, is drained into a copper vessel, where it is boiled with the hops (which provide beer with its bitter flavour), then run off for cooling and settling. After cooling, it is transferred to fermenting vessels where yeast is added, converting the sugar into alcohol. Modern beers contain about 3 to 6 per cent alcohol. After brewing, the beer is usually a finished product. At this point the beer is kegged, casked, bottled, or canned. Beers fall into two broad categories:

- *Lighter beer (lagers)*. These are made with yeast that ferments more quickly at warmer temperatures and tends to rise to the surface. Lagers use yeast that ferments more slowly at cooler temperatures and tends to settle, and they are aged at cold temperatures for weeks or months, hence the name (German, lager = storage place). Lagers are the most commonly consumed beer in the world, with brands like Budweiser, Heineken, Fosters, Carlsberg, Becks, Carling, Kronenbourg and Stella Artois.
- *Darker beer*. Included in this broad category are ales, stout and porters. Stout (and porter) are dark beers made using roasted malts or roast barley. Porter is a strong and dark beer brewed with the addition of roasted malt to give flavour and colour. Stout (today more or less identical to Guinness) is normally darker and maltier than porter and has a

more pronounced hop aroma. Porter was first recorded as being made and sold in London in the 1730s. It became very popular in the British Isles, and was responsible for the trend toward large regional breweries with tied pubs. Originally, the adjective 'stout' meant 'proud' or 'brave', but later, after the fourteenth century, 'stout' came to mean 'strong'. The first known use of the word *stout* about beer was in 1677, the sense being that a stout beer was a strong beer. The expression *Stout-Porter* was applied during the 1700s for strong versions of porter, and was used by Guinness of Ireland in 1820, although Guinness had been brewing porters since 1759. 'Stout' still meant only 'strong' and it could be related to any kind of beer, as long as it was strong: in the United Kingdom it was possible to find 'stout pale ale', for example. Later 'stout' was eventually associated only with porter, becoming a synonym of dark beer. At the end of the nineteenth century, stout porter beer (especially the so-called 'milk stout' – a sweeter version) got the reputation of being a healthy strengthening drink, so it was used by athletes and nursing women, while doctors often recommended it to help recovery. Stouts can be classed into two main categories, sweet and bitter, and there are several kinds of each. Irish stout or Dry stout is the original product, equivalent to the Guinness beer. It is very dark in colour and it often has a 'toast' or coffee-like taste. Major brands in this broad category include Murphy's (Heineken), Castle Milk Stout (SAB Miller) and of course Guinness (Diageo).

Diageo

UK-based Diageo was formed in 1997 through the merger of Guinness and Grand Metropolitan. Both companies were themselves products of earlier mergers and acquisitions – Guinness had acquired Distillers in 1986 while Grand Metropolitan had diversified from its origins as a hotel chain into spirits (IDV), food (Pillsbury), restaurants (Burger Kings) and pubs. Diageo sold off Pillsbury and Burger King and the Guinness business was integrated into the global

Table 1	Key financial figures of Diageo, 2007–09		
	2007 (£m)	2008 (£m)	2009 (£m)
Total net sales	9,917	10,643	12,283
Profit before taxation	2,095	2,015	2,093

Source: based on www.diageo.com

spirits organization. Today Diageo is a Fortune 500 Company listed on both the New York and London Stock Exchange. The firm is the world's leading premium drinks enterprise, with a broad selection of brands. It currently occupies a 30 per cent share of the global market, and owns nine of the world's top 20 spirit brands, including Smirnoff vodka, Bushmills Irish whiskey, Johnnie Walker Scotch whisky, Captain Morgan rum, Gordon's dry gin, J&B Scotch whisky, Crown Royal whiskey and Baileys cream liqueur. The portfolio also includes Guinness stout. The company has over 24,000 employees, and trades in over 180 markets around the world. Its annual turnover in the fiscal year 2009 reached £12 billion, with a total market capitalization of over £20 billion. The financial development of Diageo during the last three years is illustrated in Table 1.

Diageo Plc has one major beer brand: Guinness, which is the world's leading stout brand. However, in the world beer market the stout only accounts for 1.0 per cent of the world beer sales (see Table 2). As a result of Guinness' status, Diageo Plc's beer performance is heavily reliant on the fortunes of the Guinness brand. However, cracks have started to appear in the brand as an aggressive price increases policy was employed to mask volume declines in key markets. Diageo Plc fails to disclose operating profit figures for its beer sector or for the flagship Guinness stout brand. However, it is estimated that beer accounts for 20 per cent of company sales, while its contribution to profits is thought to be smaller, at around 15 per cent.

Diageo's top management has growing concern over the company's principal beer brand, Guinness. The company reported a volume sales decline of 2 per cent for the brand in 2009, with value sales growth of 5 per cent only being achieved as a result of aggressive price increases in its main markets. The adoption of such a strategy has raised doubts of the sustainability of brand profitability. The Guinness brand has suffered on a number of levels, being hit by deteriorating demographics, with younger drinkers turning away from stout in general, a growing preference for wine and spirits, and a shift towards off-trade consumption (buying beers in the shops and drink them at home), which puts the

on-trade (pubs and bars) Guinness at a distinct disadvantage.

One of the reasons for this shift away from traditional pub consumption towards home drinking experiences is the banning of smoking in public places, both in the United Kingdom and Ireland. Nowhere have these trends been more evident than in these key markets. In general, Diageo Plc in 2009 reported a 2 per cent decline in Guinness worldwide volume sales, while in the United Kingdom and Ireland the fall was steeper, at 3 per cent. Nevertheless, on the back of notable price rises, value growth of 4 per cent was achieved in both markets.

Guinness – an iconic Irish brand

As an adopted Irish national icon (though it is actually not Irish-owned), the Guinness brand is readily recognized throughout the world, even by non-consumers. Indeed, it is one of only a few truly global beer brands, possessing a geographic coverage that spans all international regions. Brewed in over 50 countries, the Guinness recipe is modified to suit different market tastes in type and strength, with around 20 different variants sold worldwide. Its prime line is Guinness Draught, launched in 1959 and marketed in over 70 countries. This sub-brand accounts for around 55 per cent of all Guinness sold worldwide.

Widget technology saw Guinness Draught move into cans in 1989, and into bottles in 1999. To entice younger lager drinkers to stout, Guinness Draught Extra Cold was added to its range in its core markets of the UK and Ireland in 1998. The sub-brand actually comes from the same barrel as Guinness draught but goes through a super cooler on the way to the glass, and is served at a temperature around one-third lower than regular

The Guinness Surger
Diageo plc.

Table 2　World market for beer and stout, 2008

Beer/stout 2008	Western Europe	Eastern Europe	North America	Latin America	Asia Pacific	Australia and Asia	Africa and Middle East	World total
Beer volume sales (million litres)	30,000	20,000	26,000	24,000	45,000	2,000	8,000	155,000
Stout volume sales (million litres)	637	121	122	21	88	25	720	1,600 (1.0% of total beer sales)
Brand (company) market shares	%	%	%	%	%	%	%	%
Guiness (Diageo)	80	12	86	5	64	66	30	55
Murphy's (Heineken)	8	6	3					5
Zywiec Porter (Heineken)		14						2
Kelt (Heineken)		8						1
Beamish (Heineken)	4	1						3
Carlsberg (Carlsberg)	1	1						1
Okocim Porter (Carlsberg)		4						1
Danish Royal Stout (Carlsberg)					5			
Lvivske (BBH)		12				1		
Baltica 6 Porter (BBH)		5						
Tyskie Porter (SAB Miller)		10				1		
Castle Milk Stout (SAB Miller)							64	15
Morenita (CCU)				94				1
Speight's (Lion Nathan)						12		
Monteith's (Asia Pacific Breweries)						12		
Hite Stout (Hite Brewery)					10			1
Others	7	27	11	1	21	10	6	8
Total	100	100	100	100	100	100	100	100
Beer distribution	%	%	%	%	%	%	%	%
On-trade (bars, pubs etc.)	48	22	25	39	33	26	34	34
Off-trade (retail)	52	78	75	61	67	74	66	66
Total	100	100	100	100	100	100	100	100

Source: based on Euromonitor.

Guinness. This product is generally served in more modern outlets, where people prefer their beer cooler than standard.

Other line extensions include Guinness Bitter, a dark beer primarily sold in the United Kingdom, Guinness Extra Stout, which is mainly distributed in Europe in bottles and cans and Guinness Foreign Extra Stout. The latter is a higher strength, carbonated stout with a strong oaky flavour and no head, which is distributed throughout Africa, Asia and the Caribbean. Malta Guinness, an alcohol-free beer sold in Africa, and Guinness Extra Smooth, a smoother and creamy variation on traditional Guinness Draught, complete the Guinness portfolio.

The world market for beer and stout

Although Guinness is holding 60 per cent of the world stout market the brand accounts only for 0.6 per cent (60 per cent of 1 per cent) of the total world beer market (see Table 2).

Guinness's market share has a pretty stable world market share of around 60 per cent. The three largest markets for stout are Nigeria, Ireland and UK, which together account for 40 per cent of global volume sales in 2008.

Competitors

Despite recent regional declines, the global strength of Diageo Plc's Guinness brand has left little room for other major brands to become established in stout. Its main international rivals are SAB Miller's Castle Milk Stout, Heineken with its Murphy's brand and Beamish (a former Scottish & Newcastle brand).

Castle Milk Stout (SAB Miller)

Castle Milk Stout is only present in South Africa but it is very strongly placed here. This country has a considerable base, equivalent in size to the US stout environment, and combined with relatively low consumption of stout on a global level, this means that Castle Milk Stout had a heavy influence on the global market, with a volume share of 20 per cent in 2005. The product's performance of late has been dramatic. Under the guidance of SAB Miller, the brand is by far the leading stout product in South Africa, with a share of 89 per cent, a notable leap from the 74 per cent posted in 2003. It appears that Diageo Plc's decision to cut back marketing spend and implement aggressive price increases has backfired in South Africa.

Murphy's (Heineken)

Murphy's features in most markets across western and Eastern Europe and North America, but most significantly it holds a 7 per cent volume share of the largest stout market: the United Kingdom. Here, Murphy's has exerted limited pressure on Guinness in recent years, although its own share is partially under threat, facing similar problems in appealing to younger demographics. Conversely, notable brand growth in 2004 was evident in Slovakia, while forward momentum was maintained in Italy, France, the Netherlands, Norway and Russia.

Beamish (Heineken)

Beamish remains the most popular stout after Guinness in Ireland, posting a notable increase in volume share in 2004, up from 7 per cent to 8 per cent. Beamish is less of a threat in the United Kingdom, and is also present in the smaller stout markets of Canada, Portugal, France, Spain and the Ukraine. In 2003, Beamish was also introduced to the Finnish off-trade environment. Carlsberg is another international player in stout, but its competitive position is diluted by the fragmentation of its brand portfolio, which includes Carlsberg, Danish Royal Stout and Okocim Porter.

St Patrick's Day Fashion
Everybody needs a Little Black Drink

Diageo plc.

Local brand competition

Other local brands that generate reasonable volumes include Zywiec Porter in Poland and Kelt in Slovakia. Both of these brands are owned by Heineken and contributed to the company retaining its position as the number three player in stout, with a volume share of 8 per cent in 2008. That said, it remains some way behind the two leaders. Asahi Stout and Kirin Stout in Japan are also strong localized brands. Across Eastern Europe, Asia-Pacific, Australasia and Africa and the Middle East, Guinness has to contend with strong local brands. Aside from Castle Milk Stout, SAB Miller's other key brand is Tyskie Porter, which is hugely popular in Poland. Overall, SAB Miller sits in second place in global sales of stout, reflecting the strong performance of Castle Milk Stout in its domestic market.

Guinness market shares across regions

As seen in Table 2, Guinness is the market leader in four of the seven regions: western Europe, North America, Africa and Middle East, Asia Pacific and Australia and Asia. In the remaining three regions Guinness is number two or three.

Western Europe

Focusing on stout, in western Europe Diageo Plc led every national market with the exception of Denmark and Greece. Despite this strength, the company experienced its second successive year of volume sales decline in the region. At the heart of this downward trend in 2008 was a notable volume sales decline in Ireland, at 5 per cent and stagnation in the United Kingdom. Also the other markets in the region are declining. Key to this decline is the ageing profile of stout drinkers, with younger consumers failing to connect with the product. In addition, wine and spirits have grown in popularity, taking share from beer, and momentum behind the off-trade sector has grown, placing the on-trade-focused Guinness brand at a disadvantage. The main driver of the lower growth of stout is the shift from on-trade to off-trade. In UK and Ireland around 80 per cent of Guinness sales take place in the on-trade.

Eastern Europe

The strength of local brands also poses a problem to Guinness in Eastern Europe, with limited market shares in markets such as Poland (10 per cent in 2008), the Ukraine (3 per cent) and Slovakia (4 per cent). Guinness' volume share of stout is at 12 per cent in the region, its second lowest showing, with only its presence in Latin America smaller. Notably, Diageo posted a steady increase in its volume share of stout between 2004 and 2008 as consumers enjoyed rising disposable income levels and looked to trade up from low-to-middle end local brands. In contrast, Heineken, in pole position with its standard brand (Zywiec Porter), steadily lost share over the same period.

North America

Guinness also suffered a decline in North America, with sales volume falling in 2005. Poor US beer market conditions, with a price war taking place among leading players, were the main reason behind the downbeat performance, as performance in Canada was stronger. Nevertheless, the company remained the dominant force in stout in the region, with a volume share of 86 per cent in 2005.

Latin America

In Latin America a relatively new arrival in stout is Cía de Cervecerías Unidas SA (CCU) in Chile, although its global presence is negligible. CCU is dominating the Latin American market and its entry with its Morenita brand has knocked Guinness off the top spot.

Asia-Pacific

Demand for stout is underdeveloped in Asia-Pacific, where an almost total lack of demand in the populous markets of China and India is a notable barrier to growth. The Guinness sales volume declined in Hong Kong and experienced a marked dip in Indonesia and Thailand. A key force behind Diageo Plc's decline was the success of local player Hite Brewery Company Ltd, whose Hite Stout products quickly and confidently gained volume share of stout following its entry in 2000. Given its performance to date, this product comprises a considerable threat to Diageo Plc in the region. In addition, other local players performed well in recent years, negatively affecting Diageo Plc's regional position. Despite the dip in volume share, Diageo Plc remained the number one player in stout, even maintaining the top spot in Hong Kong, where decline was at its steepest. Another source of positive momentum in 2004 was Japan, where the company took its volume share to over 40 per cent. This growth was a notable achievement given the extent of local competition from Asahi and Kirin, which both have rival products to Guinness (Asahi Stout and Kirin Stout) and both enjoy significant price advantages. In Asia Pacific the intro of ginseng-flavoured stout brands signals repositioning of stout. Examples of Ginseng Stout brands are Danish Royal Stout Ginseng (Carlsberg), Partner Stout Ginseng (Bali Hai Brewery) and ABC Exstra Stout Ginseng (Asia Pacific Breweries). These new ginseng stout brands are developed for fans who seek a full-bodied stout with additional benefits. The key end target market for this product segment is the middle-income male consumer.

Australia and Asia

This region is one of the strongest markets for Guinness, which enjoys a market share of 66 per cent in the region as a whole.

Africa and the Middle East

This regions is one of the most important for the company in terms of growth potential as the level of stout consumption is among the highest in the world and much growth is expected in the short term. The majority of Diageo's worldwide brewing facilities are in Africa where its majority-owned brewing operations such as in Kenya, Nigeria, Cameroon, Ghana and the Seychelles brew both Guinness and local brands. Guinness is also produced by third-party brewers in other African countries where volumes are not so strong.

Overall Guinness is a market leader in Africa and Middle East. Guinness' strongest markets are the markets in East Africa (Kenya, Uganda and Tanzania), though the majority of volumes are sold in Nigeria, which is the brand's second-largest market globally. For example, Guinness has a market share of 97 per cent in Kenya, while SAB Miller's strength is based on its dominance (77 per cent market share) in South Africa. Heineken is especially strong in Nigeria and Cameroon. Consequently, company performances are very reliant on local geographic conditions.

The international marketing strategy

In the following, Guinness' initiatives within the international marketing mix will be explained.

New product innovation/packaging

Diageo Plc moved its Guinness Draught into bottles in late 1999 following the development of a new 'rocket widget', which enabled Guinness to retain its distinctive foamy white head when consumed from its packaging. Presented in long-neck bottles, this line positioned Guinness alongside premium lagers and flavoured alcoholic beverages, such as Diageo Plc's popular Smirnoff Ice.

The beer market in the United Kingdom is seeing a dynamic shift away from traditional pub consumption towards home drinking experiences, partially due to the banning of smoking in public places. The impact of banning smoking in pubs in Ireland and the United Kingdom was indicating a switch from on-trade (pubs, bars) into off-trade as more people opted to smoke and drink at home.

In February 2006 the Guinness Surger was launched. It is a plug-in unit promising to deliver the perfect pint at home by sending ultrasonic sound waves through the special Guinness Draught Surger beer. By releasing this new product, Diageo is aiming to recreate the 'pub experience' in consumers' own homes, as the idea of pubs in which people can smoke will be a thing of the past. Consumers purchasing drinks for at-home occasions want to mimic the on-trade experience as much as possible, particularly in terms of presentation and quality. The new Surger gadget delivers exactly this, as well as having a 'shareability' factor to enhance consumers' at home drinking experience through the novelty of using the ultrasound device. The price in the United Kingdom is £17 for the starter kit which includes one Surger, a pint glass and two cans of Surger Beer.

Guinness Draught Surger could help Diageo to capitalize on the growing movement towards the off-trade. The product has already been released with success in Japan and Singapore, and will be the focus of a £2.5 million marketing campaign in the UK. However, the Guinness Surger Unit was withdrawn from the UK market in April 2008 and sales of the cans were withdrawn from Tesco stores.

In 2009 the Surger unit is again available in UK and worldwide, including countries such as the USA, Italy, France, Spain, Austria, Australia and Japan. Guinness Surger cans are available to licensed premises in the different sizes – UK and Spain 520ml, USA 14.9 fluid ounces, Europe 330ml, Japan 350ml and Australia 375ml.

Distribution

Diageo Plc handles its own distribution as a rule. However, in many countries, stout occupies a very small niche in the beer environment, making it uneconomical for Guinness to set up its own production and distribution network. It therefore operates in partnership with a number of local and international brewers. Sometimes the company appoints third-party distributors or agrees a joint venture for the purpose.

Distribution agreements most often include licensing and distribution agreements for beer. These include both Guinness and rival brands. For example, with Carlsberg it is allowing them the production of their beer in Ireland. In return Carlsberg helps Guinness with distribution in some countries. Japanese Sapporo beer is also produced in the Guinness breweries. As compensation, Guinness gets access to Japanese distribution.

Diageo has also entered into a three-way joint venture with Heineken and Namibia Breweries Limited in southern Africa, called Brandhouse, to take advantage of the consumer shift towards premium brands. The company is also aiming to merge its business in Ghana (Guinness Ghana Limited) with Heineken's Ghana Breweries Limited, to achieve operational synergy benefits.

Diageo terminated its rights agreement for the distribution of Bass Ale in the United States with effect from 30 June 2003. According to the original agreement Diageo had the rights to distribute Bass Ale in the US until 2016. After negotiation, the distribution rights reverted to the global brand owner, Interbrew, for £69 million.

Advertising of Guinness

Guinness advertising spend has been reduced in recent years, falling in both 2004 and 2005. In the latter, it stood at £1,023 million, compared to £1,039 million, a fall of 2 per cent. Whether this caution is a wise move in times of increased competition remains to be seen. As a largely unique product that leads its category, Guinness has historically been supported by a high degree of creative and ground-breaking marketing and advertising, beginning with the 'Guinness for

Strength' girder-man in 1934, and its long-surviving Toucan character, which ran from 1935 to 1982. Guinness has increasingly developed below-the-line campaigns to target existing and potential consumers with the development of customer relationship marketing (CRM). However, above-the-line spend in 2002 was notable, with Guinness's first ever global campaign entitled 'believe'. This focused on the concept of 'self belief' and 'belief in Guinness', and was created by BBDO. The campaign featured a logo with the V in 'believe' replaced with the Guinness harp, and was designed to reinforce brand loyalty among existing consumers and, of course, attract new ones.

Advertising in the United Kingdom and Ireland

Especially in the United Kingdom and Ireland, the Guinness marketing campaigns have been very high profile, turning the brand into one of the most successful fast-moving consumer goods in the UK, with very strong top-of-mind recall awareness. In Ireland, however, repeated attempts to reinvigorate the Guinness brand have met with limited success. In February 2004, Diageo Plc launched a new advertising campaign for Guinness in the UK called 'Out of Darkness Comes Light'. The first advert in the series – Moth – represented the start of a campaign marking a new chapter in the heritage of Guinness advertising. This advert was followed up by the Mustang execution, which has all the epic drama and scale characteristic of Guinness advertising. It was supported by a total media spend of £15 million, and first appeared on national TV in September 2004.

In 2005, Diageo Plc launched a new advertising campaign for the core Guinness brand in the United Kingdom and Ireland late in the year. The 'Evolution' campaign features an advert depicting three men in a bar taking a sip of Guinness and then being transported back in time, going back through the main stages of evolution. The new advert had a more contemporary and youthful feel than previous showings, suggesting that Diageo Plc has responded to the problem of deteriorating demographics affecting the brand.

In 2007 Diageo launched the 'Hands', a £2.5 million campaign for Guinness, which included an online presence as well as traditional TV and print executions.

Advertising in Africa

As the biggest growth markets for Guinness are African countries, the greatest marketing innovation generated by Diageo Plc is being implemented here. Guinness spent more than £25 million on advertising in Africa, where the brand commands premium pricing through its reputation. Following on from Saatchi & Saatchi's 1999 creation of character Michael Power in a series of five-minute action thriller advertisements, the concept has culminated in a full-length promotional film production shown across Africa. Guinness Nigeria shot a new Michael Power film, which was screened in 2004. In a further display of commitment to this growth region, Guinness Nigeria has worked with local communities to provide them with clean, safe water. Royalties from the Guinness-sponsored feature film 'Critical Assignment', which highlights the need for clean drinking water, have helped fund a Water of Life project.

How to attract the young consumer

Despite its previous marketing successes, Guinness is suffering from a lack of take-up among younger consumers in preference for more fashionable lagers and FABs. An interesting trend in Diageo Plc's marketing strategy was a further change in the way the company marketed its flagship Guinness brand. For a period on its Guinness.com website, the company actively encouraged consumers to mix Guinness with other products to produce various 'cocktails'. This was clearly a further effort to appeal to the youth segment given that many consumers in this age group find the taste of Guinness too bitter. Examples of mixers suggested by the company included champagne, blackcurrant juice, lime juice or curaçao, cacao and Dubonnet.

Sponsoring

The positioning of Guinness has been centred on the brand's traditional associations with sports. In 2005, Guinness made a notable investment in sports sponsorship, putting its name to the 2005 tour of the British and Irish Lions rugby union team to New Zealand and paying £20 million to sponsor the 2005–2006 season of top league domestic rugby union in the United Kingdom. In addition, the brand was the sponsor of the G-8 Summit in Gleneagles, Scotland.

In 2008 Diageo announced that Guinness would be the title sponsor for Singapore Rugby. The three-year deal sees Guinness on its sponsorship on the Guinness Premiership in the UK and Ireland, the Irish national rugby team and the club Hong Kong Sevens. In Singapore Guinness will sponsor three divisions, as well as the elite knock-out competition, the Singapore Cup.

Investments in a new Irish-theme pub concept

Guinness consumption rose partly because of the development of the Irish-theme pub. In the UK, Diageo Plc invested £13 million in 2001 in developing a new bar concept that it encouraged independent owners of Irish-theme pubs to adopt.

The idea was to make traditional pubs less cluttered and more contemporary, lighter and cleaner and thereby more appealing to women. This new concept also put a stronger focus on spirits rather than draught beer, thereby signalling that Diageo Plc saw its spirits brands driving future revenue growth rather than Guinness beer.

The top management in Diageo is in doubt as to what to do about Guinness in future. Should they continue the 'milking strategy' by withdrawing marketing resources (lowering costs) and increasing revenues (by increasing the end-consumer prices)? At least that would maximize profits over a shorter term and Diageo could use the financial resources in acquiring other beer brands. Or should Diageo instead make a long-term investment in developing the brand, by implementing new global marketing initiatives?

Sources: Wiggins, J. (2006) 'Guinness still posing slow sales problems at Diageo', *Financial Times*, 30 June; Choueke, M. (2006) 'Dark times for the black stuff?', *Marketing Week*, 15 June; Carey, B. (2006) 'Is Guinness still good for Diageo?' *Sunday Times* (London), 9 April; www.diageo.com; www.euromonitor.com.

QUESTIONS

As an international marketing consultant you are asked to give an independent assessment of Guinness' opportunities in the world beer market. You are specifically asked the following questions:

1. How would you explain the Guinness pricing strategy and the underlying assumptions about consumer behaviour when Diageo reports for 2005 that in the United Kingdom and Ireland the Guinness sales volume fell by 3 per cent, but a value growth of 4 per cent was achieved in both markets, mainly due to price increases?

2. Motivated by the success of this pricing strategy, should Diageo continue to increase the price of Guinness?

3. In Choueke (2006) an anonymous beer retail buyer comments on Guinness' decreasing sales volume:

Guinness has an older profile of drinker and with an ever-increasing availability of continental lagers and a fast-growing range of alcopops, the younger generation of drinkers simply haven't bought into it. Innovation − widgets and gadgets − will keep the brand alive for a while but where else can Diageo go? Flavoured Guinness? No thanks. It is in decline and Diageo's best minds can't do much about it. The brand may have only a couple of decades worth of life in it and I would milk it for everything before getting rid of it and concentrating on spirits.

Do you agree with this statement? Explain your reasons.

4. What elements of the Guinness international marketing strategy would you focus on in order to increase both global sales volume, value and profits?

CASE STUDY IV.3

Dyson Vacuum Cleaner: shifting from domestic to international marketing with the famous bagless vacuum cleaner

The Dyson history

It is impossible to separate the very British Dyson vacuum cleaner from its very British inventor. Together they are synonymous with innovation and legal battles against established rivals.

James Dyson was born in Norfolk in 1947. He studied furniture design and interior design at the Royal College of Art from 1966 to 1970 and his first product, the Sea Truck, was launched while he was still studying.

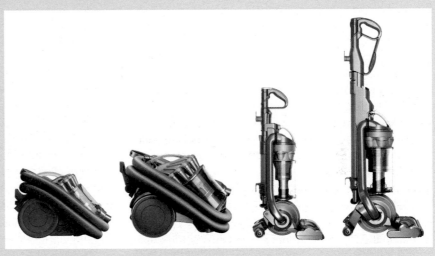

Courtesy of Dyson.

Dyson's foray into developing vacuum cleaner technology happened by chance. In 1978, while renovating his 300-year-old country house, Dyson became frustrated with the poor performance of his conventional vacuum cleaner. Whenever he went to use it, there was poor suction. One day he thought he would find out what was wrong with the design. He noted that the appliance worked by drawing air through the bag to create suction, but when even a fine layer of dust got inside, it clogged its pores, stopping the airflow and suction.

In his usual style of seeking solutions from unexpected sources, Dyson noticed how a nearby sawmill used a cyclone – a 30-foot-high cone that spun dust out of the air by centrifugal force – to expel waste. He reasoned that a vacuum cleaner that could separate dust by cyclonic action and spin it out of the airstream which would eliminate the need for both bag and filter. James Dyson set out to replicate the cyclonic system.

Over the next eight years, Dyson tried to license his dual cyclone concept to established vacuum manufacturers, only to be turned down. At least two of these initial contacts forced him to file patent infringement lawsuits, which he won in out-of-court and in-court settlements. Finally in 1985, a small company in Japan contacted him out of the blue after seeing a picture of his vacuum cleaner in a magazine. Mortgaged to the hilt and on the brink of bankruptcy, Dyson took the cheapest flight to Tokyo to negotiate a deal. The result was the G Force vacuum cleaner, priced at US$2,000, which became the ultimate domestic appliance status symbol in Japan.

In June 1993, using money from the Japanese licence, Dyson opened a research centre and factory in Malmesbury, Wiltshire. Here he developed the Dyson dual cyclone and within two years it was the fastest-selling vacuum cleaner in the UK.

Dyson was nearly bankrupted by the legal costs of establishing and protecting his patent. It took him more than 14 years to get his first product into a shop and it is on display in the Science Museum. Other products can be seen in the Victoria & Albert Museum, the San Francisco Museum of Modern Art and the Georges Pompidou Centre in Paris.

Dyson went on to develop the Root 8 Cyclone, which removes more dust by using eight cyclones instead of two. In 2000, he launched the Contra-rotator washing machine, which uses two drums spinning in opposite directions and is said to wash faster and with better results than traditional washing machines.

In 2008 the company's sales reached £700 million, roughly two-thirds of which came from outside the United Kingdom, while pre-tax profit for the year was £150 million, up 32 per cent on 2008. Almost all the sales come from vacuum cleaners – a product in which Dyson has built large sales in the United States, Japan and Australia.

Marketing of the Dyson vacuum cleaner

Dyson believes the most effective marketing tool is by word of mouth, and today the company claims 70 per cent of its vacuum cleaners are sold on personal recommendation. An enthusiastic self-publicist, Dyson believes that if you make something, you should sell it yourself, so he often appears in his own advertisements.

When a Belgian court banned Dyson from denigrating old-style vacuum cleaner bags, he was pictured wearing his trademark blue shirt and holding a Dyson vacuum cleaner in a press advertisement that had the word 'bag' blacked out several times. A note at the bottom said: 'Sorry, but the Belgian courts won't let you know what everyone has a right to know'.

Dyson has sometimes shunned advertising altogether. For example, in 1996–97 the company spent its marketing budget sponsoring Sir Ranulph Fiennes' solo expedition to Antarctica, and gave £1.5 million to the charity Breakthrough Breast Cancer.

As rivals started to manufacture their own bagless cleaners, Dyson knew he would have to advertise more aggressively and in 2000 he appointed an advertising agency to promote the £2 million business. The marketing strategy, however, remains true to Dyson's original principles, with an emphasis on information and education rather than brand-building. Moreover, it seems to be working, one in every three vacuum cleaners bought in Britain today is a Dyson. See also Table 1.

The world market for vacuum cleaners

The use of vacuum cleaners is largely related to national preferences for carpets rather than floor tiles. In many warm countries floor tiles are more usual than carpets, and these can be swept rather than vacuumed. In countries where houses are predominantly carpeted, such as in Northern Europe, Eastern Europe and North America, the number of households owning vacuum cleaners is high. In 2008 approximately 95 per cent of households owned vacuum cleaners in Belgium, Germany, Japan, the Netherlands, Sweden, the United States and the United Kingdom. Many Belgian households possess more than one vacuum cleaner, as traditional vacuum cleaners are often complemented with hand-held cleaners (cleanettes). In parts of Eastern Europe it is also common to carpet walls, which provides additional demand for vacuum cleaners.

Few vacuum cleaners are sold in China and India. Vacuum cleaners have only been available in China for ten years, but ownership has not become widespread. In India many of the rural population do not have the means for such appliances and power supply is erratic. The Asia-Pacific market for vacuum cleaners (not shown in Table 1) is 14 million units per year.

The world market for vacuum cleaners is fairly mature and stable. As average prices fell throughout 2000–08, value growth amounted to only 2 per cent overall. In 2008 the number of vacuum cleaners sold throughout the world was 85 million units. Demand is driven mainly by replacement purchases at the end of a product's life cycle (the commercial lifetime of a vacuum cleaner is about eight years), although new product developments such as bagless models spurred growth in some markets.

The most sold vacuum cleaner types are the upright and the cylinder types. The distinction between upright and cylinder vacuum cleaners became less clear in recent years, with the addition of hoses and tools to the upright version and cylinders mimicking uprights by adding turbo brushes to eradicate dust from carpets.

Cylinder, or canister, vacuum cleaners make up the majority of the global market, but do not take a strong lead, accounting for 70 per cent of European volume sales in 2008, compared with 30 per cent for upright models (see Table 1). As upright vacuum cleaners are more expensive their share is higher by value, amounting to 35 per cent of the market by value.

Generally, the sales of upright vacuum cleaners grew faster than cylinders over the five-year period from 2000 to 2008. This largely reflected trends in the US, which was the world's leading market for vacuum cleaners (especially upright vacuum cleaners). Here, the addition of new features fuelled the upright subsector, including bagless operation, HEPA (high-efficiency particulate air) filtration and self-propulsion, which are available in various combinations on models selling for less than US$200.

In other markets, such as in Eastern Europe, cylinder vacuum cleaners are the most popular type as they are more practical for use on wall carpets, which are common, for example, in Russia.

Hand-held vacuum cleaners do not play an important role in the market, and are ignored in the rest of this case study.

The market for vacuum cleaners tends to be dominated by leading white goods manufacturers. Electrolux was uncontested world leader in this sector in 2008 with a volume share of 14 per cent through its brands Eureka and Electrolux.

| Table 1 | Vacuum cleaners: market volume and market shares (2008) |

Market/%/Manufacturers (brands)	Germany	Italy	Sweden	France	Spain	UK	Netherlands		Total western Europe	United States
Total market										
Volume (million units)	6.0	2.5	0.6	3.0	0.9	7.0	1.0	+ others 3.0	24.0	35
% – types:										
Cylinder	80	60	95	90	95	35	90		70	15
Upright	20	40	5	10	5	65	10		30	85
Total	100	100	100	100	100	100	100		100	100
Market shares (%):										
BSH (Bosch-Siemens Hausgeräte)	14	–	9	–	–	–	28		8	
Electrolux (Eureka in US)	13	–	51	19	–	14	9		14	18
Miele	11	–	12	9	–	3	23		9	
Dyson Appliances	6	1	2	1	1	22	2		10	4
SEB Group (Rowenta + Moulinex)	1	18	–	22	19	–	8		7	
TTI (Hoover/Dirt devil)	15	12	–	–	–	7	–		8	30
Bissell										21
Philips	3	–	2	–	7	–	10		4	
De Longhi	–	15	–	–	–	–	–		2	
Matsushita (Panasonic)		–	8	–	21	5	–		2	
Daewoo Group		8	–	–	–	–	–		1	
Samsung		6	–	–	–	–	–		1	
Electromomésticos Solac SA		–	–	–	10	–	–		1	
Private label	8	–	15	2	5	3	3		4	5
Others	29	40	1	47	37	46	17		30	22
Total	100	100	100	100	100	100	100		100	100

Comments: In Europe and USA Hoover and Dirt Devil are manufactured by TTI Floor Care North America (Hoover) and its subsidiary Royal Appliance Manufacturing (Dirt Devil). The SEB group took over the Rowenta brand in 1988. In 2001 the SEB Group took over Moulinex SA and the SEB Group now markets the Moulinex vacuum cleaner.

Source: author's own, based on Euromonitor.

In recent years one of the most significant developments in the market is bagless technology. Dyson UK pioneered its dual cyclone technology back in 1993 and it is protected by patent, but other manufacturers were quick to develop bagless versions. In the United States, bagless vacuum cleaners increased their unit share from just 2.6 per cent in 1998 to over 20 per cent in 2008.

The western European market is rather fragmented. Dyson was some way behind Electrolux with a share of 9 per cent (see Table 1). Though Dyson's overall market share is not high it used to be one of the dominating brands in the high-priced segment.

The Asia-Pacific market for vacuum cleaners is highly concentrated, with the top five players accounting for 80 per cent of sales in 2008. These were all Japanese companies, led by Matsushita. The latter also led the Australasian market, slightly ahead of Dyson. Interestingly, Samsung did not rank among the top five Asian manufacturers in 2008, although it led the Eastern European market.

In the United States Dyson now sells 1 million units, equal to a total market share of 4 per cent. However, in the high-priced segment (US$400 – plus) Dyson (in 2008) pushed Hoover to a second place with 21 per cent of the market against Hoover's 15 per cent. Dyson is taking market shares in the high end, which Hoover used to dominate, and at the same time Hoover lost the low-cost market to non-brand Asian competitors. While not as expensive as ultra-premium lines, such as Miele and Kirby, upright models of Dyson vacuum cleaners are resolutely high-end, with models retailing for US$350–550. The company does not engage in discounting, maintaining the brand's high prices as part of an overall image of quality. Even its hand-held model retails for US$150, which is significantly higher than its competitors. In United States vacuum cleaners can be found in a growing number of retail outlets, such as Best Buy, Sears Bed, Bath & Beyond, Target and Wal-Mart.

Competitors

The following describes the five most important players in the world vacuum cleaner industry.

BSH (Bosch-Siemens Hausgeräte)

Bosch-Siemens Hausgeräte (www.bsh-group.com) was established in 1967 by the merger of the domestic appliance divisions of Robert Bosch Hausgeräte and Siemens. During the 1990s, the company was largely geared towards improving its international presence and this was achieved mainly through organic growth, with a cautious approach taken towards acquisitions (e.g. Ufesa).

Ufesa is the leading manufacturer in Spain and Portugal of small appliances such as vacuum cleaners, irons and coffee makers, and has a good export network to Latin America. The acquisition allowed BSH to improve its production and distribution arrangements.

Bosch-Siemens Hausgeräte (BSH) is entirely focused on the production and servicing of domestic electrical appliances, including large kitchen appliances and small electrical appliances.

BSH remains highly focused on western Europe, especially its domestic German market. Germany alone accounted for 28 per cent of total sales in 2008, down from 30 per cent the previous year. This was due to the difficult trading environment, which led to a 4 per cent overall decline in sales in this market.

Sales in markets outside western Europe were minimal, with North America, Eastern Europe and Asia-Pacific each accounting for 6 per cent of the total and Latin America just 3 per cent. Eastern Europe recorded above-average growth rates, especially Russia with over 21 per cent.

Sales in Latin America continued to decline, due to the ongoing economic crisis in Argentina, and both Brazil and Argentina causing significant foreign-exchange-related losses. However, double-digit growth was achieved in China, where the company saw sales rise for the fourth consecutive year.

Electrolux

Electrolux www.electrolux.com is the world's second-largest manufacturer of large kitchen appliances behind American Whirlpool, in terms of revenue derived from this activity. The company is headquartered in Sweden and produces a wide range of large kitchen appliances, as well as vacuum cleaners and heating and cooling equipment. In addition, Electrolux manufactures products outside the scope of this report, such as garden equipment, food service equipment and chainsaws.

Electrolux dates back to 1901 when its predecessor, Lux AB, was formed in Stockholm as a manufacturer of kerosene lamps. The company changed its name to Electrolux AB in 1919, following collaboration between Lux AB and Svenska Elektron AB. The company shifted into electrical appliances in 1912, when it introduced its first household vacuum cleaner, the Lux 1. In 1925, this was followed by the launch of the first Electrolux absorption refrigerator. The company was quick to expand internationally, and by the 1930s was selling refrigerators and vacuum cleaners across the globe.

Between the 1940s and the 1980s, Electrolux expanded into the areas of large kitchen appliances, floor care and garden equipment sectors through a wide range of acquisitions. In the 1990s the company worked to expand its appliance business internationally.

The company is divided into two major business areas:

1. Consumer durables, including large kitchen appliances and air conditioners, floor care products (vacuum cleaners) and garden equipment (such as lawnmowers, garden tractors and lawn trimmers).
2. Professional products, including food-service equipment, laundry equipment for apartment/house laundry rooms, launderettes, hotels and institutions, components such as compressors, forestry equipment such as chainsaws and clearing saws and other products such as landscape maintenance equipment, turf-care equipment and professional-use power cutters.

Electrolux's business is largely split between Europe and North America, which together accounted for 80 per cent of sales in the consumer durables division in 2008. The company has achieved a good balance between these regions, with similar sales levels.

Miele

Miele (www.mielevacuums.com) is a German-based, family-run company, which produces a range of premium household appliances (e.g. vacuum cleaners), commercial appliances, components and fitted kitchens.

Carl Miele and Reinhard Zinkann established Miele in Gütersloh, Germany in 1899. Since its inception the company has been focused on producing high-quality appliances at the premium end of the market.

The company began producing washing machines in 1900: vacuum cleaners and dishwashers added to the product portfolio in the 1920s. During the 1950s and 1960s the company began to produce fully automatic washing machines and dishwashers, as well as tumble dryers. The 1970s saw further advances in technology, with the launch of built-in washing machines and condenser dryers and microcomputer-controlled appliances.

Since then, they have produced a number of innovative appliances including washing machines with hand-wash programmes for woollens, and during the 1990s, vacuum cleaners with the HEPA filter and sealed system. HEPA (high-efficiency particulate air) filters are beneficial for asthma and allergy sufferers, because the HERA filter traps fine particles such as pollen which trigger allergy and asthma symptoms.

Over the past decade Miele has focused on expanding its business overseas, especially in Eastern Europe and Asia-Pacific. The company opened a branch office in Hong Kong in 1998, followed by offices in Poland and Russia, US headquarters in Princeton, New Jersey in 1999 and in 2001 it opened sales offices in Singapore and Mexico.

Miele has made few significant acquisitions through its history. Its largest acquisition was that of Imperial, a German company specializing in built-in appliances and catering equipment, in 1990.

Miele products are marketed throughout Europe and also in the United States, Canada, South Africa, Australia, Japan and Hong Kong through subsidiaries, and elsewhere in the world via authorized importers.

The company's range of domestic electrical appliances covers vacuum cleaners, large kitchen appliances such as home laundry appliances, refrigeration appliances, large cooking appliances, microwaves and dishwashers and other small appliances such as rotary irons and coffee makers. The company specializes in producing innovative products within these sectors.

As a private company, Miele does not release detailed financial results.

The company lists its highest gross overseas market as the Netherlands, followed by Switzerland, France, Austria, the United Kingdom and the United States. The United States recorded especially swift growth at double-digit rates. Double-digit growth was also achieved in Greece, Finland and Ireland, while other markets showing above average growth, included the United Kingdom and Norway. Russia also showed extremely good growth, although to date the company has only focused on Moscow and St Petersburg.

Groupe SEB

Groupe SEB of France (www.seb.com) is one of the world's leading producers of small domestic equipment. The company is entirely focused on this area, manufacturing household goods (cookware), as well as small electrical appliances such as cooking appliances (steam cookers, toasters, coffee makers and grills), home appliances (vacuum cleaners and fans), and personal care appliances (hair dryers, scales and electric toothbrushes). SEB's key brands include T-Fal/Tefal, Rowenta, Krups and SEB.

Groupe SEB's origins date back to 1857, when the tinware company Antoine Lescure was founded. The company gradually expanded its activities to include products such as kitchen utensils and zinc tubs, beginning to mechanize its production at the beginning of the twentieth century. In 1953, the company launched the first pressure cooker.

The company has since grown by acquisition. This began with Tefal in 1968, a company specializing in non-stick cookware, and continued with the acquisition of the Lyon company, Calor, a maker of irons, hair dryers, small washing machines and portable radiators in 1972. In 1973, a group structure was formed under a lead holding company, SEB SA, which was listed on the Paris Stock Exchange two years later.

Groupe SEB made a significant push into international markets when it acquired Rowenta in 1988, a German manufacturer of irons, electric coffee makers, toasters and vacuum cleaners. In 1992 and 1993, it took advantage of the opening up of Eastern Europe, setting up marketing operations to make inroads in these countries and gain a foothold in the Russian market.

In 1997–98, Groupe SEB entered South America with the acquisition of Arno, Brazil's market leader in small electrical appliances. Arno specializes in the manufacture and sale of food preparation appliances (mixers/blenders), non-automatic washing machines and fans.

In September 2001, Groupe SEB's main domestic rival, Moulinex, filed for bankruptcy. The company submitted an offer for a partial takeover of the business assets of Moulinex, for which it finally received approval by both the European Commission and the French Finance Ministry in 2002. Moulinex had purchased one of Europe's leading brands, Krups, in the early 1990s, and was a good fit with Groupe SEB's existing businesses.

Groupe SEB has stated its intention to expand in emerging markets which offer high growth potential, such as Brazil, Korea, the CIS (former Soviet Republic) countries and China, although it also sees potential for development of high added-value niche products in developed markets such as the EU, North America and Japan.

Growth was achieved in all regions in 2008, largely due to the partial acquisition in that year of Moulinex-Krups.

Whirlpool

In 2006 Whirlpool announced that it had taken over Maytag's Hoover vacuum cleaner division. Whirlpool closed its takeover of Maytag in March, after passing an extended Justice Department anti-trust review. Hoover was acquired as part of its US$1.68 billion purchase of Maytag Corp. The company operates under the premium brands Maytag, Jenn Air, and the lower-end brands Magic Chef, Amana and Admiral. It operates mainly in the United States, but has sales subsidiaries in Canada, Australia, Mexico, Puerto Rico and the United Kingdom.

Maytag Corp traces its roots back to 1893 when F.L. Maytag began manufacturing farm implements in Newton, Iowa. In order to offset seasonal slumps in demand he introduced a wooden-tub washing machine in 1907. The company diversified into cooking appliances and refrigerators after the Second World War in 1946. It introduced its first automatic washing machine in 1949, and its first portable dishwashers in 1966.

One of the most famous brands in the vacuum cleaner industry – Hoover – dates back to 1907, when it was developed by the Hoover family in Canton, Ohio. The Hoover Company began selling its products worldwide in 1921. Maytag took over the Hoover brand in 1989 when they merged with Chicago Pacific Corporation. In 1995, Maytag sold the European Hoover operations to the Italian appliance manufacturer Candy. In 2008, Hoover and Dirt Devil were taken over by TTI Floor Care Birth America and its subsidiary, Royal Appliance Manufacturing Co.

In the vacuum cleaner sector, Whirlpool operates only under the Hoover brand, which has a strong heritage and is the leading brand in the US market. Hoover manufactures a wide range of vacuum cleaners, including uprights, canisters, stick and hand-held vacuums, hard surface cleaners, extractors and other home care products.

In mid-2006 Whirlpool Corp. sold the Hoover vacuum cleaner business. The Hoover brand, with its 3,000 employees, did not fit with Whirlpool's core products – laundry, refrigeration and kitchen equipment.

Distribution of vacuum cleaners

The situation in Dyson's domestic market, the UK, is as follows.

Department stores are the most popular source of small electrical goods in the UK, with many trusted names (e.g. Co-op Home Stores and John Lewis) who are able to stock a sufficient variety of competitively priced goods to attract consumer loyalty. Their share has increased slightly over recent years, as department stores in general have become more fashionable again.

Specialist multiples have the second largest share, although not far behind are the independents which have a larger share of the small electrical appliances market than they do of large appliances. Smaller high street stores in small- and medium-sized towns attract buyers of small electrical appliances, like vacuum cleaners, because consumers are less motivated to drive to a retail park for these items, than they are say, for a fridge.

Grocery multiples, such as Tesco and Asda, sell vacuum cleaners and generally offer advantageous deals on a narrow range of goods. Catalogue showrooms such as Argos also benefited from increasing their range and from low pricing and online shopping facilities.

Distribution of vacuum cleaners has become hugely extensive, with supermarkets and grocery stores stocking the cheaper to mid-end of the market. For electrical retailers still selling smaller items, their domain lies more in the pricier, higher-end of the market.

The distribution of vacuum cleaners in most other major countries is limited principally to specialist 'household appliance' store chains and department stores.

Huge retail chains like Electric City, Best Buy and Sears increasingly dominate the distribution of vacuum cleaners in United States.

Production moved to Malaysia

In recent years, Dyson has decided to move most of its vacuum cleaner production from the United Kingdom to the Far East (Malaysia).

Although Dyson is still a leading vacuum cleaner brand, it is beginning to lose out to cheaper machines that have developed their own bagless technology. The dilemma they face is dropping its own prices or reinforcing the power and quality of the brand. The loyalty of Dyson's customers has dropped off and the company's market share in UK by volume has also decreased.

Introduction of the Dyson Airblade

In 2008 Dyson released a new type of hand dryer, the Dyson Airblade. Dyson claims that it dries hands in 10 seconds, that it is more cost-effective for energy usage than traditional hot air blower hand dryers, and is more environmentally friendly, saving 83 per cent in energy in comparison to conventional hand dryers. Based on 200 uses a day for 365 days a year, the Airblade would cost £30 to operate for that full year.

The end customers for the product are primarily hotels, restaurants, big enterprises, institutions, airports etc. In United States alone there are approximately 20 million toilets outside private homes. US paper towel sales are US$2 billion, while the hand dryer market is about US$54 million. Dyson aims to steal market share from the makers of both products.

The end price for the Dyson Airblade is approximately £1,000 (exclusive of installation and sales tax).

Courtesy of Dyson.

Dyson Airblade competition

The Dyson Airblade is similar to the Mitsubishi Jet Towel, which uses a similar design and technology. The Jet Towel has been used in Japanese bathrooms since 1997. Another UK company, Excel Dryer Ltd, have also released a similar machine; XLerator, advertised as being 98 per cent cheaper than paper towels, and more environmentally friendly. These machines are now commonly used in British supermarkets such as Tesco and Asda, replacing older, less efficient dryers such as those made by World Dryer Corporation.

An American company, American Dryer, has also developed a high-speed hand dryer with a 10-second drying time. The eXtremeAir is also economical at a cost of US$390 US. It works by blasting a user's hands with a stream of heated air at 185 mph. This breaks up the surface tension of the water for quick removal and evaporation. It uses about 80 per cent less energy than conventional hand dryers which require 2,300 watts of electrical power for 30–40 seconds.

Interestingly, a Taiwanese company, Hokwang Industries, makes high-speed hand dryer that is not only fast but also more entertaining and multifunctional. They have integrated high brightness LED lights to hand dryers to increase the ease and delight of use. The sensor of hand dryer can project a blue light which allows user to see the sensing range.

In New Zealand innovative company Eco Global markets the ecodrier which cleans the hands in under 10 seconds with four separate filter systems.

World Dryer have also released a two high-speed hand dryers. These are 'Airforce' and 'Airmax'. The 'Airmax' claims to be the quietest hand dryer in its class and to dry your hands in just 15 seconds; the 'Airforce' claims to use 80 per cent less power than a conventional hand dryer and dry your hands quickly.

Sources: www.dyson.com; www.electrolux.com; www.mielevacuums.com; www.seb.com; www.hoover.com.
Horovitz, B. (2007) 'Vacuum leader Dyson sets sights on hand dryer market' *USA Today*, 18 June 2007, http://www.usatoday.com/money/industries/manufacturing/2007-06-17-dyson-usat_N.htm; http://news.bbc.co.uk, Marsh, P. (2006), 'A 10-year struggle to clean up in the appliance market', *Financial Times*, 27 June, p. 26.

QUESTIONS

1. Until now Dyson has concentrated its efforts in the United Kingdom, the United States, Japan and Australia. In your opinion, which new international markets should be allocated more marketing resources, in order to develop them into future Dyson growth markets?

2. In the US market Dyson achieved its market share by moving into the mass retail channels, like Electric City and Best Buy. Some industry specialists are critical of this the long-term strategy for Dyson's high-priced product. Evaluate the Dyson distribution strategy in the US market.

3. Do you think that James Dyson can repeat the international vacuum cleaner success with the hand-dryer market with its Dyson Airblade? Why? Why not?

CASE STUDY IV.4

Triumph Motorcycles Ltd: rising from the ashes in the international motorcycle business

When Marlon Brando led a group of outlaw bikers in the 1950s film *The Wild One*, he rode a Triumph. It was the obvious choice back then. Britain was the biggest motorbike maker in the world and led the motorcycling world in performance and engineering innovation with such bygone makers as BSA, Matchless and Vincent, to name just a few. And Triumph was winning every race in sight. But after bad management and botched rescue attempts by successive governments Triumph went bankrupt in 1983. However, the marque is back, starring in films such as *Mission Impossible 2*. When Tom Cruise roared on to the screen on a sleek motorcycle it wasn't a Harley or a Honda but a Triumph, which is also featured in Arnold Schwarzenegger's *Terminator 3*. The Triumph bike has captured approximatcly 75 per cent of the 'Hollywood' market, one of few US markets where Triumph is the market leader.

Product segments in the motorcycle market

Motorcycles were often classified by engine capacity in three categories:

1. lightweight (50–250cc)
2. middleweight (251–650cc)
3. heavyweight (651cc and up).

Triumph's motorcycles are in the middleweight and heavyweight category only, competing mainly with companies such as Harley-Davidson, Ducati, BMW and of course the main Japanese motorcycle manufacturers.

Motorcycles were also classified by types of use, generally separated into four groups: standard, which emphasized simplicity and cost; performance, which focused on racing and speed; touring, which emphasized comfort and amenities for long-distance travel; and custom, which featured styling and individual owner customization. The standard models tended to have the smaller engines, while the performance motorcycles often had an engine capacity of more than 251cc. The touring models typically had a comfortable seating position and their engines ranged from middleweight to super heavyweight types.

Triumph Motorcycles Ltd.

History

The credit for Triumph's rebirth goes to John Bloor, a builder who bought the company's remains (the Triumph brand name and the company's designs and tooling) for about US$200,000. He has invested £80 million on, among other things, a new plant in Leicestershire. The product has been completely revamped. New engines were crucial. Most have a distinctive three-cylinder layout, which makes them more powerful than the two-cylinder bikes made in Europe and the United States, and more relaxing than the high-revving four-cylinder bikes made in Japan.

Bloor was betting on the nostalgic power of the Triumph brand. Back in the 1950s and 1960s, Triumph and Harley-Davidson were fierce rivals. The original Triumphs offered lighter weight and better handling than Harley's machines, and sales of the British bikes were stronger in the United States than they were in their home market. The bikes are also part of US folklore. Despite what flag-waving Harley guys in bars may mistakenly claim, Steve McQueen in *The Great Escape* and Marlon Brando in *The Wild One* rode Triumphs. James Dean had one too. Legend and myth and the power of branding do not come any better.

Bloor's first act as a prospective motorcycle manufacturer was to hire three employees of the original Triumph company who had been involved in developing new models. Bloor realized that the engine is everything in a motorcycle, and there is no way to make a bike with a dull motor feel red-hot to the customer. So while he outsourced other parts of the bike, he put his team of engineers and metalworkers to work designing new liquid-cooled, three- and four-cylinder engines that would save costs by sharing internal parts.

Bloor's decision to keep a three-cylinder engine from the original line-up turned out to be a great marketing move, and it has helped the company stand out from the crowd. Most other bikes use two- or four-cylinder engines. Triumph's soulful three-cylinder has won a place in the hearts of many bikers, who tend to be a discriminating bunch when it comes to how an engine feels and delivers power on the road. Three-cylinder engines are also perfect for middle-aged men who are getting back into bikes.

Today

Big-bike sales have doubled in Britain over the past five years, and the buyers are no longer youngsters needing cheap wheels but older people with the money to spend on expensive toys. Many of these born-again bikers have not touched a motorbike since their teens, and find Japanese offerings just a bit too fast and flash for their taste.

Triumph's sales have risen from 2,000 in 1991 to approximately 50,000 in 2008 – similar to the old Triumph's peak of 50,000 in the late 1960s. Most buyers now are aged between 35 and 55. US sales (which make up 27 per cent of the total) have increased since in 2001 Triumph introduced a retro-styled bike, called the Bonneville, and are now rising at an annual rate of 40 per cent. The Bonneville (a twin-cylinder, 800cc machine, priced at US$7,000–8,000) is about 85 per cent faithful to the 650cc Bonneville of yore, which was the machine to ride in the 1960s if you were not a Harley man. Further introduction of a Harley-style cruiser bike is being considered by the Triumph management team. Taking marketing cues from Harley-Davidson, Triumph also offers a line of clothing and accessories.

Growth should be consistent. Sales are rising by 15 per cent a year, putting Triumph within sight of European rivals such as BMW and Ducati. Triumph's marketing manager believes there is plenty of scope for growth in the United States, where 550,000 big bikes are sold each year. Triumph currently accounts for around 2 per cent of that, compared with 12 per cent of the British market. To grab more, it needs to exploit not just its classic name but also its old race-winning reputation.

Total sales in 2008 were approximately £255 million, the number of employees was about 550 and net profit was approximately £15 million.

Triumph offers a clothing and accessories line designed according to bike and rider style and sells its bikes in more than 20 major national markets.

Of the motorcycles Triumph produces, 56 per cent are sold in Europe, 27 per cent in the US and Canada, 3 per cent in Japan and 14 per cent in the rest of the world. The company is actively reviewing niche markets for other specialized forms of motorcycles to add to its line-up, and is keeping to the trend of dealers who stock a full range of branded motorcycle, and only motorcycles.

The downturn of the Japanese manufacturers' market shares

In 1981 Japan's motorbike industry was in a state of blissful ignorance. Its manufacturers had managed to dominate the world in not much over a decade and annual production had hit 7.4 million units. Although they did not know it, this was to be their best year.

Two decades later and Japanese manufacturers are nowhere near as dominant. While they still loom large on the global motorbike market, 1981s record domestic production has declined to just 2.4 million. This serves as a stark reminder of a painful trend for all types of Japanese manufacturers as their domestic costs have risen, their markets have matured and their rivals have sharpened their game.

In 2001 two Japanese manufacturers – Suzuki and Kawasaki – joined forces to jointly produce and develop new bikes, marking the end of the 'big four' in Japan, where they ruled alongside much bigger rivals Honda and Yamaha.

The hollowing out shift to overseas production through joint ventures and wholly owned plants has also cut into domestic production in Japan.

The Suzuki–Kawasaki tie-up also serves as a symbol for what has happened to Japan's motorbike industry in the last two decades. Once-lazy and inefficient rivals such as Ducati, BMW and Harley-Davidson have found a way of replying to the competitive threat from Japan and are clawing back market share. In Europe, for example, Japan's market share has fallen from 80 per cent to 50 per cent over five years, although numbers have risen. In the vital US market its share has fallen by 10 per cent over the past decade.

The rise and rise of the Japanese motorbike manufacturers owed as much to luck as to design.

Manufacturers were servicing a huge domestic market for many years, which generated the profits that financed the export drive. It also gave the Japanese a finely honed design and production machine that churned out faster, more reliable and better-looking bikes – and did so every year. The weak yen also made Japanese exports intensely competitive.

In addition, they were up against severely weakened domestic manufacturers in the West. Triumph, BSA and Norton in the United Kingdom, for example, were spent forces, and the country was in the middle of labour disputes that generated a lazy attitude towards design and technology, producing machines that looked old-fashioned in comparison to their Japanese rivals.

The Japanese manufacturers, perhaps complacent in their success, failed to spot a key change in the motorbike-buying world. They were too obsessed with technology and assembly quality and did not recognize that motorbikes had become consumer goods which had a brand value. Harley-Davidson led the way here with branded goods ranging from desk clocks to women's thongs, feeding hugely into profits.

Japanese manufacturers based their bikes on racing models. Undoubtedly Japanese bikes are lighter and faster, but it takes a lot of skill to ride them. Western manufacturers have been designing for people who like to ride normal bikes in a normal environment. As Japan's rivals have caught up with the technology they have also managed to inject something extra.

Ducati conveys on two wheels the kind of image its Italian counterpart, Ferrari, has on four. Triumph has capitalized on its Britishness and the appeal of the marque's previous incarnation with such models as the Bonneville. Harley-Davidson has built up an appeal for weekend rebels with US$70,000-plus salaries. BMW has combined engineering excellence with design flair.

However, to talk of the demise of the Japanese motorbike industry would be unwise. Honda remains the largest manufacturer of motorbikes in the world, but the Japanese are removing themselves from the big bike category. Honda, Yamaha and Suzuki are concentrating on 100–500cc bikes for mass production in the developing countries of Asia. The bulk of Japanese-made bikes are small and service the growing economies of Asia, where having a 50cc or 100cc bike is the first step on a transportation ladder that eventually leads to a Toyota Corolla. India and China are huge and growing markets for the Japanese and Suzuki says it hopes its new link with its smaller rival will help its efforts in China.

The alliance between Suzuki and Kawasaki has more to do with these markets than the competition in the superbike league. It allows them to pare costs considerably by jointly procuring parts and joining forces on product design, development and production. It also matches similar moves by Honda, which has reduced the number of its Japanese motorcycle production lines from five to two in recent years. While Japanese manufacturers may be facing competition at the top end of the market, motorbikes are a high-volume game – and in this game the Japanese are still the winners.

The global competitive situation today

The competitive market situation in the three main regions of the world is shown in Table 1.

Market trends

In industrialized wealthy economies such as Japan, the United States and Europe motorcycles are often purchased for recreation in addition to basic transport. In developing economies and others with low income per capita, motorcycles or smaller two-wheelers were purchased primarily for basic transport, and the market was distinctly different. Historically large touring bikes, cruisers and racers sold almost exclusively in the wealthy economies while motorcycles with small engine displacement and mopeds made up the vast majority of sales in the developing nations. Decreasing trends in the overall market in some nations were due in large part to replacement of two-wheeled vehicles by automobiles as the countries became more affluent.

Table 1	The three main market areas for heavyweight motorcycles (651cc) number of registrations 2008		
	North America	Europe	Asia/Pacific
Total industry (1,000s)	480	397	80
Market share	%	%	%
Harley-Davidson/Buell	48.0	9.6	25.0
Honda	14.3	12.3	17.8
Yamaha	9.2	13.6	12.0
Kawasaki	7.5	11.3	13.8
Suzuki	12.7	16.5	10.7
BMW	2.0	15.1	4.4
Ducati	–	5.9	3.2
Triumph	2.0	6.5	1.0
Others	4.3	9.2	12.1
Total	**100.0**	**100.0**	**100.0**

Source: adapted from Harley-Davidson Financial Report 2008, and other public sources.

The challenge

A big problem for Triumph is still the relative low unit volume of motorcycles. Triumph sells about 15 per cent of the Harley-Davidson sales volume. Being so small makes it hard to develop new bikes or to buy good components at a decent price. To maintain quality Triumph makes about a third of its components in-house, and imports many from China and Japan. That clobbers profits. In 2003 Triumph also lost money. Bloor's building business, which is quite profitable, could cover those losses, but that is not a long-term solution.

As a consequence the strategy was set for increasing sale and market share in the area of large motorcycles. In 2003 Bloor hired a McKinsey consultant, first as an advisor and, later, as a commercial director (Tue Mantoni). Among other projects, Tue has worked with the introduction of the world's biggest motorcycle: Rocket III, which has a 2,294cc motor. Now Tue has contacted you as an expert in the marketing field and you should answer the questions at the end of the case study. As Bloor thinks that Triumph's market share in North America is not satisfactory, and he considers the potential for Triumph in the United States is huge, he has collected the following information about US motorcycle consumers.

The motorcycle market in the United States

The Hollywood myth of the young and wild motorcycle rider became less and less a reality in the 1990s and beginning of 2000s, according to Motorcycle Industry Council statistics regarding heavyweight motorcycle owners (see also Table 2).

The 1990s rider was more mainstream and less likely to be a part of some counterculture motorcycle gang. 'The end of the road for today's motorcyclist is just as likely to be a boardroom as a burger joint,' said Beverly St Clair Baird, Managing Director of Discover Today's Motorcycling, a public awareness campaign of the Motorcycle Industry Council. The average motorcyclist is male, 32.5 years old, married, had attended college and earns US$50,000 – about 12 per cent more than the average US household.

The average income of the motorcyclist of the 2000s has more than doubled since 1980. In 1980 fewer than 10 per cent of riders made over US$50,000 per year: in 2005 more than 90 per cent of riders had attained that income level. Riders from the 1990s onwards were also much older. They used their bikes more for leisure and recreation than had the riders of the early 1980s. The typical rider was interested in the outdoors. In surveys about their other interests fishing and hunting

Table 2	Motorcycle owner profile in United States		
	% of total owners		
	1995	**2000**	**2005**
Age			
<17	24.6	14.9	8.3
18–24	24.3	20.7	15.5
25–29	14.2	18.7	17.1
30–34	10.2	13.8	16.4
35–39	8.8	8.7	14.3
40–49	9.4	13.2	16.3
>50	5.7	8.1	10.1
Not stated	2.8	1.9	2.0
Median age	24.0	27.1	32.0
Mean age	26.9	28.5	33.1
Marital status			
Single	51.7	47.6	41.4
Married	44.3	50.3	56.6
Not stated	4.0	2.1	2.3
Highest level of education			
Grade school	13.5	7.5	5.9
Some high school	18.9	15.3	9.5
High school graduate	34.6	36.5	39.4
Some college	17.6	21.6	25.2
College graduate	9.2	12.2	12.4
Post graduate	3.1	5.2	5.2
Not stated	3.1	1.7	2.4
Occupation of owner			
Laborer/semi-skilled	20.7	23.2	24.1
Professional/technical	18.8	19.0	20.3
Mechanic/craftsman	23.3	15.1	13.1
Manager/proprietor	8.6	8.9	9.3
Clerical/sales	9.3	7.8	6.8
Service worker	7.1	6.4	6.6
Farmer/farm labourer	4.6	5.1	2.1
Military	1.9	1.6	1.5
Other	0.0	4.6	13.1
Not stated	5.7	8.3	3.1
Household income for prior year			
<$24,999	9.1	6.9	3.4
$25,000–$49,999	13.0	9.3	4.4
$50,000–$69,999	13.9	11.6	7.8
$70,000–$89,999	12.9	12.4	15.8
$90,000–$109,999	5.5	18.3	26.4
$110,000–$149,999	5.9	14.4	19.6
>$150,000	2.4	6.1	9.9
Don't know	30.3	21.0	12.7
Median	$72,500	$78,600	$90,100

Source: based on Motorcycle Industry Council.

topped the list. Motorcycle use for commuting purposes was down 14 per cent since 1980 to only 56 per cent. The demographic profile showed that motorcyclists came from all walks of life and a variety of occupational, educational and economic backgrounds.

Motorcycle accidents and fatalities dropped by more than half between 1985 and 2005. In addition to state helmet laws, this was attributed in part to an increasing trend for rider education and training programmes. Enrolment in these programmes, sponsored by individual manufacturers and industry groups such as the Motorcycle Industry Council, rose dramatically in the 1990s and 2000s. Motorcyclists today are likely to be more skilled and responsible than the riders of the 1970s and 1980s.

Women and motorcycling

Women, though not more than 10 per cent of the US riding population, are a growing segment of the industry. The AMA (American Motorcycle Association) has had women members since 1907. In the 2005 nearly a million women in the United States rode their own motorcycles. The average female rider was almost 48 years old compared to her 32-year-old male counterpart. Of the women riders 74 per cent were married, and 44 per cent attended college. The largest segment of women riders had professional/technical careers. They belonged to a riders club and were passengers for a few years before they purchased their first bike. Most women used their motorcycles for either long-distance touring (36 per cent of riding time) or for local street use (31 per cent). Only 10 per cent of their riding time was spent commuting or running errands. More women's families positively supported their riding than the families of male riders (64 per cent vs 55 per cent); however, more men's friends than women's friends supported their riding.

Profile of the typical Harley-Davidson rider

As with the average, Harley-Davidson (H-D) has about 90 per cent male and 10 per cent female riders. However, the household average income is higher than for the average rider, about US$100,000. The manufacturer has researched the 2005 purchases of H-D motorcycles. It shows that 41 per cent previously owned a H-D; 31 per cent were competitor motorcycles and the rest (28 per cent) were new to motorcycling.

Fashion trends

Motorcycling was a major fashion trend in the 1990s. The sales of motorcycles increased 50 per cent from 1995 to 2005, and motorcycle accessories, fashions and parts followed this upward trend. Owners were making personal statements by customizing their bikes with accessories, and more than 60 per cent of all owners purchased accessories in 2005 (compared to only 30 per cent in 1985). Many non-motorcycle riders or owners invested in motorcycle fashions. Men spent more on average on motorcycle fashions than women (US$227 per year for men vs US$180 for women). Overseas motor-cyclists followed the trend as well. Motorcycle fashions and accessory sales rose in both Europe and Japan in the 1990s and 2000s.

The motorcycle market in general

Motorcycle registration requires compliance with state and federal Motor Vehicle Safety Standards. Over one-third of the nation's motorcycles were concentrated in just five states: California, Texas, New York, Florida and Ohio. Over 15 per cent of the motorcycles in the United States were in California alone. Overall, there were an average of 1.5 motorcycles per 100 people in the United States in 2000. Most motorcycles in the country were registered for on-highway use: over half of these had engine displacements over 749cc, and more than 80 per cent over 450cc.

Sources: Stuart F. Brown (2002) 'A sweet Triumph' *Fortune Small Business*, 12(3/4), pp. 48–51; Kampert, P. (2003) 'British motor-cycles "Triumphant" return – Triumph motorcycles are roaring back into the American market,' http://money.cnn.com/2003/08/04/pf/autos/triumph/index.htm; http://www.mic.org/.

QUESTIONS

1. Design a global marketing programme for Triumph, including a suggestion for the priority of the 4Ps: product, price, place and promotion.

2. How should the marketing programme for the US market differ from your suggested marketing programme in question 1?

3. A member of Triumph's management team has proposed designing a special motorcycle for women. Do you think this is a good idea?

PART I
The decision whether to internationalize
Chs 1–4

PART II
Deciding which markets to enter
Chs 5–8

PART III
Market entry strategies
Chs 9–13

PART IV
Designing the global marketing programme
Chs 14–17

PART V
Implementing and coordinating the global marketing programme
Chs 18–19

Part V Contents

Part V Case studies

PART V
Implementing and coordinating the global marketing programme

Introduction to Part V

While the first four parts of this book have considered the set-up necessary to carry out global marketing activities, Part V will discuss the implementation and coordination phase.

An essential criterion for success in selling and negotiating internationally is to be able to adapt to each business partner, company and situation. Chapter 18 therefore discusses how the international negotiator should cope with the different cultural background of its counterparts. A part of this chapter will also deal with how knowledge and learning can be transferred across borders within the company and between cooperation partners.

As companies evolve from purely domestic firms to multinationals their organizational structure, coordination and control systems must change to reflect new global marketing strategies. Chapter 19 is concerned with how organizational structures and marketing budgets (including other control systems) have to be adjusted as the firm itself and market conditions change.

CHAPTER 18
Cross-cultural sales negotiations

Contents

Case studies

Learning objectives

After studying this chapter you should be able to:

- Discuss why intercultural selling through negotiation is one of the greatest challenges in global marketing.
- Explain the major phases in a cross-cultural negotiation process.
- Discuss how BATNA can be used in international negotiation.
- Discuss how learning and knowledge transfer across borders can increase international competitiveness.
- Discuss the implications of Hofstede's research for the firm's cross-cultural negotiation.
- Explain some important aspects of intercultural preparation.
- Discuss opportunities and pitfalls with global multicultural project groups.
- Explain the complexity and dangers of transnational bribery.

18.1 Introduction

Culture is a dimension that intervenes at each stage of the negotiation. It plays a role in the way people conceive of the situation even before any discussion starts because it contributes to structuring the problem. It influences the strategic approach developed in terms of competition or cooperation.

To remain competitive and to flourish in the complex and fast-changing world of international business companies must look worldwide not only for potential markets but also for sources of high quality but less expensive materials and labour. Even small business managers who never leave their home countries will deal with markets and a workforce whose cultural background is increasingly diverse. Those managers with the skills to understand and adapt to different cultures are better positioned to succeed in these endeavours and to compete successfully in the world market.

Culture contributes to orchestrating behaviours, drawing a line between what is desirable and what is not acceptable. It conditions perception in providing meaning to what is observed, organizing and codifing communication. It influences the choice of norms for fairness that will seal the final agreement. By the importance and significance that it gives to the context, culture directly influences the negotiation process. Fundamentally, negotiation as a process which is intended to reach a goal is a process of strategic nature, taking place in a cultural context and conducted by people who are themselves cultural vectors. It would be unrealistic not to take this into account. Culture is the variable that distinguishes international negotiation from any other type. Before engaging in such a lengthy and complex negotiation process as establishing a joint venture, it is essential for an international negotiator, whether buyer or seller, to assimilate basic elements of the counterpart's culture. Such a task will enable a better understanding of what really goes on around the negotiation table and in the immediate environment, to avoid misunderstandings, to communicate more effectively, to be better equipped to solve deadlocks that may surface and to be able to diagnose the real problems.

Consequently, conducting business with people from other cultures will never be as easy as doing business at home.

In the early stages of internationalization SMEs may treat cross-cultural markets as purely short-term economic opportunities to be pursued in order to maximize short-term profit. However, learning more about the nature of culture and how it affects business practices can increase the chances of success, even in the early cross-cultural business negotiations. When people from two different cultures are conducting business making assumptions about another culture is often detrimental, and can result in miscommunication. The managers in SMEs should develop realistic assumptions based on a truthful appreciation of the culture and should refrain from any thoughts of cultural stereotyping. Exhibit 18.1 shows that cultural influences can be difficult to predict.

EXHIBIT 18.1 Giving gifts in China and Japan

A US businessman once presented a clock to the daughter of his Chinese counterpart on the occasion of her marriage, not knowing that clocks are inappropriate gifts in China because they are associated with death. His insult led to the termination of the business relationship. It is also bad to give one's Japanese counterpart gifts of greater value than those received.

Source: Hendon *et al.* (1999).

All successful international marketers have personal representation abroad: face-to-face negotiations with the customer are the heart of the sales job. Negotiations are necessary to reach an agreement on the total exchange transaction, comprising such issues as the product to be delivered, the price to be paid, the payment schedule and the service agreement.

International sales negotiations have many characteristics that distinguish them from negotiations in the domestic setting. First and foremost, the cultural background of the negotiating parties is different. Successful negotiations therefore require some understanding of each party's culture and may also require the adoption of a negotiating strategy that is consistent with the other party's cultural system. It is interesting to note that Japanese negotiators, among other things, routinely request background information on US companies and key negotiators. Japanese negotiators therefore often know in advance the likely negotiating strategies and tactics of the other side.

Two different negotiation cultures: rule-based and relationship cultures

Basically, we meet two distinctly different negotiation cultures:

1. *Rule-based negotiation cultures* are found primarily in the Western part of the world. Westerners tend to trust this system, while people elsewhere trust their friends and family. Westerners organize their business around discrete deals that are drawn up as contracts or agreements and enforced by a legal system. Rule-based cultures are universalist precisely because they are rule-based. While relationship-based cultures invest authority in human beings, rule-based cultures respect the rules for their own sake. Western rulers derive their authority from the rules they enforce and by which they are chosen, not from who they are. Rules can command this kind of respect only if they are seen as inherently logical and reasonable; but logic is universal, and rules worthy of observance are therefore viewed as universally valid.

2. *Relationship negotiation cultures* (e.g. Asian cultures), by contrast, are based primarily on loyalty and obligation to friends, family, or superiors rather than on a system of rules. There is a traditional preference for building relationships rather than making deals, and the relationship-based approach remains the more effective one today in many contexts. Bargaining across the table tends to be regarded as confrontation rather than negotiation, even when it is strictly regulated by protocol, as in Japan. Confrontational bargaining is prevalent in street markets precisely because the parties typically do not have a working relationship. This kind of bargaining is acceptable when long-term collaboration is not required. However, when undertaking the major projects on which civilization rests, it is best to develop harmony and trust among the parties rather than rely on Western-style negotiation.

Bribery tends to be more prevalent in relationship-based cultures because building a relationship requires time and effort. There is always a temptation to take a short cut. Rule-based systems, on the other hand, are particularly vulnerable to cheating. This stems from the fact that behaviour is regulated as much by respect for rules as respect for people (Hooker, 2009).

18.2 Cross-cultural negotiations

Faced with different customs, perceptions and language the most common human tendency is to stereotype the other party in a negative way. A crucial perception is knowing what to look for and thoroughly researching the characteristics of a culture before conducting negotiations. Understanding other cultures is often based on tolerance. Trust and respect are essential conditions for several cultures, e.g. the Japanese, Chinese, Mexican and most Latin American cultures. The Japanese may require several meetings before actual negotiation issues are discussed, while North Americans and north Europeans are inclined to do business as soon as possible. Culture affects a range of strategies, including the many ways they are implemented. The Israeli prefers direct forms of negotiation, and the Egyptian prefers an indirect form. The Egyptians interpret Israeli directness as aggressive, and are insulted, while the Israelis view Egyptian indirectness with impatience, and consider it insincere. This cultural difference endangers any negotiation between business people in the two countries.

Even the language of negotiation can be deceptive. Compromise for North Americans and western Europeans is equal to morality, good faith and fair play. To the Mexicans and other Latin Americans compromise means losing dignity and integrity; in Russia and the Middle East it is a sign of weakness. Furthermore, members of other cultures may regard the common Western ideal of a persuasive communicator as aggressive, superficial and insincere.

The cross-cultural negotiation process

Negotiation process
A process in which two or more entities come together to discuss common and conflicting interests in order to reach an agreement of mutual benefit.

A **negotiation process** can be defined as 'a process in which two or more entities come together to discuss common and conflicting interests in order to reach an agreement of mutual benefit' (Harris and Moran, 1987, p. 55). The negotiation process is significantly influenced by the cultures within which the negotiators (typically a buyer and a seller) have been socialized and educated. Cultural differences prevalent in the international sales negotiation process can have a tremendous impact upon the process itself as well as its outcome.

The cross-cultural negotiation process can be divided into two different parts: the non-task related interaction and task related interaction (see Figure 18.1) – each will be discussed in the following sections (Simintiras and Thomas, 1998; Simintiras and Reynolds, 2001).

Figure 18.1 shows that the cross-cultural negotiation process is very much influenced by the cultural 'distance' between seller and buyer. This perspective is further developed in Figure 18.2.

Non-task-related interaction

The non-task-related aspects of the sales negotiation process (status distinction, impression formation accuracy and interpersonal attractiveness) are considered first as it is these factors that are more relevant when establishing a relationship with the buyer; that is, *approaching* the buyer:

Status distinction

In cross-cultural negotiations it is critical that sellers and buyers understand status distinction. Status distinction is defined by interpersonal rank, age, gender, education, the position of an individual in the company and the relative position of one's company. Different cultures attach different degrees of importance to status in negotiations. High-context cultures are status-oriented and the meaning of communication is internalized in the person. The words used by negotiators in high-context cultures are not as important as the negotiator's status. The status distinctions of negotiators between high- and low-context are sources of potential problems. For example, a seller from a high-context culture negotiating with a buyer from a low-context culture is likely to attach importance to the status of the buyer. The seller expects the buyer to reciprocate this respect, but this will rarely take place.

Impression formation accuracy

This stage refers to initial contact between negotiators. The first two minutes that a salesperson spends with a prospect are the most important (the 'moment of truth'). Meeting someone

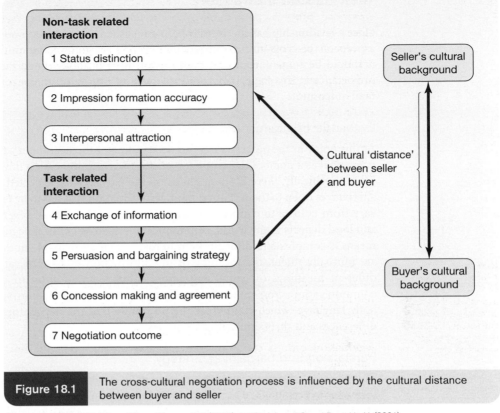

| **Figure 18.1** | The cross-cultural negotiation process is influenced by the cultural distance between buyer and seller |

Source: adapted from Simintiras, A.C. and Thomas, A.H. (1998) and Simintiras, A.C. and Reynolds, N. (2001).

for the first time, individuals have immediate feelings that precede rationalized thought processes; these feelings lead to the formation of instant opinions that are often based on minimal information. As the perceptions of the individuals from dissimilar cultures differ, the likelihood of a negotiator forming accurate impressions of the counterpart is reduced. A bad impression based on an inaccurate impression formation may also have negative effects on subsequent stages of negotiation.

Interpersonal attraction

This stage refers to the immediate face-to-face impression influenced by the feelings of attraction or liking between the buyer and seller. Interpersonal attraction can have either a positive or negative influence on the negotiation outcome. Similarity between negotiators can induce trust which leads, in turn, to interpersonal attraction. Individuals who are attracted are likely to make concessions in the bargaining process. Thus an individual negotiator may give up economic rewards for the rewards of the satisfaction derived from the relationship with an attractive partner.

Zhang and Dodgson (2007) have given an interesting character sketch of the founder of a Korean start-up IT-company, Mr. Lee:

> *We found Mr. Lee was influenced by his partners, and sometimes followed their advice – even though he knew they were not necessarily right, because he could not face losing business relations from his personal networks. (p. 345)*

Korean negotiation culture is based on Confucianism and its values permeate every aspect of society. Like other Asian countries, Korea is a society where group harmony within social networks, and company loyalty and commitment, are greatly appreciated collectivistic attributes.

Task-related interaction

Once a relationship has successfully been established between buyer and seller, the task-related aspects of the cross-cultural negotiation process are going to be more important. However, it should be remembered that even though the non-task-related factors are not of prime importance at this stage, they could still have an impact on the negotiation process and the final outcome.

Exchange of information

At this point in the process a clear understanding of the negotiator's needs and expectations is essential as a point of departure for an effective communication flow between the partners. More specifically, there is an emphasis on the participants' expected utilities of the various alternatives open to them. The amount of information that has to be exchanged explicitly will vary from culture to culture, and with the extra complexity of several thousand languages and local dialects in the world, communication in cross-cultural negotiations through verbal means is complex and difficult. Even in cases when participants understand each other and are mutually fluent, the meaning of the information exchanged can be lost as a result of different meanings of words and across cultures. In addition to difficulties with verbal communication, cross-cultural sales negotiations are subject to non-verbal problems, such as body language, which can reduce the possibility that the negotiators will understand their differences and their similarities accurately.

Persuasion and bargaining strategy

This phase of the negotiation process refers to a negotiator's attempts to modify the performance expectations of the other party through the use of various persuasive tactics. There are various styles of persuasion and each culture has its own style of persuasion. According to Anglemar and Stern (1978), there are two basic approaches to the negotiation process: *representational* and *instrumental strategies.*

When *representational strategies* are used communication is based on identification of problems, a search for solutions and the selection of the most appropriate course of action; for example, the salesperson may cooperate with the buyer and seek information on the buyer's views of the situation.

When *instrumental strategies* are used, communication involves affecting the other party's behaviour and attitudes; for example, a salesperson may influence the buyer with persuasive promises, commitments, rewards and punishments. The existence of a friendly and cooperative negotiation climate favours the use of the representational bargaining strategy.

Concession-making and agreement

This stage refers to the manoeuvring of negotiators from their initial position to a point of agreement on what is being negotiated. Negotiators from different cultures have different approaches to concession-making. For example, while in low-context cultures negotiators are likely to use logic, individuals in high-context cultures are more likely to use personalized arguments.

BATNA (best alternative to a negotiated agreement) is a term coined by Roger Fisher and William Ury in their 1981 bestseller, *Getting to Yes: Negotiating Without Giving In.* BATNAs are critical to negotiation because the negotiator cannot make a wise decision about whether to accept a negotiated agreement unless they know what the alternatives are. The BATNA is the only standard that can protect both from accepting terms that are too unfavourable and from rejecting terms that it would be in your best interest to accept. In the simplest terms, if the proposed agreement is better than the negotiator's BATNA, then the negotiator should accept it. If the agreement is not better than their BATNA, then they should reopen negotiations. If the negotiator cannot improve the agreement, they should at least consider withdrawing from the negotiations and pursuing their alternative, though the costs of doing that must be considered as well. Furthermore, the more the negotiator can learn about the BATNA of the counterpart, the better prepared they will be for negotiation. Then they will

BATNA
Best alternative to a negotiated agreement. The negotiator cannot make a wise decision about whether to accept a negotiated agreement unless they know what the alternatives are. If the proposed agreement is better than the negotiator's BATNA, then they should accept it. Having a good BATNA increases negotiation power.

be able to develop a more realistic view of what the outcomes may be and what offers are reasonable.

Having a good BATNA increases negotiating power. Therefore, it is important to improve the BATNA whenever possible. Good negotiators know when their opponent is desperate for an agreement. When that occurs, they will demand much more, knowing their opponent will have to give in. If the opponent apparently has many options outside of negotiation, however, they are likely to get many more concessions in an effort to keep them at the negotiating table. Making the BATNA as strong as possible before negotiating and making that BATNA known to the opponent will strengthen the negotiating position.

BATNA also affects the so-called 'ripeness', the time at which a dispute is ready or 'ripe' for settlement. When parties have similar ideas or 'congruent images' about what BATNAs exist, then the negotiation is ripe for reaching agreement. Having congruent BATNA images means that both parties have similar views of how a dispute will turn out if they do not agree, but rather pursue other options. In such a situation, it is often smarter for them to negotiate an agreement without continuing the disputing process, thus saving the transaction costs.

Put in other terms, a conflict becomes ripe for resolution when the parties realize that the status quo – no negotiation – is a negative sum (or 'lose–lose') situation, not a zero-sum ('win–lose') situation. To avoid the mutual loss, the negotiators must consider negotiation in an attempt to reach a positive sum (or 'win–win') outcome.

Ripeness is a matter of perception. Finding a ripe moment requires research and intelligence studies to identify the objective and subjective elements.

On the other hand, disputants may hold 'dissimilar images' about what BATNAs exist. For example, both sides may think they can win a dispute if they decide to pursue it in court or through force. If both sides' BATNAs tell them they can pursue the conflict and win, the likely result is a power contest. If one side's BATNA is indeed much better than the other's, the side with the better BATNA is likely to prevail. If the BATNAs are about equal, however, the parties may reach a stalemate. If the conflict is costly enough, eventually the parties may come to realize that their BATNAs were not as good as they thought they were. Then the dispute will again be 'ripe' for negotiation.

Negotiation outcome

Agreement is the last stage of the negotiation process. The agreement should be the starting point for the development of a deeper relationship between buyer and seller. The final agreement of a negotiation process may take the form of a gentleman's agreement, which is common in high-context cultures, or more formal contracts, which are more prevalent in low-context countries.

Implications of Hofstede's work

From Hofstede's work we see that there are differences (gaps) between national cultures. Each of four dimensions is reflected in the corporate culture patterns exhibited across countries (Hofstede, 1983). In the following, implications of Hofstede's four dimensions on the firm's international negotiation strategies will be discussed (Rowden, 2001; McGinnis, 2005).

Masculinity/femininity

Masculine cultures value assertiveness, independence, task orientation and self-achievement. Masculine culture's strategy for negotiation is usually competitive, resulting in a win–lose situation. Conflict is usually resolved by fighting rather than compromising, reflecting an ego-boosting approach. In this situation the person with the most competitive behaviour is likely to gain the most. On the other hand, feminine cultures value cooperation, nurturing, modesty, empathy and social relations, and prefer a collaborative or a compromising style or strategy to assure the best possible mutually accepting solution to obtain a win–win situation.

When negotiating, individuals from masculine countries are more likely to focus on the specifics of the agreement and not show much concern for its overall impact on the other party.

Negotiators from feminine cultures are more likely to be concerned with the agreement's aesthetics and longer-range effects; they feel that the details can be worked out later.

Uncertainty avoidance

This dimension refers to the comfort level of a person in an unclear or risky situation. High uncertainty avoidance cultures have formal bureaucratic negotiation rules, rely on rituals and standards and trust only family and friends. They require clearly defined structure and guidelines. Low uncertainty avoidance cultures prefer to work informally with flexibility. They disfavour hierarchy, and are likely to seek resolving solutions and compromises rather than the status quo.

Negotiators from high-risk avoidance cultures are likely to seek specific commitments in terms of volume, timing and requirements. Their counterparts from low-uncertainty avoidance cultures are likely to be comfortable with rough estimates of volume and timing and with constantly changing requirements. During the negotiating process, discussions around delays in new product availability, for example, might cause great concern to those high on uncertainty avoidance. On the other hand, it would be regarded by those who are low on uncertainty avoidance as an opportunity to improvise creatively.

Power distance

This dimension refers to the acceptance of authority differences between those who have power and those affected by power. High power distance is authoritarian, and protocol, formality and hierarchy are considered important. In high power distance cultures the CEO of the company is often directly involved in the negotiations and is the final decision-maker.

Business negotiations between equals (low power distance) are basically a Western concept and are not found in status-oriented societies such as Japan, Korea or Russia. Western Europeans and North Americans are normally informal and downplay status by using first names, dressing in casual attire, etc.

The Japanese dress conservatively – they always prefer dark business suits; to be dressed casually during negotiations with the Japanese would, therefore, be inappropriate. The Japanese do not believe in using first names unless in the very best of personal relationships. In Asia honours, titles and status are extremely important: address your counterparts by their proper titles. Frankness and directness are important in the Western world, but are not desirable in Asia.

The valued European handshake is often out of place in Japan, where bowing is customary. When meeting a devout Muslim, never shake with the left hand or utilize the left hand for any purpose – it is considered rude and a personal affront.

When a person from a high masculine culture negotiates with a high power distance culture conflict will most likely result if neither party makes an effort to understand the cultural balance. Competence is valued over seniority, which yields a consultative management style. Dealings between cultures with low masculinity and low power distance usually result in more cooperative and creative behaviour.

Negotiators from low power distance cultures may be frustrated by the need of negotiators from high power distance cultures to seek approvals from their supervisors. On the other hand, negotiators from high power distance cultures may feel pressured by the pace imposed by those from low power distance cultures. The key here is to understand the power distance mindset of the people that you are negotiating with. That understanding is the first step toward closing the deal and setting realistic expectations for the relationship that follows.

Individualism/collectivism

Individualistic cultures tend to put tasks before relationships and value independence highly. These cultures tolerate open conflict and place the needs of the individual over the needs of a group, community or society. In negotiations the individualistic society expects the other party to have the authority to make decisions unilaterally. In a highly individualist country such as the United States it is considered socially acceptable to pursue one's own ends without understanding the benefits for others. In contrast managers from a collectivistic culture, such as China, will seek a stable relationship with a long-term orientation, stressing above all the establishment of a personal relationship. A collectivistic society values solidarity, loyalty and strong interdependence among individuals, and the members define themselves in terms of their membership within groups. Collectivist managers assume that details in the negotiation process can be worked out and show more concern for the needs of the other party by focusing on group goals. Members of collectivist societies are irritated when members from individualistic societies promote their own positions and ideas during negotiations.

On the other hand, negotiators from individualistic societies are more likely to focus on the short term, make extreme offers and view negotiations from a competitive perspective. A critical factor in such negotiations is for each party to understand the other's main interests rather than focusing solely on its own.

Different organizational models

The British model of organization seems to be that of a village market with no decisive hierarchy, flexible rules and a resolution of problems by negotiating. The German model is more like a well-oiled machine. The exercise of personal command is largely unnecessary because the rules settle everything. The French model is more of a pyramidal hierarchy held together by a united command issuing strong rules. If we look at international buyer–seller relations, the national culture is only one level in the cultural hierarchy that will influence the behaviour of the individual buyer or seller. When members of different cultures come together to communicate, whether within the sales organization or in buyer–seller encounters, they typically do not bring the same shared values, thought patterns and actions to the situation. Common ground is typically limited. This increases the degree of uncertainty about the outcome of the interaction and can limit the efficiency and effectiveness of communication. To reduce uncertainty communicators must predict accurately how others will behave and be able to explain the behaviours of others (Bush and Ingram, 2001).

The gap model in international negotiation

In negotiation situations the most fundamental gap influencing the interaction between buyer and seller is the difference between their respective cultural backgrounds (gap 1 in Figure 18.2). This cultural distance can be expressed in terms of differences in communication and negotiation behaviour, the concepts of time, space or work patterns and the nature of social rituals and norms (Madsen, 1994). The cultural distance between two partners tends to increase the transaction costs, which may be quite high in cross-cultural negotiations.

Cultural influence on persons, and therefore international negotiations, can be analysed at various levels of society. Furthermore there is a learning 'effect' in the way that a person's cultural identity formed in one specific cultural setting will affect how they view other situations in other cultural settings. Both seller and buyer are influenced by (at least) the national and organizational culture they belong to. As seen in Chapter 7 (Figure 7.2) there are probably more levels in the understanding of individual negotiation behaviour.

The level of adaptation that is necessary is dependent on how culturally similar the seller and buyer are in the first place. However, the cultural differences between buyer and seller are likely to be less than the cultural differences between their two nations, as, to a certain extent, they will share a 'business' culture.

The influence of national culture

The national culture is the macro/societal culture that represents a distinct way of life of a group of citizens in a certain country. This national culture is composed of the norms and

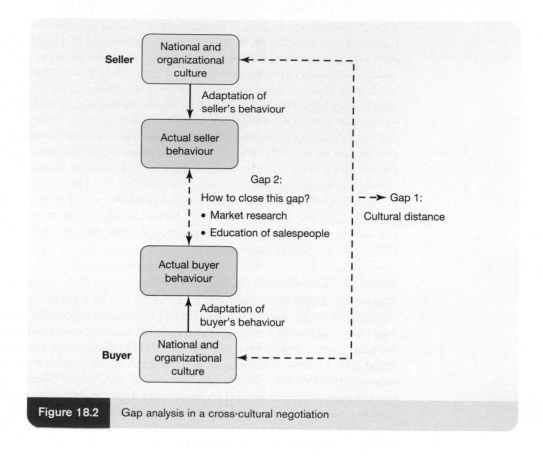

Figure 18.2   Gap analysis in a cross-cultural negotiation

values that members hold as well as their level of, for example, economic development, education system, national laws and other parts of the regulatory environment (Harvey and Griffith, 2002). All these factors play an important role in socializing individuals in a specific pattern of belief (Andersen, 2003). Therefore it is typical that when individuals encounter cultural differences in their international interactions/relationships, they tend to view people from different national cultures as strangers, that is unknown people who belong to different groups. This feeling of distance can directly impact upon trust and personal bonding, which increases the probability of conflict between seller and buyer in the negotiation process. The discussion earlier of the four dimensions of Hofstede's research gives several examples of differences in national culture and how they may affect intercultural negotiations between two partners.

The influence of organizational culture

Organizational culture is the pattern of shared behaviour, values and beliefs that provides a foundation for understanding the organizational functioning processes (Schein, 1985). When two or more organizations are negotiating with each other the relative level of consistency of core elements between organizational cultures can directly influence the effectiveness of communication and negotiation.

The overall complexity of a firm's communication environment will vary tremendously when elements of national culture and organizational culture are examined. In instances where a high level of national culture distance exists between buyer and seller and the organizational cultures are inconsistent (i.e. high interorganizational distance), the negotiation environment will be highly complex, necessitating careful planning and monitoring of the firm's intercultural negotiation strategies. Alternatively, when the national cultural distance is low and the cultures of buyer's and seller's organizations are consistent, both partners will find it easier to employ effective negotiation strategies without too much adaptation (Griffith, 2002).

In the case of a national and organizational cultural 'distance' between buyer and seller, both the buyer and especially the seller will try to adapt their own behaviour in such a way that they think is acceptable to the other party. In this way the initial gap 1 may be reduced to gap 2, through adaptation of behaviour. The extent to which the seller can adjust his behaviour to another culture's communication style is a function of their skills and experience. The necessary skills include the ability to handle stress, initiate conversation and establish a meaningful relationship.

However, neither the seller nor the buyer obtains full understanding of the other party's culture, so the final result will often still be a difference between the cultural behaviour of the seller and the buyer (gap 2). This gap can create friction in the negotiation and exchange process and hence give rise to transaction costs.

Gap 2 can be reduced through market research and the education of salespeople (see the next section). However, salespeople bring different 'baggage' with them in the form of attitudes and skills that result in different stages of intercultural awareness. The different stages of inter-cultural prepareness are highlighted in the next section. For example, if a trainer chooses to give a basic cultural awareness exercise to salespeople who are already at the acceptance stage and willing to learn about behaviour strategies, they are likely to be bored and not see the value of some types of diversity training.

Furthermore, face-to-face communication skills remain an important topic in international sales training. This is especially true in consultative selling, where questioning and listening skills are essential in the global marketing context. However, learning about cultural diversity through training programmes should help salespeople and marketing executives be better prepared to predict the behaviours they encounter with diverse customers or co-workers. Yet many salespeople are sceptical of training and question its value. In fact employees may view diversity training as simply a current fad or the 'politically correct thing to do'. However, if not prepared many salespeople may not realize the impact of cultural diversity until they encounter an unfamiliar cultural situation.

EXHIBIT 18.2 Euro Disney becomes Disneyland Resort Paris – Disney learns to adapt to European cultures

The Walt Disney Company began scouting locations for a European theme park in the mid-1980s, with France and Spain emerging as the strongest possibilities. The city of Marne-la-Vallée (about 20 miles east of Paris) eventually won the battle for the new mouse house, and in 1987 Disney created subsidiary Euro Disney. It broke ground on the $4.4 billion project the next year, and in 1989 Euro Disney went public (Walt Disney retained a 49 per cent stake).

In preparing the opening of Euro Disney in 1992, the company's first chairman proudly announced that his company would 'help change Europe's chemistry'.

However, some cross-cultural blunders occurred:

- Prior to opening the park, Disney insisted employees comply with a detailed written code regarding clothing, jewellery and other aspects of personal appearance. Women were expected to wear 'appropriate undergarments' and keep their fingernails short. Disney defended its move, noting that similar codes were used in its other parks. The goal was to ensure that guests received the kind of experience associated with the Disney name. Despite these statements the French considered the code to be an insult to French culture, individualism and privacy.

- The extension of Disney's standard 'no alcohol' policy from the United States meant that wine was not available at Euro Disney. This, too, was deemed inappropriate in a country renowned for its production and consumption of wine.

It took a series of adaptations, such as renaming the park Disneyland Resort Paris and the addition of some special attractions, to make the park profitable as of 1996.

The Disneyland Resort Paris theme park is now, Europe's top tourist attraction. Attendance has surpassed the Eiffel Tower as Europe's number 1 tourist destination with more than 12 million visits per year.

In the fiscal year 2006 Disneyland Paris drew about 12.8 million visitors: 40 per cent were from France, with 15 per cent from Belgium, Luxembourg and the Netherlands, 20 per cent from the United Kingdom, 9 per cent from Spain and 5 per cent from Germany.

For the year 2006 Disneyland Resort Paris reported revenues of €1087,7 million with consolidated net losses of €89 million. Of the total revenues 53.2 per cent came from the theme parks, 37.9 per cent came from the hotels and Disney Village, and the remaining 8.9 per cent came from real estate and other things.

The Resort features some 50 rides and attractions, more than 60 restaurants, 54 shops and plenty of live entertainment. The company also runs seven hotels, two convention centres and the Disney Village entertainment complex that links the park to the on-site hotels. Its newest park, Walt Disney Studios Park, opened in 2002. Euro Disney pays royalty and management fees to Walt Disney.

© Pawel Libera/Corbis.

Euro Disney restructured its debt in early 2005 and is renewing its focus on sales and marketing efforts. It is also planning a wide variety of upgrades to its hotels and rides: it revamped Space Mountain roller coaster in late 2005 to reopen as Space Mountain; Mission 2 and the *Toy Story 2*-themed ride Buzz Light-year Laser Blast were inaugurated in 2006.

In 2007, Disneyland Resort Paris will mark its fifteenth anniversary with an exceptional celebration. Guests will enjoy *Le Chateau de la Belle au Bois Dormant*, which will be specially decorated for the event, and Disney stories will come to life in new ways with special character experiences and new attractions and shows. In 2008, the Twilight Zone Tower of Terror will open at the Walt Disney Studios Park. In 2007 two exciting attractions are debuting in the new land called Toon Studio at the Walt Disney Studios Park. They are:

- *Crush's Coaster* – guests step through the soundstage set of Sydney Harbour, from the hit Disney/Pixar film *Finding Nemo*, and into an adventure onboard a spinning turtle shell, surfing the East Australian Current.
- *Cars Quatre Roues Rallye* – guests take a spin through the desert landscape on a wild, figure-of-eight racecourse. It's a rigorous test drive for the guests and their rookie cars, but on hand with racing tips and encouragement are the stars of the hit Disney/Pixar film *Cars* – Lightning McQueen and Mater – cheering from the sidelines over the roar of the engines.

Over the years the company has learned to cater more to European tastes, e.g. by serving foods and beverages such as sausage and wine. Disney Studios' virtual tour guides also use European actors.

Sources: Tagliabue (2000) Della Cava (1999); www.eurodisney.com; Hoovers Company Records: Euro Disney S.C.A, December 2006.
Source: Copyright © Disney.

One of the main problems frequently encountered in providing salespeople with meaningful educational experience that includes cultural diversity (distance) is the inability to provide on-location experiential learning opportunities routinely. This is due to lack of time and resources. Although desirable, in many instances one cannot take the salesperson to the culture beforehand to analyse and learn from their reactions. A viable alternative to this dilemma is to expose trainees to a simulated culturally diverse experience. The advantages of this approach are that it is more efficient and requires the active involvement of individuals, resulting in experiential learning. Simulations based on role-plays and result-oriented learning have been very successful in teaching salespeople and managers (Bush and Ingram, 2001).

Negotiating strategies

Basic to negotiating is, of course, knowing your own strengths and weaknesses, but also knowing as much as possible about the other side, understanding the other's way of thinking and recognizing their perspective. Even starting from a position of weakness there are strategies that a salesperson can pursue to turn the negotiation to their advantage.

18.3   Intercultural preparation

Many salespeople may be aware that cultural diversity is an important issue in their work environment. However, as evidenced by many stories of cultural blunders (see the example in Exhibit 18.2) salespeople may not realize the impact of diversity on their ability to predict behaviour in a selling situation. Thus individuals may progress through a kind of self-revelation about their own perceived skills and how these skills impact on their interactions with co-workers or buyers of culturally diverse backgrounds. Participating in such an experimental exercise can help sales and marketing personnel begin to understand the impact of cultural diversity in different ways.

General intercultural preparation

The following five-step approach is proposed to help firms with preparing their salespeople for coping with cultural diversities when entering different international markets (Bush and Ingram, 2001):

1. Build awareness about how cultural differences impact upon them in the sales organization.
2. Motivate salespeople and managers to rethink their behaviour and attitude towards customers.
3. Allow salespeople to examine their own biases in a psychologically safe environment.
4. Examine how stereotypes are developed, and how they can create misunderstandings between buyers and sellers.
5. Identify diversity issues that need to be addressed in the international sales organization.

This simulation may be perceived as a valuable starting point for learning about communication styles and cultural differences. Most firms realize that cultural diversity training requires much more time than expected. One of the difficulties in educating individuals about communicating between cultures or subcultures is that individuals can not be handled in only a two-hour session. Respecting and successfully interacting with members of diverse cultures is a long-term process. By participating in a long-term exercise salespeople may begin to realize that the concept of diversity goes beyond 'the right thing to do' or satisfying affirmative action requirements. Valuing diversity can also impact the bottom line of an organization.

Specific evaluation of a partner's intercultural communication and negotiation competences

To address the issues involved with the fit and reduction of 'gaps' in negotiation processes a firm must be proactive and develop specific strategies to enhance communication effectiveness. Most organizations have not formalized their management of cross-cultural communication, but at least three steps are necessary in order to improve the selling firm's cross-cultural communication and negotiation competences:

1. *Assessing communication competences of salespersons:* given the importance of a salesperson's communication competences for relationship success, it is critical that selling firms assess these persons' competences. Once the technical level (e.g. technical and standard language competences) is assessed the firm could use the above-mentioned simulation and experiential methods to gauge behavioural competences.

2. *Assessing communication competences of negotiators in the buying firm:* if possible the same procedure as in (1) should be carried out for the buyers in the foreign culture. However, it might be difficult to get this information about the negotiators in the buying firm.

3. *Matching communication and negotiation competences of buying and selling firm:* only if there is a match (and not too large a gap) between the communication competences of the two firms can they realistically expect success in the international negotiation and in the possible future relationship. Of course it should be noted that the selling firm is only able to control its internal competences, and not those of the buying firm.

This issue of communication assessment can also be integrated into the firm's partner selection and retention criteria. As the selling firm begins to integrate these communication competences into its partner selection and retention criteria it is also important that it shows flexibility and willingness to improve the existing competences in relation to its partner (the buying firm).

18.4 Coping with expatriates

Expatriates
Employees sent out from the HQ to work for the company in the foreign markets, often in its subsidiaries.

The following discussion can be applied not only to expatriate salespeople but also to other jobs in the firm based in a foreign country (e.g. an administrative position in a foreign subsidiary). Expatriate salespeople negotiating in foreign cultures often experience a culture shock when confronted with a buyer. Culture shock is experienced more intensely by **expatriates** whose cultures are most different from the ones in which they are now working. What can the management of the international firm do to minimize the risk of culture shock? The following areas should be considered (Guy and Patton, 1996).

The decision to employ an expatriate salesperson

The first major decision to make is whether the use of home country expatriates is the best choice for entering and serving foreign markets. The firm should first examine its own past experience with culture shock and sales rep adjustment in other cultures. Inexperienced firms would probably be best advised to evaluate possible agents and distributors rather than using home country expatriates. Other options for firms with their own sales force are host country or third country nationals (see also section 17.3).

The firm should try to identify the elements in the expatriate sales job that suggest potential problems with culture shock. If the job is highly technical, is located in an area with other home country nationals and involves similar tastes and lifestyles as in the home country, then the expatriate sales force may be appropriate.

If, however, the job places the expatriate salesperson in an unfamiliar job with conflicting expectations, the firm should consider other options. The chances of greater culture shock and adjustment problems increase with greater cultural distance. The greater the high-context/low-context contrast, the greater is the chance of difficulty. When entering a different culture many familiar symbols and cues are missing. The removal of these everyday reassurances can lead to feelings of frustration, stress and anxiety.

Selection of expatriates

Being an expatriate salesperson is a critical task and the selection process should be given considerable thought, not be decided too quickly. The selection should not be based primarily on the technical competence of the salesperson. Substantial emphasis must also be placed on the following attributes:

- foreign-language skills
- general relational abilities
- emotional stability
- educational background
- past experience with the designated culture
- ability to deal with stress.

Previous research (Guy and Patton, 1996) suggests that the following characteristics of the expatriate are associated with a lower level of cultural shock:

- open-mindedness
- empathy
- cultural sensitivity
- resilience
- low ego identity.

An assessment of the potential expatriate alone is not sufficient if the person has a family that will be making the move as well. Family issues that must be considered include marital stability, the overall emotional stability of family members and family cohesiveness. In-depth interviews with at least the rep's spouse and preferably other family members as well can be very useful in determining the status of these variables.

Training

Selecting the most appropriate training programme for each expatriate requires methods for classifying people into various levels of intercultural skills. Each level needs a different training programme. The initial requirement is to train the expatriate, and any accompanying family member, to know the main sociocultural, economic, political, legal and technological factors in the assigned country.

The training activities may include:

- area/country description
- cultural assimilation training
- role playing
- handling critical incidents
- case studies
- stress reduction training
- field experience
- extensive language training.

Obviously many firms will not be able to provide all the training needed in-house or through a single source, but they may need to coordinate a variety of methods and external programmes for their expatriates to take place before and during the foreign assignment.

Support

It is very important to provide a solid support network from the head office so that the expatriate is not simply left alone to sink or swim. Support during expatriate assignment may include a number of elements:

- Adequate monetary compensation or other benefits.
- Constant communication from the home base regarding ongoing operations at head office and in the assigned country/area.
- Providing opportunities for periodic travel to the home country to maintain contacts and relationships within the firm. The home base could also send copies of forthcoming job postings in which the expatriate may be interested.

The expatriate should identify and contact individuals in the host country who can become a part of the expatriate's social network. It is also important that the expatriate's spouse and family are included in a social support network.

Repatriation

Companies employing expatriates should develop an integrated career plan, identifying likely subsequent job positions and career progression. If the expatriates, during their careers, are exposed to a series of international assignments, each assignment should be selected to develop their awareness of different cultures. For example, for a UK company the first non-UK assignment would be a culturally similar or proximate country, say Germany or the United States, the next assignment might be South Africa or Australia, the next Hong Kong, then Japan and so on. In this way cultural shock is minimized, because the process encourages the ability to manage situations in more and more distant cultures.

The return of the expatriate to the home country is sometimes difficult. Lack of job guarantees is one of the most critical challenges faced by expatriates. Some months prior to return an internal position search should be started with a home visit arranged for the expatriate to meet with appropriate managers. An internal sponsor in the head office should be appointed to maintain ongoing contact and to help the expatriate secure a desirable position upon return.

Sometimes expatriated families also experience a culture shock upon returning to the home country; therefore some support is needed during repatriation. This includes spouse job-finding assistance and time to readjust before going back to work.

18.5 Knowledge management and learning across borders

Managing global knowledge that crosses the lines between business units, subsidiaries and departments that are dispersed geographically across continents is highly complex and requires consideration of different issues and factors. The global strategy exploits the knowledge of the parent organization (headquarters) through worldwide diffusion and adaptation. It strives to achieve the slogan, 'think globally but act locally', through dynamic interdependence between the headquarters and the subsidiaries. Organizations following such a strategy coordinate efforts, ensuring local flexibility while exploiting the benefits of global integration and efficiencies, as well as ensuring worldwide diffusion of innovation (Desouza and Evaristo, 2003).

A key element in knowledge management is continuous learning from experience (Stewart, 2001). In practical terms the aim of knowledge management, as a learning-focused activity across borders, is to keep track of valuable capabilities used in one market that could be used elsewhere (in other geographic markets), so that firms can continually update their knowledge without 'reinventing the wheel'. See the example in Figure 18.3 for a systematic approach to global learning from transferring best practices in the firm's different international markets.

The steps in transferring the firm's best practices to other international markets are:

1. By benchmarking (comparing) the different procedures in the firm's international markets the firm should be able to pick up best practices – in Figure 18.3 the best practices are

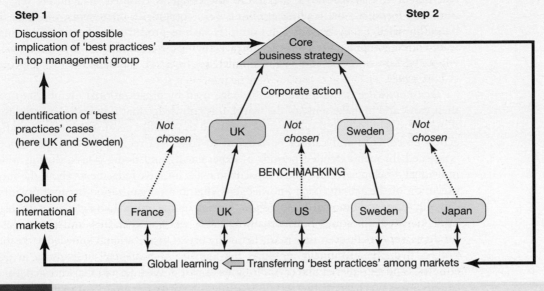

Step 1

Discussion of possible implication of 'best practices' in top management group

Identification of 'best practices' cases (here UK and Sweden)

Collection of international markets

Step 2

Core business strategy

Corporate action

Not chosen   UK   *Not chosen*   Sweden   *Not chosen*

BENCHMARKING

France   UK   US   Sweden   Japan

Global learning ⬅ Transferring 'best practices' among markets

Figure 18.3	Bottom-up learning in global marketing

found in the United Kingdom and Sweden. Subsequently, the possible implications of the best practices are discussed in the 'top management' group.

2. After the procedures for diffusion of the best practices have been established in the top management group the next step is to see if these best practices can be used elsewhere in the firm's international markets. In order to disseminate global knowledge and best practices, meetings (with representatives from all international markets) and global project groups should be established. If done successfully the benchmarking could result in a global learning process, where the different international marketing managers would select the most usable elements from the presented best practices and adapt these in the local markets.

However, as noted earlier in this chapter, knowledge developed and used in one cultural context is not easily transferred to another. The lack of personal relationships, the absence of trust and cultural distance all conspire to create resistance, frictions and misunderstandings in cross-cultural knowledge management (Bell *et al.*, 2002).

As globalization becoming a centrepiece in the business strategy of many firms – be it firms engaged in product development or providing services – the ability to manage the 'global knowledge engine' to achieve a competitive edge in today's knowledge-intensive economy is one of the keys to sustainable competitiveness. In the context of global marketing the management of knowledge is de facto a cross-cultural activity, whose key task is to foster and continually make more sophisticated collaborative cross-cultural learning (Berrell *et al.*, 2002). Of course the kind and/or the type of knowledge that is strategic for an organization and which needs to be managed for competitiveness varies depending on the business context and the value of different types of knowledge associated with it.

Explicit and tacit knowledge

New knowledge is created through the synergistic relationship and interplay between *tacit* and *explicit* knowledge.

Explicit knowledge is defined as knowledge that can be expressed formally using a system of symbols, and can therefore be easily communicated or diffused. It is either object- or rule-based. It is object-based when the knowledge is codified in symbols (e.g. words, numbers, formulas) or in physical objects (e.g. equipment, documents, models). Object-based knowledge may be found in examples such as product specifications, patents, software codes, computer databases, technical drawings, etc. Explicit knowledge is rule-based when the knowledge is codified into rules, routines, or standard operating procedures (Choo, 1998).

Tacit knowledge is the implicit knowledge used by organizational members to perform their work and to make sense of the world. It is knowledge that is uncodified and difficult to diffuse across borders and subsidiaries. It is hard to verbalize because it is expressed through action-based skills and cannot be reduced to rules and recipes. Instead tacit knowledge is learned through extended periods of experiencing and doing a task, during which the individual develops a feel for and a capacity to make intuitive judgements about the successful execution of the activity. Tacit knowledge is vital to an organization because organizations can only learn and innovate by somehow levering on the implicit knowledge of its members. Tacit knowledge becomes substantially valuable when it is turned into new capabilities, products, services or even new markets for the firm. Organizational knowledge creation is a process that organizationally amplifies the knowledge created by individuals in different countries and subsidiaries and crystallizes it as a part of the international knowledge network of the company. There are two sets of dynamics that drive the process of international knowledge amplification (Nonaka and Takeuchi, 1995):

1. converting tacit knowledge into explicit knowledge;
2. moving knowledge from the individual level to the group, organizational and interorganizational levels (across subsidiaries in different countries).

A central issue in internationalized firms concerns where knowledge is created and diffused: capabilities in creating knowledge centres of excellence may be formed in certain subsidiaries, for example, regarding specific functions such as product development or international marketing.

Global project groups

Today's business with its growing emphasis on globalization increasingly requires people to collaborate in workgroups that cross cultural and geographic boundaries. The trend to multicultural workgroups emerged as a reaction to changed economic conditions, forcing organizations to develop new structures in order to minimize costs and maximize flexibility. One consequence of these changes is that as a result of rapid knowledge growth and increasingly complex work environments more and more tasks can only be accomplished in international project groups by cooperation of functionally and culturally different experts. Based on the assumption of diversity creating value and therefore competitive advantage by bringing together different ideas and pooling knowledge, multicultural project groups have become a prevailing tendency in multinational organizations. However, the use of such groups in practice often turns out to be a lot more problematic than expected. It seems that the cognitive advantages which can be gained by a diverse workforce are counterbalanced by relational problems such as miscommunication and distrust, and therefore high turnover rates (Wolf, 2002). Nevertheless, with today's economy facing an ever-increasing need to cross all kinds of borders, the existence of culturally diverse project groups has become inevitable.

Given the communication problems and trust issues that plague ad hoc global project groups, structuring the project team is particularly critical to success. Three questions need to be addressed by the the firm's (top management Govindarajan and Gupta, 2001):

1. *Is the objective clearly defined?* One of the first concerns for any global project team must be to discuss the group's agenda explicitly and ensure that the objective/problem is defined clearly and correctly. Many project groups do not fully resolve and discuss the issues

involved and they immediately run into problems. Different framing of the same problem can produce different outcomes. Because the project group typically has members from different subsidiaries that usually compete with one another for scarce corporate resources they tend to have a high degree of internal conflict, combined with a low level of trust. As a result it is generally best to frame the problem of the project group in terms of the company's position vis-à-vis the external marketplace instead of emphasizing internal issues. An external focus encourages benchmarking, fosters creativity and provides a compelling rationale for making the tough decisions inherent in any manufacturing rationalization and workforce reduction. Given the possible communication problems in the global project group it is imperative that the members understand the agenda of the project group: the scope of the project, the expected deliverables and the timeline. Cultural and language differences may complicate the task of getting group members to agree on the agenda and the problems to be solved. Clarity is essential to promoting commitment and accountability.

2. *Choosing group members.* Another key to creating a successful global team is choosing the right group members. Two issues are of particular importance: how do you balance diversity within the team and what should be the size of the group? Normally we will see high levels of diversity. Why? First, members come from diverse cultural and national backgrounds – this refers to so-called *behavioural diversity*. Second, members generally represent subsidiaries whose agenda may not be congruent. Third, because members often represent different functional units and departments, their priorities and perspectives may differ. The last two issues refer to so-called *cognitive diversity*.

   Let us take a closer look at an example of behavioural diversity. Consider, for example, a cross-border project group in a Swedish–Chinese joint venture. The norm in most Chinese teams is that the most senior member presents the team's perspective, but in a Swedish team the most junior member typically does so. Unless the members of the team are sensitized to such differences misunderstandings can easily emerge and block communication. So behavioural diversity is best regarded as a necessary evil: something that no global project group can avoid but the effects of which the group must attempt to minimize through training in cultural sensitivity.

   Let us also take a closer look at an example of cognitive diversity. This diversity refers to differences in the substantive content of how members perceive the group's challenges and opportunities. Differences in functional backgrounds can account for substantive cognitive differences on issues of 'market pull' (preferred by people in marketing departments) and 'technology push' (preferred by people in engineering departments). Because no single member can ever have a monopoly on wisdom cognitive diversity is almost always a source of strength. Divergent perspectives foster creativity and a more comprehensive search for and assessment of options, but the group must be able to integrate the perspectives and come to a single solution.

3. *Selection of team leadership.* Structuring the leadership of a global project team involves critical decisions around three roles: the *project leader*, the *external coach* and *the internal sponsor*. The project leader plays a pivotal role in cross-border project groups. They must contribute to the development of trust between the members and maybe have the biggest stake in the outcome of the project. They must possess conflict-resolution and integration skills and expertise in process management, including diagnosing problems, assessing situations and generating and evaluating options. An external coach serves as an ad hoc member of the project group and is an expert in process more than content. The need for such a coach is likely to be high when the process-management skills of the best available project leader are inadequate. This might happen if the appointed leader has some major stake in the project's outcome, for example if a cross-border task force has to rationalize and decrease the number of subsidiaries around the world by 30 per cent. The internal sponsor of a global project group is typically a senior level executive with a strong interest in the success of the team. Among the responsibilities of the sponsor are to provide ongoing guidelines and to facilitate access to resources.

At any given time a global company will typically have many project groups working on different cross-border coordination issues. Therefore it makes sense for the company to undertake initiatives to create interpersonal familiarity and trust among key managers of different subsidiaries. For example, Unilever uses several approaches to do this – such as bringing together managers from different subsidiaries in executive development education programmes.

When a project group consists of members with distinct knowledge and skills drawn from different subsidiaries in different countries the potential for cognitive diversity is high, and this can also be a source of competitive strength. However, intellectual diversity will almost always bring with it some degree of interpersonal incompatibility and communication difficulty. Process mechanisms that recognize and anticipate such pitfalls – and integrate the best of individuals' ideas and contributions – are needed to help the project group reconcile diverse perspectives and arrive at better, more creative and novel solutions.

18.6 Transnational bribery in cross-cultural negotiations

Bribery
Involving a company from an industrialized country offering an illicit payment to a developing country's public official with perceived or real influence over contract awards. Bribery may range from gifts to large amounts of money.

On first consideration **bribery** is both unethical and illegal, but a closer look reveals that bribery is not really a straightforward issue. The ethical and legal problems associated with bribery can be quite complex. Thus the definition of bribery can range from the relatively innocuous payment of a few pounds to a minor official or business manager in order to expedite the processing of papers or the loading of a truck, to the extreme of paying millions of pounds to a head of state to guarantee a company preferential treatment. Scott *et al.* (2002) generally define bribery as 'involving a company from an industrialized country offering an illicit payment to a developing country's public official with perceived or real influence over contract awards' (p. 2).

The difference between lubrication and bribery must be established. Lubrication payments accompany requests for a person to do a job more rapidly or more efficiently. They involve a relatively small cash sum, gift or service made to a low-ranking official in a country where such offerings are not prohibited by law, the purpose being to facilitate or expedite the normal, lawful performance of a duty by that official. This practice is common in many countries. Bribery, on the other hand, generally involves large sums of money, which are frequently not properly accounted for, and is designed to entice an official to commit an illegal act on behalf of the one paying the bribe.

Another type of payment that can appear to be a bribe, but may not be, is an agent's fee. When a businessperson is uncertain of a country's rules and regulations an agent may be hired to represent the company in that country. This person will do a more efficient and thorough job than someone unfamiliar with country-specific procedures.

There are many intermediaries (attorneys, agents, distributors and so forth) who function simply as channels for illegal payments. The process is further complicated by legal codes that vary from country to country: what is illegal in one country is winked at in another and legal in a third. In some countries illegal payments can become a major business expense. Hong Kong companies report that bribes account for about 5 per cent of the cost of doing business in China. In Russia the cost is 15–20 per cent, and in Indonesia as high as 30 per cent (Gesteland, 1996, p. 93).

The answer to the question of bribery is not an unqualified one. It is easy to generalize about the ethics of political pay-offs and other types of payment; it is much more difficult to make the decision to withhold payment of money when not making the payment may affect the company's ability to do business profitably or at all. With the variety of ethical standards and levels of morality which exist in different cultures the dilemma of ethics and pragmatism that faces international business cannot be resolved until more countries decide to deal effectively with the issue.

EXHIBIT 18.3   Does bribery also cover sexual favours? The case of Lockheed Martin and a South Korean defence contract

A US court has ruled that arms maker Lockheed Martin can be sued for allegedly using sexual favours and bribes to win a South Korean defence contract. Lockheed Martin has denied the allegations.

The case was filed by the Korea Supply Company (KSC) after it lost a contract to Lockheed subsidiary Loral for the supply of an aircraft radar system to South Korea in 1996.

KSC's lawsuit claims a Loral employee, Linda Kim – a former model and singer – bribed South Korean military officers and offered sexual favours to the country's defence minister, Lee Yang Ho. He has admitted to having an 'inappropriate relationship' with Ms Kim but denies it influenced his decision-making. Ms Kim's love letters to the defence minister made headline news in South Korea after they were implicated in another bribery scandal.

The US Foreign Corrupt Practises Act forbids US companies from bribing foreign officials to influence an official act or decision.

Source: based on BBC News, 'Lockheed sex suit to go ahead', 3 May 2003, news.bbc.co.uk/go/pr/fr/-/2/hi/business/2,820,939.stm.

18.7   Summary

When marketing internationally negotiation skills are needed. Negotiation skills and personal selling skills are related. Personal selling typically occurs at the field sales force level and during formal negotiation processes. Cultural factors are critical to understanding the negotiation style of foreigners.

The negotiation process is significantly influenced by the cultures within which the negotiators (typically a buyer and a seller) have been socialized and educated. Cultural differences prevalent in the international sales negotiation process can have a tremendous impact upon the process itself as well as its outcome.

The cross-cultural negotiation process can be divided into two different parts: the *non-task-related interaction* and *task-related interaction*. The non-task-related aspects of the sales negotiation process (status distinction, impression formation accuracy and interpersonal attractiveness) are considered first as it is these factors that are more relevant when approaching the buyer. Once a contact has successfully been established, the task-related aspects of the sales negotiation process (exchange of information, persuasion and bargaining strategies and concession-making and agreement) begins.

Prior to the two partners negotiation process there is a cultural distance between them. This cultural distance causes some transaction costs, which may be quite high. To reduce the cultural distance training of the negotiators is required.

The culture shock felt by expatriates indicates that sending negotiators and salespeople to foreign markets is often difficult and complex to implement successfully. Five important areas of implementation include: (1) making the initial decision to employ an expatriate sales force, (2) identifying and selecting qualified candidates, (3) providing adequate training, (4) maintaining ongoing support and (5) achieving satisfactory repatriation.

In global knowledge management a key element is the continuous learning from experiences in different markets. In practical terms, the aim of knowledge management as a learning-focused activity across borders is to keep track of valuable capabilities used in one market that could be used elsewhere (in other geographic markets), so that firms can continually update their knowledge without reinventing the wheel.

The ethical question of what is right or appropriate poses many dilemmas for international marketers. Bribery is an issue that is defined very differently from country to country. What is acceptable in one country may be completely unacceptable in another.

CASE STUDY 18.1

Mecca Cola: marketing of a 'Muslim' cola to the European market

Until now the cola war has mainly been going on in North America and Europe. But in January 2003 a French Tunisian opened up a second front – by producing a carbonated drink named Mecca Cola, a new soft drink designed to cash in on anti-US sentiment, mainly in European markets. The new drink will be marketed in 1.5 litre bottles and 330ml cans.

Mecca Cola – a political choice

The new brand, which has a striking resemblance to Coca-Cola, is specifically intended to make a political statement. Its French label and advertising slogan translates as 'No more drinking stupid – drink with commitment'.

The creator of Mecca Cola, prominent French political activist Taoufiq Mathlouthi, claims the drink is not competition for Coke and that his campaign is not anti-American. Instead, he says, each bottle sold is a protest against the Bush administration's foreign policy. Mathlouthi promises that 10 per cent of profits will go to Palestinian causes, humanitarian aid for Palestinian children, education and preserving their heritage. Mathlouthi hopes to make Mecca Cola the soft drink of choice for anti-globalists everywhere and thus push out that icon of US capitalism, Coca-Cola.

Mr Masood Shadjareh, Chairman of the London-based Islamic Human Rights Commission, which is backing calls to shun US brands, predicted huge interest in the new cola. He told the *Guardian*:

The Muslim community is targeting Coca-Cola because people feel that the only thing they can do is hit America economically. It is not only an issue for someone like me who is an activist. I bought some fizzy drinks and my children, who are ten and twelve, found out they were products of Coca-Cola and refused to drink them. I told them I'd already paid for them, but my daughter said 'Look Daddy, it just won't go down'.

Meanwhile, some religious fundamentalists object to the use of the name of the Muslim holy city on a soft drink. There is no indication Mecca Cola or any other boycott product will do long-term harm to US multinationals, Coca-Cola and Pepsi Cola, but some US manufacturers admit the boycott is having an impact on sales. And no one denies how easy it is for consumers to express their politics by simply switching brands. Coca-Cola's comment was: 'Ultimately it is the consumer who will make the decision'. Coca-Cola insists that it is 'not affiliated with any religion or ethnic group' and does not engage in politics.

Zam Zam Cola

It is not the first time Coca-Cola has been the target of a 'buy Muslim' challenge. Zam Zam Cola, an Iranian drink named after a holy spring in Mecca, has won an enthusiastic reception in Saudi Arabia and Bahrain.

US companies such as McDonald's, Starbucks, Nike and the two cola giants admit the general 'buy Muslim' campaign is wounding them. Sales of Coca-Cola have dropped between 20 and 40 per cent in some countries. In Morocco, a government official estimates sales of Pepsi and Coca-Cola could fall by half in the north, which is a stronghold of Islamic groups.

Mecca Cola

In the United Arab Emirates, sales of the local Star Cola are up by 40 per cent over the past three months.

Zam Zam, which also produces non-alcoholic 'Islamic beer', has a long pedigree in Iran, where it was founded in 1954 and today has 47 per cent of the domestic market. For many years it was the Iranian partner of Pepsi Cola until their contract was ended after the 1979 revolution.

A Saudi firm owned by one of the kingdom's princes, Turki Abdallah al-Faisal signed an agreement with the Zam Zam Group in January 2003, giving the Saudi company exclusive distribution rights in Saudi Arabia, Egypt and a number of other Arab countries.

Zam Zam was taken over by the Foundation of the Dispossessed, a powerful state charity run by clerics, and today it employs more than 7,000 people in its 17 factories in Iran. It is now planning to build factories in the Persian Gulf.

Its cola is already exported to Saudi Arabia, Bahrain, Qatar, the United Arab Emirates, Oman, Kuwait, Afghanistan and Iraq, and the company says it will soon ship its drinks to Lebanon, Syria and Denmark – its first European client.

The marketing and internationalization of Mecca Cola

Other firms in the Middle East have tried creating different cola drinks, but none has turned its drink into a political weapon. The first businesses to sell Mecca Cola were what Mr Mathlouthi described as 'small ethnic shops in Muslim areas'. Now the drink, originally targeted at France's Muslim community, can be found on the shelves of large cash and carry supermarkets in France, Belgium and Germany. The company behind Mecca Cola says the United Kingdom is also a huge market and it already has orders to send about 2 million bottles a month to Britain.

While Coca-Cola's revenues in the Middle East represent less than 2 per cent of its global business, it is galling for Coke to lag behind Pepsi in the region. Britain's 1.8 million Muslims have only recently begun to discover a collective voice and it remains unclear whether a boycott or a 'buy Muslim' campaign will occur.

In Muslim areas of Paris the soft drink is sold for £1.20 per 1.5-litre bottle, approximately the same as its US rival Coke.

Developments 2003–2006

Riding on anti-Western anger over issues like Palestine, Iraq, Iran and Afghanistan and also the Danish Muhammed cartoons (January–February 2006), Mecca Cola achieved impressive sales in several Muslim countries. Pakistan, Algeria, Yemen, Malaysia and France are Mecca Cola's top markets. In 2006 the demand for Mecca Cola is estimated to be 1.5 million cans per month in the Gulf region alone.

In 2006 Mecca Cola (with its HQ in the United Arab Emirates) announced it would now launch coffee shops under the brand name Mecca Café to provide an alternative to established Western outlets in Muslim countries. The first coffee shop was ready to be opened at Dubai Healthcare City and would be followed by coffee shops in Kuala Lumpur in Malaysia and Pakistan's Islamabad.

Mecca Cola planned to have at least one coffee shop in every Muslim capital. After that it will discuss franchising arrangements with partners for expanding the chain.

The company had also launched a new energy drink called 'Mecca Power', based purely on halal ingredients (Husain, 2006).

Latest developments

The soft drink was introduced in 2003 with much hype targeting Arab and Muslim customers around the world, but around 2009 it silently disappeared from shelves in the UAE and Saudi Arabia.

While the brand had to be withdrawn from Saudi Arabia because the country did not allow the company to use the name 'Mecca' for its private business, the reason for its disappearance from the UAE market (where the HQ are located) remains unclear.

At the beginning of 2010 the future for Mecca Cola seems unclear.

Sources: www.mecca-cola.com; Husain, S. (2006) 'Mecca cola rides anti-west wave with café chain plan', *Gulf News*, 22 February.

QUESTIONS

1. What were the main reasons for the success of Mecca Cola around 2005?

2. What are the criteria for the successful implementation of Mecca Cola's international marketing strategies?

3. How should Taoufiq Mathlouthi prepare his sales force culturally for selling Mecca Cola to European supermarket chains?

4. Can Taoufiq Mathlouthi repeat the international Mecca Cola success with the new coffee shop chain and new energy drink Mecca Power?

CASE STUDY 18.2

TOTO: the Japanese toilet manufacturer seeks export opportunities for its high-tech brands in the United States

An average person visits the toilet 2,500 times per year, about 6–8 times per day. People spend at least three years of their lives using the toilet, and women take three times as long to use the toilet as men (www.worldtoilet.org).

Founded in 1917, Japanese toilet maker TOTO (www.toto.co.jp) is the largest toilet manufacturer in the world, producing more than 12 million toilets annually. TOTO's net sales in the financial year 2008 were $4.7 billion; with a loss of $267 million. Their total number of employees at the end of March 2009 was 24,000.

Over the years, TOTO has made a sales success in Japan. Japanese Government statistics show that the 'innovative toilet seat' that features an integrated bidet (represented by TOTO's Washlet-brand) are now installed in 69 per cent of Japanese homes compared to just 14 per cent in 1992. TOTO, which employs around 1,500 engineers, dominates this 'innovative toilet seat' market with a 50 per cent share. Its closest rival, Japan's Inax Corp., trails at 25 per cent. Numbers for Japan's overall toilet market in 'water closets' are like this: TOTO's market share is 60 per cent while Inax is about 30 per cent). However, outside Japan, TOTO's market share is only very small, with 13 per cent of TOTO's total net sales coming from overseas in 2008. The United States' market is the number one target (41 per cent of overseas sales), and China is the second (37 per cent of overseas sales).

TOTO.

US market for toilets

The United States is the largest and most competitive market in the world: in 2008 16 million toilets were sold in the US market. TOTO's sales to the US in 2008 were approximately $260 million. In 1989, TOTO began to make inroads into the US market with the establishment of TOKI KiKi USA, Inc., but in 2008 their overall market share of the US toilet market is still only very small – approximately 6 per cent.

Americans are said to move residences once every seven or eight years, creating a used-home market larger than that in Japan. As a consequence, remodelling is effectively the same level (or better) as that of new homes. Compared with Japan, the United States has stricter water conservation regulations for toilets and spurred by these regulations, industry specialists expect to see demand for replacement toilets in the future.

New housing starts are over 1.6 million annually, thanks in part to low interest rates in the US new housing market. Even when you consider the 1.1 million new housing starts in Japan, the US housing market is substantially larger in scale, and therefore has more potential. TOTO is targeting high value-added markets in the US through the kitchen/bath shop and waterworks channels, and bypassing the home improvement centre channel. Through the kitchen/bath shop and waterworks channels TOTO provides customers with services, including consulting and installation for its products. In this way TOTO is hoping to capture market shares in the high-end of the US toilet market.

TOTO penetrates the US market but is facing cultural barriers

TOTO made toilet history in 1980 when, improving on a US model that combined the bidet and the toilet seat, it produced the 'Washlet', bringing warm water to the user's nether regions. TOTO did what the

American toilet makers were reluctant to try – they brought electronics into the water closet. Top-of-the-line Washlets now came with wall-mounted control panels as complex as those of stereo systems. Their manifold buttons allow adjustment of the nozzle position, water pressure and type of spray, plus blow-drying, air purification and seat warming for those cold winter mornings. Water and seat temperatures are adjustable. The controls can also be set so the lid rises as the user approaches the Washlet. Globally, more than 20 million Washlets have been sold (mainly in Japan) since their introduction in 1980. The United States, however, is a country without a history with the bidet. Bidets – usually stand-alone fixtures used in conjunction with toilets – originated in France and have been in use throughout the southern part of Europe since the 1700s. Ironically, almost three decades ago TOTO began importing hospital-grade bidets from the United States to sell to Japan's ageing population. It soon discovered there was a larger market for the fixtures and adapted the traditional bidet into a toilet seat attachment, which fits onto existing toilet bowls.

While US consumers are just waking up to Washlets, the Japanese are going even more upmarket. TOTO's new Neorest model, Washlet integrated toilet (introduced in 2003) gets rid of the inner rim of the bowl and brings in 'the tornado flush'. The Neorest (priced at $5,200) has all the features of TOTO's Washlet, including a heated seat for cold nights, built-in back-and-front bidet with oscillating or pulsating spray massage and a warm-air dryer, all with temperature controls on a wall-mounted remote. Add to these features the smart toilet's built-in air purifier and motion sensors that detect your approach and automatically raise the lid. Males can lift the seat with the touch of a button and in doing so instruct the unit to flush with less water. Complete your business and the toilet automatically shuts the lid (while putting the seat down!) and flushes.

QUESTIONS

1. What cultural barriers would the Japanese managers from Toto meet when negotiating with American managers from building societies about new contracts for toilets in US luxury apartments?

2. Some analysts argue that tackling cultural toilet norms and barriers is not worth the effort and that Toto would be better off pulling its Washlets and Neorests out of the United States and Europe altogether and concentrating on more receptive Asian markets like China, and of course Japan. Do you agree? Why? Why not?

Sources: Toto annual and financial report 2009; Adapted from Helms. T. (2003, 'The toilet marketplace', *Supply House Times*, September 2003, pp. 72–78; www.ceramicindustry.com; www.toto.co.jp; www.worldtoilet.org.

VIDEO CASE STUDY 18.3 **Dunkin' Donuts**

download from www.pearsoned.co.uk/hollensen

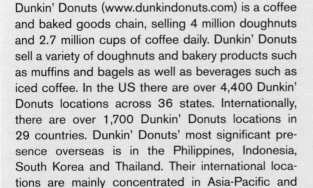

Dunkin' Donuts (www.dunkindonuts.com) is a coffee and baked goods chain, selling 4 million doughnuts and 2.7 million cups of coffee daily. Dunkin' Donuts sell a variety of doughnuts and bakery products such as muffins and bagels as well as beverages such as iced coffee. In the US there are over 4,400 Dunkin' Donuts locations across 36 states. Internationally, there are over 1,700 Dunkin' Donuts locations in 29 countries. Dunkin' Donuts' most significant presence overseas is in the Philippines, Indonesia, South Korea and Thailand. Their international locations are mainly concentrated in Asia-Pacific and Latin America.

Questions

1. Dunkin' Donuts wants to get a better market position in Europe, and set up a meeting in London with potential franchisees from different European countries in order to negotiate franchising deals that could provide a higher growth in this region. What potential dangers should the US negotiator be aware of in this kind of cross-national negotiation?

2. What is Dunkin' Donuts' value perception and positioning strategy?

3. How has Dunkin' Donuts responded to competitive changes in the global marketplace?

For further exercises and cases, see this book's website at **www.pearsoned.co.uk/hollensen**

Questions for discussion

1. Explain why the negotiation process abroad may differ from country to country.

2. You are a European preparing to negotiate with a Japanese firm for the first time. How would you prepare for the assignment if it is taking place: (a) in the Japanese headquarters; (b) in one of its European subsidiaries?

3. Should expatriate personnel be used? What are some of the difficulties they may encounter overseas? What can be done to minimize these problems?

4. Compare and contrast the negotiating styles of Europeans and Asians. What are the similarities? What are the differences?

5. What are your views on lobbying efforts by foreign firms?

6. Why is it so difficult for an international marketer to deal with bribery?

References

Andersen, P.H. (2003) 'Relationship marketing in cross-cultural contexts', in Rugimbana, R. and Nwankwo, S. (eds), *Cross-cultural Marketing*. London: Thomson, pp. 209–225.

Anglemar, R. and Stern, L.W. (1978) 'Development of a content analytical system for analysis of bargaining communication in marketing', *Journal of Marketing Research*, February, pp. 93–102.

Bell, D.B., Giordano, R. and Putz, P. (2002) 'Inter-firm sharing of process knowledge: exploring knowledge markets', *Knowledge and Process Management*, 9(1), pp. 12–22.

Berrell, M., Gloet, M. and Wright, P. (2002) 'Organizational learning in international joint ventures: implications for management development', *Journal of Management Development*, 21(2), pp. 83–100.

Bush, V.D. and Ingram, T. (2001) 'Building and assessing cultural diversity skills: implications for sales training', *Industrial Marketing Management*, 30, pp. 65–76.

Choo, C. (1998) *The Knowing Organization*. Oxford University Press, New York.

Desouza, K. and Evaristo, R. (2003) 'Global knowledge management strategies', *European Management Journal*, 21(1), pp. 62–67.

Della Cava, R.R. (1999) 'Magic kingdoms, new colonies: theme parks are staking bigger claims in Europe', *USA Today*, 17 February.

Fisher, R. and William Ury, W. (1981) *Getting to Yes: Negotiating Agreement Without Giving In*. Penguin Books, New York.

Gesteland, R.R. (1996) *Cross-cultural Business Behaviour*. Copenhagen Business School Press, Copenhagen.

Govindarajan, V. and Gupta, A.K. (2001) 'Building an effective global business team', *MIT Sloan Management Review*, Summer, pp. 63–71.

Griffith, D.A. (2002) 'The role of communication competencies in international business relationship development', *Journal of World Business*, 37(4), pp. 256–265.

Guy, B.S. and Patton, P.W.E. (1996) 'Managing the effects of culture shock and sojourner adjustment on the expatriate industrial sales force', *Industrial Marketing Management*, 25, pp. 385–393.

Harris, P.R. and Moran, R.T. (1987) *Managing Cultural Differences*. Houston, TX: Gulf Publishing Company.

Harvey, M.G. and Griffith, D.A. (2002) 'Developing effective intercultural relationships: the importance of communication strategies', *Thunderbird International Business Review*, 44(4), pp. 455–476.

Hendon, D.W., Hendon, R.A. and Herbig, P. (1999) *Cross-cultural Negotiations*, Praeger Publishers, Westport, CT.

Hofstede, G. (1983) 'The cultural relativity of organizational practices and theories', *Journal of International Business Studies*, Fall, pp. 75–89.

Hooker, J. (2009) 'Corruption from a cross-cultural perspective', *Cross Cultural Management*, 16(3), pp. 251–267.

Madsen, T.K. (1994) 'A contingency approach to export performance research', *Advances in International Marketing*, 6, pp. 25–42.

McGinnis, M.A. (2005) 'Lessons in cross-cultural negotiations', *Supply Chain Management Review*, April, pp. 9–10.

Nonaka, I. and Takeuchi, H. (1995) *The Knowledge-creating Company*. Oxford University Press, New York.

Rowden, R.W. (2001) 'Research note: how a small business enters the international market', *Thunderbird International Business Review*, 43(2), pp. 257–268.

Schein, E.H. (1985) *Organizational Culture and Leadership*. Jossey-Bass Publishers, San Francisco, CA.

Scott, J., Gilliard, D. and Scott, R. (2002) 'Eliminating bribery as a transnational marketing strategy', *International Journal of Commerce & Management*, 12(1), pp. 1–17.

Simintiras, A.C. and Reynolds, N. (2001) 'Toward an understanding of the role of cross-cultural equivalence in international personal selling', *Journal of Marketing Management*, 16(8), pp. 829–851.

Simintiras, A.C. and Thomas, A.H. (1998) 'Cross-cultural sales negotiations: a literature review and research propositions', *International Marketing Review*, 15(1), pp. 10–28.

Stewart, D. (2001) 'Reinterpreting the learning organization', *The Learning Organization*, 8(4), pp. 141–152.

Tagliabue, J. (2000) 'Lights, action in France for second Disney Park', *New York Times*, 13 February.

Wolf, J. (2002) 'Multicultural workgroups', *Management International Review*, 42(1), pp. 3–4.

Zhang, M.Y. and Dodgson, M. (2007) 'A roasted duck can still fly away: a case study of technology, nationality, culture and the rapid and early internationalization of the firm', *Journal of World Business*, 42, pp. 336–349.

CHAPTER 19

Organization and control of the global marketing programme

Contents

Case studies

Learning objectives

After studying this chapter you should be able to:

- Examine how firms build their organizational structure internationally and what roles headquarters can play.
- Identify the variables that affect the reorganization design.
- Describe and evaluate functional, geographic, product and matrix organizations as the key international structural alternatives.
- Explain the pitfalls and opportunities of global account management.
- Describe the key elements of the marketing control system.
- List the most important measures for marketing performance.
- Explain how a global marketing budget is established.
- Understand the steps in developing the global marketing plan.

19.1   Introduction

The overall objective of this chapter is to study intra-organizational relationships as part of the firm's attempt to optimize its competitive response in areas most critical to its business. As market conditions change, and companies evolve from purely domestic entities to multinationals, their organizational structure, coordination and control systems must also change.

First, this chapter will focus on the advantages and disadvantages of the main organizational structures available as well as their appropriateness at various stages of internationalization. Then the chapter will outline the need for a control system to oversee the international operations of the company.

19.2   Organization of global marketing activities

The way in which a global marketing organization is structured is an important determinant of its ability to exploit the opportunities available to it effectively and efficiently. It also determines the capacity for responding to problems and challenges. Companies operating internationally must decide whether the organization should be structured along functions, products, geographical areas or combinations of the three (a matrix). The evolutionary nature of organizational changes is shown in Figure 19.1. The following pages discuss the different organizational structures.

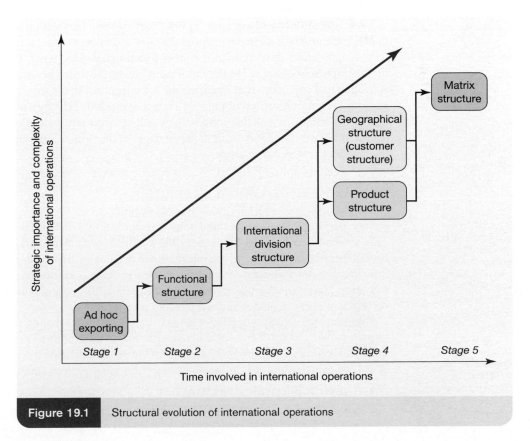

Figure 19.1   Structural evolution of international operations

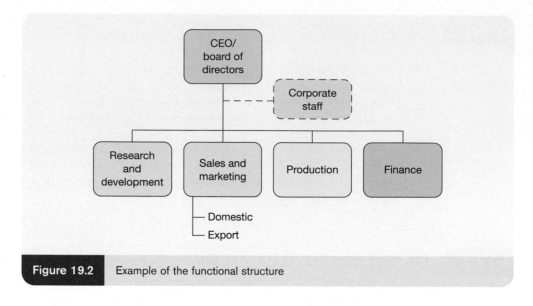

| **Figure 19.2** | Example of the functional structure |

Functional structure

Functional structure
Here the next level after top management is divided into functional departments, e.g. R&D, sales and marketing, production and finance.

Of all the approaches, the **functional structure** (Figure 19.2) is the simplest. Here management is concerned primarily with the functional efficiency of the company.

Many companies begin their international business activities as a result of having received enquiries from abroad. The company, being new to international business, has no international specialist and typically has few products and few markets. In this early stage of international involvement the domestic marketing department may have the responsibility for global marketing activities, but as the international involvement intensifies an export or international department may become part of the organizational structure. The export department may be a subdepartment of the sales and marketing department (as in Figure 19.2) or may have equal ranking with the other functional departments. This choice will depend on the importance assigned to the export activities of the firm. Because the export department is the first real step in internationalizing the organizational structure it should be a fully fledged marketing organization and not merely a sales organization. The functional export department design is particularly suitable for SMEs, as well as larger companies, that are manufacturing standardized products and are in the early stages of developing international business, having low product and area diversities.

International divisional structure

International divisional structure
As international sales grow, at some point the international division may emerge at the same level as the functional departments.

As international sales grow, at some point an **international divisional structure** may emerge. This division becomes directly responsible for the development and implementation of the overall international strategy. The international division incorporates international expertise, information flows about foreign market opportunities and authority over international activities. However, manufacturing and other related functions remain with the domestic divisions in order to take advantage of economies of scale.

International divisions best serve firms with new products that do not vary significantly in terms of their environmental sensitivity, and whose international sales and profits are still quite insignificant compared with those of the domestic divisions.

Product divisional structure

Product divisional structure
The next level after top management is divided into product division, e.g. Product A, B, C and D.

A typical **product divisional structure** is presented in Figure 19.3.

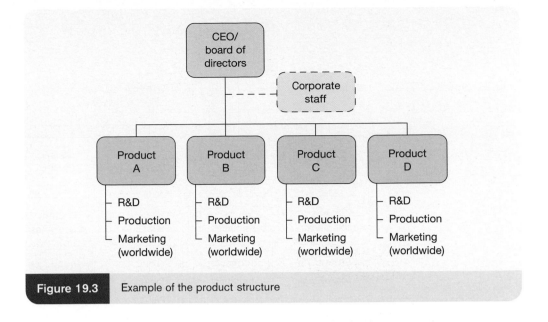

Figure 19.3	Example of the product structure

In general, the product structure is better suited to companies with more experience in international business and marketing, and with diversified product lines and extensive R&D activities. The product division structure is most appropriate under conditions where the products have potential for worldwide standardization. One of the major benefits of the approach is improved cost efficiency through centralization of manufacturing facilities for each product line. This is crucial in industries in which competitive position is determined by world market share, that in turn is often determined by the degree to which manufacturing is rationalized (utilization of economies of scale). The main disadvantages of this type of structure are:

- It duplicates functional resources: you will find R&D, production, marketing, sales force management, etc. in each product division.
- It under-utilizes sales and distribution facilities (subsidiaries) abroad. In the 'product structure' there is a tendency that marketing of products is taken care of, centrally from the homebase ('Marketing [worldwide]'). Therefore there is less need for the facilities in the local sales subsidiary.
- The product divisions tend to develop a total independence of each other in world markets. For example, a global product division structure may end up with several subsidiaries in the same foreign country reporting to different product divisions, with no one at headquarters responsible for the overall corporate presence in that country.

Geographical structure

Geographical structure
The next level after top management is divided into international divisions, e.g. Europe, North America, Latin America, Asia/Pacific and Africa/Middle East.

If market conditions with respect to product acceptance and operating conditions vary considerably across world markets, then the **geographical structure** is the one to choose. This structure is especially useful for companies that have a homogeneous range of products (similar technologies and common end-use markets), but at the same time need fast and efficient worldwide distribution. Typically, the world is divided into regions (divisions), as shown in Figure 19.4.

Many food, beverage, car and pharmaceutical companies use this type of structure. Its main advantage is its ability to respond easily and quickly to the environmental and market demands of a regional or national area through minor modifications in product design, pricing, market communication and packaging. Therefore the structure encourages adaptive

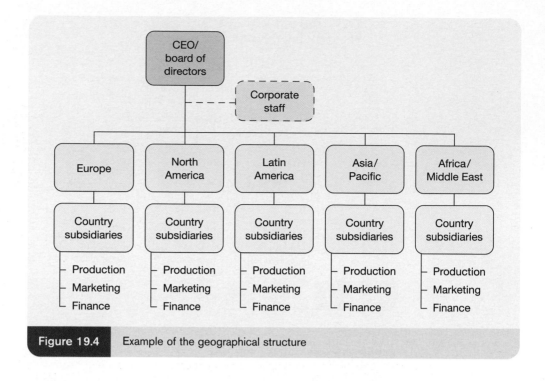

Figure 19.4 Example of the geographical structure

global marketing programmes. Moreover, economies of scale can be achieved within regions. Another reason for the popularity of this structure is its tendency to create area autonomy. However, this may also complicate the tasks of coordinating product variations and transferring new product ideas and marketing techniques from one country to another.

Hence the geographical structure ensures the best use of the firm's regional expertise, but it means a less than optimal allocation of product and functional expertise. If each region needs its own staff of product and functional specialists, duplication and also inefficiency may be the result. As indicated in Figure 19.4, the geographical structure may include both regional management centres (Europe, North America, etc.) and country-based subsidiaries.

Regional management centres

There are two main reasons for the existence of regional management centres (RMCs):

1. When sales volume in a particular region becomes substantial there need to be some specialized staff to focus on that region, to realize more fully the potential of an already growing market.
2. Homogeneity within regions and heterogeneity between them necessitate treating each important region separately. Therefore a regional management centre becomes an appropriate organizational feature.

Country-based subsidiaries

Instead of or parallel to a regional centre, each country has its own organizational unit. Country-based subsidiaries are characterized by a high degree of adaptation to local conditions. Since each subsidiary develops its own unique activities and its own autonomy, it is sometimes relevant to combine local subsidiaries with an RMC: for example, to utilize opportunities across European countries.

Firms may also organize their operations using a customer structure, especially if the customer groups they serve are very different: for example, businesses and governments.

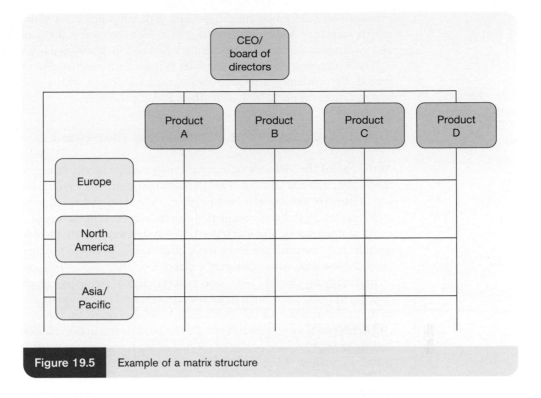

Figure 19.5   Example of a matrix structure

Catering to these diverse groups may require the concentration of specialists in particular divisions. The product may be the same, but the buying processes of the various customer groups may differ. Governmental buying is characterized by bidding, in which price plays a larger role than when businesses are the buyers. Much of what has been said about the geographical structure also applies to the customer structure.

Matrix structure

The product structure tends to offer better opportunities to rationalize production across countries, thus gaining production cost efficiencies. On the other hand, the geographical structure is more responsive to local market trends and needs, and allows for more coordination in a whole region.

Matrix structure
The next level after top management consists of two organizational structures (product and geographical areas) intersecting with each other. Results in dual reporting relationships.

Some global companies need both capabilities, so they have adopted a more complex structure: the **matrix structure**. The international matrix structure consists of two organizational structures intersecting with each other. As a consequence there are dual reporting relationships. These two structures can be a combination of the general forms already discussed. For example, the matrix structure might consist of product divisions intersecting with functional departments, or geographical areas intersecting with global divisions. The two intersecting structures will largely be a function of what the organization sees as the two dominant aspects of its environment.

The typical international matrix structure is the two-dimensional structure that emphasizes product and geography (Figure 19.5). Generally, each product division has worldwide responsibilities for its own business, and each geographical or area division is responsible for the foreign operations in its region. If national organizations (subsidiaries) are involved they are responsible for operations at the country level.

Because the two dimensions of product and geography overlap at the affiliate level, both enter into local decision-making and planning processes. It is assumed that area and product managers will defend different positions, but this will lead to tensions and creative conflict. Area managers will tend to favour responsiveness to local environmental factors, and product managers will defend positions favouring cost efficiencies and global competitiveness. The matrix structure deliberately creates a dual focus to ensure that conflicts between product and geographical area concerns are identified and then analysed objectively.

The structure is useful for companies that are both product diversified and geographically spread. By combining a product management approach with a market-oriented approach one can meet the needs both of markets and of products.

The future role of the international manager

At the end of the 1980s many internationally oriented companies adopted the transnational model (Bartlett and Ghoshal, 1989). It held that companies should leverage their capabilities across borders and transfer best practices to achieve global economies and respond to the local market. In this way companies avoided duplicating their functions (product development, manufacturing and marketing). However, it required that senior managers could think, operate and communicate along three dimensions: function, product and geography. Surely there are few such 'supermanagers' around!

In a study by Quelch (1992) one manager says of changing managerial roles: 'I am at the fulcrum of the tension between local adaptation and global standardization. My boss tells me to think global and act local. That's easier said than done' (p. 158).

There is no universal solution to the ideal profile for an international manager, but Quelch and Bloom (1996) have predicted the 'fall of the transnational manager and the return of the country manager'. They studied behaviour of country managers in different countries and concluded that the opportunities in expanding emerging markets (e.g. Eastern Europe) have to be grasped by entrepreneurial country managers. The transnational manager is better suited to stable and saturated markets, such as western Europe, with its progress towards a single market.

19.3 The global account management organization

Global account management
A relationship-oriented marketing management approach focusing on dealing with the needs of an important global customer (an account) with a global organization (foreign subsidiaries all over the world).

Global account management (GAM) can be understood as a relationship-oriented marketing management approach focusing on dealing with the needs of an important global customer (that is, an account) in the business-to-business market.

GAM can be defined as an organizational form (a person or a team) in a global supplier organization used to coordinate and manage worldwide activities, by servicing an important customer centrally from headquarters (Harvey *et al.*, 2002). See also Figure 19.6.

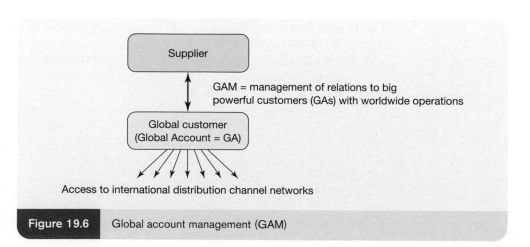

| Figure 19.6 | Global account management (GAM) |

For the small supplier enterprises that are ambitious and growth-oriented, it is imperative that they learn to find ways of engaging with large MNCs (global customers) who have the complementary resources and capabilities that can lead to, for instance, an innovative product offering being rolled out on a global scale, through the international distribution system of the global customer (global account). In other words, these small suppliers must seriously consider, as Prashantham and Birkinshaw (2008) put it, learning how to 'dance with the gorillas'.

A global account is a customer that is of strategic importance to the achievement of the supplier's corporate objectives, pursues integrated and coordinated strategies on a worldwide basis and demands a globally integrated product/service offering (Wilson and Millman, 2003).

A global account manager is the person in the selling company who represents that company's capabilities to the buying company, the buying company's needs to the selling company, and brings the two together.

The importance of GAM strategies will grow in future (Harvey *et al.*, 2002; Shi *et al.*, 2004, 2005) because of the consolidation (mergers and acquisitions [M&As] and global strategic alliances) which takes place in most industries. This development means that big multinational customers are getting even bigger and more powerful with increasing buying power. The following discusses what the supplier can do about this development.

Successful GAM often requires an understanding of the logic of both product and service management. Moreover, excellent operational level capabilities are useless if strategic level management is inferior, and vice versa – the GAM approach combines strategic and operational level marketing management.

The starting point for the following is the firm that wishes to implement GAM. Afterwards the development of GAM is regarded in a dyadic perspective.

Implementation of GAM

The firm that wants to implement successful GAM with suitable global accounts may go through the following four steps (Ojasalo, 2001):

1. identifying the selling firm's global accounts
2. analysing the global accounts
3. selecting suitable strategies for the global accounts
4. developing operational level capabilities to build, grow and maintain profitable and long-lasting relationships with global accounts.

Identifying the selling firm's global accounts

This means answering the question which existing or potential accounts are of strategic importance to us now and in the future?

The following criteria can be used to determine strategically important customers:

- sales volume;
- age of the relationship;
- the selling firm's share of customers' purchase: the new relationship marketing (RM) paradigm measures success in terms of long-term gains in its share of its customers' business, unlike mass marketing that counts wins or losses in terms of market share increases that may well be temporary (Peppers and Rogers, 1995);
- profitability of the customer to seller;
- use of strategic resources: extent of executive/management commitment.

There is a positive relation (correlation) between the criteria and the likelihood of customers' being identified as global accounts (strategic customers).

Analysing global accounts

This includes activities such as analysing:

- *The basic characteristics of a global account.* Includes assessing the relevant economic and activity aspects of their internal and external environment. This, for example, includes the account's internal value chain inputs, markets, suppliers, products and economic situation.
- *The relationship history.* Involves assessing the relevant economic and activity aspects of the relationship history. This includes volume of sales, profitability, global account's objectives, buying behaviour (the account's decision-making process), information exchange, special needs, buying frequency and complaints. Among the above-mentioned aspects, knowing/estimating relationship value plays a particularly important role. The revenues from each global account (customer lifetime value) should exceed the costs of establishing and maintaining the relationship within a certain time span.
- *The level and development of commitment to the relationship.* The account's present and anticipated commitment to the relationship is important, since the extent of the business with the account depends on that.
- *Goal congruence of the parties.* Goal congruence, or commonality of interests between buyer and seller, greatly affects their cooperation both at the strategic and operational levels. Common interests and relationship value together determine whether two companies can be partners, friends or rivals. The organization that aims its sights lower than the sort of partnership relationship an account is looking for risks losing long-term share of that account's business.
- *Switching costs.* It is useful to estimate both the global account's and the selling company's switching costs in the event that the relationship dissolves. Switching costs are the costs of replacing an existing partner with another. These may be very different for the two parties and thus affect the power position in the relationship. Switching costs are also called transaction costs and are affected by irretrievable investments in the relationship, the adaptations made and the bonds that have developed. High switching costs may prevent a relationship from ending even though the global account's accumulated satisfaction with the selling company may be non-existent or negative.

Selecting suitable strategies for the global accounts

This depends greatly on the power positions of the seller and the global account. The power structure within different accounts may vary significantly. Thus the selling company may typically not freely select the strategy – there is often only one strategic alternative to be chosen if there is a desire to retain the account.

Maybe the selling firm might prefer to avoid very powerful accounts. Sometimes the selling firm realizes that accounts which are less attractive today may become attractive in future. Thus, in the case of certain accounts, the objective of the strategy may be merely to keep the relationship alive for future opportunities.

Developing operational level capabilities

This refers to customization and development of capabilities related to the following.

Product/service development and performance

Joint R&D projects are typical between a selling company and a global account in industrial and high-tech markets. In addition, information technology (IT) applied in just-in-time production and distribution channels increases the possibilities of customizing the offering in consumer markets as well.

New products developed in a partnership are not automatically more successful than those developed in-house. However, R&D projects may bring other kinds of long-term benefits, such as access to account organization and learning. Improving capabilities for providing services to global accounts is extremely important, because even when the core product is a tangible good it is often the related services that differentiate the selling company from its competitors and provide competitive advantage.

Organizational structure

The selling company's *organizational ability* to meet the global account's needs can be developed, for example, by adjusting the organizational structure to correspond to the global account's global and local needs and by increasing the number of interfaces between the selling company and the account, and thus also the number of interacting persons. Organizational capabilities can also be developed by organizing teams, consisting of people with the necessary competences and authorities, to take care of global accounts.

Individuals (human resources)

A company's capabilities related to individuals can be developed by selecting the right people as global account managers and for global account teams, and by developing their skills. The global account manager's responsibilities are often complex and varied, and therefore require a large number of skills and qualifications, which should be taken into account in the selection and development of global account managers.

It is quite common to find that the current set of global account managers may be good at maintaining their own relationships with their contacts in the account but lack the total set of skills required to lead an account team through a transition in the account relationship. Therefore an assessment of the total desired interfaces between the seller and the customer needs to be considered. It may be that a change is required by moving the relationship from a dependency on a 1:1 relationship (between the global account manager and the chief buyer) to a network of organizational relationships spanning many different projects, functions and countries.

Information exchange

Information exchange between the selling company and a global account is particularly important in GAM. An important relationship-specific task is to search, filter, judge and store information about the organizations, strategies, goals, potentials and problems of the partners. However, this mainly depends on the mutual trust and attitudes of the parties, and on the technical arrangements. A global account's trust is something that the selling company has to earn over time by its performance, whereas the technical side can be developed, for example with IT.

Company and individual level benefits

Successful long-term GAM in a business-to-business context always requires the ability to offer both company and individual level benefits to global accounts.

Company level benefits are rational and may be either short or long term, direct or indirect, and typically contribute to the global account's turnover, profitability, cost savings, organizational efficiency and effectiveness and image. Individual level benefits in turn may be rational or emotional. From the relationship management point of view the global individual(s) is/are the one(s) with the power to continue or terminate the relationship. Rational individual level benefits contribute, for example, to the individual's own career, income and ease of job. Emotional individual level benefits include friendship, a sense of caring and ego enhancement.

The dyadic development of GAM

The Millman-Wilson model in Figure 19.7 describes and demonstrates the typical dyadic progression of a relationship between buyer and seller through five stages – Pre-GAM, Early GAM, Mid-GAM, Partnership GAM and Synergistic-GAM (Wilson and Millman, 2003).

Pre-GAM describes preparation for GAM. A buying company is identified as having key account potential, and the selling company starts to focus resources on winning some business with that prospect. Both seller and buyer are sending out signals (factual information) and exchanging messages (interactions) prior to the decision to engage in transactions. There is a need to develop networks of contacts, to gain knowledge about the customer's operations and to begin to assess the potential for relational development.

Early GAM: at this stage the selling company is concerned with identifying the opportunities for account penetration once the account has been won. This is probably the most typical sales relationship, the classic 'bow-tie'.

Adapted solutions are needed, and the key account manager will be focused on understanding more about their customer and the market in which that customer is competing. The buying company will still be market testing other selling companies. Detailed knowledge of the global customer and their core competences, the depth of the relationship and the potential for creating relation-specific entrepreneurial value are all limited at this stage. There is an increasing need for political skills to be applied as the potential of the account is identified and the global account manager is called upon to ensure that the resources of the supplier configure to best serve the needs of the customer (Wilson and Millman, 2003). The selling company must concentrate hard on product, service and intangibles – the buying company wants recognition that the product offering is the prime reason for the relationship – and expects it to work.

Mid-GAM stage: this is a transition stage between the classic 'bow-tie' and the 'diamond' of the partnership GAM stage (see Figure 19.8).

At this stage the selling company has established credibility with the buying company. Contacts between the two organizations increase at all levels and assume greater importance. Nevertheless, buying companies still feel the need for alternative sources of supply. This may be driven by their own customers' desire for choice. The selling company's offering is still periodically market tested, but is reliably perceived to be good value. The selling company is now a 'preferred' supplier.

Partnership GAM: this is the stage where benefits should start to flow. When partnership GAM is reached the selling company is seen by the buying company organization as a strategic external resource. The two companies will be sharing sensitive information and engaging in joint problem solution. Pricing will be long term and stable, but it will have been established that each side will allow the other to make a profit.

If a major disadvantage of the bow-tie of early GAM was the denial of access to customers' internal processes and to their market, the main advantage of the 'diamond' relationship is in seeing and understanding the 'opening' of the 'global account'.

Global accounts will test all the supplier company's innovations so that they have first access to, and first benefit from, the latest technology. The buying company will expect to be guaranteed continuity of supply and access to the best material. Expertise will be shared. The buying company will also expect to gain from continuous improvement. There may be joint promotions, where appropriate.

Synergistic GAM: this is the ultimate stage in the relational development model. The experience gained at the partnership stage – coordinating the team-sell, coaching the team on its interface roles – will be a good starting point for moving to synergistic GAM. The closer the relationship, the greater the knowledge about the customer and the greater the potential for creating entrepreneurial value.

The selling company understands that they still have no automatic right to the customer's business. Nevertheless, exit barriers have been built up. The buying company is confident that its relationship with the selling company is delivering improved quality and reduced cost. Costing systems become transparent. Joint research and development will take place. There

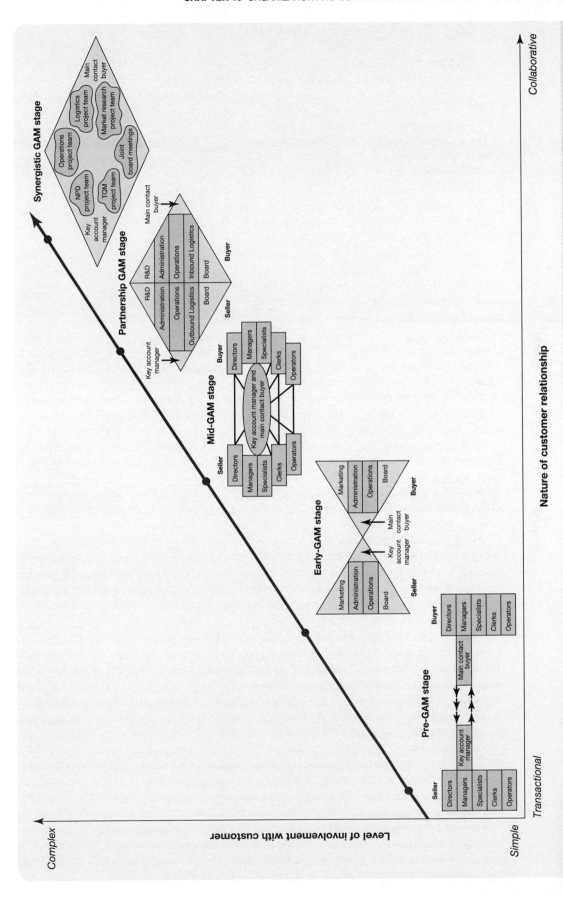

Figure 19.7   Relational development model

Source: adapted from Millman and Wilson (1995); Wilson and Millman (2003).

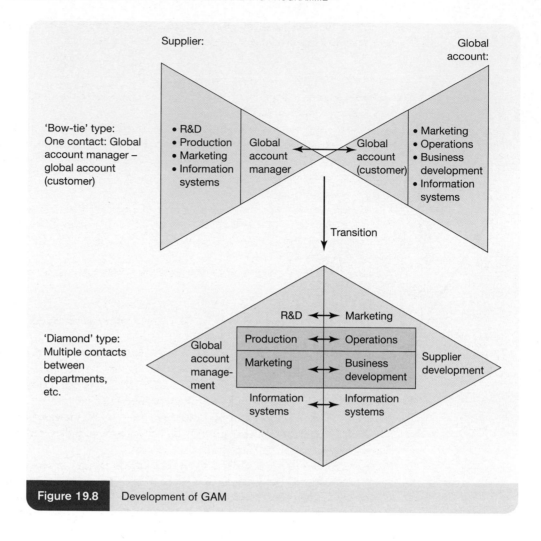

Figure 19.8 Development of GAM

will be interfaces at every level and function between the organizations. Top management commitment will be fulfilled through joint board meetings and reviews. There will be a joint business plan, joint strategies, joint market research. Information flow should be streamlined and information systems integration will be planned or in place as a consequence. Transaction costs will be reduced.

Though there are clear advantages for both partners in moving through the different GAM stages there are also pitfalls. As the contacts proliferate through the stages, so does the speed of activity – and the risk of saying and doing the wrong things. Through the stages the key account manager changes from 'super salesperson' to 'super coach'. In the last two stages the key account manager moves on to a 'super coordinator', who conducts the orchestra.

If the key account manager does not move along then the potential of losing control is great, resulting in well-meaning but misdirected individuals following their own quite separate courses.

Key account management requires process excellence and highly skilled professionals to manage relationships with strategic customers. For most companies this represents a number of revolutions. A revolution is needed in the way activity is costed and costs are attributed, from product or geographical focus to customer focus. Currently few financial or information systems in companies are sophisticated enough to support the higher levels of key account management. A transformation is needed in the way the professional with responsibility for a customer relationship is developed, from an emphasis on selling skills to management skills, including cross-cultural management skills (McDonald *et al.*, 1997).

We end this section by assessing the advantages and disadvantages by going into GAM, seen from the supplier's (seller's) point of view:

Supplier's (seller's) advantages with GAM

- Provides a better fulfilment of the customer's global need for having only one supplier of certain products and services.
- Smaller supplier enterprises often have significant complementary assets that the MNC will struggle to develop efficiently itself, for example proprietary technologies. Most large MNCs actively seek out new ideas and innovations on a worldwide basis; indeed, many believe their ability to do this is one of their key sources of competitive advantage.
- Creating barriers for competitors – given the high switching costs global competitors (to the supplier) will have difficulty in displacing the existing supplier. If the supplier becomes the preferred supplier, the customer becomes dependent on the supplier shifting power in the relationship.
- Increased sales of existing products and services through a closer relationship with the key customer.
- Facilitating the introduction of new products/services – the global account (GA) is perceived to be more willing to take on new product trials and carry a more complete product line.
- Coordination of marketing/selling activities across borders may increase the total worldwide sales value to this customer – the GAM strategy enables the supplier to coordinate global marketing programmes (i.e. standardization) while at the same time permitting local adaptation to individual country environment.
- Perceived high potential for profit increase – due to the increased sales and global coordination – development of a strategic 'fit' between the supplier and the customer increases the effectiveness of the supplying organization.
- By using the learning effects the supplier has the ability to reduce the marginal cost of creating adapted programmes for every new country/region. In this way economies of scale as well as economies of scope can be utilized through the GAM strategy.
- Through the global network of the customer the supplier might get access to new customers around the world.

Supplier's (seller's) disadvantages with GAM

- The supplier will feel pressure from the global customers to improve global consistency – they may force the supplier to institute GAM to maintain their global 'preferred' supplier status.
- *Lack of access and attention:* small enterprises have restricted access to the attention of key decision-makers in the MNC, which is very different from the situation in an MNCN–MNC relationship where the executives are equal partners. Thus with smaller suppliers there is a problem of *asymmetry in resources.* Smaller supplier enterprises lack the reputation, financial muscle and human resources of their potential partners, which is in direct contrast to the situation in a balanced MNCN–MNC relationship. Indeed, in many respects small supplier enterprises and MNCs are entirely different organizations, which makes communication and knowledge transfer extremely difficult. MNCs typically have a clear separation between line and staff roles, many functional specialists and explicit processes for every activity. Small supplier enterprises are full of generalists, many of whom perform multiple functions, and they get things done through ad hoc and informal processes (Prashantham and Birkinshaw, 2008).
- Normally the supplier would use different prices for the customer's different subsidiaries in the different countries. However, the global customer may attempt to use GAM as a means to lower prices globally, by using the argument that there should be equity/commonality of pricing throughout the global network of the customer's subsidiaries.

However, research done by Yip and Bink (2007) concludes that the suppliers' globally consistent service performance is more important than lower prices to the global cusomers. So suppliers adopting the GAM can build relationships with their global customers that go beyond price discounts.

- Pressure to 'standardize' all terms of trade on a global basis, and not just price. So GAS increasingly demand uniformity in such issues as volume discounts, transportation charges, overheads, special charges and so forth.
- The supplier's loss of GA due to major competitors utilizing the GAM strategy – the supplier may feel compelled to form a GAM team to match or counteract the strategy of key customers.
- Most often a GAM strategy is connected to the use of some kind of matrix organization. Consequently there may be multiple decision-makers in the supplier organization making the same decision from different perspectives (e.g. global vs local). The cost of managing may increase due to the parallel structures at global and local levels. Moreover, the parallel structures might slow down the decision-making process.

The organizational set-up of global account management

According to Figure 19.9 three different organizational models will be presented.

1. Central HQ–HQ negotiation model

This model shows a situation where the product in question is standardized. The customer HQ will collect the demands from the different subsidiaries around the world. Thereafter the customer will meet with the supplier and the HQ-to-HQ negotiations will take place. In this situation the customer will typically exercise significant buying power, because the supplier will not have any international organization that can offset this buying power. For the supplier, a standardized (high) quality is the condition for being invited to the discussions with the customer HQ. Subsequently, the discussion will quickly come down to a question of the 'right' price. The supplier will always be under pressure to lower the price and cut costs of producing the product package (including services).

IKEA (turnover in 2004 of €22,713 million, achieved through its 301 IKEA shops around the world), is an example of a customer that puts its furniture suppliers under constant pressure to reduce their prices and make their production more efficient, in order to reduce costs. Recently IKEA planned to reduce its distribution warehouse costs by 10 per cent per year. In order to achieve this goal they run weekly batch global-demand forecasts for each of its three major regions: North America, Asia and EMEA (Europe, Middle East and Africa). The fulfilment solution will balance demand forecasts with inventory levels and replenish accordingly through IKEA's ordering system (Scheraga, 2005). Orders may be sent to IKEA's suppliers weekly or daily, depending on how active they are with the retailer. IKEA suppliers are pressurized to deliver furniture to IKEA more frequently and more directly to its stores around the world. If a European sub-supplier of furniture wants to be a global supplier to IKEA it must now consider establishing production and assembling factories in the other two main regions of the world: North America and Asia.

2. Balanced negotiation model

In this situation the central HQ to HQ negotiation is supplemented with some decentralized and local negotiations on a country basis. Typically this will take place in the form of negotiations between the local subsidiaries of the customers and the different partners (e.g. agents) or subsidiaries of the supplier. The HQ to HQ negotiations will set the possible range of outcomes for the following negotiations on a local basis. This will allow for some degree of price differentiation across the involved countries, dependent on the degree of necessary product adaptation to local conditions. Sauer-Danfoss (www.sauer-danfoss.com) is an example of a sub-supplier working to this model (see Exhibit 19.1).

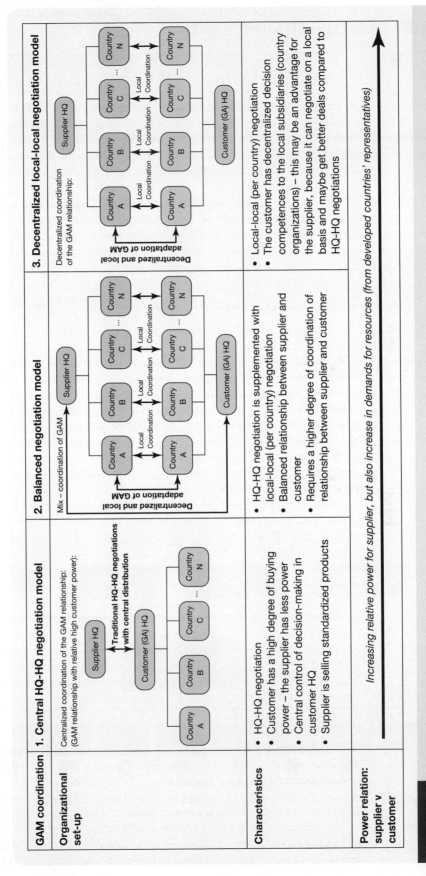

Figure 19.9   The organizational set-up in GAM

Source: different Sauer-Danfoss material (as at 2004), Hollensen (2006).

EXHIBIT 19.1 Sauer-Danfoss's GAM

Sauer-Danfoss is one of the world's leading companies for the development, production and sale of hydraulic power transmission systems – primarily for use in mobile work vehicles. Sauer-Danfoss, with more than 7,000 employees worldwide and revenue of approximately US$ 1.3 billion (2004), has sales, manufacturing and engineering capabilities in Europe, the Americas and the Asia-Pacific region. Sauer-Danfoss' key global customers (GAs) are John Deere, Case New Holland, Ingersoll-Rand, Agco and Caterpillar (see also Case 6.2).

One of Sauer-Danfoss's main global accounts (OEM customers), Case New Holland (CNH) is the number one manufacturer of agricultural tractors and combines in the world and the third-largest maker of construction equipment. Revenue in 2004 totalled $12 billion. Based in the United States, CNH's network of dealers and distributors operates in over 160 countries. CNH agricultural products are sold under the Case IH, New Holland and Steyr brands. CNH construction equipment is sold under the Case, FiatAllis, Fiat Kobelco, Kobelco, New Holland and O&K brands.

As a result of a merger in 1999 CNH is an example of consolidation on the OEM customer side. The consequence of this consolidation is that fewer than the ten largest OEM customers will represent more than half of Sauer-Danfoss's potential sales over the medium to long term. There is no doubt that the price-down pressure will continue worldwide. The global business culture trend is leading towards a more professional buying process on the customer side. This development requires a new way of structuring the Sauer-Danfoss organization, and the answer is GAM. As illustrated in the figure below. Sauer-Danfoss has met the requirements of CNH's worldwide production units by forming local production locations and GAM team groups in India, China, Poland, North America, Italy, Brazil, Germany and the United Kingdom. In partnership with CNH the GAM teams try to find more cost-effective solutions, rather than simply reduce prices. Sauer-Danfoss is following CNH into low-cost manufacturing countries, such as India and China. At all of CNH's worldwide production units there is pressure for a higher degree of outsourcing and a request for value added packages. Sauer-Danfoss tries to fulfil this requirement by supplying pre-assembled kit packages and delivering more system solutions to CNH.

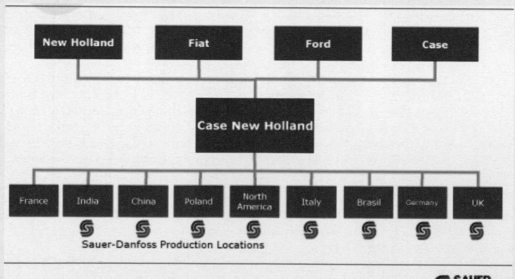

Source: different Sauer-Danfoss material (as at 2004), Hollensen (2006).

3. Decentralized local–local negotiation model

According to this model the negotiations will only take place on a local basis, partly because the supplier is often selling system solutions which require a high degree of adaptation to the different markets (countries). This means that the HQs are disconnected from the negotiation processes. A consolidation process in the customer's industry may cause this outcome. If the customer has been involved in several M&As, it will have difficulties in understanding the overall picture of the decision structures in the new merged multinational company. In such a situation the customer will tend to decentralize even important decisions to the country subsidiaries, because it has lost its overview of the whole multinational company. It can be really difficult to control and coordinate decision processes in recently merged companies. For that reason top managers will often refer the buying decisions to local decision-makers in local country subsidiaries.

This will give the supplier better opportunities for sub-optimization by negotiating only locally with a customer's country-based organizations. By using this approach the supplier may be in a better relative negotiation position and may also achieve better (higher) prices in some markets by using this model. However, the supplier may have higher costs connected to fulfilling the different requirements of the customer's local subsidiaries. Also this model requires that the supplier has an established network of subsidiaries or partners (e.g. agents) who are familiar with the product solutions of the supplier and who can offer local adapted product solutions for the customer's subsidiaries in the different countries (see Exhibit 19.2).

EXHIBIT 19.2 AGRAMKOW – working to the model 3

AGRAMKOW (www.agramkow.com) is an example of a company working to this model. AGRAMKOW (Denmark) has a goal to become one of the world's leading developers and suppliers of filling equipment for fluid refrigerants, which are used, for example, in refrigerators or in automotive air conditioners. In 2004 their total sales were approximately $35 million, of which 95 per cent was realized outside the home country (Denmark). The total number of employees is 150. AGRAMKOW's global customers (GAs) are big multinational companies like Whirlpool (USA), Electrolux (Sweden), Samsung (Korea), Haier (China), Siemens (Germany) and General Electric (USA).

It is a fact that global customers are getting fewer and bigger by mergers and acquisitions. For example, AGRAMKOW's process fluid fill system is fitted into the total production line of the refrigerator manufacturer Electrolux. AGRAMKOW has 'only' three or four subsidiaries around the world, but instead of having several subsidiaries to support the local production units of the major GAs (like in the Sauer-Danfoss case), it has transferred the values of AGRAMKOW to distributors and agents in order to turn them into partners with internalized AGRAMKOW values. The AGRAMKOW management has implemented this partner strategy by inviting all the potential partners to common seminars and meetings at the AGRAMKOW HQ in Denmark. The purpose of these meetings is to increase:

- common team spirit and commitment to the AGRAMKOW shared values and goals – this has also been achieved by including some common social activities (e.g. sport activities);
- sales skills for winning local GA business;
- technical competence for installation, integration, maintenance and repair of AGRAMKOW equipment/ solutions;
- understanding of the necessity for constant feedback to AGRAMKOW on performance and other market activities (e.g. competitor activity).

Afterwards the individual partner and their organization (e.g. the Chinese partner) is in a better position to take care of customized products, local service and customer care directed towards the local GA unit (e.g. the local Electrolux refrigerator production unit in China). This also means that AGRAMKOW has increased its relative power on the local basis towards one of its important GAs, Electrolux.

Despite this positive development there have been some difficulties in the process of turning the distributors and agents into partners. Those organizations with small turnovers of AGRAMKOW products and services have been somewhat reluctant to take part in this process (Hollensen, 2006).

In summary, the importance of GAM strategies will grow in the future because of consolidation in most industries across the world. The development of relational contracting with a large, global customer – the cooperation between a customer and a supplier into a long-term global relationship – has a number of positive outcomes. However, a great deal of learning is necessary when deciding to implement a GAM strategy because high stakes and high exit barriers accompany the implementation.

19.4 Controlling the global marketing programme

The final, but often neglected stage of international market planning, is the control process. Not only is control important to evaluate how we have performed, but it completes the circle of planning by providing the feedback necessary for the start of the next planning cycle.

Figure 19.10 illustrates the connection between the marketing plan, the marketing budget and the control system.

After building the global marketing plan, its quantification appears in the form of budgets. The budget is the basis for the design of the marketing control system that may give the necessary feedback for a possible reformulation of the global marketing plan. The marketing budgets should represent a projection of actions and expected results, and they should be capable of accurate monitoring and controlling. Indeed, measuring performance against budget is the main (regular) management review process, which may cause the feed back in Figure 19.10.

The purpose of a marketing budget is to pull all the revenues and costs involved in marketing together into one comprehensive document. It is a managerial tool that balances what needs to be spent against what can be afforded and helps make choices about priorities. It is then used in monitoring the performance in practice. The marketing budget is usually the most powerful tool with which you think through the relationship between desired results and available means. Its starting point should be the marketing strategies and plans that have already been formulated in the marketing plan itself. In practice, the strategies and plans will run in parallel and will interact.

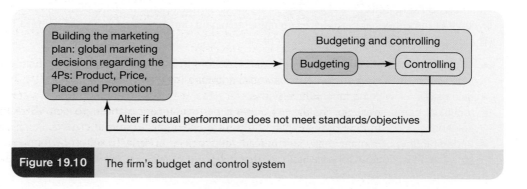

Figure 19.10 The firm's budget and control system

Unfortunately, however, 'control' is often viewed by the people of an organization as being negative. If individuals fear that the control process will be used not only to judge their performance, but as a basis for punishing them, then it will be feared and reviled.

The evaluation and control of global marketing probably represents one of the weakest areas of marketing practice in many companies. Even the organizations that are otherwise strong in their strategic marketing planning have poor control and evaluation procedures for their global marketing. There are a number of possible reasons for this: primarily, there is no such thing as a 'standard' system of control for marketing.

The function of the organizational structure is to provide a framework in which objectives can be met. However, a set of instruments and processes is needed to influence the behaviour and performance of organization members to meet the goals. The critical issue is the same as with organizational structures: what is the ideal amount of control? On the one hand, headquarters needs information to ensure that international activities contribute maximum benefit to the overall organization. On the other hand, controls should not be construed as a code of law.

The global question is to determine how to establish a control mechanism capable of early interception of emerging problems. Considered here are various criteria appropriate for the evaluation process, control styles, feedback and corrective action. These concepts are important for all businesses, but in the international arena they are vital.

Design of a control system

In designing a control system management must consider the costs of establishing and maintaining it and trade them off against the benefits to be gained. Any control system will require investment in a management structure and in systems designs.

The design of the control system can be divided into two groups dependent on the objective of control:

1. output control (typically based on financial measures)
2. behavioural controls (typically based on non-financial measures).

Output control
Regular monitoring of output, like profits, sales figures and expenditures (typically based on financial measures).

Output control may consist of expenditure control, which involves regular monitoring of expenditure figures, comparison of these with budget targets, and taking decisions to cut or increase expenditure where any variance is believed to be harmful. Measures of output are accumulated at regular intervals and typically forwarded from the foreign subsidiary to headquarters, where they are evaluated and criticized based on comparison to the plan or budget.

Behavioural controls
Regular monitoring of behaviour, like sales people's ability to interact with customers (typically based on non-financial measures).

Behavioural controls require the exercise of influence over behaviour. This influence can be achieved, for example, by providing sales manuals to subsidiary personnel or by fitting new employees into the corporate culture. Behavioural controls often require an extensive socialization process, and informal, personal interaction is central to the process. Substantial resources must be spent to train the individual to share the corporate culture: that is, 'the way things are done at the company'.

To build common vision and values managers at the Japanese company Matsushita spend a substantial amount of their first months in what the company calls 'cultural and spiritual training'. They study the company credo, the 'Seven Spirits of Matsushita', and the philosophy of the founder, Kanosuke Matsushita.

However, there remains a strong tradition of using output (financial) criteria. A fixation with output criteria leads companies to ignore the less tangible behavioural (non-financial) measures, although these are the real drivers of corporate success. However, there is a weakness in the behavioural performance measures. To date there has been little success in developing explicit links from behaviour to output criteria. Furthermore, companies and managers are still judged on financial criteria (profit contribution). Until a clear link is established it is likely that behavioural criteria will continue to be treated with a degree of scepticism.

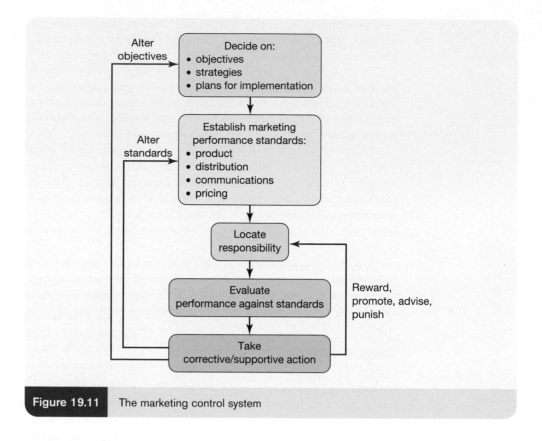

Figure 19.11 The marketing control system

We will now develop a global marketing control system based primarily on output controls. Marketing control is an essential element of the marketing planning process because it provides a review of how well marketing objectives have been achieved. A framework for controlling marketing activities is given in Figure 19.11.

The marketing control system begins with the company setting some marketing activities in motion (plans for implementation). This may be the result of certain objectives and strategies, each of which must be achieved within a given budget. Hence budgetary control is essential.

The next step in the control process is to establish specific performance standards that will need to be achieved for each area of activity if overall and sub-objectives are to be achieved. For example, in order to achieve a specified sales objective, a specific target of performance for each sales area may be required. In turn this may require a specific standard of perform-ance from each of the salespeople in the region with respect to, for example, number of calls, conversion rates and, of course, order value. Table 19.1 provides a representative sample of the types of data required. Marketing performance measures and standards will vary by company and product according to the goals and objectives delineated in the marketing plan.

The next step is to locate responsibility. In some cases responsibility ultimately falls on one person (e.g. the brand manager); in others it is shared (e.g. the sales manager and sales force). It is important to consider this issue, because corrective or supportive action may need to focus on those responsible for the success of marketing activity.

In order to be successful the people involved and affected by the control process should be consulted in both the design and implementation stages of marketing control. Above all they will need to be convinced that the purpose of control is to improve their own levels of success and that of the company. Subordinates need to be involved in setting and agreeing their own standards of performance, preferably through a system of management by objectives.

Table 19.1	Measures of marketing performance

Product	Distribution
● Sales by market segments ● New product introductions each year ● Sales relative to potential ● Sales growth rates ● Market share ● Contribution margin ● Product defects ● Warranty expense ● Percentage of total profits ● Return on investment	● Sales, expenses and contribution margin by channel type ● Percentage of stores carrying the product ● Sales relative to market potential by channel, intermediary type and specific intermediaries ● Percentage of on-time delivery ● Expense-to-sales ratio by channel, etc. ● Order cycle performance by channel, etc. ● Logistics cost by logistics activity by channel
Pricing	**Communication**
● Response time to price changes of competitors ● Price relative to competitor ● Price changes relative to sales volume ● Discount structure relative to sales volume ● Bid strategy relative to new contacts ● Margin structure relative to marketing expenses ● Margins relative to channel member performance	● Advertising effectiveness by type of media (e.g. awareness levels) ● Actual audience/target audience ratio ● Cost per contact ● Number of calls, enquiries and information requests by type of media ● Sales per sales call ● Sales per territory relative to potential ● Selling expenses to sales ratio ● New accounts per time period ● Lost accounts per time period

Source: adapted from Jobber, D. (1995) *Principles and Practice of Marketing*, published by McGraw-Hill.

Performance is then evaluated against these standards, which relies on an efficient information system. A judgement has to be made about the degree of success and failure achieved and what corrective or supportive action is to be taken. This can take various forms:

● Failure that is attributed to the poor performance of individuals may result in the giving of advice regarding future attitudes and actions, training and/or punishment (e.g. criticism, lower pay, demotion, termination of employment). Success, on the other hand, should be rewarded with praise, promotion and/or higher pay.

● Failure that is attributed to unrealistic marketing objectives and performance may cause management to lower objectives or lower marketing standards. Success that is thought to reflect unambitious objectives and standards may cause them to be raised in the next period.

Many firms assume that corrective action needs to be taken only when results are less than those required or when budgets and costs are being exceeded. In fact both 'negative' (under-achievement) and 'positive' (overachievement) deviations may require corrective action. For example, failure to spend the amount budgeted for, say, sales force expenses may indicate that the initial sum allocated was excessive and needs to be reassessed, and/or that the sales force is not as 'active' as it might be.

It is also necessary to determine such things as the frequency of measurement (e.g. daily, weekly, monthly or annually). More frequent and more detailed measurement usually means more cost. We need to be careful to ensure that the costs of measurement and the control process itself do not exceed the value of such measurements and do not overly interfere with the activities of those being measured.

The impact of the environment must also be taken into account when designing a control system:

- The control system should measure only dimensions over which the organization has control. Rewards or sanctions make little sense if they are based on dimensions that may be relevant for overall corporate performance, but over which no influence can be exerted (e.g. price controls). Neglecting the factor of individual performance capability would send the wrong signals and severely impair the motivation of personnel.
- Control systems should harmonize with local regulations and customs. In some cases, however, corporate behavioural controls have to be exercised against local customs even though overall operations may be affected negatively. This type of situation occurs, for example, when a subsidiary operates in markets where unauthorized facilitating payments are a common business practice.

Feedforward control

Feedforward control
Monitors variables other than performance – variables that may change before performance itself. In this way deviations can be controlled proactively before their full impact has been felt.

Much of the information provided by the firm's marketing control system is feedback on what has been accomplished in both financial (profits) and non-financial (customer satisfaction, market share) terms. As such, the control process is remedial in its outlook. It can be argued that control systems should be forward-looking and preventive, and that the control process should start at the same time as the planning process. Such a form of control is **feedforward control** (Figure 19.12).

Feedforward control would continuously evaluate plans, monitoring the environment to detect changes that would call for revising objectives and strategies. Feedforward control monitors variables other than performance; variables that may change before performance itself changes. The result is that deviations can be controlled before their full impact has been felt. Such a system is proactive in that it anticipates environmental change, whereas after-the-fact and steering control systems are more reactive in that they deal with changes after they occur. Examples of early symptoms (early performance indicators) are presented in Table 19.2.

Feedforward control focuses on information that is prognostic: it tries to discover problems waiting to occur. Formal processes of feedforward control can be incorporated into the business marketer's total control programme to enhance its effectiveness considerably. Utilization of a feedforward approach would help ensure that planning and control are treated as concurrent activities.

Table 19.2	Some key early performance indicators
Early performance indicators	**Market implication**
Sudden drop in quantities demanded	Problem in marketing strategy or its implementation
Sharp decrease or increase in sales volume	Product gaining acceptance or being rejected quickly
Customer complaints	Product not debugged properly
A notable decrease in competitors' business	Product gaining acceptance quickly or market conditions deteriorating
Large volumes of returned merchandise	Problems in basic product design
Excessive requests for parts or reported repairs	Problems in basic product design, low standards
Sudden changes in fashions or styles	Product (or competitors' product) causing a deep impact on the consumers' lifestyles

Source: Samli *et al.* (1993, p. 425).

Table 19.3	Types of marketing control		
Type of control	**Prime responsibility**	**Purpose of control**	**Examples of techniques/approaches**
Strategic control	Top management Middle management	To examine if planned results are being achieved	Marketing effectiveness ratings Marketing audit
Efficiency control	Line and staff management Marketing controller	To examine ways of improving the efficiency of marketing	Sales force efficiency Advertising efficiency Distribution efficiency
Annual plan control	Top management Middle management	To examine if planned results are being achieved	Sales analysis Market share analysis Marketing expenses to sales ratio Customer tracking
Profit control (budget control)	Marketing controller	To examine where the company is making and losing money	Profitability by e.g. product, customer group or trade channel

Source: adapted from Kotler, Philip, *Marketing Management: Analysis, Planning, Implementation and Control, 9th*, © 1997. Electronically reproduced by permission of Pearson Education, Inc., Upper Saddle River, New Jersey

Key areas for control in marketing

Kotler (1997) distinguishes four types of marketing control, each involving different approaches, different purposes and a different allocation of responsibilities. These are shown in Table 19.3. Here we will focus on annual plan control and profit control, since they are the most obvious areas of concern to firms with limited resources (e.g. SMEs).

Annual plan control

The purpose of annual plan control is to determine the extent to which marketing efforts over the year have been successful. This control will centre on measuring and evaluating sales in relation to sales goals, market share analysis and expense analysis.

Sales performance is a key element in annual plan control. Sales control consists of a hierarchy of standards on different organizational control levels. These are interlinked, as shown in Figure 19.13.

We can see from the diagram that any variances in achieving sales targets at the corporate level are the result of variances in the performance of individual salespeople at the operational level. At every level of sales control variances must be studied with a view to

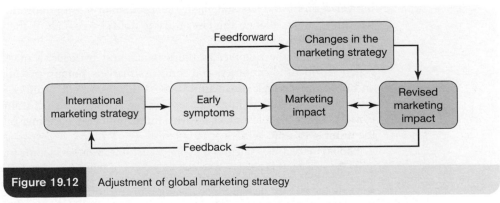

Figure 19.12	Adjustment of global marketing strategy

Source: Samli *et al.* (1993, p. 421).

| Figure 19.13 | The hierarchy of sales and control |

determining their causes. In general, variances may be due to a combination of factors in volume and/or price.

Profit control

In addition to the previously discussed control elements, all international marketers must be concerned to control their profit. The budgetary period is normally one year because budgets are tied to the accounting systems of the company. In the following section we will further explore how global marketing budgets are developed, the starting point being the GAM organization and the country-based structure of the company.

19.5 The global marketing budget

The classic quantification of a global marketing plan appears in the form of budgets. Because these are so rigorously quantified they are particularly important. They should represent a projection of actions and expected results, and they should be capable of accurate monitoring. Indeed performance against budget is the main (regular) management review process.

Budgeting is also an organization process that involves making forecasts based on the proposed marketing strategy and programmes. The forecasts are then used to construct a budgeted profit-and-loss statement (i.e. profitability). An important aspect of budgeting is deciding how to allocate the last available dollars across all of the proposed programmes within the marketing plan.

Recognizing the *customer* as the primary unit of focus, a market-based business will expand its focus to customers and countries/markets, not just products or units sold. This is an important strategic distinction because there is a finite number of potential customers, but a larger range of products and services can be sold to each customer. A business's volume is its customer share in a market with a finite number of customers at any point in time, not the number of units sold.

Global marketing strategies that affect customer volume include marketing strategies that:

- attract new customers to grow market share
- grow the market demand by bringing more customers into a market
- enter new markets to create new sources of customer volume.

All marketing strategies require *some* level of marketing effort to achieve a certain level of market share. Expenses associated with sales effort, market communications, customer service and market management are required to implement a marketing strategy designed to obtain a certain customer volume. The costs of this marketing effort are the *marketing expenses* and they must be deducted from the total contribution to produce a *net marketing contribution*.

Figure 19.14 illustrates the traditional marketing budget (per country or customer group) and its underlying determinants. From Figure 19.14 the most important measures of marketing profitability may be defined as:

$$\text{Contribution margin in \%} = \frac{\text{Total contribution}}{\text{Total revenue}} \times 100$$

$$\text{Marketing contribution margin \%} = \frac{\text{Total marketing contribution}}{\text{Total revenue}} \times 100$$

$$\text{Profit margin \%} = \frac{\text{Net profit (before taxes)}}{\text{Total revenue}} \times 100$$

$$\text{Return on assets (ROA)} = \frac{\text{Net profit (before taxes)}}{\text{Assets}}$$

If we have information about the size of assets (accounts receivable + inventory + cash + plant + equipment) we could also define:

$$\text{Return on assets (ROA)} = \frac{\text{Net profit (before taxes)}}{\text{Assets}}$$

ROA is similar to the well-known measure: ROI = return on investment.

Table 19.4 presents an example of a global marketing budget for a manufacturer of consumer goods. Included in the budget are those marketing variables that can be controlled and changed by the sales and marketing functions (departments) in the home country and in the export market. In Table 19.4 the only variable that cannot be controlled by the international sales and marketing departments is variable costs.

The global marketing budget system (as presented in Table 19.4) is used for the following (main) purposes:

- Allocation of marketing resources among countries/markets to maximize profits. In Table 19.4 it is the responsibility of the global marketing director to maximize the total contribution 2 for the whole world.
- Evaluation of country/market performance. In Table 19.4 it is the responsibility of export managers or country managers to maximize contribution 2 for each of their countries.

Note that besides the marketing variables presented in Table 19.4 the global marketing budget normally contains inventory costs for finished goods. As the production sizes of these goods are normally based on input from the sales and marketing department, the inventory of unsold goods will also be the responsibility of the international marketing manager or director. Furthermore, the global marketing budget may also contain customer-specific or country-specific product development costs, if certain new products are preconditions for selling in certain markets.

In contrast to budgets, long-range plans extend over periods from two to ten years, and their content is more qualitative and judgemental in nature than that of budgets. For SMEs shorter periods (such as two years) are the norm because of the perceived uncertainty of diverse foreign environments.

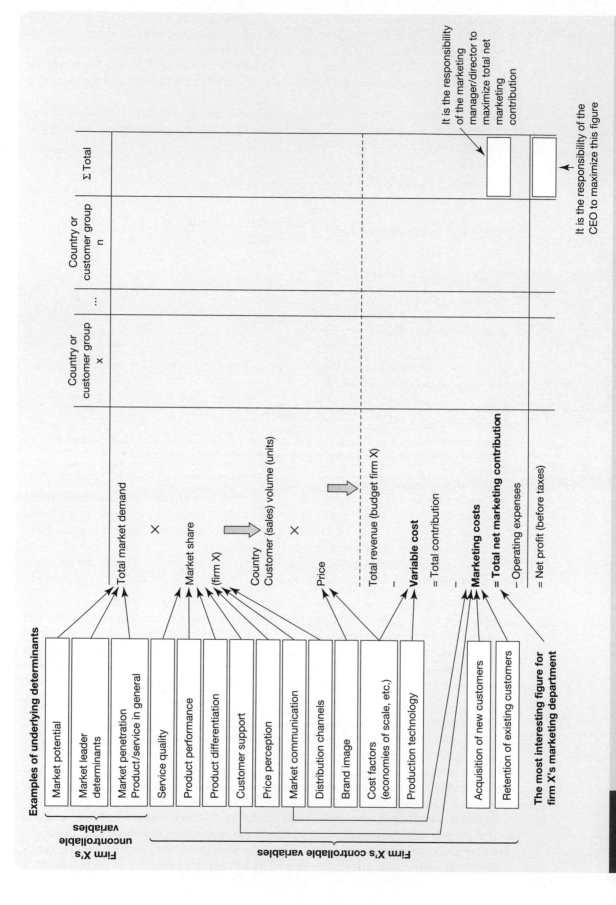

Figure 19.14 Marketing budget 200X and its underlying determinants

Table 19.4	An example of an international marketing budget for a manufacturer exporting consumer goods											

International marketing budget	Europe					America				Asia/Pacific			
	UK		Germany		France		USA		Japan		Korea		Other markets
Year = _____	A	B	A		A		A		A	B	A	B	A	B	A	B

Net sales (gross sales less trade discounts, allowances, etc.)

÷ Variable costs
= Contribution 1
÷ Marketing costs:

Sales costs (salaries, commissions for agents, incentives, travelling, training, conferences)

Consumer marketing costs (TV commercials, radio, print, sales promotion)

Trade marketing costs (fairs, exhibitions, in-store promotions, contributions for retailer campaigns)

= Σ **Total contribution 2**
(marketing contribution)

B = budget figures; **A** = actual.

Note: on a short-term (one-year) basis, the export managers or country managers are responsible for maximizing the actual figures for each country and minimizing their deviation from budget figures. The international marketing manager/director is responsible for maximizing the actual figure for the total world and minimizing its deviation from the budget figure. Cooperation is required between the country managers and the international marketing manager/director to coordinate and allocate the total marketing resources in an optimum way. Sometimes certain inventory costs and product development costs may also be included in the total marketing budget (see main text).
Source: Hollensen (2010).

19.6 The process of developing the global marketing plan

The purpose of the global marketing plan is to create sustainable competitive advantages in the global marketplace. Generally, firms go through some kind of mental process in developing global marketing plans. In SMEs this process is normally informal; in larger organizations it is often more systematized. Figure 1.2 (pp.8–11) at the start of the book offers a systematized approach to developing a global marketing plan.

19.7 Summary

Implementation of a global marketing programme requires an appropriate organizational structure. As the scope of a firm's global marketing strategy changes its organizational structure must be modified in accordance with its tasks and technology and the external environment. Five ways of structuring an international organization have been presented: functional structure, international divisional structure, product structure, geographical structure (customer structure) and matrix structure. The choice of organizational structure is affected by such factors as the degree of internationalization of the firm, the strategic importance of the firm's international operations, the complexity of its international business and the availability of qualified managers.

Control is the process of ensuring that global marketing activities are carried out as intended. It involves monitoring aspects of performance and taking corrective action where necessary. The global marketing control system consists of deciding marketing objectives, setting performance standards, locating responsibility, evaluating performance against standards and taking corrective or supportive action.

In an after-the-fact control system, managers wait until the end of the planning period to take corrective action. In a feedforward control system, corrective action is taken during the planning period by tracking early performance indicators and steering the organization back to desired objectives if it goes out of control.

The most obvious areas of control relate to the control of the annual marketing plan and the control of profitability. The purpose of the global marketing budget is mainly to allocate marketing resources across countries to maximize worldwide total marketing contribution.

CASE STUDY 19.1

Mars Inc.: merger of the European food, pet care and confectionery divisions

Mars Inc. is a diversified multifunctional company whose primary products include foods, petcare, confectionery, electronics and drinks. Owned and controlled by the Mars family, this US giant is one of the world's biggest private companies, but also one of the most secretive.

Mars' decision in January 2000 to merge its food, pet care and confectionery divisions across Europe – and eventually with headquarters in the UK – has split the marketing industry.

The most well-known brands within the three divisions are:

Martin Keane/PA/EMPICS

- foods: Uncle Ben's rice and sauces;
- pet care: Whiskas, Pedigree;
- confectionery: M&Ms, Snickers, Milky Way, Mars Bar.

Mars UK says the decision to pool the businesses was taken to strike at the company's international competitors in food and confectionery, such as Nestlé and Unilever. The move also coincides with plans to create a single European market and highlights the company's belief that its consumers' needs are the same across the continent.

However, the combination of food and confectionery with pet care is not clear to all industry observers. One industry analyst made the comment:

Generally speaking, Mars is doing the right thing by merging divisions to squeeze profits out of them. Before the advent of the euro it was acceptable to run separate companies in different European countries but not any more.

Another analyst said: 'I can't imagine it marketing all three sides of the business together. They're too different.'

The only visible benefit appears to be an improvement in distribution. Tastes across European markets are very different, whether you're selling products for animals or people.

It's all very well Mars saying it will tackle competitors such as Nestlé and Unilever, but they are only rivals in food and confectionery.

If Mars starts laying down too many controls by merging all its businesses – and therefore also its marketing and management strategies – it may streamline communications, but could lose the creativity available in different regions.

Source: McCawley (2000).

QUESTIONS

1. Discuss the two views of organizing Mars' European activities.
2. Did Mars Inc. do the right thing in your opinion?

CASE STUDY 19.2

Henkel: should Henkel shift to a more customer-centric organization?

Henkel is a multinational company headquartered in Düsseldorf, Germany. It has about 52,000 employees worldwide and counts among the most internationally aligned German-based companies in the global marketplace. The company was founded in Aachen, Germany in 1876 by the 28-year-old Fritz Henkel and two partners. Its first product was washing powder based on water-glass. In contrast to all similar products, which at that time were sold loose, this heavy-duty detergent was marketed in handy packets.

Today the company's products and technologies are distributed in approximately 125 countries around the world. Henkel has three globally operating business sectors:

Henkel.

Henkel.

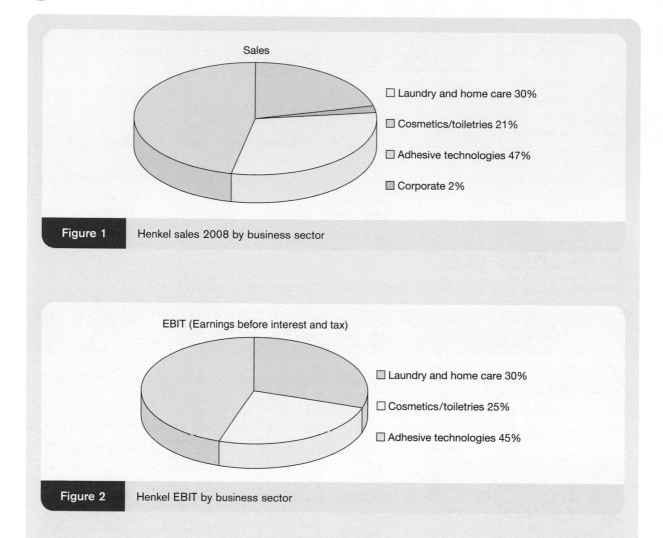

Figure 1 Henkel sales 2008 by business sector

Figure 2 Henkel EBIT by business sector

Laundry and home care has always played an important role for Henkel particularly because the company had started with a product from this business sector. It consists of household cleaning products such as laundry detergent and dishwashing liquid. One of the most well-known products is the washing powder Persil.

Cosmetics and toiletries are the second key business sector. Henkel's cosmetic division is one of the largest of its kind in the world. It consists of beauty and oral care products such as shampoo, toothpaste, hair colourants and shower gel.

The *adhesive technologies* market is where Henkel is the undisputed market leader. Here the company produces adhesives, sealants and surface treatments for consumers, craftsmen and industrial applications.

Henkel is an innovation driven company that controls a well-balanced portfolio of international, regional and local brands. The annual research and development investment is 2.7 per cent of sales. The target groups for Henkel's products are consumers, craftsmen and industrial users. Henkel's credo is to provide superior (customized) solutions and innovative technologies for the individual business-to-consumer (B2C) and business-to-business client (B2B).

Its main competitors in the laundry and home care division are Unilever, Procter & Gamble and Reckitt Benckiser. In its cosmetics and toiletries division, its competitors are Unilever, Procter & Gamble and L'Oréal.

In order to live up to this commitment Henkel's employees work closely with B2C (lead users) and B2B customers (global accounts) and focus on their current needs as well as on the challenges which they will face in the future. This customer-centric philosophy is the main reason why Henkel

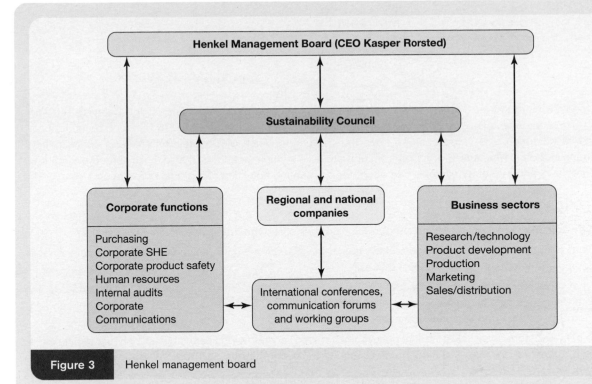

Figure 3	Henkel management board

has become a partner of choice for many leading companies.

The Henkel management board is responsible for the sustainability policy. Led by the chairman of the management board, the sustainability council, whose members are drawn from all areas of the company, steers the global sustainability activities. Henkel has successfully implemented company-wide control instruments and regional action programmes. Achievements and advances are recorded transparently and improvement measures can be aligned optimally to the respective social challenges and priorities.

Henkel-Walmart

In 2003 Walmart, the world's largest public corporation by revenue, according to Fortune Global 500 and one of Henkel's global customers increasingly demanded an intensified, global relationship. Retailers are slowly becoming more powerful than the manufacturers, because they are launching their own brands. At the same time overall trade revenues are growing due to the retailer's internationalization

strategy. Prices are slowly approaching the production costs of the products. Henkel is considering shifting its strategy from a product-centric to a more customer-centric approach. Consequently, the new CEO, Kasper Rorsted, is considering implementing a 'glocal' approach, coordinating multidimensional global processes and local/regional distribution. This is now embedded in a global account management programme with Walmart.

QUESTIONS

1. Is it a good idea to shift the Henkel organization from a more product- to a more customer-centric approach?

2. What are the challenges of being a customer-driven multinational that serves both B2B and B2C customers?

3. How can Henkel intensify the B2B relation with its key global customers?

The case is developed by: Ph.D. researcher Vlad Stefan Wulff, University of Southern Denmark.

VIDEO CASE STUDY 19.3 McDonald's

download from www.pearsoned.co.uk/hollensen

McDonald's Corporation (McDonald's) (www.mcdonalds.com) is the world's largest food service retailing chain. The company is known for its burgers and fries which it sells through 31,000 fast-food restaurants in over 119 countries. The video case explores the challenges which McDonald's may face in consolidating revenues and other financial information from operations in multiple countries. It also looks at recognizing how differing laws and monetary systems can affect the accounting activities of a global corporation.

Questions

1. Why does McDonald's use 'constant currency' comparisons when reporting its financial results?

2. What effect do the corporate income tax rates in the countries where McDonald's operates have on the income statements prepared in local offices?

3. What problems might arise if individual McDonald's restaurants were required to enter sales data directly onto the company's centralized accounting website, instead of following the current procedure of sending it through country and regional channels?

4. To help investors and analysts better assess the company's worldwide financial health, should McDonald's be required to disclose detailed financial results for every country and region? Support your chosen position.

For further exercises and cases, see this book's website at **www.pearsoned.co.uk/hollensen**

Questions for discussion

1. This chapter suggests that the development of a firm's international organization can be divided into different stages. Identify these stages and discuss their relationship to the international competitiveness of the firm.

2. Identify appropriate organizational structures for managing international product development. Discuss key features of the structure(s) suggested.

3. What key internal/external factors influence the organizational structure? Can you think of additional factors? Explain.

4. Discuss the pros and cons of standardizing the marketing management process. Is a standardized process of more benefit to the company pursuing a national market strategy or a global market strategy?

5. Discuss to what degree the choice of organizational structure is essentially a choice between headquarters centralization and local autonomy.

6. Discuss how the international organization of a firm may affect its planning process.

7. Discuss why firms need global marketing controls.

8. What is meant by performance indicators? Why does a firm need them?

9. Performance reviews of subsidiary managers and personnel are required rarely, if at all, by headquarters. Why?

10. Identify the major weaknesses inherent in the international division structure.

11. Discuss the benefits gained by adopting a matrix organizational structure.

References

Bartlett, C. and Ghoshal, S. (1989) *Managing Across Borders: The Transnational Solution*. Boston, MA, Harvard University Press.

Harvey, M., Myers, M.B. and Novicevic, M.M. (2002) 'The managerial issues associated with global account management', *Thunderbird International Business Review*, 44(5), pp. 625–647.

Hollensen, S. (2006) 'Global account management (GAM): two case studies illustrating the organizational set-up', *The Marketing Management Journal*, 16(1), pp. 244–250.

Hollensen, S. (2010) *Marketing Management – A Relationship Approach*, 2nd edn. Financial Times/Prentice Hall, Harlow.

Jobber, D. (1995) *Principles and Practice of Marketing*. McGraw-Hill, New York.

Kotler, P. (1997) *Marketing Management: Analysis, Planning, Implementation and Control*, 9th edn. Prentice-Hall, Englewood Cliffs, NJ.

McCawley, I. (2000) 'Can Mars bridge gaps in merger?' *Marketing Week*, News Analysis, 13 January.

McDonald, M., Millman, T. and Rogers, B. (1997) 'Key account management: theory, practice and challenges', *Journal of Marketing Management*, 13, pp. 737–757.

Millman, T. and Wilson, K. (1995) 'From key account selling to key account management', *Journal of Marketing Practice: Applied Marketing Science*, 1, pp. 9–21.

Ojasalo, J. (2001) 'Key account management at company and individual levels in B2B relationships', *The Journal of Business and Industrial Marketing*, 16(3), pp. 199–220.

Peppers, D. and Rogers, M. (1995) 'A new marketing paradigm: share of customer, not market share', *Harvard Business Review*, July–August, pp. 105–113.

Prashantham, S. and Birkinshaw, J. (2008) 'Dancing with gorillas: how small companies can partner effectively with MNCs', *California Management Review*, 51(1), pp. 6–23.

Quelch, J.A. (1992) 'The new country managers', *The McKinsey Quarterly*, 4, pp. 155–165.

Quelch, J.A. and Bloom, H. (1996) 'The return of the country manager', *The McKinsey Quarterly*, 2, pp. 30–43.

Samli, A.C., Still, R. and Hill, J.S. (1993) *International Marketing: Planning and Practice*. Macmillan, London.

Scheraga, P. (2005) 'Balancing act at IKEA', *Chain Store Age*, 81(6), pp. 45–46.

Shi, Linda, H., Zou, Shaoming and Cavusgil, S. Tamer (2004) 'A conceptual framework of global account management capabilities and firm performance', *International Business Review*, 13, pp. 539–553.

Shi, Linda, H., Zou, Shaoming, White, J. Cris, McNally, Regina, C. and Cavusgil, S. Tamer (2005) 'Executive insights: global account management capability: insights from leading suppliers', *Journal of International Marketing*, 13(2), pp. 93–113.

Wilson, K. and Millman, T. (2003) 'The global account manager as political entrepreneur', *Industrial Marketing Management*, 32, pp. 151–158.

Yip, G.S. and Bink, A.J.M. (2007) 'Managing global accounts', *Harvard Business Review*, September, pp. 103–111.

CASE STUDY V.1

Sony Music Entertainment: new worldwide organizational structure and the marketing, planning and budgeting of Pink's new album

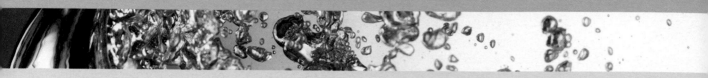

On a sunny December day in 2009 the Executive Vice President Marketing for Sony Music Entertainment (SME), Tim Prescott, gets on a plane from New York bound for London where, among other things, he is going to meet megastar Pink about the marketing campaign of her new CD release in Autumn 2010. Pink was one of BMG's best-selling artists, and Tim is looking forward to meeting the star personally.

New in his job as Executive Vice President, Tim uses the plane trip over the Atlantic to study the global music industry more thoroughly,

With a world market share of 22 per cent (Universal Music has 26 per cent) SME is still number 2 in the industry, but they can not relax – the competitors (EMI and Warner Music) are not far behind.

In August 2008 the international media and entertainment companies Sony Corporation and Bertelsmann AG announced that Sony had agreed to acquire Bertelsmann's 50 per cent stake in Sony BMG. The new music company, to be called Sony Music Entertainment Inc. (SME), became a wholly owned subsidiary of Sony Corporation of America. SME's HQ is in New York.

SME operates music labels such as Arista Records, Upstate Records, Columbia Records, Epic Records, J Records, Jive Records, RCA Records, LaFace Records and Zomba Records. The sale price was not disclosed when the deal was announced in August, but news reports valued it at $1.5 billion.

After landing in London Tim hurries to the meeting with Pink, but on the way he thinks about the new global organizational structure of Sony Music Entertainment.

In spring 2009 Sony Music Entertainment introduced a new organizational strategy for its music labels and corporate staff that would allow the company to focus on creating global music superstars who reach across geographical boundaries. The streamlining of the organization eliminates regional corporate groups in Europe, Asia and Latin American regions, and creates four new strategic groups within SME: Office of the Chairman, Label Group, Territory Management and Corporate Center. All management from the groups will report directly to the CEO, Rolf Schmidt-Holtz.

Sony Music Entertainment wants to strengthen relationships with its artists. The top management of the company thinks this structure allows its creative executives to be closer to artists, while allowing managers to better support their creative executives. Sony Music Entertainment wants an organization built on record labels with global reach. The labels and the creative executives should be able to work more closely with artists while being able to rely on effective global marketing capabilities.

Label Group will consist of US-based record labels including Arista Records, RCA Music Group, Jive/Zomba, La Face Records and RLG-Nashville, as well as Music Publishing.

Territory Management will consist of major territories and country groups, such as Japan, Germany/Switzerland/Austria, the United Kingdom, Australia and South Africa.

Reporting to the Office of the Chairman, Tim Prescott will serve as the company's highest-ranking marketing executive, overseeing global marketing campaigns for Sony Music Entertainment artists. Also reporting to the Office of the Chairman are Human Resources, Strategy and New Technology and Corporate Communications.

One of Tim's first tasks in the summer of 2009 was to create the worldwide marketing plan for the UK-singer Pink and her new album released in September 2010. Hence, at Tim's meeting with Pink in London they agree that the launch of Pink's CD should start up in the United Kingdom in an effort to get to the top of the charts as quickly as possible.

First some general information about the newest market data from the global music industry.

The world music industry in 2009

A handful of music companies (operating through several hundred subsidiaries and over a thousand labels) account for most records sold in the advanced economies. Music publishing – production and licensing of intellectual property rights – is even more concentrated.

Table 1	The global recorded music industry

Record company	Market shares (%) on the world market for recorded music (2009)
Universal Music Group	26
Sony Music Entertainment	20
EMI Group	13
Warner Music	11
Independent labels	30
Total	100 (approximately $30 billion)

Source: based on International Federation of the Phonographic Industry (IFPI), www.ifpi.com.

In 2009 the global recorded music industry was estimated at $30 billion. Total annual unit sales (CDs, music videos, MP3s) in 2009 were approximately 3 billion. The approximate market shares on the world market are shown in Table 1.

Over the past 100 years we have seen the music industry evolve through three basic stages, characterized by different technologies and different publishing organisations. Prior to the gramophone, when sheet music was the primary vehicle for disseminating popular music, the industry was dominated by music publishing houses. With the rise of recording (and subsequently broadcasting, which was driven by the availability of 'canned content'), those publishers were displaced by the record companies.

Today, increasingly the industry has involved entertainment groups that bring together a broad range of content distribution and repackaging activities – broadcast, film, video, booking and performance management agencies, records, music licensing, print publishing.

See also the value chain of the music recording industry in Figure 1.

Next some further information about the artist, Pink.

Pink – one of the best-selling pop-rock artists

Pink (Alecia Beth Moore) was born 8 September 1979 in Pennsylvania. To date she has sold over 31 million

Pink
WireImage/Getty images.

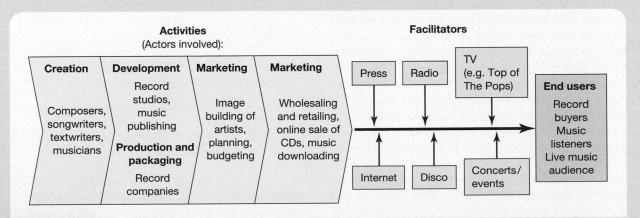

Figure 1	The value chain in the music industry

albums worldwide. Her songs are characterized by their personally rebellious tone and a statement-like strict use of the first person.

She released her first single *There You Go* and first album, the R&B-oriented *Can't Take Me Home*, in 2000 via LaFace Records, which garnered commercial success. Her more pop rock-oriented second studio album, *Missundaztood*, which began a marked shift in the sound of her music, was released in 2001, and was successful worldwide. The CD *Can't Take Me Home* was certified double platinum in the US, sold 5 million copies worldwide and produced more top 10 singles.

On the second album, Pink took her sound in a new direction and sought more creative control during the recording of her second album. She recruited Linda Perry, former singer of 4 Non Blondes (one of Pink's favourites in her teenage years). The album, named *Missundaztood* because of Pink's belief that people had a wrong image of her, was released in November 2001.

Its lead single, *Get the Party Started* (written and produced by Perry), went top five in the US and many other countries, and number one in Australia.

Pink's third and fourth studio albums went well but sales were not excellent.

Funhouse, the fifth studio album by Pink was released by LaFace Records worldwide in October 2008. Upon its release, the album reached number one on the charts in Australia, New Zealand and United Kingdom, while debuting at number two in Germany, Ireland, France and United States. The album's lead single, *So What*, was the biggest solo success of Pink's career until then, topping the charts in eleven countries so far, including her native United States, the UK, Germany and in Australia, and reaching the top five in many others. Pink has stated that this album is her most vulnerable to date. Much of the album's subject matter alludes to the fact that Moore recently separated from her husband, Carey Hart. However, they did not sign legal divorce documents: a divorce was planned but did not proceed. The first single, *So What*, opens with: 'I guess I just lost my husband/I don't know where he went' *Please Don't Leave Me* also addresses the split. The artist sums up its theme thus: 'Okay, I'm an asshole, but love me anyway.'

Funhouse became Pink's first number one album in the UK, entering at number one on 2 November 2008. It has currently been certified three times platinum with sales of over 900,000. As well as the release of the singles from *Funhouse*, other noticeable promotions which have helped the album have longevity on the charts include the first leg of her UK tour which started in April 2009 and ended in May.

In order to promote *Funhouse* a number of PR activities were performed in the second half of 2008:

Pink's *Funhouse* iPhone App was created in support of *Funhouse* and represents the first artist-themed promotional app to be made for the iPhone App platform.

On 6 November 2008 Pink performed her hit single *So What* at the MTV Europe Music Awards during a live show where 40,000 feathers were released on stage, making her unable to sing the line '*And you're a tool, so . . .*'

Pink has appeared on many talks shows to help promote the album – *The Today Show* on 28 October; *The View* on 29 October; *Late Night with Conan O'Brien* on 30 October; *CBS Early Show* on 3 November; and the *Ellen Degeneres Show* on 24 November.

Pink appeared on German talk show *Wetten, dass . .?* in December 2008.

Pink's sixth album is expected in autumn 2010.

The typical value chain for a CD

The following shows how the 'value added' of a typical CD album is split among the various players in the value chain:

	£
Retail price to consumers	12
Price to retail	9
Price to distributor	6
Price to distributor (exclusive of artist royalty)	5

For a CD single the full retail price to consumers is about £3, but when a record is being pushed hard by the record label retailers are offered big discounts in an attempt to shift units in the all-important first week. In such circumstances singles can retail for as little as 99p.

Development
In the music industry record labels will actively seek to sign up bands and artistes on long-term exclusive contracts. A key to success in development is to spot talent and to sign it up early.

Production
Production is relatively cheap in the music industry, and the cost of digital recording equipment and production of CDs is falling rapidly. Some consumers do not understand why the sale price of a CD is so much higher than the cost of producing the actual physical disc. However, as described below, there are many different activities and costs involved in creating songs and marketing the end result, the CD.

Distributors

Major distributors have a global network of branch offices to handle the sales, marketing and distribution process. Sometimes the distributors may outsource the physical distribution process.

Retail

Retailers put in orders to the wholesalers as and when albums and singles are required. In the United Kingdom the retail chains are dominated by HMV. These chains account for about 80 per cent of the market.

The costs of a hit

Singles are released with the purpose of getting to the top of the charts. The financial risks involved in mounting an attack on the UK charts have never been greater. According to research carried out by BBC News Online, securing a top ten hit in the United Kingdom in the current climate is likely to cost a minimum of £125,000. Ever-increasing amounts of financial resources are being thrown at marketing and promotion in the hope that a single will be picked up by MTV, radio and, perhaps most importantly, the major retailers, in order to secure the highest chart entry.

Biggest cost categories

Of course the most important component of a CD is the artist's effort that goes into developing the music. Artists spend a large portion of their creative energy on writing song lyrics and composing music or working with producers and A&R executives to find great songs from great writers. This task can take weeks, months, or even years. The creative ability of these artists to produce the music, combined with the time and energy they spend throughout that process, is in itself priceless. But while the creative process is priceless, it must be compensated. Artists receive royalties on each recording, which vary according to their contract, and the songwriter gets royalties too. In addition, the label incurs the costs of finding and signing new artists.

Once an artist or group has songs composed they then go into a studio and begin recording. The costs of recording, including studio fees, musicians, sound engineers, producers and others, must all be recovered by the price of the CD.

Then come marketing and promotion costs – perhaps the most expensive part of the music business today. They include increasingly expensive video clips, public relations, tour support, marketing campaigns and promotion to get the songs played. Labels make investments in artists by paying for both the production and the promotion of the album. New technology such as the Internet offers new ways for artists to reach music fans, but it still requires that some entity, whether a traditional label or another kind of company, market and promote the artist so that fans are aware of new releases.

For every album released in a given year a marketing strategy was developed to make that album stand out from the others hitting the market. Artwork must be designed for the CD box, and promotional materials (posters, store displays and music videos) developed and produced. For many artists a costly concert tour is essential to promote their recordings.

Another factor commonly overlooked in assessing CD prices is to assume that all CDs are equally profitable. In fact the vast majority are never profitable; for example, in the United States, 27,000 new releases hit the market every year. Most of these CDs never sell enough to recover costs. In the end, less than 10 per cent are profitable and, in effect, it is these recordings that finance the rest.

Marketing and promotion costs

Singles are essentially 3–4 minute adverts for CD albums. Singles' sales guarantee chart places and, in turn, radio play – and that is why music label companies persist with them. They are a kind of loss-leader for albums, where the real money is made.

The biggest expense is normally the promotional video, which for a mainstream artist starts at about £40,000 and can cost anything up to £1 million (however, this is exceptional). If the music video is to be shown on, say, MTV it has to comply with a number of requirements, which are set out by MTV (use of alcohol, sex, etc.).

It is common practice for the big retailers, for example HMV, to charge music label companies for promoting a single in their shops. This comes in the form of a 'singles pack', which guarantees a prominent position for the product in the shop. There are also bonuses to be paid to the sales force to check that the single is being properly promoted in-store.

The singles chart – compiled each week by different organizations and TV stations, such as *Top of the Pops* on the BBC, has always been the cornerstone of the UK music industry. More singles are sold in the United Kingdom than anywhere in the world – including the United States, where the album remains king. In 2000 it took an average of 118,700 sold singles to secure a number one spot in the UK chart. Since 2005 the UK singles chart has combined actual release sales with legal online downloads. Initially the proportion of digital sales to physical sales was relatively low, but now (2009) more than 80 per cent of single sales take place online. Sales via mobile phones and video downloads are also now counted.

Here are some of the basic costs for a 'typical' UK top ten single:

	£
Recording	3,500
Promotion video	100,000–150,000
Remixes (of the original single)	5,000–10,000
Merchandising	15,000
Posters	10,000
Stickers	5,000
PR (Press)	5,000
Promotion copies to radio stations, etc.	8,000
Website	20,000
Manufacturing costs (20p per CD)	10,000
Optional costs:	
Press ads	15,000
Billboard campaign	50,000
TV/radio/Internet advertising	200,000

Because of the high costs involved combined with the general decline in the sales of CDs and singles (due to the trend towards online downloading of songs), many industry insiders think the singles market cannot continue in its current form. One possible escape route is the radio-only release, where a track from an album is promoted to radio stations, but is not actually available to buy. This often happens in the United States, where there is less emphasis on singles' sales, and the singles chart is largely based on radio play.

Sources: adapted from: International Federation of the Phonographic Industry (IFPI), www.ifpi.com; www.sonymusic.com; www.sonybmg.com; RIAA, 'The costs of a CD', http://www.riaa.com/MD-US-7.cfm, 2003; BMG press release, New York, 23 January 2003; BBC News, 'Sony and BMG merger backed by EU', 19 July; BBC News, 'Sony BMG deal under new scrutiny', 13 July 2006.

QUESTIONS

1. What do you think of the change in Sony Music Entertainment's organizational structure, from a geographical structure to an artist-driven organization?

2. How would you produce a sales and marketing budget for Pink's forthcoming single and album?

3. How would you control your budgets? What key figures would you monitor?

4. Which marketing mix would you suggest to increase Sony Music Entertainment's share in the UK market, where the company has less than 20 per cent market share?

5. Discuss acquisition as a possible growth strategy.

CASE STUDY V.2

OneCafé: a 'born global' penetrates the coffee industry

OneCafé International AB was founded in September 2001 and is a packaging company. The company develops systems for brewing and serving a single cup of fresh coffee.

The background story

In 2001, Håkan Löfholm and Lars Bendix had a cup of coffee at Arlanda Airport in Stockholm. As usual, this was not a very pleasant experience, and, while reluctantly sipping their coffee, they started to wonder why there wasn't an easy way to make a cup of freshly brewed coffee.

As true entrepreneurs, Håkan and Lars couldn't stop thinking about the problem. Together they started to investigate the matter. They soon discovered that many others had tried before them, and by studying their mistakes they started to realize what problems they had to solve. One of the crucial barriers to cross was the construction of the filter bag. It had to contain the coffee, but still be able to let the water flow through without any barriers. In addition, the package had to be designed in a way that made it easy to use and dispose of without stains and leakages.

After two years of research and development, they had a fully functional prototype. At this point, they decided that it was time to make it in to a full-time commitment. Together with Frank Thygesen and Johnny Ragazzo they formed OneCafé International AB (www.onecafe.se).

Production in Uganda – being a social responsible company

Almost from the start, OneCafé realized that they needed an especially grinded coffee with superior quality. Their research led them to Africa – and to Uganda. Here OneCafé found not just coffee beans of the right quality, but also craftsmen and women with both the experience and commitment. In cooperation with them, OneCafé developed the brand, Uganda Original. This is now produced at their own plant in Uganda, Elgonia OneCafé International Ltd.

OneCafé International.

Initially, the reason for manufacturing both the coffee and the package in Uganda was to maintain a consistent grade of high quality throughout the whole production process – from bean to cup. Soon it also became a significant part of the vision that drives OneCafé: sustainable development.

With their presence in Uganda, OneCafé can actually make a difference. They can contribute to Uganda's development and ensure that the farmers get a fair part of the profit. OneCafé has also decided to work in accordance with UN's Millennium Development Goals 2015 (http://cyberschoolbus.un.org/). This means that OneCafé, among other things, strives to promote gender equality and empower women to ensure environmental sustainability and to be a part of a global partnership for development.

As an example, OneCafé supports a project to plant trees to improve the farmers' coffee production. Coffee grown without tree shade yields 2 kg beans per tree on average. By planting a tree that shadows about ten plants, the yield grows to 4 kg each, which means an extra 20 kg per year from the ten coffee plants. On addition, the beans produced are larger and of better quality. Planting trees also helps to sustain underground water sources and control of landslides.

How to brew a cup of OneCafé

OneCafé International.

Competitors

OneCafé competes with other one-cup serving systems. The competition includes several different products in different markets:

- Instant coffee (freeze- or spray-dried) e.g. Nescafé.
- 3 in 1 – single portion concepts (instant coffee, powdered milk, sugar).
- Single Pod machine systems (e.g. Senseo, Nespresso and Cafissimo).
- Coffee makers for filter brewing.
- French press (Cafétiere, Bodum).
- Teabags with instant and fresh coffee, e.g. Folgers coffee singles.
- Open filter bag solutions for placing on or in the cup, e.g. Cafusa and Rombouts.

The most similar products available are drip-in and drip-on solutions for fresh coffee (e.g. Rombouts and Cafusa). These products are most common in Japan, the UK, Belgium and Greece. However, the main competition is instant, freeze-dried coffee solutions. OneCafé is an alternative product to instant coffee products such as Nescafé.

Concerning the one-portion concept without machines, a number of established roasting companies in the USA, among them Maxwell House (Kraft Foods) and Folgers (Procter & Gamble) have discovered the single cup market. Several years ago, these companies introduced one-portion coffee, which they chose to call 'coffee singles – 100 per cent pure coffee'. The filter bag, which is basically a traditional tea bag, contains up to 50 per cent additives of instant coffee. They have not been able to produce a product made only of fresh coffee beans.

The coffee supply chain and OneCafé's role within this

The coffee supply chain process varies greatly depending on origin country and buyer. In some countries, beans are exported through government coffee boards while other countries use private exporters only. After they are shipped to the import country, coffee beans are visually inspected and test-tasted for quality through a process called 'cupping'. After passing inspection, coffee is stored in warehouses until it is shipped to roasters. Large roasters often have their own coffee buyers and procure green beans directly from producers. Large roasters also stockpile green coffee at the import warehouses to help decrease their exposure to market conditions. Conversely, smaller roasters bought coffee from independent brokers and importers who may have beans at warehouses and thus were exposed to a much larger risk of price fluctuations.

After roasters buy green coffee, the beans are shipped to roasting facilities where they are roasted until they receive their characteristic colour and aroma, and then cooled. Once the beans are cooled, roasters blend beans from different countries to balance the flavours and strengths. This process is essential because it allows for a consistent flavour even if supplies vary due to prices and availability. Roasters then package, market and distribute coffee through a variety of methods. The largest roasters grind and vacuum-pack coffee in packed bricks or cans and distribute their products through wholesale channels. These roasters can supply coffee for restaurants, airlines and hotels in addition to selling directly to consumer through retail channels. Specialty coffee, in contrast, is roasted and packaged in a manner to guarantee quality and freshness. It is sold in both whole bean and ground forms through wholesale and retail channels.

In the OneCafé case the supply chain is somewhat different (see Figure 1). Until now OneCafé has packaged directly on the spot in their own production unit, Elgonia OneCafé. However, during 2008 OneCafé developed their own packaging machine, where 55–60 OneCafé units per minute can be produced on the production line.

As illustrated in Figure 1 there are several options:

- Offer the production and packaging machine line for the big roasters on a license basis. This means that the big coffee companies could offer the OneCafé in

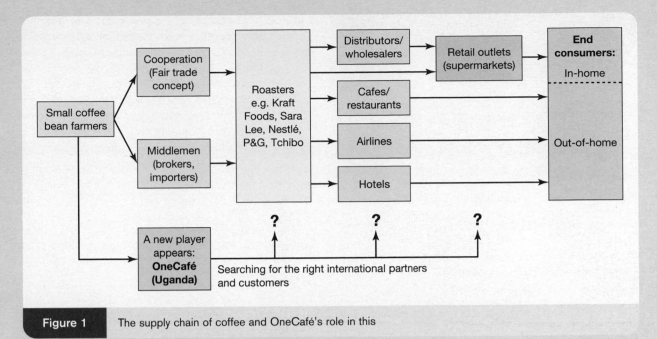

Figure 1   The supply chain of coffee and OneCafé's role in this

their product range with their own logo or as co-branding with OneCafé. This could be done for a small licensing royalty per produced unit or an annual license fee.

- OneCafé could produce the OneCafé products itself and sell them to the big roasters as an OEM-product under the roaster's logo or with OneCafé co-branding.
- OneCafé could sell its product directly to the distributors/wholesalers and/or directly to the retail chains under the OneCafé brand.
- OneCafé could sell its product directly to the retail chains under its own brands (private labels), or combined with some OneCafé co-branding.
- OneCafé could sell its product directly to the catering (food service) market under its own brand (e.g. under the hotel group name) or as co-branding with OneCafé. The possible cooperation partners would be restaurant chains, hotel chains, airline catering companies, etc.

The average retail price across borders for one 'OneCafé' is around €0.8 (the price paid by the end-consumer in the retail outlet).

Two new business opportunities come up

During 2008 two new business concepts are introduced as a direct spin-off from the original One-Café concept.

Cafe2Fly

Cafe2fly is a new product within the 'coffee-to-go' market segment.

This concept is based on a specific product idea. The 'technology' of Cafe2Fly is hidden in the patented cup lid of the cardboard cup (see the two pictures). In the top of the cup lid there is a filter, which prevents the coffee grounds coming into the mouth of the coffee drinker.

You can brew one cup of fresh coffee in the following way:

1. Pour roasted coffee into the cardboard cup.
2. Pour hot water into the cardboard cup.
3. Put the cup lid onto the cardboard cup – maybe add milk or sugar in the hole of the cup lid – stir the

How to brew a cup of Cafe2Fly: pour 15 grammes of coffee into the cardboard cup
OneCafé International

Pour hot water into the cup (85–95 degrees)

Put on the lid – you can add milk or sugar

Stir the coffee and it is ready to drink

OneCafé International

coffee with a stick (the coffee will not come out of this hole when you drink out of it).

4. Enjoy your coffee.

The process of making a cup of tea is in principle the same as with coffee.

Originally OneCafé developed its concept for coffee, but during the process it turned out that the Café2Fly concept was also suitable for tea (e.g. fruit or herbal tea). OneCafé is now seeking a partnership with a tea producer to further develop the concept.

OneCafé thinks that Cafe2Fly has market opportunities in the following segments:

- Coffee shop chains (Starbucks, Robert's Coffee, etc.).
- In retail points such as petrol stations, 7-Eleven etc.
- Fast food chains (McDonald's, Burger King etc.).
- Small food-serving points, kiosks (hot dog vans, fast-food stands, ice cream kiosks etc.).
- Food-serving areas in supermarkets.
- Events (sport, music, festivals).
- Trains, buses, airplanes, (on-board sales).
- Airports, bus stations, railway stations, cruises.

FarmMountain shops

The shop concept, FarmMountain, was developed in order to create a public awareness of OneCafé's corporate basic values, building on the history of Africa. Originally FarmMountain was not a core business for OneCafé but something that was developed due to the access to the story from Africa. FarmMountain is ongoing and still being developed. The Company's first shop opened on 26 October 2007, in a central location in Randers, Denmark.

In the shop the customer will be able to roast their own coffee once they have chosen it from a wide range of green coffee beans. Their own blend will be made of FarmMountain beans, grown in Uganda. Roasting is done under the customer's watchful eye; and finally they return home with hot, flavourful, newly roasted beans.

In addition to offering coffee varieties such as OneCafé, Cafe2fly and green, roasted/ whole or ground beans, tea, chocolate, coffee shop products and equipment will be on sale.

The management is now considering, either selling OneCafé and/or Cafe2Fly off as a separate businesses or to further develop the FarmMountain internationally though a franchising concept.

QUESTIONS

In Spring 2010 Lars Bendix is preparing one of his many trips to Uganda. He is not convinced which one(s) of the three business concepts is the most attractive to pursue. The company is still in the process of attracting foreign investors, and right now it has only got limited financial resources. On his way to Arlanda Airport, Lars tries to collect his thoughts, but he still has his doubts about what to do. He decides to call you as an international marketing expert. Before Lars returns to Sweden in one week, he would like you to prepare a report with answers to the following questions. Of course you would like to help in this situation, and you agree to prepare the report within the next week.

1. Which of the three business opportunities (the original OneCafé product, Cafe2Fly and Farm-Mountain shop) would you recommend the OneCafé management to focus on in future?

2. For the original OneCafé product: which international partners should OneCafé try to cooperate with and how? Set up a priority list of potential cooperation partners.

3. Would it be relevant for the OneCafé management to use the global account management (GAM) concept? If yes, how should it be used?

Sources: material from OneCafé (www.onecafe.se) – especially the author would like to thank one of the founders, Lars Bendix, for his valuable contribution.

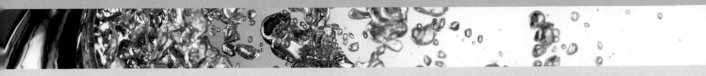

The shaving history

With over 450 million shavers sold, the Philips shaver is the best-sold electric shaver worldwide. The many millions of men who shave themselves with Philips are a fitting testimony of the quality of this excellent shaving system. Since 1939, several generations of electric shavers have been developed and introduced.

In October 1937, a Philips employee in the US wrote to the Netherlands that an electric shaver could be an interesting over-the-counter product that would fit perfectly in the Philips product range and could be sold through the radio trade. To study the idea in more detail a box filled with shavers was sent to a group of engineers in the Netherlands. When Alexandre Horowitz evaluated the electric shavers brought over from the United States, he saw possibilities for Philips and said: 'Let us see if we can make a rotating version'.

This marked the beginning of Philishave, the shaver with the one round head. The first Philishave was presented to the public at the Spring exhibition in Utrecht, the Netherlands on the 14 March 1939. The brand 'Philishave' was first registered on 5 April 1939 and the first patent was filed 31 May 1939. But before the Philishave project was well and truly off the ground, the Second World War broke out and sales fell drastically.

After the Second World War, Philishave began its slow march forward, although there was no sign of a real breakthrough. Great efforts were made to prepare the market. Shaving demonstrations ensured that more and more people could experience in person the benefits of this new system. A larger shaving head and a new design improved the product and the number of people choosing the electric shaver with the rounded head increased daily. However, the main problem of the single-headed shaver was that shaving took too long because of the shaver's relatively small surface area.

In 1947 Philips started to sell its first rotating blade electric razor in America as the Norelco shaver, designed as a brand as much as a product. 'Norelco' stood for modern, industrial, technological. Since then, the Phillips shaver is sold in United States under the Norelco name.

In their quest for shaving perfection, the developers chose the most logical solution: a model with two

Royal Philips Electronics of the Netherlands.

shaving heads, called the 'egg'. The great breakthrough came in the early fifties with this two-headed Philishave. Sales soared to unprecedented heights with the United States as undisputed leader. The new production centre in the Dutch town of Drachten was working at full speed to keep up with the explosive growth.

The 'egg' had been a great triumph, but was old-fashioned by the end of the 1950s. A new model was needed to boost sales further, which was a difficult task to say the least, as success does not repeat itself easily. The most obvious innovation was the development of a shaver with three heads. However, after a pilot in the test market New Zealand, Philips cancelled the test. A new two-head shaver nicknamed 'the pipe' became a worthy successor.

In the 1960s, decade of boundless prosperity, the demand for cars, televisions and refrigerators seemed insatiable. Philishave also profited from this surge in prosperity as production and sales soared to new heights. In addition to the standard electric shave, a new exclusive model made its entry. The wider range meant that the consumer could choose from several models and price ranges.

In 1966, the retail trade was in desperate need of a new Philishave that would surpass competition. With the Philishave '3', Philips set the tone for another generation of shavers. The milestone of the 100 millionth shaver produced was reached as early as 1970. Despite good results, the market share was regularly threatened in the 1970s. The 'battle of the shavers' was raging hard. Global annual figures continued to increase because new markets were being found, but sales in the most important countries fell catastrophically. Next to the competitive intensity and deteriorating economy, Philips discovered that the electric shaver was no longer number 1 on the wish lists of men. Management faced a difficult task ensuring a long-term top position in the market.

The solution was found in the philosophy of the wheel. This entailed a price increase, so that more money could be spent on research and promotion. More support to the retail trade and drastic product improvements would increase sales so that more money could be used for research and promotion. This was the 'philosophy of the wheel' in a nutshell. Sales rocketed in 1975, and the battle of the shavers had been decided in the favour of the triple-headed Philishave.

The 1980s heralded a new period of growth with the double action system giving a tangible better result. Electronics paved the way to greater comfort and cordless ease. Consumers were given an even wider choice as result of a significant expansion of the product line. And with special models, Philips started targeting South East Asia and the young, the shaving generations of the future.

The fall of the Berlin Wall symbolized the coming of a new era in the 1990s: an era of freedom, economic boom and opening borders. New ideas in design, development, production and marketing went further than ever before. To celebrate the production of the 300 millionth Philishave, Philips introduced a special edition with a walnut print.

In 1998 on the eve of a new millennium, Philips crossed the border between dry and wet shaving with Cool Skin. The Cool Skin was a new way of shaving with an integrated moisturising shaving emulsion. This additive from Nivea for Men prepares skin and stubble, which results in a close shave.

Between the first Philishave and the latest Philips Arcitec shaver lie 70 eventful years; years of innovation, unprecedented growth and triumphed setbacks.

Furthermore a new milestone is expected: the sale of the 500,000,000th shaver in 2007.

The world market for shaving

The world market for male shaving can be split into two main segments: electric shaving and wet shaving. The electric shaving market is dominated by Philips, followed at a distance by Braun. The wet shaving category is dominated by Gillette followed at distance by Wilkinson.

The total male shaving market worldwide is estimated at €6 billion in 2008. The wet shaving market worldwide is about twice the size of the electric shaving market. On world basis about 40 per cent mostly use dry shaving and 60 per cent mostly wet shaving. In the western world wet shaving is mainly popular among younger men whereas dry shaving is preferred by the elderly (Euromonitor).

Electric shaving is largely accepted by many millions of users because it makes you feel good and the skin really well cared for with no irritation, nicks or cuts. Furthermore, it is convenient and saves time and money.

The market for male electric shaving is estimated at €2.4 billion (40 per cent of US$6 billion) in 2008, with a market volume for the global male electric shaving of approximately 40 million units. The main regions are Europe (where Germany, the United Kingdom and France are key countries) and Asia (with China and Japan as key countries) both regions with 34 per cent of sales. The third-largest region is North America with 26 per cent. Latin America and Middle East and Africa close the loop with respectively 4 per cent and 2 per cent. See Figure 1.

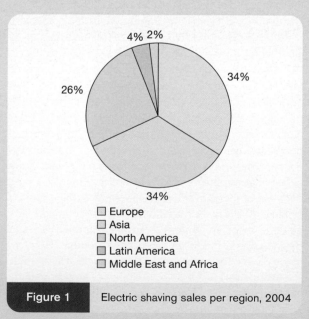

| Figure 1 | Electric shaving sales per region, 2004 |

Source: Philips DAP/Shaving & Beauty.

Competitors

Philips dominated the electronic shaving market with a 44 per cent global market share in 2004. Braun, Remington and Panasonic follow at a distance. In each of the markets local brands compete which have been clustered in the 'other/local' category (see Figure 2).

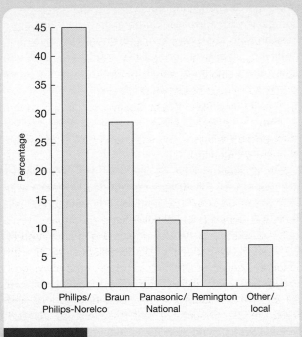

Philips and Braun are the two truly global brands competing in each of the continents, but their electric shavers are based on two different technologies. Philips only sells and markets *rotary shavers*, whereas Braun only markets *foil shavers*. Philips dominates the markets in four continents only to be the number two player in Asia Pacific. Braun is number two in Europe, Latin America and Middle East and Africa and the number three in North America and Asia Pacific. For Remington the North American market, where it has the number two position, is key, as the company does not command a substantial market position outside this region. Remington competes in both the foil and rotary segments. Panasonic competes mainly in the Asia Pacific region where it has the number one position. Local competition is also the strongest in Asia Pacific (see Table 1).

The general picture is that Philips is the global market leader, but there are regional differences. In the eastern part of Europe, Philips and Braun have a head-on competition, each having about 40 per cent of the market, whereas Philips is the clear market leader in western Europe. Also in Australia the competitive situation is different from the general trend: here Remington is the market leader.

The general trend is that Philips is gaining market share in North America at the expense of Braun and Remington. In the following there is a description of the three most important competitors.

Figure 3 looks at the advertisement budget in two key countries for Remington, Panasonic, Braun and Philips.

Braun

Braun (www.braun.com) was founded in 1921 in Frankfurt by Max Braun. The companies headquarters of Braun GmbH are in Kronberg, Germany. From 1967 to 2005 Braun was part of the Gillette Company, which has been acquired by Procter & Gamble. Braun employs around 9,000 employees worldwide and had net sales in 2004 of US$1,392 million. Its profit from operations in 2004 was US$99 million (after 2004 it is impossible to separate financial results from this part of Gillette/P&G).

The company's product range consists of 200 small electrical appliances in ten categories: electric shavers, epilators, food processors, coffee makers, irons, infrared ear thermometers, blood pressure monitors, hair care appliances, electric oral care products,

Table 1	Geographical percentage market shares				
	Europe	Asia Pacific	North America	Latin America	Middle East and Africa
Philips	54	27	47	78	79
Braun	38	24	23	18	13
Panasonic	3	29	1	–	–
Remington	4	2	28	–	4
Other	1	18	1	4	4
Total	**100**	**100**	**100**	**100**	**100**

Source: Philips DAP/Shaving & Beauty.

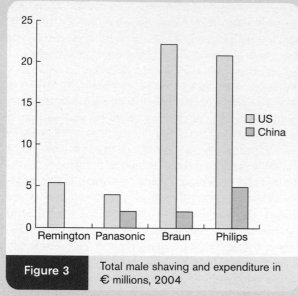

| Figure 3 | Total male shaving and expenditure in € millions, 2004 |

Source: Philips DAP/Shaving & Beauty.

clocks and calculators. Braun is market leader in foil shavers, epilators, hand blenders, infrared ear thermometers and electric oral care products. Its production takes place in seven plants in five countries: Germany, Ireland, Spain, Mexico and China. Its key shaving products are Activator, Syncro, Flex, CruZer.

With innovative solutions, Braun helps millions of modern men be well-shaved and well-groomed at all times. Braun offers a broad choice of electric shavers for a close and gentle shave. Braun foil shavers have unique pivoting shaver heads that follow facial contours to guarantee top shaving comfort. The triple shaving system sets new standards in closeness. And with the breakthrough 'Clean&Charge' shaver cleaning centre, Braun has found the ideal way to assure spick-and-span freshness every day.

Its product portfolio consists of six products: 360 complete, Syncro Pro, FreeGlider, Contour series, Tricontrol and Cruzer.

Panasonic

Panasonic (www.panasonic.com) is part of the Matsushita Corporation headquartered in Osaka, Japan. The company was founded in 1918, has annual sales of US$70 billion and employs 250,000 people. The global brand slogan 'Panasonic ideas for life' represents the commitment of Matsushita employees around the world, from R&D and manufacturing, to marketing and services, in providing products and services with value-added ideas, which enrich lives and advance society.

Panasonic focuses on its pivot action shaving system that claims to have a more comfortable shave, the sharpest blades for precise and accurate shaving and a linear motor that offers a frictionless shave.

Panasonic has no global line up as it offers different products in ranges and different range names in countries. Its product portfolio consists of six products: Lamdash, Linear smoother, Mild smoother, System smoother, TwinEx and Super razor.

Remington

Remington (www.remingtonproducts.com) is part of Spectrum Brands since 2003. Earlier the name of the company was Rayovac Corporation. The company's mission is to seek long-term growth in both sales and profits by providing innovative, high-quality products that create significant value for customers, combined with establishing long-term partnerships with customers, suppliers and employees.

The turnover in electric shaving was modest US$268 million in 2007. The company is operating with an overall loss (negative profits).

The company aims to globalize and diversify by expanding distribution in all served markets and aims to generate growth through aggressive pricing, product design and marketing innovation.

Remington introduced the world's first rotary cleaning system with titanium-coated blades and the technology to clean itself.

The company offers both a range of rotary and foil shavers. In rotary shavers the Microflex 800, Microflex 600, Microflex 400 and Microflex 200 are key series. In Foil shavers the Microscreen 700, Microscreen 500, Microscreen 300, Microscreen 100 and a travel razor are in the range. The high-end model of both ranges is also offered with a cleaning system.

Recently the sharp line between dry and wet shaving is blurring. The Philips Cool Skin system dispenses Nivea for Men shaving lotion during the shave. The system is water-resistant, so allowing its use in the shower. The shaver can be charged for 40 minutes of shaving time. On the other side, Gillette's M3Power razor (introduced in May 2004), uses a battery-powered motor to help lift whiskers, making for a better shave whether the razor is used in the shower or not.

Seasonal sales and distribution channels

Given the high price tags slapped on electric shavers and as new product developments are concentrated in the premium end, sales of electric shavers tend to be focused over the Christmas period and in connection with Father's Day. It is estimated that approximately 45 per cent of value sales are focused over the fourth quarter and these are mainly bought as gifts. Of this, it is estimated that females who purchase the products as gifts for males make 40 per cent of purchases and appealing to female consumers is, therefore, crucial over this time period. While traditional channels dominate retail distribution, volume sales through non-traditional channels such as supermarkets/hypermarkets, electrical stores and the Internet are important growth areas, particularly over the festive season (Euromonitor).

Marketing of the Philips shavers

When Philips started selling shavers, the company used small adverts in newspapers and postcards (a first form of direct mail). However, the key element was demonstrating, demonstrating and demonstrating. Furthermore, Philips has always put quality before turnover.

The flying start of the two-header in the 1950s was followed up with more advertising activities. In addition to dealer adverts in local newspapers, full page adverts began to appear in leading magazines. Radio and TV commercials further stimulated interest, as did sponsored programmes. Even in Hollywood, the shaver made its appearance in the motion picture *The Long Wait*, where actor Anthony Quinn shaved himself for an entire scene with the two headed egg, a first form of product placement that has become normal today.

In the 1960s and in line with expectations, the largest group of buyers was made up of well-established users of electric shavers that were ready for their second or third Philishave, the best shaver money could buy. Furthermore, market researchers discovered that the more expensive shavers were especially popular among female buyers that bought the shaver as a fitting gift for their boyfriends or husbands. In all the product range extensions were a success.

During the 1970s neither money nor effort were spared to promote the electric shaver. In the United States, Philips Norelco would broadcast commercials around the most popular television programmes like Ed Sullivan. Advertisements appeared in trend-setting magazines like *Time* and *Sports Illustrated*. Even the landing on the moon formed the basis of a publicity stunt. Next to shavers for the home, Philips also introduced the Carshaver to increase its potential usage.

In the 1980s Philips continued segmentation and targeted specific customer segments like the younger generations with 'New Wave Junior'. In the United States a new advertising campaign was launched, in which various sports heroes claimed that Philipshave and Norelco were tough on your beard, not on your face. In Japan, Philishave leveraged its sponsorship

North America
Royal Philips Electronics of the Netherlands.

Germany
Royal Philips Electronics of the Netherlands.

Another example is the Norelco gift advertisements for the North American market
Royal Philips Electronics of the Netherlands.

of Roger Moore in the James Bond movie *A View to a Kill.*

In the 1990s, shaving was marketed as an emotion, a daily ritual. The worldwide advertisement campaign 'For The Man Inside' emphasized this emotional side of the modern man. The famous Cobra artist Corneille painted a giant Reflex Action model in 1996. The shaver drew large crowds in a number of European cities during the Philishave moving art tour. Cool Skin is yet another striking example of the innovative power of Philishave. The products and the marketing are constantly on the move.

Philishave as a brand has undergone the necessary development. In addition to electric shavers and Cool Skin, Philips introduced beard and hair trimmers in the 1990s and moved from 'electric shaver with the round head' to a brand for male shaving and grooming.

The marketing of the latest innovation, the SmartTouch-XL, is part of the Philips brand campaign. Here a mix of online and traditional media has been used including the F1 game at http://www.attwilliams.philips.com/. Examples of the SmartTouch-XL campaigns from different regions are shown below.

From March 2006, all Philishave products will be rebranded with the Philips brand name. Philishave is one of the world's most successful brands in electric shaving. However, when a consumer enters a shop looking to buy a shaver, they tend to have Philips rather than Philishave in mind. In fact, recent research has shown that consumers' perception of the Philishave brand is different from how they think of Philips as a whole. In consumer tests on awareness levels, purchase intent and performance against brand pillars, the Philips brand received more positive feedback than Philishave. The Philishave sub-brand does not sufficiently reflect Philips' brand values today.

The introduction of the Artitec shaver

In September 2007 Philips started selling the Arcitec shaver, first in the US and Britain and later in the rest of the world. Prices range from US$169 to US$249, depending on the model. The company will not market it as aggressively in India or China:

- In India people can get a shave at the corner stand for 20 rupees, or 50 cents, so that huge market is not yet primed for a premium product like the Arcitec.

● Chinese men, the company found in its research, generally have less hair, and Asian hair tends to be rounder in shape and thicker in diameter than Caucasian hair, making it stronger but slower-growing. So the Chinese don't necessarily need a razor with three rotating blades like the Arcitec. Electric shaving is growing in popularity with young men in China, however, so Philips will launch a double-headed razor there along with the Arcitec to give customers some options.

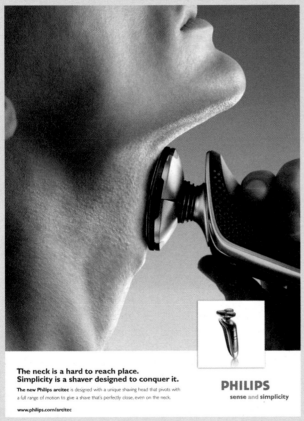

The neck is a hard to reach place.
Simplicity is a shaver designed to conquer it.
The new Philips arcitec is designed with a unique shaving head that pivots with a full range of motion to give a shave that's perfectly close, even on the neck.
www.philips.com/arcitec

PHILIPS
sense and simplicity

Courtesy of Philips Consumer Electronics/Jaap Vliegenthart (photographer)

What about female customers? Philips' research shows nearly half of electric shaver purchases are gifts, and 75 per cent of those are bought by women for men. Yet wives, girlfriends, and mums do not know much about men's razors and are terrified of choosing the wrong one. So Philips created a specific marketing campaign for female shoppers, and they uploaded video demos online through Amazon.com showing typical male shaving dilemmas, like getting at those nasty little neck hairs.

The Arcitec's packaging will represent Philips' broader attempt to unify all its products under one brand name worldwide. For decades, the company sold its products in the US under many brands, including Norelco. The Philips logo will now appear above the Norelco logo on the packaging and in the future, Philips plans to phase out the name Norelco altogether.

A sponsor-partnership with AT&T Williams

In 2006, Philips, has set up a partnership with Formula One (F1) team WilliamsF1. It is one of the most important names in sport. Both brands share a long history of innovation and technical expertise and a passion for marketing.

Frank Williams had been running various operations in Formula 1 prior to creating his own team in 1977. After meeting Patrick Head, the two formed what was then called Williams Grand Prix Engineering, now WilliamsF1. The team debuted in the 1977 Spanish Grand Prix. The team became very successful during the 1980s and 1990s, winning nine F1 Constructors' Championships and seven Drivers' Championships and becoming one of the so-called F1 'Big Three' teams (who have achieved over 100 race victories) alongside Ferrari and McLaren.

As well as new driver Nico Rosberg the WilliamsF1 Team also joined forces with Philips, naming the brand as official Male Shaving Partner.

In 2007 there was a change in name, as it was announced that AT&T would become the title sponsors for the team from the 2008 season – renaming the team to AT&T Williams. AT&T were previously involved as minor sponsors with the Jaguar and McLaren teams, but moved to Williams following McLaren's announcement of a title sponsorship deal with Vodafone, a competitor of AT&T.

In December 2007 Philips Shavers signed a new three-year sponsorship agreement with the AT&T Williams team. The agreement will run through to the end of the 2010 Formula One season, includes exclusive access to promotional collateral and an increased level of branding with the team.

The Philips Shavers brand will now appear on the back of the team's shirts as well as existing branding positions on the nose of the car and on the team's overalls.

For the 2008–9 season, AT&T Williams confirmed Nico Rosberg as one of their race drivers. However for the 2010 season, Nico Rosberg and Kazuki Nakajima have left WilliamsF1. Nico Rosberg has joined the Mercedes Grand Prix team together with Michael Schumacher as Rosberg's team-mate. In the 2010 season Rubens Barrichello and Nico Hulkenberg are driving for the WilliamsF1 team.

For the 2009–10 season Philips Shavers is still sponsor for the AT&T Williams Formula One team (http://www.attwilliams.philips.com/). Formula One is the world's single most popular annual televised sporting event with an average of 162 million TV viewers across the globe per Grand Prix. Philips has even developed its special edition AT&T Williams shaver, with a host of special features in addition to its sleek team-branded design.

In November 2009 Philips Shaver was also working with AT&T Williams on a competition to allow a Formula One fan the chance to do five laps in its race car. Part of the prize is a session in the team simulator to prove to technical director Sam Michael that the winner would be the 'top' man or woman in the hunt.

Source: http://www.attwilliams.philips.com/; 'Philishave, generations of shaving excellence, an impression of 60 years of Philishave', a publication marking the 60th anniversary of Philishave, Philips DAP Groningen, 1998; GFK, NPD and import/export figures 2004.

QUESTIONS

1. What are the key success factors (KSFs) in the male shaving market? How are they different from the female shaving market?

2. How can Philips increase the worldwide share of 'dry shaving'?

3. How will you characterize and explain the cross-national advertising 'rowing boat' campaign?

4. Who are the target groups for the:
   (a) 'rowing boat' advertising campaign
   (b) 'gift' advertising campaign

5. What is the difference in the cooperative relationship that Philips has with Nivea (Cool Skin) and that with AT&T Williams?

CASE STUDY V.4

Vipp AS: an SME uses global branding to break into the international waste bin business

In 1939 the company Vipp (www.vipp.dk) came into existence accidentally when the wife of inventor Holger Nielsen needed a solid, pedal-operated waste bin for her hairdressing salon in Randers. Later on dentists and doctors became aware of the waste bin. So, for the next 50 years, the waste bin was produced for hairdressers, clinics, petrol stations and recently also for 'designer' shops.

When Holger Nielsens died in 1992, only one other person was employed by the company. Nielsen's daughter, Jette Egelund, took over the business. In 1996 her son Kasper and her daughter Sofie joined her. Today Kasper and Sofie Egelund are co-owners of Vipp and are employed as marketing manager and graphic designer respectively.

To begin with Jette tried to find time for the family business. However, in 1995 she quit her full-time job and spent the next few years trying to convince her distributors that the Vipp bin belongs in designer shops as much as it does in dentists' practices and salons.

Jette had no business experience, but little by little she got the hang of it. She tied a bin to a suitcase carrier and set out for the export markets. In Denmark the department stores Magasin and Illum turned her away, arguing that a waste bin from Randers did not belong in their product range – they would neither own nor would they have a dentist's waste bin on their stores' shelves. Every marketing expert with whom Jette Egelund spoke gave her the same advice: to stick to her present customers – dentists, doctors, hospital wholesalers, restaurants. Believing that her father's product is a trendy, quality product, she was convinced that there would be ordinary consumers who could see the beauty of the waste bin and be willing to pay for it. If the Danes would not, the foreign countries might.

In the mid-1990s a holiday trip to London became the beginning of Vipp's internationalization process. Jette paid a visit to the international trend-setting Conran Shop. It was difficult to get the English buyers' attention, but a week after her visit Conran Shop placed an order for 30 bins for the shop in London and 35 for that in Paris. Not a large order, but having Conran Shop among one's customers is very prestigious.

At about the same time Jette attended an international design and interior fair in Frankfurt. Here a German designer fell for the bin and advised her to contact the German mail order company Manufactum. She did, and it resulted in a full-page advertisement in their catalogue and in sales growth of 30 per cent compared to the year before.

Since then the export share has increased and is now 70 per cent of today's total sales. The only thing about the Vipp waste bin that has changed over the years is the shape of the lid. To begin with the lid was produced on a lathe. In the 1950s Holger Nielsen got a hydraulic press that made it possible to produce the smooth surface.

The list of customers now includes leading design shops like Casa Shop, Illuns Bolighus and foreign design distributors such as Waterworks in New York.

Today the company has 20 employees within sales, marketing, logistics and administration. The head office and showroom are situated on Islands Brygge in Copenhagen, whereas most of the production is outsourced to external factories. The bin is available in six sizes and as a miniature. The price to the end consumer varies between €180 and €350. In addition Vipp produces a toilet brush (€140) and a laundry basket (€400). The company sells approximately 300 bins a day – both to the B2B market and to the B2C market through designer shops and lifestyle stores worldwide. Approximately 10 per cent of the total sale goes to the B2B market, mainly in Denmark. The rest goes to the B2C market all over the world, mainly through designer shops.

Competitors

Vipp AS thinks that their product is special but they accept that they may have some competitors in the design and brand-oriented segment for household products. Two of their main competitors are Brabantia (Holland) and Wesco (Germany).

Brabantia (www.brabantia.com) is one of the leading European brands in household metal articles. The company was founded in Holland in 1919 when the van Elderen family, which still owns the firm, began manufacturing a range of watering cans and other

Xylophone bin created by Dominic Wilcox
Vipp Inc.

advertising from country to country is the text being translated.

Vipp believes that its international and design-aware end customers go to the same places, read the same lifestyle magazines and want the same articles for everyday use. Therefore the company is also inspired by a brand such as Coca-Cola. The cornerstone of Vipp's radical branding strategy is the product. Marketing Manager Kasper Egelund says:

> The most important thing about branding is to have a good product. Our most important asset is that we produce the original pedal-operated waste bin that is used by dentists, hairdressers and doctors. We can rightfully say that our bin is the original pedal-operated waste bin from 1939 – no copy product can beat that. We just have to make sure to tell the story to the end customers.
>
> Source: the Danish newspaper *Erhvervsbladet*, 3 April 2003.

Today Vipp AS has a marketing budget of €300,000. Until now the marketing budget has mainly been used for frequent 'shows' of the Vipp bin in lifestyle magazines such as the Danish *Bo Bedre*.

household products. Today 30 per cent of the total Brabantia Group turnover (€150 million in 2005) is attributable to the UK market, where Brabantia has its own production and where the brand is also supported by TV commercials. The product range's profile has also been boosted by other valuable TV appearances. In the United Kingdom Brabantia has developed a national sales network through most of the well-known retail outlets, such as John Lewis and Tesco. The average price level for Brabantia's top waste bins is approximately 30 per cent below Vipp. (Wesco would be somewhere in-between Vipp and Brabantia.) In general Brabantia have broadened their distribution much more than Vipp.

Wesco (Westermann & Co. GmbH) (www.wesco.de) is a much smaller competitor than Brabantia, with only about 100 employees and a turnover of €25 million in 2005. The company was founded in 1867 as a traditional metals company. Over the years Wesco has developed its product range into cashboxes and kitchen accessories other than the waste bin. Wesco is not an international player, as are Brabantia and Vipp, but it has a strong position in the German market.

Standardized international marketing

Throughout the export markets the Vipp waste bin is sold in the same way, the only difference in the

By Anders Hviid / Vipp Inc.

Change of Vipp's international sales organization

In 2001 the company changed its sales organization. For almost five years it had ten foreign agents to manage sales outside Denmark, but now it has decided to use its own three sales representatives and a sales manager to take care of sales to retailers. Vipp will switch over to its own sales representatives as soon as the sales potential in a country can justify employing them. This already happens in the so-called A markets (Germany, Holland, Sweden, Belgium and Denmark), where the company itself manages sales and brand profiling through its own sales representatives. Its own sales force covers the A markets from HQ in Copenhagen. In these A markets the sales force tries to establish close relationships with larger and smaller designer shops in order to ensure that the proactive branding is implemented right through to the end customers. Vipp's own sales force helps the designer shops with in-store promotion and merchandising of Vipp products.

One of the reasons for the reorientation is that the company established only a very small growth in sales during the time the agents were employed. Vipp found that sales improved when its own representatives made the sales. On 31 March 2003, Kasper Egelund said to the Danish newspaper *Jyllands-posten*: 'An agent is a kind of merchant, who opens his jacket saying: "I sell everything; what do you want?" For us that leaves a good deal to be desired. Agents are not loyal to your product; they are not enthusiastic for it.'

In the so-called B markets, such as the United Kingdom or United States, the sales force visits a few key customers (retail chains), which would order larger quantities. In C markets (overseas markets) there are no active Vipp selling efforts. However, Vipp will sell to the active information-seeking customers, who will show up at exhibitions, on the telephone or on the Internet. As an exception Vipp has an importer (with a stock of waste bins and toilet brushes) in Australia, where the high transport costs make up a large percentage of the total product costs.

Special marketing events – art exhibitions

In 2005 Vipp had its first experience of the art world. The House of Vipp and 30 French artists, among them Christian Lacroix, Phillipe Starck, Chantal Thomass, Agnes B and Inès de la Fressange, raised €35,000 in Paris October 2005 for Handicap International.

In 2006 the Carrousel du Louvre in Paris has devoted one of its exhibition rooms to Vipp. The task of providing a sensuous setting went to industrial designer Mauricio Clavero. Mauricio created an artistic, luxury universe comprising such decorative elements as crystal, mosaic and light.

In 2008 Vipp exhibited some artists' works on the Vipp bin in New York (see pictures).

Jette Egelund has now handed over the daily responsibility to her two children, Sofie and Kasper. They have taken over a major responsibility of operations along with a professional management group. However, Jette Egelund still oversees the business as chairman of the board and is working from the headquarters every day.

New products have been introduced and more will follow. This year Vipp has presented the new bathroom series to complete the bathroom furnishings.

Following the exhibition in New York in 2008, the management group decided to open a showroom in New York to support the growing market in the US.

Helena Christensen and Rachel Roy at the 2008 New York 2008 exhibition
By Sara Jaye Weiss / Vipp Inc.

QUESTIONS

1. Vipp is considering increasing its marketing budget by €100,000 per year for its bin. What would be the break-even point of such an extra marketing cost? (Assume Vipp ex-works price of €80 and a contribution margin of 40 per cent.)

2. In your opinion, on which marketing activities should the €100,000 be used, and how should Vipp measure the effect of the marketing investment?

3. Discuss the pros and cons of using a company's own sales force as opposed to agents. Draw a conclusion based on your discussion.

4. Until now Vipp's sales organization has been structured in such a way that each sales representative has been responsible for some European countries. Discuss alternative ways of structuring the sales force. Conclude on this basis with 'Which external interest groups should Vipp communicate with in order to increase the long-term sales?'

5. Imagine that Vipp AS is considering online/Internet sales of its waste bin and toilet brush to end customers in B and C markets. What problems and possibilities do you see for Vipp AS in this connection?

INDEX